BIOLOGICAL PSYCHOLOGY

DON JUAN: . . . Will you not agree with me
. . . that it is inconceivable that Life,
having once produced [birds],
should, if love and beauty were her
object, start off on another line
and labor at the clumsy elephant
and hideous ape, whose grandchildren
we are?

THE DEVIL: You conclude then, that Life
was driving at clumsiness and
ugliness?

DON JUAN: No, perverse devil that you
are, a thousand times no. Life was
driving at brains—at its darling
object: an organ by which it can
attain not only self-consciousness
but self-understanding.

George Bernard Shaw
Man and Superman, Act III

BIOLOGICAL PSYCHOLOGY

An Introduction to Behavioral, Cognitive, and Clinical Neuroscience

SECOND EDITION

MARK R. ROSENZWEIG

ARNOLD L. LEIMAN

S. MARC BREEDLOVE

University of California, Berkeley

SINAUER ASSOCIATES, Inc. • Publishers
Sunderland, Massachusetts

About the cover

Section of macaque retina showing rod bipolar cells (orange) and AII amacrine cells (blue). The large rod bipolar terminals make many contacts with AII processes at the bottom of the picture. A few cone bipolar cells, terminating in the faint red band, are also stained. Courtesy of Stephen C. Massey, Department of Ophthalmology and Visual Science, University of Texas Health Science Center, Houston.

BIOLOGICAL PSYCHOLOGY:
An Introduction to Behavioral, Cognitive, and Clinical Neuroscience, Second Edition

Library of Congress Cataloging-in-Publication Data

Rosenzweig, Mark R.
   Biological psychology : an introduction to behavioral, cognitive, and clinical neuroscience / Mark R. Rosenzweig, Arnold L. Leiman, S. Marc Breedlove. – 2nd ed.
        p.   cm.
   Includes bibliographical references and index.
   ISBN 0-87893-791-9
   1. Psychobiology.   I. Leiman, Arnold L.   II. Breedlove, S. Marc.   III. Title.
QP360.R658 1999
   612.8—dc21   98-44244
                                                                  CIP

Manufactured in the United States of America

10 9 8 7 6 5 4 3 2

We dedicate this book affectionately to our wives, children, and grandchildren.
We appreciate their support and patience over the years of this project.

	M.R.R.		**A.L.L.**		**S.M.B.**		
	Janine		*Lannon*		*Cindy*		
Anne	*Suzanne*	*Philip*	*Jessica* *Timothy*	*Ben*	*Nick*	*Tessa*	*Kit*
Jim	*Kent*	*Laura*					
	Lauren	*Thomas*					
	David	*Caroline*					
	Gregory						
	Elise						

Brief Contents

Contents

PART 1
Biological Foundations of Behavior 23

PART 2
Evolution and Development of the Nervous System 133

PART 3
Perception and Action 187

PART 4
The Regulation of Behavior 315

Chapter 14   Biological Rhythms, Sleep, and Dreaming 379

PART 5
Emotions and Mental Disorders 407

Chapter 15   Emotions, Aggression, and Stress 409

Chapter 16   Psychopathology: Biological Bases of Behavior Disorders 435

PART 6
Cognitive Neuroscience 465

Preface

*A*s we write, today's newspaper announces the discovery of a gene that may account for sociability in many species. A TV program claims that a specific molecule can improve memory. Last week's newsmagazine featured an article on a "diet pill" that may help people to overcome obesity. Other recent news articles have dealt with the following questions:

- Can experience increase the capacity of the brain?
- Is sexual orientation inherited?
- How much sleep do we really need?

These are important questions, but the basic issues they address and the research being conducted to answer them cannot be reduced to "sound bites." A meaningful approach to questions like these requires an understanding of the bodily systems that underlie behavior and experience. Our aim in *Biological Psychology* is to provide a foundation that places these and other important problems in a unified scientific context.

This book explores the biological bases of our experience and behavior: the ways in which bodily states and processes produce and control behavior and cognition, and—just as important—the ways in which behavior, cognition, and the environment exert their influence on bodily systems. We treat biology in a broad sense. As in most textbooks of this sort, there is substantial coverage of the proximate, physiological underpinnings of behavior, but we have attempted to give due attention to ultimate causes by placing these discussions in an evolutionary framework whenever possible. The focus of the book is human behavior, but we include numerous discussions of other species' solutions to the problems of survival as well.

Many scientific disciplines contribute to these themes, so we draw upon the research of psychologists, anatomists, biochemists, endocrinologists, engineers, geneticists, immunologists, neurologists, physiologists, evolutionary biologists, and zoologists. In order to gain a panoramic view of the questions that concern biological psychologists, we have tried to rise above the limits of any single specialty.

Throughout, the text employs a five-fold approach to biological psychology—descriptive, comparative/ evolutionary, developmental, mechanistic, and applied/ clinical. Finally, we emphasize neuroscience research, whether conducted by psychologists or non-psychologists, that aims to inform our understanding of behavior, and we also give great attention to work that explores the remarkable plasticity of the nervous system; a final chapter drives home the particular importance of plasticity in the psychological approach to neuroscience.

In our experience, students enrolled in biological psychology courses can be quite diverse in terms of their academic backgrounds and their personal interests, so we have taken pains to make the subject as accessible as possible to the widest spectrum of students by providing both the behavioral and biological foundations for each main topic. Some students will feel comfortable skipping or skimming some of this background material, but others will benefit from studying it carefully before moving on to the core of each chapter.

We have given considerable thought to the ordering of the chapters and in this revision have made what we believe are positive changes in that regard. However, we realize that some instructors may still prefer to teach topics in a different order or to omit some chapters entirely, so we have written each chapter as a relatively self-contained unit. Recognizing that courses also vary in length from a single quarter or semester to two semesters, we wrote the text with the intent that it could be reasonably covered in a single quarter by omitting a few chapters, but the text provides enough material for a two-quarter or even a two-semester course. Specific suggestions for creating syllabi with different emphases can be found in the *Instructor's Resource Book*. For example, in a two-semester course the instructor can take advantage of the additional material cited as Special Topics and found on our Website (www.biopsychology.com). We have successfully taught the course using the book in each of these formats.

Many features of the text are designed to enhance students' mastery of the material:

- We have created what we believe is the finest full-color illustration program in any current biological psychology text. The acclaimed art program from the first edition has undergone hundreds of additions and refinements, always with a clear peda-gogical goal in mind. Data from original sources have been recast in ways that are designed to aid the student's understanding. All-new photographs of the human brain—clear, detailed, and consis-tent—are another feature of this edition.

- Each chapter opens by laying the groundwork for the content by placing it in a "real-world" context, and concludes with a concise Summary and list of Recommended Reading.
- Key terms are set in boldface type where first de-fined, and are also included in an improved, more comprehensive Glossary.
- "Boxes" describe interesting applications, important methods, sidelights, or refreshers on theoretical con-cepts relevant to biological psychology, or place the findings in the chapter in a historical perspective.
- A brand-new *Student Study Guide*, by Neil V. Wat-son of Simon Fraser University, offers a complete chapter outline, a review of general concepts, a list of study objectives, illustrations from the text with study questions, chapter tests, self-evaluation exer-cises, concept applications, and answers to ques-tions and exercises.
- Icons in the margins call attention to five special as-pects of the text:

Competing hypotheses We frequently underscore the point that science is a process, and that it advances by continually testing competing hy-potheses to account for observations. As examples in the text illustrate, sometimes further research indicates which of a group of hypotheses is correct; sometimes all the hypotheses are rejected for a new, more ade-quate hypothesis.

Important method Many of the stunning advances in neuro-science in recent years are due to the in-troduction of powerful new methods that have made it possible to make progress on previous-ly intractable problems. This icon highlights these new methods as well as more venerable research techniques.

Animal model Students are reminded of the importance of animal research in biological psycholo-gy by the identification of important ani-mal models, which often enable investigators to make progress on questions that have significant implica-tions for both human and animal welfare.

Genes and behavior The revolution in molecular biology is clarifying many of the mechanisms in-volved in genetic influences on behavior, and this icon highlights important examples.

As noted above, plasticity of the nervous system is a repeated theme in the text. This icon calls attention to particularly robust examples of plasticity.

- Two other icons integrate ancillary materials into the discussion:

Sylvius is an interactive neuroanatomy tu-torial on the CD-ROM packaged in this text. Developed by S. Mark Williams of Duke University Medical Center, it is based on stun-ning sections of one human brain. This icon identifies places in the text where reference to *Sylvius* will be of particular help in visualizing and understanding par-ticular neural structures.

Students and instructors have the option of reading additional material that en-riches the discussion on the *Student CD-ROM* or at the www.biopsychology.com Website. The Special Topics icon is a pointer to this resource.

Some of the most satisfying experiences in writ-ing—and revising—this book have been the lively and creative discussions among the three of us. Each of us has a different research focus, and each of us is in-volved in certain fields more fully than the others. Pooling our experiences and discussing the relevance of findings in one area to other aspects of biological pyschology has been a rewarding experience, and we believe that this integration of knowledge from diverse but complementary fields has enriched the book.

Acknowledgments

In preparing this book we benefited from the help of many people. These include members of the staff of Sinauer Associates: Peter Farley, Editor; Paula Noo-nan, Production Editor; Kathaleen Emerson, Ancillar-ies Editor; Christopher Small, Production Manager; Jefferson Johnson, Book Designer and Electronic Pro-duction; and Janice Holabird and Wendy Beck, Elec-tronic Production. Copy editor Stephanie Hiebert con-sistently contributed thoughtful improvements under intense deadlines. Patrick Lane, Mike Demaray, and colleagues at J/B Woolsey Associates patiently and skillfully transformed our rough sketches into the handsome and dynamic art program of this text. Mark Williams produced the *Sylvius* CD-ROM and kindly provided images for the text as well. Molly Lojo or-ganized our references and glossary with skill and cheer.

We also want to thank our past undergraduate and graduate students ranging back to the 1950s for their helpful responses to our instruction, and the colleagues who provided information and critical comments about our manuscript: Brian Derrick; Karen De Valois; Russell De Valois; Jack Gallant; Ervin Hafter; Richard Ivry; Lucia Jacobs; Dacher Keltner; Raymond E. Kesner; Joe L. Martinez, Jr.; James L. McGaugh; Frederick Seil; Arthur Shimamura; and Irving Zucker, as well as Bruno E. Will and Nicole Bonaventure, Université Louis Pasteur, Strasbourg.

We remain grateful to the reviewers whose comments helped shape the first edition, including:

Duane Albrecht, *University of Texas*

Catherine P. Cramer, *Dartmouth College*

Loretta M. Flanagan-Cato, *University of Pennsylvania*

James Gross, *Stanford University*

Wendy Heller, *University of Illinois*

Janice Juraska, *University of Illinois*

Joseph E. LeDoux, *New York University*

Michael A. Leon, *University of California, Irvine*

Randy J. Nelson, *Johns Hopkins University*

James Pfaus, *Concordia University*

Jeffrey D. Schall, *Vanderbilt University*

Dale R. Sengelaub, *Indiana University*

Matthew Shapiro, *McGill University*

Cheryl L. Sisk, *Michigan State University*

Franco J. Vaccarino, *University of Toronto*

Cyma Van Petten, *University of Arizona*

Charles J. Vierck, *University of Florida*

Walter Wilczynski, *University of Texas*

Three instructors—Stephen A Maren, University of Michigan; Neil V. Watson, Simon Fraser University; and Mark C. Zrull, Appalachian State University—acted as "diary reviewers," keeping detailed records of their teaching experience with the first edition in order to provide us with feedback toward this revision. We thank them for their careful assessment of the book and their students' reactions to it.

The following reviewers provided insightful suggestions for refining the manuscript for this edition, and we are thankful for their assistance:

Anne E. Powell Anderson, *Smith College*

Mark S. Blumberg, *University of Iowa*

Eliot A. Brenowitz, *University of Washington*

Catherine P. Cramer, *Dartmouth College*

Francis W. Flynn, *University of Wyoming*

Diane C. Gooding, *University of Wisconsin*

Janet M. Gray, *Vassar College*

Mary E. Harrington, *Smith College*

Robert J. McDonald, *University of Toronto*

Robert L. Meisel, *Purdue University*

Jeffrey S. Mogil, *University of Illinois*

Lee Osterhout, *University of Washington*

Helene S. Porte, *Cornell University*

Scott R. Robinson, *University of Iowa*

David A. Rosenbaum, *Pennsylvania State University*

Martin F. Sarter, *Ohio State University*

Robert Wickesberg, *University of Illinois*

Finally, we would like to thank all our colleagues who contribute research in biological psychology and related fields. We welcome all comments and suggestions from instructors, students, or colleagues. You may e-mail them to us at: biopsych@sinauer.com.

MARK R. ROSENZWEIG
ARNOLD L. LEIMAN
S. MARC BREEDLOVE

1 Biological Psychology: Scope and Outlook

A legend from India (retold by Thomas Mann in *The Transposed Heads*) provides a colorful introduction to the main theme of this book. In this story the beautiful Sita marries a slender, intellectual merchant, but she is also attracted to his best friend, a spirited, brawny blacksmith. One day each young man beheads himself in a temple of the goddess Kali. Sita enters the temple, looking for them, and finds them lying in pools of blood in front of the statue of Kali. Horrified, Sita prays to Kali, begging the goddess to restore the men

Francesco Clemente, *Untitled*, 1985. Gouache on paper

to life. Kali grants the wish and instructs Sita to place the heads carefully on the bodies. Sita undertakes the task with feverish energy and soon sees the men come back to life. Only then does she realize that she has placed each head on the wrong body! Now the three young people are faced with a baffling problem: Which man is Sita's spouse? The one with the intellectual's head and the muscular body? Or the blacksmith's head on the intellectual's body? The legend explores the complexities of how each head affects the body that it now controls, and how each body influences the head.

This old Hindu legend emphasizes that individual identity, personality, and talents are functions of brain–body interactions.

What Is Biological Psychology?

In this book we explore the many ways in which the structures and actions of the brain produce mind and behavior. But that is only half of our task. We are also interested in the ways that behavior in turn modifies the structures and actions of the brain. One of the most important lessons we hope to convey is that interactions between brain and behavior are reciprocal. The brain controls behavior, and in turn behavior alters the brain.

Our goal is to provide an interesting and coherent account of the main ideas and research in biological psychology, which is of great popular as well as scientific interest (Figure 1.1). Because there are so many pieces to tie together, we try to introduce a given piece of information when it makes a difference to the understanding of a subject—especially when it forms part of a story. Most important, we seek to communicate our own interest and excitement about the mysteries of mind and body.

Many Disciplines Contribute to Biological Psychology

No treaty or trade union agreement has ever defined the boundaries of biological psychology. It is a field that includes many players who come from quite different backgrounds—psychologists, biologists, physiologists, engineers, neurologists, psychiatrists, and many others. Further, it shares concepts and research approaches with many other disciplines. Figure 1.2 maps the relations of biological psychology to other disciplines. Clearly, the biological psychology umbrella is very wide.

Biological psychology is the field that relates behavior to bodily processes, especially the workings of the brain. The main goal of this area of study is to understand behavior and experience in terms of their biological substrates. Like other sciences, biological psychology is dedicated to improving the human condition. As Einstein once said in an address to students, concern for humanity and its fate must always form the chief interest of all scientific endeavor "in or-

1.1 Biological Psychology in the News
Many newspaper and magazine articles feature topics in biological psychology.

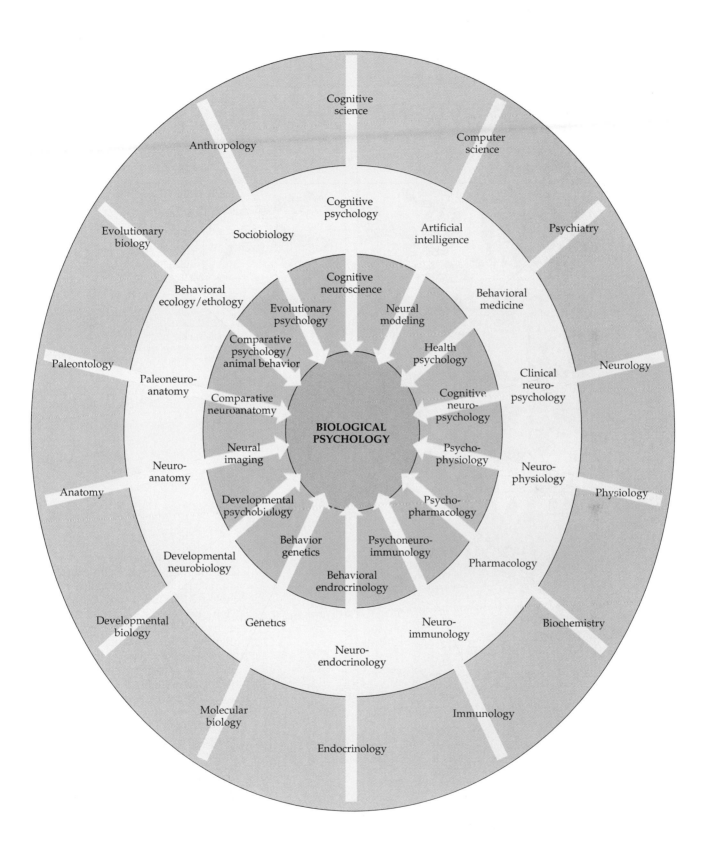

1.2 The Relations of Biological Psychology to Other Fields of Study
In this graphical representation of the relationships among biological psychology and other scientific disciplines, fields toward the center of the map are closest to biological psychology in their history, outlook, aims, or methods.

BOX 1.1   *We Are All Alike and We Are All Different*

Each person has some characteristics shared by...

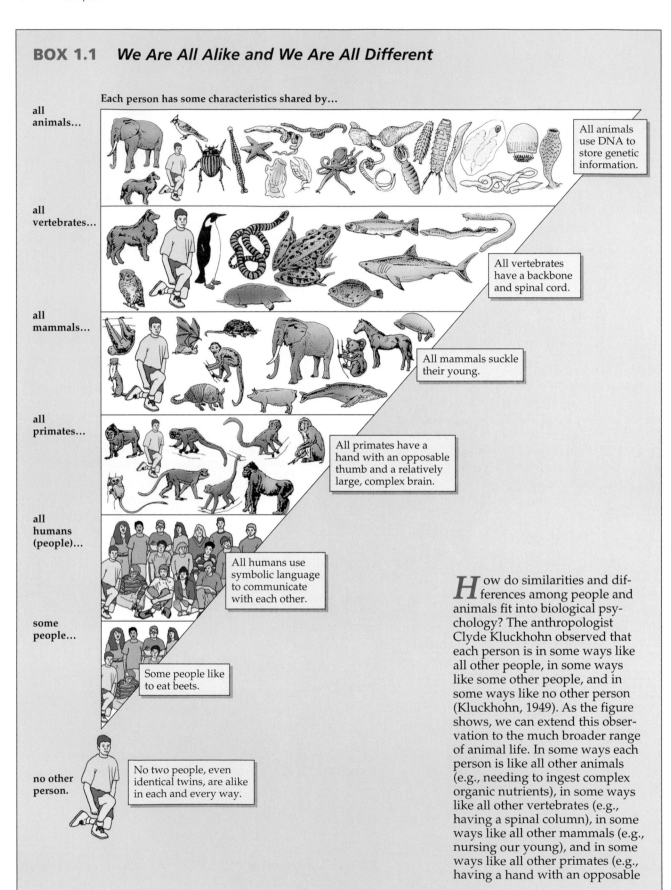

all animals...

All animals use DNA to store genetic information.

all vertebrates...

All vertebrates have a backbone and spinal cord.

all mammals...

All mammals suckle their young.

all primates...

All primates have a hand with an opposable thumb and a relatively large, complex brain.

all humans (people)...

All humans use symbolic language to communicate with each other.

some people...

Some people like to eat beets.

no other person.

No two people, even identical twins, are alike in each and every way.

*H*ow do similarities and differences among people and animals fit into biological psychology? The anthropologist Clyde Kluckhohn observed that each person is in some ways like all other people, in some ways like some other people, and in some ways like no other person (Kluckhohn, 1949). As the figure shows, we can extend this observation to the much broader range of animal life. In some ways each person is like all other animals (e.g., needing to ingest complex organic nutrients), in some ways like all other vertebrates (e.g., having a spinal column), in some ways like all other mammals (e.g., nursing our young), and in some ways like all other primates (e.g., having a hand with an opposable thumb and a relatively large, complex brain).

Whether knowledge gained about a process in another species applies to humans depends on whether we are like that species in regard to that process. The fundamental research on the mechanisms of inheritance in the bacterium *Escherichia coli* proved so widely applicable that some molecular biologists proclaimed, "What is true of *E. coli* is true of the elephant." To a remarkable extent, that statement is true, but there are also some important differences in the genetic mechanisms of *E. coli* and mammals. With respect to each biological property, researchers must determine where animals are identical and where they are different. When we seek animal models for studying human behavior or biological processes, we must ask the question, Does the proposed model really share the same sphere of identity with human beings with respect to what is being studied? We will see many cases in which it does.

Even within the same species, however, individuals differ from one another: cat from cat, blue jay from blue jay, and person from person. Biological psychology seeks to understand individual differences as well as similarities. This interest in the individual is one of the most important differences between psychology and other approaches to behavior. The lottery of heredity ensures that each individual has a unique genetic makeup (the only exception being identical twins). The way the individual's unique genetic composition is translated into bodily form and behavioral capacities is part of our story. Furthermore, each individual has a unique set of personal experiences. Therefore, the way in which each person is able to process information and store the memories of these experiences is another part of our story.

---

der that the creations of our minds shall be a blessing and not a curse." Workers in the health sciences increasingly recognize the reciprocal interactions between behavior and bodily structure and function. For example, one new area is psychoneuroimmunology, which includes studies of relations among illness, the immune system, the brain, and psychological factors.

Five Viewpoints Explore the Biology of Behavior

In our pursuit to understand the biological bases of behavior we use several different perspectives. Because each one yields information that complements the others, the combination of perspectives is especially powerful. The five major perspectives are: (1) *describing* behavior, (2) studying the *evolution* of behavior, (3) observing the *development* of behavior and its biological characteristics over the life span, (4) studying the biological *mechanisms* of behavior, and (5) studying *applications* of biological psychology—for example, to dysfunctions of human behavior.

Behavior Can Be Described according to Different Criteria

Until we describe what we want to study, we cannot get far. Depending on the goals of our investigation, we may describe behavior in terms of detailed acts or processes, or in terms of results or functions. An analytic description of arm movements might record the successive positions of the limb or the contraction of different muscles. A functional behavioral description, on the other hand, would state whether the limb was being used in walking, running, hopping, swimming, or shooting dice. To be useful for scientific study, a description must be precise and reveal the essential features of the behavior, using accurately defined terms and units.

We Can Compare Species to Find How the Brain and Behavior Have Evolved

Darwin's theory of evolution through natural selection is central to all modern biology and psychology. From this perspective emerge two rather different emphases: (1) the *continuity* of behavior and biological processes among species because of common ancestry and (2) the species-specific *differences* in behavior and biology that have evolved in adaption to different environments. At some points in this book we will concentrate on continuity—that is, features of behavior and its biological mechanisms that are common to many species. At other points, we will look at species-specific behaviors.

Continuity of behaviors and mechanisms. Nature is conservative. Bodily or behavioral inventions, once evolved, may be maintained for millions of years and may be seen in animals that otherwise appear to be very different. For example, the nerve impulse (see Chapter 3) is essentially the same in a jellyfish, a cockroach, and a human being. Some of the chemical compounds that transmit messages through the bloodstream (hormones) are also the same in diverse animals (although the same hormone may do different things in different species). Some of the sex hormones occur in all mammalian species. In such cases we share these characteristics with these species because the characteristics first arose in a shared ancestral species (Box 1.1).

But similarity of a feature between species does not guarantee that it came from a common ancestor. Similar solutions to a problem may have evolved independently in different classes of animals. For example, color vision emerged independently in insects, fish, reptiles, birds, and mammals, each group developing a slightly different way of distinguishing colors.

Species-specific behaviors.   Different species have evolved some specific ways of dealing with their environments. An earthworm's sensory endowments, for example, are quite different from those of a robin. Certain species of bat rely almost exclusively on hearing to navigate and find their prey; these species have become nearly blind. Other species of bat, however, are visually oriented, depending on their eyes to find their way around and to secure their food. Human beings use both vision and audition (hearing). However, we ignore electrical fields in the environment, while certain kinds of fish emit electrical pulses and detect the resulting electrical fields to guide locomotion.

Communicative behavior also differs greatly among species. Some species rely chiefly on visual sig-

nals, some on auditory signals, and some on olfactory (smell) signals. In many species the production of signals does not require learning but simply follows an inherited species-specific pattern. In other species, the young must learn behavior from adults. For example, some songbirds must learn their song from their parents, and even though there are many varieties of birdsong, each individual's song conforms fairly closely to the pattern of its species.

The Body and Behavior Develop over the Life Span

Ontogeny is the process by which an individual changes in the course of its lifetime—grows up and grows old. Observing the way in which a particular behavior changes during ontogeny may give us clues to its functions and mechanisms. For example, we know that learning ability in monkeys increases over several years of development. Therefore we can speculate that prolonged maturation of neural circuits is required for complex learning tasks. In rodents the ability to form long-term memories lags somewhat behind the maturation of learning ability. Young rodents

---

TABLE 1.1   *Five Research Perspectives Applied to Three Kinds of Behavior*

Research perspective	Sexual behavior	Learning and memory	Language and communication
		Kind of behavior	
1. Description			
Structural description	What are the main patterns of reproductive behavior and sex differences in behavior?	In what main ways does behavior change as a consequence of experience—for example, conditioning?	How are the sounds of speech patterned?
Functional description	How do specialized patterns of behavior contribute to mating and to care of young?	How do certain behaviors lead to rewards or avoidance of punishment?	What behavior is involved in making statements or asking questions?
2. Comparative/ evolutionary	How does mating depend on hormones in different species?	How do different species compare in kinds and speed of learning?	How did the human speech apparatus evolve?
3. Development	How do reproductive and secondary sex characteristics develop over the life span?	How do learning and memory change over the life span?	How do language and communication develop over the life span?
4. Mechanisms	What neural circuits and hormones are involved in reproductive behavior?	What anatomical and chemical changes in the brain hold memories?	What brain regions are particularly involved in language?
5. Applications	What kind of hormonal treatments can treat sexual inadequacy?	What are the prospects for a "smart pill," one that will improve abilities to learn and remember?	What kinds of treatments can aid recovery of language following stroke?

learn well but forget more quickly than older ones, suggesting that learning and memory involve different neural processes. Studying the development of reproductive capacity and of differences in behavior between the sexes, along with changes in bodily structures and processes, enables us to throw light on bodily mechanisms of sex behaviors.

Biological Mechanisms Underlie All Behavior

The history of a species tells us the evolutionary determinants of its behavior; the history of an individual tells us the developmental determinants. To learn about the mechanisms of an individual's behavior, we study his or her present bodily endowments and states. To understand the underlying "mechanisms" of behavior, we must regard the organism (with all due respect) as a "machine," made up of billions of nerve cells, or **neurons**. We must ask the question, How is this thing constructed to be able to do that?

Our major aim in biological psychology is to examine bodily mechanisms that make particular behaviors possible. For example, in the case of learning and memory, we would like to know the sequence of electrophysiological and biochemical processes that must occur between the initial capture of information and its eventual retrieval from memory. We would also like to know what parts of the nervous system are particularly involved in learning and memory. In the case of reproductive behavior, we would like to know the developmental processes in the body that produce the capacity for sexual behavior. We also want to understand the neuronal and hormonal processes that underlie reproductive behavior.

Research Can Be Applied to Human Problems

A major goal of biological psychology is to use research findings to improve the health and well-being of humans and other animals. Numerous human diseases involve malfunctioning of the brain. Many of these are already being alleviated as the result of research in the neurosciences, and the **Special topic** prospects for continuing advances in this area are good. Attempts to apply knowledge also benefit basic research. For example, the study of memory disorders in humans has pushed investigators to extend our knowledge of the brain regions involved in different kinds of memory (see Chapter 17). Table 1.1 shows how each of these perspectives can be applied to three kinds of behavior. Topic 1.1 continues this discussion of research strategies. *

---

* The icons that appear in the margins throughout the book are explained in the Preface.

Three Approaches Relate Brain and Behavior

Biological psychologists use three approaches to understand the relationship between brain and behavior: somatic intervention, behavioral intervention, and correlation. In the most commonly employed approach, **somatic intervention** (Figure 1.3*a*), the investigator alters a structure or function of the brain or body to see how this change alters behavior. In this approach, somatic intervention is the independent variable, and the behavioral effect is the dependent variable; that is, the resulting behavior depends on how the brain has been altered. For example, mild electrical stimulation of one part of her brain not only made a patient laugh, but she found whatever she happened to be looking at amusing (Fried et al., 1998). In later chapters we will describe many kinds of somatic intervention with both humans and other animals—for example:

1. A hormone is administered to some animals but not to others; various behaviors of the two groups are later compared.
2. A part of the brain is stimulated electrically, and behavioral effects are observed.
3. A connection between two parts of the nervous system is cut, and changes in behavior are measured.

The approach opposite to somatic intervention is psychological or **behavioral intervention** (Figure 1.3*b*). In this approach, the scientist intervenes in the behavior of an organism and looks for resultant changes in bodily structure or function. Here behavior is the independent variable, and change in the body is the dependent variable. Among the examples that we will consider in later chapters are the following:

1. Putting two adults of opposite sex together may lead to increased secretion of certain hormones.
2. Exposing a person or animal to a visual stimulus provokes changes in electrical activity and blood flow in parts of the brain.
3. Training animals in a maze is accompanied by electrophysiological, biochemical, and anatomical changes in parts of their brains.

The third approach to brain–behavior relations, **correlation** (Figure 1.3*c*), consists of finding the extent to which a given bodily measure varies with a given behavioral measure. Some questions we will examine later are as follows:

1. Are people with larger brains more intelligent than people with smaller brains?

(a) Manipulating the body may affect behavior

(b) Experience affects the body

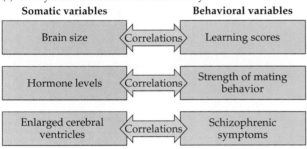

(c) Bodily and behavioral measures covary

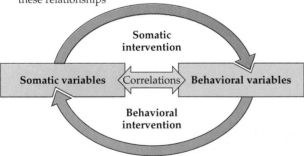

(d) Biological psychology seeks to understand all these relationships

Somatic intervention

Somatic variables ⟨Correlations⟩ **Behavioral variables**

Behavioral intervention

1.3 Three Main Approaches to Studying the Physiology of Behavior

(a) In a somatic intervention, investigators change the body structure or chemistry of an animal in some way and observe and measure any resulting behavioral effects. (b) Conversely, researchers may change an animal's behavior or its environment and try to ascertain whether the change results in physiological or anatomical changes. (c) Measurements of both kinds of variables allow researchers to arrive at correlations between somatic changes and behavioral changes. (d) Each approach enriches and informs the others.

2. Are individual differences in sexual behavior correlated with levels of certain hormones in the individuals?
3. Is the severity of schizophrenia correlated with the magnitude of changes in brain structure?

Such correlations should not be taken as proof of causal relationship. For one thing, even if a causal relation exists, the correlation does not reveal its direction—that is, which variable is independent and which is dependent. For another, two terms might be correlated only because a third factor determines the values of the two factors measured. What the existence of a correlation does indicate is that the two variables are linked in some way—directly or indirectly. Such a correlation often stimulates investigators to formulate hypotheses and to test them by somatic or behavioral intervention.

Combining these three approaches yields the circle diagram of Figure 1.3d. This diagram incorporates the basic approaches to studying relationships between bodily processes and behavior. It also emphasizes the theme (brought out in the myth of the transposed heads that was related at the beginning of this chapter) that the relations between brain and body are reciprocal; each affects the other in an ongoing cycle of bodily and behavioral interactions. We will see examples of this reciprocal relationship throughout the book.

Neural Plasticity: Behavior Can Change the Brain

This idea that there is a reciprocal relationship between brain and behavior has embedded within it a concept that is, for most people, startling. When we say that behavior and experience affect the brain, we mean that they literally, physically alter the brain. The brain of a child growing up in a French-speaking household assembles itself into a configuration that is different from the brain of a child who hears only English. That's why the first child, as an adult, understands French effortlessly while the second does not. In this case, we cannot tell you what the structural differences are exactly, but we do know one part of the brain that is being altered by these different experiences (see Chapter 19). There are numerous examples, almost all in the animal literature, in which experience has been demonstrated to affect the number or size of neurons, or the number or size of connections between neurons. This ability of the brain, both in development and in adulthood, to be changed by the environment and by experience, is called **neural plasticity**.

Today when we hear the word "plastic," we think of the class of materials found in so many modern products. But originally "plastic" meant "flexible, malleable" (from the Latin *plasticus*, "that may be molded"), and the modern materials were named plastics because they can be molded into nearly any shape.

Neural plasticity William James (1890, p. 110) described plasticity as "the possession of a structure weak enough to yield to an influence, but strong enough not to yield all at once. . . . Nervous tissue seems endowed with a very extraordinary degree of plasticity of this sort; so that we may without hesitation lay down as our first proposition the following, that the phenomena of habit in living beings are due to the plasticity of the organic materials of which their bodies are composed."

In the ensuing decades research has shown that the brain is even more plastic than James suspected. For example, parts of neurons known as dendritic spines (see Chapter 2) appear to be in constant motion, changing their shape in the course of seconds (Fischer et al., 1998). We will see many examples in this book of cases in which experience alters the structure and/or function of the brain: In Chapter 5, hearing a baby cry will cause the mother's brain to secrete a hormone; in Chapter 7, visual experience in developing kittens will direct the formation of connections in the brain; in Chapter 12, a mother rat's grooming of her pups will affect the survival of spinal cord neurons; and in Chapter 18, a sea slug learning a task will strengthen the connections between two particular neurons.

We can sometimes demonstrate in humans that experience can influence the functioning of the brain. For example, when people were asked to put their hand into moderately hot water (47°C), a part of the brain became active, presumably because of the discomfort involved (Rainville et al., 1997). But subjects who were led to believe the water would be very hot had a more activated brain than subjects who were led to believe the discomfort would be minimal (Figure 1.4), even though the water was the same temperature for all subjects. The psychological expectation affected the magnitude of the brain response. In turn, the people with the more activated brain also reported a more unpleasant experience.

Perhaps nothing distinguishes biological psychology from other neurosciences more clearly than this fascination with neural plasticity. Biological psychologists have a pervasive interest in how experience physically alters the brain and therefore affects future behavior. We will touch on this theme in almost every chapter and review some of these examples again in Chapter 20.

Biological Psychologists Use Several Levels of Analysis

Finding explanations for behavior often involves dealing with several levels of biological analysis. The units of each level of analysis are simpler in structure and organization than those of the level above. Figure 1.5 shows how we can analyze the brain into successively less complex units until we arrive at single nerve cells and their even simpler, molecular constituents.

Scientific explanations usually involve analysis on a simpler or more basic level of organization than that of the structure or function to be explained. This approach is known as **reductionism**. In principle it is possible to reduce each explanatory series down to the molecular or atomic level, though for practical reasons this extent of reductionism is rare. For example, the organic chemist and the neurochemist usually deal with large complex molecules and the laws that govern them; seldom do they seek explanations in terms of atoms.

Naturally, in all fields different problems are carried to different levels of analysis, and fruitful work is often being done simultaneously by different workers at several levels. Thus, in their research on visual perception, behavioral psychologists advance analytical descriptions of behavior. They try to determine how the eyes move while looking at a visual pattern, or how the contrast among parts of the pattern deter-

1.4 Pictures of Pain
Subjects told to expect only mild discomfort from putting their hand into 47°C water (*left*) show less activation in a particular brain region (the anterior cingulate cortex) than subjects expecting more discomfort (*right*). Areas of high activation are indicated by orange, red, and white. (From Rainville et al., 1997; courtesy of Pierre Rainville.)

tvalue
6.00
5.00
4.00
3.00

Social level:
Individuals behaving
in social interaction

Organ level:
Brain, spinal cord,
peripheral nerves,
and eyes

Neural systems level:
Eyes and visual brain regions

Brain region level:
Visual cortex

Circuit level:
Local neural circut

Cellular level:
Single neuron

Synaptic level

Molecular level

Membrane receptors

1.5 Levels of Analysis in Biological Psychology
The scope of biological psychology ranges from the
level of the individual interacting with others to
the level of the molecule. Depending on the question at hand, investigators use different techniques
to focus on these many levels, but always with an
eye toward how their findings apply to behavior.

mines its visibility. Meanwhile, other psychologists and biologists study the differences in visual endowments among species and try to determine the adaptive significance of these differences. For example, how is the presence (or absence) of color vision related to the life of a species? At the same time, other investigators trace out brain structures and networks involved in different kinds of visual discrimination. Still other neuroscientists try to ascertain the electrical and chemical events that occur at synapses in the brain during vision.

As we consider explanations of many kinds of behavior in terms of bodily events, we will point out the main levels of analysis that are currently being used to study each problem. We will also identify some of the applications of each level of research.

A Preview of the Book: Major Areas of Current Research

The accelerated pace of advances in biological psychology has provided answers to some fundamental questions and offers prospects of new productive approaches. Here are some examples of current research that will be considered in this book.

Problem: How does the brain grow, maintain, and repair itself over the life span, and how are these capacities related to the growth and development of the mind and behavior from the womb to the tomb?

By 6 months after conception, the developing human is equipped with a brain that contains billions of nerve cells organized in precise arrays with specific interconnections. The plan for development of the human brain resembles in many ways those of other mammals, and even those of all other vertebrates, but with important species specific features. Each species has to be prepared to carry out many behaviors at birth and to acquire others soon after birth. The developmental blueprint not only specifies the arrangement of most nerve cells long before birth, but it also provides for and depends on environmental influences to help shape neural development after birth.

Current Research: Brain transplants can repair damaged brains.

A short while ago brain transplants were unreal, the stuff of science fiction. Can a piece of the brain be replaced by cells derived from other animals? Can the transplanted cells be incorporated into neural circuits much as one might re-

place transistors in your radio? The prospect for this kind of intervention is especially important for many human neurological disorders characterized by nerve cell degeneration produced by disease or stroke. (**Strokes** are disorders of blood vessels—either a block or a rupture of a vessel—that destroy or cripple particular brain regions, disabling many people.)

During the 1980s, basic research showed the feasibility of brain transplants in experimental animals. A crucial finding from these studies was that cells from fetal animals are far more likely to provide successful transplants than are cells from adults. Donor tissue derived from an embryonic or fetal animal is placed on the surface of a damaged region or broken up into cells and injected into the brain. Brain-damaged animals can show functional recovery after such injections of brain transplants (Ralph and Lehman, 1991; Ridley and Baker, 1991).

The success of these demonstrations led to efforts to use transplants to remedy Parkinson's disease in afflicted humans (Figure 1.6). Parkinson's disease is characterized by many changes in movements, including tremors and slowness of actions (see Chapter 11). Injections of fetal cells or other donor tissue into some brain regions has alleviated the symptoms of Parkinson's disease in some humans (Madrazo et al., 1990). In some animal research, a brain transplant coupled with enriched experience is significantly more effective than either treatment alone in restoring function (see Chapter 18).

Problem: How does the nervous system capture, process, and represent information about the environment?

The world around us is abuzz with many energies packaged in varied ways. Only some of these become sights, sounds, touches, and smells that we can recognize and respond to. What computational activities of the brain underlie our sensory abilities? Investigators have learned much about how our world is represented in circuits and activities of the brain. Sensory stimuli—from simple touches to complex sounds and elaborate displays of color and form—are processed by many specialized brain regions. The brain's information about our world is often modified by processes such as attention. A matter of considerable interest to researchers is understanding how complex perceptual categories such as distinctive visual patterns or the sounds of language are organized in the brain.

Donor cells

Cells dispersed in solution

Cells injected into target region of patient's brain

1.6 Brain Cell Transplantation
This brain cell transplantation procedure has been employed both in humans with brain diseases and in animals in research studies.

A striking finding is the observation that some nerve cells are particularly excited by faces, as opposed to other stimuli that might involve the same amount of light and visual complexity. Figure 1.7 shows one such finding from research by Robert Desimone and colleagues (1984): Some neurons in monkeys' brains are especially excited by frontal views of the monkey face, whereas others are maximally excited by lateral views of a face. The face as a perceptual category seems organized in a distinctive way; we will discuss more about this aspect of visual processing in Chapter 10.

Problem: How does sexual orientation develop?

For the vast majority of us, a point comes in our lives, usually before adolescence, when we begin forming romantic attachments to and consider having sexual relations with certain types of people. Usually that "type" is someone of the opposite sex, but some of us are attracted to people of the same sex. Whether homosexual or heterosexual, this orientation, once formed, is rather stable, especially for males. How does this orientation come about, and what factors affect which orientation we develop?

Current Research: There are brain correlates of sexual orientation.

In every human culture, some individuals display a homosexual orientation. Cultures differ widely in their reaction to and treatment of homosexuals and have various traditional theories about why some people develop this sexual orientation. Modern research also wrestles with this problem.

The report by LeVay (1991) that the brains of heterosexual and homosexual men are slightly different in the region known as the hypothalamus has fueled the debate about whether some people are "born gay." Several other brain regions were subsequently reported to be different in gay and straight men, but despite the almost universal reaction to these studies in the media, these findings tell us nothing about whether child-rearing practices, genes, or a combination of the two

Current Research: Some nerve cells prefer faces.

Recognition of faces is very important to the social life of primates, including humans. For example, facial expression is important for the communication of emotions (see Chapter 15). Individual identity is intimately tied to distinctive facial features. Neurologists studying the effects of brain changes from stroke have described an intriguing syndrome that suggests that the brain's visual system has distinct sets of nerve cells involved with particular perceptual categories. After strokes that involve specific regions of cerebral cortex, some patients lose the ability to recognize human faces (see Chapter 19).

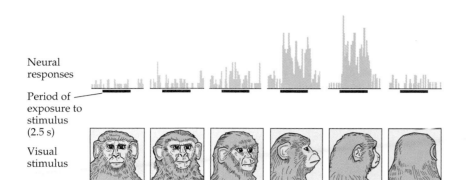

Neural responses

Period of exposure to stimulus (2.5 s)

Visual stimulus

0°   30°   60°   80°   100°   180°

1.7 A Preference for Profiles
Responses of a single monkey brain cell to different pictures of monkey heads. This nerve cell fired vigorously when the monkey was shown a lateral view of a monkey head (80° and 100°), but weakly when a frontal (0°) or near-frontal (30°) view was presented. Other cells in monkey brains respond best to full-face views. The responses outside the periods of stimulation (shown as black bars) are due to ongoing neural activity. (After Desimone et al., 1984.)

are responsible for these structural and behavioral differences. These reports are part of a long-standing series of studies investigating how the brains of male and female animals come to be different—a process in which hormones play a crucial role. In Chapter 12 we'll use these studies to help us understand the limits and opportunities for studying biological correlates of sexual orientation in humans.

Problem: What brain sites and activities underlie feelings and emotional expression?

The organization of many regions of the nervous system is influenced by neurochemicals, including hormones, and many neural circuits are activated or inhibited by chemical messages. For example, investigators are now studying both similarities in and differences between the sexes in details of brain structure and chemistry as clues to understanding why women are so much more likely than men to suffer from depression.

Current Research: Depression can be seen in the brain.

All of us from time to time feel a little low and listless, but for millions of people across the world depression is a major life-threatening psychiatric disorder. The lethality of depression is increasingly prominent in younger patients—in the form of suicide (see Chapter 16). Many different causes of depression have been suggested, including psychosocial factors, stress, and brain states. The advent of new ways of looking at the living brain has given us novel insights into the biology of this disorder. Brain scans derived from comparing normal subjects and depressed patients show striking increases in the activity of some brain regions and decreases in the activity of others.

Problem: How does the brain store information?

The ability to recollect and use the past is critical for the survival of any animal, from the most simple to the most complex. Learning and memory are among the most extraordinary abilities of human beings. Breakthrough research in this area is exploring how the brain accomplishes these feats (see Chapter 18).

Current Research: Memory can be established in a dish.

Is memory a property of the whole brain, or are there different kinds of memory devices in many different parts of the brain? One approach to this issue involves an unusual phenomenon, discovered in 1973, that still fascinates researchers. This phenomenon—called long-term potentiation—was initially detected in a brain region involved in learning and memory, the hippocampus. Researchers showed that a brief period of electrical stimulation of this area could enhance electrical activity in nerve cells for minutes or hours—a kind of memory device, since the cells seemed to "remember" that they had been stimulated. Figure 1.8 shows a dramatic example: A small piece of tissue from this region can remain alive when bathed with nutrients in a small dish. Such a tissue slice will also show long-term potentiation when electrically stimulated. Thus, a simple brain memory device can be studied in a dish.

 Important method

(a) Rat brain
Hippocampus
1 cm

(b) Slice of hippocampus in petri dish

(c) Recording electrode
Hippocampal section in recording chamber
Stimulating electrode

(d) Recording display
Microscope
Stimulator

1.8 Memory in a Dish
In a research preparation that has become important in the study of the neural bases of memory, a small slice of tissue from an area of the brain called the hippocampus, which is believed to be important for memory, is removed from the brain (a) and placed in a dish (b). A brief, intense train of stimulation is applied to the tissue with an electrode (c). Electrical recordings from the slice (d) show that the amount of electrical activity produced by subsequent stimuli is changed for a period of hours as a result of the brief train of intense stimulation. That the cells in the slice "remember" the initial stimulation in this way has led researchers to use this preparation as a model of memory formation and storage.

Problem: What are the neurobiological bases of language in humans?

Of all our attributes, none is more distinctively human than language. In the past 10 years considerable new information has been obtained about structures in the brain essential for language and brain activity during language tasks.

Current Research: Language lights up the brain.

For years, the complexity of language and the limited tools for exploring brain activity in humans prevented detailed studies of brain activities during language performance. Biological study of language was restricted largely to the

Hearing words   Seeing words

Reading words   Generating verbs

1.9 The Brain Activated by Language
These images show which brain regions were most active when subjects performed four tasks involving language. The techniques used to generate such images are described in Chapter 2. (Courtesy of Marcus Raichle.)

examination of impairments following brain injury and disease. Brain scans provide a more dynamic portrait of cortical organization and functioning during language tasks in normal subjects. Figure 1.9 shows an example of brain activity during different types of language performance, such as listening to, seeing, and speaking words.

Each of the foregoing questions will be taken up in later chapters. Some of the examples we will consider may seem almost as fantastic as the legend of the transposed heads, but these findings have led to cures for psychoses, the relief of pain, the restoration of partial sight to some blind people, and stimulation of the growth of the brain, which thereby improves the capacity to learn. These and other achievements that are now becoming familiar would have seemed unbelievable a few decades ago. As science fiction writer Arthur C. Clarke stated, "The science of one generation was the magic of the preceding one."

Neuroscience Contributes to Our Understanding of Psychiatric Disorders

One of the great promises of biological psychology is that it can contribute to the understanding and devising of treatment strategies of disorders that involve the brain. Like any complex mechanism, the brain is subject to a variety of malfunctions and breakdowns. People afflicted by disorders of the brain are not an exotic few. At least one person in five around the world currently suffers from neurological and/or psychiatric disorders that vary in severity from complete disability to significant changes in quality of life. Figure 1.10a shows the estimated numbers of U.S. residents afflicted by some of the main neurological disorders. Figure 1.10b gives estimates of the numbers of U.S. adults who suffer from certain major psychiatric disorders. The division of disorders in Figure 1.10 reflects the traditional distinctions between neurology and psychiatry, but both fields are becoming oriented more toward neuroscience.

The toll of these disorders is enormous, both in terms of individual suffering and in social costs. The National Foundation for Brain Research estimated in 1992 that direct and indirect costs of behavioral and brain disorders amount to $400 billion a year in the United States. For example, $160 billion a year is spent on the treatment of alcohol and substance abuse, and the cost for treatment of dementia (severely disordered thinking) exceeds the costs of treating cancer and heart disease combined. This high cost has impelled researchers to try to understand the mechanisms involved in these disorders and in some cases to alleviate or even to prevent them.

(*a*) Prevalence of neurological disorders

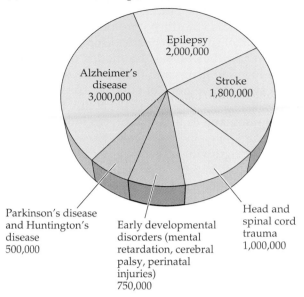

(*b*) Incidence of psychiatric disorders

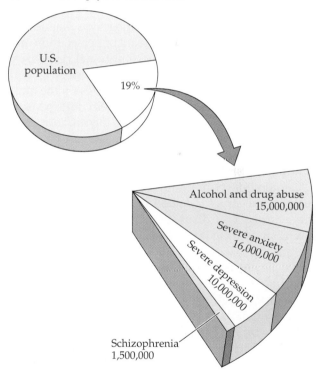

1.10 The Toll of Brain Disorders
The prevalence of neurological disorders (*a*) and psychiatric disorders (*b*) in the United States. As brain research progresses, many disorders previously characterized as psychiatric are thought to be neurological in origin.

The following are examples of research that is providing relief from some of these grave disorders—examples that will be discussed in later chapters:

1. Antipsychotic and antianxiety drugs introduced in the 1950s have enabled many patients to lead fuller

lives less haunted by the crippling consequences of intense symptoms. Studies of the effects of these drugs have also produced profound insights into the nature of some psychiatric disorders.

2. Discoveries that reveal the modes of action of habit-forming drugs and their effects on the nervous system give hope of effective cures for people addicted to drugs and of the ability to prevent lasting damage in infants born to mothers who take drugs.

3. The fastest-growing affliction in industrialized societies is Alzheimer's disease, a profound loss of cognitive abilities that strikes especially older people. Current research is exploring some of the causes and brain mechanisms of this devastating condition.

The sections that follow focus on two other examples in a little more depth.

Neuroscience Is Helping Us to Understand Schizophrenia

Some people spend the bulk of their lives plagued by hallucinations, unwarranted fears of persecution and other delusions, and blunted emotional responses. They frequently appear socially withdrawn, and many such individuals spend their lives on the margins of society. Often these people seem unresponsive to all forms of intervention, including modern drug treatments. **Schizophrenia** is the diagnostic category for this disorder, which investigators have long sought to understand as a kind of brain disease.

Contemporary brain imaging techniques have revealed some structural abnormalities in the brain that characterize this disorder from its earliest stages, commonly during late adolescence. Figure 1.11 shows changes deep within the brains of these patients that can be visualized using imaging techniques such as computerized tomography (CT) scans and magnetic resonance imaging (MRI) scans of living patients. Both techniques produce cross-sectional pictures of the living brain (see Chapter 2). These data may help pinpoint circuitry changes that underlie this disorder.

Brain Imaging Aids Understanding of Infantile Autism

The ability to visualize brain structures in living patients has also offered insights into an odd and tragic disorder that appears early in life—infantile **autism**. Unlike the usual cuddly infants, autistic children avoid eye contact with parents when held, push away from close contact, and, as they become older, seem more and more inaccessible. Their language acquisition is severely impaired, and they begin to exhibit strange automatic acts, such as incessant rocking. This disorder remains a mystery, but genetic studies reveal clear evidence of the powerful role of inheritance. Im-

1.11 Identical Twins but Nonidentical Brains and Behavior
In these images of the brains of identical twins, the fluid-filled cerebral ventricles are prominent as dark "butterfly" shapes. The twin whose brain is imaged on the right is schizophrenic, and has the enlarged cerebral ventricles that some researchers believe are characteristic of this disorder. The other twin is not schizophrenic; his brain (*left*) clearly has smaller ventricles. (Courtesy of E. Fuller Torrey.)

ages of the brains of some of these patients reveal a reduction in the size of the corpus callosum and of regions within the cerebellum (Egaas et al., 1995), a large structure in the brain associated with motor control mechanisms and with some kinds of learning.

Laboratory and Clinical Approaches Complement Each Other

Basic research and clinical practice influence each other. Basic research provides concepts and techniques that clinicians use to understand and help people with malfunctioning brains. At the same time, clinical observation of these patients provides data and stimulates the development of theories about brain mechanisms. This exchange is mutually beneficial, and the boundaries between laboratory and clinic are disappearing.

Two Brains in One Head

Research on the functions of the two cerebral hemispheres illustrates the productive interplay between laboratory and clinic. Suppose that each time a right-handed person buttoned a shirt, the person's left hand sought to unbutton it. Two separate controllers would seem to be involved, but is this possible? Most of us are saved from such frustration because information from the right and left sides of the body is integrated by pathways that connect the two sides of the brain. But what happens when these connections are severed? Can we then observe two different types of consciousness?

Although the structures of the left and right sides of the brain seem very much alike, functional differences between the cerebral hemispheres of human brains become evident after brain damage such as that resulting from a stroke. For instance, injury to certain parts of the left cerebral hemisphere can produce striking changes in speech and language, whereas injury to the right hemisphere rarely affects speech. This situation used to be described as "cerebral dominance," implying that a talkative left cerebral hemisphere dominated a mute right hemisphere.

New information about hemispheric specialization of function has come from studies of patients in whom the connections between the right and left cerebral hemispheres have been cut; these people are referred to as **split-brain individuals**. Early work with such patients in the 1930s did not reveal clear differences between the functions of the two hemispheres, because of a lack of appropriate methods of behavioral assessment. Coming from a background of animal research, Roger Sperry (1974) and his collaborators (e.g., Gazzaniga, 1992) understood how to test separately the functioning of the two hemispheres, and they found remarkable differences in humans. These results prompted Sperry to speak of separate forms of consciousness in the two hemispheres of the brain. The patients seemed literally to be of two minds. Indeed, one of Sperry's patients was seen to button a shirt with one hand and try to unbutton it with the other. For his research with split-brain subjects and other contributions, Sperry was awarded the Nobel prize in physiology or medicine in 1981.

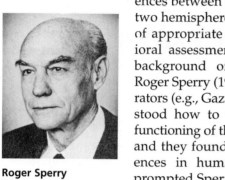

Roger Sperry
(1913–1995)

Tests have indicated similar but much more subtle differences in cognitive style of the two hemispheres even in normal humans. Whereas the left is said to be analytic and verbal, the right has been characterized as spatial and holistic. However, most researchers emphasize the integrative functioning of the hemispheres in human cognitive activities.

Animal Research Makes Vital Contributions

Because we will draw on animal research throughout this book, we should comment on some of the ethical issues of experimentation on animals. Human beings' involvement and concern with other species predates recorded history. Early humans had to study animal behavior and physiology in order to escape some species and hunt others. To study biological bases of behavior inevitably requires research on animals of other species as well as on human beings. Because of the importance of carefully regulated animal research for both human and an-

Animal model

imal health and well-being, the National Research Council (1988, 1991) undertook a study on the many uses of animals in research. The study notes that 93% of the mammals used in research are laboratory-reared rodents. It also reports that most Americans agree that animal research should continue and that this conclusion is well founded.

It makes no sense to sacrifice future human health and well-being by not using animals in research today. We owe our good health to past investigators and the animals they studied. As we decide on the future of animal research, we should keep in mind the generations who will look back at us and ask if we acted wisely.

Further improvements in human health and well-being and reduction of the disorders listed in Figure 1.10 depend on ongoing research, much of which requires animal subjects. Students of psychology usually underestimate the contributions of animal research to all the main fields of psychology because, as one study found (Domjan and Purdy, 1995, p. 501), the most widely used introductory psychology textbooks obscure the contributions of animal research, and they present major findings from animal research as if they had been obtained with human subjects.

The History of Research on the Brain and Behavior Begins in Antiquity

Although the brain has long been studied, only recently have scientists recognized the central role of the brain in controlling behavior. When Egyptian pharaoh Tutankhamen was mummified (around 1300 B.C.E.), four important organs were preserved in alabaster jars in his tomb: liver, lungs, stomach, and intestines. The heart was preserved in its place within the body. All these organs were considered necessary to ensure the pharaoh's continued existence in the afterlife. The brain, however, was removed from the skull and discarded. Although the Egyptian version of the afterlife entailed considerable struggle, the brain was not considered an asset.

Neither the Hebrew Bible (written from the twelfth to the second century B.C.E.) nor the New Testament ever mentions the brain. However, the Bible mentions the heart hundreds of times and makes several references each to the liver, the stomach, and the bowels as the seats of passion, courage, and pity. "Get thee a heart of wisdom," said the prophet.

The heart is also where Aristotle (around 350 B.C.E.), the most prominent scientist of ancient Greece, located mental capacities. We still reflect this ancient notion when we call people kind-hearted, open-hearted, hard-hearted, faint-hearted, or heartless, and when we speak of learning "by heart." Aristotle considered the brain to be only a cooling unit to lower the temperature of the hot blood from the heart. Other Greek

1.12 Leonardo da Vinci's Changing View of the Brain
In an early representation (*left*), Leonardo simply copied old schematic drawings that represented the cerebral ventricles as a linear series of chambers. Later, he made a drawing based on direct observation (*right*): After making a cast of the ventricles of an ox brain by pouring melted wax into the brain and letting it set, he cut away the tissue to reveal the ventricles' true shape.

thinkers, however, did consider the brain to be the seat of intellect and the organ that controls behavior. Thus around 400 B.C.E. Hippocrates, the great physician of Greek antiquity, wrote:

> Not only our pleasure, our joy and our laughter but also our sorrow, pain, grief, and tears rise from the brain, and the brain alone. With it we think and understand, see and hear, and we discriminate between the ugly and the beautiful, between what is pleasant and what is unpleasant and between good and evil. (*On the Sacred Disease*)

The dispute between those who located intellect in the heart and those who located it in the brain still raged 2000 years later, in Shakespeare's time: "Tell me, where is fancy bred,/Or in the heart or in the head?" (*Merchant of Venice*, Act III, Scene 2).

Around 350 B.C.E., the Greek physician Herophilus (called the Father of Anatomy) advanced our knowledge of the nervous system by dissecting bodies of both people and animals. Among other investigations, he traced spinal nerves from muscles and skin into the spinal cord. He also noted that each region of the body is connected to separate nerves. A second-century Greco-Roman physician, Galen (frequently described as the Father of Medicine), treated the injuries of gladiators and dissected some animals. He advanced the idea that animal spirits—a mysterious fluid—passed along nerves to all regions of the body. Although this concept did not advance our understanding of the nervous system, Galen provided interesting drawings of the organization of the brain. His assessment of the behavioral changes produced

by injuries to the heads of gladiators also drew attention to the brain as the controller of behavior.

Renaissance Scientists Began to Understand Brain Anatomy and Physiology

The eminent Renaissance painter and scientist Leonardo da Vinci (1452–1519) studied the workings of the human body and laid the foundations of anatomical drawing. He especially pioneered in providing views from different angles and cross-sectional representations. His artistic renditions of the body included portraits of the nerves in the arm and the fluid-filled ventricles of the brain (Figure 1.12). Descriptions of the brain by Renaissance anatomists emphasized the shape and appearance of the external surfaces of the brain, since these were the parts that were easiest to see when the skull was removed. It was immediately apparent to anyone who looked that the brain has an extraordinarily strange shape. The complexity of its visible form led to the use of an elaborate, precise vocabulary to label different regions.

In 1633, René Descartes (1596–1650) wrote an influential book (*De homine* [*On Man*]), in which he tried to explain how the behavior of animals, and to some extent of humans, could be like the workings of a machine. In addition to tackling other topics, Descartes pro-

1.13 An Early Account of Reflexes
In this depiction of an explanation by Descartes, when a person's toe touches fire, the heat causes nervous activity to flow up the nerve to the brain. There, the nervous activity is "reflected" back down to the leg muscles, which contract, pulling the foot away from the fire; the idea of activity being reflected back is what gave rise to the word "reflex." In Descartes's time, the difference between sensory and motor nerves had not yet been discovered, nor was it known that nerve fibers normally conduct in only one direction. Nevertheless, Descartes promoted thinking about bodily processes in scientific terms, and this focus led to steadily more accurate knowledge and concepts.

posed the concept of spinal reflexes and a neural pathway for them (Figure 1.13). Attempting to relate the mind to the body, he suggested that the two come into contact in the pineal gland, located within the brain. His reasons for suggesting the pineal gland were these: (1) Whereas most brain structures are double, located symmetrically in the two hemispheres, the pineal gland is single, like consciousness. (2) Descartes believed, erroneously, that the pineal gland exists only in humans and not in animals. Although this aspect of his reasoning did not hold up, Descartes did pose clearly problems of relations between mind and brain that later thinkers and investigators have continued to tackle.

As Descartes was preparing to publish his book, he learned that the Vatican had forced Galileo to renounce his teaching that Earth revolves around the sun, threatening to execute him if he did not recant. Fearful that his own speculations about mind and body could also incur the wrath of the church, Descartes withheld his book from publication, and it did not appear until 1662, after his death. Descartes believed that if people were nothing more than intricate machines, they could have about as much free will as a pocket watch and no opportunity to make

the moral choices that were so important to the church. He asserted that humans, at least, had a nonmaterial soul as well as a material body. This notion of **dualism** spread widely, and left other philosophers with the task of determining how a nonmaterial soul could exert influence over a material body and brain. Biological psychologists reject dualism and insist that all the workings of the mind can also, in theory, be understood as a purely physical process in the material world, specifically in the brain.

The Concept of Localization of Function Arose in the Nineteenth Century

Only in the nineteenth and twentieth centuries did educated people in the Western world finally accept the brain as the organ that coordinates and controls behavior. A popular notion of the nineteenth century, called **phrenology**, held that the cerebral cortex consisted of separate functional areas, or "organs," and that each organ was responsible for a behavioral faculty; faculties were qualities such as love of family, perception of color, or curiosity (Figure 1.14). Investigators assigned functions to brain regions by observing the behavior of individuals and noting, from

1.14 A Phrenological Head
In the early nineteenth century, certain "faculties," such as skill at mathematics or a tendency toward aggression, were believed to be directly associated with particular brain regions. Phrenologists used diagrams like this one to measure bumps on the skull, which they took as an indication of how fully developed each brain region was in an individual, and hence how fully that person should display particular qualities.

the shape of the skull, which underlying regions of the brain were more or less developed. The assignment of faculties to regions of the brain was arbitrary, but most opponents of the idea rejected the entire concept of localization of brain function; they insisted that the brain, like the mind, functions as a whole. Thus, one camp proclaimed the localization of function, and the opposing camp supported the unity of brain function. And since neither side had very strong evidence, debates on this question continued into the twentieth century.

Competing hypotheses

In the 1860s the French surgeon Paul Broca (1824–1880) engaged in heated discussions about the relation between language and the brain. He argued against formidable critics that language ability was not a property of the entire brain but rather was localized in a restricted brain region. The theme that psychological functions could be localized in specific brain regions was strongly advanced when Broca presented a postmortem analysis of a patient who had been unable to talk for several years.

The findings of the autopsy of the brain conducted by Broca revealed destruction of a region within the frontal portions of the brain on the left side—a region now known as *Broca's area*. The study of additional patients further convinced Broca that language expression was mediated by a specific brain region rather than reflecting the activities of the entire brain.

These nineteenth-century observations form the background for a continuing theme of research in biological psychology—notably the search for distinguishing differences among brain regions on the basis of their structure, and the effort to relate different

---

BOX 1.2   *Is Bigger Better? The Case of the Brain and Intelligence*

*D*oes a bigger brain indicate greater intelligence? This question has been the subject of lively controversy for at least two centuries. Sir Francis Galton (1822–1911), the scientist who invented the correlation coefficient, stated that the greatest disappointment in his life was his failure to find a significant relationship between head size and intelligence. But Galton didn't have the proper tools to conduct this investigation. He had to use head size (Figure A) when he really wanted to measure brain size. In addition, at the time he undertook this study, there were no good measures of intelligence. Galton had to rely on teachers' estimates of their students' intelligence, and every student knows that teachers can be quite wrong. Other investigators in the nineteenth century measured the volumes of skulls of various groups and estimated intelligence on the basis of occupations or other doubtful criteria.

The development and standardization of intelligence tests in the twentieth century provided invaluable help for one side of the question, but until recently, measures of head size still had to be used to estimate brain size for any sample of living subjects. Such studies usually showed positive but small correlations between

(A) A nineteetnth-century apparatus for head measurement

brain size and intelligence. In one review of several such studies, the correlations ranged from +0.08 to +0.22 (van Valen, 1974). The reviewer estimated that, allowing for errors in estimation of brain size and in measurement of intelligence, the true correlation between brain size and intelligence might be as high as +0.30.

The invention of noninvasive techniques to visualize and measure the brains of living subjects has made possible a direct approach to the question of relations between brain size and intelligence. A team of psychologists and other neuroscientists (Willerman et al., 1991) undertook a direct study in which they selected college students with no history of neurological problems and whose intelligence test scores were either high (IQ >130) or average (IQ <103). By excluding students with a middle range of IQ scores, the investigators wanted to increase the possibility of find-kinds of behavior to different brain regions. An additional theme emerging from these studies is the relation of brain size to ability (Box 1.2). Nineteenth-century anatomy included microscopic studies of sections of the brain. These studies revealed for the first time the shapes, sizes, and identity of nerve cells of the brain (Figure 1.15).

In 1890, *Principles of Psychology,* by William James, signaled the beginnings of a modern biological psychology. The strength of the ideas described in this book is evident by the continuing frequent citation of the work, especially by contemporary cognitive neuroscientists. In James's work, psychological ideas such as consciousness and other aspects of human experience came to be seen as properties of the nervous system, and a more complete understanding of psychological phenomena was to be achieved by the study of the nervous system. A true biological psychology began to emerge from this approach.

Modern Biological Psychology Arose in the Twentieth Century

The end of the nineteenth century and the start of the twentieth brought many important developments for biological psychology. German psychologist Hermann Ebbinghaus had shown in 1885 how to measure learning and memory in humans. In 1898, American psychologist Edward L. Thorndike showed in his doctoral thesis how to measure learning and memory in animal subjects. Early in the twentieth century, Russian physiologist Ivan P. Pavlov announced research in his laboratory on the conditioned reflex in animals.

American psychologist Shepard I. Franz (1902) sought the site of learning and memory in the brain,

ing a relationship between IQ and brain size. Brain size was measured for each student by magnetic resonance imaging (MRI). Any influence of body size on brain size was removed statistically so that it could not affect the final results. The overall result was a highly significant correlation coefficient, 0.51, with no significant difference between values for men and women. Since this correlation was probably increased by the selection for high or average IQ, the investigators applied a statistical correction and estimated that the correlation would be about 0.35 for a more representative sample.

Another independent study with normal adult subjects has borne this conclusion out (Andreasen et al., 1993). In this second study, 67 normal adult subjects were recruited through newspaper advertising and screened for neurological or psychiatric disorders, then given IQ tests. MRI scans such as those shown in Figure B were used for accurate measurement of the size of different brain regions. After correction for body size, the correlation between brain size and IQ scores was 0.38. Thus, on the basis of modern techniques, the long-standing controversy appears to have been settled in favor of a significant correlation between brain size and intelligence. Note, however, that the modest size of the correlation, while highly significant, still allows for many additional important factors as determinants of intelligence.

Historically, scientists have often misused information about brain size in racially or ethnically prejudicial ways (Gould, 1981). In fact, however, all racial groups show overlapping and widely varying brain size. (Figure A from the Bettmann Archive; Figure B courtesy of Nancy Andreasen.)

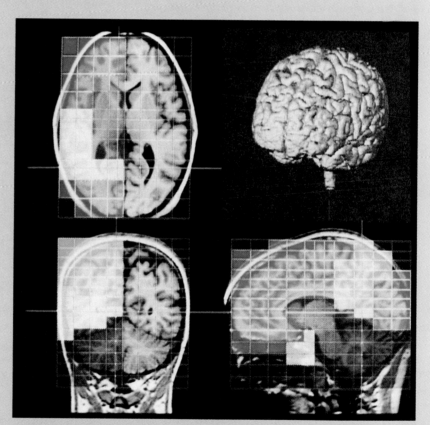

(B) Images from a modern brain measurement study

1.15 A Nineteenth-Century Anatomist's Look at Nerve Cells
These drawings of brain cells, still cited today, were made by the great Spanish anatomist Santiago Ramón y Cajal (1852–1934) on the basis of his careful observations with the microscope.

combining Thorndike's training procedures with localized brain lesions in animal subjects. This work

Karl S. Lashley
(1890–1958)

started a search for the traces of experience in the brain—a quest that Karl S. Lashley (1890–1958) referred to as the "search for the engram." Lashley studied with Franz and took over the problem of investigating the locations and mechanisms of memory functions in the brain. His approach was primarily anatomical, and he focused on assessing the behavioral effects of brain lesions. In a long career, Lashley contributed many important findings and trained many students to study the biological mechanisms not only of learning and memory, but also of perception and motivation (R. F. Thompson, 1992).

Current biological psychology bears the strong imprint of Canadian psychologist Donald O. Hebb (1904–1985), a student of Lashley. By the 1940s, electrophysiological studies of the nervous system had begun to offer tantalizing pictures of an incessantly active brain. In his book *The Organization of Behavior* (1949), Hebb showed in principle how complex cognitive behavior could be accomplished by networks of active neurons. He suggested how brain cell connections that are initially more or less random could become organized by sensory input and stimulation into

strongly interconnected groups that he called cell assemblies. His hypothesis about how neurons strengthen their connections through use became known as the *Hebbian synapse*, a topic much studied by current neuroscientists (see Chapters 17 and 18). Brief accounts of Hebb's career and contributions have been written by Peter Milner (1992, 1993).

National Data Banks and Brain Mapping Are the Foci of Contemporary Research

Within a relatively short time, neuroscientists throughout the world have amassed an enormous amount of data about how nervous systems work. This data explosion extends from the level of molecular details to the complexity of behaviors such as memory and emotions. New techniques, such as those that help identify genetic mechanisms and nervous system functioning, promise to add many more important pieces in the puzzle of the brain. Committees of neuroscientists have advocated the establishment of a major national project that wouldenable all these pieces discovered by individual researchers to be assembled in national computerized databases that would become a comprehensive blueprint of the brain:

> The committee recommends that the Brain Mapping Initiative be established with the long-term objective of developing three-dimensional computerized maps and models of the structure, functions, connectivity, pharmacology, and molecular biology of human, rat, and monkey brains across developmental stages and reflecting both normal and disease states. (Pechura and Martin, 1991)

These databases include the ability to relate integrated maps of the anatomy of the brain with maps of physiological activity and maps that relate to behavioral processes.

Recommended Reading

Ackerman, S. (1992). *Discovering the brain.* Washington, DC: National Academy Press.

Finger, S. (1994). *Origins of neuroscience.* New York: Oxford University Press.

Pechura, C. M., and Martin, J. B. (Eds.). (1991). *Mapping the brain and its functions.* Washington, DC: National Academy Press.

To keep in touch with progress in this field, you can find reviews and evaluations of research in the following publications:

Annual Review of Neuroscience. Palo Alto, CA: Annual Reviews.

Annual Review of Psychology. Palo Alto, CA: Annual Reviews.

Nature Neuroscience. New York: Nature America.

The Neuroscientist. Baltimore: Williams & Wilkins.

Trends in Neurosciences. Amsterdam: Elsevier.

PART

1

Biological Foundations of Behavior

Within your head is an information processing system, the brain, that contains at least 100 billion nerve cells. These cells are connected to one another in extremely varied and elaborate patterns. A single cell may receive connections from thousands of others. The essence of our identity is locked up in the character of these brain connections. An extensive web of nerve fibers connects the brain to every part of the body, monitoring, regulating, and modulating the functions of every bodily structure and system. The workings of this vast assembly make possible our perceptions, thoughts, movements, motives, and feelings.

Our first objective in this section is to describe the basic structures of the adult human brain—structures we share with all other humans (Chapter 2). In Chapter 3 we will discuss the electrical signals that a neuron uses to integrate information, and the chemical signals that a neuron uses to transmit information to other cells, including other neurons. Chapter 4 is devoted to a greater understanding of the chemical signals that, among other things, help us understand how drugs affect behavior. Other chemical signals are released into the bloodstream to affect neurons and other cells, and therefore behavior. These chemical signals, called hormones, are the subject of Chapter 5.

2 Functional Neuroanatomy: The Nervous System and Behavior

Collection of Whitney Museum of American Art, gift of Lincoln Kirstein.
Photograph by Jerry L. Thompson ©1966 by Whitney Museum of American Art

Pavel Tchelitchew, *Anatomical Painting*, 1946

Thoughts, feelings, perceptions, and acts—all are products of the workings of the human brain. These accomplishments depend on the architecture of the brain and the way it works. In this chapter we will discuss the structural character of the brain. The basic ways in which these structures work will be taken up in Chapters 3, 4, and 5, when we discuss electrical signals in neurons, chemical signals between neurons, and hormonal signals between the nervous system and the rest of the body.

To understand the structure of the brain we have to consider its components and the extensive network of linkages among them. These paths and circuits form the anatomical basis for information processing. This structure is a highly precise arrangement of parts; our efforts to achieve a biological understanding of behavior must start with an appreciation of the basic units of the brain, their connections, and their arrangements into networks that process information. We will try to relate the details of the architecture of the nervous system that are especially important for subsequent chapters.

On a Small Scale, the Nervous System Is Composed of Cells

In any animal, the nervous system extends throughout the body; every organ is connected to the brain. The building blocks of the entire nervous system are cells, the most important of which are the **nerve cells**, or **neurons**. Each human being has about 100 billion to 150 billion neurons; the assemblies of these building blocks into circuits are what underlie the simplest and the most complex of our abilities and talents. Each neuron receives inputs from many other nerve cells and distributes information to many other nerve cells. The integration and analysis of information are primary operations of the brain. After discussing these operations at the cellular level, we will turn to a large-scale view.

The Neuron Doctrine Defines Neurons and Their Connections

In the late nineteenth century, anatomists sought to understand the differences between human and animal brains by making microscopic studies of brain cells. They used distinctive dyes or stains that highlighted particular elements of the brain and showed that brains contain a large assembly of oddly shaped neurons (Figure 2.1). Unlike other organs, the brain exhibits an extraordinary range of variation in cell shape.

Some nineteenth-century anatomists thought that neurons were continuous with one another, forming a nearly endless series of interconnected tubes. According to this view, information in the nervous system was carried through continuous channels. However, the bril-

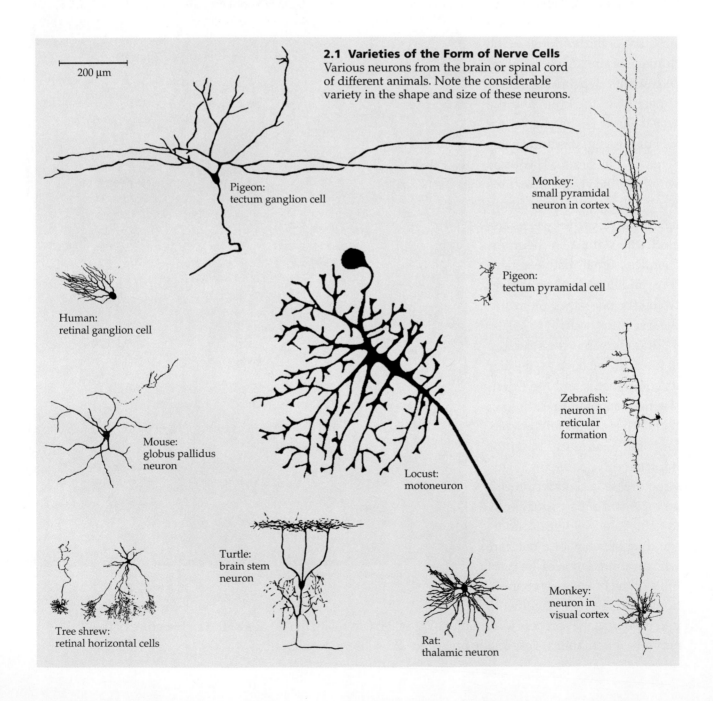

2.1 Varieties of the Form of Nerve Cells
Various neurons from the brain or spinal cord of different animals. Note the considerable variety in the shape and size of these neurons.

200 μm

Pigeon: tectum ganglion cell

Monkey: small pyramidal neuron in cortex

Human: retinal ganglion cell

Pigeon: tectum pyramidal cell

Mouse: globus pallidus neuron

Zebrafish: neuron in reticular formation

Locust: motoneuron

Turtle: brain stem neuron

Tree shrew: retinal horizontal cells

Rat: thalamic neuron

Monkey: neuron in visual cortex

Santiago Ramón y Cajal
(1852–1934)

liant Spanish anatomist Santiago Ramón y Cajal offered a convincing alternative. He presented elegant studies of nerve cells and patiently drew portraits of neurons that continue to be cited today (see Figure 1.15). Ramón y Cajal was convinced that although neurons come very close to one another (i.e., they are *contiguous*), they are not quite *continuous* with one another. He insisted that at each point of contact between neurons is a tiny gap that keeps the cells separate.

From these studies emerged a new perspective—the **neuron doctrine**. According to this doctrine, (1) the brain is composed of separate neurons and other cells that are independent structurally, metabolically, and functionally; and (2) information is transmitted from cell to cell across tiny gaps, which were later named **synapses**. By the 1950s, the high-resolution abilities of the electron microscope had fully confirmed the neuron doctrine. Nerve cells are indeed separate from each other.

Cells of another important class in the nervous system are the **glial cells** (also sometimes called glia or neuroglia). Because neurons are generally larger and they produce readily measured electrical signals, we know much more about them than about glial cells. Because we know for certain that neurons integrate information, we will be concerned mainly with neurons in this book. After describing neurons here, however, we will discuss some of the main types of glial cells and their known functions.

There Are Many Types of Nerve Cells

Neurons are remarkably diverse in shape; at least 200 geometrically distinguishable types of nerve cells are found in the brains of mammals (for some examples, see Figure 2.1). These cells are distinguished on the basis of size and shape. These differences in size and shape have implications for the ways in which neurons process and transmit information. Nerve cells are not simple relays that transmit the same information they receive. Rather, the typical neuron collects signals from several sources, integrates the information, transforms it, changes it into complex output signals, and distributes these signals to many other cells. The ways in which information is represented and processed in the nervous system are determined by the interactions of nerve cells.

Although this structural diversity vastly complicates our task in describing nerve cells, some features are common to all nerve cells. Most neurons have three distinct structural parts that are directly related to the functional properties of the cell: (1) a **cell body** region, which is defined by the presence of the nucleus; (2) extensions of the cell body called **dendrites**

(from the Greek *dendron*, "tree"), which vastly increase the receptive surface of the neuron; and (3) a single extension of another type, the **axon**. These three parts are illustrated in Figures 2.2 and 2.3.

In many neurons the axon is only a few micrometers long, but in spinal sensory and motor neurons, it can reach more than a meter in length.* For example, the giraffe has axons that are an incredible several meters long. In order for you to wiggle your toes, individual axons must carry the instructions from the spinal cord to muscles in your foot. Long fibers of sensory neurons then carry messages back to the spinal cord.

The ability to see and measure nerve cells and trace their connections is vital to solving many problems in biological psychology and neuroscience. A few of these problems are: How do neurons grow and make connections during individual development? In what ways do the nervous systems of men and women differ? What differences in nerve cells and their connections characterize Alzheimer's disease? How do nerve cells change as a consequence of learning? What changes in neurons and their connections permit recovery of function after damage to the nervous system?

Although answers to these questions depend on our ability to study nerve cells, neurons are difficult to examine and measure for several reasons. First, they are small, and their extensions (dendrites and axons) are even smaller (1 to 3 μm in diameter). Furthermore, if you cut a thin slice of brain tissue and look at it under a microscope, it is hard to see any brain cells, because they don't contrast with surrounding areas. The ability to see details of cells requires special chemical agents to make cells or parts of cells stand out from the background. Box 2.1 describes some techniques for visualizing neurons, as well as some methods used to trace pathways in the nervous system.

Important method

Neurons Can Be Classified by Shape, Size, or Function

Anatomists use the shapes of cell bodies, dendrites, and axons to classify the many varieties of nerve cells into three principal types: multipolar, bipolar, and monopolar neurons. These different types of neurons are specialized for particular kinds of interactions. **Multipolar neurons** are nerve cells that have many dendrites and a single axon (Figure 2.3a). Most of the neurons of the vertebrate brain are multipolar. **Bipolar neurons** have a single dendrite at one end of the cell

---

* The meter (m), the unit of length in the metric system, equals 39.37 inches. A centimeter (cm) is one-hundredth of a meter (10^{-2} m); a millimeter (mm) is one-thousandth of a meter (10^{-3} m); a micrometer, or micron (μm), is one-millionth of a meter (10^{-6} m); and a nanometer (nm) is one-billionth of a meter (10^{-9} m).

Dendrites

Cell body

Nucleus

Axon

Dendritic
spines

Axon
terminals

2.2 Typical Nerve Cells with Their Major Components
Many axon terminals contact dendritic spines; others contact dendrites directly.
Note that the many dendritic spines shown here would probably be occupied by
an axon terminal, but for clarity they have been left empty.

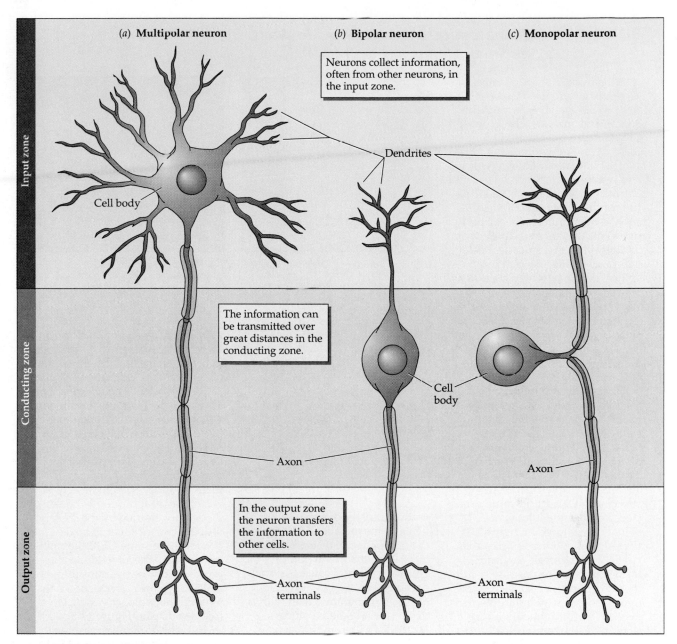

Input zone

Conducting zone

Output zone

(a) **Multipolar neuron**   (b) **Bipolar neuron**   (c) **Monopolar neuron**

Neurons collect information, often from other neurons, in the input zone.

Dendrites

Cell body

The information can be transmitted over great distances in the conducting zone.

Cell body

Axon

Axon

In the output zone the neuron transfers the information to other cells.

Axon terminals

Axon terminals

2.3 A Classification of Neurons into Three Principal Types

(a) Multipolar neurons have many dendrites extending from the cell body, and a single axon. (b) Bipolar neurons have a single dendrite extending from the cell body, and a single axon. (c) Monopolar neurons have a single branch that emerges from the cell body and extends in two directions.

and a single axon at the other end (Figure 2.3b). This type of nerve cell is found in some sensory systems, including the retina and the olfactory (smell) system. **Monopolar neurons** have a single branch (usually thought of as an axon) that, after leaving the cell body, extends in two directions (Figure 2.3c). One end is the receptive pole (the input zone), the other the output zone. Such cells transmit touch information from the

body into the spinal cord. In all three types of neurons, the dendrites are the input zone, and in multipolar cells, the cell body is also part of the input zone.

Another common way of classifying nerve cells is by size. Examples of small nerve cells are the types called granule ("grain"), spindle, and stellate ("star-shaped"). Large cells include the types called pyramidal, Golgi type I, and Purkinje. Each region of the brain is a collection of both large and small neurons. Vertebrate nerve cell bodies range from as small as 10 μm to as large as 100 μm in diameter.

A third simple classification of neurons is by function. Some neurons send their axon to a muscle or gland, and the job of these neurons is to make the muscle contract or to change the activity of the gland. Such neurons are called **motoneurons** (or motor neu-

BOX 2.1 *Neuroanatomical Methods Provide Ways to See Small Things in the Brain*

*I*n the middle of the nineteenth century, dyes used to color fabrics provided a breakthrough in anatomical analysis. Dead, preserved nerve cells treated with these dyes, known in histology as stains, suddenly become vivid, and hidden parts become evident. Different dyes have special affinities for different parts of the cell, such as membranes, the cell body, or the sheaths surrounding axons.

Golgi stains outline the full cell, including details like dendritic spines (Figure A). Golgi staining is often used to characterize the variety of cell types in a region. For reasons that remain a mystery, this technique stains only a small number of cells, each of which stands out in dramatic contrast to adjacent unstained cells.

Nissl stains outline all cell bodies because the dyes are attracted to RNA, which encircles the nucleus. Nissl stains allow us to measure cell body size and the density of cells in particular regions (Figure B). Other stains are absorbed by myelin, the fatty sheaths that surround some axons (see, for example, the sections of spinal cord shown in Figure 2.11). Exposing slices of brain tissue to particular chemicals can transform some neurotransmitters into fluorescent chemicals. Nerve cells treated in this way light up when exposed to ultraviolet light. Injecting fluorescent molecules directly into a neuron provides a Golgi-like view of its dendrites (Figure C).

Some histological techniques can reveal aspects of the dynamic

(A) Golgi stain

(B) Nissl stain

(C) Neuron injected with fluorescent dye

neurochemistry of nerve cells, particularly the metabolic processes of the cell. Cells can be manipulated into taking their own photograph—a method called **autoradiography**. For example, we might inject a living animal with radioactively labeled **2-deoxyglucose (2-DG)**. 2-DG resembles glucose enough that active cells take it up more readily than inactive cells do. But once the 2-DG is inside, it cannot be broken down, so it just sits inside even the most active neu-

rons. To create an autoradiogram, the experimenter presents the animal with a stimulus condition that results in neural activity while the 2-DG is injected. The neurons that are active during that stimulus will take up more of the radioactive 2-DG than will the inactive neurons. The experimenters then sacrifice the animal, cut thin sections of brain tissue, and place them on slides, which they cover with photographic emulsion. Radioactivity emitted by the 2-DG in the cells causes silver to be deposited—the same effect that light has on film. The silver deposition produces fine dark grains immediately above the active neurons that took up the radioactive substance (see Box 5.1 and Figure 14.3).

Improved microscopes have also broadened our understanding of the fine structure of cells. Observations using routine forms of light microscopy provide detailed resolution down to about

rons). Other neurons are directly affected by changes in the environment; they respond to light, a particular odor, or touch. These cells are **sensory neurons**. The remaining neurons, which constitute the vast majority, receive input from and send their output to other neurons. Thus they are called **interneurons**.

The Neuronal Cell Body and Dendrites Receive Information across Synapses

The diversity of neuronal shapes arises especially from the variation in the form and shape of den-

drites, the extensions that arise from the nerve cell body and branch out in highly complex ways (see Figure 2.1). The shape of the dendritic tree—the full arrangement of dendrites of a single cell—provides clues about the information processing of a particular cell. All along the surface of the dendrite are many contacts, the synapses. Most neurons receive thosands of synapses. Through the synapses information is transmitted from one neuron to the next. A synapse, or synaptic region, has three principal components (Figure 2.4):

1 to 2 μm. Smaller objects fail to deflect light particles (photons), so they cannot be detected with light. But because electrons are even smaller than photons, electron microscopy extends a hundredfold the range of structures that can be visualized, making it possible to see some of the smallest details within cells (e.g., see Figures 2.4, 2.6, and 2.7). All these forms of microscopic study are now being coupled with computers to provide rapid, automatic, quantitative assessment of particular aspects of nerve cells, such as dendrite length.

Another approach to the marking of cells of the brain is to apply immunological techniques. These techniques allow neuroanatomists to mark groups of cells that have an attribute in common, such as particular membrane components or particular proteins within a cell. This approach, known as **immunocytochemistry** because it uses immune system molecules (antibodies) to detect cells (the Greek *kytos*, from which we get the prefix "cyto-," means "hollow vessel"; "cyto-" is used to mean "cells"), is described in detail in the Appendix. Because neurons often produce distinctive proteins (immediate early gene products) when active, immunocytochemistry for those proteins is quickly replacing 2-DG as a means of determining which neurons are active during a particular behavior.

Tracing Pathways in the Brain

The cells of the brain are interconnected through a complex web of pathways. Understanding the circuits formed by these cells and their extensions required the development of techniques that clearly outline the terminals of particular cell groups or show the cells of origin of particular axon tracts. Tracing pathways in the nervous system is difficult for several reasons: (1) Axons have an even smaller diameter than cell bodies have; (2) axons from different sources look alike; and (3) fibers with different destinations often travel together over parts of their routes, making it hard to disentangle one set from the rest. Although at first glance this task of tracing neural pathways seems insurmountable—remember, our brain contains billions of neurons—anatomists were not daunted.

Classical anatomical techniques for tracing pathways rely on visualizing the products of degenerating axons. First, the cell bodies of origin are surgically damaged. Within a few days the axons of the cells begin to degenerate, and during this phase they are especially likely to accumulate silver salts. When the dying axons are exposed to silver compounds, they acquire a dark brownish black color. Examining a series of sections for the presence of such marked axons makes it possible to trace a pathway over some distance. Newer procedures accomplish the same goal by the injection of radioactively labeled amino acids into a collection of cell bodies. These radioactive molecules are taken up by the cell, incorporated into proteins, and transported to the tips of the axons. Brain sections are then coated with a sensitive emulsion as a film would be. After some time (which ranges from hours to weeks), the slides are developed and stained. If the pathway originates in the area of the injected cells, developed silver grains will be located in axons and their terminals, making the whole pathway visible.

(D) HRP-filled motoneuron

A more recent, powerful technique to determine the cells of origin of a particular set of axons employs **horseradish peroxidase** (**HRP**), an enzyme found in the roots of horseradish and many other plants. HRP catalyzes certain chemical reactions that leave a visible reaction product of dark granules. HRP acts as a tracer of pathways because it is taken up into the axon at the terminals and transported back to the cell body. After HRP is injected into one part of the nervous system, any neurons that have axon terminals there will transport the HRP back to the cell body, which can be made visible with chemical reactions (Figure D). All along the way visible reaction products are formed—akin to footprints along a pathway. (Figure A courtesy of Timothy DeVoogd; Figure C courtesy of Carla Shatz; Figure D courtesy of Dale Sengelaub.)

---

1. the **presynaptic zone**, in many instances a swelling of the axon terminal called the **synaptic bouton** ("button")
2. a specialized **postsynaptic membrane** in the surface of the dendrite or cell body
3. a **synaptic cleft**—that is, a space between the presynaptic and postsynaptic elements—which measures about 20 to 40 nm.

Detailed electron microscopic examination of the presynaptic terminal shows that it contains many small spheres, called **synaptic vesicles**. They range in size from 30 to 140 nm. These vesicles contain a chemical substance that can be released into the synaptic cleft, and this release is triggered by electrical activity in the axon. The released chemical, called a **synaptic transmitter**, or **neurotransmitter**, flows across the cleft and produces electrical changes in the postsynaptic membrane. Many different transmitters have been identified in the brain, including acetylcholine, dopamine, and glutamate, but many more remain to be discovered.

(a) Presynaptic neuron

Postsynaptic neuron

Axon hillock

Dendritic spines

Presynaptic terminal (bouton)

Mitochondrion

Synaptic vesicles

Synaptic cleft

Postsynaptic spine

Flow of information

2.4 Synapses

(a) Axons typically form a synapse on the cell body or dendrites of a neuron. On dendrites, synapses may form on dendritic spines or on the shaft of a dendrite. (b) Transmission electron micrographs and (c) freeze-fractured scanning electron micrographs provide different view of the fine structure of synapses; the colors correspond to the drawings in Part a. (Micrographs from Peters et al., 1991.)

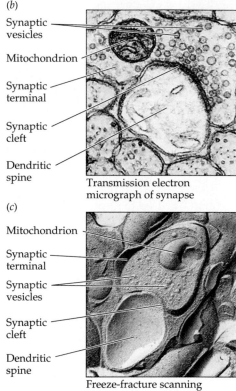

(b)
Synaptic vesicles
Mitochondrion
Synaptic terminal
Synaptic cleft
Dendritic spine

Transmission electron micrograph of synapse

(c)
Mitochondrion
Synaptic terminal
Synaptic vesicles
Synaptic cleft
Dendritic spine

Freeze-fracture scanning electron micrograph of synapse

The electrical changes in the postsynaptic membrane determine whether the postsynaptic cell will be excited or inhibited. The surface of the postsynaptic membrane is different from adjacent regions of the membrane. It contains special **receptor molecules** (often referred to simply as receptors) that capture and react to molecules of the transmitter agent (see Figure 1.5). Numerous synapses cover the surfaces of dendrites and of the cell body. This number is possible because these synaptic junctions are very small—less than 1 μm^2 each. Some individual cells of the brain have as many as 100,000 synapses, although the more common number for larger cells is around 5000 to 10,000. Synaptic contacts are particularly numerous in nerve cells that have elaborate dendrites.

Along the dendrites on many nerve cells of the brain are outgrowths called **dendritic spines** or thorns (see Figures 2.2 and 2.4). These spines give some dendrites a rough or corrugated surface. They have become the focus of considerable attention, because their structural appearance and function may be modified by experience (see Chapter 18). In some cases they seem to change shape within seconds (Fischer et al., 1998). Both the size and number of dendritic spines are affected by various treatments of an animal, such as training or exposure to sensory stimuli.

Neural plasticity

The Axon Is a Specialized Output Zone

A typical axon has several regions that are structurally and functionally distinguishable (see Figure 2.3). In multipolar neurons the axon originates out of the cell body from a cone-shaped region called the **axon hillock** (see Figure 2.4a). The electrical impulse that carries the message of each neuron to other neurons begins in the axon hillock and travels down the axon (see Chapter 3). The axon beyond the hillock is tubular, with a diameter ranging from 0.5 to 20 μm in mammals and as large as 500 μm in the "giant" axons of some invertebrates.

With very few exceptions, nerve cells have only one axon. But axons often divide into several branches, called **axon collaterals**. Because of this branching, a single nerve cell can exert influence over a wide array of other cells. Toward its ending, an axon or a collateral typically divides into numerous branches of fine diameter. At the ends of the branches (the **axon ter-**

minals), specialized structures form the synapse, the connection to the next cell. By synapsing on this target, the axon terminals are said to **innervate** (or supply neural input to) the cell. Table 2.1 compares the main structural features of axons and dendrites.

A pair of terms are used to describe axons, always in relation to a particular brain region or structure under discussion. Axons carrying information into the region are said to be **afferents**. Axons carrying information away from the brain region are called **efferents**. Every axon can be described as either an efferent from the region containing its cell body, or an afferent to the target it innervates. Most often the structure under discussion is the brain, so if you read "afferents" without any qualification, you may assume that these are axons bringing information into the brain. Similarly, unless the context provides another structure as a reference point, "efferents" refers to axons carrying commands from the brain out to the body.

The cell body manufactures proteins under the guidance of DNA in the cell nucleus (see the Appendix). Therefore proteins needed for growth and function must be transported from the cell body to distant regions in the axon. The movement of materials within the axon is referred to as **axonal transport** (Figure 2.5). Some molecules are transported along axons at a "slow" rate (1 to 3 mm per day); others are transported by a "fast" system (400 mm per day). How do substances move in axons? Investigators have observed structures in axons referred to as **microtubules** (20 to 26 nm in diameter) that look like hollow cylinders (see Figure 2.5b). There are also systems of smaller rods (10 nm in diameter) called **neurofilaments** (found only in neurons). Smaller yet are **microfilaments** (7 nm in diameter), which are found in all cells. These three molecules determine the shape of a cell, but evidence suggests that they are also involved in axonal transport. At least three types of proteins have been identified that are part of the "motor" mechanism that moves substances in conjunction with microtubules (Amos and Cross, 1997; Schnapp, 1997).

Glial Cells Support Neural Activity

Glial cells are named after the original conception of their function—that they serve as something like glue (the Greek *glia* means "glue"). Clearly, structural support—or some aspects of it—is one biological role of glial cells. Glial cells may also serve a nutritive role, providing a pathway from the vascular system to the nerve cells for delivering raw materials that neurons use to synthesize complex compounds. Unlike nerve cells, glial cells are produced throughout our lifetime. Although many aspects of the functional roles of glial cells remain a puzzle, we do know some things—and there are many other interesting ideas—about their function.

There are four classes of glial cells. One type, called an **astrocyte** (from the Greek *astra*, "star"), is a star-shaped cell with numerous extensions (or processes) in all directions (Figure 2.6a). Some astrocytes form end feet on the blood vessels of the brain. These end feet look as though they are attached to the vessels by suckerlike extensions. Extensions of astrocytes form the tough sheets that wrap around the outer surface of the brain, the dura mater. Bundles of astrocyte extensions interweave among nerve fibers, as though giving structural support. Astrocytes may also contribute to the metabolism of synaptic transmitters and may regulate the balance of ions. In addition, astrocytes release growth factors, proteins that are important in the growth and repair of nerve cells.

A second type of glial cell is the **microglial cell**. As the name suggests, microglial cells are very small. They migrate in large numbers to sites of injury or disease in the nervous system, apparently to remove debris from injured or dead cells.

The third and fourth types of glial cells—oligodendrocytes and Schwann cells—perform a vital function for nerve cells, as the next section describes.

Some Glial Cells Wrap around Axons, Forming Myelin Sheaths

Wrapped around most axons are sheaths, which are called **myelin** (Figure 2.6b), formed by nearby glial cells. The process of production of this wrapping is called **myelination**. This sheathing affects the speed of conduction of neural impulses. Anything that interferes with the myelin sheath can have catastrophic consequences for the individual, as is evident in various demyelinating diseases, such as multiple sclerosis, which is caused by loss of myelin on the axons of the brain.

Within the brain and spinal cord, the myelin sheath is formed by a type of glial cell called an **oligodendrocyte** (Figure 2.6b).

TABLE 2.1 *Distinctions between Axons and Dendrites*

Axons	Dendrites
Usually one per neuron, with many terminal branches	Usually many per neuron
Uniform diameter until start of terminal branching	Diameter tapers progressively toward its ending
Join cell body at a distinct region called the axon hillock	No hillocklike region
Usually covered with myelin	No myelin covering
Lengths from practically non-existent to several meters	Usually much shorter than axons
Along length, branches tend to be perpendicular	Along dendrites, branches occur over wide range of acute angles

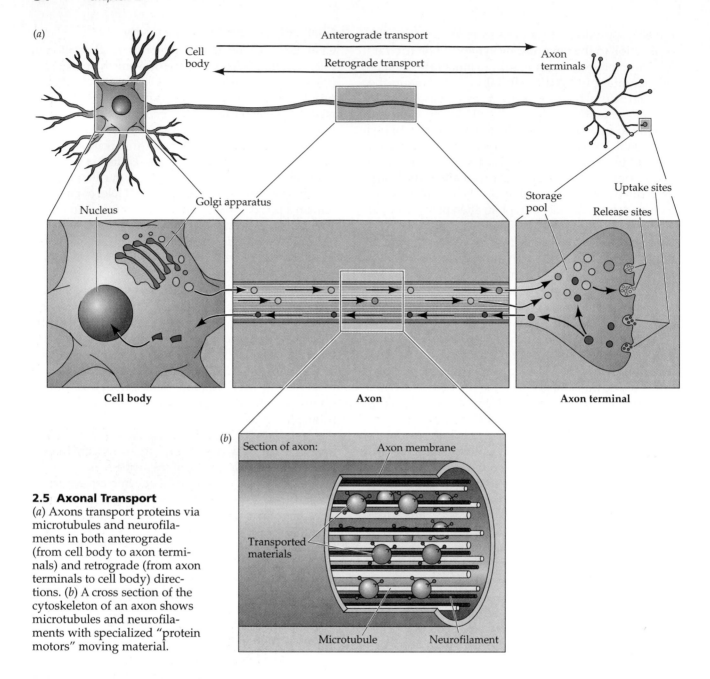

(a)

Cell body   Anterograde transport   Axon terminals
Retrograde transport

Nucleus   Golgi apparatus   Storage pool   Uptake sites   Release sites

Cell body   **Axon**   **Axon terminal**

(b) Section of axon: Axon membrane

Transported materials

Microtubule   Neurofilament

2.5 Axonal Transport

(*a*) Axons transport proteins via microtubules and neurofilaments in both anterograde (from cell body to axon terminals) and retrograde (from axon terminals to cell body) directions. (*b*) A cross section of the cytoskeleton of an axon shows microtubules and neurofilaments with specialized "protein motors" moving material.

This cell is much smaller than an astrocyte and has fewer extensions (the Greek *oligos* means "few"). The myelination provided by oligodendrocytes continues for extended periods of time in human beings—in some brain regions up to 10 to 15 years after birth, and possibly throughout life. Oligodendrocytes are also commonly associated with nerve cell bodies, especially the bodies of larger neurons. Because of this association, they are frequently regarded as satellite cells of neurons.

For axons outside the brain and spinal cord, myelin is provided by another type of glial cell—the **Schwann cell**. A single Schwann cell produces the myelin coat for a very limited length of the axon, seldom extending more than 200 μm. Hence numerous Schwann cells are needed to myelinate the length of a single axon.

Between the segments of myelin are small gaps in the coating. Such a gap, where the axon membrane is exposed, is called a **node of Ranvier** (see Figure 2.6*b*). The regularity of the wrapping is nicely illustrated in cross sections of the axon (see Figure 2.6*c*).

Many axons of very thin diameter have no close wrapping of myelin; they are commonly referred to as unmyelinated fibers or axons. Although these fibers do not have an elaborate coating, they still have a relationship with glial cells. Several axons become embedded in troughs of the Schwann cell, but without elaborate wrapping (Figure 2.7). The manner in which these glial cells surround neurons, especially the synaptic surfaces of neurons, suggests that one of their roles is to isolate receptive surfaces to prevent interactions among synapses by keeping various inputs segregated.

(a) **Astrocyte**

Capillary

(c)

Axon

Myelin

2.6 Types of Glial Cells

(a) A type of astrocyte—the protoplasmic astrocyte—contacts capillaries and is adjacent to nerve cell membranes. (b) Extensions or arms of oligodendrocytes form myelin wrapping (blue) on axons (yellow); four axons are shown in this view. (c) This colorized electron micrograph of a myelinated axon shows the many layers of the myelin sheath. (Micrograph from Peters et al., 1991.)

Oligodendrocytes

(b)

Axon

Myelin sheath

Nodes of Ranvier

Glial cells are of clinical interest because they form the principal tumors of the brain and spinal cord. Furthermore, some classes of glial cells, especially astrocytes, respond to brain injury by changing in size—that is, by swelling. This **edema** damages neurons and is responsible for many symptoms of brain injuries.

On a Large Scale, the Nervous System Consists of Central and Peripheral Divisions

To this point, we have described the basic building blocks of the nervous system—neurons and their synapses, and glial cells. Structural analysis in neuroscience research involves many different levels extending from these basic building blocks to features of an entire brain. These levels are analogous to the different views of a scene that a zoom lens can provide, ranging from close-up, intimate views of fine detail to a much broader view of interactions of different brain regions or the properties of the whole brain (see Figure 1.5).

In this section we will describe the human nervous system on a much larger scale, viewing the brain with the unaided eye. For this discussion you will need to understand the conventions that anatomists use for describing various viewpoints of the body and the brain. These conventions are described in Box 2.2.

2.7 Unmyelinated Axons Viewed by Electron Microscopy

Unmyelinated axons do not show the regular wrapping illustrated in Figure 2.6c. Instead they are embedded in the troughs of glial cells, and they are seen here in cross section as the light-colored circular shapes. The large dark area in the center of the photograph is the nucleus of a glial cell, the cytoplasm of which surrounds the axons. (From Peters et al., 1991.)

BOX 2.2 *Three Customary Orientations for Viewing the Brain and Body*

Because the nervous system is a three-dimensional structure, two-dimensional illustrations and diagrams cannot represent it completely. The brain is usually cut in one of three main planes to obtain a two-dimensional section from this three-dimensional object. It is useful to know the terminology and conventions that apply to these sections, which are shown in the figure.

The plane that bisects the body into right and left halves is called the **sagittal plane** (from the Latin *sagitta,* "arrow"). The plane that divides the body into a front (anterior) and a back (posterior) part is called by several names: **coro-**nal plane (from the Latin *corona,* "crown"), frontal plane, or transverse plane. By convention coronal sections are usually viewed from behind so that the right side of the figure represents the right side of the brain. The third main plane, which divides the brain into upper and lower parts, is called the **horizontal plane** and is usually viewed from above.

In addition, several directional terms are used. **Medial** means "toward the middle" and is contrasted with **lateral**, "toward the side." The head end is referred to by any of several terms: **anterior, cephalic** (from the Greek *kephale,* "head"), or **rostral** (from the Latin *rostrum,* "prow of a ship"). The tail end is called **posterior** or **caudal** (from the Latin *cauda,* "tail"). **Proximal** (from the Latin *proximus,* "nearest") means "near the trunk or center," and **distal** means "toward the periphery" or "toward the end of a limb" (distant from the origin or point of attachment).

Dorsal means "toward or at the back," and **ventral** means "toward or at the belly or front." In four-legged animals, such as the cat or the rat, "dorsal" refers to both the back of the body and the top of the head and brain. For consistency in comparing brains among species, this term is also used to refer to the top of

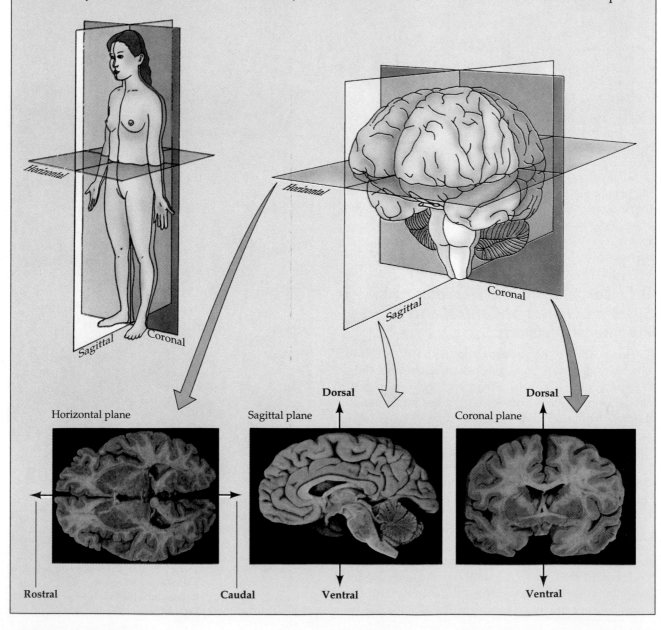

Horizontal plane

Sagittal plane

Dorsal

Ventral

Coronal plane

Dorsal

Ventral

Rostral

Caudal

the brain of a human or of a chimpanzee, even though in such two-legged animals the top of the brain is not at the back of the body. Similarly "ventral" is understood to designate the bottom of the brain of a two-legged as well as of a four-legged animal.

Although these terms may seem strange at first, they provide a means of describing anatomy without ambiguity. If you want to become adept with these terms, launch the *Sylvius* CD-ROM included in this book, or get together with a friend and quiz each oth-

er about anatomical relations. "Where's the navel? In a medial position on the ventral surface, caudal to the rib cage, and rostral to the pelvis." (Photographs courtesy of S. Mark Williams and Dale Purves, Duke University Medical Center.)

To consolidate these anatomical viewpoints, see *Sylvius*, the interactive brain atlas on the CD-ROM that accompanies this book. As you continue to read the book,

Sylvius especially the present chapter, you may wish to consult *Sylvius* for detailed views of the brain. Since the topic of this chapter is anatomy, your understanding of the text will be enhanced by using *Sylvius* throughout; however, in later chapters, the *Sylvius* icon, seen in the margin here, will be placed at points in the text where material in *Sylvius* is particularly helpful.

Figure 2.8*a* presents a view of the entire human nervous system. Examining the nervous system from this viewpoint reveals a natural subdivision into a **central nervous system (CNS)**, consisting of the brain and spinal cord (Figure 2.8*b*), and a **peripheral nervous system** (all nervous system parts that are outside the bony skull and spinal column). After

(a)

■ Central nervous system

□ Peripheral nervous system

(b)

← C1

← T1

← L1

← S1

2.8 The Central and Peripheral Nervous Systems
(*a*) This view of the nervous system is a composite of two drawings: a modern view of the central nervous system (the brain and spinal cord) is shown in blue and is superimposed on a rendering of the peripheral nervous system by the great sixteenth-century anatomist Andreas Vesalius. The peripheral nervous system courses through the body and connects all body organs and systems to the central nervous system. (*b*) The brain and spinal cord form the central nervous system. Spinal nerves are abbreviated as follows: C1, first cervical nerve; T1, first thoracic nerve; L1, first lumbar nerve; S1, first sacral nerve.

discussing the peripheral nervous system, we will turn our attention to the control center of the entire nervous system, the brain.

The Peripheral Nervous System Consists of Three Components

The peripheral nervous system consists of nerves—collections of axons bundled together—that extend throughout the body. These nerves transmit information to muscles (motor pathways) or arise from sensory surfaces (sensory pathways). Three components make up the peripheral nervous system: (1) the cranial nerves, which are connected directly to the brain; (2) the spinal nerves, which are connected at regular intervals to the spinal cord; and (3) the autonomic nervous system, which originates from both the brain

2.9 The Cranial Nerves
Bundles of axons form the 12 pairs of cranial nerves, which are conventionally referred to by the Roman numerals I through XII. This basal view of the brain (see inset for orientation) shows the cranial nerves and their primary functions.

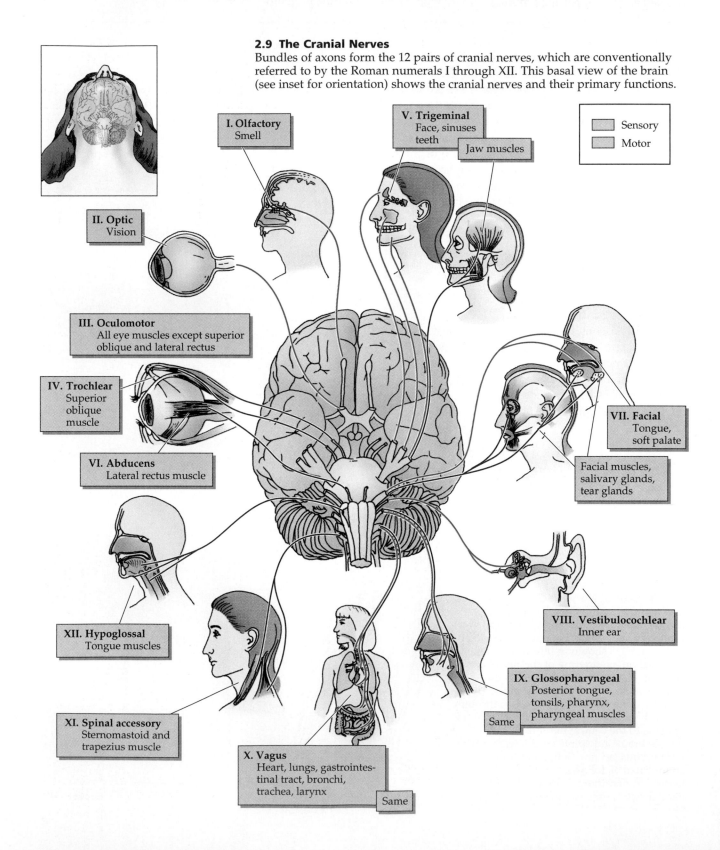

I. Olfactory
Smell

V. Trigeminal
Face, sinuses teeth

Jaw muscles

Sensory
Motor

II. Optic
Vision

III. Oculomotor
All eye muscles except superior oblique and lateral rectus

IV. Trochlear
Superior oblique muscle

VI. Abducens
Lateral rectus muscle

VII. Facial
Tongue, soft palate

Facial muscles, salivary glands, tear glands

VIII. Vestibulocochlear
Inner ear

XII. Hypoglossal
Tongue muscles

IX. Glossopharyngeal
Posterior tongue, tonsils, pharynx, pharyngeal muscles

Same

XI. Spinal accessory
Sternomastoid and trapezius muscle

X. Vagus
Heart, lungs, gastrointestinal tract, bronchi, trachea, larynx

Same

and the spinal cord. All three components inform the CNS about events in the environment and transmit commands from the CNS to the body.

The cranial nerves. The 12 pairs of **cranial nerves** in the human brain are concerned mainly with sensory and motor systems associated with the head (Figure 2.9). These nerves pass through small openings in the skull to enter or leave the brain. The cranial nerves are known both by name and by Roman numeral. Some cranial nerves are exclusively sensory pathways to the brain: the olfactory (I), optic (II), and auditory (or vestibulocochlear; VIII) nerves. Others are exclusively motor pathways from the brain: The oculomotor (III), trochlear (IV), and abducens (VI) nerves innervate (form synapses on) muscles to move the eye, the spinal accessory (XI) nerves control neck muscles, and the hypoglossal (XII) nerves control the tongue.

The remaining cranial nerves have both sensory and motor functions. The trigeminal (V), for example, serves facial sensation through some axons, but also controls chewing movements through other axons. The facial (VII) nerves control face muscles and receive taste sensation, while the glossopharyngeal (IX) nerves receive sensation from the throat and control muscles there. The vagus (X) nerve extends far from the head, running to the heart, liver, and intestines. Its long, convoluted route is the reason for its name, which is Latin for "wandering." The vagus and some other cranial nerves are also part of the parasympathetic nervous system, which we'll describe shortly.

The spinal nerves. Along the length of the spinal cord are 31 pairs of **spinal nerves**, with one member of each pair for each side of the body (Figure 2.10). These nerves join the spinal cord at regularly spaced intervals through openings in the bony structures of the spinal column. Each spinal nerve consists of the fusion of two distinct branches, called roots, which are functionally different. The **dorsal** (back) **root** of each spinal nerve consists of sensory pathways from the body to the spinal cord. The **ventral** (front) **root** consists of motor pathways from the spinal cord to the muscles.

2.10 The Spinal Cord and Spinal Nerves
(*Middle*) The spinal column runs from the base of the brain to the sacrum; a pair of nerves emerges from each level (see Figure 2.8b). (*Bottom right*) The spinal cord is surrounded by bony vertebrae and is enclosed in three membrane layers. Each vertebra has an opening on each side through which the spinal nerves pass. (*Top right*) Location of spinal cord gray matter and the white matter that surrounds it. In the gray matter are interneurons and the motoneurons that send axons to the muscles. The white matter consists of myelinated axons that run up and down the spinal column. (*Left*) Stained cross sections of the spinal cord at the cervical, thoracic, lumbar, and sacral levels. The stain turns the fatty myelin sheaths of the axons dark, so the white matter looks dark in this presentation. (Photographs from Hanaway et al., 1998.)

The name of a spinal nerve is the same as the segment of spinal cord to which it is connected: **cervical** (neck), **thoracic** (trunk), **lumbar** (small of the back), or **sacral** (bottom of the spinal column). Thus, the T12 spinal nerve is the spinal nerve that is connected to the twelfth segment of the thoracic portion of the spinal cord (see Figure 2.8*b*). Fibers from different spinal nerves join to form peripheral nerves, usually at some distance from the spinal cord.

The autonomic nervous system.   Ancient anatomists found collections of neurons outside the CNS, which we call **ganglia** (singular ganglion). Because they were outside the CNS, these neuron aggregates were named **autonomic** ("independent") **ganglia**. Today we know that the autonomic ganglia are controlled by neurons in the CNS; the autonomic nervous system actually spans both the central and the peripheral nervous systems. Autonomic neurons within the brain and spinal cord send out their axons to innervate neurons in the ganglia. These neurons, which have their cell bodies within the ganglia, in turn send their axons out to innervate all the major organs. The central neurons that innervate the ganglia are known as **preganglionic** autonomic cells; the ganglionic neurons that innervate the body are **postganglionic** autonomic cells.

The autonomic nervous system is divided into two components: the **sympathetic nervous system** and the **parasympathetic nervous system**. The preganglionic cells of the sympathetic nervous system are found exclusively in the spinal cord, specifically in the thoracic and lumbar regions. These cells send their axons a short distance to innervate a chain of ganglia running along each side of the spinal column; this chain is called the **sympathetic chain** (Figure 2.11, *left*). Cells of the sympathetic chain innervate smooth muscles in organs and in the walls of blood vessels. A convenient, if somewhat oversimplified, summary of the effects of sympathetic activation is that it prepares the body for action: Blood pressure increases, the pupils of the eyes widen, and the heart quickens.

The parasympathetic nervous system gets its name (from the Greek *para*, "around") because its preganglionic neurons are found above and below those of the sympathetic system—in the brain and the sacral spinal cord (Figure 2.11, *right*). These preganglionic cells also innervate ganglia, but parasympathetic ganglia are not collected in a chain as sympathetic ganglia are. Rather, parasympathetic ganglia are dispersed throughout the body, usually near the organ affected. For many bodily functions, the sympathetic and parasympathetic divisions act in opposite directions, and the result is very accurate control. For example, the heartbeat is quickened by the activity of sympathetic nerves during exercise, but it is slowed by the vagus nerve (part of the parasympathetic system) during rest. Sympathetic activation constricts blood vessels, raising blood pressure, while parasympathetic activation relaxes vessel walls. The functions of the autonomic nervous system are "independent" in another sense: We cannot voluntarily control the activity of this system in the same way that we can control our movements.

The Central Nervous System Consists of Brain and Spinal Cord

The spinal cord is a conduit that funnels sensory information from the body up to the brain and conveys brain motor commands out to the body. Thus we will discuss the spinal cord later when we are examining sensation (see Chapter 8) and movement (see Chapter 11). The remainder of this chapter will deal with the executive portion of the CNS: the brain.

Brain features that are visible to the naked eye.   Given the importance of the adult human brain, it is surprising that it weighs a mere 1400 g, 2% of the average body weight. However, even gross inspection reveals that what the brain lacks in weight it makes up for in intricacy. Figure 2.12 offers three views of the human brain in standard orientations. These views will be helpful in our future discussions. Viewed from the side (see Figure 2.12*a*) or from the top, the human brain is dominated by the **cerebral hemispheres** (telencephalon), which sit atop and surround the brain stem, which is continuous with the spinal cord. You can **Sylvius** see the brain in greater detail, rotate it, and zoom in on details by using the *Sylvius* brain atlas in the CD that comes with this book.

The shape of the paired cerebral hemispheres is the result of elaborate folding together of tissue. The resulting ridges of tissue, called **gyri** (singular gyrus), are separated from each other by furrows called **sulci** (singular sulcus). Such folding enormously increases

2.11 The Autonomic Nervous System ▶
The sympathetic division of the autonomic nervous system (*left*) consists of the sympathetic chains and the nerve fibers that flow from them. The parasympathetic division (*right*) arises from both the cranial and the sacral parts of the spinal cord. All preganglionic axons release acetylcholine as a neurotransmitter, as do postganglionic cells in the parasympathetic division. Sympathetic postganglionic cells use norepinephrine (noradrenaline) as a neurotransmitter. The two different postganglionic transmitters ("noradrenergic" for norepinephrine and "cholinergic" for acetylcholine) allow the autonomic nervous system to have two opposing effects on target organs.

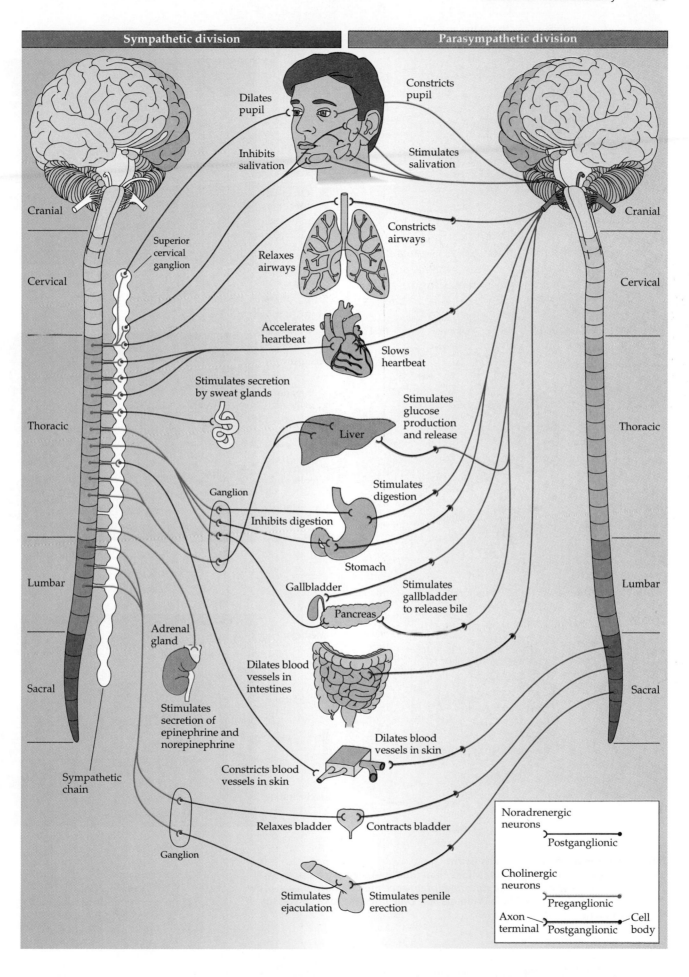

Sympathetic division

Parasympathetic division

Dilates pupil

Constricts pupil

Inhibits salivation

Stimulates salivation

Cranial

Cranial

Superior cervical ganglion

Constricts airways

Relaxes airways

Cervical

Cervical

Accelerates heartbeat

Slows heartbeat

Stimulates secretion by sweat glands

Stimulates glucose production and release

Liver

Thoracic

Thoracic

Ganglion

Stimulates digestion

Inhibits digestion

Stomach

Gallbladder

Stimulates gallbladder to release bile

Lumbar

Lumbar

Pancreas

Adrenal gland

Dilates blood vessels in intestines

Sacral

Sacral

Stimulates secretion of epinephrine and norepinephrine

Dilates blood vessels in skin

Constricts blood vessels in skin

Sympathetic chain

Relaxes bladder

Contracts bladder

Ganglion

Stimulates ejaculation

Stimulates penile erection

Noradrenergic neurons

Postganglionic

Cholinergic neurons

Preganglionic

Axon terminal

Postganglionic

Cell body

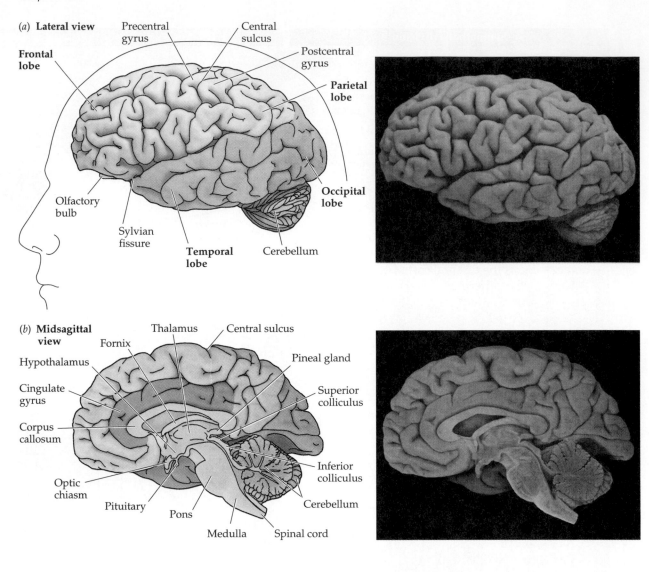

(a) **Lateral view**

Precentral gyrus
Central sulcus
Postcentral gyrus
Frontal lobe
Parietal lobe
Olfactory bulb
Occipital lobe
Sylvian fissure
Cerebellum
Temporal lobe

(b) **Midsagittal view**

Thalamus
Central sulcus
Fornix
Hypothalamus
Pineal gland
Cingulate gyrus
Superior colliculus
Corpus callosum
Inferior colliculus
Optic chiasm
Cerebellum
Pituitary
Pons
Medulla
Spinal cord

(c) **Basal view**

Temporal lobe
Mammillary body
Medulla
Olfactory bulb
Spinal cord
Frontal lobe
Cerebellum
Optic chiasm
Pons
Pituitary
Uncus

2.12 Three Views of the Human Brain
(a) Lateral view (from the side). (b) Midsagittal (midline) view. (c) Basal view (from below). On the right is a postmortem brain specimen seen from each view. (Photographs courtesy of S. Mark Williams and Dale Purves, Duke University Medical Center.)

the cerebral surface area; about two-thirds of the cerebral surface is hidden in the depths of these folds. Because the pattern of folding has many features that are common to all humans, the major divisions of the cerebral hemispheres can be labeled. The major sectors of the cerebral hemispheres are the **frontal, parietal, temporal**, and **occipital** regions, or lobes. These lobes are distinguished by colors in the left column of Figure 2.12. Some of the boundaries defined by folds are clearly marked (for example, the lateral sulcus, or **Sylvian fissure**, which demarcates the temporal lobe, and the **central sulcus**, which divides frontal from parietal lobes, are quite prominent); others (those dividing parietal from occipital and occipital from temporal lobes) are less well defined. The outer shell of the hemispheres is the **cerebral cortex** (the word "cortex" refers to the outermost layers of a structure), sometimes referred to as simply the cortex.

Whereas the cerebral hemispheres seem to serve "higher," more abstract functions—damage to the cerebrum may deprive us of speech or sight—"lower" parts of the brain regulate respiration, heart rate, and other basic functions. The occipital cortex receives information from the eyes and analyzes that information to give us sight. Most auditory information reaches the temporal lobe, and damage there can impair hearing. Touch information is integrated in a strip of parietal cortex just behind the central sulcus (the **postcentral gyrus** of the parietal lobe), while in front of the central sulcus, the **precentral gyrus** of the frontal lobe is crucial for motor control. A view from a midline position (see Figure 2.12*b*) shows a large bundle of axons called the **corpus callosum**, which connects corresponding points of the right and left cerebral hemispheres.

No matter what plane is used to section the brain (see Box 2.2), two distinct shades of color are evident (Figure 2.13). The whitish areas contain tracts that appear relatively white because of the lipid (fat) content of myelin covering the axons. Darker gray areas are dominated more by cell bodies, which are devoid of myelin. Thus, the term **white matter** refers to bundles of nerve fibers, and the term **gray matter** refers to areas that are rich in nerve cell bodies. The importance of this distinction between gray and white matter is clear in the study by Andreasen et al. (1993) noted in Box 1.2. In that study, the correlation between intelligence and the volume of gray matter in the cerebral hemispheres is much higher than that between intelligence and the volume of white matter. By sectioning the brain, we can now begin to examine the internal portions of the nervous system.

Developmental subdivisions of the brain. The complex form of the adult human brain makes it hard to understand why anatomists use terms the way they do. For example, the part of your brain closest to the back of your head is labeled as part of the forebrain. How can we make sense of this terminology? The clue to how the brain is subdivided lies in the way it develops early in life. In Chapter 7 we will consider brain development as a subject in its own right. For now we will discuss brain development in the context of categorizing brain structures.

In a very young embryo of any vertebrate, the CNS looks like a tube. The walls of this neural tube are made of cells, and the interior is filled with fluid. A few weeks after conception, the human neural tube begins to show three separate swellings at the head

(a) Horizontal section

Basal ganglia Thalamus Gray matter (cortex) White matter

Frontal poles

Occipital poles

Third ventricle Posterior horn of lateral ventricle

(b) Lateral view showing planes of section

(c) Coronal or transverse section

Corpus callosum

Basal ganglia

Caudate nucleus Putamen

Lateral ventricle Amygdala Temporal lobe

2.13 Inside the Brain
Horizontal (*a*) and coronal (*c*) sections of the human brain; the planes of section are shown in corresponding colors in the lateral view (*b*). The light color of the white matter is from the fatty myelin surrounding the axons in the major fiber tracts. Gray matter consists of cell bodies that form the outer layers of the brain and nuclei within the brain. (Photographs courtesy of S. Mark Williams and Dale Purves, Duke University Medical Center.)

end (Figure 2.14*a*): the **forebrain** (or prosencephalon), the **midbrain** (or **mesencephalon**), and the **hindbrain** (or rhombencephalon). (The term "encephalon," meaning "brain," comes from the Greek *en*, "in," and *kephale*, "head.")

Seven weeks after conception, the forebrain and hindbrain have already developed clear subdivisions. At the very front of the developing brain is the **telencephalon**, which will become the cerebral hemispheres. The other part of the forebrain is the **diencephalon** (or "between brain"), which will include regions called the thalamus and the hypothalamus. The midbrain comes next. Behind it the hindbrain has two divisions: the **metencephalon**, which will develop into the **cerebellum** ("little brain") and the **pons** ("bridge"); and the **myelencephalon**, or **medulla**. The term **brain stem** usually refers to the midbrain, pons, and medulla combined. Figure 2.14*c* shows the positions of these main structures and their relative sizes in the adult human brain. Even when the brain achieves its adult form, it is still a fluid-filled tube, but one of very complicated shape.

Each of these five main sections (telencephalon, diencephalon, mesencephalon, metencephalon, and myelencephalon) can be subdivided in turn (Figure 2.14*b*). We can work our way from the largest, most general divisions at the left of the schematic to more specific ones at the right. Within each region are aggregations of neurons called **nuclei** (singular nucleus) and bundles of axons called **tracts**. (Recall that in the periphery, aggregations of neurons are called ganglia, and bundles of axons are called nerves.) Because these nuclei and tracts are recognizable from individual to individual, and often from species to species, they have names too. You are probably more interested in the functions of all these parts of the brain than in their names, but each region serves more than one function, most functions are spread out through several structures, and ideas about function are constantly being revised by new data. Thus, having oriented you to the general organization of the brain, we will embark on just a brief look at the functions of specific parts, leaving the detailed discussion for later chapters.

Now that you've seen both small- and large-scale views of the nervous system, you can refer to Table 2.2 to compare the sizes of some important neural structures.

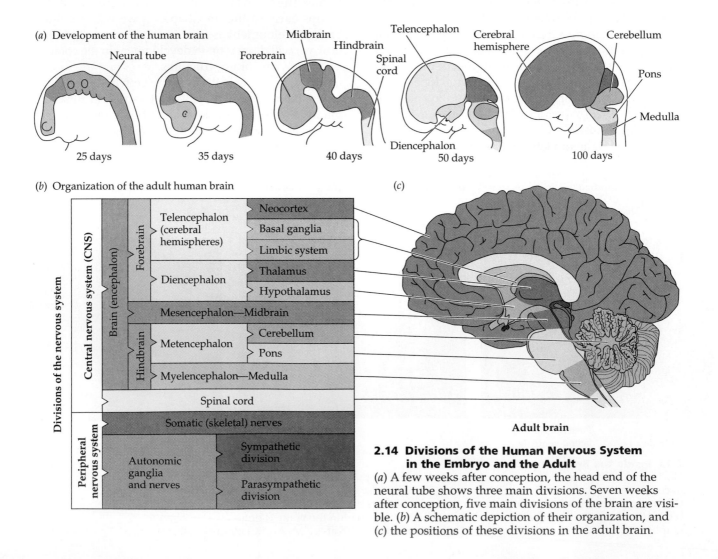

(a) Development of the human brain

Neural tube · 25 days · 35 days · Midbrain · Hindbrain · Forebrain · Spinal cord · 40 days · Telencephalon · Diencephalon · 50 days · Cerebral hemisphere · Cerebellum · Pons · Medulla · 100 days

(b) Organization of the adult human brain

(c)

Adult brain

2.14 Divisions of the Human Nervous System in the Embryo and the Adult

(*a*) A few weeks after conception, the head end of the neural tube shows three main divisions. Seven weeks after conception, five main divisions of the brain are visible. (*b*) A schematic depiction of their organization, and (*c*) the positions of these divisions in the adult brain.

TABLE 2.2 *Sizes of Some Neural Structures and the Units of Measurement and Magnification Used in Studying Them*

Structure	Size	Unit of measurement	Magnification	Observation method
Whole brain	Adult human brain measures about 15 cm from front to back	$1\text{ cm} = 10^{-2}\text{ m}$	1 (life size)	Naked eye
Cerebral cortex	Cortex of human brain is about 3 mm thick	$1\text{ mm} = 10^{-3}\text{ m}$	×10	Naked eye
Nerve cells	Large neuron cell bodies are about 100 µm (0.1 mm) in diameter	$0.1\text{ mm} = 10^{-4}\text{ m} = 100\text{ µm}$	×100 (10^2)	Naked eye / Light microscope
Parts of neurons	Large axons and dendrites are about 10 µm (0.01 mm) in diameter	$0.01\text{ mm} = 10^{-5}\text{ m} = 10\text{ µm}$	×1,000 (10^3)	Light microscope
Synapse	A synaptic ending is about 1 µm in diameter	$1\text{ µm} = 10^{-6}\text{ m}$	×10,000 (10^4)	Light microscope
Synaptic cleft	The synaptic cleft between neurons is about 20 nm across	$0.1\text{ µm} = 100\text{ nm} = 10^{-7}\text{ m}$	×100,000 (10^5)	Light microscope / Electron microscope
Neuronal membrane	A neuronal membrane is about 5 nm thick	$10\text{ nm} = 10^{-8}\text{ m}$	×1,000,000 (10^6)	Electron microscope
Ion channel	The diameter of an ion channel is about 0.5 nm	$1\text{ nm} = 10^{-9}\text{ m}$	×10,000,000 (10^7)	Electron microscope

Brain Structures Can Be Described on the Basis of Function

Although we give simple, capsule statements about functions here, later chapters take them up more fully, so concentrate now on understanding the physical layout of the parts rather than their functions. We'll look briefly at each of the five basic parts of the brain in turn and then examine the cerebral cortex in a little more detail. Although there are some single structures around the midline, such as the corpus callosum, pineal gland, and pituitary gland (see Figure

(*a*) Basal ganglia

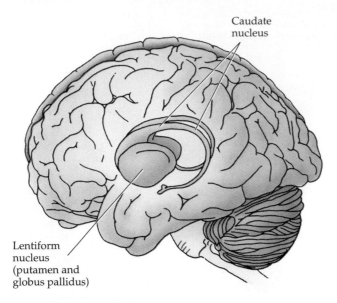

Caudate
nucleus

Lentiform
nucleus
(putamen and
globus pallidus)

(*b*) Limbic system

Cingulate
cortex

Fornix

Thalamus

Olfactory
bulb

Mammillary
body

Amygdala

Hippocampus

2.15 Two Important Brain Systems
(*a*) The basal ganglia—caudate nucleus, putamen, and globus pallidus—are important in movement. (*b*) The limbic system—hippocampus, thalamus, cingulate cortex, fornix, olfactory bulb, amygdala, and mammillary bodies—is important for emotion, learning, and memory.

2.12*b*), each of the structures we'll describe next is found in both the right and the left sides of the brain.

Within the Cerebral Hemispheres Are the Basal Ganglia and the Limbic System

The **basal ganglia** include the **caudate nucleus**, **putamen**, and **globus pallidus** deep within the telencephalon, under the cerebral cortex (Figures 2.13 and 2.15*a*). The **amygdala** (Latin for "almond," which it resembles in shape) is embedded in the temporal lobe. These four nuclei (not really ganglia, despite the unfortunate name "basal ganglia") send axons back and forth to innervate one another, forming a neural system. The basal ganglia are very important in motor control, as we will see in Chapter 11.

The term **limbic system** is a loosely defined designation for a widespread group of brain nuclei (Figure 2.15*b*) that innervate each other to form a network intimately involved in mechanisms of emotion and learning. The **hippocampus** (from the Greek *hippokampos*, "seahorse," which it resembles in shape) and the **fornix** form two arcs under the surface of the hemispheres. Other components of the limbic system include a strip of cortex called the **cingulate gyrus**, the amygdala (which is also a part of the basal ganglia), and the **olfactory bulb**. The rest of the limbic system is found in the diencephalon (see the next section), including the hypothalamus and the nipple-shaped **mammillary bodies** (see Figure 2.12*c*).

The Diencephalon Is Divided into Thalamus and Hypothalamus

The uppermost portion of the diencephalon is the **thalamus**, seen in the center of the adult brain in Figures 2.13*a* and 2.14*c*. The thalamus is a complex cluster of nuclei that act as way stations to the cerebral cortex. Almost all sensory information enters the thalamus, where neurons send that information to the overlying cortex. The cortical cells in turn innervate the thalamus, perhaps to control which sensory information is transmitted.

Because it is under the thalamus, the second part of the diencephalon is known as the **hypothalamus** (Figure 2.12*b*). The hypothalamus is relatively small but is packed with many distinct nuclei that have vital functions. The hypothalamus has been implicated in hunger, thirst, temperature regulation, reproductive behaviors, and much more. The hypothalamus also controls the pituitary gland, which in turn controls almost all hormone secretion, as we'll learn in Chapter 5.

The Midbrain Forms the Top of the Brain Stem

Within the midbrain are groups of neuronal cell bodies that send their axons out to form cranial nerves. For example, the cell bodies of motoneurons that send their axons to form the oculomotor nerve (III, controlling many eye movements) are clustered together in the midbrain, forming the oculomotor nucleus. Other such cranial nerve nuclei are found throughout the brain stem. Two pairs of bumps are visible on the dorsal surface of the midbrain; the more rostral pair are the **superior colliculi** (singular colliculus), and the caudal pair are the **inferior colliculi** (Figure 2.12*b*). The superior colliculi receive visual information; the inferior colliculi receive information about sound.

Also found in the midbrain is a distributed network of neurons collectively referred to as the **reticular formation** (from the Latin *reticulum*, "network"). The reticular formation stretches from the midbrain down to the medulla. Many varied functions have been attributed to different parts of this loose aggregation of neurons, including sleep and arousal, temperature regulation, and motor control.

The Cerebellum Is Attached to the Pons

The lateral, midline, and basal views in Figure 2.12 show the cerebellum. Like the cerebral hemispheres, the cerebellum includes an elaborately folded surface sheet; in this case the folds are very close together. The arrangement of cells within the sheet is relatively simple (Figure 2.16). A middle layer is composed of a single row of large, multipolar neurons called **Purkinje cells**, after the anatomist who first described their elaborate fan-shaped dendritic patterns. All along the surface of these dendrites are numerous dendritic spines. An outer, "molecular" layer is composed of an orderly array of axons that runs parallel to the surface; hence they are called **parallel fibers**. In the depths beneath the Purkinje cells is a huge collection of small **granule cells**, whose axons form the parallel fibers of the surface. The cerebellum plays a role in motor coordination and some types of learning.

Immediately below (ventral to) the cerebellum, contributing to the brain stem, is the **pons** (see Figure 2.12*a* and *c*). The pons includes regions involved in motor control and sensory analysis, including several cranial nerve nuclei. Information from the ear first enters the brain in the pons. The pons also contains several groups of neurons that send their axons down to affect the spinal cord, primarily to regulate movement.

The Medulla Maintains Vital Body Functions

The medulla forms the bottom of the brain stem and marks the transition from brain stem to spinal cord. Within the medulla are the XI and XII cranial nerve nuclei—cell bodies of neurons that control the neck and tongue muscles, respectively. The reticular formation, which we first saw in the midbrain, stretches through the pons and ends in the medulla. The medulla also contributes to the regulation of breathing and heart rate, so **lesions** (tissue damage) there are often fatal. Several groups of medullary neurons send their axons down the spinal cord to communicate with neurons there. Axons from the rest of the brain that reach down to affect the spinal cord must also pass through the medulla.

The Cerebral Cortex Serves Many Functions

Neuroscientists have long argued that understanding human cognition depends on unraveling the structure and fundamental functions of the cerebral cortex. In fact, by accepting electrical silence of the cortex as a criterion for defining death, many governments now define human life in terms of the workings of the cerebral cortex. The cerebral cortex is estimated to contain 50 billion to 100 billion neurons. If the cerebral cortex were unfolded, it would occupy an area of about 2000 cm^2 (315 square inches) or a square about 45 cm (18 inches) on a side. How are these cells arranged? How do the arrangements allow for particular feats of human information processing?

The neurons of the cerebral cortex are arranged in distinct layers—a laminar form of organization. Cell body and axon stains, such as those illustrated in Figure 2.17*a*, show six distinct layers in most of the cerebral cortex. (In Chapter 6 we'll discuss the three types of cerebral cortex.) Each **cortical layer** is distinct because it consists either of groups of cells of particular sizes, or of patterns of dendrites or axons. For example, the outermost layer, layer 1, is distinct because it has few cell bodies, while layer 3 stands out because of the many neurons with large cell bodies. The relative thickness of the layers varies across the cerebral cortex, suggesting a division of the cortex into subregions defined in terms of differences in the aggregation of nerve cells. Researchers have developed maps of these subregions of the cerebral cortex based on dif-

2.16 Arrangement of Cells within the Cerebellum

Large Purkinje cells dominate the cerebellum. Innervation between the various types forms a very consistent pattern. Cells depicted in black inhibit the actions of other cells.

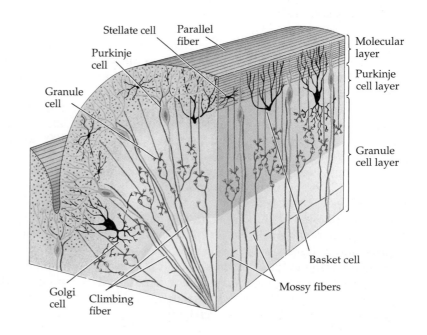

(a) Six layers of cortex

(b) A single pyramidal neuron

Apical
dendrite

Cell
body

Basal
dendrites

Axon

100 μm

400 μm

2.17 Layers of the Cerebral Cortex
(a) The six layers of cortex can be distinguished with stains that reveal all cell bodies (*left*), or with stains that reveal a few neurons in their entirety (*right*). (b) A single pyramidal cell enlarged about 200 times. (c) Regions of the cortex as delineated in a classic cytoarchitectonic map by Korbinian Brodmann (1909).

(c) Cytoarchitectonic map of regions of the cortex

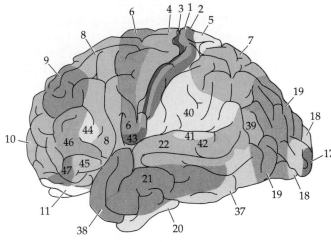

neurons of the cortex appear to be arranged in columns perpendicular to the layers, as we'll see shortly.

The variation in thickness of the different layers of cerebral cortex is related to differences in their functions. Incoming sensory fibers from the thalamus terminate especially in layer 4, so this layer is particularly prominent in regions that represent sensory functions. In fact, in part of the visual cortex in the occipital lobe, layer 4 is so prominent that it appears to the naked eye as a stripe in sections cut through this area. For this reason part of the visual cortex is known as striate ("striped") cortex. Fibers that leave the cerebral cortex arise especially from layer 3, which is particularly prominent in the main motor regions of the cortex. Layer 3 is also characterized by especially large pyramidal cells.

Cortical columns. Some brain regions have distinctive geometric arrangements of cells that can function as information processing units. Visible in the cortex are columns of nerve cells that extend through the entire thickness of the cortex, from the white matter to the surface. In humans these **cortical columns** are about 3 mm deep and about 400 to 1000 μm in diameter (Mountcastle, 1979). Within such a column, the functional connections among cells (synaptic connections) are mainly in the vertical direction, but there are also some horizontal connections. The human cerebral cortex contains about a million cortical columns, which are thought to be the functional modules of cortical operations. In Chapter 10 we will discuss in some detail the cortical columns that analyze visual stimuli.

Vernon Mountcastle

ferences in cell density, sizes and shapes of cortical neurons, and intracortical connection patterns. Figure 2.17*c* is a map based on these criteria. Divisions based on these structural criteria also seem to define functional zones such as sensory and motor zones. The numbered cortial regions in Figure 2.17*c* are known as **Brodmann's areas**; we will refer to them by number in later chapters. For example, in Chapter 10 we will refer to area 17, the primary visual area at the occipital (posterior) pole of the brain.

The most prominent kind of neuron in the cerebral cortex—the **pyramidal cell** (Figure 2.17*b*)—usually has its cell bodies in layers 3 to 5. One dendrite of each pyramidal cell (called the **apical dendrite**) usually extends to the outermost surface of the cortex. The pyramidal cell also has several dendrites (called **basal dendrites**) that spread out horizontally from the cell body. Frequently

Connections among cortical regions are mainly tracts of axons (Figure 2.18). Some of these connections are short pathways that loop beneath the cortex to nearby cortical regions; others travel longer distances through the cerebral hemispheres. The largest of these pathways is the corpus callosum, through which run connections between corresponding points on the two hemispheres. Longer links between cortical regions involve multisynaptic chains of neurons that loop through subcortical regions such as the thalamus and the basal ganglia.

The Brain Is Well Protected and Has an Abundant Blood Supply

Within the bony skull and vertebrae, the brain and spinal cord are surrounded by three protective sheets of tissue called **meninges** (see Figure 2.10). The outermost sheet is a tough envelope called the **dura mater** (in Latin, literally "hard mother"). The innermost layer, called the **pia mater** (Latin for "tender mother"), adheres tightly to the surface of the brain and follows all its contours. (The term *mater*, "mother," reflects the medieval belief that these tissues gave birth to the brain.) The delicate, weblike membrane between the dura mater and the pia mater is called the **arachnoid** (literally, "spiderweblike"). Space within the arachnoid is filled with **cerebrospinal fluid** (**CSF**), a clear, colorless liquid.

The Cerebral Ventricles Are Chambers Filled with Fluid

Inside the brain is a series of chambers filled with CSF (Figure 2.19). These cavities form what is known as the **ventricular system**. A highly vascular (full of blood vessels) portion of the lining of the ventricles, called the **choroid plexus**, secretes cerebrospinal fluid, essentially by removing blood cells from plasma. CSF has at least two main functions:

1. It acts mechanically as a shock absorber for the brain. Because the brain floats in CSF as the head moves, movements of the head do not result in forceful shifting of the brain inside the skull cavity.
2. It mediates between blood vessels and brain tissue in the exchange of materials, including nutrients.

Short tracts arch between nearby areas of the cortex.

Several long tracts run in an anterior—posterior direction.

Long projection fibers run to and from the cerebral cortex. Some go through the corpus callosum connecting homologous regions of the two hemispheres.

Corpus callosum

2.18 Cortical Tract Connections among Cortical Regions

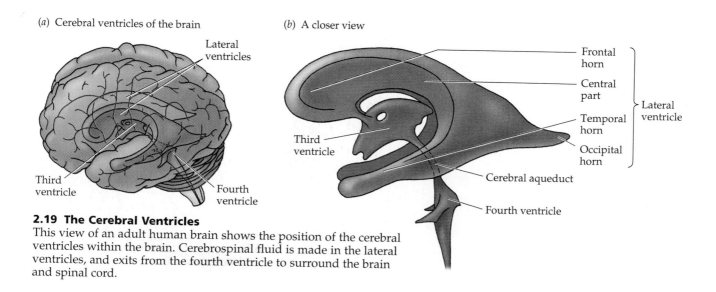

(*a*) Cerebral ventricles of the brain

Lateral ventricles

Third ventricle

Fourth ventricle

(*b*) A closer view

Frontal horn

Central part

Temporal horn

Occipital horn

Lateral ventricle

Third ventricle

Cerebral aqueduct

Fourth ventricle

2.19 The Cerebral Ventricles
This view of an adult human brain shows the position of the cerebral ventricles within the brain. Cerebrospinal fluid is made in the lateral ventricles, and exits from the fourth ventricle to surround the brain and spinal cord.

Each hemisphere of the brain contains a **lateral ventricle** (ventricles 1 and 2) that has a complex shape. CSF forms in the lateral ventricles and flows from them into the **third ventricle**, which is located in the midline and continues down a narrow passage, to the **fourth ventricle**, which lies anterior to the cerebellum. Just below the cerebellum is a small aperture, through which CSF leaves the ventricular system to circulate over the outer surface of the brain and spinal cord. CSF is absorbed back into the circulatory system through large veins beneath the top of the skull.

The Brain Has an Elaborate Vascular System

Because the brain works intensely, it has a strong metabolic demand for its fuels, oxygen and glucose. Having very little reserve of either fuel, the brain depends critically on its blood supply to provide them. Blood is delivered to the brain via two main channels, the carotid arteries and the vertebral arteries (Figure 2.20).

The common **carotid arteries** ascend the left and right sides of the neck. The internal carotid artery enters the skull and branches into anterior and middle cerebral arteries, which supply blood to large regions of the cerebral hemispheres. The **vertebral arteries** ascend along the bony vertebrae and enter the base of the skull. They join together to form the **basilar artery**, which runs along the ventral surface of the brain stem. Branches of the basilar artery supply blood to the brain stem and to posterior portions of the cerebral hemispheres.

At the base of the brain, the carotid and basilar arteries join to form a structure called the **circle of Willis**. This joining of vascular paths may provide some needed "backup" if any of the main arteries to the brain should be damaged or blocked by disease. The common term "stroke" refers to changes in the flow of blood in the brain produced by blockage or rupture of blood vessels, or by reduced flow due to heart impairment. Stroke is among the most common life-threatening disorders of humans.

The very fine capillaries that branch off from small arteries deliver nutrients and other substances to brain cells and remove waste products. This exchange in the brain is quite different from exchanges between blood vessels and cells in other body organs. Capillaries in the brain offer much greater resistance to the passage of large molecules across their walls than do capillar-

(a) Basal view of brain

Internal carotid artery

Circle of Willis

Vertebral artery

Basilar artery

Anterior cerebral artery

Middle cerebral artery

Posterior cerebral artery

(b) Midsagittal view

(c) Lateral view

2.20 The Blood Supply of the Human Brain
The anterior, middle, and posterior cerebral arteries—the three principal arteries that provide blood to the cerebral hemispheres—are depicted here in views of the basal (a), midsagittal (b), and lateral (c) surfaces of the brain. The basilar and internal carotid arteries form a circle at the base of the brain known as the circle of Willis.

ies elsewhere. The brain is thus protected from exposure to some substances found in the blood. We refer to this protective mechanism as the **blood–brain barrier**. This barrier results from the tight fit between the cells that make up the walls of capillaries (endothelial cells) in the brain, which thus do not readily let through large molecules. The blood–brain barrier may have evolved to protect the brain from substances that other organs can tolerate.

Newer Imaging Techniques Allow Us to Look into the Living Human Brain

Researchers have long sought ways to peer into the living human brain to see structures and how they work in different behavioral states. An ordinary X-ray of the head reveals an outline of the skull with little or no definition of brain tissue. Since the X-ray density of all parts of the brain is very similar, there is little contrast between regions of the brain. To provide contrast between brain tissue and blood vessels, investigators inject dyes into blood vessels. The resultant X-ray pictures—called **angiograms**—provide an outline of the vascular paths of the brain and are useful in describing vascular disease, such as stroke.

Important method

Developments in computers and computer programs since the mid-1970s have enabled us to integrate many different X-ray views into a portrait that enhances small differences in density and resembles a cross section of the brain. These portraits are referred to as tomograms (from the Greek *tomos*, "cross-cut" or "section," and *gramma*, "record" or "picture"). Producing **computerized axial tomograms** (**CATs**), or **CT** (computerized tomography) **scans**, involves moving an X-ray source in an arc around the head. The patient lies on a table, and the patient's head is then inserted into the middle of a doughnut-shaped ring (Figure 2.21*a*). An X-ray source is moved in a circular path around the head, at each position delivering a small amount of X-radiation, which passes through the head. The amount of this radiation that is absorbed within the head depends on the density of the tissue. A ring of detectors opposite the X-ray source analyzes the amount of X-radiation that has passed through the head. The X-ray tube and detectors are then moved to a new position, and the process is repeated until a composite picture can be constructed by a computer on the basis of the many X-ray views from different angles around the head.

Figure 2.21*a* shows a typical CT scan of one level of the brain. Each picture element (or pixel) in the final portrait is the result of a complex mathematical analysis of this small brain region viewed from many different angles. The spatial resolution of this technique has now been improved to the point where relatively small changes, such as shrinkage of a gyrus, can be visualized. Figure 2.21*a* illustrates the use of CT in the study of the behavioral effects of stroke. This technique has enabled observation of cerebral cortical changes or differences in Alzheimer's disease, schizophrenia, dyslexia, and many other disorders.

CT has been a most valuable tool, although a newer approach, **magnetic resonance imaging** (**MRI**), has become a robust competitor. MRI generates pictures that reveal some structural details in the living brain without exposing the patient to X-rays (Andreasen, 1989). MRI uses radio waves and other magnetic energy. The patient lies within a large magnet (Figure 2.21*b*), and the molecular effect of applied magnetic fields is registered by a coil detector, from which successive outputs are analyzed by computer. The resultant image can display extremely small changes in the brain, such as the loss of myelin around groups of axons, a symptom that is characteristic of demyelinating diseases. With this technique, structural abnormalities have been studied intensively in humans of all ages and conditions.

Images of the physiological functioning of the brain were first provided by a technique called **positron emission tomography** (**PET**) (Figure 2.21*c*). To obtain images of the functional state of the brain, radioactive chemicals are injected into the blood vessels. These radioisotopes travel to the brain, and their emission can be assessed by detectors outside the body. Computerized analysis of these data reveals the differential uptake and use of the chemicals in various brain regions. The most commonly used substance is a type of radioactive glucose that is taken up into different brain regions according to their levels of metabolic activity. A color transform of this information yields a striking picture that highlights areas of intense metabolic response (see Figure 2.21*c*) (Holcomb et al., 1989). Using this technique, we can generate metabolic maps of the brain during states such as attention, movements, responses to sensory stimuli, and decision making. Special techniques can identify brain regions that are activated by specific stimuli or tasks (Box 2.3). In addition, we can identify regions that are abnormal in metabolic responses even if they are structurally intact.

Each technique that we have described here has limitations in terms of speed (temporal resolution), sharpness (spatial resolution), or cost, but more powerful machines and new techniques are being used to improve brain imaging. For example, a new experimental PET device has much greater spatial resolution, because it uses about 120,000 detectors instead of the 18,000 in most PET machines. In the case of MRI, much greater speed has now been achieved using a technique called **functional MRI** (**fMRI**) or fast MRI. This technique is based on the use of high-powered, rapidly oscillating magnetic-field gradients and improved, powerful computation. A refinement of fMRI technique now allows scientists to detect oxygen consumption by active brain regions, providing an fMRI

(*a*) Computerized tomography (CT)

Normal

Stroke victim

(*b*) Magnetic resonance imaging (MRI)

Horizontal view

Coronal view

(*c*) Positron emission tomography (PET)

Normal

Alzheimer's patient

2.21 Visualizing the Living Human Brain
(*Left column*) The procedures of, and (*middle and right columns*) images obtained from, three important brain imaging techniques. (*a*) CT scans can be used in studying brain organization and language. The CT scans shown here are from a normal patient and from a stroke patient; the stroke lesion is visible as a large yellow area. (*b*) MRI images are notable for their great detail, as seen in these horizontal and coronal sections of a normal human brain. Note the clarity in the definition of gyri and sulci of the cerebral cortex. (*c*) PET scans show levels of metabolic activity in the brain, as in these images from a normal human and an Alzheimer's patient; note the greater level of activity in the normal brain. The clinical convention is to display such images reversed, as though you were looking at the patient's face, with the left hemisphere on the right, and the right hemisphere on the left. For clarity, in this text we will always show the left side of the brain on the left and the right hemisphere on the right.

BOX 2.3 *Isolating Specific Brain Activity*

Many illustrations in this and later chapters show PET scans of brain activity specifically related to brain disorders or cognitive processes. Usually most of the brain is active, so isolating specific activity requires special procedures. The PET scan shown at the upper left in the figure here (labeled "Visual stimulus") was made while a person looked at a fixation point surrounded by a flickering checkerboard ring; the scan next to it ("Control") was made while a person looked at a fixation point alone. In a comparison of the two, it is hard to see differences, but subtracting the control values from the stimulation values yields a difference figure such as that shown at the upper right ("Difference image"); in this scan, it is easy to see that the main difference in activity is in the posterior part of the brain (the visual cortex).

The PET scans in the middle row are difference images for five individuals who performed the same two stimulation and control tasks. Averaging these five scans results in the mean difference image for all five subjects shown at the bottom. Such images yield more reliable results than individual images, but they lack some of the specificity of the individual images.

All the PET images shown in this book are difference images, usually made from scans of a single individual's brain. When you see brain function images in this book or in the popular press, note whether they are direct scans or difference images; if the latter, note whether they show values for an individual or for the mean of a group. (PET scans courtesy of Marcus Raichle.)

Visual stimulus   Control

Brain scans are made while a subject is in a control condition, and while he or she is exposed to an experimental stimulus or performs a task. The difference in brain activity in the scans can be computed and represented as a color-coded "difference image" that shows the areas of the brain that were most active during the experimental condition.

Resulting brain activity   Difference image

Difference images from several subjects can be added together and averaged…

…to arrive at a "mean difference image" that shows the most active brain areas for all subjects in an experiment.

Mean difference image

---

portrait of activity. Current imaging methods respond to changes in blood flow that start about 2 seconds after sensory stimulation and take about 7 seconds to reach a peak. Because this is much slower than neural responses, some investigators combine brain imaging with recordings of electrical activity of the brain, using imaging to locate activity and electrical responses to time it (e.g., Snyder et al., 1995).

Other investigators are using light to make images of brain activity within the head (Gratton et al., 1998; Vrillinger and Chance, 1997). Recently, investigators have found that near-infrared light (wavelengths 700–1000 nm) passes through skin, scalp, and skull, and penetrates into the brain. When such light is transmitted into the brain and detectors pick up the reflections at various nearby sites, the responses reflect the activity of cortical regions. Some components of the optical responses reflect the electrical signals of neurons, and other components reflect blood flow. The relatively low expense and small size of the optical imaging apparatus may allow many more laboratories to use brain imaging in their research. Optical studies could be done with young children or children with attention deficits who will not lie still in an MRI magnet or a PET scanner. They could also be used to monitor patients at bedside.

To investigate many problems of biological psychology, imaging provides convergent evidence with studies of naturally occurring or experimental brain lesions. Each of these kinds of investigation helps to overcome limitations on the other source of evidence. Furthermore, "remarkable progress in brain imaging techniques does not compete with the psychological analysis of behavior but instead places a new premium upon the thoughtfulness and accuracy of such analysis" (Gabrieli, 1998, p. 89). We will see many examples of brain imaging in later chapters.

Summary

1. The nervous system is extensive—monitoring, regulating, and modulating the activities of all parts and organs of the body.

2. Nerve cells (neurons) are the basic units of the nervous system. The typical neuron of most vertebrate species has three main parts: (1) the cell body, which contains the nucleus; (2) dendrites, which receive information; and (3) an axon, which carries impulses from the neuron. Because of the variety of functions they serve, neurons are extremely varied in size, shape, and chemical activity.

3. Neurons make functional contacts with other neurons, or with muscles or glands, at specialized junctions called synapses. At most synapses a chemical transmitter liberated by the presynaptic terminal diffuses across the synaptic cleft and binds to special receptor molecules in the postsynaptic membrane.

4. The axon is the specialized output zone of the nerve cell and is generally tubular, branching at the end into many collaterals. Axonal transport is the movement of materials within the axon.

5. Glial cells serve many functions, including the breakdown of transmitters, the production of myelin sheaths around axons, the exchange of nutrients and other materials with neurons, and the removal of cellular debris.

6. The nervous system of vertebrates is divided into central and peripheral nervous systems.

7. The central nervous system (CNS) consists of the brain and spinal cord. The main divisions of the brain can be seen most clearly in the embryo. These divisions are the forebrain (telencephalon and diencephalon), the midbrain (mesencephalon), and the hindbrain (metencephalon and myelencephalon).

8. The peripheral nervous system includes the cranial nerves, spinal nerves, and autonomic ganglia. The autonomic nervous system consists of the sympathetic nervous system, which tends to activate the body for action, and the parasympathetic nervous system, which tends to have an effect opposite to that of the sympathetic system.

9. The human brain is dominated by the cerebral hemispheres, which include the cerebral cortex, an extensive sheet of folded tissue. The cerebral cortex is responsible for higher-order functions such as vision, language, and memory. Other neural systems include the basal ganglia, which regulate movement; the limbic system, which controls emotional behaviors; and the cerebellum, which aids coordination and some kinds of learning.

10. The brain and spinal cord are protected by coverings of tissue called meninges and by cerebrospinal fluid (CSF), which surrounds and infiltrates the brain (via cerebral ventricles) to act as a shock absorber.

11. The blood system of the brain is an elaborate array of blood vessels that deliver nutrients and other substances to the brain. The walls of the blood vessels in the brain provide a barrier to the flow of large, potentially harmful molecules into the brain.

12. Modern techniques make it possible to visualize the anatomy of the living human brain and regional metabolic differences using external monitoring devices. These techniques include computerized axial tomography (CT scans), positron emission tomography (PET scans), and magnetic resonance imaging (MRI).

Recommended Reading

Brodal, P. (1992). *The central nervous system: Structure and function.* New York: Oxford University Press.

Hanaway, J., Woolsey, T. A., Gado, M. H., and Roberts, M. P. (1998). *The brain atlas.* Bethesda, MD: Fitzgerald Science.

Mai, J. K., Assheuer, J., and Paxinos, G. (1997). *Atlas of the human brain.* San Diego, CA: Academic Press.

Martin, J. H. (1996). *Neuroanatomy: Text and atlas* (2nd ed.). Stamford, CT: Appleton & Lange.

Posner, M. I., and Raichle, M. E. (1997). *Images of mind.* San Francisco: Freeman.

Posner, M. I., and Raichle, M. E. (Eds.) (1998). National Academy of Sciences Colloquium on Neuroimaging of Human Brain Function. *Proceedings of the National Academy of Sciences, U.S.A., 95:3,* 736–939.

Shepherd, G. (1991). *Foundations of the neuron doctrine.* New York: Oxford University Press.

Stewart, M. G. (1992). *Quantitative methods in neuroanatomy.* New York: Wiley-Liss.

3 Neurophysiology: Conduction, Transmission, and Integration of Neural Signals

As you read this page, light stimulates your eye and starts a barrage of signals that travel along nerve cells to your brain. At the same time, recollections are summoned about the connections between what you are reading and memories and thoughts of related ideas. In both cases, circuits of neurons in the brain provide the biological substrates for these experiences. What are the elementary signals of nerve cells? How do these signals speed along axons and move across the synaptic gaps between neurons? How can neural circuits process information? In this chapter, we describe the basic electrical signals of nervous systems and the physicochemical basis of these electrical events. Understanding how nerve cells conduct signals prepares us to consider how information is transmitted from one neuron to another and how information is processed in different kinds of circuits.

Piet Mondrian, *Broadway Boogie Woogie*, 1942–43

Electrical Signals Are the Vocabulary of the Nervous System

One of the most powerful developments in animal evolution was the electrical signaling of neurons. This innovation appears in animals as diverse as human beings, insects, and jellyfish—in fact, in almost all multicellular animals. These neural signals underlie the whole range of thought and action, from composing music or solving a mathematical problem to feeling an itch on the skin and swatting a mosquito.

The nervous system uses three different kinds of electrical events:

1. Neurons show a **resting potential**, or **membrane potential**, when they are inactive. This small electrical difference between the inner and outer surfaces of the membrane results from the separation of electrically charged particles called **ions**. (An ion is an atom or molecule in a solution that has acquired an electrical charge by gaining or losing one or more electrons.) Most other kinds of cells, such as muscle cells and blood corpuscles, also have membrane potentials. Nerve cells are unique because changes in their resting potential are signals that can be transmitted and integrated in complex ways.

2. **Nerve impulses**, or **action potentials**, are brief, propagated changes that travel rapidly along the axons of neurons. These changes are conducted in chain reaction fashion, maintaining a uniform size as they advance, and they enable axons to serve as channels for rapid communication.

3. **Local potentials**, or **graded potentials**, are initiated at postsynaptic sites and vary in size and duration. Rather than being actively propagated, they spread passively, so the amplitude of such a potential decreases progressively as it moves farther from its site of origin. These potentials are also called **postsynaptic potentials**. Interaction among graded postsynaptic potentials is a basic mechanism by which the nervous system processes information.

Let's consider the characteristic states of the neuron at rest and during activity. These electrical potentials can be thought of as the basic vocabulary of the nervous system. Knowing the vocabulary, we can understand how information is communicated and processed in the nervous system.

The Resting Potential of Neurons Can Be Measured

A few simple experiments reveal the characteristics of electrical potentials in nerve cells. The initial experimental setup (Figure 3.1a) includes an axon placed in a bathing fluid that resembles **extracellular fluids** that normally surround the cells of our body, a pair of electrodes—the one with a very fine tip is called a **microelectrode**—and attached devices to amplify, record,

and display electrical potentials. As long as the microelectrode remains outside the axon, there is zero potential difference between the microelectrode tip and a large reference electrode placed at some distance from the axon in the bath. (There are no differences in potential between any two electrodes placed in the extracellular medium, because the distribution of ions in the extracellular fluid is uniform, or homogeneous.)

When the electrode penetrates the membrane of the axon (Figure 3.1b), we see a sudden drop in potential to a level of –60 to –80 millivolts (mV). That is, the inside of the axon is electrically negative with respect to the outside. This difference (which represents the membrane, or resting, potential) demonstrates that the axonal membrane separates charges. The composition of intracellular fluid differs from that of the extracellular fluid. We will see how that difference is created when we discuss ionic mechanisms in the next section.

This hypothetical experiment would be hard to perform with just any axon. Most axons of mammals are less than 20 μm in diameter and quite difficult to pierce with an electrode. But nature provided neurophysiologists with an extraordinary solution to this problem: the giant axons of invertebrates, especially those of the squid. Squid axons can attain a diameter of 1 mm, so thick and apparent to the unaided eye that observers originally thought these axons must be part of the circulatory or urinary system. Electrodes in the form of glass tubes tapering to a sharp point about 0.2 μm in diameter can be inserted into a giant axon without altering its properties or activity. The membrane seems to seal around the inserted electrode tip.

Ionic Mechanisms Maintain the Resting Potential

Why is there a membrane potential? To answer this question, we have to understand the difference in distribution of charged particles—ions—between the inside and outside of the nerve cell membrane. In addition, we will consider the various physical and chemical forces that act at the membrane of the nerve cell. These forces include (1) **concentration gradients**—ions move from regions of high concentration to regions of low concentration, (2) **electrical forces**—like charges repel and opposite charges attract, and (3) **selective permeability** of nerve cell membranes—some ions can pass through the nerve cell membrane more readily than others.

To begin, consider the distribution of ions on both sides of the simplified and idealized neural membrane in Figure 3.2. Inside the cell is a high concentration of large protein ions, each with a considerable negative charge. These ions provide most of the negative charges inside the cell. There is also a high concentration of potassium ions (K^+), each of which has a positive electrical charge. The internal concentrations of sodium (Na^+) and chloride (Cl^-) ions are low. Because of their negative charges, the protein and chloride ions are called **anions**. Positively charged ions, such as K^+

(a) Zero potential difference when the two electrodes are in the bath

Reference electrode

Recording electrode

mV

Amplifier

(b) When the recording electrode enters the axon, a negative potential difference is seen

mV

Amplifier

Microelectrode

Inside axon

3.1 Measuring the Resting Potential

and Na$^+$, are called **cations**. The cell membrane contains many specialized small pores or channels through which the potassium ions can flow in or out relatively easily but that are not permeable to the other ions. At rest the nerve cell membrane is most permeable to potassium ions, much less permeable to sodium ions, and even less permeable to the large protein anions.

The negative charge of the protein ions trapped inside the cell, combined with the relative permeability of the membrane to K$^+$ primarily account for the resting potential of neurons. If we place such a neuron (with its high concentration of K$^+$ ions inside) in a solution that mimics its natural "environment," such as

3.2 Distribution of Ions inside and outside a Neuron

Most potassium ions (K$^+$) are found inside the neuron; most sodium (Na$^+$) and chloride (Cl$^-$) ions are in the extracellular space. These ions are exchanged through specialized channels in the cell membrane. The large, negatively charged protein molecules stay inside the neuron and account for much of the negative resting potential.

Key

	= Na$^+$	= K$^+$	= Cl$^-$	= Ca^{2+}	= Anion
Outside cell	440	20	560	10	few
Inside cell	50	400	40–150	0.0001	many

blood plasma or extracellular fluid (which has a low concentration of K^+ ions), the K^+ ions will exit the cell. The reason is that substances in solution move from regions of high concentration to regions of low concentration, unless there is a barrier to prevent them. In the absence of other forces, potassium ions tend to move out of the cell, because their concentration is 20 times greater inside than outside. Because the membrane of the axon is impermeable to large anions, they stay inside the cell. So the movement of positively charged K^+ ions leaving the cell creates a difference in electrical potential across the membrane, with a net negative charge inside the cell. But when the potential difference across the membrane becomes large enough, the net outflow of positive ions stops, because the positive ions outside repel each other but are attracted to the negative ions inside.

At this point, the tendency of the K^+ ions to flow from the regions of high concentration inside the cell is exactly balanced by the negative charge that attracts them inside. This potential is called the **potassium equilibrium potential** and is so predictable according to the laws of physical chemistry that it can be calculated using an equation, called the *Nernst equation.* The Nernst equation represents the voltage that develops when a semipermeable membrane separates different concentrations of ions. It predicts that the potential across the squid axon membrane will be about –75 mV, relative to the outside. The actual value is about –70 mV.

The predicted value differs from the observed value because the membrane is not absolutely impermeable to Na^+ ions. Small numbers of Na^+ ions leak in gradually through channels for sodium ions that open spontaneously and briefly, and this inward movement of Na^+ tends to reduce the membrane potential. The reduced potential, in turn, causes more potassium ions to move out. Eventually the leakage would cause the concentrations inside and outside the cell to become the same, and the membrane potential would disappear. But the neuron prevents this by actively pumping sodium out of the cell and potassium into the cell just rapidly enough to counter the leakage. Thus, maintaining the membrane potential, which is necessary for the neuron to be ready to conduct impulses, demands metabolic work by the cell. In fact, most of the energy expended by the brain—whether waking or sleeping—is thought to be used to maintain the ionic gradients across neuronal membranes.

A Threshold Amount of Depolarization Triggers an Action Potential

The experiments that we will describe in this section require a source of electrical stimulation. To talk about these experiments, we must add two terms to our vocabulary: **Hyperpolarization** is an increase in membrane potential (greater negativity inside the membrane in comparison with the outside); **depolarization** is a reduction of the membrane potential (decreased negativity inside the neuron). The stimulator in these experiments will provide hyperpolarizing or depolarizing electrical pulses to the axon, and we will see how such stimuli affect the membrane potential.

Figure 3.3 displays the changes in membrane potential that occur in response to successively stronger stimulus pulses. The application of *hyperpolarizing* stimuli to the axonal membrane results in responses that almost mirror the "shape" of the stimulus pulse (see Figure 3.3*b*). These responses passively reflect the stimulus, with distortions at the leading and trailing edges resulting from an electrical property of the membrane: its *capacitance,* or the ability to store electrical charges. If we placed several fine electrodes at successive positions along the axon and applied a hyperpolarizing pulse, we would see another important attribute of biological potentials in a conducting medium: The responses are progressively smaller at greater and greater distances from the stimulus site. A simple law of physics describes this relationship: In a conducting medium, the size of a potential decays as a function of the square of the distance. Since the amplitudes of these responses decline with distance, they are examples of local or graded potentials.

If we apply a series of *depolarizing* pulses (see Figure 3.3*c*), the membrane response to the initial few stimuli is a series of depolarizing changes—decreases in the resting potential—with some distortions. These again are local, graded responses. However, the situation changes suddenly when the stimulus depolarizes the cell to –50 mV or so. At this potential, known as the **threshold**, a rapid, brief (0.5 to 2.0 ms) response is provoked: the action potential or nerve impulse. This response is a brief change in the membrane potential that momentarily makes the inside of the membrane positive with respect to the outside; it is sometimes called an **overshoot**. This action potential will propagate down the axon, as we'll discuss a little later.

What happens when we increase the level of depolarizing stimuli in successive pulses until they are well above threshold? This experiment displays another significant property of axonal membranes: With further increases in depolarizing stimulation, the amplitude of the nerve impulse does not change. The size of the nerve impulse is thus independent of stimulus magnitude. This characteristic is referred to as the **all-or-none property** of the nerve impulse. However, increases in stimulus strength are represented in the axon by changes in the frequency of nerve impulses rather than in the amplitude. Thus with stronger stimuli, more nerve impulses are produced, but the size of each impulse remains the same.

If we continue the experiment on this axon by applying either very strong stimuli or stimulating pulses that are closely spaced in time, we observe another im-

(a)

(b) Hyperpolarizing stimuli

(c) Depolarizing stimuli

Responses

Responses

Action potential

Overshoot

Depolarizing responses

Threshold

Hyperpolarizing responses

Subthreshold responses

Resting potential

Afterpotential

3.3 Effects of Hyperpolarizing and Depolarizing Stimuli on a Neuron

(*a*) The experimental setup. (*b*) Increasing the strength of hyperpolarizing stimuli leads to greater hyperpolarization of the neuron. (*c*) Increasing the strength of depolarizing stimuli leads to increasing depolarization of the neuron until the threshold is reached and an action potential is generated.

portant property of axonal membranes. As we offer the beleaguered axon more and more stimuli, we note an upper limit to the frequency for nerve impulse activity, at about 1200 impulses per second. (Many neurons have even slower maximum rates of response.) The same underlying property is shown in experiments in which we compare the effects of varying the interval between two successive stimuli; that is, we space our stimuli closer and closer together until, at a particular brief interval, only the first pulse elicits a nerve impulse. In this case the axon membrane is said to be **refractory** (unresponsive) to the second stimulus. For a short while after the initiation of a nerve impulse the membrane is totally insensitive to applied stimuli. This period is called the **absolute refractory phase** and is followed by a period of reduced sensitivity, the **relative refractory phase**.

A closer look at the form of the nerve impulse shows that the return to baseline is not simple. Rather, many axons show oscillations of potential following the nerve impulse. These changes are called **afterpotentials** (or "undershoots"), and they are related to ion movements that we'll describe shortly.

Ionic Mechanisms Underlie the Action Potential

In the previous section we noted that when the membrane potential or voltage is changed by about 15 mV in a positive direction (depolarized), the membrane potential suddenly shifts in an explosive manner to a point at which the inside of the cell becomes transiently positive relative to the outside. The membrane potential then rapidly falls to somewhat less than the resting potential and then returns to the resting level. Why does this happen? It used to be thought that the action potential resulted from a momentary increase in membrane permeability to all ions that causes the membrane potential to drop to zero, but Nobel prize–winning research with the squid axon by English neurophysiologists Alan Hodgkin and Andrew Huxley revealed that an overshoot briefly makes the inside of the neuron positive with respect to the outside (see Figure 3.3c).

The amplitude of this overshoot is determined by the concentration of sodium ions (Hodgkin and Katz, 1949), even though sodium does not affect the resting potential. At the peak of the nerve impulse, the potential across the membrane approaches that predict-

Alan Hodgkin
(1914–1998)

Andrew F. Huxley

ed by the Nernst equation with respect to the concentration of sodium ions: about +40 mV. At this potential, the concentration gradient pushing Na$^+$ ions in is exactly balanced by the positive charge pushing them out.

In its resting state the neural membrane can be thought of as a "potassium membrane," since it is permeable only to K$^+$ and the potential is about that of the potassium equilibrium potential. The active membrane, however, is a "sodium membrane," permeable mainly to Na$^+$, so the membrane potential briefly tends toward the sodium equilibrium potential. Thus the action potential occurs during a sudden shift in membrane properties, which revert quickly to the resting state.

What causes the changes from K$^+$ permeability to Na$^+$ permeability and back again? A reduction in the resting potential of the membrane (depolarization) increases Na$^+$ permeability. This depolarization can be thought of as "opening gates" in pores, or ion channels, that pass from the inside to the outside of the membrane (Figure 3.4). Some gates or channels admit Na$^+$ but no other ions. As some sodium ions enter the neuron, the resting potential is further reduced, causing still more Na$^+$ channels to open. Thus the process accelerates until all barriers to the entry of Na$^+$ are removed, and sodium ions rush in. This process is an example of positive feedback, which we'll discuss in more detail later in the chapter. The increased permeability to Na$^+$ lasts less than a millisecond in some neurons; then a process of inactivation blocks the Na$^+$ channels. By this time the membrane potential has reached the sodium equilibrium potential of around +40 mV. Now positive charges inside the nerve cell tend to push potassium ions out, and the permeability to K$^+$ also increases, so the resting potential is soon restored.

The absolute and relative refractory phases also can be related to these changes in membrane permeability to ions. When the Na$^+$ channels have opened completely during the rise of the nerve impulse, further stimulation does not affect the course of events. During inactivation of the Na$^+$ channels, when stimulation cannot reopen them, the action current falls off.

Thus, during the rising and falling phases of an action potential, the neuron is *absolutely* refractory to elicitation of a second impulse. While K$^+$ ions are flowing out and the resting potential is being restored, the neuron is *relatively* refractory.

Why do sodium channels open when the cell is depolarized, and why do they close again less than a millisecond later? The application of special techniques has enabled a more complete picture of the dynamics of ion channels. The following sections present a brief look at this research.

Ion Channels Are Gated Rapidly

Because changes in the permeability of the nerve membrane to Na$^+$ and K$^+$ during the nerve impulse are so important, many investigators study the mechanisms that control these events. One problem is finding the molecular bases of the voltage sensors in the axon membrane that trigger the changes; another is locating the "gates" in the ionic channels. Gating (opening and closing) is thought to involve rearrangements in the shape or positions of charged molecules that line the channel. Making such changes requires the expenditure of energy. Minute electrical currents across the membrane seem to be related to the molecular rearrangements that open or shut gates in ion channels; these currents have been called **gating currents**.

As we will see, some ion channels are gated mainly by changes in the electrical potential across the neuronal membrane and are thus referred to as **voltage-gated channels**; other ion channels are gated chiefly by chemical substances that bind to their outer surfaces. We will discuss these ion channels later in the chapter. Axon membranes are studded with special voltage-gated sodium channels that open in response to depolarization, then automatically close again within a millisecond (Figure 3.5). These voltage-gated channels allow axons to produce the action potential. The molecular structure of each sodium channel allows it to be in (1) a resting state, or (2) an activated state in which the channel is open, or (3) an inactivated state in which the channel is closed and cannot be activated by depolarization. Thus, for each sodium channel there is an **activation gate** that is closed when the membrane is resting and opened with depolarization and an **inactivation gate** that is open in a resting state and closes slowly with depolarization.

In general, the cell bodies and most dendrites do not conduct action potentials, and this lack of conduction can be explained in terms of the kinds of membrane channels they contain. Although the cell body and den-

3.4 Receptors and Channels

Neuronal membranes are studded with receptors and channels that consist of several large protein molecules linked together, floating in the fatty layers of the membrane.

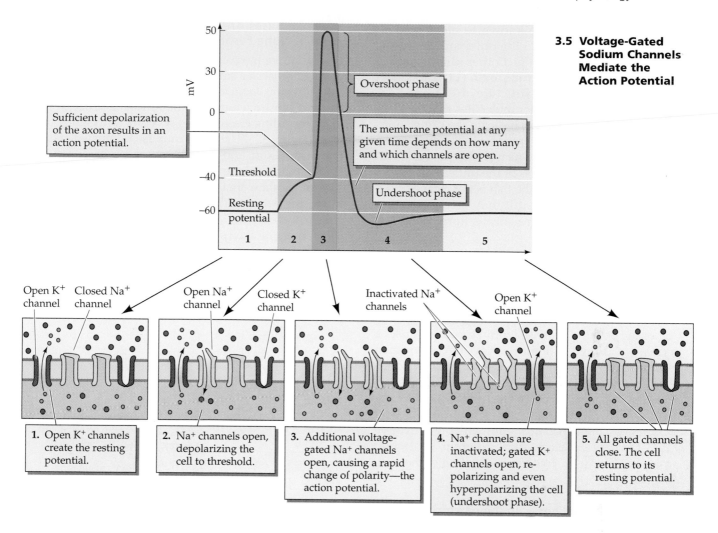

3.5 Voltage-Gated Sodium Channels Mediate the Action Potential

Sufficient depolarization of the axon results in an action potential.

Overshoot phase

The membrane potential at any given time depends on how many and which channels are open.

Undershoot phase

Threshold

Resting potential

Open K+ channel Closed Na+ channel

Open Na+ channel Closed K+ channel

Inactivated Na+ channels

Open K+ channel

1. Open K+ channels create the resting potential.

2. Na+ channels open, depolarizing the cell to threshold.

3. Additional voltage-gated Na+ channels open, causing a rapid change of polarity—the action potential.

4. Na+ channels are inactivated; gated K+ channels open, re-polarizing and even hyperpolarizing the cell (undershoot phase).

5. All gated channels close. The cell returns to its resting potential.

drites have ion channels that are gated by certain chemicals, and they can therefore be stimulated chemically, they have few voltage-gated channels. For this reason, a change in electrical potential cannot regenerate itself over the surface of the cell body by affecting voltage-gated channels in the adjacent stretch of cell membrane. The same is true for most dendrites. However, axons have voltage-gated ion channels and thus are electrically excitable.

How Can We Study Ion Channels?

Let's look briefly at present concepts of the structure of ion channels and then consider how investigators have been able to determine these structures. The membrane is a double layer of lipids whose fatty nature tends to repel water. Because ions in water or body fluids are usually surrounded by clusters of water molecules, they cannot easily pass through neuron membranes. Instead, they penetrate the cell through special channels, the inner surfaces of which do not repel water (see Figure 3.4).

Important method

The ion channels in neuron membranes are too tiny to be seen in detail even with the electron microscope. How then can investigators determine their structures

and modes of operation? Three main techniques have been used, providing more complete knowledge about ion channels. Molecular genetic analysis of potassium and sodium channels in a variety of cells including muscles and neurons has yielded a detailed portrait of ion channel structure and function. Some of these studies have come from the scrutiny of abnormalities in sodium and potassium channel function that underlie particular human diseases. For example, some heritable muscle disorders characterized by loss of muscle tone or paralysis involve abnormalities in the sodium channels of muscle that include an impairment of the inactivation gate for sodium (S. C. Cannon, 1996). These studies reveal that multiple genes encode the structure and function of ion channel proteins. Other researchers use pharmacology or patch clamp techniques, which we describe next.

Pharmacological techniques. Pharmacological experiments use certain toxins of animal origin to block specific ion channels—some affecting the activation gate near the outer end of the channel, and others inhibiting the inactivation gate at the inner end of the channel. By specifically blocking only some channels, these toxins make it easier to study the remaining channels.

Two animal toxins are known to block sodium channels when applied to the outer surface of the membrane; they do not affect other kinds of channels. These toxins are **tetrodotoxin (TTX)** and **saxitoxin (STX)**. The size and structure of TTX and STX, together with those of other molecules that do or do not alter Na$^+$ permeability, indicate the dimensions of the sodium channel. Tetrodotoxin is found in the ovaries of the puffer fish, which is esteemed as a delicacy in Japan. If the ovaries of the puffer fish are not removed properly and if the fish is not cleaned with great care, people who eat it may be poisoned by TTX, which prevents their neurons from producing action potentials.

In contrast to toxins that act at a site near the outer surface of the membrane, certain local anesthetics act at a different site, which is accessible only from inside the membrane. Whereas the action of local anesthetics is temporary and wears off, the introduction of the enzyme pronase within the axon causes a permanent change. Pronase destroys the inactivation gate that normally shuts the Na$^+$ channel. Two kinds of scorpions have evolved venoms that block neural conduction. The venom of the *Leiurus* scorpion impairs the inactivation gate; the venom of the *Centruroides* scorpion specifically impairs the activation gate. Thus, it is clear that different molecular processes control the two kinds of gating of the sodium channel.

Patch clamp recordings.   In the **patch clamp** technique, a small patch of membrane is sealed by suction to the end of a micropipette, enabling investigators to record currents through single membrane channels (Figure 3.6). Erwin Neher and Bert Sakmann were awarded the Nobel prize in 1991 for devising this technique. Patch clamp recordings have been made not only in nerve cells but also in glial cells and muscle cells. The recordings show that the channels open abruptly and remain open only briefly (see Figure 3.6, bottom). Opening of some channels is made more likely by changes in voltage; these are the voltage-gated channels we described earlier. As we have seen, one example is the voltage-activated sodium channel that is responsible for the rising phase of the nerve impulse. This type of channel responds extremely rapidly. Channels of the other main family respond to chemical substances applied to the surface of the cell; their responses are slower than those of the voltage-gated channels. Examples of these *chemically gated channels* will come up a little later in this chapter when we discuss what happens at synapses.

Erwin Neher (left)
Bert Sakmann (right)

Nerve Impulses Are Propagated in All-or-None Fashion

Now that we have explored the characteristics of a nerve impulse at a single location on the axon, we can ask how the axon communicates nerve impulses along its entire length. To examine this process, we place recording electrodes at several points along the axon (Figure 3.7). The nerve impulse is initiated at one end of the axon, and recordings are made with electrodes placed along the length of the axon. These recordings show that the nerve impulse appears with increasing delays at the successive positions along the length of the axon. The nerve impulse initiated at one location on the axon spreads in a sort of chain reaction along the length, traveling at speeds that range from less than 1 m/s in some fibers to more than 100 m/s in others.

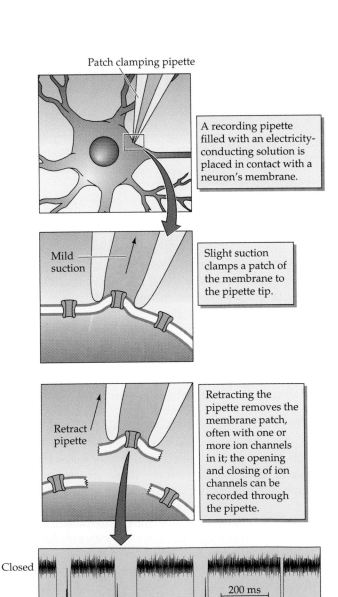

Patch clamping pipette

A recording pipette filled with an electricity-conducting solution is placed in contact with a neuron's membrane.

Mild suction

Slight suction clamps a patch of the membrane to the pipette tip.

Retract pipette

Retracting the pipette removes the membrane patch, often with one or more ion channels in it; the opening and closing of ion channels can be recorded through the pipette.

Closed

200 ms

Open

3.6 Patch Clamp Recording from a Single Ion Channel

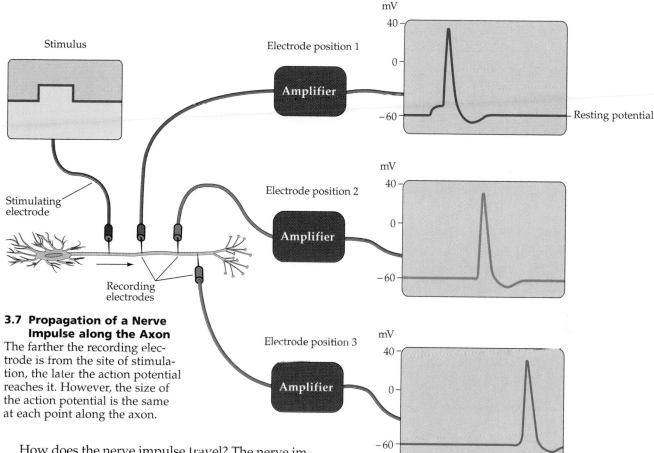

3.7 Propagation of a Nerve Impulse along the Axon
The farther the recording electrode is from the site of stimulation, the later the action potential reaches it. However, the size of the action potential is the same at each point along the axon.

How does the nerve impulse travel? The nerve impulse is a change in membrane potential that is regenerated at successive axon locations. It spreads from one region to another because the flow of current associated with this small and rapid change in potential depolarizes and thus stimulates adjacent axon segments. That is (as we noted earlier), the nerve impulse regenerates itself at successive points along the axon. An analogy is the spread of fire along a row of closely spaced matches. When one match is lit, the heat associated with its flame can be hot enough to start fire in an adjacent match and so on along the row. Voltage-gated sodium channels open when the axon is depolarized to threshold. In turn, the influx of sodium ions—the movement into the cell of positive charges—depolarizes the adjacent segment of axon membrane and therefore opens new gates for the movement of sodium ions.

The axon normally conducts impulses in only one direction because the action potential starts at the **axon hillock**, the place where the axon emerges from the cell body. As the action potential progresses along the axon, it leaves in its wake a stretch of refractory membrane. Propagated activity does not spread from the hillock back over the cell body and dendrites, because the membrane of the cell body and of most dendrites does not produce a regenerated impulse.

If we record the conduction speed of impulses in axons that differ in diameter, we see that the rate of conduction varies with the diameter of the axon. In mammals, relatively large, heavily myelinated fibers are found in sensory and motor nerves. In these neurons conduction speed ranges from about 5 m/s in axons that are 2 µm in diameter to 120 m/s in axons that are 20 µm in diameter. Although once thought to be as great as the speed of light, the highest speed of neural conduction is "only" about one-third the speed of sound in air. This relatively high rate of conduction aids the speed of sensory and motor processes (Figure 3.8).

The myelin sheathing on the larger mammalian nerve fibers greatly speeds conduction. The myelin is interrupted by the **nodes of Ranvier**, small gaps spaced about every millimeter along the axon (see Figure 2.6). Since the myelin insulation offers considerable resistance to the flow of ionic currents, the impulse jumps from node to node. This process is called **saltatory conduction** (from the Latin *saltus*, "a leap or jump") (Figure 3.8*b*). The evolution of rapid saltatory conduction in vertebrates has given them a major behavioral advantage over invertebrates, in which axons are unmyelinated and mostly small in diameter, and thus slow in conduction.

One exception to this rule is that many invertebrates have a few giant axons, which mediate behaviorally significant motor responses, such as escape movements. In the invertebrate as in the vertebrate, the speed of conduction increases with axon diameter.

(a) Slow (10 meters per second) conduction of action potential along unmyelinated axon

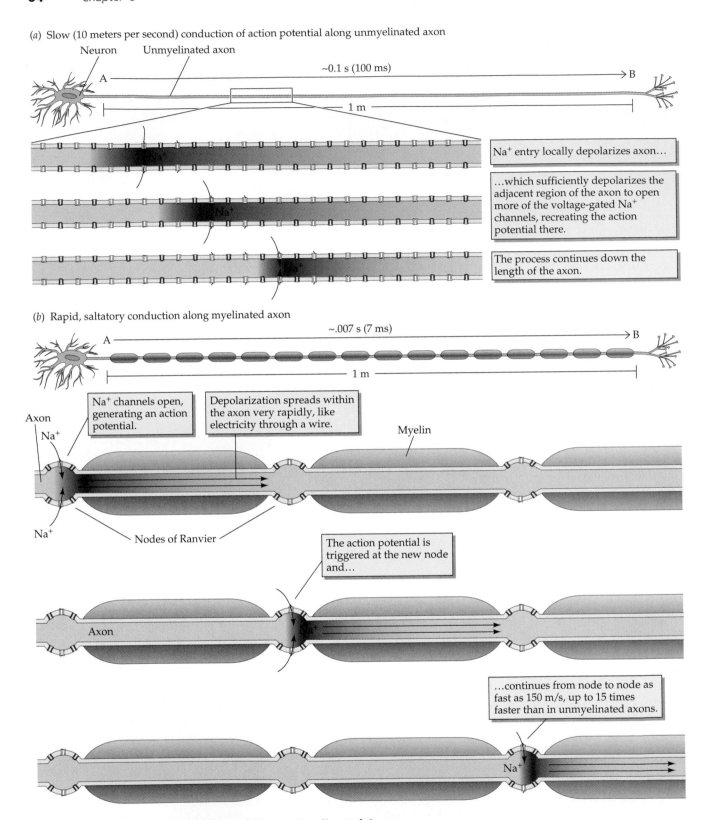

Neuron   Unmyelinated axon

~0.1 s (100 ms)

A   B

1 m

Na⁺ entry locally depolarizes axon…

…which sufficiently depolarizes the adjacent region of the axon to open more of the voltage-gated Na⁺ channels, recreating the action potential there.

The process continues down the length of the axon.

(b) Rapid, saltatory conduction along myelinated axon

~.007 s (7 ms)

A   B

1 m

Na⁺ channels open, generating an action potential.

Depolarization spreads within the axon very rapidly, like electricity through a wire.

Myelin

Axon

Na⁺

Na⁺   Nodes of Ranvier

The action potential is triggered at the new node and…

Axon

…continues from node to node as fast as 150 m/s, up to 15 times faster than in unmyelinated axons.

Na⁺

3.8 Conduction along Unmyelinated Versus Myelinated Axons

The giant axon of the squid has an unusually high rate of conduction for an invertebrate, but the rate still is only about 20 m/s, about the rate of small myelinated neurons with diameters of only 5 µm. To conduct impulses as fast as a myelinated vertebrate axon does, an unmyelinated invertebrate axon has to have 10 times the diameter and thus 100 times the volume. It has been estimated that at least 10% of the volume of the human brain is occupied by myelinated axons. To maintain the conduction velocity of our cerebral neurons without the help of myelin, our brains would have to be ten times as large as they are.

The importance of myelin sheathing in promoting rapid conduction of neural impulses helps explain why myelination is an important index of maturation of the nervous system (see Chapter 7). It also helps explain the gravity of diseases that attack myelin, such as **multiple sclerosis**. With this disease, the body mounts an immune response against its own myelin, resulting in both motor and sensory impairments, including slowing of movements and loss of sensory abilities.

In Synaptic Transmission, the Activity of Presynaptic Axon Terminals Elicits Postsynaptic Potentials

Neurons communicate with one another at synapses. Until the early 1920s, vigorous dispute characterized discussions about the nature of communication across synapses in the nervous system. The big issue was whether synaptic communication was electrical or chemical: Either the electrical nerve impulse directly stimulates the adjacent cell, or the neuron secretes a substance that excites the adjacent cell. Attempts to prove various forms of the electrical or the chemical hypothesis provoked lively controversies for a century.

Competing hypotheses

Then one night in 1921, Otto Loewi awoke from a dream in which he thought of an experiment that might answer the question. He excitedly scribbled some notes and returned to sleep. In the morning he was disappointed to find his notes indecipherable. When he had the dream again, Loewi got dressed and went straight to his lab to complete the relatively simple experiment. He electrically stimulated the vagus nerve in a frog, which he knew would slow its heart rate. He then took the fluid bathing that heart and applied it to another, unstimulated heart. This second heart also slowed its beating, showing that stimulation of the first heart had released a chemical into the fluid. Loewi eventually proved that the chemical inhibiting the heart was acetylcholine—the first demonstrated **neurotransmitter** (or **transmitter**), a chemical released by a neuron to affect a postsynaptic cell. We will discuss transmitters further in this chapter and in Chapter 4. Although most synapses use a chemical signal such as acetylcholine, eventually it was found that the nervous system also employs electrical synapses (Box 3.1).

Postsynaptic (local) potentials are studied with a setup like that shown in Figure 3.9. During the 1950s and 1960s, experiments on synaptic transmission in mammals involved spinal motoneurons because they are large and many characteristics of their inputs were known. The receptive surface of each spinal motoneuron has many synaptic connections. By selecting the presynaptic cell to stimulate, investigators can see how the motoneuron responds to inputs from these varied connections. The responses of the presynaptic and postsynaptic cells are shown on the same graphs in Figure 3.9 for easy comparison of their time relations.

Stimulation of an excitatory presynaptic neuron leads to an all-or-none action potential in the presynaptic cell. In the postsynaptic cell, after a brief synaptic delay, a small local depolarization is seen. This postsynaptic membrane depolarization is known

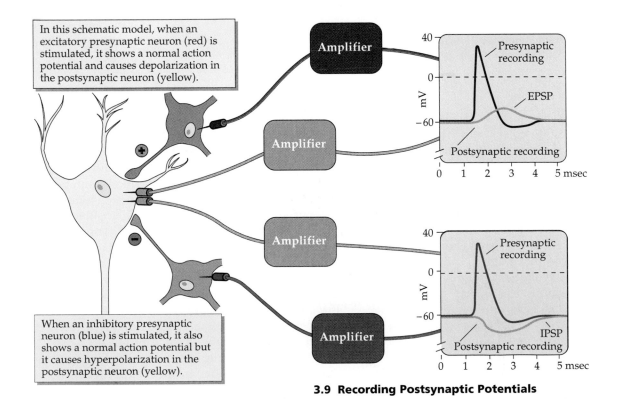

In this schematic model, when an excitatory presynaptic neuron (red) is stimulated, it shows a normal action potential and causes depolarization in the postsynaptic neuron (yellow).

When an inhibitory presynaptic neuron (blue) is stimulated, it also shows a normal action potential but it causes hyperpolarization in the postsynaptic neuron (yellow).

3.9 Recording Postsynaptic Potentials

BOX 3.1 *Electrical Synapses Work with No Time Delay*

Although most synapses require a chemical substance to mediate synaptic transmission, all species that have been investigated in this regard also have some purely electrical synapses. At **electrical synapses** the presynaptic membrane comes even closer to the postsynaptic membrane than it does at chemical synapses; the cleft measures only 2 to 4 nm (see Figure A). In contrast, the gap is 20 to 40 nm at chemical synapses. At electrical synapses, the facing membranes of the two cells have relatively large channels that allow ions to flow from one neuron into the other (Figure B). As a consequence, the flow of electrical current that is associated with nerve impulses in the presynaptic axon terminal can travel across the presynaptic and the postsynaptic membranes.

Transmission at these synapses closely resembles conduction along the axon. Electrical synapses therefore work with practically no time delay, in contrast to chemical synapses, where the delay is on the order of a millisecond—slow in terms of neurons. Because of the speed of their transmission, electrical synapses are frequently found in neural circuits that mediate escape behaviors in invertebrates. They are also found where many fibers must be activated synchronously, as in the vertebrate oculomotor system. (Figure A courtesy of Constantino Sotelo.)

(A) Electron micrograph of an electrical synapse

(B) Diagram of an electrical synapse

Neuron 1

Neuron 2

3.5 nm

20 nm

4.2 nm

Ions pass freely between cells

---

as an **excitatory postsynaptic potential** (**EPSP**) because it pushes the postsynaptic cell closer to the threshold for an action potential. Generally the combined effect of many excitatory synapses is required to elicit an action potential in a postsynaptic neuron. If excitatory postsynaptic potentials are elicited almost simultaneously by many neurons that converge on the motor cell, these potentials can summate and produce a depolarization that reaches the threshold and triggers an action potential. Note that there is a delay: In the fastest cases, the postsynaptic depolarization begins about half a millisecond after the presynaptic impulses. This delay was important evidence that the postsynaptic effect is not just a weakened reflection of the presynaptic action current, because a purely electrical response would not show such a delay.

The action potential of an inhibitory presynaptic neuron looks exactly like that of the excitatory pre-

synaptic fiber; neurons have only one kind of propagated signal. But the *postsynaptic* local potentials show opposite polarities. When the inhibitory neuron is stimulated, the postsynaptic signal is an *increase* of the resting potential. This hyperpolarization is inhibitory for the motoneuron—it decreases the probability that the neuron will fire an impulse—so it is called an **inhibitory postsynaptic potential** (**IPSP**). Although we have been paying more attention to excitation, inhibition also plays a vital role in neural processing of information. Just as driving a car requires brakes as well as an accelerator, neural switches must be turned off as well as on. The nervous system treads a narrow path between overexcitation, leading to seizures, and underexcitation, leading to coma and death.

Whether a neuron fires off an action potential at any given moment is decided by the relation between the number of excitatory and the number of inhibitory (*a*) Excitatory inputs cause the cell to fire

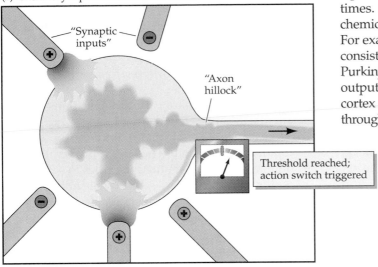

"Synaptic inputs"

"Axon hillock"

Threshold reached; action switch triggered

(*b*) Inhibition also plays a role

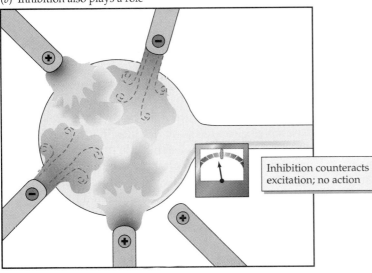

Inhibition counteracts excitation; no action

(*c*) The cell integrates excitation and inhibition

Additional excitation overcomes inhibition; action switch triggered

3.10 Physical Model of Spatial Summation in a Postsynaptic Cell

signals it is receiving, and it receives many of both at all times. Some neurons and some synaptic transmitter chemicals are specialized to send inhibitory messages. For example, the entire output of the cerebellar cortex consists of messages from the large Purkinje cells. The Purkinje cell axons send only inhibitory messages to the output nuclei deep in the cerebellum, so the cerebellar cortex exercises all of its effects on the rest of the brain through inhibition. The terminals of the Purkinje cell axons use the synaptic transmitter gamma-aminobutyric acid (GABA), as do many other cells. A measure of the importance of inhibition is the estimate that GABA is present at about 40% of the synapses in the brain. In later chapters we will see specific neural circuits that involve inhibition—circuits for perception, motor control, and emotion.

Temporal Summation and Spatial Summation Integrate Synaptic Inputs

Synaptic transmission and impulse conduction not only communicate signals but also integrate and transform messages in ways that make complex behavior possible. This means that the nerve cell, with its synaptic inputs, is able both to summate and to subtract input signals. These operations are possible because of the characteristics of synaptic inputs, the way in which the neuron integrates the postsynaptic potentials, and the trigger mechanism that determines whether a neuron will fire off an impulse.

As we have seen, the postsynaptic potentials that are caused by the action of transmitter chemicals can be either depolarizing (excitatory) or hyperpolarizing (inhibitory). These EPSPs and IPSPs spread passively over the neuron from their points of origin on dendrites and on the cell body. The trigger mechanism for mammalian neurons is located at the initial segment of the axon, which in mammalian multipolar neurons is the axon hillock. Thus what determines whether the postsynaptic neuron will fire off an action potential is whether depolarization reaches the critical threshold at the axon hillock.

The physical model in Figure 3.10 is analogous to information processing by the nerve cell. Here the cell body is represented by a metal disc. For simplicity, no dendrites are shown, and all input endings are on the cell body. The presynaptic terminals are represented by tubes through which blasts of hot or cold air can be delivered; hot air represents excitatory synaptic action, and cold air inhibitory synaptic action. The axon hillock contains a thermostat. If the temperature rises above a critical temperature (the threshold), the thermostat closes a circuit and triggers a propagated impulse.

Suppose impulses arrive at two excitatory endings, as shown in Figure 3.10*a*. The pulses of hot air are delivered, causing local heating of the cell body. This heat spreads out over the disc, dissipating as it spreads so that only a small proportion of the heat reaches the axon hillock. Yet the two together push the hillock region to threshold. Figure 3.10*b* shows what happens when blasts of cold air are also delivered. The resultant local cooling also spreads passively, so the change of temperature diminishes as it travels. Since some tubes cool and others warm the hillock, these effects partially cancel each other. Thus the net effect is the difference between the two: The neuron subtracts the IPSP from the EPSP.

If two excitatory terminals are activated simultaneously, their effects sum at the hillock: The neuron adds postsynaptic potentials that have the same sign. The summation of potentials across the cell body is called **spatial summation**. Only if the overall result of all the potentials is sufficient to raise the hillock temperature to the threshold level is an impulse triggered (Figure 3.10*c*). Usually the convergence of excitatory messages from many presynaptic fibers is required to fire off a neuron.

Postsynaptic effects that are not absolutely simultaneous can also be summated, since the effects last for a few milliseconds. The closer they are in time, the greater the overlap and the more complete the summation, which in this case is called **temporal summation**. Even successive impulses arriving at the same terminal can produce postsynaptic effects that summate. Thus although the impulses are all-or-none, the postsynaptic effect can be graded in size: A rapid barrage of impulses produces a larger postsynaptic potential than a single impulse does.

Dendrites have been omitted from Figure 3.10 for simplicity, but they add to the story. Dendrites augment the receptive surface of the neuron and increase the amount of input information the neuron can handle. The farther out on a dendrite a potential is produced, the less effect the potential will have on the trigger zone for action potentials—the axon hillock. When the potential arises at a dendritic spine, its effect is further reduced because it has to spread down the shaft of the spine. Thus information arriving at various parts of the neuron is weighted in terms of the distance and path resistance to the axon hillock.

We have mentioned many properties of action and synaptic potentials. Table 3.1 summarizes these properties and notes the principal similarities and differences among the three kinds of neural potentials.

The Sequence of Transmission Processes at Chemical Synapses

The sequence of events during chemical synaptic transmission, shown in Figure 3.11, includes the following main steps:

1. The nerve impulse propagates into the presynaptic axon terminal.
2. A change in voltage-gated calcium channels in the axon terminal leads to the movement of calcium ions into the axon terminal.
3. Calcium causes synaptic vesicles to fuse with the presynaptic membrane.
4. Fused vesicles release their transmitter molecules into the synaptic cleft.
5. Some transmitter molecules bind onto special receptor molecules in the postsynaptic membrane.
6. Binding of the transmitter molecules to distinct receptor molecules leads—directly or indirectly—to the opening of ion channels in the postsynaptic membrane; the resulting flow of ions alters the polarization of the postsynaptic neuron. If the depolarization is sufficient to reach the threshold of the postsynaptic neuron, it will fire an action potential at its axon hillock.
7. Synaptic transmitter is inactivated or removed rapidly from the synaptic cleft, so the transmission is brief and accurately follows the presynaptic input signal.

Let's review these steps in a little more detail. As we noted in Chapter 2, synaptic vesicles are located within the axon terminal of the presynaptic neuron. These vesicles are small globules that range from 30 to 140 nm in diameter. From the time they were discovered in electron micrographs in the 1950s, synaptic vesicles were linked with chemical transmission, and they have since been demonstrated to store packets of the chemical transmitter used at the synapse. As is true of chocolates in a box, the size and shape of the vesicles provide clues to the identity of the transmitters they contain. Researchers used to believe that any given neuron uses only a single transmitter, but many end boutons have been found to contain two or more kinds of vesicles and transmitters.

In Chapter 2 we also learned that the synaptic cleft is the space between the presynaptic and postsynap-

TABLE 3.1	**Characteristics of Electrical Signals of Nerve Cells**	
Type of signal	**Signaling role**	**Typical duration (ms)**
Action potential (neural impulse)	Conduction along a neuron	1–2
Excitatory postsynaptic potential (EPSP)	Transmission between neurons	10–100
Inhibitory postsynaptic potential (IPSP)	Transmission between neurons	10–100

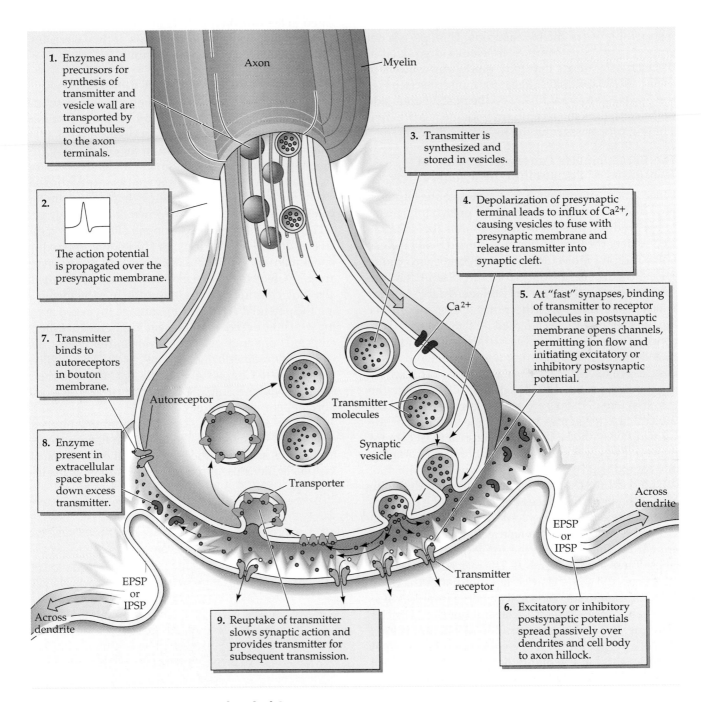

1. Enzymes and precursors for synthesis of transmitter and vesicle wall are transported by microtubules to the axon terminals.

2. The action potential is propagated over the presynaptic membrane.

3. Transmitter is synthesized and stored in vesicles.

4. Depolarization of presynaptic terminal leads to influx of Ca^{2+}, causing vesicles to fuse with presynaptic membrane and release transmitter into synaptic cleft.

5. At "fast" synapses, binding of transmitter to receptor molecules in postsynaptic membrane opens channels, permitting ion flow and initiating excitatory or inhibitory postsynaptic potential.

7. Transmitter binds to autoreceptors in bouton membrane.

8. Enzyme present in extracellular space breaks down excess transmitter.

9. Reuptake of transmitter slows synaptic action and provides transmitter for subsequent transmission.

6. Excitatory or inhibitory postsynaptic potentials spread passively over dendrites and cell body to axon hillock.

Axon

Myelin

Ca^{2+}

Autoreceptor

Transmitter molecules

Synaptic vesicle

Transporter

Transmitter receptor

EPSP or IPSP

Across dendrite

EPSP or IPSP

Across dendrite

3.11 Steps in Transmission at a Chemical Synapse

Amplitude	Character	Mode of propagation	Ion channel opening	Channel sensitive to:
Overshooting, 100 mV	All-or-nothing, digital	Actively propagated, regenerative	First Na^+, then K^+, in different channels	Voltage (depolarization)
Depolarizing, from less than 1 to more than 20 mV	Graded, analog	Local, passive spread	Na^+–K^+	Chemical (neurotransmitter)
Hyperpolarizing, from less than 1 to about 15 mV	Graded, analog	Local, passive spread	K^+–Cl^-	Chemical (neurotransmitter)

tic neurons. Only about 20 to 40 nm separate the facing membranes of the two neurons. This space is not empty; it contains complex molecules organized in distinctive patterns that may guide transmitters to their postsynaptic sites. Receptor molecules (see Figure 3.4) are clustered thickly on the postsynaptic side of the cleft; thus the receptor membrane has different staining properties from the rest of the membrane.

The Nerve Impulse Causes the Release of Transmitter Molecules into the Synaptic Cleft

When a nerve impulse reaches a presynaptic terminal, how does it cause vesicles near the presynaptic membrane to discharge their contents into the synaptic cleft, where the transmitter molecules quickly diffuse to the receptor molecules on the other side (see Figure 3.11)? The arrival of the nerve impulse at the presynaptic terminal causes calcium ions (Ca^{2+}) to enter the terminal. The greater the influx of Ca^{2+}, the greater the number of vesicles released by the impulse. If the concentration of Ca^{2+} in the extracellular fluid is reduced, fewer Ca^{2+} ions enter the terminal and fewer vesicles are released. Most synaptic delay is caused by the processes related to the entrance of Ca^{2+} into the terminal. Small delays are also caused by diffusion of the transmitter across the cleft and reaction of the transmitter with the receptor. The structural components of the synaptic vesicle membrane are complex; one component is a protein called synaptotagmin that can bind calcium. Other vesicle components deal with the mechanism that places the vesicle in the right position for release of its contents (Matthews, 1996).

All the vesicles for a given transmitter in a synapse appear to contain about the same number of molecules of transmitter chemical. The release of each vesicle causes the same change in potential in the postsynaptic membrane. Normally a nerve impulse causes release of the contents of several hundred vesicles at a time. But if the concentration of calcium is lowered at a synapse, only a few vesicles are released per impulse, and the size of unit depolarizations can then be measured. The number of molecules of transmitter per vesicle is probably in the tens of thousands.

The presynaptic terminal normally produces and stores enough transmitter to ensure that it is ready for activity. Intense stimulation of the neuron reduces the number of vesicles, but soon more vesicles are produced to replace those that were discharged. Neurons differ in their ability to keep pace with a rapid rate of incoming signals. The production of the transmitter chemical is governed by enzymes that are manufac-

tured in the neuron cell body and transported actively down the axons to the terminals. If they were not, synaptic function could not continue.

Receptor Molecules Recognize Transmitters

The action of a key in a lock is a good analogy to the action of a transmitter on a receptor protein. Just as a particular key can open different doors, a particular chemical transmitter can lead to the opening of different channels in the neural membrane. At excitatory synapses where it is the transmitter, **acetylcholine (ACh)** fits into "recognition sites" in **receptor molecules** located in the postsynaptic membrane (Figure 3.12). This binding of ACh opens channels successively for Na^+ and K^+ ions, as Hodgkin and Huxley had shown for neural excitation. At inhibitory synapses, ACh opens a different door; it opens channels allowing chloride ions (Cl^-) to enter, thereby increasing the potential across the membrane (hyperpolarizing it). Thus, the receptor protein is different at different kinds of synapses. Other transmitter chemicals (such as norepinephrine, glycine, and GABA, which we discuss in Chapter 4) must fit like keys into their specific locks; see Table 4.1 for a list of the most important neurotransmitters.

The lock-and-key analogy is strengthened by the observation that various chemicals can fit onto receptor proteins and block the entrance of the key. Some of the preparations used in this research resemble the in-

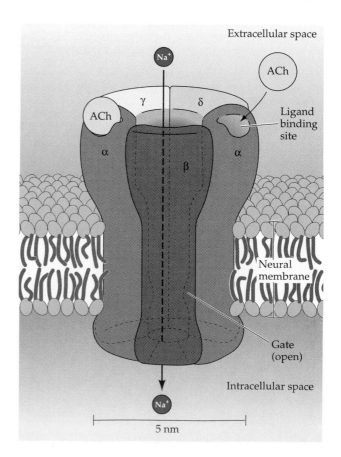

3.12 A Nicotinic Acetylcholine Receptor
Each nicotinic ACh receptor consists of five subunits. Two of the subunits have ligand-binding sites that normally bind ACh molecules but also bind nicotine and other "nicotinic" drugs. The ACh molecule and Na^+ ions are enlarged for diagrammatic purposes.

gredients of a witch's brew. Two blocking agents for ACh are poisons: curare and bungarotoxin. Curare is the arrowhead poison used by native South Americans. Extracted from a plant, it greatly increases the efficiency of hunting: If the hunter hits any part of the prey, the arrow's poison soon paralyzes the animal. Bungarotoxin is a lethal poison produced by the bungarus snake of Taiwan. This toxin has proved very useful in studying acetylcholine receptors because a radioactive label can be attached to it without altering its action. With such labeling, it is possible to investigate the number and distribution of receptor molecules at synapses, as well as details of the binding of transmitter to receptor.

Another poison, muscarine, mimics the action of ACh at some synapses. This poison is extracted from the mushroom *Amanita muscaria*. Molecules such as muscarine and nicotine that act like a transmitter at a receptor are called **agonists** (from the Greek *agon,* "contest, struggle") of that transmitter. Similarly, molecules that interfere with or prevent the action of a transmitter, as curare or bungarotoxin block the action of ACh at nicotinic receptors, are called **antagonists**.

Just as there are master keys that fit many different locks, there are submaster keys that fit a certain group of locks, and keys that fit only a single lock. Similarly, some chemical transmitters bind to several different receptor molecules, and others bind to only one. ACh acts on at least four kinds of receptors. Nicotinic and muscarinic are the two main kinds of cholinergic receptors (all ACh receptors are referred to as **cholinergic**). Nicotinic cholinergic receptors are found at synapses on skeletal muscles and in autonomic ganglia. Muscarinic cholinergic receptors are found on organs innervated by the parasympathetic division of the autonomic system (e.g., the heart muscle, the intestines, and the salivary gland). Most ACh receptors in the brain are muscarinic. Most nicotinic sites are excitatory, but there are also inhibitory nicotinic synapses, and there are both excitatory and inhibitory muscarinic synapses, making at least four kinds of acetylcholine receptors. The existence of many types of receptors for each transmitter agent appears to be a device to produce specificity of action in the nervous system.

Molecular genetic analysis has enabled researchers to generate a structural portrait of the nicotinic ACh receptor. Because many nicotinic ACh receptors are found in the electric organ of eels, it was possible to isolate from such organs the messenger RNA for these receptors. Large amounts of the corresponding DNA could then be cloned, and the sequence of nucleotides that convey the information of the DNA could be determined. From this sequence, the amino acid structure of the receptor could be deduced, enabling the construction of models of the three-dimensional structure of the nicotinic ACh receptor (see Figure 3.12) (Stroud and Finer-Moore, 1985).

The receptor resembles a lopsided dumbbell with a tube running down its central axis. The handle of the dumbbell spans the cell membrane (which is about 6 nm thick); the larger sphere extends about 5 nm above the surface of the membrane into the extracellular space, and the smaller sphere extends about 2 nm inside the cell. The sides of the ion channel (the tube that runs through the handle) consist of five subunits arranged like staves in a barrel. Two units bind to ACh and are alike; the other three are all different. Both ACh-binding sites must be occupied for the channel to open. The genes for each of the four types of subunits have been isolated (Mishina et al., 1984), and neuroscientists have been able to assemble complete or incomplete receptors to study how they work.

After the structure of the nicotinic ACh receptor was determined, similar analyses were carried out for other receptors, including receptors for some of the synaptic transmitter molecules that we will be considering later, such as GABA, glycine, and glutamate. Several of these receptors resemble each other, suggesting that they all belong to the same family and have a common evolutionary origin.

The number of receptors for a given transmitter in a region of the brain varies widely. Quantifying changes in the number of receptors has provided valuable insights, showing, for example, when various transmitter systems become active in fetal life and how the number of receptors changes over the life span. The number of receptors remains plastic in adults: Not only are there seasonal variations, but many kinds of receptors show a regular daily variation of 50% or more in number, as we will see when we take up daily rhythms in Chapter 14. The numbers of some receptors have been found to vary with the use of drugs (see Chapter 16). Chapter 18 describes how the number of some receptors increases with activity.

Recognition of Transmitters by Receptors Gates Ion Channels

The recognition of transmitter molecules by receptor molecules leads to gating of ion channels in two different ways. **Ionotropic receptors** (Figure 3.13*a*) directly control an ion channel. When they bind to the released transmitter, the ion channel opens and ions flow across the membrane. (Ionotropic receptors are also known as chemically gated or **ligand-gated ion channels**, because a chemical that binds a receptor is called a **ligand**.) **Metabotropic receptors** (Figure 3.13*b*) recognize the synaptic transmitter, but they do not directly control ion channels. Instead, they activate molecules known as **G proteins**.

"G protein" is a convenient designation for proteins that bind the compounds guanosine diphosphate (GDP) and guanosine triphosphate (GTP) and other guanine nucleotides. Sometimes the action of a G protein itself opens an ion channel, but in other cases, the G protein activates another, internal chemical

(a) Ligand-gated ion channel (fast, ionotropic)

Ions

1. Neurotransmitter binds.

Neurotransmitter

Outside cell

Inside cell

2. Channel opens.

3. Ions flow across membrane.

(b) G protein–coupled receptor (slow, metabotropic)

1. Neurotransmitter binds.

Neurotrans-mitter

Receptor

4. Ion channel opens.

α β γ

G protein

α

2. G protein is activated.

3. G protein subunits or intracellular messengers modulate ion channels.

Ions

5. Ions flow across membrane.

3.13 Two Types of Chemical Synapses

signal to affect ion channels. If we think of the transmitter as the first signal or messenger at the synapse, then in this type of synapse the G protein–activated substance within the cell is a second messenger. The **second messenger**, which is a chemical (such as cyclic AMP, diacylglycerol, or arachidonic acid) that is made more plentiful by G protein action, amplifies the effect of the first messenger and can initiate processes that lead to changes in electrical potential at the membrane. In many cases second messengers also lead to biochemical changes within the neuron.

Since about 80% of the known neurotransmitters and hormones activate cellular signal mechanisms through receptors coupled to G proteins, this device is very important (Birnbaumer et al., 1990). The G protein is located on the inner side of the neural membrane. When a transmitter molecule binds to a receptor that is coupled to a G protein, parts of the G protein complex dissociate (i.e., separate from each other). One part, called the alpha subunit, migrates away within the cell and modulates the activity of its target molecules. Depending on the type of cell and receptor, the target may be a second-messenger system, or an enzyme that works on an ion channel, or an ion pump. Many combinations of different receptors with different G proteins have already been identified, and more are being discovered at a rapid pace (Gudermann et al., 1997; Kobilka, 1992). For more information on modulation of channel function by G proteins, see Topic 3.1.

 Special topic

Table 3.2 summarizes the characteristics of the two different types of chemical synapses.

The Action of Synaptic Transmitters Is Stopped Rapidly

When a chemical transmitter such as ACh is released into the synaptic cleft, its postsynaptic action is not only prompt, but usually very brief as well. This brevity ensures that the message is repeated faithfully. Such accuracy of timing is necessary in many neural systems—for example, to ensure rapid changes of contraction and relaxation of muscles in coordinated behavior. The prompt cessation of transmitter effects is achieved in one of two ways: (1) Some transmitters are rapidly broken down and thus inactivated by a special enzyme, a process known as **degradation**. (2) Other transmitters are rapidly cleared from the synaptic cleft by being taken up into the presynaptic terminal, a process known as **reuptake**; reuptake not only cuts off the synaptic activity promptly, but also allows the terminal to recycle transmitter molecules.

In an example of the first instance, the enzyme that inactivates ACh is acetylcholinesterase (AChE). Acetylcholinesterase hydrolyzes (breaks down) ACh very rapidly into choline and acetic acid, and these products are recycled (at least in part) to make more ACh in the end bouton. AChE is found especially at synapses, but also elsewhere in the nervous system. Thus, if any ACh escapes from a synapse where it is released, it is unlikely to survive and reach other synapses, where it could start false messages.

TABLE 3.2 *Characteristics of the Two Main Kinds of Chemical Synapses*

	Ionotropic ("fast")	Metabotropic ("slow")
Characteristics		
Coupling of receptor to ion channel	Direct	Indirect; often uses G protein and/or second messenger
Speed of transmission	Fast	Slow[a]
Duration of response	Brief	Longer[a]
Examples of transmitters	ACh (at nicotinic receptor) Glycine, glutamate, GABA	ACh (at muscarinic receptor) Norepinephrine, dopamine, glutamate Neuropeptides
Names	Directly coupled	Indirectly coupled
	Fast	Slow
	Ligand-activated	G protein–coupled, or second messenger–coupled
	Ionotropic (directed toward ion flow)	Metabotropic (directed toward chemical events within the neuron)

[a] Especially for neuropeptide transmitters.

Norepinephrine and dopamine are examples of transmitters whose activity is terminated mainly by reuptake. In these cases, special receptors for the transmitter are located on the presynaptic axon terminal. These receptors, usually called **transporters**, take up the transmitter molecules and return them to the interior of the axon terminal, thus preventing them from making further contact with the postsynaptic receptors. Once taken up into the presynaptic terminal, some of the transmitter molecules are inserted into vesicles and can be released in response to further nerve impulses. The reuptake mechanism has been implicated in some kinds of mental illness (see Chapter 16).

At this point in our discussion, we should note that many of the neurophysiological properties of nerve cells we have discussed in this chapter show great variability (see Box 3.2).

The Evolution of Ion Channels, Synapses, and Transmitters

Many investigators are interested in comparative aspects and the evolution of ion channels, synapses, and transmitters (Arbas et al., 1991; see also Hille, 1992). For example, certain voltage-gated ion channels for K^+ and Ca^{2+} are found in plants and in unicellular animals as well as in multicellular animals and thus

---

BOX 3.2 *Nerve Cells Vary in Their Signaling*

The picture of nerve cell signals that we have presented to this point is a portrait of a typical cell operating under baseline conditions. Exceptions to these usual properties give the nervous system additional flexibility in information processing. To provide a sense of the diversity of neuron "lifestyles," here are a few of many such exceptions:

- Some nerve cells have very short axons or no axons at all. These cells communicate with other cells only via local electrical potentials and not via nerve impulses.
- Nerve cells differ in impulse threshold, the amount of depolarization necessary for initiating a nerve impulse.

- Nerve cells vary in the relationship between magnitude of depolarization and rate of nerve impulse firing. For some neurons, small increments in depolarization produce large changes in nerve impulse firing; for others the slope of the relation is shallower.
- The form of the action potential (e.g., the rate of rise and the duration) differs among neurons.
- Neurons differ in responses of synapses to successive nerve impulses. Some synapses show facilitating effects; that is, the size of successive synaptic potentials grows. In contrast, at other synapses the successive responses become smaller and smaller. Both of these effects show that the history of recent use affects what happens at a

synapse. This memorylike device of the synapse may be related to broader behavioral states such as learning and memory.
- Neurons differ in pacemaker-like activity. Some cells are autorhythmic, regularly generating nerve impulses independently of synaptic inputs. These cells may be especially important in controlling rhythmic behaviors.
- Temperature affects the rate of firing of some neurons, allowing them to act as internal temperature sensors.
- Neurons are influenced by hormones and neuromodulators (called neuromodulators because by themselves they do not produce significant neural effects; usually they change the way a neuron responds to a transmitter).

3.14 The Sequence and Timing of Events in the Knee Jerk Reflex

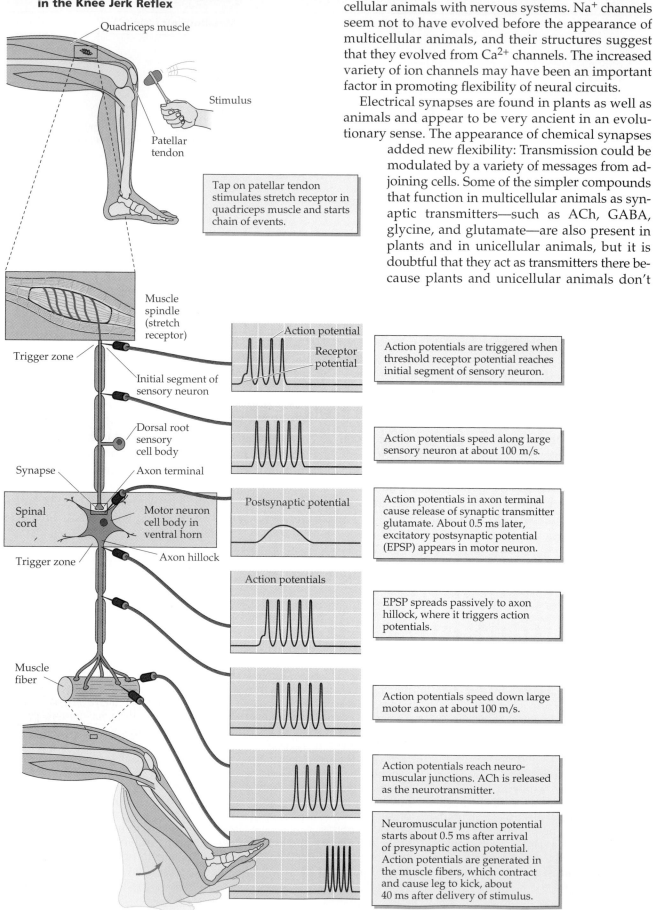

Quadriceps muscle

Stimulus

Patellar tendon

Tap on patellar tendon stimulates stretch receptor in quadriceps muscle and starts chain of events.

Muscle spindle (stretch receptor)

Trigger zone

Initial segment of sensory neuron

Dorsal root sensory cell body

Synapse

Axon terminal

Spinal cord

Motor neuron cell body in ventral horn

Trigger zone

Axon hillock

Muscle fiber

Action potential

Receptor potential

Action potentials are triggered when threshold receptor potential reaches initial segment of sensory neuron.

Action potentials speed along large sensory neuron at about 100 m/s.

Postsynaptic potential

Action potentials in axon terminal cause release of synaptic transmitter glutamate. About 0.5 ms later, excitatory postsynaptic potential (EPSP) appears in motor neuron.

Action potentials

EPSP spreads passively to axon hillock, where it triggers action potentials.

Action potentials speed down large motor axon at about 100 m/s.

Action potentials reach neuro-muscular junctions. ACh is released as the neurotransmitter.

Neuromuscular junction potential starts about 0.5 ms after arrival of presynaptic action potential. Action potentials are generated in the muscle fibers, which contract and cause leg to kick, about 40 ms after delivery of stimulus.

must have evolved before the appearance of multicellular animals with nervous systems. Na⁺ channels seem not to have evolved before the appearance of multicellular animals, and their structures suggest that they evolved from Ca^{2+} channels. The increased variety of ion channels may have been an important factor in promoting flexibility of neural circuits.

Electrical synapses are found in plants as well as animals and appear to be very ancient in an evolutionary sense. The appearance of chemical synapses added new flexibility: Transmission could be modulated by a variety of messages from adjoining cells. Some of the simpler compounds that function in multicellular animals as synaptic transmitters—such as ACh, GABA, glycine, and glutamate—are also present in plants and in unicellular animals, but it is doubtful that they act as transmitters there because plants and unicellular animals don't have nervous systems. The transmitter functions these substances provide in multicellular animals probably evolved from and superseded their functions in plants and unicellular animals. The inhibitory ligand-gated receptors (for GABA and glycine) appear to have evolved from the excitatory nicotinic ACh receptor. The neuropeptide transmitters appear to have arisen first in multicellular animals. Thus, in communication of information in the body, as for other functions, evolution has proceeded by conserving and "tinkering with" the available raw material.

Neurons and Synapses Combine to Make Circuits

Now that we have discussed the basic properties of neurons and synapses, it is time for an initial look at how they can be connected together into circuits to perform important functions such as conveying messages and processing information. The use of the term "circuit" for an assemblage of neurons and their synaptic interconnections is an analogy to electrical or electronic circuits, in which an arrangement of components (such as resistors, capacitors, transistors, and their connecting wires) accomplishes a particular function such as amplification, oscillation, or filtering. Electrical or electronic circuits can represent signals in either analog or digital ways—that is, in terms of continuously varying values or in terms of integers. Neurons also have both analog signals (graded potentials) and digital signals (all-or-none action potentials). The nervous system comprises many different types of neural circuits that accomplish basic functions in cognition, emotion, and action— all the categories of behavior and experience. For now we will take up just three basic types of neural circuit: (1) the neural chain, (2) the feedback circuit, and (3) the oscillator circuit.

The Simplest Neural Circuit Is the Neural Chain

The first neural circuit that investigators proposed was the linking of neurons together in a chain. From the seventeenth century until well into the twentieth century, most attempts to understand behavior in neural terms were based on chains of neurons, which do account for some behaviors. For example, the basic circuit for the stretch reflex, such as the **knee jerk reflex**, consists of a sensory neuron, a

motor neuron, and a single synapse where the sensory neuron joins the motor neuron. Hundreds or thousands of such circuits work in parallel to enable the stretch reflex. Figure 3.14 shows the sequence and timing of events in the knee jerk reflex. Note that this reflex is extremely rapid: Only about 40 ms elapse between the stimulus and the initiation of the response. Several factors account for this rapidity: (1) Both the sensory and the motor axons involved are of large diameter and thus conduct rapidly; (2) the sensory cells synapse directly on the motor neurons; and (3) both the central synapse and the neuromuscular junction are fast synapses.

For some purposes, the afferent (input) parts of the visual system can be represented as a neural chain (Figure 3.15*a*). In reality, the retina contains many kinds of neural circuits, which we discuss in Chapter 10. A more accurate schematic diagram of the visual system (Figure 3.15*b*) brings out two other features of many neural circuits: **convergence** and **divergence**. In many parts of the nervous system, the axons from large numbers of neurons converge on certain cells. In the human eye, about 100 million receptor cells concentrate their information down on about 1 million ganglion cells; these ganglion cells convey the information from the eye to the brain. Higher in the visual system there is much divergence: The 1 million axons of the optic nerve communicate to billions of neurons in several different specialized regions of the cerebral cortex.

(*a*) The visual system represented as a neural chain

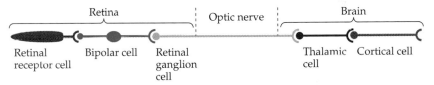

(*b*) A more realistic representation, showing convergence and divergence

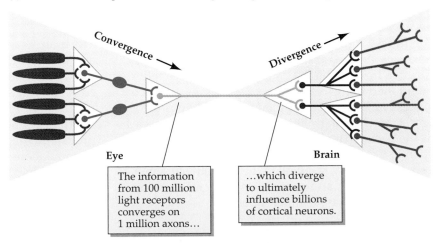

3.15 Two Representations of Neural Circuitry
(*a*) Simple representation of the input part of the visual system. (*b*) A more complex representation, illustrating convergence and divergence.

(a) Negative feedback loop within a single cell

Excitatory synapse
Inhibitory synapse
Negative feedback loop

(b) Negative feedback loop through interneuron

Interneuron
Negative feedback loop

3.16 Negative Feedback Circuits
(a) Within a single cell. (b) Including interneurons.

The Feedback Circuit Is a Regulator

In a feedback circuit, part of the output is "fed back" to the input. There are two types of feedback circuits: positive and negative. In **positive feedback circuits**, the effect of the output is to sustain or increase the activity of the initial input; in **negative feedback circuits**, the output inhibits the activity of the initial input. In some feedback circuits, a branch of the axon of a neuron loops back and contacts the same neuron (Figure 3.16a). In others, one or more intermediate neurons form the feedback loop (Figure 3.16b).

Feedback circuits were first discovered in the nervous system in the 1940s, and psychologist Donald O. Hebb (1949) pointed out their relevance for psychological and neuroscience theory. For example, a positive feedback circuit can be used to sustain neural activity, which can contribute to maintaining a motivational state or to forming the cellular basis of memory. Negative feedback circuits help regulate many body functions by maintaining relatively constant conditions. A thermostat is an example of a negative feedback device; many neural circuits in the body function in the same basic manner. The stretch reflex, mentioned in the previous section, serves as part of a negative feedback system in maintaining posture as you stand. Swaying a little to the front causes muscles in the back of the leg to stretch; the leg muscles respond by contracting, bringing the body again to the vertical. Similarly, swaying to the back stretches muscles in the front, and again the stretch reflex brings about the necessary compensation.

The Oscillator Circuit Controls Rhythmic Behavior

Many kinds of behavior are rhythmic, and their cycles differ in duration from short to long—from beating of

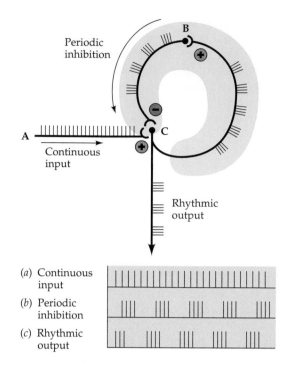

Periodic inhibition

B

A
Continuous input

C

Rhythmic output

(a) Continuous input

(b) Periodic inhibition

(c) Rhythmic output

3.17 A Simple Oscillator Circuit
A continuous series of action potentials from neuron A is modulated by inhibitory interneuron B into rhythmic output from cell C.

the heart, breathing, walking, sleeping, and waking, to annual migration. Some neurons, mostly in invertebrates, show inherent spontaneous rhythmicity of activity: The frequency of neural impulses of such a "pacemaker" cell waxes and wanes in regular alternation. Rhythmic wing beating in some insects is controlled by such oscillation. In both invertebrates and vertebrates, however, oscillatory activity usually depends on circuits of neurons. Figure 3.17 shows a simple **oscillator circuit**.

Gross Electrical Activity of the Human Brain

The brain is a large collection of separate elements, and the electrical activity of thousands of cells working together adds up to potentials that can be recorded even at the surface of the skull. Recordings of electrical activity in the brain that are made with large electrodes either on the scalp or within the brain can present useful glimpses of the simultaneous workings of populations of neurons. Investigators divide brain potentials into two principal classes: those that appear spontaneously without specific stimulation and those that are evoked by particular stimuli.

Electroencephalograms Measure Spontaneous Brain Potentials

A recording of spontaneous brain potentials is called an **electroencephalogram** (EEG), or more informally,

(a) Electroencephalogram

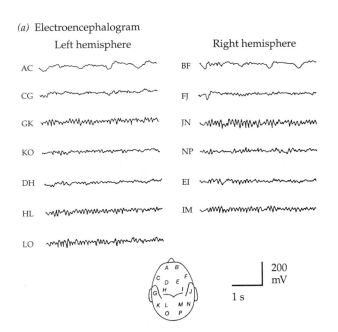

Left hemisphere　　　　　Right hemisphere

AC

CG

GK

KO

DH

HL

LO

BF

FJ

JN

NP

EI

IM

200 mV

1 s

"brain waves" (Figure 3.18*a*). As we will see in Chapter 14, EEG recordings of a sleeping person allow investigators to distinguish different kinds and stages of sleep. Brain potentials also provide significant diagnostic data—for example, in distinguishing forms of seizure disorders (see Box 3.3). They also provide prognostic data—for example, predictions of the functional effects of brain injury. In most states of the United States, EEGs are used to determine death according to the legal definition.

New developments in computer technology yield detailed quantitative analyses of brain potentials, buoying hopes for even greater clinical applications, especially in psychiatry. One such system of analysis and display of brain potentials is **brain electrical activity mapping** (**BEAM**) (F. H. Duffy et al., 1992; F. H. Duffy et al., 1979). Figure 3.18*b* shows an example of a BEAM display.

Event-Related Potentials Measure Changes Resulting from Discrete Stimuli

Gross potential changes evoked by discrete stimuli—usually sensory stimuli, such as light flashes or clicks—are called **event-related potentials** (**ERPs**) (Figure 3.18*c*). In the usual experiment to study this phenomenon, ERPs in a series are averaged to obtain a reliable estimate of stimulus-elicited brain activity. Sensory-evoked potentials have distinctive characteristics of wave shape and latency that reflect the type of stimulus, the state of the subject, and the site of recording. Subtler psychological processes, such as expectancy, appear to influence some characteristics of evoked potentials.

Computer techniques enable researchers to record brain potentials at some distance from the sites at which they are generated. Such recording is akin to the ability of a sensitive heat detector to pick up minute sources of heat that are located at a distance. An example that has attracted considerable research and clinical attention is "auditory-evoked brain stem potentials" (see Figure 3.18*c*). The neural generators of these waves are located far from the site of recording—in the auditory nerve and successive levels of the auditory brain stem pathways. These responses provide a way to assess the neural responsiveness of the brain stem and especially its auditory pathways. For example, decreases in the amplitude of certain waves or increases in their la-

(b) BEAM images

CONVENTIONAL 2D MAP (18 CHANNELS)

HIGH RESOLUTION 3D MAP WITH MRI (124 CHANNELS)

EEG Systems Laboratory & Sam Technology

(c) Event-related potentials

N_1

CNV

P_2

I　II　III　IV V　VI

N_o　N_a　N_b

P_o

P_a　P_1

N_1

N_2

P_2

P_3

−1000　　−500　　0　　　+10　　+100　　+1000 ms

Contingent negative variation

Brain stem responses

Midlatency components

Task-related potentials

Warning signal　　　Stimulus

3.18 Gross Potentials of the Human Nervous System
(*a*) Electroencephalogram (EEG). (*b*) Brain electrical activity mapping (BEAM). (*c*) Event-related potentials (ERPs).

BOX 3.3 Seizure Disorders

*E*pilepsy (from the Greek *epilepsia*, a form of the verb meaning "to seize") has provoked wonder and worry since the dawn of civilization. The seizures that accompany this disease have spawned, through the ages, much speculation about the cause—from demons to gods. Consequently, people afflicted with this disease have sometimes been shunned, sometimes exalted. Epidemiological studies indicate that 30 million people worldwide suffer from epilepsy. Since epilepsy affects so many people, the origin and possible cures of this disease are an important focus of research.

What causes seizures? The electrical character of nervous system signals offers the special biological advantages of rapid communication and the ability to generate, receive, and integrate a wide array of messages. However, this fundamental property also comes at a price. In addition to the high metabolic demands of nerve cells is the potential cost of seizures. Because of the extensive connections among its nerve cells, the brain can generate massive waves of intense nerve cell activity that seem to involve almost the entire brain. A **seizure** is

the synchronized excitation of large groups of nerve cells. These unusual electrical events in the brain have a wide array of possible causes, including trauma or injury to the brain, as well as chemical changes derived from metabolic faults or exposure to toxins.

Several types of seizure disorders can be distinguished both behaviorally and neurophysiologically. Generalized seizures are characterized by loss of consciousness and symmetrical involvement of body musculature. **Grand mal seizures** exhibit an EEG pattern that is evident at many places in the brain (Figure A). The behavior connected with this state is dramatic. The person loses consciousness, and the muscles of the entire body suddenly contract, producing stiff limbs and body. This tonic phase of the seizure is followed 1 to 2 minutes later by a clonic phase consisting of sudden alternating jerks and relaxation of the body.

Minutes or hours of confusion and sleep follow. When nonprofessionals refer to epilepsy, they generally mean grand mal seizures.

(A) Grand mal seizure

(B) Petit mal seizure

tency have been valuable in detecting hearing impairments in very young children and noncommunicative persons. Hidden hearing deficits in children who were initially diagnosed as autistic have been revealed in this manner. Another use of these brain stem–evoked potentials is in the assessment of brain stem injury or damage, such as that produced by tumors or stroke.

Long-latency components of scalp-recorded ERPs tend to reflect the impact of information processing variables, such as attention, decision making, and other complex psychological dimensions. Another way of contrasting these events with short-latency events, such as the brain stem potentials, is to compare the sorts of factors that affect them. The later potentials are influenced more by endogenous factors, such as attention. In contrast, short-latency responses are more determined by exogenous factors; they are more determined by stimulus, so dimensions like stimulus intensity have a far more profound effect on early components of ERPs than on longer-latency components.

Although it is difficult to determine which brain region produced a given component of the ERP, such changes are detected quickly, within a fraction of a sec-

ond. In contrast, computer-coordinated imaging of brain activity, such as functional MRI (see Chapter 2), indicates clearly which brain region is active, but because such imaging techniques must average activity over seconds or minutes, they are much slower than ERPs. Perhaps the greatest promise for future research is a melding of the two techniques—using ERPs to detect changes in brain activity rapidly, and using fMRI or PET scans to indicate where those changes originate within the brain (Abdullaev and Posner, 1998; Snyder et al., 1995).

As noted in Chapter 2, another promising new technique projects near-infrared light onto a person's head. Some of the light penetrates the scalp and skull, and sensitive monitors surrounding the head can detect how that light is scattered (Villringer and Chance, 1997). Two types of changes in the brain affect the light scattering: slow changes in blood flow (such as those detected by fMRI) and rapid changes in membrane potentials (such as those detected by ERP). Since the equipment for this method is much less expensive than the equipment required by fMRI or PET, in the future we may see more studies using light scattering.

Petit mal seizures are a more subtle variant of generalized seizures. This condition is revealed by a distinctive electrical pattern in EEG recordings, called the spike-and-wave pattern, that lasts 5 to 15 seconds (Figure B). Periods of such unusual electrical activity can occur many times a day. During these periods the person is unaware of the environment and later cannot recall events that occurred during the petit mal episode. Behaviorally, the person does not show unusual muscle activity, except for a cessation of ongoing activity and sustained staring.

The prime ingredients needed for the development and maintenance of a seizure are as follows:

1. The capacity of membranes in some "pacemaker" neurons to develop intense activity either in response to synaptic input or spontaneously. A pacemaker for seizure activity might emerge from membrane damage that results in exaggerated ion conductances for calcium, sodium, or potassium. Giant excitatory synaptic potentials may also cause intense cell activities that lead to seizures.

2. A selective loss of inhibitory processes (in many, but not all, types of seizures). Drugs that reduce the effectiveness of GABA, the most common inhibitory transmitter, are potent seizure producers.

3. Excitatory circuits that propagate excessive neuronal discharges to other regions.

Frequent storms of electrical activity that invade the brains of epileptics may leave many marks, including some psychological and behavioral changes. Clinical neurologists have suggested a connection between one type of seizure disorder—temporal lobe epilepsy—and certain personality attributes (Trimble, 1991). Some researchers argue that emotional changes observed in these disorders are a direct result of frequent activation by seizures of emotional circuits in the temporal lobe. Others believe that emotional changes arise as a result of psychological responses to the social trauma of having a life with unpredictable seizures. Some patients with temporal lobe seizures exhibit striking and varied aggressive behavior.

Hindler (1989) described a person in whom strong aggression was elicited by the laughing of an infant, which appeared to trigger odd olfactory sensations and other features of temporal lobe seizure activity.

Seizures can occur in the brains of many nonhuman creatures. Spontaneous seizures characterize some animals—for example, some breeds of dog, especially beagles. One interesting model of seizure disorders uses repeated direct electrical stimulation of brain regions to provoke epileptic seizures. This process of establishing seizures is referred to as **kindling** (McNamara, 1984). To establish seizure activity in this model, an electrical stimulus that is too weak to cause a seizure on its own is delivered directly through implanted electrodes to a particular brain site in the animal. Over a period of days, this brief stimulus comes to produce both behavioral changes and signs of seizure activity in a progressive manner. Eventually seizures appear spontaneously. The phenomenon of kindling may be relevant to the finding that some human patients develop multiple foci for the initiation of seizures as a result of a history of seizure activity (Morrell, 1991).

Summary

1. Nerve cells are specialized for receiving, processing, and transmitting signals.

2. Neural signals are changes in the resting potential, which is the normal small difference in voltage between the inside and outside of the cell membrane.

3. The different concentrations of ions inside and outside the neuron—and especially of potassium ions (K^+)—account for the resting potential. The inside of the neuron is about −60 to −70 mV compared to the outside. The resting membrane is mainly permeable to potassium ions and is thus a "potassium membrane."

4. A propagated nerve impulse, also called an action potential, travels the length of the axon without diminishing in amplitude; the impulse is regenerated by successive segments of the axon.

5. Reduction of the resting potential (depolarization of the membrane) makes the axon membrane more permeable to sodium ions (Na^+); that is, channels open that admit mainly Na^+. If this depolarization reaches a threshold value, the membrane becomes briefly a "sodium membrane," and the axon becomes briefly more positive inside than outside. Depolarization of a stretch of membrane stimulates the adjacent stretch of membrane to depolarize, so the action potential sweeps along the axon.

6. Postsynaptic (local) potentials spread very rapidly, but they are not propagated. Thus they diminish in amplitude as they spread passively along dendrites and the cell body.

7. Excitatory postsynaptic potentials (EPSPs) are depolarizing (they decrease the resting potential) and make it easier for the neuron to generate an action potential. Inhibitory postsynaptic potentials (IPSPs) are hyperpolarizing (they increase the resting potential) and make it harder for the neuron to fire.

8. Cell bodies process information by integrating (adding algebraically) postsynaptic potentials across their surfaces.

9. A propagated nerve impulse is initiated at the axon hillock when the excess of EPSPs over IPSPs reaches threshold.

10. During the action potential, the neuron cannot be excited by a second stimulus; it is absolutely refractory.

11. Some synapses use electrical transmission and do not require a chemical transmitter. At these electrical

synapses, the cleft between presynaptic and post-synaptic cells is extremely narrow.

12. At most synapses the transmission of information from one neuron to another requires a chemical transmitter that diffuses across the synaptic cleft and binds to receptor molecules in the postsynaptic membrane. Because the transmitter binds to the receptor, it is called a ligand.

13. At some synapses, the receptor molecule responds to recognition of a transmitter by opening an ion channel within its own structure. At other synapses, the binding of a transmitter molecule to a receptor molecule leads to opening of channels through the activity of G proteins and second messengers.

14. Evidence for the evolution of ion channels, synapses, and transmitters has been obtained from comparative studies. For example, certain ion channels and electrical synapses are found in plants as well as animals, but Na^+ channels and neuropeptide transmitters appear to have arisen first in multicellular animals.

15. Neurons and synapses can be assembled into circuits that process information. Three basic kinds of neural circuit are the neural chain, the feedback circuit, and the oscillator circuit.

16. The summation of electrical changes over millions of nerve cells can be detected by electrodes on the scalp. This electroencephalography (EEG) can reveal rapid changes in brain function, especially in response to a brief, controlled stimulus that evokes an event-related potential (ERP).

Recommended Reading

Hall, Z. W. (Ed.). (1992). *An introduction to molecular neurobiology.* Sunderland, MA: Sinauer.

Kandel, E. R., Schwartz, J. H., and Jessell, T. M. (1995). *Essentials of neural science and behavior.* Norwalk, CT: Appleton & Lange.

Nicholls, J. G., Martin, A. R., and Wallace, B. G. (1992). *From neuron to brain* (3rd ed.). Sunderland, MA: Sinauer.

Purves, D., Augustine, G. J., Fitzpatrick, D., Katz, L. C., LaMantia, A. S., and McNamara, J. O. (1997). *Neuroscience.* Sunderland, MA: Sinauer.

Shepherd, G. M. (Ed.). (1994). *The synaptic organization of the brain* (3rd ed.). New York: Oxford.

4 Psychopharmacology: Neurotransmitters, Drugs, and Behavior

Most drugs affect the brain and behavior by changing synaptic transmission. To begin our discussion about drugs and the nervous system, we review the varieties of transmitters, many of which we mentioned in Chapter 3. Then we consider examples of how drugs affect the nervous system and behavior. We also discuss drug dependency, and the information that neuroscientists can offer to help deal with the personal and social problems associated with substance abuse.

As far back as we can trace human history, people have tasted, sipped, chewed, or swallowed all kinds of substances—animal, vegetable, and mineral. From these experiences, people have learned to consume some substances and shun others. Social customs and dietary codes evolved to protect people from consuming harmful substances. This long history of

Fred Tomaselli, *Brain with Flowers*, 1990–1997
Cannabis leaves, LSD, photos, acrylic, and resin on wood

seeking, testing, and using different substances came not only from the need for nourishment but also from the desire to relieve pain, control anxiety, and pursue pleasure. Human consumption of drugs is so pervasive that one investigator characterizes human beings as "drug-taking animals" (B. E. Leonard, 1992). But we are not alone in this activity; "almost every species of animal has engaged in the natural pursuit of intoxicants" (R. K. Siegel, 1989, p. viii).

The Search for Chemical Transmitters

Identifying the different synaptic transmitter agents and understanding how they act are continuing quests. Table 4.1 summarizes the various classes of currently known transmitters, some of which we mentioned in the previous chapter. Some of the amine transmitters—including acetylcholine, norepinephrine, and epinephrine (adrenaline)—were recognized as transmitters in the 1940s. Beginning in the 1950s, investigators discovered that some amino acids, the building blocks of proteins, also act as transmitters at some synapses; these amino acid transmitters include glutamate, glycine, and GABA, among others. In the 1970s, investigators recognized that many peptides—short strings of amino acids—could be synaptic transmitters; some examples are the endogenous opioids, oxytocin, substance P, and vasopressin. As the search continued, the number of probable synaptic transmitters grew from a few to several dozen, and new discoveries continue to bring surprises. Among the most startling of these discoveries was the evidence that the simple gas nitric oxide (NO) appears to serve as a messenger between neurons, although not in the usual synaptic sense (Ignarro, 1991; Moncada et al., 1991).

What does it take for a substance to be considered a transmitter? The criteria come from the view of synaptic transmission that we discussed in Chapter 3. To prove that a particular substance is the chemical transmitter at a particular synapse, we must demonstrate the following:

1. The chemical exists in the presynaptic terminals.
2. The enzymes for synthesizing the transmitter exist in the presynaptic terminals or, in the case of the peptides, in the cell body.
3. The transmitter is released when nerve impulses reach the terminals, and in sufficient quantities to produce normal changes in postsynaptic potentials.
4. Specific receptors exist on the postsynaptic membrane for the released transmitter.
5. Experimental application of appropriate amounts of the chemical at the synapse produces changes in postsynaptic potentials.
6. Blocking release of the substance prevents presynaptic nerve impulses from altering the activity of the postsynaptic cell.

Substances that satisfy the criteria for transmitters include acetylcholine, norepinephrine, dopamine, serotonin, GABA, glutamate, and others (see Table 4.1 for others). There is considerable evidence that several other substances are transmitters, but most investigators want to see even more evidence before they are convinced. Even if a substance is known to be a transmitter in one location, it may be hard to prove that it acts as a transmitter at another location where it is found.

For example, acetylcholine was long accepted as a transmitter agent in the peripheral nervous system (its role at the vertebrate neuromuscular junction was well known; see Chapter 11), but it was harder to prove that it serves as a transmitter in the central nervous system as well. Now it is recognized that acetylcholine is widely distributed in the brain, and its possible relationship to the cognitive deficits seen in Alzheimer's disease is the subject of much current work. About 30 small peptides have been identified within sensory and autonomic neurons and in several CNS pathways. Considering the rate at which these substances are being discovered and characterized, it would not be surprising if there turned out to be several hundred different peptides conveying information at synapses in different subsets of neurons.

TABLE 4.1	*Some Synaptic Transmitters and Families of Transmitters*
Family and subfamily	**Transmitters and transmitter candidates**
Amines	
Quaternary amines	Acetylcholine (ACh)
Monoamines	*Catecholamines*
	Norepinephrine (NE)
	Epinephrine (adrenaline)
	Dopamine (DA)
	Indoleamines
	Serotonin (5-hydroxy-tryptamine; 5-HT)
	Melatonin
Amino acids	Gamma-aminobutyric acid (GABA)
	Glutamate
	Glycine
	Histamine
Neuropeptides	
Opioid peptides	*Enkephalins*
	Met-enkephalin
	Leu-enkephalin
	Endorphins
	Beta-endorphin
	Dynorphins
	Dynorphin A
Peptide hormones	Oxytocin
	Substance P
	Cholecystokinin (CCK)
	Vasopressin
	Neuropeptide Y (NPY)
	Hypothalamic releasing hormones

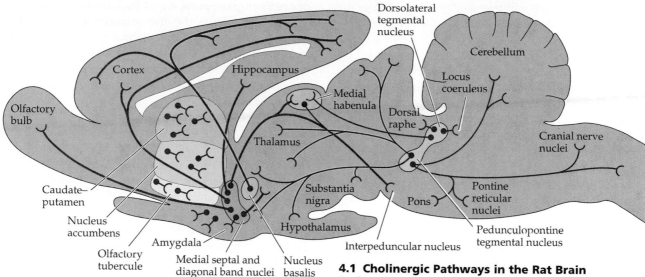

4.1 Cholinergic Pathways in the Rat Brain
In this sagittal view, the nuclei containing cell bodies of neurons that release acetylcholine are indicated by different colors; the projections of axons from these neurons are indicated by red lines. Because they use acetylcholine as a transmitter, these neurons are said to be cholinergic. (After Butcher and Woolf, 1986.)

Neurotransmitter Systems Form a Complex Array in the Brain

The neurochemical complexity of the brain has become more evident as techniques such as immunocytochemistry (see Box 2.1) have provided a more complete appreciation of the location of these substances within the nervous system and the multiplicity of ways in which they interact. Although at one time in the recent past it was thought that each nerve cell contained only one transmitter, we now know that some nerve cells contain more than one transmitter—a phenomenon known as neurotransmitter *coexistence* or *colocalization*. In this section, we present maps showing where some neurotransmitters are found in the brain, and the character of receptors for these transmitters.

Acetylcholine Was the First Neurotransmitter to Be Identified

Acetylcholine (ACh), the chemical at work in Otto Loewi's classic experiment (see Chapter 3), was the first chemical substance to be known as a neurotransmitter. The development of techniques to measure small quantities of enzymes involved in the synthesis of ACh demonstrated the role of this compound as a transmitter in the brain. Figure 4.1 shows the distribution of ACh-containing (**cholinergic**) nerve cell bodies and their projections.

Several distinct clusters of cholinergic cells are apparent. The basal forebrain includes a major group of cholinergic cells in the medial septal nucleus, the diagonal band of Broca, the nucleus basalis of Meynert, and the substantia innominata. These cholinergic cells project to the hippocampus and amygdala, among other sites. Cells in this group are often destroyed in Alzheimer's disease, which suggests an important role for cholinergic neurons in learning and memory, as will be discussed in Chapter 18.

This role of ACh is especially emphasized by the deleterious effects on learning and memory of the cholinergic antagonist scopolamine, a substance that blocks some ACh receptors. (Remember that the term "antagonist" refers to substances that bind to receptors but fail to initiate synaptic effects and therefore can block the action of a neurotransmitter; the term "agonist" refers to substances that bind to the receptors of a transmitter and initiate some of its effects.) A behavioral role of ACh in the regulation of sleep has been suggested by several observations, including the clustering of cholinergic cells in the brain stem that control some aspects of sleep states. Box 4.1 describes how neurons synthesize ACh and other transmitters.

In Chapter 3 we noted that there are two broad classes of ACh receptors in the peripheral and central nervous systems: nicotinic and muscarinic receptors. Within each of these two groups are subgroups of receptor types. Most nicotinic receptors throughout the brain are primarily excitatory, responses occur rapidly, and these receptors can be blocked by curare. Muscarinic receptors have slower responses when activated and can be either excitatory or inhibitory; they can be blocked by atropine or scopolamine. Muscarinic receptors are G protein–coupled (metabotropic) receptors (see Figure 3.13 and Table 3.2).

Five Monoamines Act as Neurotransmitters

There are two principal classes of **monoamines**: catecholamines and indoleamines. The **catecholamine** neurotransmitters are dopamine, epinephrine, and norepinephrine, which we discuss next. The **indoleamines** are melatonin and serotonin. In the sections that follow, we will take a closer look at three of these monoamines: dopamine, norepinephrine, and serotonin.

Dopamine. Almost a million nerve cells in the human brain contain **dopamine** (**DA**). The locations of these cells and their projections in rat brain are shown in Figure 4.2. Dopaminergic neurons are found in several main groups; Figure 4.2 focuses on two of these groups: the mesostriatal system and the mesolimbocortical system.

The **mesostriatal system**, as the name indicates, originates from the substantia nigra and nearby tegmental areas (in the midbrain, or mesencephalon) and ascends as part of the medial forebrain bundle to innervate the striatum: the caudate nucleus, putamen, and globus pallidus (see Figure 4.2*a*). Although this group contains relatively few nerve cells, a single axon can give rise to thousands of synapses. Degeneration of this system, through loss of neurons either with aging or illicit drug use, can result in the resting tremors

or even complete paralysis of Parkinson's disease (see Chapter 11). Thus the mesostriatal DA system is thought normally to play a crucial role in motor control. Another component of this system innervates the olfactory tubercle and the nucleus accumbens—both important in the effects of various psychostimulants, such as cocaine.

The **mesolimbocortical system** originates in a midbrain region designated A10 (see Figure 4.2*b*), and projects to the limbic system (amygdala, septum, hippocampus) and the cortex. This pathway has been implicated in various theories that schizophrenia is mediated by overstimulation of DA pathways (see Chapter 16).

Several subtypes of DA receptors have been discovered and have been labeled D_1, D_2, D_3, D_4, and D_5, numbered in the order of their discovery. The D_1 and D_5 receptors are similar to each other but quite different from the D_2, D_3, and D_4 receptors, all three of which resemble each other. Drugs that are DA agonists or antagonists often act differentially with respect to this ar-

---

BOX 4.1   *Pathways for Neurotransmitter Synthesis*

Many of the most studied neurotransmitters, including the amine hormones, must be synthesized through the use of specialized enzymes. Therefore we can gain some ideas about where these transmitters are produced by finding out where the associated enzymes occur. For example, the enzyme choline acetyltransferase (ChAT) causes a choline molecule to combine with an enzyme (acetyl coenzyme A, or acetyl CoA) to produce a molecule of ACh:

Acetyl CoA + choline
$$\downarrow \text{ChAT}$$
ACh + coenzyme A

The enzyme acetylcholinesterase (AChE) breaks down the ACh, leaving choline and acetic acid:

ACh
$$\downarrow \text{AChE}$$
Choline + acetic acid

Thus by noting where ChAT and AChE are found, we can make inferences about where ACh might be made and released, respectively. In fact, AChE is very widely

distributed, but ChAT is found primarily in the cell bodies indicated in Figure 4.1.

All of the catecholamine transmitters (norepinephrine, epinephrine, and dopamine) are produced in successive steps in the same synthetic pathway, starting with the amino acid tyrosine and using several different enzymes:

Tyrosine
$$\downarrow \text{Tyrosine hydroxylase}$$
L-dopa
$$\downarrow \text{Aromatic L-amino acid decarboxylase}$$
Dopamine
$$\downarrow \text{Dopamine } \beta\text{-hydroxylase}$$
Norepinephrine
$$\downarrow \text{Phenylethanolamine } N\text{-methyltransferase}$$
Epinephrine

Only neurons that possess the enzyme tyrosine hydroxylase have the capacity to produce these catecholamine transmitters. A neuron without tyrosine hyroxylase cannot.

The indoleamine serotonin is produced from the amino acid tryptophan in two chemical steps:

Tryptophan
$$\downarrow \text{Tryptophan hydroxylase}$$
5-Hydroxytryptophan (5-HTP)
$$\downarrow \text{Aromatic L-amino acid decarboxylase}$$
5-Hydroxytryptamine (5-HT; serotonin)

All of the monoamines (dopamine, norepinephrine, epinephrine, serotonin, and melatonin) are inactivated to a great extent by reuptake through the presynaptic transporters for each, but they are also enzymatically degraded. Most of the initial degradation of monoamines is carried out by a class of enzymes known as monoamine oxidases (MAOs).

Neuropeptides are synthesized like any other peptide or protein—through transcription of a gene and translation of messenger RNA (mRNA), so we can find neurons making those transmitters by looking for the appropriate mRNA transcript—through the use of Northern blots or in situ hybridization (see the Appendix).

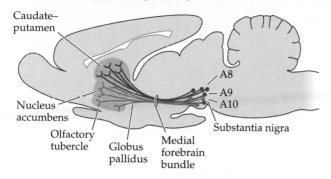

(a) Dorsal mesostriatal (nigrostriatal; blue) and ventral mesostriatal (green) dopamine systems

Caudate–putamen

A8
A9
A10

Nucleus accumbens

Olfactory tubercle
Globus pallidus
Medial forebrain bundle
Substantia nigra

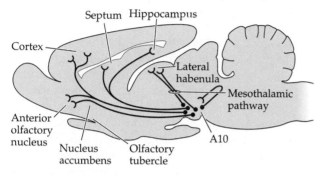

(b) Mesolimbocortical and mesothalamic dopamine systems

Septum Hippocampus

Cortex

Lateral habenula
Mesothalamic pathway

Anterior olfactory nucleus

A10

Nucleus accumbens
Olfactory tubercle

4.2 Dopaminergic Pathways in the Rat Brain
The neurons in the pathways represented in these sagittal views release dopamine and thus are called dopaminergic. (After Feldman et al., 1997.)

ray of receptor types. For example, haloperidol is a potent **antipsychotic** and is a DA receptor antagonist with a nearly 100-fold selectivity for D_2 over D_1 receptors. In fact, there is a strong correlation between the effectiveness of antipsychotics for relieving symptoms of schizophrenia and their tendency to bind D_2 receptors. The antipsychotic drugs (also known as neuroleptics) have revolutionized the treatment of schizophrenia because they greatly reduce many of the symptoms that prevent patients with this condition from living on their own

(see Chapter 16). In addition, a rich research literature (e.g., Nader et al., 1997) connects DA to reward and reinforcement; the D_2 receptor subtype seems to have a special role in these behaviors.

Norepinephrine.   Neurons that release **norepinephrine (NE)** are organized into three main clusters in the brain stem: the **locus coeruleus** complex in the pons, the lateral tegmental system of the midbrain, and the dorsal medullary group (Figure 4.3). Because norepinephrine is also known as noradrenaline, NE-producing cells are said to be **noradrenergic.** The output of the noradrenergic locus coeruleus cells extends broadly throughout the cerebrum, including the cerebral cortex and thalamic nuclei. In addition, it projects prominently to the cerebellum and spinal cord. Because of this wide distribution of projection paths, noradrenergic cells of the locus coeruleus are believed to modulate many behavioral and physiological processes.

◉ **Sylvius**

Serotonin.   The second class of monoamines—the indoleamines—consists of melatonin and serotonin. Here we will discuss serotonin. **Serotonin** is abbreviated **5-HT** because its chemical name is 5-hydroxytryptamine. Large areas of the brain are innervated by **serotonergic** fibers, although 5-HT cell bodies are relatively few and are concentrated in the brain stem (most are found in the **raphe nuclei** near the midline). Figure 4.4 shows the distribution of cell bodies and fibers that release 5-HT in the rodent brain. Humans have about 200,000 serotonergic cells, a minuscule number compared with the billions of nerve cells. However, tracts and fibers that release 5-HT extend throughout the brain.

The most prominent serotonergic pathway emerges from the dorsal raphe nuclei, a site that is involved in the control of sleep states (see Chapter 14). Drugs that modify some aspect of 5-HT activation seem especially prominent as antidepressants; Prozac is an example (see Chapter 15). At least 15 types of 5-HT receptors have been described.

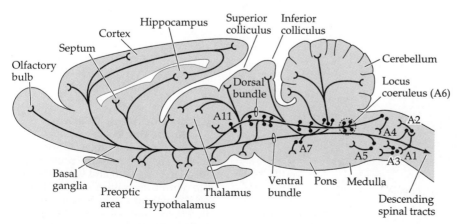

Hippocampus
Superior colliculus
Inferior colliculus
Cortex
Septum
Olfactory bulb
Cerebellum
Dorsal bundle
Locus coeruleus (A6)
A11
A2
A4
A7
A5
A3 A1
Basal ganglia
Preoptic area
Hypothalamus
Thalamus
Ventral bundle
Pons Medulla
Descending spinal tracts

4.3 Noradrenergic Pathways in the Rat Brain
The neurons shown in this sagittal view release norepinephrine as a transmitter. (After Feldman et al., 1997.)

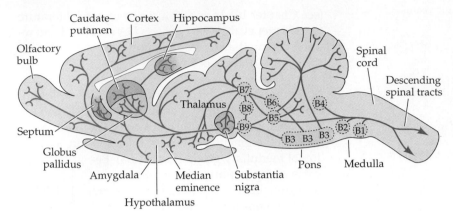

4.4 Serotonergic Pathways in the Rat Brain
The neurons in the numbered nuclei identified in this sagittal view release serotonin (5-HT) and thus are said to be serotonergic. (After Feldman et al., 1997.)

Some Amino Acids Act as Neurotransmitters

The most common transmitters in the brain are members of a chemical class called amino acids. In this group there are two prominent excitatory amino acids—**glutamate** and **aspartate**—and two prominent inhibitory amino acids—**gamma-aminobutyric acid (GABA)** and **glycine**. These transmitters are distributed throughout the central nervous system. Glutamate is the most common excitatory transmitter, and GABA is the major inhibitory transmitter in the brain.

GABA receptors are divided into three large classes (designated $GABA_A$, $GABA_B$, and $GABA_C$), each exhibiting quite different properties. By mixing and matching various subunits, the brain may normally make hundreds of different GABA receptors. Receptors in the $GABA_A$ class contain a chloride channel and include several distinct binding sites, as we'll see later. $GABA_A$ receptors are ionotropic receptors (recall that ionotropic receptors react quickly because they contain an ion channel; see Figure 3.13), and therefore mediate fast inhibitory postsynaptic potentials. The drug sensitivities of $GABA_B$ receptors differ from those of $GABA_A$ receptors, and $GABA_B$ receptors are coupled to a G protein. In other words, $GABA_B$ receptors are metabotropic receptors, in contrast to the ionotropic $GABA_A$ receptors. $GABA_C$ receptors are ionotropic with a chloride channel, but they differ in subunit structure from other GABA receptors. Neural inhibition is the dominant story about GABA, and it is there-

fore not surprising that drugs that block the actions of GABA are potent seizure provokers.

Glutamate transmission employs a group of ionotropic receptors referred to as AMPA, kainate, and NMDA receptors (their names refer to drugs that act as selective agonists). Because NMDA-type glutamate receptors are active in a fascinating model of learning and memory (see Chapter 18), they have been studied very closely (see Box 4.2). There are also several metabotropic glutamate receptors (that act more slowly because they work through second messengers to affect channels). Glutamate is associated with an interesting feature of synaptic transmission called **excitotoxicity**, a phenomenon in which prolonged depolarization produced by glutamate kills neurons. This condition can arise with neural injury and amplify the effects of injury or stroke.

Many Peptides Function as Neurotransmitters

Many different peptides are found in the brain; those that have a prominent role as neurotransmitters include (1) opioid peptides (peptides that can mimic opiate drugs such as morphine), including met-enkephalin, leu-enkephalin, beta-endorphin, and dynorphin; (2) a group of peptides found in the gut and spinal cord or brain, including substance P, cholecystokinin (CCK), neurotensin, neuropeptide Y (NPY), and others; and (3) pituitary hormones such as oxytocin and vasopressin (Figure 4.5), among others. Many of these peptides act as neurotransmitters at certain synapses, but they also act as hormones (see Chapter 5).

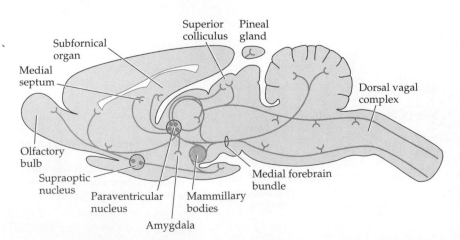

4.5 Oxytocinergic Pathways in the Rat Brain
In addition to their roles as hormones released from the posterior pituitary, oxytocin and vasopressin are neurotransmitters in the brain and spinal cord. The neurons identified in this sagittal view release oxytocin. (After Feldman et al., 1997.)

BOX 4.2   *A Star among Receptor Molecules*

Because of its special role in many kinds of information processing, the NMDA receptor is getting star treatment; it is the subject of thousands of recent research articles, more than 100 review articles in the past few years (e.g., Daw et al., 1993), and a symposium volume (Watkins and Collingridge, 1994). The NMDA receptor is one of the two main kinds of receptors activated by glutamate, which is a major excitatory synaptic transmitter found in all parts of the nervous system. The name "NMDA receptor" reflects the fact that this receptor is especially sensitive to the glutamate agonist *N-methyl-D-aspartate*. The other main kind of glutamate receptor is the AMPA receptor, which is particularly sensitive to the glutamate agonist α-amino-3-hydroxy-5-methyl-4-isoxazole-propionic acid.

The NMDA receptor acts differently from most receptor molecules because it is both ligand-gated and voltage-sensitive. When the NMDA receptor is activated, Ca^{2+} ions flow through its central channel into the neuron. But only very small amounts of Ca^{2+} flow through the NMDA receptor at the resting potential of –75 mV or at any membrane potential between –75 and –35 mV. The reason for the low Ca^{2+} conductance at these membrane potentials is that magnesium ions (Mg^{2+}) block the NMDA channel, as the left panel of the figure illustrates.

Sufficient activation of AMPA receptors or other excitatory receptors in the same neuronal membrane can partially depolarize the membrane to less than –35 mV. This depolarization removes the Mg^{2+} block (right panel of the figure); the NMDA receptor now responds actively to glutamate and admits large amounts of Ca^{2+} through the channel. The Ca^{2+} starts a cascade of effects resulting in more AMPA receptors, described in more detail in Chapter 18. Thus, the NMDA receptor is fully active only when it is gated by a combination of voltage and its ligand. Patch clamp studies show that activation of NMDA receptors usually has a relatively slow onset and a prolonged effect (up to 500 ms), whereas non-NMDA receptors at the same synapse act rapidly and their channels remain open only a few milliseconds at a time.

We can study the contributions of NMDA receptors by observing which functions are impaired or abolished by an NMDA antagonist. One such agent is aminophosphonovalerate (APV), which antagonizes the binding of glutamate to the NMDA receptor. Experiments with APV demonstrate that NMDA receptors are not needed for the normal flow of synaptic messages. But when the activity of other receptors reaches a relatively high level and partially depolarizes the membrane, NMDA receptors amplify and prolong the synaptic activity.

Because of these special properties, NMDA receptors play a wide variety of important roles. In later chapters we will see examples of how the NMDA receptor is involved in visual, auditory, and pain perception; in regulating motor and circulatory functions; and in fostering memory formation.

Research on Drugs Ranges from Molecular Processes to Effects on Behavior

The subject of neuropsychopharmacology—how drugs affect the nervous system and behavior—is vast and changing at a rapid pace. Our coverage of this topic will necessarily be brief and incomplete. A more complete discussion is available in recent textbooks (e.g., Feldman et al., 1997) and in Topic 4.1, Technical Matters: Drug Measurement and Testing.

Special topic

The range and complexity of neuropsychopharmacology is suggested by the different meanings of the Greek word *pharmakon*, which is the root of "pharmacology." *Pharmakon* has three principal meanings: (1) "a charm"—that is, an object thought to have a magical effect, (2) "a poison," and (3) "a remedy or medicine." We also use the term "drug" in different ways. One common meaning is "a medicine used in the treatment of a disease" (e.g., a "prescription drug," or an "over-the-counter drug"). Quite a different meaning of "drug," but also a common one, is "a psychoactive agent," especially an addictive one—that is, a drug of abuse. The shared meaning of these usages is a substance that, taken in relatively small amounts, has clear effects on experience, mood, emotion, activity, and/or health.

Some drugs originally evolved in plants, probably to discourage animals from eating the plants (see Topic 4.2, Where Do Drugs Come From? An Evolutionary Story). One example is the morphine produced by the opium poppy (Figure 4.6). Almost all the drugs of interest to psychologists are those that reliably alter behavior, and these drugs usually act on particular classes of neurotransmitter receptors, as we discuss next.

Special topic ↗

To understand how drugs work, we must use many levels of analysis—from molecules to behavior and experience (see Figure 1.4). Because drugs exert their effects at the molecular level, but have profound effects on behavior, we will encounter these different levels of analysis in this chapter.

Here are some basic questions about drugs we will address:

1. Many drugs have been found to act on receptor molecules. What are the natural compounds—the keys—that fit into the receptor locks?
2. Many drugs are effective because they alter neural conduction or synaptic transmission. What are prominent examples of such effects?
3. Repeated use of a drug can make a given dose either less effective or more effective. What accounts for these changes with repeated use?

Drugs Fit like Keys into Molecular Locks

To change the functioning of a cell, molecules of a drug must reach and interact with one or more constituents of the cell. The first component the drug encounters is the cell membrane. Some drugs are effective because they interact with lipid molecules in the membrane, but most drugs of interest to biological psychology react with specialized receptor molecules. Receptor molecules are proteins that may be situated either in the cell membrane—as are the receptor molecules in the postsynaptic membrane that we considered in Chapter 3—or inside the membrane—as are the receptors for certain hormones that we will consider in Chapter 5.

Perhaps the most compelling single principle of neurotransmitters and their receptors is that a given neurotransmitter may normally act on several different receptors. We've seen this already in the case of GABA receptors: This single compound, GABA, may act on hundreds of different receptors. Apparently natural selection tinkers with the structure of receptors more often than with transmitters. The resulting multiplicity of receptors offers an opportunity for pharmacological approaches because **synthetic** (human-made) compounds can be devised to affect some of the receptors that are normally activated by a neurotransmitter, but not others. Thus there is always

4.6 The Source of Opium and Morphine
The opium poppy flower and seedpod.

a great deal of interest in which version of a receptor is the target of a given drug.

Drug molecules do not seek out particular receptor molecules; rather, drug molecules spread widely throughout the body, and when they contact receptor molecules with the specific shape that fits the drug molecule, the two molecules bind together briefly and begin a chain of events. The lock-and-key analogy is often used for this binding action, as we mentioned in the previous chapter. But now we have to think of keys (drug molecules) trying to insert themselves in all the locks (receptor molecules) in the neighborhood; each key unlocks only a particular set of doors.

Where a drug appears to bind to receptor molecules, investigators try to find the endogenous substance that is the natural ligand for that receptor. (**Endogenous** means occurring naturally within the body. Drugs are **exogenous** substances; that is, they are introduced from outside the body.) In some cases, such as the opioids, the key was identified before the structure of the lock was determined. In other cases, such as the receptor for the active ingredient of marijuana, the lock was identified before the endogenous key was found. Once the drug or transmitter (the key) binds to the receptor (the lock), it somehow alters the shape of the receptor to set off a chain of events, often the flow of ions across the postsynaptic membrane. But the binding is usually temporary, and when the drug or transmitter breaks away from the receptor, the receptor resumes its unbound shape and ion flow stops.

Drug–Receptor Relations Vary in Specificity

The tuning of drug molecules to a receptor is not absolutely specific. That is, a particular drug molecule may bind strongly with one kind of receptor molecule, more weakly with some others, and not at all with many others. A drug molecule that has more than one kind of action in the body may do so because it affects more than one kind of receptor molecule. For example, we saw in Chapter 3 that the transmitter ACh acts at both nicotinic and muscarinic synaptic receptor molecules. Some drugs combat anxiety at low doses without producing sedation (relaxation, drowsiness), but at higher doses they cause sedation, probably because at those doses they activate another type of receptor molecule.

Some drug molecules will bind to the receptor for a long time; others bind for only a short time. All other things being equal, the drug that binds for a long time will have a greater effect because it will activate the receptor longer. The compound that binds to the receptor longer is said to have a greater **binding affinity** (or, simply, **affinity**) for the re-

Important method

ceptor. In principle you would like to know how long a given drug molecule binds to a receptor molecule, but in practice it is easier to measure binding affinity in a different way. Continuous addition of molecules of the drug to a solution containing those receptors eventually produces a concentration of drug that binds half of the receptors present. At this point, for every drug molecule that is released by a receptor, another molecule will bind to another receptor. If the drug has a very high affinity (and therefore binds to the receptor for a relatively long time), then a very low concentration of drug molecules will be sufficient to bind half the receptors present. So pharmacologists tend to speak of a drug's affinity for the receptor in terms of the concentration of drug needed to bind half the receptors. The lower this concentration is, the greater the drug's affinity.

Note that the binding of a ligand with a receptor molecule does not necessarily mean that the ligand *activates* the receptor. In some cases a particular ligand (call it ligand A) merely occupies the receptor site and prevents another kind of ligand (ligand B) from activating the receptor; in this case, substance A is the antagonist of substance B. If substance C works like B on the same receptor molecules, C is an agonist of B. Agonists act in the same way; antagonists act in opposite ways (Figure 4.7).

Drugs Affect Each Stage of Neural Conduction and Synaptic Transmission

Almost all the behavioral effects that we discuss in this chapter are caused by the activities of drugs on synaptic events and processes and on neural conduction. Table 4.2 explains how certain drugs affect the major steps in neural conduction and synaptic transmission (see Figure 3.11). In the discussion that follows we'll comment on some of these agents and their effects, as well as on related effects of other agents.

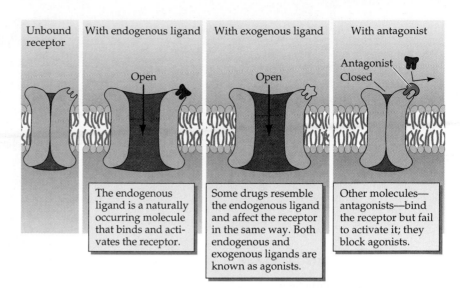

4.7 Drugs Act as Either Agonists or Antagonists

Drugs Affect Presynaptic Events

If axonal transport is inhibited by a drug (e.g., colchicine), enzymes that are manufactured in the cell body are not replaced in the presynaptic terminals. Since enzymes are needed to manufacture transmitter chemicals and vesicle walls, such drugs prevent replenishment of the transmitter agent as it is used up and cause synaptic transmission to fail. Although the drug reserpine does not interfere with the synthesis of transmitters, it does inhibit the storage of catecholamine transmitters (dopamine, epinephrine, and norepinephrine) in vesicles. Even if a presynaptic terminal has an adequate supply of transmitter stored in vesicles, various agents or conditions can prevent the release of transmitter when a nerve impulse reaches the terminal. A low concentration of calcium (Ca^{2+}) in the extracellular fluid is such a condition: Under these circumstances, too little Ca^{2+} enters to cause the release of transmitter.

Specific toxins prevent the release of specific kinds of transmitter (de Paiva et al., 1993; see Table 4.2 for examples). For instance, botulinum toxin, which is formed by bacteria that multiply in improperly canned food, poisons many people each year by blocking the release of ACh. The botulinum toxin binds to specialized receptors in nicotinic cholinergic neural membranes and is transported into the cell, where it blocks Ca^{2+}-dependent release of transmitter (McMahon et al., 1992). A related bacterial product, tetanus toxin, acts similarly, blocking activity at inhibitory synapses and causing strong involuntary contractions of muscles (McMahon et al., 1992). Tetanus is an acute, often fatal disease characterized by strong contractions of muscles, especially those of the neck and jaw; this condition is also called lockjaw.

Other agents stimulate or facilitate the release of certain transmitters. For example, the venom of the

TABLE 4.2 *The Effects of Drugs on Certain Neural Processes*

Neural process	Drug effects
Axonal processes	
Transport of proteins between cell body and axon terminals	Colchicine impairs formation and maintenance of microtubules.
Conduction of action potentials	Tetrodotoxin and saxitoxin block ion channels and prevent conduction.
Synthesis and storage of synaptic transmitters	
Transport of transmitter precursors into nerve terminal	Hemicholinium blocks uptake of choline, a precursor of ACh.
Synthesis of transmitters catalyzed by enzymes	Alpha-methyl-*para*-tyrosine inhibits tyrosine hydroxylase, thus preventing synthesis of the catecholamine transmitters (see Box 4.1).
Uptake of transmitters into vesicles	Reserpine inhibits uptake of transmitters into vesicles.
Release of synaptic transmitters	
Release of transmitters from vesicles by calcium-dependent mechanisms	Calcium channel blockers (e.g., verapamil) inhibit release of transmitters.
Release of transmitters by calcium-independent mechanisms	Amphetamines stimulate release of catecholamine transmitters and enhance the release caused by action potentials.
	Black widow spider venom causes overrelease, and thus depletion, of ACh.
Modulation of the release of some transmitters by presynaptic receptors	Adenosine blocks release of catecholamine transmitters; caffeine competes with adenosine for presynaptic receptors, thus preventing its inhibitory effects.
	Binding of opioids to presynaptic receptors decreases release of ACh, norepinephrine, and dopamine.
Activity of transmitters in the synaptic cleft	
Inactivation of ACh by the enzyme acetylcholinesterase (AChE)	Drugs such as physostigmine inhibit AChE and prolong the activity of ACh at the synapse.
Inactivation of catecholamine transmitters by reuptake into the presynaptic terminal	Cocaine and amphetamine inhibit reuptake mechanism, thus prolonging synaptic activity.
Events in postsynaptic neurons	
Alteration of the number of receptor molecules	Alcohol increases number of receptors for inhibitory transmitter GABA.
	Tricyclic antidepressants reduce number of cate-cholamine receptors.
Activation of receptor molecules	Antipsychotic drugs block some dopamine receptors. LSD is an agonist at some serotonin receptors. Curare blocks nicotinic ACh receptors.
Activation of second messengers	Lithium inhibits the second messenger cyclic AMP (see Chapter 3).

black widow spider exaggerates the release of ACh. The stimulant drug amphetamine facilitates the release of catecholamine transmitters, as well as inhibiting their reuptake, which further increases their synaptic action. Caffeine has an excitatory effect because it competes with a neuromodulator. (**Neuromodulators** are compounds that are not transmitters themselves, but act on presynaptic receptors to affect the release of transmitter.) Caffeine blocks the presynaptic receptor for the neuromodulator adenosine.

Since adenosine normally inhibits the release of catecholamine transmitters, caffeine acts to increase catecholamine stimulation and induce an arousing effect.

Where does adenosine normally come from? It appears that at least some catecholaminergic synapses release adenosine along with the neurotransmitter. The adenosine binds to receptors on the same presynaptic terminal that released it, so we say that the adenosine acted on **autoreceptors.** It may seem odd that a neuron that is releasing transmitter would also release a neuromodulator to inhibit transmitter release, but this type of complicated modulation of transmitter release may be the rule, not the exception.

Drugs Affect Postsynaptic Events

Postsynaptic receptor molecules can be blocked by various drugs. For example, curare blocks nicotinic ACh receptors. Since the synapses between nerves and skeletal muscles are nicotinic, curare paralyzes all skeletal muscles, including those used in breathing. Behavior can be disrupted not only by blocking but also by prolonging transmitter–receptor action. Agents that inhibit the enzyme acetylcholinesterase (AChE) allow ACh to remain active at the synapse and alter the timing of synaptic transmission. Effects can range from mild to severe, depending on the anti-AChE agent and its dosage.

The drug physostigmine has temporary and reversible anti-AChE effects. Mild doses of it are used in certain medical conditions when ACh action at neuromuscular junctions is weak and inadequate. On the other hand, some organic phosphorus compounds, such as diisopropyl fluorophosphate (DFP), are potent and persistent inhibitors of AChE. DFP is the active ingredient in certain insecticides, which must be used with caution because they are highly toxic to human beings.

Drugs That Affect the Brain Can Be Divided into Functional Classes

Of the many drugs that affect the brain, several draw special attention because they contribute to social distress and personal disasters. These drugs are often classified on the basis of their effects on the brain. We will briefly review some of the major features of these substances.

Opiates Help Relieve Pain

Opium has a long history of human use that stretches back to the Stone Age. It is a mixture of many substances. Morphine, the major active substance in opium, was extracted from poppy flower seedpods (see Figure 4.6) in pure form at the start of the nineteenth century. Morphine continues to be used medically as a very effective **analgesic** (painkiller), but it also has a strong potential for addiction. Many people have become addicted to morphine and to an artificially modified form of morphine—heroin (diacetylmorphine).

Candace Pert

In 1973, pharmacologists Candace Pert and Solomon Snyder found that opiate drugs such as morphine bind to receptor molecules that are concentrated in certain regions of the brain (C. B. Pert and Snyder, 1973). Other investigators published similar findings in the same year. Opiate

receptors are found especially in the limbic and hypothalamic areas of the brain, and they are particularly rich in the locus coerulcus and in the gray matter that surrounds the aqueduct in the brain stem (the **periaqueductal gray**) (Figure 4.8). Injection of morphine directly into the periaqueductal gray causes analgesia, indicating that this is a region where morphine acts to reduce pain perception (see Chapter 8). Refined analyses showed

Solomon Snyder

that the opiate receptors are located in postsynaptic membranes, but investigators still did not know either the structure of the opiate receptors or the identity of their endogenous ligand(s). They began an intensive search for natural substances in the body that would normally bind to the opiate receptors. In other words, they were looking for the natural keys that fit the lock of the opiate receptors.

In 1975, pharmacologists John Hughes and Hans Kosterlitz announced that they had isolated from pig brain two similar peptides that bind to the opiate receptor. They called these substances **enkephalins** (from the Greek *en*, "within," and *kephale*, "head"). Soon afterward, the same enkephalins were found in the brains of other mammals. Research with animal subjects demonstrated that enkephalins relieve pain

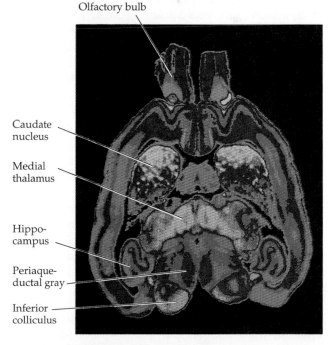

4.8 Distribution of Opiate Receptors in the Rat Brain
Opiate receptors are widely distributed in the brain (areas of highest binding are shown in yellow, orange, and red), but they are concentrated in the medial thalamus and in some brain stem areas—the locus coeruleus, the periaqueductal gray, and the raphe nuclei. (Courtesy of Miles Herkenham, National Institute of Mental Health.)

and are addictive. Only a small part of the enkephalin molecule is the same as the morphine molecule; this common part is what binds to the opioid receptor. Further research uncovered whole families of what are called **endogenous opioids**—that is, opioids that are found naturally in the brain. One of these families consists of compounds called *endorphins*, a contraction of "endogenous morphine"—literally, "the brain's own morphine."

On the other side of the transmitter–receptor story, investigators have sought to find the structure of each kind of opioid receptor molecule—that is, the structure of the lock that is opened by the opioids and opiates. Three main kinds of opioid receptor were hypothesized, because different drugs bind each type most strongly: the delta, kappa, and mu opioid receptors. In 1992 the detailed structure of the delta opioid receptor was first announced (Evans et al., 1992), and this finding was soon followed by discovery of the structures of the kappa (Yasuda et al., 1993) and mu (J. B. Wang et al., 1993) receptors. The structures of all three opioid receptors resemble those of other G protein–coupled receptors, which we discussed in Chapter 3.

Marijuana Has a Wide Array of Effects

More people in the United States use **marijuana** than any other illegal drug (U.S. Department of Health and Human Services, 1991). Many investigators have studied marijuana and its effects. Marijuana is obtained from a plant, *Cannabis sativa* (Figure 4.9), which also furnishes other preparations, such as hashish. The main active ingredient in marijuana and hashish is the compound **tetrahydrocannabinol** (**THC**), which was extracted and identified in 1964 (Gaoni and Mechoulam, 1964). THC, marijuana, hashish, and related preparations are called **cannabinoids**. Their effects on experience are highly variable among individuals, from stimulating and causing hallucinations to inducing relaxation, or sometimes initially causing almost no effect at all. Continued use of marijuana often causes addiction, although many people start using it without being aware of this potential. Smoking marijuana can also contribute to respiratory diseases, similar to the effects of smoking cigarettes. Some proponents of marijuana for medicinal purposes tout it as a natural substance, but nature has produced many toxic substances in both plants and animals.

In the case of marijuana, investigators deciphered the structure of the receptor molecule before they discovered the endogenous ligand—the body's own marijuana. For years after THC was discovered, its mode of action was not known. Some researchers thought it might pass through the neural membrane and affect intracellular metabolism. Investigators tried to locate THC receptors by placing THC, tagged with a radioactive tracer, onto slices of brain and observing where the THC accumulated. But THC

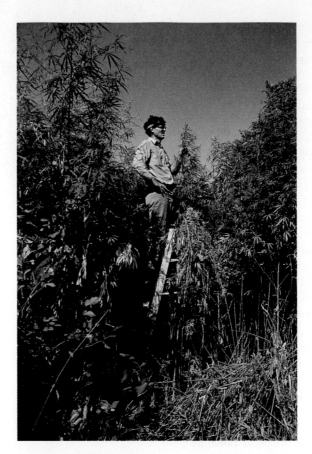

4.9 Marijuana Harvest
Although growing marijuana is illegal in the United States, this plant has been estimated to be the largest cash crop in several states. This field is located in Kansas.

turned out to be a "sticky" molecule that binds nonspecifically to surfaces all through the brain. This case is an example of one molecule binding to another without activating it.

In subsequent experiments, scientists used a synthetic THC-like compound that has a more specific affinity for THC receptors. With this ligand they found that the receptor molecules for THC are indeed located in neuronal membranes (Devane et al., 1988). High concentrations occur in the substantia nigra, the hippocampus, the cerebellar cortex, and the cerebral cortex (Figure 4.10); other regions, such as the brain stem, show few of these receptors. Soon after these experiments, other investigators found the sequence of amino acids in the receptor molecule by cloning the gene of rats (Matsuda et al., 1990) and of humans (Gerard et al., 1991), enabling them to infer that the receptor molecule is a G protein–coupled receptor. But the natural substance in the body that might normally bind to this receptor was still unknown.

In 1992, investigators isolated an endogenous compound in brain tissue that binds to the THC receptor and that has at least some of the properties of THC (Devane et al., 1992). In the hope that they had found an endogenous equivalent to marijuana, the discov-

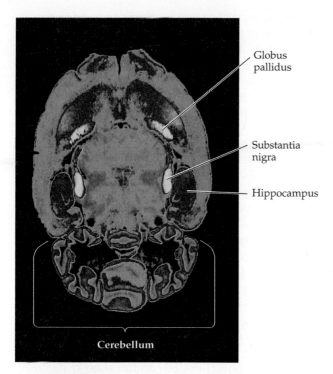

4.10 Distribution of Cannabinoid Receptors in the Rat Brain
Areas of highest binding are indicated by yellow, orange, and red in this horizontal section. (Courtesy of Miles Herkenham, National Institute of Mental Health.)

erers named this compound **anandamide** (from the Sanskrit *ananda,* "bliss"). Further research showed that anandamide and THC produce several of the same effects—reduced sensitivity to pain, hypothermia, hypomotility, and catalepsy—and these effects vary with dosage and route of administration (P. B. Smith et al., 1994). If this substance really is the endogenous equivalent of THC, the discovery will allow researchers to identify the neurons that produce the substance and to study their functions in the nervous system; up to now, the mechanism(s) of the action of marijuana have not been clear.

Recently, a more abundant endogenous ligand for the cannabinoid (marijuana) receptor has been discovered (Stella et al., 1997). It was isolated from intestinal tissue and found to be present in the brain in amounts 170 times greater than anandamide. Identification of this ligand will also aid in the search for other drugs that have the clinical effects of marijuana (painkilling, lowering blood pressure, combatting nausea, and lowering eye pressure in glaucoma) without causing an emotional "high" and will help reveal the neural circuits and processes involved in producing the psychological effects of marijuana.

Alcohol Acts as a Depressant

Alcohol has traveled the full route of human history, no doubt because it is so easily produced by fermentation, which can readily occur when fruit or grains are left standing in a warm damp place. Alcohol is the most commonly used psychoactive substance and frequently serves as the day's tension reducer. The action of alcohol on the nervous system is biphasic: An initial stimulant phase is followed by a more prolonged depressant phase. Maintained use of alcohol can damage nerve cells; cells of the superior frontal cortex, Purkinje cells of the cerebellum, and hippocampal pyramidal cells show particularly prominent pathological changes. These degenerative effects of chronic alcohol use may be due to a secondary consequence of alcoholism—poor diet. Chronic alcoholics may suffer severe thiamine deficiency, which can lead to neural degeneration and Korsakoff's syndrome.

Using new methods to measure neurodegeneration, Kril et al. (1997) reported that frontal lobes of alcoholics—especially superior frontal association cortex—are the regions most affected by chronic alcohol use. However, some of the anatomical changes that are evident in the brains of chronic alcoholics may be reversible with abstinence. For example, chronic exposure to alcohol in experimental rats reduces the number of synapses on cerebellar neurons, but this number is restored to control levels after a period of recovery (Dlugos and Pentney, 1997). In humans, MRI studies of short-term effects of abstinence show an increase in the volume of cortical gray matter and a reduction in ventricular volume (Figure 4.11; Pfefferbaum et al., 1995).

Neural plasticity

The nature of this reversibility remains a puzzle. It is clearly not due to rehydration, and it may well be a form of neural plasticity. PET scans also reveal a restorative effect in alcoholics who abstain from drinking. A return in glucose utilization by the frontal cortex to normal levels is evident in alcoholics who are abstinent for 1 month. This metabolic change in the brain is also related to an improvement in neuropsychological tests that are sensitive to the the functioning of the frontal lobe (Johnson-Greene et al., 1997). The destructive effects of alcohol are mediated probably by the breakdown products of alcohol—aldehydes—rather than by the direct effects of alcohol on nerve cells (Seil et al., 1977).

Interactions between alcohol and GABA are a prominent basis of the effects of alcohol on the brain; alcohol activates the $GABA_A$ receptor–coupled chloride channel, which increases postsynaptic inhibition. Alcohol also affects other transmitters. For example, low doses of alcohol stimulate dopamine pathways, and the resulting increase in dopamine may be related to the euphoriant properties of alcohol. Opiate antagonists such as naloxone suppress alcohol consumption in rats (Froehlich et al., 1990), a finding that suggests the possible involvement of opioid receptors in the mediation of alcohol effects.

Several researchers have argued that there is a strong hereditary component to alcoholism; this hy-

(a) Anterior cortical gray matter

(b) Lateral ventricles

MRI session

4.11 Effects of Alcohol on the Brain
MRI studies of alcoholics show that abstaining from alcohol for 30 days (a) increases the volume of cortical gray matter and (b) decreases the volume of the lateral ventricles. (After Pfefferbaum et al., 1995.)

pothesis is supported by some human studies and selective breeding experiments in rats. In humans, 20 to 50% of the sons of alcoholics and 3 to 8% of the daughters become alcoholics themselves. Rates of alcoholism in the first-degree relatives of alcoholics are several times higher than are rates for the general population.

Genes and behavior
An 8-year longitudinal study of healthy young men revealed that a family history of alcoholism is associated with a threefold increased risk for alcohol abuse or dependence (Schuckit and Smith, 1997).

Two types of alcoholism have been described by Cloninger (1987): Type 1 alcoholism results from genetic predispositon coupled with environmental exposure to heavy drinking; type 2 arises regardless of environmental background. Brain wave patterns may differ between these two groups, although this finding has become quite controversial.

Anxiolytics Combat Anxiety

Most of us occasionally suffer feelings of vague dissatisfaction or apprehension that we call anxiety, but here we will be concerned with the disabling emo-

tional distress that resembles abject fear and terror. Severe anxiety that prevents people from carrying on normal daily activities is estimated to afflict about 8% of adult Americans. These clinical states of anxiety include phobias—such as the fear of taking an airplane or even of leaving the house—and frank attacks of panic. We will take up anxiety and its mechanisms more fully in Chapter 16; here we will consider briefly some drugs that are used to combat anxiety and ways of measuring their effects.

Many substances have been used to combat anxiety. Such substances are called **anxiolytics** (from "anxiety" and the Greek *lyein*, "to loosen or dissolve"). One substance that has long been used as an anxiolytic is alcohol. Alcohol decreases anxiety in some people, but it has some quite undesirable consequences, such as neuropsychological impairments with excessive use and a strong potential for addiction. Opiates and barbiturates have also been used to relieve anxiety, but they seem to sedate or, in higher doses, to produce stupor rather than being true anxiolytics.

In the early 1960s, an effective new family of anxiolytics was found: the **benzodiazepines**. Benzodiazepines are some of the most frequently prescribed drugs, especially diazepam (trade name Valium). They bind strongly to receptors that appear to be found exclusively within the central nervous system. Benzodiazepine receptors are associated with and appear to enhance the activity of a subset of receptors for the inhibitory transmitter GABA, thus producing larger inhibitory postsynaptic potentials than would be caused by GABA working alone. In fact, there are several different binding sites on GABA receptors, some that facilitate and some that inhibit the effect of GABA (Figure 4.12). Note that the benzodiazepine does not bind to the same site on the receptor as does the transmitter GABA. In this case we say that the benzodiazepine is a **noncompetitive ligand**—it affects the activation of the receptor without competing with the transmitter for its binding site.

Just as in the case of the opioid narcotics, neuroscientists have been searching for a natural substance in the nervous system that binds to the so-called benzodiazepine receptor—an endogenous ligand for the receptor—but the quest continues and already has taken a great deal longer than the search for the enkephalins and endorphins took. Some investigators have suggested that the endogenous ligand is the neurohormone allopregnanolone, which is derived from the hormone progesterone. This neurohormone is induced and released as a consequence of stress; it has a calming effect. Allopregnanolone binds to GABA receptors and increases the effectiveness of GABA. In turn, GABA inhibits the release of corticotropin-releasing hormone, which triggers stress responses. Thus, allopregnanolone may be an endogenous anxiolytic substance whose actions can be mimicked by the benzodiazepine drugs. Meanwhile, other endoge-

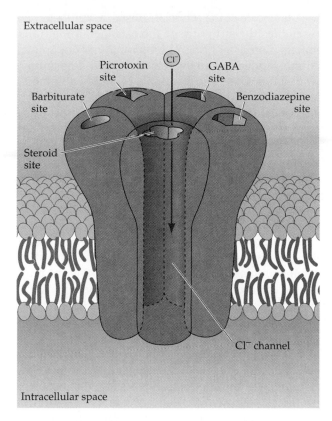

Extracellular space

Picrotoxin site

Cl⁻

GABA site

Barbiturate site

Benzodiazepine site

Steroid site

Cl⁻ channel

Intracellular space

4.12 The GABA Receptor Has Many Different Binding Sites

nous ligands have also been proposed for the complex benzodiazepine receptor, and the search continues (Alho et al., 1994; Purdy et al., 1992). Of course, some drugs may have no endogenous counterpart. By pure chance alone, a drug molecule may happen to bind to part of a receptor that does not normally interact with any compound.

Because antianxiety drugs have some potential for addiction, investigators continue to try to develop anxiolytic agents that may have little or no risk for addicting their users. To screen drugs for possible improved anxiolytic effectiveness, investigators need animal models of anxiety. The problem of finding valid animal models for human states and conditions has engendered much thought and discussion on the part of academics, clinicians, and industrial practitioners (Geyer and Markou, 1995; Willner, 1991). We cannot delve deep into this topic here, but Topic 4.3, Animal Models Aid the Search for Antianxiety Drugs, looks at an animal model for anxiety.

 Animal model

 Special topic

Stimulants Increase the Activity of the Nervous System

The degree of activity of the nervous system is determined by competing excitatory and inhibitory influences. Stimulants are drugs that tip the balance to-

ward the excitatory side; they therefore have an alerting, activating effect. Many naturally occurring and artificial stimulants are widely used; examples include amphetamine, nicotine, caffeine, and cocaine. Some stimulants act directly by increasing excitatory synaptic potentials. Others act by blocking normal inhibitory processes; one example we've seen already is the blocking of adenosine by caffeine.

Cocaine. **Cocaine** is an alkaloid that comes from the leaves of the coca shrub, which is indigenous to Bolivia, Colombia, and Peru. The people in these countries chew coca leaves or drink a tea brewed from the leaves to increase endurance, alleviate hunger, and promote a sense of well-being. This use of coca leaves does not seem to cause problems. However, the indigenous material has been transformed by scientific and technological modifications into addictive forms such as cocaine powder and crack cocaine crystals.

Cocaine was isolated in 1859 and came into use in the 1890s as a local anesthetic and to relieve depression, until it was found to be addictive. It was widely used as a psychostimulant until 1932, when it gave way to **amphetamine**, which acts much like cocaine but was easier to obtain (amphetamine was sold in inhalers for nasal congestion and some people cracked open the inhaler to get the drug). When legal restrictions on amphetamine raised its price in the 1960s, cocaine use rose again. Many users inhale cocaine powder, which enters the bloodstream and takes effect rapidly by this route.

Crack cocaine is a smokable form of cocaine that appeared in the mid-1980s. Because cocaine in this form enters the blood and the brain even more rapidly, crack cocaine is even more addictive than cocaine powder. Cocaine seems to block monoamine transporters, especially those for NE (norepinephrine) (Figure 4.13), blocking reuptake of the transmitters and therefore boosting their effects.

Some children are initially exposed to cocaine while in the womb, and there has been widespread fear that exposure during fetal life might produce irreversible harm to the development of brain and behavior. The pendulum of scientific view swings widely on this topic. An initial fear that severe developmental impairments occurred in children who were exposed to crack during their fetal life gave way to the view that the social and intellectual impairments are more a function of social and economic deprivation of the mother.

A recent meeting has provided more information for discussion of this topic (Vogel, 1997). Although the home environment of children who were exposed to cocaine prenatally has potent effects on intellectual development, fetal exposure to cocaine also impairs intellectual growth to some extent. Some cocaine-related developmental effects are decreased ability to focus attention as an infant and heightened threshold for arousal. In rabbits exposed to cocaine, dendrites in the

Cortex
Caudate
Putamen
Amygdala

4.13 Cocaine Binding Sites in the Monkey Brain
This autoradiograph of a coronal section shows the distribution of cocaine binding. Areas of highest binding are shown by orange and yellow. (Courtesy of Bertha K. Madras.)

anterior cingulate area grow 30 to 50% longer and weave extensions through several planes (Levitt et al., 1997). These rabbits also show inefficient transmission involving some dopamine receptors.

Nicotine and amphetamine. Like cocaine, tobacco is native to the Americas, where European explorers first encountered smoking. When smoking tobacco was introduced to England in the sixteenth century, King James banned it, but he was unable to prevent its growing use. However, tobacco was not used widely until about 1880, when a technological innovation in curing tobacco made it seem mild and thus it could be readily inhaled in cigarettes (W. Bennett, 1983). Exposed to the large surface of the lungs, the **nicotine** from cigarettes enters the blood and brain much more rapidly than does nicotine from pipe tobacco or cigars or from chewing tobacco or snuff. Taking nicotine in this way is strongly rewarding and may be more addictive than smoking tobacco in cigars or pipes is. Let's look a little more closely at the effects of nicotine on the body and the mechanisms by which nicotine produces these effects.

The stimulant nicotine activates one class of ACh receptors, which, as we learned in Chapter 3, are called nicotinic receptors. Most nicotinic receptors are found at neuromuscular junctions and in neurons of the autonomic ganglia, but many are also present in the central nervous system. When nicotine is absorbed through the action of smoking or chewing tobacco, it increases the heart rate, both directly, by stimulating sympathetic ganglia, and indirectly, by stimulating the adrenal gland to release the hormone epinephrine. Nicotine also increases blood pressure, secretion of hydrochloric acid in the stomach, and motor activity of the bowel. These neural effects, quite apart from the effects of tobacco tar on the lungs, contribute to the unhealthful consequences of heavy and prolonged use of tobacco products.

A molecule of the artificial substance amphetamine resembles the structure of the catecholamine transmitters (norepinephrine, epinephrine, and dopamine). Amphetamine causes the release of these transmitters from the presynaptic terminals even when no nerve impulse arrives at the terminals, and it potentiates the effects of nerve impulses in causing the release of transmitters. After catecholamine transmitter molecules reach the synaptic cleft, amphetamine enhances their activity in two ways: (1) by blocking the reuptake of catecholamines into the presynaptic terminal, and (2) by competing with the catecholamines for the enzyme that inactivates them (monoamine oxidase).

These effects of amphetamine prolong the presence of the catecholamine transmitters in the synaptic cleft, thus increasing their effectiveness. The stimulant cocaine is similar to amphetamine in blocking the reuptake of catecholamines, but it does not have the other synaptic effects of amphetamine. Although first synthesized in 1887, amphetamine did not become widely abused until the late 1930s.

Because amphetamine stimulates and enhances the activity of the catecholamine transmitters, it has a variety of behavioral effects. On a short-term basis, it produces heightened alertness and even euphoria, and wards off boredom. Its short-term use can promote sustained effort without rest or sleep and with lowered fatigue. Although a person may be able to accomplish more work and feel more confident by using amphetamine, most studies show that the quality of work is not improved by the drug; it appears to increase motivation but not cognitive ability. The activity of amphetamine at synapses of the autonomic nervous system may also produce annoying side effects, including high blood pressure, tremor, dizziness, sweating, rapid breathing, and nausea.

Prolonged use of amphetamine causes **tolerance**— the progressive loss of effectiveness of a drug that is administered repeatedly. Often tolerance develops because the number of receptors is reduced by repeated stimulation with the drug. Thus larger and larger doses of the drug are needed to achieve the same effect. Continued amphetamine intake at higher doses often leads to sleeplessness, severe weight loss, and general deterioration of mental and physical condition. It may lead to symptoms that closely resemble those of paranoid schizophrenia: compulsive, agitated behavior and irrational suspiciousness. In fact, some users of amphetamine have been diagnosed as schizophrenic by doctors who did not know about their use of the drug. Study of the syndrome resulting from amphetamine abuse has led to hypotheses about schizophrenia and possible therapy for it, as we will see in Chapter 16.

Interestingly, repeated use of some drugs can lead to the opposite of tolerance—**sensitization**. In that case, the same dose of drug has a *greater* effect with repeated use. Some people develop sensitivity to cocaine, especially after a period of abstinence, perhaps because the number of monoamine receptors increases (Peris et al., 1990).

Hallucinogenic Drugs Alter Sensory Perception

Some drugs alter sensory perception, often in striking or dramatic ways, and produce peculiar experiences and even psychotic behavior. These drugs are termed **hallucinogens**—agents that cause hallucinations. But some investigators feel that the term "hallucinogen" is not appropriate, because whereas a hallucination is a perception that takes place *without* sensory stimulation, hallucinogens such as LSD, mescaline, and psilocybin alter or distort perceptions. The effects of LSD and related substances are predominantly visual and can become frightening. Users often see fantastic pictures with intense colors, and they are often aware that these strangely altered perceptions are not real events.

Hallucinogenic agents are chemically diverse; several have been found to affect one or another of the amine synaptic transmitter systems. For example, mescaline, the drug extracted from the peyote plant, affects the norepinephrine system. LSD and psilocybin act on one kind of serotonin receptor. Other hallucinogens, such as muscarine, found in some mushrooms, affect the ACh system.

LSD (*l*ysergic *a*cid *d*iethylamide) was synthesized in 1938 by Albert Hofmann, a Swiss pharmacologist, who was looking for new therapeutic agents. Because tests with animals did not appear to show effects, he put the compound aside. Then one day in 1943, Dr. Hofmann experienced a peculiar dreamlike, almost drunken state. When he closed his eyes, fantastic pictures of intense color and extraordinary plasticity seemed to surge toward him. The state lasted about 2 hours. Correctly suspecting that he had accidentally ingested a small amount of LSD, Hofmann began to investigate the compound again. LSD proved to be amazingly potent; a fraction of a milligram was enough to induce hallucinations.

In the 1950s, many investigators worked on LSD, hoping it would provide a useful model of psychosis that would suggest clues about the biochemical processes in mental illnesses. The structure of LSD resembles that of serotonin, and LSD was soon found to act on serotonin receptors, but the mechanism by which LSD evokes hallucinations is still unknown. Many former users of LSD have reported flashbacks—that is, experiences as if they had taken a dose of drug, even though they are drug-free. These episodes can follow even brief use of LSD, but it is not yet clear whether they reflect permanent neural changes or a special form of memory.

Phencyclidine (commonly known as **PCP** or "angel dust") was developed in 1956 as a potent analgesic and anesthetic agent. It was soon dropped from use in anesthesia because patients reported effects such as agitation, excitement, delirium, hostility, and disorganization of perceptions. PCP is often sold illegally as a hallucinogen. Toxic reactions include the "four Cs":

Low doses of PCP may produce (1) combativeness and (2) catatonia (a condition that may include stupor, stereotyped behavior, mania, and either rigidity or extreme flexibility of the limbs). Overdoses of PCP result in (3) convulsions or coma that may last for days and (4) confusion that may last for weeks. As with amphetamine, users sometimes develop a psychotic condition that resembles schizophrenia, so PCP may provide a useful chemical model of schizophrenia (see Chapter 16).

PCP antagonizes the NMDA receptor, perhaps at a special binding site (see Figure 4.16), and it stimulates the release of the transmitter dopamine (Gorelick and Balster, 1995). Research continues to attempt to find the brain circuits specifically affected by PCP. Ketamine is a less potent NMDA antagonist that is used as an anesthetic agent with nonhumans. PET studies of the effects of ketamine on the brains of healthy volunteers showed focal increases of metabolic activity in the prefrontal cortex (Breier et al., 1997). Administration of this substance also produced transient psychotic symptoms in this group.

Some "Recreational" Drugs May Have Long-Term Effects

The dangers of drug use widely heralded in public health campaigns usually focus on short-term changes. In these discussions we have all heard of the hallucination-inducing properties of mescaline, PCP, and LSD. Similarly, we all know about the heroin "rush," the cocaine "high," and the many other relatively short-term effects of recreational drugs described in newspapers, magazines, and textbooks. But do these drugs have enduring effects that persist well beyond a period of hours or days? Do these drugs have toxic effects that change brain physiology and anatomy?

This question is a difficult topic to study, requiring a lot of patience. Many factors intervene in the period following drug use, and it is quite difficult to attribute relatively long-term changes to an acute use of these substances. Nevertheless, some ominous findings indicate that brain changes produced by recreational drugs may persist for months (McCann et al., 1997).

For some of us, "ecstasy" is an exalted state of being; for others, the term is the street name for the hallucinogenic amphetamine derivative **MDMA** (3,4-*m*ethylene*d*ioxy*m*eth*a*mphetamine). For a short period, MDMA enjoyed popularity as an adjunct to psychotherapy. In nonhumans, this drug produces persistent effects on serotonin-producing neurons: prolonged reduction in serotonin metabolites and the serotonin transporter. In addition, fine serotonin axons are damaged, but cell bodies in the brain stem are spared. This effect is partially illustrated in Figure 4.14, which shows a marked reduction in serotonin axons in **Animal model**

the neocortex and hippocampus of a squirrel monkey treated with MDMA 18 months earlier. These changes

4.14 Long-Term Effects of a Single Dose of "Ecstasy" on the Monkey Brain
Serotonin axons in the dorsal neocortex of (*left*) a control squirrel monkey and (*right*) a squirrel monkey treated with a single dose of MDMA 18 months earlier. (Courtesy of George Ricaurte.)

may be related to the persistent psychiatric and cognitive effects, including memory disturbances, that are seen in cases of MDMA use.

The widespread use of cocaine and the accompanying progressive debility of habitual users has provoked many studies of the long-term effects of this substance. Cocaine can provoke an acute stroke and long-term alterations in cerebral blood flow (Holman et al., 1993). Decreases in cerebral glucose metabolism are evident for several months after cocaine use is discontinued. Although cocaine has a strong impact on dopamine neurons, it is not regarded as a dopamine neurotoxin.

The intoxication produced by PCP may also include neurotoxic effects on hippocampal neurons and related limbic system cells. Given over several days to experimental animals, PCP produces extensive degeneration of the limbic system, including sites in the hippocampus and the cingulate gyrus. Perhaps the most pervasive neurotoxin is not a drug at all, but environmental lead (see Topic 4.4, Lead Toxicity Impairs Intelligence).

Special topic

Drug Abuse Is Pervasive

Substance abuse and addiction have become a social problem that afflicts millions of people and disrupts the lives of their families, friends, and associates. The whole community is affected because (1) many people who use tobacco, alcohol, and other drugs die prematurely; (2) substance abusers commit crimes and cause traffic accidents, fires, and other social disorders; (3) the costs of helping addicts control their dependence and abuse and of controlling drug trafficking are high; and (4) many babies whose mothers used psychoactive substances (including alcohol and nicotine) during pregnancy are born with brain impairments.

To gain some perspective on the relative importance of dependence on different substances as causes of death, consider these figures: Smoking is estimated to cause about 432,000 deaths annually in the United States—20% of all U.S. deaths—more than 100,000 of which are from lung cancer (Figure 4.15). Further evidence of the toxicity of smoking is the recent finding that among people 55 years and older, it doubles the risk of dementia, especially of Alzheimer's disease (Ott et al., 1998). About 125,000 deaths annually in the United States are associated with the use of alcohol, many of them resulting from traffic accidents caused by drinking. Illegal drugs are estimated to cause about 20,000 deaths annually in the United States, and about 8000 more are attributed to drug-associated AIDS (Institute for Health Policy, Brandeis University, 1993, pp. 32–37; Mathias, 1994). Even if the number of deaths caused by illegal drugs has been underestimated, it is clear that the legal drugs—nicotine and alcohol—exact a far larger social cost than do illegal drugs.

The differences in mortality caused by these substances are related to the frequency of use. About half of all Americans use alcohol in a given month, according to a nationwide household survey by the U.S. Department of Health and Human Services. Some authorities consider about 10% of the total population to be alcoholic (Helzer, 1987). About 27% smoke cigarettes in a given month, and about 15% report smoking a pack or more a day. Only about 7% report using any illegal drug in a month. Marijuana is the most widely used illegal drug; about 5% report use in a month, and about 1% report daily use. About 0.9% report using cocaine (including crack) in a given month.

In addition to frequency of use, the differences in mortality are related to the risks associated with the particular type of substance being used (U.S. Congress, Joint Economic Committee, 1988). Among each million persons who smoke, about 3000 are expected to die annually as a consequence of smoking; among each million who consume alcohol, only about 540 are expected to die annually from drinking. (Illegal drugs were not included in this series of estimates.) Thus, although more people use alcohol in a given month

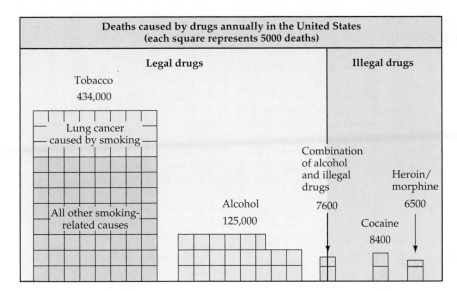

Deaths caused by drugs annually in the United States (each square represents 5000 deaths)	
Legal drugs	**Illegal drugs**

Tobacco
434,000

Lung cancer caused by smoking

All other smoking-related causes

Alcohol
125,000

Combination of alcohol and illegal drugs
7600

Heroin/morphine
6500

Cocaine
8400

4.15 Deaths Caused by Drugs
The number of deaths caused annually in the United States by the legal drugs tobacco and alcohol far exceeds the number caused by illegal drugs. On the other hand, illegal drugs tend to kill people at a younger age. (After Mathias, 1994.)

than smoke cigarettes, exposure to active smoking is a much greater risk factor than is drinking alcohol (U.S. Department of Health and Human Services, 1991). The use of alcohol and cigarettes is broadly distributed across adult ages, but the use of marijuana and cocaine is confined mainly to the 18-to-34 age group. Almost as many females as males use alcohol and cigarettes, but only half as many females as males use marijuana or cocaine.

In the discussion that follows, we will examine the mechanisms of drug abuse, the different approaches to understanding drug abuse, how individuals vary in their vulnerability to drug abuse, and how drug abuse can be prevented and treated.

The Mechanisms of Drug Abuse Have Been Studied Extensively

For more than a century, scientists have been investigating substance dependence. Although much has been learned, many mysteries remain, and fully effective means to combat dependence and abuse have yet to be discovered. Physiological, behavioral, and environmental mechanisms for substance dependence have been proposed and investigated; some investigators put more emphasis on one or another of these types of mechanisms (Glantz and Pickens, 1992).

We will consider different kinds of mechanisms, taking examples mainly from dependence and abuse related to cocaine, the opiate drugs (such as morphine and heroin), nicotine, and alcohol, because these substances have been studied the most thoroughly. Scientists and clinicians engaged in this field have developed specific terminology that does not always coincide completely with the way the public uses terms related to substance dependence, substance abuse, and addiction. Box 4.3 clarifies some of this terminology.

Although we are concerned mainly with substance abuse by humans, many cases have been reported in which animals in the wild administer addictive sub-

stances to themselves and even become dependent on them (R. K. Siegel, 1989). For example, elephants have been observed becoming repeatedly intoxicated by eating fermented fruits. When confined to game preserves, elephants accept alcohol, and when their space is restricted, which presumably is stressful, they increase their drinking. Baboons consume tobacco in the wild, and intoxicating mushrooms are eaten by cattle, reindeer, and rabbits. These observations suggest that the propensity for drug use and possibly even addiction is widespread among animals. In fact, numerous laboratory investigations with animal subjects have revealed important facts about the bases of substance dependence.

Because addictive substances are no exception to the general rule that drugs produce multiple effects, it is difficult to determine which mechanisms are most important in producing dependence. For example, cocaine has the following major characteristics: (1) It is a local anesthetic; (2) its administration promptly leads to pleasurable feelings, so it is a rewarding agent; and (3) it is a psychomotor stimulant, enhancing activity at synapses that use catecholamine transmitters, speeding the heart rate, and evoking other circulatory responses, which sometimes prove fatal.

Opiate drugs, such as morphine, also have a variety of effects, including but not limited to the following: (1) They lead to predominance of parasympathetic activity and depression of the activity of the heart and respiratory system; (2) they quickly have a pleasurable and rewarding effect; (3) their use leads to development of tolerance, so dosages must be increased to maintain effects; and (4) they lead to development of strong physical dependence—that is, after repeated use, abstinence from the drug causes a severe withdrawal syndrome.

The withdrawal syndrome is so striking that some investigators have proposed that development of dependence is the basic characteristic of addiction. Oth-

---

BOX 4.3 *The Terminology of Substance-Related Disorders*

*F*or definitions of mental disorders, psychiatrists, psychologists, and neuroscientists rely on the *Diagnostic and Statistical Manual of Mental Disorders* (fourth edition), often called DSM-IV (American Psychiatric Association, 1994; all page numbers cited in this box refer to this manual). What the public usually calls addiction, the DSM-IV calls **substance-related disorders**. Within this category, **dependence** is a more severe disorder than **abuse**.

The essential feature of dependence on psychoactive substances (e.g., alcohol, tobacco, cocaine, marijuana) is "a cluster of cognitive, behavioral, and physiological symptoms indicating that the individual continues use of the substance despite significant substance-related problems" (p. 176). To be diagnosed as dependent, a person must meet at least three of seven criteria, four of which are the following:

1. The substance is often taken in larger amounts or over a longer period than intended.

2. The persistent desire or efforts to cut down or control substance use are unsuccessful.

3. Much time is devoted to activities necessary to procure the substance (e.g., visiting multiple doctors or driving long distances), to use the substance (e.g., chain-smoking), or to recover from its effects.

4. Important social, occupational, or recreational activities are abandoned or reduced because of substance use.

We list these criteria only to give you an indication of the symptoms of substance-related dependence. Diagnosis should be left to qualified experts.

The severity of dependence varies from mild to moderate to severe. A person exhibiting mild dependence has few, if any, symptoms beyond the three required to make the diagnosis, and the symptoms result in only mild impairment in work or in usual social activities or relationships with others. Severe dependence is evidenced by many symptoms,

which markedly interfere with work or with usual social activities or relationships.

When the criteria for dependence have not been met, but there is evidence of maladaptive patterns of substance use that have persisted at least 1 month or have occurred repeatedly, the diagnosis is substance abuse. Some examples of situations in which a diagnosis of abuse is appropriate are as follows (p. 182):

1. A student has substance-related absences, suspensions, or expulsion from school.

2. A person is repeatedly intoxicated with alcohol in situations that are hazardous—for example, when driving a car, operating machinery, or engaging in risky recreations such as swimming or rock climbing.

3. A person has recurrent substance-related legal problems—for example, arrests for disorderly conduct, assault and battery, or driving under the influence.

---

ers insist that the only property that is shared by all habit-forming drugs is the strong reward (R. A. Wise, 1992). Still others argue that addiction is an attempt to adapt to chronic distress of any sort (Alexander and Hadaway, 1982). The cause of addiction is an area of current controversy, and we cannot survey it thoroughly here, let alone present a simple conclusion, but we will indicate some of the main findings and positions.

Different Approaches Compete to Help Us Understand Drug Abuse

Attempts to explain drug abuse and addiction have changed widely during the last 2 centuries. The different explanations have different implications for our understanding of behavior and for treatment of addiction, and some explanations are better suited to one or another phase of drug abuse, as we'll see. Each explanation continues to be used by some people.

The moral model. The earliest approach to explaining drug abuse was to blame the drug user for lack of moral character or lack of self-control. Explanations of this sort often have a religious character and hold that only divine help will free a person from addiction.

Applications based on the moral model have been effective. For example, the temperance movement in the United States, beginning around the 1830s, is estimated to have cut per capita consumption of alcohol to about one-third its level in the period from 1800 to 1820 (Rorabaugh, 1976).

The disease model. The disease model for addiction arose in the latter part of the nineteenth century, partly from concern about the abuse of drugs such as opium and morphine that were prescribed by physicians and included in many popular remedies. In this view, the person who abuses drugs requires medical treatment rather than moral exhortation or punishment. This view also justifies spending money on research on drug abuse in the same way that money is spent on other diseases. It is still not clear, however, what kind of a disease addiction is, or how a disease causes people to take psychoactive drugs.

Usually the term "disease" is reserved for a state in which we can identify an abnormal physical or biochemical condition; examples include the presence of an infectious agent, such as the syphilis bacterium, damage to brain tissue such as that found in Parkin-

→ **Competing**
→ **hypotheses**

son's disease, or under- or overproduction of various hormones (see Chapter 5). Investigators have not been able to find such an abnormal physical or biochemical condition in the case of drug addiction (although mounting evidence suggests that some people are more susceptible to addiction, as we'll see later). Nevertheless, this approach continues to appeal to many. In 1995, celebrating the twenty-fifth anniversary of the U.S. National Institute on Alcohol Abuse and Alcoholism, Director Enoch Gordis stated that ultimately scientific research will lead to "better treatment, better diagnosis, better prevention, and the putting to rest of the notion that alcoholism isn't a disease" (Azar, 1995).

The physical dependence model.

The physical dependence model is based on the unpleasant **withdrawal symptoms** that often occur when a person stops taking a drug that he or she has used frequently, especially at high doses. The specific withdrawal symptoms depend on the drug. For example, the withdrawal symptoms of morphine include irritability, tremor, loss of appetite, and elevated heart rate and blood pressure. Waves of goosebumps occur, and the skin resembles that of a plucked turkey, which is why abrupt withdrawal without any treatment is called "cold turkey." Some of the user's physiological functions appear to have adapted to the actions of the drug, and withdrawing the drug, or even reducing its dosage, appears to disturb these aspects of functioning. Withdrawal symptoms can be suppressed quickly (within 15 to 20 minutes in the case of morphine) by administration of the substance to which the person is addicted. This model provides an explanation of why addicts work compulsively to get drugs: to avoid or overcome withdrawal effects.

The physical dependence model seems to work well for maintenance of dependence on alcohol and opiate drugs, and it has become widely accepted. However, it does not explain why abusers acquire the drug habit in the first place. Furthermore, some investigators questioned the generality of this explanation when they found that powerful addictions could be formed to drugs such as cocaine that do not cause physical symptoms upon withdrawal. Rather than abandon the dependence model, however, some investigators then proposed that there is psychological dependence on drugs as well as physical dependence. But whereas physiological withdrawal symptoms provide evidence for physical dependence on drugs, the so-called psychological dependence is defined by the *absence* of physiological symptoms. Clearly a better explanation is needed.

The cellular mechanisms model.

The existence of addiction to nicotine, alcohol, cocaine, heroin, and other drugs indicates that reward centers of the brain can be activated by chemicals that have highly selective effects; it also suggests that other chemical agents can be found or synthesized to reverse aspects of addiction (Korenman and Barchas, 1993). In fact, research has already yielded many agonists, antagonists, and modulators of some commonly abused drugs. A symposium and publication summarize much of the progress in (1) understanding molecular sites of drug action, (2) localizing drug effects in the brain, and (3) attempting to relate the molecular and cellular changes to drug abuse (Korenman and Barchas, 1993).

The positive reward model.

The positive reward model of addictive behavior arose from animal research that was started in the 1950s (McKim, 1991), and it has been tested in humans. Before the 1950s, researchers believed that animals could not become addicted to drugs. Most of them did not know of observations that wild animals consume psychoactive substances in nature, and they thought (incorrectly) that animals were not capable of learning an association that spanned the

Important method

15 to 20 minutes between an injection and relief from withdrawal symptoms. Then a few simple technological and procedural breakthroughs made it possible for laboratory animals to perform tasks that led to self-administration of a drug through a fine flexible tube implanted into a vein (Figure 4.16).

The first investigators to use this technique believed that physical dependence was necessary if animals were to administer drugs to themselves. Therefore they first made rats or monkeys dependent on morphine by giving them repeated injections over a period of days before giving them the opportunity to press a lever that caused delivery of morphine through the implanted tube. The animals quickly learned to respond, and it appeared that the drug infusion was acting as a typical experimental reward, such as food or water (Thompson and Schuster, 1964).

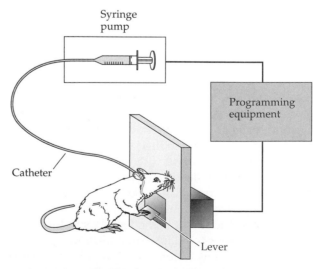

4.16 Experimental Setup for Self-Administration of a Drug by an Animal

Subsequent experiments by psychopharmacologist Charles R. Schuster demonstrated that animals that had not been made dependent would self-administer doses of morphine so low that no physical dependence ever developed (Schuster, 1970). Colleagues in the same laboratory also showed that monkeys would press a lever to self-administer cocaine and other stimulants that do not produce marked withdrawal symptoms (Pickens and Thompson, 1968). The self-administration of drugs by animals has become a frequently used research method and has many advantages, as well as some disadvantages (Koob, 1995).

Charles R. Schuster

These and other studies clearly contradict the assumptions of both the disease model and the physical dependence model of drug addiction. Although physical dependence may be an important factor in the consumption of some drugs, it is not necessary for self-administration and cannot serve as the sole explanation for drug use. Furthermore, these studies indicate that the acquisition of drug self-administration can be interpreted according to principles that govern behavior controlled by positive rewards (operant conditioning theory; see Box 17.1), thus precluding the need to consider drug self-administration a disease. Many investigators conclude that this model accounts much better for drug addiction than does the model of physical plus psychological dependence. Knowledge of the mechanisms of reward and reward circuits in the brain has also advanced greatly since the 1950s.

People Differ in Their Vulnerability to Drug Abuse

The positive reward model of addiction does not try to account for the fact that most people who try addictive drugs do not become addicted. Under some circumstances, even prolonged use is not accompanied by addiction. For example, medical patients who have been given regular doses of opiates to relieve pain during treatment show very low rates of use or abuse after release from the hospital. Of Vietnam veterans who had become addicted to heroin overseas, only 12% relapsed to dependence within 3 years after their return. Many investigators have tried to determine which factors in individuals and in their environments may account for vulnerability to the development of drug abuse (Glantz and Pickens, 1992).

The subject is complicated, because different factors appear to operate for transitions between different conditions—from nonusers to moderate users to abusers to former abusers to relapse. In addition, factors appear to differ among different drugs of abuse. Some of the most revealing investigations of this subject are longitudinal studies, which follow individuals from infancy on, giving psychological tests and interviews at regular intervals. Some of these longitudinal studies have related personality variables and life experiences to drug use and abuse. Unfortunately, such longitudinal studies are rare because they are expensive to conduct and they yield information only slowly. Factors that have been demonstrated to be significant, at least for some drugs, fall into several categories:

1. *Biological factors.* Sex is such a variable; males are more likely to abuse drugs than are females. There is also evidence for genetic predisposition: Having an alcoholic biological parent makes drug abuse more likely, even in the case of children adopted away soon after birth (Cadoret et al., 1986).
2. *Personal characteristics.* Characteristics related to drug abuse include aggressiveness and the tendency to act out emotional states. Characteristics that appear to discourage drug abuse include good school achievement, high educational goals, and religiousness. Age and maturity are important factors; youthful drug use often terminates in the midtwenties, when individuals assume adult roles of employment and marriage.
3. *Family situation.* Factors related to drug abuse include divorce of parents and having an antisocial sibling. Strong ties to parents protect against drug abuse.
4. *Social and community factors.* A high prevalence of drug use in the community, especially by the peer group, predisposes an individual toward drug abuse.

The greater the number of risk factors that apply, the more likely an individual will abuse alcohol or marijuana (Brook et al., 1992). Furthermore, these risk factors do not necessarily operate independently; in some cases they interact. For example, individuals who have high childhood ratings of aggression show a fairly strong tendency to move from moderate to heavy use of marijuana; the degree of social deviance of their peers has only a moderate effect, as the upper curve in Figure 4.17 shows. Individuals with low ratings of aggression, however, are much more likely to be influenced in marijuana abuse by the social deviance of their peers, as the lower curve in Figure 4.17 demonstrates. Although in this study only 2% of individuals with low aggression moved to heavy marijuana use if their peers were low in deviancy, those whose peers were high in deviancy had a 25% chance of moving to heavy use (Brook et al., 1992).

The multiplicity of factors, the interactions among some of them, and the changing social conditions and attitudes toward drugs all complicate research. A review of etiology (causes) and treatment of addictive behaviors calls attention to attempts to integrate biological, psychological, and sociological approaches in a biopsychosocial model of drug use and abuse (Marlatt, 1992). Another model that includes individual dif-

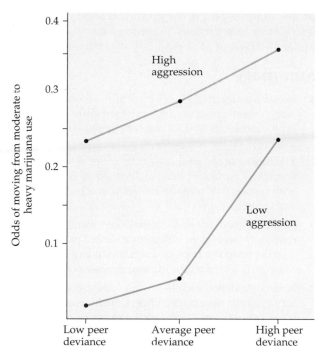

4.17 Social and Personality Factors in Marijuana Use
Individuals who rate low in aggression are not likely to use marijuana if they do not associate with socially deviant peers, but they are much more likely to use marijuana if their peers are socially deviant. (After Brook et al., 1992.)

ferences in vulnerability to drugs is the developmental psychopathology model (Glantz, 1992).

Drug Use, Abuse, and Dependence Can Be Prevented or Treated in Multiple Ways

Because drug use, abuse, and dependence cause many personal and social problems, health professionals and investigators have worked to develop a variety of ways to prevent or treat these conditions. Several of these methods are related to the various models used to explain drug use that we described earlier. For example, in keeping with the moral model, which employs exhortations such as "Just Say No," many people do abstain, and many others do not go beyond initial trials of cigarettes, alcohol, or illicit drugs. Even among those who become addicted, many overcome their problems without outside help (Peele and Brodsky, 1991): Investigators report that more than 90% of ex-smokers (S. Cohen et al., 1989) and about half of former problem drinkers (Institute of Medicine, 1990) appear to have quit on their own.

A recent review proposed several categories of medication that may aid in the treatment of drug addiction (Nathan and Gorman, 1998), including the following:

1. *Drugs for detoxification,* including those that are especially directed toward the control of withdrawal syndromes. Examples include benzodiazepines, methadone, and drugs that suppress central adrenergic activity (e.g., clonidine).

2. *Agonists of drugs that produce common addiction states.* The prime example in this category is methadone, which is a mu opiate receptor agonist that constrains the craving for heroin. Unlike heroin, methadone does not affect cognition and alertness, and it may be easier to withdraw from than other opiates, such as heroin, are.

3. *Antagonists to the addictive drug.* The administration of drugs that are specific antagonists for opiate receptors (e.g., naltrexone) can block the effects of opiate injections. Most addicts apparently prefer methadone to naltrexone because methadone produces a mild opioid effect.

4. *Anticraving medications,* including several substances that especially affect the desire for alcohol. Examples include several antidepressants and several substances that are at the animal-testing stage of development.

5. *Medication that blocks alcohol metabolism.* For alcohol abuse, some therapists prescribe the drug disulfiram (trade name Antabuse). This substance produces an accumulation of acetaldehyde, a toxic metabolite of alcohol that can be quite unpleasant. A person who takes this medication suffers unpleasant physiological reactions if he or she drinks alcohol; thus the effects of drinking are negative rather than rewarding.

The positive reward model attributes abuse and dependence to the extremely rewarding properties of drugs that many people experience, so investigators have attempted either to reduce or abolish the reward provided by a drug or to disconnect the reward from some of the noxious side effects of the drug. Here are a few examples: Smokers who fear the withdrawal symptoms if they quit smoking "cold turkey" can use nicotine chewing gum or nicotine skin patches while they attempt to quit smoking. The nicotine still has harmful effects on the body, but at least the lungs escape the effects of tobacco smoke. Moreover, nicotine delivered through gum or skin patches is less addictive than cigarette smoke is, because these methods do not deliver pulses of nicotine as rapidly to the brain as smoking does (Figure 4.18). Antianxiety drugs can also be used to reduce withdrawal symptoms.

The psychiatric or psychological models and the biopsychosocial models of substance abuse have inspired a variety of psychological and behavioral therapies. Many of these types of treatment appear to help at least some substance abusers, but no single approach appears to be uniformly effective (Institute of Medicine, 1990). Rates of relapse remain high, and many studies show that a majority of clients in abstinence programs return to using the psychoactive substance within a year after completing a course of treatment. Research breakthroughs are therefore badly

4.18 The Rise in Nicotine Concentrations Varies with the Method of Use
These curves show concentrations during the first 2 hours after tobacco is ingested in various forms. Note how much more rapidly the concentration rises after smoking a cigarette than after chewing tobacco. (After W. Bennett, 1983.)

needed to overcome the painful and costly problems of drug abuse and dependence.

Could people be immunized against drug abuse? Charles Schuster (1970) found that they could immunize a monkey against continuing to self-administer heroin (Bonese et al., 1974). The monkey had been trained to self-administer low doses of heroin and cocaine on alternate sessions. Then the monkey was immunized by injection of morphine bound to a protein. (Recall that heroin is a form of morphine.) In later sessions, the monkey continued to self-administer cocaine but soon no longer took heroin. Apparently the antibody that had been produced in response to immunization reduced the concentration of the drug to a level at which it was no longer addictive. Another

promising prospect is the administration of antibodies to overdose victims to remove circulating drug molecules (Fox et al., 1996).

Summary

1. Because many drugs work by acting on receptor molecules, investigators search for the structure of the receptor molecules and for the endogenous substances that work on the receptors.

2. The tuning of receptor molecules is not absolutely specific. A particular drug molecule may act strongly with one kind of receptor molecule and more weakly with others.

3. Repeated use of some drugs produces tolerance: An increasingly larger dose is need to achieve a particular effect. Repeated use of other drugs produces sensitization: The effects with the same dosage increase with use.

4. Some stimulants, such as nicotine, imitate an excitatory synaptic transmitter. Others, such as amphetamine, cause the release of excitatory synaptic transmitters and block the reuptake of transmitters. Still others, such as caffeine, block the activity of an inhibitory neuromodulator.

5. Substances that are used to combat anxiety, such as the benzodiazepines, are called anxiolytic drugs. The benzodiazepines synergize the activity of the inhibitory transmitter GABA at some of its receptors.

6. Some drugs are called hallucinogens because they alter sensory perception and produce peculiar experiences. Different hallucinogens act on different kinds of synaptic receptors, and it is not yet clear what causes the hallucinogenic effects.

7. Drug abuse and addiction are being studied intensively, and several models have been proposed: the moral model, the disease model, the physical dependence model, the cellular mechanisms model, and the positive reward model.

8. The study of psychopharmacology using animal subjects is useful because many species of animals consume psychoactive substances in nature, and their responses to many substances are similar to those of humans.

Recommended Reading

Bloom, F. E., and Kupfer, D. (Eds.). (1995). *Psychopharmacology: The fourth generation of progress.* New York: Raven.

Cooper, J. R., Bloom, F. E., and Roth, R. H. (1996). *The biochemical basis of neuropharmacology* (7th ed.). New York: Oxford University Press.

Feldman, R. S., Meyer, J. S., and Quenzer, L. F. (1997). *Principles of neuropsychopharmacology.* Sunderland, MA: Sinauer.

Glantz, M., and Pickens, R. (1992). *Vulnerability to drug abuse.* Washington, DC: American Psychological Association.

Julien, R. J. (1998). *A primer of drug action* (8th ed.). New York: Freeman.

5 *Hormones and Behavior*

Yayoi Kusama, *Seeds*, © circa 1958–1960

T he cells of the body communicate via chemicals, a major class of which is hormones. Without regular supplies of some hormones, our capacity to behave would be seriously impaired; without others, we would soon die. Deficiency or excess of some hormones can result in striking changes in our cognitive and emotional behavior. Tiny amounts of some hormones can markedly modify our moods and our actions, our inclination to eat or drink, our aggressiveness or submissiveness, and our reproductive and parental behavior. Furthermore, hormones do more than influence adult behavior: Early in life they help determine the development of body form. Later in life the changing outputs of some endocrine glands and the body's changing sensitivity to some hormones are prominent aspects of aging.

In this chapter we will consider the mechanisms by which hormones accomplish their functions, the main endocrine glands and their hormones, and examples of hormonal influences on physiology and on behavior. After presenting a brief history of discoveries relevant to hormones and their actions, we will compare the ways in which the endocrine and nervous systems communicate and coordinate function. Later chapters will include detailed discussion of the behavioral aspects of hormone activities.

Hormones Act in a Great Variety of Ways throughout the Body

In general, **hormones** (from the Greek *horman*, "to excite") are chemicals secreted into the bloodstream by specialized cells and carried to other parts of the body, where they act on specific target tissues to produce specific physiological effects. Specialists who study hormones are known as endocrinologists because many hormones are produced by **endocrine glands** (from the Greek *endon*, "within," and *krinein*, "to secrete"), so called because they release their hormones within the body. **Exocrine glands** (the Greek *exo* means "out"), such as the tear glands, the salivary glands, and the sweat glands, secrete their products through ducts to the outside of the body. Whereas exocrine glands are also called duct glands, endocrine glands are ductless.

Endocrine glands come in a variety of sizes, shapes, and locations in the body (Figure 5.1). Although the endocrine glands and their hormones are important, today's definition of "hormone" is more inclusive, recognizing that other tissues, such as the heart and kidneys, secrete compounds known as hormones. Even plants, which have no endocrine glands, use chemical signals that are considered to be hormones.

Our Current Understanding of Hormones Developed in Stages

Communication within the body and the integration of behavior were considered the exclusive province of the nervous system until the beginning of the twentieth century, when investigators became aware that the

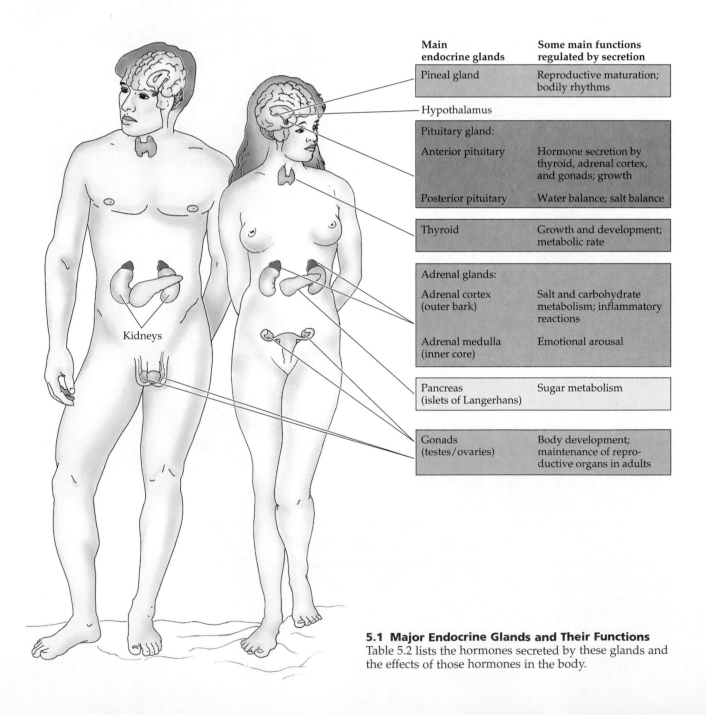

Main endocrine glands	Some main functions regulated by secretion
Pineal gland	Reproductive maturation; bodily rhythms
Hypothalamus	
Pituitary gland:	
Anterior pituitary	Hormone secretion by thyroid, adrenal cortex, and gonads; growth
Posterior pituitary	Water balance; salt balance
Thyroid	Growth and development; metabolic rate
Adrenal glands:	
Adrenal cortex (outer bark)	Salt and carbohydrate metabolism; inflammatory reactions
Adrenal medulla (inner core)	Emotional arousal
Pancreas (islets of Langerhans)	Sugar metabolism
Gonads (testes/ovaries)	Body development; maintenance of reproductive organs in adults

Kidneys

5.1 Major Endocrine Glands and Their Functions
Table 5.2 lists the hormones secreted by these glands and the effects of those hormones in the body.

endocrine system is also important for these functions. However, the role of such body fluids was anticipated in several ancient civilizations in which endocrine glands were eaten to modify health or behavior. Ancient societies also noted some of the behavioral and physiological changes from obvious endocrine pathology, such as the disfiguring enlargement of the thyroid called goiter.

In the fourth century B.C.E., Aristotle accurately described the effects of **castration** (removal of the testes) in birds, and he compared the behavioral and bodily effects with those seen in eunuchs (castrated men). Although he did not know what mechanism was involved, clearly the testes were important for the reproductive capacity and sexual characteristics of the male. This observation was consistent with the ancient Greek emphasis on body humors, or fluids, as an explanation of temperament and emotions. It was believed that these fluids—phlegm, blood, yellow bile (also known as choler), and black bile—all interacted to produce health or disease (Figure 5.2). The notion of body fluids as the basis of human temperament lingered into the nineteenth century, when terms such as "phlegmatic" (sluggish), "bilious" (ir-

ritable), and "choleric" (hot-tempered) to describe people entered the language.

The first major endocrine experiment was carried out in 1849 by German physiologist Arnold Adolph Berthold. When Berthold castrated young roosters, they showed declines in both reproductive behavior and secondary sexual characteristics, such as the rooster's comb (Figure 5.3). Berthold observed that replacement of one testis into the body cavity restored both the normal behavior of these roosters and their combs. They began crowing and showed usual sexual behaviors. Because the nerve supply to the testis had not been reestablished, Berthold concluded that the testes release a chemical into the blood that affects both male behavior and male body structures. Today we know that the testes make and release the hormone testosterone, which exerts these effects.

The French physiologist Claude Bernard helped set the stage in the nineteenth century for the emergence of endocrinology as a science. Bernard stressed the importance of the internal environment ("internal milieu") in which cells exist and emphasized that this environment must be carefully regulated. As he put it, a constant *internal* body environment is necessary for independent activity in the *external* environment. This idea was later embedded in the concept of homeostasis advanced by American physiologist Walter B. Cannon in the 1920s. **Homeostasis** is the maintenance of a relatively constant internal environment by an array of mechanisms in the body. Clinical and experimental observations starting in the late nineteenth century showed the importance of several glands—including the thyroids, the adrenal cortex, and the pituitary—for maintaining this constant environment inside our bodies.

The Granger Collection, New York

5.2 The Four Humors
A medieval representation of the ancient view that four basic body fluids, or humors, flowed through the body and that excess amounts of these fluids result in particular temperaments. (*Clockwise from top left*) An excess of black bile was said to cause melancholia; phlegm, sluggishness; blood, a highly changeable temperament; choler or yellow bile, irascibility and anxiousness.

	Group 1	Group 2	Group 3
Appearance of immature roosters			
Manipulation	None	Remove testes	Remove testes and reimplant one in abdomen
Appearance of adult roosters			
Comb and wattles:	Normal	Small	Normal
Mount hens?	Yes	No	Yes
Aggressive?	Yes	No	Yes
Crowing?	Normal	Weak	Normal

5.3 The First Experiment in Behavioral Endocrinology
Berthold's nineteenth-century experiment demonstrated the importance of hormones for behavior. Left undisturbed (Group 1), young roosters grow up to have large red wattles and combs, to mount and mate with hens readily, and to fight one another and crow loudly. Animals whose testes were removed during development (Group 2) displayed neither the appearance nor the behavior of normal roosters as adults. However, if one of the testes was reimplanted into the abdominal cavity immediately after its removal (Group 3), the rooster developed normal wattles and normal behavior. Because the reimplanted testis was in an abnormal body site, disconnected from normal innervation, and yet still affected development, Berthold reasoned that the testes release a hormonal signal that has widespread effects.

Vincent du Vigneaud

Frederick Sanger

Rosalyn Yalow

Techniques developed in the twentieth century have enabled scientists to identify many different hormones. Several Nobel prizes have been awarded for the determination of the structure of hormones. For example, Vincent du Vigneaud received the 1955 Nobel prize in chemistry for synthesizing the hormones oxytocin and vasopressin. Frederick Sanger received the same award in 1958 for establishing the chemical structure of insulin. The discovery of a sensitive technique (called radioimmunoassay, or RIA) for measuring small quantities of hormones (see Box 5.1) earned Rosalyn Yalow the Nobel prize in 1977. These techniques, together with earlier ones, give us a powerful set of tools to analyze the reciprocal relations between hormones and behavior.

Organisms Use Several Types of Chemical Communication

The following are some categories of chemical signals in the body, classified according to the form of their communication or delivery:

1. *Synaptic communication.* This form of communication was described in Chapters 3 and 4. In synaptic transmitter function (sometimes called **neurocrine** func-

tion), the released chemical signal diffuses across the synaptic cleft and causes a change in polarization of the postsynaptic membrane (Figure 5.4*a*). Typically, synaptic transmitter function is highly localized.

2. *Autocrine communication.* In **autocrine** communication a released or secreted hormone acts on the releasing cell itself and thereby affects its own activity (Figure 5.4*b*). An example of autocrine function is seen in nerve cells that have autoreceptors that are affected by the released synaptic transmitter molecules and thus monitor their own activity. In this case, the signal molecule serves both an autocrine and a synaptic transmitter function.

3. *Paracrine communication.* In **paracrine** regulation or communication, the released chemical signal diffuses to nearby target cells through the intermediate extracellular space (Figure 5.4*c*). The strongest impact is on the nearest cells.

4. *Endocrine communication.* In **endocrine** regulation and communication, the chemical signal is a hormone released into the bloodstream and taken up selectively by target organs, which may be quite far away (Figure 5.4*d*). We will see later that some neurons release hormones into the bloodstream in this manner.

5. *Pheromone communication.* Hormones can be used to communicate not only within an individual, but also from one individual to another. **Pheromones** (from the Greek *pherein,* "to carry") are hormones produced by one individual and then released outside the body to affect other individuals of the same species (Figure 5.4*e*). For example, many species of

(*a*) Neurocrine function (synaptic transmission)

Neuron

(*b*) Autocrine function

Autocrine cell

(*c*) Paracrine function

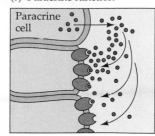

Paracrine cell

(*d*) Endocrine function

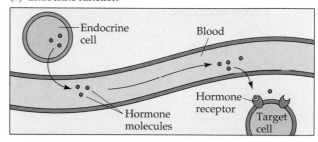

Endocrine cell

Blood

Hormone receptor

Target cell

Hormone molecules

(*e*) Pheromone function

(*f*) Allomone function

5.4 Chemical Communication Systems

(*a*) In synaptic transmitter (neurocrine) communication, a chemical signal is released from the presynaptic terminal of the neuron and binds to receptor molecules on a post-synaptic target cell. (*b*) Autocrine mechanisms are the feedback effects of a chemical signal on the very cell from which it was released. Some synaptic transmitters are also autocrine signals in that they affect receptors on the presynaptic terminal (autoreceptors). (*c*) In paracrine communication, chemical signals diffuse through extra-cellular space to nearby target cells. The strongest effects are produced in the nearest cells. (*d*) Endocrine glands produce chemical signals and release them into the bloodstream. Effects are produced in the body wherever receptors for the hormone are found. (*e*) Pheromones carry a message from one individual of the species to other individuals. Often pheromones indicate whether the individual emitting them is ready to mate. (*f*) Allomones are produced by individuals of one species to communicate with (and affect the behavior of) individuals of other species. Even plants communicate with animals via allomones.

ants produce a wide variety of pheromones that are used to communicate the presence of intruders in the nest, or to mark the trail that leads to a rich food source. Dogs and wolves urinate on various landmarks to designate their "territory"; other animals smell the pheromones in the urine and either respect or challenge the territory. In Chapter 12 we'll discuss evidence of pheromones that may synchronize menstrual cycles in women.

6. *Allomone communication.* Some chemical signals are released by members of one species and affect the behavior of individuals of another species (W. L. Brown, 1968). These hormones are called **allomones** (from the Greek *allos*, "other"). Allomones can carry messages between animal species or from plants to animals (Figure 5.4*f*). Flowers exude scents to attract insects and birds in order to distribute pollen. Other plant agents inhibit insect growth hormones, thus interfering with the life cycle of potential predators. Skunks may produce the best-known allomone of all.

Hormones Act According to Ten General Principles

Although there are some exceptions, the following rules are general principles of hormone action:

1. Hormones frequently act in a gradual fashion, activating behavioral and physiological responses long after concentrations of hormone in the blood have fallen.

2. When hormones alter behavior, they tend to act by changing the intensity or probability of evoked behaviors, rather than acting as a switch to turn behaviors on or off regardless of context.

3. Both the quantities and types of hormone released are influenced by environmental as well as endogenous factors. The relationship between behavior and hormones is clearly reciprocal; that is, hormones change behavior and behaviors change hormone levels or responses. For example, high levels of testosterone are related to aggression, and in some species males who lose in aggressive encounters show a reduction in testosterone levels, while the winners in these bouts show little change in testosterone levels. This example shows the reciprocal relation between somatic and behavioral events that we discussed in Chapter 1 (see Figure 1.3).

4. Each hormone has multiple effects on different tissues, organs, and behaviors; conversely, a single type of behavior or physiological change can be affected by many different hormones (Figure 5.5).

5. Hormones are produced in small amounts and often are secreted in bursts. This "pulsatile" secretion

Hormone A Hormone B Hormone C

Action A1

Action A2

Action A3 Action B1 Action C2

A process regulated by several hormones

5.5 Multiplicity of Hormone Action
A single hormone often has multiple effects (e.g., hormones A and C in this illustration) on several different groups of target cells. Similarly, a single process or body organ (yellow box) may be affected by several hormones.

pattern is sometimes crucial for the small amount of hormone to be effective.

6. The levels of many hormones vary rhythmically throughout the day, and many hormonal systems are controlled by circadian "clocks" in the brain, as we'll see in Chapter 14.

7. Hormones affect metabolic processes in most cells, including the buildup and breakdown of carbohydrates, lipids, and proteins. In this sense, hormones trigger long-term metabolic change.

8. Hormones interact; the effect of one hormone can be markedly changed by the actions of another hormone.

9. The chemical structure of a given hormone is similar in all vertebrates, but the functions served by that hormone can vary across species.

10. Hormones can affect only cells that possess a receptor protein that recognizes the hormone and alters cell function. Among different vertebrates, the same brain regions often possess the same hormone receptors.

Neural versus hormonal communication. There are four main differences between neural and hormonal communication:

1. *Neural communication* works somewhat like a telephone system: Messages travel over fixed channels to precise destinations. The anatomical connections between neurons determine the transmission of information from one cell to another. In contrast, *hormonal communication* works more like a TV broadcasting system: Many different endocrine messages spread throughout the body and can then be picked up by scattered cells that have receptors for them. Some hormones broadcast rather locally; for instance, the hypothalamus sends hormones only a few millimeters through the blood vessels to the anterior pituitary gland. Other hormones broadcast

throughout the body, but because cells in only a particular organ have the proper receptors, these hormones influence only that organ.

2. Whereas neural messages are rapid and are measured in milliseconds, hormonal messages are slower and are measured in seconds and minutes.

3. Most neural messages are "digitized," all-or-none impulses. Hormonal messages are analog—that is, graded in strength.

4. Neural and hormonal communication also differ in terms of voluntary control. You cannot, at a command, increase or decrease the output of a hormone or a response mediated by the endocrine system, but you can voluntarily lift your arm, blink your eyelids, or perform many other acts under neuromuscular control. This distinction between neural and hormonal systems, however, is not absolute. Many muscular responses cannot be performed or changed at will, even though they are under neural control. An example is heart rate, which is regulated by the vagus nerve and can meet changing demands during exercise or stress, but which only very few people can alter promptly and directly on command. Later in this chapter we will note examples of conditioned responses that are controlled by hormones: the milk letdown response mediated by oxytocin during breast-feeding, and the early release of insulin during eating.

Similarities in neural and hormonal communication. In spite of the differences outlined in the previous section, the neural and hormonal systems show important similarities. The nervous system uses specialized biochemical substances (neurotransmitters) to communicate across synaptic junctions in much the same way that the endocrine system uses hormones (Figure 5.6). Of course, the distance traveled by the chemical messengers differs enormously in the two cases: The synaptic cleft is only about 30 nm (30 $\times 10^{-9}$ m) wide, but hormones may travel a meter or so from the site of secretion to the target organ. Nevertheless, the analogy between chemical transmission at synapses and hormonal communication holds up in several specific respects:

1. The neuron produces its particular transmitter chemicals and stores them for later release, just as an endocrine gland stores its hormones for secretion.

2. Neurons are stimulated, usually by other neurons, to produce an action potential that causes the presynaptic terminal to release transmitter into the

(a) Neurocrine communication (synaptic transmission)

(b) Endocrine communication

(c) Neuroendocrine communication

5.6 Neuroendocrine Cells Blend Neuronal and Endocrine Mechanisms

(a) Neurons communicate with other neurons or muscle cells or glands, and signal transmission is determined by the pattern of anatomical connections. (b) Endocrine signals are transmitted through the bloodstream and are recognized by appropriate receptors in specific locations in the body. (c) Neuroendocrine (neurosecretory) cells are the interface between neurons and endocrine glands. They receive neural signals from other neurons and secrete a hormone into the bloodstream. In this way electrical signals are converted into hormonal signals.

A look at the neurons in the hypothalamus that synthesize hormones and release them into the bloodstream will highlight the similarities between neuronal and hormonal communication. These so-called **neurosecretory** (neuroendocrine) **cells** make it hard to draw a firm line between neurons and endocrine cells (see Figure 5.6c). In fact, some investigators believe that the endocrine glands may have evolved from neurosecretory cells (Norman and Litwack, 1987).

Findings that certain chemicals—either hormonal peptides or **neuropeptides** (peptides used by neurons)—in vertebrates are also found in single-celled organisms have led to a different hypothesis: that both the nervous system and the endocrine system are derived from chemical communication systems in our remote single-celled ancestors (LeRoith et al., 1992). Much current research is devoted to determining the functions of peptide compounds in the brain (Björklund et al., 1992; Koob et al., 1990). Some peptides are used as neurotransmitters. On the other hand, since peptides typically have a slower onset of effect and a longer duration of action than do other transmitters, it has been suggested that they often act as **neuromodulators** (see Chapter 4), substances that alter the reactivity of cells to specific transmitters.

Competing hypotheses

Hormones Can Be Classified by Chemical Structure

Most hormones fall into one of three categories: protein hormones, amine hormones, or steroid hormones. Like all other proteins, **protein hormones** are composed of strings of amino acids (Figure 5.7a). (Recall that a peptide is simply a small protein—i.e., a short string of amino acids. In this chapter we will refer to both protein and peptide hormones as protein hormones.) Different protein hormones consist of different combinations of amino acids. **Steroid hormones** are composed not of amino acids, but of four interconnected rings of carbon atoms (Figure 5.7b). Different steroid hormones vary in the number and kinds of atoms attached to the rings. This structure allows steroids to dissolve readily

synaptic cleft. Similarly, endocrine glands are stimulated to secrete hormones into the bloodstream, some glands responding to neural messages and others to chemical messages.

3. There are many different synaptic transmitter chemicals, and there are many different hormones. In fact, more and more chemicals are being found to serve as both. Examples are norepinephrine and epinephrine, which act as transmitters at many brain synapses but are also secreted as hormones by the adrenal gland.

4. The synaptic transmitter reacts with specific receptor molecules at the surface of the postsynaptic membrane. Similarly, hormones react with specific receptor molecules, either on the surface or in the interior of their target cells; most organs do not have receptors for a given hormone and therefore do not respond to it.

5. Often when hormones act on receptor molecules on the cell surface, a second messenger is released within the target cells to bring about changes within the cell. This process has been studied extensively in the endocrine system. Some neural effects also involve the release of second messengers in the postsynaptic neuron. Moreover, the same chemicals act as second messengers in both the nervous and the endocrine systems.

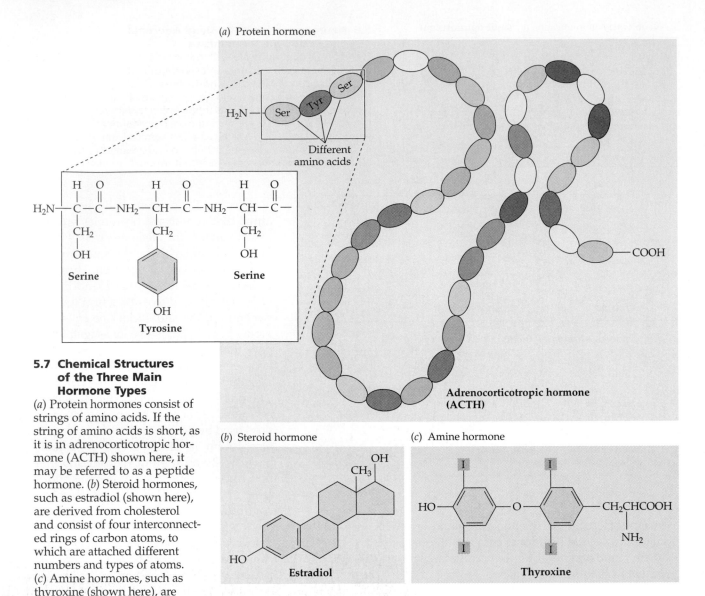

(a) Protein hormone

H₂N— Ser — Tyr — Ser —

Different amino acids

Adrenocorticotropic hormone (ACTH)

— COOH

Serine

Tyrosine

Serine

(b) Steroid hormone

Estradiol

(c) Amine hormone

Thyroxine

5.7 Chemical Structures of the Three Main Hormone Types
(a) Protein hormones consist of strings of amino acids. If the string of amino acids is short, as it is in adrenocorticotropic hormone (ACTH) shown here, it may be referred to as a peptide hormone. (b) Steroid hormones, such as estradiol (shown here), are derived from cholesterol and consist of four interconnected rings of carbon atoms, to which are attached different numbers and types of atoms. (c) Amine hormones, such as thyroxine (shown here), are modified single amino acids.

in lipids, so they can cross cell membranes easily. The distinction between protein and steroid hormones is important because these two classes of hormone interact with different types of receptors and by different mechanisms. **Amine hormones** are compounds composed of a single amino acid (hence their alias, "monoamine" hormones) that have been modified into a related molecule (Figure 5.7c). Table 5.1 gives examples of each class of hormones.

Hormones Act on a Wide Variety of Cellular Mechanisms

Later in the chapter we will be considering the effects of specific hormones on behavior. In preparation for that discussion, let's look briefly at three aspects of hormonal activity: the effects of hormones on cells, the mechanisms by which hormones exercise these effects, and the regulation of hormone secretion.

Hormones Affect Cells by Influencing Their Growth and Activity

By influencing cells in various tissues and organs, hormones affect many everyday behaviors in humans and other animals. Hormones exert these far-reaching effects by (1) promoting the proliferation, growth, and differentiation of cells, and (2) modulating cell activity. Early developmental processes are promoted by various hormones—for example, the thyroid hormones. Without these hormones, fewer cells are produced in the brain, and mental development is stunted. Although cells proliferate and differentiate mainly during early development in the brain, hormones cause cells in some organs to divide and grow at later stages of life, too. For example, male and female hormones cause secondary sex characteristics to appear during adolescence: breasts and broadening of the hips in women, and facial hair and enlargement of the Adam's apple in men.

In cells that are already differentiated, hormones can modulate the rate of function. For example, thyroid hormones and insulin promote the metabolic activity of most of the cells in our body. Other hormones modulate activity in certain types of cells. For example, luteinizing hormone (a hormone from the anterior pituitary gland) promotes the secretion of sex hormones by the testes and ovaries.

Hormones Initiate Actions by Binding to Receptor Molecules

The three classes of hormones exert their influences on target organs in two different ways:

1. Protein hormones bind to specific receptors (proteins that recognize only one hormone or class of hormones). Such receptors are usually found *on the surface* of target cell membranes and, when stimulated by the appropriate hormone, cause the release of a second messenger in the cell. (As we saw in Chapter 3, the release of a second messenger can also be caused by some synaptic transmitters.) Protein hormones exert their effects by using this mechanism to alter proteins that already exist within the cell. Most amine hormones also act via surface receptors and second messengers, but as we'll see, the thyroid hormones are an exception.

2. Steroid hormones pass through the membrane and bind to specific receptor proteins *inside* the cell. The steroid–receptor complex then binds to DNA in the nucleus of the cell. This binding affects the transcription of specific genes, increasing the production of some proteins and decreasing the production of others. Hence, these hormones act by affecting gene expression and thereby altering the production of proteins (see the Appendix).

Let's look at these two main modes of action in a little more detail and examine the ways in which hormones affect cellular function.

Protein and amine hormones act rapidly. What characteristic of a cell determines whether it responds to a particular protein hormone? Some proteins manufactured by a cell become integrated into the membrane, such as the neurotransmitter receptors discussed in Chapters 3 and 4. Part of the receptor protein faces the outside of the cell to interact with extracellular chemical signals, while other parts of the protein remain inside the cell. Some of these proteins serve as receptors for protein hormones rather than for neurotransmitters. Thus, only cells that produce the appropriate receptor proteins and insert them into the membrane will respond to a specific hormone. Hormone receptors can increase or decrease in number, and these changes are sometimes referred to as up-regulation and down-regulation, respectively. Sometimes continuous exposure to a specific hormone results in fewer receptors to bind the hormone to a cell; in other cases the reverse happens.

When a hormone binds to the extracellular portion of the receptor, the receptor molecule changes its overall shape. The alteration in the intracellular portion of the receptor then changes the internal chemistry of the cell, often by activating a second messenger (Figure 5.8a).

One second-messenger compound—cyclic adenosine monophosphate, commonly referred to as **cyclic AMP** or **cAMP**—transmits the messages of many of the peptide and amine hormones: It

TABLE 5.1	*Major Classes of Hormones*
Class	**Hormone**
Protein hormones	Adrenocorticotropic hormone (ACTH)
	Follicle-stimulating hormone (FSH)
	Luteinizing hormone (LH)
	Thyroid-stimulating hormone (TSH)
	Growth hormone (GH)
	Prolactin
	Insulin
	Glucagon
	Oxytocin
	Vasopressin (arginine vasopressin, AVP; antidiuretic hormone, ADH)
	Releasing hormones, such as: Corticotropin-releasing hormone (CRH) Gonadotropin-releasing hormone (GnRH)
Amine hormones	Epinephrine (adrenaline)
	Norepinephrine (NE)
	Thyroid hormones
	Melatonin
Steroid hormones Gonadal	Estrogens (e.g., estradiol)
	Progestins (e.g., progesterone)
	Androgens (e.g., testosterone, dihydrotestosterone)
Adrenal	Glucocorticoids (e.g., cortisol)
	Mineralocorticoids (e.g., aldosterone)

5.8 Two Main Mechanisms of Hormone Action

(*a*) Protein hormone receptors are found in the cell membrane. When the hormone binds to the receptor, a second-messenger system is activated, which affects different cellular processes. (*b*) Steroid hormones diffuse passively into cells. Inside target cells are large receptor molecules that bind to the steroid hormone. The steroid–receptor complex then binds to DNA, causing an increase in the production of some gene products and a decrease in the production of others.

(*a*) Protein hormone action

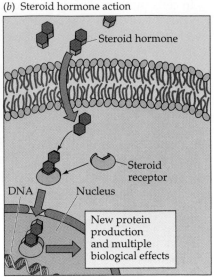

(*b*) Steroid hormone action

may seem surprising that the same second messenger can mediate the effects of many different hormones, but recall from Chapter 3 that the same kind of neural impulses can convey all sorts of neural messages. This situation is similar: A change in cAMP levels can cause very different outcomes depending on which cells are affected, on which part of a cell is affected, and on the prior biochemical activity inside the cell. Other widespread second-messenger compounds include cyclic guanosine monophosphate (cGMP) and phosphoinositides.

The specificity of hormonal effects is determined in part by the selectivity of receptors; only a few cells produce the receptor that recognizes and reacts to the hormone, and only those cells respond. For example, adrenocorticotropic hormone (ACTH) interacts with receptors on the membranes of cells in the adrenal cortex, and in these cells an increase in cAMP leads to the synthesis and release of other hormones.

Protein hormones usually act relatively rapidly, within seconds to minutes. (Although rapid for a hormone, this action is much slower than neural activity.) There can also be prolonged effects. For example, ACTH promotes the proliferation and growth of adrenal cortical cells, thereby increasing the long-term capacity to sustain production of their hormones.

Steroid hormones act slowly. Steroid hormones typically act more slowly than protein hormones, requiring hours to take effect. The specificity of action of steroid hormones is determined by the receptors that reside inside target cells. A large "superfamily" of steroid receptor genes has been discovered (Ribeiro et al., 1995). Some of these receptors are orphans; that is, we don't yet know which steroid hormone binds them.

Steroid hormones pass in and out of many cells in which they have no effect. If there are appropriate re-

ceptor proteins inside, however, these receptors bind to the hormone, and the receptor–steroid complex then binds to DNA, so they become concentrated in the nuclei of target cells (Figure 5.8*b*). Thus, as Box 5.1 describes, one can study where a steroid hormone is active by observing where radioactively tagged molecules of the steroid are concentrated. For example, when tagged estrogen is administered into the circulatory system, it accumulates not only in the reproductive tract (as you might expect), but also in the nuclei of some neurons throughout the hypothalamus. By altering protein production, steroids have a slow but often long-lasting effect on the development or adult function of cells. We will discuss such effects of steroids further in Chapter 12.

Steroids may be able to affect cells in other ways. For example, evidence suggests that estrogen, in addition to its slow, long-lasting action, can have a rapid, brief effect on some neurons. This rapid effect may involve a separate class of steroid receptors in the membrane of these neurons (Wehling, 1997). This membrane mechanism may be a way of modulating neural excitability in reproductive behavior. Such multiple mechanisms of hormonal activity are now a subject of intense study.

Feedback Control Mechanisms Regulate the Secretion of Hormones

One of the major features of almost all hormonal systems is that they don't just manufacture a hormone; they also detect and evaluate the effects of the hormone. Thus, secretion is usually monitored and regulated so that the rate is appropriate to ongoing activities and needs of the body. The basic control used is a negative feedback system: Successful output of the hormone "feeds back" to inhibit the drive for more hormone.

Figure 5.9*a* diagrams the simplest kind of system that regulates hormones. An endocrine cell releases

BOX 5.1   *Techniques of Modern Behavioral Endocrinology*

To establish that a particular hormone affects behavior, investigators usually begin with the type of experiment that Berthold performed in the nineteenth century: observing the behavior of the intact animal, then removing the endocrine gland and looking for a change in behavior (see Figure 5.3). Berthold was limited to this type of experiment, but modern scientists have many additional options available. Let's imagine we are investigating a particular effect of hormones on behavior to see how we might proceed.

Which Hormone?

First, the investigator must carefully observe the behavior of several individuals, seeking ways to classify and quantify the different types of behavior and place them in the context of the behavior of other individuals. For example, most adult male rats will try to mount and copulate with a female placed in their cage. Sometimes (about every fourth day) the female will respond to the male's advances by lifting her rump and pushing her tail to one side, allowing the male to mate with her. At such times the female is said to be receptive to the male. If the testes are removed from the male rat, he will eventually stop copulating with a female, even if she is receptive. We know that one of the hormones produced by the testes is testosterone. Is it the loss of testosterone that causes the loss of male copulatory behavior? To explore this question, we purchase some synthetic testosterone, inject it into castrated males, and observe whether the copulatory behavior returns. (It does.)

Next, we might examine individual male rats and ask whether the ones that copulate a lot have more testosterone circulating in their blood than those who copulate only a little. Thus, we measure individual differences in the amount of copulatory behavior, take a sample of blood from each individual, and measure levels of testosterone. To take this measure we use **radioimmunoassy (RIA)**, a technique that uses an antibody that binds to a particular hormone.

By adding many such antibodies to each blood sample and measuring how many of the antibodies find a hormone molecule to bind, we can estimate the total number of molecules of the hormone per unit volume of blood. (We won't go into detail here about how we determine the number of antibodies that bind to hormone.)

It turns out that individual differences in the sexual behavior of normal male rats (and normal male humans) do not correlate with differences in testosterone levels in the blood. In both rats and humans, a drastic loss of testosterone, as after castration, will result in a gradual decline in sexual behavior. Among normal males, however, everyone appears to make more than enough testosterone to maintain sexual behavior, so something else must modulate this behavior. In other words, the hormone acts in a permissive manner: It permits the display of the behavior, but something else determines how much of the behavior each individual exhibits.

Where Are the Target Cells?

What does testosterone do to permit this behavior? One step toward answering this question is to ask another question: Which parts of the brain are normally affected by this hormone? We have two methods at our disposal.

First, we might inject a castrated animal with testosterone that has been radioactively labeled (one or more of the atoms in the molecule has been replaced with a radioactive atom). After waiting about an hour for the testosterone to accumulate in the brain regions that have receptors for the hormone, we would sacrifice the animal, remove the brain, freeze it, cut thin sections from it, and place the thin sections on photographic film. If the tissue is left in place for a few months, enough radioactive

(A) Androgen autoradiogram

particles from the testosterone will hit the film to expose it. We develop the film to learn which brain regions accumulated testosterone. This method is known as *autoradiography* because the tissue "takes its own picture" with radioactivity (see Box 2.1).

When the labeled hormone is a steroid like testosterone, the radioactivity accumulates in the nuclei of brain cells and leaves small black specks on the film (Figure A). When the radiolabeled hormone is a protein hormone, the radioactivity accumulates in the membranes of cells and appears in particular layers of the brain. Computers can generate color maps that highlight regions with high densities of receptors (Figure B).

The second method for detecting hormone receptors is immunocytochemistry. In this method we use antibodies that recognize either the hormone (Figure C), or the hormone receptor. This method allows us to map the distribution of hormone receptors in the brain. We put the antibodies on slices of brain tissue, wait for them to bind to the receptors, wash off the unbound antibodies, and use chemi-

(B) Oxytocin autoradiogram

BOX 5.1 *(continued)*

cal methods to visualize the antibodies by creating a tiny dark spot at each antibody. When the antibodies recognize a steroid receptor, chemical reactions cause a brown coloration in the nuclei of target brain cells.

What Happens at the Target Cells?

Once we have used either autoradiography or immunocytochemistry (or, better yet, both) to identify brain regions that have receptors for the hormone, those regions become candidates for the places at which the hormone works to change behavior. Now we can take castrated males and implant tiny pellets of testosterone into one of those brain regions. We use RIA to ensure that the pellets are small enough that they have no effect on hormone levels in the blood. Then we ask whether the small implant in that brain region

restores the behavior. If not, then in other animals we can implant pellets in a different region or try placing implants in a combination of brain sites.

It turns out that such implants can restore male sexual behavior in rats only if they are placed in the medial preoptic area (mPOA) of the hypothalamus. Thus we have found so far that testosterone does something to the mPOA to permit individual males to display sexual behavior. Now we can examine the mPOA in detail to learn what changes in the anatomy, physiology, or protein production of this region are caused by testosterone. We have more or less caught up to modern-day scientists

(C) Vasopressin fibers in septum of intact (*left*) and castrated (*right*) rats revealed by immunocytochemistry

who work on this very question. Some of the preliminary answers will be discussed in Chapter 12. (Figure B courtesy of Bruce McEwen; Figure C courtesy of Geert DeVries.)

(a) **Autocrine feedback**   (b) **Target cell feedback**   (c) **Brain regulation**   (d) **Brain and pituitary regulation**

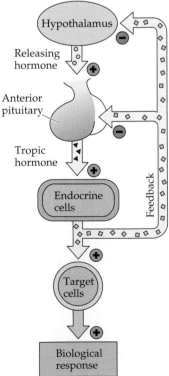

5.9 Endocrine Feedback Loops

(a) In the simplest type of negative feedback control, an endocrine gland releases a hormone that not only acts on a target, but also feeds back in an autocrine fashion to inhibit further hormone secretion. (b) The hormone from the endocrine gland acts on target cells to produce a specific set of biological effects. The consequences of these effects may be detected by the endocrine gland, inhibiting further hormone release. (c) In many feedback systems the brain becomes involved. The hypothalamic region drives the endocrine gland via either neural or hormonal signals. The target organ signals the brain to inhibit this drive. (d) Highly complex feedback mechanisms involve the hypothalamus and the anterior pituitary as well as the endocrine gland. Feedback regulation may involve a variety of routes and hormones.

a hormone that acts on target cells, but the same hormone also feeds back to inhibit the gland that released it—an autocrine response.

In other cases, the endocrine cell reacts not to its own hormone, but to the biological response the hormone elicits from the target cells (Figure 5.9*b*). The character of this response is monitored by some cells in the circuit. If the initial effects are too small, additional hormone is released. Thus, for example, the hormone insulin helps control the level of glucose circulating in the blood in the following way: After a meal, glucose from the food enters the bloodstream and extracellular fluid, causing insulin to be released from the pancreas. The insulin causes extracellular glucose to enter muscle and fat cells and stimulates them to use the glucose. As the level of glucose in the blood falls, the pancreas secretes less insulin, so a balance tends to be maintained. Thus, insulin is normally self-limiting: The more that is secreted, the more glucose that is pulled out of circulation and the lower the call for insulin. This negative feedback action of a hormone is like that of a thermostat, and just as the thermostat can be set to different temperatures at different times, the set points of a person's endocrine feedback systems can be changed to meet varying circumstances. We'll encounter negative feedback effects again in Chapter 13.

A more complex endocrine system includes the hypothalamus as part of the circuit that controls an endocrine gland (Figure 5.9*c*). This control may be exerted through a neural link, as in control of the adrenal medulla. The secretion of epinephrine by the adrenal medulla affects target cells, and the negative feedback goes directly to the hypothalamus, bypassing the endocrine gland (adrenal medulla) and reducing the demand for further hormone output.

An even greater degree of complexity is encountered when the anterior pituitary becomes involved (Figure 5.9*d*). As we'll see, several anterior pituitary hormones affect the secretion of other endocrine glands; all of these pituitary hormones are called **tropic hormones**. ("Tropic," pronounced with a long "o" as in "toe," means "directed toward.") The hypothalamus uses another set of hormones, called **releasing hormones**, to control the pituitary release of tropic hormones. Thus, the brain's releasing hormones affect the pituitary's tropic hormones, which affect the release of hormone from another endocrine gland. Feedback in this case goes from the hormone of the endocrine gland to both the hypothalamus and the anterior pituitary (Figure 5.10).

Each Endocrine Gland Secretes Specific Hormones

We will restrict our account in this chapter to some of the main endocrine glands, their hormones, and some of the principal effects of those hormones. Our treatment must be simplified because a thorough treatment would fill an entire book (e.g., Hadley, 1996). Table 5.2 gives a more complete listing of hormones and their functions. Keep in mind that most hormones have more functions than are mentioned here and that several hormones may act together to produce effects in the same target cells.

The Pituitary Gland Releases Many Important Hormones

Resting in a depression in the base of the skull is the **pituitary gland** (see Figure 5.1), about 1 cm³ in volume and weighing about 1 g. The hypothalamus sits just

5.10 An Example of Complex Endocrine Regulation
The brain funnels information to the hypothalamus, which then controls the anterior pituitary, which in turn stimulates the thyroid gland. Note that three hormones and at least four cell groups are interacting in this instance.

TABLE 5.2   *Main Endocrine Glands, Their Hormone Products, and Principal Effects of Their Hormones*

Gland	Hormones	Principal effects
Posterior pituitary (storage organ for certain hormones produced by hypothalamus)	Oxytocin	Stimulates contraction of uterine muscles; stimulates release of milk by mammary glands
	Vasopressin (AVP; antidiuretic hormone, ADH)	Stimulates increased water reabsorption by kidneys; stimulates constriction of blood vessels
Anterior pituitary	Growth hormone (GH)	Stimulates growth
	Thyroid-stimulating hormone (TSH)	Stimulates the thyroid
	Adrenocorticotropic hormone (ACTH)	Stimulates the adrenal cortex
	Follicle-stimulating hormone (FSH)	Stimulates growth of ovarian follicles and of seminiferous tubules of the testes
	Luteinizing hormone (LH)	Stimulates conversion of follicles into corpora lutea; stimulates secretion of sex hormones by gonads
	Prolactin	Stimulates milk secretion by mammary glands
Hypothalamus	Releasing hormones	Regulate hormone secretion by anterior pituitary
	Oxytocin; vasopressin	*See under* Posterior pituitary
Pineal	Melatonin	Regulates seasonal changes; regulates puberty
Adrenal cortex	Glucocorticoids (corticosterone, cortisol, hydrocortisone, etc.)	Inhibit incorporation of amino acids into protein in muscle; stimulate formation and storage of glycogen; help maintain normal blood sugar level
	Mineralocorticoids (aldosterone, deoxycorticosterone, etc.)	Regulate metabolism of sodium and potassium
	Sex hormones (especially androstenedione)	Regulate facial and body hair
Gonads		
Testes	Androgens (testosterone, dihydrotestosterone, etc.)	Stimulate development and maintenance of male primary and secondary sexual characteristics and behavior
Ovaries	Estrogens (estradiol, estrone, etc.)	Stimulate development and maintenance of female secondary sexual characteristics and behavior
	Progestins (progesterone)	Stimulate female secondary sexual characteristics and behavior; maintain pregnancy
Thyroid	Thyroxine, triiodothyronine	Stimulate oxidative metabolism
	Calcitonin	Prevents excessive rise in blood calcium
Pancreas	Insulin	Stimulates glycogen formation and storage
	Glucagon	Stimulates conversion of glycogen into glucose
Mucosa of duodenum	Secretin	Stimulates secretion of pancreatic juice
	Cholecystokinin (CCK)	Stimulates release of bile by gallbladder
	Enterogastrone	Inhibits secretion of gastric juice
Pyloric mucosa of stomach	Gastrin	Stimulates secretion of gastric juice
Heart	Atrial natriuretic peptide	Promotes salt loss in urine

above it. The term "pituitary" comes from the Latin *pituita*, "mucus," reflecting the outmoded belief that waste products dripped down from the brain into the pituitary, which secreted them out through the nose. (The ancients may have thought you could literally "sneeze your brains out.") The pituitary used to be referred to as the "master gland," a reference to its regulatory role in regard to several other endocrine glands. But this gland is itself enslaved by the hypothalamus above it, as we'll see.

Sylvius

The pituitary gland consists of two main parts: the **anterior pituitary**, or adenohypophysis, and the **posterior pituitary**, or neurohypophysis. The term "hypophysis" comes from the Greek *hypophyein,* "to grow beneath," referring to the fact that the pituitary is situated under the brain. The adenohypophysis originates from glandular tissue (the Greek *aden* means "gland"). The neurohypophysis derives from neural tissue. The anterior and posterior pituitary are completely separate in function.

The pituitary is connected to the hypothalamus by a thin piece of tissue called the pituitary stalk (see Figure 5.11). The stalk contains many axons and is richly supplied with blood vessels. The axons extend only to the posterior pituitary, which we will consider next. The blood vessels, as we will see later, transmit information exclusively to the anterior pituitary.

The posterior pituitary. The posterior pituitary gland contains two principal hormones: **oxytocin** and **arginine vasopressin** (**AVP**, often called just **vasopressin**). Neurons in various hypothalamic nuclei, especially the supraoptic nucleus and the paraventricular nucleus, synthesize these two hormones and transport them along their axons to the axon terminals. Nerve impulses in these hypothalamic neurosecretory cells travel down the axons in the pituitary stalk and reach the axon terminals in the posterior pituitary, causing release of the hormone from the terminals into the rich vascular bed of the neurohypophysis. The axon terminals abut capillaries (small blood vessels), allowing the hormone to enter circulation immediately (Figure 5.11).

Some of the signals that activate the nerve cells of the supraoptic and paraventricular nuclei are related to thirst and water regulation, which we will discuss in Chapter 13. Secretion of AVP increases blood pressure by causing blood vessels to contract. AVP is also known as *antidiuretic hormone* (*ADH*) because it inhibits the formation of urine (which is the effect that defines an antidiuretic as such). This action of AVP helps conserve water. In fact, the major physiological role of AVP is its potent antidiuretic activity; it exerts this effect with less than one-thousandth of the dose needed to alter blood pressure. But because the name "vasopressin" was the first one applied to the hormone, that is the preferred name. AVP also acts as a neurotransmitter for some neurons that project within the brain.

Oxytocin is involved in many aspects of reproductive and parental behavior. One of its functions is to stimulate contractions of the uterine muscles and thus hasten birth (the word "oxytocin" is derived from the Greek *oxys,* "rapid," and *tokos,* "childbirth"). In fact, injections of oxytocin (or the synthetic version, Pitocin) are frequently used to accelerate delivery when prolonged labor threatens the health of the fetus.

Oxytocin also triggers the **milk letdown reflex**, the contraction of cells in the mammary glands. The mech-

Hypothalamus

Paraventricular nucleus

Neuroendocrine cell bodies in the hypothalamus produce oxytocin or vasopressin.

Supraoptic nucleus

Optic chiasm

Pituitary stalk

Axons from these neurons pass through the pituitary stalk...

Capillaries

...and synapse on the capillaries of the posterior pituitary. When an action potential arrives at a terminal, oxytocin or vasopressin is released from the terminal directly into the bloodstream.

Posterior pituitary hormones
Oxytocin
Vasopressin

5.11 The Posterior Pituitary

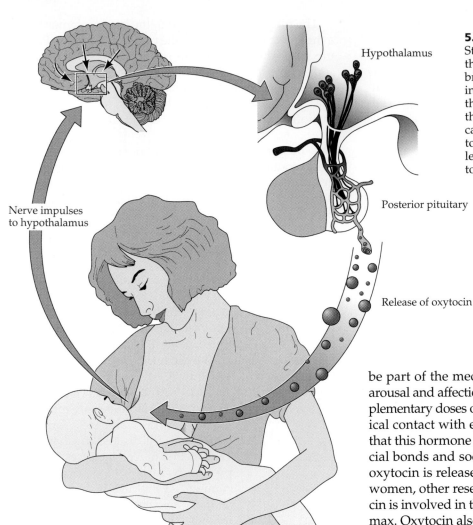

Hypothalamus

Posterior pituitary

Release of oxytocin

Nerve impulses
to hypothalamus

5.12 The Milk Letdown Reflex
Stimulation of the mother's nipple by the infant's suckling response produces brain activity in the mother that results in inputs to the hypothalamus. Cells there produce and release oxytocin from the posterior pituitary. The oxytocin causes the cells of the mammary glands to contract, thereby releasing milk. The letdown reflex may become conditioned to occur when the baby cries.

be part of the mechanism that mediates both sexual arousal and affectionate responses. Rodents given supplementary doses of oxytocin spend more time in physical contact with each other. Carter (1992) suggested that this hormone is important in the formation of social bonds and social attachment. Because a burst of oxytocin is released during orgasm in both men and women, other researchers have suggested that oxytocin is involved in the pleasurable feelings of sexual climax. Oxytocin also serves as a neurotransmitter from hypothalamic cells (see Figure 4.5), projecting widely through the nervous system. Its elaborate role is reflected in the broad distribution of receptors for this hormone in the brain.

The anterior pituitary. Different cells of the anterior lobe of the pituitary synthesize and release different tropic hormones, which we'll discuss in the next section. Synthesis and release of the tropic hormones, however, are under the control of releasing hormones, as we mentioned earlier. The releasing hormones are made by cells of the hypothalamus. We will briefly note some of the properties of these hypothalamic releasing hormones before further considering anterior pituitary actions.

Hypothalamic Releasing Hormones Govern the Anterior Pituitary

Neurons that synthesize different releasing hormones reside in different regions of the hypothalamus; like the neurons that produce oxytocin and vasopressin, these cells are considered neuroendocrine, or neurosecretory, cells. The axons of the neuroendocrine cells converge on the median eminence just above the pituitary stalk. This region contains an elaborate profusion of capillaries that form the **hypothalamic–pituitary portal system**. Axons

anism that mediates this phenomenon is a good example of the interaction of behavior and hormone release. When an infant or young animal first begins to suckle, the arrival of milk at the nipple is delayed by 30 to 60 s. This delay is caused by the sequence of steps that precede letdown. Stimulation of the nipple activates receptors in the skin, which transmit this information through a chain of neurons and synapses to hypothalamic cells that contain oxytocin. Once these cells have been sufficiently stimulated, the hormone is released from the posterior pituitary and travels via the vascular system to the mammary glands, where it produces a contraction of the cells surrounding the storage sites for milk, thus resulting in the availability of milk at the nipple (Figure 5.12). For human mothers this reflex response to suckling frequently becomes conditioned to baby cries, so milk appears promptly at the start of nursing.

Neural plasticity

Another perspective on this hormone, best summarized by the newspaper headline "A Potent Peptide Prompts an Urge to Cuddle," has emerged (Angier, 1992). Oxytocin is active in both sexes and appears to

5.13 The Anterior Pituitary

in this area contain large granules filled with hormones, which are released not into a synapse, but into the capillaries, where blood carries the releasing hormone a short distance into the anterior pituitary. The blood supply of the anterior pituitary thus contains many different releasing hormones that cause various anterior pituitary cells to change the rate at which they release their tropic hormone (Figure 5.13).

The same kinds of controls apply for all the anterior pituitary hormones: Neuroendocrine cells in the hypothalamus make one releasing hormone or another, transport it down their axons to the median eminence, and when an action potential arrives at the terminals, dump the releasing hormone into the hypothalamic–pituitary portal system. When the releasing hormones reach the anterior pituitary, they cause the cells there to release more or less tropic hormone into the bloodstream. Thus the hypothalamic releasing hormones are an important control element in the regulation of secretions of endocrine organs throughout the body (Table 5.3). Cutting the pitu-

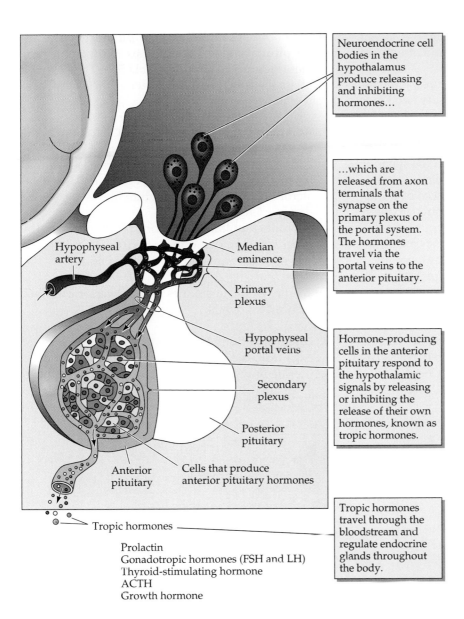

Neuroendocrine cell bodies in the hypothalamus produce releasing and inhibiting hormones…

…which are released from axon terminals that synapse on the primary plexus of the portal system. The hormones travel via the portal veins to the anterior pituitary.

Hypophyseal artery

Median eminence

Primary plexus

Hypophyseal portal veins

Secondary plexus

Posterior pituitary

Anterior pituitary

Cells that produce anterior pituitary hormones

Hormone-producing cells in the anterior pituitary respond to the hypothalamic signals by releasing or inhibiting the release of their own hormones, known as tropic hormones.

Tropic hormones
Prolactin
Gonadotropic hormones (FSH and LH)
Thyroid-stimulating hormone
ACTH
Growth hormone

Tropic hormones travel through the bloodstream and regulate endocrine glands throughout the body.

TABLE 5.3 *Control and Effects of Anterior Pituitary Hormones*

Releasing hormone	Tropic hormone affected	Main target of tropic hormone	Hormones secreted by target
Thyrotropin-releasing hormone (TRH)	Thyroid-stimulating hormone (TSH)	Thyroid	Thyroid hormones (thyroxine and triiodothyronine)
Gonadotropin-releasing hormone (GnRH)	Follicle-stimulating hormone (FSH)	Testes Ovaries	Testosterone Estrogens
	Luteinizing hormone (LH)	Testes Ovaries	Testosterone Progesterone
Corticotropin-releasing hormone (CRH)	Adrenocorticotropic hormone (ACTH)	Adrenal cortex	Glucocorticoids Mineralocorticoids
Somatocrinin (stimulates) Somatostatin (inhibits)	Growth hormone (GH)	Throughout body	Somatomedin peptides from liver
Prolactin-inhibiting factor (may be dopamine) Prolactin-releasing peptide	Prolactin	Mammary glands	None identified

itary stalk interrupts the blood vessels and the flow of releasing hormones and leads to profound atrophy of the pituitary.

The neuroendocrine cells that synthesize the releasing hormones are themselves subject to two kinds of influences:

1. They receive *neural impulses* (either excitatory or inhibitory) from other brain regions via the synaptic contacts of these cells in the hypothalamus. In this manner the endocrine system is influenced by a wide range of neural signals originating from both internal and external events. Thus, the outputs of endocrine glands can be regulated in accordance with ongoing events and can be conditioned by learning.

2. They are directly affected by *circulating messages,* such as other hormones (especially hormones that have themselves been secreted in response to tropic hormones), and by blood sugar and products of the immune system. In other words, these neuroendocrine cells are not shielded by a blood–brain barrier. (The blood–brain barrier was discussed in Chapter 2.)

Tropic hormones of the anterior pituitary. The anterior pituitary gland secretes six main tropic hormones (Figure 5.14; see also Table 5.2). The first two regulate the function of the adrenal cortex and thyroid gland:

1. **Adrenocorticotropic hormone (ACTH)** controls the production and release of hormones of the adrenal cortex. The adrenal cortex in turn releases steroid hormones. The levels of ACTH and adrenal steroids show a marked rhythm in the course of a day (see Chapter 14).

2. **Thyroid-stimulating hormone (TSH)** increases the release of thyroid hormones from the thyroid gland and markedly affects thyroid gland size.

Two other tropic hormones of the anterior pituitary influence the gonads:

3. **Luteinizing hormone (LH)** stimulates the release of eggs from the ovary in females and prepares the uterine lining for the implantation of a fertilized

5.14 Secretions of the Anterior Pituitary
Hormones produced in the anterior pituitary include tropic hormones, which control endocrine glands, and hormones that directly affect other body organs, such as bones.

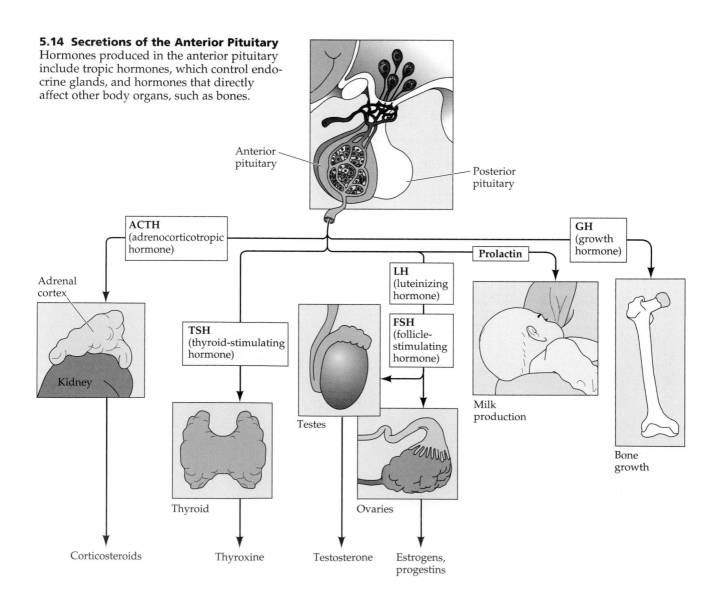

egg. In males, LH stimulates interstitial cells of the testes to produce testosterone.

4. **Follicle-stimulating hormone (FSH)** stimulates the secretion of estrogens in females and of testosterone in males. It also influences both egg and sperm production.

The two remaining tropic hormones control milk production and body growth:

5. **Prolactin** is named after its role of promoting mammary development for lactation in female mammals. In other vertebrates prolactin plays other roles; for example, in ringdoves it promotes the secretion of crop milk, which parents feed to their chicks.
6. **Growth hormone (GH;** also known as somatotropin or somatotropic hormone) acts throughout the body to influence the growth of cells and tissues by affecting protein metabolism. The daily production

and release of GH are especially prominent during the early stages of sleep. In fact, some sleep stages are required for the release of growth hormone. Several other factors influence the release of growth hormone, including a decrease in blood sugar, starvation, exercise, and stress (see Box 5.2).

Let's consider three of the target organs stimulated by tropic hormones of the anterior pituitary: the adrenal gland, the thyroid gland, and the gonads. Each of these glands secretes hormones of its own in response to the pituitary tropic hormones.

Two Divisions of the Adrenal Gland Produce Hormones

Resting on top of each kidney is an **adrenal gland**, which secretes a large variety of hormones (Figure 5.15). In mammals, the adrenal structure is divided into two major portions. In many nonmammalian vertebrates, these two portions are separate glands. In

---

BOX 5.2 *Stress and Growth: Psychosocial Dwarfism*

Genie had an extremely deprived childhood. From the age of 20 months until the age of 13 years, she was isolated in a small, closed room, and much of the time she was tied to a chair. Her disturbed parents provided food, but nobody held Genie or spoke to her. When she was released from her confinement and observed by researchers at the age of 13 years 9 months, her size made her look as if she were only 6 or 7 years old (Rymer, 1993).

Other less horrendous forms of family deprivation have also been shown to result in failure of growth. This syndrome is referred to as **psychosocial dwarfism** to emphasize that the growth failure arises from psychological and social factors mediated through the CNS and its control over endocrine functions (W. H. Green et al., 1984). When such children are removed from stressful circumstances, many begin to grow rapidly. The growth rates of three such psychosocial dwarfs, before and after periods of emotional deprivation, are shown in the figure (arrows indicate when each child was removed from the abusive situation). These children seem to have compensated for much of the growth deficit that occurred during prolonged stress periods.

How do stress and emotional deprivation impair growth? Growth impairments appear to be mediated by changed outputs of several hormones, including growth hormone (GH), cortisol, and other hormones, called **somatomedins** (which are normally released by the liver in response to GH). GH and the somatomedins normally stimulate cell growth; high levels of cortisol inhibit growth.

Some children with psychosocial dwarfism show almost a complete lack of release of GH, which may be caused by an absence of the releasing hormone somatocrinin from the hypothalamus (Brasel and Blizzard, 1974). Disturbed sleep has also been suggested as a cause of this failure (L. I. Gardner, 1972), because GH is typically released during certain stages of sleep, as we will see in Chapter 14, and children under stress show disturbed sleep patterns. Other children who exhibit psychosocial dwarfism show normal levels of GH but low levels of somatomedins, and these hormones, along with GH, appear to be necessary for normal growth. Still other psychosocial dwarfs show elevated levels of steroids (probably as a result of stress) that

inhibit growth. Some affected children show none of these hormonal disturbances. Thus, there may be other routes through which emotional factors influence growth.

Growth is an example of a process that involves many factors—hormonal, metabolic, and dietary—and can therefore malfunction in a variety of ways. Cases of psychosocial dwarfism are more common than once was thought, and investigators who study this syndrome are calling for further awareness of and attention to it (W. H. Green et al., 1984). For Genie, relief came in time to restore much of her body growth, but her mental development remained severely limited; she never learned to say more than a few words, and she now lives in an institution.

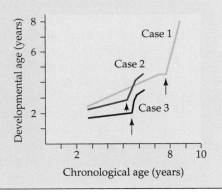

5.15 The Adrenal Gland

Situated above the kidneys, each adrenal consists of an outer layer (the cortex) and an inner layer (the medulla). The main hormones of the cortical portion are cortico-steroids, mineralocorticoids, and sex steroids (androgens and estrogens). The cells of the adrenal medulla release epinephrine and norepinephrine as a result of stimulation by the sympathetic nervous system.

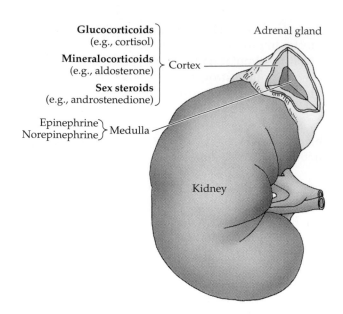

mammals, the outer bark of the gland, the **adrenal cortex**, is composed of distinct layers of cells, each producing different steroid hormones; this portion is about 80% of the gland. The core of this gland is the **adrenal medulla**, really a portion of the sympathetic nervous system because it is richly supplied with nerves from the autonomic ganglia.

The adrenal medulla releases amine hormones—**epinephrine** (adrenaline) and **norepinephrine** (noradrenaline)—in response to nerve impulses of the sympathetic nervous system. In Chapter 4 we saw that epinephrine and norepinephrine are also synaptic transmitters at certain sites in the nervous system.

The adrenal cortex produces and secretes a variety of steroid hormones, collectively called the **adrenocorticoids** (or adrenal steroids). One subgroup is the **glucocorticoids**, so named because of their effects on the metabolism of carbohydrates, including glucose. Hormones of this type, such as **cortisol**, increase the level of blood glucose. They also accelerate the breakdown of proteins. In high concentrations, glucocorticoids have a marked anti-inflammatory effect; that is, they inhibit the swelling around injuries or infections. This action normally results in the temporary decrease of bodily responses to tissue injury. However, high levels of glucocorticoids can destroy nerve cells, as we'll see shortly and in Chapter 15. Glucocorticoids can also affect appetite and muscular activity.

A second subgroup of adrenal steroids is the **mineralocorticoids**, so named because of their effects on ion concentrations in some body tissues, especially the kidneys. The primary mineralocorticoid hormone is **aldosterone**, which acts on the kidneys to retain sodium and thus reduces the amount of urine produced, conserving water. This action maintains a homeostatic equilibrium of ions in blood and extracellular fluids.

The adrenal cortex also produces **sex steroids**. The molecular structure of these hormones is very similar to that of the other adrenal steroids. The chief sex hormone secreted by the human adrenal cortex is **androstenedione**; it contributes to the adult pattern of body hair in men and women (see Topic 5.1, Sexual Awakening). In some females the adrenal cortex produces more than the normal amounts of sex hormones, causing a more masculine appearance (see Chapter 12).

Special topic

The level of circulating adrenal cortical hormones is regulated in several steps (Figure 5.16). The importance of the pituitary hormone ACTH can be demonstrated simply: Removal of the pituitary in animals results in shrinkage of the adrenal cortex and drastically reduced hormone secretion from the adrenal gland. ACTH promotes steroid synthesis in the adrenal gland; cortisol is secreted by the adrenal cortex only when ACTH is present.

Adrenal steroids in turn exert a negative feedback effect on ACTH release. As the level of adrenal cortical hormones increases, the secretion of ACTH is suppressed, so the output of hormones from the adrenal cortex diminishes. When the levels of adrenal steroids fall, the pituitary ACTH-secreting cells are released from suppression, and the concentration of ACTH in the blood rises, leading to increased output of adrenal cortical hormones.

A prominent influence on ACTH secretion is stress, both physiological and psychological. **Stress** is defined as any factor that throws us out of homeostatic balance. Such factors include unusual physiological states, such as exposure to extreme cold or heat, and an array of threatening psychological states. A complex array of physiological changes is elicited by stressors; foremost among them is the activation of pathways from the brain to the hypothalamus, the outputs of which lead to activation of the pituitary. As we have noted, hormones released from the pituitary include ACTH, which triggers the release of glucocorticoids from the adrenal cortex. Robert Sapolsky (1992) has found that high levels of glucocorticoids released during stress can kill nerve cells in the hippocampus. (Stress and ACTH are discussed further in Chapter 15.)

Thyroid Hormones Regulate Growth and Metabolism

Situated just below the vocal apparatus in the throat is the **thyroid gland** (see Figure 5.1). This gland produces and secretes several hormones. Two of these—**thyroxine** and **triiodothyronine**—are usually referred to as

5.16 Regulation of Adrenocorticoid Hormones

The level of circulating adrenal cortical hormones is regulated in several steps that involve both corticotropin-releasing hormone from the hypothalamus and adrenocorticotropic hormone secreted by the anterior pituitary.

Corticotropin-releasing hormone (CRH)

Hypothalamus

Anterior pituitary

Adrenocorticotropic hormone (ACTH)

Feedback

Adrenal cortex

Several hormones, including glucocorticoids, mineralocorticoids, and sex steroids

Different target organs

thyroid hormones; a third—*calcitonin*—promotes calcium deposition in bones and will not be discussed further. Certain thyroid cells produce these hormones, and a saclike collection of cells called the thyroid colloid stores them.

The thyroid is unique among endocrine glands because it stores large amounts of hormone and releases it slowly; normally the thyroid has at least 100 days' supply of hormones. Although thyroid hormones are amines—derived from amino acids—they behave like steroids. They bind to specialized receptors (part of the steroid receptor superfamily) found inside cells. The thyroid hormone–receptor complex then binds to DNA and regulates gene expression.

Figure 5.10 shows the control network for regulating thyroxine levels in blood. The major control is exerted by *thyroid-stimulating hormone* (TSH) from the anterior pituitary gland. The secretion of TSH by the

pituitary is controlled by two factors. The dominant factor is the negative feedback from thyroid hormones circulating in the blood; they directly inhibit the pituitary, reducing TSH release. Second, **thyrotropin-releasing hormone** (TRH) produced by the hypothalamus stimulates the release of TSH from the pituitary. When the level of circulating thyroid hormone falls, both TRH and TSH are secreted; when TSH reaches the thyroid gland, it stimulates the production and release of thyroid hormones.

Knowledge of the feedback controls of thyroid output often helps in diagnosing undersecretion (hypothyroidism) or oversecretion (hyperthyroidism) of the thyroid gland—relatively common disorders. Hypothyroidism is often caused by reduced responsiveness of the thyroid gland to TSH. At first the hypothalamus and pituitary react to this lack of response by producing more and more TSH to bring thyroid hormone levels up to normal. Physicians can sometimes detect the increased TSH levels before levels of thyroid hormones have fallen appreciably.

Thyroid hormones are the only substances produced by the body that contain iodine, and their manufacture is critically dependent on the supply of iodine. In parts of the world where foods contain little iodine, many people suffer from hypothyroidism. In such cases the thyroid gland enlarges, driven by higher and higher TSH levels. In the attempt to produce more thyroid hormones, the gland swells, producing a **goiter**. The addition of a small amount of iodine to salt—producing "iodized salt"—is now a widespread practice designed to prevent this condition.

The major role of the thyroid is to regulate metabolic processes, especially carbohydrate use. The thyroid hormones also influence growth; this function is especially evident when thyroid deficiency starts early in life. Besides stunted body growth and characteristic facial malformation, thyroid deficiency produces a marked reduction in brain size and cellular structure (branching of axons and dendrites is reduced). This state, called **cretinism**, is accompanied by mental retardation.

The Gonads Produce Steroid Hormones

Almost all aspects of reproductive behavior, including mating and parental behavior, depend on hormones. Since Chapter 12 is devoted to reproductive behavior and physiology, at this point we will only briefly note relevant hormones and some pertinent aspects of anatomy and physiology. Female and male **gonads** (ovaries and testes, respectively; see Figure

5.1) consist of two different subcompartments—one to produce hormones and another to produce gametes (eggs or sperm). Hormone production is critical for triggering both reproductive behavior in the brain and gamete production in the gonads.

The testes.   Within the **testes** are several cell types. Interspersed among the sperm-producing cells (the Sertoli cells) are the Leydig cells, which produce and secrete the hormone **testosterone**. Testosterone and other male hormones are called **androgens** (from the Greek roots *andr-*, "man," and *gen-*, "to produce, create"). The production and release of testosterone are regulated by luteinizing hormone from the anterior pituitary. LH in turn is controlled by a hypothalamic releasing hormone, **gonadotropin-releasing hormone (GnRH)**.

Testosterone controls a wide range of bodily changes that become visible at puberty, including changes in voice, hair growth, and genital size. Levels of testosterone vary during the day in adult males, although the connection between these daily rhythms and behavior remains a mystery. In species that breed only in certain

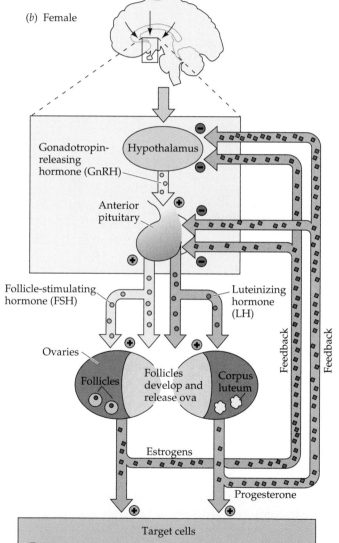

5.17 Regulation of Gonadal Steroid Hormones
(*a*) In males the principal gonadal steroid secreted is testosterone. (*b*) The female gonad produces two classes of steroids: estrogens and progestins.

seasons of the year, testosterone has especially marked effects on appearance and behavior—for example, the antlers and fighting between males that are displayed by many species of deer. Figure 5.17*a* summarizes the regulation of testosterone secretion.

The ovaries. The paired female gonads, the **ovaries**, also produce both the mature gametes (ova [singular ovum], or eggs) and hormones. However, hormonal secretion by the ovary is more complicated than by the testes. Ovarian hormones are produced in cycles, the duration of which varies with the species. Human ovarian cycles last about 4 weeks; rat cycles last only 4 days.

The ovary produces two major classes of steroid hormones: **estrogens** (from the Greek *oistros*, "gadfly or frenzy," and *gen-*, "to produce, create") and **progestins** (from the Latin *pro*, "favoring," and *gestare*, "to bear"). The most important estrogen is **estradiol**; the most influential progestin is **progesterone**. Ovarian production of these hormones is controlled by two tropic hormones of the anterior pituitary, FSH and LH. The release of these tropic hormones is controlled by GnRH from the hypothalamus (Figure 5.17*b*).

Relations among gonadal hormones. All three classes of sex hormones—androgens, estrogens, and progestins—have closely related chemical structures. They and the adrenal steroids are all derived from cholesterol, and all have the basic structure of four interconnected carbon rings (see Figure 5.7*b*). Furthermore, estrogens are synthesized from androgens, and androgens are synthesized from progestins. Different organs differ in the relative amounts of these hormones they produce. For example, whereas the testis converts only a relatively small proportion of testosterone into estradiol, the ovary converts most of the testosterone it makes into estradiol. No steroid is found exclusively in either males or females; rather the two sexes differ in the proportion of these steroids. Some of the testosterone that enters brain cells is converted within those cells to estradiol, as we'll see in Chapter 12.

The Pineal Gland Secretes Melatonin

The **pineal gland** sits atop the brain stem and in mammals is overlaid by the cerebral hemispheres (Figure 5.18*a*). Whereas other brain structures are paired (left and right), the pineal gland is a single structure. This unique aspect of the pineal may explain why the seventeenth-century philosopher René Descartes proposed that it could contain the soul.

Today we know that the pineal is innervated by the sympathetic nervous system, specifically by the superior cervical ganglion (see Figure 5.18*a*). In response to the activity of cells in this ganglion, the pineal releases an amine hormone called **melatonin**. The melatonin receptor seems to reside in cell membranes and is similar to receptors for peptide hormones. In many vertebrate species, the pineal secretion of melatonin controls whether animals are in breeding condition. Melatonin is released almost exclusively at night (Figure 5.18*b*).

5.18 Regulation of the Pineal Gland (*Inset*) The pea-shaped pineal gland sits close to the floor of the third ventricle, atop the brain stem. (*a*) Innervated by the sympathetic nervous system, specifically the superior cervical ganglion, the pineal releases melatonin. (*b*) Melatonin is released almost exclusively during the night in a wide variety of vertebrates, including humans. (After Reppert et al., 1979; photograph courtesy of S. Mark Williams and Dale Purves, Duke University Medical Center.)

In seasonally breeding mammals such as hamsters, the lengthening nights of autumn affect activity in the superior cervical ganglion, which in turn causes the pineal to prolong its nocturnal release of melatonin. The hypothalamus responds to the prolonged exposure to melatonin by becoming extremely sensitive to the negative feedback effects of gonadal steroids. Consequently, less and less GnRH is released, resulting in less gonadotropin release, as well as atrophy of the gonads. Lesion of the pineal prevents such regression, whereas prolonged treatment of normal animals with melatonin induces gonadal regression. In fact, one of the earliest hints of pineal function was the report that a boy with a tumor that was destroying the pineal reached puberty early in life.

In birds, light from the environment penetrates the thin skull and reaches the pineal gland directly. Photosensitive cells in the pineal gland monitor daily light durations. In several reptile species the pineal is close to the skull and even has an extension of photoreceptors providing a "third eye" in the back of the head. These photoreceptors do not form images but act as simple photocells, monitoring day length to regulate seasonal functions. In both birds and mammals the return of gonadal function is independent of melatonin secretion; after a fixed period of time the hypothalamus becomes less sensitive to the negative feedback effects and the gonads grow and become functional again no matter what the day length or amount of melatonin secretion.

Humans are not, strictly speaking, seasonal breeders, but melatonin has been implicated in our daily cycles, such as sleep rhythms. Like other vertebrates, we release melatonin at night, and administering melatonin has been reported to induce sleep sooner at night. In fact, many recent studies indicate a role for melatonin in the timing of sleep. For example, melatonin has been used for treatment of jet lag. Petrie et al. (1993) studied the use of melatonin in an international airplane cabin crew. Some of the crew were given melatonin 3 days before international travel and continued to receive it for 5 days after their return home. Other crew members received melatonin for 5 days after the flight. Both groups were compared to a placebo control. Jet lag, with its associated changes in alertness, was reported to be diminished for the group receiving melatonin only after the shift in time zone. Other studies have shown that melatonin administered to humans shifts circadian rhythms (Lewy et al., 1992; Sack et al., 1992).

The Pancreas Secretes Two Main Hormones

Throughout the **pancreas** (which is located in the back of the abdominal cavity; see Figure 5.1) are clusters of cells called **islets of Langerhans**, which secrete hormones directly into the bloodstream. These endocrine cells are intermingled with other cells that perform an exocrine function, secreting digestive enzymes (such as bile) into ducts leading to the gastrointestinal tract.

Hormones secreted by the islets of Langerhans include **insulin** and **glucagon**, both of which have potent and frequently reciprocal effects on glucose utilization. Insulin is produced in one type of cell within the islets (beta cells), and glucagon is secreted by another type (alpha cells).

Both nonneural and neural factors regulate the release of insulin. The level of glucose in the bloodstream, monitored by cells of the islets of Langerhans, is a critical determinant. As the level of blood sugar rises above a certain concentration, insulin is released. Among the effects of insulin are increased glucose uptake in some tissues, such as muscle, and reduced output of glucose from the liver. These effects lower blood glucose levels. As noted earlier, this reaction is a direct, negative feedback effect that does not involve a tropic hormone from the pituitary.

The effects of insulin directly antagonize those of glucagon, which increases blood glucose levels. Figure 5.19 summarizes the hormonal regulation of insulin and glucagon. In addition, there is paracrine action between adjacent alpha and beta cells of the islets of Langerhans; that is, glucagon and insulin can oppose each other locally within the pancreas, as well as by the endocrine route. The reciprocal action of insulin and glucagon helps keep blood glucose levels within the range necessary for proper functioning of the brain and other organs (see Chapter 13).

The release of insulin is also controlled by neural impulses that arrive at the pancreas via the parasympathetic vagus nerve. When a person eats, insulin is released even before glucose reaches the bloodstream. This early release occurs in response to taste stimulation in the mouth. (Other stimuli that are normally associated with eating can also cause the release of insulin.) Cutting the vagus nerve in experimental animals prevents the early release of insulin in response to the taste of food, but it does not interfere with the later response to glucose in the bloodstream, showing that the conditioned response operates via the nervous system.

Hormones Affect Behavior in Many Different Ways

As we mentioned earlier, endocrine influences on structural or functional states frequently involve the interaction of several different hormones. In this section we will consider briefly some hormonal effects on homeostasis and on learning and memory; these effects are mediated by several endocrine systems. Hormonal effects on growth are considered in Box 5.2, and hormonal influences on reproductive behavior are discussed in Chapter 12.

Hormones Help Maintain Homeostasis

Many body mechanisms have evolved to ensure the relative constancy of the internal environment. Hor-

5.19 Regulation of Blood Glucose Levels

Both glucagon and insulin are released by the pancreas, and each affects the availability of glucose in circulation (*a* and *b*). Normally, both hormones are at work in a reciprocal fashion (*c*).

(*a*) **Regulation by glucagon**

(*b*) **Regulation by insulin**

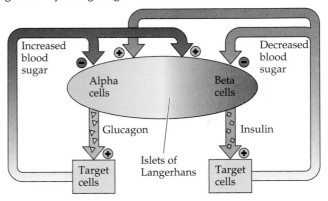

(*c*) **Regulation by both glucagon and insulin**

mones play major roles in regulating many basic homeostatic processes, such as those that govern the distribution of ions and fluids and those that control the concentration of glucose in the blood and the brain.

Consider the regulation of glucose in the blood as an example of the hormonal role in homeostasis. Between meals, the normal concentration of glucose in blood varies between 80 and 130 mg per 100 ml. Some hormones—for example, glucagon, growth hormone, and cortisol—lead to an increase in glucose concentration in the blood. Insulin causes a decrease in glucose concentration in the blood. The balance among these hormones maintains the glucose concentration of blood within a range that provides for maximal production of energy in a variety of circumstances. The level of blood sugar itself also inhibits the secretion of some hormones.

Failure in these controls has major consequences for body organs. In diabetes mellitus, a disorder characterized by insulin deficiency, glucose levels rise. These high blood levels of glucose (hyperglycemia) can produce pathological changes in body tissues leading to symptoms such as diabetic blindness. Such destruction of tissue may arise from the use of metabolic pathways that yield unusual metabolic products.

Homeostatic mechanisms of glucose regulation are particularly prominent during periods of stress or strong exercise. Hormonal changes accompanying these states enhance the release of glucose from the liver. If insufficient glucose is released, however, the central nervous system is unable to produce its full response. Glucose release is part of the alarm reaction, the prompt fight-or-flight response of the body to any stressor. Prolonged stress leads to long-term reactions that involve several other hormones. Hormonal mechanisms in homeostatic systems of water balance, energy balance, and body weight will be taken up in Chapter 13.

Hormones Can Affect Learning and Memory

Hormones affect both the early development of capacities to learn and remember, and the efficient use of these capacities after they have formed. Thyroid hormones, as already indicated, are important in the early development of the nervous system. Insufficient thyroid secretion results in fewer synaptic connections than usual, leading to cretinism.

Experimental studies have given us more information about this condition: If a drug that inhibits thyroid function is administered to infant rats, the results are a decrease in the formation of cortical synapses, as well as significantly impaired learning ability. Giving such experimental cretin rats enriched experience as they grow has been reported to diminish their behavioral deficiencies to a large extent (Davenport, 1976). (The effects of enriched experience on the brain will be discussed further in Chapter 18.)

 Animal model

The ability of juvenile or adult animals to learn and remember can be affected by the hypothalamic hormones ACTH, AVP, and oxytocin, as well as by particular fractions or analogs of these hormones, and by the catecholaminergic hormones of the adrenal medulla: norepinephrine and epinephrine (McGaugh, 1992; Schulteis and Martinez, 1992). Whether these compounds are acting as hormones or as neurotransmitters to affect learning is unknown.

One hypothesis being tested in this research is that the emotional aspects of a learning situation affect the release of hormones, and the hormones present during the period following training modulate the formation of memory; that is, the pleasure or pain or stress involved in an episode of learning will, through hormonal aftereffects, help determine how well the situation is remembered. Such hormonal effects may be important in reinforcing learning during crucial situations.

Endocrine Pathology Can Produce Extreme Effects on Human Behavior

Both deficient and excessive hormone secretion are associated with a variety of human physiological, anatomical, and behavioral disorders (Erhardt and Goldman, 1992). Some of these disorders have long been known, especially those that include either marked behavioral changes or anatomical abnormalities. Table 5.4 lists an array of hormonal disorders and their associated cognitive, emotional, and psychiatric changes.

Many hormonal disorders resemble psychiatric disorders. For example, parathyroid deficiency results in calcium deposition in the basal ganglia and a symptom portrait that resembles a severe psychotic state, schizophrenia. Patients with excessive thyroid release frequently appear intensely anxious; those with decreased thyroid release may show cognitive impairments and depression. Recently, researchers discovered an inherited form of attention deficit disorder in children that involves decreased sensitivity to thyroid hormone (Hauser et al., 1993). Excessive release of glucocorticoids by the adrenal cortex, **Cushing's syndrome**, is accompanied by many bodily and psychological changes, including fatigue, depression, unusual distribution of hair, and other autonomic changes. Several studies have indicated that affective changes, especially depression, frequently long precede other physiological effects of excessive cortisol secretion. In some people who take excessive amounts of glucocorticoids, such as athletes, psychiatric symptoms can emerge that include periods of intense psychotic behavior.

Hormonal and Neural Systems Interact to Produce Integrated Responses

Although we have focused on the endocrine system in this chapter, the endocrine system participates in interactions with many other organs, including, of course, the brain. Figure 5.20 incorporates the endocrine system into a larger schema of reciprocal relations between body and behavior. Let's examine some of these relations.

Incoming sensory stimuli elicit nerve impulses that go to several brain regions, including the cerebral cortex, cerebellum, and hypothalamus. Behavioral responses bring further changes in stimulation. For example, the person may approach or go away from the original source of stimulation, and this action will alter the size of the visual image, the loudness of sound,

TABLE 5.4 *Hormonal Disorders and Associated Cognitive, Emotional, and Psychiatric Disorders*

Hormonal disorder	Impaired cognition	Anxiety	Depression	Psychosis and delirium
Hyperthyroidism	+	++	+	+
Hypothyroidism	+	+	++	++
Hypercortisolism	+	++	++	++
Hypocortisolism	—	+	++	++
Panhypopituitarism[a]	—	+	++	++
Hyperparathyroidism	+	+	++	++
Hypoparathyroidism	?	++	+	++
Hyperinsulinism	+	++	—	++
Hypoinsulinism	+	—	—	+

Note: +, sometimes; ++, often.
[a]Undersecretion of all or nearly all anterior pituitary hormones.

and so forth. Meanwhile the endocrine system is altering the response characteristics of the person. If evaluation of the stimulus calls for action, energy is mobilized through hormonal routes. The state of some sensory receptor organs may also be altered, thus modifying further processing of stimuli.

Many behaviors require neural and hormonal coordination. For example, when a stressful situation is perceived through neural sensory channels, hormonal secretions prepare the individual to make energetic responses. The muscular movements for the fight-or-flight response are controlled neurally, but the required energy is mobilized through hormonal routes. Another example of neural and hormonal coordination is the milk letdown response (see Figure 5.12).

Four kinds of signals from one cell to another are possible in a system that has both nerve cells and endocrine cells: neural-to-neural, neural-to-endocrine, endocrine-to-endocrine, and endocrine-to-neural. All four kinds of signals can be found in the courtship behavior of the ringdove (M. B. Friedman, 1977). The visual stimulation and perception of a male dove that sees a female involve (1) neural-to-neural transmission. The particular visual stimulus activates (2) a neural-to-endocrine link, which causes some neurosecretory cells in the male's hypothalamus to secrete GnRH. (3) Endocrine-to-endocrine signals cause increased production and release of the hormone testosterone in response to the GnRH. Testosterone, in turn, alters the excitability of some neurons through (4) an endocrine-to-neural link and thus causes the male to display courtship behavior. The female dove responds to this display, thus providing new visual stimulation to the male and further neural-to-neural signals within his brain.

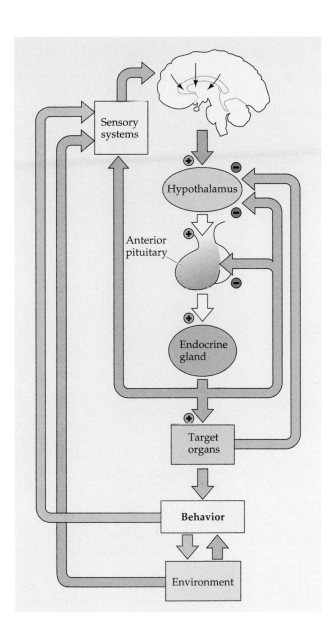

5.20 The Reciprocal Relations between Hormones and Behavior

increases the level of thyroxine in the circulation. Putting animals in a cold environment increases their thyroid activity, and keeping them there increases the size of the thyroid gland. On the other hand, physical stresses, pain, and unpleasant emotional situations decrease thyroid output, probably by modulating the secretion of TRH from the hypothalamus.

Summary

1. Hormones are chemical compounds that act as signals in the body. They are secreted by endocrine glands or specialized cells into the bloodstream and are taken up by receptor molecules in target cells.

2. Neural communication differs from hormonal communication in that neural signals travel rapidly over fixed pathways, whereas hormonal signals spread more slowly and throughout the body.

3. Neural and hormonal communication systems have several characteristics in common: Both utilize chemical messages; the same substance that acts as a hormone in some locations is a synaptic transmitter in others. Both systems manufacture, store, and release chemical messengers. Both use specific receptors and may employ second messengers.

4. Some hormones have receptors in a wide variety of cells and can therefore influence the activity of most cells in the body. Others have receptors in only certain special cells or organs.

5. Hormones act by promoting the proliferation and differentiation of cells and by modulating the activity of cells that have already differentiated.

6. Protein and amine hormones bind to specific receptor molecules at the surface of the target cell membrane and activate second-messenger molecules inside the cell. Steroid hormones pass through the membrane and bind to receptor molecules inside the cell.

7. A negative feedback system monitors and controls the rate of secretion of each hormone. In the simplest case, the hormone acts on target cells, leading them to change the amount of a substance they release; this change in turn regulates the output of the endocrine gland.

8. Several hormones are controlled by a more complex feedback system: A releasing hormone from the hypothalamus regulates the release of an anterior pituitary tropic hormone, which in turn controls secretion by an endocrine gland. In this case, feedback of the endocrine hormone acts mainly at the hypothalamus and anterior pituitary.

9. Endocrine influences on structures and functions often involve more than one hormone, as in growth, homeostasis, metabolism, and learning and memory.

10. Many behaviors require the coordination of neural and hormonal components. Messages may be transmitted in the body via neural-to-neural, neural-to-endocrine, endocrine-to-endocrine, or endocrine-to-neural links.

Our circle schema in Figure 5.20 helps reveal how we discover relations between endocrine activity and behavior. The level of circulating hormones can be altered by chemical intervention, which can affect behavior. For example, since cortisone was introduced as a drug in 1949, occasional cases of Cushing's syndrome have appeared in patients who had been given this glucocorticoid in doses that caused an oversupply of the hormone. In another example, removal of the adrenals and subsequent deprivation of aldosterone in experimental animals causes excretion of salts, which greatly increases the animals' preference for salty water. In fact, rats lacking adrenal glands show an amazing preference for even very dilute salt solutions.

Experiential interventions may also cause rapid changes in the output of many endocrine glands. For example, the output of thyroid hormone responds to many environmental influences. Starting to exercise

Recommended Reading

Becker, J. B., Breedlove, S. M., and Crews, D. (Eds.). (1992). *Behavioral endocrinology.* Cambridge, MA: MIT Press.

Greenspan, F. S., and Strewler, G. J. (1997). *Basic and clinical endocrinology* (5th ed.). Stamford, CT: Appleton & Lange.

Hadley, M. E. (1996). *Endocrinology* (4th ed.). Englewood Cliffs, NJ: Prentice Hall.

Nelson, R. J. (in press). *An introduction to behavioral endocrinology* (2nd ed.). Sunderland, MA: Sinauer.

Norris, D. O. (1997). *Vertebrate endocrinology* (3rd ed.). San Diego, CA: Academic Press.

Wilson, J. D., and Foster, D. W. (1992). *Williams textbook of endocrinology* (8th ed.). Philadelphia: Saunders.

PART 2

Evolution and Development of the Nervous System

*P*art 2 presents two viewpoints and two timescales for the development of brain and behavior. Chapter 6 considers the evolution of the brain and behavior over millions of years. Chapter 7 takes up the growth of the individual over the months and years of the life span. Both viewpoints contribute to our understanding of development, somewhat as an architect and a contractor make different but essential contributions to building a house.

The architect brings to the construction of houses the sort of perspective that evolution brings to the construction of animals. The information in the architect's plan is analogous to the information in the genome. In preparing plans, the architect calls on a long history of hard-won knowledge about structures that meet basic human needs. The contractor's perspective is more like that of the developing individual, using the plans to construct a particular house—translating the abstract information of the blueprints into a practical, working structure. The contractor's judgment and interpretation are necessary, so two houses built by different contractors from the same blueprint will not be identical.

The architect tries to foresee some of the problems of construction and to build safety factors into the plans, so that small deviations or errors will not seriously impair the safety or utility of the building. But the architect also relies on the contractor to fill in details and to improvise when external conditions require it. So too has the evolutionary wisdom distilled in the genome come to rely on the environment and experience to guide the construction of the developing brain.

6 Evolution of Brain and Behavior

*I*n this chapter we consider the intriguing story of how brains and behavior have evolved. Research on this topic focuses on many species of animals, both extant and extinct. Since we share many biological and behavioral features with all other animals, it is not surprising that our search to understand ourselves leads us to study apes, monkeys, carnivores, rodents, birds, and amphibians. The brains of all these vertebrates reveal the same basic plan as ours, although in some ways theirs are simpler and in some ways theirs differ distinctively.

The quest to understand the nervous system has also led to the study of animals that are quite different from us—invertebrates, and even single-celled animals. But de-

Alexis Rockman, *The Bounty*, 1991

scribing, cataloging, and understanding the relationships between the nervous system and behavior in even a small fraction of Earth's inhabitants would be an awesome (and dull) task unless we had a rationale beyond mere completeness. As we'll see, studying and comparing well-chosen species throw much light on the principles of organization of nervous systems.

This chapter reflects two major traditions in biology. One is to discover the *diversity* of animal forms (including the structure of the nervous system) and to understand the relationships among species. The second major tradition is to study *relationships between form and function*, which we now understand in the context of adaptation and natural selection. That is, we compare different species to see how the design of bodies and brains changes as they adapt to environmental demands.

Why Should We Study Other Species?

One old-fashioned reason for comparing species was human centered, based on the question, Why does the human being end up on top of the animal order? This human-centered perspective was properly criticized, because it implicitly pictured other animals as incomplete "little humans," a view that no modern scientists see as valid. It also embraced the old idea that animals vary along a single scale from simple to complex, whereas scientists now see a multibranching set of radiations. Today we see that comparisons of different species provide clues about our evolutionary history—the **phylogeny** of humans.

A phylogeny (from the Greek *phylon*, "tribe, kind," and *genos*, "birth") is the evolutionary history of a particular group of organisms; it is often represented as a "family tree" that shows which species may have given rise to others. (Some scientists prefer to say bush rather than tree, because the phylogeny branches so extensively.) Comparisons among extant animals, coupled with fragmentary but illuminating data from fossil remains, stimulate concepts about the history of the human body and brain, and the forces that shaped them. Figure 6.1 shows a recent attempt to reconstruct the family tree of apes and humans. This diagram shows humans and chimpanzees as being more closely related to each other than either is to the gorilla. Not all investigators agree about the branching pattern, but all agree that all three species are closely related. We will say more about phylogenies a little later in the chapter.

No animal is simply sitting around providing researchers with the details of human biological history; rather, each species is busily engaged in satisfying its needs for survival, which must include an active interchange with the environment. Species with varying biological histories show different solutions to the dilemmas of survival and reproduction. In many cases, adaptations to particular ecological niches can be related to differences in brain structure. Understanding the neural structures and mechanisms that mediate specific behaviors in various other animals can provide a new perspective and intriguing clues about the neural bases of human behavior. For example, some relatively simple animals show changes in behavior that arise from experience. Understanding how the nervous systems of these simpler animals form and store memories is providing insights into the workings of more complex animals, including human beings, as we will see in Chapter 18.

How Closely Related Are Two Species?

The attempt to construct the family trees of animals raises the question, How can we find out how closely related two species are? Some basic knowledge of this topic is important for the examples that we will consider later in this chapter and in other chapters.

Early Views of Classification and Evolution

People have probably always classified the animals they saw around them and realized that some forms resemble each other more closely than others. The contact between Europe and the Americas beginning in 1492 prompted European scholars to question how best to classify the many newly discovered animals. In the mid-eighteenth century the Swedish biologist Carolus Linnaeus (1707–1778) proposed the basic sys-

6.1 Family Tree of Apes and Humans
This tree was derived from measurements of differences between pairs of species in samples of their genetic material—molecules of deoxyribonucleic acid (DNA). To see how different two species are in their genetic endowments, trace the lines from the two members of the pair to the point that connects them, and match the point with the scale at the top. For example, the line from humans and the line from chimpanzees converge at point f, so the DNA of humans and of chimpanzees differs by only about 1.6%. The DNA of humans and of chimpanzees, in turn, differs from that of the gorilla (point e) by about 2.3%. The scale at the bottom gives the estimated number of millions of years since any pair of species shared a common ancestor. Thus, humans and chimpanzees diverged from a common ancestor about 7 million years ago. (After M. Goodman et al., 1990; Horai et al., 1995; Sibley and Ahlquist, 1987; Sibley et al., 1990.)

Table 6.1 *Classification of Some Species of Animals*

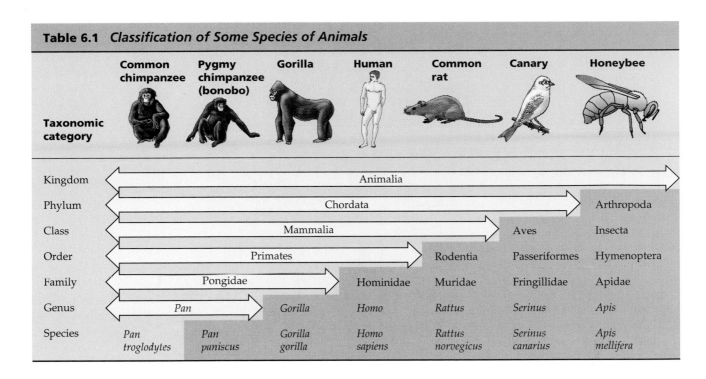

Taxonomic category	Common chimpanzee	Pygmy chimpanzee (bonobo)	Gorilla	Human	Common rat	Canary	Honeybee
Kingdom	Animalia						
Phylum	Chordata						Arthropoda
Class	Mammalia					Aves	Insecta
Order	Primates				Rodentia	Passeriformes	Hymenoptera
Family	Pongidae			Hominidae	Muridae	Fringillidae	Apidae
Genus	Pan		Gorilla	Homo	Rattus	Serinus	Apis
Species	Pan troglodytes	Pan paniscus	Gorilla gorilla	Homo sapiens	Rattus norvegicus	Serinus canarius	Apis mellifera

tem we use today. In Linnaeus's system each species is assigned two names, the first name identifying the genus and the second name indicating the species. Both names are always italicized, and the genus name is capitalized. According to this system, the modern human species is *Homo sapiens;* Table 6.1 shows the classifications of some other species.

The different levels of classification in Table 6.1 are illustrated and defined in Figure 6.2. Each successively broader category above the species level takes in more and more animals, so the members of the higher categories show increasing variety. (Here's an aid to remembering the succession of classifications in Table 6.1: *k*indly *p*ut *c*lothes *o*n, *f*or *g*oodness *s*ake.) Linnaeus classified animals mainly on the basis of gross anatomical similarities and differences; the classification of animals did not at the start imply anything about evolution or common ancestry.

Until about 200 years ago, it was generally believed that each species had been created separately. Then, at about the time of Linnaeus, some naturalists—students of animal life and structure—began to have doubts. For example, some naturalists observed that the limb bones of all mammals, no matter what the animal's way of life, are remarkably similar in many details (Figure 6.3). If these species had been specifically created for different ways of locomotion, the naturalists reasoned, they should have been built on different plans rather than all being modifications of a single plan.

The idea of evolution slowly became more acceptable as naturalists adopted it and as nineteenth-century geologists showed that Earth had been changing for millions of years. The fossils discovered early in the

nineteenth century and the inclusion of fossilized species in the Linnaean system provided additional evidence for evolution. But a plausible mechanism for evolution was lacking. Early in the nineteenth century the French naturalist Jean-Baptiste de Lamarck promoted the idea of evolution and proposed that organisms **Competing hypotheses** evolve through the gradual accumulation of characteristics acquired by individuals throughout life as they exercise and stretch their bodies. But this idea proved to be incompatible with later discoveries about genetic inheritance.

Half a century after Lamarck, in 1858, Charles Darwin and Alfred Russel Wallace announced the hypothesis of **evolution by natural selection.** Darwin and Wallace each had hit upon the idea independently, and Darwin had been accumulating much evidence to support it ever since, as a young naturalist, he had voyaged on the HMS *Beagle* to South America and the Galapagos Islands in 1831 to 1835. In 1859, Darwin published his revolutionary book *On the Origin of Species by Means of Natural Selection.* The hypothesis he stated was based on three main observations and one important inference. The facts were these: (1) Individuals of a given species are not identical, (2) some of this variation is heritable (i.e., can be inherited), and (3) not all offspring

Charles Darwin (1809–1892)

Alfred Russel Wallace (1823–1913)

KINGDOM. All living beings can be divided into five kingdoms: **animals**, plants, fungi, bacteria, and protists. **Animalia**. Approximately 1 million species of animals are known. The total number of existing species has been estimated to be as high as 30 million.	Animals
PHYLUM (plural phyla). The main—and most inclusive—subdivision of a kingdom; a group of similar, related classes. Some phyla are **Chordata**, Mollusca, and Arthropoda. Chordata differ from the other phyla by having an internal skeleton. **Chordata**. Approximately 40,000 species	Chordates
CLASS. The main subdivision of a phylum; a group of similar, related orders. Some classes within the phylum Chordata are **Mammalia**, Aves (birds), and Reptilia. Mammals are characterized by production of milk by the female mammary glands and by hair for body covering. **Mammalia**. Approximately 4300 species	Mammals
ORDER. The main subdivision of a class; a group of similar, related families. Some orders of the class Mammalia are **Carnivora** (meat eaters such as dogs, cats, bears, weasels, etc.) and Primates (humans, monkeys, and apes). **Carnivora**. Approximately 235 species	Carnivores
FAMILY. The main subdivision of an order; a group of similar, related genera. Some families in the order Carnivora are **Canidae** (dogs, foxes, and related genera) and Felidae (domestic cats, lions, panthers, and related genera). Family names always end in -idae. **Canidae**. Approximately 35 species	Canids
GENUS. The main subdivision of a family; a group of similar, related species. Some genera in the family Canidae are *Canis* (dogs, coyotes, two species of wolves, four species of jackals) and *Vulpes* (ten species of foxes). *Canis*. 8 species	Dogs, wolves, coyotes, jackals
SPECIES. The basic (most specific) unit of taxonomic classification, consisting of a population or set of populations of closely related and similar organisms capable of interbreeding. The domestic dog is the species *Canis familiaris*. There are about 400 breeds of dogs, all considered to belong to one species. *Canis familiaris*. 1 species	Domestic dogs

6.2 Linnaean Classification of the Domestic Dog

survive. The inference was that the variations among individuals affect the probabilities that they will survive and reproduce.

Darwin knew about variability from his studies of many species of plants and animals. As a naturalist and a pigeon fancier, he saw close parallels between artificial selection by breeders, which can produce differences in a few generations, and selection in nature, which may be less sharply defined but which can work over many generations.

The concept of evolution by natural selection has become one of the major organizing principles in all the life sciences, directing the study of behavior and its mechanisms, as well as the study of morphology (form

6.3 Homology
Bones of the same sort are shown here in the same color in all species. The sizes and shapes of the bones have evolved so that they are adapted to widely different functions: skilled manipulation in humans, locomotion in dogs, swimming in seals, flying in bats. The similarities among the sets of bones reflect descent from a common ancestor.

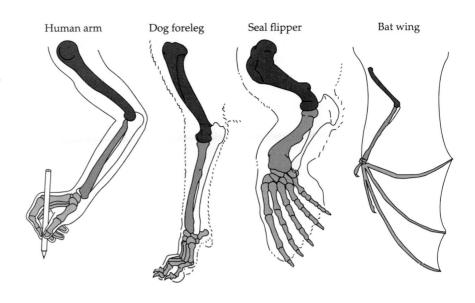

Human arm   Dog foreleg   Seal flipper   Bat wing

and structure). Darwin (1859, p. 113) wrote prophetically that because of his work, "Psychology will be based on a new foundation, that of the necessary acquirement of each mental power and capacity by gradation"— that is, through evolution.

Modern Evolutionary Theory Combines Natural Selection and Genetics

A gap in Darwin's theory was that he could not specify the source of the variation upon which natural selection acts or the mechanism by which biological inheritance works. A major step to round out the theory of evolution was accomplished by the pioneering work of an Austrian monk and botanist, Gregor Johann Mendel (1822–1884). On the basis of his research with pea plants, Mendel published the laws of inheritance in an obscure journal in 1866 (Mendel, 1866/1967). Only in 1900 were these laws brought into prominence and related to evolution when they were rediscovered independently by the Dutch biologist Hugo de Vries (1848–1935) and two other European biologists. Each of these investigators searched the scientific literature for any anticipation of his discovery and was surprised to find Mendel's papers. Each then heralded Mendel's discovery and reported his own work only as confirmation.

De Vries went beyond Mendel in an important respect: Working with primroses, he found that occasionally a new variety would arise spontaneously and then perpetuate its characteristics in successive generations. In 1901, de Vries pointed out that in such cases evolution could occur by sudden jumps, or **mutations**, as he called these changes. (Nowadays, scientists deliberately induce mutations in plants and animals, as we will discuss in Box 7.3.) Thus de Vries discovered that evolution is not only the slow process that Darwin hypothesized; it can also occur rapidly. In 1905 the English biologist William Bateson (1861–1926) proposed the term **genetics** for the study of the mechanisms of inheritance, thus recognizing a new discipline.

Although the study of genetics started with plants such as the pea and the primrose, investigators soon began to study organisms that reproduce more rapidly and that have other advantages for investigation. An example is the fruit fly *Drosophila,* whose generation time is 10 days and whose salivary glands produce giant **chromosomes** visible under a light microscope. (Chromosomes [from the Greek *chroma,* "color," and *soma,* "body"] are rod-shaped structures in the nucleus of each cell that bear genetic information. Since 1882 it had been known that chromosomes replicate themselves during cell division, but the significance of this phenomenon did not become apparent until Mendel's work was rediscovered.) Many of the findings about genetic mechanisms made with *Drosophila* and even with bacteria hold true for larger organisms, such as humans, that reproduce much more slowly.

By the 1940s, scientists realized that nucleic acids are the instruments of genetic inheritance. In 1953 Francis Crick and James D. Watson announced that the structure of the DNA molecule is a double helix. This discovery led in turn to the cracking of the genetic code, a topic taken up in the Appendix. Crick and Watson were awarded the Nobel prize in physiology or medicine in 1962.

Both gradual evolutionary changes and larger evolutionary processes, such as the formation of new species, can now be understood in the light of modern evolutionary theory, which combines Darwin's hypothesis of natural selection with modern genetics and molecular biology. Further insights continue to be added by research in these and related fields, such as developmental biology, paleontology, and systematic biology.

Newer Methods Aid in Classifying Animals and Inferring Evolution

The field of **taxonomy** (from the Greek *taxis,* "arrangement"), or classification, of animals is an ongoing endeavor. Taxonomists continue to be challenged as previously unknown animals are discovered, as new techniques become available, and as new concepts arise. They disagree about how some species are clas-

Competing hypotheses

sified and about the best overall methods of classification. For example, some of the relationships among apes and humans are being debated. You may have noticed that Figure 6.1 and Table 6.1 differ in their placement of human beings. Figure 6.1, which is based on differences between samples of DNA, shows the chimpanzees closer to humans than to gorillas in their genetic endowment; Table 6.1, which is based on body measurements, puts both chimpanzees and gorillas in the family Pongidae (the great apes), whereas humans are traditionally placed in their own family, Hominidae. The difference between these two classifications of primates remains unresolved.

In addition to the patterns in gross anatomy that Linnaeus used, more recent developments help us classify animals and make inferences about their evolution. One such development is the recognition that fossils can be used to trace the families of many living species into the remote past and to clarify some classifications. The fossil record has been invaluable, but it is still very incomplete; important fossils are being discovered every year. The fossil record also reveals many extinct species. For example, it is estimated that since birds first evolved about 150 million years ago, a total of about 150,000 species of birds have existed, but only about 9,000 exist today (Sibley and Ahlquist, 1990).

A more recent aid to classification is the development of molecular techniques that allow us to study genetic material and to measure genetic variation with precision. Analysis of genetic material—fragments of DNA molecules—from many species has confirmed many classifications and improved others. Furthermore, quantification of the amount of difference between base pairs in DNA samples from two species allows investigators to estimate the genealogical distance between them. (The method used in this quantification—nucleic acid hybridization—is described briefly in the Appendix.) Thus, DNA analyses and comparisons help in constructing phylogenetic trees, such as the one in Figure 6.1.

In addition, DNA appears to change at a relatively steady average rate in all lineages of a given order of animals (Hillis et al., 1996). Thus the proportion of differences between DNA samples from two species can be used as a "molecular clock" to estimate how long ago they diverged from a common ancestor. The absolute times on the horizontal axis in Figure 6.1 should be considered with caution, however, because scientists disagree about the calibration of the molecular clocks. This debate does not lessen the value of the *relative* time periods; that is, the overall picture appears to be accurate even if future research expands or con-

tracts the timescale. Recently, small fragments of DNA have been obtained from insects fossilized in amber as long as 40 million years ago, helping us discriminate among possible lines of descent of some modern insects and to test further the "clock" of changes in DNA over time (Poinar, 1994). A fictionalized version of this technique helped make millions of dollars for the writer and producer of the movie *Jurassic Park*.

Another way of studying relationships among species uses the forms and numbers of the chromosomes, which differ among species. Study of the numbers, forms, and staining patterns of chromosomes in 120 species of primates has enabled investigators to produce a family tree of the primates (Richard and Dutrillaux, 1997). (For more on this study, see Topic 6.1, Chromosomes.) The tree based on the analysis of chromosome patterns is very similar to that obtained independently on the basis of samples of DNA, thus strengthening our confidence in the results.

 Special topic

At present, investigators use both morphological and molecular analyses to determine the evolutionary relationships among animals. It is difficult to classify animals that resemble each other strongly in some characteristics but differ strongly in others. Instances in which responses to similar ecological features bring about similarities in behavior or structure among animals that are only distantly related (that differ in genetic heritage) are referred to as **convergent evolution**. For example, the body forms of a tuna and a dolphin resemble each other because they each evolved for efficient swimming, even though the tuna is a fish and the dolphin is a mammal descended from terrestrial ancestors. A resemblance that is due to such convergence rather than to common ancestry is called an **analogy**. By contrast, a **homology** is a resemblance based on common ancestry, such as the similarities in forelimb structures of mammals that we described earlier (see Figure 6.3).

Comparative Methods Help Us Study the Biological Mechanisms of Behavior

Comparisons of behavior and of neural mechanisms across different kinds of animals and across different ecological niches are common in biological psychology and related disciplines. We use such comparisons in every chapter of this book. Some of this research is done under natural, or field conditions, some under controlled laboratory conditions. Although studying only one species may yield important information, comparing two or more carefully chosen species or a large representative sample of species leads to a much deeper understanding of the phenomena being observed, because the evolutionary framework provides additional explanatory power. Let's look at a few examples.

Some Ways of Obtaining Food Require Bigger Brains Than Others

Most species of animals spend much of their time and energy in the pursuit of food, often using elaborate strategies. Researchers have found that the strategies that different species employ to obtain food are correlated to brain size and structure. For example, mammals that eat food distributed in clusters that are difficult to find tend to have brains larger than those of related species whose food is rather uniformly distributed and easy to find. Within several families of mammals, species that eat leaves or grass have brains that are relatively smaller than those of species that feed on fruit or insects that are distributed less densely and less uniformly. This relationship has been found among families of rodents, insectivores (such as shrews and moles), lagomorphs (such as rabbits and pikas; Clutton-Brock and Harvey, 1980), and primates (Mace et al., 1981).

Finding novel ways of obtaining food is related to the size of the forebrain in different orders of birds (L. Lefebvre et al., 1997). Investigators collected accounts of novel behavior from several ornithological journals (e.g., magpies digging up potatoes, house sparrows searching car radiator grilles for insects, crows dropping palm nuts in the path of cars that ran over and opened them). Separate data sets were prepared for North America and the British Isles, and the numbers of innovations differed among bird orders in a similar fashion in both geographic zones. The brain measures were taken from museum specimens. In both the geographic areas, the frequency of innovations is related to the relative size of the forebrain. The results suggest a directional selection for increased size of the forebrain to cope with environmental challenges and opportunities in new, flexible ways. (Another example, relating brain size in bat species to techniques of locating food, is described in Topic 6.2, Bat Brain Evolution.)

Special topic

Some behavioral adaptations have been related to differences in relative sizes of certain structures within the brain. For example, some species of bat find their way and locate prey by hearing; others rely almost entirely on vision. In the midbrain, the auditory center (the inferior colliculus) is much larger in bats that depend on hearing; bats that depend on sight have a larger visual center (the superior colliculus). Families of birds that store bits of food for later use (e.g., the acorn woodpecker, Clark's nutcracker, or the black-capped chickadee) have a larger hippocampus relative to the forebrain and to body weight than do families of birds that do not store food (Sherry, 1992). This difference has been found among both North American species (Figure 6.4) and European species.

We will see in Chapters 17 and 18 that the hippocampus is important for memory formation, and in some species especially for spatial memory, which is

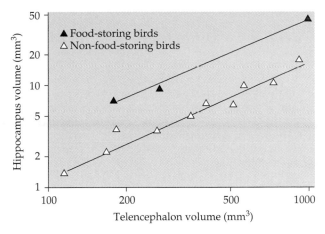

6.4 Food-Storing in Birds as Related to Hippocampal Size

Food-storing species of birds have twice as large a hippocampus in relation to their forebrain (the telencephalon) as do species that do not store food. Note that both axes are logarithmic. (After Sherry et al., 1989.)

needed to recover stored food. The families of birds that store food are no more closely related to each other than they are to other, non-food-storing families and subfamilies of birds. Thus, food storers are not all descendants of an ancestral species that stored food and that also happened to possess a large hippocampus. Rather, the evidence suggests that a large hippocampus is necessary for successful storage and recovery of food, and that several families of birds show convergent evolution for these attributes (Sherry, 1992).

Investigators have pushed this analysis further by asking the following question: Among closely related species of birds that all store food, but in which some species depend more on stored food than others, is there a relationship between the amount of storing and the relative size of the hippocampus? The answer is yes for species of corvids (including jays and nutcrackers) (Basil et al., 1996) and for species of parids (including chickadees and titmice) (Hampton et al., 1995). So even within closely related species, reliance on storing and recovering food appears to have been a selection pressure that has led to larger hippocampal size.

Box 6.1 provides other examples of solutions that different species employ to solve the dilemmas of adaptation. As a general rule, the relative size of a brain region is a good guide to the importance of the function of that region for the adaptations of the species. In this sense "more is better," but even small brain size is compatible with some complex behavior, as we will see in many instances in this book. Our understanding of how these differences in size and structure of the brain promote behavioral specializations should help us understand the neural basis of human behavior. For example, the size of some regions in the human temporal lobes seems to be related to language function (see Chapter 19).

BOX 6.1 *Differences in Brain Maps Match Differences in Lifestyles*

*I*n mammals, differences in organization of the cerebral cortex are related to differences in behavioral function, as the example in the figure shows. The North American raccoon and its Central and South American relative, the coati, are similar in appearance, and both belong to the family Procyonidae. Whereas the coati uses olfaction (smell) as much as touch, the raccoon uses touch much more than smell.

As the figure shows, the brains of the two animals reflect these differences. The raccoon cortex contains a large area representing the forepaw but only a tiny area representing the nose and snout; in contrast, the coati cortex has as large an area for the snout as for the paw.

Related research shows the differential sizes of cortical representations in animals that use especially vision (with a large visual cortex), or audition (with a large auditory cortex), or touch (with a large somatosensory cortex). Differential expansion of parts of the tactile area has been found depending on whether an animal feels chiefly with its mouth and snout, with its hands, or with its tail. By some estimates, about one-fourth of the human neocortex is involved in vision (see Figure 10.18).

Similarly, in the midbrain the superior colliculus, a visual center, is larger in visual animals, while the inferior colliculus, an auditory center, is larger in animals that rely on hearing.

Cortical representations of forepaw and snout

Relating Birdsong to Brain Structure

In recent years songbirds that are able to learn their songs (rather than inheriting them) have become a model for studies of vocal learning. Of the 23 orders of birds, only three learn their songs: the perching birds (Passeriformes), such as canaries, mockingbirds, and crows; the hummingbirds (Trochiliformes); and the parrots (Psittaciformes). Vocal learning in these species is necessary for reproduction—for example, for attracting mates and defending territory. The other birds that sing or call develop their species-specific vocalizations even if they are raised in isolation and do not hear another bird. The three orders of birds that learn their songs include more species than all the 20 other orders together, suggesting that plasticity of brain and behavior permits extensive specialization for different ecological niches and consequently a greater variety of species.

A phylogenetic tree of the 9000 species of living birds has been constructed on the basis of comparisons of the DNA of many different species (Sibley and Ahlquist, 1990). This family tree shows that the three orders that exhibit vocal learning are not closely related and have not shared a common ancestor for tens of millions of years. In fact, each of the orders with vocal learning is more closely related to some orders that do not learn their song than to the other orders that do learn their songs. These relationships suggest that innate, unlearned development of vocalization is the primitive condition and that song learning is an example of convergent evolution in the three relevant orders—perching birds, hummingbirds, and parrots (Brenowitz, 1991b).

In the 1970s, investigators began to study the brains of canaries to determine which structures govern their singing (Nottebohm et al., 1976). This and subsequent research (which we will take up in some detail in Chapter 19) revealed a special network of interconnected forebrain nuclei that are specialized for learning and controlling song. These nuclei contain receptors for gonadal sex hormones, and the hormones modulate the development and activity of this song control system in the brain. By now, this hormone-sensitive system of forebrain nuclei has been found in at least 47 species of songbirds, including the five (out of six) main families of songbirds that have been studied in this way (Brenowitz, 1991b). Furthermore, a comparative study of song repertoire size in 40 species of songbirds revealed that the species that are capable of learning larger numbers of songs have larger forebrain song control centers than do species that cannot acquire as many songs (DeVoogd et al., 1994). Only a few orders of birds with innate development of vocalization have been inspected for the presence of this forebrain system, and none have shown it. Research indicates that the forebrain song system of parrots is essentially similar to that of the perching birds (Durand et al. 1997, 1998).

 Neural plasticity

Thus, by investigating the brain structures of a relatively small number of species that have been carefully chosen for their phylogenetic relationships and their song ability, researchers are making important progress toward understanding the evolution of birdsong. If investigators had studied an equal number of species chosen at random among the 9000 current species of birds, the results would have been much less informative and less able to yield general conclusions.

Box 6.2 gives further answers to the question, Why should we study particular species? Recent examinations of comparative and evolutionary investigations in psychology are provided by Shettleworth (1993a,b), Timberlake (1993), and Kamil (1994).

Nervous Systems Differ Widely in Structure

Having compared aspects of the nervous systems of a few species, let's look more broadly at the variety of nervous systems of a few phyla of animals. Figure 6.5 shows the gross anatomy of the nervous system of some representative animals.

Invertebrates Show Enormous Diversity

Most of the animals on Earth are invertebrates, animals without backbones. (In fact, the order Coleoptera [the beetles] contains far more animal species than any other, so it's been said that, to a first approximation, every species is a beetle!) The invertebrates far exceed vertebrates in many ways, including number, diversity of appearance, and variety of habitat. Whereas invertebrates make up 17 phyla, the vertebrates are only a part of the phylum Chordata (the chordates). The

---

BOX 6.2 *Why Should We Study Particular Species?*

With all the species available, why should we choose certain ones for study? Investigators usually follow several criteria in selecting species for study. The following are several reasons for choosing a particular species:

1. *Outstanding features.* Some species are "champions" at various behaviors and abilities, such as sensory discrimination (e.g., the acute auditory localization of the owl, or the extremely fine visual acuity of the eagle) or control of movement (e.g., the flight behavior of the housefly). These abilities are often linked to highly specialized neuronal structures. Such structures incorporate and optimize particular neuronal designs that may be less conspicuous in organisms that lack these superior capacities (Bullock, 1984, 1986). Study of such species may yield general principles that apply to other species.

2. *Convenience.* Some species, such as the laboratory rat, are particularly convenient for study because they breed well in the laboratory, are relatively inexpensive to maintain, are not rare or endangered, have relatively short life spans, and have been studied extensively already, so there is a good base of knowledge about them at the outset. In addition, they may serve as good models because their morphology and behavior show clear relationships to other species. Other species are convenient because they offer advantages for certain methods of study. For example, some mollusks have relatively simple nervous systems that aid in tracing neural circuits. The fruit fly *Drosophila* is excellent for genetic studies because it has a relatively simple genome and a short time period between generations; furthermore, investigators have been increasingly impressed by the large number of DNA sequences that *Drosophila* shares with mammals, including humans (R. Lewis, 1998).

3. *Uniqueness.* Species that exhibit unusual behavior and/or morphology help illuminate particular issues. For example, the female spotted hyena appears to have a penis and is dominant over the smaller male. This sex "reversal" is caused by unusual hormonal adaptations (see Chapter 12).

4. *Comparison.* Close relationships between species that behave very differently enable the testing of hypotheses. For example, whereas in some closely related species of rodents the home ranges of males and females differ in size, in others they do not. Comparison of these species tests whether differences in maze-solving ability are associated with the size of the home range and with the size of the hippocampus (see Chapter 17).

5. *Preservation.* Studies of rare and/or endangered species can help preserve these animals. Because of their predicament, these species are seldom studied in the laboratory, but they may be investigated in field studies or in zoos.

6. *Economic importance.* Species that are economically important include agricultural animals (e.g., sheep), animals that furnish valuable products (e.g., fish), predators on agricultural animals (e.g., wolves), or destroyers of crops (e.g., elephants). Studying these animals can provide information that helps increase production and/or decrease losses.

7. *Treatment of disease.* Some species are subject to the same diseases as other species and therefore are valuable models for investigation (here we focus on diseases of the nervous system and endocrine [hormonal] system). Examples include certain kinds of mice, which provide a model for the behavior and anatomy of Down syndrome (see Chapter 7); baboons and certain breeds of dogs, which are prone to seizures (see Chapter 3); several breeds of dogs that are afflicted by narcolepsy (see Chapter 14); some strains of rodents that provide models for depression (see Chapter 16); and monkeys, which are susceptible to a drug that can cause Parkinson's disease in humans (see Chapter 11; W. T. McKinney, 1988).

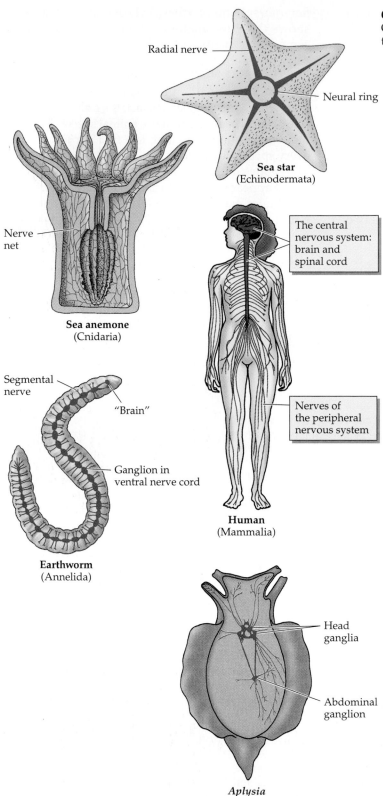

Radial nerve

Neural ring

Sea star
(Echinodermata)

Nerve net

Sea anemone
(Cnidaria)

Segmental nerve

"Brain"

Ganglion in ventral nerve cord

Earthworm
(Annelida)

The central nervous system: brain and spinal cord

Nerves of the peripheral nervous system

Human
(Mammalia)

Head ganglia

Abdominal ganglion

Aplysia
(Mollusca)

6.5 A Comparative View of Nervous Systems

Gross anatomy of the nervous system in representative animals from five phyla.

tems and the great varieties of behavioral adaptation they display. Simplicity of structure has not ruled out some forms of behavior, such as some types of learning and memory, that are also seen in more complex organisms. Furthermore, invertebrates possess elaborate sensory systems that permit detection of some stimuli with exquisite sensitivity. Every conceivable niche on land, sea, or air has been successfully exploited by one or more invertebrate species.

A leading researcher in comparative neurosciences, Theodore H. Bullock (1984, p. 473), asserts, "We cannot expect truly to comprehend either ourselves or how the nervous system works until we gain insight into this range of nervous systems, from nerve nets and simple ganglia in sea anemones and flatworms to the optic lobes of dragon flies, octopuses, and lizards to the cerebral cortex in primates." Faced with the enormous complexity of the vertebrate brain, with its billions of nerve cells, researchers have turned instead to the nervous systems of some invertebrates that have only hundreds or thousands of neurons. An exhaustive description of the "wiring diagram" of the nervous system and how it relates to behavior may be possible with these invertebrates. Complex aspects of behavior, such as memory and species-typical eating or aggressive behaviors, have been explored in an exciting manner in several invertebrates that have become laboratory favorites.

Theodore H. Bullock

With all the diversity of invertebrate nervous systems, we cannot select a few as "representative," but we will describe some features of the nervous systems of mollusks and insects in preparation for our treatment of research on these animals in later chapters.

abundance of invertebrates is clearly demonstrated by the following estimate: For each person on Earth, there are at least 1 billion insects, which are just one type of invertebrate.

Neuroscientists focus on certain invertebrates because of the relative simplicity of their nervous sys-

***The mollusk* Aplysia.** Slugs, snails, clams, and octopuses are a few of the almost 100,000 species of mollusks. These soft-bodied animals display an enormous range of complexity in both body and behavior. Some mollusks, such as the octopus, show excellent problem-solving capabilities; other mollusks exist in a near parasitic form. The head end of a mollusk usually consists of a mouth, tentacles, and eyes. The typical structure also includes a footlike appendage and a visceral section that is frequently covered by a protective envelope called the mantle. A simple marine mollusk, *Aplysia*, has gained considerable notoriety because it has been used extensively in cellular studies of learning and memory (see Chapter 18). Here we review briefly the principal structures of the nervous system of *Aplysia*.

Animal model

The nervous system of *Aplysia* consists of four paired ganglia at the head end that form a ring around the esophagus (Figure 6.6a). Below these head ganglia is a fused abdominal ganglion. The ganglia are interconnected by tracts. One head ganglion innervates the eyes and the tentacles; a second head ganglion inner-

vates the mouth muscles. The other two paired ganglia innervate the foot. The abdominal ganglion controls such major visceral functions as circulation, respiration, and reproduction. Comprehensive research by Eric Kandel and his collaborators has led to detailed maps of **identifiable neurons** in these ganglia, especially the abdominal ganglion. (These cells are called identifiable because they are large and similar from one *Aplysia* to the next, so investigators can recognize them and give them code names.) Because the nervous system of *Aplysia* includes many identifiable cells (Figure 6.6b), it has become possible to trace the circuits that mediate various behaviors in this animal. Work with *Aplysia* has also provided much detailed understanding of the molecular basis of learning (Kandel et al., 1986; Krasne and Glanzman, 1995), supporting the view that simpler invertebrate nervous systems can provide useful models for examining complex features of the human brain.

Insect nervous systems. Insects, of which there are more than 1 million living species, are remarkable in the animal kingdom for color, form, and presence in a great variety of habitats. The life cycle of many insects includes striking morphological changes (e.g., from caterpillar to butterfly) that not only affect the external form of the animal but also involve a resculpturing of the nervous system. The sensory organs of insects display great variety and sensitivity. Success in the battle for survival has affected this group of animals in many distinctive ways, and it is easy to appreciate why neuroscientists have focused much research on the neural mechanisms of the behavior of insects. In spite of the diversity of insect body form, the central nervous systems of insects are remarkably similar: They vary "astonishingly little from the most primitive to the most advanced" (Edwards and Palka, 1991, p. 391).

The gross outline of the adult insect nervous system consists of a brain in the head end and ganglia in each body segment behind the head (Figure 6.7). Bundles of axons connect ganglia to the brain. The number of ganglia varies; in some insects all the ganglia of the chest and abdomen fuse into one major collection of cells. In other insects there are as many as eight ganglia in a chain. The brain itself contains three ma-

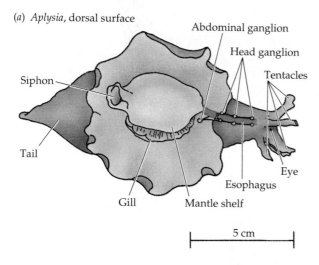

(a) *Aplysia*, dorsal surface

- Abdominal ganglion
- Head ganglion
- Tentacles
- Siphon
- Tail
- Eye
- Esophagus
- Gill
- Mantle shelf

⊢ 5 cm ⊣

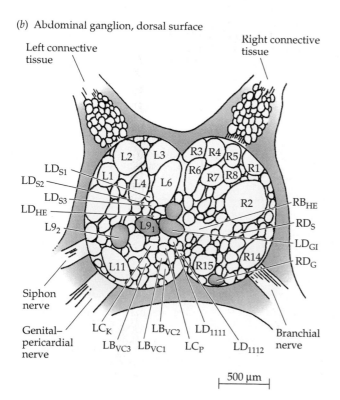

(b) Abdominal ganglion, dorsal surface

Left connective tissue — Right connective tissue

L2, L3, R3, R4, R5, R6, R7, R8, R1
LD$_{S1}$, L1, L4, L6, R2, RB$_{HE}$
LD$_{S2}$, RD$_{S}$
LD$_{S3}$, L9$_1$, LD$_{GI}$
LD$_{HE}$, L9$_2$, R14, RD$_{G}$
L11, R15
Siphon nerve
Genital–pericardial nerve — LC$_K$, LB$_{VC3}$, LB$_{VC2}$, LB$_{VC1}$, LD$_{1111}$, LC$_P$, LD$_{1112}$ — Branchial nerve

⊢ 500 µm ⊣

6.6 The Nervous System of *Aplysia*

The sea snail *Aplysia* has a relatively simple nervous system with large identifiable neurons, which has made it a popular species in research on the neural basis of learning and memory. (a) Dorsal view of the entire organism. The neural ganglia and connecting nerve cords are shown in yellow. (b) Dorsal view of an abdominal ganglion, with several identified neurons labeled. Neurons that are in the circuit involved in habituation, a learned decreased response to a repeated stimulus, are shown in pink. (Part *a* after Kandel, 1976; *b* from Frazier et al., 1967.)

jor compartments: the protocerebrum, deutocerebrum, and tritocerebrum. The most complex part of the insect brain is the protocerebrum, which consists of a right and a left lobe, each continuous with a large optic lobe, an extension of the compound eye. Within the optic lobe are distinct masses of cells that receive input from the eye as well as from the brain. Electrical stimulation of sites within the protocerebrum of various insects elicits complex behaviors.

The relative sizes of different components of the protocerebrum differ among insects, and some of these variations may be particularly relevant to behavioral variations. For example, a portion of the protocerebrum called the corpus pedunculatum is especially well developed in social insects, and the behavior of these animals tends to be more elaborate than that displayed by solitary insects.

One prominent feature of the nerve cord of insects is **giant axons**—fibers much bigger in diameter than most. The properties of these giant fibers have been explored in some interesting studies, using many different orders of insects (Edwards and Palka, 1991). These insects have receptive organs (the cerci) in the tail that can be excited by movement of the air; these receptors connect to giant interneurons with very large axons that ascend the nerve cord to the head. Along the way, these axons excite some motor neurons. This system originated to allow insects to escape from predation by retreating rapidly. In many insects (e.g., cockroaches) this system still functions as an escape system; in other insects the cerci and the connections of the giant interneurons have been modified so that they also play a role in reproductive behavior (in crickets) or help regulate flight maneuvers (in grasshoppers). Whatever its function in a particular species, the basic organization and cellular composition of this system appears to have remained the same for a very long time, perhaps as long as 400 million years (Edwards and Palka, 1991).

All Vertebrate Nervous Systems Share Certain Main Features

After a brief look at the basic features of vertebrate nervous systems, we will compare some of their main features with those of molluscan and insect nervous systems. The following are main features of the vertebrate nervous system, some of which are illustrated in Figure 6.5:

1. *Development from a hollow dorsal neural tube* (see Chapters 2 and 7).
2. *Bilateral symmetry.* (The human cerebral hemispheres are not quite identical anatomically or functionally, as we'll see in Chapters 18 and 19; see Box 19.3 for a discussion of this and other exceptions.)
3. *Segmentation.* Pairs of spinal nerves extend from each level of the spinal cord.
4. *Hierarchical control.* The cerebral hemispheres control or modulate the activity of the spinal cord.
5. *Separate systems.* The central nervous system (brain and spinal cord) is clearly separate from the peripheral nervous system.
6. *Localization of function.* Certain functions are controlled by certain locations in the central nervous system.

Presumably vertebrates have all of these features in common because they descended from a common ancestor that possessed the same neural features.

Anatomical examination of the brains of many classes of the 10,000 to 20,000 vertebrate species have revealed that vertebrates with larger bodies tend to possess larger brains. No matter what the size, however, all vertebrate brains have the same major subdivisions. The main differences among vertebrates are the absolute and relative sizes of different regions.

A comparison of human and rat brains illustrates basic similarities and differences (Figure 6.8). Each of the main structures in the human brain has a counter-

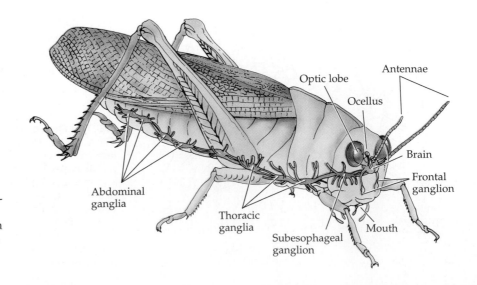

6.7 The Nervous System of a Typical Insect
In insects, the brain with its subdivisions is linked via bundles of axons (connectives) to groups of ganglia in the thorax and abdomen. The brain, connectives, and ganglia are shown here in purple.

Optic lobe
Antennae
Ocellus
Brain
Frontal ganglion
Mouth
Subesophageal ganglion
Thoracic ganglia
Abdominal ganglia

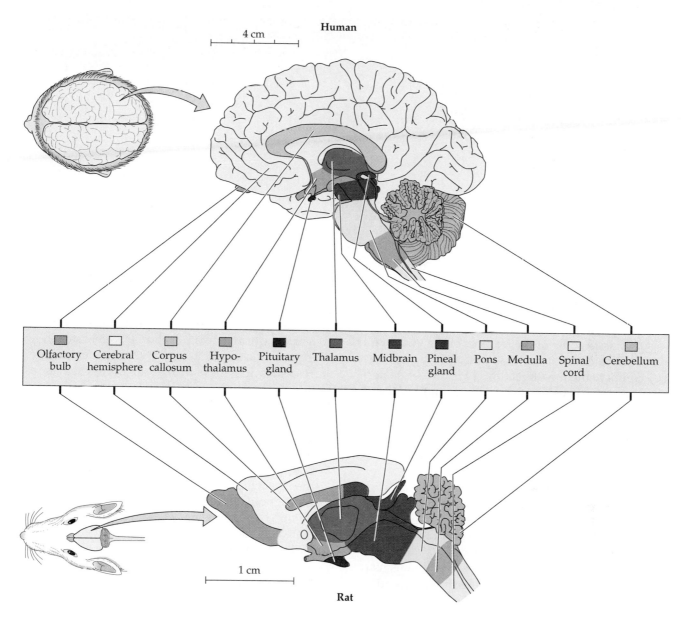

6.8 Human and Rat Brains Compared
Midsagittal views of the right hemisphere of human and rat brains; the rat brain has been enlarged about six times in linear dimensions in relation to the human brain. In both brains, the main structures are the same, and they have the same topological relations to each other. Note, however, that the cerebral hemispheres are relatively much larger in the human brain, whereas the rat has a relatively larger midbrain and olfactory bulb.

part in the rat brain. This comparison could be extended to much greater detail, down to nuclei, fiber tracts, and types of cells. Even small structures in the brains of one mammalian species are found to have exact correspondence in the brains of others. All mammals also have similar types of neurons and similar organization of the cerebellar cortex and the cerebral cortex.

The differences between the brains of humans and the brains of other mammals are mainly quantitative; that is, they concern both actual and relative sizes of the whole brain, brain regions, and brain cells. Whereas the brain of an adult human being weighs about 1400 g, that of an adult rat weighs a little less than 2 g. In each case the brain represents about 2% of total body weight. The cerebral hemispheres occupy a much greater proportion of the brain in the human than in the rat, and the surface of the human brain shows prominent gyri and fissures, whereas the rat cerebral cortex is smooth and unfissured. The rat has, relatively, much larger olfactory bulbs than the human. This difference is probably related to the rat's much greater use of the sense of smell. The size of neurons also differs significantly between human and rat; in general, human neurons are much larger than rat neurons. In addition, there are great differences in the extent of dendritic trees. Figure 6.9 gives some examples of size differences among neurons of different species.

Mouse   Rat   Dog   Cow   Horse   Human

6.9 The Same Kind of Neuron in Different Species
These pyramidal neurons from the motor cortices of different mammals are all drawn to the same scale. (After Barasa, 1960.)

200 μm

Vertebrate Nervous Systems Differ from Those of Invertebrates

To summarize some of the features of the vertebrate nervous system that we have described up to now, let's compare them with features of invertebrate nervous systems, focusing specifically on mollusks and insects:

1. *Basic plan.* All vertebrates and most invertebrates have a basic plan that consists of a central nervous system and a peripheral nervous system.
2. *Brain.* All vertebrates and many invertebrates, including mollusks and insects, have brains. The general evolutionary trend in both vertebrates and invertebrates is toward increasing brain control over ganglia at lower levels of the body.
3. *Number of neurons.* Whereas vertebrate brains usually have many neurons devoted to information processing, invertebrate brains usually have fewer but larger and more complicated neurons that manage key integrative processes.
4. *Identifiable neurons.* Some of the large invertebrate neurons are identifiable. In contrast, there are very few cases of identifiable neurons in vertebrates.
5. *Ganglion structure.* Vertebrate ganglia have the cell bodies on the inside and the dendrites and axons on the outside. Ganglia in invertebrate nervous systems have a characteristic structure: an outer rind that consists of monopolar cell bodies and an inner core that consists of the extensions of the cell bodies forming a dense neuropil (a network of axons and dendrites).
6. *Axons and neural conduction.* Many axons of mammalian neurons are surrounded by myelin, which helps them conduct impulses faster than the unmyelinated invertebrate axons (see Chapter 2). Many invertebrates have a few giant axons to convey messages rapidly in escape systems; vertebrates, with their generally rapid neural conduction, do not have such giant axons.

7. *Structural changes.* The structure of the nervous system undergoes large-scale changes in some invertebrates during metamorphosis. Vertebrates show important changes in neural structure during development, but these changes are not as dramatic as the changes during invertebrate metamorphoses.
8. *Location in the body.* In vertebrates, the central nervous system is encased in the bony skull and spinal column. In many invertebrates the nervous system is built around the digestive tract.
9. *Constancy.* The basic structure and connections of the insect nervous system have remained similar throughout hundreds of millions of years, even though body forms have varied greatly. The vertebrate nervous system has also maintained the same basic structure for hundreds of millions of years of evolution. Although differences in body form are less extreme among the vertebrates than among the insects, nevertheless many evolutionary changes have taken place in vertebrate brains.

The Evolution of Vertebrate Brains Can Be Related to Changes in Behavior

During the course of evolution, the characteristics of the nervous system have changed progressively. One especially prominent change during the last 100 million years has been a general tendency for the brain size of vertebrates to increase, and the brains of our human ancestors have shown a particularly striking increase in size during the last 2 million years. How, then, has the evolution of the brain been related to changes in behavioral capacity?

Present-Day Animals and Fossils Reveal Evolution of the Brain

We could learn more about the evolution of the brain by studying the brains of fossil animals. But brains themselves do not fossilize—at least, not literally. Two methods of analysis have proved helpful. One is to use the cranial cavity of a fossil skull to make a cast of the brain that once occupied that space. These casts (called **endocasts**) give a reasonable indication of the size and shape of the brain.

The other method is to study present-day animals, choosing species that show various degrees of similarity to (or difference from) ancestral forms. Although no modern animal is an ancestor of any other living form, some present species resemble ancestral forms more closely than others do. For example, present-day salamanders are much more similar to vertebrates of 300 million years ago than are any mammals. Among the mammals, some species, such as the opossum, resemble fossil mammals of 50 million years ago more than do other species, such as the dog. Thus, a species such as the opossum is said to retain primitive or ancestral states of particular anatomical features. Anatomists who study the brains of living species can obtain far more detailed information from such species than from endocasts, because they can investigate the internal structure of the brain: its nuclei, fiber tracts, and the circuitry formed by connections of its neurons.

We must be careful not to interpret the evolutionary record as if it were a linear sequence. The main classes of vertebrates in Figure 6.10, for example, represent different lines or radiations of evolution that

have been proceeding separately for at least 200 million years. Thus a particular evolutionary development may not have been available to mammals even if it occurred before the first mammals appeared. For example, among the sharks, some complex forms long ago evolved much larger brains than primitive sharks had, but the evolution of large brains in sharks cannot account for the large brains of mammals. The line of descent that eventually led to mammals had separated from that of the sharks before the large-brained sharks evolved. Let's consider some examples of changes in the size and organization of vertebrate brains.

Through Evolution, Vertebrate Brains Have Changed in Both Size and Organization

Recent research shows that even the living vertebrate that has the most primitive features—the lamprey (a kind of jawless fish)—has a more complex brain than it used to be given credit for. The lamprey has not only the basic neural chassis of spinal cord, hindbrain, and midbrain, but also a diencephalon and a telencephalon. Its telencephalon has cerebral hemispheres and other subdivisions that are also found in the mammalian brain. So all vertebrate brains appear to have these regions. One difference in basic brain struc-

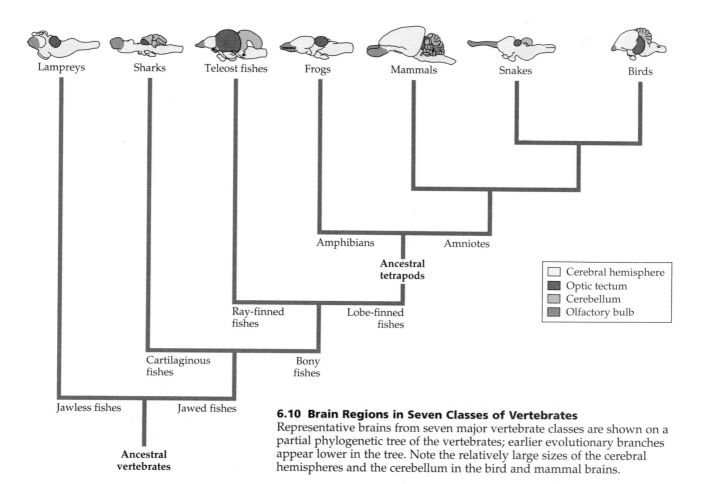

6.10 Brain Regions in Seven Classes of Vertebrates
Representative brains from seven major vertebrate classes are shown on a partial phylogenetic tree of the vertebrates; earlier evolutionary branches appear lower in the tree. Note the relatively large sizes of the cerebral hemispheres and the cerebellum in the bird and mammal brains.

ture between the lamprey and other vertebrates is that the cerebellum in the lamprey is very small and may consist of only some brain stem nuclei. The evolution of large cerebellar hemispheres in birds and mammals appears to be a case of parallel evolution from the small cerebellum in their common reptilian ancestor; the increased size of the cerebellum may be related to increased complexity of sensory processing and increased motor agility.

The differences among the brains of vertebrate species, then, lie not in the existence of basic subdivisions, but in their relative size and elaboration. At what stages of vertebrate evolution do various regions of the brain first become important? Large paired optic lobes in its midbrain probably represent the lamprey's highest level of visual integration. In bony fishes, amphibians, and reptiles, the relatively large optic tectum in the midbrain is the main brain center for vision (see Figure 6.10). In birds and mammals, however, complex visual perception requires an enlarged telencephalon.

Reptiles were the first vertebrates to exhibit relatively large cerebral hemispheres. Reptiles were also the first vertebrates to have a cerebral cortex, but their cortex has only three layers, unlike the six-layered neocortex of mammals. Part of the cortex in reptiles appears to be homologous to the hippocampus in mammals. The hippocampus in mammals has three layers and is called **archicortex** (from the Greek *archi-*, "ancient") because it is extremely old in an evolutionary sense.

Some mammals that have primitive traits, such as the opossum, have a relatively large **paleocortex** (from the Greek *palai-*, "old," but not as old as *archi-* implies); this and related structures are grouped under the name **limbic system.** (This system was introduced in Chapter 2. We will take up the limbic system in Chapter 15 in connection with emotion and motivation, and in Chapters 17 and 18 in connection with learning and memory.) In humans, the olfactory bulb is part of the paleocortex.

All mammals have a six-layered **neocortex** (from the Greek *neos*, "new"). In more recent mammals the neocortex accounts for more than half the volume of the brain. In many larger mammals the neocortex is deeply fissured, so a large cortical surface covers the brain. In more recent mammals, the cortex is the structure mainly responsible for many complex functions, such as the perception of objects. Regions of the brain that were responsible for perceptual functions in less encephalized animals—such as the midbrain optic lobes (in the lamprey) or the midbrain optic center (in the frog)—have in present-day mammals become visual reflex centers or way stations in the projection pathway to the cortex. (We will refer to the neocortex in almost every chapter, from Chapter 8 on, in connection with not only perception but also complex cognitive functions.)

Evolution of brain size.   The brain is sometimes said to have increased in size with the appearance of each succeeding vertebrate class shown in Figure 6.10, but that statement is wrong in several respects. For one thing, there are exceptions among the present-day representatives of the various classes; for example, birds appeared later than mammals but do not have larger brains. For another, the generalization arose from the old way of viewing vertebrate evolution: as one linear series of increasing complexity rather than as a series of successive radiations.

If we compare animals of similar body size, there is considerable variation in brain size within each line of evolution. For example, within the ancient class of jawless fishes, the hagfishes, which are more recent members of that class, possess forebrains that are four times as large as those of lampreys of comparable body size. The increase of brain size in relation to behavioral capacity has been studied most thoroughly in the mammals.

The encephalization factor.   The study of brain size is complicated by the wide range of body sizes. What relation holds between the size of the body and that of the brain? A general relationship was found first for present-day species and then applied successfully to fossil species. This function turns out to be useful in finding relationships between brain and behavioral capacities.

We humans long believed our own brains to be the largest of all brains, but this belief was upset in the seventeenth century when the elephant brain was found to weigh three times as much as our own. Later, whale brains were found to be even larger. These findings puzzled scholars who took it for granted that human beings are the most intelligent of animals and therefore must have the largest brains. To address this apparent discrepancy, they proposed that brain **Competing hypotheses** weight should be expressed as a fraction of body weight. On this basis humans outrank elephants, whales, and all other animals of large or moderate body size. But a mouse has about the same ratio of brain weight to body weight as a human, and the tiny shrew outranks a human on this measure. Without trying to prove that one species or another is "brainiest," we would like to know how much brain is needed to control and serve a body of a given size. From a comparative point of view, what is the general relation between brain size and body size?

When we plot brain weights and body weights for a large sample of mammals, we see some generalities (Figure 6.11a). All the plot points fall within a narrow polygon. Since both scales are logarithmic, the graph encompasses a great variety of animal sizes, and departures from the general rule tend to be minimized. The line drawn through the center of the polygon has a slope of about 0.69 (Harvey and Krebs, 1990).

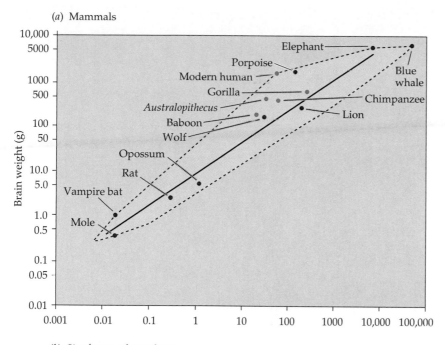

(a) Mammals

6.11 Relation between Brain Weight and Body Weight

(a) Brain weight related to body weight in several mammal species. Note that both axes are logarithmic, so the graph includes a wide range of brain weights and body weights. A polygon has been drawn to connect the extreme cases and include the whole sample. The diagonal line shows the basic relationship, with brain weight related to the 0.7 power of body weight. (b) Brain weight plotted against body weight for various species in six classes of vertebrates. Each class is represented by a polygon that includes a large sample of species in that class. The other classes of animals fall below the mammals, reflecting the fact that relative brain weight to body weight is smaller in those classes; they are less "brainy" than the mammals. (Part *a* after H. Stephan et al., 1981; *b* after Jerison, 1991.)

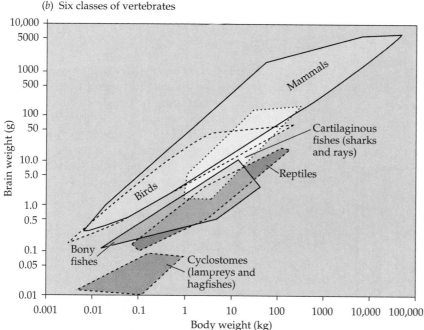

(b) Six classes of vertebrates

jay) has a brain that weighs about 1 g, but a fish or a reptile of the same body weight has a brain that weighs only a little more than 0.1 g; a 100 g lamprey has a brain that weighs only about 0.03 g.

To take into account the variation both between classes and within classes, we need a measure of vertical distance above or below the diagonal line on the graph. This distance is usually called *k* and is different for each class and for each species. Because *k* indicates the relative amount of brain, it is called the **encephalization factor.** The greater the encephalization factor for a species, the higher its value is above the diagonal line for its class. In Figure 6.11a the point for humans is farther above the diagonal than the point for any other species. In terms of the encephalization factor, human beings rate higher than any other species. Figure 6.12 gives the values of the encephalization factor for several mammalian species.

Brain size has been studied in many species of mammal, both living and fossil. These studies have yielded clues about some selection pressures that have led to larger brains. For example, you may have heard the statement that dinosaurs became extinct because of the inadequacy of their small ("walnut-sized") brains (see Figure 6.13). Is this true? Examination of endocasts of dinosaur brains and use of the equation that relates brain weight (which can be estimated from

Let's test the generality of this rule by examining the relation between brain weight and body weight for six vertebrate classes (Figure 6.11b). In each class except the mammals, the data yield a diagonal area with a slope of about three-fourths, so the relationship between brain weight and body weight is similar for all classes of vertebrates. But notice that the diagonal areas are displaced from each other vertically in Figure 6.11b: The mammals are highest, the bony fishes and reptiles clearly lower, and cyclostomes (e.g., the lamprey) the lowest. This configuration reflects the fact that these classes have successively less brain weight for a body of the same size. Thus, a mammal or a bird that weighs about 100 g (e.g., a rat or a blue

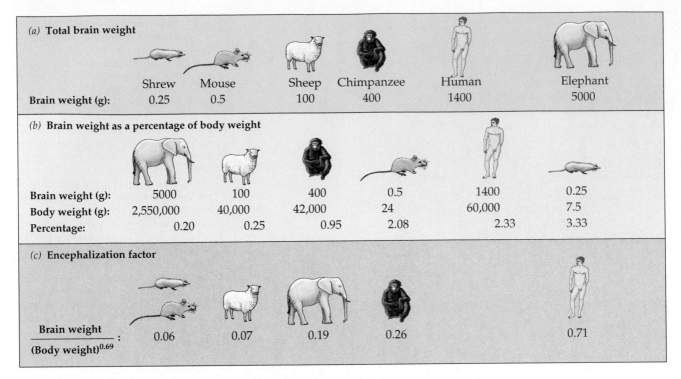

(a) Total brain weight

	Shrew	Mouse	Sheep	Chimpanzee	Human	Elephant
Brain weight (g):	0.25	0.5	100	400	1400	5000

(b) Brain weight as a percentage of body weight

	Elephant	Sheep	Chimpanzee	Mouse	Human	Shrew
Brain weight (g):	5000	100	400	0.5	1400	0.25
Body weight (g):	2,550,000	40,000	42,000	24	60,000	7.5
Percentage:	0.20	0.25	0.95	2.08	2.33	3.33

(c) Encephalization factor

$\dfrac{\text{Brain weight}}{(\text{Body weight})^{0.69}}:$	0.06	0.07	0.19	0.26	0.71

6.12 Who Is the Brainiest?
For this sample of small to large mammals, the answer depends on what measure is used: (a) total brain weight, (b) brain weight as a percentage of body weight, or (c) the encephalization factor. For each measure the animals are ranked from lowest value to highest value.

THE FAR SIDE   By GARY LARSON

"The picture's pretty bleak gentlemen . . . The world's climates are changing, the mammals are taking over, and we all have a brain about the size of a walnut."

6.13 Was the Dinosaur Being Too Modest?

brain volume) to body weight show that dinosaur brain weights fit the relationship for reptiles shown in Figure 6.11*b*. For example, the brain of *Tyrannosaurus rex* probably weighed about 700 g—only half the size of the human brain, but much heavier than a walnut and appropriate for a reptile of its size—so it seems unlikely that dinosaurs perished because of a lack of brains (Jerison, 1991).

Brain size evolved as a whole. As the brain has evolved, it has shown adaptive size changes both in specific regions and overall; this adaptation illustrates both the specificity and the continuity among species that we mentioned in Chapter 1. Certain capabilities, such as food foraging or birdsong, have been linked to sizes of particular brain regions, as we saw earlier in this chapter. In contrast, some other capabilities are related to overall neocortical volume rather than to the volume of any particular region of cortex; this relationship suggests that the amount of cortex devoted to some capabilities could increase only as the result of an increase in total cortical volume, although this seems like an inefficient and expensive way to increase the tissue related to a specific function.

The conclusion that changes occur in the overall size of the brain rather than in specific brain regions is consistent with the concept that overall developmental factors and programs (which we will consider in Chapter 7) severely constrain the magnitude of local adaptations. Supporting this conclusion is the recent finding that if the weight of the brain of any mammalian species is known, the weight of each of its parts can be predicted (Finlay and Darlington, 1995).

In this study the investigators compiled published data on sizes of the main parts of the brain in 131 species of mammals—insectivores, bats, prosimians, and simians (including *Homo sapiens*). Their data set had the advantages, for comparative study, of including a large number of species, a wide range of ecological niches (including terrestrial, arboreal [tree-dwelling], burrowing, amphibious, and flying), a wide range of body weights (2 to 105,000 g) and brain sizes (60 to 1,252,000 mm^3), and the fact that the 11 brain divisions measured constitute the entire brain. Because of the wide range of sizes, the logarithms of the sizes were used in the analyses.

In logarithmic scales, the size of each brain structure, except for the olfactory bulb, showed a highly linear relation to brain weight. The size of each structure, except the olfactory bulb, correlated 0.96 or higher with total brain size; for the olfactory bulb the correlation was only 0.70. Thus, for all parts of the brain except the olfactory bulb, a simple rule relates the size of the particular structure to total brain size.

Although the different parts of the brain increase regularly in size as total brain size increases, different parts increase at different rates from the others. In a series of mammalian brains from small to large, the medulla increases relatively little as brain weight grows, the cerebellum keeps pace with brain weight, and the neocortex grows the most of all the parts; Figure 6.14 shows examples. Thus the proportion of brain devoted to each part differs in important ways from small to large brains.

The fact that the brain shows overall developmental constraints does not contradict the existence of some specific size adaptations of brain structures. For one thing, the brain divisions analyzed by Finlay and Darlington are relatively large, and most of them contain subdivisions that may vary in their development. Thus, for example, one of the brain divisions in their study is the metencephalon, which includes both the inferior colliculus and the superior colliculus; as we have mentioned, the inferior colliculus is larger in animals that depend mainly on audition, whereas the superior colliculus is larger in animals that rely on vision. So although general constraints on development are strong, specific adaptations of brain regions can occur.

Hominid brains evolved relatively rapidly. Valuable information about evolutionary relationships between brain and behavior comes from the study of hominids—primates of the family Hominidae—of which humans (*Homo sapiens*) are the only living species. This approach is intriguing for the light it sheds on our distant ancestors, and it helps us understand how the body adapts to the environment through natural selection.

The structural and behavioral features that we consider characteristic of humans did not develop simultaneously (Falk, 1993). Our large brain is a relatively late development. According to one estimate, the trunk and arms of hominids reached their present form about 10 million years ago. (Note that the time span of human evolution and the dates of fossils have been altered by recent methods of dating. Not all authorities agree on these dates; they should be considered only approximate.) Hominids began walking on two feet more than 3.5 million years ago, and the oldest stone tools date back to about 2.6 million years ago (Figure 6.15).

The early tool users were bipedal hominids called australopithecines. Endocasts of their skulls show a

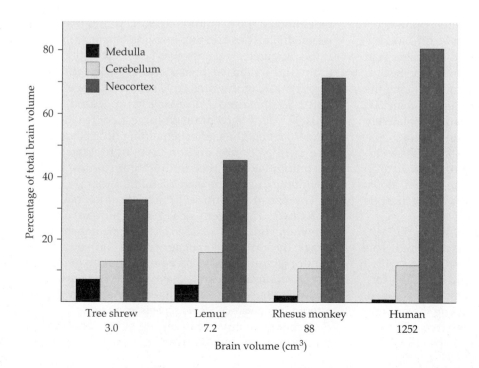

6.14 Changes in the Apportionment of Brain Regions among Primates
This graph shows the percentage of brain volume occupied by three different parts of the brain in four different primates. As the size of the brain increases, different parts of the brain increase at different rates. The size of the neocortex increases steadily as a proportion of brain size, while that of the cerebellum stays about the same, and the relative size of the medulla decreases. This generalization holds for all primates. (Data from H. Stephan et al., 1981.)

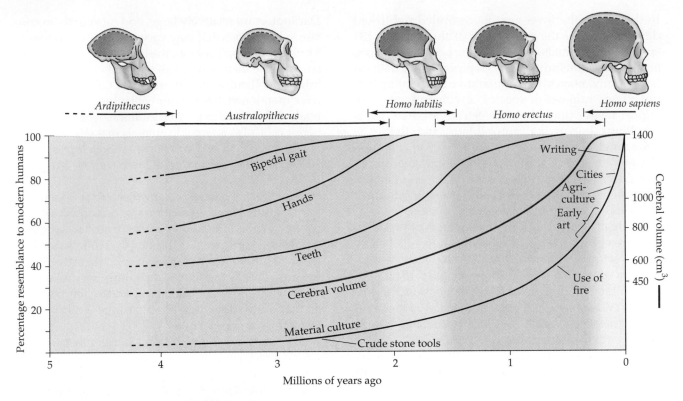

6.15 Aspects of Hominid Evolution
The bipedal (two-footed) gait was similar to that of modern humans even in *Australopithecus*, but cerebral volume reached its current size only in *Homo sapiens*. High culture (art, agriculture, cities, writing) emerged only relatively recently and was not associated with any further change in brain size. (After Tobias, 1980; updated with the assistance of Tim White.)

brain volume of about 350 to 400 cm³, about the size of the modern chimpanzee brain. Chimpanzees do not make tools from stone, although they collect stones to use as tools. But the australopithecines made and used crude stone tools in hunting and in breaking animal bones to eat. The ability to use tools reduced the selection pressure to maintain large jaws and teeth, and hominid jaws and teeth thus became steadily smaller than the ape's and more like those of modern human beings. Even though the brain did not grow much among the australopithecines, never becoming larger than 600 cm³, they were successful animals, lasting—relatively unchanged—until about 1.5 to 2 million years ago. Examination of ancient campsites suggests that these early hominids lived in small nomadic groups of 20 to 50 individuals. They hunted and gathered plant foods. This life of hunting and gathering was a new lifestyle that was continued by later hominids.

About 1.5 to 2 million years ago, when the australopithecines died out, *Homo erectus* appeared. This early representative of the genus *Homo* started with a cranial capacity of about 700 cm³ and a smaller face than *Australopithecus* had. As *Homo erectus* developed, the brain became steadily larger, reaching the present-day volume of about 1400 cm³, and the face continued to become smaller. *Homo erectus* made elaborate stone

tools, used fire, and killed large animals. Fossils and tools of *Homo erectus* are found throughout three continents, whereas those of the australopithecines are found only in Africa. *Homo erectus* may have represented a level of capacity and of cultural adaptation that allowed the hominids to expand into new environmental niches and to overcome barriers that kept earlier hominids in a narrower range. Evolution of the brain and increased behavioral capacity advanced rapidly during the time of *Homo erectus* (see Figure 6.15). By the time *Homo sapiens* appeared, about 200,000 years ago, brain volume had reached the modern level. Thus, after remaining little changed in size during about 2 million years of tool use by the australopithecines, the hominid brain almost tripled in volume during the next 1.5 million years.

The size of the human brain now appears to be at a plateau. The recent changes in human lifestyle shown in Figure 6.15—such as the appearance of language, the introduction of agriculture and animal husbandry (about 10,000 years ago), and urban living (the last few thousand years)—have all been accomplished and assimilated by a brain that does not seem to have altered in size since *Homo sapiens* appeared.

A change in any organ during evolution suggests that the change confers advantages with respect to the survival of the individuals in that environment. A rapid change, as in the size of the hominid brain, implies strong advantages for survival. Can we then determine in what ways the evolution of the human brain accompanied and made possible certain changes in human behavior?

Unfortunately, we cannot directly examine the brains of australopithecines. All we have is the information about size and external shape that endocasts afford. Chimpanzees have brains of about the same size and shape as australopithecine brains, but chimpanzees have never been seen to fashion a stone tool, even crudely. They catch small game, but not in the frequent manner that is suggested by the collections of bones of prey found in association with australopithecine tools and fossils. Thus, behavioral evidence suggests that the australopithecine is our closer relative, further advanced toward human culture than is the chimpanzee. Keeping in mind that the brain organization of the australopithecine probably also differed somewhat from that of the chimpanzee, let's see how the modern human brain differs from that of the chimpanzee to give us some clues about the evolution of the hominid brain.

Prominent differences between the organization of the brain of *Homo sapiens* and that of the chimpanzee include the following:

1. The human brain has larger motor and sensory cortical areas devoted to the hands.
2. In both the human brain and the chimpanzee brain, parts of the limbic system are involved in vocalization. However, the human brain shows, in addition, large neocortical regions devoted to the production and perception of speech. Nonhuman primates have relatively smaller neocortical regions controlling vocalization.
3. For speech, manual dexterity, and other functions, the human brain shows striking hemispheric specialization of functions. In the chimpanzee the two hemispheres seem more equivalent in function.
4. The primary sensory regions of the cortex are somewhat greater in the human than in the chimpanzee. But the main expansion in the human cortex lies outside these sensory regions. Deacon (1997) estimates that the human **prefrontal cortex** (that is, the cortex anterior to the motor cortex) is about twice the size that would be predicted in an ape with a brain as large as a human's. The development of the prefrontal cortex permitted more varied and more elaborate processing of information and may have underlain the emergence of symbolic thinking.

In trying to account for the evolution of the human brain and for the special capabilities of *Homo sapiens*, different theorists have emphasized different behavioral traits: "Dexterity and tool use, language, group hunting, various aspects of social structure, and the ability to plan for the future have all been proposed as primary in the cascade of changes leading to the constellation of traits we now possess" (Finlay and Darlington, 1995, p. 1583). From their analysis of the evolution of the mammalian brain, Finlay and Darlington suggest that the multiple facets and rapid rate of human evolution may be explained by the fact that large primates are on the part of the curve relating neocortex weight to brain weight where small increases in brain weight are associated with large increases in neocortex weight. Selection for any single cognitive ability might therefore cause, in parallel, greater processing capacity for all the other abilities. Finlay and Darlington (1995, p. 1583) suggest that the neocortex, as a general-purpose processor, may allow "the organism to take advantage of the extra brain structure in ways not directly selected for during evolution." Charles Darwin (in F. Darwin, 1888, p. 169) made almost the same point in the nineteenth century:

> In many cases, the continued development of a part—for instance the beak of a bird or the teeth of a mammal—would not aid the species in gaining its food, or for any other object; but with man we can see no definite limit to the continual development of the brain and mental faculties, as far as advantage is concerned.

The survival advantage of larger brains does not hold only for human beings, or primates, or mammalian predators and prey. It would even be too limited to maintain, as Shaw's Don Juan does in the epigraph at the beginning of this book, that large brains are the specialty of the mammalian line. Within each line of vertebrate evolution relative brain size varies: The more recently arrived species usually has the larger encephalization factor. Furthermore, in each vertebrate line it is the dorsal part of the telencephalon that has expanded and differentiated in the species with more elaborated capabilities. We will discuss the expansion in size of the prefrontal cortex in Chapter 19 (see Figure 19.17*b*). As we find more such common responses to selection pressures, they may reveal the "rules" of how nervous systems adapt and evolve.

A large brain is expensive. Having a large brain entails costs as well as benefits for human beings and other large-brained animals. Growth of a large brain requires a long gestation period, which is a burden on the mother, and childbirth is difficult because of the large size of the baby's head. Much of the growth of the brain continues during the years after birth, which means prolonged dependence of the infant and prolonged parental care. Although the brain makes up only about 2% of our total adult body weight, it accounts for about 15% of our cardiac output and metabolic budget when we are at rest. These percentages decrease when the body is active, because muscles increase their demands, but even then the energy requirements of the brain remain high.

The genetic specifications of the brain require more than half of the human genome, because there are so many kinds of brain cells and connections. These complex genetic messages are vulnerable to accidents; many of the known disorders of behavior are related to mutations of single genes. The evolution of large brains is especially remarkable when viewed in the context of these costs.

Summary

1. Studies of the classification of animals help determine how closely different species are related. Knowing this relationship, in turn, helps us interpret similarities and differences in the behavior and structure of different species.

2. Comparative studies of the nervous system help us understand the evolution of the nervous system, including the human brain. They also provide a perspective for understanding species-typical behavioral adaptations.

3. The nervous systems of invertebrate animals range in complexity from a simple nerve net to the complex structures of the octopus. The nervous systems of certain invertebrates may provide a simplified model for understanding some aspects of vertebrate nervous systems.

4. Some of the distinctive features of invertebrate nervous systems include large, identifiable monopolar neurons and large axons that are frequently components of circuits mediating rapid escape behaviors.

5. The main divisions of the brain are the same in all vertebrates. Differences among these animals are largely quantitative, as reflected in differences in the relative sizes of nerve cells and brain regions.

6. Size differences in brain regions among various mammals are frequently related to distinctive forms of behavioral adaptation.

7. Evolutionary changes in brain size are apparent in comparisons of fossils and contemporary animals.

8. The brain size of a species must be interpreted in terms of body size. The overall rule for vertebrates is that brain weight is proportional to the 0.7 power of body weight.

9. Some animals have larger brains and some have smaller brains than is predicted by the general relation between brain and body weights; that is, they differ in encephalization factor. Humans, in particular, have larger brains than would be predicted from their body size.

10. Within each of the lines of vertebrate evolution, relative brain size varies, and the more recently evolved species usually have the larger encephalization factors.

11. The human brain, as compared to brains of nonhuman primates, has larger motor and sensory cortical areas devoted to the hands, larger cortical regions devoted to the production and perception of speech, a larger proportion of the brain devoted to varied and elaborate processing of information, and striking hemispheric specializations of function.

12. Research that compares the behavior and structure of species, in relation to their phylogeny, is being applied in many ways to understanding biological bases of behavior and to improving the health and well-being of humans and other animal species.

Recommended Reading

Alcock, J. A. (1998). *Animal behavior: An evolutionary approach* (6th ed.). Sunderland, MA: Sinauer.

Butler, A. B., and Hodos, W. (1996). *Comparative vertebrate anatomy: Evolution and adaptation.* New York: Wiley-Liss.

Futuyma, D. J. (1998). *Evolutionary biology* (3rd ed.). Sunderland, MA: Sinauer.

Krebs, J. R., and Davies, N. B. (Eds.) (1997). *Behavioral ecology: An evolutionary approach.* Cambridge, MA: Blackwell Science.

Li, W., and Graur, D. (1991). *Fundamentals of molecular evolution.* Sunderland, MA: Sinauer.

Mayr, E., and Ashlock, P. D. (1991). *Principles of systematic zoology* (2nd ed.). New York: McGraw-Hill.

Shettleworth, S. A. (1993a,b). *Cognition, evolution, and behavior.* New York: Oxford University Press.

7 Life-Span Development of the Brain and Behavior

Age puts its stamp on the behavior of all animals. Although the pace, progression, and orderliness of changes are especially prominent early in life, change is a feature of the entire span of life. Shakespeare put it well in his play *As You Like It* when he said

> . . . from hour to hour, we ripe and ripe,
> And then, from hour to hour, we rot and
> rot . . .

In this chapter we will describe the features of adult brains that we introduced in Chapters 2 and 3 in terms of their progress through life from the womb to the tomb. The fertilization of an egg leads to a body with a brain that contains billions of neurons with an incredible number of connections. The pace of this process is extraordinary: During the height of prenatal growth of the human brain, 250,000 neurons are added per minute. Our discussion of this developmental process will range wide: We will describe the emergence of nerve cells, and the formation of their connections, as well as the roles of genes and of experience in shaping the emerging nervous system.

Salvador Dali, *Galatea of the Spheres*, 1952

Growth and Development of the Brain Are Orderly Processes

The journey from fertilized egg to mature organism is exceedingly complicated. Picture, if you can, the number of neurons in the mature human brain. Recent estimates suggest that there are about 100 billion neurons and at least as many glial cells. Neurons include many cell types, and they form a vast array of connections. The number of synapses on a single large neuron ranges in the thousands, and the overall number of connections in the brain is about 100 trillion. These numbers alone suggest that the growth and development of the brain are massively complex. In addition to existing in great numbers, these elements are arranged into distinct, ordered, species-typical patterns.

Brain Weight and Volume Change from Birth to Old Age

One measure of brain development is the weight of the brain at different stages of life. Weight can be considered a summary of many developmental processes. A study by Dekaban and Sadowsky (1978) gives a definitive portrait of the weight of the human brain over the life span. They measured the brains of 5826 people, selected from more than 25,000 cases from several cities. Figure 7.1 shows the changes with age in the weight of the brain in males and females. Note the rapid increase during the first 5 years. Brain weight is at its peak from about age 18 to about age 30, after which it declines gradually.

The Brain Emerges from the Neural Tube

A new human being begins when a sperm about 60 μm long penetrates the wall of an egg cell 100 to 150 μm in diameter. The fertilized egg, or **zygote**, has 46 chromosomes, which contain the complete genetic recipe for the development of a new individual.

(A summary of the life cycle of cells, including a discussion of the basic genetic materials and how they direct cell activities, is provided in the Appendix. More complete details about cell activities and heredity are provided in comprehensive biology texts such as W. K. Purves et al., 1998.) Rapid cell division begins the developmental program. Within 12 hours after conception the single cell has divided into two cells, and after 3 days these two cells have become a small mass of homogeneous cells, like a cluster of grapes, about 200 μm in diameter.

Within a week the emerging human embryo shows three distinct cell layers (Figure 7.2*a*). These layers are the beginnings of all the tissues of the embryo. The nervous system will develop from the outer layer, called the **ectoderm** (from the Greek *ektos,* "out," and *derma,* "skin"). As the cell layers thicken, they grow into a flat oval plate. In the ectodermal level of this plate, uneven rates of cell division form a groove—the primitive streak—which will form the midline. At the head end of the groove, a thickened collection of cells forms 2 weeks after fertilization. Ridges of ectoderm continue to bulge on both sides of the middle position. The groove between them is called the **neural groove** (Figure 7.2*b*).

The pace of events now increases. The neural ridges come together to form the **neural tube** (Figure 7.2*c*). At the anterior part of the neural tube, three subdivisions become apparent. These subdivisions correspond to the future **forebrain** (prosencephalon, consisting of the telencephalon and the diencephalon), **midbrain** (mesencephalon), and **hindbrain** (rhombencephalon, consisting of the metencephalon and the myelencephalon) discussed in Chapter 2 (Figure 7.2*d*). The interior of the neural tube becomes the cerebral ventricles of the brain, the central canal of the spinal cord, and the passages that connect them.

By the end of the eighth week, the human embryo shows the rudimentary beginnings of most body or-

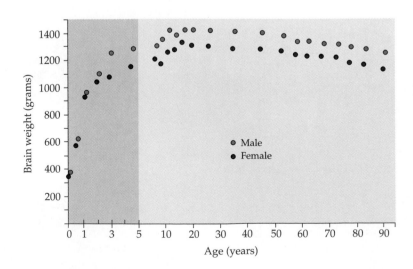

7.1 Human Brain Weight as a Function of Age

Note that the age scale on this graph has been expanded for the first 5 years in order to show data more clearly during this period of rapid growth. (After Dekaban and Sadowsky, 1978.)

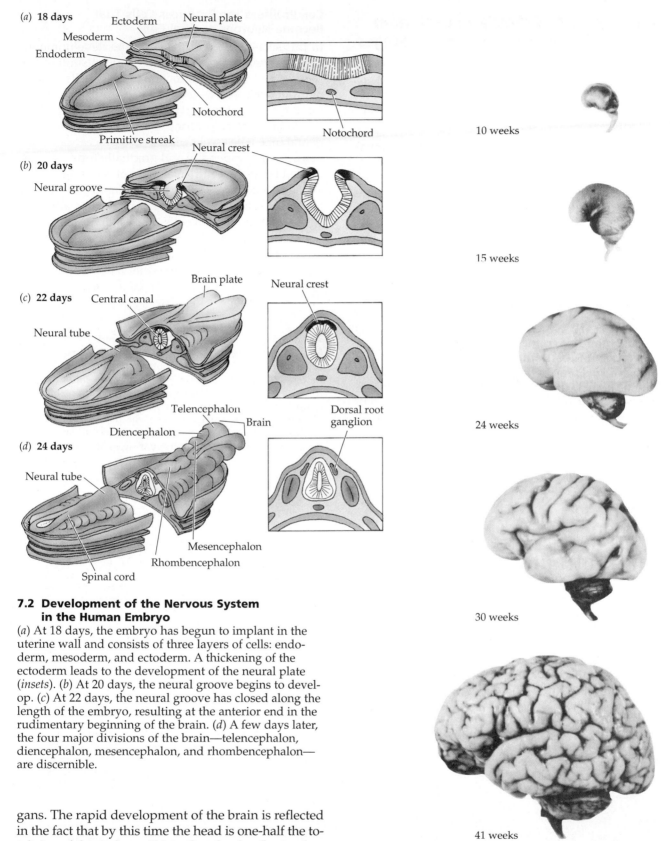

7.2 Development of the Nervous System in the Human Embryo

(*a*) At 18 days, the embryo has begun to implant in the uterine wall and consists of three layers of cells: endoderm, mesoderm, and ectoderm. A thickening of the ectoderm leads to the development of the neural plate (*insets*). (*b*) At 20 days, the neural groove begins to develop. (*c*) At 22 days, the neural groove has closed along the length of the embryo, resulting at the anterior end in the rudimentary beginning of the brain. (*d*) A few days later, the four major divisions of the brain—telencephalon, diencephalon, mesencephalon, and rhombencephalon—are discernible.

gans. The rapid development of the brain is reflected in the fact that by this time the head is one-half the total size of the embryo. (Note that the developing human is called an **embryo** during the first 10 weeks after fertilization; thereafter it is called a **fetus**.) Figure 7.3 shows the prenatal development of the human brain from weeks 10 through 41.

7.3 Development of the Brain in the Human Fetus
Lateral views of the human brain (shown at one-third size) at several stages of fetal development. Note the gradual emergence of gyri and sulci. (From Larroche, 1977.)

Development of the Nervous System Can Be Divided into Six Distinct Stages

From a cellular viewpoint it is useful to consider brain development as a sequence of distinct stages, most of which occur during prenatal life. Here we'll name these stages, and in the discussion that follows we will take up each stage in succession:

1. *Neurogenesis,* the mitotic division of nonneuronal cells to produce neurons.
2. *Cell migration,* the massive movements of nerve cells or their precursors to establish distinctive nerve cell populations (nuclei in the CNS, layers of the cerebral cortex, etc.).
3. *Differentiation* of cells into distinctive types of neurons.
4. *Synaptogenesis,* the establishment of synaptic connections as axons and dendrites grow.
5. *Neuronal cell death,* the selective death of many nerve cells.
6. *Synapse rearrangement,* the loss of some synapses and development of others, to refine synaptic connections.

This sequence is portrayed in Figure 7.4. The six stages proceed at different rates and times in different parts of the nervous system. Some of the stages may overlap even within a region.

Cell Proliferation Produces Cells That Become Neurons or Glial Cells

In this section we will focus on the developmental stages of neurons specifically. Glial cells follow the same sequence. The production of nerve cells is called **neurogenesis**. Nerve cells themselves do not divide, but the cells that will give rise to neurons begin as a single layer of cells along the inner surface of the neural tube. These cells divide (in a process called **mitosis**; see the Appendix) and gradually form a closely packed layer, the **ventricular zone** of cells (Figure 7.5). These cells continue to divide, giving rise to "daughter" cells, which also divide. All neurons and glial cells are derived from cells that originate from such ventricular mitosis. Eventually some daughter cells leave the ventricular zone and begin expressing genes that transform the cell into either a neuron or a glial cell. These two types of cells separate early in the ven-

7.4 Six Stages of Neural Development
(*a*) Cells of the neural tube divide to provide progeny cells. (*b*) The cells produced migrate to their appropriate region. (*c*) The cells differentiate to become either a neuron or a glial cell. (*d*) Neurons extend their axons and dendrites to form many synapses with one another. (*e*) Many neurons normally die early in development. (*f*) Many of the synapses initially formed will later be retracted, while other, later-appearing synapses form.

(*a*) Mitosis (neurogenesis)

(*b*) Migration

(*c*) Differentiation

(*d*) Synaptogenesis

(*e*) Cell death

(*f*) Synapse rearrangement

(a)

(b)

(c)

Outer surface

| This cell will differentiate into a neuron. |

Marginal zone

Ventricular zone

Inner surface   Mitosis   Time →

| This cell undergoes a second round of mitosis. |

7.5 Proliferation of Cellular Precursors of Neurons and Glial Cells

(a) A small section of the wall of the neural tube at an early stage of embryonic development. Only ventricular (V) and marginal (M) layers are visible. (b) Later an intermediate (I) layer develops as the wall thickens. (c) Nuclei (within their cells) migrate from the ventricular layer to the outer layers. Some cells, however, return to the ventricular zone and divide, and the resulting daughter cells migrate to the outer layers, repeating the cycle.

tricular zone. In most mammals neural cells in the ventricular layer continue to form until birth; very few are added after birth, although some nerve cells are added to some brain regions after birth.

Each part of an animal's brain has a species-characteristic "birth date." That is, there is an orderly chronological program for brain development, and it is possible to state the approximate days during development on which particular cell groups stop dividing. Of course, given the complexity of vertebrate brains, it is difficult to trace individual cell develop-

ment from the initial small population of ventricular cells. Descendants disappear in the crowd. However, in some simpler invertebrate nervous systems that have very few neurons, mitotic lineages can be traced more easily and completely.

A favorite animal of researchers who study the lineage of nerve cells is the nematode *Caenorhabditis elegans*, a tiny worm that has only 302 nerve cells. Because the body of *C. elegans* is almost transparent (Figure 7.6a), researchers have been able to map the origins of each nerve cell, and they have identified several of the genes that control the paths of neural development (Wolinsky and Way, 1990). By observing the successive cell divisions of a *C. elegans* zygote, investigators can predict exactly the fate of each cell in the adult—whether it will be a sensory neuron, muscle cell, skin cell, and so on—on the basis of its mitotic "ancestors."

Whereas cell fate in *C. elegans* is a highly determined and stereotypical result of mitotic lineage (Figure 7.6b), in vertebrates the paths from cell origins to the completed nervous system are more complex. New techniques, such as the injection of substances that act as markers or the use of induced mutations, have shown that in vertebrates the paths of development include more local regulatory mechanisms. The hallmark of vertebrate development is that cell fate is affected by **cell–cell interactions** as cells sort themselves out and take on the fate that is appropriate in the context of what neighboring cells are doing. Thus, vertebrate development is less determined intrinsically; that is, it is more subject to environmental signals and, as we'll see, experience.

Traditionally, investigators of nervous system development believed that most mammals have at birth all the nerve cells they will ever have. Researchers have usually attributed the postnatal growth of human brain weight to growth in the size of neurons, branching of dendrites, elaboration of synapses, increase in myelin, and addition of nonneural (glial) cells. Within recent years, this belief has been modified, primarily because it now appears that small neurons are added for a period after birth and, in some cases, even in adulthood (E. Gould et al., 1998).

All the large neurons the brain will ever contain are indeed present at birth, but in regions around the brain ventricles, the ventricular zone (see Figure 7.5), mitotic division continues after birth. Several regions of the rat brain, including the olfactory bulb and the hippocampus, appear to add small neurons derived from the ventricular zone. In fact, it is now well established that nerve cells of the olfactory end organ are normally replaced throughout life. This process involves a set of cells adjacent to olfactory receptor cells that become neurons, perhaps in response to the ongoing death of olfactory nerve cells (Jacobson, 1991).

The dogma that no new neurons are added to the adult nervous system is strongly challenged by excit-

(a)

7.6 Cell Fate in a Simple Organism

(*a*) A montage of photomicrographs showing the transparent body of *C. elegans*. (*b*) The mitotic lineage of cells that give rise to the body of the adult *C. elegans*; nervous system cells are highlighted in blue. The structure and function of every cell can be predicted from its mitotic lineage. Such mitotic determination of cell differentiation does not seem important to the development of vertebrates. (Part *a* courtesy of Erik Jorgensen and Howard Hughes Medical Institute; *b* after Pines, 1992.)

(b)   Zygote

Shaded areas represent neural cells.

The end of each line represents one of the 987 cells of the adult *C. elegans*.

ing research on the neural basis of birdsong (discussed in Chapters 12 and 19). Briefly, birdsong development in males of some species is under hormonal control, dependent on the hormone testosterone. In earlier research, Nottebohm (1980) determined the parts of the bird brain that are responsible for song learning and performance. During the course of this work, he noted that at least one part of the relevant brain circuit for birdsong is large in spring and shrinks to half that size in the fall. This seasonal change in the size of the brain region is related to male hormone levels and singing behavior (Nottebohm, 1991).

Competing hypotheses

Some of this seasonal variation in the size of the brain region responsible for birdsong is accounted for by seasonal variations in dendritic length and branching. However, Nottebohm has also presented evidence that new neurons are added throughout life. New cells form in the ventricular zone, migrate to the nearby vocal control brain region, and there differentiate into neurons. These observations suggest the need to reexamine the belief that the adult brain does not add new neurons. At the very least such renewed research could offer a better understanding of the conditions that lead to the usual cessation of neuron addition in adulthood.

New Nerve Cells Migrate

Neurons of the developing nervous system are always on the move. At some stage the cells that form in the ventricular layer through mitotic division move away, in a process known as **cell migration**. The cells acquire short extensions at the "head" and "tail" ends. Some descriptions of migrating cells compare them to a trail of active ants (Figure 7.7). In primates, by the time of birth almost all presumptive nerve cells have completed their migration, but in rats, cells that will become neurons continue to migrate in some regions for several weeks following birth.

Cells do not move in an aimless, haphazard manner. Information about the guidance of cell migration comes from studies using radioactive substances that become incorporated into the cell before migration. These substances "tag" the cell so that it can be fol-

 Important method

lowed and its migratory paths clearly outlined. Many elegant studies by Rakic (reviewed in Rakic, 1985) show that some cells in the developing brain move along the surface of a particular type of glial cell that appears early. Like spokes (radii) of a wheel, these **radial glial cells** extend from the inner to the outer surfaces of the emerging nervous system (Figure 7.8). The radial glial cells act as a series of guide wires, and the

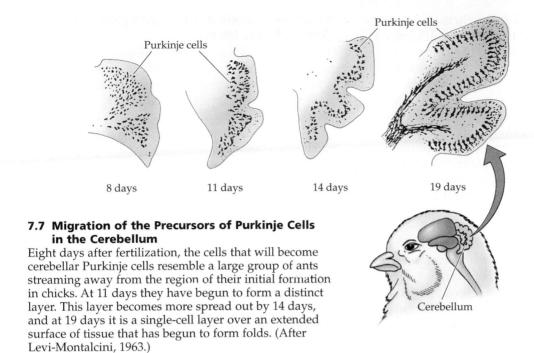

7.7 Migration of the Precursors of Purkinje Cells in the Cerebellum

Eight days after fertilization, the cells that will become cerebellar Purkinje cells resemble a large group of ants streaming away from the region of their initial formation in chicks. At 11 days they have begun to form a distinct layer. This layer becomes more spread out by 14 days, and at 19 days it is a single-cell layer over an extended surface of tissue that has begun to form folds. (After Levi-Montalcini, 1963.)

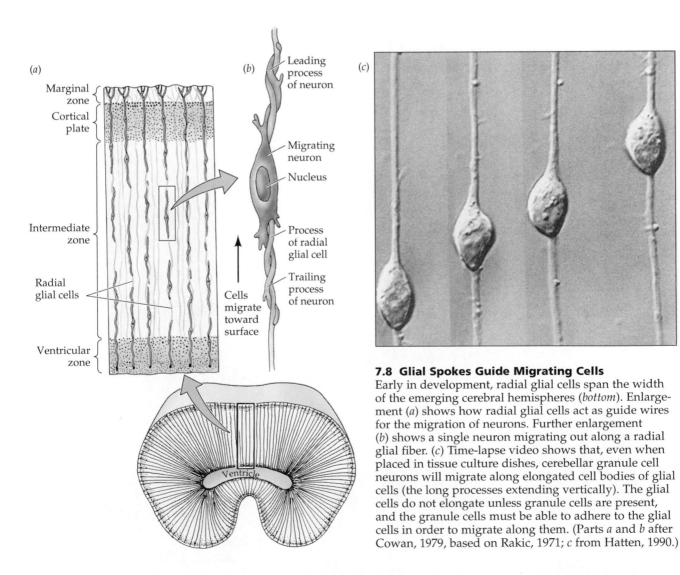

7.8 Glial Spokes Guide Migrating Cells

Early in development, radial glial cells span the width of the emerging cerebral hemispheres (*bottom*). Enlargement (*a*) shows how radial glial cells act as guide wires for the migration of neurons. Further enlargement (*b*) shows a single neuron migrating out along a radial glial fiber. (*c*) Time-lapse video shows that, even when placed in tissue culture dishes, cerebellar granule cell neurons will migrate along elongated cell bodies of glial cells (the long processes extending vertically). The glial cells do not elongate unless granule cells are present, and the granule cells must be able to adhere to the glial cells in order to migrate along them. (Parts *a* and *b* after Cowan, 1979, based on Rakic, 1971; *c* from Hatten, 1990.)

newly formed cells creep along them. One article about this process is titled "Riding the Glial Monorail" (Hatten, 1990). A striking image of this process observed **in vitro** (in a laboratory dish) is shown in Figure 7.8c. Some cells that form later migrate in a different manner, attracted to the surfaces of neurons (Rakic, 1985).

Failures in the mechanism of cell migration result in either a vastly reduced population of neurons or a disorderly arrangement and, not surprisingly, behavioral disorders. The migration of cells and the outgrowth of nerve cell extensions (dendrites and axons) involve various chemicals. Molecules that promote the adhesion of developing elements of the nervous system, and thereby guide migrating cells and growing axons, are called **cell adhesion molecules (CAMs)**. Knowledge about CAMs and other components of the extracellular matrix surrounding developing cells is important for understanding the major steps in neural development (Reichardt and Tomaselli, 1991). CAMs may also guide axons to regenerate when they are cut in adulthood (Box 7.1). The single-file appearance of nerve cell precursors during cell migration (see Figure 7.8a) is followed by the aggregation, or grouping, of cells in a manner that foreshadows the nuclei of the adult brain that we discussed in Chapter 2. For example, cells of the cerebral cortex and cerebellar cortex become arranged in layers during fetal development, and these groupings are the beginnings of the defined regions of the brain.

Neocortical Layers Are Formed by Successive Waves of New Neurons

The developmental assembly of each region of the brain follows a precise timetable; many parts of the schedule appear to rely on mutual interactions of cells in the developing region. To show how regions may acquire characteristic orderly forms, let's take the cerebral cortex as an example. The billions of neurons in the human neocortex are arranged in six layers, and the cells of each layer differ in form and size.

Examination of the closed neural tube of a human embryo at the end of the third week after fertilization reveals a zone of dividing cells all around the inner surfaces—the ventricular zone (see Figure 7.5). Intense cell division continues to produce cells that will in time become the neurons of the cerebral cortex. This rapid proliferation continues until the sixth month of fetal life, by which time the cerebral cortex has its full complement of neurons.

As shown in Figure 7.9, formation of the cell layers in the cerebral cortex is a regular process. Cells that form along the ventricular zone migrate away from it. Each new cell migrates beyond those born earlier.

7.9 Cerebral Cortex Tissue in Early Development of Humans
These representations of cerebral cortex show the extent of neural connections at birth (*a*), at 3 months of age (*b*), and at 2 years of age (*c*). Numerals refer to the six cortical layers. (From Conel, 1939, 1947, 1959.)

(*a*) Newborn

(*b*) Three-month-old

(*c*) Two-year-old

Thus, the inner layer (layer VI) has the "oldest" neurons, and the youngest neurons are in the outermost layer (layer I). Cells within each layer that will become the large neurons are born first; smaller cells are born slightly later. Migration time—the interval between cell birth and arrival of the cell at its final position—becomes progressively longer, taking only a few hours for layer VI and about 5 days for the last group of new

---

BOX 7.1   *Degeneration and Regeneration of Nervous Tissue*

When a mature nerve cell is injured, it can regrow in several ways. Complete replacement of injured nerve cells is rare in mammals, but the figure illustrates two characteristic forms of degeneration and regeneration in the mammalian peripheral and central nervous systems. Injury close to the cell body of a neuron produces a series of changes that result in the eventual destruction of the cell. This process is called **retrograde degeneration** (*left*; 2 and 3). If the injured neuron dies, the target cells formerly innervated by that neuron may show signs of transneuronal degeneration (4).

Cutting through the axon also produces loss of the distal part of the axon (the part separated from the cell body). This process is called Wallerian degeneration or **anterograde degeneration** (*right*; 2 and 3). The part of the axon that remains connected to the cell body may regrow. Severed axons in the peripheral nervous system regrow readily. Sprouts emerge from the part of the axon that is still connected to the nerve cell body and advance slowly toward the periphery (4). Cell adhesion molecules (CAMs) help guide the regenerating axons. Some animals have an enviable advantage. After an injury to the brain, several fish and amphibians appear to be able to regenerate large parts of the brain itself.

From an experimental point of view, our interest in regeneration of the nervous system lies principally in the fact that regeneration involves processes that seem similar to original development. Studying regeneration may thus increase our understanding of the original processes of growth of the nervous system. From a therapeutic viewpoint, these studies may help scientists learn how to induce repair and regrowth of damaged neural tissue in humans.

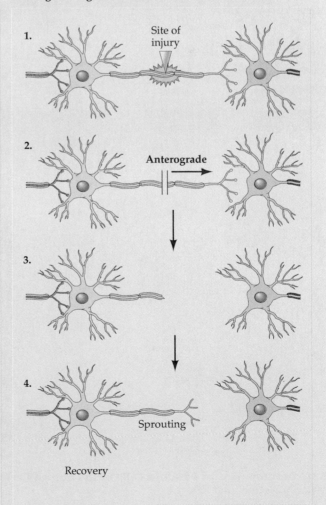

Retrograde degeneration

1. Site of injury
2. Retrograde
3. Atrophy
4. Transneuronal degeneration

Anterograde degeneration

1. Site of injury
2. Anterograde
3.
4. Sprouting

Recovery

cortical cells. The most intense phase of dendritic growth and synapse formation in the cerebral cortex occurs after birth.

Cells in Newly Formed Brain Regions Differentiate into Neurons

Newly arrived cells in the brain bear no more resemblance to mature nerve cells than they do to the cells of other organs. Once they reach their destinations, however, the cells begin to use ("express") particular genes to make the particular proteins a neuron needs. This process of **differentiation** allows the cell to acquire the distinctive appearance of neurons that are characteristic of their particular region. Figure 7.10 shows the progressive unfolding of Purkinje cells of the cerebellar cortex. Outgrowths from the dendrites of these cells appear soon after the cells have aligned into a single row. Slowly more and more branches form, progressively expanding the receptive surface of the Purkinje cell.

What controls differentiation is not completely understood, but two classes of influence are known. First,

intrinsic self-organization is an important factor; both granule cells and Purkinje cells in tissue culture grow in a typical manner, although they are deprived of **Genes and behavior**
some normal connections (Seil et al., 1974). When a cell shows characteristics that are independent of neighboring cells, we say it is acting in a **cell-autonomous** manner. In cell-autonomous differentiation, presumably only the genes within that cell are directing events. Some examples exist in the nervous system.

It has been shown repeatedly, however, that the neural environment also greatly influences nerve cell differentiation. In other words, neighboring cells are a second major influence on the differentiation of neurons. In vertebrates (unlike the case of the nematode *C. elegans*), young neural cells seem to have the capacity to become many varieties of neurons, and the particular type of neuron that a cell becomes depends on where it happens to be and what its neighboring cells are. For example, consider spinal motoneurons—cells in the spinal cord that send their axons out to control muscles. Motoneurons are large, multipolar cells found in the left and right sides of the spinal cord in the ventral horn of gray matter. Motoneurons are among the first recognizable neurons in the spinal cord and send their axons out early in fetal development. How do these cells "know" they should express motoneuron-specific genes and grow into motoneurons?

Experiments that examine the late divisions giving rise to motoneurons make it clear that the cells are not attending to mitotic lineage (Leber et al., 1990). Instead, some spinal cells are directed to become motoneurons under the influence of other cells lying just ventral to the developing spinal cord—in the **notochord**, a rodlike structure that forms along the midline (see Figure 7.2*a*). If we insert an additional length of notochord *above* the spinal cord, cells begin differentiating into motoneurons on each side of the spinal cord near the extra notochord (Roelink et al., 1994). The notochord releases a protein messenger (which has been identified and playfully named "sonic hedgehog") that diffuses to the spinal cord and directs some (but not all) cells to become motoneurons (Figure 7.11).

12th fetal week	15 weeks	18 weeks	22 weeks
28 weeks	32 weeks	35 weeks	Birth

100 μm

11 months postnatal   Adult

7.10 Development of Purkinje Cells in the Human Cerebellum (After N. Zecevic and Rakic, 1976.)

7.11 The Induction of Spinal Motoneurons
Spinal motoneurons normally cluster in the ventral region on either side. The notochord (green circle at bottom) lies just beneath the spinal cord and secretes a protein called sonic hedgehog. The concentration of this protein in the ventral spinal cord induces those cells to develop as motoneurons (gold). Another protein (blue) is expressed only in the dorsal spinal cord. (Courtesy of Thomas Jessell.)

The influence of one set of cells on the fate of neighboring cells is called **induction**; the notochord induces some spinal cord cells to differentiate into motoneurons. Induction of this sort has been demonstrated many times in the developing vertebrate body and, more recently, in the brain. Another way to describe the situation is that there is extensive cell–cell interaction, each cell taking cues from its neighbors. The idea of cells influencing each other's differentiation may make the entire affair seem very complex, as it is.

One consequence of this system, however, is that cells differentiate into the type of neuron that is appropriate for that brain region; thus cell–cell interaction coordinates development—directing differentiation to provide the right type of neuron for each part of the brain. Another consequence of the reliance of development on cell–cell interactions such as induction is that if a few cells are injured or lost, other cells will "answer the call" of inducing factors and fill in for the missing cells.

This phenomenon can be observed in any vertebrate and many invertebrate embryos from which some cells have been removed. For example, if cells are removed early enough from a developing limb bud in a chick embryo, other cells pitch in, and by the time the chick hatches, the limb looks normal—with no parts missing. Embryologists refer to such adaptive responses to early injury as **regulation**: The developing animal compensates for missing or injured cells. Because cell fate is so tightly coupled with mitotic lineage in *C. elegans*, this organism shows little or no regulation. If a cell in *C. elegans* is killed (with a laser through the microscope), no other cells take its place; the animal must do without that cell.

The Axons and Dendrites of Young Neurons Grow Extensively and Form Synapses

The biggest changes in brain cells early in life take place in the branches and connections among neurons. There are huge increases in the length of dendrites, which seem to involve processes akin to those involved in the growth of axons. Collectively these processes are known as **synaptogenesis**. At the tips of both axons and dendrites are **growth cones**, swollen ends from which extensions emerge (Figure 7.12*a*). The very fine outgrowths, called **filopodia** (singular filopodium), are spikelike, while the sheetlike extensions are called **lamellipodia** (singular lamellipodium). Both the filopodia and lamellipodia seem to adhere to the extracellular environment, and then contract to pull the growth cone (leaving the growing axon or dendrite behind it) in a particular direction. The fact that dendrite growth cones have been found in adult animals suggests that dendrites continue to elongate and change throughout life in response to functional demands.

What guides axons along the paths they take? A long-standing notion is that axons are guided by chemicals released or secreted by the target nerve cells or other tissues, such as muscles (C. S. Goodman, 1996; Tessier-Lavigne and Placzek, 1991). The axon growth cone responds to the concentration gradient of this chemical that provides directional guidance. This view, formally labeled the *chemotropic guidance of axons,* is illustrated in Figure 7.12*b* and *c,* which show the ability of a chemical to act as an attractant for growing sensory neurons. A large body of work examining the way in which axons from the eye regenerate and find their original brain targets in amphibians also implicates chemotropic guidance of axons. Other chemical signals seem to guide axons by repelling the growth cones of some cells but not others (Keynes and Cook, 1992). Dendritic growth is also affected by both intrinsic factors and cell–cell interactions, especially the approach of axons from other cells (T. H. Brown et al., 1992).

The molecular biology of axonal and dendritic growth has been studied in detail, and many different substances have been implicated in this process. Early in development the growing axon and dendrite contain different proteins, suggesting that the nerve cell acquires a basic polarity—the axonal end and the dendritic end—at the earliest stages of development. How the cell body directs the appropriate molecules to each end is an area of intensive study.

Synapses form at an increasingly rapid rate, particularly on dendrites (Figure 7.13). In many nerve cells, synapses form at dendritic spines. The spines themselves proliferate rapidly after birth. These connections can be affected by postnatal experience, as we will see in Chapter 18. To support the metabolic needs of the expanded dendritic tree, the nerve cell body greatly increases in volume.

Why is a synapse created at any single site on a neuron or other targets such as muscle? Undoubtedly some type of chemical recognition bonds a presynaptic ending to a particular postsynaptic site; the molecular features of this recognition mechanism are slowly unfolding.

The Death of Many Neurons Is a Normal Part of Development

As strange as it may seem, **neuronal cell death** is a crucial phase of brain development, especially during embryonic stages. This developmental stage is not unique to the nervous system. Naturally occurring cell death, also called **apoptosis** (from the Greek *apo*, "away from," and *ptosis*, "act of falling"), is evident as a kind of sculpturing process in the emergence of other tissues in both animals and plants (Oppenheim, 1991). In the nervous system, however, the number of cells that die during early development is quite large. In some regions of the brain and spinal cord, most of the nerve cells die during prenatal development. Figure 7.14 illustrates the magnitude of this developmental phenomenon. The proportion of nerve cells that die varies from region to region and ranges from 20 to 80% of the cells. Naturally occurring neuronal cell death was first described by Viktor Hamburger (1958) in chicks, in which about half the originally produced spinal motoneurons die before the chicks hatch.

Viktor Hamburger

7.12 Growth Cones Form at the Tip of Growing Axons and Dendrites

(*a*) The fine, threadlike extensions shown here are filopodia, which find adhesive surfaces and pull the growth cone, and therefore the growing axon, to the right. (*b*) Target cells release a chemical that creates a gradient (dots) around them. Growth cones orient to and follow the gradient to the cells. (*c*) The extensions visible here are growing out of a sensory ganglion (left) toward their normal target tissue. (Part *a* courtesy of Paul Bridgman; *b* after Tessier-Lavigne et al., 1988; *b* and *c* courtesy of Marc Tessier-Lavigne.)

Several factors influence this massive cell death in the nervous system. The extent of cell death is regulated in part by factors associated with the synaptic targets of cells. Reduction of the size of the synaptic target invariably reduces the number of surviving

(*a*)

(*b*)

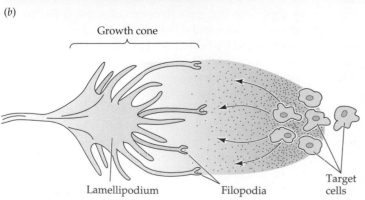

Growth cone

Lamellipodium   Filopodia   Target cells

(*c*)

(a) Rat visual cortex

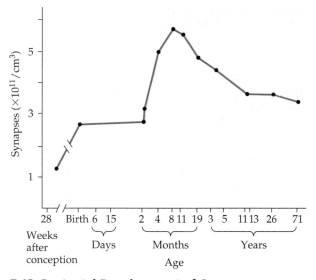

(b) Human visual cortex

7.13 Postnatal Development of Synapses
The rate of synapse development in rat visual cortex (a) and human visual cortex (b). In humans, note the decline in the density of synapses after the first year of life. (Part a after Blue and Parnavelas, 1983; b from Huttenlocher et al., 1982.)

that a fatal defect is not the cause of their normal death. In fact, evidence suggests that all cells carry **death genes**—genes that are expressed only when a cell "decides" to die (Johnson and Deckwerth, 1993; Peter et al., 1997; L. M. Schwartz, 1992). The genes seem to encode for enzymes that cut up DNA and proteins, presumably so that the constituents can be recycled.

Afferents (axons that provide synaptic input to a neuron) exert some influence on neuron death during development. Reducing afferent input significantly increases neuronal death in various nervous system regions (Oppenheim, 1991). Some of this effect may be mediated by the afferents that are exciting the neurons—perhaps active neurons are more likely to survive. Sometimes hormones in general circulation affect cell death. Nerve cell death in moth nervous systems is triggered by the same hormones that produce the transformation from caterpillar to moth (Truman, 1983; Weeks and Levine, 1990). The Mauthner cell (a specialized cell in the medulla) of

(a) Chick spinal motoneurons

(b) Human spinal motoneurons

7.14 Many Neurons Die during Normal Early Development
The pattern of neuronal cell death in spinal motoneurons of chicks (a) and humans (b). Many neuronal populations show a similar pattern of apoptosis. (Part a from Hamburger, 1975; b from Forger and Breedlove, 1987.)

nerve cells. For example, if the leg of a tadpole is removed early in development, many more developing spinal motoneurons die than if the leg had remained in position. Conversely, grafting on an extra leg—a technique that is possible with chicken embryos and tadpoles—appreciably reduces the usual loss of cells; in this instance, the mature spinal cord has more than the usual number of neurons.

These observations suggest that the target of a developing population of nerve cells influences the survival of these neurons and that the neurons are *competing* for something in order to survive. These results also suggest that some of the cells that would have died in the absence of the extra leg are capable of performing the job of motoneurons, so we can conclude some amphibians changes as a result of the secretion of thyroid hormones. The cell degenerates as the animal's lifestyle changes from aquatic to terrestrial. In Chapter 12 we will note the importance of certain sex hormones in controlling cell death in the spinal cord of mammals. But the most important factor regulating neuronal cell death seems to be competition among neurons.

According to one view, neurons compete for connections to target structures (other nerve cells or end organs, such as muscle). Cells that make adequate synapses remain; those without a place to form synaptic connections die.

Competing hypotheses

Another view is that the cells compete not just for synaptic sites, but for a chemical that the target structure makes and releases. Neurons that receive enough of the chemical survive; those that do not, die.

Such target-derived chemicals are called **neurotrophic factors** (or simply trophic factors) because they act as if they "feed" the neurons to help them survive (in Greek, *trophe* means "nourishment"). The neurotrophic factor that was the first to be identified keeps developing sympathetic neurons alive, as we'll discuss next. It is widely assumed that there are many neurotrophic factors, each specifically maintaining a particular population of neurons during a period of neuronal cell death.

Neurotrophic Factors Allow Neurons to Survive and Grow

More than 30 years ago, investigators discovered a substance—called **nerve growth factor** (**NGF**)—that markedly affects the growth of neurons in spinal ganglia and in the ganglia of the sympathetic nervous system (Bothwell, 1995; Levi-Montalcini, 1982). If NGF was administered to a chick embryo, it caused the formation of sympathetic ganglia with many more cells than usual. These cells were also larger and had many extensive processes (Figure 7.15).

The discovery of NGF earned Rita Levi-Montalcini and Stanley Cohen the Nobel prize in physiology or medicine in 1986. Originally, NGF was found in a variety of unusual places, including the salivary glands of mice, certain skin tumors, and the venom of a snake. Later, precise biochemical techniques revealed that NGF is normally produced by various target organs during development. NGF is taken up by the axons of sympathetic neurons innervating the organs and transported back to the cell body, and it prevents some of the sympathetic neurons from dying. The amount of NGF produced by targets during development is roughly correlated with the amount of sympathetic innervation the targets receive in adulthood. This relationship suggests that differing degrees of cell death, controlled by ac-

Rita Levi-Montalcini

7.15 Effects of Nerve Growth Factor
If NGF is added to the solution bathing a spinal ganglion grown in isolation outside the body (in vitro), neuronal processes grow out in an exuberant, radiating fashion. (From Levi-Montalcini, 1963.)

cess to NGF, match the sympathetic innervation to each target. NGF was the first neurotrophic factor to be identified.

Part of the interest in NGF arose from the possibility that there were more neurotrophic factors, each one affecting the survival of a particular cell type during a specific developmental period. After the discovery of NGF, investigators began searching for other neurotrophic factors. One such factor, purified from the brains of many animals, was named **brain-derived neurotrophic factor** (**BDNF**). The gene for BDNF turned out to be very similar to the gene for NGF. Investigators used molecular techniques to search for other NGF-related molecules and found several more.

The family of NGF-like molecules was named the neurotrophin family. The two most recently described members are called neurotrophin-3 and -4 (numbers 1 and 2 were reserved for NGF and BDNF, respectively). Neurotrophic factors that are unrelated to NGF also have been found, including ciliary neurotrophic factor (named after its ability to keep neurons from ciliary ganglia alive in vitro). The exact role of these various factors (and other neurotrophic factors yet to be discovered) in keeping neurons alive is under intense scientific scrutiny (Lewin and Barde, 1996).

Synaptic Connections Are Refined by Synapse Rearrangement

Just as not all the neurons produced by the developing individual are kept into adulthood, so too some of the synapses formed early in development are later retracted. Originally this process was described as synapse elimination, but later studies found that although some original synapses are lost, new synapses are also formed. Thus a more accurate term is **synapse**

rearrangement or synaptic remodeling. In most cases synapse rearrangement takes place after the period of cell death, so the two processes are not directly related.

For example, as we learned already, about half of the spinal motoneurons that form die later (see Figure 7.14). By the end of the cell death period, each surviving motoneuron innervates many muscle fibers, and every muscle fiber is innervated by several motoneurons. But later the surviving motoneurons retract many of their axon collaterals, until each muscle fiber comes to be innervated by only one motoneuron. Then each motoneuron enlarges the remaining synapse.

Similar events have been documented in several neural regions, including the cerebellum (Mariani and Changeux, 1981), the brain stem (Jackson and Parks, 1982), the visual cortex (Hubel et al., 1977), and several autonomic ganglia (Lichtman and Purves, 1980). Each ganglion cell originally receives a few synapses from each of several axons. Then some synapses are retracted while others form, until each ganglion cell receives many synapses from only a single source.

There is a large net loss of synapses in the cerebral cortex of developing monkeys (Rakic et al., 1986). After reaching a peak about 3 months after birth, by 3 years of age the number of synapses declines to approximately two-thirds of the maximal number. The magnitude of synapse loss seems the same throughout the four cerebral lobes. Whether there is a net loss of synapses in human cerebral cortex during development has not been addressed. What determines which synapses are kept and which are lost? Although we don't know all the factors, one important influence is neural activity (see Box 7.2 for an example).

Later in this chapter we'll see cases in which active synapses are maintained and inactive synapses are retracted in the mammalian visual system. Perhaps electrical activity increases the ability of a neuron to take up neurotrophic factors. In Chapter 8 we'll review evidence that synapse rearrangement in the cerebral cortex can continue throughout life. The studies we will describe show that active use of a particular finger leads to an expansion of the cerebral cortical regions responding to that finger. This expansion could be due to the retraction of some synapses and the formation of others.

Glial Cells Are Produced throughout Life

As already noted, glial cells develop from the same populations of immature cells as neurons. The factors that determine whether a cell differentiates into a neuron or a glial cell remain unknown. Unlike neurons, glial cells continue to be added to the nervous system throughout life. (Sometimes the process becomes aberrant, resulting in glial tumors, or gliomas, of the brain.) Glial cells continue to be produced for a longer period than neurons are produced, and glial cell production peaks later in the developmental process. In fact, the most intense phase of glial cell proliferation in many animals occurs after birth, when glial cells are added from immature cells located in the ventricular zones.

Glial Cells Myelinate Axons Mostly after Birth

The development of sheaths around axons—the process of myelination (Figure 7.16)—greatly changes the rate at which axons conduct messages (see Figure

7.16 Myelin Formation
The repeated wrapping of a Schwann cell cytoplasm around an axon results in a many-layered sheath that insulates the axon electrically, speeding the conduction of electrical signals along its length.

Schwann cell

Axon

Nucleus

BOX 7.2   *The Frog Retinotectal System Demonstrates Intrinsic and Extrinsic Factors in Neural Development*

*I*n the 1940s, Roger Sperry began a series of experiments that seemed to emphasize the importance of intrinsic factors, such as genes, for determining the pattern of connections in the brain. If the optic nerve that connects an eye to the brain is cut in an adult mammal, the animal is blinded in that eye and never recovers. In fish and amphibians such as frogs, however, the animal is only temporarily blinded; in a few months the axons from the eye (specifically, from the so-called ganglion cells of the retina) reinnervate the brain (specifically the dorsal portion of the midbrain, called the tectum) and the animal recovers its eyesight. When food is presented on the left or right, above or below, the animal flicks its tongue accurately to retrieve it. Thus, either (1) the retina reestablishes the same pattern of connections to the tectum that was there before surgery and the brain interprets visual information as before, or (2) the retina reinnervates the tectum at random, but the brain learns how to interpret the information presented in this new pattern.

Several lines of evidence have established that the first hypothesis is correct. One such piece of evidence is that the first-arriving retinal axons sometimes pass over uninnervated tectum to reach their original position. In the classic

(A) Two possible mechanisms of chemoaffinity

case illustrating this phenomenon, the optic nerve was cut and the eye was rotated 180°; when the animal recovered eyesight, it behaved as if the visual image had been rotated 180°: It moved to the left when trying to get food presented on the right, and it flicked its tongue up when food was presented below. The only explanation for this behavior is that the retinal axons had grown back to their original positions on the tectum, ignoring the rotation of the eye. Furthermore, once the

original connections were reestablished, the brain interpreted the information as if the eye were in its original position. Even years later, the animals had not learned to make sense of information from the rotated eye.

Sperry proposed the **chemoaffinity hypothesis** to explain how retinal axons know which part of the tectum to innervate. Suppose each retinal cell and each tectal cell has a specific chemical identity—an address of sorts. Then each retinal cell need only

---

3.8). Myelination has a strong impact on behavior, since it profoundly affects the velocity of the nerve impulse and thereby affects the temporal order of events in the nervous system. Disorders that disrupt myelin in adulthood (such as multiple sclerosis) have devastating effects.

In humans, the earliest myelination in the peripheral nervous system is evident in cranial and spinal nerves about 24 weeks after conception. But the most intense phase of myelination occurs shortly after birth. Furthermore, some investigators believe that myelin can be added to axons throughout life. The first nerve tracts in the human nervous system to become myelinated are in the spinal cord. Myelination then spreads successively into the hindbrain, midbrain, and forebrain. Within the cerebral cortex, sensory zones are

myelinated before motor zones; correspondingly, sensory functions mature before motor functions.

Growth and Development of the Brain Reflect the Interaction of Intrinsic and Extrinsic Factors

Many factors influence the emergence of the form, arrangements, and connections of the developing brain. One influence is genes, which direct the production of every protein the cell can make. In the nematode *C. elegans*, genes are almost the only factors affecting development; the cells somehow keep track of their mitotic lineage and then simply express the genes that are appropriate for the cell fate that their lineage directs. Genes are a major influence on all development, including that seek out the proper address in the tectum and the entire pattern will be reestablished; many chemical cues (represented by many colors in Figure A, *left*) or only a few (two colors in Figure A, *right*) may be involved.

Several preparations indicated that there are limits to how accurately retinal cells can find their original target, but there is one dramatic demonstration: When retinal cells are placed in culture dishes, their axons grow and show preferences. The axons of ganglion cells from lateral retina prefer to grow over cell membranes from rostral tectum (their normal target) rather than over cell membranes from caudal tectum (Bonhoeffer and Huf, 1985). Axons from medial retina, however, show no preference. Thus evidence suggests that chemical cues direct the retinal axons to the roughly appropriate region of tectum.

The most recent evidence indicates that, having arrived at the roughly appropriate region of tectum, retinal connections are fine-tuned by extrinsic factors, specifically by experience. Normally each retina innervates only the tectum on the opposite side. When implantation of a third eye forces two retinas to innervate a single tectum (Figure B, *top*), they each do so in the same rough pattern, but they segregate; axons from one retina predominate in one area and axons from the other

(B) A three-eyed frog has two eyes innervating the left tectum

retina predominate in neighboring tectum, so there are alternating stripes of innervation from the two eyes (Figure B, *bottom*).

This segregation depends on activity (Constantine-Paton et al., 1990). If neural activity in one eye is silenced (by injection of drugs), it loses its connections to the tectum and the other eye takes over, innervating the entire tectum. If both eyes are silenced (by the animal's being kept in the dark), neither eye predominates, their axons fail to segregate in the tectum,

and the detailed pattern of innervation fails to appear. Thus, the retinotectal system appears to reestablish the original pattern of innervation in two steps: (1) Chemical cues bring retinal axons to the approximately correct region of tectum. (2) The neural activity of the retinal cells, normally driven by patterned visual stimulation, directs these axons to innervate or maintain innervation of the precise tectal region. (Figure B courtesy of Martha Constantine-Paton.)

---

of the vertebrate brain. An animal that has inherited an altered gene will make an altered protein, which will affect any cell structure that includes that protein. Thus, every neuronal structure, and therefore every behavior, can be altered by changes in the appropriate gene(s). It is useful to think of genes as *intrinsic* factors—that is, factors that originate within the developing cell itself. All other influences we can consider *extrinsic*—that is, originating outside of the developing cell.

Genes and behavior

What are the extrinsic factors? For mammals, which depend on nutrients supplied from the mother during development, an important extrinsic factor is whether the fetus is provided with the nutrients needed to carry out the genetic instructions. As we'll see, the lack of nutrients or the presence of chemicals that interfere with

the delivery of nutrients can have a profound effect on brain development.

Another important class of extrinsic factors for all vertebrates is cell–cell interactions: Whether a cell expresses a particular gene, takes a particular shape, or performs a particular task may depend on whether neighboring cells exert an inductive influence. The recognition that cell–cell interactions are very important for brain development led to the discovery of another extrinsic factor—neural activity.

As we'll see, sometimes the electrical activity of a neuron can affect the fate of other cells (whether they live or die) and can determine whether or not synapses are maintained. Finally, the ability of neural activity to direct brain development identifies another influence—experience.

TABLE 7.1 *Intrinsic and Extrinsic Factors That Affect Neural Development*

Factors	Examples of effects
Intrinsic factors (genes)	
Chromosomal aberrations	Down syndrome, fragile X syndrome
Single-gene effects	Phenylketonuria, various *Drosophila* mutants, Tay-Sachs disease
Extrinsic factors	
Nutrients	Malnutrition
Drugs, toxins	Fetal alcohol syndrome
Cell–cell interactions	
Induction directs differentiation	Motoneuron differentiation induced by notochord
Trophic factors direct cell death or synapse loss	Developing sympathetic neurons spared by NGF from death
Neural activity affects synapse maintenance and loss	
Non-sensory-driven	Eye segregation in layer 4 cortex before birth
Sensory-driven (experience)	Ocular dominance outside layer 4 after birth
Birth process in mammals	Hypoxia-induced mental retardation

First, the developing organism's own behavior generates sensory experience. Furthermore, events in the environment (sounds, lights, odors, and so on) also affect the activity of sensory neurons; in several cases the activity of the sensory neurons determines which synapses are maintained and which are lost. In this way experience can alter the connections of the developing brain, thereby affecting an individual's behavior in adulthood. Table 7.1 lists these intrinsic and extrinsic factors and some of the examples we'll use to illustrate each.

Genes Are the Intrinsic Factors That Influence Brain Development

Psychologists have shown the importance of genetic factors in a variety of behaviors in many species, including humans (Rende and Plomin, 1995). Of course, genes do not work in isolation. Development should be viewed as the interaction of genetic instructions with the other, extrinsic influences we mentioned in the previous section.

Identical genes, different nervous systems. One breeding technique produces genetically identical animals, called **clones**, which used to be known mainly in science fiction and horror films. But life imitates fiction. While the sheep Dolly was the first successfully cloned mammal, she was not the first animal to be cloned. Using grasshopper clones, C. Goodman (1979) compared the uniformity and variability in the growth and development of different neurons. Although the basic shape of larger cells showed considerable uni-

Genes and behavior

formity, many neurons of cloned grasshoppers showed differences in neural connections between these genetically identical individuals.

Similar results were derived from a tiny crustacean, the daphnia, well known to aquarium owners (Macagno et al., 1973). Female daphnia can reproduce without fertilization by males, and lines of genetically identical female offspring are the result. The daphnia eye contains exactly 176 sensory neurons, which make synaptic contacts with exactly 110 neurons of the optic ganglion. Furthermore, a particular sensory neuron makes contact with only a few specific neurons in the ganglion. But the exact number of synapses established between a particular sensory neuron and a specific neuron in the ganglion can vary by more than threefold between individual daphnia clones. Even between the right and left sides of the eye of an individual, where there are symmetrically placed "twin" neurons, one twin neuron may form more synapses than the other. Thus, both within and between individual daphnia, neurons encoded by the same genes differ in the number of their synaptic connections. Presumably, the variations are due to variation in extrinsic factors.

Among vertebrates, identical neurons for comparing synaptic connections among twins are harder to find. But some fish have identifiable neurons—Mauthner cells—and some of these fish reproduce as daphnia do; that is, females produce daughters that are genetically identical to each other and to their mother. Each fish has a single giant Mauthner cell on each side of the brain. Although the pattern of dendritic branching of the Mauthner cells is similar from individual to individual among clones, there are individual differences in the detail of branching and of synapses. Thus, the finding in daphnia can be extended at least to the Mauthner cells in the fish brain (Levinthal et al., 1976).

No direct observations of this sort have been made for humans, but identical human twins often differ in size at birth, and presumably their brains differ at least as much as do those of inbred mice. Some indirect evidence indicates that for human identical twins the branching pattern of nerve endings in the skin must differ. For example, even identical twins show some differences in their fingerprints, although their prints are more similar than are those of fraternal twins. Further differences between the nervous systems of identical twins may be caused by responses to differential experiences, as we will see in Chapters 17 and 18 when we consider the effects of experience and learning on the anatomy of the nervous system. Indeed, in several places in this book we'll find that human identical twins do not always share such traits as schizophrenia (see Figure 1.11), sexual orientation, or depression, and these differences between twins cannot be attributed to the genome.

Now we can consider several terms that aid the discussion of intrinsic and extrinsic factors. The sum of all the intrinsic, genetic information an individual has is its **genotype** or **genome**. The sum of all the physical characteristics that make up an individual is its **phenotype**. Your genotype was determined at the moment of fertilization and remains the same throughout your life. But your phenotype changes constantly, as you grow up and grow old and even, in a tiny way, with each breath. Phenotype is determined by the interaction of genotype and extrinsic factors, including experience. Thus twins that have identical genotypes do not have identical phenotypes, because they have not received identical extrinsic influences. Because their nervous system phenotypes are somewhat different, twins do not behave exactly the same. A related term, **congenital**, is often misunderstood to mean "inherited," but really it refers to a character that is "present at birth," whether inherited or not.

Effects of mutations.   Sometimes a rare animal inherits a sudden change in genetic structure, a **muta-**

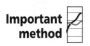

Important method **tion**, that is related to marked anatomical or physiological change. Researchers can increase the frequency of mutations by exposing animals to chemicals or radiation that produce changes in genes.

Mutants—animals that display these changes—are interesting to study because their changed genetic characteristics may be quite specific and striking. For example, Greenspan et al. (1980) described mutants of the fruit fly *Drosophila* that seemed normal in every way except that they had memory problems. These mutants—affectionately labeled *dunce, amnesiac,* and

turnip—either failed to learn or could learn but forgot rapidly. Biochemical deficits in these mutants (due to mutations that render specific genes and therefore specific proteins ineffective) may account for the failures of memory (Dudai, 1988). The strength of research on *Drosophila* mutants derives from the wealth of specific mutations, each one involving a distinct defect in part of the fly's nervous system (Hall and Greenspan, 1979). For example, a lethal *Drosophila* mutant, *Notch,* has an enlarged nervous system because too many precursor cells are produced.

Many mutations in mice affect the nervous system. In these animals special defects appear during development of the nervous system. Some mice fail to produce particular brain regions. Others show specific anatomical derangements, such as a failure to myelinate or to arrange cells in their characteristic alignments. Mutants of one group that is especially intriguing to researchers all have single-gene mutations that affect the postnatal development of the cerebellum. The names of these mutant animals—*reeler, staggerer,* and *weaver*—reflect the locomotor impairment that characterizes them. Figure 7.17 illustrates the impact of these mutations on the size and arrangement of the cerebellum.

The cerebellum of *reeler* (see Figure 7.17c) shows an abnormal positioning of cells. There are no characteristic layers in the cerebellum, hippocampus, or cerebral cortex. Strangely, although cells of these regions are in abnormal positions, many connections among these cells are appropriate (Caviness, 1980). The cerebellum of *weaver* (see Figure 7.17b) has far fewer granule cells than a normal cerebellum (see Figure 7.17a), which arises from a failure of granule cells to migrate properly. The granule cells from *weaver* mice fail to make the CAM that would allow them to attach to and migrate along glial cells; therefore they fail to reach their appropriate levels and the cerebellum fails to develop the normal laminar (layered) organization. Today scientists sometimes deliberately delete or introduce a particular gene in mice in order to study the effect of that gene on the nervous system (Box 7.3).

Despite the importance of genes for nervous system development, understanding the genome alone could never enable an understanding of the developing brain, because, as we'll see next, experience also directs developing neurons.

Experience Is an Important Influence on Brain Development

The young of many species are born in a highly immature state, both anatomically and behaviorally. For example, in humans the weight of the brain at birth is only one-fourth of its adult weight. Infants of such species are totally dependent on their parents. In these species developments in brain and in behavior seem to vary together. The successes and failures of early

(a) Normal   (b) *weaver*   (c) *reeler*

7.17 Cerebellar Mutants among Mice
(a) The cerebellum in a normal mouse at three levels of magnification (×25, ×66, and ×250, from bottom to top). (b) Comparable views in the mutant *weaver*. Note the almost complete absence of granule cells, while the alignment of Purkinje cells (arrows) is normal. (c) Sections from the cerebellar mutant *reeler*. Marked derangement of the customary layering of cells is evident. Both mutants show overall shrinkage of the cerebellum. (From A. L. Leiman, unpublished observations.)

experience can affect the growth and development of brain circuits.

Varying an individual's experience during early development has been found to alter many aspects of behavior, brain anatomy, and brain chemistry (E. L. Bennett et al., 1964; Gottlieb, 1976; Rosenzweig and Bennett, 1977, 1978). The altered behavior itself indicates that the early experience affected brain development. Some experimental treatments—for example, the early administration of sex hormones—can determine whether the organism develops into the male or the female body type (see Chapter 12). Can experience have an equally striking role?

Neural plasticity

In one classic experiment, male mallard ducklings were raised for their first 8 to 10 weeks with other duck species. As mature drakes, they were given the choice of mating with mallard ducks or with ducks of the species with which they had been raised. Whereas all mallards reared with mallards choose mallards as mates, about two-thirds of the experimental animals chose the other species (Schutz, 1965). The animals seem to have imprinted on their foster parents as the appropriate type of sexual target. Normally such sexual imprinting would result in a sexual partner of the same species.

The effects of experience on development can be negative or positive. For instance, prenatal exposure to certain sounds can hasten hatching time in quail embryos (Gottlieb, 1976). Early recognition of species and of parental vocalizations depends on the embryo's being exposed to specific kinds of auditory stimulation before the chick hatches (W. G. Hall and Oppenheim, 1987).

Visual Deprivation Can Lead to Blindness

The role of experience in guiding neural development is best understood in the visual system. Some people do not see forms clearly with one eye, even though the eye is intact and a sharp image is focused on the retina. Such impairments of vision are known as **amblyopia** (from the Greek *amblys*, "dull, blunt," and *ops*, "eye"). Some people with this disorder have a "lazy eye," one that is turned inward (cross-eyed) or outward. Children born with such a misalignment see a double image rather than a single fused image. If the deviated eye is not surgically realigned early in childhood, vision becomes impaired. By the time an untreated person reaches the age of 7 or 8, pattern vision in the deviated eye is almost completely suppressed. Realignment of the eyes in adulthood does not restore acute vision to the turned eye.

The inability in these cases to correct the problem in adulthood is quite striking, since throughout the person's development light enters this eye in a normal manner and the nerve cells of the eye continue to be excited. Similar misalignment of the eyes, when it appears for the first time in adulthood, produces double vision, a condition that shows no change with further aging. These clinical observations of humans suggest

BOX 7.3   *Transgenic and Knockout Mice*

*I*n the text we have discussed several instances in which animals with mutations in specific genes can offer clues about the role of genes in development and brain function. Until recently the only types of mutants one could study were the very rare cases of spontaneous mutations or mutations caused by animals being treated with radiation or chemicals to increase the rate of mutation. Unless very small, short-lived animals like *Drosophila* were the subject of the research, this process was tedious because very few of the induced mutations would be in the gene of interest.

Among the many new tools brought to us by the revolution in molecular biology is *site-directed mutagenesis*—the ability to cause a mutation in a particular gene. Researchers using this technique must know the sequence of nucleotides in the gene of interest. Then they can use the tendency of complementary nucleotides to hybridize with that part of the gene to induce changes (see the Appendix for a refresher on hybridization). The easiest change to make is total disruption of the gene, making it nonfunctional. If you do this in special embryonic mouse cells, there are ways to introduce the manipulated gene into the testes or ovaries of a developing mouse. That mouse can then produce offspring that are missing one copy of the gene and, through inbreeding, grandchildren missing *both* copies of the gene. We call the resulting animal a **knockout mouse** because the gene of interest has been "knocked out."

By following the development of knockout mice, we can obtain clues about the role of particular genes in normal animals. For example, the motoneurons of brain-derived neurotrophic factor (BDNF) knockout mice survive despite the absence of BDNF (Sendtner et al., 1996), so we know that trophic factor is not crucial for motoneuron survival. On the other hand, some parasympathetic ganglia fail to form in BDNF knockout mice (Erickson et al., 1996), suggesting that these neurons depend on BDNF for survival. As we'll see in Chapter 18, several genes suspected of playing a role in learning have been knocked out in mice, and the resulting animals indeed show deficits in learning.

There are some problems in interpreting such results, because the missing gene may have contributed only very indirectly to the learning process, or the animal's poor performance may have been due to a distraction caused by the knockout. For that matter, even identical behavior by animals that do not possess the gene does not prove that the gene is unimportant for behavior. Perhaps the developing animal, in the absence of that gene, somehow has compensated for the loss and found a new way to solve the problem. This would be another example of the embryonic regulation that is so common in vertebrate development.

In other cases, a functional, manipulated copy of a gene can be introduced into the mouse. Such animals are called **transgenics** because a gene has been transferred into their genome. This approach is often used in order to understand genetic disorders. For example, in Chapter 11 we'll learn that when a human gene that causes severe motor impairments is transferred into mice, the mice develop very similar symptoms to those that appear in humans. It may be possible to study the disease more closely in these mice and test possible therapies. So far, knockout and transgenic animals have one limitation: They possess the genetic manipulation from the moment of conception and in every cell in the body. The next challenge for molecular neurobiologists will be to knock out or replace a gene in an animal after it has reached adulthood, or to replace or knock out the gene in only one region of the brain. Already some limited successes have been reported, and more are sure to come.

---

that unusual positioning of the eyes during early development changes neural connections in the brain. (However, the connections may change further even in adults if the weak eye is exercised sufficiently [Romero-Apis et al., 1982].) We'll discuss amblyopia in more detail in Chapter 10.

Understanding the cause of amblyopia in people has been greatly advanced by visual-deprivation experiments with animals. These experiments revealed startling changes related to disuse of the visual system during early critical periods. Depriving animals of light to both eyes (**binocular deprivation**) produces structural changes in visual cortical neurons: a loss of dendritic spines and a reduction in synaptic density. Cragg (1975) emphasized that these effects are most extensive during the early period of synaptic development in the visual cortex (Figure 7.18).

If deprivation is maintained for several weeks during development, when the animals' eyes open, they will be blind. Although light enters their eyes and the cells of the eyes send messages to the brain, the brain seems to ignore the messages, and the animals are unable to detect visual stimuli. If the deprivation lasts long enough, the animals are never able to recover eyesight. Thus, early visual experience is crucial for the proper development of vision. There appear to be **sensitive periods** during which these manipulations of experience can exert long-lasting effects on the system. After the sensitive period, the manipulations have little or no effect. The exact timing of the sensitive period depends on the manipulation exerted and the species examined.

Even subtle manipulations of visual experience have profound effects on the developing visual sys-

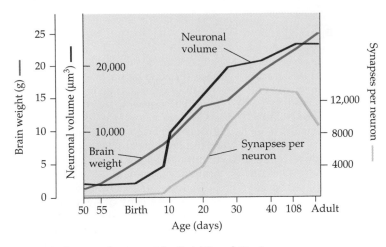

7.18 Brain Development in Cat Visual Cortex
Synaptic development is most intense from 8 to 37 days after birth, a period during which visual experience can have profound influence. Note that brain weight and cell volume rise in a parallel fashion and precede synaptic development. Note also the decline in synapse numbers after 108 days of age—evidence of synapse rearrangement. (After Cragg, 1975.)

tem. Pioneering work by Hubel and Wiesel, who shared the Nobel prize in physiology or medicine in 1981, showed that depriving only one eye of light (**monocular deprivation**) produces profound structural and functional changes in the thalamus and visual cortex. Monocular deprivation in an infant cat or monkey causes the deprived eye not to respond when the animal reaches adulthood.

Animal model

The effect of visual deprivation can be illustrated graphically by an **ocular dominance histogram**, which portrays the strength of response of a brain neuron to stimuli presented to either the left or the right eye. Normally, most cortical neurons (except those in layer IV; Figure 7.9) are excited equally by light presented to either eye (Figure 7.19a). Few neurons are activated solely by inputs to one eye. Monocular deprivation early in development results in a striking shift in this graph; most cortical neurons respond only to input from the nondeprived eye (Figure 7.19b). In cats the susceptible period for this effect is the first 4 months of life. In rhesus monkeys the sensitive period extends to age 6 months. After these ages visual deprivation has little effect.

The mechanisms proposed for this phenomenon bring us to a possible understanding of the forms of amblyopia we have described. During early development, synapses are rearranged in the visual cortex, and axons representing input from each eye "compete" for synaptic places. Active, used synapses become effective connections and predominate over inactive, disused synapses. Thus, if one eye is "silenced," synapses carrying information from that eye are retracted while synapses derived from the other eye are maintained. In Chapter 18 we will see that the

maintenance of active synapses and retraction of inactive synapses may also play a role in learning and memory.

Researchers offer a similar explanation for amblyopia produced by misalignment of the eyes. Hubel and Wiesel (1965) produced an animal replica of this human condition by cutting muscles on one side of the eye in young cats. The ocular dominance histogram of these animals reveals that the normal binocular sensitivity of visual cortical cells is greatly reduced (Figure 7.19c). A much larger proportion of visual cortical cells are excited by stimulation of either the right or the left eye than in control animals. This effect occurs because after surgery visual stimuli falling on the misaligned eyes no longer provide simultaneous, convergent input to the cells of the visual cortex.

The competitive interaction between the eyes results in a paradox: Brief deprivation of both eyes can have less of an effect on neuronal connections than an equal period of deprivation to only one eye (compare panels a, b, and d in Figure 7.19). Presumably the binocular deprivation keeps both eyes on an equal footing for driving cells into the visual cortex, so the predominantly binocular input to the cortical cells is retained.

Early Exposure to Visual Patterns Helps Fine-Tune Connections in the Visual System

At birth the visual cortex is quite immature, and most synapses have yet to form. Evidence cited in the previous sections shows that profound disuse results in changes in both structure and response of visual pathways. The modifiability of the developing brain is also evidenced when animals are exposed to certain visual patterns during early development.

Neural plasticity

Experiments in which visual patterns are manipulated early in an animal's life have used patterns such as horizontal or vertical lines (Blakemore, 1976), a field of such stripes seen through goggles (H. V. B. Hirsch and Spinelli, 1971), or small spots of light (Pettigrew and Freeman, 1973). In each case, experimenters try to ensure that the animals are exposed to visual stimuli of only one particular type. Then the animals' behavioral responses and/or their brain responses to the visual stimuli are recorded. The question is whether the animals can see stimuli they were exposed to during a sensitive developmental period better than they see novel stimuli. Although controversial (Movshon and van Sluyters, 1981), the results suggest that visual experiences during the critical early periods of life can modify the responses of nerve cells in the visual cortex. The effects are more subtle than those seen with complete deprivation, but the ability of animals to detect visual stimuli of a particular, general pattern (e.g.,

(*a*) **Normal**

(*b*) **Monocular deprivation**

(*c*) **One eye deviated**

(*d*) **Binocular deprivation**

7.19 Ocular Dominance Histograms
Cells in the visual cortex of adult cats that respond *only* to stimulation of the opposite eye are class 1 cells. Cells that respond *mainly* to stimulation of the opposite eye are class 2. Cells that respond equally to either eye are class 4. Cells responding only to stimulation of the eye on the same side are class 7, and so on. (*a*) Normal adult. (*b*) After monocular deprivation through the early critical period. (*c*) After early deviation of one eye—that is, squint. (*d*) After binocular deprivation. (After Hubel and Wiesel, 1965; Wiesel and Hubel, 1965.)

tion of BDNF causes the dendrites of neurons in visual cortex to shrink (McAllister et al., 1997), suggesting that this neurotrophic factor normally favors the retention of synapses. So perhaps presynaptic uptake of neurotrophic factors depends on synaptic activity, such that inactive synapses wither for lack of neurotrophic factor.

Experiences in Other Senses Also Affect Neural Development

Development of the brain also can be affected by early manipulation of nonvisual sensory inputs—a mouse's whiskers, for

horizontal lines versus vertical lines) depends on their exposure to such visual patterns during development. These experience-dependent effects are probably mediated by synapse rearrangement within the visual cortex. The sensitive period for these effects is roughly the same as for monocular deprivation.

One popular notion is that neurotrophic factors may be playing a role in experience-driven synapse rearrangement. For example, if the postsynaptic cells are making a limited supply of a neurotrophic factor, and if active synapses take up more of the factor than inactive synapses take up, then perhaps the inactive axons retract for lack of neurotrophic factor. If this were the case, then providing all the presynaptic axon terminals with excess neurotrophic factor might delay synapse rearrangement in response to manipulations of visual experience. Indeed, Cabelli et al. (1995) found that infusions of BDNF or neurotrophin-4 into kitten visual cortex inhibited the formation of ocular dominance columns. Neither NGF nor neurotrophin-3 had this effect. Conversely, interfering with the ac-

example. Thomas Woolsey and collaborators (T. A. Woolsey and Wann, 1976; T. A. Woolsey et al., 1981) found a unique clustering of nerve cells in a region of the cerebral cortex of the mouse that receives input from the whiskers. The arrangement of whiskers on the skin is distinctive. They are aligned similarly for all animals of the same species. The region of the cortex in which the whiskers are represented contain clusters of cells, called **whisker barrels** because the way they are arrayed makes them look like barrels squeezed together in the cortex. The layout of these cortical barrels corresponds to the map of the whiskers (Figure 7.20). If a whisker is cut a few days after birth, sensory information from that whisker is silenced (because the shortened whisker doesn't brush against anything) and its cortical barrel does not develop. Furthermore, the whisker barrels that represent adjacent, intact whiskers tend to be enlarged, as if expanding at the expense of their neighboring whisker (see Figure 7.20*c* and *d*). Thalamic neurons relaying this whisker

Neural plasticity

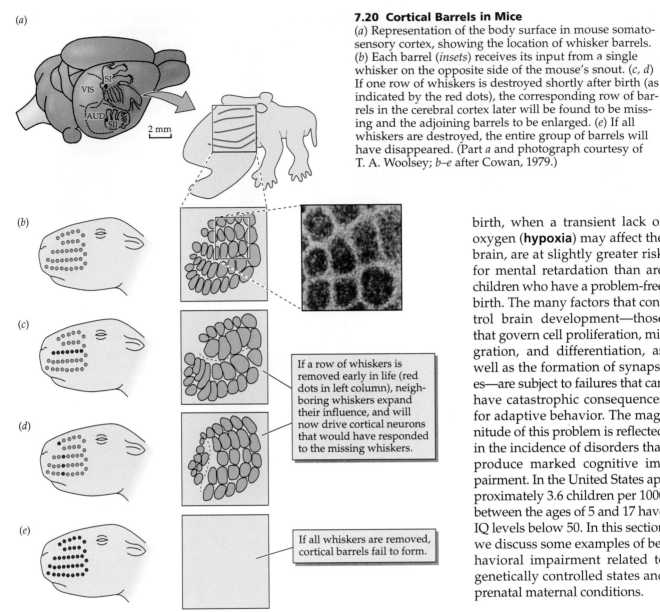

(a)

(b)

(c)

(d)

(e)

If a row of whiskers is removed early in life (red dots in left column), neighboring whiskers expand their influence, and will now drive cortical neurons that would have responded to the missing whiskers.

If all whiskers are removed, cortical barrels fail to form.

7.20 Cortical Barrels in Mice
(a) Representation of the body surface in mouse somatosensory cortex, showing the location of whisker barrels. (b) Each barrel (*insets*) receives its input from a single whisker on the opposite side of the mouse's snout. (c, d) If one row of whiskers is destroyed shortly after birth (as indicated by the red dots), the corresponding row of barrels in the cerebral cortex later will be found to be missing and the adjoining barrels to be enlarged. (e) If all whiskers are destroyed, the entire group of barrels will have disappeared. (Part *a* and photograph courtesy of T. A. Woolsey; *b–e* after Cowan, 1979.)

birth, when a transient lack of oxygen (**hypoxia**) may affect the brain, are at slightly greater risk for mental retardation than are children who have a problem-free birth. The many factors that control brain development—those that govern cell proliferation, migration, and differentiation, as well as the formation of synapses—are subject to failures that can have catastrophic consequences for adaptive behavior. The magnitude of this problem is reflected in the incidence of disorders that produce marked cognitive impairment. In the United States approximately 3.6 children per 1000 between the ages of 5 and 17 have IQ levels below 50. In this section we discuss some examples of behavioral impairment related to genetically controlled states and prenatal maternal conditions.

Some Genetic Disorders Have Widespread Effects on the Nervous System

Examples of genetically controlled states that cause developmental disorders focus on the actions of mutant genes and chromosomal abnormalities. Many metabolic disorders profoundly affect the developing brain, and some appear very early in life. In this category are 100 to 200 different disorders involving disturbances in the metabolism of proteins, carbohydrates, or lipids. Characteristically, the genetic defect is the absence of a particular enzyme that controls a critical biochemical step in the synthesis or breakdown of a vital body product. Enzymatic deficits can affect the brain in two ways: Either (1) certain compounds build up to toxic levels, or (2) compounds needed for function or structure fail to be synthesized.

An example of the first type of deficit is **phenylketonuria (PKU)**, a recessive hereditary disorder of protein metabolism that at one time resulted in many mentally retarded people. One out of 50 persons is a

information to the cortex are also being remodeled by the changes in experience (Zantua et al., 1996).

We have given only a few examples of the many experiments showing that sensory stimuli influence the development of the brain with respect to both structure and function (Katz and Shatz, 1996). The effects differ depending on variables such as age of the subject, duration of the experience, and type of stimulation.

Maldevelopment of the Human Brain Impairs Behavior

Because the processes that guide development of the human brain are so multiple, intricate, and complex, there are many ways in which they can go wrong. Children who experience complicated delivery at carrier; one in 10,000 births is an affected victim. The basic defect is the absence of an enzyme necessary to metabolize phenylalanine, an amino acid that is present in many foods. The brain damage caused by phenylketonuria is probably due to an enormous buildup of phenylalanine.

Genes and behavior

The discovery of PKU marked the first time that an inborn error of metabolism was associated with mental retardation. Nowadays there are screening methods, required by law throughout the United States and in many other countries, that assess the level of phenylalanine in children a few days after birth. Early detection is important because brain impairment can be prevented by a diet low in phenylalanine. Recent evidence suggests that such dietary control of phenylketonuria is critical during early years, especially before age 2, and that the diet can be relaxed during adulthood. However, behaviorally normal mothers with PKU have a high percentage of mentally retarded offspring. This result may be related to the mother's phenylalanine levels, but dietary treatment during pregnancy does not seem to reduce the fetal effects (Kolodny and Cable, 1982). The mechanism leading to mental retardation may thus be more complex than the original hypothesis of phenylalanine excess suggested (G. N. Thompson and Halliday, 1990).

New syndromes that probably involve inherited metabolic disorders are constantly being discovered. Recently, researchers have become interested in a disorder called **Williams syndrome**. Patients with this disorder have largely intact linguistic functioning, a large vocabulary, and very fluent speech. Yet they also show clear mental retardation on standard IQ tests: They have great difficulty in copying a pattern of blocks or assembling a picture from its parts (Lenhoff et al., 1997). MRI studies reveal a selective effect on brain development. Patients who suffer from Williams syndrome show reduced cerebral size, but normal cerebellar and subcortical structure (Jernigan et al., 1993). An autopsy of one such patient revealed increased cell packing and abnormally clustered and oriented neurons throughout the brain (Galaburda et al., 1994).

A common form of cognitive disorder resulting from a chromosomal abnormality is **Down syndrome**. The disorder associated with 95% of these cases is an extra chromosome 21 (for a total of three). This disorder is strikingly related to the age of the mother at the time of conception: For women over 45 years of age, the chance of having a baby with Down syndrome is nearly 1 in 40 (Karp, 1976). The behavioral dysfunctions are quite varied. Most individuals who have Down syndrome have a very low IQ, but some rare individuals attain an IQ of 80. Brain abnormalities in Down syndrome also vary.

Animal model Biopsies of the cerebral cortex of Down syndrome sufferers show abnormal formation of dendritic spines. A mouse model that involves an extra chromosome re-

sults in structural and behavioral changes that are analogous to Down syndrome in humans (C. J. Epstein, 1986). Investigation of this model is providing valuable insights into how the extra chromosome causes the structural and behavioral abnormalities associated with Down syndrome (Siarey et al., 1997).

Very likely, the most frequent cause of inherited mental retardation is the condition **fragile X syndrome**, which is produced by a fragile site on the X chromosome. At the end of the long arm of the X chromosome is a site that seems prone to breaking because the DNA there is unstable (Yu et al., 1991). Persons with this abnormality have a modified facial appearance, including elongation of the face, large prominent ears, and a prominent chin. A wide range of cognitive impairments—from mild to severe retardation— is associated with this syndrome (Baumgardner et al., 1994). The disorder is more common in males than in females.

The molecular basis of fragile X syndrome provided a surprise for geneticists because it demonstrated that we don't always pass on a faithful copy of our DNA to our offspring. The fragile site in the DNA consists of the same three nucleotides (CGG; see the Appendix for a review of nucleotides) repeated over and over. Most people have only 6 to 50 of these **trinucleotide repeats** at this site (Laxova, 1994). But during the production of sperm or eggs, the number of repeats sometimes changes, so a father who had only 50 trinucleotide repeats may provide 100 repeats to his daughter. People who have between 51 and 200 of the CGG repeats are themselves unaffected, but if their children receive more than 200 repeats, they will display fragile X syndrome. No one knows why the number of repeats changes from one generation to the next or what determines whether more or fewer repeats will appear (Paulson and Fischbeck, 1996). Trinucleotide repeats are also at the heart of another genetically based behavioral disorder—Huntington's disease (see Chapter 11).

Exposure to Drugs during Pregnancy Can Impair Neural Development

Even in the protected environment of the womb, the embryo and fetus are not immune to what is taking place in the mother's body. Maternal conditions such as viral infection, exposure to drugs, and malnutrition are especially likely to result in developmental disorders in the unborn child. Concern with the maternal environment as a determinant of brain development has spawned a new field: **behavioral teratology**. (Teratology—from the Greek *teras*, "monster"—is the study of malformations.) Investigators in this field are especially concerned with the pathological behavioral effects of drugs ingested during pregnancy.

Although researchers have only recently proven the potential of alcohol to affect fetal growth and development, there is a long history of concern about alcohol and pregnancy, dating back to classical Greek and Roman times. Aristotle warned that "foolish, drunken . . .

women . . . bring forth children like unto themselves, morose and languid" (cited in Abel, 1982). By now, the wisdom of this observation (if not the misogyny) is well supported by abundant research. About 40% of children born to alcoholic mothers show a distinctive profile of anatomical, physiological, and behavioral impairments known as **fetal alcohol syndrome** (**FAS**) (Abel, 1984; Colangelo and Jones, 1982).

Prominent anatomical effects of fetal exposure to alcohol include distinctive changes in facial features (e.g., a sunken nasal bridge, and altered shape of the nose and eyelids) and stunted growth. Few of these children catch up in the years following birth (Colangelo and Jones, 1982). The most common problem associated with FAS is mental retardation, which varies in severity. No alcohol threshold has yet been established for this syndrome, but it can occur with relatively moderate intake during pregnancy. In addition to mental retardation, children with fetal alcohol syndrome show other neurological abnormalities, such as hyperactivity, irritability, tremulousness, and other signs of motor instability (Figure 7.21). Even children of alcoholic mothers who do not show physical symptoms and are therefore not diagnosed as FAS often have neurophysiological impairments (Mattson et al., 1998).

Researchers have yet to establish whether these effects are mediated mainly by alcohol, by its toxic metabolites, or by the effects of alcohol on the metabolic health and nutrition of the mother. (Effects of malnutrition are discussed in Topic 7.1, Brain Development Requires Proper Nutrition). This syndrome

Special topic

may not be distinctive to alcohol; heavy use of marijuana seems to exert a similar effect on fetal growth and development (Hingson et al., 1982).

7.21 Abnormal Brain Development Associated with Fetal Alcohol Syndrome
A brain from an FAS infant (*left*) compared to a brain from a normal infant of the same age (*right*). The FAS brain shows microcephaly, fewer cerebral cortical gyri, and the presence of a sheet of ectopic (abnormally migrated) glia over the surface of the left hemisphere. (Courtesy of S. Clarren.)

The Brain Continues to Change As We Grow Older

The passage of time brings us an accumulation of joys and sorrows—perhaps riches and fame—and a progressive decline in many of our abilities. Although slower responses seem inevitable with aging, many of our cognitive abilities show little change during the adult years, until we reach an advanced age. What happens to brain structure from adolescence to the day when we all become a little forgetful and walk more hesitantly? Does the structure of the brain change continuously throughout the life span of any animal?

Changes in the structure of the brain with aging can be viewed at different levels, from subcellular structures to overall brain morphology. Brain weight declines with age, but some people have questioned the relevance of aging to these weight changes, since it is hard to distinguish changes due to aging from changes that arise from disease states shortly before death. An excellent study that eliminated such confounding factors (see Figure 7.1) showed that changes are very small up to the age of 45, after which time the weight of the brain begins to decline significantly. The course of these changes is the same for men and women, even though women generally live 7 to 10 years longer than men. Data also emphasize that aging is a variable state. Declines are evident in many people, and exaggerated in some. To some investigators this variability emphasizes the genetic contribution to aging and reinforces the idea that if you want to live long, choose parents and grandparents who have lived long.

Another measure used in studies of brain aging is the number of neural and glial cells in particular volumes of tissue. Investigators map specific regions and count the number of cells in various areas, using tissue taken from people who have died at different ages. These studies suggest that cell changes begin as early as the third decade of life and are specific to particular regions. Even more noticeable than the decrease in the number of cells is the loss of synaptic connections, which is especially prominent in the frontal cortical regions. However, growth cones can be found in the dendritic terminals of cortical cells of old people, suggesting that some forms of synaptic plasticity continue throughout life.

Memory Impairment Correlates with Hippocampal Shrinkage during Aging

In a recent study of healthy and cognitively normal people, aged 55 to 87, investigators asked whether mild impairment in memory is specifically related to reduction in size of the hippocampal formation (HF) or is better explained by generalized shrinkage of brain tissue (Golomb et al., 1994). (In Chapter 18 we'll see that the HF is implicated in memory formation.) Loss of HF tissue has been reported in cases of mild Alzheimer's disease and in elderly individuals who

7.22 Hippocampal Shrinkage Correlates with Memory Decline in Aging
(*Left*) Plane of MRI images illustrating the variables tested for correlation with memory decline in normal aged people. (*Right*) The hippocampal formation is shaded red, the supratemporal gyrus is orange, and the space between brain and skull is yellow-green. Only shrinkage of the hippocampal formation correlated with memory decline. (From Golomb et al., 1994.) (MRI courtesy of James Golomb.)

show cognitive impairment (Convit et al., 1993; de Leon et al., 1993; Killiany et al., 1993), but it is unclear to what extent atrophy of the HF can account for milder declines in memory that many neurologically healthy older people experience.

In one study, volunteers took a series of memory tests and were scored for both immediate recall and delayed recall. A series of ten coronal MRI images for each subject was measured for three variables (Figure 7.22): (1) volume of the HF; (2) volume of the supratemporal gyrus, a region that is close to the HF and is known to shrink with age but has not been implicated in memory; and (3) volume of the subarachnoid cerebrospinal fluid (that is, the fluid-filled space between the interior of the skull and the surface of the brain), which yields a measure of overall shrinkage of the brain. Immediate memory showed very little decline with age, but delayed memory did decline. When effects of sex, age, IQ, and overall brain atrophy were eliminated statistically, HF volume was the only brain measure that correlated significantly with the delayed memory score.

Of course, brain regions not included in this study also may correlate with memory, so other areas of the brain should be included in future measurements. In addition, the techniques of this experiment did not allow the researchers to measure small regions, such as the entorhinal cortex, that animal experiments show are also important for memory.

Two regions of the motor system show how different the effects of aging can be. In the motor cortex a type of large neuron—the Betz cell—starts to decline in number by about age 50, and by the time a person reaches age 80, many of these cells have shriveled away (Scheibel et al., 1977). In contrast, other cells involved in motor circuitry—for example, those in an area of the brain stem called the inferior olive—remain about the same in number through at least 8 decades of life.

PET scans of elderly people add a new perspective to aging-related changes. Studies of normal cases reveal that cerebral metabolism remains almost constant. This stability is in marked contrast to the decline of cerebral metabolism in Alzheimer's disease, which we will consider next.

Alzheimer's Disease Is Associated with a Decline in Cerebral Metabolism

Since 1900, the population of people over the age of 65 in the United States has increased dramatically. By the year 2000, at least 30 million Americans will be in this age group. Most people reaching this age lead happy, productive lives, although at a slower pace than they did in earlier years. In a growing number of elderly people, however, age has brought a particular agony—the disorder called **Alzheimer's disease**, named after the neurologist who first described a type of **dementia** (drastic failure of cognitive ability, including memory failure and loss of orientation) appearing before the age of 65. Alzheimer's disease is sometimes called senile dementia. Almost 2 million Americans suffer from Alzheimer's disease, and the progressive aging of our population means that these ranks will swell in the next 20 to 40 years. This disorder is found worldwide (with almost no geographic differences), and its frequency increases exponentially with aging (Rocca et al., 1991).

Alzheimer's disease is characterized by a progressive decline in intellectual functioning. It begins as a loss of memory of recent events. Eventually this memory impairment becomes all-encompassing, so extensive that Alzheimer's patients cannot maintain any form of conversation, because both the context and prior information are rapidly lost. They cannot answer simple questions such as, What year is it? Who is the president of the United States? or Where are you now? Cognitive decline is progressive and relentless. In time, patients become disoriented and easily lose themselves in familiar surroundings. Very commonly, this drastic loss of cognitive functioning is unaccompanied by any other readily apparent mark of debility, such as loss of motor coordination.

Observations of the whole brain of Alzheimer's patients reveal striking cortical atrophy, especially in frontal, temporal, and parietal areas. Studies on brain metabolism of these patients are especially revealing. PET scans following the administration of a radioactive form of glucose show marked reduction of metabolism in posterior parietal cortex and some portions of the temporal lobe (Figure 7.23). A substantial decline in

(a) Normal   *(b)* Alzheimer's

7.23 Alzheimer's Patients Show Reduced Activity in the Brain
When compared with normal elderly subjects (*a*), patients with Alzheimer's disease (*b*) show less widespread brain activation in PET scans. The dots in part *b* highlight regions where this difference is particularly apparent. (Courtesy of John Mazziotta.)

glucose utilization seems to precede the emergence of more severe cognitive impairments (Foster et al., 1984).

Microscopic studies of the brains of Alzheimer's patients reveal characteristic cellular changes. For example, the basal forebrain nuclei seem to disappear in Alzheimer's patients (Figure 7.24*a*). Some cells show abnormalities of neurofilaments called **neurofibrillary tangles**, which are abnormal whorls of filaments that form a tangled array in the cell. Studies of tissue also show strange patches of degenerating axon terminals and dendrites, termed **senile plaques** (Figure 7.23*b*). Contained within each plaque is a substance called **β-amyloid**, an unusual protein that arises from cleavage of a much larger protein (Selkoe, 1991). The number of senile plaques is directly related to the magnitude of cognitive impairment. Plaques of amyloid deposits are found in Alzheimer's patients in frontal and temporoparietal cortex, the hippocampus, and associated limbic system sites.

A gene called *ApoE* (for "apolipoprotein E") has been associated with Alzheimer's disease (Strittmatter and Roses, 1996). The most common forms of the gene are *ApoE2*, *ApoE3*, and *ApoE4*. Everyone has two copies of the gene, but people who have one or two copies of the *ApoE4* version are at much higher risk for Alzheimer's. How the different versions of the *ApoE* gene contribute to development of senile plaques or neurofibrillary tangles remains unknown.

Two Timescales Are Needed to Describe Brain Development

In the introduction to this second part of our book, we warned that Chapters 6 and 7 would present two very different timescales for the development of brain and behavior—the eons of evolution versus the days and years of ontogeny. These different timescales are analogous to the different but equally essential contributions of an architect and a contractor in building a house.

7.24 Alzheimer's Patients Show Structural Changes in the Brain
(*a*) Location of basal forebrain nuclei in the brain and distribution of their axons, which use acetylcholine as a neurotransmitter. These cells seem to disappear in Alzheimer's patients. (*b*) Neurofibrillary tangles (flame-shaped objects) and senile plaques (darkly stained clusters) in the cerebral cortex of an aged Alzheimer's patient. (From Roses, 1995; micrograph courtesy of Gary W. Van Hoesen.)

(a)

Cerebral cortex

Basal forebrain nuclei

Hippocampus

(b)

In preparing his plans, the architect calls on a long history of human knowledge about structures that meet basic human needs. These plans incorporate hard-won information gathered over the centuries. Similarly, our genes carry a basic plan that has worked for millions of generations. The contractor's perspective is more like that of a developing individual. He must use the general plans of the architect to construct a particular house here and now. As he builds, the contractor's judgment and interpretation are necessary, so two houses built from the same blueprints will not be identical, just as two monozygotic twins will show differences. In fact, even the best architects rely on contractors to adjust and improvise to make their plans work. Similarly, the information in our genome relies on extrinsic factors such as experience to determine the fine wiring of the nervous system. This analogy is extended in Topic 7.2, The Architect and the Contractor.

Genes and behavior

Neural plasticity

Special topic

Long ago, well before the common ancestor to all the vertebrates emerged, developing animals began relying on cell–cell interactions to adjust the fate of individual cells on the basis of their position in the organism as a whole. Once this strategy was adopted, it was only a matter of time before the fate of some neurons would be affected by neural activity. So neural activity began determining which synapses and neurons would be retained and which would be eliminated. Eventually, it would be the neural activity derived from sensory neurons—experience itself—that would affect these decisions. That is how we humans came to have a nervous system so malleable, so plastic, that we can write, read, and think about our own origins.

Summary

1. Early embryological events in the formation of the nervous system include a sequence of six cellular processes: (1) the production of nerve cells (neurogenesis); (2) the movement of cells away from regions of mitotic division (cell migration); (3) the acquisition, by these cells, of distinctive neuronal forms (cell differentiation); (4) the establishment of synaptic connections (synaptogenesis); (5) the selective loss of some cells (neuronal cell death); and (6) the selective rearrangement of previously formed synapses.

2. Fetal and postnatal changes in the brain include the myelination of axons by glial cells and the development of dendrites and synapses by neurons. Although in humans most neurons are present at birth, most synapses develop after birth and may continue developing into adulthood.

3. In simple animals such as the nematode *Caenorhabditis elegans*, neural pathways and synapses form according to an innate, genetic plan that specifies the precise relations between growing axons and particular target cells. In more complicated animals, however, including all vertebrates, genes do not exert such rigid control on specific neural connections.

4. Among the many determinants of brain development are (1) genetic information and (2) a multitude of extrinsic factors, such as neurotrophic factors, nutrition, and experience.

5. Experience affects the growth and development of the nervous system. Three possible explanations for this influence are that experience (1) induces and modulates the formation of synapses; (2) maintains synapses that are already formed; and (3) determines which neurons and synapses will survive and which will be eliminated.

6. Maldevelopment of the brain can occur as a result of genetically controlled disorders. Some are metabolic disorders, such as phenylketonuria; others, such as Down syndrome, are related to disorders of chromosomes.

7. Impairments of fetal development that lead to mental retardation can be caused by the use of drugs such as alcohol or marijuana during pregnancy.

8. The brain continues to change throughout life. Old age is accompanied by the loss of neurons and synaptic connections in some regions of the brain. In some people the changes are more severe than in others; pathological changes characterize the condition known as Alzheimer's disease.

Recommended Reading

Brown, M. C., Hopkins, W. G., and Keynes, R. J. (1991). *Essentials of neural development*. Cambridge, England: Cambridge University Press.

Cowan, W. M., Jessell, T. M., and Zipursky, S. L. (1997) *Molecular and cellular approaches to neural development*. New York: Oxford University Press.

Gilbert, S. F. (1997). *Developmental biology* (5th ed.). Sunderland, MA: Sinauer.

Jacobson, M. (1991). *Developmental neurobiology*. New York: Plenum.

Purves, D., and Lichtman, J. W. (1985). *Principles of neural development*. Sunderland, MA: Sinauer.

PART 3

Perception and Action

*L*ight from the sun warms our skin and stimulates our eyes. A chorus of sounds, ranging from the songs of insects to the hearty performances of opera singers stimulates our ears. Winds bend the hairs on the skin and carry substances that lead to a sense of pleasant or unpleasant odors. The food we eat affects receptors in the mouth, the stomach, and the brain. All about us a wide range of energies and substances excites our senses and supplies our brains with a vast array of information about many external and internal happenings. The success of any animal—including humans—in dealing with the tasks of survival depends on its ability to construct reliable representations of some of the physical characteristics of its environment. In most cases, however, sensory systems are not slavish, passive copiers and reflectors of impinging stimuli—quite the contrary. Evolutionary success calls for far more selective action. For any species, sensory systems construct only partial and selective portraits of the world.

Sensory inputs to the brain do not merely provide "pictures in the head"; they often incite the individual to act. Consider the simple case of a sound that occurs suddenly: Our eyes almost automatically turn toward the source of the sound. Some movements are not directly driven or triggered by sensory events but reflect intrinsic programs of action, which may involve sensory inputs only as modulators. How information is processed in both perceptual (addressed in Chapters 8 through 10) and motor (Chapter 11) systems is our theme in Part 3.

8 *General Principles of Sensory Processing, Touch, and Pain*

*A*ll around us are many different types of energy that affect us in various ways. Some molecules traveling through the air cause us to note particular odors. We detect waves of compression and expansion of air as sounds. Our abilities to detect, recognize, and appreciate these varied energies depend on the characteristics of sensory systems. These systems include receptors specialized to detect specific energies and the neural pathways of the spinal cord and the brain that receive input from these receptors. For each species, however, certain features of surrounding energies have become especially significant for adaptive success. For example, the bat darting through the evening sky is specially equipped to detect ultrasonic cries. Most humans, on the other hand, are hardly able to detect such sounds. Some snakes, such as boa constrictors, have infrared sensing organs that enable them to generate a heat-sensitive image of their surroundings, thus enabling them to locate potential prey. Each species has distinctive windows on the world based on the energy sensitivities of its receptors and on how its nervous system processes information from the receptors. In our discussion of the workings of sensory systems, we will first consider some of the basic principles of sensory processing and then examine how particular sensory systems work.

Gregory Thompson, *Expulsion from the Garden*, 1985

Sensory Processing

All Sensory Systems Follow the Same Basic Plan

The basic plan of all sensory systems begins at the sites where energies impinging on the body are converted into a form that activates nerve cells. All animals have specialized body parts that are particularly sensitive to some forms of energy. These body parts—**sensory receptor organs**—act as filters of the environment: They detect and respond to some stimuli but not others. Furthermore, receptors convert energy into the language of the nervous system—electrical signals.

In any animal, sensory information is processed by a system of codes. These codes are rules that translate attributes of a stimulus, such as intensity, into activity of nerve cells. Knowing these codes, the experimenter should be able to look at a pattern of nerve impulses and distinguish between a beautiful sunset and a tasty bit of food. Of course, we are only slowly gaining understanding of sensory coding, and up to now our knowledge has been restricted mainly to simple dimensions of stimuli, such as color and spatial location.

Sensory systems are complex because sensory-evoked neural activity involves many different brain regions. The way an event is represented varies in different brain regions, because each region does not merely passively reflect the barrage of neural inputs, but actively processes these inputs. This processing can be described as filtering, abstracting, and integrating, all of which affect the way in which events are represented in the brain.

It is useful to consider some ideal properties of sensory systems from both biological and engineering perspectives. These perspectives help us understand the characteristics of sensory systems, the evolutionary forces that have generated them, and the costs and benefits of various sensory mechanisms. The sections that follow describe some of the optimal features and some realistic compromises.

A Sensory System Requires Different Receptors to Discriminate among Forms of Energy

The types of energies and the range of substances in the world are quite broad. Different kinds of energy, such as light and sound, need different receptors to convert them into neural activity, just as taking a photograph requires a camera, not an audiotape recorder. We gain information by distinguishing among types of stimulus energy. We may appreciate the poet who writes, "The dawn came up like thunder," but most of the time we want to know whether a sudden dramatic sensory event was auditory or visual, a touch or a smell. Furthermore, different senses furnish us with quite different information: We may see a car hurtling toward us, hear the whine of a mosquito circling us, or smell gas escaping, but we might not hear the car until it is too late, and we would not smell the mosquito or see the gas. Thus, our model sensory system should provide us with the means of detecting and distinguishing among different forms of energy.

The pioneer physiologist Johannes Müller explored this requirement of sensory systems early in the nineteenth century. He proposed the doctrine of **specific nerve energies**, which states that the receptors and neural channels for the different senses are independent and operate in their own special ways. For example, no matter how the eye is stimulated—by light or mechanical pressure or by electrical shock—the resulting sensation is always visual. Müller formulated his hypothesis before the nature of nervous transmission was known. Today, we know that the messages for the different senses—such as seeing, hearing, touching, sensing pain, and sensing temperature are kept separate and distinct not by the use of different "nerve energies," but by the use of separate nerve tracts. It would be costly for each animal species to be sensitive to all the kinds of energy in its environment. Each species therefore has evolved the sensory detectors it needs to respond to certain forms of stimulation. Even the external appearance of receptor organs differs markedly among species (Figure 8.1).

A Sensory System Should Discriminate among Different Intensities of Stimulation

Many forms of energy have a broad range of intensities. For example, a sonic boom brings to the ear millions of times more energy than the tick of a watch, and sunlight at noon has 10 million times more energy than the wan light of the first quarter moon. The optimal visual sensory system would be able to represent stimulus values over these broad ranges so that the viewer could always discriminate accurately, neither groping in the dark nor being blinded by the glare of intense light. However, because sensitivity to very feeble stimuli may require highly specialized, and therefore costly, sensory detectors, we must settle for a realistic lower limit.

If the system is to respond to a wide range of intensities, it should be sensitive to differences in intensity; that is, it should be able to provide large responses for small changes in the strength of a stimulus. The absolute value of a stimulus is seldom of major adaptive significance. In most instances the important signal for survival is a change in the stimulus. We respond mainly to changes—whether they are changes in intensity, quality, or location of the stimulus.

A Sensory System Should Respond Reliably

In a reliable sensory system, the relation between any signal in the external or internal environment and the response of the sensory system to that signal is con-

8.1 Variety of Eyes
(*a*) The compound eyes of a tabanid fly are specially adapted for detecting motion. (*b*) The panther chameleon can move its eyes independently. (*c*) The eyes of the Philippine tarsier are specialized for nocturnal foraging. (*d*) The eyes of the American bald eagle are specialized for high acuity.

sistent. Imagine your confusion if a cold stimulus randomly elicited the responses cold, warm, painful, and slippery. To establish useful representations of the world, our sensory system must produce the same sensations for the same stimuli. A customary way to improve the reliability of a system is to increase the number of its components. Using several different circuits to process the same stimulus (parallel processing) is a conventional way to ensure reliability. The backup plans that ensure reliability in engineering designs generally provide such "fail-safe" options. Increasing the number of components in biological systems, however, comes at greater metabolic expense and may compromise speed.

A Sensory System Should Respond Rapidly

Optimal adjustment to the world requires that sensory information be processed rapidly. As a driver, you have to perceive the motion of other cars swiftly and correctly to avoid collisions. Similarly, it does not do a predator much good to recognize prey unless it can do so both rapidly and accurately. Thus, we have come up against a conflict between optimal properties: They must be able to respond both reliably and rapidly.

A Sensory System Should Suppress Extraneous Information

Have you ever tried to hold a conversation on a dance floor? Could you hear anything besides the overwhelming input of the music? This example illustrates a paradox. In describing the optimal sensory system, we have emphasized the need for exquisite sensitivity and reliability, but now we argue that this extraordinary system should also be able to ignore some of the world. From moment to moment, particular stimuli may be especially important, while other stimuli fade into insignificance. The fragrance of perfume may be quite compelling in an intimate situation, but it may go undetected when we are reading a road map. As we will see, different sensory devices suppress stimuli in different ways. Such devices include varying the response thresholds, adaptation, and different forms of direct and indirect controls.

How are the optimal properties that we have just discussed realized in the sensory systems of human beings and other species? What compromises has natural selection settled upon? Let's examine some basic features of all actual sensory systems.

TABLE 8.1   *Classification of Sensory Systems*

Type of sensory system	Modality	Adequate stimuli
Mechanical	Touch	Contact with or deformation of body surface
	Hearing	Sound vibrations in air or water
	Vestibular	Head movement and orientation
	Joint	Position and movement
	Muscle	Tension
Photic	Seeing	Visible radiant energy
Thermal	Cold	Decrement of skin temperature
	Warmth	Increment of skin temperature
Electrical	(No common name because humans do not have this sense)	Differences in density of electrical currents
Chemical	Smell	Odorous substances dissolved in air or water in the nasal cavity
	Taste	Substances in contact with the tongue or other taste receptor; in mammals the categories of taste experience are sweet, sour, salty, bitter
	Common chemical	Changes in CO_2, pH, osmotic pressure

Different Species Detect Different Aspects of the World with Similar Sensory Systems

From the physicist's point of view, the stimuli that animals detect are forms of physical energy or chemical substances that can be defined and described by measures of physics and chemistry. For example, a sound meter can be used to measure the intensity of an acoustic stimulus. But, as we have said, not all the forms of physical energy that the physicist or chemist can describe are necessarily potential stimuli for an animal. Some forms of energy, such as radio waves, cannot be detected by the sensory systems of any existing animal.

Table 8.1 classifies sensory systems, identifying the kinds of stimuli related to each system. An **adequate stimulus** is the type of stimulus for which a given sensory organ is particularly adapted. The adequate stimulus for the eye is photic (light) energy; although mechanical pressure on the eye or an electrical shock can stimulate the retina and produce sensations of light, these are not adequate stimuli for the eye.

Sensory Systems of Particular Animals Have a Restricted Range of Responsiveness

For any single form of physical energy, the sensory systems of a particular animal are quite selective. For example, humans do not hear sounds in the frequency range above 20,000 hertz (Hz), a range we call ultrasonic. To a bat, however, air vibrations of 50,000 Hz would be sound waves, just as vibrations of 10,000 Hz would. The range of hearing for larger mammals is

even lower than that of humans. Figure 8.2 compares the auditory ranges of some animals. In the visual realm, too, some animals can detect stimuli that humans cannot. For example, bees see in the ultraviolet range of light.

Sensory Processing Begins in Receptor Cells

Detection of energy starts with the properties of **receptor cells**. A given receptor cell is specialized to detect particular energies or chemicals. Upon exposure to a stimulus, a receptor cell converts the energy into a change in the electrical potential across its membrane. Changing the signal in this way is called **sensory transduction** (devices that convert energy from one form to another are known as transducers, and the process is called transduction). Receptors are transducers that are the starting points for the neural activity that leads to sensory perception. Figure 8.3 shows some different receptor cells in skin. We will look at these types in more detail later in the chapter.

Most receptors are associated with nerve endings. For example, various kinds of corpuscles are associated with nerve endings in the skin. The eye has specialized receptor cells that convert photic energy into electrical charges that stimulate the fibers of the optic nerve. The inner ear has specialized hair cells that transduce mechanical energy into electrical signals that stimulate the fibers of the auditory nerve.

Across the animal kingdom, receptors offer enormous diversity. A wide array of sizes, shapes, and forms reflects the varying survival needs of different animals. For some snakes, detectors of infrared radiation are essential, and several species of fish depend

8.2 Do You Hear What I Hear?

(a) Auditory sensitivity ranges of three mammals. (b) Auditory sensitivity ranges of many species of fish, birds, and mammals. Note that the species within a class detect a similar range of frequencies. For a discussion of the measurement of sound, see Box 9.1.

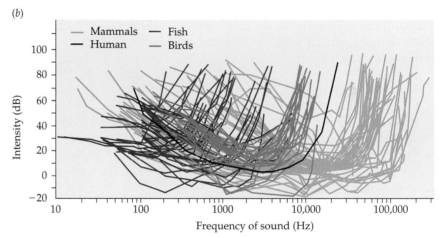

on receptors of electrical energy. Evolutionary processes have led to the emergence of specialized sensors attuned to the inputs or signals that are characteristic of particular environmental niches. Thus, we can view receptors as embodying strategies for success in particular worlds.

The Initial Stage of Sensory Processing Is a Change in Electrical Potential in Receptor Cells

The structure of a receptor determines the forms of energy to which it will respond. In all cases the steps between the impact of energy at a receptor and the initiation of nerve impulses in a nerve fiber leading away from the receptor involve local changes of membrane potential; these are referred to as **generator potentials**. (In most instances, the generator potential resembles the excitatory postsynaptic potentials discussed in Chapter 3.) These electrical changes are the necessary and sufficient conditions for generating nerve impulses. They are part of the causal link between stimulus and nerve impulse.

The details of the generator potential process were explored by Loewenstein (1971) in an elegant study

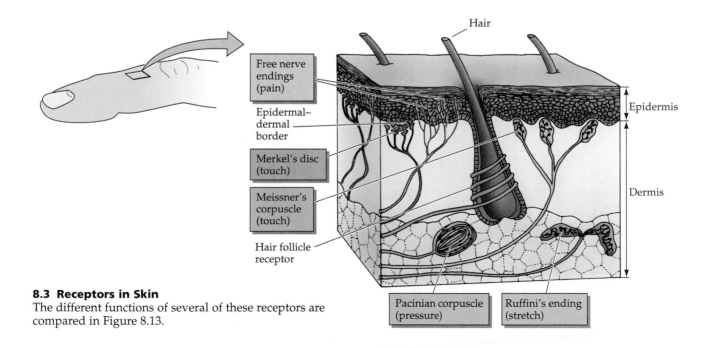

8.3 Receptors in Skin
The different functions of several of these receptors are compared in Figure 8.13.

on a receptor called the **Pacinian corpuscle**. This receptor is found throughout the body in skin and muscle but is especially prominent in tissue overlying the abdominal cavity. It is made of a neural fiber that enters a structure that resembles a tiny onion consisting of concentric layers of tissue separated by fluid (Figure 8.4*a*).

Mechanical stimuli delivered to the corpuscle produce a graded electrical potential with an amplitude that is directly proportional to the strength of the stimulus. When this electrical event reaches sufficient amplitude, the nerve impulse is generated. Careful dissection of the corpuscle, leaving the bared axon terminal intact, shows that this graded potential—the generator potential—is initiated in the nerve terminal. Pressing the corpuscle bends this terminal, which leads to the generator event. The sequence of excitatory events is as follows:

1. Mechanical stimulation deforms the corpuscle.
2. This deformation leads to mechanical stretch of the tip of the axon.

3. Mechanical effects open pores in the axonal membrane allowing sodium ions to enter (Figure 8.4*b*).
4. When the generator potential reaches threshold amplitude, it can elicit nerve impulses (Figure 8.4*c*).

Let's now examine the sensory events that stimuli elicit at sensory receptors.

Sensory Information Processing Is Selective and Analytical

Thinkers in ancient Greece believed that the nerves were tubes through which tiny bits of stimulus objects traveled to the brain, there to be analyzed and recognized. Even after gaining accurate knowledge of neural conduction in the twentieth century, many investigators thought that the sensory nerves simply transmitted accurate information about stimulation to the brain centers. Now, however, it is clear that the sense organs and peripheral sensory pathways convey only limited—even distorted—information to the centers. A good deal of selection and analysis takes place in the peripheral sensory pathways. In the discussion that follows we will examine some basic aspects of this processing: coding, sensory adaptation, suppression, receptive fields, and attention.

(*a*) Innervation of Pacinian corpuscle

(*b*)

8.4 Structure and Function of the Pacinian Corpuscle
(*a*) The Pacinian corpuscle surrounds an afferent nerve fiber ending. (*b*) When the nerve membrane is at rest, the ion channels are too narrow to admit sodium (Na$^+$) ions. Pressure on the corpuscle stretches part of the neuron membrane, enlarging the ion channels and permitting the entry of Na$^+$, which initiates an action potential. (*c*) The neuron shows increasing response to stimuli of increasing intensity.

(*c*)

Sensory Events Are Represented by Neural Codes

Information about the world is represented in the circuits of the nervous system by electrical potentials in single nerve cells or groups of cells. We have already considered the first step in this process—the transformation of energy at receptors (i.e., transduction). Now we must ask the question, How are these events represented in the neural pathways? In some manner electrical events in nerve cells "stand for" or represent stimuli impinging on an organism. This system of representation is often referred to as **coding**. (A code is a set of rules for translating information from one form to another. For example, we can code a message in English for telegraphic transmission, by using the set of rules that make up the dot–dash Morse code.) Sensory information can be encoded into all-or-none action potentials according to several criteria: the frequency of the impulses, the rhythm in which clusters

of impulses occur, and so forth. Here we will examine possible neural representations of the intensity, quality, position, and pattern of stimuli.

Stimulus intensity. We respond to sensory stimuli over a wide range of intensities. Furthermore, within this range we can detect small differences of intensity. How are different intensities of the same stimulus represented in the nervous system? Within a single nerve cell the frequency of nerve impulses can represent stimulus intensity (Figure 8.5a). However, only a limited range of different sensory intensities can be represented in this manner. As we noted in Chapter 3, the maximal rate of firing for a single nerve cell, obtained under highly artificial conditions, is about 1200 impulses per second. Most sensory fibers do not fire more than a few hundred impulses per second. The number of differences in intensity that can be detected in vision and hearing is much greater than this code can offer. Therefore, variations in the firing rate of a single cell simply cannot account for the full range of intensity perception.

Multiple nerve cells acting in a parallel manner provide a broader range for coding the intensity of a stimulus. As the strength of a stimulus increases, new nerve cells are "recruited"; thus intensity can be represented by the number of active cells. A variant of this idea is the principle of intensity coding called **range fractionation** (Figure 8.5b). According to this hypothesis, a wide range of intensity values can be accurately noted in the nervous system by cells that are "specialists" in particular segments or fractions of an intensity scale. This mode of stimulus coding requires an array of receptors and nerve cells with a wide distribution of thresholds, some with very high sensitivity (lower thresholds) and others with much lower sensitivity (higher thresholds).

(*a*) Response rate versus stimulus intensity for three neurons with different thresholds

(*b*) Simulation of responses for the three neurons

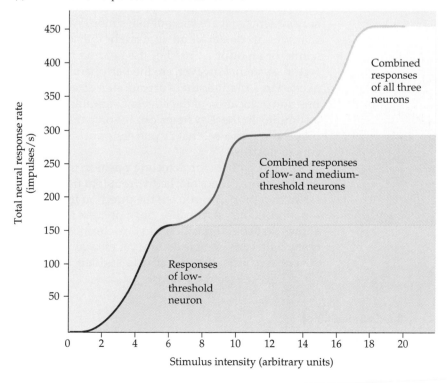

8.5 Intensity Coding

(*a*) Rate of firing in three nerve cells, each with a different threshold: low, medium, or high. Each cell varies its response over a fraction of the total range of stimulus intensities. (*b*) Although none of these nerve cells can respond faster than 150 times per second, the sum of all three can vary in response rate from 0 to 450 impulses per second, accurately indicating the intensity of the stimulus.

Stimulus type.   Within any sensory modality, we can readily discriminate many qualitative differences among stimuli. For example, we can discriminate among wavelengths of light, frequencies of sound, and a variety of skin sensations, such as touch, warmth, cold, and pain. What kind of coding underlies these qualitative differences? An important part of the answer is the concept of **labeled lines**. This view states that particular nerve cells are, at the outset, labeled for distinctive sensory experiences (Figure 8.6). Neural activity in this "line" provides the basis for our detection of the experience. Its qualities are predeter-

mined. Major separation of sensory experiences into modalities clearly involves labeled lines; stimulation of the optic nerve, for instance, always yields vision and never gives us sounds or touch sensations. But controversy surrounds the coding for submodalities, as is particularly evident in vision. For example, there does not seem to be a separate labeled line for each discriminable color, although a few main kinds of retinal receptors respond preferentially to some parts of the visible spectrum, as we'll see in Chapter 10.

Stimulus location.   The position of an object or event, either outside or inside the body, is an important feature of the information that a person or animal gains by sensory analysis. Some sensory systems reveal this information by the position of excited receptors on the sensory surface. This feature is most evident in the visual and **somatosensory** ("body sensation") systems.

Seeing the position of an event or object and feeling the site of a stimulus on the skin both depend on which receptors are excited. Each receptor in either system activates pathways that convey unique positional information. In these systems the spatial properties of a stimulus are represented by labeled lines that uniquely convey spatial information. In both the visual and the tactile system, cells at all levels of the nervous system—from the surface sheet of receptors to the cerebral cortex—are arranged in an orderly, maplike manner. The map at each level is not exact but reflects both position and receptor density. Thus, more cells are allocated to the spatial representation of sensitive, densely innervated sites like the fovea of the eye, or skin surfaces like the lips, than to sites that are less sensitive, such as the periphery of the eye or the skin of the back.

Information about location is not restricted to sensory systems that are laid out like a map. We all know that we can detect quite accurately the source of a sound or an odor. In neither the hearing nor the olfactory system, however, are the peripheral receptors excited in a manner that corresponds directly to the position or location of the relevant stimulus. Locating a stimulus in these systems can involve unilateral or bilateral receptors—that is, one ear or nostril or both ears or nostrils.

The mechanism for detecting position using bilateral receptors differs markedly from that using a unilateral receptor. Can you tell the direction from which a sound comes if you use only one ear? Research shows that sound position can be determined unilaterally with considerable accuracy if the sound lasts for several seconds, but not if it is sudden and brief.

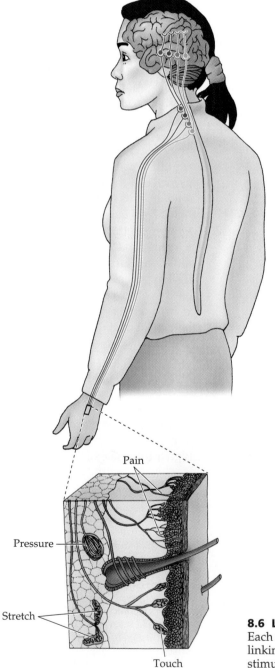

Pain

Pressure

Stretch

Touch

8.6 Labeled Lines
Each receptor (stretch, pressure, pain, touch) has a distinct pathway linking the receptor surface to the brain, so different qualities of skin stimulation can be communicated to distinct places in the brain.

Monaural (one-ear) detection of sound location depends on head movements; it is a sampling, in successive instants, of sound intensity—similar to radar scanning. Some animals with movable external ears (like the cat) can substitute movements of the external ear for head movements. Monaural detection of stimulus location also depends on short-term memory, since successive stimuli are compared for intensity.

With bilateral receptor systems—the two ears or the two nostrils—the relative time of arrival of the stimulus at the two receptors, or the relative intensity, is directly related to the location of the stimulus. For example, the only time when both ears are excited identically is when the sound source is equidistant from the ears, in the median plane of the head. As the stimulus moves to the left or right, receptors of the left and right sides are excited asymmetrically. Our auditory localization circuits allow us to judge accurately whether a sound source is slightly to the right or left of center when the difference in time of stimulus arrival at the two ears is only a few millionths of a second. Specialized nerve cells that receive inputs from both left and right ears and measure stimulus disparities between left and right are discussed in Chapter 9.

Stimulus identity. Being able to recognize stimuli requires the ability both to perceive patterns of stimulation and to recall patterns that have been learned previously. Usually these abilities go together, but in some cases of brain damage, they become divorced. In Chapter 19, for example, we will consider some rare cases of people who can see and describe faces but who can no longer recognize familiar faces.

Receptor Response Can Decline with Maintained Stimuli

Many receptors show progressive loss of sensitivity when stimulation is maintained. This process is called **adaptation**. We can demonstrate adaptation by recording nerve impulses in a fiber leading from a receptor. Observations of the time course of nerve impulses show a progressive decline in the rate of discharges as the stimulus is continued (Figure 8.7). In terms of adaptation, there are two kinds of receptors: **Tonic receptors** show a slow or nonexistent decline in the frequency of nerve impulses as stimulation is maintained. In other words, these receptors show relatively little adaptation. **Phasic receptors** show a rapid fall in the frequency of nerve impulses.

Adaptation means that there is a progressive shift in perception and neural activity away from accurate portrayal of maintained physical events. Thus, the nervous system may fail to register neural activity even though the stimulus continues. Such a striking discrepancy does not imply a weakness in the integrity of receptors; rather it emphasizes the significance of changes of state as the effective properties of stimuli. Adaptation is a form of information suppression that prevents the nervous system from becoming overwhelmed by stimuli that offer very little "news" about the world. For example, the pressing of a hair on the leg by pants may be continuous, but we are saved from a constant neural barrage from this stimulus by several suppression mechanisms, including adaptation.

The bases of adaptation include both neural and nonneural events. For example, in some mechanical receptors, adaptation develops from the elasticity of the receptor cell itself. This situation is especially evident in the Pacinian corpuscle that detects mechanical pressure. Maintained pressure on a corpuscle results in an initial burst of neural activity and a rapid fall to almost nothing. The size of this receptor enables experimenters to remove the corpuscle (the accessory cell) and apply the same constant stimulus to the terminal region of the sensory nerve fiber—that is, to bend the tip of the neuron. In this instance, maintained mechanical stimulation produces a continuing discharge of nerve impulses. This result suggests that for this receptor, adaptation is a mechanical property of the nonneural component, the corpuscle. In some receptors, adaptation reflects a change in the generator potential of the cell. Changes in this electrical property of a receptor may be produced by ionic changes that result in hyperpolarization.

Sensory Inputs Can Be Suppressed

We have noted that successful adaptation and survival do not depend on exact copying of external and internal stimuli. Rather, our success as a species demands

(a) Weak stimulus

(b) Moderate stimulus

(c) Strong stimulus

0   1   2 s

8.7 Sensory Adaptation
The rate of firing of this neuron, the receptive field for which is located on the fifth finger, is rapid when the stimulus (whether weak, moderate, strong) is first applied, but then adapts, slowing to a steady rate. (After Knibestol and Valbo, 1970.)

that our sensory systems accentuate, from among the many things happening about us, the important changes of stimuli. Without selectivity we would suffer from an overload of information and would end up with a confusing picture of the world. In addition to minimizing sensory overload, the suppression of some sensory inputs may reduce the metabolic expense of nervous system activities.

Information in sensory systems is constrained or suppressed in at least two ways. In many sensory systems, accessory structures can reduce the level of input in the sensory pathway. For example, closure of the eyelid reduces the level of illumination that reaches the retina. In the auditory system, contraction of the middle-ear muscles reduces the intensity of sounds that reach the cochlea. In this form of sensory control, the relevant mechanisms change the intensity of the stimulus before it reaches the receptors.

A second form of information control involves neural connections that descend from the brain to lower levels in the sensory pathway, in some cases as far as the receptor surface. For example, higher centers in the pain system (discussed later in this chapter) send axons down the spinal cord, where they can inhibit incoming pain signals. Such central modulation of sensory input is also evident in the auditory system, where a small group of cells in the brain stem send axons along the auditory nerve to connect with the base of the receptor cells. Stimulation of this pathway can dampen sounds in a more selective manner than the action of middle-ear muscles can.

Successive Levels of the CNS Process Sensory Information

Sensory stimulation leads to responses and perceptions. How? In brief, different levels and regions of the brain process information from receptor surfaces in different ways. These sites of information processing are located along pathways that lead from the sensory surface to the highest levels of the brain, and each sensory system has its own distinctive pathways. Specifically, pathways from receptors lead into the spinal cord or brain stem, where they connect to distinct clusters of nerve cells. These cells, in turn, have axons that connect to other nerve cell groups. Eventually the pathway terminates in sets of neurons in regions of the cerebral cortex. Each sensory modality—such as touch, vision, or hearing—has a distinct collection of tracts and stations in the brain that are collectively known as the sensory or afferent pathway for that modality.

Each station in any pathway is thought to accomplish a basic aspect of information processing. For example, there is important information processing at the spinal level. Painful stimulation of the finger will lead to reflex withdrawal of the hand, which is mediated by spinal circuits. At the brain stem level, other circuits can turn the head toward the source of stimulation. Presumably the most complex aspects of sensory repre-

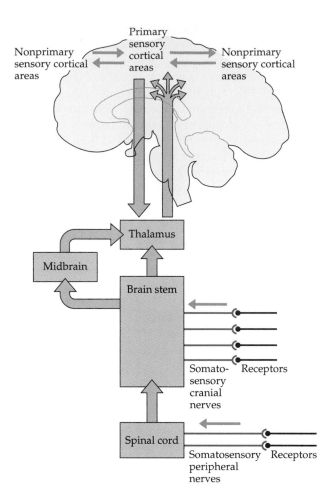

8.8 Levels of Somatosensory Processing

sentations are at the level of the cerebral cortex. A major goal of contemporary studies of sensory processing is to understand the transformations of signals at each level in afferent pathways within the nervous system.

As sensory information enters the nervous system, it travels in divergent pathways, so there is more than one representation of that modality at each level of the nervous system (Figure 8.8). For several senses, information reaches the thalamus before being relayed to the cortex; the somatosensory system is one example. Figure 8.9 shows six different somatosensory regions in the monkey cortex. Each of them is a full, orderly representation of either the body surface or deep body tissues. Neurophysiologist Clinton Woolsey was a pioneer in mapping these somatosensory regions. Similar collections of maps are found at different levels of the auditory and visual pathways. One way of studying these brain maps is to record the receptive fields of the cells that constitute them. Let's take a closer look at the different levels of sensory representation in the central nervous system.

Clinton Woolsey (1904–1993)

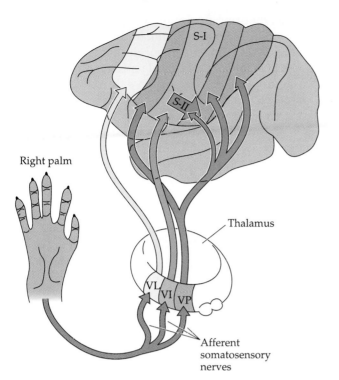

Right palm

Thalamus

VL
VI VP

Afferent
somatosensory
nerves

8.9 Thalamic Relays

Some of the connections between thalamus and cortex in the somatosensory system of monkeys. Different divisions of the thalamus—ventrolateral (VL), ventralis intermedius (VI), and ventroposterior (VP) send axons to different somatosensory regions of the cerebral cortex. (After Merzenich and Kaas, 1980.)

Receptive fields of sensory neurons.   The **receptive field** of a sensory neuron consists of the stimulus region and the features that cause that cell to alter its firing rate. To determine the receptive field of a neuron, investigators record its electrical responses to a variety of stimuli to learn what makes the activity of the cell change from its resting rate (Figure 8.10).

Important method

Such experiments show that receptive fields have either an excitatory center and an inhibitory surround or an inhibitory center and an excitatory surround.

Receptive fields differ also in size and shape, and in the quality of stimulation that activates them. For example, some cells respond preferentially to light touch, while other cells fire most rapidly in response to painful stimuli. Much of the earlier work on receptor field properties of cerebral cortical somatosensory cells was done by Vernon Mountcastle. Although we have taken these examples from neurons in the cortex, receptive fields have been studied for cells at all levels, and we will see examples in other brain regions later in this chapter and in the next two chapters.

Regions of the cerebral cortex.   Several lines of evidence indicate that the different cortical areas that represent the same receptive surface receive different inputs, process the information differently, and make different contributions to perceptual experiences

(a) Experimental setup

Amplifier A   **Amplifier B**

Receptive field
for cortical
neuron A

Receptive field
for cortical
neuron B

(b) Cortical cell with receptive field on forelimb

Forelimb

Touch in center of
receptive field excites

Touch in surround
inhibits

Touch outside receptive
field has no effect
(spontaneous activity)

Period of
stimulation

Cortical neuron A

(c) Cortical cell with receptive field on tail

Tail

Touch in center of
receptive field excites

Touch in surround
inhibits

Touch outside receptive
field has no effect

Period of
stimulation

Cortical neuron B

8.10 Identifying Somatosensory Receptive Fields

Procedures used to record from somatosensory neurons of the cerebral cortex. Changes in the position of the stimulus affect the rate of neural impulses. Neuron A responds to touch on a region of the forepaw; neuron B, only a few millimeters away in the somatosensory cortex, responds to stimulation of the tail. The receptive fields of these neurons include an excitatory center and an inhibitory surround, but other neurons have receptive fields with the reverse organization—inhibitory centers and excitatory surrounds.

(Miyashita, 1993; Zeki, 1993). The evidence for different inputs is that these areas receive fibers from different divisions of the thalamus (see Figure 8.9) and that the maps, although orderly, differ in internal arrangement. Some geographic maps exaggerate a particular aspect; for example, the "New Yorker's map of the United States" magnifies New York while shrinking the rest of the country. Similarly, we'll see that cortical representations of the body surface always enlarge the representation of the hand.

In somatosensory cortical regions, one area (S-I in Figure 8.9) maps the opposite side of the body. Another area (S-II) maps both sides of the body in registered overlay; that is, the left-arm and right-arm representations occupy the same part of the map, and so forth. Neurons within some somatosensory maps are most sensitive to stimulation of the skin surface, others to muscles and joints; moreover, some neurons are sensitive to stationary stimuli, others to movement (Mountcastle, 1984).

Different cortical regions probably are simultaneously processing different aspects of perceptual experience, but the details of this processing are not yet known. In spite of this specialization, it would be incorrect to suppose that a given cortical sensory region receives a packet of information and processes it without further communication with other brain regions. For one thing, the cortical and thalamic regions exchange information back and forth. For another, the different cortical regions for a given modality communicate by fibers that make subcortical loops.

Even though each sensory modality is represented by several topographically organized cortical fields that all have direct thalamic input, there are reasons for referring to one field as primary for each sense: The primary area is the main source of input to the other fields for the same modality, even though these other fields also have direct thalamic inputs. Discovering the separate and joint contributions of different sensory regions to perception remains a challenge. Recent findings do not conform to a strict hierarchical model with its schema of primary, secondary, and association areas.

Plasticity in cortical maps. At one time most researchers thought that cortical maps were fixed and invariant among all members of the same species. Contemporary researchers offer a quite different perspective on cortical sensory maps, emphasizing the variability in maps that is attributable to experience. The results of three experiments illustrate the plasticity of sensory representation (Merzenich and Jenkins, 1993). In the first, the receptive field of a monkey's hand was mapped in detail in the somatosensory cortex (Figure 8.11a). Then the nerve to the thumb and index finger was severed. After a few weeks, remapping the same somatosensory cortex revealed that the area representing these fingers had shrunk, while the areas

of the neighboring fingers had expanded into their former territory (Figure 8.11b). In the second experiment, the middle finger was surgically removed. This treatment expanded the cortical representation of each adjacent finger (Figure 8.11c). In a third experiment, the monkey was trained to maintain contact with a rotating disc with one or two fingers in order to obtain food rewards. After several weeks of training, the hand area was mapped again, and the trained fingers were found to have considerably enlarged representations over their previous areas (Figure 8.11d).

Neural plasticity

More recent studies of plasticity in the primary somatosensory cortex of monkeys show that training animals in tasks that require skilled use of digits appears to expand cortical sectors involved in this task (Xerri et al., 1996). In addition, receptive fields of the frequently stimulated digits were smaller than those observed for control digits; that is, somatosensory cells showed increase spatial resolution following training experiences. Similar findings were noted by these researchers in rats exposed to differential tactile experience. Rats exposed to a more enriched somatosensory experience showed enlargement of forepaw representation in the primary somatosensory cortex.

In a review of the topic of plasticity of sensory representation, Kaas (1991) reached the following conclusions:

1. Cortical maps in all sensory systems can change with experience and use.
2. Such plasticity of cortical maps has been found in a wide range of mammalian species, indicating that adult plasticity is a feature of all mammalian brains.
3. Sensory maps at both lower and higher levels in the nervous system show changes with use and disuse, but changes are more dramatic at higher levels, possibly because changes accumulate along the sensory pathways and because the higher levels may have greater potential for plasticity.
4. Some changes in cortical maps occur after weeks or months of use or disuse; they may arise from the production of new synapses (sprouting) or the loss of others. On the other hand, some changes are so rapid, occurring within hours, that they may arise from changes in the strength of existing synapses. Rapid changes in cortical maps may also result from a loss of sustained inhibition of some synapses; these changes could be thought of as the unmasking of synaptic effects that are normally suppressed.

Sensory Systems Influence One Another

Many research observations and individual experiences show that the use of one sensory system influences perception derived from another sensory system (Stein and Meredith, 1993). For example, cats often do not respond to birds unless they can both see

(a) Representation of the left hand in primary somatosensory cortex in right hemisphere of monkey brain

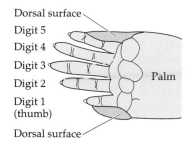

Dorsal surface
Digit 5
Digit 4
Digit 3
Digit 2
Digit 1 (thumb)
Dorsal surface

Palm

Body
Posterior   Face   Anterior

Details of cortical map
(D5 = Digit 5, etc.)

(b) Experiment 1

Nerve from thumb (D1) and index finger (D2) severed.

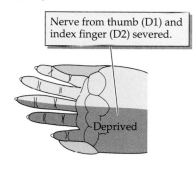

Deprived

Immediately after severing the nerve, the areas representing D1 and D2 are unresponsive to stimuli.

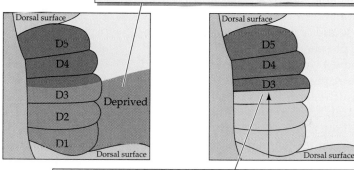

Five months later, the representation of the dorsal surface has expanded into the region that formerly represented D1 and D2.

(c) Experiment 2

D3 surgically removed.

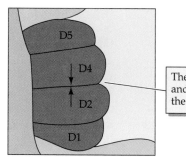

The areas representing D2 and D4 expand and replace the representation of D3.

(d) Experiment 3

Monkey trained to keep two fingers in contact with rotating stimulus disk.

Stimulus disk

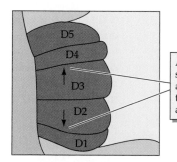

Areas representing stimulated digits expand and replace part of the areas that formerly represented adjacent digits.

8.11 Plasticity of Somatosensory Representations
(After Merzenich and Jenkins, 1993.)

and hear them; neither sense alone is sufficient to elicit a response (Meredith and Stein, 1983). Such intersensory effects are evident in even the simplest of invertebrates. Many sensory areas in the brain do not represent exclusively a single modality but show a mixture of inputs from different modalities. Individual sensory cells may also respond to stimuli of more than one modality. Some "visual" cells, for instance, also respond to auditory or tactile stimuli. Stimuli converge in such polymodal cells, providing a mechanism for intersensory interactions.

Recently investigators have found that many brain cells show very different responses to stimulation of two or more modalities than to stimulation of only one modality. This interaction can take any of several forms. For example, some cells respond only weakly or not at all to a sound or a light but respond strongly when both are presented at once. Some cells that respond to light show a weaker response when a sound is also presented. Although studies of such intersensory effects are much more demanding than are studies of single stimuli, because many different combinations of stimuli must be tested, such investigation is important to our understanding of some perceptual effects.

Attention.   William James in 1890 wrote, "Everyone knows what attention is. It is the taking possession by the mind in clear and vivid form one out of what seem several simultaneous objects or trains of thought." In fact, however, not everyone agrees about the definition of **attention**. This important aspect of sensory processing has a multiplicity of meanings.

One view emphasizes the state of alertness or vigilance that enables animals to detect signals. In this view, attention is a generalized activation that attunes us to inputs. According to another view, attention is the process that allows the selection of some sensory inputs

from among many competing ones. Some investigators view attention in a more introspective manner, arguing that it is a state of mental concentration or effort that makes it possible to focus on a particular task. As you can see, a notion that may seem self-evident to some has considerable complexity.

Certain regions of the cerebral cortex have been particularly implicated in attention, as evidenced by the impairment of attention in people and animals with localized cortical damage and by recordings of electrical activity of cells in different cortical regions while animals attend to stimuli or await stimuli in order to obtain rewards. One cortical region that appears to play a special role in attention is a part of the posterior parietal lobe. Many cells here are polymodal. Some of them are especially responsive when a trained monkey is expecting the appearance of a stimulus (Mountcastle et al., 1981). Lesions of this area in monkeys result in inattention or neglect of stimuli on the opposite side. (In Chapter 19 we will see that this symptom is especially severe in people with lesions of the right parietal lobe.) The frontal eye fields seem to be involved in attentive visual exploration of space. The posterior part of the cingulate cortex (around the posterior part of the corpus callosum) has been implicated in motivational aspects of attention. These three cortical areas have especially prominent anatomical connections with each other, and each receives strong input from sensory fibers (Mesulam, 1989).

PET studies have provided important data about brain regions involved in spatial attention in humans. Figure 8.12 shows activation in the anterior cingulate cortex (especially on the right side) during a task involving a shift in spatial orientation (Gitelman et al., 1996; Nobre et al., 1997). This region has been hypothesized to play a significant role in an "executive" attention system (Posner and Raichle, 1994).

Touch and Pain

Touch Includes a Variety of Sensations

Skin envelops our bodies and provides a boundary with our surroundings. This delicate boundary harbors an array of receptors that enable us to detect and discriminate among many types of impinging stimuli. All forms of touch, from the most delicate movement of a single hair to the most forceful pressing of the flesh, are recorded by receptors on the skin. Among primates, an important aspect of skin sensations is the active manipulation of objects by the hands, which enables identification and use of various shapes. The ability to detect differences in temperature adds to the versatility of the skin. More complex aspects of skin sensations are evident in the worlds of pain with which we are all too familiar. After examining how skin senses work—looking specifically at sensory receptors in the skin, at how sensory information from the skin is transmitted to the

8.12 Brain Regions Activated When We Are Attending Functional MRI images of a subject cued to expect a stimulus in a particular portion of the visual field shows right-hemisphere activation in the cingulate cortex in midsagittal (left) and frontal (right) views. Areas of highest activation are shown in yellow. CG = cingulate gyrus; CS = cingulate sulcus. (Courtesy of Darren Gitelman.)

brain, and at how that information is processed in the brain—we will discuss pain.

Many Different Skin Sensations Arise from All over the Body

Touch is not just touch. Careful studies of skin sensations using a variety of stimuli reveal that qualitatively different sensory experiences can be provoked by skin excitation. Examples include pressure, vibration, tickle, "pins and needles," and more complex dimensions, such as smoothness or wetness. Skin sensations vary not only qualitatively but also spatially across the extent of the body surface. For example, studies on the "two-point" threshold reveal spatial discrimination differences on the body surface. The two-point threshold is a measure of how far apart two points, such as the tips of two pencils, must be in order to be perceived as separate points. As the two points of the pencils are brought closer together on the body surface, they are perceived as one point. Some parts of the body, such as the lips and fingers, have very low two-point thresholds (they can detect two points even when the points are quite close together); other parts, such as the back or leg, have very high two-point thresholds, detecting the two points as only one when the points are still relatively far apart.

Skin Is a Complex Organ That Contains a Variety of Sensory Receptors

The average person has about 1 to 2 m² (10 to 20 square feet) of skin. Skin is not a simple structure but is made up of three separate layers; the relative thickness of each layer varies over the body surface. The outermost layer—the **epidermis**—is the thinnest and varies most widely, ranging from a very flexible, relatively thick layer on the surface of the hands and feet to the delicate outer layer of the eyelid. Each day millions of new cells are added to the outermost layer. The middle layer—the **dermis**—contains a rich network of nerve fibers and blood vessels, in addition to a network of connective tissue that is rich in the protein collagen, which gives skin its strength. The character of skin is further complicated by other specialized outgrowths, such as hair or feathers, claws, hooves, and horns. The innermost layer—**subcutaneous tissue**—contains fat cells, which act as thermal insulators and cushion internal organs from mechanical shock.

Within the skin are several receptors that have distinctive shapes (Figure 8.13; see also Figure 8.3). We have already mentioned the Pacinian corpuscles,

8.13 Properties of Skin Receptors Related to Touch
(*Top*) Type of skin receptor; (*middle*) size and type of receptive field; (*bottom*) electrophysiological response. (*a*) Meissner's corpuscles innervate fast-adapting nerve fibers with small receptive fields. (*b*) Merkel's discs innervate slow-adapting fibers with small receptive fields. (*c*) Pacinian corpuscles innervate fast-adapting fibers with large receptive fields. (*d*) Ruffini's endings innervate slow-adapting fibers with large receptive fields. (After Valbo and Johansson, 1984.)

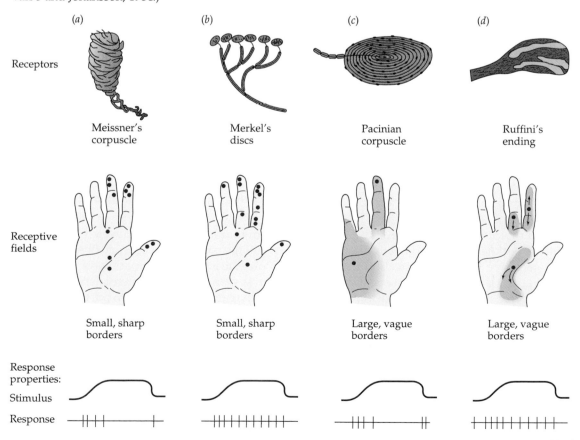

TABLE 8.2 *Fibers That Link Receptors to the CNS*

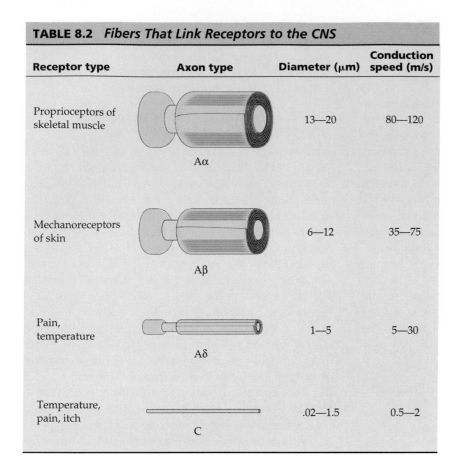

Receptor type	Axon type	Diameter (μm)	Conduction speed (m/s)
Proprioceptors of skeletal muscle	Aα	13—20	80—120
Mechanoreceptors of skin	Aβ	6—12	35—75
Pain, temperature	Aδ	1—5	5—30
Temperature, pain, itch	C	.02—1.5	0.5—2

fibers of different diameters and therefore different speeds of conduction (Table 8.2).

Within the smooth skin of the hand are an estimated 17,000 tactile units of four main types, which are distinguished by the size and shape of their receptive fields and various functional properties, such as the response to maintained stimulation (adaptation) (Valbo and Johansson, 1984). Two of these groups of peripheral nerve fibers have small receptive fields that are especially dense at the fingertips. One of these two groups shows rapid adaptation to maintained skin indentation (see Figure 8.13a); the other group continues to respond as mechanical stimulation is maintained (see Figure 8.13b). Each of these groups is believed to involve a different end-organ receptor in the skin.

The other two main groups of fibers have very large receptive fields; some of these receptive fields may encompass an entire finger. The fibers with large receptive fields are also subdivided into two groups: a fast-adapting subgroup (see Figure 8.13c) and a slow-adapting subgroup (see Figure 8.13d). The slow-adapting nerve fibers with large receptive fields are also especially responsive to stretch and therefore to mechanical stimuli that move across the skin in particular directions. Fast-adapting fibers have very low thresholds to mechanical stimuli. In fact, a single nerve impulse in some of these fibers can lead to touch perception. A single brief electrical stimulus can also be detected.

which are found deep within the dermis and are the largest receptors in some skin areas, around muscles and joints, and within the gut. Pacinian corpuscles are fast-responding receptors whose excitation is delivered to fast-conducting nerve fibers (see Figure 8.13c). The Pacinian corpuscles respond to vibration of the skin and deep pressure. Other receptors, called **Meissner's corpuscles** (see Figure 8.13a), are especially densely distributed in skin regions where sensitive spatial discrimination is possible, but these receptors respond poorly to vibrating stimuli. The regions where Meissner's corpuscles predominate include the fingertips, tongue, and lips. Also found in these regions are oval-shaped receptors called **Merkel's discs** (Figure 8.13b), which are sometimes found in bundles that are especially sensitive to touch. Detection of pain, heat, and cold at the skin has been associated with the activation of free **nerve endings**. **Ruffini's endings** detect stretching of the skin (see Figure 8.13d).

Some investigators, however, have cautioned against readily equating sensory categories and distinct structural classes of receptors. The psychological categories of skin sensations were developed independently of receptor types, and it is not yet clear whether these two can be related to each other in a simple way. Receptors are linked to the central nervous system by

Two Pathways Carry Sensory Information from the Skin to the Brain

Inputs from the skin surface are directed to the spinal cord. Within the cord, somatosensory fibers ascend to the brain in at least two major pathways: (1) the dorsal column system and (2) the anterolateral (spinothalamic) system (Figure 8.14). Inputs to the **dorsal column system** enter the spinal cord and ascend to the medulla, where they synapse. The axons of postsynaptic cells form a fiber bundle that crosses in the brain stem to the opposite side and ascends to a group of nuclei of the thalamus. Outputs of the thalamus are directed to postcentral cortical regions referred to as the somatosensory cortex. The **anterolateral**, or **spinothalamic**, **system** has a different arrangement. Inputs from

8.14 Somatosensory Pathways
(*Left*) General view of the system including ascending spinal tracts, thalamic relay, and primary cortical representation. (*Right*) The spinal tracts in greater detail, including crossed and uncrossed spinal pathways. All afferent messages cross before reaching the thalamus.

the skin to this system synapse on cells in the spinal cord, whose axons cross to the opposite side and ascend in the anterolateral columns of the spinal cord. At least some of the input to this system mediates pain and temperature sensations.

The skin surface can be divided into bands, or **dermatomes**, according to which spinal nerve carries the most axons from each region (Figure 8.15*a*). A dermatome (from the Greek *derma*, "skin," and *tomos*, "section") is a strip of skin innervated by a particular spinal root. The pattern of dermatomes is hard to understand in an upright human, but we must remember that erect posture is a recent evolutionary development in mammals. The mammalian dermatomal pattern evolved among our quadrupedal (four-legged) ancestors. Thus, the dermatomal pattern becomes clear when depicted on a person in a quadrupedal posture (Figure 8.15*b*). There is also a modest amount of overlap between dermatomes (Figure 8.15*c*).

The cells in all brain regions concerned with somatic sensation are arranged according to the plan of the body surface. Thus, each region is a map of the body in which the relative areas devoted to body regions reflect the density of body innervation. Since

many fibers are involved with the sensory surface of the head, especially the lips, a particularly large number of cells are concerned with the head; in contrast, far fewer fibers innervate the trunk, so the number of cells that represent the trunk is much lower (Figure 8.16).

Cortical Columns Show Specificity for Modality and Location

We saw in Chapter 2 that the cerebral cortex is organized into vertical columns of neurons; in this section we will examine the functional significance of these cortical columns. It had long been known that the cortex contains large functional regions, such as the somatosensory areas and the visual areas, and that each of these regions is a sort of map of the sensory world. Then, in pioneering work begun in the 1950s, Mountcastle (1984) mapped the receptive fields of individual neurons in somatosensory cortex using microelectrodes. This work revealed that each cortical cell not only has a precise receptive field, but also responds to only one submodality. For example, a particular cell responds only to a given kind of stimulation, such as light touch, and another cell responds only to deep pressure. Furthermore, Mountcastle found to his surprise that, within a given column of neurons, all the cells respond to the same location and quality of stimulation. All the columns in a band

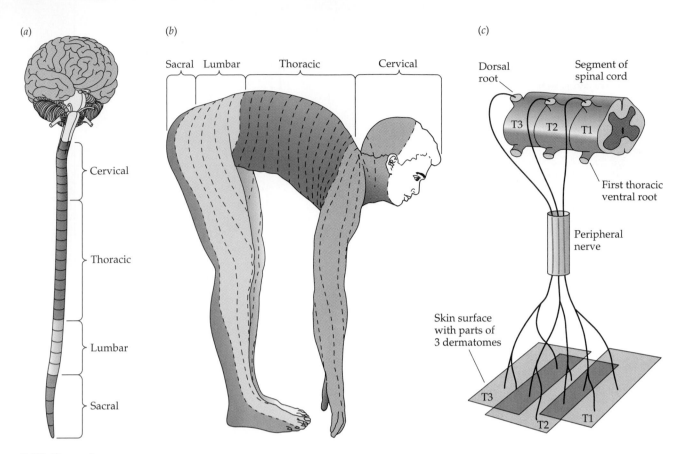

(a)

(b) Sacral Lumbar Thoracic Cervical

(a) Cervical — Thoracic — Lumbar — Sacral

(c) Dorsal root · Segment of spinal cord · T3 T2 T1 · First thoracic ventral root · Peripheral nerve · Skin surface with parts of 3 dermatomes · T3 T2 T1

8.15 Dermatomes
(a) Bands of skin send their sensory inputs to different dorsal roots of the spinal cord. Each dermatome is the section of the skin that is innervated primarily by a given dorsal root of the spinal cord. (b) Side view of the human body in quadrupedal position. Here the pattern of dermatomes is color coded to correspond to the spinal regions in *a*, and it appears more straightforward than it would in the erect posture. (c) Adjacent dorsal roots of the spinal cord collect sensory fibers from overlapping strips of skin, so the boundaries between the dermatomes overlap.

of adjacent columns respond to the same quality of stimulation, and another band of columns is devoted to another kind of stimulation (Figure 8.17).

Each column extends from the surface of the cortex (layer I in Figure 8.17) down to the base of the cortex (layer VI). Area 3b of the cortex receives input from both fast-adapting and slow-adapting receptors near the surface of the skin. Each type of receptor feeds information to a different cortical column. Moving the stimulation to a slightly different region on the skin shifts the excitation to a different cortical column. Area 3a of cortex contains cells that respond to stimulation of the stretch receptors in the muscles, and within area 3a each change in location means stimulation of a different column. Thus, the columns code for both location and quality of stimulation.

In Chapters 9 and 10 we will see that the auditory and visual areas of the cerebral cortex have a similar kind of columnar organization. The discovery of the columnar organization of sensory cortex has been

called "perhaps the most important single advance in cortical physiology in the past several decades" (Kandel et al., 1991).

Neural Maps at Several Levels Represent the Body Surface

The surface of the body is represented at each level of the somatosensory nervous system by an organization of nerve cells that provides a spatial map of the body surface. The first stage of this map of body position is the organization of individual dermatomes at a spinal level. Although individual dermatomes overlap to some extent, they are arranged in an orderly fashion along the length of the spinal cord. At various levels of the brain, the surface of the body is again represented by an orderly map of nerve cells. Thus, the sensory topography of relevant thalamic cells and cortical areas reflects body topography.

The extreme detail of somatosensory system mapping of certain body surfaces is shown in work on rodents (R. M. Harris and Woolsey, 1983). Sections of rat somatosensory cortex obtained by slicing the cortex in a plane tangential to the surface reveal some unusual groupings of cells in circular patterns. Successive sections of tissue in the same plane resemble the sides of a barrel; thus, these groupings were named cortical barrels. The wall of each barrel consists of tightly

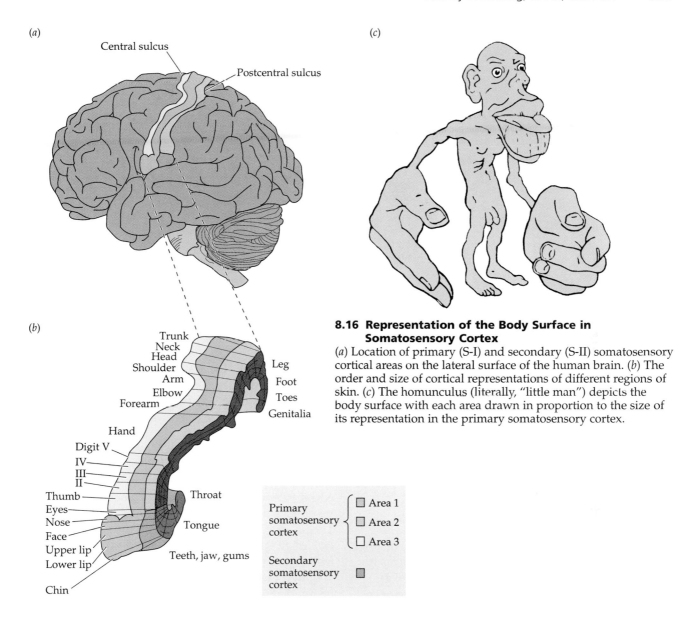

8.16 Representation of the Body Surface in Somatosensory Cortex

(*a*) Location of primary (S-I) and secondary (S-II) somatosensory cortical areas on the lateral surface of the human brain. (*b*) The order and size of cortical representations of different regions of skin. (*c*) The homunculus (literally, "little man") depicts the body surface with each area drawn in proportion to the size of its representation in the primary somatosensory cortex.

packed cell bodies surrounding a less dense area. Electrical recordings of cells in the cortical barrels of a rat revealed the startling fact that each barrel is activated by one whisker on the opposite side of the head. Further, the layout of whiskers on the face of the animal corresponds to the layout of barrels in the cortex. Whiskers are important to a rodent's ability to find its way through narrow passages in the dark. In Chapter 7 we noted the importance of intact facial whiskers for the development or maintenance of cortical barrels. Rats from which the whiskers were removed early in life did not form cortical barrels (see Figure 7.20).

Neural plasticity

This form of somatosensory cortical plasticity may involve sprouting and retraction of axonal processes (Elliott et al., 1996). The involvement of GABA in the plasticity of cortical barrels is suggested by the observations of increased GABA synapses during the period of barrel plasticity (Micheva and Beaulieu, 1996). The role of cholinergic inputs to cortical barrels is indicated by observations of reduced barrel plasticity in acetylcholine-depleted animals (Baskerville et al., 1997).

Somatosensory Perception of Objects Requires Active Manipulation

The functions of the somatosensory cortex in discriminating forms have been studied in monkeys in two ways: (1) The effects of lesions in this region have been observed. (2) Responses of individual neurons have been recorded while the monkeys' hands were stimulated. Lesions impaired the ability of the animal to discriminate the form, size, and roughness or smoothness of tactile objects (Norsell, 1980). Each of these impairments could be localized to a subregion of somatosensory cortex: Lesions in one area affected mainly the discrimination of texture, lesions in a

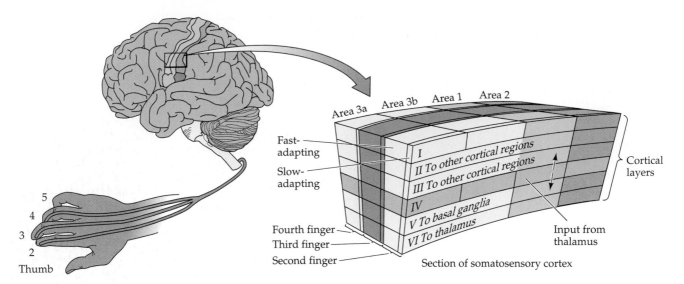

8.17 Columnar Organization of the Somatosensory Cortex
This region of somatosensory cortex represents some of the fingers of the right hand. The different regions of somatosensory cortex—Brodmann's areas 3a, 3b, 1, and 2—receive their main inputs from different kinds of receptors. Area 3b receives most of its projections from the superficial skin, including both fast-adapting and slow-adapting receptors; these projections are represented in separate cortical columns or slabs. Area 3a receives input from receptors in the muscle spindles. The cortex is organized vertically in columns and horizontally in layers. In layer IV, input from the thalamus arrives at the cortex. (After Kaas et al., 1979.)

second area impaired mainly the discrimination of angles, and lesions in a third area affected all forms of tactile discrimination (Randolf and Semmes, 1974).

Temporal and spatial aspects of touch have been studied using complex stimuli (Darian-Smith et al., 1980). In this research, metal strips of varied widths and spacing were moved at different rates of speed under the fingertips of monkeys while recordings were made from sensory nerves. No single fiber could give an accurate record of each ridge and depression in the stimulus, but the ensemble of fibers provided an accurate representation.

Spatial discrimination of more complex stimuli has been studied in a similar way, using stimuli such as Braille dots or other small forms. Cells in the somatosensory cortex were classified in these studies according to the characteristics of their receptive fields (Iwamura and Tanaka, 1978). About one-fourth of the cells responded to simple pressure stimulation of points on the skin. Another fourth responded best to specialized stimulation of the skin (e.g., movement of a probe or a narrow band or rod). Another fourth of the cells could be activated either by stimulation of the skin or by movement of one or more finger joints. About one-eighth of the cells responded specifically

to manipulation of joints. The remainder of the cells could not be activated when the experimenter stimulated either skin or joints, but some of these cells responded strongly when the animal grasped an object and manipulated it.

Some of these "active touch" cells had highly specific response characteristics. For example, one unit responded actively when the monkey felt a straight-edged ruler or a small rectangular block, but it did not respond when the monkey grasped a ball or bottle. The presence of two parallel edges appeared to be crucial for effective activation of this cell. The same electrode penetration identified another cell that responded best when the monkey grasped a ball and responded well to a bottle, but did not respond at all when the monkey manipulated a rectangular block.

Grasping objects causes complex patterns of stimulation of skin receptors and joint receptors. This information about skin and joint stimulation must reach many cortical units. Apparently different cells require particular combinations of input if they are to respond. These units with complex receptive fields in the somatosensory cortex are somewhat like the units with complex auditory or visual receptive fields that we will learn about in Chapters 9 and 10.

PET studies have shown that in humans the posterior part of the parietal cortex is activated during exploration of objects by touch (Roland and Larson, 1976). This result was obtained by the recording of blood flow in the cortex under three conditions:

1. The experimenter moved the passive hand of the observer over the stimulus object.
2. The person moved his or her hand energetically but did not touch an object.
3. The person explored an object by touch.

THE HUMAN PINCUSHION WHO INCURS CONSTANT
RISKS OF BLOOD POISONING.

The earliest scientific report of a person with congenital insensitivity to pain was of a man working in the theater, like the man shown here, as a "human pincushion." (Culver Pictures, Inc.)

Case descriptions note that the bodies of such people show extensive scarring from injuries to fingers, hands, and legs (Manfredi et al., 1981). One little girl had deliberately knocked out most of her teeth by 8 years of age and had to be instructed to leave her teeth alone (Rasmussen, 1996). The first clinically reported person with congenital insensitivity to pain worked on the stage as a "human pincushion" (Figure 8.18) (Dearborn, 1932). Many people with this disorder die young, frequently from extreme trauma to the body. These cases suggest that pain guides adaptive behavior by indicating potential harm. Pain is so commonplace for most of us that we easily forget its guiding role: The experience of pain leads to behavior that removes the body from a source of injury.

Advances in human pain research, including the development of effective drug intervention, depend to a great extent on basic research using other animals. In addition, understanding pain in animals offers a distinctive insight into their adaptive behaviors. Comparative observations of pain behavior in humans and other animals led Dennis and Melzack (1983) to argue that pain serves three purposes:

1. Short-lasting pain causes us to withdraw from the source, often reflexively, thus preventing further damage.
2. Long-lasting pain promotes behaviors such as sleep, inactivity, grooming, feeding, and drinking that promote recuperation.
3. The expression of pain may serve as a social signal to other animals. For example, screeching after a painful stimulus may have significant adaptive value by signaling the potential of harm to genetically related members of the same species or eliciting certain care-giving behavior from others—such as grooming, defending, and feeding—that could mean the survival of the victim.

Human Pain Can Be Measured

In some parts of the world, people endure, with stoic indifference, rituals (including body mutilation) that would cause most other humans to cry out in pain. Incisions of the face, hands, arms, legs, or chest; walking on hot coals; and other treatments clearly harmful to the body can be part of the ritual. Comparable experiences are also seen in more ordinary circumstances, such as the occasions when a highly "excited" athlete continues to play a game with a broken arm or leg. Learning, experience, emotion, and culture all seem to affect pain in striking ways.

Only in the last of these conditions was there specific activation of the posterior parietal cortex, suggesting that this region is particularly involved in active touch.

Pain Is an Unpleasant but Adaptive Experience

Pain has been defined as "an unpleasant sensory and emotional experience associated with actual or potential tissue damage, or described in terms of such damage." Because of its capacity to be unpleasant and cause great suffering, it may be difficult to imagine a "biological role" for pain. But clues to the adaptive significance of pain can be gleaned from the study of rare individuals who never experience pain. The **congenital insensitivity to pain** that such people display is probably inherited, since the pain insensitivity syndrome is sometimes seen in siblings (E. Hirsch et al., 1995), and one version of insensitivity has been traced to a defect in a gene for a receptor to nerve growth factor (Indo et al., 1996), suggesting that pain fibers in these individuals fail to grow out for lack of response to a neurotrophic signal.

Genes and behavior

Some people who display this insensitivity can discriminate between the touch of the point or head of a pin but experience no pain when pricked with a pin.

Detailed psychological studies of the experience of pain further emphasize its complexity. The mere terms "mild" and "intense" are inadequate to describe the sensation that is distinctive to a particular disease or injury. Furthermore, in order to assess the need for pain relief intervention, some kind of quantitative measurement is necessary (Chapman et al., 1985). For example, Melzack (1984) has provided a detailed quantitative rating scale that examines the language of pain.

This rating scale—called the McGill Pain Assessment Questionnaire—consists of a list of words arranged into classes that describe three different aspects of the pain experience: (1) the sensory–discriminative quality, (2) the motivational–affective (emotional) quality, and (3) an overall cognitive evaluative quality (Figure 8.19). Patients are asked to select the set of words that best describes their pain, and within the selected sets, to identify the word that is relevant to their condition. Quantitative treatment of this scale includes adding up the number of selected words and the rank value.

Important method

One of the interesting aspects of the scale is that it can distinguish among pain syndromes, meaning that patients use a distinctive constellation of words to describe a particular pain experience. For example, data obtained from different groups of patients show that the pain of toothache is described differently from the pain of arthritis, which in turn is described differently from menstrual pain. The simple query by a physician "Is the pain still there?" may soon be replaced by a more detailed analysis that will provide better clues about the effectiveness of procedures used to control the suffering of pain.

Pain Information Is Transmitted through Special Neural Systems

Contemporary studies of pain mechanisms have described the characteristics of receptors in the skin that transmit pain information and the relevant pathways of the central nervous system. Many unknowns remain in our understanding of pain pathways, and research continues to elaborate on the complexity of the distribution of neural activity initiated by pain stimuli. In this section we will discuss some features of peripheral and central nervous system pathways that mediate pain.

Peripheral origins of pain information.   In most cases the initial stimulus for pain is the partial destruction of or injury to tissue adjacent to certain nerve fibers. This tissue change results in the release of a chemical substance or substances that most likely activate pain fibers in the skin. Various substances have been suggested as the chemical mediators of pain, including neuropeptides, serotonin, histamine, various proteolytic (protein-metabolizing) enzymes, and prostaglandins—a group of unusual hormones (Figure 8.20). This area of research is very important because it may lead to the development of new pain relief drugs that act at the periphery.

Are some peripheral receptors and nerve fibers specialized for the signaling of noxious stimulation? Over the years this question has generated considerable controversy. Some researchers have argued that there are no specialized receptors or fibers that respond to noxious stimulation; they suggest instead that pain is initiated by a pattern of stimulation of a broad class of peripheral afferent fibers. Other researchers have argued that pain involves a specialized class of afferent fibers that conduct more slowly. Perl (1980) clarified this issue by showing that there are two classes of peripheral afferent fibers that respond to noxious stimulation.

One class (type **Aδ fibers**; see Table 8.2) includes large-diameter, myelinated, high-threshold receptors. Because of the large axon diameter and myelination, these fibers report very quickly. When you stub your toe, the first, sharp pain you feel is conducted by these fibers. A second class of pain receptors of the skin consists of thin, unmyelinated fibers (called **C fibers**; see Table 8.2). These fibers conduct slowly and adapt slowly, providing us with the second wave of pain—the dull, lasting ache in that darned toe.

Another indication that there are specialized pain fibers in the periphery comes from studies of capsaicin, the ingredient that makes chili peppers spicy. When investigators isolated the receptor that is bound by capsaicin, they found that the receptor also responds to sudden increases in temperature (Caterina et al., 1997). So the reason that chili peppers taste "hot" appears to be that the capsaicin in the peppers activates channels in the body that normally detect noxious heat. Paradoxically, rubbing capsaicin into the skin overlying arthritic joints brings some pain relief, perhaps because overactivated pain fibers temporarily run out of transmitter. Thus, contemporary re-

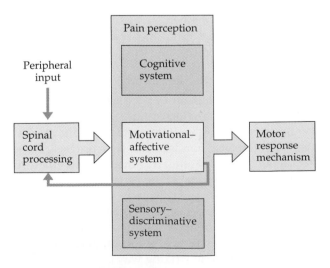

8.19 The Multifaceted Character of Pain

8.20 Peripheral Mediation of Pain
When the skin is injured, activity of the peripheral nervous system causes the local release of various substances.

Damaged cells release substances that excite nerve endings.

Action potentials generated in the periphery can reflexively excite blood vessels and other cells to produce inflammation.

Information enters dorsal horn of spinal cord and is relayed to brain.

Pain fibers release substance P and glutamate as a neuromodulator in spinal cord.

search has clearly established that there are specific groups of nociceptors—receptor cells that respond selectively to noxious stimulation. Information about pain is then transmitted in specialized pain fibers.

Special CNS pathways mediate pain. In the central nervous system, special pathways mediate pain. Afferent fibers from the periphery that carry nociceptive information probably use glutamate as a neurotransmitter to excite cells, but they also release the neuromodulator substance P in the superficial layers of the dorsal horn. Substance P is a neuropeptide (the "P" originally stood for "peptide") that plays a crucial role in pain perception. Injection of capsaicin into the skin provides a specific painful stimulus that leads to the release of substance P in the dorsal horn of the spinal cord. There the postsynaptic neurons take up the substance P and begin remodeling their dendrites; investigators have speculated that this neural plasticity later affects pain perception (Mantyh et al., 1995, 1997).

Further evidence that substance P plays a role in pain comes from experiments with knockout mice that lack either the gene for the precursor to substance P (Cao et al., 1998) or a gene for the substance P receptor (Felipe et al., 1998). (See Box 7.3 to review experimental techniques using knockout mice.) These mice are unresponsive to certain kinds of intense pain. Interestingly, they still responded to mildly painful stimuli, suggesting that other signals, perhaps the glutamate neurotransmitter, can carry that information. The dorsal horn neurons that receive this information send their axons across the midline and up the spinal cord to terminate in several nuclei of the thalamus.

Several other pain pathways have been identified within the spinal cord. The pain response properties of various parts of these pathways have been clearly

established; as with peripheral labeled lines (see Figure 8.6), cells at different levels of the CNS respond preferentially to intense mechanical stimuli and other noxious stimuli. Several distinct tracts in the spinal cord ascend to the brain carrying pain information (Figure 8.21). Especially prominent among these are the spinothalamic tracts.

The pain information is eventually integrated in the **cingulate cortex**. Recall from Chapter 1 that the cingulate cortex is much more likely to be activated by a stimulus if people are led to believe that the stimulus will be painful (see Figure 1.4). A sensory illusion further confirms the role of the cingulate cortex in pain perception: Placing your hand over alternating pipes of cool and warm (not hot) water produces the sensation of pain, as though the pipes were hot. This is a wonderful illustration that "pain is in the brain," because no tissue is actually being damaged. The cingulate cortex is also activated in people experiencing this illusory pain (Craig et al., 1996).

Pain Can Be Controlled by a Variety of Mechanisms and Pathways

Relief from the suffering of pain has long been a dominant concern of humans. Throughout history different remedies have been offered. One interesting, puzzling aspect of pain pathways is that their interruption reduces pain perception only temporarily. After a pathway in the spinal cord is cut, pain is diminished, but returns after an interval of weeks or months. The usual way of interpreting these data is that nociceptive input from the remaining intact pathways becomes abnormally effective. Pain relief received renewed attention after the publication of an insightful paper by Melzack and Wall (1965). They suggested that pain is subject to many modulating in-

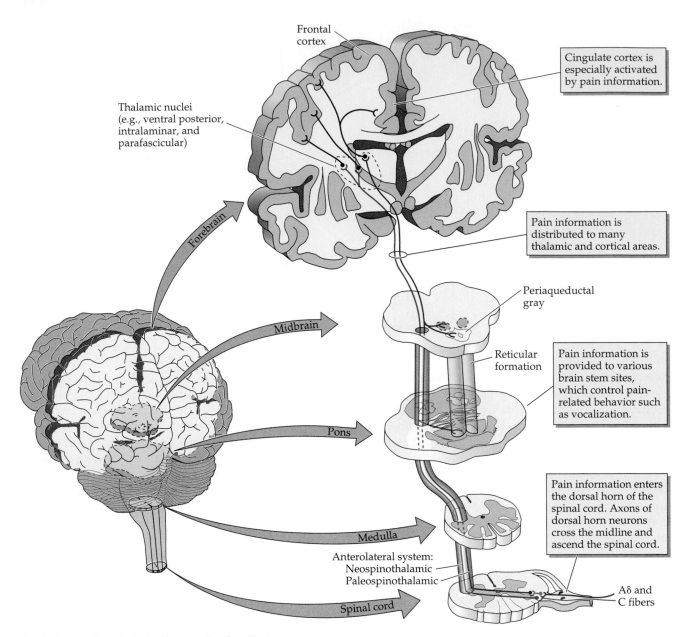

8.21 Ascending Pain Pathways in the CNS
Pain sensation travels from its origin to the brain via the spinal cord.

Ronald Melzack

P. D. Wall

fluences, including some that can close spinal "gates" controlling the flow of pain information from the spinal cord to the brain.

Additional control is exerted by higher centers in the pain system, which send axons down the spinal cord, where they terminate on the first synapses of the pain system in the superficial layers of the dorsal horn. The modulatory signals above the spinal cord can inhibit the transmission of incoming pain impulses. The discovery of the brain's power to control the flow of pain signals has inspired many new approaches for the alleviation of pain. In the sections that follow, we will discuss some of these strategies, which are examples of the interaction between basic research and application.

Opiate drugs. Over the centuries opium has been exploited for its pain-relieving effects. For years researchers attempted to determine how opiate drugs—drugs derived from or related to opium—control pain; finally they successfully showed that the brain contains natural opiatelike substances, or opioids. This finding suggested that the brain has built-in mechanisms to control the transmission of pain information. In effect, the brain might modulate pain in a manner akin to that produced by exogenous opiates such as morphine. Several classes of endogenous opioids have now been discovered (see Chapter 4), and various ideas about how these substances affect the circuitry of pain information have been presented (Basbaum and Fields, 1984).

Early observations showed that stimulation of the **periaqueductal gray** area of the brain stem in rats (see Figure 8.21) produces potent **analgesia** (loss of pain sensation; from the Greek roots *an-*, "not," and *algesis*, "feeling of pain"). Injection of opiates into this area also relieves pain, suggesting that the region contains synaptic receptors for opiatelike substances. Neural inputs to the periaqueductal gray area are diverse, including axons that arise from some cerebral cortical sites, the amygdala, and the hypothalamus. Most important is a strong input from the spinal cord, which presumably delivers nociceptive information.

According to the model of the control of pain transmission in the spinal cord by the brain stem proposed by Basbaum and Fields (1978, 1984), excitation of periaqueductal gray neurons leads via endorphin-containing axons to the stimulation of neurons in the medulla. These medullary neurons have serotonin-containing axons that innervate the spinal cord and inhibit neurons that transmit information from the periphery. In this way, pain information is blocked by a direct gating action in the spinal cord. Electrical stimulation of the descending tract elicits inhibition of the response of spinal cord sensory relay cells to noxious stimulation of the skin. Figure 8.22 shows both the ascending pain communication system and the descending pain control system. Considerable evidence supports this model, including the anatomical and physiological demonstration of pathways that descend from the brain stem to various levels of the spinal cord.

In addition to their beneficial pain-relieving effects, opiates and other analgesics (painkillers) often produce side effects such as confusion, drowsiness, vomiting, constipation, and depression of the respiratory system. Now that we know the circuitry of the pain relief system, why give large doses of the drug systemically (i.e., throughout the body)? Instead, physicians can now administer very small doses of opiates directly to the spinal cord to relieve pain, thus avoiding many of the side effects. The drugs can be administered epidurally (just outside the spinal cord's dura mater) or intrathecally (between the dura mater and the spinal cord). Both routes are somewhat invasive and therefore are restricted to surgical anesthesia, childbirth, or the management of severe chronic pain (Landau and Levy, 1993).

In the clinical context there have been long-standing concerns about the use of morphine and other opiates for the relief of pain because of their addictive potential. Low doses and infrequent use have been the common standard. However, a recent report of the Agency for Health Care Policy and Research urges swift and aggressive use of painkillers after surgery to relieve pain and speed recovery. Several studies show that the danger of addiction from the use of morphine to relieve surgical pain had been vastly overexaggerated (Melzack, 1990); it is now estimated to be no more than 0.04% (Brownlee and Schrof, 1997). Moreover, once chronic pain develops, it is extremely difficult to overcome, so the best approach is to prevent the onset of chronic pain by early, aggressive treatment.

Other, nonopioid analgesics may be available soon. For example, a drug isolated from frog skin, called epibatidine, is a very potent analgesic that seems to act on nicotinic cholinergic receptors in the dorsal horn of the spinal cord (Bannon et al., 1998).

Stimulation of the skin. Human history is filled with examples of the use of strange techniques to achieve relief from pain. One of the more unusual procedures is the administration of electrical currents to the body. Centuries ago this technique included the application of electric fish or eels to sites of pain. More recently, a procedure called **transcutaneous electrical nerve stimulation** (**TENS**) has gained prominence as a way to suppress certain types of pain that have proven difficult to control. In TENS treatment, electrical pulses are delivered through electrodes attached to the skin, which excite nerves that supply the region that hurts. The stimulation itself produces a sense of tingling rather than pain. In some cases dramatic relief of pain can outlast the duration of stimulation by a factor of hours. The best touch relief is produced when the electrical stimulation is delivered close to the source of pain.

TENS has been especially successful in the treatment of patients whose pain is derived from peripheral nerve injuries. The analgesic action of this technique is at least partially mediated by endogenous opioids, since administration of **naloxone**, an opioid antagonist, partially blocks this analgesic action. Recall, for example, the last time you stubbed your toe. In addition to a string of expletives, a frequent result of such incidents is the self-administration of skin stimulation; that is, you react by vigorously rubbing the injured area, which brings a little relief.

Placebos. The search for relief from pain has led people to consume many unusual substances; even chemically inert pills have been reported to alleviate pain in many patients. The term **placebo** (from the Latin for "I shall please") has been applied to such inert substances or other treatments that have no obvious direct physiological effect. Whenever a placebo appears to alleviate pain, investigators try to determine the indirect effects of the placebo treatment or of the circumstances in which it was administered.

(a) Ascending pain communication pathways

(b) Descending pain modulation pathways

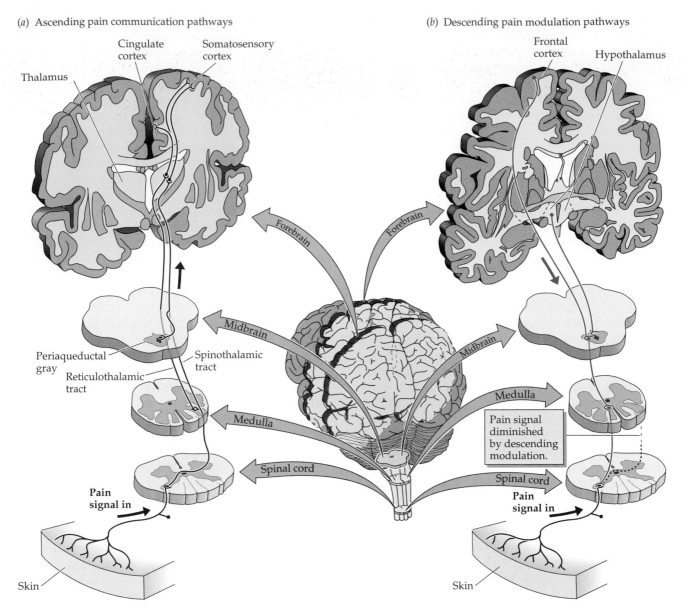

8.22 Ascending and Descending Pain Pathways
Pain sensation is projected up to the brain (a), but the brain can inhibit these signals to control pain (b). (After Basbaum and Fields, 1984.)

Research has yielded striking observations providing clues about why placebos relieve pain in some patients. In one study, J. D. Levine et al. (1978) used volunteer subjects who had just had their wisdom teeth extracted—an especially painful procedure that one could expect to make some people miserable. These patients were told that they were being given an analgesic but were not told what kind. Some of these patients received morphine-based drugs, and some were given saline solutions—the placebo. One out of three patients given the placebo experienced pain relief. (Morphine produced relief in most of the patients but, as has been shown before, not in *all* patients.) To explore the mechanisms of the placebo effect, the re-searchers gave naloxone to other patients who were also administered the placebo. Recall that naloxone blocks the effects of both exogenous opiates and endogenous opioids, or opiatelike substances. Patients given the placebo and naloxone did not experience pain relief; this result implies that placebo relief of pain is mediated by an endogenous opioid system.

A critical analysis of studies of the mechanisms of placebo effects by Grevert and Goldstein (1985) has pointed to some deficiencies in these studies. Factors such as suitable control groups and the dose level of naloxone have proved critical in placebo research. Furthermore, we now know that there are several types of opioid receptors in the brain, and the affinity of naloxone for these various receptors is quite different. Thus, a negative effect of naloxone administration is not definitive in excluding the possible mediation of endogenous opioids. Moreover, in a study designed to deal with criticisms of previous placebo research, Grevert et al. (1983) showed that naloxone did not completely prevent placebo-induced analgesia but rather reduced the effectiveness of a placebo. The results suggest that both opioid and nonopioid mechanisms contribute to placebo analgesia; the same conclusion comes from studies of stress-induced analgesia that we will discuss shortly. Future studies dealing with this phenomenon will increase our understanding of the multifaceted character of pain relief.

Acupuncture. The earliest description of pain relief from **acupuncture** is at least 3000 years old. In some acupuncture procedures, the needles are manipulated once they are in position; in other instances electrical or heat stimulation is delivered through the inserted needles. The points at which needles are inserted are related to the locus of pain and some of the characteristics of the pain condition.

Acupuncture has gained popularity, but detailed clinical assessments indicate that only some people achieve continued relief from chronic pain. At least part of the pain-blocking character of acupuncture appears to be mediated by the release of endorphins (Tang et al., 1997). Administering opioid antagonists such as naloxone prior to acupuncture blocks or reduces its pain control effects. More research is needed in clinical settings to identify the limits of this type of pain control. Animal models of the procedures used with human patients are also promoting an understanding of this ancient but enduring remedy.

Stress. A deer fleeing from an encounter with a mountain lion would do well to ignore any pain from injuries for the moment. Sometimes people badly hurt in traumatic circumstances report little or no immediate pain, suggesting that the injured deer indeed feels no pain. Inhibition of pain has been shown in many laboratory situations that involve unusual treatments, such as electrical stimulation of the brain. Such studies demonstrate the existence of pain control circuitry, but they do not provide information about the customary ways in which inhibitory systems are activated.

What conditions normally activate endorphin-mediated pain control? To answer this question, researchers have examined pain inhibition that might arise in stressful circumstances. Some researchers have suggested that stress induces activation of the brain systems that produce analgesia when pain threatens to overwhelm effective coping strategies. Studies concerned with how pain might control pain itself have revealed some new perspectives on mechanisms that mediate these effects.

Researchers found that exposure of rats to mild foot shock produced analgesia. Many other forms of stress, such as swimming in cold water, also produced inhibition of pain responses. Other observations suggested that such stress-induced analgesia is mediated by endogenous opioids in the brain. In fact, the analgesia produced by stress was similar in several re-

spects to that produced by opiates (Bodnar et al., 1980). Like opiates, repeated exposure to stress resulted in declining analgesic effectiveness. In addition, cross-tolerance is observed between opiates and stressors; that is, diminished analgesia to repeated stress is accompanied by reduced pain inhibition by opiate drugs. However, antagonists to opiates, such as naloxone, have had variable effects on stress-induced analgesia, suggesting that some part of stress-induced analgesia is not mediated by endogenous opioids. More recent research has explored this theme more completely.

John Liebeskind—who was for many years a leading researcher in the area of pain—and his colleagues studied rats in stress situations that consisted of inescapable foot shock (Terman et al., 1984). Different groups of rats were exposed to different regimens of foot shock, and changes in pain threshold were assessed by a technique called the tail-flick test. This assessment is a measure of the level of radiant heat that produces a quick flick of a rat's tail away from the

John Liebeskind
(1935–1997)

heat. In these studies the role of endogenous opioids was assessed by the administration of an opiate antagonist—naltrexone.

In this experimental situation, the stress of inescapable shock produces an increase in tail-flick latency, which shows that the shock stress produces an analgesic effect. However, administration of naltrexone produces a curious complication. When analgesia is produced by short periods of foot shock, naltrexone reverses the analgesic response, a result demonstrating that the source of analgesia is an opioid system in the brain. However, antagonists to opiates have little effect on stress-induced analgesia if the duration or intensity of foot shock is altered. This finding demonstrates that stress activates both an opioid-sensitive analgesic system and a pain control system that does not involve opioids. Relatively precise parameters of the stress-inducing stimuli seem to determine which system is activated.

Similar elements are probably involved in both of these pain control circuits, since spinal lesions disrupt both forms of stress-induced analgesia. But the pathways must be separated to some extent, for some brain stem lesions can affect the opiate-mediated analgesia without affecting the nonopiate-mediated analgesia (Terman et al., 1984). These findings are very important in suggesting clinical strategies for pain relief intervention in humans. Further research should clarify whether additional forms of pain relief are controlled by other circuits.

Table 8.3 summarizes the many types of pain relief strategies and interventions, including surgical and pharmacological strategies, psychological brain and

Table 8.3 *Summary of Types of Pain Relief Intervention*

Measure	Mechanism	Limitations/comments
Psychogenic		
Placebo	May activate endorphin-mediated pain control system	Sometimes inhibited by opiate antagonists
Hypnosis	Alters brain's perception of pain	Control unaffected by opiate antagonists
Stress	Both opioid and nonopioid mechanisms	Clinically impractical and inappropriate
Cognitive (learning, coping strategies)	May activate endorphin-mediated pain control system	Limited usefulness in severe pain
Pharmacological		
Opiates	Bind to opioid receptors in periaqueductal gray and spinal cord	Severe side effects due to binding in other brain regions
Spinal block	Drugs block pain signals in spinal cord	Avoids side effects of systemic administration
Anti-inflammitory drugs	Block prostaglandin and leukotriene synthesis at site of injury	Major side effects
Aspirin	Blocks prostaglandin synthesis at site of injury	Does not block leukotriene synthesis
Stimulation		
TENS/mechanical	Tactile or electrical stimulation of large fibers blocks or alters pain signal to brain	Segmental control; must be applied at site of pain
Acupunture	Seems similar to TENS	Sometimes affected by opiate antagonists
Central gray	Electrical stimulation activates endorphin-mediated pain control systems, blocking pain signal in spinal cord	Control inhibited by opiate antagonists
Surgical		
Cut peripheral nerve cord		
Rhizotomy	Create physical break in pain pathway	Considerable risk of failure or return of pain
Cord hemisection		
Frontal lobotomy		

spinal cord stimulation, and sensory stimulation. The elusive nature of pain is evident in this range of potential interventions, some of which reflect desperation in the face of great anguish. Of course, the persistence of pain often leads to the testing of new tools, some of which are readily denounced as quackery. However, some techniques that elicit initial skepticism may come back with better evidence.

For example, recently researchers examined the potential pain relief provided by magnets (Vallbona et al., 1997). Small magnets slightly stronger than the ones on your refrigerator door were strapped to sensitive pain-generating areas of the body. In the control condition, inactive magnets were strapped over painful areas in other patients. A marked reduction in scores on a pain questionnaire were evident in the group that was exposed to the active as opposed to inactive magnets. No ready explanation of this effect was provided by these researchers, but other researchers have shown that somatosensory-evoked potentials elicited by pain-related stimuli are reduced when subjects are exposed to oscillating magnetic fields (Sartucci et al., 1997).

Summary

Sensory Processing

1. A sensory system furnishes selected information to the brain about internal and external events and conditions. It captures and processes only information that is significant for the particular organism.

2. Ideal sensory systems discriminate among some of the available forms of energy, respond over a wide range of intensities, are highly sensitive to a change of stimuli, respond reliably and rapidly, and suppress unwanted information.

3. Stimuli that some species detect readily have no effect on other species that lack the necessary receptors.

4. Some receptors are simple free nerve endings, but most include cells that are specialized to transduce particular kinds of energy.

5. Energy is transduced at sensory receptors by the production of a generator potential that stimulates the sensory neurons.

6. Coding translates receptor information into patterns of neural activity.

7. In adaptation, the rate of impulses progressively decreases as the same stimulation is maintained. This decline is slow in the case of tonic receptors but rapid for phasic receptors. Adaptation protects the nervous system from redundant stimulation.

8. Mechanisms of information suppression include accessory structures, descending pathways from neural centers to the receptor, and central circuits.

9. The receptive field of a cell is the stimulus region that changes the response of the cell.

10. The succession of levels in a sensory pathway is thought to allow for different and perhaps successively more elaborate kinds of processing.

11. Attention is the temporary enhancement of certain sensory messages during particular states of the individual.

Touch and Pain

1. The skin contains several distinct types of receptors that have specific sensitivities. Inputs from the skin course through distinct spinal pathways, including the dorsal column system and the anterolateral (spinothalamic) system.

2. The surface of the body is represented at each level of the somatosensory system, and at the level of the cerebral cortex are multiple maps of the body surface.

3. Pain guides adaptive behavior by providing indications of harmful stimuli. Pain is a complex state that is strongly influenced by cultural factors and many aspects of individual experience.

4. Pain sensation is subject to many controlling or modulating conditions, including circuitry within the brain and spinal cord that employs opioid synapses. One component in the modulation of pain is made up of the descending pathways arising in the brain that inhibit incoming neural activity at synapses within the spinal cord.

5. Pain control has been achieved by the administration of drugs (including placebos), electrical and mechanical stimulation of the skin, acupuncture, and surgery, among other methods.

Recommended Reading

Carli, G., and Zimmerman, M. (Eds.). (1996). *Towards the neurobiology of chronic pain*. Amsterdam: Elsevier.

Fields, H. L. (1988). *Pain*. New York: McGraw-Hill.

Franzen, O., Johanson, R., and Terneius, L. (Eds.). (1996). *Somesthesis and the neurobiology of the somatosensory cortex*. Boston: Birkhauser.

Johnson, K. O., Hsiao, S. S., and Twombly, I. A. (1995). Neural mechanisms of tactile form recognition. In M. S. Gazzaniga (Ed.), *The cognitive neurosciences* (pp. 253–269). Cambridge, MA: MIT Press.

Kruger, L. (1996). *Pain and touch*. San Diego, CA: Academic Press.

Stein, B., and Meredith, M. A. (1993). *The merging of the senses*. Cambridge, MA: MIT Press.

Valbo, A. B. (1995). Single-afferent neurons and somatic sensation in humans. In M. S. Gazzaniga (Ed.), *The cognitive neurosciences* (pp. 237–253). Cambridge, MA: MIT Press.

Wall, P. D., and Jones, M. 1991. *Defeating pain: The war against a silent epidemic*. New York: Plenum.

Hearing, Vestibular Perception, Taste, and Smell

Photograph courtesy of PaceWildenstein

Lucas Samaras, *Untitled*, February 16, 1961. Pastel on paper, 13" × 10"

You exist only because your ancestors had keen senses that allowed them to find food and to avoid predators and other dangers. In this chapter we continue our consideration of sensory worlds by discussing the perception of signals from distant sources, including hearing (audition) and smell (olfaction). We will also explore two related sensory systems: (1) the vestibular system, which detects orientation and movement of the body, and which is related to the auditory system, and (2) the sense of taste, which, like smell, is a chemical sense. Recent discoveries have greatly expanded our understanding of both receptor mechanisms and central processing, especially in audition and olfaction. Both of these senses are extremely acute, and we will explore some of the special mechanisms that make them so sensitive. We begin with hearing, because audition evolved from special mechanical receptors related to the somatosensory elements we discussed in Chapter 8.

Hearing

Hearing is an important part of the adaptive behavior of many animals. For humans, the sounds of speech form the basic elements of languages and therefore of social relations. Helen Keller, who was both blind and deaf, said, "Blindness deprives you of contact with things; deafness deprives you of contact with people."

The sounds of any single language are only a small subset of the enormous possibilities for sounds that can be produced by human vocal cavities. The sounds produced by animals—from insects to whales—also have a wide range of complexity. The adaptive successes of many animals are linked to their ability to make and perceive these sounds, with which they probe the environment. For example, the melodic songs of male birds and the chirps of male crickets attract females of their species. The grunts, screeches, and burbly sounds of primates signal danger or the need for comfort or satisfaction. Owls and bats exploit the directional property of sound to locate prey and avoid obstacles in the dark. Whales communicate with each other using sounds that can travel hundreds of miles in the ocean. Unlike sights, sounds can turn corners and go around obstacles, and they work as well in the dark as in the light.

Your auditory system can detect rapid changes of sound intensity (measured in **decibels**, **dB**) and frequency (measured in **hertz**, **Hz**). Box 9.1 describes the basic principles of sound. In fact, the speed of auditory information processing is so good that the analysis of frequency by the human ear rivals that of modern

---

BOX 9.1   *The Basics of Sound*

Sound is a repetitive change in the pressure of a particular medium, commonly air or water. In air the change arises because air particles are moved by a vibrating mechanical system, such as the glottis of the larynx in speech, the cone of a loudspeaker, or a tuning fork. In the latter case, as the tuning fork moves away from a resting position, it compresses air particles, causing the air pressure to rise above atmospheric pressure. As the tuning fork swings to the other side of its resting position, air particle density is briefly reduced with respect to atmospheric pressure. A single alternation of compression and expansion of air is called one cycle. Figure A illustrates the changes in the spacing of air particles produced by a vibrating tuning fork.

Because the sound produced by a tuning fork has only one frequency of vibration, it is called a pure tone and can be represented by a sine wave. A pure tone is described physically in terms of two measures:

1. **Frequency**, or the number of cycles per second, measured in hertz (Hz). For example, middle A on a piano has a frequency of 440 Hz.
2. **Amplitude**, or intensity—the distance of particle movement in a defined period of time, usually measured as pressure, or force per unit area, in dynes per square centimeter (dyn/cm²).

(A) Amplitude and frequency of sound waves

Vibrating body (tuning fork)

Compression and expansion of air molecules produced by the tuning fork's vibration

Amplitude: Sine wave representation of the pressure waves above

Wavelength, one cycle

Greater amplitude of movement

Amplitude doubled; frequency same as above

Greater frequency of movement

Amplitude same as original; frequency doubled

Wavelength, one cycle

Most sounds are more complicated than a pure tone. For example, a sound made by a musical instrument contains a fundamental frequency and harmonics. The *fundamental* is the basic frequency, and the *harmonics* are multiples of the fundamental. Thus, if the fundamental is 440 Hz, the harmonics are 880, 1320, 1760, and so on. When different instruments play the same note, they differ in the relative intensities of the various harmonics; this difference is what gives each instrument its characteristic sound quality, or **timbre**. Any complex pattern can be analyzed into a sum of sine waves, a process called **Fourier analysis** after the French mathematician who discovered it. (We will see in Chapter 10 that Fourier analysis can also be applied to visual patterns.) Figure B shows how a complex, square electronic gadgets. Your ear is also as sensitive as possible to weak sounds at frequencies in the range from 1000 to 2000 Hz. If it were any more sensitive, you would be distracted by the noise of air molecules bouncing against each other in your ear canal.

Each Part of the Ear Performs a Specific Function in Hearing

How do the small vibrations of air particles become the speech, music, and other sounds we hear? By shaping the mechanical forces that act on auditory end organs, the peripheral components of the auditory system determine the beginnings of auditory perception. In this section we discuss these initial stages of auditory processing.

The External Ear Captures, Focuses, and Filters Sound

Sound waves are collected by the external ear, which consists of the part we readily see, called the **pinna** (plural pinnae; Latin for "wing"), and a canal that leads to the eardrum (Figure 9.1). The external ear is a distinctly mammalian characteristic, and mammals show a wide array of ear shapes and sizes. The acoustic properties of the external ear are important because its shape physically transforms sound energies. The "hills and valleys" of the pinna modify the character of sound that reaches the middle and inner ear. Some frequencies of sound are enhanced; others are dimmed. For example, the shape of the human ear especially increases the efficiency of sounds in the frequency range of 2000 to 5000 Hz, a range that is im-

wave (*b*) can be analyzed into component sine waves of different frequencies. Using only the fundamental (*c*) and two harmonic frequencies (*d*, *e*), we can come close to restructuring the square wave (*f*). By using additional frequencies, we could eventually duplicate the square wave perfectly.

Most animals produce sound. Hearing enables humans to detect energies that we and other animals produce, either for communication or incidentally to other activities. Since the ear is sensitive to a huge range of sound pressures, sound *intensity* (a measure of the difference between two pressures) is usually expressed in decibels (dB), a logarithmic scale. The definition of a decibel is as follows:

$$N(\text{dB}) = 20 \log P_1/P_2$$

where *N* is the number of decibels and P_1 and P_2 are the two pressures to be compared. The common reference level, or threshold, in hearing studies (P_2 in the notation above) is 0.0002 dyn/cm²; this is the least amount of pressure necessary for an average human observer to hear a 1000 Hz tone. In this scale a whisper is about ten times as intense as 0.0002 dyn/cm², and a jet airliner 500 feet overhead about a million times as intense. In decibel notation the whisper is about 20 dB above threshold, and the jetliner is about 120 dB above threshold. Normal conversation is about 60 dB above the reference level.

(B) Fourier analysis

(*a*) Part of a black and white grid

(*b*) Stimulus intensity across the grid, a square wave

High

Low

(*c*) Fundamental frequency

(*d*) Third harmonic, ⅓ amplitude

(*e*) Fifth harmonic, ⅕ amplitude

(*f*) Sum of (*c*) + (*d*) + (*e*)

portant for speech perception. The shape of the external ear is also important in sound localization—that is, identifying the direction and distance of the source of a sound (discussed later in this chapter).

Few humans can move their ears, but many other mammals have an elaborate set of muscles associated with the external ear, enabling them to change the shape of the pinna and to point it toward the source of sound. Animals with acute auditory localization abilities, such as bats, have especially mobile ears. Of course, animals with mobile ears have to take into account the position of the pinna when interpreting sounds around them. Information about the position of the external ear in such animals is conveyed to the auditory pathways in several forms, including feedback information from receptors in the muscles around the pinna.

The Middle Ear Concentrates Sound Energies

Between the external ear and the receptor cells of the inner ear is a group of structures, including bones and muscles, that constitute the **middle ear** (see Figure 9.1*c*). A chain of three tiny bones, or **ossicles**, connects the eardrum (**tympanic membrane**) at the end of the ear canal to an opening of the inner ear called the **oval window**. These ossicles are the smallest bones in the body; they are called the **malleus** (hammer), the **incus** (anvil), and the **stapes** (stirrup). Small displacements of the tympanic membrane move the chain of ossicles. These bones help the minute mechanical forces of air particles perform the difficult task of compressing the fluid in the inner ear by focusing the pressures from the relatively large tympanic membrane onto the small oval window. This arrangement vastly amplifies the sound pressure so that it is capable of stimulating the fluid-filled inner ear.

9.1 The Human Ear

(a) **Orientation in the head**

External ear (pinna)

(b) **The auditory structures enlarged**

Inner ear

Facial nerve

Middle ear

Auditory nerve

Cochlea

Ear canal   Tympanic membrane (eardrum)   Ossicles   Eustachian tube
Round window

(c) **The middle ear**

Nerve to tensor tympani (from mandibular branch of trigeminal nerve)

Tensor tympani muscle

Malleus

Incus

Tympanic membrane (eardrum)

Stapes

Oval window

Facial nerve   Branch to stapedius muscle   Stapedius muscle   Round window

The mechanical linkage of the ossicles is not fixed; it is modulated by two muscles in ways that improve auditory perception and protect the delicate inner ear from loud, potentially damaging sounds. One of these muscles, the **tensor tympani** (see Figure 9.1*c*), is attached to the malleus, which is connected to the tympanic membrane. The other muscle of the middle ear is attached to the stapes and thus is called the **stapedius**. When activated, these muscles stiffen the linkages of the middle-ear bones, thus limiting the effectiveness of sounds. The muscles of the middle ear are activated by sounds that are 80 to 90 dB above a person's hearing threshold—about as loud as a noisy street. When a loud sound occurs, the stapedius muscle starts to contract about 200 ms later.

The muscles of the middle ear also become active during body movement, swallowing, and vocalization; they are the reason we hear few of the sounds produced by the workings of our own bodies. In some animals, activation of these muscles prevents damage to receptors from very loud, self-produced vocalizations (Avan et al., 1992). For example, some birds and bats (and some babies) produce vocalizations at intense levels of sound pressure; activation of the stapedius muscle dramatically reduces the effect of the vocalization on the animal's own auditory receptors. In the case of sounds produced by our own body, the stapedius muscle contracts automatically just *before* the sound-producing movement. People whose middle-ear muscles have been damaged by disease complain about the annoying loudness of sounds they formerly ignored.

The Inner Ear Transduces Mechanical Energy into Neural Activity

The complex structures of the **inner ear** (Figure 9.2) convert sound into neural activity. To understand how the inner ear accomplishes this transduction, let's look at the details of the inner ear. In mammals the auditory portion of the inner ear is a coiled structure called the **cochlea** (from the Greek *kochlos*, "snail") (see Figure 9.2*a* and *b*). The human cochlea is embedded in the temporal bone of the skull and is a marvel of miniaturization. In an adult, the cochlea measures only about 4 mm in diameter—about the size of a pea. Unrolled, the cochlea would measure about 35 to 40 mm in length.

The region nearest the oval-window membrane is the base of the spiral; the other end, or top, is referred to as the apex. Along the length of the cochlea are three parallel canals: (1) the **tympanic canal**, (2) the **vestibular canal**, and (3) the **middle canal** (see Figure 9.2*c*). Because the entire structure is filled with noncompressible fluid, movement within the cochlea in response to a push on the oval window requires the presence of a movable outlet membrane. This membrane is the **round window**, which separates the tympanic canal from the middle ear (see Figure 9.1*c*).

The principal elements for converting sounds into neural activity are found on the **basilar membrane**, a flexible structure that separates the tympanic canal from the middle canal (see Figure 9.2*c*). This membrane vibrates in response to sound. It is about five times wider at the apex of the cochlea than at the base, even though the cochlea itself narrows toward its apex. Within the middle canal and atop the basilar membrane is the **organ of Corti**—the collective term for all the elements involved in the transduction of sounds. The organ of Corti includes three main structures: (1) the sensory cells (hair cells), (2) an elaborate

9.2 Structures of the Inner Ear

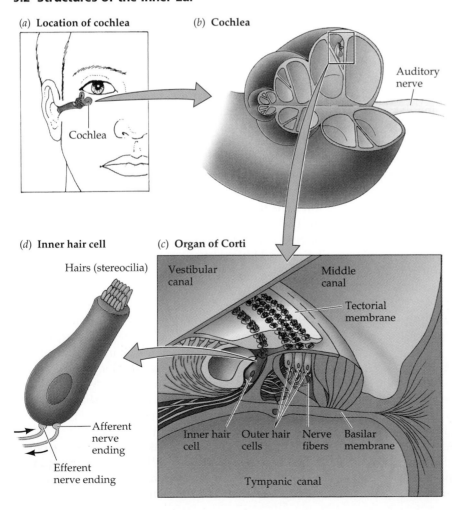

(*a*) **Location of cochlea**

Cochlea

(*b*) **Cochlea**

Auditory nerve

(*d*) **Inner hair cell**

Hairs (stereocilia)

Afferent nerve ending

Efferent nerve ending

(*c*) **Organ of Corti**

Vestibular canal

Middle canal

Tectorial membrane

Inner hair cell

Outer hair cells

Nerve fibers

Basilar membrane

Tympanic canal

9.3 Auditory Nerve Fibers and Synapses in the Organ of Corti

(*a*) Synaptic connections to the inner hair cells and the outer hair cells. (*b*) Hypothesized synaptic transmitters in the organ of Corti.

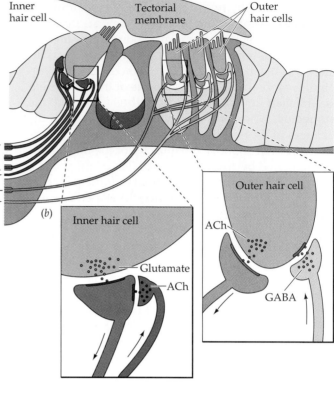

Nerve fibers:
1. Afferent, to cochlear nucleus of brain stem
2. Efferent, from lateral superior olivary nucleus
3. Afferent, to cochlear nucleus
4. Efferent, from medial superior olivary nucleus

framework of supporting cells, and (3) the terminations of the auditory nerve fibers (see Figure 9.2*c* and *d*).

Each ear contains two sets of sensory cells, a single row of about 3500 **inner hair cells** (IHCs; called "inner" because they are closer to the central axis of the cochlea) and about 12,000 **outer hair cells** (OHCs) in three rows (see Figure 9.2*c*). The IHCs are flask shaped, and the OHCs are cylindrical, with a diameter of approximately 5 μm and a length of 20 to 70 μm. From the upper end of each hair cell protrude tiny hairs whose length ranges from 2 to 6 μm (see Figure 9.2*d*). Each hair cell has 50 to 200 of these relatively stiff hairs, which are called **stereocilia** (singular stereocilium; from the Greek *stereos*, "solid," and the Latin *cilium*, "eyelid") or simply cilia. The heights of the stereocilia increase progressively across the hair cell, so the tops approximate an inclined plane. Atop the organ of Corti is the **tectorial membrane** (see Figure 9.2*c*). The stereocilia of the OHCs extend into indentations in the bottom of the tectorial membrane.

Auditory nerve fibers contact the base of the hair cells (see Figure 9.2*d*). Each IHC is associated with 16 to 20 auditory nerve fibers; relatively few nerve fibers contact the many OHCs. In fact, the nerve fibers running from the IHCs account for 90 to 95% of the afferent auditory fibers, suggesting that the IHCs convey most of the information about sounds to the brain.

The OHCs have a different function: *modulating* acoustic stimulation. They send messages out the auditory nerve to the CNS, but they are also contacted by efferent nerve fibers from the CNS. When these efferent nerve fibers are excited, the OHCs change their length, thereby influencing the mechanics of the cochlea. Changes in length of the OHCs during the basic responses to sound sharpen the tuning to different frequencies, as we will see later in this chapter

(Ashmore, 1994). The IHCs also receive efferent messages, perhaps to inhibit some of the input from loud sounds. Further evidence of the different roles of the inner and outer hair cells comes from studies of a mutant strain of mice that lack IHCs but have normal OHCs; these mice appear to be deaf (Deol and Gluecksohn-Waelsch, 1979).

Synapses in the Organ of Corti Convey Messages to and from the Brain

The organ of Corti has four kinds of synapses and nerve fibers. Two of these (1 and 3 in Figure 9.3*a*) are afferents that convey messages from the hair cells to the brain; the other two (2 and 4 in Figure 9.3*a*) are efferents that convey messages from the brain to the hair cells. Different synaptic transmitters are active at each type of synapse (Figure 9.3*b*) (Eybalin, 1993).

Sounds Produce Waves of Fluid in the Cochlea

When the stapes moves in and out as a result of acoustic vibrations, it exerts varying pressure on the fluid of the vestibular canal, which in turn causes oscillating movements of the basilar membrane. Late in the nineteenth century, it was suggested that the cochlea might be "tuned"; that is, that different parts of the basilar membrane might be affected by different frequencies of auditory stimulation.

In the 1930s and 1940s the Hungarian scientist Georg von Békésy tested this hypothesis, using ingenious physical techniques to make direct observations on cochleas that had been surgically removed from

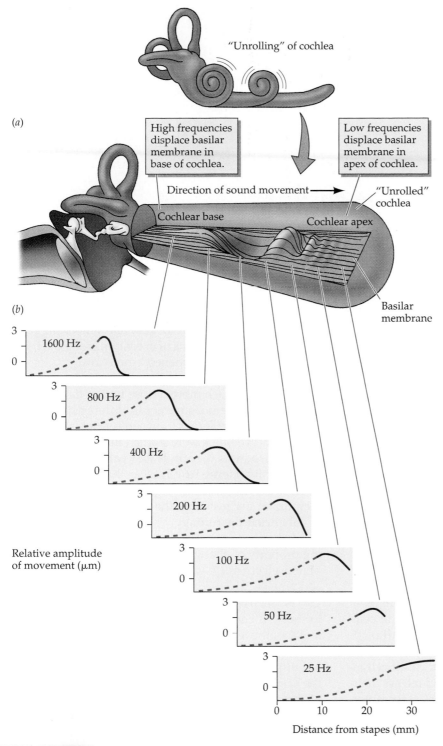

(a)

"Unrolling" of cochlea

High frequencies displace basilar membrane in base of cochlea.

Low frequencies displace basilar membrane in apex of cochlea.

Direction of sound movement ⟶

"Unrolled" cochlea

Cochlear base

Cochlear apex

Basilar membrane

(b)

1600 Hz

800 Hz

400 Hz

200 Hz

100 Hz

50 Hz

25 Hz

Relative amplitude of movement (μm)

Distance from stapes (mm)

9.4 Basilar Membrane Movement for Sounds of Different Frequencies

In this illustration the basilar membrane is represented as uncoiled. (*a*) Displacement of the basilar membrane peaks at the cochlear base for high frequencies and at the apex for low frequencies. (*b*) As the frequency (Hz, or cycles/s) of stimulation decreases, the position of the peak of membrane movement is displaced progressively toward the apex of the cochlea.

the displacement of the basilar membrane peaks in the region where the basilar membrane is narrow—the base of the cochlea. For low-frequency stimuli the amplitudes of membrane displacement peak at the widest portion of the basilar membrane—the apex—as modern techniques confirm (Ashmore, 1994).

The Hair Cells Transduce Auditory Vibrations into Electrical Signals

Modern techniques reveal intimate details of the principal elements of transduction—the hair cells (Hudspeth, 1989, 1992). The movements of fluid in the cochlea, excited by sounds, produce vibrations of the basilar membrane. These vibrations bend the hair cell cilia that are inserted into the tectorial membrane (see Figure 9.2*c*). Recordings from isolated individual hair cells showed that very small displacements of hair bundles cause rapid changes in ionic channels of the stereocilia. These changes initiate excitation of the hair cells and then of the afferent axons.

The ion channels in the stereocilia are the subject of much recent work. They are believed to be gated by mechanical energy, as are those in touch receptors (see Chapter 8), but the gates in the channels for hearing are also specialized for rapid response: They can open and close thousands of times per second. This rapidity rules out the use of second messengers, which are found in receptors for smell, taste, and sight (as we'll see later in this chapter and in Chapter 10).

The number of channels per hair cell has been estimated by measurements of the variability of response

Georg von Békésy
(1890–1972)

cadavers or dead animals. Békésy, who ultimately won the Nobel prize for his work, found that sounds initiate traveling waves that sweep along the basilar membrane, and the site of the largest amplitude of displacement of the basilar membrane depends on the frequency of the stimulus (Figure 9.4). For high frequencies

(a)

Tip links

(b)

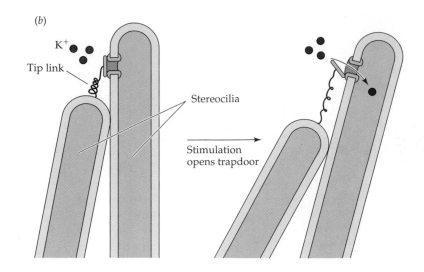

K⁺

Tip link

Stereocilia

Stimulation opens trapdoor

9.5 How Auditory Stimulation Affects the Stereocilia on Cochlear Hair Cells

(a) Micrograph of stereocilia, showing tip links as thread-like structures. *(b)* A model of hair cell stimulation proposed by Hudspeth (1992). (Micrograph courtesy of A. J. Hudspeth.)

in relation to the size of response. These measures suggest that there are only about 100 ion channels per hair cell, or about one or two per stereocilium. Comparing the recordings from different parts of the cell indicates that some ion channels are near the top of the cilia. Fine, threadlike fibers called **tip links** run along the tips of the stereocilia (Figure 9.5*a*).

According to one model (Hudspeth, 1997), a sound that makes the hair cells sway only a small percentage of their width increases the tension on the elastic tip links and pulls open a "trapdoor," opening the ion channel, which closes again in a fraction of a millisecond as the hair cell sways back (Figure 9.5*b*). Opening of the channels allows an inrush of potassium (K^+) ions and a rapid depolarization of the entire hair cell. This initial depolarization leads to a rapid influx of calcium ions (Ca^{2+}) at the *base* of the hair cell, which causes synaptic vesicles in the base of the hair cell to fuse with the presynaptic membrane and release their chemical contents—probably the synaptic transmitter glutamate—from the base of the hair cell, and stimulate the afferent nerve fiber.

The ion pores in the cilia are large and do not discriminate among kinds of ions. They let even small organic molecules pass through, which is why some drugs, such as aspirin and antibiotics, can impair hair cells by attacking their mitochondria. Susceptibility to this kind of damage of the receptor is inherited maternally, as are the mitochondria.

Active Electromechanical Processes in the Cochlea Enhance Frequency Discrimination

As Georg von Békésy realized, the broad peaks of tuning for different frequencies that he observed along the basilar membrane (see Figure 9.4) are not sharp enough to account for our ability to discriminate frequencies only 2 Hz apart. Békésy and others suggested that the broad patterns of excitation along the basilar membrane are "sharpened" somehow.

Even in the 1940s, recordings from auditory nerve fibers showed much more precise tuning than Békésy had found in his measurements of the basilar membrane. The **tuning curves** (or receptive fields) of single auditory nerve fibers were studied through recordings of their responses to sounds that varied in frequency and intensity (Figure 9.6). The fact that auditory nerve fibers are tuned much more precisely than the basilar membrane suggests that the cochlea itself has a way of enhancing the tuning.

We mentioned earlier that OHCs show the surprising property of changing length when they are stimulated electrically—an electromechanical response (Brownell et al., 1985). Hyperpolarization causes the OHCs to lengthen, while depolarization causes them to shorten. These changes, which amount to as much as 4% of the length of the cell, occur almost instantaneously. Investigators hypothesize that these mechanical responses of the OHCs amplify the movements of the basilar membrane and thereby sharpen its tuning (Ashmore, 1994; Hubbard, 1993). Other evidence of the active nature of the cochlea is that the ear can emit sounds (see the next section).

But while each neuron responds to a very precise frequency at its threshold, as more intense stimuli are used the neuron responds to a broader range of frequencies. For example, the fiber shown in red in Figure 9.6 has its "best frequency" at 1200 Hz; that is, it responds to a very weak tone at 1200 Hz. When sounds are 20 dB stronger, however, the fiber responds to any frequency from 500 to 1800 Hz. Thus, an auditory nerve fiber is not a labeled line of the sort we discussed in Chapter 8; that is, it does not respond to just one frequency of stimulation. If the brain received a signal from only one such fiber, it would not

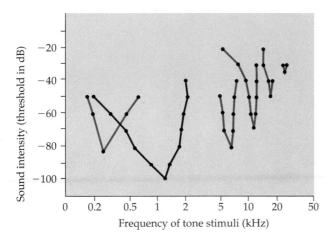

9.6 Examples of Tuning Curves of Auditory Nerve Cells
The curves are obtained by measurement of neural responses to sounds of different intensities and frequencies. These curves are threshold measurements. Illustrated here are responses of six neural units recorded from the auditory nerve of the cat. (After Kiang, 1965.)

be able to tell whether the stimulus was a weak tone of 1200 Hz or a stronger tone of 500 or 1800 Hz or any frequency in between.

The ability to discriminate frequencies is even sharper at higher stations of the auditory nervous system, as Békésy hypothesized. At the medial geniculate nucleus and the auditory cortex, neurons are excited by certain frequencies and inhibited by neighboring frequencies. This interplay of excitation and inhibition further sharpens the frequency responses, allowing us to discriminate very small frequency differences.

The Ears Emit Sounds as Part of the Hearing Process

The cochlea is not only the first stage in the analysis of sounds; in most people it also *produces* sounds. If you make a brief sound—a click or a short burst of tone—in the external ear canal, a few milliseconds later a similar sound comes back from the inner ear. This is not just an echo from the eardrum or middle ear, although such echoes exist. The cochlea produces this sound. The sounds the cochlea produces in response to acoustic stimulation are called **evoked otoacoustic emissions (EOAEs)**. They occur in all people who have normal hearing and are thought to reflect the active participation of the cochlea in hearing.

In addition to evoked otoacoustic emissions, the ears of many people also produce continuous low-level sounds at one or more frequencies; these sounds are called **spontaneous otoacoustic emissions (SOAEs)** (Kemp, 1979; Zurek, 1981). These spontaneous emissions are usually less than 20 dB above threshold; they can be detected by sensitive microphones in quiet environments, but the people who produce these sounds do not perceive them. About two-thirds of women

and half of men under 60 produce SOAEs (McFadden, 1993a). Since they are observed in infants as well as in adults, SOAEs don't seem to require prior auditory experience. Usually people who have SOAEs have more sensitive hearing than persons without them, and in most people the right ear (which is more likely than the left ear to produce SOAEs) has a slightly lower threshold for sound than the left ear has (McFadden, 1993b).

McFadden (1993b) reported a startling finding: Women who have a twin brother show significantly fewer SOAEs, and weaker EOAEs, than singleton females or females who have a female twin. McFadden suggests that the reason for the lower incidence of SOAEs in females with male twins is that in the womb, the female is exposed to androgens secreted by the male—a prenatal masculinizing effect (see Chapter 12). Because lesbians have weaker EOAEs than heterosexual women (McFadden and Pasanen, 1998), these evoked potentials are unexpectedly being related to human sexual orientation.

Evoked otoacoustic emissions may aid the screening of young children, especially newborns, for hearing impairments. Several studies have shown that EOAEs can be observed in human infants and that this technique is as useful as a commonly used electrophysiological technique for detecting hearing impairments (Doyle et al., 1997; Nozza, et al., 1997). The electrophysiological technique employed to compare with otoacoustic emissions is known as **auditory-evoked potentials**, like those we mentioned in Chapter 3. These electrical responses are obtained from an electrode on the scalp and include a series of waveforms generated at successive places in the auditory pathway that extends from cochlea to cortex.

Auditory System Pathways Run from the Brain Stem to the Cortex

On each side of the human head, about 30,000 to 50,000 auditory fibers from the cochlea make up the auditory part of the eighth (vestibulocochlear) cranial nerve. Recall that most of these afferent fibers are carrying messages from the IHCs, each of which stimulates several nerve fibers. Input from the auditory nerve is distributed in a complex manner to both sides of the brain (Figure 9.7). Each auditory nerve fiber divides into two main branches as it enters the brain stem. Each branch goes to separate groups of cells in the dorsal and ventral **cochlear nuclei.**

The output of the cochlear nuclei also travels via multiple paths. One set of paths goes to the **superior olivary nuclei,** which receive inputs from both right and left cochlear nuclei. The bilateral input to this set of cells is the first level for **binaural** (two ears) **interaction** of afferents in the auditory system and is therefore of primary importance for mechanisms of auditory localization, which we'll discuss shortly. Several other parallel

9.7 Auditory Pathways of the Human Brain

View from the front of the head, showing the first binaural afferent interactions in the brain stem and increasing binaural interaction at higher levels of the auditory system.

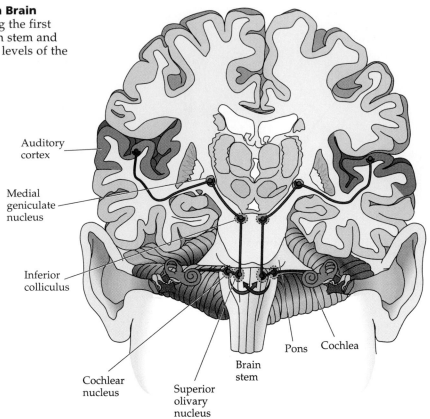

paths converge on the **inferior colliculus**, which is the auditory center of the midbrain. Outputs of the inferior colliculus go to the **medial geniculate nucleus** of the thalamus. At least two different pathways from the medial geniculate extend to several auditory cortical areas.

Sylvius ⊙

At each level of the auditory system, from cochlea to auditory cortex, a major feature is that the neurons are arranged in an orderly map that reflects the frequencies of stimuli; cells responsive to high frequencies are located at a distance from those responsive to low frequencies. This mapping of neural regions of the auditory system according to stimulus frequency is called **tonotopic organization**. To find the representation of a frequency in the inferior colliculus

Important method ▨

of the cat, investigators injected an animal with 2-deoxyglucose (2-DG) and then exposed it to a tone of a particular frequency. 2-DG is taken up by cells as though it were glucose, but 2-DG is not metabolized, so it remains in the cells. The neurons that are most active at the time 2-DG is injected take up more 2-DG than other cells, so postmortem processing reveals the regions of greatest activity (Figure 9.8).

The auditory cortex of many animals has been studied, and these studies have

enabled us to map the extent and character of responses to auditory stimulation. Most animals seem to have several auditory cortical fields. Merzenich et al., (1993) suggest that input to each region of auditory cortex includes both a tonotopically arranged system and a second, nontonotopic system projected

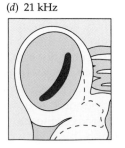

9.8 Mapping Auditory Frequencies in the Cat Inferior Colliculus

(*a*) Lateral view of the cat brain, showing the plane of the section in *b* through the inferior colliculi. (*b*) Transverse section through the inferior colliculus. (*c*, *d*) Location of the cells labeled with 2-DG via 2000 Hz stimulation (*c*), and 21,000 Hz stimulation (*d*). (*e*) Complete tonotopic mapping. (After Serviere et al., 1984.)

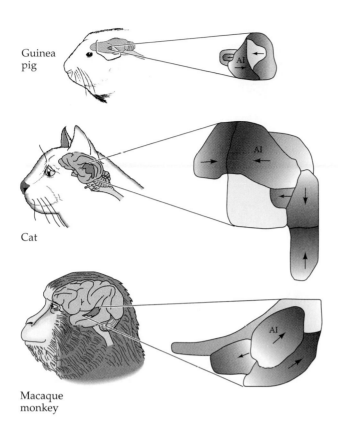

Guinea pig

Cat

Macaque monkey

9.9 Tonotopic Organization of Auditory Cortical Regions in Three Species of Mammals
The arrows show the direction of tonotopic representation, from low to high frequencies. (After Merzenich et al., 1993.)

from other subcortical areas. That is, different fields of the auditory cortex may be specialized for location of sounds in space, movement of sound sources, perception of species-specific sounds, and so on (Figure 9.9). In the next chapter we will see that different visual cortical areas specialize in representation of color, movement, and object recognition.

The human auditory cortex has been studied with noninvasive imaging techniques, including positron emission tomography (PET) and functional magnetic resonance imaging (fMRI). Stimulation with pure tones or noise activates chiefly the primary auditory cortex on the superior temporal lobe (Figure 9.10*a*). Speech activates this and other auditory areas (Figure 9.10*a* and *b*). As in other mammals, the human primary auditory area is tonotopically organized.

Two Main Theories Describe How We Discriminate Pitch

Most of us can discriminate very small differences in frequency of sound over the entire audible range—from 20 Hz to 15,000 or even 20,000 Hz. The ability to detect a change in frequency is usually measured as the **minimal discriminable frequency difference** between two tones. The detectable difference is about

2 Hz for sounds up to 2000 Hz; above these frequencies it grows larger. Note that "frequency" and "pitch" are not synonymous terms. **Frequency** describes a *physical property* of sounds (see Box 9.1); **pitch** relates solely to sensory *experience*—that is, the responses of subjects to sounds. There are many reasons to emphasize this distinction, including the fact that frequency is not the sole determinant of pitch experience (at some frequencies, sounds seem to increase in pitch as they become more intense), and changes in pitch do not precisely parallel changes in frequency.

How do we account for the ability to discriminate pitches? Two main theories have been offered. One, described as **place theory**, argues that our perception of pitch depends on where the sound causes maximal displacement of the basilar membrane. Place, according to this view, also includes which neurons are stimulated in the central auditory pathways; that is, particular nerve cells receive excitation from a particular part of the basilar membrane and therefore respond to particular stimulus frequencies.

➡️ **Competing hypotheses**

The alternative theory, commonly known as **volley theory**, emphasizes the relations between the frequency of auditory stimuli and the pattern or timing of neural discharges. According to this perspective, the firing pattern of a single nerve cell reveals the frequency of the stimulus, because each time the stimulus changes frequency, the pattern of neuronal discharge is altered. The crudest representation of this idea suggests a one-to-one relationship; that is, a 500 Hz tone is represented by 500 nerve impulses per second, and a 1000 Hz tone stimulating the same neuron is represented by a frequency of 1000 nerve impulses per second. In both cases the firing of the nerve impulse is "phase-locked" to the stimulus; that is, it occurs at a particular portion of the cycle. Such a phase-locked representation can be accomplished more accurately by several fibers than by a single fiber—hence the term "volley," as in a volley of nerve impulses. Are these views—place and volley theories—necessarily antagonistic? No. In fact, the contemporary view of pitch perception incorporates both perspectives.

As place theory predicts, the region of maximal vibration along the basilar membrane varies with the frequency of the stimulus: A change of frequency is accompanied by a change in the region of maximal disturbance (see Figure 9.4). The relations between the location of maximal displacement on the basilar membrane and frequency of the stimulus are considerably sharper than Georg von Békésy originally observed, especially for sounds above 1000 Hz (Rhode, 1984). For complex sounds with several frequency components, the cochlea accomplishes a sort of Fourier analysis (see Box 9.1), with the different frequencies represented by peaks of vibration at different places along the basilar membrane. The accuracy of such place representation of auditory frequency has improved over the course of evolution as the basilar

(a)

Subject 1   Subject 2

Noise

Speech sounds

(b) Listening to words   1   2   3   4   5

1
2
3
4
5

9.10 Responses of the Human Auditory Cortex to Random Sounds versus Speech

(a) fMRI scans of the cerebral hemispheres show that pure tones or noise (*top*) activate chiefly the primary auditory area on the superior aspect of the temporal lobe, while listening to speech sounds (*bottom*) activates other auditory cortical regions as well as the primary auditory area. (b) Lateral (*left*) and horizontal (*right*) PET scans show that listening to words activates not only several regions of the cerebral cortex but also regions of the thalamus and the cerebellum. The numbered horizontal lines in the left panel correspond to the levels of the horizontal sections in the right panel. (Part *a* from Binder et al., 1994, courtesy of Jeffrey Binder; *b* from Posner and Raichle, 1994, courtesy of Marcus Raichle.)

membrane has lengthened and the number of hair cells and auditory nerve fibers has increased.

On the other hand, an abundance of neurophysiological data suggest that pitch sensation also involves temporal patterns of nerve discharge, as volley theory predicts. Thus, single neurons may be able to convey frequency information for a broad range of frequencies. In these experiments the measurement of temporal pattern is usually the distribution of the intervals between the nerve impulses elicited by a stimulus. A neuron can be said to code the frequency of the sound if this distribution is either the same as the interval between successive cycles of the sound or an integral multiple of it. This kind of coding is quite prominent at frequencies below about 1500 Hz, although it has also been noted for sounds with frequencies up to 4000 Hz.

So the frequency properties of a sound can be coded in two ways: (1) the distribution of excitation among cells—that is, place coding or tonotopic representation—and (2) the temporal pattern (volley) of discharge in cells extending from the auditory nerve to the auditory cortex. With complex sounds, such as speech, that contain mixtures of frequencies, the auditory system makes a partial Fourier analysis, so we respond to the presence of different frequencies in a complex sound. For example, we discriminate vowel sounds because each vowel sound has its own characteristic frequency bands, and the relative intensities of different harmonic frequencies (see Box 9.1) help us identify musical instruments.

One Ear Can Localize Sounds, but Two Ears Can Do It Better

Under special circumstances—when sounds are of long duration and the head is free to move—**monaural detection** (using one ear) of acoustic sources is almost as good as **binaural detection** (using two ears). Normally, however, we use two ears to locate the position of a sound source, with great accuracy (within about 1°). This ability usually depends on the interaction of neural messages from the two ears.

What features of the stimulus are important for binaural localization? Two main binaural cues for auditory localization are (1) the difference in sound *intensity* at the two ears and (2) the difference in the *time of arrival* of sound at the two ears. More complex binaural differences also play a part, such as the frequency spectrum and phase differences. Stimuli that

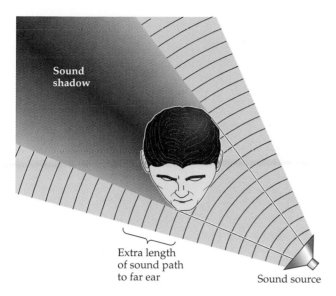

9.11 Cues for Binaural Hearing
The two ears receive somewhat different information from sound sources located to one side or the other of the observer's midline. The head blocks frequencies greater than 1000 Hz, producing binaural differences in sound intensity. Sounds also take longer to reach the more distant ear, resulting in binaural differences in time of arrival.

differ at the two ears are called **dichotic stimuli**. Early in the twentieth century, some investigators stressed the importance of intensity differences in dichotic stimuli, while others emphasized time differences. As often happens, both were correct. The idea that we use both intensity differences and arrival distances to localize sound is known as the **duplex theory**.

Some sounds show intensity differences at the two ears because the head casts a sound shadow (Figure 9.11). The sound frequencies that are effectively blocked depend on the size of the head, since low-frequency sounds have long waves that go around the head. At low frequencies, no matter where sounds are presented in the horizontal plane, there are virtually no intensity differences between the ears. For these frequencies, differences in times of arrival are the principal cues for sound position. At higher frequencies, the sound shadow cast by the head produces significant binaural intensity differences. We cannot tell by monitoring our own performance that we are using one cue to localize high-frequency sounds and another cue to localize low-frequency sounds. In general we are aware of the results of neural processing but not of the processing itself.

How are the binaural features of an acoustic environment analyzed by the nervous system? There are many opportunities for binaural interaction at various levels of the brain stem—regions where single nerve cells receive inputs derived from both ears, including the superior olivary complex. Cells within the superior olivary region are particularly sensitive to binaur-

al differences of time or intensity. The inferior colliculus also receives binaural inputs from several brain stem nuclei.

Are there neurons at the inferior colliculus that respond to some sound positions but not others? The answer differs depending on the species. In mammals, little evidence supports this idea (Masterton and Imig, 1984). One might conclude either that the detection of acoustic position is the product of the summation of many cells active in particular spatial and temporal patterns, or that sounds are localized at a higher level, such as the cortex.

Middlebrooks and Pettigrew (1981) tested for spatial selectivity in cortical neurons of the cat, using a setup like that shown in Figure 9.12*a*. About half the neurons showed some spatial selectivity (Figure 9.12*b*). Some of these neurons responded to a sound that originated anywhere in the opposite hemifield. Other location-sensitive neurons had relatively small receptive fields that responded only to sounds at a particular location on the side of the opposite ear. There was no indication of a systematic map of sound space in cats, but such mapping does occur in the brain of the owl.

In the owl, which uses accurate auditory localization to hunt at night, detailed and elaborate neural representations of auditory space are found. In the avian equivalent to the inferior colliculus (the tectum), some cells are arranged in a roughly spherical representation of space; that is, each space-specific cell has a receptive field that includes sounds coming from a small cone of space centering on the owl's head. Successive cells in the nucleus represent neighboring regions of auditory space (Knudsen, 1984b; Knudsen and Konishi, 1978).

In the owl tectum ("roof," or dorsal part of the midbrain), both auditory and visual space are represented, and the maps for the two senses correspond closely (Knudsen, 1982). Most cells in this region respond to both auditory and visual stimuli, and all of the auditory cells respond specifically to spatial direction. In most cases the visual receptive field of a cell is enclosed within the auditory receptive field of the same cell. Perhaps this close alignment of auditory and visual maps of space provides signals for motor responses with regard to the position of the stimulus. A little later in this chapter we will see how early experience affects auditory maps in the owl tectum.

The Auditory Cortex Performs Complex Tasks in the Perception of Sound

Most investigators of hearing, from the late nineteenth century until recently, believed that auditory sensation and discrimination depend on the auditory cortex. The noncortical auditory nuclei were considered to be mere relay stations or stepping-stones in a pathway to

(a)

(b)

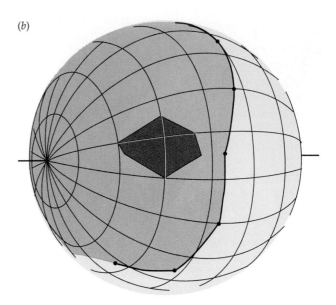

9.12 Spatial Sensitivity of the Auditory Neurons in Cat Cortex

(*a*) A loudspeaker emitting sound was moved along the surface of an imaginary sphere with a radius of 1 m while the responses of individual neurons were recorded. (*b*) About half the neurons showed some spatial sensitivity. Of these neurons, half responded to sounds that originated anywhere in the opposite hemifield (brown), and the other half showed relatively small receptive fields, responding only to sounds at a particular location on the side of the opposite ear (light blue). (After Middlebrooks and Pettigrew, 1981.)

the cortex (Masterton, 1993). Clinical and experimental neurology seemed to support this idea. Patients with injury to the auditory cortex and animals with extensive lesions of the auditory cortex often appeared to ignore sounds, but little attempt was made to determine what such patients or animals could hear or discriminate. Even after such attempts were made with experimental animals, beginning in the 1940s, the unexpected results were long resisted.

Careful experiments combining surgical removal of auditory cortex and behavioral testing showed that cats do not *need* auditory cortex to discriminate intensity (Raab and Ades, 1946; Rosenzweig, 1946), frequency (Butler et al., 1957), or duration of tones (for a review, see Neff and Casseday, 1977). If the auditory cortex is not involved in these basic kinds of auditory discrimination, then what *does* it do?

Auditory neuroscientists once relied on physically simple but unnatural pure tones (Masterton, 1993, 1997). Most of the sounds in nature are brief and change rapidly—such as vocalizations of animals, footsteps, snaps, crackles, and pops—and the auditory nervous system likely evolved to deal with such sounds. Indeed, most central auditory neurons habituate rapidly to continuous sound, ceasing to respond after only a few milliseconds, but brief sounds or

abrupt onsets of sound usually evoke responses from a wide array of neurons from the cochlear nuclei to the auditory cortex. Ablation of auditory cortex in cats does impair discrimination of temporal *patterns* of sound (Neff and Casseday, 1977). Similarly, in monkeys, bilateral ablation of the auditory cortex impairs the ability to discriminate species-specific vocalizations (Heffner and Heffner, 1989).

We mentioned earlier that listening to speech activates both primary auditory cortex and auditory association areas in humans, which is consistent with the idea that auditory cortex is required to process complex patterns of sound. Interestingly, the same regions are activated when normal subjects try to lip-read—that is, to understand someone by watching their lips without auditory cues (Calvert et al., 1997)—a result that suggests that auditory cortex also integrates other, nonauditory, information with sounds.

If the different regions of auditory cortex are not required for discriminating frequency, why are many of them tonotopic in their layout? Since the cochlea responds to different frequencies in a regular manner along its length, perhaps it is orderly and economical for the afferent projections from the cochlea to maintain a tonotopic distribution through the successive stations of the nervous system. Any other kind of projection would require crossing of fibers and more complex, and thus more expensive, organization. But auditory brain regions that are tonotopic in one dimension can represent aspects such as space or movement in the other dimension, or even complex aspects such as species-specific vocalizations.

Experience Affects Auditory Perception and the Auditory Pathways

Aspects of auditory discrimination and the neural circuits involved in hearing change as we grow. At birth the human infant has diverse hearing abilities. In fact, good evidence suggests that the fetus responds to sounds. Postnatal developments involve elaborate structural changes throughout auditory pathways. Accompanying these changes are progressive improvements in the perception of complex sounds, such as speech. Since the world after birth is filled with a complex array of sounds, it is reasonable to ask whether experience in some way shapes or modulates the forming of connections in the auditory system.

One fascinating demonstration of the role of early auditory experience comes from studies of musicians (Pantev et al., 1998). The evoked brain activity, as measured by magnetic imaging, from musicians and nonmusicians was identical in response to pure tones. But if, instead of pure tones, the more complex and musically relevant sounds from a piano were used, musicians displayed a greater brain response than did nonmusicians. Now maybe these people became musicians because their brains were more responsive to complex tones to begin with. However, there was a significant correlation between the magnitude of brain response to piano tones and the age at which the musicians began studying music. The earlier the musician had begun her studies, the greater the brain response to piano tones. This result suggests that it is indeed the exposure to musical training that affects brain auditory responsiveness.

Neural plasticity

Another aspect of auditory experience that is especially amenable to study is auditory localization. At birth, many animals show a coarse ability to localize sounds. Human infants often move their eyes toward the side where a sound stimulus occurs. Changes in the size of the ears and head, however, change the character of information used for auditory localization, and various studies have shown that animals improve their localization abilities as they mature.

The role of auditory experience in the development of sound localization is implied by observations in bilaterally deaf children who were fitted with different types of hearing aids (Beggs and Foreman, 1980). The children in one group were given a hearing aid that delivered the same sounds to both ears. In a second group children were fitted with a separate hearing aid for each ear, so that they experienced dichotic stimuli. Both groups experienced impoverished auditory environments. When examined years later, the children who had been fitted with dichotic hearing aids were able to localize sounds with significantly greater accuracy than that shown by the children who had experienced comparable overall levels of sounds but were deprived of dichotic stimuli.

Knudsen and colleagues (1984) performed some elegant studies using an especially acute binaural perceiver—the owl. To assess the impact of early deprivation of binaural inputs, the investigators placed a plug in one ear of the owl, which reduced sound intensity in that ear by 20 to 40 dB. This treatment was applied to owls of various ages. When the plug was first placed in the ear, the animal made large localization errors to the side of the open ear. For example, if a sound was made directly in front of the owl, the owl responded as if the sound had come from the side of the open ear—presumably because the sound was more intense in that ear, which would normally mean that it came from that side.

Adult animals never seemed to adjust to the ear plug, but owls that were younger than 8 weeks at the time of plugging slowly began to compensate for the distortion produced by the blockage of one ear. Then, when the ear plugs were removed, these animals made large localization errors to the opposite side. Knudsen and Knudsen (1985) showed the critical role of vision in this process of adjustment of auditory localization. Barn owls with one ear plugged did not correct their auditory localization errors if deprived of vision. Furthermore, if owls were fitted with prisms that deviated vision by 10° (Figure 9.13), the adjustment of auditory localization was matched to this visual error.

Neurophysiological studies of these owls reveal some features of the underlying mechanisms (Knudsen, 1985). As we mentioned earlier, within the tectum of barn owls are nerve cells that are bimodal; that is, they respond to both visual and auditory stimuli. These neurons are selective for sound source locations and visual spatial information. The auditory and visual spatial sensitivities are similarly aligned; that is, they correspond to approximately the same positions in space. So either a sound or a visual cue in one location will activate neurons in a particular region of the tectum.

9.13 Special Glasses Show the Role of Vision in Auditory Localization
This young owl has had prisms fitted over its eyes to deviate vision by about 10° to the side. At first, it will make mistakes when reaching for a visual target, but eventually it will learn to adapt to the prisms. The neurons in its tectum will also adapt, so now neurons excited by a sound from a particular location in space will also be excited by visual stimuli presented 10° to the left of that location. (Courtesy of Eric Knudsen.)

When the correspondence between auditory localization cues and visual position is changed by the use of an ear plug in young owls, an interesting finding is noted. Even though correspondence was altered by the ear plug, when tested months later, the auditory receptive fields aligned well with the visual receptive fields. But removal of the ear plug caused the cells' most sensitive auditory receptive areas to shift away from the alignment with the visual fields of a nerve cell. These changes in auditory spatial tuning did not occur in an adult animal that had been similarly treated, which suggests that this experience-dependent process involves a critical period during early development. These changes might arise from either structural modifications of growing neural circuits or from modulations of synaptic effectiveness.

The latter possibility is supported by the results of a follow-up study (Knudsen, 1998) of owls, like those already discussed, which had been fitted with prisms for a period and then allowed to recover without prisms during development. Unlike normal owls, these developmentally manipulated owls could learn to compensate when the prisms were put on again in adulthood. It's as though the abnormal connections made during the exposure to the prisms early in life had persisted, and could be reawakened by adult experience.

Maps of mammalian auditory areas also show plasticity. For example, monkeys were trained by means of a food reward to perform a difficult auditory frequency discrimination task. After several months of training, the cortical surface area representing the frequency band in which they had learned to discriminate had increased. Other subjects that heard the same tones but were not required to engage in the discrimination task did not develop an enlarged representation for these frequencies (Recanzone et al., 1993).

Making a localized lesion in the cochlea of an adult guinea pig increases the thresholds of neurons in certain cortical regions; these regions represent the sound frequencies corresponding to the damaged part of the cochlea (Robertson and Irvine, 1989). A month after the lesions are made, however, the neurons in the affected regions of the cortex respond with normal sensitivity to sound frequencies adjacent to those transduced by the damaged part of the cortex. Thus, the auditory cortical map remains plastic even in adult mammals. Further aspects of the plasticity of auditory cortex are described in Chapter 18. In fact, the plasticity of the mammalian cortex appears to be a major aspect of auditory cortex function.

Neural plasticity

Deafness Is a Major Disorder of the Nervous System

There are about 18 million cases of deafness or hearing impairment in the United States (Travis, 1992). These disabilities range in severity from occasional difficulties in speech perception (a drop in sensitivity of 41 to 55 dB between 500 and 2000 Hz) to the inability to hear anything (a 90 dB drop between 500 and 2000 Hz). In this section, after looking at the different kinds of deafness, we will discuss a promising treatment for deafness.

Different Kinds of Deafness Have Different Causes

Many severe hearing impairments arise early in life and impair language acquisition. There are three general categories of deafness:

1. **Conduction deafness** arises when disorders of the outer or middle ear prevent vibrations from auditory stimuli from reaching the cochlea.
2. **Sensorineural deafness** results from disorders of the cochlea or the eighth-nerve fibers conducting information from the cochlea to the brain.
3. **Central deafness** is due to disorders in brain auditory regions.

The conditions that cause sensorineural deafness are quite varied and include hundreds of hereditary disorders (Pennisi, 1997), metabolic dysfunctions, exposure to toxic substances, trauma, and loud sounds. The end result is the same: Auditory nerve fibers are unable to become excited in a normal manner. E. D. Lynch et al. (1997) isolated a gene responsible for sensorineural deafness in a large family in Costa Rica. This deafness starts at 10 years of age and results in total bilateral deafness by the age of 30. **Genes and behavior** The defective gene normally encodes one of the structural proteins that stiffen the hair cells. Other genetic forms of deafness involve other genes that control hair cell structure.

Drug-induced deafness results from the toxic properties of a group of antibiotics that includes streptomycin and gentamicin. The **ototoxic** (ear-damaging) properties of streptomycin were discovered because this antibiotic is remarkably effective in the treatment of tuberculosis. There was a tremendous price to pay for the cure: Many patients showed severe cochlear and/or vestibular damage. In some patients, streptomycin produced total, irreversible loss of hearing caused by the almost complete destruction of hair cells in the cochlea. Generally the highest frequencies are the first to be affected, because the basal region of the cochlea is especially susceptible.

Noise-induced hearing impairments also involve primarily inner-ear mechanisms. Noise pollution and the advent of recreational sounds—such as those derived from intense music, motorcycles and other loud engines, and especially the firing of guns—have made hearing loss a prominent problem and have given **audiologists** (hearing therapists) and **otologists** (ear doctors) a lot of business (W. W. Clark, 1991).

The cochlea can be damaged by exposure to intense sudden sounds or to chronic sounds of high intensity. The initial histological changes in the inner ear involve primarily hair cells, and the outer hair cells are more susceptible to sound trauma than are the inner cells. The progression of changes with continued sound exposure leads in some individuals to destruction of the organ of Corti and the nerve fibers that innervate it. Loud sounds coupled with the use of some over-the-counter drugs such as aspirin can have profound effects on hearing (McFadden and Champlin, 1990). The hearing loss caused by chronic use of aspirin can be impressive—a reduction of up to 40 dB for high tones, coupled with the development of **tinnitus**, a sensation of noises or ringing in the ears (Brien, 1993).

Can damaged hair cells be regrown in mammals? Although fish and amphibians produce hair cells throughout life and are thus able to replace damaged hair cells, mammals traditionally were thought to be incapable of regenerating hair cells. But later findings call this traditional idea into question. First, researchers discovered that birds can regenerate hair cells damaged by acoustic overstimulation or by ototoxic chemicals (Cotanche, 1987). Later, chemical stimulation was found to induce the regeneration of hair cells in cultures of the organ of Corti that had been surgically removed from young rats (P. P. Lefebvre et al., 1993). Because increasing the availability of cyclic AMP aids hair cell regeneration in chickens (Corwin and Oberholtzer, 1997), it may be possible one day to chemically induce hair cell regeneration in mammals.

Neural plasticity

Central deafness (hearing loss caused by brain lesions or impairments) is seldom a simple loss of sensitivity (Bauer and Rubens, 1985). An example of the complexity of changes in auditory perception following cerebral cortical damage is **word deafness**, a disorder in which people show normal speech and hearing for simple sounds but cannot recognize spoken words. Some researchers have suggested that the basis of word deafness is an abnormally slow analysis of auditory inputs. Another example of central deafness is **cortical deafness**, in which patients have difficulty recognizing both verbal and nonverbal auditory stimuli. Cortical deafness is a rare syndrome that arises from a bilateral destruction of inputs to the auditory cortex.

Case reports by Y. Tanaka et al. (1991) show deafness when strokes appear to interrupt all of the projection fibers (white matter) from the medial geniculate nucleus to the various auditory cortical regions. These patients still show various acoustic reflexes mediated by the brain stem—such as bodily responses to environmental sounds—although they deny hearing the sounds they react to. In contrast, patients with bilateral destruction of only the primary auditory cortex often have less severe hearing loss; presumably, other auditory cortical regions maintain hearing.

Electrical Stimulation of the Auditory Nerve Can Alleviate Deafness

Researchers have tried to restore hearing in profoundly deaf individuals by directly stimulating the auditory nerve with electrical currents (Loeb, 1990; J. M. Miller and Spelman, 1990). Progress in the development of **cochlear implants** that deliver such electrical stimulation has been rapid.

Who gains by the use of such devices? In several types of sensorineural hearing loss, including those caused by ototoxic drugs and childhood meningitis, the damage that produces deafness involves the hair cells. Although the hair cells may be completely destroyed, the electrical excitability of the auditory nerve often remains unchanged. Some of the most enthusiastic recipients of this clinical aid are patients who became deaf before acquiring language (Loeb, 1990). However, some deaf people and advocates of the deaf oppose the use of such prostheses (Crouch, 1997). They believe that deaf people should accept their disability and use sign language to communicate, rather than become imperfect hearers. Nevertheless, analytical studies reveal an increase in speech perception with continued use of cochlear prostheses (Skinner et al., 1997).

What kinds of sensory responses does electrical stimulation of the auditory nerve provoke? The usual technique employed in these studies is the insertion of a small group of wires through the cochlea to the endings of the auditory nerve. In these patients electrical stimulation produces pitch sensations that are partially related to the tonotopic organization of the cochlea. Unfortunately, the effective number of channels is limited by technical factors, so the range of frequencies that can be excited is also limited. With successive technical advances, the number has increased from 6 different frequencies to 20, but this range is still very limited compared with the range of frequencies we appreciate in normal hearing. Dynamic range is also limited, because intensities of electrical stimulation barely above the thresholds for sound produce discomfort.

Nevertheless, when stimulation is controlled by the sounds picked up by a microphone, the resulting pattern of electrical stimulation of the auditory nerve greatly facilitates some acoustically mediated behaviors and aids speech perception. For example, this treatment makes it possible to distinguish voiced and unvoiced speech sounds (e.g., "v" and "f"), which cannot be distinguished in lip-reading. Auditory excitation produced by cochlear electrical stimulation in deaf individuals markedly increases the metabolic rate of the auditory cortex of these patients, as revealed by PET studies (J. Ito et al., 1993). This finding indicates that such electrical stimulation may activate the speech comprehension systems of the auditory cortex.

Vestibular Perception

The vestibular system provides information about the force of gravity on the body and the acceleration of the head. When you go up in an elevator, you feel the acceleration clearly. When you turn your head or ride in a car going around a tight curve, you feel the change of direction. If you are not used to these kinds of stimulation, sensitivity to motion can make you "seasick." The receptors of the vestibular system inform the brain about mechanical forces, such as gravity and acceleration, that act on the body.

9.14 Peripheral Structures of the Vestibular System

(*a*) Position of the vestibular apparatus in the temporal bone. (*b*) Orientation of the semicircular canals, the utricle, and the saccule. (*c*) Receptor surface of the saccule and the utricle, showing otolith crystals. (*d*) Hair cells in the utricle or saccule. (*e*) An ampulla, or end, of a semicircular canal. (*f*) Hair cells in the ampulla.

The Receptor Mechanisms for the Vestibular System Are in the Inner Ear

The receptors of the vestibular system lie within the inner ear next to the cochlea. (The term "vestibular" comes from the Latin *vestibulum*, "entrance hall," and reflects the fact that the system lies in hollow spaces in the temporal bone.) In mammals, one portion of the vestibular system consists of three **semicircular canals**, fluid-filled tubes, each oriented in a different plane (Figure 9.14*a* and *b*). The three canals are connected at their ends to a saclike structure called the **utricle** (literally, "little uterus"). Lying below the utricle is another small fluid-filled sac, the **saccule** ("little sac").

Receptors in these structures, like those of the auditory system, are groups of hair cells whose bending leads to the excitation of nerve fibers. In each semicircular canal, the hair cells are in an enlarged region, the **ampulla** (plural ampullae), that lies at the junction between each canal and the utricle (Figure 9.14*b* and *e*). Here the cilia of the hair cells are embedded in a gelatinous mass (Figure 9.14*c*). The orientation of the hairs is quite precise and determines the kind of mechanical force to which they are especially sensitive.

The three semicircular canals are at right angles to each other; thus, one or another detects angular acceleration in any direction. The receptors in the saccule and utricle respond to static positions of the head. Small bony crystals on the gelatinous membrane, called **otoliths** (from the Greek *ot-*, "ear," and *lithos*, "stone"), increase the sensitivity of these receptors to movement (Figure 9.14*c* and *d*). At the base of the hair

cells in these receptors are nerve fibers connected much like those that connect auditory hair cells.

Evolution Has Shaped the Auditory and Vestibular End Organs

The long evolutionary history of the auditory–vestibular system is better known than that of other sensory systems because the receptors are encased in bone, which can fossilize (van Bergeijk, 1967; E. G. Wever, 1974). It is generally accepted that the auditory end organ evolved from the vestibular system. In turn, the vestibular system evolved from the **lateral-line system**, a sensory system found in many kinds of fish and some amphibians. The lateral-line system is an array of receptors along the side of the body; tiny hairs emerge from sensory cells in the skin. These hairs are embedded in small gelatinous columns called **cupulae** (singular cupula), like those in mammals (Figure 9.14*e* and *f*).

In aquatic animals with lateral-line systems, movements of water in relation to the body surface stimulate these receptors so that the animal can detect currents of water and movements of other animals, prey, or predators. Information from the lateral line helps schools of fish stay in formation; each fish feels the currents made by the others. A specialized form of lateral-line organ is the lateral-line canal, a groove that partially encloses the cupulae. It is speculated that the first semicircular canals developed from a stretch of lateral-line canal that migrated into the body. This development gave the animal a sensor for turns to the right or left, and this receptor, being away from the surface of the body, was free of effects of stimulation of the skin. Sensitivity to change of direction was optimized when the canal developed into a roughly circular form.

From the vestibular system that arose out of the lateral-line system evolved the auditory system (Figure 9.15). Animals that have more advanced characteristics show longer auditory ducts with greater numbers of hair cells and auditory nerve fibers. Presumably this larger system is the basis for the excellent ability to discriminate frequencies and auditory patterns.

Nerve Fibers from the Vestibular Portion of the Vestibulocochlear Nerve Synapse in the Brain Stem

The structural arrangements of brain pathways dealing with vestibular excitation reflect its close connection to muscle adjustments in the body. Nerve fibers from the vestibular receptors enter lower levels of the brain stem and synapse in a group of nuclei, called the **vestibular nuclei**. Some of the fibers bypass this structure and go directly to the cerebellum, a center for motor control. The outputs of the vestibular nuclei are

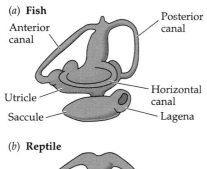

(*a*) **Fish**

Anterior canal

Posterior canal

Utricle

Horizontal canal

Saccule

Lagena

(*b*) **Reptile**

Utricle

Saccule

Lagena

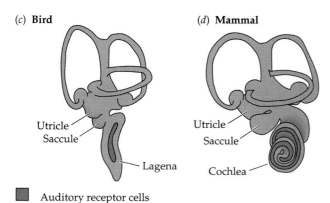

(*c*) **Bird**

Utricle

Saccule

Lagena

(*d*) **Mammal**

Utricle

Saccule

Cochlea

■ Auditory receptor cells

9.15 Evolution of the Vestibular and Auditory End Organs

complex, as is appropriate to their influences on the motor system. These outputs go to the motor nuclei of the eye muscles, the thalamus, and the cerebral cortex, among others.

Some Forms of Vestibular Excitation Produce Motion Sickness

There is one aspect of vestibular activation that many of us would gladly lose. Certain types of body acceleration—such as those we experience as a passenger in an oceangoing boat, an airplane, a car, or an amusement park ride—can produce distress known as **motion sickness**. Caloric stimulation—the pouring of warm water into one ear canal—produces the same effect by initiating movements of inner ear fluids that simulate mechanical stimulation. Motion sickness is caused especially by low-frequency movements that an individual cannot control. For example, passengers in a car may suffer from motion sickness, but the driver does not.

One major theory of motion sickness—**sensory conflict theory**—says that the malady arises from contradictory sensory messages, especially a discrepancy between vestibular and visual information. For instance, as an airplane suddenly moves up, the vestibular system is excited but the eyes see the constancy of the plane's interior; the resulting disorientation is distressing (Benson, 1990).

Why do we experience motion sickness? The experimental psychologist Michel Treisman (1977) hypothesized that the sensory conflict of some conditions of motion sets off responses that evolved to rid the body of swallowed poison. According to this hypothesis, discrepancies in sensory information from various modalities signal danger and cause dizziness and vomiting to eliminate potentially toxic food. Such a response has obvious significance for preservation of life, although it is not helpful as a response to movements of vehicles. A person whose vestibular system has been destroyed by toxic drugs or by side effects of antibiotics does not experience motion sickness.

The Chemical Senses: Taste and Smell

Sensitivity to chemical stimuli in the environment is vital for the survival of organisms throughout the animal kingdom. The sense of taste provides an assessment of foods (Lindemann, 1995): Sweet indicates high-calorie foods; salty and sour relate to important aspects of homeostasis; and bitter warns of toxic constituents. Many animals also use chemical sensitivity to detect the odor trails of other animals, thus informing themselves about prey and predators and guiding themselves to mates. This section will show examples of the many roles of the chemical senses—taste and smell—in guiding behavior.

We start our review of the chemical senses with taste, which is somewhat simpler and in some ways has been more thoroughly investigated than smell. Smell is a more complicated and puzzling chemical sense, although recent discoveries are greatly increasing our understanding of olfaction.

Chemicals in Tastants Elicit Taste Sensations

Humans Detect Four Basic Tastes

Because we recognize many substances by their distinct flavor, we tend to think that we can discriminate many tastes. But humans detect only four basic tastes: salty, sour, sweet, and bitter. (We can qualify that limitation a bit, because, as we will see, there is probably more than one sweet taste, and there are probably several bitter tastes.) The sensations aroused by foods such as an apple, a steak, or an olive are *flavors* rather than simple tastes; they involve smell as well as taste. Block your nose, and a potato tastes the same as an apple. Our ability to respond to many odors—it is estimated that humans can detect more than 10,000 different odors and can discriminate as many as 5000 (Ressler et al., 1994)—is what produces the complex array of flavors that we normally think of as tastes. Most mammals share the four basic tastes that humans discriminate, but members of the cat family have only three: Cats are not sensitive to sweet. Other animals may have more tastes than humans do.

The ability to taste many substances is already well developed at birth. Even premature infants show characteristic responses to different tastes, sucking in response to a sweet substance but trying to spit out a bitter substance. Newborns seem to be relatively insensitive to salty tastes, but a preference for mildly salty substances develops in the first few months. This preference does not seem to be related to experience with salty tastes but probably indicates maturation of the mechanisms of salt perception (Beauchamp et al., 1994).

Tastes Excite Specialized Receptor Cells on the Tongue

In mammals, most taste receptor cells are located on small projections from the surface of the tongue; these little bumps are called **papillae** (singular papilla; Latin for "nipples"). Each papilla holds one or more clusters of 50 to 150 cells, which are the **taste buds** (Figure 9.16a). At the surface end of the taste bud is an opening, the taste pore. The taste cells extend fine cilia into the taste pore, which come into contact with **tastants** (substances that can be tasted). Not all the sensory cells in taste buds signal taste sensations; some are pain receptors, responding to stimuli such as "hot" red pepper, and others are touch receptors. With a life span of only 10 to 14 days, taste cells are constantly

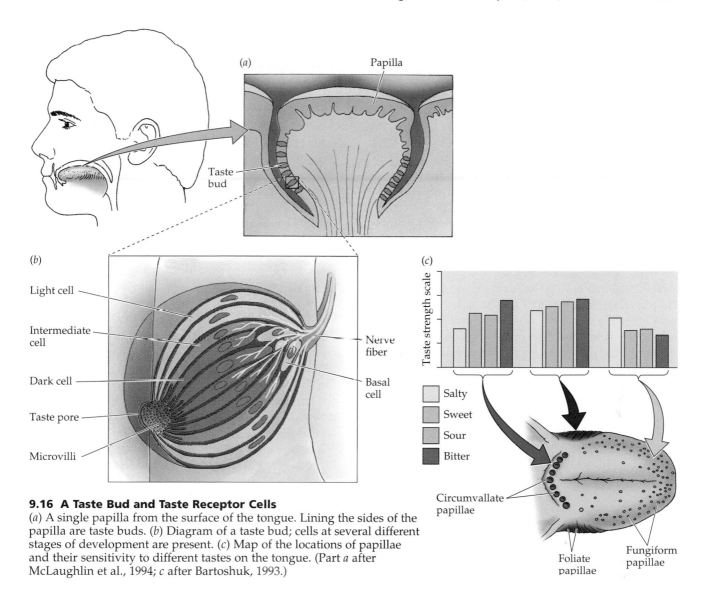

9.16 A Taste Bud and Taste Receptor Cells
(*a*) A single papilla from the surface of the tongue. Lining the sides of the papilla are taste buds. (*b*) Diagram of a taste bud; cells at several different stages of development are present. (*c*) Map of the locations of papillae and their sensitivity to different tastes on the tongue. (Part *a* after McLaughlin et al., 1994; *c* after Bartoshuk, 1993.)

being replaced. A single taste bud has receptor cells that are at many different stages of development (Figure 9.16*b*).

There are three kinds of taste papillae; Figure 9.16*c* shows their distribution on the tongue. The most numerous are **fungiform papillae**, which resemble button mushrooms in shape (*fungus* is Latin for "mushroom"). There are hundreds of fungiform papillae on the tongue, but the numbers vary greatly among individuals. A fungiform papilla usually contains only a single taste bud. Each of the few **circumvallate papillae** and **foliate papillae** contains several taste buds.

Many books show a map of the tongue indicating that each taste is perceived mainly in one region (sweet at the tip of the tongue, bitter at the back, and so on), but Linda Bartoshuk (1993, p. 253), a specialist in taste psychophysics, states that this map is erroneous: "The [usual] tongue map has become an enduring scientific myth." Work of Collings (1974) and Yanagisawa et al. (1992) shows that all four basic tastes can be perceived anywhere on the tongue

where there are taste receptors. The areas do not differ greatly in the strength of taste sensations they mediate (see Figure 9.16*c*).

Different Cellular Processes Transduce the Four Basic Tastes

The tastes salty and sour are evoked when taste cells are stimulated by simple ions acting on ion channels in the membranes of the taste cells. Sweet and bitter tastes are perceived by specialized receptor molecules and communicated by second messengers. We will examine the mechanisms of each taste, proceeding from simple to complex.

Salty. Sodium ions (Na^+) are transported across the membranes of taste cells by sodium ion channels. Blocking these channels with a drug prevents the salty taste of sodium chloride in both humans and rats; facilitating the passage of Na^+ across the membrane with another drug intensifies salty tastes (Schiffman et al., 1986). The entry of sodium ions partially depolarizes the taste cells and causes them to release neurotransmitters that stimulate the afferent neurons that relay the information to the brain.

Sour. An acid tastes sour, whether it is a simple inorganic compound, such as hydrogen chloride, or a more complex organic compound, such as lactic acid. The property that all acids share is that each releases a hydrogen ion (H^+). The hydrogen ions block potassium channels in cell membranes, preventing the release of potassium ions (K^+) from taste cells. The buildup of K^+ in the cell leads to depolarization and to neurotransmitter release. The afferent fibers stimulated by these taste cells report the acidic stimulation to the brain.

Sweet. The molecular mechanisms in the transduction of sweet and bitter tastes are more complex than those responsible for salty and sour tastes. There are good reasons to believe that sweet and bitter tastants stimulate specialized receptor molecules on membranes of the taste cells, causing a cascade of internal cellular events involving G proteins and second messengers. These receptors are probably like the slow, metabotropic synaptic receptors we considered in Chapter 3. A novel G protein α subunit has been isolated in taste cells (McLaughlin et al., 1994). Investigators have not yet identified the receptor molecules for sweet or bitter tastes. A variety of molecules taste sweet, and psychophysiological experiments show that there is probably more than one kind of sweet taste.

Bitter. Bitter sensations are evoked by even more different tastants than are sweet sensations. The bitter taste of many toxic substances—such as nicotine, caffeine, strychnine, and morphine—provided strong evolutionary pressure to develop a high sensitivity to bitterness. Different bitter substances can be discriminated from each other—in psychophysical work with human tasters (McBurney et al., 1972) and with animal subjects (Lush, 1989)—suggesting that there is more than one receptor for bitterness.

Further evidence of the existence of multiple receptors for bitterness is the specific inability of some individuals to taste certain bitter substances. For example, about 25% of people in the United States cannot taste the chemical phenylthiocarbamide (PTC) and the related compound 6-*n*-propylthiouracil (PROP), even though they can taste other bitter substances. Family genetic studies have suggested that the ability to taste PTC and PROP requires a gene that can take two forms (alleles), *T* and *t*. Individuals with the *T* allele can taste these substances. Individuals with two *tt* alleles are nontasters. Those carrying one of each allele (*Tt*) are tasters, which is why the *T* gene is called dominant.

Psychophysical evidence indicates that the tasters can be divided into two groups: medium tasters and supertasters—the latter representing about 25% of the total population (Bartoshuk et al., 1992). This breakdown suggests the possibility that medium tasters have one dominant allele, *Tt*, and supertasters have two dominant alleles, *TT*. Supertasters perceive stronger taste intensities not only from some bitter compounds but also from some sweet compounds (Bartoshuk et al., 1992). Counts of the number of taste buds in people with varying sensitivity to PROP show that nontasters have the fewest taste buds (averaging 96 per square centimeter) on the tongue tip, medium tasters an intermediate number (averaging 184), and supertasters the most (averaging 425; Reedy et al., 1993). These differences are striking, but numbers of taste buds alone cannot explain the observation that supertasters experience only certain substances more intensely than do medium tasters (Bartoshuk and Beauchamp, 1994).

Neural Coding for Tastes Is Complex

Since different taste cells appear to be responsible for each of the four main tastes, it might seem obvious that each afferent axon from the taste buds carries information about only one taste. This idea is known as the labeled-line hypothesis, or **specific-pathway hypothesis.** (Recall our discussions of labeled lines for the skin senses in Chapter 8 and for auditory frequencies earlier in this chapter.) According to another hypothesis, **pattern coding**, each axon responds to some extent to more than one taste, and taste discrimination requires central processing based on relative activity coming from different afferent axons.

Recording from individual taste axons shows that each axon responds to a low concentration of one taste stimulus but also responds to higher concentrations of other tastes (Pfaffmann et al., 1979). For example, one axon responds most readily to sweet stimuli but also responds to a concentrated salty or bitter solution. Thus, the fact that this cell is active does not tell whether it is responding to a dilute sugar solution or a strong salt solution. Only central analysis of the *pattern* of responses across several neurons reveals the identity of the stimulus. This situation is similar to what we saw in audition: The response of a single axon can be evoked by a weak stimulus at its best frequency or by stronger stimuli anywhere in a broad range.

Taste Information Is Transmitted to Several Parts of the Brain

The **gustatory system** (from the Latin *gustare*, "to taste") extends from the taste receptor cells through brain stem nuclei and the thalamus to the cerebral cortex (Figure 9.17). Each taste cell transmits information to several afferent fibers, and each afferent fiber receives information from several taste cells. The afferent fibers run along three different cranial nerves—the facial (VII), glossopharyngeal (IX), and vagus (X) nerves (see Figure 2.9). The gustatory fibers in each of

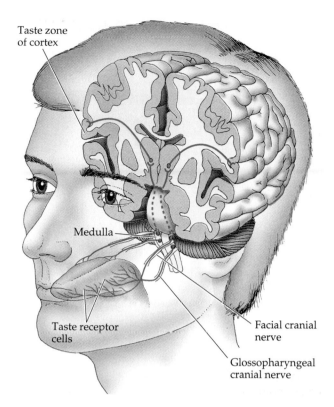

Taste zone
of cortex

Medulla

Taste receptor
cells

Facial cranial
nerve

Glossopharyngeal
cranial nerve

9.17 Anatomy and Main Pathways of the Human Gustatory System

these nerves run to the medulla. Here they synapse with second-order gustatory fibers that run to the ventral posterior medial nucleus of the thalamus. After another synapse, third-order gustatory fibers run to the cortical taste areas in the somatosensory cortex.

Chemicals in the Air Elicit Odor Sensations

We have already noted that many aspects of an animal's world are determined by chemicals carried in the air. Information about human abilities to detect and identify odors comes from a survey sponsored by *National Geographic Magazine* that elicited responses from more than 1.5 million individuals (Gilbert and Wyslocki, 1987). Scents were affixed to pages of the magazine and were released when the paper surface was scratched. Readers were asked to detect the odors, to identify them, and to mail in response sheets. Six odors were presented as a sample of some aspects of the wide variety of odors that humans can detect.

Half the respondents were able to detect all six odors, and only about 1% were unable to smell three or more samples. But there was widespread partial **anosmia** (odor blindness): Thirty-five percent of the respondents could not detect androsterone (sweat), and 29% could not detect galaxolide (musk); most individuals who could not detect one of these odors

could not detect the other either. Women were slightly better than men in both detecting and identifying odors. The ability to detect odors declined somewhat with age. This age-related drop was greatest in the elderly people who rated mercaptans—the foul smell added to natural gas—as extremely unpleasant, indicating a possible danger for elderly people. Smokers showed a dulled sense of smell; they found pleasant odors to be less pleasant and unpleasant odors less unpleasant than nonsmokers did.

The Sense of Smell Starts with Receptor Neurons in the Nose

In humans, a sheet of cells called the **olfactory epithelium** lines the dorsal portion of the nasal cavities and adjacent regions, including the septum that separates the left and right nasal cavities (Figure 9.18). Within the olfactory epithelium of the nasal cavity are three types of cells: receptor neurons, supporting cells, and basal cells. At least 6 million olfactory receptor neurons are found in the 2 cm^2 area of human olfactory epithelium; in many other mammals this number is an order of magnitude greater; for example, rabbits have about 40 million receptor neurons in the olfactory epithelium.

Each receptor cell has a long slender apical dendrite that extends to the outermost layer of the epithelium, the mucosal surface. There numerous **cilia** emerge from the **dendritic knob** and extend along the mucosal surface. At the opposite end of each bipolar olfactory receptor cell, a fine unmyelinated axon, which is among the smallest-diameter axons in the nervous system, runs to the olfactory bulb (which we will discuss shortly).

In contrast to many other receptor neurons in the body, olfactory receptor neurons are constantly degenerating and being replaced by new receptor cells, even in adults (Costanza, 1991). It is easy to understand why they degenerate; these neurons are in direct contact with the external environment and are therefore exposed to a wide array of irritants, such as chemicals and viruses. But we do not yet understand exactly how they are replaced. After an olfactory receptor cell degenerates, an adjacent basal cell differentiates into a neuron and extends dendrites to the mucosal surface and an axon into the brain. **Neural plasticity**

Thus, the olfactory system is constantly being rewired; the functional capability of these new connections has been clearly demonstrated in both behavioral and electrophysiological studies of animals with completely regenerated olfactory epithelium. Investigators are trying to determine how these neurons can regenerate while those in most other parts of the nervous system cannot. A related unresolved question is how the new neurons are able to establish the correct connections in the olfactory bulb.

9.18 Anatomy and Main Pathways of the Human Olfactory System

The schematic diagram at lower right indicates the main olfactory pathways in the brain.

Odorants Excite Specialized Receptor Molecules on Olfactory Receptor Cells

Odorants enter the nasal cavity during inhalation and especially during periods of sniffing; they also rise to the nasal cavity from the mouth when we chew food. The direction of airflow in the nose is determined by complex curved surfaces called **turbinates** that form the nasal cavity (see Figure 9.18). Airborne molecules initially encounter the fluids of the mucosal layer, which contain binding proteins that transport odorants to receptor surfaces (Farbman, 1994). These stimulus-binding proteins have been found in a wide array of animals, including insects and mammals. The viscosity (stickiness) of the mucous layer determines how rapidly odorants reach the cilia of olfactory receptor cells (Kinnamon and Cummings 1992).

The odorant stimulus then interacts with receptor sites located in the **olfactory cilia** and the dendritic knob of the receptor cells. These receptors are members of a superfamily of G protein–linked receptors. Interactions with the receptor trigger the synthesis of second messengers, including cyclic AMP (cAMP) and inositol trisphosphate (IP$_3$). Cyclic AMP opens a cation channel (Brunet et al., 1996) to elicit the gener-

ator current that depolarizes the olfactory receptor cell, and the depolarization, in turn, leads to action potentials.

This sensory transduction process, portrayed in Figure 9.19, is similar to the activation of other sensory systems, such as those for sweet and bitter tastes, and those in the eye (see Chapter 10). A specific G protein is used by all the olfactory receptors, because mice in which the gene for this particular G protein is knocked out are generally anosmic (Belluscio et al., 1998). In other cases the second messenger is IP$_3$, which opens calcium channels, depolarizing the olfactory receptor cell (Anholt, 1993).

Discoveries in the 1990s have strongly supported the hypothesis that there are many specific olfactory receptor molecules (Buck, 1996; Buck and Axel, 1991). This research has revealed a large, novel family of genes for G protein receptors expressed in the olfactory epithelium. Each of these receptor molecules has seven regions that are believed to span the cell membrane, and these molecules are synthesized only in

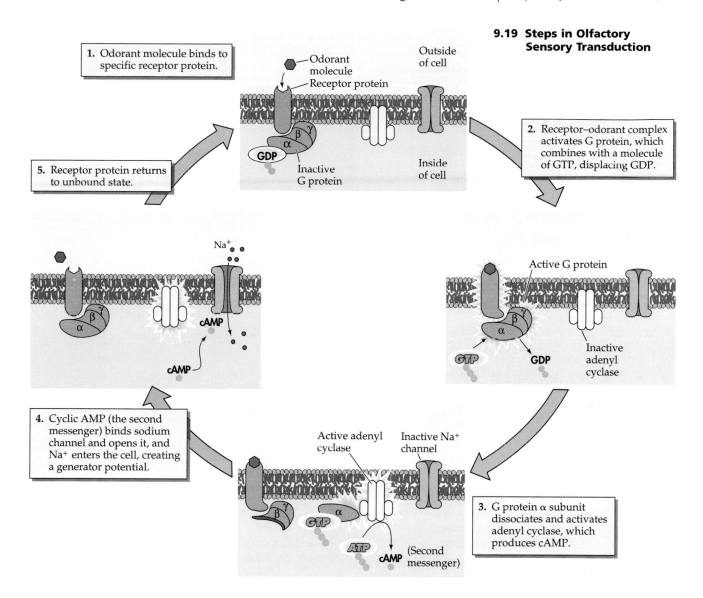

9.19 Steps in Olfactory Sensory Transduction

1. Odorant molecule binds to specific receptor protein.

2. Receptor–odorant complex activates G protein, which combines with a molecule of GTP, displacing GDP.

3. G protein α subunit dissociates and activates adenyl cyclase, which produces cAMP.

4. Cyclic AMP (the second messenger) binds sodium channel and opens it, and Na⁺ enters the cell, creating a generator potential.

5. Receptor protein returns to unbound state.

the olfactory receptor cells and not in the neighboring supporting cells or basal cells. The members of this family of receptors are diverse, although they have certain regions in common. There are subfamilies whose members are very similar and may recognize subtle differences between structurally related odorants. Zhao et al. (1998) proved that these proteins are indeed odor receptors, by transfecting rat olfactory epithelial cells with a gene to produce more copies of one of the proteins, and demonstrating that as a result the animal was more sensitive to a particular set of odorants.

The human genome is estimated to contain about 500 to 1000 different odorant receptor genes (Ressler et al., 1994). Comparisons with the estimated 5000 odors that humans can discriminate suggest that each odorant receptor interacts with a small number of different odorants. Although some odorants may be "recognized" by a single kind of receptor molecule, most odorants probably are recognized by a combination of a few different kinds of receptor molecules. Neurons

that express the same receptor gene are not closely clustered in the olfactory epithelium, but they are limited to distinct regions of the epithelium (Figure 9.20). Each subfamily of receptors is synthesized in several different bands of the epithelium (Vassar et al., 1993).

Olfactory Axons Connect with the Olfactory Bulb, Whose Output Projects to Several Brain Regions

The numerous axons of the olfactory nerve terminate in a complex structure at the anterior end of the brain called the **olfactory bulb** (see Figure 9.18). The olfactory bulb is organized into many roughly spherically shaped neural circuits called **glomeruli** (singular glomerulus). The intrinsic circuitry within these glomeruli contributes to an elaborate feedback control and modulation of olfactory bulb activity. Rats have about 900 glomeruli on each side, and olfactory receptors expressing a particular receptor protein will innervate with precision only one of these glomeruli.

Sylvius

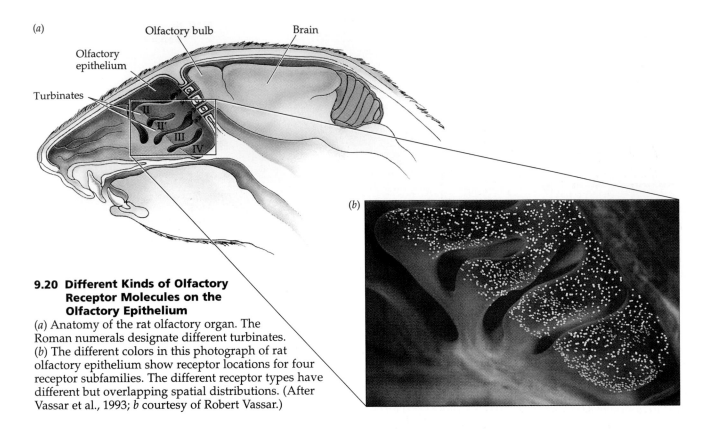

(a)

Olfactory bulb

Brain

Olfactory epithelium

Turbinates

II
II'
III
IV

(b)

9.20 Different Kinds of Olfactory Receptor Molecules on the Olfactory Epithelium
(a) Anatomy of the rat olfactory organ. The Roman numerals designate different turbinates. (b) The different colors in this photograph of rat olfactory epithelium show receptor locations for four receptor subfamilies. The different receptor types have different but overlapping spatial distributions. (After Vassar et al., 1993; b courtesy of Robert Vassar.)

So there appears to be a topographic distribution of smells in the bulb, but so far we don't understand the relationship between neighboring glomeruli.

Recall that olfactory receptors are continually being replaced and that the new receptors must reestablish contact with the brain. Experiments with knockout mice suggest that the olfactory receptor proteins help guide the innervating axons to the proper target. Disruptions of the receptor protein prevent newly generated olfactory receptor axons from reaching their normal glomerulus (F. Wang et al., 1998). The olfactory bulb, in relation to the rest of the brain, is much smaller in humans than in animals such as rats that depend extensively on olfaction (compare Figures 9.18 and 9.20).

Outputs from the olfactory bulb extend to prepyriform cortex, the amygdala, and the hypothalamus, among other brain regions. Functional MRI studies of human brain activation suggest that the prepyriform cortex is activated during sniffing, whether or not an odor is present (Sobel et al., 1998), apparently because the airflow induced by sniffing provides somatosensory stimulation. On the other hand, when an odor is present, orbitofrontal cortex is activated, whether or not the person sniffs. So the sniffing that accompanies olfactory exploration may help activate particular brain pathways. Note that the olfactory system is the only sensory system in vertebrates that does not synapse in the thalamus on its way to the cortex.

Many Vertebrates Possess a Vomeronasal System

Many vertebrates have a second chemical detection system that appears to specialize in detecting **pheromones**, the odor signals or trails that many animals secrete (see Chapter 5). This **vomeronasal system** (see Box 9.2), as it is called, is present in most terrestrial mammals, amphibians, and reptiles, and consists of a **vomeronasal organ** of epithelial cells near the olfactory epithelium. Rodents have a family of receptor proteins that are similar to, but distinct from, the receptor proteins in the olfactory epithelium that we discussed earlier. The vomeronasal system is usually said to be absent or vestigial in fishes, birds, and higher primates, including humans (M. Halpern, 1987). However, there is evidence—both anatomical (D. T. Moran et al., 1991) and electrophysiological (Monti-Bloch et al., 1994)—of a vomeronasal system in adult humans (see Chapter 12).

The report that extracts of human sweat, when applied to the upper lip of women, can adjust their menstrual cycle by 1 to 2 days (Stern and McClintock, 1998) suggests that humans detect pheromones. The donor sweat was gathered from other women, and depending on where the donors were in their menstrual cycles, the recipients' cycle was either accelerated or retarded in response. Sex pheromones enable males of many species to discriminate ovulating from nonovulating females, and mothers and their off-

BOX 9.2 *Why Do Snakes Have Forked Tongues?*

*T*he forked tongue of snakes has intrigued people for millennia, inspiring many hypotheses about its function (Schwenk, 1994). In many cultures and religions the forked tongue symbolizes malevolence and deceit. The first person known to inquire about the functional significance of the forked tongue was Aristotle; he suggested that this feature would double the pleasure of gustatory sensations. By the beginning of the twentieth century, the consensus was that the snake's tongue is a tactile organ; that is, the snake uses it to tap the ground much as a blind person uses a cane.

In 1920, L. G. Browman suggested what seemed to be a winning hypothesis: When the snake retracts its tongue, the tips (or tines) of the forked tongue are inserted into openings on both sides of the roof of the mouth; through these openings chemical stimuli reach special olfactory organs—the vomeronasal organs (VNOs). These organs are highly developed in snakes, lizards, and many mammals. They are a second olfactory system that appears to have evolved specifically to detect pheromones, the chemical signals that animals secrete as messages to other animals of their species. (We will refer to the VNOs and pheromones again in Chapter 12, on sex.)

Browman suggested that the forked tongue flicks out, picking up chemical signals, and then delivers these signals to the VNOs. Later demonstrations that cutting the vomeronasal nerve reduces the frequency of tongue flicks (M. Halpern et al., 1997) fit this hypothesis. But X-ray movie studies of tongue flicks in snakes and lizards with forked tongues disproved the hypothesis; they showed that when the tongue is withdrawn into the mouth, it enters a sheath and the tips do not go into the openings to the VNOs (Gillingham and Clark, 1981). In-

stead, the chemical molecules are deposited on pads at the bottom of the mouth, and closing the mouth presses the pads and molecules against the VNO openings.

If the tongue is not forked to fit into the VNOs, then what function could the forked shape serve? Schwenk (1994) proposed a solution that encompasses observations from several fields—animal behavior, ecology, sensory physiology, and neuroanatomy. He hypothesized that the forked tongue allows the snake to sense chemical stimuli at two points simultaneously, thereby giving it the ability to detect gradients in an odor trail. Obtaining two simultaneous readings enhances the ability of the snake to follow pheromone trails accurately, as depicted in the figure. This ability is important in seeking both prey and mates.

This accurate spatial chemical perception is like other systems for spatial perception that are based on simultaneous stimulation of two separated sense organs—for example, auditory localization, which depends on differential stimulation at the two ears, as we discussed earlier in this chapter. Similarly, the use of the two eyes permits stereovision (see Chapter 10).

Several kinds of evidence support the hypothesis that forked tongues evolved as chemosensory edge detectors to enhance the ability to follow odor trails:

(1) Snakes and lizards spread the tines of their tongue apart when they retrieve odor molecules, then draw the tines together when retracting the tongue. The greater the distance between sampling points, the better the animals sample a chemical gradient.
(2) Whereas lizards with forked tongues forage widely, lizard species without forked tongues tend not to forage widely.
(3) Forked tongues have evolved independently at least twice in different families of reptiles (Schwenk, 1994), indicating their value as an adaptation. (4) In the snake nervous system, each tine of the tongue projects to a nucleus in the other side of the brain, and the two nuclei are linked across the two hemispheres. This arrangement is similar to the anatomy of auditory centers in mammals and birds that permits the computation of binaural differences and mediates auditory localization.

Species in other orders have also evolved paired chemical receptors to guide individuals to mates or prey. For example, male gypsy moths have large, elaborate, odor-detecting antennae with which they track potential mates over large distances. And the ant nest beetle has spoon-shaped antennae extending from each side of the head with which it detects and follows the pheromones of the ants that are its food.

spring recognize each other through airborne cues. Many of the cues are emitted in urine and distinctive body glands.

The role of olfaction in human social behavior is less obvious. Humans have distinctive odors, as shown by the ability of police dogs to readily distinguish one person from another, but do people respond to human odors? Human infants recognize their mothers by odors of the breast, and human mothers can distinguish the odors of their babies from others. In contrast to other animals, humans show no clear role for pheromones in their copulatory behavior, but the allure of perfumes and colognes provides a clue that humans might not be all that different from other animals (Takagi, 1989). (In fact, "Pheromone" is the name of a perfume.) The role of odors in mediating the emotional tone of humans is well documented. Some odors provoke a sense of comfort and others can be distressing, especially the odors of substances that could produce food poisoning.

Olfaction Displays Some Cognitive Aspects

Some animals have species-specific responses to certain odors, such as pheromones, but human responses to odor are learned. From a whiff, we can often identify and name an odorant, an ability that depends on learning. Adult rats readily learn in a laboratory apparatus to choose the correct side on the basis of odor cues (Staubli et al., 1995). Rat pups develop an attraction to artificial odors that are paired with reinforcing stimuli like those they receive from maternal care; such reinforcing stimuli include grooming and infusions of milk or sucrose solution into the mouth (Caza and Spear, 1984; Leon et al., 1978).

The pairing of a reinforcing tactile stimulus and an unfamiliar odor, peppermint, resulted in enhanced uptake of 2-deoxyglucose in certain glomeruli in the olfactory bulb of rat pups (Sullivan and Leon, 1986). The enhanced uptake was associated with a 21% enlargement of the individual glomeruli affected (Woo and Leon, 1987). None of these changes occurred in the bulbs of animals exposed **Neural plasticity** to the peppermint odor alone or to the tactile stimulation alone. Thus training results in measurable, localized changes in the olfactory bulb.

Summary

Hearing

1. The external ear captures, focuses, and filters sound. The sound arriving at the tympanic membrane (eardrum) is focused by the ossicles of the middle ear onto the oval window to stimulate the fluid-filled inner ear (cochlea).

2. Sound arriving at the oval window causes traveling waves to sweep along the basilar membrane of the inner ear. For high-frequency sounds, the largest displacement of the basilar membrane is at the base of the cochlea, near the oval window; for low-frequency sounds, the largest amplitude is near the apex of the cochlea.

3. The organ of Corti has both inner hair cells (about 3500 in humans) and outer hair cells (about 12,000 in humans). The inner hair cells convey most of the information about sounds; each is associated with about 20 nerve fibers. The outer hair cells amplify the movements of the basilar membrane in response to sound, thus sharpening the frequency tuning of the cochlea.

4. Vibration of the hair cells causes the opening and closing of ion channels, thereby transducing mechanical movement into changes in electrical potential. These changes in potential stimulate the nerve cell endings that contact the hair cells.

5. Discrimination of auditory frequency involves two kinds of neural coding: For low frequencies, each cycle of the sound can be represented by nerve impulses (volley theory); higher frequencies are represented mainly by the site of maximal stimulation along the basilar membrane (place theory).

6. At each level of the auditory system, sound frequencies are mapped in an orderly succession; this is called tonotopic mapping.

7. Auditory localization depends on differences in the sounds arriving at the two ears. For low-frequency sounds, differences in time of arrival at the two ears are especially important. For high-frequency sounds, differences in intensity are especially important.

8. Sound experiences early in life can influence later auditory localization and the responses of neurons in auditory pathways. Experiences later in life can also lead to changes in responses of auditory neurons.

9. Deafness can be caused by pathological changes at any level of the auditory system. Conductive deafness consists of impairments in the transmission of sound to the cochlea that are produced by changes in the external or middle ears. Sensorineural deafness arises in the cochlea or auditory nerve. Central deafness arises in the brain.

10. Some forms of deafness can now be alleviated by direct electrical stimulation of the auditory nerve by an implanted prosthesis (a cochlear implant) that records and transforms acoustic stimuli.

Vestibular Perception

1. The receptors of the vestibular system lie within the inner ear next to the cochlea. In mammals the vestibular system consists of three semicircular canals, the utricle, and the saccule.

2. Within each of these structures, the receptors, like those of the auditory system, are groups of hair cells whose bending leads to the excitation of nerve fibers.

3. The vestibular system appears to have evolved from the lateral-line system, found in many kinds of fish and some amphibians. It is generally accepted that the auditory end organ evolved from the vestibular system.

The Chemical Senses: Taste and Smell

1. Humans detect only four main tastes: salty, sour, sweet, and bitter.

2. In mammals, most taste receptor cells are located in clusters of cells called taste buds. The taste cells extend fine cilia into the taste pore of the bud, where tastants come into contact with them. The taste buds are situated on small projections from the surface of the tongue called papillae.

3. The tastes of salty and sour are evoked by simple ions acting on ion channels in the membrane of taste cells. Sweet and bitter tastes are perceived by specialized receptor molecules and communicated by second messengers.

4. Each taste axon responds most strongly to one taste but also to other tastes. Taste discrimination requires central processing based on relative activity coming from different afferent axons.

5. Each taste cell transmits information to several afferent fibers, and each afferent fiber receives information from several taste cells. The afferent fibers run along cranial nerves to brain stem nuclei. The gustatory system extends from the taste receptor cells through brain stem nuclei to the thalamus and then to the cerebral cortex.

6. In contrast to the ability detect only four tastes, humans can detect thousands of different odors. Many species depend more on smell than humans do; such species have more olfactory receptor cells, larger olfactory bulbs, and lower thresholds for odorants.

7. Each olfactory receptor cell is a small bipolar cell whose dendrites extend to the olfactory epithelium in the nose. The fine, unmyelinated axon runs to the olfactory bulb. An olfactory receptor cell dies after about 2 weeks and is replaced by an adjacent basal cell.

8. There is a large family of odor receptor molecules. Each of these receptor molecules has seven transmembrane regions and utilizes G proteins and second messengers.

9. Neurons that express the same receptor gene are not closely clustered in the olfactory epithelium, but they are limited to distinct regions of the epithelium. Each subfamily of receptors is synthesized in several different bands of the epithelium.

10. The axons of the olfactory nerve terminate in the olfactory bulb. The projection from the epithelium to the bulb maintains a zonal distribution for different kinds of receptor molecules.

11. Outputs from the olfactory bulb extend to prepyriform cortex, the amygdala, and the hypothalamus, among other brain regions.

12. Many responses to odors are learned, even by young animals. Training results in measurable, localized anatomical and physiological changes in the olfactory bulb.

Recommended Reading

Altschuler, R. A., Bobbin, R. P., Clopton, B. M., and Hoffman, D. W. (Eds.). (1991). *Neurobiology of hearing: The central auditory system.* New York: Raven.

Bartoshuk, L. M., and Beauchamp, G. K. (1994). Chemical senses. *Annual Review of Psychology, 45,* 419–449.

Buck, L. B. (1996). Information coding in the vertebrate olfactory system. *Annual Review of Neuroscience, 19,* 517–545.

Ciba Foundation. (1993). *The molecular basis of taste and smell.* New York: Wiley.

Farbman, A. I. (1992). *Cell biology of olfaction.* Cambridge, England: Cambridge University Press.

Hildebrand, J. G., and Shepherd, G. M. (1997). Mechanisms of olfactory discrimination: Converging evidence for common principles across phyla. *Annual Review of Neuroscience, 20,* 595–631.

Masterton, R. B. (1993). Neurobehavioral studies of the central auditory system. *Annals of Otology, Rhinology, and Laryngology, Supplement, 168,* 31–34.

Popper, A. N., and Fay, R. R. (Eds.). (1992). *The mammalian auditory pathway: Neurophysiology.* New York: Springer.

Yost, W. A. (1994). *Fundamentals of hearing* (3rd ed.). New York: Plenum.

10

Vision: From Eye to Brain

Vision plays a key role in our lives and those of many other animals. Even animals that inhabit relatively dark ecological niches—such as owls, bats, and deep-sea fish—need information from light receptors. Some invertebrates are so greedy for light that they have multiple light receptors scattered about the body, and some amphibians have photoreceptors directly in their brain.

The visual *perceptions* of each species depend on how their eyes and brains evolved to process information about the spatial distribution of

Mary Joan Waid, *Dream Series V*, 1983

various wavelengths of light. Different kinds of processing allow us to see the form, color, position, and distance of objects in the visual field. Research on visual information processing is one of the most active fields of biological psychology and neuroscience, as it should be, since about one-fourth of the human cerebral cortex is devoted to visual analysis and perception. Our aim is to convey some of the major challenges, accomplishments, and excitement of this field.

After introducing some of the main phenomena of visual perception, we will examine the bases of vision—structures and functions of the visual system, from the eye to the cerebral cortex. Different parts of the brain process different aspects of visual perception, as we will see from experiments using brain imaging during perception and from evidence connecting specific impairments of vision with brain lesions.

Vision Provides Information about the Form, Color, Location, and Movement of Objects

Although we're familiar with vision because we use it every day, some features of visual perception are not immediately apparent. Some of these features are surprising, but a good grasp of the visual system (which we will discuss shortly) helps us understand many of these phenomena.

Perception of Form and Identification of Objects Are Complex Accomplishments

The whole area that you can see without moving your head or eyes is called your **visual field.** In a single glance, you can perceive the details of objects accurately only in the center of your visual field. We are usually not aware of this phenomenon because we move the direction of our gaze rapidly as we scan a scene or read a line of print. Thus we build up a sort of collage of detailed views. But try keeping your eyes fixed on a letter in the center of a line and then attempt to read a word in the opposite column. You'll find it difficult because **visual acuity** (the sharpness of vision) falls off rapidly from the center of the visual field toward the periphery. This difference in acuity across the visual field is the reason your gaze has to jump from place to place in a line as you read.

If a stimulus suddenly appears away from the center of the visual field, we shift our direction of view, placing the new stimulus in the center of the visual field, where we can see it clearly. When we examine the circuitry of the retina and of higher stations of the visual system a little later, we will learn why vision is so much more acute in the center of the visual field. Most of us don't have to worry about having acute vision only in the center of our visual field, but many older people have a condition (called macular degeneration) in which the receptor cells at the center of the retina degenerate; such people are left with at best only the fuzzy, indistinct vision of the peripheral visual field. Experts estimate that 6.3 million older Americans will develop macular degeneration by the year 2030.

If we examine the visual field of each eye separately, we find a **blind spot** about 16° to the temporal (lateral) side of the fixation point. This blind spot is relatively large, about 5° in diameter. (The full moon is about 0.5° in diameter.) Use Figure 10.1 to find the blind spot in the visual field of your right eye. The reason for the blind spot is that the fibers of the optic nerve exit the eye in a region called the **optic disc** (Figure 10.2) about 16° to the *nasal* (nose) side of the retinal center. Because there are no receptors in this region, nothing can be seen in the corresponding *temporal* part of the visual field. The optic disc on the nasal side of the retina causes the blind spot in the temporal side of the visual field because the pupil and the lens reverse the retinal

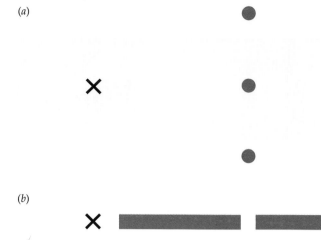

(a)

(b)

10.1 The Blind Spot

To locate your blind spot, hold the page about 10 to 12 cm (4 to 5 inches) away. Close your left eye and focus your right eye on the X. In (a), the middle dot on the right should disappear. In (b), when you place the gap at your blind spot, you will see a solid line rather than a broken line. (You may need to adjust the page closer or farther away to locate your blind spot.)

image, left to right, as Figure 10.2 shows; the retinal image is also inverted top to bottom.

The blind spot does not appear as a dark spot; it is simply a region from which we cannot obtain visual information. Find your blind spot again using Figure 10.1a and place a pencil so that its center runs vertically through the blind spot. Do you see a gap in the pencil where it intersects the blind spot? No. You receive no information from the blind spot, yet you perceive a complete pencil—your perceptual system fills in from the surrounding area. If you place the gap in the line in Figure 10.1b in your blind spot, you will see the line as complete because the gap is invisible. Similarly, if you keep your left eye closed and look at a uniform area or most patterns with your right eye, you will not be aware of any discontinuity in the region of the blind spot. An isolated stimulus, however (such as the dot in Figure 10.1a), may disappear in the blind spot. King Charles I of England is said to have amused himself by "beheading" some courtiers in this way.

We perceive a simple form like a triangle or recognize the face of a friend so rapidly and easily that we do not appreciate that these are exceedingly complex events that require processing in several parts of the brain. Most of the forms we see are embedded in complicated fields of objects; separating out a particular form for attention and identification requires practice and skill. It has been very difficult to achieve even primitive object recognition with artificial systems such as computers. Furthermore, recognition requires more than the accurate perception of objects. For example, as we will see in Chapter 19, some people with brain damage lose their ability to recognize familiar faces, even though they can still describe them accurately.

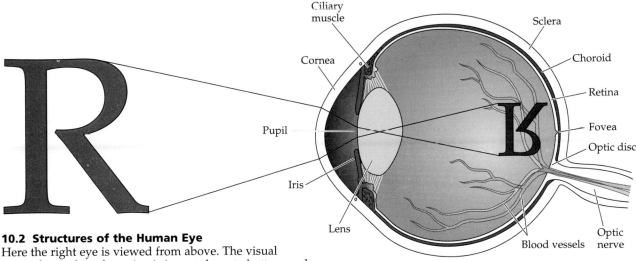

10.2 Structures of the Human Eye
Here the right eye is viewed from above. The visual image focused on the retina is inverted top to bottom and reversed right to left. The gap in the retina where the optic nerve leaves the eyeball is the optic disc.

Consider the complexity of visual perception at the level of the nervous system: Each photoreceptor at each instant is in a particular state of membrane polarization, which is signaled to the neural units by a certain rate of transmitter release. In effect, each receptor is signaling a quantitative index of excitation that can be represented by a number. The nervous system takes in, about three times per second, a number from each of the approximately 100 million photoreceptors, and it faces the stupendous task of trying to figure out what in the outside world could have produced that particular array of values.

Figure 10.3 illustrates a much simpler example of such a task. The numbers in this array represent shades of gray from darkest (2) to lightest (9). As you inspect this grid, you may notice that the lighter shades appear mainly in the upper half of the array, but you don't perceive a form. Now look at Figure 10.4, which shows the shades of gray that correspond to the numbers in the array in Figure 10.3—the form leaps out. Your nervous system processes those data to achieve the perception in an instant. How the nervous system processes so much data so quickly is the staggering problem that confronts anyone who tries to understand vision. We will consider current research and theories that attempt to resolve this absorbing question.

Color Is Created by the Visual System

For most of us, the visible world has several distinguishable hues: blue, green, yellow, red, and their intermediates. For about 8% of human males and about 0.5% of females, however, some of these color distinctions are either absent or at least less striking. Although the term "color blindness" is commonly used to describe impairments in color perception, most people with impaired color vision distinguish *some*

hues. Complete color blindness in humans is extremely rare, although it can be caused by brain lesions. Animals exhibit different degrees of color vision. Many species of birds, fish, and insects have excellent color vision. Humans and Old World monkeys also have an excellent ability to discriminate wavelengths, but many other mammals (e.g., cats) cannot discriminate wavelengths very well. We'll see more about the distribution of color vision among mammals later in this chapter.

```
9 9 8 8 8 8 8 8 8 8 8 8 8 8 8 8 8 8 8 8 8 8 8 8 8 8 8 7 7 6
9 9 8 8 9 8 9 8 8 8 8 8 8 6 5 7 7 9 5 7 8 8 8 8 8 8 7 7 7 7
9 9 8 9 9 9 9 9 9 9 9 7 4 3 3 3 3 4 4 6 8 8 8 8 8 7 7 7 7
9 9 8 8 9 9 9 9 9 9 8 5 3 3 4 4 3 3 3 4 4 3 6 8 8 8 8 8 7 7 7
9 9 9 8 8 8 8 8 7 4 3 3 3 8 9 9 6 4 3 3 3 3 3 4 8 8 7 7 7 7 7
9 9 9 8 8 8 8 8 4 3 3 6 9 9 9 9 8 6 4 3 3 3 4 8 8 8 7 7 7 7
9 9 9 9 8 8 8 6 4 3 4 9 9 9 9 9 9 9 8 4 3 4 4 6 7 7 7 7 7 7
9 9 8 8 8 8 8 5 3 3 6 9 9 9 9 9 9 9 6 4 5 5 5 7 7 7 7 7 7
9 9 8 8 8 8 8 4 2 3 8 8 9 9 9 9 9 9 9 8 6 6 4 6 7 7 7 7 7
9 9 8 8 8 8 8 2 2 3 6 7 9 9 9 9 9 9 8 8 9 8 6 4 4 6 7 7 7 7
9 9 8 8 8 8 4 3 2 3 4 6 7 8 5 4 5 7 8 8 8 8 6 3 4 6 6 7 7 7
9 9 8 8 8 8 3 3 5 4 2 6 8 6 4 4 3 4 8 6 3 4 3 4 4 7 6 6 7 7 7
9 9 8 8 8 7 4 6 6 4 3 7 7 5 6 4 4 6 8 5 3 3 3 5 7 7 7 7 7 6
9 9 8 8 8 7 7 4 7 4 8 3 8 8 7 6 5 8 8 8 5 4 4 7 7 6 6 6 6 6
9 8 8 7 7 7 7 4 6 7 7 3 5 7 8 7 7 7 7 8 6 5 5 6 6 6 6 6 6 6
9 8 7 7 7 7 7 6 4 7 6 4 3 5 6 7 7 6 7 7 7 6 6 4 6 5 6 6 6 6 6
9 8 7 7 7 7 7 7 5 5 3 4 3 4 4 6 6 6 5 3 4 3 4 4 5 5 5 5 5 6 5
9 8 7 7 7 7 6 6 5 2 4 4 6 5 5 6 7 7 4 2 3 2 5 5 5 5 5 5 5 5
9 8 7 7 6 6 6 7 6 4 4 4 6 6 6 5 5 3 2 4 5 5 5 5 5 5 5 5 5 5
9 7 7 7 7 6 6 6 6 6 5 3 3 6 6 5 6 4 3 4 2 4 5 5 5 5 5 5 5 5
9 7 7 7 7 6 6 6 6 5 4 2 4 4 3 5 5 6 5 3 2 3 5 5 5 5 5 5 5 5
9 7 7 7 7 6 6 6 6 4 6 2 2 2 2 2 3 3 2 2 2 4 5 5 5 5 5 5 4 5 4
9 7 7 7 6 7 6 6 6 5 2 7 5 2 2 2 2 2 2 2 2 4 5 5 5 5 5 5 4 4 4
9 7 7 7 7 7 6 7 6 3 2 4 7 6 2 2 2 2 2 4 5 5 5 5 5 5 5 4 5 4
9 7 7 7 7 6 4 2 2 2 2 7 7 6 5 3 2 2 4 5 4 5 5 5 5 5 5 4 4 5 4
9 7 7 7 6 2 2 2 2 2 2 4 6 4 3 6 6 6 6 6 2 4 5 5 5 5 4 4 4 5 4
9 7 6 3 2 2 2 2 2 3 3 2 2 2 3 2 2 2 2 2 3 2 2 5 5 5 5 4 4 4 5 4
8 4 2 2 2 2 2 2 3 3 3 3 3 3 3 3 3 2 2 2 2 2 2 4 4 5 4 4 5 5 4
8 2 2 2 2 2 2 2 3 3 3 2 2 2 4 3 3 4 2 2 2 2 2 2 3 4 5 5 4
8 2 2 2 2 2 2 2 3 3 3 2 2 3 3 5 4 3 2 2 2 2 2 2 2 2 3 4 5 5
6 2 2 2 2 2 2 2 2 2 2 2 2 2 2 3 7 6 6 5 5 5 3 2 2 2 2 2 2 3
6 2 2 2 2 2 2 2 2 2 2 2 2 2 2 2 4 6 6 6 6 6 2 2 2 2 2 2 2 2
```

10.3 Can You Identify the Subject?
This array of numbers represents the point-to-point illumination of a picture, from darkest (2) to lightest (9).

10.4 The Subject of Figure 10.3

A patch of light has other aspects besides hue. The color solid shown in Figure 10.5 illustrates the basic dimensions of our perception of light when the visual system is adapted to daylight illumination; the figure is deliberately asymmetrical, for reasons we will mention. The three dimensions of color are as follows:

1. **Brightness,** which varies from dark to light; it is the vertical dimension in Figure 10.5. The middle plane of the figure is tipped up for yellow and down for blue because yellow in the spectrum is perceived as lighter and blue as darker than the other hues.
2. **Hue,** which varies continuously around the color circle through blue, green, yellow, orange, and red. (Hue is what most people mean when they say "color.")
3. **Saturation,** which varies from rich full colors at the periphery of the color solid to gray at the center. For example, starting with red at the periphery, the colors become paler toward the center, going through pink to gray. Yellow is shown closer to the central axis than the other saturated hues because yellow is perceived as less saturated than the other spectral hues.

It is important not to equate *perception* of a particular hue with a particular *stimulus*—a wavelength of light—because, depending on the intensity of illumination and on the surrounding field, a patch illuminated by a particular wavelength is seen as various different hues. As illumination fades, the blues in a painting or a rug appear more prominent and the reds appear duller, even though the wavelength distribution in the light has not changed. In addition, the hue perceived at a particular point is strongly affected by

the pattern of wavelengths and intensities in other parts of the visual field.

Brightness Is Created by the Visual System

The brightness dimension of visual perception is also created by the visual system rather than being determined entirely by the amount of illumination reflected. Figure 10.6 presents two examples as illustration. The enhancement of the boundaries of the bars in Figure 10.6a, which are uniformly gray but look as though the color varies in brightness, is based on a neural process called **lateral inhibition**. Lateral inhibition occurs where the neurons in a region, in this case, retinal cells, are interconnected, either through their own axons or by means of intermediary neurons (interneurons), and each neuron tends to inhibit its neighbors (Figure 10.6c). Lateral inhibition occurs in the skin senses, too; if you press the end of a ruler against the skin of your forearm, for example, you will probably feel the pressure at the corners of the ruler more strongly than the pressure along the line of contact.

In Figure 10.6b, two patches that clearly differ in brightness *reflect the same amount of light*. If you use your hands to cover the surrounding pattern to the left and right of the two patches, then they appear the same. How are such puzzling effects produced? Although the contrast effect in Figure 10.6a is determined, at least in part, by interactions among adjacent retinal cells, the two areas indicated in Figure 10.6b are

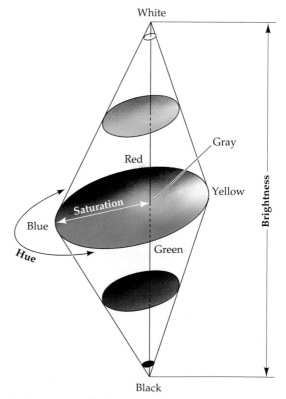

10.5 The Color Solid
This diagram illustrates the three basic dimensions of the perception of light: brightness, hue, and saturation.

(a)

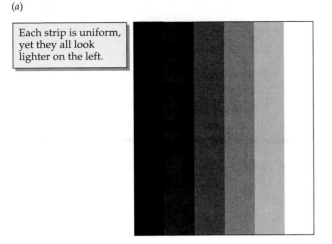

Each strip is uniform, yet they all look lighter on the left.

(b)

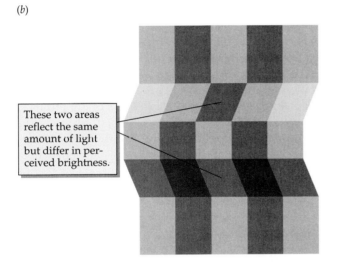

These two areas reflect the same amount of light but differ in perceived brightness.

(c)

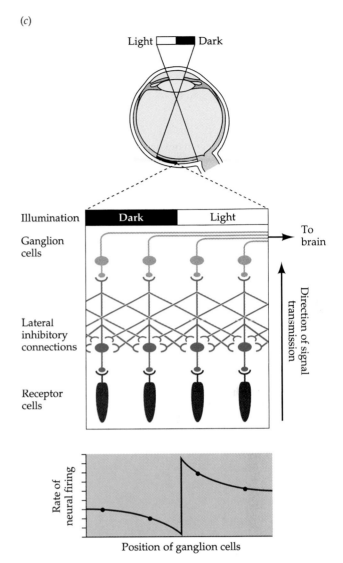

10.6 Context Affects the Perception of Brightness
(a) Although each of the four central bars is uniform in color, each appears lighter on the left and darker on the right. *(b)* Shading around a patch of light affects the perception of brightness. For example, even though the two indicated patches are the same shade of gray, one appears darker than the other. If you don't believe this, view the two patches through two holes 2 cm apart. *(c)* A circuit of neurons in the retina can explain how lateral inhibition sharpens the contrasts in part *a*. (Part *b* from Adelson, 1993.)

not adjacent, so the effect must be produced higher in the visual system (Adelson, 1993).

Motion Can Enhance the Perception of Objects

Movement enhances the visibility of objects, which is an important adaptation in the visual system because predators and prey both must be sensitive to moving objects in order to survive. In the periphery of our visual field, we may not be able to see stationary objects, but we can detect motion. Visibility is aided by motion only within a range of angular displacement that is appropriate to the locomotion of animals. Anything that moves faster is a blur or may be invisible, as is a bullet

speeding by. Anything that moves too slowly—such as the hands of a clock—is not seen as moving, although we can note from time to time that it has changed position. A succession of still pictures, presented at the proper rate, can cause apparent motion, as in motion pictures. The investigation of apparent visual motion by psychologist Max Wertheimer in the 1920s led to the Gestalt movement in psychology. Perception of motion is analyzed by special areas of the brain, as we will see later in this chapter.

The Eye Is Both an Optical Device and a Neural Organ

The eye is an elaborate structure with optical functions (capturing light and forming detailed spatial images) and neural functions (transducing light into neural signals and beginning the processing that enables us to perceive objects and scenes). The optical functions of the eye require both internal and external muscles under delicate neural control. The eye transduces light into neural activity through a series of steps in receptor cells of the retina, starting with photochemical transformations. Our examination of the eye will lead us to a discussion about how this elaborate organ evolved.

The Vertebrate Eye Acts in Some Ways like a Camera

Our ability to discriminate visual objects and scenes depends on numerous structures and processes. First among these are the structures and processes that enable the eye to form relatively accurate optical images on the light-sensitive cells of the retina. (Box 10.1 describes some of the features of the optical stimulus.) Accurate optical images are necessary for us to be able to see the shapes of objects; that is, light from a point on a target object must end up as a point—rather than a blur—in the retinal image. Without optical images, light-sensitive cells would be able to detect only the presence or absence of light and would not be able to see forms, just as exposing photographic film to light outside a camera will not produce an image of the surroundings.

To produce optical images, the eye has many of the features of a camera, starting with a lens to focus light (see Figure 10.2). Light travels in a straight line until it encounters a change in the density of the medium, which causes light rays to bend. This bending of light rays, called **refraction**, is the basis of such instruments as eyeglasses, telescopes, and microscopes. The

cornea of the eye, the curvature of which is fixed, bends light rays, and is primarily responsible for forming the image on the retina. The lens, the shape of which is controlled by the **ciliary muscles** inside the eye, makes further adjustments. As the degree of contraction of the ciliary muscles varies, the lens focuses images of nearer or farther objects so that they form sharp images on the retina; this process of focusing is called **accommodation**.

In many people the shape of the eyeball prevents the lens from bringing images into sharp focus on the retina. Eyeglasses or contact lenses can correct such conditions. As mammals age, their lenses become less elastic and therefore less able to change curvature to bring nearby objects into focus. Humans correct this problem by wearing bifocal, trifocal, or continuously variable eyeglasses, in which segments of the lens refract differently, permitting accurate viewing at various distances.

The amount of light that enters the eye is controlled by the size of the **pupil**, just as the aperture controls the light that enters a camera. The pupil is an opening in the structure called the **iris** (see Figure 10.2). In Chapter 2 we mentioned that dilation of the pupils is controlled by the sympathetic division of the autonomic system, and constriction by the parasympathetic division. Since both divisions usually are active, pupil size reflects a balance of influences.

BOX 10.1   *The Basics of Light*

*T*he physical energy to which our visual system responds is a band of electromagnetic radiation. This radiation comes in very small packets of energy called **quanta** (singular quantum). Each quantum can be described by a single number, its **wavelength** (the distance between two adjacent crests of vibratory activity). The human visual system responds only to quanta whose wavelengths lie within a very narrow section of the total electromagnetic range, from about 400 to 700 nm, as the figure shows. Such quanta of light energy are called **photons** (from the Greek *phos*, "light"). The band of radiant energy visible to animals may be narrow, but it must provide for accurate reflection from the surface of objects in the size range that matters for survival. Radio waves are good for imaging objects of astronomical size; X rays penetrate below the surface of objects.

Each photon is a very small amount of energy; the exact

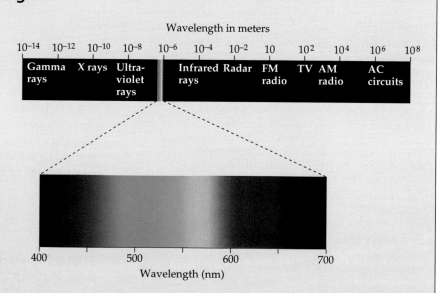

amount depends on its wavelength. A single photon of wavelength 560 nm contains only a tiny amount of energy. A 100 W (watt) light bulb gives off only about 3 W of visible light; the rest is heat. But even the 3 W of light amounts to 8 quintillion (8×10^{18})

photons per second. When quanta within the visible spectrum enter the eye, they can evoke visual sensations. The exact nature of such sensations depends both on the wavelengths of the quanta and on the number of quanta per second.

During an eye examination, the doctor may use a drug to block acetylcholine transmission in the parasympathetic synapses of your iris; this drug relaxes the sphincter muscle fibers and permits the pupil to open widely. One drug that has this effect, belladonna (which is Italian for "beautiful lady"), got its name because it was thought to make a woman more beautiful by giving her the wide-open pupils of an attentive person. Some drugs, such as morphine, stimulate the sympathetic division; intensely constricted pupils are a sign of overdose of such drugs.

The movement of the eyes is controlled by the **extraocular muscles**, three pairs of muscles that extend from the outside of the eyeball to the bony socket of the eye; fixating (focusing on) still or moving targets requires delicate control of these muscles. Eye movements are discussed further in Chapter 11.

Visual Processing Begins in the Retina

The first stages of the processing of visual information occur in the **retina**, the receptive surface inside the back of the eye (Figure 10.7a). The retina is only 200 to 300 μm thick—not much thicker than the edge of a razor blade—but it contains several types of cells in distinct layers (Figure 10.7b). The receptive cells are modified neurons; some are called **rods** because of their relatively long, narrow form, others are called **cones** (Figure 10.7c). The rods and cones release neurotransmitter molecules that modulate the activity of the **bipolar cells** that synapse with them (Figure 10.7f). The bipolar cells in turn connect with **ganglion cells**. The axons of the ganglion cells form the **optic nerve**, which carries information to the brain. **Horizontal cells** and **amacrine cells** (see Figure 10.7f) are especially significant nerve cells in interactions within the retina. The horizontal cells contact both the receptor cells and the bipolar cells; the amacrine cells contact both the bipolar and the ganglion cells. An example of interaction in the retina is lateral inhibition (see Figure 10.6c).

The rods, cones, bipolar cells, and horizontal cells generate only graded local potentials; they do not generate or conduct action potentials. These cells affect each other through the *graded* release of neurotransmitters in response to *graded* changes in electrical potentials. The amacrine cells and the ganglion cells, on the other hand, do conduct action potentials. Because the ganglion cells have action potentials and are relatively large in size, they were the first retinal cells to have their activity recorded electrically. From the receptive cells to the ganglion cells an enormous number of data converge and are compressed; the human eye contains about 100 million rods and 4 million cones, but there are only 1 million ganglion cells to transmit that information to the brain. The multitude of retinal cells and the connections among them permit a great deal of information processing in the eye.

Studies of human sensitivity to light reveal the existence of two different functional systems corresponding to the two different populations of receptors (rods and cones) and associated neural elements in the retina. One system works in dim light and involves the rods and highly convergent neural processing; this system is called the **scotopic system** (from the Greek *skotos*, "darkness," and *ops*, "eye"). The scotopic system does not respond differentially to wavelengths, which is the basis for the saying "at night, all cats are gray."

The other system requires more light and involves much more detailed neural processing; in some species, it shows differential sensitivity to wavelengths, enabling color vision. This system involves the cones and is called the **photopic system** (which, like "photon," comes from the Greek *phos*, "light"). At moderate levels of illumination, both rods and cones function, and some ganglion cells receive input from both types of receptors. Having these two systems enables us to see over a wide range of light intensities. Table 10.1 summarizes the characteristics of the photopic and scotopic systems.

TABLE 10.1 *Properties of the Human Photopic and Scotopic Visual Systems*

Property	Photopic system	Scotopic system
Receptors[a]	Cones	Rods
Approximate number of receptors per eye	4 million	100 million
Photopigments[b]	Three classes of cone opsins; the basis of color vision	Rhodopsin
Sensitivity	Low; needs relatively strong stimulation; used for day vision	High; can be stimulated by weak light intensity; used for night vision
Location in retina[c]	Concentrated in and near fovea; present less densely throughout retina	Outside fovea
Receptive field size and visual acuity	Small in fovea, so acuity is high; larger outside fovea	Larger, so acuity is lower

[a]Cones and rods are illustrated in Figure 10.7c.
[b]Figure 10.23 shows the spectral sensitivities of the photopigments.
[c]See Figure 10.11.

(*a*) Cross section of eye

(*b*) Cross section of retina

Optic nerve fibers

Ganglion cell layer

Bipolar cell layer

Rod and cone cell layer

Pigmented epithelium

(*c*) Photoreceptors

Cone cell

Rod cell

(*d*) Synaptic connections at base of rod

(*e*) Outer segments of rod

(*f*) Neural connections in retina

Ganglion cell

Amacrine cell

Flat bipolar cell

Invaginating bipolar cell

Horizontal cell

Rod cell

Direction of signal transmission

10.7 Anatomy of the Retina

(*a*) The eye in cross section, showing the location of the retina. (*b*) Cross section of the retina, showing its layered structure. (*c*) Structure of a single rod and a single cone. (*d*) Synaptic connections at the base of a rod. (*e*) Outer segments of a rod. (*f*) Synaptic connections of rods to other retinal cells. Note the two classes of bipolar cells—those that make invaginating connections to photoreceptors (penetrating into a pouch in the receptor membrane) and those that make flat connections. The invaginating bipolar cells depolarize to an increase of light intensity; the bipolar cells with flat connections depolarize to a decrease of light intensity.

The extraordinary sensitivity of rods and cones is the result of their unusual structure and biochemistry. A portion of their structure, when magnified, looks like a large stack of pancakes or discs (see Figure 10.7*e*). The stacking of discs increases the probability of capturing quanta of light, an especially important function, since light is reflected in many directions by the surface of the eyeball, the lens, and the fluid media inside the eye. The reflection and absorption of light at all these surfaces means that only a fraction of the light that strikes the cornea actually reaches the retina.

The quanta of light that strike the discs are captured by special photopigment receptor molecules. In the rods this photopigment is **rhodopsin** (from the Greek *rhodon,* "rose," and *opsis,* "vision"). Cones use a few main photopigments, as we will see later. All the photopigments in the eye consist of two parts: **retinal** (an abbreviated form of *retinaldehyde,* which is vitamin A aldehyde) and **opsin.** (From this point forward the noun "retinal," standing for the molecule, will be printed in small capital letters—RETINAL—to distinguish it from the adjective "retinal," meaning "pertaining to the retina.") The pioneering studies of George Wald (1964) established the chemical structure of rhodopsin and the related visual pigments of the cone receptors, earning him the 1967 Nobel prize in physiology or medicine. The visual receptor molecules span the membranes of receptor discs and have structures that are similar to those of the G protein–coupled receptor molecules for synaptic transmitters that we discussed in Chapter 3.

When light activates a rhodopsin molecule, the RETINAL dissociates rapidly from the opsin, revealing an enzymatic site on the opsin molecule. The activated opsin combines rapidly with many molecules of the G protein transducin (Figure 10.8). Transducin in turn acts through an enzyme, phosphodiesterase (PDE), to transform cyclic GMP (cyclic guanosine monophosphate) to 5'-GMP. In the dark, cyclic GMP holds channels for sodium ions (Na^+) open; light stimulation initiates a cascade of events that closes Na^+ channels. Capture of a single quantum of light, under dim light conditions, can lead to the closing of hundreds of sodium channels in the photoreceptor membrane and block the entry of more than 1 million Na^+ ions (Schnapf and Baylor, 1987). Closing the Na^+ channels creates a hyperpolarizing generator potential (Figure 10.8*b*). This change of potential represents the initial electrical signal of activation of the visual pathway. The size of the photoreceptor potential determines the amount of synaptic transmitter released.

It may seem puzzling at first that light stimulation hyperpolarizes vertebrate retinal photoreceptors, since sensory stimulation depolarizes most other receptor cells. But remember that the visual system responds to *changes* in light. Either an increase or a decrease in light intensity can stimulate the visual system, and hyperpolarization is just as much a neural signal as is depolarization. And just as stimulation of rhodopsin hyperpolarizes the rods, stimulation of the cone pigments hyperpolarizes the cones.

Photoreceptors Excite Some Retinal Cells and Inhibit Others

Each cone in the central retina connects to four bipolar cells (Figure 10.9). Two are **midget bipolar cells**, which connect to just this one cone; the other two are **diffuse bipolar cells**, which connect to several neighboring cones as well. In the dark, the photoreceptor is depolarized and steadily releases its synaptic transmitter, probably glutamate. This transmitter depolarizes (excites) one midget cell and one diffuse bipolar cell, but it hyperpolarizes (inhibits) the other midget cell and diffuse bipolar cell (Daw et al., 1989).

We saw in Chapter 3 that the same neurotransmitter can have opposite effects when it acts at different chemical receptor molecules in the neuronal membrane; the retinal bipolar cells are an example. Some agonists of glutamate stimulate one class of bipolar cells—the **on-center bipolar cells**, which respond with depolarization to light in the center of their receptive field—without affecting the **off-center bipolar cells**, which respond to light offset from the center of their receptive field. Other agonists of glutamate, acting at different membrane receptor molecules, have the reverse action: They depolarize off-center bipolar cells and hyperpolarize on-center bipolar cells.

Normally in the dark the photoreceptor transmitter depolarizes the bipolar cells that report "light off," or "dark," to ganglion cells, which relay the message to higher visual centers. At the same time, the same photoreceptor transmitter hyperpolarizes the other bipolar cells and prevents them from reporting "light on." When a particular region of the retina is illuminated, some bipolar cells that were being hyperpolarized by the photoreceptor transmitter are now released from hyperpolarization, so they depolarize and report "light" to the ganglion cells. The stimulated ganglion cells then fire nerve impulses and report "light" to higher visual centers.

A small stimulus in a particular part of the visual field affects only those visual cells whose receptive field is in the corresponding part of the retina. A mosaic of receptive fields covers the whole retina, except for the blind spot. Similarly, as we saw in Chapter 8, different somatosensory receptive fields serve different parts of the body surface (see Figure 8.10), and the ensemble covers the whole body.

Retinal ganglion cells normally fire at a low rate in the absence of stimulation. If you are in a place with no light, you don't see "black." You see a sort of dim flickering, which is caused by the spontaneous activity of the retinal ganglion cells. As we will see in more detail later, some ganglion cells fire more impulses when illumination increases, some fire at a higher rate when illumination decreases, and some fire in response to both increases and decreases.

Different Mechanisms Enable the Eyes to Work over a Wide Range of Light Intensities

Many sensory systems have to work over wide ranges of stimulus intensity, as we learned in Chapter 8. This is certainly true of the visual system: A very bright light is about 10 billion times as intense as the weakest lights we can see (Figure 10.10). At any given time, however, we can discriminate over a range of light intensity that is only about one-fifth the size of the total range. Let's discuss the mechanisms by which the eye adapts to the prevailing level of illumination.

One way the visual system deals with a large range of intensities is by adjusting the size of the pupil. In bright light the pupil contracts quickly to admit only

(a) Rod photoreceptor

Rod cell outer segment

Amplifier

Microelectrode

Rod cell inner segment

Light

10.8 Light Causes Photoreceptors to Hyperpolarize
A rod photoreceptor (a) is hyperpolarized by light stimulation, as shown in (b). (c) The hyperpolarization is caused by a cascade of neurochemical events that enormously multiply the effect of each photon captured by a receptor cell.

(b) Stimulation hyperpolarizes receptor

Light flash

Electrical potential (mV)

−35 Dim light

−45 Medium light

−55 Bright light

0   100   200
Time (ms)

(c) Photochemical amplification of stimulus

1. Light stimulation of a molecule of rhodopsin activates about 500 molecules of the G protein transducin. This activation causes a GTP molecule to replace the GDP molecule that binds to a subunit of transducin.

2. The activated G protein activates a phosphodiesterase (PDE).

3. Each PDE molecule hydrolyzes more than 2000 molecules of cGMP, reducing its concentration.

Outer-segment membrane

5′-**GMP**

cGMP

Open Na⁺ channel

Na⁺

Na⁺

Closed Na⁺ channel

Light

Rhodopsin

Disc membrane

Transducin

γ
β
α

GTP   GDP

α
GTP

PDE

Disc

4. The reduction in cGMP leads to closure of Na⁺ channels and hyperpolarization of the receptor. One photon of light can block the entry of more than 1 million Na⁺ molecules.

Inside rod cell   Outside cell

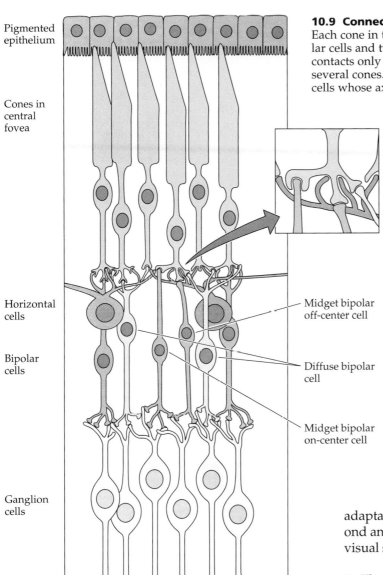

Pigmented epithelium

Cones in central fovea

Horizontal cells

Bipolar cells

Ganglion cells

Axons of optic nerve

Midget bipolar off-center cell

Diffuse bipolar cell

Midget bipolar on-center cell

10.9 Connections of Cones to Bipolar Cells

Each cone in the central retina is connected to two midget bipolar cells and two diffuse bipolar cells. Each midget bipolar cell contacts only one cone, but each diffuse bipolar cell contacts several cones. The bipolar cells contact the retinal ganglion cells whose axons form the optic nerve.

coarse. The eye solves this problem by having receptors *adapt* to the prevailing level of illumination; that is, each receptor adjusts its sensitivity to match the average level of ambient illumination. Thus the visual system is concerned with *differences*, or *changes*, in brightness, not with the absolute level of illumination.

At any given time a photoreceptor operates over a range of intensities of about 100-fold; that is, it is completely depolarized by a stimulus about one-tenth the ambient level of illumination, and a light ten times more intense than the ambient level will completely hyperpolarize it. The fact that the sensitivity of the visual receptors adapts to the level of illumination means that the receptors can shift their whole range of response to work around the prevailing level of illumination. Further adaptation occurs in the ganglion cells and the lateral geniculate nucleus, and probably at higher levels too.

Three main factors help account for the adaptation of sensitivity in the receptor cells; the second and third of these mechanisms are specific to the visual system:

1. *The role of calcium.* Probably the most important factor is one shared by other sensory modalities—the role(s) of calcium (Ca^{2+}) ions (Pugh and Lamb, 1990). When intracellular Ca^{2+} ions are bound ex-

about one-sixteenth as much light as when illumination is dim. Although rapid, this pupil response cannot account for the billionfold range of visual sensitivity. Another mechanism for handling different light intensities is *range fractionation*; that is, different receptors—some with low thresholds and others with high thresholds—handle different intensities. Figure 8.5 illustrated this mechanism for the somesthetic system.

The visual system uses this mechanism by dividing the receptors into two systems: the scotopic (rod) and photopic (cone) systems (see Table 10.1). But additional range fractionation would carry an unacceptable cost: If, at a particular light level, several sets of receptors were not responding, acuity would be impaired. If only a fraction of the receptors responded to the small changes of light intensity around a given level, the active receptors would be spaced apart from each other in the retina, and the "grain" of the retina would be

Intensity of light reflected from objects (lamberts)

Cone vision
Rod vision

10
1
10^{-2}
10^{-5}
10^{-9}

Dazzling light; bright sun on snow
Outdoors in full sunlight
Outdoors under a tree on a sunny day
Comfortable indoor illumination; night sports events
Threshold for perception of color; bright moonlight
Threshold when dark-adapted

10.10 The Wide Range of Sensitivity to Light Intensity

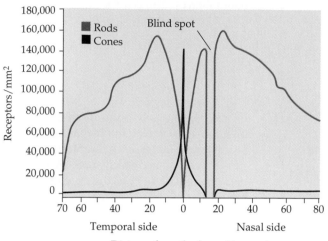

(a) Distributions of rods and cones across the retina

Temporal side   Nasal side

Distance from the fovea (degrees)

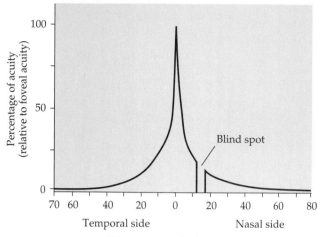

(b) Variation of visual acuity across the retina

Temporal side   Nasal side

Distance from the fovea (degrees)

10.11 Frequencies of Retinal Receptors and Visual Acuity
(a) Distribution of rods and cones across the retina. (b) The variation of visual acuity across the retina reflects the distribution of cones. (c) In the fovea, light reaches the cones without having to pass through other layers of cells.

(c) Cross section of the central retina

perimentally and thus made unavailable for reactions, the visual system can no longer adapt to higher levels of illumination.

2. *The balance between* RETINAL *and opsin.* When the photoreceptor pigment is split apart by light, its two components—RETINAL and opsin—slowly recombine, so the balance between the rate of breakdown of the pigment and its rate of recombination determines how much photopigment is available at any given time to respond to stimulation by light. If you go from bright daylight into a dark theater, it takes several minutes until enough rhodopsin becomes available to restore your dark vision.

3. *The availability of retinal chemicals for transduction.* Several retinal chemicals are required for transduction. They tend to be abundant at low levels of illumination but increasingly rare at higher levels of illumination, so increasing numbers of photons are required to activate them and hyperpolarize the receptors (Pugh and Lamb, 1993).

Acuity Is Best in Foveal Vision Because of the Dense Array of Cones in the Fovea

We noted early in this chapter that acuity is especially fine in the center of the visual field and falls off rapidly toward the periphery. Reasons for this difference have been found in the retina and successive lev-

els of the visual system, each of which is a detailed map of the visible world. Although the neural maps preserve the *order* of the visual field, each map emphasizes some regions at the expense of others; that is, each map is topographic. One reason that the maps are topographic is that the concentration of receptors in the center of the retinal surface is denser than that of the periphery (Figure 10.11a). The central region, called the **fovea** (Latin for "pit"), has a dense concentration of cones, and in this region light reaches the cone without having to pass through other layers of cells (Figure 10.11c). These structural arrangements provide for maximal acuity in the fovea.

The data on cone concentration in Figure 10.11a come from a classic study by Østerberg (1935), but they are based on only one retina. More recently Curcio et al. (1987) measured four other retinas. Østerberg's data fall in the same range, but the four retinas differed by as much as three to one in the number of cones per square millimeter in the fovea. Very likely this variation is related to individual differences in visual acuity. Species differences in visual acuity are also related to the density of cones in the fovea. For example, hawks, whose acuity is much greater than that of humans, have much narrower and more densely packed cones in the fovea than humans do. In the human retina, both cones and rods increase their diameter toward the periphery.

The rods show a different distribution from the cones; they are absent in the fovea but are more numerous than cones in the periphery of the retina. They are the most concentrated in a ring about 20° away from the center of the retina. That is why, if you want to see a dim star, you do best to search for it about 20° away from your central gaze. Not only are the rods more sensitive to dim light than the cones, but input from more rods converges on ganglion cells in the scotopic system, further increasing its sensitivity to weak stimuli. As mentioned earlier, there are no rods or cones in the optic disc (the "blind spot"), where the axons of the ganglion cells leave the retina and where blood vessels enter the retina.

A major part of the projection of visual space onto the topographic brain maps is devoted to the foveal region (Figure 10.12*a*) (Tootell et al., 1982). Although the **primary visual cortex** (abbreviated **V1**) of the macaque

is located on the lateral surface of the occipital area, the human V1 is located mainly on the medial surface of the cortex (Figure 10.12*b*). The fact that, as in the monkey, about half of the human V1 is devoted to the fovea and the retinal region just around the fovea does not mean that our spatial perception is distorted. Rather, this representation makes possible the great acuity of spatial discrimination in the central part of the visual field. Our acuity falls off about as rapidly in the horizontal direction as in the vertical direction, but species that live in open, flat environments (such as the cheetah and the rabbit) have fields of acute vision that extend farther horizontally than vertically.

Sylvius

Studying the regions of blindness caused by brain injuries reveals the extreme orderliness of the mapping of the visual field. If we know the site of injury in the visual pathway, we can predict the location of such a perceptual gap, or **scotoma** (plural scotomata), in the visual field. Although the word "scotoma" comes from the Greek *skotoma*, meaning "to darken," a scotoma is not perceived as a dark patch in the visual field; rather it is a spot where nothing can be per-

10.12 Maps of the Primary Visual Cortex

(*a*) A pattern of flickering lights (*left*) was shown in a macaque's visual field, and a map of the visual field was revealed by autoradiography in a flattened section of the primary visual cortex (*right*). (*b*) Maps of human visual cortex derived from fMRI measurements show primary visual cortex as the innermost yellow band on each medial view. (Part *a* from Tootell et al., 1988; *b* from Tootell et al., 1998; both courtesy of Roger Tootell.)

(*a*) Macaque

> The small central region of the visual field projects to a large part of primary visual cortex.

1 cm

(*b*) Human

Right hemisphere   **Left hemisphere**

ceived, and usually rigorous testing is required to demonstrate its existence.

Within a scotoma, a person cannot perceive visual cues, but in some cases some visual discrimination in this region is still possible; this paradoxical phenomenon has been called "blindsight." In other cases, stimuli that cannot be seen within a scotoma affect judgments of stimuli outside it (Stoerig and Cowey, 1997). For more on such effects, see Topic 10.1, "Blindsight" and Perceptual Effects of Stimuli in Scotomata. Blindsight may also be related to the phenomenon of "hemispatial neglect"—neglect of the side opposite to an injured cerebral hemisphere—which we will discuss in Chapter 19.

Special topic

When we look at a complex organ like the eye of a mammal, an octopus, or a fly, it is hard at first to understand how it could have evolved. But inspection of different living species reveals a gradation from very simple light-sensitive cells to increasingly complex organs with focusing devices. Phylogenetic studies indicate that eyes evolved independently in several different phyla (see Box 10.2).

Neural Signals Travel from the Retina to Several Brain Regions

The results of visual processing in the retina *converge* on the ganglion cells, from which they then *diverge* to several brain structures (see Figure 3.15*b*). The optic nerves, which are made up of the axons of the ganglion cells in each eye, convey visual information to the brain (Figure 10.13). In all vertebrate animals, some or all of the axons of each optic nerve cross to the opposite cerebral hemisphere.

The optic nerves cross at the **optic chiasm** (named from the Greek letter χ [chi] because of its crossover shape), which is located just anterior to the stalk of the pituitary gland. In humans, axons from the half of the retina toward the nose (the nasal retina) cross over to the opposite side of the brain. The half of the retina toward the side of the head (the temporal retina) projects its axons to its own side of the head. Proportionally more axons cross over in animals, such as rodents, that have laterally placed eyes with little binocular overlap *Sylvius*

BOX 10.2 *Eyes with Lenses Have Evolved in Several Phyla*

Phylogenetic studies indicate that some of the steps in the evolution of eyes with lenses, like those of a mammal or an octopus, were the following (Land and Fernald, 1992):

1. Concentrating light-sensitive cells into *localized groups* that serve as photoreceptor organs (Figure A). Animals with such photoreceptor organs have better chances of surviving and reproducing than do similar animals with scattered receptor cells, because photoreceptor organs facilitate responding differently to stimuli that strike different parts of the body surface.

2. Clustering light receptors at the bottom of *pitlike or cuplike depressions* in the skin (Figure B). Animals with this adaptation can discriminate better among stimuli that come from different directions. They also perceive increased contrast of stimuli against a background of ambient light.

3. Narrowing the top of the cup into a *small aperture* so that, like a pinhole camera, the eye can focus well (Figure C).

4. Closing over the opening with *transparent skin* or filling the cup with a transparent substance (Figure D). This covering protects the eye against the entry of foreign substances that might injure the receptor cells or block vision.

5. Forming *a lens* either by thickening the transparent skin or by modifying other tissue in the eye (Figure E). This adapta-

in their fields of vision. After they pass the optic chiasm, the axons of the retinal ganglion cells are known collectively as the **optic tract.**

Most axons of the optic tract terminate in the **lateral geniculate nucleus (LGN)**, which is the visual part of the thalamus. Most of the axons of postsynaptic cells in the LGN form the **optic radiations**, which terminate in the visual areas in the **occipital cortex** at the back of the brain. In addition to the primary visual cortex (V1) shown in Figures 10.12 and 10.13, numerous surrounding regions of the cortex are also largely visual in function (see Figure 10.18). The primary visual cortex is often called the **striate cortex** because a broad stripe or striation is visible in anatomical sections through this region; the stripe represents layer 4 of the cortex where the optic radiation fibers arrive.

Inputs from the two eyes converge at the cortical level, making binocular effects possible. Visual cortical areas outside the striate cortex are sometimes called extrastriate cortex. As Figure 10.13 shows, the visual cortex in the right cerebral hemisphere receives its input from the left half of the visual field, and the visual cortex in the left hemisphere receives its input from the right half of the visual field. Because of the orderly mapping of the visual field (known as retinotopic mapping) at the various levels of the visual system, damage to parts of the visual system can be diagnosed from defects in perception of the visual field.

Figure 10.13 shows that some axons leave the optic tract to reach sites other than the LGN. Some retinal ganglion cells send their optic-tract axons to the superior colliculus in the midbrain. In Chapter 8 we saw that cells in the deeper layers of the superior colliculus form maps of visual, somatosensory, and auditory space, as well as of the motor system—and that all these maps are aligned with each other.

The superior colliculus helps coordinate rapid movements of the eyes toward a target. Other ganglion cells send relatively small bundles of optic-tract axons to nuclei in the hypothalamus that are involved in the control of daily cycles of behavior, which we will discuss in Chapter 14. Optic-tract axons from still other ganglion cells go to the midbrain nuclei that regulate the size of the pupil and help coordinate the

---

tion improves the focusing of the eye while allowing the aperture to be relatively large to let in more light; thus, vision can be acute even when light is not intense.

The only requirement for the evolution of eyes to begin appears to be the existence of light-sensitive cells. Natural selection then favors the development of auxiliary mechanisms needed to improve vision. Many kinds of cells show some light sensitivity, and different phyla have modified different types of cells for specialized photoreceptors. The most common starting point has been cells of epidermal (skin) origin, but some lines (including our chordate vertebrate ancestors) derived their visual receptors from cells of neural origin. All known visual systems use a light-receptor molecule similar to rhodopsin, indicating a basic similarity among them.

Phylogenetic studies of the structure and development of eyes led investigators to conclude that eyes evolved independently in many different phyla (Salvini-Plawen and Mayr, 1970). A competent optical system with a lens, however, has evolved in only six of the 33 phyla of multicellular animals. These few phyla have been very successful; they account for about 96% of known species of multicellular animals. An effective optical system may have contributed to this success (Land and Fernald, 1992).

The fact that the cephalopods (such as squid and octopus) evolved a visual system that in many ways resembles that of vertebrates (from fish to humans) suggests that there are major constraints on the development of a visual system for a large, rapidly moving animal. Let's look at some of the major similarities and differences between the eyes of cephalopods and those of vertebrates. In both, the eyes are relatively large, allowing for many receptors and the ability to gather large amounts of light. The incoming light is regulated by a pupil and focused by a lens. In both cephalopods and vertebrates, three sets of extraocular muscles move the eyeballs.

An important difference in eye structure is the organization of the retina. In the vertebrate eye, light must travel through neurons and blood vessels to reach the receptors, and the area where the neural axons and blood vessels enter and leave the retina forms the blind spot. In cephalopods the organization is more efficient in some respects: Light reaches the receptors directly, and the neurons and blood vessels lie *behind* the receptors; thus there is no blind spot. The detailed structure of the receptor cells is quite different in cephalopods and vertebrates. In addition, the visual stimulus causes depolarization of cephalopod (and most invertebrate) retinal receptor cells, but it causes hyperpolarization of fish and mammalian retinal receptors.

The major similarities between cephalopod and vertebrate eyes have often been cited as examples of convergent evolution, showing ways in which similar functions can be achieved with different structures and processes, starting from different origins. Recent research suggests, however, that the eyes of all seeing animals share at least one important genetic feature: The compound eye of the fruit fly *Drosophila*, the vertebrate eye, and the cephalopod eye all develop using genes of the *Pax* family. The finding that highly homologous molecules are key regulators of eye development in different phyla argues that eyes in all phyla share a common origin (Zuker, 1994).

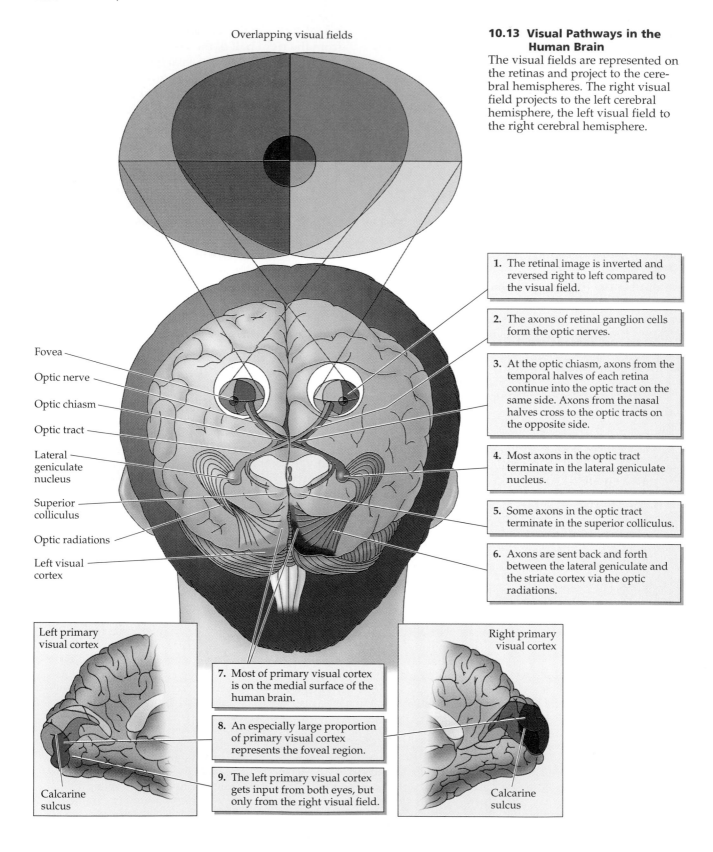

Overlapping visual fields

10.13 Visual Pathways in the Human Brain
The visual fields are represented on the retinas and project to the cerebral hemispheres. The right visual field projects to the left cerebral hemisphere, the left visual field to the right cerebral hemisphere.

Fovea

Optic nerve

Optic chiasm

Optic tract

Lateral geniculate nucleus

Superior colliculus

Optic radiations

Left visual cortex

1. The retinal image is inverted and reversed right to left compared to the visual field.

2. The axons of retinal ganglion cells form the optic nerves.

3. At the optic chiasm, axons from the temporal halves of each retina continue into the optic tract on the same side. Axons from the nasal halves cross to the optic tracts on the opposite side.

4. Most axons in the optic tract terminate in the lateral geniculate nucleus.

5. Some axons in the optic tract terminate in the superior colliculus.

6. Axons are sent back and forth between the lateral geniculate and the striate cortex via the optic radiations.

Left primary visual cortex

Right primary visual cortex

7. Most of primary visual cortex is on the medial surface of the human brain.

8. An especially large proportion of primary visual cortex represents the foveal region.

9. The left primary visual cortex gets input from both eyes, but only from the right visual field.

Calcarine sulcus

Calcarine sulcus

movements of the eyes. Some of the midbrain visual nuclei also project axons to the cerebellum, where the activity maps visual space.

Investigators have found several cortical areas for each sensory modality, and most of these areas are laid out in an orderly topographic map of the receptor surface (C. N. Woolsey, 1981a, 1981b, 1981c). Examination of the cortex of the macaque (an Old World monkey) reveals more than 30 visual areas, each of which is a topographic representation of the retina (see Figure 10.18). Evidence is accumulating that different cortical regions work in parallel to process different aspects of visual perception, such as form, color, location, and movement, as we will take up later in this chapter.

Investigators use a variety of techniques to map the visual system: anatomical tracing of fibers, electrophysiological recording of activity evoked by specific kinds of visual stimulation, PET and other noninvasive measures of regional activity in the brain, and experimental and clinical lesions of the visual system. Integrating the findings from these techniques provides us with our current understanding of the structure and functions of the visual system.

Neurons at Different Levels of the Visual System Have Very Different Receptive Fields

Spots of light that are lighter or darker than surrounding areas are sufficient to activate cells in the retina or LGN, but many cells in the visual cortex are more demanding and respond only to more complicated stimuli. The nature of the receptive field of a cell gives us good clues about its function(s) in achieving various aspects of perception. In this research, investigators ask to what extent we can understand certain phenomena of visual perception on the basis of properties of neurons at a given level in the nervous system. Moreover, we want to know to what extent other phenomena require combinations or circuits of cells instead of just properties of individual neurons. In the next sections we will see some cases in which neurons at lower levels in the visual system seem to account for particular perceptual phenomena and other cases in which solutions need to be sought at higher levels in the visual system.

Stephen Kuffler
(1913–1980)

Horace Barlow

Neurons in the Retina and the LGN Have Concentric Receptive Fields

Two scientists discovered the main features of the receptive fields of vertebrate retinal ganglion cells independently within a few months of each other: Stephen Kuffler (1953), studying the cat, and Horace Barlow (1953), studying the frog. They recorded from single ganglion cells while they moved a small spot of light across the receptive field, keeping the animal's eye still. Results showed that the receptive fields of retinal ganglion cells are concentric, consisting of a roughly circular central area and a ring around it. Similar results were later obtained for retinal bipolar cells, but whereas the responses of the bipolar cells are changes in polarization (depolariza-

tion or hyperpolarization), the responses of the ganglion cells are nerve impulses.

Ganglion cells were studied before bipolar cells because they are larger and make easier targets for recording. Both bipolar cells and ganglion cells have two basic types of retinal receptive fields: **on-center/off-surround** (Figure 10.14*a*) and **off-center/on-surround** (Figure 10.14*b*). The center and its surround are always antagonistic and tend to cancel each other's activity. These effects explain why uniform illumination of the visual field is less effective in activating a ganglion cell than is a well-placed small spot or a line or edge passing through the center of the cell's receptive field. Later work found that the receptive fields of ganglion cells in the cat are actually elongated (Hammond, 1974), and that different cells respond selectively to different orientations of stimulation (Thibos and Levick, 1985). In primates, however, the ganglion cells do not appear to show orientation specificity.

Although the visual mechanisms of cats have been studied extensively, cats have little or no color vision, so we will focus on research with primates, which possess good color vision as well as good form vision. Investigators who study primate visual systems take the organization of the LGN as their key. The anatomy of the primate LGN is different from that of the cat. Whereas the LGN of the cat has only four layers, the primate LGN has six layers (Figure 10.15). Figure 10.15 shows why the structure is called geniculate: The layers are bent like a knee, for which the Latin word is *genu*.

The four dorsal, or outer, layers of the primate LGN are called **parvocellular** (from the Latin *parvus*, "small") because their cells are relatively small. The two ventral, or inner, layers are called **magnocellular** (from the Latin *magnus*, "large") because their cells are large. Most of the neurons in the magnocellular layers have relatively large receptive fields, the input of which can be traced back to the diffuse retinal bipolar cells that contact several neighboring photoreceptor cells. Many magnocellular neurons do not show differential wavelength responses; that is, they are not involved in color discrimination. The neurons of the parvocellular layers have relatively small receptive fields, the input of which is derived from the midget bipolar cells; these neurons discriminate wavelengths.

The LGN cells of all six layers have concentric receptive fields. At the LGN, stimulation of the surround becomes relatively more important than it is at the retina, so it is harder to stimulate an LGN cell with uniform illumination of the visual field. At the cerebral cortex it is even more difficult to arouse a response by altering the overall illumination.

Discovery of the difference between the parvocellular and magnocellular neurons of the primate LGN led investigators to take a fresh look at primate ganglion cells; they found two main types (A. G. Leventhal, 1979; Perry et al., 1984). The two types are sometimes called

(*a*) An on-center / off-surround cell

(*b*) An off-center / on-surround cell

10.14 Receptive Fields of Retinal Cells

In primates, each retinal bipolar cell and each retinal ganglion cell has a concentric receptive field, with antagonistic center and surround. Here cells are shown responding to narrower or broader beams of light. Bipolar cells respond by changes in local membrane potentials; ganglion cells respond with action potentials. (*a*) An on-center/off-surround cell is excited by an increase of illumination in the center of its receptive field and inhibited by an increase of illumination in the surround. (*b*) Changes in illumination have the opposite effects on an off-center/on-surround cell.

M and P ganglion cells because they project their axons, respectively, to the *m*agnocellular or *p*arvocellular layers of the LGN. The M ganglion cells are relatively large cells with large dendritic fields that contact many bipolar cells; consequently they have large receptive fields. The M ganglion cells can detect stimuli with low contrast and are sensitive to motion; they respond transiently, and they have large-diameter axons that conduct very rapidly. M ganglion cells make up about 10% of the primate retinal ganglion cells.

About 80% of the primate retinal ganglion cells send their axons to the P layers of the LGN. These P ganglion cells are relatively small and have small dendritic and receptive fields. Several properties of the P ganglion cells distinguish them from the M ganglion cells:

1. The P cells require high contrast to be stimulated, and they are relatively insensitive to motion.
2. Most P ganglion cells show differential responses to different wavelengths, so they provide a basis for color vision.
3. P cells have sustained, or tonic, responses.

The remaining 10% of the primate ganglion cells, which are neither M nor P type, will not concern us here.

Neurons in the Visual Cortex Have Varied and Complicated Receptive Fields

The next level of the visual system, the primary visual cortex, provided a puzzle. Neurons from the LGN

Coronal section

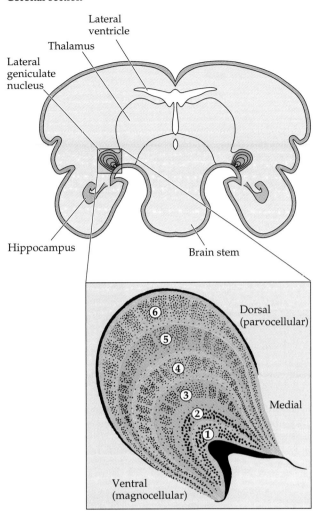

10.15 Cross Section of the Monkey Lateral Geniculate Nucleus
In the four dorsal (parvocellular) layers, the cells are relatively small; in the two ventral (magnocellular) layers, the cells are relatively large. Cells with input from the opposite eye are located in layers 1, 4, and 6 (pink); cells with input from the eye on the same side are located in layers 2, 3, and 5 (blue).

send their axons to cells in the primary visual cortex (V1), but the spots of light that are effective stimuli for LGN cells are not very effective at the cortical level. After much unfruitful work, success in stimulating cortical visual cells was finally announced in 1959: David Hubel and Torsten Wiesel reported that visual cortical cells require more specific, elongated stimuli than those that activate LGN cells. Most cells in area V1 respond best to lines or bars in a particular position and at a particular orientation in the visual field (Figure 10.16b). Some cortical cells also require movement of the stimulus to

David Hubel

make them respond actively. For some of these cells, any movement in their field is sufficient; others are even more demanding, requiring motion in a specific direction (Figure 10.16c). For this and related research, Hubel and Wiesel were awarded the Nobel prize in physiology or medicine in 1981. The success of this research also led many researchers to accept the theoretical model proposed by Hubel and Wiesel, but

Torsten Wiesel

challenges have emerged. Let's examine a few more of Hubel and Wiesel's findings and look at their theoretical model.

Hubel and Wiesel categorized cortical cells into three main classes according to the types of stimuli required to produce maximum responses. So-called **simple cortical cells** responded best to an edge or a bar of a particular width and with a particular orientation and location in the visual field. These cells were therefore sometimes called bar detectors or edge detectors. Like the simple cells, **complex cortical cells** had elongated receptive fields, but they also showed some latitude for location; that is, they responded to a bar of a particular size and orientation anywhere within a particular area of the visual field. **Hypercomplex cortical cells** had inhibitory areas at the two ends; that is, the best response occurred if the bar was of limited length, and extending the length beyond this limit reduced the response. Later work showed that even simple and complex cortical cells possess this property, at least to some extent.

Hubel and Wiesel's theoretical model can be described as hierarchical; that is, more complex events are built up from inputs of simpler ones. For example, a simple cortical cell can be thought of as receiving input from a row of LGN cells, and a complex cortical cell can be thought of as receiving its input from a row of simple cortical cells. Other theorists extrapolated from this model of Hubel and Wiesel, suggesting higher-order circuits of cells to detect any possible form. Thus it was suggested that by integration of enough successive levels of analysis, a unit could be constructed that would enable a person to recognize his or her grandmother, and such hypothetical "grandmother cells" were frequently mentioned in the literature. According to this view, any time such a cell was excited, up would pop a picture of one's grandmother. This hypothesis was given as a possible explanation for facial recognition.

Critics soon pointed out problems with the hierarchical model—some of a theoretical nature, others arising from empirical observations. For one thing, a "grandmother-recognizing" circuit would require vast numbers of cells, perhaps even more than the number available in the cerebral cortex. Although each successive stage in the hierarchy is built on the preceding

Examples of receptive fields of brain cells:

10.16 Receptive Fields of Cells at Various Levels in the Cat Visual System
Microelectrode recordings reveal that cells differ greatly in their receptive fields. (*a*) Visual cells in the thalamus (LGN) have concentric receptive fields. (*b*) Visual cells in the cerebral cortex may show orientation specificity or respond only to motion, or (*c*) they may respond only to motion in a particular direction.

one, Hoffman and Stone (1971) found that the complex cells had slightly *faster* responses. The hierarchical theory, however, requires the simple cells to respond earlier. Furthermore, complex cells were found to receive direct input from LGN cells, whereas the hierarchical theory would have them obtain input from simple cortical cells.

Competing hypotheses

At the same time that difficulties with this model were being shown (e.g., by J. Stone et al., 1979), an alternative model was emerging, which we will describe next. The contest between these models is still not settled, however. Chilling the cortex of a cat, which inhibited interneurons, did not affect the orientation tuning of simple cortical cells, but it silenced most complex cortical cells tested, all of which lacked monosynaptic connections to the LGN (Ferster et al., 1996). These observations support the hierarchical model. For more on this question, see Topic 10.2, What Accounts for Orientation Selectivity of Neurons in the Primary Visual Cortex?

Special topic

Most Cells in the Primary Visual Cortex Are Tuned to Particular Spatial Frequencies
Concepts of pattern analysis in terms of lines and edges at various orientations have largely given way to what is known as the **spatial-frequency filter model**. To discuss this model, we must become familiar with a way of regarding spatial vision that is quite different from our intuitive thinking (R. L. De Valois and De Valois, 1988; Westheimer, 1984). By the spatial fre-

quency of a visual stimulus, we mean the number of light/dark (or color) cycles it shows per degree of visual space. For example, Figure 10.17*a* and *b* differ in the spacing of the bars; Figure 10.17*a* has twice as many bars in the same horizontal space and is therefore said to have double the spatial frequency of Figure 10.17*b*. The spatial-frequency technique applies Fourier analysis (see Box 9.1) or linear systems theory rather than analyzing visual patterns into bars and angles.

In Box 9.1, we saw that we can produce any complex, repeating auditory stimulus by adding together simple sine waves. Conversely, using Fourier analysis, we can determine which sine waves would be needed to make any particular complex waveform. The same principle of Fourier analysis can be applied to visual patterns. If the dimension from dark to light is made to vary according to a sine wave function, the result is visual patterns like the ones in Figure 10.17*c* and *d*. A series of dark and light stripes, like those in Figure 10.17*a* and *b*, can be analyzed into the sum of a visual sine wave and its odd harmonics—that is, multiples of the basic frequency.

A complex visual pattern or scene can also be analyzed by the Fourier technique; in this case frequency components at different angles of orientation are also used. A given spatial frequency can exist at any level of contrast; Figures 10.17*c* and *d* show examples of high and low contrast, respectively. To reproduce or perceive the complex pattern or scene accurately, the system has to handle all the spatial frequencies that are present in it. If the high frequencies are filtered out, the small details and sharp contrasts are lost; if the low frequencies are filtered out, the large uniform areas and gradual transitions are lost. Figure 10.17*e–g* shows how the filtering of spatial frequencies affects a photograph. The photograph is still recognizable after the high visual frequencies are filtered out (Figure 10.17*f*) or when the low frequencies are filtered out (Figure 10.17*g*). (Similarly, speech is still recognizable, although it sounds distorted, after either the high audio frequencies or the low frequencies are filtered out.)

F. W. Campbell and Robson (1968) suggested that the visual system includes many channels that are tuned to different spatial frequencies, just as the auditory system has channels for different acoustic frequencies. The term "channel" is used here to mean a mechanism that accepts or deals with only a particular band or class of information. A particular radio or television station transmits its information through an assigned channel or band of wavelengths; to receive this information, you must tune your receiving device to the particular channel.

The suggestion that the nervous system has different spatial-frequency channels was soon supported by results of experiments on selective adaptation to visual frequency (Blakemore and Campbell, 1969; Pantle and Sekuler, 1968). In these experiments a person spent a minute or more inspecting a visual grating with a given spacing (or spatial frequency), such as those in Figure 10.17*a* and *b*. Looking at the grating

(*a*) High-frequency
square wave

(*b*) Low-frequency
square wave

(*c*) High-contrast
sinusoidal spatial grating

(*d*) Low-contrast
sinusoidal spatial grating

10 cycles

5 cycles

(*e*)   (*f*)   (*g*)

10.17 Spatial Frequencies
(*a, b*) The spacing between dark and light stripes shows that part *a* has double the spatial frequency of part *b*. (*c, d*) Visual grids with sinusoidal modulation of intensity: (*c*) high contrast; (*d*) low contrast. (*e–g*) A photograph of Groucho Marx subjected to spatial filtering: (*e*) normal photograph; (*f*) high spatial frequencies filtered out; (*g*) low spatial frequencies filtered out. (Parts *e–g* courtesy of John Frisby.)

(a) Macaque brain, lateral view

(c) Visual areas in the macaque cortex, unfolded view

(b) Macaque brain, medial view

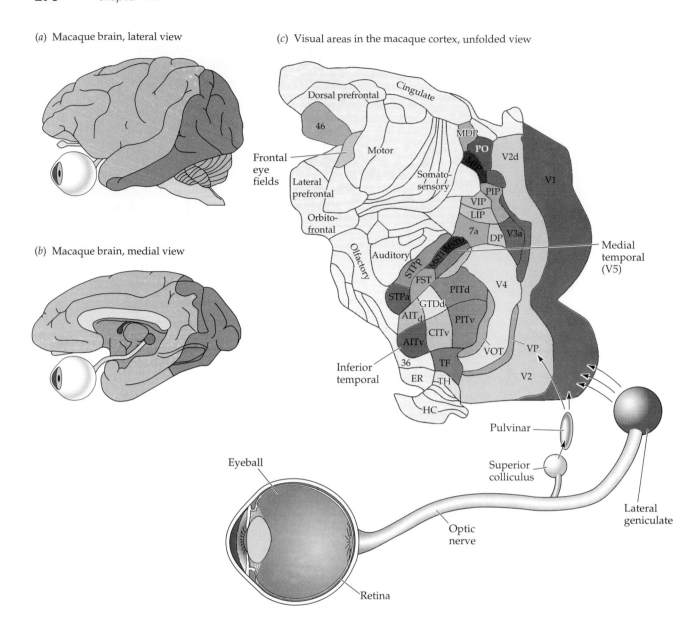

(d) Visual areas in the human occipital cortex, "flattened" by computational techniques

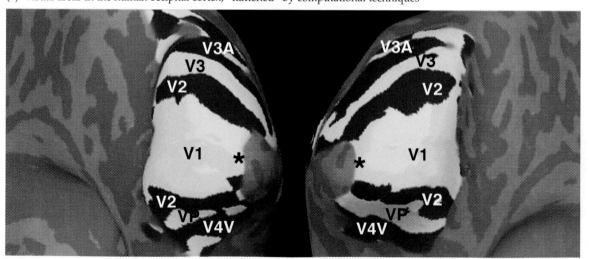

◀ 10.18 Main Visual Areas in the Monkey and Human Brain

(*a*, *b*) Macaque visual areas in occipital and temporal cortex are labeled in pink. Part *c* shows all the known visual areas of the macaque cortex in color. (*d*) Using computational techniques, the occipital regions of human brain shown in Figure 10.12*b* were "inflated," flattening the brain and bringing sulci in the cortex to the surface, which reveals the relative size and extent of various cortical visual areas (see text). The black asterisks identify the representation of the center of the fovea. (Parts *a*–*c* adapted from Van Essen and Drury, 1997; *d* from Tootell et al., 1998; courtesy of Roger Tootell.)

made the cells that are tuned to that frequency adapt (become less sensitive). Then the person's sensitivity to gratings of different spacings was determined. The results showed that sensitivity to the subsequent gratings was depressed briefly at whatever frequency the person had adapted to. According to Russell De Valois and Karen De Valois (1980, p. 320), the suggestion of multiple spatial frequency channels

> had revolutionary impact because it led to entirely different conceptions of the way in which the visual system might function in dealing with spatial stimuli. It suggests that rather than specifically detecting such seminaturalistic features as bars and edges, the system is breaking down complex stimuli into their individual spatial frequency components in a kind of crude Fourier analysis.

The responses of cortical cells to spatial-frequency stimuli were found to be tuned more accurately to the dimensions of spatial-frequency grids than to the widths of bars (R. L. De Valois et al., 1977; Hochstein and Shapley, 1976; Maffei and Fiorentini, 1973). The concept of multiple spatial-frequency channels does not require a thorough Fourier analysis of the optical image (Westheimer, 1984). In fact, the receptive field of a cortical cell typically shows only an excitatory axis and one clear band of inhibition by the surround on each side, but the spacing of these components shows the frequency tuning. The spatial-frequency approach has proved useful in the analysis of many aspects of human pattern vision (K. K. De Valois et al., 1979). The images of high-definition TV are transmitted in terms of spatial frequencies.

Neurons in the Visual Cortex beyond Area V1 Have Complex Receptive Fields and Contribute to the Identification of Forms

Area V1 is only a small part of the cortex devoted to vision. Area V1 sends axons to other visual cortical areas, including areas that appear to be involved in the perception of form: area V2, area V4, and the inferior temporal area (see Figure 10.18*c*). Some of these extrastriate areas also receive direct input from the LGN. The receptive fields of the cells in many of these extrastriate visual areas are even more complex than those in cells of

area V1. As Figure 10.18*a*–*c* reflects, on the basis of anatomical, physiological, and behavioral investigations with macaque monkeys, we know that at least 32 distinct cortical areas are directly involved in visual function (Van Essen and Drury, 1997; Van Essen et al., 1992).

The visual areas of the human brain have been less thoroughly mapped than those in the monkey brain, and mainly by neuroimaging, which does not have as fine spatial resolution as the electrophysiological recording used in the monkey brain. The general layout appears to be similar in the two species, although fewer specific visual regions have been mapped in the human (Figure 10.18*d*). There are important differences in *proportions* of cortical areas between the two species. In the macaque monkey, the occipital lobe occupies 32% of the neocortex and the frontal lobe 26%; in the human, the occipital lobe occupies 19% and the frontal lobe 36%. Whereas the 32 areas that are largely or entirely visual in function occupy 54% of the surface of the macaque neocortex, the visual areas account for only about 23% of human neocortex. We will discuss only a few of the main visual cortical areas and their functions.

Area V2 is adjacent to V1, and many of its cells show properties similar to those of V1 cells. Many V2 cells can respond to illusory contours, which may help explain how we perceive contours such as the boundaries of the upright triangle in Figure 10.19 (Peterhans and von der Heydt, 1989). Clearly such cells respond to complex relations among the parts of their receptive field. Some V1 cells can also respond to illusory contours (Grosof et al., 1993), but this feature is more common in area V2, which shows that the perception of illusory contours begins at a lower level in the visual system than investigators expected.

Area V4 receives axons from V2 and has cells that give their strongest responses to the sinusoidal frequency gratings that we discussed in the previous sec-

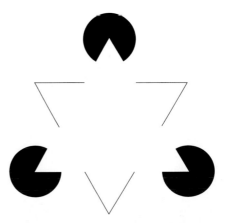

10.19 A Geometric Figure with "Illusory" or "Subjective" Contours

Cells have been found in visual cortical areas that respond to illusory contours such as those of the upright triangle shown here. These contours thus have neurophysiological meaning.

tion. Many V4 cells respond even better, however, to concentric and radial stimuli, such as those in Figure 10.20a (Gallant et al., 1993). Investigators suggest that these V4 cells show an intermediate stage between the spatial-frequency processing in V1 and V2 cells and the recognition of pattern and form in cells of the inferior temporal area. Area V4 also has many cells that respond preferentially (most strongly) to wavelength differences, as we will see later in this chapter when we discuss color vision.

Area V5 appears to be specialized for the perception of motion, as we will also discuss later in this chapter. The inferior temporal visual cortex (IT) has many cells that respond best to particular complex forms, including forms the subject has learned to recognize. We saw one example in Figure 1.6: a cell that responded best to a monkey face in lateral view. Because many cells in the IT have highly specific receptive fields, it is hard to find the exact stimuli that can activate a particular cell. Experimenters start by presenting many three-dimensional animal and plant objects (Desimone et al., 1984; K. Tanaka, 1993). When a stimulus elicits a strong response, the experimenters then simplify the image by sequentially removing parts of the features to determine the necessary and sufficient features for maximal activation of the cell.

Most cells in the IT do not require a natural object such as a face to activate them; instead they require moderately complex shapes, sometimes combined with color or texture, such as those in Figure 10.20b. K. Tanaka (1993) reports that the IT has a columnar organization like that of V1 (as we will see shortly), with adjacent cells often having similar receptive fields. He proposes that simultaneous activation of tens of such cells may be sufficient to specify a natural object. The complex receptive fields in the IT probably develop through experience and learning. When a monkey was trained for a year to discriminate a set of 28 moderately complex

shapes, 39% of the cells in the anterior IT gave a large response to some of these shapes, whereas in control monkeys only 9% of the cells responded strongly to these forms (Kobatake and Tanaka, 1994).

Neural plasticity

The prefrontal cortex also contains a restricted region of neurons that are activated by faces but not by other visual stimuli, as found both by noninvasive recording of human subjects (Ungerleider et al., 1998) and by electrical recording of neurons in the monkey brain (Scalaidhe et al., 1997). These neurons receive connections from the superior temporal sulcus and adjacent cortex on the inferior temporal gyrus. These findings indicate that the ventral visual pathway that processes stimulus identification extends from the primary visual cortex through temporal cortical regions to the prefrontal cortex.

Recognition of familiar objects requires more than accurate perception of forms. As we will see in Chapter 19, some people with brain damage caused by strokes can describe familiar faces accurately but can no longer recognize them. The existence of specific deficits after brain damage suggests that particular abilities or skills depend on particular regions of the brain that are not required for other kinds of ability or performance. In subsequent chapters we will consider other dissociations between abilities that depend on different brain regions.

10.20 Complex Stimuli Evoke Strong Responses in Visual Cortex

(a) These concentric and radial stimuli evoke maximal responses from some cells in visual cortical area V4. The stimuli that evoked the highest response rates (see scale bar) are shown in red and orange. (b) Twelve examples of the critical features of stimuli that evoke maximal responses from cells in the anterior inferior temporal area. (Part a from Gallant et al., 1993, courtesy of Jack Gallant; b from K. Tanaka, 1993, courtesy of Keiji Tanaka.)

(a)

1.1   62.0

(b)

Area V1 Is Organized in Columns

Area V1 is organized into columns with a richness of representation unimagined only a few years ago. More complicated than the organization of the somatosensory cortex (see Chapter 8), the primary visual cortex has separate representations for at least four dimensions of the visual stimulus: (1) location in the visual field, with larger, finer mapping of the central region of the visual field than of the periphery; (2) orientation; (3) color; and (4) ocular dominance (**ocular dominance columns, ODCs**, are alternating bands or stripes of cells that represent each of the two eyes separately).

ODCs were first discovered by electrophysiological recording of the receptive fields of individual neurons when one eye or the other was stimulated by visual targets. This recording revealed the existence of elongated bands of cells that respond preferentially (i.e., more strongly) to stimulation of one eye. Each band is about 0.5 mm wide. A given point in the visual field elicits responses in adjacent ODCs. The ocular dominance is especially clear in the broad layer 4 of area V1, where each cell responds to only one eye. Above and below layer 4, most cells respond to stimulation of both eyes, so ocular dominance is expressed less strongly than in layer 4.

Anatomical tracing techniques that proliferated beginning in the 1970s furnished additional information about ODCs. For example, when a small dose of radioactive amino acid is injected into one eye, some of it is transported along neurons, crossing synapses and reaching the visual cortex. Autoradiographic examination of the cortex then reveals parallel bands of radioactivity in layer 4 that correspond to the ODCs of the injected eye. Activation of neurons *outside* layer 4 was demonstrated by the use of the 2-deoxyglucose (2-DG) autoradiographic technique described in Box 2.1.

In these experiments, a monkey had one eye covered and the other eye open while radioactive 2-DG was administered. Subsequent autoradiography of the cortical tissue showed not only bands about 350 μm wide in layer 4, but also dots of radioactivity about 150 μm wide in the other layers, indicating responses to stimulation of the one eye. These dots ran along the centers of the ocular dominance columns. The presence of these dots shows that some of the neurons in other layers of the columns are also mainly monocular.

Techniques of optical imaging of cortical activity (T. Bonhoeffer and Grinvald, 1991; Tsó et al., 1990) allow us to see the ocular dominance columns in the primary visual cortex of an awake monkey when visual patterns are presented to one eye (Figure 10.21*a* and *b*). The imaging is based on small changes in the light reflected from the cortex during activity. These changes are of two types:

Important method

(1) changes in blood volume, probably in the capillaries of the activated area; and (2) changes in cortical tissue, such as the movement of ions and water or the expansion and contraction of extracellular spaces. Experimenters can combine optical imaging with electrophysiological recording to obtain visual guidance for placing microelectrodes in particular parts of ODCs. Figure 10.21*b* shows the ODCs that were activated when one eye was stimulated. The investigators suggest that this recording technique will prove useful as a mapping tool in human neurosurgery.

The ocular dominance columns develop during the first 4 months in the cat and during the first 6 months in the macaque monkey. As we saw in Chapter 7, both eyes must be exposed to the visual environment if each eye is to obtain its own cortical representation (see Figure 7.19). Up to the age of 3 or 4 months, human infants are unimpressed by stereograms (pairs of pictures showing somewhat different left-eye and right-eye views that most adult observers perceive as a three-dimensional view). At the age of 3 or 4 months, however, most infants are captivated by stereograms (Held, 1993). Presumably, before that age the cortex is unable to separate the information from the two eyes, because it reaches the same cortical neurons.

Within the ocular dominance columns are narrower **orientation columns** 30 to 100 μm in diameter. Microelectrode recording has shown that all the cells within each orientation column share the same preference for stimuli at a given orientation within the visual field (Figure 10.21*c* and *d*). As the recording electrode is moved from one orientation column to the next, the preferred axis of orientation shifts by about 10°. That is, in one column all the cells are "tuned" to upright stimuli (at an orientation of 0°); in an adjacent column, all cells respond best to stimuli at 10° from the vertical; in the next column, at 20°; and so forth. In Figure 10.21*d* we see the indications of activity at the surface of the cortex produced by stimuli of four different orientations (see Figure 10.21*c*). Inspection reveals regularly spaced "pinwheels" in which responses to the different stimulus orientations pivot around a center.

Also within the ocular dominance columns of primate visual areas are vertical "blobs" (sometimes called "pegs") that can be seen when the tissue is stained to reveal the enzyme cytochrome oxidase. Early experiments suggested that the blobs were related to color vision (Hendrickson, 1985; Livingstone and Hubel, 1984), but later work has cast doubt on this hypothesis. Quantitative studies show that neurons in the blobs cannot be readily distinguished from neurons outside the blobs on the basis of either chromatic tuning (Lennie et al., 1990) or orientation tuning (A. G. Leventhal et al., 1995). In addition, even nocturnal primates, whose retinas are poor in cones, and cats, which have little or no color vision, have blobs; and cone-rich rodents, such as ground squirrels, do *not* have blobs.

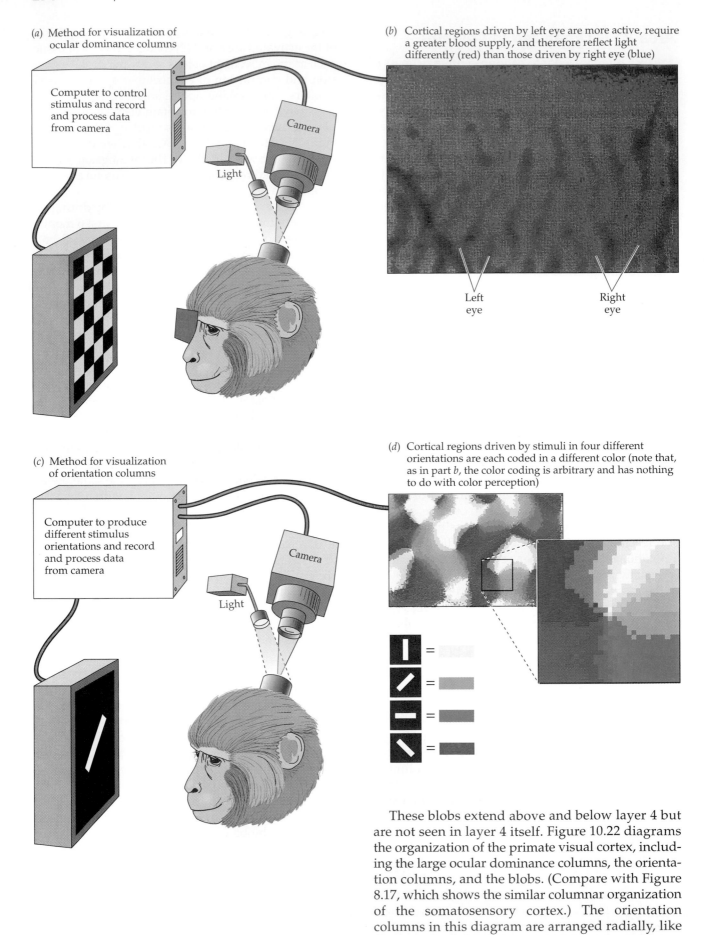

(a) Method for visualization of ocular dominance columns

Computer to control stimulus and record and process data from camera

Camera

Light

(b) Cortical regions driven by left eye are more active, require a greater blood supply, and therefore reflect light differently (red) than those driven by right eye (blue)

Left eye

Right eye

(c) Method for visualization of orientation columns

Computer to produce different stimulus orientations and record and process data from camera

Camera

Light

(d) Cortical regions driven by stimuli in four different orientations are each coded in a different color (note that, as in part b, the color coding is arbitrary and has nothing to do with color perception)

These blobs extend above and below layer 4 but are not seen in layer 4 itself. Figure 10.22 diagrams the organization of the primate visual cortex, including the large ocular dominance columns, the orientation columns, and the blobs. (Compare with Figure 8.17, which shows the similar columnar organization of the somatosensory cortex.) The orientation columns in this diagram are arranged radially, like the "pinwheels" in Figure 10.21d. Some investigators (*a*) In a method for visualization of ODCs, a camera records changes in light reflected from the cortex when the monkey views a twinkling checkerboard with one eye. Small differences in reflected light are amplified, and intensity is coded by color (red for strong intensity, blue for weak). (*b*) After the recording is processed, ODCs for the active eye are seen as red stripes. (*c*) In a method for visualization of orientation columns, stimuli at different orientations (vertical, horizontal, diagonal) are presented to reveal groups of neurons that respond most strongly

to a particular orientation. The stimuli are usually black or white, but here they are color coded to correspond to color-coded responses to four different orientations combined into a single pattern (*d*). Although the pattern at first seems disorderly, closer inspection reveals several regions at which all four orientations converge in a "pinwheel" pattern (inset). Note that the foci of pinwheels occur at regular intervals, that each orientation is represented only once within a pinwheel, and that the sequence of orientations is consistent across pinwheels. (Adapted from T. Bonhoeffer and Grinvald, 1991; *b* and *d* courtesy of A. Grinvald.)

suggest that the orientation columns are laid out in a rectangular arrangement, like city blocks; this question is not yet settled.

Color Vision Depends on Special Channels from the Retinal Cones through Cortical Area V4

For most people, different hues are a striking aspect of vision. The system for color perception appears to have at least three stages (R. L. De Valois and De Valois, 1993). The first stage involves the cones, the retinal receptor cells that are specialized to respond to certain wavelengths of light. The second stage is the processing of this information by neurons in the local circuits of the retina, leading to retinal ganglion cells that are excited by light of some wavelengths

and inhibited by light of other wavelengths. The ganglion cells send the wavelength information via their axons to both the magnocellular and parvocellular layers of the LGN; from there this information goes to area V1, from which it is relayed to other visual cortical areas. The third stage of color perception takes place in the cortex.

Color Perception Requires Receptor Cells That Differ in Their Sensitivities to Different Wavelengths

At the start of the nineteenth century, scientists first hypothesized that three separate kinds of receptors in the retina provide the basis for color vision. This **trichromatic hypothesis** (from the Greek *tri-*, "three," and *chroma*, "color") was endorsed in 1852 by the great physiologist-physicist Hermann von Helmholtz

10.22 Organization of the Primate Striate Cortex
Two partial ODCs representing the left and right eyes. Blobs extend vertically through layers 1 to 3 and 5 to 6 of the ODCs. Small columns represent the preferred orientations of groups of cells; these orientation columns radiate out from the centers of the blobs. The orientation is color coded here, as in Figure 10.21. For simplification, this diagram does not represent spatial frequency (higher spatial frequencies are represented at the edges of the blocks and lower frequencies in the centers), nor does it represent the spectrally opponent cells (which we'll discuss shortly) that occur irregularly in the columns.

and became the dominant position. Helmholtz predicted that blue-sensitive, green-sensitive, and red-sensitive cones would be found, that each would be sharply tuned to its part of the spectrum, and that each type would have a separate path to the brain. The color of an object would be recognized, then, on the basis of which color receptor was activated. This system would be like the mechanisms for discriminating touch and temperature on the basis of which skin receptors and labeled neural lines are activated (see Chapter 8).

Competing hypotheses   Later in the nineteenth century, the physiologist Ewald Hering proposed a different explanation. He argued, on the basis of visual experience, that there are three opposed pairs of colors—blue and yellow, green and red, and black and white—and that three physiological processes with opposed positive and negative values must therefore be the basis of color vision. As we will see, both this **opponent-process hypothesis** and the trichromatic hypothesis are encompassed in current color vision theory, but neither of the old hypotheses is sufficient by itself.

Measurements of photopigments in cones have borne out the trichromatic hypothesis in part. Each cone of the human retina has one of three classes of pigments. These pigments do not, however, have the narrow spectral distributions that Helmholtz predicted. The color system that Helmholtz postulated would have given rather poor color vision and poor visual acuity. Color vision would be poor because only a few different hues could be discriminated; within the long-wavelength region of the spectrum there would be only red, and not all the range of hues that we see. Acuity would be poor because the grain of the retinal mosaic would be coarse; a red stimulus could affect only one-third of the receptors. (Actually, acuity is as good in red light as it is in white light.)

The human visual system does not have receptors that are sensitive to only a narrow part of the visible spectrum. Two of the three retinal cone pigments give some response to light of almost any wavelength. The pigments have different *peaks* of sensitivity, but the peaks are not as far apart as Helmholtz predicted. As Figure 10.23 shows, the peaks occur at about 420 nm (in the part of the spectrum where we usually see blue under photopic conditions), about 530 nm (where most of us see green), and about 560 nm (where most of us see yellow-green). Despite Helmholtz's prediction, none of the curves peaks in the long-wavelength part of the spectrum, where most of us see red (around 630 nm).

Under ordinary conditions almost any visual object stimulates at least two kinds of cones, thus ensuring high visual acuity and good perception of form. The spectral sensitivities of the three cone types differ from each other, and the nervous system detects and processes these differences to extract the color infor-

10.23 Spectral Sensitivities of Human Photopigments
Each pigment has a peak sensitivity, but responds to a wide range of wavelengths.

mation. Thus, certain ganglion cells and certain cells at higher stations in the visual system are color-specific, even though the receptor cells are not. Similarly, visual receptors are not form-specific, but form is detected later in the visual centers by comparison of the outputs of different receptors.

Since the cones are not color detectors, the most appropriate brief names for them can be taken from their peak areas of wavelength sensitivity: "short" (S) for the receptor with peak sensitivity at about 420 nm, "medium" (M) at 530 nm, and "long" (L) at 560 nm. There are roughly equal numbers of M and L receptors, but far fewer S receptors; this difference explains why acuity is much lower with short-wavelength illumination than in the other parts of the visible spectrum.

The genes for wavelength-sensitive pigments in the retina have been located on human chromosomes, and the amino acid sequences for the cone pigments have been determined (Nathans, 1987). The similarities in structure of the three genes suggest that they are all derived from a common ancestral gene. In particular, the genes for the medium- and long-wavelength pigments occupy adjacent positions on the X chromosome and are much more similar to each other than either is to the gene for the short-wavelength pigment on chromosome 6.

The fact that humans and Old World monkeys have both M and L pigments, whereas most New World monkeys have only a single longer-wavelength pigment, suggests that the M and L pigments differentiated recently in evolutionary terms. Furthermore, the genes for the M and L pigments are variable among individuals, and particular variants in these pigment genes correspond to variants in color vision, so-called color blindness. Thus, detailed examination of a person's photopigment genes can now show whether the person has normal color vision or has one of the recognized deficiencies of color discrimination. In animal experiments, antibodies that have been developed for the S, M, and L cones can be dyed distinctively, making it relatively easy to locate the different kinds of cones and to study their distribution over the retina (Wikler and Rakic, 1990).

The fact that the genes for the M and L pigments are on the X chromosome explains why defects of color vision are much more frequent in human males than in human females. Because males have only one X chromosome, a mutation in the genes for the M or L pigments can impair color vision. But if a female has a defective photopigment gene in one of her two X chromosomes, a normal copy of the gene on the other X chromosome can compensate. Only very rarely do both of a female's X chromosomes have defective genes for color receptors.

Genes and behavior

Some Retinal Ganglion Cells and Parvocellular LGN Cells Show Spectral Opponency

Recordings made from retinal ganglion cells in Old World monkeys, which can discriminate colors as humans with normal color vision do, reveal the second stage of processing of color vision. Most ganglion cells and cells in the parvocellular layers of the LGN fire in response to some wavelengths and are inhibited by other wavelengths. Leading this research are Russell De Valois and Karen De Valois, whose results provide much of the information in this discussion.

Russell De Valois

Karen De Valois

Figure 10.24*a* shows the response of a parvocellular LGN cell as a spot of light centered on the receptive field of the cell is changed from one wavelength to another. Firing is inhibited by wavelengths from about 420 to 600 nm, then stimulated from about 600 nm on. A cell exhibiting this response pattern is called a plus L/minus M cell (+L/–M). Since two regions of the spectrum have opposite effects on the cell's rate of firing, this is an example of a spectrally opponent cell. Figure 10.24 shows examples of responses of the four main kinds of spectrally opponent cells.

Each spectrally opponent ganglion cell presumably receives input from two or three different kinds of cones through bipolar cells. The connections from at least one type of cone are excitatory, and those from at least one other type are inhibitory (Figure 10.25). The spectrally opponent ganglion cells thus record the difference in stimulation of different populations of cones. For example, a +M/–L cell responds to the difference

10.24 Responses of the Four Main Types of Spectrally Opponent Cells in the Monkey LGN

Each type is excited by one band of wavelengths and inhibited by another.

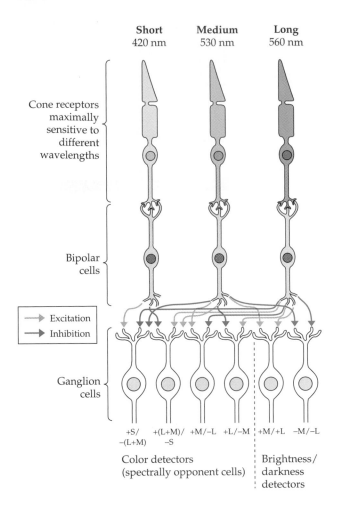

Short
420 nm

Medium
530 nm

Long
560 nm

Cone receptors
maximally
sensitive to
different
wavelengths

Bipolar
cells

→ Excitation
→ Inhibition

Ganglion
cells

+S/
–(L+M)

+(L+M)/
–S

+M/–L +L/–M

+M/+L –M/–L

Color detectors
(spectrally opponent cells)

Brightness/
darkness
detectors

**10.25 A Model of the Connections of the
Wavelength Discrimination Systems
in the Primate Retina**
The connections from the cones yield four kinds of spectrally opponent ganglion cells, as well as ganglion cells
that detect brightness or darkness. (After De Valois and
De Valois, 1980.)

in the excitation of M and L cones. (Recall from Chapter 3 that a neuron can process information by subtracting one input from another; spectral opponency is
an example of such information processing.)

Although the peaks of the sensitivity curves of the
M and L cones are not very different (see Figure
10.23), the M-minus-L *difference* curve (see Figure
10.24b) shows a clear peak around 500 nm (in the
green or blue-green part of the spectrum). The L-mi-
nus-M difference function (see Figure 10.24a) shows a
peak around 650 nm (in the reddish orange part of the
spectrum). Thus, +M/–L and +L/–M cells yield distinctly different neural response curves.

The spectrally opponent neurons are the second
stage in the system for color perception, but they still
cannot be called color cells, for the following reasons:
(1) They send their outputs into many higher circuits—for detection of form, depth, and movement, as
well as hue; and (2) their peak wavelength sensitivi-

ties do not correspond precisely to the wavelengths
that we see as the principal hues.

In addition to the four kinds of spectrally opponent
ganglion cells, Figure 10.25 diagrams the presumed
inputs of ganglion cells that detect brightness and
darkness. The brightness detectors receive stimulation
from both M and L cones (+M/+L); the darkness detectors are inhibited by both M and L cones (–M/–L).

In the monkey LGN, 70 to 80% of the cells are spectrally opponent; in the cat, very few spectrally opponent cells are found—only about 1%. This difference
explains the ease with which monkeys discriminate
wavelengths and the difficulty of training cats to discriminate even large differences in wavelength.

Some Visual Cortical Cells and Regions Appear to Be Specialized for Color Perception

In the cortex, spectral information appears to be used
for various kinds of information processing. Forms are
segregated from their background by differences in
color or intensity (or both). The most important role
that color plays in our perception is to denote which
parts of a complex image belong to one object and
which belong to another. Some animals use displays
of brightly colored body parts to call attention to
themselves, but color can also be used as camouflage.

Some spectrally opponent cortical cells contribute
to the perception of color, providing the third stage of
the color vision system. R. L. De Valois and De Valois
(1993) have suggested how adding and subtracting
the outputs of spectrally opponent ganglion cells
could yield cortical cells that are perceptually opponent: red versus green, blue versus yellow, and black
versus white. The spectral responses of these cells correspond to the wavelengths of the principal hues
specified by human observers, and their characteristics also help explain other color phenomena.

Visual cortical region V4 is particularly rich in col-
or-sensitive cells. Evidence that this area is normally
involved in the perception of color in humans comes
from studies using positron-emission tomography
(PET). Area V4 is activated when subjects view colored stimuli but not when they view black-and-
white stimuli (Zeki et al., 1991). Rare human patients
have lost color vision completely after sustaining
brain lesions that included area V4 (A. R. Damasio et
al., 1980; Zeki, 1993). One poignant case is an artist
who could no longer see the hues in the impression-
ist paintings he had once admired (Sacks and
Wasserman, 1987); he could still make black-and-
white sketches, but he could no longer paint in col-
or. Such lack of color vision is called **achromatopsia**
(from the Greek *a-*, "without"; *chroma*, "color"; and
opsis, "vision"). Since each half of the visual field is
seen by the opposite side of the brain, unilateral
damage to area V4 can cause loss of color vision in
half of the visual field (a condition called hemiachromatopsia) (Kölmel, 1988).

Most Mammalian Species Have Some Color Vision

In 1942, Gordon Walls concluded from a survey that within the mammals, color vision is by no means widespread, and this conclusion has been repeated in many books and articles. A much more extensive survey by Gerald Jacobs (1993), however, indicates that almost all mammals probably have at least some degree of color vision, which he defines as the ability to discriminate among stimuli that differ in wavelength distributions of spectral energy. Among mammals, only certain primates have good trichromatic color vision (i.e., based on three classes of cone photopigments), but many species have dichromatic color vision (based on two classes of cone pigments). Most so-called color-blind humans have dichromatic vision and can distinguish short-wavelength stimuli (blue) from long-wavelength stimuli (not blue).

The ability of animals to discriminate visual cues on the basis of wavelength can be measured by behavioral tests (Neitz et al., 1989). Indirect approaches include measuring the electrical responses of the eye to flashes of different stimuli (Goldsmith, 1986; Neitz and Jacobs, 1984) or measuring the pigment in individual photoreceptors (Bowmaker, 1984; J. S. Levine and MacNichol, 1982). No species that possesses multiple cone pigments has been found to lack the central **Important method** neural mechanisms for using them in color vision. In a few species, all three of the methods mentioned here have been used to study color vision, and because in these test cases the results of the three methods agreed, clear evidence from any one of these methods is accepted as proof of color vision.

On the basis of his survey, G. H. Jacobs (1993) suggested that it is better to think of a continuum of color capabilities rather than use an all-or-none criterion, and he proposed that four categories cover all mammalian species:

1. *Excellent trichromatic color vision* is found in diurnal primates such as humans and the rhesus monkey (*Macaca mulatta*).
2. *Robust dichromatic color vision* is found in species that have two kinds of cone photopigments and a reasonably large population of cones. Examples of such species are the dog and the pig.
3. *Feeble dichromatic color vision* occurs in species that have two kinds of cone pigments but only a small population of cones. Examples are the domestic cat and the coati (*Nasua nasua*).
4. *Minimal color vision* is possessed by species that have only a single kind of cone pigment and that must rely on interactions between rods and cones to discriminate wavelength. Examples are the owl monkey (*Aotes trivirgatus*) and the raccoon (*Procyon lotor*).

When both diurnal and nocturnal species of a given taxonomic family have been tested for color vision (e.g., the coati and the raccoon), the diurnal species (in this case the coati) usually has the better color vision. (For more on measurement of color vision in animals and a table showing categories of color vision in several species, see Topic 10.3, Color Vision in Some Mammalian Species.) **Special topic**

Investigators uncovered a perplexing problem in attempts to characterize the color vision of squirrel monkeys (*Saimiri sciureus*). Monkeys of this species showed a great deal of variability among individuals when they took behavioral tests of color vision: About half were dichromats (among this group there were six different kinds of red–green vision), but the other half were trichromats. After puzzling over the data, the investigators found an unexpected pattern: All the male squirrel monkeys were dichromats, and about four-fifths of the females were trichromats (G. H. Jacobs, 1984; Jacobs et al., 1993). Imagine the arguments about choices of clothing and interior decoration if all men were dichromats and most women were trichromats!

Perception of Visual Motion Is Analyzed by a Special System That Includes Cortical Area V5

Some retinal ganglion cells respond preferentially to a certain *direction* of motion of objects; for example, certain ganglion cells respond to stimuli that move to the left but not to stimuli that move to the right (Barlow and Levick, 1965). Investigators have hypothesized that the direction-selective responses require retinal circuits involving both excitation and inhibition: Whereas movement in the preferred direction stimulates excitatory units before inhibitory units, movement in the nonpreferred direction reaches inhibitory units first.

Motion is analyzed by the cortex, partly in regions close to those that control eye movements. All the neurons in area V5 (also called the medial temporal area in the monkey; see Figure 10.18) respond to moving visual stimuli, but they do not respond differentially to the wavelength of stimulation. A variety of studies provide converging evidence that area V5 is specialized for the perception of motion and direction of motion. PET scan studies of human subjects show that moving stimuli, rather than colored stimuli, evoke responses in area V5.

When monkeys are trained to report the direction of perceived motion, experimental lesions of area V5 impair their performance, at least temporarily (Newsome et al., 1985). Electrical stimulation of clusters of V5 neurons with similar preferred directions of motion can affect the monkeys' judgments of direction of motion: Weak stimulation biases the judgments toward the preferred direction of the neurons (Salzman et al., 1992); stronger stimulation impairs performance, presumably because its effects spread to neurons representing all directions of motion (Murasugi et al., 1993).

One striking report described a woman who had lost the ability to perceive motion after a stroke that had damaged the medial temporal region, area V5, of her brain (Zihl et al., 1983). The woman was unable to perceive continuous motion and saw only separate, successive positions. This impairment led to many problems in her daily life. She had difficulty crossing streets because she could not follow the positions of automobiles in motion: "When I'm looking at the car first, it seems far away. But then, when I want to cross the road, suddenly the car is very near." She complained of difficulties in following conversations because she could not see the movements of speakers' lips. And she had trouble pouring tea into a cup because the fluid appeared to be frozen; she could not stop pouring at the right time because she was unable to see the movement in the cup as the fluid rose. Except for her inability to perceive motion, this woman's visual perception appeared to be normal.

Are the Many Cortical Visual Areas Organized Into Two Major Systems?

Many investigators have wondered why primate visual systems contain so many distinct regions. Research we have just discussed indicates that certain regions specialize in processing different attributes or dimensions of visual experience (such as shape, location, color, motion, and orientation). But the number of visual fields—over 30—is larger than the number of basic attributes. Perhaps the reason the number of separate visual regions that have been found is so much greater than the number of regions for any other sensory modality is simply that investigators, being visually oriented primates themselves, have lavished special attention on the visual system.

Competing hypotheses However, some investigators (e.g., Schiller, 1996) have claimed that many of the visual regions overlap in function and that neurons in many regions perform several different tasks rather than analyzing a single attribute. Others (e.g., Orban et al., 1996) suggest that a particular attribute is processed in different areas along with other attributes (e.g., motion and color in one area, motion and form in another, and so on). Such multiple representation of different attributes within an area might help account for the large number of visual areas, as well as for the multifunctional properties of neurons.

Other workers have suggested that the many cortical visual areas can be grouped into two major systems. Earlier work with hamsters led to the hypothesis that there are two visual systems: One, for identification of objects, involves especially the visu-

al cortex; the other, for location of objects, involves especially the superior colliculus (G. Schneider, 1969).

This hypothesis was later extended to primates, drawing on research on localized brain lesions in monkeys. Mishkin and Ungerleider (1982) proposed that primates have two main cortical processing streams, both originating in primary visual cortex: a ventral processing stream responsible for visual identification of objects, and a dorsal stream responsible for appreciating the spatial location of objects and visual guidance of movement toward objects. These processing streams were called, respectively, the "what" and the "where" streams. PET studies as well as brain lesions in patients indicate that the human brain also possesses what and where visual processing streams similar to those found in monkeys (Figure 10.26a) (Ungerleider et al., 1998). In the ventral stream, including regions of the occipitotemporal, inferotemporal, and inferior frontal areas, information about faces becomes more specific as one proceeds farther forward. PET studies show that whereas general information about facial features and gender are extracted more posteriorly, the more anterior parts of the stream provide representations of individual faces (Courtney et al., 1996).

Leslie Ungerleider

Mortimer Mishkin

Later came the suggestion that the ventral processing stream, which is mainly responsible for analysis of form and color and for recognition of objects, is an extension of the parvocellular (P) pathway, whereas the dorsal processing stream, mainly responsible for perception of location, depth, and movement, is an extension of the magnocellular (M) system (Livingstone and Hubel, 1988). From the LGN, the P and M divisions were thought to project to different layers and areas of the cerebral cortex (Figure 10.26b). In area V1, the P and M projections are segregated but intertwined with each pathway leading to a different region of layer 4 in area V1. In area V2 as well, the M and P systems occupy separate but intermixed small regions. It was proposed that beyond area V2 the two systems segregate completely—the P pathway going to inferotemporal regions of the cortex, the M pathway to parietal regions.

In a recent review of this topic, Merigan and Maunsell (1993, p. 370) stated, "The notion of parallel visual subsystems has been broadly disseminated and popularized . . . and has quickly become **Competing hypotheses** widely accepted, owing in part to its great explanatory power and its appealing simplicity." But these

(a) Broad locations of the ventral and dorsal pathways in the human brain

(b) The magnocellular and parvocellular pathways, from the retina to the higher levels of the visual cerebral cortex

Dorsal stream: spatial location

Occipital lobe

Ventral stream: object vision, faces

Frontal lobe

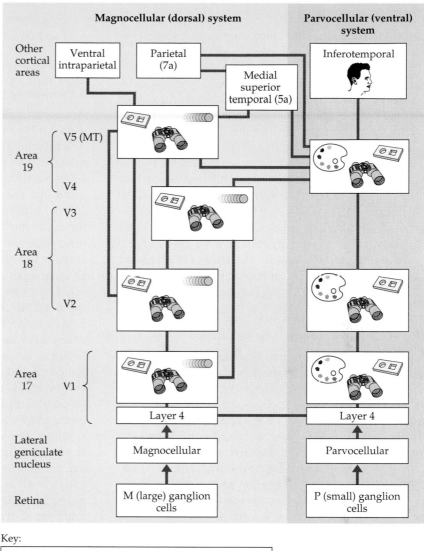

10.26 Parallel Processing Pathways in the Visual System
(a) Broad locations of the ventral (what) and dorsal (where) pathways. (b) The magnocellular (dorsal) and parvocellular (ventral) pathways, from the retina to the higher levels of the visual cerebral cortex. These pathways are separate at the lower levels of the visual system, but they show increasing overlap at the higher levels. (Part a courtesy of Leslie Ungerleider.)

reviewers point out that increasing evidence—anatomical, neurophysiological, and behavioral—suggests that the two systems overlap and intermingle considerably, beginning in layer 4b of V1, and the systems become increasingly merged at higher levels, so the idea of separate cortical M and P pathways has to be abandoned.

Genetic and Environmental Factors Interact to Determine Some Aspects of Visual Development

The main pathways of the visual system appear to be determined genetically. For example, some features of cellular anatomy and neurochemistry of the monkey visual cortex develop even without input from the photoreceptors (Kuljis and Rakic, 1990). However, many aspects of the visual system develop in interaction with the environment and visual experience.

We discussed this topic in Chapter 7, where we considered the effects of depriving one or both eyes of light during the first months after birth (see Figure 7.19). In Chapter 7 we also considered the misalignment of the two eyes ("lazy eye"), which can lead to the condition called **amblyopia,** in which acuity is poor in one eye even though the eye and retina are normal. We'll learn more about amblyopia and other effects of early experience in the next and final section of this chapter.

Visual Neuroscience Can Be Applied to Alleviate Some Visual Deficiencies

Vision is so important that many investigators have sought ways to prevent impairment, to improve inadequate vision, and to restore sight to the blind. In the United States, half a million people are blind. Recent medical advances have reduced some causes of blindness but have increased blindness from other causes. For example, improved treatment resulting in the increased survival of diabetics does not overcome all effects of this disease, one of which in many cases is blindness, and diabetes causes half the cases of blindness in the United States. In the discussion that follows we will first consider ways of avoiding impairment of vision. Then we will take up ways of exercising and training designed to improve an impaired visual system. Finally, we will take a brief look at two ways of partially overcoming blindness: (1) bypassing nonfunctioning eyes by stimulating the visual cortex directly; and (2) substituting another sense for vision.

Impairment of Vision Often Can Be Prevented or Reduced

Studies of the development of vision in children and other animals show that most cases of amblyopia are avoidable and that the incidence of **myopia** ("nearsightedness") can be reduced. Amblyopia develops if the two eyes are not aligned properly. In such cases, during the first few years of life the child tends to suppress the information that arrives from one eye to the cortex, and that eye becomes functionally blind. If the weak eye is given regular practice, by occlusion of the good eye, then vision can be preserved in both eyes. The balance of the eye muscles may need to be surgically adjusted to bring the two eyes into better alignment.

Myopia develops if the eyeball is too long, forcing the eye to focus objects in front of the retina rather than on the retina. Considerable evidence suggests that myopia occurs when children spend much time looking at targets close up rather than at objects far away (Marzani and Wallman, 1997). Before civilization, most people spent most of their time looking at objects far away, such as predators, prey, sources of water, and so on. Thus they kept the eye relaxed most of the time. Now, however, people spend long periods of time gazing at objects close at hand, such as books and computer screens. This constant close focusing requires that the lens be kept thick (unrelaxed). The eye tends to compensate by elongating to make focusing easier, thus causing progressive myopia. Preventive steps can be taken, especially during childhood and adolescence:

1. Read only in adequate light—enough that you can hold the book as far away as possible and still discern the words.

2. Avoid small type.
3. If you already have a prescription for myopia and you can read without using glasses, do so, because the glasses force you to thicken your lens more, thus accelerating the problem.

Increased Exercise Can Restore Function to a Previously Deprived or Neglected Eye

Attempts to alleviate amblyopia by training have produced mixed results and a great deal of controversy. The treatment recommended most often is, beginning at as early an age as possible, giving the weak eye extensive training and experience while obstructing the good eye (American Academy of Ophthalmology, 1994). (Although we follow the usual practice in referring to the "good" eye and the "weak" eye, the difference lies not in the eyes but in the higher visual centers to which they send their neural messages. Even in an eye deprived of experience of visual patterns, the retinal cells often have normal receptive fields.) Children with amblyopia often wear a patch or opaque contact lens over their good eye to force use of the weak eye.

Some investigators (e.g., Epelbaum et al., 1993) have concluded that only treatment during the first few years of life can be effective. Others report considerable improvement, even with adults, if they exercise the weak eye sufficiently and if the amblyopia is not too severe. One study reported considerable recovery from long-standing amblyopia when the good eye was lost or severely damaged (Romero-Apis et al., 1982). In all eight patients in this study, aged 16 to 69 at the time they lost their good eye, the vision in the amblyopic eye improved markedly, thus revealing plasticity of the adult brain.

A remarkable study by Chow and Stewart (1972) encouraged much subsequent work on rehabilitation, even in adult animals and people. Chow and Stewart studied kittens, depriving one or both eyes of pattern vision for about the first 20 months after birth—longer than the critical period for development of visual function (from about 3 to 12 weeks of age). When a unilaterally deprived kitten was then tested for pattern perception with the previously deprived eye, it showed almost no discrimination on formal tests and it was not able to guide its locomotion visually, although it performed well using its other eye.

The investigators then undertook an intensive program of rehabilitation with some of the kittens. They "gentled" and petted these animals frequently to keep them working on the demanding program. Over time the kittens developed some pattern discrimination with the previously deprived eye, and they could use it to guide their locomotion. Furthermore, recovery of vision was accompanied by morphological changes in the LGN. After monocular de-

Neural plasticity

privation, the LGN cells that had received input from the deprived eye were about one-third smaller than those that had been stimulated by pattern vision. When the previously deprived eye was retrained, the difference in size of LGN cells disappeared. Electrical recording showed that retraining also increased the number of binocular cells (those that respond to stimulation of either eye) in the visual cortex, in comparison with kittens that were not retrained. Such animal research, as well as research with human patients, provides encouraging examples for programs of rehabilitation (Bach-y-Rita, 1992).

The evidence for continuing plasticity in the visual system is consistent with similar evidence from the somesthetic system, presented in Chapter 8, and from the auditory system, presented in Chapter 9. Evidence of plasticity in other parts of the adult nervous system will be presented in Chapter 18.

Some Approaches Can Partially Overcome Blindness

In Chapter 9 we saw that when the hair cells of the cochlea do not function, a prosthetic device can be implanted to stimulate the auditory nerve directly. Some investigators are trying to do something comparable to overcome blindness, by stimulating the visual cortex with an array of electrodes. This approach bypasses not only the nonfunctional eyes but also the visual centers up to the level of the cortex and so eliminates processing at those levels of the brain.

Substituting another sense for vision is another way to overcome some of the handicaps of blindness. Braille reading is an example. A more ambitious attempt of this sort is to use an optical scanning device and feed the output to a series of raised points that can be detected by the fingers. Some blind people have learned to use such a device in order to "see" their environment (Bach-y-Rita, 1992). For more on these efforts to overcome blindness, see Topic 10.4, Ways of Partially Overcoming Blindness.

 Special topic

Summary

1. The perception of forms and the recognition of objects are complex accomplishments that require processing in many parts of the visual system.

2. The vertebrate eye is an elaborate structure that forms detailed and accurate optical images on the receptive cells of the retina.

3. Many different phyla have independently evolved photoreceptor organs; several have evolved eyes with lenses to focus light.

4. Visual information processing begins in the retina, where cells that contain photopigments capture light and initiate neural activity. Two kinds of retinal receptor cells, rods and cones, are the initial stages of two systems—the scotopic (dim light) and photopic (bright light) systems, respectively.

5. Each receptor reports only how strongly it has been excited, so at any given instant the visual nervous system receives an enormous array of quantitative information and has to determine what patterns in the outside world could have produced a particular set of "numbers." About one-fourth of our neocortex is devoted to this computation.

6. Brain pathways of the visual system include the lateral geniculate nucleus in the thalamus, the primary visual cortex (striate cortex, or V1), and other cortical regions. Some axons of retinal ganglion cells extend to the superior colliculus in the midbrain.

7. Recordings from cells at successively higher levels in the visual system reveal that the receptive fields change in two main ways: (1) They become larger (occupy larger parts of the visual field), and (2) they require increasingly specific stimuli to evoke responses.

8. The cortex contains several visual areas, each presenting a topographic map of the visual field, but each processing one or more different aspects of visual information, such as form, color, or movement.

9. For the perception of visual patterns and forms, the stimulus pattern is analyzed at the primary visual cortex according to the orientation and spatial frequency of stimuli.

10. Like the somatosensory and auditory cortices, the primary visual cortex is organized in columns perpendicular to the surface. Columns and groups of columns provide separate representations of the two eyes, of the angular orientation of stimuli, of position in the visual field, and of color.

11. In both cats and primates, parallel magnocellular and parvocellular projective systems from the retina to the brain mediate different aspects of visual projection, but these systems show increasing overlap in the cortical visual areas.

12. The ability to locate visual stimuli in space is aided by detailed spatial maps at every level of the visual system.

13. The discrimination of hue in Old World primates and in humans depends on the existence of three different cone photopigments and on the fact that retinal connections yield four different kinds of spectrally opponent retinal ganglion cells.

14. Clinical evidence supports the concept of parallel processing, because genetic anomalies or injury to the brain may impair some aspects of visual perception while leaving others intact. An example is achromatopsia (the inability to see hues).

15. The main pathways of the visual system appear to be determined genetically, but many aspects of the visual system develop in interaction with the environment and visual experience.

16. Attempts to treat amblyopia work best when retraining starts early in life, but success with some older patients demonstrates that the visual nervous system remains plastic even in adults.

17. Approaches to aiding the blind include bypassing nonfunctioning eyes by stimulating the visual cortex directly and substituting another sense (touch or audition) for vision.

Recommended Reading

De Valois, R. L., and De Valois, K. K. (1988). *Spatial vision.* New York: Oxford University Press.

Kaiser, P. K., and Boynton, R. M. (1996). *Human color vision.* Washington, DC: Optical Society of America.

Rodieck, R. W. (1998). *The first steps in seeing.* Sunderland, MA: Sinauer.

Wandell, B. A. (1995). *Foundations of vision.* Sunderland, MA: Sinauer.

Zeki, S. (1993). *A vision of the brain.* London: Blackwell.

11 *Movements and Actions*

*O*ur movements and acts seem effortless; we hardly think about what it takes for us to reach out and pick up an object, walk across a room, or even talk. It just happens. But even everyday movements require an intricate sequence of muscle activity. Think, for example, of all the muscles involved when you say a single word. The tongue, larynx, throat, lips, chest, and diaphragm must work in a highly coordinated manner to produce even the simplest speech sound. And there is little room for error if you are to be understood. The difference between saying "time" and "dime," for example, depends mainly on whether your vocal cords are relaxed or tensed during the start of the word.

What enables us to perform the movements and acts that make up our behavior? Any coordinated movement implies that there are underlying neural mechanisms for choosing the appropriate muscles and how they should act. These mechanisms require motoneurons to be activated in the proper order. Voluntary behavior adds another level of complexity: how the initial idea for a movement or act is translated into the selection of muscles. This process must involve at some places in the nervous system a plan for action—a motor plan.

We begin our discussion by looking at movements and their coordination from different points of view—the behavioral view, the control systems view, and especially the neurobiological view.

Marcel Duchamp, *Nude Descending a Staircase*, 1912

The Behavioral View

Crawling, walking, flying, and swimming are some of the many ways to move from one place to another. Close analysis of different animals offers some notions about the underlying mechanisms of these behaviors. For example, the vigorous, regular beating of insect or bird wings suggests that the nervous system contains a rhythm generator, an oscillator. The varied gaits of four-legged animals suggest that different oscillators are coupled in precise but flexible ways to produce co-ordinated movement. The great versatility of learned movements in humans shows the range of complex adjustments made possible by the motor system.

Movements and Actions Can Be Classified into Categories

Efforts to classify movements began with the distinction between the "machinelike" actions of nonhuman animals and the "voluntary" behavior of humans. In the seventeenth century the philosopher René Descartes emphasized this distinction, and in the eighteenth and nineteenth centuries it was advanced by discoveries of the basic properties of the spinal cord. By the nineteenth century, scientists knew that the dorsal roots of the spinal cord serve sensory functions and that the ventral roots contain motor fibers; connections between the two seemed to provide the basis for simple movements.

Sir Charles Sherrington
(1857–1957)

In the late nineteenth and early twentieth centuries the British physiologist Charles Sherrington conducted extensive studies of spinal animals (animals whose spinal cord has been disconnected from the brain). He showed that skin stimulation, such as pinching, provokes simple acts such as limb withdrawal. Many such observations led him to argue that the basic units of movement are **reflexes**, which he defined as simple, highly stereotyped, and unlearned responses to external stimuli. He showed that the magnitude of a reflex is directly related to the intensity of the stimulus. Sherrington's work ushered in an era of intensive attempts to identify the different reflexes and to chart their pathways in the nervous system, particularly in the spinal cord. Some reflexes involve only pathways in the spinal cord linking dorsal and ventral roots; others involve longer loops connecting spinal cord segments to each other, or to brain regions.

Are reflexes the basic units of more complex movements and acts? Can every act be broken down into reflexes? The reflex perspective appropriately invited criticism when it tried in a rather simple fashion to explain complex behaviors. For instance, Sherrington thought that complex acts were simply combinations of simpler reflexes strung out in a particular temporal order. The limitations of this perspective are apparent in attempts to analyze complex sequences of behavior, such as speech, in reflex terms. For example, explanations of speech in terms of reflexes are based on the claim that the movements and sounds associated with each element of speech provide the stimuli that instigate the next element. If this were true, speech would be a series of stimulus–response units chained together, each response triggering the next.

On the contrary, it appears that the speaker has a plan in which several units (speech sounds) are placed in a larger pattern. Sometimes the units are misplaced, although the pattern is preserved: "Our queer old dean," said English clergyman William Spooner, when he meant, "Our dear old queen." Or "You hissed all my mystery lectures." (Spooner was so prone to mix up the order of sounds in his sentences that this type of error is called a spoonerism.) Such mistakes reveal a plan: The speaker is anticipating a later sound and executing it too soon. A chain of reflexes would not be subject to such an error.

Notions of a **motor plan**, or motor program, have been strongly advanced by researchers in this field, although not without calls for elaboration of these terms (Rosenbaum, 1991). They are loose metaphors that convey the view that complex movements and acts are controlled and produced by a set of commands to muscles that is completely established *before* an act occurs. Feedback from movements may inform the motor program about how the execution is unfolding (Pearson, 1993). Examples of this kind of internal plan for action range from skilled movements, such as piano playing, to a wide repertoire of simple escape behaviors of animals such as crayfish.

Table 11.1 gives a scheme for classifying movements and acts that focuses on their functional properties rather than on their exact muscle relations. We can use this table to distinguish between movements and acts. Simple reflexes include brief, unitary activities of muscle that we commonly call **movements**. These events are discrete, in many cases limited to a single part of the body, such as a limb. The lower parts of the table list complex, sequential behaviors, frequently oriented toward a goal. Different movements of several body parts might be included in such behavior. These more complex events we distinguish as **acts**, or action patterns.

Movements and Acts Can Be Analyzed and Measured in a Variety of Ways

Movements and acts are readily visible in motion pictures, and high-speed photography provides an intimate portrait of even the most rapid events. To deal with the large amounts of data furnished by high-speed photography, methods of simplification or numerical analysis have been devised. Photographic techniques such as multiple exposures offer simple

TABLE 11.1   *A Classification of Movements and Acts*

Movements	Examples
Simple reflex	Stretch, knee jerk, sneezing, startle, eye blink, pupillary contraction
Posture and postural changes	Standing, rearing, lying, balancing, sitting, urination posture
Sensory orientation	Head turning, touching, eye fixation, sniffing, ear movement, tasting
Acts	
Locomotion	Walking, creeping, running, crawling, swimming, stalking, flying, hopping
Species-typical action patterns	
Ingestion	Tasting, chewing, biting, sipping, drinking
Courtship display	Sniffing, chasing, retreating
Escape and defense	Hissing, spitting, submission posture, cowering
Grooming	Washing, preening, licking
Gestures	Grimacing, tail erection, squinting, tooth baring, smiling
Acquired skills	Speech, tool use, dressing, painting, sculpting, driving a car, sports, dancing

portraits of human movement. Continuing developments in computer graphic simulation techniques also provide striking examples of the representation of movements. For example, the world of sports uses detailed analyses of athletic acts (Figure 11.1). The data that generate these portraits are either time-lapse photographs or information derived from sensors attached at joints. Computer programs process digitized photos to help quantify the performance, thereby enabling detailed measurement of the positions of different body parts in successive instants.

 Important method   Another approach to the fine-grain analysis of movements is to record the electrical activity of muscles, a procedure referred to as **electromyography (EMG)**.

Since the contraction of muscles involves electrical potentials generated by the muscle fibers, fine needle electrodes placed in a muscle or electrodes placed on the skin over a muscle can provide electrical indications of muscle activity (Figure 11.2). If electrodes are placed over many different muscles, we get an electrical portrait of the contraction of the muscles involved in a distinct act, including the progressive buildup and decay of their activity. This technique is useful in diagnosing neuromuscular disorders. As we noted earlier, human speech requires exceedingly precise muscle control; for more on this subject, see Topic 11.1, Vocalization.   **Special topic**

The Control Systems View

Engineering descriptions of the regulation and control of machines provide a useful way of looking at the mechanisms that regulate and control our movements. In designing machines, engineers commonly encounter two problems: (1) accuracy—how to prevent or minimize error; and (2) speed—how to accomplish a task quickly and efficiently. Two forms of control mechanisms—closed-loop and open-loop—are commonly employed to optimize performance according to these criteria.

In **closed-loop control mechanisms**, information flows from whatever is being controlled back to the

11.1 Digitized Movement
Computerized representation of a runner's movements.

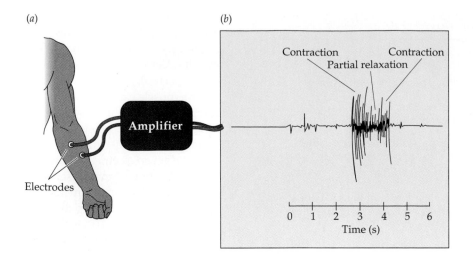

(a)

(b)

Amplifier

Electrodes

Contraction   Contraction
Partial relaxation

0 1 2 3 4 5 6
Time (s)

11.2 Electromyography
(a) Electrodes on the arm detect action potentials that trigger contraction in underlying muscles. (b) The resulting electromyogram shows activity with contraction and relaxation.

device that controls it. The control of endocrine secretion, which we discussed in Chapter 5, is a closed-loop mechanism (see Figures 5.9 and 5.10). We can consider a more complex example of a closed-loop system: someone driving a car. In this case the variable being controlled is the position of an automobile on the road (Figure 11.3). Continuous information is provided by the driver's visual system, which guides corrections. Slow, sustained movements, sometimes called **ramp movements** (or smooth movements) are usually closed-loop in character, continuously guided by feedback.

The only way the car could stay on the road without feedback control (e.g., if you were driving with your eyes closed) would be with the aid of accurate memory of all the turns and bends in the road. But the car would not be able to deal with anything new, such as other moving cars. Such a memory system could be considered a form of open-loop control. **Open-loop control mechanisms** do not involve external forms of feedback; output is measured by a sensor, but the activity is preprogrammed. Open-loop controls are needed in systems that must respond so rapidly that no time is available for the delay of a feedback path-

(a) Feedback control while driving

1. The car veers to the left

2. Overcorrection turns the car to the right

3. The target position is achieved

(b)

Control signal

Error signal

Error detector

Controller

Command

Controlled system

Output

Feedback signal

Transducer

11.3 A Closed-Loop System
(a) Example of feedback control in auto driving. (b) Formal description of closed-loop systems. In the example in part a, the controlled system is the automobile. The input to the controlled system is the position of the steering wheel; the output is the position on the road. The transducer is an element that measures output, and the error detector measures differences between actual output and desired output (control signal). In this example the transducer (the visual system), error detector (the perceptual system), and controller (the muscles) all refer to properties of the person driving the car. The actual position of the car is compared with its desired position on the road, and the driver makes corrections to minimize the discrepancy. Closed-loop systems emphasize accuracy and flexibility at the expense of speed.

way. For example, once a baseball pitcher begins throwing a fastball, the pitch is completed no matter what the sensory feedback. Such open-loop movements are called **ballistic movements**. Because there is no feedback, open-loop systems need other ways to reduce error and variability. They must anticipate potential error. In living systems, prior learning may be the basis for accurate anticipation (see Box 11.1).

BOX 11.1   *Movements and Acts Are Shaped and Modified by Learning*

We don't have to learn how to withdraw a hand from a hot stove, or how to breathe or swallow. These and many other acts are highly stereotyped, "involuntary" reflexes; no aspect of a person's attention changes their essential character. In contrast, we need explicit training to play tennis, use a keyboard, and perform many other trivial to extraordinary acts. The characteristics of these acts are highly variable and frequently idiosyncratic, and they show considerable variability among individuals. These acts are commonly referred to as "voluntary" motor skills. How are such skills acquired? A comprehensive review of motor learning has been provided by Ivry (1993), who notes that many variables affect skill acquisition or motor learning. This variability may account for why there are so many theoretical views in this field.

A simple example, in which a single subject performs the task of using a joystick to move a cursor on a screen to follow a moving spot of light, helps focus issues in motor learning. Large errors are evident in the initial trials; the subject is slow to change course and overshoots the path of the spot. On successive presentations of this simple stimulus, the subject tracks the spot faster and with very few errors. What has happened during the acquisition of this motor skill? According to Paul Fitts (Fitts and Posner, 1967), a pioneer in the modern study of motor learning, there are three stages in skill acquisition:

1. *The cognitive stage.* Thoughts are developed about different features of the task and the effects of actions.

2. *The associative stage.* Trial-and-error solutions are attempted and successful strategies are defined.

3. *The automatic stage.* Acts are performed with little conscious recognition, and variability in performance is reduced. In this stage, behavior relies less on continuous feedback, and it has become more "open-loop" in character.

Another view about skill acquisition is that it involves the development of a **schema** for action—the formation of some kind of higher-level program. The performance of any skilled movement shows that several types of information are essential to the acquisition of a motor skill. One model of skill learning (Keele and Summers, 1976) posits that input to muscles is provided by a hypothetical movement program in the brain that directs the timing and force of neural outputs to muscles (the motor outflow). Feedback from receptors in joints, and other modes of information about movements—visual or auditory—are matched to a model of skilled performance, as the figure shows.

Feedback information thus provides input about errors, which are gradually reduced. In some cases the need for monitoring the movement is eliminated; that is, Fitts's third stage is reached. At this stage in the learning of a skilled movement, the subject becomes unaware of the act; execution is automatic. Faster performance becomes possible because feedback control loops have less impact.

Eye Movements Make Use of Visual Feedback

Special topic Visual feedback plays an important role in controlling the **extraocular muscles** (see Topic 11.2, Extraocular Muscles), which move your eyes. But you may not appreciate that your eyes move in three quite different ways, each of which combines open-loop and closed-loop characteristics.

1. As you read this line of type, you make quick eye movements to transfer your gaze from one fixation point to another. These quick, accurate movements are called **saccades** (French for "twitch" or "jerk"), or **saccadic movements**. You also make use of saccades when you direct your attention to a stimulus that appears suddenly in the periphery of your visual field. The superior colliculi play a role in controlling saccades.

2. Even when you try to keep your eyes still they always show fine, involuntary, to-and-fro movements. In cases of dizziness or some diseases, the eye may show large oscillatory movements, a condition called **nystagmus**. The fine normal oscillatory movements are called **physiological nystagmus** (in this case "physiological" means "normal"). Physiological nystagmus has an important function: If an image is held absolutely stationary on the retina by artificial means (such as a special small projector mounted on a contact lens), the image fades out in a minute or less because the visual system adapts rapidly to constant stimulation. Physiological nystagmus moves the eye enough to prevent such adaptation, so we are not bothered by images fading from view as we try to gaze steadily at them. (A woman who could not move her eyes was forced to constantly move her head in order to see [Gilchrist et al., 1997]).

3. When your gaze smoothly and continuously follows a moving object, you are making use of **pursuit movement**. Feedback is required to keep the gaze close to the target. Some people are unable to perform smooth, accurate pursuit movements; their gaze undershoots, then overshoots, the moving position of the target. This deficiency appears to be linked to schizophrenia (D. L. Levy et al., 1993), as we will discuss in Chapter 16. The smooth pursuit is made possible by the visual feedback guiding the extraocular muscles. The basal ganglia are thought to provide the signals allowing for the ramp movements underlying smooth pursuit.

The Neurobiological View

Adaptive acts are enabled by instructions generated by neural processing in the brain and spinal cord; these instructions in turn lead to neural activity in motoneurons connected to muscles. Neuroscientists have

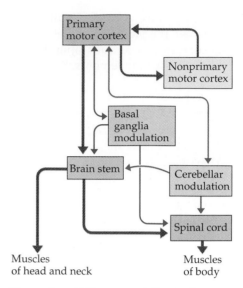

11.4 Hierarchy of Movement Control
The primary motor cortex receives information from other cortical areas and sends commands to the brain stem, which passes commands to the spinal cord. Both the cerebellum and the basal ganglia provide adjustments to these commands.

distinguished several different levels of hierarchically organized motor control systems:

1. The *skeletal system* and the muscles attached to it determine which movements are possible.
2. The *spinal cord* controls those muscles in response to sensory information. In the simplest case, this may be a reflexive response. The spinal cord also implements motor commands from the brain.
3. The *brain stem* integrates motor commands from higher levels of the brain and transmits them to the spinal cord. The brain stem also relays sensory information about the body from the spinal cord to the forebrain.
4. Some of the main commands for action are initiated in the *primary motor cortex.*
5. The areas adjacent to motor cortex, *nonprimary motor cortex,* initiate another level of cortical processing.
6. Other brain regions—the *cerebellum and basal ganglia*—modulate the activities of these hierarchically organized control systems.

We will examine each of these levels of control in more detail. This organizational scheme, outlined in Figure 11.4, will guide the order of our discussion.

The Skeletal System Enables Particular Movements and Precludes Others

Some properties of behavior arise from characteristics of the skeleton and muscles themselves. For example, the length, form, and weight of the limbs shape an animal's stride. The skeletal system of any vertebrate

(a) Ellipsoidal joint (wrist)

(b) Ball-and-socket joint (hip)

(c) Hinge joint (knee)

11.5 Joints and Movements

Shown next to each joint is an enlarged mechanical model that indicates the kinds of movements the joint can perform. (*a*) The wrist joint moves in two principal planes: lateral and vertical. (*b*) The hip joint is a "universal" joint, moving in all three planes. (*c*) The knee joint has a single plane of motion.

timing of behavior and the forces that can be generated; the rate and force of muscular contractions limit some responses.

A muscle is composed of thousands of individual muscle fibers. The contraction of muscle fibers leads to movements or to the maintenance of position according to the ways in which the muscle is mechanically attached to a bone or bones. The arrangement around a typical joint is illustrated in Figure 11.6. Muscles are connected to bone by **tendons**. Around a joint, different muscles are arranged in a reciprocal fashion: When one muscle group contracts (shortens), the other is extended; that is, the muscles are **antagonists**. Muscles that act together are said to be **synergists**. Coordinated action around a joint may require one set of motoneurons to be excited while the antagonistic set of motoneurons is inhibited. The limb can be locked in position by co-contraction of the opposed muscles.

consists of many separate bones of different shape, weight, and length. Through painful experience we know that bones themselves do not bend, although their shape may change as the result of sustaining unusual use or weight. The primary sites for bending are the joints, where bones meet. Figure 11.5 illustrates the human skeleton and shows examples of some joints and their possible movements. Some joints, such as the hip, are almost "universal" joints, permitting movement in many planes. Others, like the elbow or knee, are more limited and tolerate little deviation from the principal axis of rotation.

Muscles Control the Actions of the Skeletal System

Our bare skeleton must now be clothed with muscles. The distribution of muscles in the body—their size and how they attach to bones—is a direct indication of the forms of movement they mediate. By contracting (under instructions from motoneurons), some muscles produce forces that sustain body weight, whereas others produce movement around a joint. In contrast, some muscles do not act on the skeleton at all; examples include the muscles that move the eyes, lips, and tongue and those that contract the abdomen. Muscles have springlike properties that influence the

The molecular machinery of muscles. Each muscle fiber is made up of many filaments of two kinds arranged in a regular manner (Figure 11.7*a*). Bands of relatively thick filaments alternate with bands of thinner filaments, giving the fibers a striped appearance. The thick and thin filaments (made up of the complex proteins **myosin** and **actin**, respectively) always overlap. Contraction of the muscle increases the overlap: The filaments slide past each other, shortening the overall length of the muscle fiber (Figure 11.7*b*).

Muscle types. Many of the muscles in your body, such as your heart, are not under your direct control. Because of their appearance, these muscles are called **smooth muscle**, and because their contractions are regulated by the autonomic nervous system, we will not discuss them further. Rather, we will concern ourselves with a second class of muscle, called **striated muscles** (because they have a striped appearance), which are under voluntary control.

(a)   (b)

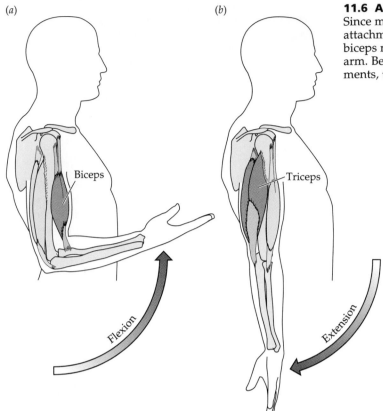

Biceps

Triceps

Flexion

Extension

11.6 Arrangement of Muscles around the Elbow
Since muscles exert force only by contracting, muscle attachments determine the resulting movement. (*a*) The biceps muscle flexes the arm. (*b*) The triceps extends the arm. Because these two muscles mediate opposite movements, they are known as antagonists.

Because of the varying tasks they perform, different muscles require different speeds, precision, strength, and endurance. Matched to these requirements are at least two main types of striated muscle fibers: "fast" and "slow." Eye movements, for example, must be quick and accurate so that we can follow moving objects and shift our gaze from one target to another. But fibers in the extraocular muscles do not have to maintain tension for long periods of time, because some fibers relax while others contract. The extraocular muscles are therefore made up of **fast muscle fibers**. In leg muscles, fast fibers react promptly and strongly but fatigue rapidly; they are used mainly for activities in which muscle tension changes frequently, as in walking or running. Mixed in with the fast muscle fibers are **slow muscle fibers**, which are not as strong but have greater resistance to fatigue; they are used chiefly to maintain posture.

Neural Messages Reach Muscle Fibers at the Neuromuscular Junction

Once a motoneuron has integrated all the information bombarding it through hundreds or thousands of synapses (Figure 11.8*a*), it may produce an action potential. As the axon splits into many branches near the target muscle (Figure 11.8*b*), each branch carries an action potential to its terminal, which then (in vertebrates) releases **acetylcholine (ACh)**. Then all the mus-

cle fibers innervated by that motoneuron respond to the ACh by producing action potentials of their own. The action potentials travel along each muscle fiber, permitting sodium (Na^+) and calcium (Ca^{2+}) ions to enter and then trigger the molecular changes that produce contraction.

The region where the motoneuron terminal and the adjoining muscle fiber meet—and produce distinctive structures for communication—is called the **neuromuscular junction** (Figure 11.8*c* and *d*). The neuromuscular junction is large and very effective: Almost every action potential that reaches the axon terminal releases enough ACh to cause a large enough depolarization (called an **end-plate potential**) in the muscle fiber to produce an action potential. Thus, normally every action potential in the motoneuron elicits a contraction in the postsynaptic fiber. In vertebrates, muscles can only be excited (by ACh), so the only way to prevent a muscle from contracting is to inhibit its motoneuron and prevent it from sending an action potential to the neuromuscular junction. Because it is large and accessible, the neuromuscular junction is a very well studied synapse, and much of what we know about synapses and synaptic plasticity was first established at the neuromuscular junction.

Even though the neuromuscular junction is a large and reliable synapse, its properties can change with use. All of us are familiar with muscle fatigue from extended use; some of the reduced responsiveness of the fatigued muscle is due to diminished effectiveness of neuromuscular junctions. Another well-known example of neural plasticity is **posttetanic potentiation**. When a rapid series of action potentials (a tetanus) is induced in a motor nerve, the neuromuscular junctions are altered for a period so that subsequent single action potentials cause a stronger end-plate potential in the muscle. This potentiation is caused by a buildup of Ca^{2+} ions in the presynaptic terminal and therefore the release of more ACh. The study of several types of neuromuscular-junction plasticity led to other studies of synaptic plasticity that may underlie learning, as will be discussed in Chapter 18.

Early in embryogenesis, young muscle fibers have ACh receptors along their entire length, so application of ACh anywhere along the fiber causes a response.

(a)

Muscle

Tendons

Nuclei

Each muscle fiber is a single, large cell with many nuclei.

Muscle fiber (10–100 μm diameter)

Myofibril

Actin (5 nm diameter)

Myosin (10 nm diameter)

Myofilament

(b)

Actin

Start

1. Muscle action potential begins at neuromuscular junction, causing wave of depolarization and release of Ca^{2+}.

ADP + P

Resting myosin fibril with ADP bound to head

Ca^{2+}

5. ATP is hydrolyzed, and myosin heads return to resting position.

Myosin head

ADP

6. If Ca^{2+} remains available, the cycle repeats and muscle contraction continues.

2. Ca^{2+} exposes myosin binding sites on actin filament; myosin heads bind to actin; ADP is released.

4. ATP binds to myosin, causing it to release actin.

ATP

ATP

ADP

3. Power stroke: Myosin head changes position; filaments slide past one another.

11.7 The Composition of Muscles and the Mechanism of Muscle Contraction

(a) Views of muscle fibers at progressively greater magnifications, from life-size to 2 million times life-size. *(b)* How actions of myosin and actin cause muscle contraction. Adding a phosphate molecule to adenosine diphosphate (ADP) converts it to adenosine triphosphate (ATP).

(a)
Astrocyte processes
Oligodendrocytes
Giant boutons
Boutons
Axon
Myelin sheath
Dendrites

(b)
Gray matter: dorsal horns
Dorsal root (sensory)
Spinal nerve
Muscle fiber
Ventral horns
Lateral horn
Axon of motoneuron
Ventral root (motor)
Biceps muscle
Nerve

(c)
Neuromuscular junctions

(d)
Axon terminal branch
Axon
Motor end plate
Muscle fiber nucleus
Muscle fiber

11.8 Motoneurons and Neuromuscular Junctions

(a) Each motoneuron receives thousands of synapses from other neurons. (b) Spinal motoneurons send their axons out the ventral roots to the periphery. Near the muscle each axon splits into several collaterals, each of which innervates a separate muscle fiber within the muscle. A single motoneuron, together with all the muscle fibers controlled by that motoneuron, constitutes a motor unit. (c, d) Axon terminals innervate muscle fibers at the neuromuscular junction. (Part a from Poritsky, 1969.)

But as the growing axon tip (the growth cone; see Figure 7.12) from a motoneuron contacts the fiber, ACh receptors migrate from other parts of the muscle fiber to cluster opposite the axon tip. (Remember that receptors and ion channels "float" in the fatty membrane of cells.) From this point on, the muscle fiber preferentially inserts additional ACh receptors beneath the motoneuron terminal at the newly formed neuromuscular junction. Vertebrate motoneurons sometimes also release other chemicals, including peptides such as calcitonin gene–related peptide. Perhaps these peptides tell the muscle fiber where to insert ACh receptors (Laufer and Changeux, 1989).

In adults, if muscle fibers are denervated (i.e., deprived of a nerve supply, as when the motor nerve to the muscle is cut), the muscle fibers again produce ACh receptors along their entire length. Thereafter the fibers are said to show **denervation supersensitivity** because contractions can be produced by the application of ACh anywhere along the fiber, as in the embryo. Once the regenerating motoneuron axons reach the muscle fiber, the fiber again provides ACh receptors only at the point of contact.

Another interesting aspect of the development of the neuromuscular junction is that early in life, every muscle fiber is contacted by several motoneurons (Redfern, 1970). During a postnatal period of **neuro-muscular synapse elimination**, however, all motoneurons withdraw some of their terminal branches until every muscle fiber is innervated by only a single motoneuron. Many researchers are studying how the motoneurons and muscle fibers eliminate just the right number of synapses to accomplish this task (C. L. Jordan et al., 1988; Purves, 1988). The net result is that each motoneuron has exclusive control of a pool of muscle fibers, enabling finely graded contractions of muscles. For more information on this subject, see Topic 11.3, Fetal Activity.

Special topic

The ratio of motor axons to muscle groups affects the precision of the control of movements. Fine neural control results when each axon connects to only a few muscle fibers. To understand this concept better, let's look at the motor unit. The **motor unit** consists of a single motor axon and all the muscle fibers it innervates (see Figure 11.8c). The **innervation ratio** is the ratio of motor axons to muscle fibers. High innervation ratios characterize muscles involved in fine movements, like those of the eye (1:3 ratio). Muscles that act on large body masses such as those of the leg have low innervation ratios of one neuron to several hundred muscle fibers (1:300); thus, the same call for contraction goes to hundreds of leg muscle fibers at the same time.

The Motoneuron Integrates Information from the Brain and Spinal Cord

Muscles contract because motoneurons of the spinal cord and cranial nerve nuclei initiate neural activity that travels along motor axons to muscles. These motoneurons are the **final common pathway** that links the activity of the rest of the spinal cord and brain to our many muscles. Because they respond to inputs from so many sources, motoneurons often have very widespread dendritic fields, and they are the largest cells in the spinal cord. Furthermore, motoneurons must respond to a tremendous variety of synaptic transmitters, both excitatory and inhibitory.

Motor cells of the spinal cord are not uniform in size or electrophysiological properties. Large motoneurons have axons of wide diameter and therefore conduct impulses faster. In general, small motoneurons innervate slow muscles and are more easily excited by synaptic currents; therefore they are activated before large motoneurons (Jones et al., 1994). Large motoneurons innervate fast muscles and tend to respond after small cells because, being large, they are less readily excited by synaptic currents. Their discharge characteristics are more phasic or abrupt. All spinal levels contain both large and small motoneurons.

Sensory Feedback from Muscles, Tendons, and Joints Monitors Movements

To produce rapid coordinated movements of the body, the integrative mechanisms of the brain and spinal cord must have information about the state of the muscles, the positions of the limbs, and the instructions being issued by the motor centers. This kind of information about body movements and positions is called **proprioceptive** (from the Latin *proprius*, "own," and *recipere*, "to receive").

The sequence and intensity of muscle activation are monitored by sensory receptors, which report the state of muscles and joints to circuits that initiate and guide movements. Several kinds of sensory receptors can provide information about the state of muscle length or contraction. Two major kinds of receptors are **muscle spindles**, which lie in parallel with the muscle fibers (Figure 11.9*a* and *c*), and **Golgi tendon organs**, which lie in series with muscles, one end attached to tendon, the other to muscle (Figure 11.9*a* and *b*). The mechanical sensitivities of the spindles and tendon organs differ. The stretching of a muscle, which occurs in most movements, activates especially the spindles and transiently the tendon organs. The shortening of a muscle during contraction activates the tendon organs because they lie in series with the muscle. Together these two kinds of receptors transmit to the central nervous system a range of information about muscle activities.

Classic studies in physiology, especially those of Sherrington, emphasized the importance of these receptors for movement. Mott (1895) and Sherrington (1898) showed that after they cut the afferent fibers from muscles, monkeys failed to use the deafferented limb, even if the efferent connections from motoneurons to muscles were preserved. The deafferented limb is not paralyzed, since it can be activated (the motoneurons still innervate the muscles), but lack of information from the muscle leads to relative disuse. So the monkey can flex a deafferented limb in response to a visual signal to avoid a shock to the body, even though during free behavior the arm looks paralyzed.

Although deafferenting one forearm leads to apparent paralysis of that limb, the result is quite different if both forearms are deafferented. In the latter case the monkey recovers coordinated use of its forearms over a few months (Taub, 1976). When one limb is deafferented, the monkey makes do with the other, but when both are deafferented, the monkey has to learn to use them and is able to do so. Even if only one arm is deafferented, forced use of it can lead to the return of coordinated use of the two arms.

This effect was shown in experiments in which the hand of the intact limb was placed inside a ball, which prevented the monkey from grasping objects with the hand but allowed finger movements and thus prevented atrophy. Slowly the deafferented limb gained dexterity, and over several weeks fine movements like those needed for feeding were achieved. After several months the ball on the intact hand was removed, and the monkey made coordinated movements of both limbs. However, if the forced usage lasted less than 4 months, movements of the deafferented limb subsequently regressed rapidly.

The portrait of deafferentation in humans provides some striking insight into the significance of sensory feedback. One patient suffered loss of sensory input from muscles, joints, and skin, but his motor functions were spared (Marsden et al., 1984). He engaged in a wide range of manual activities, including repetitive alternating hand movements and some grasping movements. A striking example of preserved motor skills was his ability to drive his manual-transmission car. In contrast, fine movements of the fingers, such as writing or fastening buttons, were drastically impaired. In addition, acquiring new movements of the hand was quite difficult. For example, after buying a new car, the patient found he was unable to acquire the arm movements necessary to drive it and had to revert to his old car. Thus, sensory feedback is an important ingredient in skilled performance and in motor learning.

People who lose their proprioceptive sense can sometimes compensate by using other sensory modalities for feedback. For example, two deafferented pa-

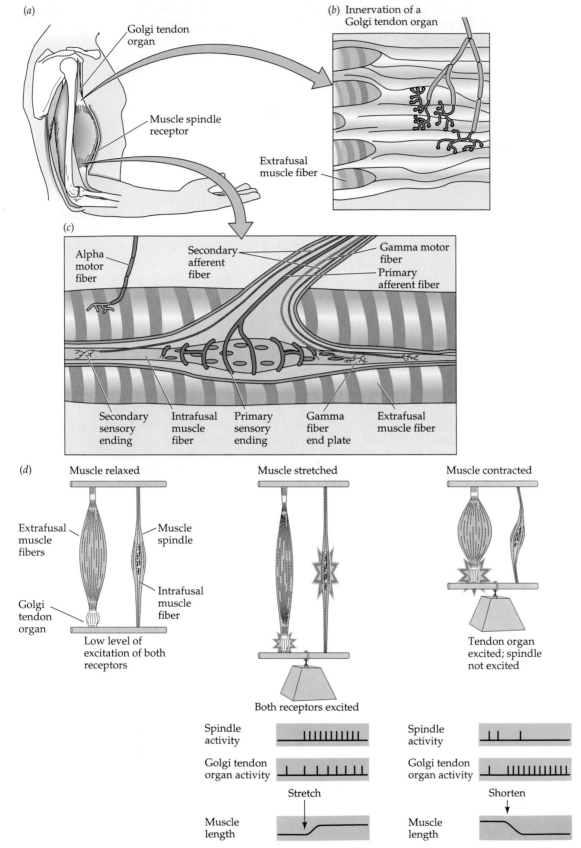

(a)

Golgi tendon organ

Muscle spindle receptor

(b) Innervation of a Golgi tendon organ

Extrafusal muscle fiber

(c)

Alpha motor fiber

Secondary afferent fiber

Gamma motor fiber

Primary afferent fiber

Secondary sensory ending

Intrafusal muscle fiber

Primary sensory ending

Gamma fiber end plate

Extrafusal muscle fiber

(d)

Muscle relaxed

Extrafusal muscle fibers

Muscle spindle

Golgi tendon organ

Intrafusal muscle fiber

Low level of excitation of both receptors

Muscle stretched

Both receptors excited

Muscle contracted

Tendon organ excited; spindle not excited

Spindle activity

Golgi tendon organ activity

Stretch

Muscle length

Spindle activity

Golgi tendon organ activity

Shorten

Muscle length

11.9 Muscle Receptors

(a) Location of muscle spindles in the body of the muscle and of Golgi organs in the tendons. (b) Typical sensory ending of a Golgi tendon organ. (c) Typical structure of a muscle spindle. Two types of receptor endings are shown: primary and secondary. Gamma motor fibers control a contractile portion of the spindle. (d) The excitation of muscle receptors when a load is imposed.

tients were found to rely heavily on visual feedback to allow them to walk, and to pick up objects (Nougier et al., 1996). In fact, there may be channels of visual information to the motor system of which we are unaware. A patient with damage to the visual cortex could not report whether a slot was vertical or horizontal, yet when she was asked to insert a card in the slot, she consistently rotated her hand to put the card in smoothly. Similar experiments suggest that even neurologically intact people sometimes use visual cues of which they are unaware to guide their movements (Goodale and Haffenden, 1998).

The muscle spindle.   The muscle spindle of vertebrates is a complicated structure consisting of both afferent and efferent elements (see Figure 11.9*c*). The spindle gets its name from its shape—a sort of cylinder that is thicker in the middle and tapers at its two ends. The Latin for "spindle," *fusus,* is used to form adjectives referring to the muscle spindle; thus the small muscle fibers *within* each spindle are called **intrafusal fibers**, and the ordinary muscle fibers that lie *outside* the spindles are referred to as **extrafusal fibers**.

The muscle spindle contains two kinds of receptors: **primary sensory endings** (also called annulospiral endings) and **secondary sensory endings** (also called flower spray endings). These endings are related to different parts of the spindle (see Figure 11.9*c*). The primary ending wraps in a spiral fashion around a region called the nuclear bag (the central region of the intrafusal fiber). The secondary endings terminate toward the thin ends of the spindle.

How do these elements become excited? Suppose a muscle is stretched, as when a load is placed on it. For example, if you were trying to hold your arm straight out in front of you, palm up, and someone put a book in your hand, that would put an additional load on your biceps. Your arm would move down transiently, stretching the biceps muscle. The muscle spindle would also stretch, and the resulting deformation of the endings on the spindle would set up nerve impulses in the afferent fibers. These afferents inform the spinal cord, and the spinal cord then informs the brain about the muscle stretch and therefore about the load imposed (see Figure 11.9*d*).

Two important factors affect the stretch of the muscle. One is the *rate of change* of muscle length. In our example the rate of change is jointly a function of the weight of the load and the rate at which the load is applied. The second factor is the *force* you must continually exert with the muscle to prevent dropping the load. In our example this force is a function only of the weight of the book. The different receptor elements of the muscle spindle are differentially sensitive to these two features of muscle length changes. The primary (central) endings show a maximum discharge early in stretch and then adapt to a lower discharge rate. In contrast, the secondary (distal) endings are maximally sensitive to maintained length and are slow to change their rate during the early phase of stretch. Because of this differential sensitivity, the primary endings are called *dynamic* and the secondary endings are called *static* indicators of muscle length. This distinction probably arises from the difference in how these receptors are embedded in the spindle rather than from a difference in the nerve fibers themselves.

Regulation of muscle spindle sensitivity.   Muscle spindles not only help maintain posture; they also coordinate movement. Spindles are informed of planned and ongoing actions through innervation by special motoneurons that alter the tension within the spindle and thus control the sensitivity of its receptors. These motoneurons are called **gamma efferents**, or gamma motoneurons, to distinguish them from the faster-conducting **alpha motoneurons**, which go to extrafusal muscle fibers (see Figure 11.9*c*). The cell bodies of gamma efferents are found in the ventral horns of the spinal cord.

The gamma efferent axon fibers connect to a contractile region of the spindle (called the myotube region). The activity in the gamma fibers causes a change in the length and tension of the spindle, which modifies its sensitivity to changes in the length of adjacent extrafusal muscle fibers. Hence the number of impulses elicited in the spindle afferents is a function of two factors: (1) muscle stretch, and (2) the resting tension in the muscle spindle.

How do the gamma efferents help coordinate movements? Suppose that instead of continuing to hold your arm out straight ahead, you move your forearm up and down. If the muscle spindle had only one fixed degree of internal tension, it could not help monitor and coordinate this movement. As the forearm moves up, the extrafusal and intrafusal fibers both shorten. Shortening the spindle, as we have noted, removes the tension, so the sensory endings should no longer respond. But the real situation is more complicated and more effective. As the muscle shortens, the gamma efferents must correspondingly increase the tension on the intrafusal fibers, if they are to maintain their sensitivity. One reflection of the importance of the gamma efferent system is the fact that about 30% of all efferent fibers are gamma efferents (the rest are alpha motoneurons).

The muscle spindles are responsive primarily to *stretch;* the other receptors that respond to muscle tension—Golgi tendon organs—are especially sensitive to muscle *contraction,* or shortening. Golgi tendon organs are rather insensitive to passive muscle stretch because they are connected in series with an elastic component (see Figure 11.9*d*). They detect overloads that threaten to tear muscles and tendons. Stimulation of these receptors inhibits the motoneurons supplying the muscles that pull on the tendon and thus, by relaxing the tension, prevents mechanical damage.

Movements Are Controlled at Several Nervous System Levels

The nerve cells directly responsible for excitation of muscle are the motoneurons in the ventral region of the spinal cord and in the brain stem nuclei of several cranial nerves. (See Figures 2.9 and 2.10 for the anatomy of the cranial nerves and spinal cord.) This is the simplest level in the neural control of motoneurons. Firing patterns of these cells determine the onset, coordination, and termination of muscle activity. To understand the physiology of movement, we need to know the source of the inputs to motoneurons. A variety of influences converge on the motoneurons. Some arise solely at the spinal level from muscle afferents and the intrinsic circuitry of the spinal cord. Other influences are directed to motor cells from several brain pathways. This is another reason that spinal and cranial motoneurons are called the final common pathway.

Spinal Reflexes Mediate "Automatic" Responses

One way to study spinal mechanisms is to sever the connections between the brain and the spinal cord (producing a spinal animal) and then observe the forms of behavior that can be elicited below the level of the cut. (All voluntary movements that depend on brain mechanisms are lost, of course, as is sensation from the regions below the cut.) Immediately after the cord is severed, there is an interval of decreased synaptic excitability in spinal cord neurons because they are isolated from brain communication. This condition is known as **spinal shock**. The period may last for months in humans, although for cats and dogs, it may last only a few hours. During this period no reflexes mediated by the spinal cord can be elicited by either skin stimulation or excitation of muscle afferents.

As spinal shock fades, various kinds of reflexes can be elicited; their properties help us understand the basic functional organization of the spinal cord. The spinal animal can show various stretch reflexes that may function well enough to support its weight standing for brief periods. Stimulation of the skin of a spinal animal can also elicit reflex effects, which can be readily demonstrated in a spinal cat or dog by intense stimulation of the toe pad. This stimulation results in abrupt withdrawal of the stimulated limb, a response called the **flexion reflex**. Unlike the stretch reflex, which involves a monosynaptic pathway, as we'll see in the next section, the flexion reflex is controlled by a multisynaptic pathway within the spinal cord. Other reflexive behaviors evident in the spinal animal include bladder emptying and penile erection. Thus, some very basic properties of movement are

"wired in" to the organization of the spinal cord itself and do not require the brain.

The behavior of the spinal animal also reveals the presence of pattern generator circuits in the spinal cord, which we'll describe later in this chapter. For example, mechanical stimulation of the feet or electrical stimulation of the spinal cord can elicit rhythmic movements of the legs. If the cut is high on the spinal cord, the alternating movements of the limbs are coordinated as in walking; this coordination indicates that the pattern generators for the different limbs are linked within the spinal cord (P. Grillner et al., 1991).

Spinal reflexes do not usually function in isolation. They are integrated and modulated by the activity of brain circuits. Control of movements involves **selective potentiation** of spinal neural circuits; that is, the activity of certain spinal circuits is enhanced by the brain, while the activity of other spinal circuits is inhibited.

The stretch reflex. A good example of automatic control at the spinal level is the **stretch reflex**—the contraction that results when a muscle stretches. The physiological condition for muscle stretch can be readily understood under conditions of an imposed weight or load. For example, in Figure 11.10 a weight (disturbance) added to the hand imposes sudden stretch on muscle 1 (M1). Such a disturbance can be imposed on many joints simply by the weight of the body. The circuit that keeps us from dropping the load or simply falling from the weight of our body is one that links muscle spindles and the relevant muscles. The simplest depiction of the events portrayed in Figure 11.10 is the following (steps 1 to 3 we already saw when we described the activity of the muscle spindle):

1. A disturbance is imposed.
2. The muscle is stretched.
3. Afferent elements of the muscle spindle are excited.
4. Excitatory synaptic potentials in motoneurons are produced by muscle spindle afferents. (These afferents connect directly—that is, monosynaptically—to the motoneurons that control the stretched muscle.)
5. The muscle is stimulated by motoneuron output, contracting to oppose muscle stretch.

This sequence describes a simple negative feedback system that tends to restore the limb to its "desired" position. Additional influences exerted by activation of the muscle spindle system include inhibition of the motoneurons that supply the antagonistic muscle (M2). Two synapses are involved. Thus, in the situation illustrated in Figure 11.10, spindle information terminates on the interneuron whose output goes to the motoneuron that supplies M2, at which junction inhibitory postsynaptic activity is pro-

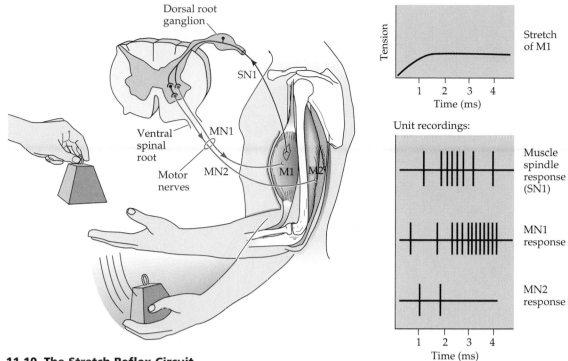

11.10 The Stretch Reflex Circuit
MN1 is the motor nerve to muscle 1 (M1) and MN2 is the motor nerve to muscle 2 (M2), an antagonist to muscle 1. SN1 is the sensory nerve from the muscle spindle of M1. Characteristic responses at different stages in the circuit are shown at right.

duced. During this action, then, the spindle excites the stretched muscle (and its synergists) and inhibits the antagonistic muscles. The relaxation of antagonistic muscles ensures that they are not injured by the sudden movement. A familiar example of the stretch reflex is the knee jerk used in medical examinations to test the integrity of the neural circuit just described (see Figure 3.14).

Pathways from the Brain Control Different Aspects of Movements

Pathways from the brain to cranial and spinal motoneurons are many and complex (Figure 11.11). Complex movements clearly involve programs of the brain, which are a major focus of research. (Refer to Figure 11.4 to review the relations of major brain regions associated with the control of movement.) Some pathways deliver discrete information; for example, the vestibulospinal tract provides important information about head position, and this information influences postural muscles to adjust the body.

Ideas about the different roles of each pathway in integrating and controlling movement have relied heavily on observations of changes in posture and locomotion produced by natural or experimental interferences in the brain. Clinical data from people with brain damage have generated useful anatomical and functional distinctions between two major divisions of the motor system: the pyramidal and extrapyramidal motor systems.

The **pyramidal system** (or **corticospinal system**) consists of the neuron cell bodies within the cerebral cortex and their axons, which pass through the brain stem, forming the pyramidal tract to the spinal cord (see Figure 11.11a). Many of these cell bodies are located in the primary motor cortex, the cortical region just anterior to the central sulcus (see Figure 11.12a).

⊙ *Sylvius*

The pyramidal tract is most clearly seen where it passes through the anterior aspect of the medulla. In a cross section of the medulla, the tract is a wedge-shaped anterior protuberance (pyramid) on each side of the midline. The pyramidal tract consists of large-diameter (and therefore fast-conducting) axons and is a relatively recent development in evolution. It has been likened to a superhighway pushed through after the network of local routes had been established. Lesions of the pyramidal system deprive the patient of the ability to move individual joints and limbs.

In addition to the corticospinal outflow through the pyramidal tract, many other motor tracts run from the forebrain to the brain stem and spinal cord. Since these tracts are outside of the pyramids of the medulla, they and their connections are called the **extrapyramidal system**. In general, lesions of the extrapyramidal system do not prevent movement of individual joints and limbs, but they do interfere with spinal reflexes, usually exaggerating them. Information flows from the extrapyramidal system to the spinal cord through two principal pathways—the

Frontal cortex

(a)

Cerebral cortex

Upper medulla

Lower medulla

Spinal cord

Pyramid of medulla

Decussation of pyramidal tract

Ventral cerebrospinal tract

Lateral cerebrospinal tract

(b)

Brain stem seen in posterior view of human brain

Oculomotor nucleus: most external eye muscles

Abducens nucleus: lateral rectus muscle of eyeball

Accessory motor nucleus: sternomastoid muscle, trapezius muscle

Brain stem reticular formation

Trigeminal nucleus: jaw muscles

Facial nucleus: muscles of the face

Superior and inferior salivary nuclei

Motor nucleus of vagus: heart, lungs, bronchi, trachea, larynx, gastrointestinal tract

11.11 Spinal Tracts

(a) In the pyramidal (or corticospinal) motor system, most of the fibers cross to the opposite side in the medulla (at the decussation of the pyramidal tract) and descend the spinal cord in the lateral cerebrospinal tract. *(b)* Brain stem nuclei of cranial nerves and the brain stem reticular formation, as viewed from the rear. The corresponding cranial nerves are shown in Figure 2.9.

reticulospinal and rubrospinal tracts. The extensive pool of interconnected neurons called the reticular formation modulates various aspects of movements. Some zones of the reticular formation facilitate movements; other zones are inhibitory. These effects are transmitted in descending tracts known as **reticulospinal tracts** that arise from the reticular formation and connect to spinal interneurons, where they influence the excitability of spinal motor circuitry (see Figure 11.15). Some neurons of the reticular formation also help regulate the activation of muscles responsible for breathing. The second extrapyramidal outflow originates from the midbrain's red nucleus and so is called the **rubrospinal tract** (the Latin *ruber* means "red") (see Figure 11.15).

Also found in the brain stem are cranial motor nuclei whose axons innervate muscles of the head and neck (see Figure 11.11*b*).

Primary Motor Cortex Is an Executive Motor Control Mechanism

In humans, brain injuries involving the primary motor cortex produce partial paralysis on the side of the body opposite the brain lesion. This disturbance is greatest in distal muscles, such as those of the hand. Humans with these lesions are generally disinclined to use the affected limb.

Because human lesions arise from accidental injury or disease, they are usually not limited to a single neural system. The symptoms of corticospinal injury and the complexity of the observed changes may arise in part from loss of adjacent motor control systems. In other primates, experimental lesions restricted to the

pyramidal tracts produce similar changes, although the overall picture is less severe. Six weeks after bilateral interruption of the pyramidal tracts, monkeys can run, climb, and reach accurately for food. The persistent deficits they display are a limited ability in individual finger movements and an overall tendency for slower-than-normal movements. Although they have difficulty releasing food from the hand, they can readily release their grip while climbing. In mammals other than primates, the impairments following pyramidal lesions are even less severe.

What do the species differences in these deficits mean in terms of the overall role of the corticospinal system? This problem has plagued many investigators, and definitive answers have not yet been found. In attempts to provide answers, investigators have made recordings from pyramidal cells during various movements and have closely examined the anatomical relations between the motor cortex and other levels of movement control systems. We will consider briefly some of the ideas emerging from these studies.

In the late nineteenth century, several experimenters showed that electrical stimulation of some regions of the cerebral cortex could elicit body movements, particularly flexion of the limbs. These early findings—and the results of other converging experiments—helped scientists develop maps of movements elicited by cortical stimulation. Figure 11.12*b* shows a map of the human **primary motor cortex**.

The largest motor regions in these maps are devoted to the most elaborate and complex movements in any species. For example, humans and other primates have extremely large cortical fields concerned with hand

(a) Lateral view of brain showing location of primary motor cortex

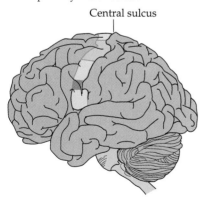

Central sulcus

(b) Representation of the body in primary motor cortex

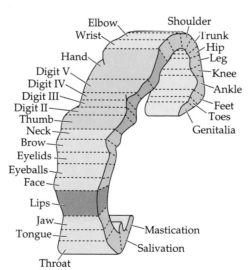

Elbow, Wrist, Hand, Digit V, Digit IV, Digit III, Digit II, Thumb, Neck, Brow, Eyelids, Eyeballs, Face, Lips, Jaw, Tongue, Throat

Shoulder, Trunk, Hip, Leg, Knee, Ankle, Feet, Toes, Genitalia

Mastication, Salivation

(c) Motor homunculus

11.12 Human Primary Motor Cortex
(*a*) Lateral view of the human brain, showing the location of primary motor cortex. (*b*) The sequence and sizes of regions controlling motor responses of different parts of the body. (*c*) The proportions of this homunculus show the relative sizes of motor representations of parts of the body.

(a)

Five separate trials

Target appears   Movement begins

(b)

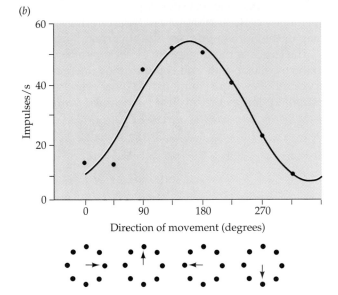

11.13 Directional Tuning of Motor Cortex Cells
(a) Activity of a single neuron during arm movement toward a target in eight different directions; each horizontal record in the eight blocks of data represents one of five trials. Note that this cell consistently fires before the arm moves in the direction from 90° to 180° to 270°, and is silent before movements in the other directions. (b) The average frequency of discharge during the interval before movement in the various directions. (From Georgopoulos et al., 1982.)

The motor cortex–pyramidal tract system may be the executive mechanism for voluntary movements. According to this view, the motor cortex represents particular kinds of movement, especially fine movements of the limbs, and the activation of these cells commands the excitation of relevant spinal and cranial motoneurons. In primates the pyramidal tract has some monosynaptic connections with spinal motoneurons, but most pyramidal tract neurons influence spinal motoneurons through polysynaptic routes and share control of these motor cells with other descending influences.

The functional properties of motor cortex neurons have been studied by analysis of recordings made from these cells during movements. In some experiments monkeys are trained to make particular movements such as reaching or pressing levers, while activity from single motor cortex cells is monitored (Evarts et al., 1984). For some types of movement—especially those involving gross movements of a limb, in contrast to the fine movements of a hand—it is very

movements. "Colonies" of cells are related to particular muscle groups, and they seem to form vertical columns in the cortex (Ghez et al., 1991), an organizational principle similar to that of cortical sensory systems (see Chapter 10). About one-third of the human pyramidal tract fibers originate in the so-called motor area of the cortex. Another one-fifth come from the postcentral gyrus (somatosensory cortex). The remaining pyramidal fibers arise from many other cortical regions. Thus control of motor function is dispersed among cortical areas, leading to controversies about the boundaries of the primary motor cortex (Rothwell, 1994).

difficult to see a relationship between the firing pattern of a single cell and measures of movement.

Apostolos Georgopoulos has focused on the properties of *populations* of motor cortex neurons (Georgopoulos et al., 1993). He recorded from the motor cortex neurons of monkeys that were trained to make free arm movements in eight possible target directions (Figure 11.13*a*). Many cells changed their firing rates according to the direction of the movement, and for any one cell, discharge rates were highest in a particular direction (Figure 11.13*b*). Although different cells prefer different directions, each cell carries only partial information about the direction of reaching. When the activity of several hundred neurons is combined, their overall vector shows a good relation to the actual direction of the reaching arm. Given the millions of neurons in this region, a larger sampling would presumably provide an even more accurate prediction (Georgopoulos et al., 1993).

Apostolos Georgopoulos

Nonprimary Motor Cortex Aids Motor Sequencing

Recordings of single nonprimary motor cortex neurons in awake monkeys have shown that many nerve cells in nonprimary motor cortex change their discharge rate just before the onset of conditioned movements, such as pressing a key in response to a sensory stimulus. Some nerve cells in these regions also respond to a sensory stimulus without evidence of elicited movement (S. P. Wise and Strick, 1984). Such data suggest that these regions are involved in the sensory guidance of movements, or that they represent higher-level intentions for movement. Favoring the latter hypothesis is the fact that nonprimary motor cortical areas are especially active during the preparation of skilled movements, typically sequences of movements.

Nonprimary motor cortex consists of two main regions: the **supplementary motor cortex**, which lies mainly on the medial aspect of the hemisphere, and the **premotor cortex**, which is anterior to the primary motor cortex (Figure 11.14). Patients with unilateral lesions of premotor cortex retain fine motor control of the fingers but are impaired in the stability of stance and gait and in the coordination of the two hands. Patients with bilateral damage to the supplementary motor cortex are unable to move or speak voluntarily, although some automatic and reflex movements remain. These long-lasting effects suggest that this region is involved in the conception and initiation of movement and movement sequences (Freund, 1984).

Studies of localized cerebral blood flow and metabolism reveal that in simple tasks, such as keeping a spring compressed between two fingers of one hand, blood flow increases markedly in the hand area of the opposite primary motor cortex (Roland, 1980, 1984). Increasing the complexity of motor tasks to a sequence of behaviors extends the area of blood flow increase to the supplementary motor cortex. Finally, when subjects mentally *rehearse* the complex movement sequence, the enhanced blood flow is restricted to the supplementary motor cortex.

Whereas the supplementary motor cortex is especially activated during *internally* generated finger sequences, the premotor cortex is activated when motor sequences are guided *externally* by stimuli (Larsson et al., 1996)—a distinction that is also revealed by recordings of neuronal activity in behaving monkeys (Halsband et al., 1994).

11.14 Human Motor Cortical Areas
The primary motor cortex lies just anterior to the central sulcus. Anterior to the primary motor cortex are the premotor cortex and the supplementary motor cortex, which together make up the nonprimary motor cortex.

(*a*) Lateral view — Supplementary motor cortex — Primary motor cortex — (*b*) Medial view

Premotor cortex

Another distinction between supplementary motor cortex and premotor cortex is suggested by a study in which people learned the same sequence of finger movements under two conditions. In one condition the subjects soon became aware of the repeating sequence and began anticipating the next finger movement. In the other condition, subjects were distracted by another task and therefore never became aware of the repeating sequence, but nevertheless they learned it (as evidenced by their improved performance). Thus both groups learned to perform the same sequence of finger movements, but different brain regions were activated in these two conditions.

Neural plasticity The undistracted subjects, explicitly aware of the sequence they were learning, showed activation of the premotor cortex, but the distracted subjects, unaware that they were (implicitly) learning the sequence, showed activation of the supplementary motor cortex (Hazeltine et al., 1997). Perhaps, then, the premotor cortex participates in *explicit* motor learning while the supplementary motor cortex mediates *implicit* motor learning.

A subset of premotor neurons are also activated when objects are brought close to the monkey's face or hand. If the lights are then turned out, some of these neurons continue to fire even if the object is silently moved, suggesting to Charles Gross and colleagues (Graziano et al., 1997), that the cells are coding for where the monkey *thinks* the object is. When the lights are turned back on and the monkey sees the object gone, the neurons cease firing. Such neurons may help us reach out for objects that are no longer visible.

Charles Gross

The Basal Ganglia Modulate Movements

The **basal ganglia** include a group of interconnected forebrain nuclei—the caudate nucleus, putamen, and globus pallidus. Closely associated with these structures are some nuclei in the midbrain— **Sylvius** the substantia nigra and subthalamic nucleus. Figure 11.15 shows the locations and major connections of these structures (see also Figure 2.15*a*). The caudate nucleus and putamen together are referred to as the **striatum**.

Each of these structures has subcomponents whose characteristics and connections have been described in detail (Graybiel, 1995). These structures receive input from wide areas of the cerebral cortex and send much of their output right back to the cerebral cortex in what can be described as a cortex–basal ganglia–cortex loop. Lesions of these regions in humans produce movement impairments that seem quite different from those that follow interruption of the pyra-

midal system. We will discuss these impairments later in the chapter.

Inputs to the basal ganglia come from an extensive region of the cerebral cortex, as well as from thalamic nuclei and the substantia nigra. The sources of inputs suggest a subdivision of the basal ganglia into two major systems. One includes the caudate nucleus, whose inputs are especially derived from frontal association cortex. The other system includes the putamen; inputs to this system come from sensorimotor cortical zones. Lesions within these subdivisions have different effects (DeLong et al., 1984). Lesions of the caudate impair relatively complex behavior; lesions in the putamen have more exclusively motor impairments, affecting the strength and rate of response, rather than the direction of response.

Animal studies of the basal ganglia use both lesions and recordings of single neurons during motor responses (DeLong et al., 1984). Each structure of the basal ganglia contains a topographic representation of body musculature. Studies suggest that the basal ganglia play a role in determining the amplitude and direction of movement rather than affecting the initiation of actions. The basal ganglia networks thus seem to modulate the patterns of activity initiated in other brain circuits that control movements, such as motor and premotor cortical systems (see Figure 11.4). Experiments also indicate that basal ganglia are especially important in the generation of movements influenced by memories, in contrast to those guided by sensory control (Evarts et al., 1984). This point is also emphasized by Graybiel et al. (1994), who indicate that the multiple loops that connect the basal ganglia and neocortex are important in sensorimotor learning.

The Cerebellum Affects Programs, Timing, and Coordination of Acts

The cerebellar cortex in higher vertebrates is a sheet with many folds. This brain structure is found in almost all vertebrates. In some vertebrate groups its size varies according to the range and complexity of movements. For **Sylvius** example, the cerebellum is much larger in fish with extensive locomotor behavior than it is in less active fish; it is also large in flying birds, as compared with bird species that do not fly.

Recall from Chapter 2 that the outer layers of the cerebellum are called the cerebellar cortex and are dominated by a sheet of large multipolar cells called Purkinje cells (see Figure 2.16). All output of the cerebellar cortex travels via the axons of Purkinje cells, all of which synapse with the deep cerebellar nuclei. At these synapses they produce only inhibitory postsynaptic potentials. Hence, all the circuitry of the extensive cortical portion of the cerebellum, which also includes 10 billion to 20 billion granule cells in humans, guides movement by inhibiting neurons.

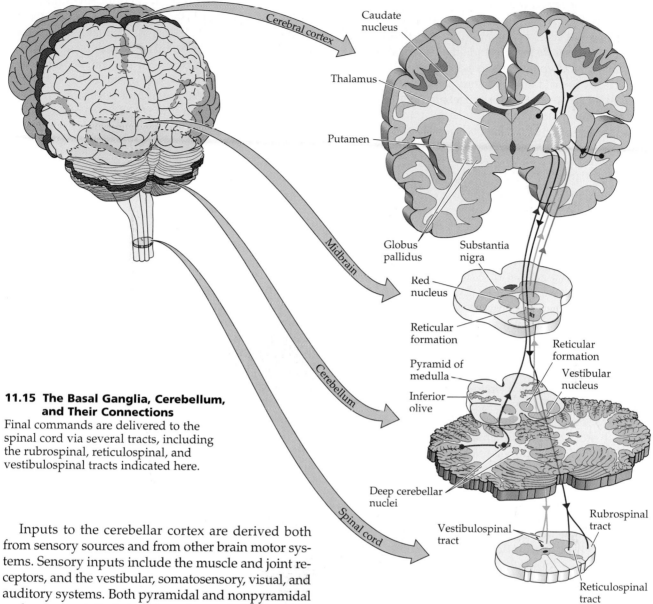

Caudate
nucleus

Thalamus

Putamen

Globus
pallidus

Substantia
nigra

Red
nucleus

Reticular
formation

Reticular
formation

Pyramid of
medulla

Vestibular
nucleus

Inferior
olive

Deep cerebellar
nuclei

Vestibulospinal
tract

Rubrospinal
tract

Reticulospinal
tract

Cerebral cortex

Midbrain

Cerebellum

Spinal cord

11.15 The Basal Ganglia, Cerebellum, and Their Connections
Final commands are delivered to the spinal cord via several tracts, including the rubrospinal, reticulospinal, and vestibulospinal tracts indicated here.

Inputs to the cerebellar cortex are derived both from sensory sources and from other brain motor systems. Sensory inputs include the muscle and joint receptors, and the vestibular, somatosensory, visual, and auditory systems. Both pyramidal and nonpyramidal pathways contribute inputs to the cerebellum and in turn receive outputs from the deep nuclei of the cerebellum. Thus, the cerebellum receives elaborate information both from systems that monitor movements and from systems that execute movements. For this reason the cerebellum has long been believed to play a role in the feedback control of movements. It has also been suggested that the cerebellum elaborates neural "programs" for the control of skilled movements, particularly rapid, repeated movements that become automatic. This role of the cerebellum in the acquisition and retention of learned motor responses will be discussed in Chapter 18.

Various theories and experiments have suggested that cerebellar circuitry includes memorylike devices that might be important for motor learning. Masao Ito (1987) has de-

Masao Ito

scribed a long-term depression of Purkinje cell activity that occurs when both the climbing-fiber and parallel-fiber inputs to these cells are stimulated together (see Topic 11.4, Cerebellar Circuitry). The depression of firing can last as long as 1 hour. This kind of memory change in the cerebellar cortex might be important for adaptive changes that involve interactions between the vestibular and visual systems, such as those that accompany the changing orientation of the head.

 Special topic

Endogenous Oscillators Drive Many Repetitive Movements

However it is accomplished, most locomotion is rhythmic. For all animals, moving about consists of repetitive cycles of the same act, be it the beating of wings or the repetitive swinging of legs. In Chapter 3 we presented an example of a basic neural circuit that could act as an **endogenous oscillator** (see Figure 3.17), generating regularly repeating sequences of behavior. Do the repetitive cycles of locomotion reflect such endogenous oscillators that provide the basic locomotor programs that motoneurons obligingly obey?

Early theories did not favor endogenous oscillators, emphasizing instead the role of sensory feedback and a reflex chain. According to this view, each act provides the sensory feedback from muscles that stimulates the next component. As with Sherrington's attempt to reduce complex behavior to a series of reflexes (which we discussed earlier in this chapter), this explanation is inadequate. Later experiments showed that eliminating the sensory feedback in locomotor acts such as walking or flying did *not* affect the basic rhythmic aspect of the act.

We now know that rhythmic movements are generated by mechanisms within the spinal cord. These endogenous rhythms are normally modulated by feedback, but they can function independently of brain influences or afferents. The term **central pattern generator** has been used to refer to the neural circuitry responsible for generating rhythmic patterns of behavior as seen in walking. Typically neurons in a central pattern generator circuit display reciprocal inhibitory innervation.

Central pattern generation in locomotor rhythms has been studied by Grillner and colleagues (P. Grillner et al., 1991; S. Grillner, 1985). Their electromyographic records of hindlimb muscles of cats with spinal cord section and dorsal root cuts reveal a "walking" pattern that lasts for seconds when a single dorsal root is briefly stimulated electrically. This response has been referred to as **fictive locomotion**; for more on the subject, see Topic 11.5, Fictive Locomotion.

Special topic ↗

Outputs from spinal motoneurons also show different types of coordination that are variants of typical locomotor patterns, like galloping. The activity of the relevant muscles shows phase relations similar to characteristic muscle time differences observed in the movements of intact animals. Three intact adjacent spinal segments provide the minimal amount of spinal processing necessary for generation of part of the locomotor rhythm. Thus, the brain does not generate the essential rhythm in the spinal cord, but it may control the onset of the rhythm and provide corrections arising from other influences registered by the brain.

Disorders of Muscle, Spinal Cord, or Brain Can Disrupt Movement

Many metabolic conditions can affect the chemistry and structure of muscle. In Chapter 5 we noted that several hormones—especially thyroid hormones—affect muscle chemistry and function. Chronically low levels of thyroid hormone produce muscle weakness

and slowness of muscle contraction. Several muscle diseases are particularly mysterious, seemingly involving biochemical abnormalities that lead to structural changes in muscle; these disorders are referred to as **muscular dystrophy**. As the name implies, a symptom that the various muscular dystrophies share is the wasting away of muscles. Many muscular dystrophies are hereditary; because of recent advances, Duchenne's muscular dystrophy is the best understood.

Duchenne's muscular dystrophy strikes almost exclusively boys, beginning at the age of about 4 to 6 years and leading to death within a decade. Pedigrees suggested that the disorder is a simple Mendelian trait—caused by a single gene, in this case carried on the X chromosome. When researchers began examining the X chromosomes in members of families afflicted with the disorder, they found that a single gene was indeed abnormal in all the boys carrying the disorder, and on one of the two X chromosomes carried by their mother, but was normal in the fathers and in all unafflicted brothers.

The gene and its normal protein product were named **dystrophin**. In some ways the name is unfortunate, because this protein, when normal, does *not* lead to dystrophy. Dystrophin is normally produced in muscle cells and may play a role in regulating internal calcium (Ca^{2+}) stores. Because females have two X chromosomes, even if one carries the defective copy of the dystrophin gene, the other X chromosome can still produce normal dystrophin. But about half the sons of such females will receive the defective gene and will be afflicted with the disease. No one knows why the defective dystrophin protein shows no effects during the first few years of life. Mice with a mutation in this gene also show normal muscle function early in life and dystrophy in adulthood, but unlike humans with Duchenne's, the mice recover without intervention.

 Genes and behavior

Results from studies of the gene that encodes dystrophin suggest a very promising therapy for Duchenne's muscular dystrophy. Since females who carry the defective gene on only one of their X chromosomes are unafflicted by the disease, administering dystrophin protein to afflicted boys may enable their muscles to function properly. The fact that muscles are particularly willing to accept new genes facilitates such treatment; sometimes the mere injection of messenger RNA for dystrophin causes muscle cells to translate the RNA and produce the protein for a while (Barr and Leiden, 1991). Other gene therapies may lead to the permanent establishment of a functional dystrophin gene in the muscles of Duchenne's patients.

The Immune System May Attack Neuromuscular Junctions

Movement disorders involving the neuromuscular junction include a variety of reversible poison states.

For example, snake bites can cause neuromuscular blocks because the venom of some highly poisonous snakes contains substances (such as bungarotoxin, which we discussed in Chapter 3) that block post-synaptic receptor sites for acetylcholine.

Studies on the mechanisms of action of this venom have led directly to an understanding of one of the more debilitating neuromuscular disorders, **myasthenia gravis** (from the Greek *mys*, "muscle," and *asthenes*, "weak"; and the Latin *gravis*, "grave" or "serious"). This disorder is characterized by a profound weakness of skeletal muscles. The disease often first affects the muscles of the head, producing symptoms such as drooping of the eyelids, double vision, and slowing of speech. In later stages, paralysis of the muscles that control swallowing and respiration can become life-threatening. Basic research in animals and continuing studies in human patients have established that antibodies directed against acetylcholine receptors cause these changes. Apparently myasthenic patients spontaneously develop these antibodies, which attack their own postsynaptic membranes (A. G. Engel, 1984).

Spinal Cord Pathology Causes Some Motor Impairments

Pathological changes in motoneurons also produce movement paralysis or weakness. Virus-induced destruction of motoneurons—for example, by the disease polio—was once a frightening prospect, especially in the United States and western Europe. Polioviruses destroy motoneurons of the spinal cord and, in more severe types of the disease, cranial motoneurons of the brain stem. Since the muscles can no longer be called on to contract, they atrophy.

War, sports, and accidents cause many forms of human spinal injuries that result in motor impairment. Injuries to the human spinal cord commonly develop from forces to the neck or back that break bone and compress the spinal cord. If the spinal cord is severed completely, immediate paralysis results, and reflexes below the level of injury are lost—a condition known as **flaccid paralysis**. Flaccid paralysis generally results only when a considerable stretch of the spinal cord has been destroyed. When the injury severs the spinal cord without causing widespread destruction of tissue, reflexes below the level of injury frequently become excessive because the intact tissue lacks the dampening influence of brain inhibitory pathways.

The hope of reconnecting the injured spinal cord no longer seems as far-fetched as it once did. **Neural plasticity** Months after the lamprey spinal cord is severed, these animals can swim again without any therapeutic intervention (S. Cohen et al., 1989), but they seem unique among vertebrates in this regard. In rats, implants of peripheral nerve or fetal nervous tissue may provide a "bridge" across the injury to allow reconnection of the spinal cord (Bernstein-Goral and Bregman, 1993).

Recall from Chapter 9 that CNS neurons of a special population are continuously produced throughout life and send out new axons—the olfactory receptors. When Y. Li et al. (1997) took glial cells (called ensheathing cells) from the olfactory bulb and used them as a bridge across spinal cord cuts in rats, the corticospinal axons regenerated across the injury and the animals eventually regained use of their forepaws. Providing neurotrophic factors such as neurotrophin-3 to severed spinal cord axons also seems to promote regeneration (H. Cheng et al., 1996; Grill et al., 1997). These observations buoy the hope that regeneration in the injured spinal cord of humans will become possible (Waxman and Kocsis, 1997).

Brain Stem Pathology Causes Some Motor Impairments

In the late 1930s, the sad end of the brilliant baseball career of New York Yankees star Lou Gehrig brought public awareness to an unusual degenerative disorder in which the motoneurons of the brain stem and spinal cord are destroyed and their target muscles waste away. This syndrome is formally known as **amyotrophic lateral sclerosis** (**ALS**), although journalists more commonly refer to it as Lou Gehrig's disease. The plight of the late Senator Jacob Javits (1904–1986) drew attention to the personal struggles that accompany this disease, which progressively paralyzes a person while leaving intellectual abilities intact. Characteristic symptoms at the start of the disorder depend on the level of the nervous system at which motoneuron destruction begins (Tandan and Bradley, 1985). The origins of the disease remain a mystery, but a wide range of causal factors is under investigation, including premature aging, toxic minerals, viruses, immune responses, and endocrine dysfunction.

About 10% of ALS cases are hereditary; that is, there is a clear family history of the disease, indicating that gene defects are involved. The pedigrees of several afflicted families indicate a single-gene disorder. The particular gene has been isolated (Andersen et al., 1995) and found to encode an enzyme—copper/zinc superoxide dismutase—that can convert highly reactive compounds (carrying what chemists call a free radical) into more ordinary compounds that can react in only a few ways. Some investigators speculate that this enzyme protects the muscles and/or motoneurons from the cellular damage that free radicals might cause. Thus, the nonhereditary cases of ALS might stem from the buildup of similar damage from other sources, and this damage may accumulate despite the efforts of such enzymes. But this plausible hypothesis appears to have been disproved by an experimental test.

 Genes and behavior

When scientists produced transgenic mice that, in addition to their own normal copies of the enzyme, carried a copy of the defective human gene, these animals displayed an ALS-like syndrome (Gurney et al., 1994). Their muscles wasted away and their motoneurons died, leading to an early death. Presumably the normal genes continued to protect these animals from free-radical damage, yet they succumbed to the disease. Thus the abnormal gene may actively damage part of the neuromuscular system. These molecular genetic changes may also lead to high levels of the transmitter glutamate (Dean, 1994). In high concentrations this excitatory amino acid can cause neurons to die.

Cerebral Cortex Pathology Causes Some Motor Impairments

Motor impairments that follow strokes or injury to the human cerebral cortex are familiar to clinical investigators. The most common change is a paralysis or partial paralysis (paresis) of voluntary movements on one side of the body, usually the result of injury to the cerebral cortex of the hemisphere opposite the side of the body displaying symptoms. In addition, affected patients show some spasticity, especially increased rigidity in response to forced movement of the limbs. The spasticity reflects the exaggeration of stretch reflexes. Abnormal reflexes occur, such as the flaring and extension of the toes elicited by stroking the sole of the foot (the Babinski reflex). In the months following cerebral cortical injury, the clinical picture changes. The initial paralysis slowly diminishes, and some voluntary movements of the proximal portion of limbs return, although fine motor control of fingers is seldom regained. As we noted previously, in humans the symptoms are more severe than in many other mammals.

Damage to nonmotor zones of the cerebral cortex, such as some regions of parietal or frontal association cortex, produces more complicated changes in motor control. Box 11.2 describes one such condition—apraxia.

BOX 11.2   *Sometimes I Can Move, Sometimes I Can't*

A patient is seated in front of an examiner who is assessing the impact of a recent stroke. Simple inquiries reveal a startling deficit. When asked to smile, our patient is unable, although he certainly attempts to. If asked to use a comb placed in front of him, he seems unable to figure out what to do. But things aren't as simple as they might appear. At one point in the discussion our patient spontaneously smiles, and at another point he retrieves a comb from his pocket and combs his hair with ease and accuracy.

Our patient is displaying a syndrome called **apraxia** (from the Greek *a-*, "not," and *praxis*, "action"). Apraxia is the inability to carry out certain acts even though paralysis or weakness is not evident and comprehension and motivation are intact. Apraxia was first described by the nineteenth-century neurologist Hughlings Jackson, who noted that some patients could not protrude their tongue on command even though they could use it in a variety of spontaneous acts such as speech, licking their lips, and eating. Apraxia is a symptom of a variety of disorders, including stroke, Alzheimer's disease, and developmental disorders of children.

Neurologists studying stroke patients have discovered several different types of apraxia. **Ideomotor apraxia** is characterized by the inability to carry out a simple motor activity in response to a verbal command (e.g., "smile," or "use this comb"), even though this same activity is readily performed spontaneously. Some researchers emphasize that this type of apraxia is characterized by the inability to select responses, arrange them in an appropriate order, and orient them properly; these processes are crucial in gestures. Other researchers emphasize the connection between this disorder and aphasia (disturbances of language that follow injury or diseases of the cerebral hemispheres).

Ideational apraxia is an impairment in the carrying out of a *sequence* of actions that are components of a behavioral script, although each element or step can be done correctly. A patient was asked to go through the sequence of acts to light a candle with a match. Although she was unable to comply with this request, when the lights went out during a storm she found a candle and lit it (Kosslyn et al., 1992). Such patients have difficulty pushing a

button, then pulling a handle, then depressing a switch in sequence when asked (see the figure), but they can do each of these tasks in isolation.

One anatomical explanation of apraxia focuses on the disconnection of primary motor areas from nonprimary motor areas. Other anatomical interpretations emphasize the importance of injury to parietal areas, which include representations of various sensory features of actions.

Parkinson's Disease Results from Lack of Stimulation of the Basal Ganglia

Diseases of the basal ganglia can produce a variety of effects, some almost opposite to others. Some disorders reflect release from the constraints that the basal ganglia usually impose on motor control. In the absence of these constraints, the activity initiated by other brain regions appears unchecked and yields dramatic, persistent excesses of movement. Other basal ganglia disorders produce slowness of movement and marked changes in muscle tone.

Almost 200 years ago, physician James Parkinson noted a small group of people on the streets of London who moved quite slowly, showed regular tremors of the hands and face while at rest, and walked with a rigid bearing. Another feature of what is now known as **Parkinson's disease** is a loss of facial muscle tone, which gives the face a masklike appearance. Parkinson's patients also show few spontaneous actions and have great difficulty in all motor efforts, no matter how routine. These changes are progressive and may take years to reach a maximally disabled state.

Parkinson's patients show progressive degeneration of dopamine-containing cells in the substantia nigra of

 Special topic

the brain (see Topic 11.6, Dopamine Loss with Age). The loss of cells in this area is continuous; symptoms appear only after a major loss (Figure 11.16). The causes of this disorder remain a mystery, although the discovery of a form of the disorder induced by illicit drugs (described in Box 11.3) has suggested to some researchers that subtle exposures to toxins over a prolonged period underlie the development of the disorder (Tetrud et al., 1994).

Most cases of Parkinson's disease are probably not inherited, but in one large Italian family Parkinson's disease develops in members who inherit a defective copy of the gene that encodes α-synuclein (Polymeropoulos et al., 1997), a protein normally expressed in the basal ganglia. Researchers hope that determining how this defective protein causes Parkinson's in this family will suggest clues to the onset of nonhereditary Parkinson's.

For years, there was no treatment for Parkinson's disease. A pharmacological therapy emerged from the discovery in the late 1960s that Parkinson's patients show a loss of dopamine levels in the substantia nigra, which projects to the corpus striatum. This treatment was the administration of a precursor to dopamine to enhance the dopamine levels of surviving cells. The substance, called **L-dopa**, markedly reduces symptoms in Parkinson's patients, including a decrease in tremor and an increase in the speed of movements.

Although L-dopa can reverse some symptoms of Parkinson's disease, nerve cell degeneration in the

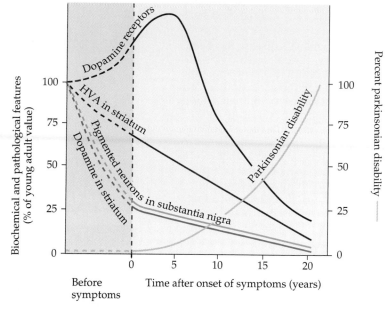

11.16 Relations between Parkinson's Disease and Dopamine

Initially, increased production of dopamine receptors compensates for the loss of dopamine cells. But continued loss of cells eventually leads to declines in striatal dopamine levels and a worsening of parkinsonian symptoms. Dotted lines represent estimates based on values obtained in aging, nonparkinsonian patients. HVA (homovanillic acid) is a primary metabolite of dopamine. (After Jankovic and Calne, 1989.)

substantia nigra is relentless. Since the cell bodies in the brain stem degenerate, dopamine-containing terminals in the caudate nucleus and putamen also disappear. Eventually, too few dopamine-containing neurons remain in the substantia nigra to be influenced by the intake of L-dopa.

Until recently, no treatments to address this terminal condition were available. By the 1980s, however, researchers had begun to use transplants of dopamine-containing cells as a form of treatment in humans. Initially they transplanted dopamine cells of the adrenal gland into the cerebral ventricles of patients. It was believed that these cells would act as a "chemical factory" and release dopamine into the surrounding area, which includes the caudate nucleus. But clinical benefits with this intervention were minimal.

The refinement of techniques led to the transplantation of human fetal cells derived from the brain stem (see Figure 1.6). Direct injection of these cells into the corpus striatum (Figure 11.17) (Peschanski et al., 1994) produces remarkable symptom relief in some Parkinson's patients. In addition to improving the quality of movements, this graft increases the efficacy of L-dopa treatment. Animal research on such grafts indicates that these fetal brain stem cells become integrated into the circuitry of the corpus striatum; thus, transplants result in a rewiring of the damaged brains in addition

BOX 11.3   *The Frozen Addicts*

*P*arkinson's disease has been very difficult to study because until recently it was not possible to find or produce a similar disorder in laboratory animals. Sloppy synthesis of illegal drugs led to the first valuable model of Parkinson's disease. This saga began when several drug addicts were admitted to a hospital in California with an unusual array of symptoms. Especially puzzling was the fact that although they were in their twenties, they presented an unmistakable portrait of Parkinson's disease, which is usually restricted to people 50 or older. The movements of these young patients were slow, they had tremors of the hands, and their faces were frozen without expression. In addition, the diagnosis of Parkinson's disease in these cases was confirmed by the therapeutic response to the drug L-dopa.

All of these drug addicts had recently used a "home-brewed" synthetic form of heroin. That fact, coupled with the recollection of a report of an unusual disorder that had arisen from a laboratory accident several years earlier, led to the conclusion that the synthetic heroin contained a neurotoxin that produced brain damage typical of Parkinson's disease (Kopin and Markey, 1988; Langston, 1985).

Moving step by step in a trail that resembles a detective story, researchers pieced together what had happened. Chemical studies led to the identification of a contaminant in the synthetic heroin, now known as MPTP (an abbreviation of a much longer chemical name). Many addicts have been exposed to this substance, but relatively few come down with this parkinsonian disorder. Patients with symptoms show a decline in dopamine concentrations in the brain, as revealed by PET scan (top panel of the figure) (W. R. Martin and Hayden, 1987).

The injection of MPTP into various research animals yielded a startling result: Although rats and rabbits showed only minimal and

Preoperative

13 months postoperative

PET scans of a patient suffering from MPTP-induced Parkinson's disease before and after a therapeutic transplant.

transient motor impairments, monkeys were as sensitive to the toxin as humans are, developing a permanent set of motor changes identical to those of humans with Parkinson's disease. Furthermore, the sites of damage in the brain were identical to those in the frozen addicts and in Parkinson's patients.

MPTP accumulates in the substantia nigra and caudate nucleus because it binds selectively to a form of the enzyme monoamine oxidase (MAO), which is plentiful in these regions. MPTP interacts with this enzyme to form a highly toxic metabolite: MPP^+. Researchers have suggested that the natural pigment neuromelanin, found in the substantia nigra, accounts for the selectivity of damage produced by MPTP (S. H. Snyder and D'Amato, 1985). They have shown that MPP^+ binds with special affinity to this pig-

ment. Thus, cells with neuromelanin accumulate MPP^+ to toxic levels, and since cells of the substantia nigra contain large amounts of the pigment, they are particularly vulnerable to the destructive impact of MPP^+. In other parts of the brain, MPP^+ levels decline following exposure; in contrast, MPP^+ levels in substantia nigra cells may continue to increase for some time following exposure. In view of this binding mechanism, differences among species become more comprehensible. Nigral cells of monkeys and humans have pigment, while those of rodents are unpigmented.

Monkeys can be protected against the toxic effects by oxidase inhibitors and certain other drugs (D'Amato et al., 1987). This drug model has already resulted in new drug treatments that hold considerable promise for human sufferers. For example, the MAO inhibitor deprenyl slows the progression of Parkinson's disease. Discovering a primate model of this disease opened an exciting set of research opportunities that is removing the shroud of mystery that has enveloped Parkinson's disease. Primate experiments have also provided an opportunity to test other therapies, such as neural transplants. This research has led to apparently successful transplants in human patients (bottom panel of the figure), including some of the original frozen addicts.

Some researchers have speculated that Parkinson's disease in humans arises from exposure to an unknown toxin. In two cases involving laboratory workers, MPTP-induced disease arose from either inhalation of or skin contact with MPTP, suggesting that brief and almost trivial contact with MPTP is sufficient to begin the disease. Some environmental toxins, such as certain herbicides, may provide exposure to MPP^+ (S. H. Snyder and D'Amato, 1986). (Figures courtesy of J. William Langston.)

Patient 3

Patient 4

Preengraftment   1 year   3 years

11.17 Brain Implants to Treat Parkinson's Disease
The injection of human fetal cells into patients with Parkinson's disease led to increased dopamine receptors (coded in yellow and red) in the striatum 1 and 3 years later, as these PET scans reveal. (From Lindvall et al., 1994.)

to the effects they produce by the release of synaptic transmitter. Such transplants appear to have helped patients who suffer from drug-induced Parkinson's disease (see Box 11.3). Because there are ethical problems with the use of fetal cells, however, some researchers hope to produce cells that are genetically engineered to make dopamine; these cells may substitute for fetal cells as effective donor grafts.

An aspect of Parkinson's disease that might be independent of the degree of motor impairment is the appearance of cognitive and emotional changes. Some Parkinson's patients show marked cognitive decline during the course of their illness (Cummings, 1995). Depression in Parkinson's patients is also common; some researchers have attributed it to the consequences of diminished movement capabilities and the general stress of such incapacity. Other researchers have attributed this depression to a diminished responsiveness of the serotonergic system (Sano et al., 1991).

Depressed Parkinson's patients show lower levels of the metabolites of serotonin than do nondepressed Parkinson's patients. Reduced activity in prefrontal cortex in these patients also suggests that their altered mood is associated with frontal lobe impairments. Studies of mood and emotions in Parkinson's patients have laid the groundwork for research on the role of basal ganglia in emotional regulation in psychiatric disorders, which we will consider in Chapter 16.

Huntington's Disease Is Characterized by Excessive Movement Caused by Deterioration of the Basal Ganglia

George Huntington was a young physician whose only publication (1872) was a description of a strange motor affliction of a nearby family. He correctly noticed that this disorder was inherited, passed from generation to generation. We now know that **Huntington's disease** is transmitted by a single dominant gene, so each child of a victim has a 50% chance of developing the disease.

 Genes and behavior

The first symptoms of this disease are subtle behavioral changes: clumsiness, twitches in fingers and the face. Subtlety is rapidly lost as the illness progresses; a continuing stream of involuntary jerks engulfs the entire body. Aimless movements of the eyes, jerky leg movements, and writhing of the body turn the routine challenges of the day into insurmountable obstacles. Worse yet, as the disease progresses, marked behavioral changes include intellectual deterioration, depression, and in a minority of patients, a psychotic state that resembles schizophrenia. Both memory disruption and changes in visuospatial organization are common in this disorder (Shoulson, 1992). In some patients, cognitive and emotional changes may appear many years before obvious motor impairments do (N. S. Wexler et al., 1991). Huntington's disease usually develops over a period of 15 to 20 years.

The neuroanatomical basis of this disorder is the profound, progressive destruction of the basal ganglia, especially the caudate nucleus and the putamen (Figure 11.18). Several types of cells are particularly vulnerable, including neurons that contain the transmitter GABA. Perhaps death of these cells results from a transmitter or transmitterlike substance in the brains of patients. One model for the progression of motor symptoms emphasizes the destruction of inhibitory circuitry as the essential characteristic of the disorder (N. S. Wexler et al., 1991). Acetylcholine-containing neurons are relatively spared.

Because the symptoms of Huntington's disease usually first appear between the ages of 30 and 45 years, many victims have children before knowing whether they will ultimately contract the disease. Until quite recently this meant continuing generations of ravaged individuals. After losing her mother to this disease, psychologist Nancy Wexler pieced together a pedigree map of more than 10,000 individuals, including more than 300 Huntington's patients, from a community in Venezuela. After years of work, she and her collaborators (including David Housman, James Gusella, and Venezuelan physician Ernesto Bonilla) were able to pinpoint the gene, on chromosome 4, that is responsible for the disorder (Gusella and MacDonald, 1993).

Nancy Wexler

The function of the protein is still unknown, but the nature of the mutation in this gene (called *HD* for Huntington's disease) provides unexpected insight into the inheritance of Huntington's disease. In afflicted individuals the *HD* gene is interrupted by a series of three nucleotides—CAG—repeated over and over (see the Appendix). This **trinucleotide repeat** can vary in length; if there are fewer than 30 repeats, no symptoms appear, but if there are 38 or more trinucleotide repeats in the *HD* gene, the person will develop Huntington's disease (A. B. Young, 1993). The longer the string of trinucleotide repeats, the earlier in life Huntington's disease symptoms commence. When the repeats are carried by the mother, the gene with its repeats is copied faithfully in eggs and transmitted to the offspring, but in the production of sperm, a father may transmit more or fewer repeats than he himself carries. Unfortunately, it is more common for the father to transmit more repeats than fewer repeats. Thus, in some cases an asymptomatic father may transmit Huntington's disease to his offspring.

How does carrying a copy of *HD* with extended repeats cause degeneration of the striatum and the

Genes and behavior

Lateral ventricles

11.18 Neuropathology in Huntington's Disease A coronal section through the brain of a Huntington's patient shows marked enlargement of the ventricles caused by atrophy of the neighboring caudate nucleus and putamen. Compare this section to the coronal section of a normal brain in Figure 2.13c, where the caudate and putamen are clearly visible. (Courtesy of W. W. Tourtellotte.)

symptoms of Huntington's disease? One hypothesis was that only striatal cells normally make the protein encoded by *HD* (which has been named **huntingtin**), so only these cells die when it is defective. But huntingtin, whether normal or defective, is produced not just in the striatum, but throughout the brain, by both neurons and glial cells. Huntingtin is also made in the muscles, liver, pancreas, and testes (A. B. Young, 1993). Thus, the reason that the defective *HD* gene affects only striatal cells remains a mystery.

A second protein has been found to bind huntingtin and is called HAP-1 (for huntingtin-associated protein) (X. Li et al., 1995). HAP-1 is found primarily in the brain (X. Li et al., 1996) and binds the mutant version of huntingtin even more tightly than the normal version, so perhaps this increased binding kills striatal neurons. Study of the function of HAP-1 and normal and defective huntingtin proteins in laboratory animals may suggest future therapies.

The example of Huntington's disease, with its increased movements, demonstrates the major role that inhibition plays in normal motor control. Without adequate inhibition, a person is compelled to perform a variety of unwanted movements. A milder loss of inhibition is caused by variations in the glycine receptor (the amino acid glycine is also a neurotransmitter, usually inhibitory). People who inherit a mutant, less effective form of the glycine receptor (Rajendra et al., 1994) display a lifelong exaggeration of the startle response (Shiang et al., 1993).

Cerebellar Damage Leads to Many Motor Impairments

Since the cerebellum modulates many aspects of motor performance, it is not surprising that its impairment leads to many abnormalities of behavior. These symptoms permit an examiner to identify with considerable accuracy what part of the cerebellum is involved (Dichgans, 1984).

A relatively common lesion of the cerebellum results from a tumor that usually occurs in childhood. The tumor damages a part of the cerebellum—the vermis—that has close connections to the vestibular system and therefore causes disturbances of balance. The patient walks as if drunk and has difficulty even standing erect. Often patients afflicted in this way place their feet widely apart in an attempt to maintain balance. The abnormalities usually involve the legs and trunk but not the arms.

Normally the world seems to hold still as we walk because movements of our eyes compensate for movements of the head. Some patients with lesions of the cerebellum, however, see the world around them move whenever they move their heads. If normal subjects wear prismatic lenses, they learn to compensate for the new relationship between movement of the eyes and perceived change of direction. Patients with lesions of the vestibular part of the cerebellum cannot make this adjustment, suggesting that this part of the cerebellum is important for such learning.

Some alcoholic patients show degeneration of the cortex of the anterior lobe of the cerebellum. When this region is damaged, abnormalities of gait and posture are common. The legs show **ataxia** (loss of coordination), but the arms do not. Loss of coordination and swaying indicate that the patient is not compensating normally for the usual deviations of position and posture. Several investigators have proposed that the cerebellum works like a comparator in a negative feedback circuit, comparing ongoing movements with target levels and sending corrective instructions to overcome any departures from planned values. (Such a feedback system is diagrammed in Figure 11.3b.) The cerebellar cortex has motor and sensory maps of the body that are in register (i.e., that are perfectly superimposed), which may allow the comparison of ongoing acts with planned positions and motions of body parts.

Difficulties of motor coordination are common after damage to the lateral aspects of the cerebellum. One such problem is called **decomposition of movement**, because gestures are broken up into individual segments instead of being executed smoothly. A patient who had this problem after damage to his right cerebellar hemisphere described his condition in this way: "The movements of my left hand are done subconsciously, but I have to think out each movement of my right arm. I come to a dead stop in turning and

have to think it out before I start again." Thus the cerebellum is needed not to initiate acts or to plan the sequence of movements, but to facilitate activation and to "package" movements economically (Brooks, 1984).

Summary

1. Two broad categories of motor activity—movements and acts—are divided into subcategories. Reflexes are movements; more complex motor behaviors are acts. Complex acts suggest the existence of a motor plan.

2. Reflexes are patterns of relatively simple and stereotyped movements that are elicited by stimulation of sensory receptors; their amplitude is proportional to the intensity of the stimulation.

3. Many reflexes are controlled by closed-loop, negative feedback circuits. Some behaviors are so rapid, however, that they are controlled by open-loop systems; that is, the pattern is preset and does not respond to feedback.

4. The extraocular muscles are controlled by feedback that produces three different types of eye movements: saccades, physiological nystagmus, and pursuit movements.

5. Motor control systems are organized into a hierarchy that consists of the skeletal system and associated muscles, the spinal cord, the brain stem, and various parts of the brain, including the primary and nonprimary motor cortices, the cerebellum, and the basal ganglia.

6. Muscles around a joint work in pairs. Antagonists work in opposite ways; synergists work together. Muscle consists of thick and thin protein filaments that slide past each other to contract the muscle. Smooth muscles, such as the heart, are under involuntary control; striated muscles are under voluntary control.

7. Muscle contractions are regulated by neural impulses that travel over motor nerve fibers (axons from motoneurons) and reach muscle fibers at the neuromuscular junction.

8. The final common pathway for impulses to skeletal muscles consists of motoneurons, whose cell bodies in vertebrates are located in the ventral horn of the spinal cord and within the brain stem. The motoneurons receive impulses from a variety of sources, including sensory input from the dorsal spinal roots, other spinal cord neurons, and descending fibers from the brain.

9. Muscle spindles and Golgi tendon organs—sensory receptors in the muscles and tendons, respectively—transmit a wide range of information about muscle activities to the central nervous system. The sensitivity of the muscle spindle can be adjusted by efferent impulses that control the length of the muscle spindle. This adjustment allows flexible control of posture and movement.

10. Circuits within the spinal cord underlie the spinal reflexes, which can occur even when the cord is cut and connections to the brain are severed.

11. When a muscle is stretched, a reflex circuit often causes contraction, which works to restore the muscle to its original length; this response is called the stretch reflex. The stretch of the muscle is detected by muscle spindles.

12. The corticospinal tract is especially well developed in primates and is mainly involved in controlling fine movements of the extremities. Its fibers originate mainly in the primary motor cortex and adjacent regions, and they run directly to spinal motoneurons or to interneurons in the spinal cord. Nonprimary motor cortex helps control the sequence of movements.

13. Brain regions that modulate movement include the basal ganglia (caudate nucleus, putamen, and globus pallidus), some major brain stem nuclei (substantia nigra, thalamic nuclei, and red nucleus), and the cerebellum.

14. Movement disorders can result from impairment at any of several levels of the motor system: muscles, neuromuscular junctions, motoneurons, the spinal cord, brain stem, cerebral cortex, basal ganglia, or cerebellum. The characteristics of the movement disorders depend on and permit diagnosis of the locus of impairment.

Recommended Reading

Requin, J., and Stelmach, G. E. (Eds.). (1991). *Tutorials in motor neuroscience.* Dordrecht, Netherlands: Kluwer.

Rosenbaum, D. A. (1991). *Human motor control.* San Diego, CA: Academic Press.

Rothwell, J. (1994). *Control of human voluntary movement* (2nd ed.). London: Chapman and Hall.

Stein, P. S. G., Grillner, S., and Selverston, A. I. (1998). *Neurons, networks, and motor behavior.* Cambridge, MA: MIT Press.

The Regulation of Behavior

So far, we have reviewed the basic structure and function of the nervous system, the specialized organs that gather information about the environment, and the specialized motor systems that allow us to respond to that information. Now we come to a problem—given the information we have, which response should we make? The number of possible responses is, for all practical purposes, infinite. But natural selection favors some responses in one situation, other responses in others. From the point of view of natural selection, a food deprived animal should eat, an animal that's lost water should drink, an animal that is not adapted to function in darkness should sleep at night, and so on. When an animal consistently displays the same response, even in slightly inappropriate circumstances, we can infer that the animal is motivated to make that response. Of course the brain is pivotal in making the decision about which response to make. To some extent, we can find the different brain regions that are involved in deciding whether to reproduce (Chapter 12), eat, drink, seek shelter (Chapter 13), sleep (Chapter 14), be afraid, panic, or fight (Chapter 15). In each of these cases, we catalog the situations that usually elicit a particular response from members of a particular species, and ask which brain regions are required for the response to be elicited, which brain regions are activated by the situation, and how various responses are integrated. As we'll see, many brain regions are involved in each of these responses, which is a recurring theme in this book.

12

Sex: Evolutionary, Hormonal, and Neural Bases

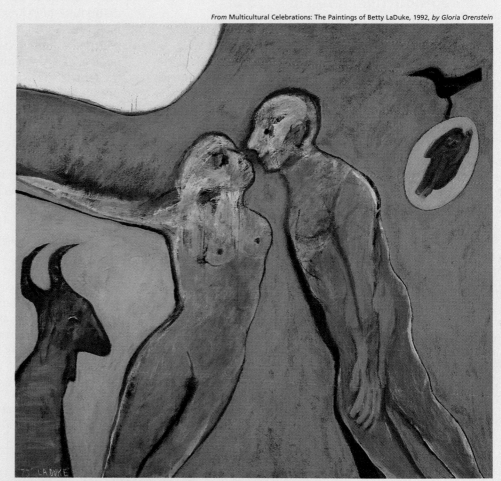

From Multicultural Celebrations: The Paintings of Betty LaDuke, 1992, by Gloria Orenstein

Betty LaDuke, *India: Inside the Taj,* 1975

Sexuality is such an important part of our lives that we take for granted some of its most basic properties—for example, that two and only two sexes are required for reproduction, that in most species males are somewhat larger and more aggressive than females, and that an adult human is, in some core sense, either a man or a woman. In this chapter we will learn that there are exceptions to each of these rules. We divide the chapter into three main sections: (1) First we'll review sexual behaviors, which includes the sex act itself, copulation. (2) Next, the bewildering variety of sexual behaviors across species (and within our own species) will lead us to consider why such a messy and confusing process as sexual reproduction evolved. We'll find that sexual reproduction eventually gave rise to two sexes, which can sometimes be remarkably divergent in structure and behavior. (3) The evolution of two different sexes will lead us to the final topic, sexual differentiation—the process by which an individual's body and brain develop in a male or female fashion.

Sexual Behavior

We wish we could explain exactly why and how humans and other animals engage in the "three Cs"—courting, copulating, and cohabiting—but very little practical knowledge of such matters exists, as James Thurber and E. B. White lamented in 1929 (Figure 12.1). You may feel that there has been little improvement in the years since. Two main barriers have blocked our understanding of sexual behavior: (1) a deep-seated reluctance within our culture to disseminate knowledge about sexual behavior and (2) the remarkable variety of sexual behaviors in existence.

Reproductive Behavior Can Be Divided into Four Stages

Sexual attraction is the first stage in bringing the male and female together (Figure 12.2). In many species an individual is attractive to others, and is itself attracted to others, only when its body is ready to reproduce. We can gauge how attractive a female is by observing how males respond to her—how rapidly they approach, how hard they work to gain access to her, and so on. The same measures show how attractive a male is to females. By manipulating the appearance of females, we can deduce which features males find attractive.

Such methods have demonstrated that in many species of apes and monkeys the male is attracted by the sight of the female's "sex skin," which swells under the influence of steroid hormones—estrogens. Most male mammals are also attracted by particular odors emitted by females of their species; in many cases such odors are also the result of the action of estrogens. Thus estrogens simultaneously instigate the release of eggs (ovulation) and attract males to fertilize them. In many species, estrogens also stimulate the production of vaginal lubricants to facilitate copulation. Of course, the female may find some of the males that approach her unattractive and refuse to mate with them. Despite a few descriptions of what may or may not be rape in nonhuman animals, for most species copulation is not possible without the female's active cooperation.

If the animals are mutually attracted, they may progress to the second stage of reproductive behavior: **appetitive behaviors** (behaviors that establish, maintain, or promote sexual interaction). A female mammal that engages in such behaviors is said to be **proceptive**: She may approach males, remain close to them, or show alternating approach and retreat behavior. In rats, the female may run away from the male with a distinctive hopping and darting gait, to which the male often responds by mounting the female. Male appetitive behaviors usually consist of staying near the female. In many mammals the male may sniff around the female's face and vagina. Male birds may engage in elaborate songs or nest-building behaviors.

If both animals display appetitive behaviors, they may progress to the third stage of reproduction: **copulation**, also known as coitus. In many vertebrates, including all mammals, copulation begins when the male puts his penis inside the female's vagina—a behavior referred to as **intromission**. Then the male ejaculates, rhythmically squirting a fluid mixture called semen inside the female. The semen contains reproductive cells called sperm for reproduction.

After one bout of copulation the animals will not mate again for a period of time, which is called the **refractory phase**. The refractory phase varies from minutes to months, depending on the species and circumstances. Many animals show a shorter refractory phase if they are provided with a new partner, a phenomenon known as the **Coolidge effect**.

12.1 Sex According to Thurber and White
In *Is Sex Necessary?* (1929), James Thurber and E. B. White explain, "It is customary to illustrate sexology chapters with a cross section of the human body. The authors have chosen to substitute in its place a chart of the North Atlantic, showing airplane routes. The authors realize that this will be of no help to the sex novice, but neither is a cross section of the human body." If you insist on a cross section, see Figure 12.7.

12.2 Stages of Reproductive Behavior

Interaction between male and female partners in sexual reproduction is extensive, progressing in four stages: sexual attraction, appetitive behavior, copulation, and postcopulatory behavior. The postcopulatory phase (pink background) includes a temporary decrease in the sexual attractiveness of the partner and inhibition of appetitive behavior. (After Beach, 1977.)

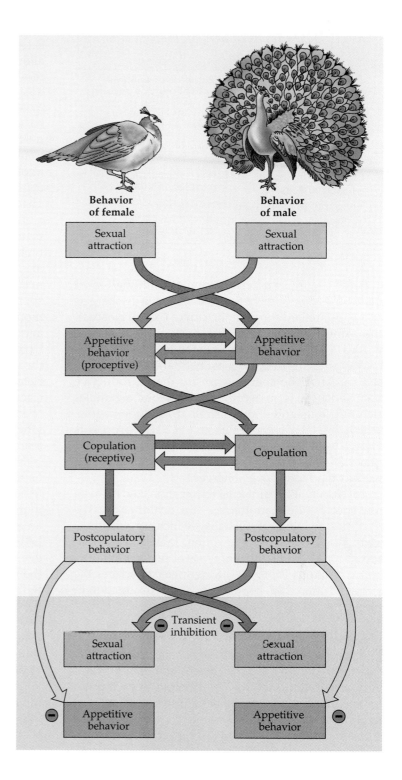

The female often appears to choose whether or not copulation will take place; when she is willing to copulate she is said to be **sexually receptive**, **in heat**, or **in estrus**. In some species, the female may show proceptive behaviors days before she will participate in copulation itself. In that case she is said to be proceptive but not (yet) receptive (see Figure 12.2). Usually females are receptive only during periods when mating is likely to result in reproduction. Because most animals are seasonal breeders (see Chapter 14), females thus are usually receptive only during the breeding season, which varies considerably from species to species. Many species, such as salmon, octopus, and cicadas, reproduce only once, during a single season at the end of life.

Finally, the fourth stage of reproductive behavior consists of **postcopulatory behaviors**. These behaviors are especially varied across species. In some mammals—dogs and southern grasshopper mice, for example—the male's penis swells so much after ejaculation that he can't remove it from the female for a while (10 to 15 minutes in dogs), and the animals are said to be in a **copulatory lock** (Dewsbury, 1972). (Despite wild stories you may have heard or read, humans do not experience copulatory lock, not even with Viagra.) Postcopulatory behaviors also include parental behaviors, which are discussed in Topic 12.4, Parental Care.

Copulation Brings Gametes Together for Reproduction

Sexually mature females are animals that can produce **gametes** called eggs, or **ova** (singular ovum); sexually mature males produce gametes called **sperm**. Successful reproduction requires a sperm cell to contact and fuse with an egg cell, a process known as **fertilization**. The resulting single cell is called a fertilized egg, or **zygote**, and will eventually divide and grow to make a new individual.

For many vertebrates, fertilization takes place outside the female's body, a process known as **external** **fertilization**. In most fishes and frogs, for example, males and females release their gametes in water, where fertilization takes place. In some fishes, such as guppies and swordtails, the male uses a modified fin to direct his sperm to swim into the female's body, where the sperm fertilize the female's eggs. Such **internal fertilization**, a feature of all mammals, birds, and reptiles, allows the zygotes to remain moist even in a desert, and the resulting offspring may gain nutrients from the mother.

TABLE 12.1	*Types of Sexual Reproduction in Animals*
Type	**Examples of animals that follow this pattern**
External fertilization (requires aquatic environment)	Many invertebrates, fishes, amphibians
Internal fertilization	
Oviparity (laying of fertilized eggs)	Insects, birds, many reptiles, monotremes
Viviparity (live birth)	Some fishes, reptiles, all mammals except monotremes

Birds use internal fertilization even though most male birds do not have a penis. Semen is discharged and eggs are laid through the **cloaca** (plural cloacae), the same passage through which birds eliminate wastes. The female squats low; the male mounts her back, pushes his cloaca against hers, and squirts in the semen. After the sperm swim up the reproductive tract and fertilize an ovum, the female bird assembles rich nutrients and a tough shell around the zygote, which she later extrudes as an egg. This process is known as **oviparity**. In live birth, or **viviparity**, the zygote develops extensively within the female until a well-formed individual emerges.

All mammals use internal fertilization, and all but a few species (the monotremes—the echidnas and the platypus of Australia—which are oviparous) give birth to live young. Table 12.1 summarizes the different types of sexual reproduction. Topic 12.1, Ringdoves, describes the stages of courtship, copulation, and reproduction in ringdoves.

 Special topic

Copulation in Rats Is a Brief Interlude

Like most other rodents, rats do not engage in lengthy courtship, nor do the partners tend to remain together after copulation. Rats are attracted to each other largely through odors. Females are spontaneous ovulators; that is, even when left alone they ovulate every 4 to 5 days. For a few hours during each cycle, the female seeks out a male and displays proceptive behaviors—hopping and darting, which we mentioned earlier, and ear wiggling. Both animals produce vocalizations at frequencies too high for humans to detect but audible to each other.

These behaviors prompt the male to mount the female from the rear, grasp her hind flanks with his forelegs, and rhythmically thrust his hips. If the female is receptive, she stands still and assumes a posture that allows intromission: She lifts her head and rump and moves her tail to one side. This posture is called **lordosis** (Figure 12.3). Once intromission is achieved, the male rat makes a single thrust, lasting half a second or so, and then springs back off the female. During the next 6 to 7 minutes the male and female will orchestrate seven to nine such intromissions; then, instead of a springing dismount, the male will raise the front half of his body up for a second or two while he ejaculates. Then he falls backward off the female.

The male almost immediately begins grooming his penis with his tongue and forepaws, while the female typically remains still for a few minutes before grooming her vagina. The male pays little attention to the female for the next 5 minutes or so until, often in response to the female's proceptive behaviors, he will mount for another round of multiple intromissions and another ejaculation. In other rodent species, intromission may be accompanied by more prolonged thrusting, or the penis may swell to form a copulatory lock. The northern pygmy mouse has only a single ejaculation during a mating session. In some rodent species a male and a female live together before and long after copulation; such animals are said to form **pair bonds**.

Hormones play an important role in rat mating behaviors. Testosterone increases the male's interest in females, causes him to mount them more rapidly and more often, and allows him to achieve ejaculation. If an adult male rat is **castrated** (has his testes removed), he will stop ejaculating within a few weeks and will eventually stop mounting receptive females. Although testosterone disappears from the bloodstream within a few hours after castration, whatever effects the hormone had on the nervous system take several days to dissipate. Treating a castrated male with testosterone eventually restores mating behavior; thus testosterone is an example of a steroid that has an **activational effect** on behavior.

Interestingly, although male rats differ considerably in the vigor with which they mate with a receptive female, blood levels of testosterone clearly are not responsible for these differences. Evidence of this effect

12.3 Copulation in Rats
The raised rump and deflected tail of the female (the lordosis posture) make intromission possible. (After Barnett, 1975.)

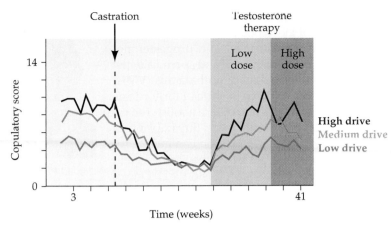

12.4 Androgens Permit Male Copulatory Behavior

Although androgens have an effect, hormone level does not completely determine the amount of sex behavior, even in rodents. After castration caused the sex activity of male guinea pigs to decrease, the same amount of testosterone was given to each animal, beginning at week 26. Each group returned to the level of sex activity it had exhibited before castration. Doubling the amount of hormone at week 36 did not increase the mating activity of any group. (After Grunt and Young, 1953.)

comes from experiments in which many male rats are classified on the basis of how often they mount females. Among scientists, such males (rats, we mean) are referred to as either "studs" or "duds." These groups show no significant differences in blood testosterone levels. Furthermore, when castrated males are given identical amounts of testosterone, the former studs remain studs and the duds are still duds. This effect was first demonstrated for male guinea pigs (Figure 12.4). In fact, a very small amount of testosterone—one-tenth the amount normally produced by the animals—is enough to maintain the mating behavior of stud rats. Thus, since all rats make more

testosterone than is required to maintain their copulatory behavior, something else appears to be responsible for individual differences in mating activity.

Adult female rats release eggs (**ovulate**) every 4 or 5 days. Estrogens secreted at the beginning of this **ovulatory cycle** facilitate the proceptive behavior of the female rat, and the subsequent production of progesterone increases proceptive behavior and permits lordosis (Figure 12.5). An adult female whose ovaries have been removed will show neither proceptive nor receptive behaviors, and neither estrogen nor progesterone treatment alone will restore them. However, 2 days of estrogen treatment followed by a single injection of progesterone will, about 6 hours later, make the female rat proceptive and receptive for a few hours. One reason the rat must receive estrogen before progesterone is that the estrogen causes the brain to make progesterone receptors. Without estrogen pretreatment, the brain cannot respond to the progesterone.

Female rats ovulate spontaneously, and males maintain high testosterone levels throughout the breeding season, whether a partner is present or not. The animals see very little of each other outside the 30 minutes or so taken up with copulation. However, the multiple intromissions before an ejaculation are not mere idle dawdling on the part of the male. If a male rat ejaculates the first time he enters the female (say, because a researcher arranged for him to enter another female several times first), the female which receives his sperm will not become pregnant. Only if the female receives enough vaginal stimulation from multiple intromissions will her brain later cause the release of prolactin at a crucial stage for maintaining pregnancy. In this instance, then, the behavior of one rat (the male) affects the hormonal secretions of its mate.

Neural Circuitry of the Brain Regulates Reproductive Behavior

Most of what we know about the neural circuitry underlying reproductive behaviors comes from animal models, especially rats. That literature indicates that the hypothalamus and steroid hormones play a central role in regulating copulatory behavior, and as

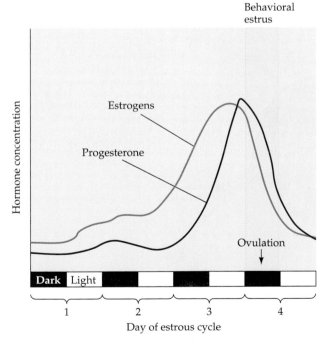

12.5 Rat Ovulatory Cycle

Changes in hormone levels indicate when the female rat will display lordosis. This behavioral receptivity, or estrus, occurs after the animal has been exposed first to estrogens, then to progesterone. In spontaneous ovulators such as rats, the cycle of hormone secretion will repeat unless eggs are fertilized. In that case, the embryos secrete hormones to interrupt the cycle and maintain pregnancy.

we'll see, there's reason to believe that this is true of humans as well.

Steroids Act on the Hypothalamus to Promote Female Receptivity

Recall that female rats display the lordosis response, indicating that they are sexually receptive, during only one night of their 4- to 5-day ovulatory cycle, and that we can induce this receptivity in female rodents by injecting them with estradiol for a few days, then injecting them with progesterone. Donald Pfaff (1997) of The Rockefeller University has exploited this steroid sensitivity of the lordosis response to map out the neural centers that mediate this behavior.

Steroid autoradiography indicated that the hypothalamus contains a center for estrogen- and progesterone-sensitive neurons, and specifically the **ventromedial hypothalamus (VMH)** was found to be crucial for lordosis because lesions there abolish the response. Furthermore, tiny implants of estradiol in the brain can induce receptivity, but only if they are placed in the VMH region (Lisk, 1962). One of the actions of estrogen treatment is to increase the size of the dendritic trees of VMH neurons within 48 hours (Meisel and Luttrell, 1990).

Donald Pfaff

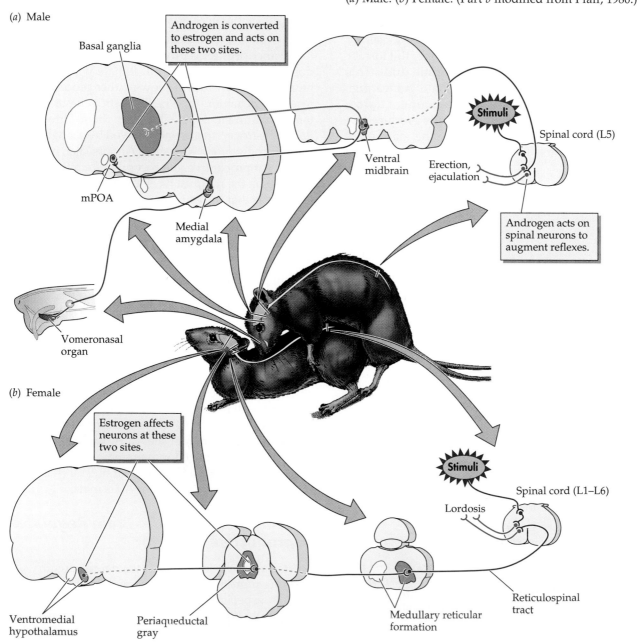

12.6 Neural Circuits for Reproduction in Rodents
(a) Male. (b) Female. (Part b modified from Pfaff, 1980.)

(a) Male

Basal ganglia

Androgen is converted to estrogen and acts on these two sites.

Stimuli

Spinal cord (L5)

Ventral midbrain

Erection, ejaculation

mPOA

Medial amygdala

Androgen acts on spinal neurons to augment reflexes.

Vomeronasal organ

(b) Female

Estrogen affects neurons at these two sites.

Stimuli

Spinal cord (L1–L6)

Lordosis

Reticulospinal tract

Ventromedial hypothalamus

Periaqueductal gray

Medullary reticular formation

The VMH sends axons to the gray region of the midbrain, where again lesions greatly diminish lordosis. The periaqueductal gray neurons project to the medullary reticular formation, which in turn projects to the spinal cord via the reticulospinal tract. In the spinal cord the sensory information provided by the mounting male evokes the motor response of lordosis. Thus the role of the VMH is to monitor steroid hormone concentrations and, at the right time in the ovulatory cycle, activate a multisynaptic pathway that induces the spinal cord to show a lordosis response that is otherwise absent (Pfaff 1997). Figure 12.6*a*, based on Pfaff's many studies, schematically represents this neural pathway and the steroid-responsive components.

Androgens Activate a Neural System for Male Reproductive Behavior

Steroid hormones also activate male copulatory behavior in rodents, and again the sites of steroid action provided important clues revealing the neural circuitry involved. The hypothalamic **medial preoptic area** (**mPOA**) is chock-full of steroid-sensitive neurons, and lesions of the mPOA abolish male copulatory behavior in a wide variety of vertebrate species (Meisel and Sachs, 1994). Furthermore, mating can be reinstated in castrated males by small implants of androgen in the mPOA but not in other brain regions. A small nucleus within the mPOA is larger in male rats than in females, as we'll see later in this chapter. Neurons in the mPOA send their axons to the ventral midbrain via the medial forebrain bundle. From the ventral midbrain, information goes to the basal ganglia (presumably to coordinate mounting behaviors) and, through a diffuse multisynaptic pathway, to the spinal cord. The spinal cord, in turn, mediates the various reflexes of intromission and ejaculation.

Surprisingly, when testosterone activates the mPOA in an adult male rat, it does so after being converted to estrogen, which then acts on estrogen receptors. On the other hand, the activation of androgen receptors in the periphery and spinal cord is what induces the intromission and ejaculation reflexes.

We can gather information about male copulatory neural systems also by investigating a sensory system that activates male arousal in rodents—the vomeronasal system. The **vomeronasal organ** (see Chapter 9) of the male detects pheromones (see Chapter 5) from receptive females that arouse the male, as evidenced by penile erections. The vomeronasal information reaches the medial amygdala, where lesions will abolish penile erections in response to receptive females (Kondo et al., 1997). The medial amygdala in turn sends axons to the mPOA. So the mPOA appears to integrate sensory information, such as pheromones and, when conditions are correct, to coordinate the motor patterns of copulation. Figure 12.6*b* summarizes the neural circuitry for male rat copulatory behavior.

We will see later that androgens, acting perhaps on the hypothalamus and/or the medial amygdala, activate sexual arousal in humans as well.

Human Reproduction Brings Gametes Together

In women, the ovaries release an egg every 28 days or so. The released egg enters the adjacent **fallopian tube**, the walls of which have specialized hairs, or cilia, that wave back and forth, moving the egg into the **uterus** (Figure 12.7*a*). The walls of the uterus are specialized to allow implantation of a developing embryo and support the **placenta**, which will nourish the embryo and fetus. If the egg is to result in a baby, it must be fertilized in the fallopian tube; thus, copulation must take place during a particular phase of the cycle or the zygote will not have enough time to divide to form an embryo that is sufficiently developed to implant into the walls of the uterus. If not implanted, the embryo will drift into the connecting vagina and outside the body.

(*a*) Female

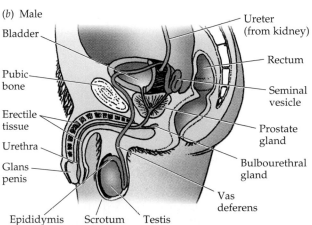

(*b*) Male

12.7 Adult Human Reproductive Anatomy
(*a*) Female. (*b*) Male. For an interesting chart of the North Atlantic, see Figure 12.1.

Surrounding the opening of the human vagina are folds of skin known as **labia** (singular labium), and rostral to the vaginal opening is a mound of tissue called the **clitoris** (plural clitorides). This region surrounding the vaginal opening is sometimes called the **vulva** (plural vulvae). In all mammals the walls of the uterus thicken before ovulation to allow implantation of a newly formed embryo. In some mammals, including humans and dogs, so many cells lining the walls of the uterus are shed between ovulations that a visible flow of cells and blood exits through the vagina—a process known as **menstruation**. In most mammals, however, many fewer cells are shed and there is no visible flow. Thus, although all vertebrate species have ovulatory cycles (the periodic release of eggs), only a few mammalian species display menstrual cycles.

In males, the sperm are produced in the **testis** (plural testes) and mature in the adjacent, crescent-shaped **epididymis** (plural epididymides) (Figure 12.7b). Attached to the epididymis is a small tube called the **vas deferens** (plural vasa deferentia). Muscles lining the vas deferens contract to propel sperm to the **urethra**, a tube that travels through the penis to reach the outside. (The urethra also connects to the bladder and conducts urine outside the body.) At the point at which the vasa deferentia from the left and right testes join with the urethra, several glands are attached: The **seminal vesicles** produce and store a cloudy, viscous fluid; the **prostate**, which encircles the urethra at this point, produces a clear, astringent fluid; and other glands contribute other fluids. During copulation, sperm are expelled from the epididymis via the vas deferens and mixed with these various fluids in the urethra; the mixture (semen) is expelled from the penis during ejaculation.

The Hallmark of Human Sexual Behavior Is Diversity

For as long as humans have written, they have written about sex. But little scientific information was available about human sexual behavior until the 1940s, when biology professor Alfred Kinsey began to ask friends and colleagues about their sexual histories. Kinsey constructed a standardized set of questions and procedures to obtain information for representative samples of the U.S. population categorized by sex, age, religion, and education. Eventually he and his collaborators were able to publish extensive surveys (based on tens of thousands of respondents) of the sexual behavior of American males (Kinsey et al., 1948) and females (Kinsey et al., 1953). Controversial in their time, these surveys indicated that nearly all men masturbated, that college-educated people were more likely to engage in oral sex than were noncollege-educated people, that many people had at one time or other engaged in homosexual behaviors, and that as much as 10% of the population preferred homosexual sex. Although recently it has been suggest-

ed that the last figure is an overestimate, these surveys revealed much about human sexual behavior.

A further step is to make behavioral and physiological observations of people engaged in sexual intercourse or masturbation, but such studies are perilous for a scientist: John B. Watson, the founder of behaviorism, attempted such studies in the early 1920s, and the ensuing scandal cost him his professorship. After Kinsey's surveys were published, however, physician William Masters and psychologist Virginia Johnson began a large, well-known project of this kind (1965, 1966, 1970; Masters et al., 1994) that greatly increased our knowledge about the physiological responses in various parts of the body during intercourse, their time courses, and their relations to what is experienced.

Among most mammalian species, including nonhuman primates, the male mounts the female from the rear, but among humans, face-to-face postures are most common. A great variety of coital postures have been described, and many couples vary their postures from session to session or even within a session. This variety of reproductive behaviors, both within and between individuals, is a characteristic that differentiates humans from all other species.

Masters and Johnson (1966) summarized the typical response patterns of men and women as consisting of four phases: increasing excitement, plateau, **orgasm** (the extremely pleasurable sensations experienced by most men during ejaculation and by most women during copulation), and resolution (Figure 12.8). In spite of the basic similarity, there are some typical differences between male and female responses.

One important difference is the greater variety of commonly observed sequences in women. Whereas men have only one basic pattern, women have three typical patterns (see Figure 12.8b). The second main difference between the sexes is that most men, but not women, have an absolute refractory phase following orgasm (see Figure 12.8a). That is, most men cannot achieve full erection and another orgasm until some time has elapsed, the length of time varying from minutes to hours, depending on individual differences and other factors. Many women, on the other hand, can have multiple orgasms in rapid succession.

Male sexual response pattern.   In males, sexual excitement mounts in response to stimulation, which may be mental or physical or both, and is accompanied by the penis being engorged with blood, making it erect. The rate of rise of excitement varies with many factors, and what may enhance excitement in some men may reduce excitement in others. If stimulation continues, the level of excitement reaches a high plateau, which many people seek to extend as long as possible. Eventually a reflexive orgasmic response is triggered and accompanied by ejaculation. Then excitement gradually dissipates and the penis loses its erection during the resolution phase. Usually the excitement phase and the

(a) Male

(b) Female

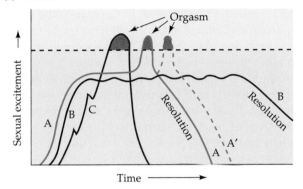

12.8   Human Sexual Response Cycles

These diagrams are schematic and do not represent a particular physiological measure, although heart rate varies in roughly this manner. The patterns vary considerably from one individual to another. (*a*) The typical male pattern, which includes an absolute refractory phase after orgasm. (*b*) Three patterns often observed in women. (After Masters and Johnson, 1966.)

resolution phase are the longest parts of the cycle. Typically the plateau phase lasts only a few minutes, the orgasm less than a minute.

Female sexual response patterns.   The most common pattern in women (pattern A in Figure 12.8*b*) is similar to the male pattern. During the excitement phase the clitoris, like the penis, swells by congestion of blood vessels. Furthermore, vaginal secretion of lubricating fluids is increased, and the muscles surrounding the vagina relax. As in males, orgasm is marked by rhythmic muscular contractions—in women, of the muscles surrounding the vagina. Stimulation of the clitoris facilitates orgasm in most women. Women and men differ in their temporal patterns of response. Women are usually somewhat slower than men to reach orgasm during intercourse and have no absolute refractory phase.

Two other patterns are common in women. In pattern B, the high level of excitement of the plateau phase does not quite trigger an orgasmic release; after a prolonged plateau period, sexual excitement grad-

ually dissipates. In pattern C, the woman experiences a rapid and explosive arrival at orgasm, with only brief plateau and resolution phases. Orgasm in this pattern tends to be both longer and more intense than in pattern A.

Multiple factors influence sexual behavior.   The similarities and differences in sexual responses exemplify the generalization of Chapter 1 that in some ways each person is like all other people, in some ways like some other people, and in some ways like no other person. The existence of differences among groups and individuals does not contradict or lessen the value of research into biological determinants of such behavior. Some behavioral differences are related to differences in genetic makeup; some may be related to differences in hormone levels. But some are certainly due to differences in experience and learning; sexual therapy, for example, usually consists of helping the person relax, recognize the sensations associated with coitus, and learn the behaviors that produce the desired effects in both partners (see Topic 12.2, Sexual Complaints). Masturbation during adolescence, rather than being harmful as suggested in previous times, may help avoid sexual problems in adulthood. As in other behaviors, practice, practice, practice helps. Sexual behavior may also aid overall health, since epidemiological studies indicate that men who have frequent sex tend to live longer than men who do not (Davey-Smith et al., 1997).

Some Diseases Can Be Transmitted through Sexual Behavior

We feel compelled to include in any discussion of human sexuality a reminder that many serious diseases, including syphilis and gonorrhea, can be communicated through sexual intercourse. The **human immunodeficiency virus**, or **HIV**, can be passed through genital, anal, or oral sex and causes **acquired immune deficiency syndrome** (**AIDS**), an insidious, fatal disease. Proper use of **condoms** (rubber sheaths fitted over the penis to trap semen) during sexual intercourse can prevent the transmission of HIV. Condoms can also be effective birth control devices, preventing unwanted pregnancies that lead to serious social and moral problems.

Hormones Play Only a Permissive Role in Human Sexual Behavior

Recall that in male rodents a little bit of testosterone must be in circulation for the male to initiate mating, but additional testosterone has no effect on the vigor of mating. Consequently, there is no correlation between the amount of androgens produced by an individual and his tendency to copulate. The same relations seem to hold for human males. Some boys fail to undergo puberty because an inability to release gonadotropins prevents the testes from being stimulated to make testosterone. To develop normally, these males must be treated with synthetic androgens.

These males, as well as men who have lost their testes as the result of cancer or accidents, have made possible double-blind tests (where neither subjects nor investigator know which subjects are receiving the drug and which are receiving a placebo) of whether androgens affect human copulatory behavior. These studies indicate that androgens indeed stimulate sexual activity in men (J. M. Davidson et al., 1979). As with testosterone in rats, blood levels below normal were sufficient for this effect, and no one has ever found a correlation between systemic androgen levels and sexual activity among men who have some level of androgens. Low androgen levels sometimes cause infertility in men and may be due to reduced release of gonadotropin-releasing hormone or of gonadotropins, or reduced sensitivity of the testes to gonadotropins. In men over 60 years old, testosterone levels gradually decline as gonadotropin levels rise, indicating that the decline is in gonadal function. The anti-impotence drug sildenafil (Viagra) has no effect on androgens, but acts directly on tissue in the penis to promote erection by inhibiting a second-messenger enzyme (phosphodiesterase-5) (Boolell et al., 1996).

You might be surprised to learn that androgens may also activate sexual interest in women. Some women report reduced interest in sex after menopause. There are many possible reasons for such a change, including several hormonal changes. As we mentioned earlier, estrogens increase a woman's ability to produce lubricants, and indeed estrogen treatment of menopausal women aids lubrication, but it does not change their interest in sex. On the other hand, a very low regimen of androgens is sometimes reported to revive menopausal women's interest in sexual relations.

Competing hypotheses

There have been several attempts to determine whether women's interest in or participation in sexual behavior varies with the menstrual cycle. Some researchers have found a slight increase in sexual behavior around the time of ovulation, but the effect is small, and several studies have failed to see any significant change in interest in sex across the menstrual cycle.

Pheromones Both Prime and Activate Reproductive Behaviors

When steroid hormones from the gonads affect the brain to activate mating behavior, the activation is not absolute; individuals are simply more likely to engage in mating behaviors when gonadal steroid levels are adequate. This activation can be thought of as communication between the gonad and the brain: By producing steroids to make gametes, the gonads also inform the brain that the body is ready to mate. This signaling takes place inside the individual, but hormones can also provide information between animals.

For example, during ovulation, female goldfish produce a hormone called F prostaglandin. Some F prostaglandin escapes the female's body and passes through the water to a male. The F prostaglandin is detected by the male and stimulates his mating behavior (Sorensen and Goetz, 1993). The most likely scenario for the evolution of this relationship is that long ago females released F prostaglandin only as a by-product of ovulation, but because the presence of the hormone conveyed important information about the female's condition, natural selection favored males who detected the hormone and began courting in response to the signal.

As we learned in Chapter 5, a chemical that is released from one individual and affects another individual is called a **pheromone**. In the case of the goldfish, a single chemical acts both as a hormone (in the female) and as a pheromone. This pheromone quickly activates another individual's behavior, but other pheromones act more gradually. In these slower cases the pheromone is said to **prime** the potential mate for copulation. Even very simple unicellular organisms, such as yeasts, prepare each other for mating by releasing and detecting pheromones (S. Fields, 1990).

Because most mammals do not live in an aquatic environment, pheromones must either pass through the air (so-called volatile chemicals) or must be passed by contact between individuals. The olfactory system may detect some such signals, but an accessory sensory system—the vomeronasal system—has developed specifically to detect pheromones (see Chapter 9). The **vomeronasal organ** consists of specialized receptor cells near but separate from the olfactory epithelium. These sensory cells detect pheromones and send electrical signals to the accessory olfactory bulb in the brain.

Two well-characterized pheromonal systems in mammals are the activation of aggression in mice and the blocking of pregnancy in several rodent species. Male mice placed in a cage together will often fight; pheromones in the urine of one mouse determine whether the other mouse will attack. If one of the mice is a female or a male that has been castrated, the normal male mouse will not attack. If the castrated male is smeared with urine from an intact male (or from a female who has been injected with androgens), however, other males will attack him. Thus, circulating androgens appear to cause chemical(s) to be released in the urine (Novikov, 1993), and other male mice can detect this signal. Male mice attack only mice that produce these pheromones, because only these mice are rivals for mating with females.

Pheromones in the urine of male mice can accelerate puberty in young females (Drickamer, 1992; M. A. Price and Vandenbergh, 1992) and can halt pregnancy in mature females (Brennan et al., 1990). Female mice can even identify an individual male by the particular mix of pheromones in his urine. When prairie voles mate, the female is exposed to pheromones from her mate's mouth and urine. If she is then isolated and has urine from that male or any other male applied to her snout, pregnancy will be blocked; the fetuses are resorbed by the female and she is soon ready to mate again. Yet if the female remains with the original male from copulation on, pregnancy continues, apparently because the female is careful not to apply her mate's urine to her vomeronasal organ (Smale et al., 1990). The female not only distinguishes males by their pheromones, but remembers which male mated with her and avoids using his urine to interrupt pregnancy. Resorption of the young in the presence of a new male may be an attempt to make the best of a bad situation: If her original mate is gone, she may be better off beginning a new litter with a different male.

Do Pheromones Synchronize Menstrual Cycles in Women?

Martha McClintock (1971) reported that women residing together in a college dormitory were more likely to have their menstrual cycles in synchrony than would be expected by chance; that is, women who spend more time with each other are more likely to menstruate at the same time. McClintock hypothesized that pheromones passing between the women serve as a signal of the ovulatory cycle, enabling synchronization.

It has been difficult to prove that women show menstrual synchrony, but most studies confirm this idea (Weller and Weller, 1993). Whether the synchronization relies on social signals or pheromonal signals between the women has been even more difficult to determine. Perhaps the most compelling evidence that pheromones play some such role is that the menstrual cycles in women who have extracts of sweat from other women applied to their upper lip are accelerated or delayed to synchronize with the cycles of the women from whom the sweat was extracted (Stern and McClintock, 1998).

Competing hypotheses

Why Are There Two Sexes?

Having talked about sex and some of its many complications, we may wonder how such an outlandish system ever got started. In fact, many animals come in two sexes. Author William Tenn (1968) imagined an exotic animal species that has seven different sexes. The sexes have wildly divergent bodies and behavior, allowing each to occupy a particular ecological niche, including both predator and prey. One problem with such an arrangement is reproduction: How do members of each of the seven sexes get together for mating when some are predators, some prey? One of the seven sexes is highly adapted for the tricky diplomacy of arranging suitable orgies. In real life, no creatures have more than two sexes, so perhaps even natural se-

lection cannot solve diplomatic problems involving more than two parties. As we'll see next, however, species with only one sex reproduce perfectly well. Why should any species bother with two?

Sexual Reproduction Helps Combine Beneficial Mutations

If in a given population of animals one individual has a very rare, *beneficial* mutation, the mutation can be spread to other individuals in only two ways. One way is for that individual to make clones of itself, to give birth to individuals that have only its genes, including the mutated one. In unicellular organisms this process is known as **fission**, the simple splitting of one individual cell into two. In multicellular animals this process is known as **parthenogenesis** (from the Greek *parthenos*, "virgin," and *genos*, "birth"; the Parthenon was a temple to the virgin goddess Athena). If the mutation is especially useful, future generations will consist mostly of this individual's progeny. Eventually other beneficial mutations may arise. Thus it is possible for a species to evolve without sexual reproduction.

But consider the other method of spreading the new gene—sexual reproduction. In this process the original holder of a helpful new gene produces offspring that have both the new gene and genes from other individuals. Some of those other genes may also be beneficial. By reproducing sexually, many beneficial genes, each arising from different individuals, can come together in later individuals. This mixing of beneficial genes certainly generates biological diversity. But evolutionary theorists still debate about why any particular individual, if capable of either parthenogenesis or sexual reproduction, would benefit by producing offspring that carry only half of its genes.

Some animals can reproduce by either method. Aphids, the small green insects that probably infest your garden every year, reproduce by parthenogenesis when there is ample food and favorable conditions for growth and unchecked reproduction. When conditions worsen, though, the aphids begin sexually reproducing, effectively swapping genes to produce offspring that begin migrating away, looking for a more hospitable environment. Perhaps the advantage of reproducing sexually is that, despite cutting in half your gene contribution to the next generation, you enhance the chance of at least some offspring surviving by producing new combinations of genes that might better survive the new conditions.

Nevertheless, parthenogenesis has been documented to occur on rare occasions in some vertebrate species, such as chickens and turkeys, and there are several species of whiptail lizards in the southwestern United States in which all individuals are females that reproduce exclusively via parthenogenesis (Figure 12.9a) (Crews, 1994). Aquarium fanciers know a species of tropical fish, the Amazon molly (Figure

(a)

(b)

(c)

12.9 Are Males Necessary?
Whiptail lizards (*a*) and Amazon mollies (*b*) are two of the rare vertebrate species that reproduce by parthenogenesis. All individuals are females who produce daughters with only the mother's genes. Nevertheless, these animals exhibit mock mating behaviors (such as those displayed by these lizards) that greatly resemble the mating behaviors of related species that reproduce sexually. (*c*) In the cichlid fish *Haplochromis burtoni,* the presence of large, brightly colored males (*bottom*) inhibits the development of other males, which remain small and dull colored (*top*). (Part *a* courtesy of David Crews; *b* courtesy of Michael Ryan; *c* courtesy of Russell Fernald.)

12.9*b*), that consists solely of females reproducing by parthenogenesis. Apparently, then, nothing inherent in the vertebrate body requires sexual reproduction, but this method of reproduction among vertebrates is so pervasive that it must convey some advantage.

But even sexual reproduction does not require that animals come in two different sexes. In many sexually reproducing species, each individual produces both sperm and eggs, and sex consists of donating sperm to a partner while accepting sperm in return. Individuals that can reproduce as either males or females are called **hermaphrodites** (from *Hermes* and *Aphrodite,* the Greek gods who exemplified masculinity and femininity, respectively). Although hermaphrodites, such as the sea slug *Aplysia,* are common among the invertebrates, very few vertebrates (and all of them are fishes) are true hermaphrodites. Early in the evolution of our prevertebrate ancestors, the male and female roles became so divergent that the sexes eventually split—some individuals reproducing exclusively via sperm, while others produced only eggs.

In many species of fish, individuals may spend some parts of their life behaving and reproducing as females and other parts of their life reproducing in a male fashion. Although these individuals never produce both sperm and eggs *at the same time,* they may be regarded as "serial" hermaphrodites. In some cases the switch in sex has obvious reproductive advantages:

Competing hypotheses

Most such fish reproduce as females when young and switch to the more aggressive, territorial behavior needed to reproduce as males only after they grow large enough to compete with others (Francis, 1992). In other fishes, social stimuli may drive the sexual switch.

For example, if you remove all the males from a tank of black molly fish (related to but different from Amazon mollies), one of the females, usually the largest, will transform into a male and successfully reproduce as that sex.

In a process that is probably related to this transformation, the African cichlid *Haplochromis burtoni* (Figure 12.9*c*), has two kinds of males. Older, larger males defend a feeding territory and mate with the females there. As long as such a male is present, younger males remain small, inconspicuously colored and sexually inactive. But if the older male is removed, the small males become aggressive and one of them eventually transforms into a larger, gaudily colored male that mates with the harem. The male that undergoes this change is usually the largest, and the change is accompanied by reduced serotonin levels in the brain (Winberg et al., 1997) and increased release of gonadotropin-releasing hormone (Fernald, 1995), driving the testes to increase steroid production. Since any male is capable of this change (as can be shown when one removes all larger males) but only one male at a time completes the transformation, the social interactions between the males must accelerate the change in one and inhibit the change in the others.

Neural plasticity

Table 12.2 reviews the various reproductive strategies.

Males and Females Often Adopt Different Reproductive Strategies

When our ancestors began reproducing through separate male and female individuals, the two sexes came to diverge in form and behavior (Figure 12.10). Today many species are **sexually dimorphic**, the term Darwin

TABLE 12.2 *Reproductive Strategies of Animals*

Type of reproduction	Strategy	Examples of animals that use the strategy
Asexual	Fission	Unicellular animals
	Parthenogenesis (virgin birth)	
	Obligatory	Amazon mollies, some whiptail lizards
	Occasional	Aphids
Sexual	Hermaphroditism (each individual produces sperm and eggs)	
	Simultaneous	Many invertebrates (e.g., *Aplysia*)
	Serial	Some fishes
	Gonochorism (separate sexes; each individual produces either sperm or eggs)	
	Sexually monomorphic	Many birds (e.g., seagulls, ringdoves)
	Sexually dimorphic	Most mammals

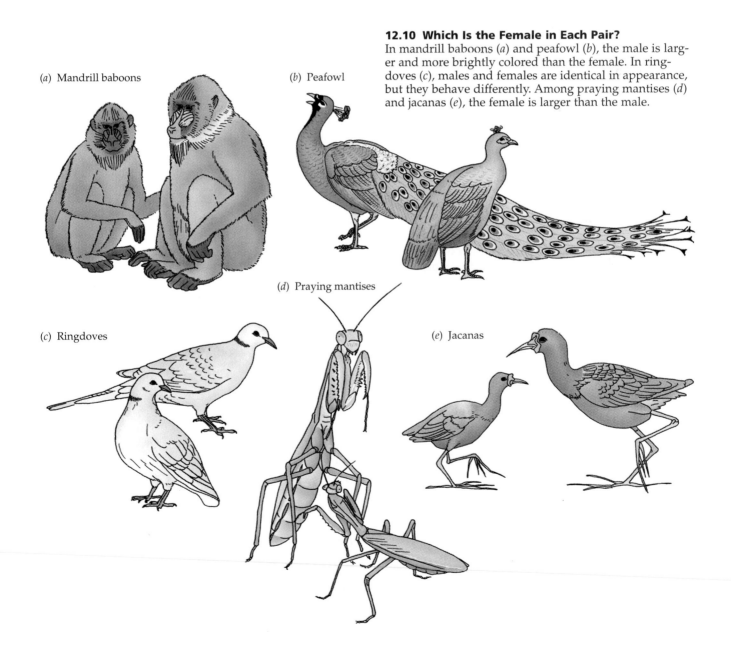

12.10 Which Is the Female in Each Pair?
In mandrill baboons (*a*) and peafowl (*b*), the male is larger and more brightly colored than the female. In ringdoves (*c*), males and females are identical in appearance, but they behave differently. Among praying mantises (*d*) and jacanas (*e*), the female is larger than the male.

(*a*) Mandrill baboons

(*b*) Peafowl

(*c*) Ringdoves

(*d*) Praying mantises

(*e*) Jacanas

12.11 Male Gametes Are Small and Cheap, Female Gametes Large and Expensive

Sperm cluster around an ovum, magnified about 1,920 times. Note that sperm are much smaller than ova, and are therefore easier to produce.

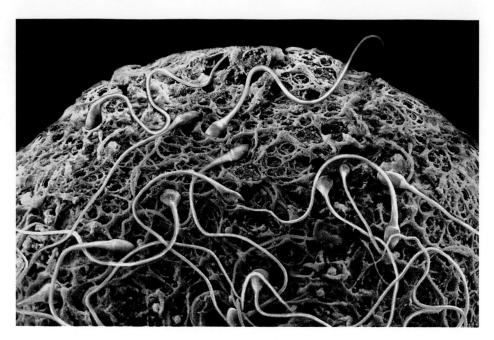

used to describe species in which males and females have very different bodies. Species in which the sexes look very similar are referred to as sexually monomorphic, despite the fact that they are different internally—for example, in the production of eggs or sperm.

The most obvious sexual dimorphism is the larger body size of males in many vertebrate species (see Figure 12.10*a* and *b*). Later in this chapter we will learn that the nervous systems of rats, humans, and other vertebrates also display sexual dimorphism. One example of sexual dimorphism that appears to have had profound effects on vertebrate evolution is the difference in the size of male gametes (sperm) and female gametes (ova).

Male gametes are small and cheap; female gametes are large and expensive. Figure 12.11 demonstrates the difference in size between male and female gametes—a well-known fact—but the difference in cost is less familiar. Every animal must gain scarce resources to live, including nutrients to support growth. Unless individuals budget their use of nutrients and energy wisely, they cannot succeed at reproduction. An individual specialized for producing sperm can produce many millions of gametes for the same cost, in terms of nutrients and energy, as that of a single egg.

Because of the low cost of producing sperm, a single male individual can gather enough energy and nutrients to produce sufficient sperm to inseminate millions of females, potentially providing the entire next generation. Females, on the other hand, must be more selective in order to reproduce successfully. Females that carefully nurture their costly eggs (in whatever manner is appropriate for that species) reproduce more often than less cautious females and come to predominate in future generations. One of the most important ways that females of any species can nurture their egg investments is to choose a mate carefully. Males that carry many beneficial genes are more likely to provide the female's offspring with favorable genes. Therefore, females that discover and mate with such males should come to predominate in future

generations, while females that mate indiscriminately will have fewer descendants.

The difficulty for a female, of course, is how to determine whether a potential mate has beneficial genes. Until recently, she could not count on training in molecular biology. Instead, the female must closely observe the appearance and behavior of the male. A vigorous, healthy male must be doing something right, and in general, an unhealthy looking male is more likely (although by no means certain) to carry harmful genes. On the other hand, inseminating a female is rarely dangerous to a male (except for species such as black widows and preying mantises, in which the female kills the male after mating, and with respect to sexually transmitted diseases). Even if the offspring do not survive, ample sperm will be left for the next female.

From this perspective, **courtship** is a period during which the female indirectly assesses the genetic makeup of a male to judge his suitability as a mate. For mammalian females, which carry their young in utero for a prolonged period and then provide milk for an additional time, the investment in each fertilized egg is tremendous, and therefore the pressure to select a good mate is intense. In most vertebrates, nearly all the females who reach reproductive age manage to mate, but only a minority of the males who reach reproductive age succeed in mating. Some interesting exceptions to this pattern are described in the next section.

Mating Systems Can Be Classified into Four Basic Types

The mating strategies of males and females across species can be classified into four different mating systems: promiscuity, polygyny, polyandry, and monogamy. These different systems seem to be related to species differences in the investment of males and females in their offspring.

1. *Promiscuity.* Recall that among mammals, most females are very selective in mating and most males never mate. Thus, a few males are doing most of the mating, and since the number of males and females is roughly equal, these males must be mating with more than one female. But most female mammals also mate with more than one male. Such a mating system, in which animals mate with several partners and do not establish long-lasting associations, is called **promiscuity**.

2. *Polygyny.* With some animals, such as elephant seals and gorillas, a long-lasting association between mates develops—one male mating with a group of females (a harem). Each female mates with only one male, but that male mates with several females. This system is called **polygyny** (from the Greek *polys*, "many," and *gyne*, "woman").

3. *Polyandry.* Much more rare than polygyny are cases of **polyandry** ("many husbands"; the Greek *aner* means "man"), in which each female of the species mates with several males, but each male mates with only one female. The jacana (see Figure 12.10*e*) is an example of a polyandrous species; in this species the females compete for mates. The females are larger and more colorful than the males, and they defend the nest site from other females. Once the female jacana lays the eggs, she departs, leaving the male to incubate the eggs and raise the young. The term **polygamy** ("many spouses"; the

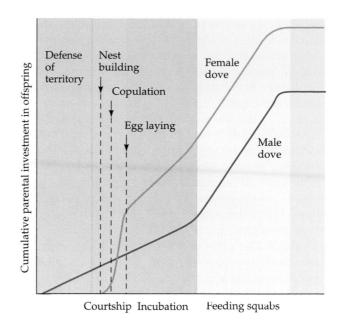

12.13 Parental Investment in Offspring
Hypothetical curves of the cumulative investment of a female and a male ringdove in their offspring throughout the reproductive cycle. Both parents incubate eggs and feed hatchlings. (Adapted from Erickson, 1978, and Trivers, 1985.)

Greek *gamos* means "marriage") is sometimes used to refer to polygyny and polyandry collectively. (Bigamy means "having two spouses.")

4. *Monogamy.* **Monogamy** ("one spouse") is the mating system characterized by one male and one female forming a breeding pair and mating exclusively (or almost exclusively) with one another. Monogamy is far more common among birds than among mammals (Figure 12.12). It has been suggested that because birds have a high metabolic rate and their young tend to be very immature at hatching, a single parent could not provide enough food for the chicks to survive (Figure 12.13). In that case, males that did not care for eggs and chicks would make little or no contribution to the next generation; thus, the development of monogamy would be expected.

Different human cultures have adopted each of these mating systems except promiscuity (see Topic 12.3, Human Mating Patterns). **Special topic**

Sexual Selection Accentuates Differences between the Sexes

As we learned in Chapter 6, Charles Darwin was the first to recognize that competition between males and the tendency of females to be very selective in mating affect the course of natural selection. He coined the term **sexual selection** to refer to the selective pressures

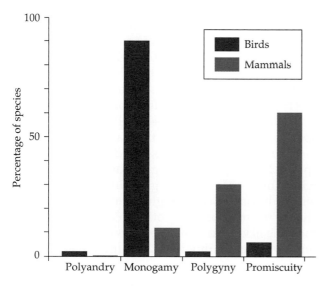

12.12 Mating Systems in Mammals and Birds
These estimates of mating-system types show that birds are far more likely than mammals to be monogamous. (Estimates for birds are based on data from Lack, 1968; estimates for mammals from Daly and Wilson, 1978. Both should be regarded as only rough estimates.)

that each sex exerts on the other. Darwin regarded sexual selection as a special type of natural selection and used the concept to explain certain features that were not easy to explain on the basis of natural selection alone. For example, why do male lions have manes, male birds of paradise display elaborate tail feathers, and male moose sport enormous antlers? These features do not seem to help the animal gather food, elude predators, or find shelter. Indeed, in many cases they seem to hinder those functions.

The only advantage Darwin could imagine these features might confer on animals was in procuring mates. Why? Because members of the other sex display a preference for mates with those features. Darwin also realized that sexual selection, by exerting *different* selective pressures on males and females, would impel the two sexes to diverge more and more in their appearance. Thus, sexual reproduction provides the pressure to select mates with advantageous genes. In some insect species the sexes are so dimorphic that zoologists originally classified them as different species. Of course, there is a limit to the influence of sexual selection, because other selective pressures also apply. A male who is overly ornamented, for example, may be unable to find food or evade predators (Figure 12.14), activities that are crucial for survival.

In sexual selection, individuals who demand that potential partners display certain characteristics or perform certain behaviors before mating benefit by passing genes that favor such behaviors on to their offspring. Once a particular species begins showing such partiality—for manes on male lions, elaborate

tails on birds, balding in men, and so on—the prejudice tends to be self-perpetuating. For example, once a population of females comes to favor mating with maned lions, a female who mates with a male without a mane leaves her offspring (especially her sons) at a distinct disadvantage. Natural selection thus favors the maintenance of such mating preferences. There is considerable debate about the extent to which sexual selection has shaped human reproduction (Box 12.1).

One interesting way in which females of several species enforce these demands is in the control of ovulation (the physical release of an egg from the ovary so that it can be fertilized). In frogs, for example, exposure to courting males facilitates ovulation in the female; the more such behavior the males display, the more eggs are released and made available for fertilization. Rats provide another example, as we saw earlier. In other species, courtship and/or copulation is *required* for ovulation. In lions, only very vigorous copulation over several days will induce the female to ovulate. The reproductive physiology of lionesses enforces strict evolutionary pressure on male behavior.

In both the parthenogenetic whiptail lizards and the Amazon mollies that we discussed earlier, closely related species reproduce sexually, and in these sexual species courtship and mating behaviors facilitate ovulation. Some remnant of this courtship-facilitated ovulation must remain in the parthenogenetic females, because they too will release more eggs if they are courted and go through mating behavior. But whom do you mate with when there are only females of your species? With whiptail lizards, females take turns mating with one another. A given female may play the role of a male one moment—wrapping her body around the other female, pressing their cloacae together, biting her neck, and so on—and play the role of a female later (see Figure 12.9a). Two females in a cage alone will literally take turns. Such mock mating increases the number of eggs released and laid.

The Amazon mollies "mate" not with one another, but with males of the closely related sailfin molly species. These males court Amazons, insert their modified fin into the female, and deposit sperm. The sperm do not fertilize the eggs, but the Amazon will release more eggs and later give birth to more daughters for having gone through the mock mating. Why should the male sailfins bother? Perhaps the cost to the male is very low, and perhaps the rehearsal will improve later mating with a sailfin female. But an-

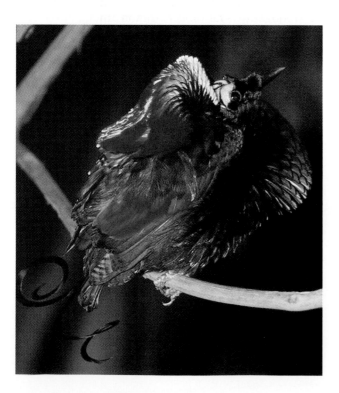

12.14 Results of Sexual Selection
A colorful tail display by a male Wilson's bird of paradise. Although such bright colors and elaborate feathers may interfere with the bird's ability to avoid predators, they definitely attract female birds of paradise.

BOX 12.1   *Evolutionary Psychology*

Speculation about selective pressure on reproductive behavior in various animals leads inevitably to questions about the extent to which our own behaviors have been affected by the difference between male and female reproductive strategies. Are women inherently more selective than men about choosing mating partners? Such a difference could be a result of the tremendous investment in time, energy, and resources that a female mammal must make in each offspring. Are men more promiscuous than women? It's easy to imagine that the low cost of producing sperm (and the potential for a man to expend no energy on child rearing)

might favor such behavior. Do romantic relationships tend to sour after about 7 years? If so, is this because, in earlier evolutionary times, it took about that long to rear a child and thus when that period ended it would be time to find a new mate in case the first mate had some genetic deficits that might be passed on to the offspring? Is there an "ideal" ratio of hip size and height that indicates maximal fertility in women? Do men in all cultures regard such a ratio as most attractive?

Such speculations have given rise to a lively and controversial field called evolutionary psychology (Barkow et al., 1992; Buss and Malamuth, 1996). It's easy to spin

plausible tales about how evolution might have shaped our behavior, but the challenge for these theorists is to come up with ways to test (and potentially disprove) these hypotheses. Such an enterprise is especially daunting when ethical considerations mean you can never manipulate the variables ("Let's see, I'd like you to marry that person over there and then I'll ask you some questions 7 years from now"), but must rely on correlations and surveys. But the drive to understand human mating behavior is so strong that we can expect more workers to enter this field. It remains to be seen whether they can prove or disprove any of these ideas.

---

other reason that has been suggested is that sailfin females, seeing the male mate with another female (of either species), may regard him as more attractive and may thus be more likely to mate with him (Schlupp et al., 1994).

 Special topic   A final, important stage of reproduction in many vertebrates is parental care of the offspring (Topic 12.4, Parental Care).

Sexual Differentiation

For species such as our own, in which the only kind of reproduction is sexual reproduction (so far), and in which sexual selection has generated sexual dimorphism, each individual must become either a male or a female to reproduce. **Sexual differentiation** is the process by which individuals develop either male or female bodies and behavior. In mammals this process begins before birth and continues until the individual becomes capable of reproducing.

The Sex of an Individual Is Determined Early in Life

For mammals sex is determined at the time of conception, when a sperm penetrates the egg and contributes either a Y chromosome or an X chromosome. From that point on, the path of sexual differentiation is set. We will describe that path and its occasional exceptions shortly. Mammals that receive an X chromosome from their father will become females; those who receive a Y chromosome will become males. (The mother always contributes an X chromosome.) Males

are said to be the **heterogametic** sex because they have two different **sex chromosomes** (XY), while females are **homogametic** (XX). In birds the females are heterogametic. The sex of some reptiles is determined by sex chromosomes; in other reptile species the factor determining whether an individual will develop as a male or female is the temperature at which the egg is incubated.

No matter what the mechanisms, the developmentally early event that normally decides whether the individual will become a male or female is known as **sexual determination**. In vertebrates the first visible consequence of sexual determination is in the **gonads**. Very early in development each individual has a pair of indifferent gonads, glands that vaguely resemble both testes and ovaries. During the first month of gestation in humans, the indifferent gonads begin changing into either ovaries or testes.

Sex Chromosomes Direct Sexual Differentiation of the Gonads

In mammals the Y chromosome contains a gene called the *SRY* gene (sex-determining *r*egion on the *Y* gene) that is responsible for the development of testes. If an individual has a Y chromosome, the cells of the indifferent gonad begin making the Sry protein. The Sry protein causes the cells in the core of the indifferent gonad (the medulla) to proliferate at the expense of the outer layers (the cortex), and the indifferent gonad develops into a testis. If the individual has no Y chromosome (or if it has a Y chromosome but the *SRY* gene is defective), no Sry protein is produced, and the indifferent gonad takes a different course: Cells of the cortical layers proliferate more than those of the medullary layers, and an ovary forms. (In reptiles that lack sex chromosomes, the temperature at which the egg is incubated appears to determine whether or not an *SRY*-like gene product is made.) For all vertebrates, this early decision of whether to form testes or ovaries has a domino effect, setting off a chain of events that result in either a male or a female.

Genes and behavior

Gonadal Hormones Direct Sexual Differentiation of the Rest of the Body

The most important way the gonads influence sexual differentiation is through their hormonal output. Developing testes produce several hormones, while ear-ly ovaries produce very little hormone. If other cells of the embryo receive the testicular hormones, they begin developing masculine characters; if the cells are not exposed to testicular hormones, they develop feminine characters.

We can chart masculine or feminine development by examining the structures connecting the gonads to the outside of the body. The conduits that allow gametes to exit the body are quite different in males and females (see Figure 12.7), so the proper development of these structures is crucial for sexual reproduction. At the embryonic stage, all individuals have the precursor tissues that could form either the female or the male apparatus. For example, the early fetus has a

12.15 Sexual Differentiation in Humans
(a) Undifferentiated fetus. (b) Male and (c) female fetus at 8 weeks of gestation. (d) Male and (e) female at 15 weeks of gestation.

genital tubercle that can form either a clitoris or a penis, as well as two sets of ducts that connect the indifferent gonads to the outer body wall: the **wolffian ducts** and the **müllerian ducts** (Figure 12.15*a*). The early fetus has both sets of ducts, but in females the müllerian ducts develop into the fallopian tubes, uterus, and inner vagina (Figure 12.15*c* and *e*), and only a remnant of the wolffian ducts remains. In males, hormones secreted by the testes orchestrate the converse outcome: The wolffian ducts develop into epididymis, vas deferens, and seminal vesicles (Figure 12.15*b* and *d*), while the müllerian ducts shrink to mere remnants.

The development of the wolffian ducts is promoted by the steroidal androgen testosterone; the shrinkage of the müllerian ducts is caused by the protein hormone **müllerian regression hormone (MRH)**. If there is no testis to produce testosterone and MRH, the wolffian ducts fail to develop and the müllerian ducts develop unimpeded. Testosterone also masculinizes other, nonwolffian-derived structures. Testosterone causes tissues around the urethra to form the prostate gland. Furthermore, testosterone acts on the epithelial tissues around the urethra to form a scrotum and penis. These effects are aided by the local conversion of testosterone into another steroidal androgen, dihydrotestosterone (DHT). The epithelial

cells have the enzyme 5-α-reductase to convert testosterone to DHT, and the DHT binds the androgen receptors even more readily than testosterone, resulting in greater gene activation and further masculine development. Without steroidal androgens, the prostate fails to form and the external skin grows into the female labia and clitoris (Figure 12.16).

Departures from the Orderly Sequence of Sexual Differentiation Result in Predictable Changes in Development

Some people have only one sex chromosome—a single X. Such genetic makeup (referred to as XO) results in **Turner's syndrome**—an apparent female with poorly developed but recognizable ovaries, as you would expect since no *SRY* gene is available. So the role of the sex chromosomes is to determine the sex of the gonad; gonadal hormones then drive sexual differentiation of the rest of the body. Figure 12.17 charts the series of events in mammalian sexual differentiation.

Sometimes XX individuals with well-formed ovaries are exposed to androgen in utero, and depending on the degree of exposure, they may be masculinized. For example, most fetal rats develop in the uterus sandwiched between two siblings. If a female is surrounded by brothers, some of the androgen from the siblings

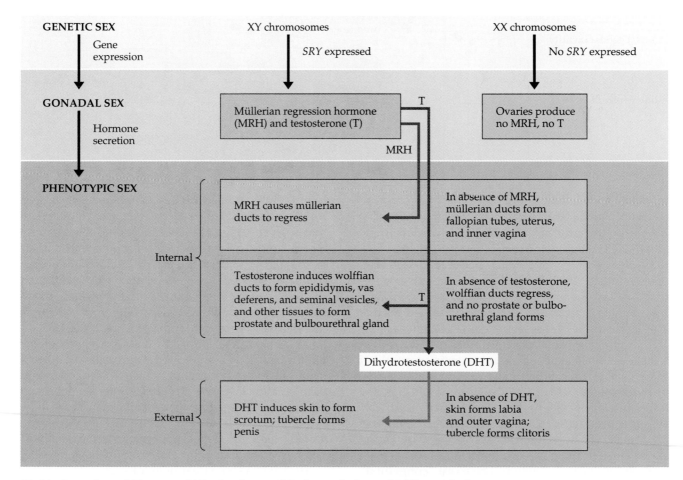

12.16 Genetic and Hormonal Mechanisms of Embryonic Sexual Differentiation

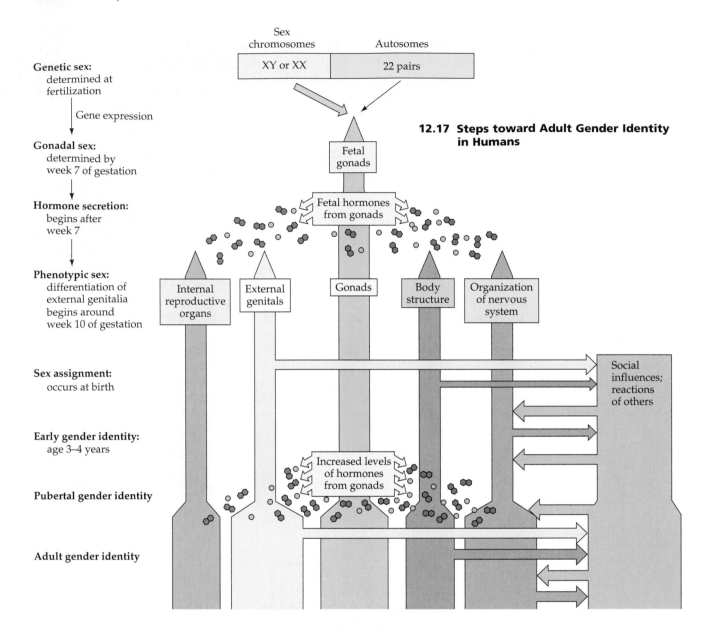

12.17 Steps toward Adult Gender Identity in Humans

Genetic sex: determined at fertilization

Gene expression

Gonadal sex: determined by week 7 of gestation

Hormone secretion: begins after week 7

Phenotypic sex: differentiation of external genitalia begins around week 10 of gestation

Sex assignment: occurs at birth

Early gender identity: age 3–4 years

Pubertal gender identity

Adult gender identity

Sex chromosomes — XY or XX

Autosomes — 22 pairs

Fetal gonads

Fetal hormones from gonads

Internal reproductive organs | External genitals | Gonads | Body structure | Organization of nervous system

Social influences; reactions of others

Increased levels of hormones from gonads

---

must reach the female because, although her gross appearance will be feminine at birth, her anogenital distance (the distance from the tip of the phallus to the anus) will be slightly greater (i.e., more malelike) than that of a female developing between two sisters (Clemens et al., 1978). In Chapter 9 we saw an example of a similar phenomenon in humans: Women who have a male twin produce otoacoustic emissions that are slightly more typical of males than of females.

In humans several genetic mutations can result in a female who is exposed to androgen in utero. What these various conditions, known as **congenital adrenal hyperplasia** (**CAH**), have in common is that the adrenal glands fail to produce sufficient corticosteroids, producing instead considerable amounts of androgens. (The condition is called adrenal hyperplasia because at birth the adrenal glands are swollen from excessive cell division. The word "congenital" means "present at birth.")

In XX individuals with this condition, the androgen levels produced are usually intermediate between those of normal females and males, and the newborn has an "intersex" appearance—a phallus that is intermediate in size between a normal clitoris and a normal penis, and skin folds that resemble both labia and scrotum (Figure 12.18). Sometimes the opening of the vagina fails to form (although the internal portion of the vagina is present), and sometimes the urethra opens somewhere along the base or length of the phallus (rather than below the clitoris as in normal females). Such individuals are readily recognizable at birth because, even in severe cases in which penis and scrotum are well formed, no testes are present in the "scrotum." The ovaries of such individuals, as you would expect, are normal and remain in the abdomen. The müllerian duct structures are fully developed.

The controversial treatment for such individuals is surgical correction of the external appearance and

12.18 An Intersex Phenotype
Genitalia of newborn girls with congenital adrenal hyperplasia (CAH). (Courtesy of John Money.)

medication to inhibit androgen production by the adrenals. But there is a growing view that surgery should be postponed until the individuals reach adulthood so that they can make informed decisions about whether to have surgery and what gender role to follow (see Topic 12.5, John/Joan). CAH females are much more likely to be described by their parents (and themselves) as "tomboys" than are other girls. In adulthood, most CAH females describe themselves as heterosexual, but they are somewhat more likely to report a homosexual orientation than are other women.

In rats and other mammals, experimenters have deliberately exposed developing females to androgenic steroids, and the results are quite uniform: Given sufficient testosterone during development, XX individuals will form wolffian duct structures: prostate, scrotum, and penis. Because the testosterone has no effect on müllerian ducts, these structures—fallopian tubes, uterus, and (internal) vagina—also develop. The gonads develop as ovaries, apparently ignoring the androgens. As we will see later in the chapter, the adult behavior of such androgenized females provided the first clues that early androgens could masculinize the brain as well as the body.

A Defective Androgen Receptor Can Block the Masculinization of Males

An interesting demonstration of the influence of androgens on sexual differentiation is provided by the condition known as **androgen insensitivity**. The gene for the androgen receptor is found on the X chromosome. An XY individual whose X chromosome has a

defective androgen receptor gene is incapable of producing the androgen receptor and is therefore unable to respond to androgenic hormones. The gonads of such people develop as normal testes, and the testes produce MRH, which inhibits müllerian duct structures, and plenty of testosterone. In the absence of working androgen receptors, however, the wolffian ducts fail to develop and the external epithelia form labia and a clitoris. Such individuals look like normal females at birth and at puberty develop breasts. (Breast development in humans appears to depend on the ratio of estrogenic to androgenic stimulation at puberty, and since androgen-insensitive individuals receive little androgenic *stimulation*, the functional estrogen-to-androgen ratio is high.)

Androgen-insensitive individuals may be recognized when their menstrual cycles fail to commence, because neither ovaries nor uterus are present to produce menstruation. Such women are infertile and, lacking a müllerian contribution, may have a slightly shallow vagina, but otherwise they look like other women (Figure 12.19) and, as we'll see next, behave like other women. At the end of this chapter we will describe another mutation that causes some people to appear to change their sex (without surgery) at adolescence.

How Should We Define Gender—by Genes, Gonads, Genitals, or the Brain?

Most humans are either male or female, and whether we examine their chromosomes, gonads, external genitalia, or internal structures, we will see a consistent pattern: Each will be either feminine or masculine in character. Behavior is much more difficult to define as feminine or masculine. The only behavior

12.19 A Woman with Testes
Although this person has the male XY chromosome pattern and therefore testes (undescended), she also has complete androgen insensitivity. Therefore her body has developed in a feminine fashion. (Courtesy of John Money.)

Gonadal Hormones Direct Sexual Differentiation of the Brain and Behavior

As scientists began discovering that testicular hormones direct masculine development of the body, behavioral researchers found evidence for a similar influence on the brain. In 1959, Phoenix, Goy, Gerall, and Young described the effect of fetal hormones on the sexual behavior of guinea pigs. Recall that a female guinea pig, like most rodents, normally displays the lordosis posture in response to male mounting for only a short period around the time of ovulation, when her fertility is highest. If a male mounts her at other times, she does not show lordosis. An experimenter can induce the female to display lordosis by injecting ovarian steroids in the sequence they normally follow during ovulation—giving her estrogens for a few days and then progesterone. A few hours after the progesterone injection, the female will display lordosis in response to male mounting.

Phoenix and collaborators knew that when the same regimen of steroids was given to an adult male guinea pig, whether or not he was allowed to keep his testes, he almost never showed lordosis in response to mounting males. In the 1959 study, the experimenters exposed female guinea pigs to testosterone in utero. As adults, these females did not show lordosis. Even if their ovaries were removed and they were given the steroidal regimen that reliably activated lordosis in normal females, these fetally androgenized females did not show lordosis. In response to these data, William C. Young and his colleagues proposed the **organizational hypothesis**: The same testicular steroids that masculinize the genitalia also masculinize the developing brain and thereby permanently alter behavior. This **organizational effect** of steroid hormones stood in contrast with the activational effect we mentioned earlier (such as when adult females are given estrogens and progesterone to activate lordosis).

William C. Young
(1899–1965)

displayed *exclusively* by one sex is childbirth. Even behaviors that are very rarely displayed by members of a sex (e.g., sexual assault by women or breast-feeding by men) occur sometimes. As for behaviors that can be measured and made amenable to experimental study in humans or other animals, we have to resort to group means and statistical tests to see the differences. A given individual will almost always display some behaviors that are more common in the opposite sex.

Androgen-insensitive individuals show us that even morphological features can be confusing criteria by which to judge sex (see Figure 12.19). Androgen-insensitive humans have a male chromosome and testes. Like most males, they do not have fallopian tubes or a uterus, but they do have a vagina and breasts, and in many respects they behave like females. They dress like females, are attracted to and marry males, and perhaps most important, even after they learn the details of their condition, they call themselves women (Money and Ehrhardt, 1972).

As we will see next, parts of the brain are also typically different between the sexes in humans and other animals. In androgen-insensitive rats, some brain regions are masculine and others are feminine. Thus, from a scientific standpoint we cannot regard an animal, especially a human, as simply masculine or feminine. Rather, we must specify which structure or behavior we mean when we say it is typical of females or of males.

Whereas steroids have an organizational influence only during early development and the effect is permanent, in adulthood they exert an activational effect, temporarily influencing behavior. Steroids have an organizational effect only when present during a **sen-**

Neural plasticity

sitive period. The exact boundaries of the sensitive period of development depend on which behavior and which species is being studied. For rats, which are **altricial** (born in an immature state), androgen given just after birth (the **neonatal** period) can affect later behavior; guinea pigs, which are **precocial** (born in a relatively mature state), must be exposed to androgens **prenatally** (before birth) for adult behavior to be affected.

Early Testicular Secretions Result in Masculine Behavior in Adulthood

The organizational hypothesis provides a unitary explanation for sexual differentiation: The same steroidal signal that masculinizes the body (androgen) also masculinizes parts of the brain, ensuring that an individual's behavior usually is appropriate for its sex. From this point of view the nervous system is just another type of tissue listening for the androgenic signal that will instruct it to organize itself in a masculine fashion. If the nervous system does not detect androgen, it will organize itself in a feminine fashion. In fact, outside of the gonads and müllerian ducts, all tissues that develop differently in males and females have been shown to do so under the influence of androgenic steroids. This is one of the functions that steroid hormones, with their capacity to infiltrate the entire body, can fulfill: sending a single message to disparate parts of the body to coordinate an integrated response.

What was demonstrated originally for the lordosis behavior of guinea pigs has been observed in a variety of vertebrate species and for a variety of behaviors. Female rats must also display lordosis for mating to take place; experiments have shown that exposing female rat pups to testosterone either just before birth or during the first 10 days after birth greatly reduces their lordosis responsiveness as adults. Such results explain the previous findings that adult male rats

Competing hypotheses show very little lordosis even when given estrogens and progesterone. Male rats that are castrated during the first week of life, however, display very good lordosis responses after a treatment of estradiol plus progesterone in adulthood. In rats, many behaviors were shown to be consistent with the organizational hypothesis: Animals exposed to either endogenous or exogenous androgens early in life behaved like males, while animals not exposed to androgens early in life behaved like females.

Some sex differences in behavior seem indifferent to early exposure to androgens. For example, male rhesus monkeys yawn more often than females, but this behavior seems to be the result of adult exposure to androgens. If rhesus males are castrated in adulthood, they yawn about as often as normal females, and treating adult females with androgens activates yawning. Exposure to androgens during development has no effect on later yawning behavior, so this sex difference in behavior seems to respond solely to activational rather than to organizational effects of androgens.

In other cases, androgens seem to be needed both in development (to organize the nervous system to enable the later behavior) and in adulthood (to activate that behavior). For example, as we learned earlier, the copulatory behavior of male rats can be quantified in terms of how often they mount a receptive female and how often such mounting results in intromission. Androgens must be present in adulthood to activate this behavior: Adult males that have been castrated stop mounting in a few weeks; injecting them with testosterone eventually restores masculine copulatory behavior. Such androgen treatment has some effect on adult female rats as well, causing them to mount other females more often, but they rarely manage intromission of their phallus (the clitoris) into the stimulus female's vagina.

To see the full range of masculine copulatory behavior in a female rat, you must treat her with androgens just before birth, just after birth, and in adulthood. Such females not only mount receptive females, but they achieve intromissions regularly and ejaculate a sperm-less fluid (Ward, 1969)! Conversely, castrating a male rat at birth will result in very few intromissions later, no matter how much androgen you give in adulthood.

Thus, masculine copulatory behavior in rats and several other rodent species seems to depend on both organizational and activational influences of androgens. An early criticism of this conclusion was offered by Frank Beach (1971), who pointed out that the failure of females and neonatally castrated male rats to achieve intromission could well be due to the small size of the phallus rather than any differences in the nervous system. Indeed, there is remarkable correlation between the size of the penis and intromission success in male rats castrated at various ages (Beach and Holz, 1946). Thus, although there is excellent evidence that steroids present at birth masculinize the body, Beach found no proof that they masculinize the brain. However, an unexpected development soon made it clear that steroids do indeed organize the developing nervous system of rodents to display male copulatory behavior, as we will see next.

Frank Beach (1911–1988)

The Estrogenic Metabolites of Testosterone Masculinize the Nervous System and Behavior of Rodents

Soon after the organizational hypothesis was published, some researchers reported a paradoxical finding. When newborn female rats were treated with small doses of estrogens, they failed to show lordosis behavior in adulthood (Feder and Whalen, 1965). In fact, a very small dose of estrogen, as little as 10 μg, could permanently masculinize these behaviors, whereas achieving the same effect with testosterone required a higher dose (100 to 1000 μg). The fact that a steroid such as estrogen, regarded as a "female hormone," could have such a profoundly masculinizing influence on later behavior was very puzzling. The results were especially strange because during development all rat fetuses are exposed to high levels of estrogen that originate in the mother and cross the placenta. If estrogens masculinize the developing brain, why aren't all females masculinized by maternal estrogens?

A closer look at the synthesis of steroid hormones reveals the explanation. The major androgen (testosterone) and the major estrogen (estradiol) differ by only one molecule. In fact, testosterone is often used as a precursor for the manufacture of estradiol in the ovary. In a single chemical reaction, called aromatization, the enzyme **aromatase** converts testosterone to estradiol and other androgens to other estrogens. The ovaries normally contain a great deal of aromatase, and the brain was found to have high levels of aromatase as well. From this evidence arose the **aromatization hypothesis**, which suggested that testicular androgens enter the brain and are converted there into estrogens, and that these estrogens are what masculinize the developing nervous system.

Why, then, aren't the brains of females masculinized by maternal estrogens? A protein found in the plasma of rat fetuses, called **α-fetoprotein**, binds estrogens and prevents them from entering the brain. Although both male and female fetuses produce α-fetoprotein, this protein does not bind androgens. The male rat is masculinized when his testes produce testosterone, which traverses the bloodstream (unimpeded by α-fetoprotein), and enters the brain, where aromatase converts the testosterone to an estrogen, the estrogen binds to estrogen receptors, and the steroid–receptor complex regulates gene expression to cause the brain to develop in a masculine fashion (Figure 12.20). If no androgens are present, no estrogens reach the brain, and the fetus develops in a feminine fashion. A lack of aromatase seems to play a role in the unusual sexual differentiation of the spotted hyena (Box 12.2).

The aromatization hypothesis, as proposed by Frederick Naftolin and further investigated by Bruce McEwen and their colleagues, was soon shown to apply even to masculine copulatory behavior in rats. If male rats were castrated at birth, they would grow up to have a small penis and to show few intromissions even when given testosterone in adulthood. If the males were castrated at birth and given the androgen dihydrotestosterone (DHT), which cannot be converted into an estrogen, as

Bruce McEwen

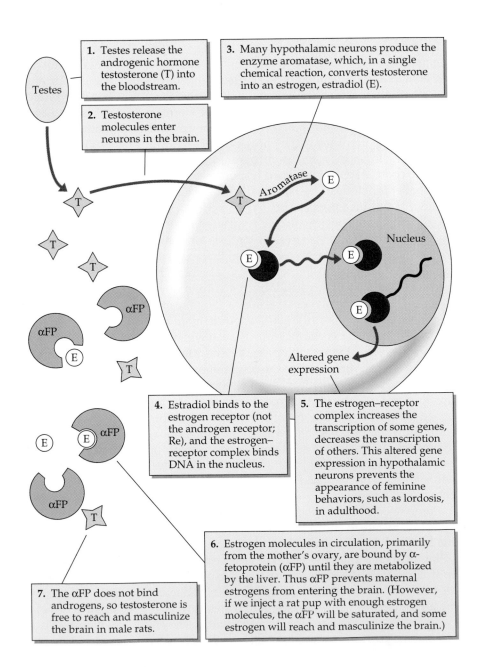

1. Testes release the androgenic hormone testosterone (T) into the bloodstream.

2. Testosterone molecules enter neurons in the brain.

3. Many hypothalamic neurons produce the enzyme aromatase, which, in a single chemical reaction, converts testosterone into an estrogen, estradiol (E).

Nucleus

Altered gene expression

4. Estradiol binds to the estrogen receptor (not the androgen receptor; Re), and the estrogen–receptor complex binds DNA in the nucleus.

5. The estrogen–receptor complex increases the transcription of some genes, decreases the transcription of others. This altered gene expression in hypothalamic neurons prevents the appearance of feminine behaviors, such as lordosis, in adulthood.

6. Estrogen molecules in circulation, primarily from the mother's ovary, are bound by α-fetoprotein (αFP) until they are metabolized by the liver. Thus αFP prevents maternal estrogens from entering the brain. (However, if we inject a rat pup with enough estrogen molecules, the αFP will be saturated, and some estrogen will reach and masculinize the brain.)

7. The αFP does not bind androgens, so testosterone is free to reach and masculinize the brain in male rats.

12.20   The Aromatization Hypothesis

BOX 12.2   *The Paradoxical Sexual Differentiation of the Spotted Hyena*

Scientists of antiquity believed that spotted hyenas were hermaphrodites. The mistake is understandable because the female hyena has a clitoris that is as large as the penis of males (as the figure shows), and like males, she urinates through her phallus. What's more, she appears to have no vagina, because during mating the male puts his penis inside the tip of her clitoris and later the pups come into the world through the clitoris.

A group of scientists in Berkeley, California, has begun to understand how this remarkable situation could come about. Since hyenas are born with this sexually monomorphic exterior (although females tend to have larger bodies than do males), either both sexes are exposed to prenatal androgens, or their epithelial tissues develop in the masculine fashion whether or not androgens are present. Studies of steroid metabolism in the hyena placenta suggest the former situation. In other mammals the placenta rapidly aromatizes androgens into estrogens; this conversion may be a way to protect mother and female fetuses from androgens produced by fetal males. (Remember that in rodents a plasma protein prevents circulating estrogens from masculinizing the brain.) But the spotted hyena placenta is remarkably deficient in the aromatase enzyme (Licht et al., 1992).

Because the hyena mother produces large amounts of the androgen androstenedione (Glickman et al., 1987), and the placenta fails to convert the androstenedione to estrogens, all the fetuses receive considerable amounts of androgens, which may account for their masculine appearance. One test of

this hypothesis would be to see whether the placenta of the striped hyena (in which females do not have a masculine appearance) has enzymatic activities more like other mammals than like the spotted hyena.

Is the spotted hyena brain affected by these early androgens? Possibly, because females grow faster than males and are more aggressive than males. The social lives of hyenas center around the adult females. All adult females are dominant over all males, which means that females always get to eat first and, except during the breeding season, do not tolerate males coming close to them. There is also a dominance hierarchy among the females, and the daughters of high-ranking females tend to get first access to food and other resources. Thus there is considerable selective pressure for females to be aggressive, especially with other females.

One of the remarkable findings from captive-bred hyenas is that

female pups begin fighting immediately after birth. They are born with teeth and use them to attack their siblings. Female pups are very aggressive, especially toward a sister. At Berkeley, investigators intervene to prevent serious injury, but field studies indicate that in the wild it is very common for one pup to kill its sibling (L. G. Frank et al., 1991). It remains to be seen whether this extreme aggression is due to prenatal stimulation of the brain with androgens.

Even if the extreme aggressiveness of the female hyena is due to fetal androgens, females do mate with males, so their brains have not been made permanently unreceptive (as would happen in prenatally androgenized rats). Just the same, mating in the spotted hyena is a tense affair, as the female seems to just barely tolerate the male's proximity, and the male alternates between approaching and retreating from his more powerful mate. (Photograph courtesy of Stephen Glickman.)

---

adults they would have a penis of normal size, but would still show few or no intromission behaviors when given androgens. On the other hand, males castrated as newborns and treated with estrogens achieve intromission regularly when treated with androgens as adults, despite having a very small penis (no larger than in untreated castrated males).

Thus Frank Beach's playful explanation of why female rats achieve few intromissions—"you can't be a carpenter if you don't have a hammer"—was disproved. Rather, early testicular secretions seemed to organize the developing nervous system to masculinize later behavior. This idea was amply confirmed later, when sex differences in the structure of the nervous system were found.

Several Regions of the Nervous System Display Prominent Sexual Dimorphism

Because male and female rats behave differently, researchers assumed that their brains were different, and the organizational hypothesis asserted that early androgens masculinize the developing brain. But these neural differences can be very subtle; the same basic circuit of neurons connected together will produce very different behavior if the strength of the myriad synapses varies. However, sex differences in the *number* of synapses were identified in the preoptic area (POA) of the hypothalamus as early as 1971 (Raisman and Field, 1971). As we will see in the discussion that follows, later demonstrations of sexual dimorphism in the nervous system would include differences in the number, size, and shape of neurons, as well as the number of synapses.

Song control regions in male songbirds. Fernando Nottebohm and Arthur Arnold were studying the brain regions that control singing in canaries and zebra finches when they noticed something unexpected. Brain sections from males and females showed that the nuclei that control song are *much* larger in males than in females (see Figure 19.3) (Nottebohm and Arnold, 1976). Measuring the sections revealed that the nuclei are five to six times larger in volume in males (which produce elaborate songs) than in females (which produce only simple calls). Let's briefly discuss these brain nuclei and their sexual dimorphism.

Birds produce song through a specialized muscular organ called the **syrinx**, which is wrapped around the air passage. The muscles of the syrinx control the frequency of sounds produced by changing the tension of membranes around the air passage. These muscles are controlled by motoneurons of the twelfth cranial nerve (the cranial nerve that controls the tongue in mammals). The corresponding nucleus receives most of its innervation from a brain nucleus called the robustus archistriatum (RA). The RA receives most of its innervation from a nucleus that is both literally and organizationally higher, the higher vocal center (HVC). Lesions of the HVC abolish complex song in canaries and zebra finches, and electrical stimulation of the nucleus elicits song snippets. Lesions of the RA also severely disrupt song, as you would expect from the circuitry we've described.

As the organizational hypothesis would suggest, the early action of steroid hormone masculinizes the brains of zebra finches: Exposing a hatchling female to either testosterone or estradiol will cause the HVC and the RA to be larger in adulthood. If such a female is also given testosterone as an adult, the nuclei will become larger still, and she will sing much like a male zebra finch does (Gurney and Konishi, 1979). Female zebra finches treated with androgen only in adulthood do not sing. Thus in zebra finches, early hormone *organizes* a masculine song system, and adult hormone *activates* the system to produce song.

The song of canaries is also affected by androgens, but in this species early steroids seem unimportant. A female canary will begin singing after a few weeks of androgen treatment in adulthood. Androgens also cause the HVC and the RA to become larger in volume and the dendrites of neurons in those regions to grow, making new synaptic connections. This difference in hormonal control of song in zebra finches and canaries may relate to the ecological niche occupied by each.

Zebra finches, originally from the Australian desert, are opportunistic breeders; they are ready to breed at any time of the year, awaiting rainfall that will provide additional food. Canaries are seasonal breeders; their reproductive apparatus (including the testes) shuts down in the fall. Therefore, male canaries have high androgen levels in spring and summer and low androgen levels in fall and winter. With this ebb and flow of androgens, singing and the volume of the HVC and the RA also vary: The nuclei grow in the spring as the animal resumes courtship singing and shrink in the fall as singing declines. Unlike zebra finches, which have only a single, relatively simple song, male canaries produce many, highly elaborate songs, learning additional songs each spring. Thus we can think of male canaries as having brains that remain sensitive to the organizational influences of androgens even in adulthood, and this continual reorganization may help them produce large repertoires to gain a mate.

The preoptic area of rats. The discovery that the brains of songbirds display such obvious sexual dimorphism inspired researchers to look for other neural sex differences. The laboratory of Roger Gorski examined the preoptic area (POA) of the hypothalamus in rats because of an earlier report that the number of synapses in this region was different in males and females and because lesions of the POA disrupt ovulatory cycles in female rats and reduce copulatory behavior in males. Sure enough, there was an easily identifiable nucleus within the POA, and this nucleus was three to five times larger in volume in males than in females (Gorski et al., 1978). This nucleus, dubbed the **sexually dimorphic nucleus of the POA (SDN-POA)**, was so much more prominent in male rats that Gorski and colleagues could tell male from female brain sections just by glancing at the slides without a microscope (Figure 12.21). Yet, despite intense anatomical study of this brain region for almost a century, no one had noticed the SDN-POA until the birdsong work inspired a search.

Like the song control nuclei in zebra finches, the SDN-POA conformed beautifully to the organizational hypothesis: Males castrated at birth had much smaller SDN-POAs in adulthood, while females androgenized at birth had large, malelike SDN-POAs as

Rat brain

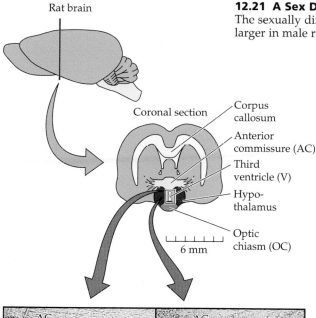

Coronal section

Corpus callosum

Anterior commissure (AC)

Third ventricle (V)

Hypo-thalamus

Optic chiasm (OC)

6 mm

Male

Female

12.21 A Sex Difference in the Hypothalamus
The sexually dimorphic nucleus of the preoptic area (SDN-POA) is much larger in male rats than in females. (Courtesy of Roger Gorski.)

SDN-POA, despite their feminine exterior, because their estrogen receptors are normal.

The function of the SDN-POA is still not completely understood. Lesions of the SDN portion of the POA in rats cause only a slight, temporary decline in male copulatory behavior. A similarly obvious sexually dimorphic nucleus has been described and studied in gerbils (Yahr and Gregory, 1993), and lesions of this SDN-POA significantly reduce the typical scent-marking behavior of male gerbils.

The spinal cord in mammals. The birdsong work inspired a search for sexual dimorphism in the spinal cord, where neural elements controlling sexual response should be different for males and females. In rats, for example, the striated bulbocavernosus (BC) muscles (absent in females) that surround the base of the penis are innervated by motoneurons in the **spinal nucleus of the bulbocavernosus (SNB)** (Figure 12.22). Male rats have about 200 SNB cells, but females have far fewer motoneurons in this region of the spinal cord.

There has been considerable progress in understanding how the sexual dimorphism in the SNB system develops. On the day before birth, female rats have BC muscles attached to the base of the clitoris that are nearly as large as those of males and that are innervated by motoneurons in the SNB region (Rand and Breedlove, 1987). In fact, a few days before birth, females have as many SNB cells as males do (Nordeen et al., 1985). In the days just before and after birth, however, many SNB cells die, especially in females, and the BC muscles of females die. A single injection of androgen delivered to a newborn female rat will

adults. Castrating male rats in *adulthood,* however, did not alter the size of the SDN-POA, and neither did treating adult females with androgens. Thus, testicular androgens somehow alter the development of the SDN-POA, resulting in a nucleus permanently larger in males than in females. Later experiments demonstrated that testosterone converted to estrogens in the brain masculinizes the SDN-POA, so this nucleus conforms to the aromatization hypothesis as well. For example, androgen-insensitive rats have a masculine

12.22 Sexual Dimorphism in the Spinal Cord
The spinal nucleus of the bulbocavernosus (SNB) consists of large, multipolar motoneurons. Male rats (*a*) have more SNB cells (arrows) than do females (*b*).

(*a*) Male rat

(*b*) Female rat

permanently spare some SNB motoneurons and their muscles. Castration of newborn males, accompanied by prenatal blockade of androgen receptors, causes the BC muscles and SNB motoneurons to die as in females. Similarly, androgen-insensitive rats have very few SNB cells and no BC muscle, so aromatization seems to be unimportant for masculine development of this system.

Androgen acts on the BC muscles to prevent their demise, and this sparing of the muscles causes the innervating SNB motoneurons to survive (Fishman et al., 1990; C. L. Jordan, Breedlove, and Arnold, 1991). Recall from Chapter 7 that about half of all the spinal motoneurons produced early in development normally die, that the death of the motoneurons can be prevented if they are provided with enough muscle target, and that the muscles are thought to provide a neurotrophic factor to keep the appropriate number of motoneurons alive into adulthood. For SNB motoneurons the neurotrophic factor may resemble ciliary neurotrophic factor (CNTF), because in mice with the receptor for CNTF knocked out, SNB motoneurons die in males despite the presence of androgens (Forger et al., 1997).

All male mammals have BC muscles, but in nonrodents their motoneurons are found in a slightly different spinal location and are known as **Onuf's nucleus**. The rat studies suggest that Onuf's nucleus should be sexually dimorphic—that males should have more Onuf's motoneurons than females do. Surprisingly, most female mammals retain a BC muscle into adulthood. For example, in women the BC surrounds the opening of the vagina, and contractions of the BC slightly constrict the opening (hence the muscle is sometimes referred to as the constrictor vestibule in women). Nevertheless, the BC is larger in men than in women, and men have more Onuf's motoneurons than women have (Forger and Breedlove, 1986).

The rat studies suggest that the sexual dimorphism in Onuf's nucleus is the result of androgenic action on the muscles that rescues motoneurons from death. Motoneuron counts in the human spinal cord indicate that we all normally lose some of these motoneurons before the twenty-sixth week of gestation (see Figure 7.14*b*) (Forger and Breedlove, 1987), a time during which male fetuses produce androgen.

Social Influences Affect Sexual Differentiation of the Nervous System

The SNB system offers an illuminating example of how social factors can mediate the masculinization produced by steroids. Newborn rat pups can neither urinate nor defecate on their own; the mother (dam) must lick the anogenital region of each pup to elicit a spinal reflex to empty the bladder and colon. (Incidentally, the dam ingests at least some of the wastes and thereby receives pheromones from the pups that affect the composition of her milk as the pups mature. Another reason not to be a rat!) Celia Moore and colleagues noticed that dams spend more time licking the anogenital region of male pups than of females. If the dam is made temporarily anosmic (unable to smell) by chemical treatment of the olfactory epithelium (see Chapter 9), she licks all the pups less and does not distinguish between males and females. Males raised by anosmic mothers thus receive less anogenital licking, and remarkably, fewer of their SNB cells survive the period around birth (C. L. Moore et al., 1992). The dam's stimulation of a male's anogenital region helps to masculinize his spinal cord.

Neural plasticity

On the one hand, this masculinization is still an effect of androgens, because the dam detects male pups by smelling androgen metabolites in their urine. On the other hand, this effect is clearly the result of a social influence: The dam treats a pup differently because he's a male and thereby masculinizes his developing nervous system. Perhaps this example illustrates the futility of trying to distinguish "biological" and "social" influences.

What about humans? Humans are at least as sensitive to social influences as rats are. In every culture most people treat boys and girls differently, even when they are infants. Such differential treatment undoubtedly has some effect on the developing human brain and contributes to later sex differences in behavior. Of course, this is a social influence, but testosterone instigated the influence when it induced formation of a penis. If prenatal androgens have even a very subtle effect on the fetal brain, then older humans interacting with the baby might detect such differences and treat the baby differently. Thus, originally subtle differences might be magnified by early social experience. Such interactions of steroidal and social influences are probably the norm in the sexual differentiation of human behavior. Much controversy surrounds the debate over whether hormones or social influences determine sexual orientation (Box 12.3).

Do Early Gonadal Hormones Masculinize Human Behaviors in Adulthood?

Since men and women behave differently, something about them, probably something about their brains, must be different. The only remaining question is whether men and women behave differently because they are raised in a culture that treats them differentially or because they develop with different biological processes, which might be immune to cultural influences. These are not mutually exclusive hypotheses. In fact, because sex roles vary in different societies (and have changed dramatically in our own society in the

Competing hypotheses

BOX 12.3 *What Determines a Person's Sexual Orientation?*

Some people develop romantic attachments to and yearn to have sex with a person of the same sex. Researchers have offered two explanations for this sexual orientation. Some suggest that infants observe the adults around them and use them as role models for their later sexual orientation as homosexual or heterosexual; sometimes, by accident or circumstance, they choose to model the opposite sex. Others believe that something happens to the fetal brain to determine later orientation ("some people are born gay").

For them, it is tempting to explain homosexual behavior as an example of the organizational action of early steroids that has been demonstrated in animals. After all, the more androgens the young male rat receives neonatally, the more male copulatory behaviors he'll display as an adult. Furthermore, by depriving a male rat of androgens at birth, we can be sure that (with adult steroid treatment) he will display lordosis (a female behavior) in response to another male in adulthood. Superficially, the behavior of the male rat deprived of androgens at birth resembles homosexual behavior, but all we have measured is which sexual motor pattern the animal will display.

A neonatally androgenized animal will mount any rat—male or female. A female rat given estrogens and progesterone will display the lordosis posture in response to mounting by any rat—or in response to the investigator's hand! In other words, the animals show these behaviors regardless of who or what their partner is. In contrast, we humans are much more concerned about what sort of partner we have than about the particular sexual behavior we perform. It is possible to measure what sort of rat companion a given rat would like to have available, but such studies paint a more complicated picture. There is more variability in steroid effects on a rat's partner preference than on lordosis or mounting behaviors.

Simon LeVay (1991) reported that the POA (preoptic area) of humans contains a nucleus (the third interstitial nucleus of the anterior hypothalamus, or INAH-3) that is

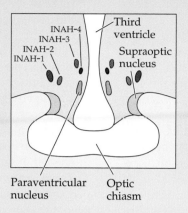

Paraventricular nucleus   Optic chiasm

larger in men than in women and larger in heterosexual men than in homosexual men (see the figure). For the public, this sounds like strong evidence that sexual orientation is "built in." Those of us studying biological psychology, however, know that early experience can alter the structure of the brain to have an influence on later behavior (see Figure 2 in the Afterword).

It's possible, then, that early social experience affects the development of INAH-3 to determine later sexual orientation. Furthermore, sexual experiences as an adult could affect INAH-3 structure, so the smaller nucleus in some homosexual men may be the result of their homosexuality, rather than vice versa. LeVay himself was careful to point out these alternatives, but most journalists know so little about the brain that they have never quite caught on. Michael Gorman (1994) suggested that the popular media also focused on LeVay's findings because they could be interpreted as conforming to a popular but very much oversimplified view of gay men—that they are like women.

The reports that sexual orientation is heritable (J. M. Bailey and Bell, 1993) also do little to resolve the controversy. Estimates are that about half the variability in sexual orientation is due to differences in the genome, which leaves ample room for early social influences. Indeed, this evidence strongly indicates that both genetic and environmental influences affect sexual orientation in humans. Each member of a very select subpopulation of homosexual men—pairs of homosexual brothers—is likely to have inherited the same region of their X chromosome from their

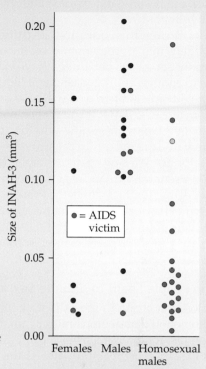

mother (Hamer et al., 1993). But even in this subpopulation there are exceptions; that is, some of the homosexual brothers received from their mother different genes from that region of the X, so coinheritance of those genes could not account for their being alike. Finally, monozygotic twins, who have exactly the same genes, do not always have the same sexual orientation (Buhrich et al., 1991).

From a political viewpoint, the controversy—whether sexual orientation is determined before birth or determined by early social influences—is irrelevant. Many religions practiced in Western culture regard homosexuality as a sin that some people choose to commit, and this view forms the prime basis for laws and prejudices against homosexuality. But scientists representing each viewpoint agree that sexual orientation, especially in males, is set very early in life—by age 4 or so. Almost all homosexual and heterosexual men report that from the beginning their interest and romantic attachments matched their adult orientation (see Topic 5.1, Sexual Awakenings). Furthermore, despite sometimes heroic efforts, no one has come up with a reliable way to change a man's sexual orientation (LeVay, 1996).

past few decades), there seems little doubt that society affects sexual differentiation of the brain and behavior. But do prenatal steroids alter the adult behavior of humans?

Answering this question is difficult. Prenatal androgens may or may not act on the brain, but they certainly act on the periphery. If we expose a female fetus to enough androgen, she will look entirely male on the outside at birth and will be treated by family and society as a male. If she (?) behaves as a male in adulthood, we won't know whether that's because of what androgens did to the outside of the body or to the brain. We saw earlier that CAH females, exposed prenatally to androgen, play more like boys than normal females do. Is the reason for this difference in behavior that androgens directly masculinized their brains or that, with their ambiguous genitalia, they or their parents have some doubts about their "real" gender?

Some People Seem to Change Sex at Puberty

We close this chapter with a discussion of a fascinating phenomenon that demonstrates again the difficulty of distinguishing prenatal from social influences.

A rare genetic mutation affects the enzyme (5-α-reductase) that converts testosterone to dihydrotestosterone (DHT). If an XY individual cannot produce this enzyme, the internal structures still develop in a masculine fashion. Testes develop, müllerian ducts regress, and wolffian duct structures, under the influence of testosterone, are masculinized. The genital epithelium, however, which normally possesses 5-α-reductase, is unable to amplify the androgenic signal by converting the testosterone to the more active DHT. Consequently, the phallus is only slightly masculinized and resembles a large clitoris, and the genital folds resemble labia, although they contain the testes. There usually is no vaginal opening.

Babies in a particular village in the Dominican Republic occasionally are born with this type of appearance (Figure 12.23). These children seem to be regarded as girls in the way they are dressed and raised (Imperato-McGinley et al., 1974). At puberty, however, the testes increase androgen production and the external genitalia become more fully masculinized. The phallus grows into a recognizable penis, the body develops narrow hips and a muscular build, without breasts, and the individuals begin acting like young men. The villagers have nicknamed such individuals *guevedoces*, meaning "eggs (testes) at 12 (years)." These men never develop facial beards, but they usually have girlfriends, indicating that they are sexually interested in women.

There are two possible explanations for why these people raised as girls would later behave as men. First, prenatal testosterone may have masculinized their brains; thus despite being raised as girls, when they reach puberty, their brains lead them to seek out girls for mates. This explanation suggests that the social influences of growing up—assigning oneself to a gender and mimicking role models of that gender, gender-specific playing and dressing—are unimportant for later behavior and sexual orientation. An alternative explanation is that early hormones have no effect—that this culture simply recognizes and teaches children that some people can start out as girls and change to boys later. If so, then the social influences on gender role development might be completely different in this society from those in ours, and it is not possible to state with certainty whether prenatal hormonal influences or early social influences are more important for sexual differentiation of human behavior.

The reports of sexual dimorphism in the adult human brain, often touted as proof of the predominance of "biological" influences, do not really address the issue. Despite the absence of any airtight demonstrations that prenatal hormones directly affect human brain and behavior, it seems likely that hormones have at least some effect on the developing brain and

Competing hypotheses

(*a*) Newborn

(*b*) Adolescent

12.23 *Guevedoces*
In the Dominican Republic some individuals, called *guevedoces*, are born with ambiguous genitalia (*a*) and are raised as girls. At puberty, however, the phallus grows into a recognizable penis (*b*), and the individuals begin acting like young men. (Courtesy of Julianne Imperato-McGinley.)

that society reinforces and accentuates sex differences in humans.

Summary

Sexual Behavior

1. Reproductive behaviors are divided into four stages: attraction, appetitive behaviors, copulation, and postcopulatory behaviors, including parental behaviors in some species.

2. The brain governs the time at which the organism should reproduce and uses protein hormones to induce the gonads to produce gametes. The gonads in turn produce steroid hormones that activate the brain to increase the probability of reproductive behaviors.

3. In humans, very low levels of testosterone are required for either men or women to display a full interest in mating, but additional testosterone has no additional effect. Therefore there is no correlation between circulating androgen levels and reproductive behaviors in men. Nor is there any strong correlation between copulatory behavior and stage of the menstrual cycle in women.

4. Human copulatory behavior is remarkably varied. Attempts at classification of the stages of copulation in humans suggest that most men show a single pattern while most women display one of three basic patterns of sexual response. For both sexes, the four basic stages of the sexual response pattern are (1) increasing excitement, (2) plateau, (3) orgasm, and (4) resolution.

Why Are There Two Sexes?

1. Sexual reproduction brings together in a single individual the beneficial mutations that arose in separate individuals.

2. In some species, sexual reproduction has led to the evolution of individuals specialized to reproduce as either a male or a female. Sexual differentiation during development then allows males and females to develop different bodies and brains.

3. Male and female vertebrates make different investments in their offspring; consequently, most males of most species are promiscuous and most females of most species are very discriminating in choosing mates. This situation leads to sexual selection pressures that can over time exaggerate sexual dimorphism.

4. There are four different types of mating systems: promiscuity (both sexes mate with multiple partners), polygyny (each male mates with multiple females), polyandry (each female mates with multiple males), and monogamy (a single male and a single female form a lasting bond).

Sexual Differentiation

1. In vertebrates, genetic sex (determined by the presence or absence of a Y chromosome in mammals) determines whether testes or ovaries will develop, and hormonal secretions from the gonads determine whether the rest of the body, including the brain, will develop in a feminine or masculine fashion. In the presence of testicular secretions a male will develop; in the absence of testicular secretions a female will develop.

2. The brains of vertebrates are masculinized by the presence of testicular steroids during early development. Such organizational effects of steroids permanently alter the structure and function of the brain and therefore permanently alter the behavior of the individual.

3. Among the prominent sexual dimorphisms in the nervous system (including the song system of birds, the sexually dimorphic nucleus of the preoptic area in rats, and the spinal nucleus of the bulbocavernosus in mammals), gonadal steroids have been shown to alter characteristics such as neuronal size, neuronal survival, dendritic growth, and synapse elimination to engender sex differences in neural structure and in behavior.

4. Several regions of the human brain are sexually dimorphic. However, we do not know whether these dimorphisms are generated by fetal steroid levels or by sex differences in the early social environment. Neither do we know whether any of the identified sex differences in neural structure are responsible for any sex differences in human behavior.

5. There seems to be no reliable animal model of sexual orientation, which is such a salient aspect of human experience. However, all research indicates that sexual orientation is determined early in life and, especially in men, is not a matter of individual choice.

Recommended Reading

Becker, J. B., Breedlove, S. M., and Crews, D. (1992). *Behavioral endocrinology.* Cambridge, MA: MIT Press.

Blum, D. (1997). *Sex on the brain.* New York: Viking Penguin.

Fausto-Sterling, A. (1985). *Myths of gender.* New York: Basic Books.

Gerall, A. A., Moltz, H., and Ward, I. L. (1992). *Handbook of behavioral neurobiology: Vol. 11, Sexual differentiation.* New York: Plenum.

LeVay, S. (1996). *Queer science.* Cambridge, MA: MIT Press.

Nelson, R. J. (in press). *An introduction to behavioral endocrinology* (2nd ed.). Sunderland, MA: Sinauer.

13 Homeostasis: Active Regulation of Internal States

Museum Boijmans Van Beuningen, Rotterdam

Salvador Dali, *Couple with their Heads Full of Clouds*, 1936

*I*n 1998 a California woman was sentenced to 2 years probation because her daughter, at age 13 and weighing 680 pounds, had died of complications from obesity. Authorities charged the mother with child endangerment because for the last year of her life, the daughter had not seen a physician and had lain on the floor, unable to reach the bathroom or keep herself clean. Some onlookers complained that the mother's punishment was too lenient; others felt she should never have been charged at all. Everyone agrees that the daughter's refusal to attend school or leave the house at all was due to the shame she felt about her weight. Clearly, then, this young girl fervently wished not to be fat. The daughter had tried many diets, yet she steadily gained weight throughout her too-short life.

In a related tragedy, some college wrestlers trying to lose weight quickly just before a tournament followed the traditional route of warming themselves to sweat and lose fluid, but they went too far and died of heart attack. In this chapter we'll learn that our body temperature, weight, and fluid balance are carefully regulated by a web of internal processes. We are not normally even aware of these processes, yet the nervous system is intimately involved in every stage.

Homeostasis Maintains Internal States within a Critical Range

Because warmth, water, and food are vital and scarce, elaborate physiological systems have evolved in the body to monitor and maintain them. One hallmark of all three systems is redundancy: There are several different means of monitoring our stores, of conserving remaining supplies, and of shedding excesses. Therefore the loss of function of one part of the system can be compensated for by the remaining portions. This redundancy helps keep us alive, but it also makes it difficult for us to figure out how the body regulates temperature, water balance, and food intake. Another hallmark of these three regulatory systems is that each one exploits the organism's behavior to regulate and to acquire more heat, water, or food. This chapter will show that all three regulatory systems—for body temperature, water balance, and food intake—are **homeostatic**; that is, they maintain relatively constant values.

The nervous system coordinates these regulatory systems. The brain closely monitors temperature, water supply, and nutrient supply, and uses a variety of neural and hormonal mechanisms to keep them within the critical range. If we have a surplus of any of the three, our bodies have ways to shed the excess, usually without our being aware of it. But when supplies are running out, we must display active behaviors to gain more; the nervous system initiates these behaviors.

If we are losing body heat, our nervous system directs us to seek warmth. When our internal water supplies are low we seek water, and when our internal nutrient supplies are low we seek food. Our conscious experience is that we feel cold, thirsty, or hungry, respectively. Other animals are unable to use words to tell us how they feel, so for the rest of this chapter we will assume that an animal that seeks water is thirsty, and that an animal seeking food is hungry. Probably such animals feel much the same way we do when we say we are thirsty or hungry, but we will not be addressing that issue. Without making any assumptions about the animal's experience, we will say that an animal seeking shelter has an internal drive to conserve heat, an animal seeking water has an internal drive (thirst) for water, and an animal seeking food has an internal drive (hunger) for food. In each case the animal is showing **motivated behavior**—behavior designed to achieve a particular goal. The particular behaviors they display may vary depending on the circumstances but nevertheless serve the goal of gaining warmth, water, or food.

The homeostatic mechanisms that regulate temperature, body fluids, and metabolism are primarily **negative feedback** systems. That is, in each case a desired value or zone is established; this desired value is called the **set point**, by analogy with the setting of a thermostat (Figure 13.1). (We already discussed negative feedback systems in connection with neural circuits in

Chapter 3 and the regulation of hormone secretion in Chapter 5.) A drop in temperature below the set point activates the thermostat, which turns on the heating system. When the thermostat registers a sufficient rise in temperature, it turns off the heating system. (Note that there is a small range of temperature between the "turn on" and "turn off" signals; otherwise the heating system would be going on and off very frequently. Thus there is really a **set zone** rather than a set point.)

The setting of the thermostat can be changed; for example, it can be turned down at night to save energy. The body temperature for most mammals and birds is usually held within a narrow range—about 36 to 38°C (97 to 100°F)—though the set zone can be altered depending on overall conditions and current goals of the organism. Our bodies also integrate the demands for nutrients and water to result in a set range of body weight that is often remarkably narrow. Later in the chapter we will see examples of animals vigorously defending their body weight—maintaining a particular weight in the face of physiological challenges.

Unavoidable Losses Require Us to Gain Heat, Water, and Food

The regulation of internal resources is complicated by the fact that staying alive requires us to give up some of them. Because external temperatures rarely hover at 37°C (98.6°F) for long, we must actively heat or cool

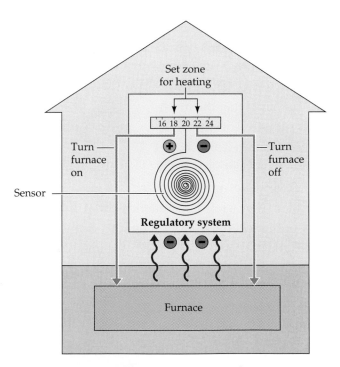

13.1 Negative Feedback
The thermostatically controlled heating system found in homes is an example of a negative feedback system. All such systems have a sensor (in this example a thermometer) to monitor the variable and a device (in this example the furnace) to change the variable. By changing the variable (e.g., by heating the room) the device sends a negative feedback signal to the sensor, turning it off.

our bodies. We lose water vapor with each breath, and through sweating, and because various biochemical processes produce waste chemicals that can be eliminated only with a little water, through urination. Food provides us with energy and nutrients (chemicals needed for growth, maintenance, and repair of the body), but our behavior uses up energy and incurs wear and tear on our bodies, so more energy and nutrients are continuously needed. Our homeostatic mechanisms are constantly challenged by these unavoidable losses (sometimes called obligatory losses), which require us to gain and conserve heat, water, and food constantly.

Important Body Variables Are Maintained through Redundant Homeostatic Systems

For guaranteed performance of vital mechanical and electrical functions, NASA designed space capsules with multiple monitoring units and with parallel systems or backup devices. This redundancy ensures that the failure of one unit or system is not lethal, since other systems can guarantee the same objective. Evolution has similarly endowed the human body with multiple systems. This endowment has complicated researchers' efforts, because interfering with one or another mechanism often produces little or no effect, since parallel or alternative mechanisms assume the burden. For example, unlike most homes, the body has at least three different thermostats; when one is not working, the others continue to regulate temperature. For water regulation there are two different, fairly independent cues that warn the brain when we need to drink. As for eating, no single brain center controls either hunger or its opposite—satiety.

Temperature Regulation

Body Temperature Is a Critical Condition for All Biological Processes

As the interior of a cell cools, chemical reactions slow down. The enzyme systems of mammals and birds are most efficient within a narrow range around 37°C. At lower temperatures, reactions slow down, and some stop altogether. At higher temperatures, protein molecules fold together improperly and thus do not function as they should. At very high temperatures, the amino acids that form proteins begin to break apart and fuse together more or less at random, and we say that the tissue is "fixed" (or, if it is edible tissue, we say it is "cooked"). Brain cells are especially sensitive to high temperatures. A very prolonged, high fever can cause brain centers that regulate heart rate and breathing to die, thus killing the patient.

At very low temperatures, the bilipid layers that make up cellular membranes become so disrupted by the formation of ice molecules that they cannot reform even when thawed. Some animals that cannot avoid subfreezing temperatures—shrimplike krill (Figure 13.2*a*) in the Arctic Ocean, for example—produce "antifreeze" consisting of special molecules that disrupt the formation of ice crystals and prevent damage to membranes (Ahlgren et al., 1988). Arctic ground squirrels (Figure 13.2*b*), however, achieve body temperatures below 0°C during hibernation and apparently do not have antifreeze molecules in their plasma (B. M. Barnes, 1989). How they avoid the formation of ice crystals is not yet understood.

(a)

(b)

13.2 Braving the Cold
Arctic krill (*a*) and golden-mantled ground squirrels (*b*) are two species that sometimes have body temperatures below 0°C. The krill produce an "antifreeze" in body fluids to prevent ice crystals from forming in cell membranes. The ground squirrels do not have such antifreeze; how they avoid the formation of damaging ice crystals is unknown.

Some Animals Generate Heat, Others Must Obtain Heat from the Environment

For centuries it has been recognized that mammals and birds differ from other animals in the way they regulate body temperature. Our ways of characterizing the difference have become more accurate and meaningful over time, but popular terminology still reflects the old division: Mammals and birds are called warm-blooded; all other creatures are called cold-blooded. But this classification is misleading. A fence lizard or a desert iguana—both of which are "cold-blooded"—usually has a body temperature only a degree or two below ours, so it is not really "cold."

The set of terminology that next came into vogue distinguished animals that maintain a constant body temperature, called homeotherms (from the Greek *homos*, "same," and *therme*, "heat"), from those whose body temperature varies with their environment, called poikilotherms (from the Greek *poikilos*, "varied"). This classification also proved inadequate, because some mammals (homeotherms) vary their body temperatures during hibernation. Furthermore, many invertebrates in the depths of the ocean (poikilotherms) never experience a change in the chill of the deep waters, so their body temperatures remain quite constant.

In modern terms we distinguish between endotherms and ectotherms. **Endotherms** (from the Greek *endon*, "within") regulate their body temperature chiefly by internal metabolic processes. **Ectotherms** (from the Greek *ektos*, "outside") get most of their heat from the environment. Most ectotherms do regulate their body temperature, but through behavioral means, such as moving to favorable sites or changing their exposure to external sources of heat. Endotherms (mainly mammals and birds) also choose favorable environments, but primarily they regulate body temperature by making internal adjustments. Whether an animal is an ectotherm or an endotherm, if it is placed in a laboratory situation where there is a gradient of temperature from warm to cold, it will spend most of its time at its preferred environmental temperature. The preferred temperature differs from species to species.

The Advantages of Endothermy Come at a Cost

No one knows whether endothermy arose in a common ancestor of the birds and mammals or arose separately in these two lines. What we do know is that endotherms pay substantial costs for maintaining a high body temperature and keeping it within narrow limits. Much food must be obtained and metabolized, elaborate regulatory systems are required, and departures of body temperature of a few degrees in either direction impair functioning. What benefits led to the evolution of such a complicated and costly system in comparison with that of the ectotherms, who get along with somewhat lower mean body temperatures and have more tolerance for changes in body temperature?

An increased capacity to sustain a high level of muscular activity over prolonged periods may have been the principal gain in the evolution of endothermy (A. F. Bennett and Ruben, 1979). A person's metabolic rate (or heat production) can rise almost tenfold between resting and very strenuous exercise (see Table 13.1). A tenfold increase above the resting level is about the greatest that vertebrates have been known to achieve, whether ectotherms or endotherms. Ectotherms are capable of such bursts of high activity for only a few minutes; in this case anaerobic metabolism—chemical reactions that do not require oxygen—contributes most of the energy. A high level of anaerobic metabolism can be maintained for only a few minutes; then the animal must rest and repay the oxygen debt. Ectotherms can escape from and sometimes even pursue endotherms over short distances, but in a long-distance race the endotherm will win. Probably the capacity for internal thermoregulation evolved along with an increasing capacity to sustain a high level of muscular activity through aerobic metabolism.

Endotherms Generate Heat through Metabolism

The utilization of stored food in the body is known as **metabolism**. Because the breaking of chemical bonds in metabolic processes releases energy as heat, all living (and thus metabolizing) tissues produce heat. The unit of heat is a kilocalorie (kcal); 1 kcal is enough heat to raise the temperature of a liter of water 1°C. An adult human may generate 600 kcal per hour when exercising strenuously, but only 60 kcal per hour when resting.

When the body is at rest, about a third of the heat it generates is produced by the brain. As body activity increases, the heat production of the brain does not rise much, but that of the muscles can increase nearly tenfold, so when we are active our bodies produce a much higher percentage of the heat we generate. Like mechanical devices, muscles produce a good deal of heat while they are accomplishing work. Muscles and gasoline engines have about the same efficiency; each produces about four or five times as much heat as mechanical work. Some of the main ways the human body gains, conserves, and dissipates heat are shown in Figure 13.3.

The rate of heat production can be adjusted to suit conditions, particularly in certain organs. Deposits of brown adipose tissue (also called **brown fat**) are found especially around vital organs in the trunk and around the cervical and thoracic levels of the spinal cord. These fat cells look brown because they are full of mitochondria that break down molecules and produce heat. Under cold conditions the sympathetic ner-

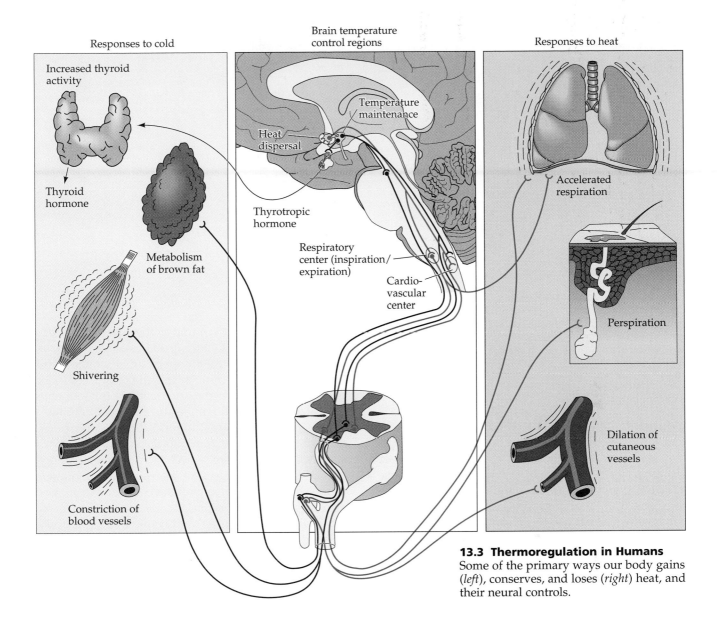

Responses to cold

Brain temperature control regions

Responses to heat

Increased thyroid activity

Thyroid hormone

Metabolism of brown fat

Shivering

Constriction of blood vessels

Temperature maintenance

Heat dispersal

Thyrotropic hormone

Respiratory center (inspiration/expiration)

Cardio-vascular center

Accelerated respiration

Perspiration

Dilation of cutaneous vessels

13.3 Thermoregulation in Humans
Some of the primary ways our body gains (*left*), conserves, and loses (*right*) heat, and their neural controls.

vous system stimulates metabolism within the brown-fat cells, producing heat.

A more conspicuous means by which heat is generated is muscular activity. At low temperatures, nerve impulses cause muscle cells to contract out of synchrony, producing shivering rather than coordinated movements. Humans start to shiver when their body temperature approaches 36.5°C. This response spreads from facial muscles to the arms and legs. The fivefold increase in oxygen uptake that accompanies extreme shivering shows how metabolically intense this response is.

Body Size and Shape Affect Heat Production and Heat Loss

Heat production is closely related to the surface area of the body, because heat is exchanged with the environment primarily at the surface of the body. A big animal like an elephant has relatively little skin surface compared with the volume of its body; a small animal like a canary has a large surface-to-volume ratio. As volume increases, the ratio of surface to volume decreases (Figure 13.4a). A high surface-to-volume ratio means a greater capacity to dissipate heat. You may have noticed that small food items such as peas cool off faster than large objects such as baked potatoes. The reason is that the surface-to-volume ratio of the potato is much lower than that of the pea.

Table 13.1 shows the body sizes of several species of mammals in terms of weight, surface area, and heat production. Smaller animals, because of their larger surface-to-volume ratio, lose heat more rapidly to the environment, so they must produce more heat in relation to body size than larger animals do. For example, from the data of Table 13.1, we see that it takes 20 cats to equal the weight of a human, but the 20 cats together produce twice the heat of the single person. (That's why we have to buy so much cat

Length of side	3	6	12
Surface area	54	216	864
Volume	27	216	1728
Surface-to-volume ratio	2:1	1:1	1:2

3.8:1	2.0:1

13.4 Surface-to-Volume Ratios
(*a*) For a given shape, the ratio of surface to volume of a solid decreases as the volume increases. (*b*) However, forms with different shapes can have very different surface areas, even if the volume is the same, as it is for the two figures shown here.

food!) Small mammals also tend to maintain body temperatures slightly higher than those of large mammals, and they lose heat more easily than larger mammals do. Large animals, on the other hand, lose heat more slowly and thus have lower metabolic rates per gram of body weight.

The effect of surface-to-volume ratio on heat conservation is evident in the distribution of species across environments. Within a group of closely related mammals or birds, for example, those living in cold climates are larger than those in warm environments. Even in a temperate zone, though, a very small mammal like the shrew has to eat almost incessantly to meet its metabolic needs.

Shape also affects the conservation of heat and therefore energy. The humanoid form in Figure 13.4*b*

has exactly the same volume as the squat figure beside it, but the more slender form has almost twice as much surface area as the compact form. Because of its lower surface-to-volume ratio, the more compact body conserves heat better and therefore is better able to protect its internal temperature in a cold climate. Among human groups, taller, more slender body forms have evolved in the Tropics, and shorter, stockier physiques are more typical of colder regions (Figure 13.5). Migrations and the intermingling of human groups blur this tendency, and of course other factors also influence stature, as the pygmies of tropical Africa illustrate. Among many animal groups, body appendages such as the ears are smaller in arctic species than in related tropical species (Figure 13.6). Smaller appendages mean a lower surface-to-volume ratio and thus less heat loss.

Fur of mammals and feathers of birds are special adaptations of the skin that insulate the body from the environment. In cold environments large mammals usually have a thick coat of fur, but thick fur on small animals would interfere with their locomotion. To in-

---

TABLE 13.1   *Body Size and Heat Production of Some Birds and Mammals*

				Energy output per day		
Species	**Body weight (kg)**	**Body surface (m²)**	**Surface-to-weight ratio (m²/kg)**	**Total (kcal)**	**Per unit of body weight (kcal/kg)**	**Per unit of body surface (kcal/m²)**
Canary	0.016	0.006	0.375	5	310	760
Rat	0.2	0.03	0.15	25	130	830
Pigeon	0.3	0.04	0.13	30	100	670
Cat	3.0	0.2	0.07	150	50	750
Human	60	1.7	0.03	1500	25	850
Elephant	3600	24	0.007	47,000	13	2000

(a)

13.5 Adaptations to Extreme Climates
Adaptations to climates include changes in behavior, physiology, and anatomy. Compare, for example, an Eskimo from arctic Alaska (*a*) with a Nilotic inhabitant of tropical Africa (*b*).

(b)

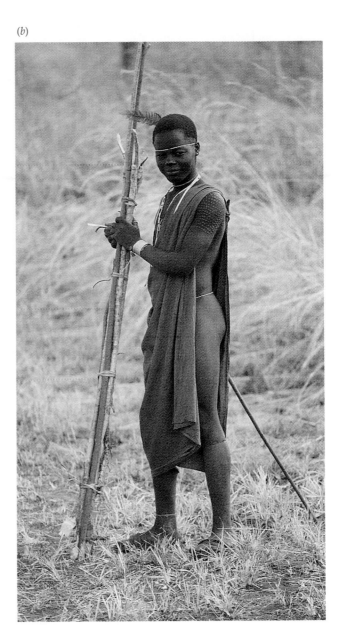

sulate properly, fur or feathers must be kept in good condition—one reason why many mammals and birds spend a great deal of time grooming and preening. For an animal like the sea otter, which spends its life in cold water, insulation is vital; even a small area of matted fur allowing heat loss could be fatal. Most species of birds have a preen gland or oil gland near the base of the tail; the bird uses its beak to distribute

13.6 Adaptations of Appendages to Climate
Variation in the size of the external ear in foxes from arctic (*a*), temperate (*b*), and tropical (*c*) climates.

(a)

(b)

(c)

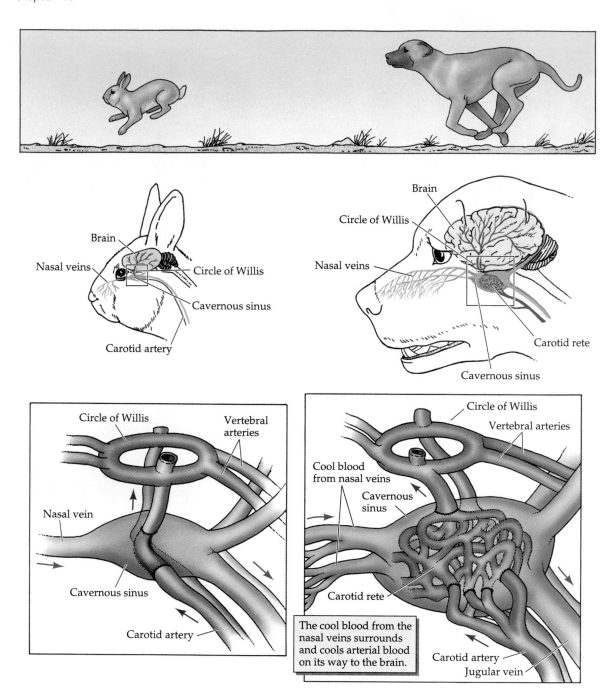

13.7 Exertion Overheats Some Animals More Than Others

Exercise produces heat, but some species, such as the dog, have a special heat exchange system to prevent the brain from overheating (*bottom right*). Human anatomy is more like that of the rabbit (*left*). (From Karasawa et al., 1997).

oil from the gland to dress the feathers and waterproof them. Of course, sometimes an animal needs to lose heat, and different species have different adaptations for doing so (Figure 13.7).

Which Behaviors Can Adjust Body Temperature?

Ectotherms generate little heat through metabolism and therefore must rely heavily on behavioral methods to regulate body temperature. The marine igua-

na of the Galápagos Islands eats seaweed underwater for an hour or more at a time (occasionally coming up for air) in water that is 10 to 15°C cooler than its preferred body temperature. After feeding, the iguana emerges and lies on a warm rock to restore its temperature. While warming up, it lies broadside to the sun to absorb as much heat as possible (Figure 13.8a). When its temperature reaches 37°C, the iguana turns to face the sun and thus absorb less heat, and it may extend its legs to keep its body away from warm surfaces (Figure 13.8b).

(a)

(b)

13.8 Behavioral Control of Body Temperature
(*a*) A Galápagos marine iguana, upon emerging from the cold sea, raises its body temperature by hugging a warm rock and lying broadside to the sun. (*b*) Once its temperature is sufficiently high, the iguana reduces its surface contact with the rock and faces the sun to minimize its exposure. These behaviors afford considerable control over body temperature. (Photographs by Mark R. Rosenzweig.)

Many other ectotherms regulate their temperature in similar ways. Some snakes, for example, adjust their coils to expose more or less surface to the sun and thus keep their internal temperature relatively constant during the day. Bees regulate the temperature inside the hive by their behavior, keeping the temperature in the brood area at 35 to 36°C. When the air temperature is low, the bees crowd into the brood area and shiver, thus generating heat. When the air temperature is high, the bees reduce the temperature in the brood area by fanning with their wings and by evaporative cooling.

Even endotherms such as mammals and birds control their exposure to the sun and to hot or cold surfaces to avoid making excessive demands on their internal regulatory mechanisms. In hot desert regions many small mammals, such as the kangaroo rat, remain in underground burrows during the day and appear above ground only at night, when the environment is relatively cool. Humans have devised many cultural practices to adapt to conditions of cold or heat. For example, Eskimo learned to design clothing that insulates well but permits the dissipation of heat through vents. Other Eskimo cultural adaptations include the design of efficient shelters, sharing of body heat, choice of diet, and use of seal oil lamps (E. F. Moran, 1981).

The behavioral thermoregulatory responses of ectotherms and endotherms can be divided into three categories:

1. Changing exposure of the body surface—for example, huddling or extending limbs
2. Changing external insulation—for example, by using clothing or nests
3. Selecting a surrounding that is less thermally stressful—for example, by moving to the shade or into a burrow

Humans seldom wait for the body to get cold before putting on a coat. We anticipate homeostatic signals on the basis of experience. As any parent will tell you, shivering reflects a lapse of intelligent behavior.

Young Birds and Mammals Need Help to Regulate Body Temperature

Fetuses maintained in the mother's body and fertilized eggs rely on their parents to provide warmth and regulate temperature. Most birds keep their eggs warm by using a specially vascularized area of skin (the brood patch), which transfers heat efficiently to the eggs. Even after hatching or birth, the young of many species cannot regulate their temperature very well, mostly because they are small (and lose heat quickly) and have limited energy resources. So they must continue to be protected by their parents.

Rat pups are born without hair, which makes it difficult to maintain body temperature when exposed to cold. The rat mother keeps her pups protected in a warm nest, and this response of the mother is related to her own thermoregulation. As shown in Figure 13.9*a*, rat pups are able to generate heat from brown fat deposits such as that between the shoulder blades from birth (Blumberg et al., 1997).

Nonetheless, one problem for newborn rats is insulating their hairless bodies to conserve the heat they generate. They huddle together and vary their positions in the huddle in accordance with changes in temperature (Figure 13.9*b*). Rectal temperatures and

(a)

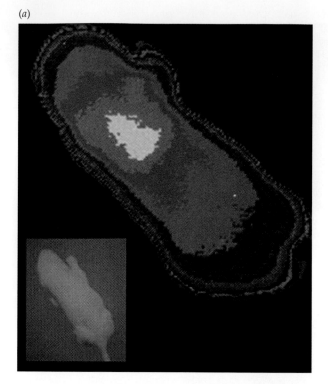

(b) High temperature   Low temperature

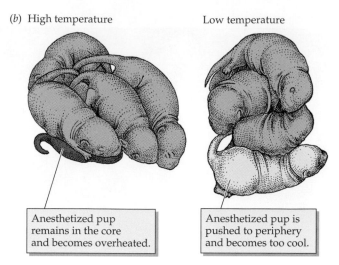

Anesthetized pup remains in the core and becomes overheated.

Anesthetized pup is pushed to periphery and becomes too cool.

13.9 Physiological and Social Thermoregulation
(a) Infrared thermograph of the dorsal surface of a week-old rat pup; the inset photograph shows the orientation of the pup. Areas of highest heat production are coded in orange and yellow, and the prominent yellow "hot spot" between the shoulder blades overlies a depot of brown fat, a thermogenic (i.e., heat producing) organ found in the young of nearly all mammals studied thus far (it is also found in adults, especially in hibernators such as ground squirrels). When rat pups are placed in a cold environment, they begin producing heat using brown fat. (b) Rat pups also use behavioral mechanisms to conserve heat. Animals push to the center of a litter to gain heat and move to the periphery to cool off. Thus an anesthetized pup will be left in the center during high temperatures and pushed to the periphery when temperatures are low. (Part a courtesy of Mark S. Blumberg; b after Alberts, 1978.)

oxygen consumption were measured in pups of different ages placed in a cool chamber (23 to 24°C), either singly or in a group of four. In 5-day-old rats, the temperature of the isolated pups fell below 30°C in less than an hour; those in the group maintained their temperatures above 30°C for 4 hours (Alberts, 1978). Huddling also significantly reduced oxygen consumption. The form of the huddle changes according to ambient temperatures; it is loose in warm temperatures but tightly cohesive in the cold. Each pup frequently changes positions in the clump, sometimes positioned inside and at other times at the periphery, effectively regulating its temperature. In effect, pups share the costs and benefits of this group activity. Thus, early in the rat's development its thermoregulation benefits from social interaction.

Some Endotherms Survive by Letting Their Body Temperature Plummet

All endotherms show some variation in body temperature. There's usually a daily fluctuation in body temperature that constitutes a circadian rhythm, which we'll discuss in Chapter 14. When we are ill we may have a fever. This fever is brought on by the body to help fight off infection (see Topic 13.1, Fever Is an Important Ally to Combat Infection). But some endotherms occupy habitats with extreme seasonal variations in temperature. For example, golden-mantled ground squirrels in the far north survive long, cold winters by staying in their burrow, curling up in a tight ball, and allowing their body temperature to plummet. An animal in this state, called **torpor**, is cold

Special topic

to the touch and appears not to breathe, but it does take a breath every few moments or so. Its heart still beats, but only very slowly.

No one knows how these animals evolved the ability to survive this drop in body temperature, which would certainly kill a human, but it seems clear that they save a great deal of energy while in torpor. The state does not last the entire winter; once a week or so the animals arouse from torpor by raising their body temperature, move about the burrow, check on the outside conditions, and if things look grim, reenter torpor. The arousal episode requires energy but lasts less than an hour, so the animals save a good deal of energy over the winter (Heldmaier and Ruf, 1992). Reduced glucose availability, which indicates a shortage of available energy, can trigger an episode of torpor (Dark et al., 1994).

The Brain Monitors and Regulates Body Temperature

The nervous system controls and regulates all the processes of heat production and heat loss, sometimes with assistance from the endocrine system. What parts of the nervous system are active in these processes?

In the 1880s physiologists found that small lesions in the hypothalamus of dogs elevated body temperature. Barbour (1912) manipulated the temperature of the hypothalamus in dogs by implanting silver wires. When the wires were heated, body temperature fell; when the wires were cooled, body temperature rose. These results suggested that body temperature is monitored in the hypothalamus and that when temperature there departs in either direction from the desired level, compensatory actions are triggered. In the 1950s, electrical recording from single cells revealed that some changed their discharge rate in response to small increases or decreases of brain temperature; these cells are scattered throughout the preoptic area (POA) and the anterior hypothalamus.

Lesion experiments in mammals indicate that there are different sites for two kinds of regulation: (1) regulation by locomotor and other behaviors common to both endotherms and ectotherms, and (2) physiological regulation characteristic of endotherms. Lesions in the lateral hypothalamus of rats abolished behavioral regulation of temperature but did not affect the autonomic thermoregulatory responses such as shivering and vasoconstriction (Satinoff and Shan, 1971; van Zoeren and Stricker, 1977). On the other hand, lesions in the POA of rats impaired the autonomic responses but did not interfere with such behaviors as pressing levers to turn heating lamps or cooling fans on or off (Satinoff and Rutstein, 1970; van Zoeren and Stricker, 1977). This is a clear example of parallel circuits for two different ways of regulating the same variable.

Receptors at the surface of the body also monitor temperature. If you enter a cold room, you soon begin to shiver—long before your core temperature falls. If you enter a hot greenhouse or a sauna, you begin to sweat before your hypothalamic temperature rises. The skin provides information to central circuits, which promptly initiate corrective action in anticipation of a change in core temperature.

Does the Body Have a Single Master Thermostat?

It would be simple to think that a single integrating center accounts for thermoregulation. However, evidence has accumulated to suggest that a single thermostat is inadequate to account for all the facets of thermoregulation. For one thing, as we saw in the previous section, there appear to be different brain sites for behavioral and autonomic regulation of temperature. Even two thermoregulatory circuits may not be sufficient.

Competing hypotheses

For example, W. W. Roberts and Mooney (1974) warmed small sites in the diencephalon and mesencephalon of rats. Normally a rat exposed to increasing heat shows successive potentiation of three different responses: First it grooms, then it moves about actively, and finally it lies quietly in a sprawled-out position. Grooming allows the rat to lose heat by evaporation of saliva from the skin, activity normally helps the rat locate a cooler spot, and sprawling out helps the rat dissipate heat without generating more heat through activity. Local heating of the brain does not produce this sequence; instead, each of these behaviors tends to be elicited by the heating of a different brain region. These observations are not consistent with the hypothesis of a single thermostat.

In addition, there seems to be a hierarchy of thermoregulatory circuits, some located at the spinal level, some centered in the midbrain, and others in the hypothalamus, including the POA. For example, spinal animals (in which the brain is disconnected from the spinal cord) can regulate body temperature somewhat, indicating that a temperature monitor is available to the spinal cord and/or the body. Such animals die in extended cold or heat, however, because they do not respond until body temperature deviates 2 to 3°C from normal values.

Satinoff (1978) suggested that the thermal set zones are broader in "lower" regions of the nervous system (Figure 13.10). The thermoregulatory systems at the "highest" level—the hypothalamus—have the narrowest neutral zones, and they normally coordinate and adjust the activity of the other systems. This

13.10 Multiple Thermostats in the Nervous System Thermoneutral zones of thermoregulatory systems are narrower at the higher levels of the nervous system than at the lower levels. (After Satinoff, 1978.)

(*a*) Hypothalamus   (*b*) Brain stem   (*c*) Spinal cord

Response — Core temperature (°C)

13.11 Basic Elements of Mammalian Thermoregulatory Systems

Afferents

Skin surface
Body core
Hypothalamus

Neural regions

Spinal cord
Brain stem
Hypothalamus

Effectors

Behavioral responses
Shivering
Heat seeking/avoiding
  behaviors

Autonomic responses
Vasoconstriction/dilation
Sweating
Respiration
Brown fat stimulation
Thyroid hormone secretion

arrangement can give the impression of a single system, although in reality there are multiple interlinked systems. Figure 13.11 summarizes the basic thermoregulatory system: Receptors in the skin, body core, and hypothalamus detect temperature and transmit that information to three neural regions (spinal cord, brain stem, and hypothalamus). If body temperature moves outside the set zone, each of these neural regions can initiate autonomic and behavioral responses to return body temperature to the set zone.

Fluid Regulation

Our Cells Evolved to Function in Seawater

The first living creatures on Earth were single-celled organisms that arose in the sea. In this setting—a large body of water with fairly uniform concentrations of salts and minerals—most basic cellular reactions evolved, including DNA production and replication, the manufacture of proteins from amino acids, and the storing and harnessing of chemical energy from ATP. These various reactions evolved by natural selection to proceed efficiently only in a particular concentration of salt water. For these creatures, maintaining the proper concentration of salts in the water was effortless: They simply let seawater inside the cell membrane and let it out again. But when multicellular animals began coming out of the water, they either had to evolve all new cellular processes to work without water or they had to bring the water with them. Only the latter solution (no pun intended) was feasible.

Land animals had to prevent dehydration (excessive loss of water) so that their cells would work properly. Thus, they needed a more or less watertight outer layer of cells, and they had to maintain the proper concentration of salts and other molecules in the water. The composition of the fluid inside your body, once proteins and the like have been removed, is still similar to that of seawater. During evolution, diversity has arisen across species in the concentration of salt in plasma. For example, in closely related fish species,

those that inhabit fresh water have a lower salt concentration in the plasma than those that inhabit seawater. For a given species, if the concentration of molecules is altered even a small amount, the most basic cellular functions cease working properly and the animal dies. A very few species, such as salmon, have adaptations that allow them to live in fresh water at hatching, to grow up in salt water, and to return again to fresh water to breed.

We cannot seal ourselves from the outside world, hoarding our "precious bodily fluids" without alteration. For one thing, completely watertight outer layers are difficult to make and cumbersome. Of more importance, many body functions require that we use up some water (and some salt molecules), as, for example, when we produce urine to rid ourselves of waste molecules. Furthermore, giving up some water molecules can be a very good way to shed excess body heat, as we saw in the discussion of temperature regulation. We are obliged to lose some water molecules, and therefore we are obliged to get some more (Table 13.2). Once we begin relinquishing and replacing our body's water, we must monitor and regulate the composition of body fluid to maintain basic cellular processes in order to live.

The Water in Our Body Moves Back and Forth between Two Major Compartments

Most of our water is contained within the billions of cells that make up our body; this is the intracellular compartment. But some fluid is outside of our cells, in the extracellular compartment. The extracellular compartment can be subdivided into the fluid between cells (interstitial fluid) and blood plasma (the protein-rich fluid that carries red and white blood cells). By convention, water in the stomach or elsewhere in the

TABLE 13.2	*Average Daily Water Balance of an Adult Human*
Source	**Quantity (l)**
Approximate intake	
Fluid water	1.2
Water content of food	1.0
Water from oxidation of food	0.3
Total	**2.5**
Approximate output	
Urine	1.4
Evaporative loss	0.9
Feces	0.2
Total	**2.5**

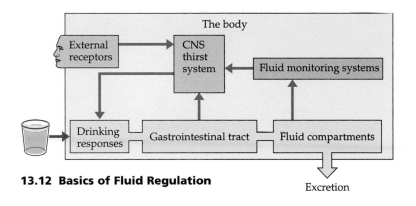

13.12 Basics of Fluid Regulation

uted throughout the beaker. If the water is hot, the dye molecules spread out more quickly. If we divide the beaker of water in half with a solid barrier that is impermeable to water and dye and we put the dye in the water on one side, the molecules distribute themselves only within that half. If we divide the beaker with a barrier that impedes dye molecules only a little, then the dye first distributes itself within the initial half and then slowly invades and distributes itself across both halves. In this case we say the barrier is permeable to the dye. A barrier such as a cell membrane that is permeable to some molecules but not others is referred to as **semipermeable**.

Before we look at what happens with semipermeable membranes, let's review a few terms. The liquid in our discussion of membranes is referred to as a **solvent**. The solid (e.g., salt) dissolved in the solvent is called a **solute**. A semipermeable membrane that allows water to pass through it but prevents the passage of salt (NaCl) molecules demonstrates the principles of osmosis (Figure 13.13). If salty water is on one side of the semipermeable membrane and pure water on the other, the motion of the salt molecules pulls in water from the other compartment. The tendency to equalize salt concentrations across the membrane causes some of the water molecules to overcome gravity, raising the level of the liquid on the salt side (see Figure 13.13c).

Put another way, molecules have a tendency to spread out—to move *down* concentration gradients

gastrointestinal tract is considered to be outside the body—in neither of these compartments. Water must leave the gastrointestinal tract and enter the body before we can make use of it. Similarly, water that has reached the bladder cannot be returned to the body and so is effectively outside the body as well. Figure 13.12 presents a simplified version of the basic systems that regulate fluid intake. Water continually migrates between the intracellular and extracellular compartments. To understand the forces driving this migration, we must understand osmosis.

Osmosis is the passive movement of molecules from one place to another. The motive force behind osmosis is the constant vibration and movement of molecules. If we put a drop of food coloring in a beaker of water, the molecules of dye meander about because of this jiggling until they are more or less uniformly distrib-

13.13 Osmosis
Water passes through a semipermeable membrane in whichever direction is necessary to maintain an equal concentration on both sides. Water moves in the same way between compartments in the human body.

Equal concentration of solute on both sides, so no net change.

Add water to one side.

Water molecules pass through semipermeable membrane, leading to equal concentration of solute on both sides. Concentration of solute is lower (on both sides) than it was before.

Add salt (NaCl) to one side.

Water molecules on left cross membrane to reach equal solute concentration on both sides.

(from an area of greater concentration to an area of lower concentration). We referred to this tendency in Chapter 3 to explain the movement of ions during generation of the action potential. In the case we have outlined here, in which the semipermeable membrane blocks the passage of salt molecules, the water molecules are moving into the compartment where they are less concentrated (because the salt molecules are there). The force that pushes or pulls water across the membrane (the force that the solutes exert on the membrane that is impermeable to them) is called **osmotic pressure**.

Cell membranes are not as passive as you might think; they strongly resist the passage of some molecules and allow other molecules to pass freely. Recall from Chapter 3, for example, that neurons normally allow very few sodium (Na^+) ions to pass through their membrane unless the voltage-sensitive Na^+ channels are opened, beginning the action potential. We refer to the concentration of solute in a solution as **osmolality**. Normally the concentration of NaCl in the extracellular fluid of mammals is about 0.9% (weight to volume, which means there's about 0.9 g of NaCl for every 100 ml of water). A solution with this concentration of salt is called physiological saline and is described as **isotonic**, having the same concentration of salt as mammalian fluids have. A solution with more salt is **hypertonic**; a solution lower in salt is **hypotonic**.

Before being administered, injected drugs are usually mixed in isotonic solution rather than in pure water because if pure water were injected into a muscle, the water would be pulled inside cells (which are filled with ions) by osmotic pressure and would rupture the cells. At the other extreme, if hypertonic saline were injected, water would be pulled out of the cells, and that too could prove lethal. These fates could befall any cells exposed to water of the wrong tonicity, so it is crucial

that we prevent the fluid surrounding our cells from becoming either too concentrated or too dilute.

The Extracellular Fluid Compartment Serves as a Buffer

The volume of a cell probably can change slightly as proteins are made or degraded, or as new membrane is added. At any one time, however, each cell has a particular volume and is filled with enzymes and other proteins. Because these proteins cannot pass through the cell's external membrane, the cell needs to take in enough water molecules to keep the internal concentrations of salts and proteins within the range at which biochemical reactions run smoothly.

Normally water molecules can pass out of the cell freely, but if a process such as osmotic pressure forces water into the cell too quickly, it will rupture and die. Viewed this way, the extracellular fluid is a "buffer"—a reservoir that provides and accepts water molecules so that cells can maintain proper internal conditions. The nervous system is responsible for ensuring that the extracellular compartment has about the right amount of water and solute to allow cells to absorb or shed water molecules readily, as conditions dictate.

Two Internal Cues Trigger Thirst

In addition to acting as a buffer, the extracellular fluid is an indicator of conditions in the intracellular compartment. In fact, the nervous system carefully monitors the extracellular compartment to determine whether we should seek water. Two cues indicate that more water may be needed: low extracellular volume (**hypovolemic thirst**) and high extracellular solute concentration (**osmotic thirst**). We'll consider each in turn.

13.14 Two Kinds of Thirst
(a) Hypovolemic thirst is triggered by the loss of blood or other body fluids (such as through diarrhea or vomiting) that contain both solutes and water. In this case, extracellular fluid is depleted without the solute concentration being changed in either the intracellular or the extracellular compartments, so there is no osmotic pressure to push water from one compartment to the other. (b) Osmotic thirst is triggered when the total volume of water is constant, but a sudden increase in the amount of solute in the extracellular compartment (as after a very salty meal) exerts osmotic pressure that pulls water out of the intracellular compartment.

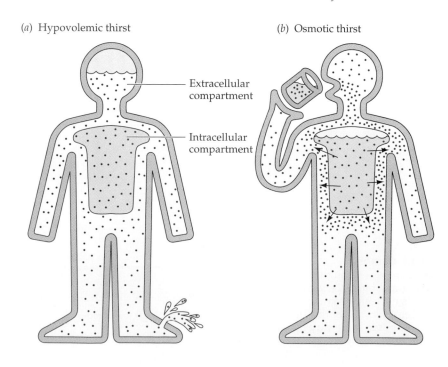

(a) Hypovolemic thirst (b) Osmotic thirst

Extracellular compartment

Intracellular compartment

Hypovolemic Thirst Is Triggered by a Loss of Water Volume

The example of hypovolemic thirst that is most easily understood is one we hope you never experience— serious blood loss (hemorrhage). Any animal that loses a significant amount of blood has a lowered total blood volume. Thus, blood vessels that would normally be full and slightly stretched no longer contain their full capacity. Blood pressure drops, and the individual (unless unconscious) becomes thirsty. Note that losing water from blood loss (or from diarrhea or vomiting) does not change the concentration of the extracellular fluid, because salts and other ions are lost with the fluid. Rather, only the *volume* of the extracellular fluid is affected in these instances (Figure 13.14*a*). However, continued loss in the extracellular compartment leads to fluid passing out of the intracellular compartment. So when the brain is informed of the initial drop in extracellular volume (by pressure receptors in major blood vessels and the heart known as **baroreceptors**) it initiates thirst to replace the water and salt hunger to replace salts.

The role of vasopressin.   When baroreceptors detect a drop in blood pressure (probably by detecting change in the tension in artery walls), they communicate that information through the autonomic nervous system. Selective potentiation of certain autonomic responses counteracts that drop in pressure. The sympathetic portion of the autonomic nervous system stimulates muscles in the artery walls to constrict, which reduces the size of the vessels, compensating for the reduced volume. The brain also receives information from the autonomic nervous system and in response releases the peptide hormone vasopressin from the posterior pituitary gland. The vasopressin further constricts blood vessel walls and instructs the kidneys to reduce the flow of water to the bladder. The latter function explains why this hormone is sometimes called antidiuretic hormone (ADH), as we saw in Chapter 5. (A diuretic is a substance that causes excessive urination.)

In the disease **diabetes insipidus**, the production of vasopressin ceases, and the kidneys retain less water; they send more urine to the bladder, and that urine is very pale and dilute (insipid). A consequence of all this urination is that the person is chronically thirsty and must drink a lot of water. Treatment with vasopressin

 Animal model relieves the symptoms. Some rats have a mutation that keeps them from producing functional vasopressin. These Brattleboro rats (so called because they were first isolated in Brattleboro, Vermont) show the symptoms of diabetes insipidus (Figure 13.15). (Note that when people talk about diabetes, they usually do not mean diabetes insipidus, but are referring to diabetes mellitus, which we'll discuss later in this chapter).

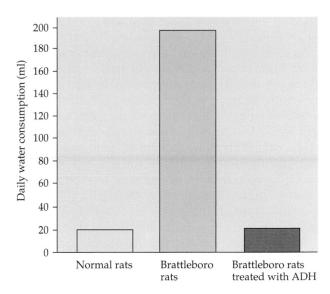

13.15 Inherited Diabetes Insipidus in Rats
Unable to produce vasopressin (ADH), Brattleboro rats urinate profusely and so must drink a lot of water. Treatment with ADH corrects this condition, which is known as diabetes insipidus.

The renin–angiotensin system.   The kidneys also detect the reduced blood flow accompanying hypovolemia and release a hormone called renin into the circulation, triggering a cascade of hormones (Figure 13.16). The renin reacts with a protein called angiotensinogen to form the protein angiotensin I. The angiotensin I is converted to **angiotensin II**, which seems to be the active product. (The first demonstrated effect of this protein was to increase blood pressure, which is how it got its name: from the Greek

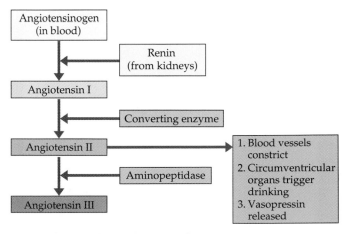

13.16 The Angiotensin Cascade
A drop in blood volume is detected by the kidneys. The kidneys then release renin, which catalyzes the conversion of angiotensinogen (already present in blood) into angiotensin I. Angiotensin I is converted into angiotensin II (the most biologically active of the angiotensins) and angiotensin III.

angeion, "blood vessel," and the Latin *tensio,* "tension or pressure.")

Angiotensin II has several water-conserving actions. In addition to constricting blood vessels, angiotensin II triggers the release of vasopressin. In addition, very low doses of angiotensin II injected into the preoptic area are extremely effective in eliciting drinking, even in animals that are not deprived of water (A. N. Epstein et al., 1970). When administered to rats that had been deprived of food but not water, angiotensin II caused them to stop eating and start drinking; thus, its effect is highly specific. It appears, then, that angiotensin II can also act on the brain to trigger the sensation of thirst, prompting the animal to drink.

Where in the brain does angiotensin II act? Although the original work found the preoptic area to be the most sensitive site, it was difficult to see how angiotensin II could reach receptors in this region, since the protein does not penetrate the blood–brain barrier. Attention then focused on the **circumventricular organs**. As their name suggests, these organs lie in the walls of the cerebral ventricles (Figure 13.17). The blood–brain barrier is somewhat "leaky" in these regions, so the neurons there have access to blood proteins that other brain regions never see. The circumventricular organs also contain receptor sites that can be affected by substances in the cerebrospinal fluid, and information about stimulation of these sites is carried by axons of the circumventricular cells into other parts of the nervous system.

The neurons in one of these regions, the subfornical organ, rapidly respond to intravenous injections of angiotensin II by showing increased metabolic activity (Kadekaro et al., 1989) and expressing IEG (immediate early gene) products (Lebrun et al., 1995). Thus, the subfornical organ may be one of the brain sites responding to angiotensin II by triggering thirst. There is

Competing hypotheses

some doubt about whether angiotensin II regulates thirst in normal situations, because reductions in blood volume that induce thirst do not always produce a measurable change in the concentration of angiotensin II in the blood (S. F. Abraham et al., 1975; Stricker, 1977). Of course, there may be more subtle changes in the concentration or distribution of angiotensin II that are not detected by present blood measures.

Osmotic Thirst Is Triggered by a Change in the Concentration of Extracellular Fluid

A more common way to trigger thirst than by loss of blood is by loss of water, through respiration, perspiration, or urination. Although some salt is lost along with the water, generally more water is lost. Thus, in addition to the reduction in volume of the extracellular fluid, which triggers the responses described in the previous section, the solute concentration of the extracellular fluid increases. The result is that water is pulled out of cells as the body tries to balance the concentrations of the intracellular and extracellular compartments. The solute concentration can be increased without an accompanying increase in volume—for example, by intake of salty food. Such an increase in solute concentration triggers a thirst that is independent of extracellular volume: osmotic thirst (see Figure 13.14*b*). Osmotic thirst causes us to seek water to protect the intracellular compartment from becoming so depleted of water that its cells are damaged.

In the 1950s it was shown that injecting a small amount of hypertonic (salty) solution into regions of the hypothalamus causes animals to start drinking. This observation suggested that some hypothalamic cells might be **osmoreceptors**—that is, cells that respond to changes in osmotic pressure. Electrical recordings from single nerve cells have revealed osmotically responsive neurons spread widely throughout the preoptic area, the anterior hypothalamus, the supraoptic nucleus, and the organum vasculosum of the lamina terminalis (OVLT), a circumventricular organ (see Figure 13.17). Perhaps these cells themselves detect the change in osmolality and are themselves osmoreceptors, or perhaps they are informed by other, true osmoreceptors. If there are neuronal osmoreceptors, they may be more "elastic" than other cells and change their rate of firing based on whether they are full (when the extracellular fluid concentration is normal) or "deflated" (when more concentrated extracellular fluid draws water out of the cell). Any osmoreceptor cells may also reside among the circumventricular organs, including the OVLT and the subfornical organ, where the blood–brain barrier is weak.

In any case, the neural circuits through which osmoreceptors trigger drinking have yet to be fully defined. The two types of thirst (hypovolemic and osmotic), the two fluid compartments (extracellular and intracellular), and the multiple methods to conserve

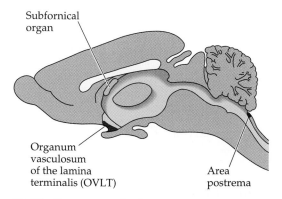

13.17 Circumventricular Organs
The circumventricular organs, here seen in a midsagittal view of the rat brain, mediate between the brain and the cerebrospinal fluid (blue). The blood–brain barrier is weak in the subfornical organ and the OVLT, so neurons there can monitor the osmolality of blood.

13.18 A More Complete View of Fluid Regulation
This more detailed version of Figure 13.12 depicts the sizes of the fluid compartments in proportion to their relative volumes. Most of our water is in the intracellular compartment, and these systems work to protect that compartment from change.

counteract our thirst (hypovolemic or osmotic). Normally all the signals—blood volume, osmolality, moisture in the mouth, estimates of the amount of water we've ingested that's "on the way"—register agreement, but the cessation of one signal alone will not stop thirst; in this way animals ensure against dehydration.

Homeostatic Regulation of Salt Is Required for Effective Regulation of Water

Animals may travel great distances to eat salt (Figure 13.19), and the sodium (Na^+) is particularly important to fluid balance. The reason is that we cannot maintain water in the extracellular compartment without solutes; if the extracellular compartment contained pure water, osmotic pressure would drive it into the cells, killing them. The number of Na^+ ions we possess primarily determines how much water we can retain. Thus, thirsty animals may prefer slightly salty water (as long as it's hypotonic) over pure water, and this preference may be adaptive for conserving water. Some Na^+ loss is inevitable, as during urination. But when water is at a premium, when an animal is thirsty, the body tries to conserve Na^+ in order to retain water. The mineralocorticoid, steroid hormone **aldosterone** is crucial to Na^+ conservation. Like vasopressin, aldosterone acts directly on the kidneys, but aldosterone induces the kidneys to conserve Na^+ (while vasopressin acts to conserve water). Aldosterone conserves some sodium to aid water retention, but animals must find salt in their diets to survive.

Since some Na^+ aids water retention, you might think that seawater would quench thirst—but it doesn't. Seawater is hypertonic—it has too much Na^+. We lose some water each day without Na^+ (through our skin, with our breathing) and that sodium-free water must be replaced. Adding isotonic water will not help restore the water-to-sodium ratio. If we could excrete lots of sodium ions in our urine, we could drink seawater, use some of the water molecules to replace the day's loss, and excrete the excess salt. But our kidneys cannot excrete enough additional Na^+ in the urine to allow this.

water make for a fairly complicated system for the regulation of water (Figure 13.18).

We Don't Stop Drinking Just Because Our Throat and Mouth Are Wet

Although plausible, the most obvious explanation of why we stop drinking—that our previously dry throat and mouth are now wet—is quite wrong. In one test of this hypothesis, thirsty animals were allowed to drink water but had the water diverted out of the esophagus through a small tube. They remained thirsty and continued drinking. Thus, we conclude that moistening the mouth is not sufficient to stop the behavior of drinking or the sensation of thirst. Furthermore, we stop drinking before water has left the gastrointestinal tract and entered the extracellular compartment. Somehow we monitor how much water we have ingested and stop in *anticipation* of correcting the extracellular volume and/or osmolality. Experience may teach us and other animals how to gauge accurately whether we've ingested enough to

Competing hypotheses

13.19 Hungry for Salt
Rabbits that inhabit sodium-deficient habitats, such as these rabbits living in alpine regions of Australia, will devour wooden pegs impregnated with sodium. Rabbits in sodium-rich habitats ignore such pegs. (From Denton, 1982.)

Marine mammals have found a means of excreting excess salt, via kidneys that can produce very concentrated urine. Many species of desert rodents can produce highly concentrated urine to help conserve water. Some seabirds, including gulls and petrels, have specialized salt glands near the nostrils that can excrete highly concentrated salt solutions (Schmidt-Nielsen, 1960); thus, they can drink seawater. Perhaps most impressive are the fishes (e.g., salmon) that can adapt to either a saltwater or a freshwater environment.

Food and Energy Regulation

Feast or famine—these are poles of human experience. We are so dependent on food for energy and for building and maintaining our bodies that hunger is a compelling motive and flavors are powerful reinforcements. The need to eat shapes our daily schedules and molds our activities. Our newspapers are full of food-related information—news of successes or failures of food crops; famines and droughts; laws and treaties governing the import and export of foods; hunger strikes; recipes and articles about food; advertisements for restaurants and kitchen appliances; effects of diet and obesity on health; clinics to treat weight problems. A major part of any economy is devoted to the raising, processing and preparing, packaging, transporting, and distributing of food. Although much of our involvement with food has purely human cultural aspects, our basic reliance on food for energy and nutrition is shared with all other animals. In the remainder of this chapter we will look at the general needs and physiological regulation of feeding and energy expenditure, as well as some species-specific aspects of food-related behavior and regulation.

Nutrient Regulation Requires the Anticipation of Future Needs

The regulation of eating and of body energy is intimately related to the regulation of body temperature and water, which we have already considered, but it is more complicated. One reason for the greater complexity is that food is needed not only to supply energy but also to supply nutrients. **Nutrients**, in the technical meaning of the term, are chemicals that are not used as sources of energy but that are required for the effective functioning of the body; for example, they are needed for the growth, maintenance, and repair of body structures. We do not know all the nutritional requirements of the body—even for humans. Of the 20 amino acids found in our bodies, nine are difficult or impossible for us to manufacture, so we must find them in our diet. These nine are thus called essential amino acids. Similarly, we must obtain a few fatty acids from food. Other nutritional requirements include about 15 vitamins and several minerals.

One reason that eating and nutrient regulation are complicated is that no animal can afford to run out of energy or nutrients; there must be a reserve on hand at all times. If the reserves are too large, though, mobility (for avoiding predators or securing prey) will be compromised. Thus, the neurobiology of feeding requires us to understand how the organism *anticipates* the need for energy and nutrients, as well as how these resources are moved in and out of various body reservoirs. For the cells of the body to receive and use vital nutrients, ingested food must be converted into simpler chemicals. These simpler substances are the products of **digestion**, a series of mechanical and chemical processes that take place in the digestive tract.

Most of Our Food Is Used to Provide Us with Energy

All the energy we need to move, think, breathe, and maintain body temperature is derived in the same way: It is released as the chemical bonds of complex molecules are broken to form smaller, simpler compounds. In a sense we "burn" food just as a car burns gasoline for energy. To raise body temperature we release the bond energy as heat. For other bodily processes, such as those in the brain, the energy is utilized by more sophisticated biochemical processes. In either case we assess the amount of energy used in terms of calories. (Recall that in physics, a calorie is the amount of energy it takes to raise the temperature of 1 ml of water by 1°C.) When nutritionists talk about calories in food, they are describing the potential energy available. Unfortunately, what a nutritionist calls a calorie is actually 1000 calories (a kilocalorie) as defined by physicists. By convention, nutritionists simply leave off the "kilo-" prefix. To avoid confusion, we will use "kilocalories" (kcal) as defined in physics. We can gauge metabolic rate, the amount of energy we use during a given period, in terms of kilocalories per day (kcal/day).

Some of the energy in food cannot be converted to metabolizable form and is instead excreted. In a study of metabolism in the laboratory rat, about 75% of the ingested energy became available for use in bodily functions (Corbett and Keesey, 1982). The available energy is used in one of three activities:

1. *Processing of newly ingested food.* Typically both metabolic rate and heat production rise just after a meal, and this rise has been interpreted as reflecting energy used to process food. The energy utilization for processing food amounts to about 8%.
2. *Basal metabolism.* The greatest part of the energy— about 55%—is used for maintaining body heat and other resting functions, such as neural potentials.
3. *Active behavioral processes.* Only about 12 to 13% of the energy is spent on this function. In an environment more conducive to activity than the small metabolic chamber used to take these measurements in the laboratory, the percentage of energy spent on active behavioral processes probably would be larger.

It used to be thought that only the expenditure of energy for active behavioral processes showed much elasticity and that basal metabolism and heat production caused by feeding were fixed. In fact, the rate of basal metabolism is known to follow a rule, de-

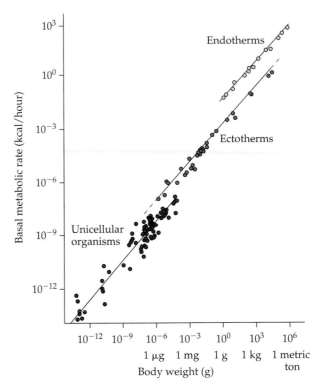

13.20 Relation between Body Size and Metabolism Over a wide range of body weights, basal metabolic rate increases in a very regular, predictable fashion. However, endotherms have a higher metabolic rate than ectotherms of a similar body weight. (After Hemmingsen, 1960.)

vised by Max Kleiber (1947), that relates energy expenditure to body weight:

$$kcal/day = 70 \times weight^{0.75}$$

where weight is expressed in kilograms. This rule has been shown to apply from the largest mammals to mice—a range in size greater than 3000 to 1 (Figure 13.20). Interestingly, this rule holds across species but not within species, which warns us that body weight is only one factor affecting metabolic rate.

Within a species, an animal's basal metabolic rate may depart significantly from the value predicted by Kleiber's equation. For example, food-deprived people have lower basal metabolism, as well as a lower weight. In fact, severe restriction of caloric intake affects metabolic rate much more than it affects body weight. Animal studies show similar disproportions (Keesey and Corbett, 1984). Thus the resting rate of energy expenditure is "basal" really only for animals and people who are in energy balance. The expenditure of energy at rest drops substantially below "normal" (the level predicted by Kleiber's formula) when body weight is reduced from the normally maintained level. Such adjustments in the rate of energy expenditure play a significant role in maintaining energy balance and in keeping an individual's body weight relatively constant (Keesey and Powley, 1986).

13.21 Why Losing Weight Is So Difficult
After 7 days on a diet of 3500 kcal/day, the intake of six obese subjects was restricted to 450 kcal/day, a drop of 87%. However, basal metabolism also declined, by 15%, so after 3 weeks body weight had declined by only 6%. (After Bray, 1969.)

Since people and animals adjust their energy expenditures in response to under- or overnutrition, they tend to resist either losing or gaining weight. This tendency helps explain why it is so difficult for some people to lose weight and for others to gain (Figure 13.21). The relation between metabolic rate and body weight may also indicate when an individual is at his physiologically normal target weight (Keesey and Corbett, 1984). Only at this weight will the person's resting metabolism be at the level predicted by Kleiber's equation. A lower metabolic rate than predicted by the equation indicates that the person is below his physiologically normal weight. People who hold their weight down by dieting may remain hypometabolic as long as their weight stays below the level that they used to maintain, and thus they must continue dieting to maintain a body weight that would be normal for someone else of similar stature.

Carbohydrates Provide Energy for Body and Brain

What molecules provide energy to the body, and how does the body regulate that energy? Large carbohydrate molecules can be broken down into simple carbohydrates, including sugars. The most important sugar used by our body is **glucose**. In fact, the brain is quite dependent on glucose for energy, while the rest of the body can use both glucose and more complicated molecules, such as fatty acids, for energy. Because a readily available supply of glucose is crucial for brain function and for survival, the liver stores glucose by combining excess glucose molecules to form a more complex carbohydrate called **glycogen**.

When the concentration of glucose molecules in circulation falls, the liver can convert the glycogen back into glucose molecules and release them into circulation as needed. This shuttling of energy supplies back

and forth is controlled by two protein hormones from the pancreas: **Glucagon** promotes the breakdown of glycogen to glucose; **insulin** promotes the conversion of glucose into glycogen (Figure 13.22). Thus the pancreatic hormones determine the balance of ready energy (glucose) from a short-term energy source (glycogen). (Recall from Chapter 5 that glucagon and insulin are secreted from the alpha and beta cells, respectively, of the islets of Langerhans within the pancreas.)

For long-term energy storage, we use fat, maintained in fat cells, which form what is known as **adipose tissue**. Fat molecules are large and complicated. You may think of them as the result of the joining together of many different sugars and other small molecules into a large molecule that is not soluble in water. Fat either comes directly from our food or is manufactured in the body from glucose and other nutrients. If the glycogen store becomes depleted, our body can convert fat into fatty acids to supply energy to the body and into glucose to provide energy to the brain.

When a human or any other animal is deprived of food, little or no energy is stored in fat deposits. When an animal eats liberally, some of the energy is laid down in fat supplies so that it will be available in the

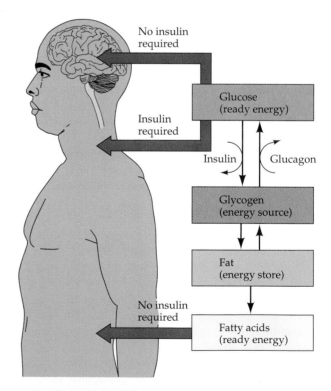

13.22 The Role of Insulin in Energy Utilization
The body can make use of either fatty acids or glucose for energy, while the brain can make ready use of only glucose. So the brain requires a constant supply of glucose, which it can use without the aid of insulin. On the other hand, the body can make use of glucose only with the aid of insulin, so in the absence of insulin our bodies must use fatty acids for energy.

future. The factors that regulate how much energy is stored in fat are not well understood. As we will see later, however, considerable evidence suggests that the body maintains its level of fat in the face of all but the most extreme diet restrictions and regains fat after the surgical removal of fat stores.

Insulin Is Crucial for the Regulation of Body Metabolism

We've already mentioned the importance of insulin for converting glucose into glycogen. Another important role of insulin is enabling the body to use glucose. Most cells regulate the import of glucose molecules via **glucose transporters** that span the cell's external membrane and bring glucose molecules from outside the cell into the cell for use. The glucose transporters must interact with insulin in order to function. (Brain cells are an important exception; they can use glucose without the aid of insulin.) Each time you eat a meal, the foods are broken down and glucose is released into the bloodstream. Most of your body requires insulin to make use of that glucose, so three different, sequential mechanisms stimulate insulin release.

First, the stimuli from food (sight, smell, and taste) evoke a conditioned release of insulin in anticipation of glucose arrival in the blood. This release, because it is mediated by the brain, is called the *cephalic phase* of insulin release. Next, during the *digestive phase,* food entering the stomach and intestines causes them to release gut hormones, some of which stimulate the pancreas to release insulin. Finally, during the *absorptive phase,* glucose enters the bloodstream, and special cells in the liver, called **glucodetectors** (or glucostats), detect this circulating glucose and signal the pancreas to release insulin.

Neural plasticity

The newly released insulin allows the body to make use of some of the glucose immediately, and other glucose is converted into glycogen. The liver and the pancreas communicate via the nervous system. Autonomic afferents from the liver deliver nerve impulses up the **vagus nerve** to synapse in the **nucleus of the solitary tract** (**NST**) in the brain stem. So information from glucodetectors in the liver travels up the vagus nerve to the NST. The information is then relayed to other brain regions, such as the hypothalamus, informing the brain of circulating glucose levels and contributing to hunger, as we'll discuss later. Efferent fibers carry signals from the brain stem back out the vagus nerve to the pancreas. These efferent fibers modulate insulin secretions from the pancreas.

Lack of insulin causes the disease **diabetes mellitus**. In Type I (or juvenile-onset) diabetes mellitus, the pancreas stops producing insulin. Although the brain can still make use of glucose from the diet, the rest of the body cannot and is forced to use energy from fatty acids. The result is that lots of glucose is left in the bloodstream because the brain cannot use it all, and the lack of insulin means there is no way to put it into glycogen storage. Some of the glucose is secreted into the urine, making the urine sweet; hence the name "diabetes mellitus" (the Latin root *mell-* means "honey"); in contrast, diabetes insipidus (which we discussed earlier in the chapter) gets its name from the dilute, uncolored urine that it produces (the Latin *insipidus* means "bland").

Untreated Diabetics Eat Ravenously yet Lose Weight

The body did not evolve to gather all its energy efficiently from fatty acids, so an untreated Type I diabetic is chronically undernourished. Although untreated diabetics eat a great deal, because their bodies cannot make much use of the food, they lose weight anyway. Tissues begin showing signs of degradation as a result of relying so heavily on the less efficient fatty acids for energy. The urine, in addition to being sweet, is also copious as the kidneys try to dump the excess glucose; consequently, untreated diabetics are also chronically thirsty. Finally, the excess glucose in circulation may itself damage some tissues, including the retina, as mentioned in Chapter 10.

The treatment is obvious: provide exogenous insulin by injection. Unfortunately, insulin normally is not secreted just once during the day. The pattern of secretion across the day is complex and varies depending on what is eaten, when it is eaten, and what other behaviors are displayed. Thus, exogenously providing the proper amount of insulin at the proper time is tricky.

There has long been evidence that Type I diabetes has a genetic component, and recent research indicates that many different genes affect the probability of developing diabetes. One hypothesis suggests that diabetes is an autoimmune disorder—that diabetics produce **Genes and behavior** antibodies that attack their own pancreatic cells, stopping the insulin supply. Why would this happen? After all, the immune system is supposed to help us. Scientists have found that some viruses that cause upper respiratory infections have a protein that resembles glutamic acid decarboxylase (GAD). When this viral protein is injected into mice, some of the mice produce antibodies that recognize both the viral protein and their own GAD. Because GAD is found on the surface of the pancreatic cells, the antibodies attack and destroy the cells, leading to a loss of insulin and the development of diabetes. Some strains of mice are much more likely to suffer these effects of viral exposure than others (Atkinson et al., 1994). Some people exposed to this virus may produce antibodies to defeat the virus that also destroy their own insulin source.

Supporting this theory are experimental results showing that some people in the early stages of diabetes have circulating antibodies that recognize GAD (Atkinson and Maclaren, 1994). Many different genes could influence whether a person makes these particular antibodies. If this hypothesis proves correct, it may be possible to inoculate children with other proteins from these viruses so that when they are exposed to the virus, they already have antibodies to defeat the infection without making the harmful antibodies.

Another, more common type of diabetes mellitus is called Type II, or adult-onset, diabetes. This milder version can be caused either by a gradually decreasing sensitivity to insulin or by gradually decreasing production of the hormone. This condition is far more common in obese people, and because the individuals still produce some insulin, it can usually be treated by reduction of the amount of glucose in the diet and by administration of a drug that stimulates the pancreas to produce more insulin, without the need to resort to insulin injections.

Despite Its Importance, Insulin Is Not the Sole Signal for Either Hunger or Satiety

Given the crucial role of insulin in mobilizing and distributing food energy, you might think that the brain monitors circulating insulin levels to decide when it is time to eat and when it is time to stop eating. For example, if the insulin level is high, there

Competing hypotheses

must be food in the pipeline and the fat stores will be increased, so the brain might produce the sensation of satiety so that we stop eating. If insulin levels are low, the brain might signal hunger to impel us to find food and eat. Experiments have shown that forcing an animal's blood insulin levels to be low causes it to become hungry and eat a large meal. If moderate levels of insulin are injected, the animal eats much less. These results suggest that insulin is a satiety signal.

Investigators tested this simple hypothesis by injecting a large amount of insulin into animals. But rather than appearing satiated, the animals responded by eating a large meal. High insulin levels direct much of the glucose into fat storage, which means that there is effectively less glucose in circulation for the brain. The brain learns of this functional glucose deficit from glucodetectors in the brain (probably in one or more of the circumventricular organs; see Figure 13.17) and the liver (which communicates to the NST via the vagus nerve). Is circulating glucose signaling satiety and hunger to the brain? Certainly this information plays a role normally, but it can't be the only source of information, because untreated diabetics have very high levels of circulating glucose, yet they are chronically hungry.

Studies of diabetic rats provide more evidence that insulin is not the only satiety signal. Like untreated human diabetics, these rats eat a great deal.

But if the rats are fed a high-fat diet, they eat normal amounts (M. I. Friedman, 1978), probably because their body can make immediate use of the fatty acids without the aid of insulin. Thus, circulating levels of insulin and glucose contribute to hunger and satiety, but they are not sufficient to explain those states entirely. Somehow the brain integrates insulin and glucose levels with other sources of information to decide whether to initiate eating. This seems to be the theme of hunger research—that the brain integrates many different signals rather than relying exclusively on any single signal to trigger hunger. Another of the cues the brain may use to signal satiety is discussed next.

Do Peptide Hormones in the Gut Signal Satiety?

We mentioned earlier that when food arrives in the stomach and intestines, these organs release several peptide hormones. Among them is **cholecystokinin (CCK)**. The release of CCK is especially pronounced if the food has a high content of fat and/or proteins. CCK seems to have widespread effects, including stimulating the pancreas to release insulin, a function we alluded to earlier. Thus, CCK meets the first criterion for a circulating satiety signal: Levels are high when food is already in the intestines and low when the intestines are empty (J. Gibbs and Smith, 1986). CCK also acts as a neurotransmitter in the brain, so we know that some neurons respond to CCK and that circulating CCK could communicate satiety to the brain. When CCK is administered to humans, however, they report experiencing nausea and even vomiting (Miaskiewicz et al., 1989). Apparently exogenous CCK acts on the intestines themselves, increasing muscular contractions and thus producing cramping and nausea.

Does CCK make rats nauseated? It's difficult to know because, for one thing, rats cannot vomit, even when they are very sick. But one indication that exogenous CCK may make rats nauseated is that pairing a new food with CCK treatment causes rats to avoid the food in the future (Chen et al., 1993). This phenomenon, called **taste aversion** (which is described in the next section), indicates that the CCK makes the rats uncomfortable and that they avoid the food thereafter under the (mistaken) assumption that the food was responsible for the unpleasant feelings.

We must interpret the effects of exogenous CCK on food intake with some suspicion: CCK may make rats feel nauseated rather than satiated, but of course the normally secreted CCK triggered by a meal does not cause us to feel nauseated. Therefore the amount of CCK and/or the corelease of presently unidentified compounds must prevent the production of nausea. Whether the endogenously released CCK, alone or in conjunction with other intestinal hormones, contributes to the sensation of satiety remains to be seen.

13.23 Taste Aversion
A blue jay immediately before (*a*) and a few minutes after (*b*) eating a monarch butterfly and becoming sick from the toxins these butterflies contain. The animal regurgitates the butterfly, wipes its beak repeatedly, and will in the future avoid eating other monarchs. (Courtesy of Lincoln Brower.)

Experience Protects Us from Toxins in Food

Learning has a profound effect on the feeding behavior of animals. We've already mentioned the cephalic phase of feeding, during which the stimuli of food evoke a conditioned release of insulin so that we will make quick use of the food. Another example of conditioning is the preference that many species show for foods to which they were exposed during development. Normally such a preference would be adaptive. Some moths prefer to lay their eggs on the leaves of whichever plant they ate as a caterpillar. This choice seems sensible: If it was good enough to enable me to survive to adulthood, it should do for my offspring.

Neural plasticity

One can influence the food preferences of adult rats by exposing them to the food as nursing pups. Rats normally prefer plain water over garlic-flavored water, but if a rat mother has only garlic-flavored water to drink, she will drink it. Her offspring, nursing for the first 21 days of their life, will prefer garlic water over plain. This preference is strengthened if the pups also are exposed to such water just after weaning (Capretta et al., 1975). Similarly, many adult humans prefer the cuisine they were fed by their parents while growing up.

Another important means by which experience shapes feeding is conditioned taste aversion, which we mentioned in our discussion of CCK in the previous section. A young, inexperienced blue jay will readily snap up and eat a monarch butterfly. Score one for the blue jay. A few minutes later, however, the bird will vomit up the butterfly and wipe its bill repeatedly as if to remove any traces (Figure 13.23). That bird will eat other butterflies, but it will not eat another monarch (Wiklund and Sillén-Tullberg, 1985), even when hundreds are available. Score several hundred for the monarchs.

Why does the blue jay vomit up the monarch? The reason is that the monarch, as a caterpillar, fed on milkweed and gathered from that plant toxins that of-

fend other caterpillars, but that monarch caterpillars tolerate. The toxins remain in the adult's body and also offend birds, making them nauseated. The bird learns to associate the monarch with illness and, to avoid becoming ill again, avoids that food from that point forward.

Investigated by John Garcia, conditioned taste aversion is sometimes referred to as the Garcia effect. The results of Garcia's original work, which involved making rats sick by using X-rays (Garcia et al., 1955), were only very slowly accepted by scientists in the 1960s because the learning psychologists then believed that any stimulus could be paired with any other stimulus equally well, and that repeated trials would be necessary for the animal to associate one stimulus with the other. The assertion that animals could learn, with a single trial, to avoid food associated with illness,

John Garcia

but would require many trials to avoid food associated with foot shock, was a heresy. Another reason for the hesitation was the common belief that the interval between presentation of the stimuli could not exceed seconds if the association was to be made (see Chapter 17), but the illness effects in Garcia's studies appeared minutes to hours after ingestion.

We now know that animals from snails to humans readily associate food with illness that occurs even hours later and use this learning ability to avoid poisons. The selective advantage of this propensity seems obvious. A related phenomenon is **neophobia**, the avoidance of new things—in this case new foods. Rats are quite reluctant to eat any new food, and when they do eat the food, they tend to eat a small amount and wait a period before eating more. If they become ill after the first sample, conditioned taste aversion prevents them from taking more.

There Is Apparently No Single Satiety Center or Single Hunger Center in the Brain

Just as no single molecule in the bloodstream always triggers hunger or satiety, it appears that no single brain region has exclusive control of these sensations. Discoveries of the early 1950s gave support for a time to a *dual-center hypothesis* of the control of eating. According to this theory, the hypothalamus contained the primary control centers for hunger and satiety: A hunger center in the lateral hypothalamus (LH) facilitated eating, and a satiety center in the ventromedial hypothalamus (VMH) inhibited eating. Information from all the other brain regions, and from other factors (such as circulating hormones) that influence eating, were presumed to funnel into and to act through these hypothalamic control centers. Further research aimed at filling in the details of this picture soon dethroned the hypothalamic regions from their exclusive status, and even the concept of a center or centers was challenged, as we will see.

The Ventromedial Hypothalamus Appeared for a Time to Be the Satiety Center

Occasionally a person develops a pathologically voracious appetite and rapidly becomes obese. In the nineteenth century, physicians found that some such patients had tumors at the base of the brain. In 1940, Hetherington and Ranson reported that bilateral lesions of the ventromedial hypothalamus (Figure 13.24) cause rats to become obese. VMH lesions produced obesity in all the species that were tested—monkeys, dogs and cats, several species of rodents, and some species of birds.

The VMH was promptly called a satiety center because destroying it seemed to prevent animals from ever being satiated with food, but this characterization was soon seen to be inadequate. Destruction of the VMH does not simply cause the rats to become feeding machines. Rather, the eating habits of VMH-lesioned rats are still controlled both by the palatability of food and by body weight, but these controls are no longer exerted in normal ways. If palatable food of high caloric content is available, VMH-lesioned rats typically show two phases of weight gain.

Animal model

At first they show an amazing increase in consumption, eating two or three times as much as normal; this condition is called **hyperphagia** (from the Greek, *hyper*, "over," and *phagein*, "to eat"). Body weight shoots up—a stage called the dynamic phase of weight gain (Figure 13.25). But after a few weeks, weight stabilizes at an obese level, and food intake is not much above normal; this stage is called the static phase of obesity. Once animals have reached this new weight, they seem to display normal satiety in response to their food. Since the VMH is gone from

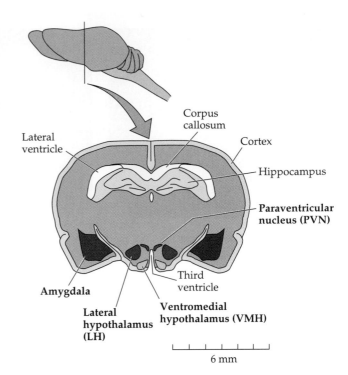

13.24 Brain Regions Implicated in the Regulation of Eating

these animals, it cannot be responsible for their satiety; therefore it seems likely that some other brain regions normally contribute to satiety.

Some observations indicate that the obese VMH-lesioned rat regulates its weight at a new target value. If an obese rat in the static phase is force-fed, its weight will rise above the plateau level; but when it is again allowed to eat on its own, body weight returns to the plateau level (see Figure 13.25). Similarly, after an obese rat has been deprived of food and has lost weight, when given free access to food, it will regain its plateau level. Furthermore, the plateau body weight also depends on the palatability of the diet. If VMH-lesioned rats are kept on a diet of laboratory chow pellets (rather than a high-fat diet), their weight does not rise much above that of control animals. If the food is adulterated with quinine to make it bitter, the body weight of the VMH-lesioned rats may fall *below* that of controls (Sclafani et al., 1976). These results suggest that VMH-lesioned rats are finicky and therefore show exaggerated reactions to palatability.

There are several hypotheses about how VMH lesions exert these effects. The VMH-lesioned animals release more insulin than control animals do (Weingarten et al., 1985), so the hyperphagia may be caused by, or at least augmented by, the increased insulin, which, as we mentioned earlier, tends to induce eating. Furthermore, the main effect of VMH lesions may be caused by the disruption of axons coming from the **paraventricular nucleus** (**PVN**). These PVN axons normally synapse on brain stem nuclei that regulate the

Competing hypotheses

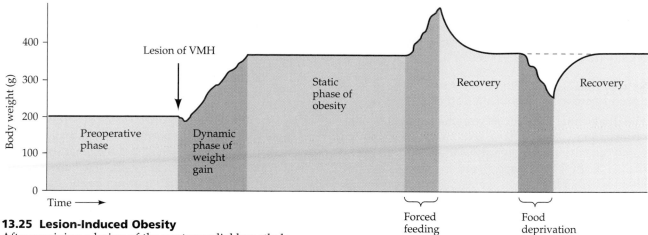

13.25 Lesion-Induced Obesity
After receiving a lesion of the ventromedial hypothalamus (VMH), rats overeat and gain weight until they reach a new, higher body weight, which they defend in the face of either forced feeding or food deprivation. Thus they continue to regulate body weight, but at a higher set point. (After Sclafani et al., 1976.)

parasympathetic vagus nerve. Because the vagus innervates and receives afferents from both the pancreas and the liver, it seems increasingly likely that "VMH lesions" are disrupting parasympathetic regulation.

The Lateral Hypothalamus Appeared for a Time to Be the Hunger Center

In 1951, Anand and Brobeck announced that bilateral destruction of the lateral hypothalamus (LH) causes rats or cats to stop eating. This refusal to eat, known as aphagia, was so severe in some cases that animals died of starvation even when their usual food was present. The investigators proposed that the LH contains a feeding center and that the VMH normally acts as a brake on feeding by inhibiting the LH.

Two important features of the effects of LH damage soon emerged (Teitelbaum and Stellar, 1954). First, the rats refused not only to eat but also to drink (they showed adipsia as well as aphagia). If the experimenters placed a bit of food or a drop of water on the

Competing hypotheses

lips or in the mouth of the rat, it spat out the food or water as if it were distasteful. Second, the aphagia and adipsia were not necessarily permanent. A few rats began to eat and drink spontaneously after about a week. Most rats would eventually eat spontaneously if they were kept alive meanwhile by having food and water pumped through a tube directly into the stomach. Thus, just as VMH destruction does not abolish all inhibition of eating, LH destruction does not permanently prevent eating and drinking. Therefore, another brain region must be able to monitor feeding and signal satiety in LH-lesioned rats. Presumably this other region contributes to satiety in normal animals.

Recovered LH-lesioned rats regulate their new body weight with precision. The larger the size of the

LH lesion, the lower the target level of body weight. If food is restricted, the weights of LH-lesioned and control rats fall in parallel, and the predeprivation level is regained when free access to food is restored (Figure 13.26). Similarly, if the only food available is eggnog (year round!), both lesioned and control rats gain weight in parallel; and when the usual diet is restored, both groups fall to their previous level. When food is adulterated with quinine, the LH-lesioned rats again show changes in parallel with normal controls (Keesey and Boyle, 1973). (Recall that VMH-lesioned rats displayed an exaggerated reaction to quinine.) Thus the LH-lesioned rats are said to defend a lowered weight target or set point (Keesey, 1980).

Human beings may become emaciated if they suffer from lesions or tumors of the lateral hypothalamus. Bilateral damage to the LH through accident or disease is rare, but even unilateral damage to the LH sometimes

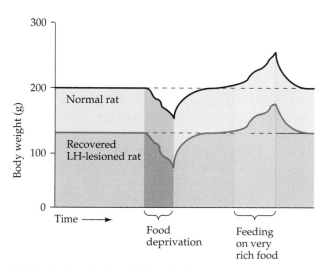

13.26 Lesion-Induced Weight Loss
Both normal rats and rats that have recovered from lesions of the lateral hypothalamus (LH) regulate body weight quite well. The LH-lesioned rats regulate around a lowered target weight, but in parallel with normal rats. (After Keesey and Boyle, 1973.)

produces aphagia and adipsia. Cases of anorexia (absence of appetite) induced by LH lesions in humans are about one-fourth as frequent as cases of hypothalamic obesity (L. E. White and Hain, 1959).

Satiety and Hunger Functions Are Spread across Several Brain Regions

The dual-center hypothesis was challenged by many observations. As we have seen, animals exhibited some capacity for hunger and satiety despite losing the LH or the VMH, respectively. Controversies arose about whether the lesions were effective because they destroyed integrative centers, as originally believed, or because they interrupted fiber tracts that passed through these regions (Marshall et al., **Competing** 1974). In addition, many brain regions **hypotheses** outside the hypothalamus were found to be involved in the regulation of feeding behavior, and they do not contribute solely by their connections to the hypothalamus. Among the regions whose destruction impairs the regulation of feeding are the amygdaloid nuclei, the frontal cortex, and the substantia nigra. Taken together, these data suggest that hunger and satiety are not centered in any single brain region, but that a network of cells distributed across the brain is responsible for these functions.

Scientists have become increasingly aware that peripheral structures, notably the liver, also play a crucial role in monitoring energy and nutrient balance and signaling the brain to activate or inhibit eating. We saw earlier that the liver detects glucose levels, and experiments indicate that the liver also detects circulating levels of fatty acids and communicates both kinds of information through the vagus nerve to the NST. For example, cutting the vagus nerve disrupts feeding responses to manipulations of circulating glucose and fatty acids (e.g., Tordoff et al., 1991). From the brain stem NST, this information reaches the hypothalamic nuclei and enters the brain's hunger system.

Genes Can Affect Target Weight

Genes can cause a high target weight. For example, mice that receive two copies of the gene called *obese* (abbreviated *ob*) regulate their body weight at a high level, as you might have guessed from the gene's name **Genes and** (Figure 13.27). These mice have **behavior** larger and more numerous fat cells than their heterozygous littermates (*ob/+*; the plus sign indicates the wild-type, normal allele). The fat mice (*ob/ob*), maintain their obesity even when given a diet

strongly adulterated with quinine or when required to work hard to obtain food (Cruce et al., 1974).

When the mouse *ob* gene was cloned, it was named **leptin** (from the Greek *leptos*, "thin"). We now understand that *obese* mice have defective genes for leptin. Normally only fat cells produce leptin, and then secrete the protein into the bloodstream (Zhang et al., 1994). Leptin receptors have been identified in the choroid plexus, the cortex, and the hypothalamus, especially the lateral hypothalamus and the supraoptic, arcuate, and paraventricular nuclei (Hakansson et al., 1998). Thus the brain may monitor circulating leptin levels to measure and regulate total body fat (Box 13.1). If so, the defect in leptin may underreport body fat, leading the animal to overeat, especially high-fat or sugary foods.

Injecting the obese (*ob/ob*) mice with normal leptin causes them to lose weight dramatically (Halaas et al., 1995), and injections directly to the hypothalamus are even more effective (Campfield et al., 1995). Behavioral genetic analyses indicate a strong genetic contribution to obesity in humans (representing the effect of many genes, not just one; R. A. Price and Gottesman, 1991), but variation in the leptin protein does *not* appear to play a role in human obesity. Examination of the leptin gene from thousands of obese people detected only two people with mutant leptin—a pair of cousins, one a 64-pound, 2-year-old boy and the other a 190-pound, 8-year-old girl (Montague et al., 1997). Furthermore, obese people, on average, secrete *more* leptin than do thin people. So perhaps what distinguishes obese people from others is a relative insensitivity to leptin rather than an insufficiency of the protein. Nevertheless, injecting leptin also caused normal mice to lose weight, so such treatment may alleviate human obesity no matter what the cause.

Certainly none of the present dietary, surgical, or pharmacological interventions reliably reverse obesity for long periods of time. A few individuals improve; many others do not. Furthermore, some of the most effective synthetic drugs for the treatment of

13.27 Inherited Obesity
A single obese (*ob/ob*) mouse weighs more than two of his normal (heterozygote, *ob/+*) siblings. (Courtesy of Jeffrey Friedman.)

BOX 13.1 *Body Fat Stores Are Tightly Regulated, Even after Surgical Removal of Fat*

We've seen that animals maintain a fairly constant body weight, even when given more food than they can eat, and that various lesions may change the body weight the animal defends, but they do not abolish weight regulation completely. Certainly most of us who have tried dieting can attest that our body seems to know how much it wants to weigh, despite our efforts.

Ample evidence suggests that body fat is carefully regulated. Perhaps the most striking demonstration is in golden-mantled ground squirrels. In the wild, these animals show a seasonal variation in body weight. Every spring, as the food supply increases, the animals fatten up considerably. You might think that this extreme seasonal variation in body weight is simply the result of having food available at some times but not others. But when these squirrels are brought into the laboratory, they continue

to show an annual rhythm in body weight, even when food is always available (Figure A) (I. Zucker, 1988). (We'll discuss annual cycles further in Chapter 14.)

Experimenters can increase or decrease the squirrels' body weight either by force-feeding the animals or by restricting their food. When food is abundant, the squirrels eat just enough to achieve not the body weight they had before the manipulation, but the body weight that is appropriate for the present point in their annual cycle. The return to their normal body composition is not simply a matter of altering diet. The way the squirrels partition what they eat—how much goes into fat, how much goes into glycogen, how much is defecated—also returns to normal. For example, they lower their metabolic rate during the fattening phase so that more food can be shuttled into fat (Dark, 1984).

Golden-mantled ground squirrels show a seasonal cycle also for

body fat. Although some of the fat can be surgically removed, after the surgery, just as with body weight, the animals eat until they regain, with remarkable precision, the amount of fat they would have had at that season without surgery (Figure B) (Dark et al., 1984). Interestingly, some of the body fat depots from which fat was removed cannot regenerate new fat cells, but when such a nonregenerating depot is removed, other fat depots increase production in compensation, restoring the animal's total body fat. Needless to say, these results are not encouraging to humans considering liposuction. Usually the fat simply returns after the procedure, which itself is not without risks. The brain of humans, and certainly that of ground squirrels, appears able to measure body fat and alter appetite to maintain a particular amount of fat.

(A) Annual body weight cycles of 3 ground squirrels with free access to food

(B) Surgical fat removal has only a transient effect on body weight

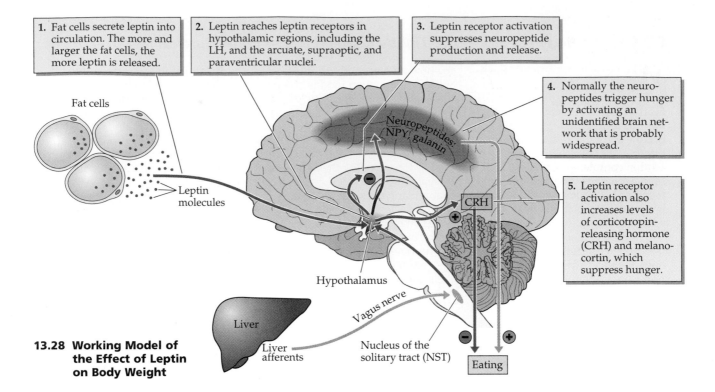

1. Fat cells secrete leptin into circulation. The more and larger the fat cells, the more leptin is released.

2. Leptin reaches leptin receptors in hypothalamic regions, including the LH, and the arcuate, supraoptic, and paraventricular nuclei.

3. Leptin receptor activation suppresses neuropeptide production and release.

4. Normally the neuropeptides trigger hunger by activating an unidentified brain network that is probably widespread.

5. Leptin receptor activation also increases levels of corticotropin-releasing hormone (CRH) and melanocortin, which suppress hunger.

Fat cells

Leptin molecules

Neuropeptides: NPY, galanin

CRH

Hypothalamus

Liver

Vagus nerve

Liver afferents

Nucleus of the solitary tract (NST)

Eating

13.28 Working Model of the Effect of Leptin on Body Weight

obesity in the past have been found to have serious, life-threatening side effects (Cannistra et al., 1997; McCann et al., 1997).

Brain Peptides May Mediate Some of the Signals for Hunger

Once the brain receives the leptin signal, it suppresses the production and release of several peptide neurotransmitters, including neuropeptide Y (NPY) and galanin (Sahu, 1998). Perhaps, then, these peptides normally trigger hunger, and leptin suppresses hunger by inhibiting the peptides (Seeley and Schwartz, 1997). Several lines of evidence support this model.

Most hypothalamic NPY is made by neurons of the **arcuate nucleus** (one of the centers that has receptors to leptin), which send their axons to other hypothalamic

Animal model

sites, including the PVN. When NPY is infused into the hypothalamus, rats that seemed satiated begin eating again (Stanley et al., 1989). In contradiction of the idea that the lateral hypothalamus is a hunger center, NPY infusions are most effective in other nearby hypothalamic sites, such as the PVN (Leibowitz, 1991). When animals are deprived of food and lose weight, NPY levels increase in the PVN (Sahu et al., 1988). Such animals are certainly hungry, and the increased hypothalamic NPY may be responsible for that sensation.

Another animal model of obesity is the Zucker strain of rats (L. M. Zucker and Zucker, 1961). Zucker rats have a defective leptin receptor and show little or no response to injections of leptin (al-Barazanji et al., 1997). Because they are insensitive to leptin, Zucker rats have more hypothalamic NPY than do normal

rats (Sanacora et al., 1990), which might explain their exaggerated appetite. In addition to suppressing several neuropeptides, leptin increases levels of corticotropin-releasing hormone (CRH), melanocortin, and neurotensin in the hypothalamus, so those peptides may normally suppress eating (Figure 13.28).

Two newly discovered neuropeptides may also be involved in hunger. Named **orexins** (from the Greek *oregein*, "to desire"), these peptides are normally produced only in the lateral hypothalamic area (Figure 13.29). When orexins are injected into the hypothalamus of rats, the animals eat four to six times more

13.29 Neuropeptides That Induce Hunger?
In situ hybridization indicates that orexin mRNA (bright spots) is made only in the lateral hypothalamus. Infusion of orexin into this region causes rats to eat more food. (Courtesy of Masashi Yanagisawa.)

13.30 Changing Ideals of Female Beauty
Supermodel Kate Moss (*a*) and *Helena Fourment as Aphrodite* (as depicted by the Flemish painter Rubens circa 1630) (*b*) exemplify ideal feminine forms of their respective eras. Some people have suggested that our modern weight-conscious notions of female beauty are responsible for some cases of anorexia nervosa and bulimia.

(a)

(b)

food than control rats. Conversely, depriving rats of food increases the production of orexins in the hypothalamus. Whether orexins are affected by circulating leptin levels has not been investigated.

Anorexia Nervosa and Bulimia Are Life-Threatening Eating Disorders

Some young people become obsessed with their body weight and become extremely thin—usually by eating very little and sometimes also regurgitating food, taking laxatives, or drinking large amounts of water to suppress appetite. This condition, which is more common in adolescent girls and women than in males, is called **anorexia nervosa**. Usually the menstrual cycle of female anorexics is disrupted or stops altogether. The name of the disorder indicates (1) that the patients have no appetite ("anorexia") and (2) that the disorder originates in the nervous system ("nervosa"). But the disorder is so poorly understood that both of these assumptions could be mistaken.

Competing hypotheses

For example, anorexics sometimes think about food a good deal, and physiological evidence suggests that they respond even more than normal subjects to the presentation of food (Broberg and Bernstein, 1989), so their appetite may be normal or even exaggerated. Yet they deny themselves food. The idea that anorexia is primarily a nervous disorder stems from the distorted body image of the patients (they may consider themselves fat when others see them as emaciated) and from the fact that their diet is self-imposed.

Bulimia (or bulimia nervosa, from the Greek *boulimia*, "great hunger") is a related disorder. Like anorex-

ics, bulimics may believe themselves fatter than they are, but they periodically gorge themselves, usually with "junk food," and then either vomit the food or take laxatives to avoid weight gain. Also like anorexics, bulimics may be obsessed with food and body weight, but not all bulimics become emaciated. Both disorders can be fatal, because in each case the patient's lack of nutrient reserves damages various organ systems and/or leaves the body unable to battle otherwise mild diseases.

Our present culture emphasizes that women, especially young women, must be thin to be attractive. It has been suggested that anorexics and bulimics are the victims of a mismatch between what their biological makeup wants them to weigh and what society expects them to weigh (Figure 13.30). In earlier times, however, when plump women were considered the most beautiful (witness Renaissance paintings), some women still fasted severely and may have been anorexics. The origins of these disorders are still elusive, and to date, the available therapies cure only a minority of patients.

Summary

1. The nervous system plays a crucial role in maintaining the homeostasis that the body requires for proper functioning. Temperature, fluid concentration, chemical energy, and nutrients must all be maintained within a critical range.

2. Several mechanisms that normally act in synchrony can be dissociated experimentally, revealing a redundancy of physiological methods that ensure homeostasis.

Temperature Regulation

1. Endotherms generate most of their body heat through the metabolism of food; ectotherms obtain most of their body heat from the environment. Both endotherms and ectotherms regulate body temperature, but ectotherms depend more on behaviors to capture heat rather than on internal heat-generating mechanisms.

2. Endotherms can remain active longer than ectotherms can, but endotherms are also obliged to gather more food than ectotherms do to generate their body warmth.

3. Body size and shape drastically affect the rate of heat loss. Small endotherms have a higher metabolic rate, using more energy (per gram of body weight) than large endotherms use.

4. Several regions of the nervous system monitor and help regulate body temperature, including the preoptic area of the hypothalamus and the spinal cord.

Fluid Regulation

1. Our cells function properly only when the concentration of salts and other ions (the osmolality) of the intracellular compartment of the body is within a critical range. The extracellular compartment is a source of replacement water and a buffer between the intracellular compartment and the outside world.

2. Thirst can be triggered either by a drop in the volume of the extracellular compartment (hypovolemic thirst) or by an increase in the osmolality of the extracellular compartment (osmotic thirst). Either signal indicates that the volume or osmolality of the intracellular compartment may fall outside the critical range. Because of the importance of osmolality, we must regulate salt intake in order to regulate water balance effectively.

3. A drop in blood volume triggers at least three responses: (1) Baroreceptors in the major blood vessels detect any volume drop and signal the brain via the autonomic nervous system. (2) The brain in turn releases vasopressin from the posterior pituitary, and the vasopression reduces blood vessel volume and the amount of water lost through urination. (3) The kidneys release renin, providing circulating angiotensin II, which reduces blood vessel volume to maintain blood pressure and may also signal the brain that the blood volume has dropped.

Food and Energy Regulation

1. Our digestive system breaks down food and uses most of the food for energy, especially because we are endotherms. The brain must have glucose for energy; the body can use either glucose or fatty acids as fuel.

2. Although brain cells can use glucose directly, body cells can import glucose only with the assistance of insulin secreted by the pancreas. Insulin also promotes the storage of glucose in fat. Another pancreatic hormone, glucagon, mobilizes fats to release glucose.

3. Manipulations of either glucose or insulin can affect whether an animal experiences hunger, but experimental studies have indicated that neither glucose nor insulin alone can be the single indicator of hunger or satiety. The nervous system integrates information about these compounds and others, such as the fat indicator leptin, to determine whether an animal should eat.

4. Within the nervous system are several regions that seem to contribute to the sensations of hunger or satiety, but an animal can regulate body weight reasonably well even when it lacks one of these regions. Thus there seems to be no single brain center for either satiety or hunger.

5. Powerful genetic and seasonal factors influence body weight, and body weight is very tightly regulated around a set zone, despite extensive dietary, behavioral, or surgical interventions.

Recommended Reading

Bray, G. A., Bouchard, C., and James, W. P. T. (1998). *Handbook of obesity.* New York: Dekker.

Le Magnen, P. (1991). *Neurobiology of feeding.* New York: Academic Press.

Milton, A. S. (Ed.). (1994). *Temperature regulation: Recent physiological and pharmacological advances.* Basel, Switzerland: Birkhauser.

Ramsay, D. J., and Booth, D. (Eds.). (1991). *Thirst: Physiological and psychological aspects.* London: Springer.

14 Biological Rhythms, Sleep, and Dreaming

Private collection, courtesy Tibor de Nagy Gallery, New York

He made the moon for the seasons;
The sun knows the place of its setting.
Thou dost appoint darkness and it
* becomes night*
In which all the beasts of the forest
* crawl about.*
The young lions roar after their prey
And seek their food from God.
When the sun rises they withdraw
And lie down in their dens.

— Psalm 104:19–23

A ll living systems show repeating, predictable changes over time. The frequency of these oscillations varies from rapid, such as brain potentials, to slow, such as annual changes like hibernation. Daily rhythms, the first topic of this chapter, have an intriguing "clocklike" regularity. Other rhythms range from minutes to seconds, and some extend from a month to years. One familiar and important daily rhythm is the sleep–waking cycle:

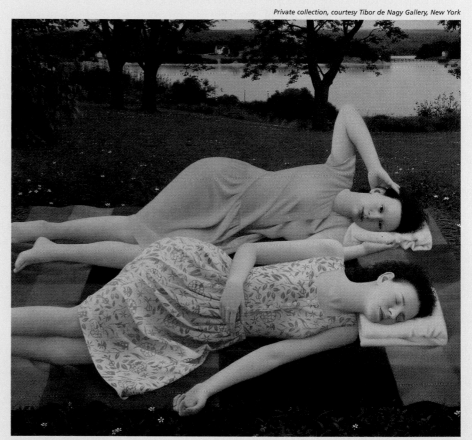

Brett Bigbee, *Two Women*, 1990–1992

By age 60, most humans have spent 20 years asleep. (Some, alas, on either side of the classroom podium.) Since sleep accounts for so large a slice of our lives, it is surprising that the behavioral and biological features of sleep remained unstudied for so long. Since the early 1960s, however, sleep has been a major focus of investigation in biological psychology.

Sleep is not just nonwaking, but rather the interlocking of elaborate cyclical processes, an alternation of several different states. The behavioral correlates of these different sleep states range from tiny finger twitches to a galaxy of images and dreams. In this chapter we'll discuss biological rhythms and patterns of sleep in human beings and other animals, the factors that influence sleep patterns, and the physiological events of sleep.

Biological Rhythms

Many Animals Show Daily Rhythms in Activity and Physiological Measures

Most functions of any living system display a rhythm of approximately 24 hours. Since these rhythms last about a day, they are called **circadian rhythms** (from the Latin *circa*, "about," and *dies*, "day"). By now circadian rhythms have been studied in a host of creatures at behavioral, physiological, and biochemical levels. One favorite way to study circadian rhythms in the laboratory takes advantage of the penchant of rodents to run in activity wheels (Figure 14.1a). A switch attached to the wheel connects to a microcomputer that registers each complete revolution.

The activity rhythm of a hamster in a running wheel is displayed in Figure 14.1b. Like most other rodents, hamsters are **nocturnal**—active during the dark periods. Humans and most other primates are **diurnal**—active during the day. Almost all other physiological measures—hormone levels, body temperature, drug sensitivity—change across the course of the day. These circadian activities show extraordinary precision: The beginning of activity may vary only a few minutes from one day to another. For humans who attend to watches and clocks, this regularity may seem uninteresting, but other animals also display remarkable regularity. They are attending to a "biological clock."

Circadian Rhythms Are Generated by an Endogenous Clock

If a hamster is placed in a constantly darkened environment, it continues to show a daily rhythm in wheel running and other measures, despite the absence of a light–dark cycle, suggesting that the animal has an internal clock to regulate these activities. On the other hand, even though the low level of light is constant, the animal may detect other external cues (e.g., outside noises, temperature, barometric pressure) about the time of day. Arguing for the internal clock, however, is the fact that the hamster shows a bit of imprecision in its cycle: Activity starts a few minutes later each day, so eventually the hamster is active while it is daytime outside (see Figure 14.1b, bottom). The animal is said to be **free-running**, maintaining its own

14.1 How Activity Rhythms Are Measured
(*a*) Typical setup for a single hamster: a running wheel monitored by an event recorder. Each revolution of the wheel produces a brief pen deflection, which forms a dark vertical mark on the slowly moving paper. The paper strips are cut up and each subsequent day's activity aligned underneath. (*b*) Normally, a hamster becomes active shortly after the start of the dark phase of the daily cycle and remains active during the dark period. After several weeks the optic tract in such a hamster was severed (asterisk), but fibers from the eye to the hypothalamus were spared. The hamster was subsequently active earlier each day, but still in synchrony with the light–dark cycle. When placed in constant dim light (*bottom*), the hamster became active a few minutes later each day. This "free-running" activity rhythm indicates that the hamster has an endogenous clock that has a period slightly greater than 24 hours. (After I. Zucker, 1976; based on Rusak and Zucker 1975.)

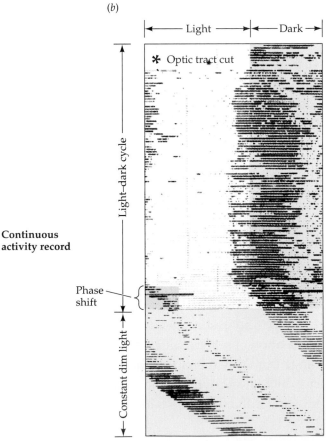

(*a*)

(*b*)

cycle, which in the absence of external cues, is not exactly 24 hours long.

The free-running period is the animal's natural rhythm. (A **period** is the time between two similar points of successive cycles, such as sunset to sunset.) Since this free-running period does not quite match the period of Earth's rotation, it cannot simply be reflecting an external cue but must be generated inside the animal. So the animal has some sort of endogenous oscillator, which we can call a clock, and in the hamster this clock runs a bit slow.

The internal clock can be set by light. If we expose a free-running nocturnal animal to periodic light and dark, the onset of activity soon becomes synchronized to the beginning of the dark period. The shift of activity produced by a synchronizing stimulus is referred to as a **phase shift** (see Figure 14.16, *middle*), and the process of shifting the rhythm is called **entrainment**. Any cue that an animal uses to synchronize its activity with the environment is called a **zeitgeber** (German for "time giver"). In the laboratory, light acts as a powerful zeitgeber. Because light stimuli can entrain circadian rhythms, the endogenous oscillatory circuit must have inputs from the visual system, as we'll discuss shortly. In humans, circadian rhythms probably are also entrained by social stimuli.

Circadian Rhythms Allow Animals to Anticipate Changes in the Environment

Why are circadian rhythms valuable to an organism? The major significance of circadian rhythms is that they synchronize behavior and body states to changes in the environment. The cycle of light and dark during the day has great significance for survival. For example, picture the small nocturnal rodent who can avoid many predators during the day by remaining hidden, and who moves about hurriedly in the dark. An endogenous clock allows animals to *anticipate* periodic events, such as the appearance of darkness, and to engage in appropriate behavior before conditions change. A snack in the den at the end of the day may prepare the animal for a long night of foraging. In other words, circadian rhythms provide the temporal organization of an animal's behavior. Biological clocks allow for resource partitioning: Diurnal animals are adapted for obtaining food during the daytime, and thus do not compete with nocturnal animals, whose adaptations favor an active life during dark periods.

An Endogenous Circadian Clock Is Located in the Hypothalamus

Where in the body is the clock (or clocks) that drives circadian rhythms, and how does it work? One way to establish the locus of circadian oscillators is to remove different organs and examine behavioral or physiological systems for any changes in circadian organiza-tion. A pioneer in the field, Curt Richter, suggested that the brain is the site of the relevant oscillators because removing various endocrine glands had little effect on the free-running rhythm of blinded rats (Richter, 1967). Although Richter did show that gross hypothalamic lesions appeared to interfere with circadian rhythms, he did not pursue this work anatomically.

In 1972, two groups of researchers clearly showed that a small region of the hypothalamus—the **suprachiasmatic nucleus** (**SCN**) (see Figure 14.4)—is the location of the circadian oscillator. The SCN gets its name from its location above the optic chiasm. F. K. Stephan and Zucker (1972) showed that lesions of the SCN interfere with circadian rhythms of drinking and locomotor behavior (Figure 14.2), and R. Y. Moore and Eichler (1972) showed that such lesions interfere with daily rhythms of adrenal steroid secretion.

Irving Zucker

The clocklike activity of the SCN is also revealed in metabolic studies using autoradiographic techniques (see Box 2.1). Figure 14.3 shows the circadian variation in the metabolic activity of the SCN. This metabolic tracing technique has also revealed some properties of fetal circadian clocks. In both rats and monkeys, the fetal SCN shows a regular circadian rhythm of metabolic activity as revealed by the 2-deoxyglucose autoradiographic technique. In these

Robert Y. Moore

studies, pregnant animals were injected with 2-deoxyglucose, and the metabolic activity of the SCN of both the parent and the fetal animals was measured. In rat fetuses a circadian rhythm is evident in the SCN shortly after it forms, well before birth. Unidentified signals from the mother appear to synchronize fetal SCN activity (Reppert, 1985). Maternal control continues for a short time following birth.

Although researchers do not yet know the source of the maternal entrainment signal, they have eliminated some candidates. The fetal rhythm survives removal of the mother's pineal, adrenal, pituitary, thyroid, and ovaries. If the maternal SCN is lesioned early in gestation, however, the SCN metabolic activity of the fetuses is temporally scattered; a circadian rhythm remains, but different fetuses in the same uterus are no longer in synchrony with each other. This evidence reinforces the view that the fetal clock is entrained by the mother.

Important method

Studies of **brain explants**—small pieces of brain tissue isolated from the body—reveal some fascinating properties of the SCN. Brain slices containing the SCN are placed in a dish with fluids resembling the extracellular environment of the brain and provided with a mixture of oxygen and carbon dioxide gases to permit

Light — Dark

Light–dark cycle

Constant dim light

* Lesion

Phase shift

14.2 The Effect of Lesions in the SCN
Circadian rhythms in the animal whose activity is plotted here were normal and synchronized to the light–dark period before an SCN lesion was made (asterisk). After the lesion the animal showed some daily rhythms in activity in synchrony with the light–dark cycle, but when placed in continuous (dim) light, its activity became completely random, indicating that the lesion had eliminated the endogenous rhythm. Note that the lesioned animal does not show a free-running rhythm of activity, but is arrhythmic, running at very different times each day. (From I. Zucker, 1976; based on Rusak and Zucker 1975.)

have photoreceptors outside the eye that are part of the mechanism of light entrainment. For example, the pineal gland of some amphibians is itself sensitive to light and helps entrain circadian rhythms to light. Because the skull over the pineal is especially thin in some amphibian species, we can think of them as having a primitive "third eye" in the back of their head. In some birds, circadian rhythms can be entrained by light even if the eyes are removed, so other photosensitive receptors must be involved in entrainment. In birds too, the pineal possesses these receptors, which detect daylight through the skull. In mammals, however, retinal pathways clearly mediate photoentrainment, because severing the optic nerves ends the role of light in circadian rhythms of all varieties.

In early experiments with rodents, lesions of the primary visual cortex and accessory pathways did not alter entrainment to a light–dark cycle, although these animals appeared "blind" and showed no indication of visually guided orientation or discrimination behavior. Robert Moore (1983) established the existence of a direct retinohypothalamic pathway—retinal ganglion cells that project out of the optic chiasm to synapse within the SCN (Figure 14.4). Lesions of this tiny pathway interfere with photic (light-induced) entrainment. A pathway from the lateral geniculate nucleus to the SCN may also facilitate photic entrainment (Rusak and Boulos, 1981).

approximately normal metabolic activities. Electrical recordings from these slices indicate that cells of the SCN show discharge rates that are synchronized to the light–dark cycle the animal had previously experienced. This is striking evidence for the endogenous character of the circadian oscillators in the SCN.

Circadian oscillations are also evident in the neural activity of the isolated SCN—an SCN still inside an animal, but isolated from other brain areas by knife cuts (a hypothalamic "island") (S. T. Inouye, cited in Turek, 1985). Evidence suggests that the neurotransmitter GABA helps generate the rhythm within the SCN (see Topic 14.1, Circadian Rhythm in GABA Receptor Function). As we'll see shortly, transplants of the SCN from one animal to another have proved that the SCN generates a circadian rhythm.

Special topic

In Mammals, Light Information from the Eyes Reaches the SCN Directly

What pathways entrain circadian rhythms to light–dark cycles? The pathway varies depending on the species (Rusak and Zucker, 1979). Some vertebrates

(a) Light phase   (b) Dark phase

SCN

14.3 Circadian Rhythm in the Metabolic Activity of the SCN
Autoradiograms of coronal sections of rat brains. (a) In a section taken from an animal during a light phase, greater metabolic activity in the SCN is represented by the darkly stained regions at the base of the brain. (b) This dark staining is not evident in a section taken from an animal during a dark phase. (From W. J. Schwartz et al., 1979.)

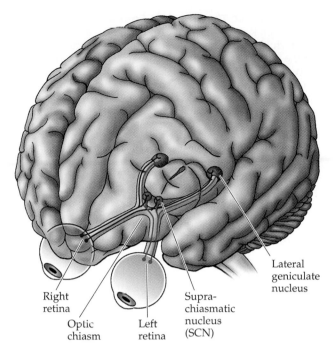

14.4 The Retinohypothalamic Pathway in Mammals
This pathway carries information about the light–dark cycle in the environment to the SCN. The information synchronizes, or entrains, the endogenous daily rhythm to external conditions. For clarity of synaptic connections, the SCN is shown proportionately larger than other features.

An exciting recent finding indicates that light information can also reach the brain *without* passing through the eyes. S. S. Campbell and Murphy (1998) applied light to the back of the knees of some human subjects and were able to shift the circadian rhythm in body temperature and melatonin secretion. Which cells in this region detect the light, and how they convey that information to the brain, are questions that remain unknown. Recently discovered photoreceptor cells distributed throughout the body of the fruit fly display a circadian rhythm in gene expression, and light can shift that rhythm independently in each cell (Plautz et al., 1997).

Figure 14.5 provides a schematic outline of the circadian system, including entrainment components.

Transplants Prove That the SCN Produces a Circadian Rhythm

Ralph and Menaker (1988) found a male hamster that exhibited an unusually short free-running activity rhythm in constant conditions. Normally hamsters free-run at a period slightly longer than 24 hours, but this male showed a period of 22 hours that was stable for 3 weeks. The researchers bred this male and, by studying his offspring, concluded that he possessed a mutation that affected the endogenous circadian rhythm. Animals with two copies of the mutation had an even shorter period—20 hours. The mutation was named *tau*, after the Greek symbol used by scientists to represent the period of a rhythm. All these animals could be entrained to a normal 24-hour light–dark period; only in constant conditions was their endogenous circadian periodicity revealed.

Dramatic evidence that this endogenous period is contained within the SCN was provided by transplant experiments. Hamsters with a lesioned SCN were placed in constant conditions; as expected, they showed arrhythmicity in activity (Figure 14.6, upper middle) (Ralph et al., 1990). Then the investigators transplanted into the hamsters an SCN taken from a fetal hamster with two copies of the mutant *tau* gene. About a week later the hamsters that had received the transplants began showing a free-running activity rhythm again, but the new rhythm matched that of the donor SCN: It was 19.5 hours rather than the original 24.05.

Reciprocal transplantations gave comparable results: The endogenous rhythm always matched the genotype of the *donor* SCN, further demonstrating that the circuitry that produces this circadian rhythmicity is within the SCN. The SCN may enforce circadian periodicity through hormone secretion, since a transplanted SCN can restore circadian rhythms even if the tissue is encapsulated to prevent nerve connections but allow hormone release (see Topic 14.2, SCN Transplants Can Act through Secretory Factors) (Silver et al., 1996).

Scientists have discovered a mouse mutant that, while able to entrain to a light–dark rhythm, fails to

14.5 Schematic Model of the Components of a Circadian System

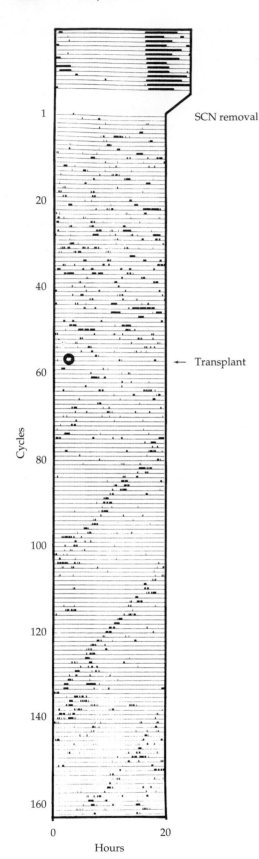

SCN removal

Transplant

Cycles

Hours

14.6 Brain Transplants Prove That the SCN Contains a Clock

A wild-type hamster, when kept in constant dim light, displayed an endogenous circadian rhythm, 24.05 hours in duration (*top*). After the SCN was lesioned, the animal became arrhythmic. Later, an SCN from a fetal hamster with two copies of the *tau* mutation was transplanted into the adult hamster (circle). Soon thereafter the adult hamster began showing a free-running activity rhythm of 19.5 hours, matching the SCN of the donor animal. This response to the transplant showed that the period of the clock is determined within the SCN. (From Ralph et al., 1990.)

display an endogenous circadian rhythm—that is, to free-run—in constant dim light (Vitaterna et al., 1994). These mice have a mutation in a gene that was named *Clock* (*c*ircadian *l*ocomoter *o*utput *c*ycles *k*aput). The *Clock* gene is found on the fifth chromosome, and only animals that have both copies of their *Clock* gene disrupted show severe arrhythmicity in constant conditions. If only one copy of the gene is disrupted, the animals free-run for a few days but then suddenly stop showing any circadian rhythmicity (Figure 14.7). The circadian oscillator in fruit flies can be studied through powerful genetic analysis (see Topic 14.3, Genetic Dissection of Circadian Rhythms).

Special topic

The SCN Is Not the Only Endogenous Oscillator

The work on biological rhythms that we have mentioned to this point shows that at least one major circadian oscillator in the brain governs multiple circadian systems, especially motor activity. Is this the *only* master oscillator? No. Examining measures other than wheel running reveals some free-running and entrained rhythms even after suprachiasmatic lesions.

14.7 When the Endogenous Clock Goes Kaput

This homozygous *Clock/Clock* mouse showed a normal circadian rhythm when given normal light cues (LD). When put in constant dim light conditions (DD), it maintained an activity period of 27.1 hours for the first 10 days but then lost circadian rhythmicity. Note, however, that an ultradian rhythm (i.e., a rhythm that has a frequency of more than once a day) with a period of just over 5 hours remains. (From Takahashi, 1995.)

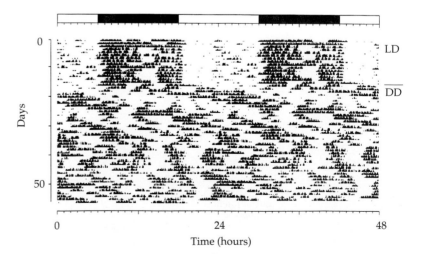

Days

LD

DD

Time (hours)

14.8 Controversial Evidence That Humans Have Two Clocks
In this human subject, bed-rest episodes (black) and body temperature (yellow) were entrained to a 24-hour day–night cycle on days 1 to 5. When the person was placed in temporal isolation, both rhythms free-ran but maintained synchrony until day 35, then spontaneously desynchronized. After day 35 the period of the body temperature rhythm shortened, and that of the rest–activity cycle lengthened, indicating that these two rhythms rely on different clocks. (From Czeisler et al., 1980.)

Moore-Ede (1982) suggested that the circadian timing system of mammals consists of two master pacemakers that drive many other secondary, passive oscillators. He hypothesized that there are two categories of circadian rhythms, each driven by a different master oscillator, one of which is found in the SCN. This suggestion was based on the desynchronization of various circadian rhythms that occurs in humans when they live (temporarily) in isolation without time cues such as daily light–dark cycles (Figure 14.8). Researchers interpreted such desynchronization as the spontaneous uncoupling of two internal clocks. The issues of oscillators and the function that each controls continue to be a major focus of current research on circadian rhythms.

Many Biological Events Display Rhythms Shorter Than a Day

Among the many diverse rhythmic biological events, a large group have periods that are shorter than those of circadian rhythms. Such rhythms are referred to as **ultradian** (designating a frequency greater than once per day), and their periods are usually from several minutes to hours. Ultradian rhythms are seen in such behaviors as bouts of activity, feeding, sleep, and hormone release. These ultradian rhythms may be superimposed on a circadian rhythm. Some more complex human behaviors also display ultradian rhythms.

Human subjects isolated from cues about time of day, or some in their normal environment, show a 90-minute cycle of daydreaming that is characterized by vivid sensory imagery (Lavie and Kripke, 1981). Ultradian rhythms in the performance of various tasks

may reflect fluctuations in alertness, which may account for the ultradian rhythm in the performance of poorly motivated subjects (Broughton, 1985). One indication of an ultradian rhythm in alertness is that EEG indices of alertness (as defined later in this chapter) vary in an ultradian rhythm. The periods of ultradian rhythms seem to be correlated with measures such as brain and body size: More rapid cycles are typical of smaller animals (Gerkema and Daan, 1985).

Destruction of the SCN, which destroys the circadian timing of activity in voles, does not affect their ultradian feeding rhythms. However, lesions to other hypothalamic areas break up ultradian rhythmicity. These areas include parts of the rostral and basal hypothalamus. Interestingly, an ultradian periodicity remains after the loss of the circadian rhythm in a *Clock/Clock* mouse (see Figure 14.7). These findings indicate that separate clocks control circadian and ultradian rhythms. We still do not know whether all ultradian rhythms reflect the operation of a single clock, or many different oscillators separately control a variety of ultradian events. Sleep cycles show an ultradian character, as we'll see later in the chapter.

Animals Use Circannual Rhythms to Anticipate Seasonal Changes

Recall that many animals display a seasonal cycle in body weight (see Chapter 13). Many other behaviors of animals are also characterized by annual rhythms. Some of these rhythms are driven by exogenous factors, such as food availability and temperature. In the laboratory, however, many annual rhythms, including body weight, persist under constant conditions. As with circadian rhythms in constant light, animals in isolation show free-running annual rhythms of a period not quite equal to 365 days. Thus there also seems to be an endogenous **circannual** oscillator.

This realm of research obviously requires considerable patience. Such rhythms are sometimes called **infradian** because their frequency is less than once per day. (A familiar infradian rhythm is the 28-day human menstrual cycle.) The relevance of annual rhythms to human behavior is becoming evident in striking seasonal disorders of behavior (see Chapter 16).

The possibility that the SCN controls circannual rhythms of ground squirrels maintained in constant conditions of photoperiod and temperature was assessed by I. Zucker et al. (1983). These researchers measured activity rhythms, reproductive cycles, and body weight cycles of animals that were free-running in both their circadian and their circannual rhythms. SCN lesions clearly disrupted circadian activity cycles, but in at least some animals these lesions did *not* affect circannual changes in body weight and reproductive status. Circannual cycles, then, do not arise from a transformation of circadian rhythms (e.g., simply counting 365 circadian cycles), and they seem to involve an oscillatory mechanism that is separate from the SCN.

Sleeping and Waking

Most of us enjoy a single period of sleep starting late in the evening and lasting until morning. The onset and termination of sleep seem synchronized to many external events, including light and dark periods. What happens to sleep when all the customary synchronizing or entraining stimuli are removed? One way to get away from such stimuli is to find deep caves and to spend weeks there with all cues to external time removed. Under such conditions a circadian rhythm of the sleep–waking cycle remains evident, although the biological clock slowly shifts from 24 to 25 hours. In other words, people have free-running periods just as a hamster does in constant dim light (Figure 14.9) (R. A. Wever, 1979). The free-running period of a little more than 24 hours indicates that humans have an endogenous circadian clock shaped by evolutionary forces that is very similar to the customary 24-hour rhythm. External cues then entrain this endogenous rhythm to 24 hours. The animal research already cited suggests that the relevant timer is the SCN.

14.9 Humans Free-Run Too
These sleep–waking patterns were recorded in a subject who, after 5 days, was isolated from cues about the time of day for the next 77 days. During this period the subject drifted away from a 24-hour daily cycle, getting the equivalent of 74 "nights" of sleep. (From Weitzman et al., 1981.)

You may think of sleep as a simple event in your life, but for biological psychologists sleep is a remarkably complex, multifaceted set of behaviors. We devote the remainder of the chapter to this fascinating phenomenon.

Human Sleep Exhibits Different Stages

Sleep seems to be characterized by the absence of behavior—a period of inactivity with raised thresholds to arousal by external stimuli. Sleep research gained momentum in the 1930s when experimenters found that brain potentials recorded from electrodes on the human scalp (by **electroencephalography**, or **EEG**; see Figure 3.18) provided a way to define, describe, and classify levels of arousal and states of sleep. This measure of brain activity is usually supplemented with recordings of eye movements and muscle tension (**electromyography**, or **EMG**). These methods later revealed two main classes of sleep: **slow-wave sleep** (**SWS**) and **rapid-eye-movement sleep**, or **REM sleep** ("REM" rhymes with "gem") (Aserinsky and Kleitman, 1953). In humans, slow-wave sleep can be divided further into four distinct stages.

Sleep ←

Subject requests sleep ↗

What are the electrophysiological distinctions that define different sleep states? To begin, the pattern of electrical activity in the fully awake, vigilant person is a desynchronized mixture of many frequencies dominated by waves of relatively fast frequencies (greater than 15 to 20 cycles per second, or hertz [Hz]) and low amplitude, sometimes referred to as beta activity. When you relax and close your eyes, a distinctive rhythm appears, consisting of a regular oscillation at a frequency of 9 to 12 Hz, known as the **alpha rhythm**. As drowsiness sets in, the amplitude of the alpha rhythm decreases, and the EEG shows events of much smaller amplitude and irregular frequency (Figure 14.10).

This stage 1 sleep is accompanied by a slowing of heart rate and a reduction of muscle tension. Many subjects awakened during this stage do not acknowledge that they have been asleep, even though they failed to respond to instructions or signals. This period usually lasts several minutes and gives way to stage 2 sleep, which is defined by 12 to 14 Hz waves called **sleep spindles** that occur in periodic bursts (see Figure 14.10).

Someone in stage 2 sleep is quite unresponsive to the external environment, and under the closed eyelids the eyes may roll about slowly. In the early part of a night of sleep, this stage leads to stage 3 sleep, which is defined by the appearance of spindles mixed with large-amplitude, very slow waves (so-called **delta waves**, about one per second). Stage 4 sleep, which follows, is defined by the presence of delta waves at least half the time.

After about an hour, the time usually required for progression through these stages, with a brief return to stage 2, something totally different occurs. Quite abruptly, scalp recordings display a pattern of small-amplitude, high-frequency activity similar in many ways to the pattern of an awake individual (see Figure 14.10, bottom), but tension in the postural neck muscles has disappeared. If you see a cat sleeping in the sitting, "sphinx" position, it cannot be in REM sleep; in REM it will be sprawled limply on the floor. As we'll see later, this flaccid muscle state appears despite intense activity in brain motor centers because brain stem regions are profoundly inhibiting motoneurons. Because of this seeming contradiction—the brain waves look awake, but the musculature is flaccid and unresponsive—another name for this state is *paradoxical sleep.*

Breathing and pulse rates become fast and irregular. The eyes now show rapid movements under the closed lids, giving this stage its most used name— REM, or rapid-eye-movement, sleep. Once you've entered REM sleep, many distinctive physiological changes occur while you remain recumbent and, in terms of common behavioral descriptions, decidedly asleep. It is during REM sleep that we experience vivid dreams.

Thus, the EEG portrait shows that sleep consists of a sequence of states instead of just an "inactive" period. Table 14.1 compares the properties of slow-wave sleep and REM sleep.

Waking

Stage 1

Vertex spike

Stage 2

Sleep spindles

Stage 3

Stage 4

REM

1 sec

14.10 Electrophysiological Correlates of Waking and Sleep
These are the characteristic EEG patterns seen during different stages of sleep in humans. The sharp wave called a vertex spike appears during stage 1 sleep. Brief periods of sleep spindles are characteristic of stage 2 sleep. Deeper stages of slow-wave sleep show progressively more large, slow delta waves. Note the similarity of activity during waking, stage 1 sleep, and REM sleep. (After Rechtschaffen and Kales, 1968.)

TABLE 14.1 *Properties of Slow-Wave and REM Sleep*

Property	Slow-wave	REM
Autonomic activities		
Heart rate	Slow decline	Variable with high bursts
Respiration	Slow decline	Variable with high bursts
Thermoregulation	Maintained	Impaired
Brain temperature	Decreased	Increased
Cerebral blood flow	Reduced	High
Skeletal muscular system		
Postural tension	Progressively reduced	Eliminated
Knee jerk reflex	Normal	Suppressed
Phasic twitches	Reduced	Increased
Eye movements	Infrequent, slow, uncoordinated	Rapid, coordinated
Cognitive state	Vague thoughts	Vivid dreams, well organized
Hormone secretion		
Growth hormone secretion	High	Low
Neural firing rates		
Cerebral cortex	Many cells reduced and more phasic	Increased firing rates; tonic (sustained) activity
Event-related potentials		
Sensory-evoked	Large	Reduced

Sleep Stages Appear in a Pattern during the Night's Sleep

Many people have exposed their sleep life to researchers in sleep laboratories. The bedroom in the experimental setup differs little from the usual sleep environment except for the presence of many wires. These wires lead to an adjacent room, where machines record brain waves and experimenters observe. The subject goes to sleep in a usual way, except that electrodes are pasted in position on the person's scalp. In addition, electrodes near the eye record eye movements, and the tension of muscles is noted by electrical recordings from the skin surface above muscles. Although the onset, pattern, duration, and termination of sleep are affected by many variables, a certain regularity allows a portrait to be drawn of the typical sleep pattern of adults.

The total sleep time of young adults usually ranges from 7 to 8 hours, and 45 to 50% of sleep is stage 2 sleep. REM sleep accounts for about 20% of total sleep. A typical night of adult human sleep shows repeating cycles about 90 to 110 minutes long, recurring four or five times in a night (Figure 14.11). These cycles change in a subtle but regular manner through the night. Cycles early in the night are shorter and are characterized by greater amounts of stages 3 and 4 SWS. The latter half of a typical night of sleep is bereft of stages 3 and 4. In contrast, REM sleep is typically more prominent in the later cycles of sleep. The first REM period is the shortest, sometimes lasting only 5 to 10 minutes; the last REM period just before awaking may last 40 minutes.

REM sleep is normally preceded by stage 2 SWS (except in infants and in a disorder called narcolepsy, which we will describe at the end of the chapter). Brief arousals occasionally occur immediately after a REM period, and you may shift your posture at this transition (Aaronson et al., 1982). The sleep cycle of 90 to 110 minutes has been viewed by some researchers as the manifestation of a basic ultradian rest–activity cycle (Kleitman, 1969); cycles of similar duration occur during waking periods. Recall that cycles of daydreaming during waking have an interval of approximately 90 minutes (Lavie and Kripke, 1981). Many other psychological and physiological properties show a 90- to 110-minute cycle, including eating and drinking, play behavior of children, and changes in heart rate (D. B. Cohen, 1979).

Some Humans Sleep Remarkably Little, yet Function Normally

The portrait of human sleep shows many variations. Some differences can be clearly related to maturational status, functional states like stress, the effects of drugs, and many other external and internal states. Some departures from the "normal" state of human sleep can be

14.11 A Typical Night of Sleep in a Young Adult
Note the progressive lengthening of REM episodes (blue) and the loss of stage 3 and 4 sleep as the night goes on. (After Kales and Kales, 1970.)

quite marked, including unusual people who hardly sleep at all. These cases are more than just folktales. Dement (1974) described a Stanford University professor who slept only 3 to 4 hours a night for more than 50 years and died at age 80.

Reports of nonsleeping humans verified by scientific observations are quite rare. After searching for that exotic type of person and about to give up the quest, sleep researcher Ray Meddis (1977) finally found a cheerful 70-year-old retired nurse who said she had slept little since childhood. She was a busy person who easily filled up her 23 hours of daily wakefulness. During the night she sat on her bed reading or writing, and at about 2:00 A.M. she fell asleep for an hour or so, after which she readily awakened. For her first 2 days in Meddis's laboratory, she did not sleep at all because it was all so interesting to her. On the third night she slept a total of 99 minutes, and her sleep contained both SWS and REM sleep periods. Later her sleep was recorded for 5 days. On the first night she did not sleep at all, but on subsequent nights she slept an average of 67 minutes. She never offered complaints about not sleeping more and did not feel drowsy during either the day or the night. Meddis described several other people who sleep either not at all or for about 1 hour per night. Some of these people report having parents who slept little.

Other people sleep longer than the normal 7 to 8 hours per night. Such "long sleepers" have more REM and stage 2 sleep, resulting from extra sleep cycles. In some human cultures a nap in the late afternoon is common—the siesta. Modern industrial societies may inhibit a natural tendency (shared with many other primates) to nap during the day.

We Do Our Most Vivid Dreaming during REM Sleep

One exciting aspect of the psychobiology of sleep is the thinking and imagery that accompany sleep. We can record the EEG of subjects, awaken them at a particular stage—1, 2, 3, 4, or REM—and question them about thoughts or perceptions immediately prior to awakening. Early data strongly indicated that dreams were restricted largely to REM sleep. Subjects reported dreams 70 to 90% of the time when they were awakened in this stage—in contrast to an incidence of 10 to 15% for non-REM sleep periods.

At first, the rapid eye movements characteristic of this period were even thought to be related to "viewing" dream scenes. In other words, if you were dreaming of watching a Ping-Pong match, your eyes would reveal the rapid to-and-fro movement of real-life observations of such a match. This scanning theory of eye movements during REM dreams now seems unlikely, because there are many differences between the characteristics of eye movements during actual viewing of scenes and those of REM sleep.

Although all studies report a large percentage of dream reports upon awakening from REM sleep, some investigators have increasingly questioned whether REM is the sole sleep state associated with dreams. In response to careful, more persistent questioning, subjects can report dreams upon awakening from non-REM sleep, especially stage 2 sleep. Dream reports of REM sleep are characterized by visual imagery, whereas the dream reports of non-REM sleep are of a more "thinking" type. REM dreams are apt to include a story that involves odd perceptions and the sense that "you are there" experiencing sights, sounds, smells, and acts. Subjects awakened from non-REM sleep report thinking about problems rather than seeing themselves in a stage presentation.

Cartwright (1979) has shown that the dreams of these two states are so different that judges reading a dream description can indicate the sleep state from which it arose with 90% accuracy. REM sleep dreams during the first half of the night are oriented toward reality. The dreams incorporate the day's experience, and the sequence of events is ordinary. Dreams during the second half of sleep are more unusual and less readily connected with the day's events, becoming more emotionally intense and bizarre. Dreams of depressed patients are emotionally bland, with very reduced activity and mood.

Terrifying dreams have become the subject of close scrutiny (Hartmann, 1984). **Nightmares** are defined as long, frightening dreams that awaken the sleeper from REM sleep. They are occasionally confused with **night**

14.12 Night Terror
Although this 1791 painting by
Henry Fuseli is called *The Nightmare*,
it more aptly illustrates night terror,
as the demon crushes the breath
from his victim.

terror, which is a sudden arousal
from stage 3 or 4 SWS marked by
intense fear and autonomic activation. In night terror the sleeper does
not recall a vivid dream but may remember a sense of a crushing feeling on the chest, as though being
suffocated (Figure 14.12). Night terrors, common in children during
the early part of an evening's sleep,
seem to be a disorder of arousal.

Nightmares are quite prevalent,
and some people are especially
plagued by them. At least 25% of
college students report having at least one nightmare
per month. (A common one, shared with Freud, is suddenly remembering a final exam that is already in
progress.) Medications that enhance the activity of
dopamine systems, such as L-dopa, also make nightmares more frequent. Individuals who experience frequent nightmares may be a more creative group, with
"loose" personal boundaries (Hartmann, 1984). Perhaps these people are prone to either a greater or a
more rapid activation of dopamine systems.

The Sleep of Different Species Provides Clues about the Evolution of Sleep

Behavioral and EEG descriptions of sleep states let us
make precise comparisons of different sleep stages in
a variety of animals. This ability has resulted in the
description of sleep in a wide assortment of mammals
and to a lesser extent in reptiles, birds, and amphibians (S. S. Campbell and Tobler, 1984). Species differ
widely in various measures of sleep. What factors
control the timing and periodic properties of sleep?

Not All Mammals Display REM Sleep

The amount of daily life occupied by sleep and the
percentage of sleep devoted to REM sleep for a variety
of animals are shown in Figure 14.13. We can make
several generalizations. All the mammals that have
been investigated thus far, with the exception of the
echidna (spiny anteater) and the dolphin, display both
REM and SWS. The spiny anteater is an egg-laying
mammal, a **monotreme**, that shows prolonged SWS

but no REM sleep. The only other monotreme is the platypus, which does have
REM sleep (see Topic 14.4, REM Sleep in
the Platypus) (J. M. Siegel et al., 1997).

 **Special
topic**

A near rival for antiquity among existing mammals is the opossum—a **marsupial** (i.e., an animal
that is born at a very early developmental stage and
spends a period of its development in a pouch). The
other mammals, including humans, are so-called **placental mammals**. Marsupials such as the opossum
display both SWS and REM sleep with EEG characteristics that are not distinguishable from those of
placental mammals. Among the other vertebrates,
only birds display clear signs of both SWS and REM
sleep. These comparisons suggest that SWS and
REM sleep developed more than 150 million years
ago in an ancestor common to birds and mammals.
Reports that reptiles may display a REM-like sleep
support this hypothesis.

Sleep in marine mammals (dolphins, whales, and
seals) is especially intriguing because these animals
must continually emerge at the surface of the water to
breathe. Sleep in the dolphin is characterized by the
complete absence of REM sleep periods, and SWS on
only one side of the brain at a time (Mukhametov,
1984). It's as if one whole hemisphere is asleep while
the other is awake. Figure 14.14 shows EEG data that
illustrate this unusual phenomenon. During these periods of "unilateral sleep," the animals continue to
come up to the surface to breathe; hence their sleep is
not characterized by relative motor immobilization.
Some seals show REM sleep and normal (bilateral)
SWS, usually when they are out of the water.

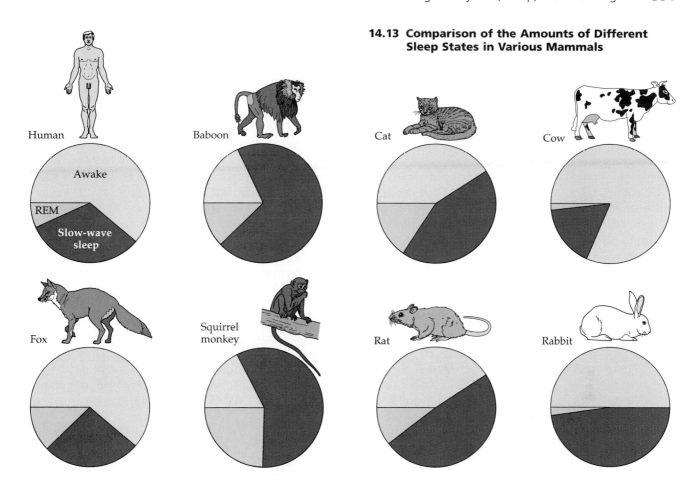

14.13 Comparison of the Amounts of Different Sleep States in Various Mammals

14.14 Sleep in Marine Mammals
(*a*) EEG patterns in right (R) and left (L) brain hemispheres in a porpoise from recording of roughly symmetrical areas of the parietal cortex. (*b*) Diagrams of EEG stages in right (R) and left (L) brain hemispheres of a bottle-nosed dolphin during a 24-hour session. The two cerebral hemispheres seem to "take turns" sleeping. (From Mukhametov, 1984.)

Vertebrate Species Differ in Their Patterns and Types of Sleep

A **sleep cycle** is a period of one episode of SWS followed by an episode of REM sleep. For the laboratory rat, one sleep cycle lasts an average of 10 to 11 minutes; for humans, one cycle lasts 90 to 110 minutes. Across species, cycle duration is inversely related to metabolic rate; that is, small animals, which tend to have high metabolic rates (see Chapter 13), have short sleep cycles. Large species have long sleep cycles.

Demands other than high metabolic rate can also cause short cycles. Some birds, such as the swift and the sooty tern, sleep briefly while gliding. The swift spends almost all its time in the air, except during the nesting season, and the sooty tern spends months flying or gliding above water, never alighting, catching fish at the surface. Sleep cycles must of necessity be short in such birds, if they sleep at all. Except for some such seabirds, all vertebrates appear to show (1) a circadian distribution of activity, (2) a prolonged phase of inactivity with (3) raised thresholds to external stimuli, and (4) a characteristic posture during inactivity. Many invertebrates also have clear periods of behavioral quiescence that include heightened arousal thresholds and distinctive postures (Hartse, 1989).

Our Sleep Patterns Change across the Life Span

In any mammal the characteristics of sleep–waking cycles change during the course of life. These changes are most evident during early development. In fact, the characteristic EEG picture of different stages of SWS is not evident until 5 or 6 years of age in humans. After this age, EEG data can be classified into stages just as adult EEG data are. Even infant sleep, however, can be generally classified into SWS and REM sleep. SWS of infants is characterized by slower EEG patterns, strong sucking, and irregular respiration. REM sleep is defined by phasic increases in respiration accompanying bursts of eye movements, EEG patterns of very low amplitude, facial grimacing, and occasional smiles. Let's look at the changing sleep patterns over the life span.

Mammals Sleep More during Infancy Than in Adulthood

A clear cycle of sleeping and waking takes several weeks to become established in human infants (Figure 14.15). A 24-hour rhythm is generally evident by 16 weeks of age. Infant sleep is characterized by short-

er sleep cycles than those of adulthood. These features of the sleep of infants seem to be due to the relative immaturity of the brain. For example, premature infants have even shorter cycles than do full-term children. Some animals born in an advanced state of development (precocial animals), such as the guinea pig, show a more mature sleep pattern at birth. The sleep patterns of mentally retarded children are different from those of normal children, with fewer eye movements during sleep and reduced amounts of REM sleep (Petre-Quadens, 1972).

Infant mammals show a large percentage of REM sleep. For example, Figure 14.16 shows that in humans within the first 2 weeks of life, 50% of sleep is REM sleep. The percentage of REM sleep is even greater in premature infants: About 80% of the sleep of infants born after only 30 weeks gestation is REM sleep. Unlike normal adults, human infants can move directly from an awake state to REM sleep. By about 4 months of age, REM sleep is entered through a period of SWS. REM sleep of infants is quite active, accompanied by muscle twitching, smiles, grimaces, and vocalizations. Perhaps the increased movement during infant REM is due to an immature ability to

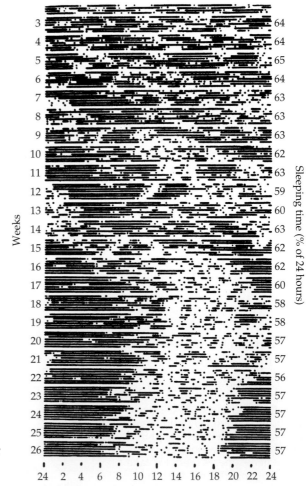

14.15 The Trouble with Babies
A stable pattern of sleep consolidated at night does not appear until about 16 weeks of age. The dark portions indicate time asleep, the blank portions time awake. (From Kleitman and Engelmann, 1953.)

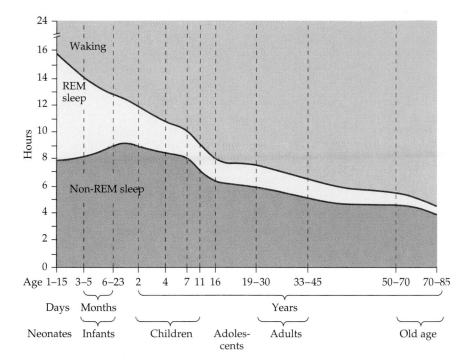

14.16 Human Sleep Patterns Change with Age
Early in life we sleep a great deal, and about half of sleep time is spent in REM sleep. By adulthood, we average about 8 hours of sleep a night, 20% of which is in REM. (After Roffwarg et al., 1966.)

(compare with Figure 14.11). Lack of sleep, or insomnia (which we will discuss at the end of this chapter), is a common complaint of the very elderly (Miles and Dement, 1980), although daytime naps may contribute to nighttime sleep difficulties.

The most dramatic progressive decline is in stages 3 and 4 sleep; amounts of these stages in persons of age 60 are only 55% of what they are at age 20. The decline of stages 3 and 4 SWS starts quite early in life, perhaps as early as the third decade (Bliwise, 1989). By age 90, all sleep of stages 3 and 4 has disappeared. This decline in stages 3 and 4 sleep in the aged may be related to diminished cognitive capabilities. An especially marked reduction of stages 3 and 4 characterizes the sleep of aged humans who show senile dementia. An age-associated decrease in stages 3 and 4 SWS is also seen in other mammals.

Are the changes in the sleep patterns of the elderly directly related to the aging process? A study by Reynolds et al. (1985) examining healthy seniors showed REM features comparable to those of young adults. Webb (1992) emphasized the wide range of variability in the sleep of aged individuals, although a central difference between the young and the old is the older person's inability to *maintain* sleep, which causes their sleep "dissatisfaction." In Chapter 18 we'll see that there are also individual differences among rats and humans in brain anatomy and chemistry with aging and that some of these differences are correlated with declines in learning ability.

inhibit motoneurons and mask activation of brain motor centers. These behaviors during REM do not seem to be related to the events of the day; rather they seem to be endogenously generated (Challamel et al., 1985).

The preponderance of REM sleep early in life suggests that this state provides stimulation that is essential to maturation of the nervous system, but this hypothesis has not been developed in any detail. A hypothesis we'll consider shortly is that REM sleep is important for the consolidation of long-term memories. Since infancy is a time of much learning, this hypothesis may account for the large amount of REM sleep early in life.

Most People Sleep Appreciably Less as They Age

The parameters of sleep change more slowly in old age than in early development. Figure 14.17 shows the pattern of a typical night of sleep in an elderly person. A decline in the total amount of sleep is evident, as is an increase in the number of arousals during a night

14.17 Typical Pattern of Sleep in an Elderly Person
Recordings of sleep in the elderly are characterized by frequent awakenings, absence of stage 4 sleep, and a reduction of stage 3 sleep. Compare this recording with the young-adult sleep pattern shown in Figure 14.11. (After Kales and Kales, 1974.)

Manipulating Sleep Reveals an Underlying Structure

Sleep is affected by many environmental, social, and biological influences. From one viewpoint, though, sleep is an amazingly stable state: Major changes in our waking behavior have only a minor impact on subsequent sleep. But some conditions do produce major shifts in sleep measures. The effects of sleep deprivation on sleep are especially interesting because they give insight into the underlying mechanisms of sleep.

Sleep Deprivation Drastically Alters Sleep Patterns

Most of us at one time or another have been willing or not-so-willing participants in informal **sleep deprivation** experiments. Thus, most of us are aware of the effect of partial or total sleep deprivation: It makes us sleepy. The study of sleep deprivation is also a way to explore the potential regulatory mechanisms of sleeping and waking. Most of the studies concern **sleep recovery**, asking questions such as, Does a sleep-deprived organism somehow keep track of the amounts and types of lost sleep? When the organism is given the opportunity to compensate, is recovery partial or complete? Can you pay off sleep debts? How many days of recovery sleep are necessary for compensation?

The effects of sleep deprivation. Early reports from sleep deprivation studies emphasized a similarity between instances of "bizarre" behavior provoked by sleep deprivation and features of psychosis, particularly schizophrenia. Partial or total sleep deprivation has been examined in the hope that it might illuminate some aspects of the genesis of psychotic behavior. A frequent theme in this work has been the functional role of dreams as a "guardian of sanity." But examination of schizophrenic patients does not seem to confirm this view. For example, these patients can show sleep–waking cycles similar to those of normal adults, and sleep deprivation does not exacerbate their symptoms.

The behavioral effects of prolonged, total sleep deprivation vary appreciably and may depend on some general personality factors and on age. In several studies employing prolonged total deprivation—205 hours (8.5 days)—some subjects showed occasional episodes of hallucinations. But the most common behavior changes noted in these experiments are increases in irritability, difficulty in concentrating, and episodes of disorientation. During each deprivation day, the effects are more prominent in the morning; by late afternoon and early evening, the subjects seem much less affected by the accumulating sleep loss. The subject's ability to perform tasks is best described by L. C. Johnson (1969, p. 216): "His performance is like a motor that after much use misfires, runs normally for a while, then falters again." Tasks that elicit strong motivation and are brief in duration may show almost no impairment, even with prolonged sleep deprivation.

Stages of sleep during recovery

14.18 Sleep Recovery after 11 Days Awake
(After Gulevich et al., 1966.)

Sleep recovery. Figure 14.18 provides data on sleep recovery in a young man following 11 days of sleep deprivation. No evidence of a psychotic state was noted, and the incentive for this unusually long act of not sleeping was simply the young man's curiosity. Researchers got into the act only after the subject started his deprivation schedule, which is the reason for the absence of predeprivation sleep data.

In the first night of sleep recovery, stage 4 sleep shows the greatest relative difference from normal. This increase in stage 4 sleep is usually at the expense of stage 2 sleep. However, the rise in stage 4 sleep during recovery never completely makes up for the deficit accumulated over the deprivation period. In fact, the amount is no greater than for deprivation periods half as long. REM sleep after prolonged sleep deprivation shows its greatest recovery during the second postdeprivation night. Eventually, the REM debt comes closer to being paid off.

Experiments of the early 1970s dealing with the "repayment of sleep debts" involved short-term deprivation effects—either total sleep deprivation or, more usually, REM deprivation. Investigators achieved the latter condition by forcefully awakening a subject whenever EEG signs of REM sleep appeared. These short-term, early REM deprivation studies showed generally that in postdeprivation recovery sessions subjects made up for the loss of REM sleep in the form of REM episodes of longer-than-normal duration. With more prolonged REM deprivation, the debt is paid off somewhat differently. Recovery of the number of hours of REM sleep is not complete. REM recovery may also involve another form of compensation—greater intensity; REM sleep in recovery nights is more "intense" than normal, with more rapid eye movements per period of time.

At Least Three Interacting Neural Systems Underlie Sleep

At one time sleep was regarded as a passive state, as though most of the brain simply stops working while we sleep, leaving us unaware of events around us. We now know that sleep is an active state mediated by at least three interacting neural systems: (1) a forebrain system that by itself can display SWS; (2) a brain stem system that activates the forebrain into wakefulness; (3) a pontine system that triggers REM sleep.

The role of the forebrain. The most straightforward evidence for the three sleep systems comes from experiments in which the brain is transected—literally cut into two parts, an upper part and a lower part. The entire brain can be isolated from the body by an incision between the medulla and the spinal cord. This preparation was first studied by the Belgian physiologist Frédéric Brémer (1935), who called it the isolated brain, or **encéphale isolé**. The EEGs of these animals showed signs of waking that alternated with signs of sleeping (Figure 14.19). During EEG-defined wakeful periods, the pupils were dilated and the eyes followed moving objects. During EEG-defined sleep, the pupils were small, as is characteristic of normal sleep. (Brémer did not distinguish between SWS and REM sleep; this distinction was not discovered until the 1950s. But we now know that REM sleep can also be detected in the isolated brain.) Where are the centers that mediate wakefulness and sleep in the encéphale isolé?

If in other animals the transection is made higher along the brain stem, in the midbrain, a very different result is achieved. Brémer referred to such preparations as an isolated forebrain, or **cerveau isolé**, and he found that the EEG from the brain in front of the cut displayed constant SWS (see Figure 14.19). We now know that the isolated forebrain does not show REM sleep, so it appears that the forebrain alone can generate SWS with no contributions from the lower brain regions.

The **basal forebrain**, in the ventral frontal lobe and anterior hypothalamus, appears to be crucial for SWS. Lesions in that region can abolish SWS, and electrical stimulation of the basal forebrain can induce SWS activity (Sterman and Clemente, 1962). Conversely, the region between these two transections—the medulla, pons, and lower midbrain—contains the other two sleep centers: one for activating the forebrain from sleep into wakefulness, and another for triggering REM sleep, each of which we will discuss in the next section.

The reticular formation. In the late 1940s, Brémer's experiments were reinterpreted on the basis of experiments in which the extensive region of the brain stem known as the **reticular formation** (Figure 14.20) was

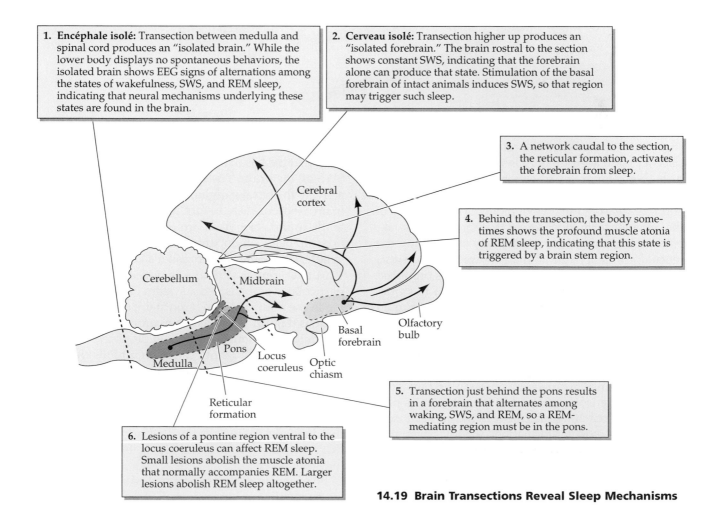

1. **Encéphale isolé:** Transection between medulla and spinal cord produces an "isolated brain." While the lower body displays no spontaneous behaviors, the isolated brain shows EEG signs of alternations among the states of wakefulness, SWS, and REM sleep, indicating that neural mechanisms underlying these states are found in the brain.

2. **Cerveau isolé:** Transection higher up produces an "isolated forebrain." The brain rostral to the section shows constant SWS, indicating that the forebrain alone can produce that state. Stimulation of the basal forebrain of intact animals induces SWS, so that region may trigger such sleep.

3. A network caudal to the section, the reticular formation, activates the forebrain from sleep.

4. Behind the transection, the body sometimes shows the profound muscle atonia of REM sleep, indicating that this state is triggered by a brain stem region.

5. Transection just behind the pons results in a forebrain that alternates among waking, SWS, and REM, so a REM-mediating region must be in the pons.

6. Lesions of a pontine region ventral to the locus coeruleus can affect REM sleep. Small lesions abolish the muscle atonia that normally accompanies REM. Larger lesions abolish REM sleep altogether.

Cerebral cortex

Cerebellum

Midbrain

Medulla

Pons

Locus coeruleus

Optic chiasm

Basal forebrain

Olfactory bulb

Reticular formation

14.19 Brain Transections Reveal Sleep Mechanisms

14.20 The Brain Stem Reticular Formation
This system is thought to activate the rest of
the brain.

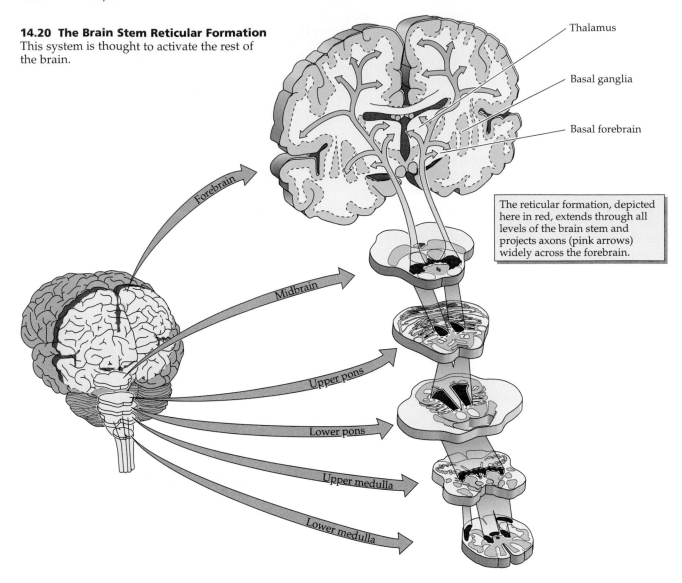

Thalamus

Basal ganglia

Basal forebrain

The reticular formation, depicted
here in red, extends through all
levels of the brain stem and
projects axons (pink arrows)
widely across the forebrain.

Forebrain

Midbrain

Upper pons

Lower pons

Upper medulla

Lower medulla

stimulated electrically. The reticular formation consists of a diffuse group of cells whose axons and dendrites course in many directions, extending from the
medulla through the thalamus. Giuseppe Moruzzi
and Horace Magoun (1949), pioneers in the study of
the reticular formation, found that they could awak-
en sleeping animals by electrically stimulating the
reticular formation; the animals showed rapid arousal
(see Figure 14.19). Lesions of these regions produced
persistent sleep in the animals, although this phenomenon was not observed if the lesions interrupted
only the sensory pathways in the brain stem.

The effects noted by Brémer were now interpreted
as arising not from loss of sensory input alone, but
from the interruption of an activating system within
the brain stem. This mechanism remained intact in
the encéphale isolé animal, but its output was precluded from reaching the cortex in the cerveau isolé
animal. The "reticular formation" school argued that
waking results from activity of brain stem reticular
formation systems and that sleep is the passive result
of a decline in activity in the reticular formation. As
we mentioned already, however, good evidence sug-

gests that the basal forebrain region actively imposes
SWS on the brain. The reticular formation seems to
activate the basal ganglia, thalamus, and basal forebrain. Neurons there in turn release dopamine, which
tends to increase brain arousal, although the relationship between dopamine and brain arousal is not
simple, since other factors can also come into play.

Michel Jouvet (1967), a major sleep researcher,
particularly emphasized a system of neurons cours-
ing in the midline of the brain stem, called the **raphe
nucleus** (Figure 14.21). These neurons use the neurotransmitter serotonin, and Jouvet proposed that serotonin release throughout the brain inhibits the reticular formation, therefore promoting sleep, especially
SWS. For example, the drug parachlorophenylala-
nine (PCPA) blocks the synthesis of serotonin, producing a decrease in transmitter levels and a reduction in sleep, although repeated administration of
PCPA becomes progressively less effective in reducing sleep levels.

Pharmacological enhancement of serotonin activity frequently prolongs sleep. Serotonin activity can

14.21 The Raphe Nucleus, Locus Coeruleus, and Their Projections

Locus coeruleus neurons (blue) are found in the dorsal pons, use norepinephrine as a neurotransmitter, and project axons widely throughout the brain.

Cortex

Midbrain

Upper pons

Lower pons

Locus coeruleus

Upper medulla

Neurons of the raphe (red) are located along the brain stem midline, use serotonin as a neurotransmitter, and project axons widely throughout the brain.

Lower medulla

be enhanced by direct injection of the transmitter into the cerebral ventricles or by the use of drugs that enhance serotonin concentrations—for example, by the administration of the precursor tryptophan. However, the broad controlling role once attributed to serotonin in neurochemical models of sleep must now be tempered by the recognition that other transmitters also seem to be part of the sleep story (Table 14.2).

The pons. Different cuts through the brain stem that are intermediate to the cerveau isolé and encéphale isolé make it clear that the pons is crucial for REM sleep. If a cut is made below the pons, the rostral brain (still connected to the pons) displays REM sleep alternating with SWS (see Figure 14.19). Conversely, if the cut is made just rostral to the pons, leaving the

pons attached to the caudal nervous system (medulla and spinal cord), then the caudal half of the animal shows REM sleep (J. M. Siegel, 1994).

You might wonder how we can recognize REM sleep in animals with a transected brain stem. We can monitor REM sleep caudal to the transection by monitoring muscle tone. The profound muscle relaxation (atonia) seen during REM sleep is never seen outside that state. Alternating periods of such atonia are good evidence that REM sleep is being induced. For monitoring REM sleep rostral to the transection, researchers rely on a specific EEG phenomenon that is seen only in REM. During that state, **PGO waves** ("PGO" stands for *p*ons, *g*eniculate, and *o*ccipital cortex) arise from the pons and reach the occipital cortex (Figure 14.22).

(*a*) Slow-wave sleep

(*b*) REM sleep

PGO spikes

2 s

14.22 PGO Waves Associated with REM Sleep in Cats
Bursts of PGO waves or spikes are especially prominent in recordings from the lateral geniculate such as these, but only during REM sleep.

Other methods pinpointed the region of the pons that is important for REM sleep. Lesions of a small region just ventral to the locus coeruleus abolish REM sleep (see Figure 14.19) (L. Friedman and Jones, 1984). Electrical stimulation of this same region, or pharmacological stimulation of this region with cholinergic agonists, can induce or prolong REM sleep. Finally, monitoring of neuronal activity in this region reveals some neurons that seem to be active only during REM sleep (J. M. Siegel, 1994). So the pons seems to have a REM sleep center.

Small lesions that destroy only a part of this pontine REM center indicate that part of this region is specialized to produce the profound muscle atonia of REM. This motor inhibition depends on influences descending from the brain to the spinal cord, because reflexes during sleep are not depressed if the spinal cord has been disconnected from the brain. Recordings from spinal motoneurons during REM sleep reveal powerful inhibitory postsynaptic potentials (IPSPs) that prevent the motoneurons from reaching threshold and producing an action potential. Thus the subject's muscles are not just relaxed, but flaccid. This loss of muscle tone during REM sleep can be abolished by small lesions ventral to the locus coeruleus, suggesting that this region plays a role in uncoupling the motor system during sleep (Morrison, 1983).

Cats with such lesions seem to act out their dreams. After a bout of SWS, the EEG from the cats becomes desynchronized as it does during waking and REM sleep, and the animals stagger to their feet. Are they awake or in REM sleep? They move their heads as though visually tracking moving objects (that aren't there), bat with their forepaws at nothing, and ignore objects that are present. This behavior is also accompanied by PGO waves, as already mentioned, that occur only during REM sleep in intact animals. In addition, the cats' "inner eyelid," the translucent nictitating membrane, partially covers the eyes. Thus, although the cats appear to be in REM sleep, motor activity is not inhibited by the brain. Many cells in this region, like the cells of the locus coeruleus itself, use norepinephrine as a neurotransmitter.

Some Hormones Normally Are Secreted during Sleep

Daily rhythms are apparent in the secretion of many hormones, including various pituitary hormones. A specific link to sleep processes has been established for growth hormone, which, in addition to being involved in growth processes, participates in governing the metabolism of proteins and carbohydrates. The highest concentrations of growth hormone in blood are evident during sleep (Figure 14.23). Growth hormone is released normally only during SWS, particularly stages 3 and 4.

The exact nature of the control or regulation of hormone release by sleep remains to be explored. For instance, is SWS the exclusive causal condition for

TABLE 14.2 *Neurotransmitter Alterations That Affect Sleep and Arousal*

Neurotransmitter	Site of cell bodies	Manipulation	Effects on sleep
Serotonin	Raphe nuclei	Increase	Promotes sleep
		Decrease	Reduces sleep
Norepinephrine	Locus coeruleus	Increase	Promotes waking, inhibits REM sleep
		Lesions	Abolish loss of muscle tone in REM sleep
Dopamine	Basal ganglia	Increase	Arousal
		Decrease	Biphasic effects on sleep
Acetylcholine	Basal forebrain	Increase	Induces REM
		Decrease	Suppresses REM

14.23 Growth Hormone Is Secreted While We Sleep
These recordings of the patterns of sleep and of growth hormone release in two different subjects show the correlation between SWS and release of this hormone. (After Y. Taka-hashi, 1979.)

growth hormone release? And how are these events synchronized? Studies suggest that growth hormone may have direct effects on the brain and thus influence sleep (J. V. Martin et al., 1985). As we saw in Chapter 5, the hormone melatonin is secreted by the pineal during the dark period in vertebrates, in both nocturnal and diurnal species (see Figure 5.18*b*); some evidence suggests that melatonin can aid the induction of sleep in humans. Topic 14.5, The Search for Sleep-Promoting Substances, discusses the search for substances in general circulation that might promote sleep.

 Special topic

What Are the Biological Functions of Sleep?

Why do most of us spend one-third of our lifetime asleep? Furthermore, why is sleep divided into two dissimilar states with distinct physiological attributes? The functions of sleep are a subject of great debate; our discussion here emphasizes only the major ideas. Keep in mind that the proposed functions or biological roles of sleep are not mutually exclusive; sleep may play many roles. As with other processes, sleep may have acquired more than one function during evolution. The four functions most often ascribed to sleep are as follows:

 Competing hypotheses

1. Energy conservation
2. Predator avoidance
3. Body restoration
4. Learning aid

None of these four proposed functions has yet been proved, and no theory has been proposed to explain why some people who sleep very little show apparently normal intellect and personality.

Sleep Conserves Energy

We consume less energy when we sleep. For example, SWS is marked by reduced muscular tension, lowered heart rate, reduced blood pressure, and slower respiration. Reduced metabolic processes are also related to the characteristic lowered body temperature of sleep. This diminished metabolic activity during sleep suggests that one role of sleep is to conserve energy. From this perspective sleep enforces the cessation of ongoing activities and thus ensures rest.

We can see the importance of this function by looking at the world from the perspective of small animals. Small animals have very high metabolic rates, so activity for them is metabolically expensive. Demand can easily outstrip supply. Periods of reduced activity can be especially valuable if they occur when food is scarce. Some support for the view that sleep conserves energy can be seen in comparative sleep data, which reveal a high correlation between total amount of sleep per day and waking metabolic rate. Small animals sleep more than large species (see Figure 14.14). The energy savings may not be as great as you might think, however, since at least part of sleep, such as the phasic events of REM sleep, is characterized by intense metabolic expenditure.

Sleep Helps Animals Avoid Predators

Intense evolutionary pressures have generated a variety of tactics for avoiding predators. Diurnal animals are well adapted to survive in the daytime; nocturnal animals are adapted for surviving the night. Meddis (1975) suggests that sleep helps animals stay out of harm's way during the part of the day when each is most vulnerable to predation. In this manner, sleep can enable effective sharing of an ecological niche—survival without becoming a meal. From a similar perspective, F. Snyder (1969) suggested that REM sleep is a periodic quasi-arousal to make sure the sleep site is still safe.

Sleep Restores the Body

If someone asked you why you sleep, chances are you would answer that you sleep because you're tired. Indeed, one of the proposed functions of sleep is simply the rebuilding or restoration of materials used during waking, such as proteins (Moruzzi, 1972). The release of growth hormone during SWS, which we mentioned earlier, supports a restorative hypothesis. Hartmann (1973) suggests that there are two types of restorative needs that sleep deals with differently: physical tiredness and the tiredness associated with emotional activation.

Surprisingly, the restorative perspective is only weakly supported by research. A simple way to test this idea is to look at the effects of changes in presleep activity on the duration or cycle of sleep. Can intense metabolic expenditure during the day influence sleep duration? For most people, exercise may cause them to fall asleep more quickly, but not to sleep longer. On the other hand, prolonged and total sleep deprivation, either forced on rats or as a result of inherited pathology in humans, interferes with the immune system and leads to death (Box 14.1). So the widespread belief that sleep helps us recover from illness is well supported by animal research.

Animal model

Sleep Appears to Aid Learning

Every now and then we are confronted with newspaper reports and advertisements that herald a new technique or gadget that will enable us to learn during sleep. The appeal of such possibilities is overwhelming to some people, including those who begrudgingly accept sleep as a necessary interference with the pursuit of knowledge and those who sport the fantasy that information can be transmitted by the deep embrace of a book. More seriously, sleep is a state in which many neurons are active. Can we learn during this state? Even if we can't learn during sleep, can sleep help us consolidate what we learned in the preceding period of wakefulness? If so, then sleep deprivation may interfere with learning. Students participating in the ritual of overnight cramming for exams would want to know. Conversely, do the learning experiences of a day influence the pattern of the subsequent night's sleep?

Only simple learning occurs during sleep. The idea that we can learn while sleeping is a controversial area beset with many conflicting claims (Aarons, 1976). The only overall conclusion one can confidently draw from a large range of studies is that if you are relying on acquiring and retaining complex information during sleep, you should find a backup system (Druckman and Bjork, 1994). Although several nonhuman experiments indicate that simple conditioned responses can be acquired during various sleep stages, evidence of people learning verbal materials while asleep is quite modest.

Studies that ensured that the subjects were asleep during presentation of verbal material—by recording EEG patterns, muscular potentials (EMG), and eye movements—provided no convincing evidence that people could recall the material later when awake. Until recently, all such experiments used explicit recall or recognition; that is, the subjects were asked to recall or recognize the material. Investigators of learning now differentiate recall from *implicit* memory—that is, memory that is revealed through performance. (We will take up this distinction further in Chapter 17.)

A type of implicit memory is seen in priming in which recent use of a word makes it more likely that the subject will offer that word in a response. For example, subjects listen to a list of paired words in which the first word is a homophone (e.g., "hair" or "hare") and the other word provides context for one of the spellings (e.g., "tortoise"). In the recall test given 10 minutes after the presentation, the subjects are asked to spell words from a list that includes the homophones presented earlier. Subjects who hear the word pairs in the waking state show clear priming effects: They are significantly more likely to spell the homophones in accordance with the context word (in our example, "hare"), but subjects who hear the words either during REM sleep or stage 2 SWS show no evidence of priming (Wood et al., 1992). Thus it appears that neither explicit nor implicit memories for verbal material form during sleep.

Some less complicated forms of learning are possible in both humans and other animals, as shown by habituation experiments in which a stimulus is repeated without consequence for a period of time. For example, if a sudden loud sound is presented during SWS, the subject—human or cat—will show EEG signs of arousal. Repetition of the stimulus makes the arousal result less likely. In some sense this response is not learning during sleep, since arousal is produced. However, this phenomenon indicates that the novelty of a stimulus can be detected in the sleeping state.

A peculiar property of dreams is that, unless we tell them to someone or write them down soon after waking, we tend to forget them (Dement, 1974). It is probably beneficial that most dreams are never stored in long-term memory, since it would be counterproductive to store permanent traces of events that might not be accurate descriptions of the world. Perhaps one of the roles of the SWS that follows REM episodes is to provide the neural condition that precludes lasting storage of the events of REM periods. Or perhaps the random, incoherent chain of events in most dreams makes them difficult to consolidate or retrieve.

Consolidation of material learned while awake. In 1924, Jenkins and Dallenbach reported an experiment that continues to provoke research. They trained some subjects in a verbal learning task at bedtime and tested them 8 hours later on arising from sleep, and they

BOX 14.1 *Sleep Deprivation Can Be Fatal*

*"Sleep that knits up the
ravell'd sleave of care"*

— *William Shakespeare,*
Macbeth, Act II, Scene 2

Although some people seem to need very little sleep, most of us feel the need to sleep 7 to 8 hours a night. In fact, sustained sleep deprivation in rats causes them to increase their metabolic rate, lose weight, and, within an average of 19 days, die (Everson et al., 1989). Allowing them to sleep prevents their death.

After the fatal effect of sleep deprivation had been shown, researchers undertook studies in which they terminated the sleep deprivation before the fatal end point and looked for pathological changes in different organ systems. No single organ system seems affected in chronically sleep-deprived animals, but early in the deprivation they develop sores on their bodies. These sores seem to be the beginning of the end; shortly thereafter the rats' plasma reveals infections from a host of bacteria, which probably enter through the sores (Everson, 1993). These bacteria are not normally fatal for rats, because the rats' immune system and body defenses keep the bacteria in check, but severely sleep-deprived rats fail to develop a fever in response to these infections. In fact, the animals show a *drop* in body temperature, which probably speeds bacterial infections, which in turn leads to diffuse organ damage.

The decline of these severely sleep-deprived rats is complicated, but if the sequence of events we have described is responsible for their death, then we should ask why the skin develops the sores that permit bacteria to enter. One observation is that the skin of these rats fails to show an inflammatory response to the infections. Inflammation is the local dilation of blood vessels, which enables greater blood flow and thus allows more immune cells to reach and attack an infection. Signs of inflammation include a reddening of the skin, a rise in local temperature, and swelling. We have no idea how sleep deprivation impairs inflammatory response, but such response is crucial for maintaining the integrity of our skin. So perhaps Shakespeare's folk theory of the function of sleep, quoted above, isn't so far from the truth.

What about the rare humans who sleep only 1 or 2 hours a night? Why aren't their immune systems and inflammatory responses compromised? We don't know, but since the distinguishing trait of these people is that they don't *need* much sleep, perhaps their immune system and inflammatory response don't need much sleep either. Or perhaps the small amount of sleep they have almost every night is more efficient at doing whatever sleep does.

Some unfortunate humans inherit a defect in the gene for the prion protein, and although they sleep normally at the beginning of their life, in midlife they simply stop sleeping—with fatal effect. People with this disease, called **fatal familial insomnia**, die 7 to 24 months after the insomnia begins (Medori et al., 1992). Autopsy reveals degeneration of the thalamus; this lesion may be responsible for the insomnia (Manetto et al., 1992). (Recall that electrical stimulation of the thalamus can induce sleep in animals.) As in sleep-deprived rats, the humans seem not to have obvious damage to any single organ system. Perhaps these patients die *because* they are chronically sleep-deprived. Research with rats certainly supports the idea that prolonged insomnia is fatal.

---

trained other subjects early in the day and tested them 8 hours later (with no intervening sleep). The results showed better retention when a period of sleep intervened between a learning period and tests of recall. What accounts for such an effect?

Several differing psychological explanations have been offered. One suggests that during the waking period between learning and recall, diverse experiences interfere with accurate recall. Sleep during this interval appreciably reduces interfering stimulation. A second explanation notes that memory tends to decay and that this relentless process is simply slower during sleep. These two explanations posit sleep as a passive process in consolidating memory.

Competing hypotheses

A third explanation emphasizes an active, functional contribution of sleep to learning. This view says that sleep includes processes that consolidate the learning of waking periods (Kavanu, 1997). Sleep is then seen as providing the conditions to allow a firm "printing" of enduring memory traces. A possible neurophysiological correlate of such consolidation has been described in the rat hippocampus (see Topic 14.6, Hippocampal Unit Activity and Sleep) (M. A. Wilson and McNaughton, 1994).

Special topic

Ekstrand et al. (1977) compared the magnitude of memory loss in three groups, all of whom had learned lists of paired associates. Group 1 learned a list in the evening and was tested for retention after an interval of 8 hours of no sleep; group 2 slept for half the night, was then awakened and learned the list, and had 4 more hours of sleep before retention testing; group 3 learned the list, slept 4 hours, and was then awakened and tested for retention. Group 2 showed the best recall. The experimenters' interpreted these results to mean that SWS favors retention, but other interpretations are possible. Idzikowski (1984) showed that 8 hours of sleep (16 hours after learning) leads to better verbal retention than no sleep does. A control experiment showed that this effect was not due to the stress of sleep deprivation (Horne, 1985).

Many animal studies have explored the notion that sleep is important for learning and retention (C. Smith, 1985). One approach has been to examine the qualitative and quantitative character of sleep following training experiences. The most consistent finding in this type of study is that the amount of REM sleep increases considerably after learning. In several studies the increased REM sleep occurred immediately at the onset of sleep following training. Increases in the amount of REM sleep result either from longer REM episodes or from more frequent REM episodes. In a few experiments studying exposure to enriched environment, not only REM but also SWS was enhanced. If learning extends over several days, the increase in REM sleep is largest during the steepest part of the learning curve (Bloch, 1976).

The functional significance of increases in REM sleep following learning has been explored by inducing REM sleep deprivation. Subjects in these studies are deprived of REM sleep during the period in which REM increments are normally seen after learning. As short a period as 3 hours of such deprivation retards the rate of learning in some cases (C. Smith, 1985). REM sleep deprivation following learning has also produced results open to more than one interpretation.

This kind of study is difficult to perform because REM sleep deprivation entails many physiological changes that might overwhelm more subtle effects that are pertinent to learning and associated phenomena. Some of the tasks employed may be too simple to require the REM mechanism. Or perhaps only certain types of learning processes are sensitive to REM deprivation. For example, in humans certain "perceptual" learning tasks, such as learning to discriminate different textures visually, show little improvement in a single training session but show considerable improvement 8 to 10 hours after the session.

Karni et al. (1994) found that if people were deprived of REM sleep after a session, they failed to show improvement the next day. In contrast, depriving them of only SWS had no effect. So perhaps REM sleep is important only for very particular types of tasks. Lavie's report (1996) of a person with a brain stem injury that seemed to eliminate REM, but did not prevent him from completing his education, further challenges the idea of a central role for REM in learning.

Perhaps "we dream in order to forget," speculated Crick and Mitchison (1983), who brought to the study of REM sleep some concepts of information theory and computer science. The essence of their argument is that REM sleep is a period of reverse learning, in which false or irrelevant memories that are routinely accumulated during the day are erased—a kind of mental housecleaning. According to this theory, the cerebral cortex is a rich matrix of interconnected cells that might become overloaded with bizarre or unusual associations. REM sleep weakens the irrelevant synapses by "zapping" them.

Psychiatrists Allan Hobson and Robert McCarley (1977) considered dreams an innocent by-product of basic bodily restorative processes with no significance by themselves. From the perspective of their "activation synthesis" hypothesis, there is no way to accomplish the biological role of sleep without the "accidental" provocation of dreams. Certain brain stem regions produce phasic activation that affects the visual cortex. This activation excites visual cortical neurons to produce the perceptual elements of a dream. These random bursts are synthesized by the cognitive activity of the dreamer, so upon awakening she or he remembers a narrativelike weaving together of the disparate elements.

Sleep Disorders Can Be Serious, Even Life-Threatening

The peace and comfort of regular, uninterrupted sleep each day may occasionally be disturbed by occurrences such as inability to fall asleep, prolonged sleep, or unusual awakenings. The assessment of sleep is a major focus of sleep disorder clinics, which have become common in major medical centers. The Association for Sleep Disorder Clinics provides a forum for analysis of research needs and accomplishments. Table 14.3 lists the main diagnostic classes of sleep disorders and gives examples of each (American Academy of Neurology, 1992; Weitzman, 1981).

Some Minor Dysfunctions Are Associated with Sleep

Among the dysfunctions associated with sleep are several events that are more common in children than in adults. **Somnambulism** (sleepwalking) can consist of getting out of bed, walking around the room, and appearing awake. In most children these episodes last a few seconds to minutes, and the child usually does not remember the experience. Because such episodes occur during stages 3 and 4 SWS, they are more common in the first half of the night (when those stages predominate). The belief that sleepwalkers are acting out a dream is not supported by data (Parkes, 1985). The main problem is the inability of sleepwalkers to awaken into full contact with their surroundings.

SWS is also related to two other common sleep disorders in children—night terrors (mentioned earlier) and **sleep enuresis** (bed-wetting). Most people grow out of somnambulism, night terrors, or sleep enuresis without intervention, but pharmacological approaches can be used to reduce the amount of stages 3 and 4 sleep (as well as REM time) while increasing stage 2 sleep. For sleep enuresis, some doctors prescribe a nasal spray of the hormone vasopressin (antidiuretic hormone) before bedtime, which decreases the amount of urine collecting in the bladder.

REM sleep can aggravate some health problems. Intense activation of autonomically innervated vis-

TABLE 14.3 *A Classification of Sleep Disorders*

1. *Disorders of initiating and maintaining sleep (insomnia)*
    Ordinary, uncomplicated insomnia
        Transient
        Persistent
    Drug-related insomnia
        Use of stimulants
        Withdrawal of depressants
        Chronic alcoholism
    Insomnia associated with psychiatric disorders
    Insomnia associated with sleep-induced respiratory impairment
        Sleep apnea
2. *Disorders of excessive drowsiness*
    Narcolepsy
    Drowsiness associated with psychiatric problems
    Drug-related drowsiness
    Drowsiness associated with sleep-induced respiratory impairment
3. *Disorders of sleep–waking schedule*
    Transient disruption
        Time zone change by airplane flight (jet lag)
        Work shift, especially night work
    Persistent disruption
        Irregular rhythm
4. *Dysfunctions associated with sleep, sleep stages, or partial arousals*
    Sleepwalking (somnambulism)
    Sleep enuresis (bed-wetting)
    Night terror
    Nightmares
    Sleep-related seizures
    Teeth grinding
    Sleep-related activation of cardiac and gastrointestinal symptoms

After Weitzman, 1981.

ceral organs during REM sleep can increase the severity of impairments. Gastric ulcer patients secrete 3 to 20 times more acid during REM episodes than do normal subjects, and many ulcer patients report intense pain that awakens them from sleep. Cardiovascular patients experience similar attacks of illness. Hospital reports show that cardiac patients are most likely to die between the hours of 4:00 and 6:00 A.M., the period of most intense and prolonged REM episodes. Kales (1973) found that 32 out of 39 episodes of angina (chest pain caused by artery disease) occurred during REM episodes. Appropriate medical care for some patients thus might include measures intended to reduce REM sleep.

Insomniacs Have Trouble Falling Asleep or Staying Asleep

Almost all of us experience an occasional inability to fall asleep, and a very few individuals die apparently because they stop sleeping altogether (see Box 14.1).

But many people persistently find it difficult to fall asleep and/or stay asleep as long as they would like. Estimates of the prevalence of **insomnia** from surveys range from 15% of the adult population of Scotland to one-third of the people in Los Angeles (Parkes, 1985). Insomnia is commonly reported by people who are older, female, or users of drugs like tobacco, coffee, and alcohol. Insomnia seems to be the final common outcome for various situational, neurological, psychiatric, and medical conditions. It is not a trivial disorder; adults who regularly sleep for short periods show a higher mortality rate than those who regularly sleep 7 to 8 hours each night (Wingard and Berkman, 1983).

Sometimes there is a discrepancy between a person's reported failure to sleep and EEG indicators of sleep. This discrepancy has been labeled *sleep state misperception* (McCall and Edinger, 1992). People with this condition report that they did not sleep even when they showed EEG signs of sleep and failed to respond to stimuli during the EEG-defined sleep state. Other insomniacs show less REM sleep and more stage 2 sleep than normal sleepers. No differences are evident in the amounts of stages 3 and 4 sleep.

Situational factors that contribute to insomnia include shift work, time zone changes, and environmental conditions such as "novelty" (that hard motel bed). Usually these conditions produce transient **sleep-onset insomnia**—a difficulty in falling asleep. Drugs and neuro-logical and psychiatric factors seem to cause **sleep-maintenance insomnia**—a difficulty in remaining asleep. In this type of insomnia, sleep is punctuated by frequent nighttime arousals. This form of insomnia is especially evident in disorders of the respiratory system.

In some people, respiration becomes unreliable during sleep. Respiration in such people can cease or slow to dangerous levels; blood levels of oxygen show a marked drop. This syndrome, called **sleep apnea**, arises from either the progressive relaxation of muscles of the chest, diaphragm, and throat cavity or changes in the pacemaker respiratory neurons of the brain stem. In the former instance, relaxation of the throat obstructs the airway—a kind of self-choking. This mode of sleep apnea is common in very obese people, but it also occurs, often undiagnosed, in nonobese people. Each episode of apnea arouses the person enough to restore breathing, but the frequent nighttime arousals make these people sleepy in the daytime. Insertion of a removable tube in the throat can restore a normal sleep pattern and eliminate excess daytime sleepiness. For others, breathing through a special machine maintains air pressure in their airways and prevents the collapse.

Investigators have speculated that **sudden infant death syndrome** (**SIDS**, or crib death) arises from sleep apnea as a result of a reduction in the brain stem neural activity that normally paces respiration. Continuous monitoring of the sleep of infants at risk for crib death can save the lives of some children.

Although Many Drugs Affect Sleep, There Is No Perfect Sleeping Pill

Throughout recorded history humans have reached for substances to enhance the prospects of sleep. Early civilizations discovered substances in the plant world that induce sleep (Hartmann, 1978). Ancient Greeks used the juice of the poppy to obtain opium and used products of the mandrake plant that we recognize today as scopolamine and atropine. The preparation of barbituric acid in the mid-nineteenth century by the discoverer of aspirin, Adolph von Bayer, began the development of an enormous number of substances—barbiturates—that continue to be used for sleep dysfunctions. Unfortunately, none of these substances can provide a completely normal night of sleep in terms of time spent in various sleep states such as REM sleep, and none of them remains effective when used repeatedly.

Most modern sleeping pills seem to activate GABA receptors, inhibiting broad regions of the brain. But reliance on sleeping pills, including the currently popular benzodiazepine triazolam (Halcion), poses many problems (Rothschild, 1992). Viewed solely as a way to deal with sleep problems, current drugs fall far short of being a suitable remedy for several reasons.

First, continual use of sleep medication causes these substances to lose their sleep-inducing properties, and this declining ability to induce sleep frequently leads to increased dosages that are self-prescribed and pose a health hazard. A second major drawback in the use of sleeping pills is that they produce marked changes in the pattern of sleep, both during the period of drug use and for a period following drug use that may last for days. Most commonly, during the initial phase of drug use REM sleep is reduced, especially during the first half of a night of sleep. A gradual adaptation to drug use is evident in the return of REM sleep with continued use of sleeping pills. Sudden withdrawal of sleeping pills results in a period of REM rebound with an intensity that many people experience as unpleasant and that may lead to a return to reliance on sleeping pills. A final major problem in the frequent use of sleeping pills is their impact on waking behavior. A persistent "sleep drunkenness" coupled with drowsiness, despite intense efforts at maintaining vigilance, may impair productive activity during waking hours.

These problems have led to the development of other biochemical approaches to the treatment of sleep disorders. Because melatonin is normally released from the pineal at night (see Figure 5.18*b*), the administration of exogenous melatonin has been suggested to aid the onset of sleep. In fact, melatonin does have a weak hypnotic effect soon after administration (Chase and Gidal, 1997), perhaps because it causes a lowering of body temperature, reducing arousal and causing drowsiness (Dawson and Encel, 1993). Mendelson (1997) remains unconvinced that melatonin really helps insomnia, but it does seem to reduce the effects of jet lag (Arendt et al., 1997). There are at least two different melatonin receptors, and only one of them seems to mediate the effects of melatonin on circadian rhythm (see Topic 14.7, Melatonin Receptors) (D. Liu et al., 1997), so drugs that can selectively activate that particular melatonin receptor will probably be developed.

▸ **Special topic**

Another approach to treating sleep disorders is to promote increases in the concentration and release of neurotransmitters that may be involved in sleep induction. Hartmann (1978) emphasized serotonin as an important transmitter in this process. Serotonin levels in the brain can be strongly influenced by the administration of tryptophan, which is a precursor in the synthesis of serotonin. Low doses of the precursor under double-blind conditions (neither experimenters nor subjects know which subjects receive the drug and which take the control until after the study is over) reduced sleep latency without changing the basic pattern of sleep in humans (Hartmann, 1978). Larger doses, however, can lead to other health problems. Meanwhile, Grandmother's suggestion to drink a glass of warm milk before bed may be sound, since milk is a source of tryptophan.

Narcoleptics Are Always Sleepy

Although some of us might find it difficult to consider excessive sleeping an affliction, many people are either drowsy all the time or suffer sudden attacks of sleep. In these cases sleep is not viewed as welcome rest but rather as an encumbrance that endangers and compromises the quality of life.

One of the largest groups of patients found at sleep disorder clinics consists of people who suffer from narcolepsy. **Narcolepsy** is an unusual disorder in which the patient is afflicted by frequent, intense attacks of sleep, which last 5 to 30 minutes and can occur at any time during the usual waking hours. Uncontrollable attacks of sleep occur several times a day—usually about every 90 minutes (Dantz et al., 1994). Narcoleptics feel drowsy most of the time.

Individuals with this sleep disorder are distinguished by the appearance of REM sleep at the onset of sleep. In fact, the duration of a narcoleptic attack is similar to the usual period of a REM sleep episode. At

(a) (b)

(c) (d)

14.24 Narcolepsy in Dogs
A narcoleptic dog that suffers cataplexy when excited is offered a food treat (*a*), becomes wobbly (*b*), lies down (*c*), and finally falls limply to the floor (*d*). (Courtesy of Seiji Nishino.)

night, however, narcoleptics exhibit a relatively normal sleep pattern. Some investigators consider this disorder to be the result of a brain stem dysfunction in which a waking mechanism fails to suppress the brain stem centers that control REM sleep.

Many narcoleptics also show **cataplexy**, a sudden loss of muscle tone, leading to collapse of the body *without* loss of consciousness. These episodes, like narcoleptic attacks, are triggered by sudden, intense emotional stimuli, including both laughter and anger. At sleep onset, some narcoleptics report **sleep paralysis**, which includes the (temporary) inability to move or talk; in this state they may experience sudden sensory hallucinations. This disorder usually manifests itself between the ages of 15 and 25 years and continues throughout life. No structural changes in the brain have been connected to narcolepsy. Several studies have shown a familial factor; one human narcolepsy susceptibility gene has been identified and is an immune-related gene (Mignot et al., 1993).

Several strains of dogs have been shown to exhibit the properties of narcolepsy (Aldrich, 1993). These animals show sudden motor inhibition (cataplexy) and

 Animal model very short latencies to sleep onset (Figure 14.24). Many instances of sleep-onset REM episodes are evident, just as in human narcoleptics. Cataplexy in these animals is suppressed by the same drugs that are used to treat human cataplexy. These narcoleptic dogs have abnormally high acetylcholine receptor levels in the pons (Aldrich et al., 1993). Moreover, inducing cataplexy in these animals (by offering very desirable food) causes

an increase in the release of acetylcholine in the pontine reticular formation (Reid et al., 1994). The mutant gene at work in one of these narcoleptic strains of dogs has been named *canarc*, and as with the human gene for narcolepsy, the *canarc* gene seems to be a part of the immune system (Mignot et al., 1991). How an alteration of the immune system could lead to narcolepsy remains a mystery, but a relationship between the immune system and sleep is not a new concept.

Summary

Biological Rhythms

1. Many living systems show circadian rhythms that can be entrained by environmental stimuli, especially light. These rhythms synchronize behavior and body states to changes in the environment.

2. Neural pacemakers in the suprachiasmatic nucleus (SCN) of the hypothalamus are the basis of many (but not all) circadian rhythms. The basis of light entrainment in many cases is a pathway from the retina to the SCN.

3. Rhythms shorter than 24 hours (ultradian rhythms) or longer than 24 hours (infradian rhythms) are evident in both behavior and biological processes. The underlying mechanism does not involve clocks in the SCN.

Sleep and Waking

1. During sleep, almost all mammals alternate between two main states, slow-wave sleep (SWS) and rapid-eye-movement (REM) sleep.

2. Human SWS shows several stages defined by EEG criteria that include bursts of spindles and persistent

trains of large, slow waves. During SWS, muscle tension, heart rate, respiratory rate, and temperature decline progressively.

3. REM sleep is characterized by a rapid EEG of low amplitude—almost like the EEG during active waking behavior—and intense autonomic activation, but the postural muscles are flaccid because of profound inhibition of motoneurons.

4. In adult humans, SWS and REM sleep alternate every 90 to 110 minutes. Smaller animals have shorter sleep cycles and spend more overall time asleep.

5. Mental activity does not cease during sleep. Vivid perceptual experiences (dreams) are frequently reported by subjects awakened from REM sleep; reports of ideas or thinking are often given by subjects awakened from SWS.

6. The characteristics of sleep–waking cycles change during the course of life. Mature animals sleep less than the young, and REM sleep accounts for a smaller fraction of their sleep.

7. The prominence of REM sleep in infants suggests that REM sleep contributes to development of the brain and to learning.

8. Deprivation of sleep for a few nights in a row leads to impairment in tasks that require sustained vigilance. During recovery nights following deprivation, the lost SWS and REM sleep are partially restored over several nights.

9. Many brain structures are involved in the initiation and maintenance of sleep. Particular emphasis has been placed on brain stem structures, including the reticular formation, the raphe nucleus, and the locus coeruleus.

10. Researchers have suggested several biological roles for sleep, including conservation of energy, avoidance of predators, restoration of depleted resources, and consolidation of memory.

11. Since memory formation is impaired when sleep deprivation—particularly REM sleep deprivation—follows learning sessions, sleep may aid the consolidation of memory. Little or no new learning, however, can take place during sleep.

12. Sleep appears to promote health, since prolonged sleep deprivation or insomnia fatally compromises the ability of an individual to combat infection.

13. Sleep disorders fall into four major categories: (1) disorders of initiation and maintenance of sleep (e.g., insomnia); (2) disorders of excessive drowsiness (e.g., narcolepsy); (3) disorders of the sleep–waking schedule; and (4) dysfunctions associated with sleep, sleep stages, or partial arousals (e.g., sleepwalking).

14. Many drugs used to induce sleep inhibit REM sleep during the first few nights. When the drug is withdrawn, there is a rebound increase of REM sleep on the following nights. No pill repeatedly provides a normal night of sleep.

Recommended Reading

Carskadon, M. A. (Ed.). (1993). *Encyclopedia of sleep and dreaming.* New York: Macmillan.

Cooper, R. (Ed.). (1994). *Sleep.* New York: Chapman & Hall Medical.

Kryger, M. K., Roth, T., and Dement, W. C. (Eds.). (1999). *Principles and practice of sleep medicine* (3rd ed.). New York: Saunders.

Pressman, M. R., and Orr, W. C. (Eds.). (1997). *Understanding sleep: The evaluation and treatment of sleep disorders.* Washington, DC: American Psychological Association.

Schwartz, W. J. (Ed.). (1997). *Sleep science: Integrating basic research and clinical practice.* Basel, Switzerland: Karger.

Takahashi, J. S. (1995). Molecular neurobiology and genetics of circadian rhythms in mammals. *Annual Review of Neuroscience, 18,* 531–554.

PART 5

Emotions and Mental Disorders

S o far in this text we have discussed a wide variety of behaviors that individuals display in particular circumstances, and in each case the behaviors seem adaptive to those circumstances. We detect stimuli that surround us, drink when body fluids are low, eat when energy supplies are depleted, sleep at night when moving about may be dangerous. It is a little more difficult to understand why we are sometimes angry, terrified, or joyful, but these emotions are clearly an important part of our lives. Chapter 15 takes up research that attempts to explain how emotions are generated and what body mechanisms are involved. Some emotions are indeed adaptive, even if we sometimes resent experiencing them. Other emotionally based behaviors are clearly not adaptive, and thus are referred to as disorders. It will not help us to survive or reproduce if we hear voices that are not present, are driven to suicide by depression, or persistently relive dreadful memories. Chapter 16 deals with the origin of these and other disorders and the modest means we have available to combat them.

15 Emotions, Aggression, and Stress

Edvard Munch (1863–1944), *Melancholy*, 1894–1895

*T*he sound of unexpected footsteps in the eerie quiet of the night brings fear to many of us. But the sound of music we enjoy and the voice of someone we love summon feelings of warmth. For some of us, feelings and emotions can become vastly exaggerated; fears can become paralyzing attacks of anxiety and panic. No story about our behavior is complete without consideration of the many events in a single day that involve feelings.

The psychobiological study of emotions has progressed in several directions. One traditional area focuses on bodily responses during emotional states, especially changes in facial expression, and visceral responses such as changes in heart rate. The study of brain mechanisms related to emotional states has especially emphasized fear and aggression, because both are important for human existence. Another focus of research on emotion is maladaptive activation related to stress, such as that which accompanies some health impairments. Emotions are closely identified with many aspects of mental disorders, since marked emotional changes are among the more striking characteristics of many of these conditions. We explore the connections between emotions and mental disorders in Chapter 16.

What Are Emotions?

The complicated world of emotions includes a wide range of observable behaviors, expressed feelings, and changes in body state. This diversity—that is, the many meanings of the word "emotion"—has made the subject hard to study. For many of us emotions are very personal states, difficult to define or identify except in the most obvious instances. Is the hissing cat frightened, angry, or perhaps enjoying tormenting its solicitous but apprehensive owner? Moreover, many aspects of our emotions seem unconscious even to us. So for many years emotions were neglected as a field of study, but there has been a significant renaissance of interest in this fascinating topic.

Emotions Have Three Different Components

There are at least three components of emotion:

1. *Feeling.* Emotion is a feeling that is private and subjective. Humans can report an extraordinary range of states, which they say they "feel" or experience. These reports of subjective experience may or may not have overt indicators.
2. *Physiological arousal.* Emotion is a state of physiological arousal—an expression or display of distinctive somatic and autonomic responses. This emphasis suggests that emotional states can be defined by particular constellations of bodily responses. The physiological arousal that accompanies emotion allows us to examine emotion in nonhuman animals as well as in human beings.
3. *Actions.* Emotions are actions commonly deemed "emotional," such as defending or attacking in response to a threat. This aspect of emotion is especially relevant to Darwin's view of the functional roles of emotion. He suggested that emotions have an important survival role because they aid in generating appropriate reactions to "emergency" events in the environment, such as the sudden appearance of a predator.

Psychologists Have Defined Different Categories of Emotion

An ongoing discussion about the study of human emotions focuses on whether a basic core set of emotions underlies the more varied and delicate nuances of our world of feelings. From a biological perspective, one reason for interest in this question is the possibility that distinctly separate brain systems are related to different parts of this core set. Plutchik (1994) suggests that there are eight basic emotions grouped in four pairs of opposites: (1) joy/sadness, (2) acceptance/disgust, (3) anger/fear, and (4) expectation/surprise. In Plutchik's view, all other emotions are derived from combinations of this basic array, which he believes is quite similar across all human societies. Table 15.1 presents this classification of emotions.

The number of emotions, how discrete they are, and their relation to cognitive activities remain active topics of psychological theorizing (Oatley and Jenkins, 1996). In general, a biological approach to emotions has emphasized a group of discrete, core emotions for which there seems to be a basis for comparisons both across human cultures and between humans and other animals.

Broad Theories of Emotion Emphasize Bodily Responses

In many emotional states, we can sense our heart beating fast, our hands and face feeling warm, our palms sweating, and a queasy feeling in our stomach. Strong emotions are nearly inseparable from activation of the skeletal-muscle and/or autonomic nervous systems. Common expressions capture this association: "with all my heart," "hair standing on end," "a sinking feeling in the stomach." Several theories have tried to explain the especially close tie between the subjective psychological phenomena we know as emotions and the activity of visceral organs controlled by the autonomic nervous system. Folk psychology suggests that the autonomic reactions are caused by

TABLE 15.1 *A Classification of Emotions*

Emotional pair	Intensity					
	"Positive" emotions			"Negative" emotions		
	High	Medium	Low	High	Medium	Low
Joy/Sadness	Ecstasy	Joy	Happiness	Grief	Sadness	Pensiveness
Acceptance/disgust	Adoration	Affection	Regard	Loathing	Disgust	Boredom
Anger/fear	Rage	Anger	Annoyance	Terror	Fear	Apprehension
Expectation/surprise	Vigilance	Expectation	Alertness	Amazement	Surprise	Distraction

Based on Plutchik, 1994.

the emotion: "I was so angry my hands were shaking," as though the anger produced the shaking.

The James–Lange Theory Considers Emotions to Be the Perception of Bodily Changes

William James, the leading figure in American psychology around the start of the twentieth century, turned the folk psychology idea on its head, suggesting that the emotions we experience are caused by the bodily changes. From this perspective we experience fear because we perceive the bodily activity triggered by particular stimuli. About the same time that James was developing his theories of emotion, a Danish physician, Carl Lange, proposed a similar view, which he boldly stated as follows: "We owe all the emotional side of our mental life, our joys and sorrows, our happy and unhappy hours, to our vasomotor system. If the impressions which fall upon our senses did not possess the power of stimulating it, we would wander through life, unsympathetic and passionless, all impressions of the outer world would only enrich our experience, increase our knowledge, but would give us neither care nor fear" (Lange, 1887).

The James–Lange theory thus emphasizes peripheral physiological events in emotion. Different emotions feel different because they are generated by a different constellation of physiological responses. The theory initiated many studies that attempted to link emotions to bodily responses, a focus of lasting interest in the field. Questions such as "What are the responses of the heart in love, anger, fear?" continue to form a prominent part of the biological study of emotions. Although the James–Lange theory initiated this research, it has not survived critical assessment.

Competing hypotheses

The Cannon–Bard Theory Emphasizes Central Processes

The simplicity of the James–Lange theory presented ready opportunity for experimental assessment. Physiologists Walter Cannon and Philip Bard studied relations between the autonomic nervous system and emotion, and offered strong criticism of the James–Lange theory. For Cannon and Bard the autonomic changes accompanying strong emotions seemed very much the same, whether the emotion experienced was anger, fear, or great surprise. Cannon (1929) emphasized that these bodily reactions (increased heart rate, glucose mobilization, and other effects) are an emergency response of an organism to a sudden threatening condition, producing maximal activation of the sympathetic nervous system. So the function of emotion is to help us deal with a changing environment (Levenson, 1994).

But for Cannon and Bard, it is the brain's job to decide what particular emotion is an appropriate response to the stimuli. According to this view, the cerebral cortex simultaneously decides on the appropriate emotional response and activates the sympathetic system so that the body is ready for either fight or flight, as the brain decides. The Cannon–Bard theory provoked many studies of the effects of brain lesions and electrical stimulation on emotion.

Stanley Schachter Proposed a Cognitive Interpretation of Stimuli and Visceral States

Like Cannon and Bard, Stanley Schachter (1975) also emphasized cognitive mechanisms in emotion, suggesting that individuals interpret visceral activation in terms of the eliciting stimuli, the surrounding situation, their cognitive states, and experience. According to Schachter, emotional labels (e.g., anger, fear, joy) depend on the interpretations of a situation—interpretations that are controlled by internal cognitive systems.

Competing hypotheses

In a famous experiment (Schachter and Singer, 1962), people were injected with epinephrine (adrenaline) and told either that there would be no effect or that their heart would race. People who were warned of the reaction reported no emotional experience, but some people who were not forewarned experienced an emotion when their body responded to the drug, as would be predicted by the James–Lange theory (bodily reactions are experienced as emotion) but not the Cannon–Bard theory (the cortex separately activates emotion and the bodily reaction).

However, the *particular* emotion experienced could be affected by whether a confederate in the room acted angry or happy. The unsuspecting subjects injected with epinephrine were much more likely to report feeling angry when in the presence of an "angry" confederate, and more likely to report feeling elated when with a "happy" confederate. These findings contradict the James–Lange prediction that a different constellation of autonomic reactions would instigate feelings of anger or euphoria. Subjects injected with placebo were much less likely to report an emotional experience, no matter how the confederate behaved.

Thus, an emotional state is the result of an interaction between physiological activation and cognitive interpretation of that arousal. According to this view, emotion depends not only on the interaction of arousal and cognitive appraisal but also on the perception that a causal connection exists between physiological arousal and emotional cognition (Reisenzein, 1983). Figure 15.1 compares these different theories of emotion.

Schachter's theory has not been without critics. For example, the theory asserts that physiological arousal is "nonspecific," affecting only the intensity of a perceived emotion but not its quality, yet each different emotion seems to exhibit a specific pattern of autonomic arousal (Cacioppo et al., 1993). When subjects were asked to pose facial expressions distinctive for particular emotions, autonomic patterns of the subjects were different for several emotions, such as fear and sadness (Levenson et al., 1990).

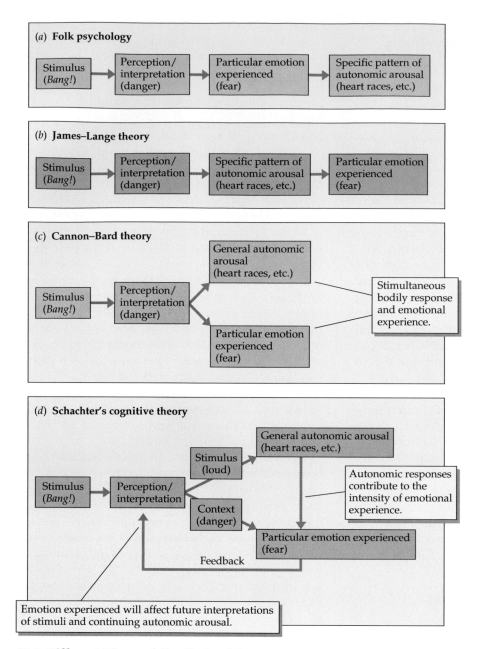

15.1 Different Views of the Chain of Events in Emotional Responses

(*a*) Folk psychology suggests that emotions cause the body to react. (*b*) James and Lange suggested that the bodily response might evoke the emotional experience. (*c*) But Cannon and Bard insisted that the brain had to interpret the situation to decide which emotion is appropriate. (*d*) Schachter attempted to reconcile these views by suggesting that the intensity of emotion can be affected by the bodily responses and that the brain continuously assesses the situation.

Facial Expressions Reveal Emotional States

Our bodies indicate emotions in many ways. Overt expressions of emotion are evident in posture, gesture, and facial expression; all these dimensions are well cultivated by actors and actresses. The human face, which is hard to hide from view, is a ready source of information. Its elaborate and finely controlled musculature provides for an enormous range of expressions, thus enhancing the prospect for communication. In this section we discuss the variety of facial expressions and their neural control.

Facial Expressions Have Complex Functions in Communication

In his book *The Expression of the Emotions in Man and Animals* (1872), Charles Darwin cataloged the facial expressions of humans and other animals and emphasized the universal nature of these expressions. He noted especially that facial expressions are connected to distinctive emotional states both in humans and in nonhuman primates. In part he viewed facial expressions as information communicated to other animals.

Paul Ekman

Paul Ekman has provided rich insight into the properties of facial expressions. He and his collaborators have developed an array of analytical tools that enable objective description and measurement of facial expressions among humans of different cultures (Ekman et al., 1981, 1983). Analyses of facial expressions reveal that both static features and rapidly changing features of the face (the latter produced by facial muscles) provide information.

How many different emotions can be detected in facial expressions? According to Ekman (1973), there are distinctive expressions for anger, sadness, happiness, fear, disgust, surprise, and contempt (Figure 15.2). Dacher Keltner has argued that embarrassment should be added to the list (Keltner and Buswell, 1996). Facial expressions of these emotions are interpreted similarly across many cultures. No explicit training is needed to interpret the expressions in any of these cultures.

Cross-cultural similarity is also noted in the production of expressions specific to particular emotions. For example, people in a preliterate New Guinea society, when displaying particular emotions, show facial expressions like those of people in industrialized societies. This "universality" hypothesis of facial expression has come under strong criticism. Fridlund

(1994) suggests that universal expressions do not account for the full complement of human facial expressions. Cultural differences may emerge in culture-specific display rules, which stipulate social contexts for facial expression. For example, Russell (1994) found significant differences across cultures in the recognition of some emotional states from facial expressions (Figure 15.3). Some anthropologists have suggested that cultures that prescribe rules for facial expression and control and enforce those rules by cultural conditioning might mask the universal property of facial expressions. A model of this process is presented in Figure 15.4. The remaining controversy focuses on the extent to which culture affects the facial display of emotion.

Facial displays are usually regarded as expressions or indicators of emotion; each primary emotion is said to be connected to a pattern of facial-muscle activation. However, Fridlund (1994) suggests that faces may not reflect emotions per se, but may serve to communicate in a social context. According to Fridlund, a major role of facial expression is "paralinguistic"; that is, the face is accessory to verbal communication, perhaps providing emphasis and direction in conversation. For example, Gilbert et al. (1986) showed that subjects display few facial responses to odor when smelling alone but significantly more in a social setting. In support of the social-display role of facial expression, Kraut and Johnston (1979) noted

Anger

Sadness

Happiness

Fear

Disgust

Surprise

Contempt

15.2 Universal Facial Expressions of Emotion
According to Paul Ekman and colleagues, the seven basic emotional facial expressions shown here are displayed in all cultures. Other workers suggest embarrassment should be added to the list. (Courtesy of David Matsumoto.)

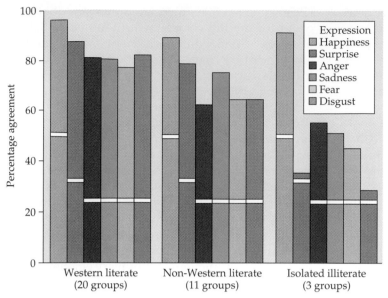

15.3 Cultural Differences in Recognizing Facial Expressions of Emotion
Within Western literate groups there is widespread agreement about the emotions accompanying photographs of facial expressions (*left*). But people from isolated illiterate groups (*right*) are much less likely to agree with our judgments of some facial expressions, especially those of surprise and disgust. The white horizontal bars indicate the percentage agreement you would expect by chance alone. (From Russell, 1994.)

that bowlers seldom smile when making a strike, but they frequently smile when they turn around to meet the faces of others watching them.

Facial expression in nonhuman primates permits the study of cross-species emotional displays. Redican (1982) described distinctive primate expressions labeled as (1) grimace, perhaps analogous to human expressions of fear or surprise; (2) tense mouth, akin to human expressions of anger; and (3) play face, similar in form to the human smile. In nonprimates the range of facial expressions is more limited, since the muscles of the face resemble a continuous sheet of poorly differentiated muscles.

Facial Expressions Are Mediated by a Set of Muscles, Two Cranial Nerves, and Varied CNS Pathways

How are facial expressions produced? Within the human face is an elaborate network of finely innervated muscles whose functional roles in addition to facial expression include production of speech, eating, and respiration, among others. Facial muscles can be divided into two categories: (1) Superficial muscles attach to facial skin (Figure 15.5). They act as sphincters, changing the shape of the mouth, eyes, or nose, for example, or they pull on their attachment to the skin. One superficial facial muscle, the frontalis muscle, wrinkles the forehead and raises the eyebrow. (2) Deep facial muscles attach to skeletal structures of the head. These muscles enable movements such as chewing. An example of a deep muscle is the masseter, a powerful jaw muscle.

Human facial muscles are innervated by two cranial nerves: (1) the facial nerve, which innervates the superficial muscles of facial expression; and (2) the trigeminal nerve, which innervates muscles that move the jaw. Studies of the facial nerve reveal that the right and left sides are completely independent. As Figure 15.5 shows, the main trunk of the facial nerve divides into an upper and lower division shortly after entering the face. These nerve fibers originate in the brain stem in a region called the nucleus of the facial nerve. Distinct subgroups of neurons within this nucleus form specific branches of the facial nerve, which in turn connect to distinct segments of the face. Within the facial-nerve nucleus, cells that control the muscles of the lower face are clearly separated from those that control the muscles of the upper face.

The face is represented extensively in the human motor cortex (see Figure 11.12). The cerebral cortex innervates the facial nucleus both bilaterally and unilaterally: The lower half of the face receives input from the opposite side of the cortex; the upper half receives

15.4 Model for Emotional Facial Expressions across Cultures

Facial muscles

Branches of the facial nerve

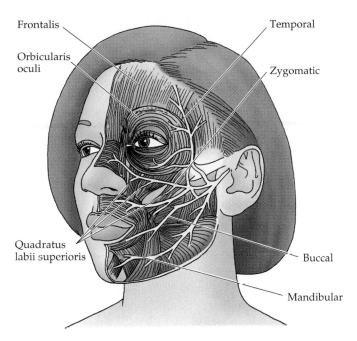

15.5 Facial Muscles and Their Neural Control

input from both sides. This pattern of innervation is evident in our ability to produce one-sided movements of the lips (the unilateral movement of an eyebrow is a more exotic talent shared by few).

Some investigators suggest that the brain control of voluntary facial movements is very different from that of facial movements induced by emotion (Rinn, 1984). Whereas voluntary activation of the facial-nerve nucleus is achieved through the corticospinal system, emotional activation of the face is presumed to involve subcortical systems. Support for this view comes from studies of patients who have sustained unilateral damage to the motor cortex. Such patients are unable to retract the corner of the mouth opposite to the damaged hemisphere when asked to do so, but both corners retract during a period of spontaneous, happy laughter or amusement. The reverse syndrome follows damage to subcortical regions such as the basal ganglia, as in Parkinson's disease. Such patients are able to move the facial muscles voluntarily, but they lose spontaneous emotional expression of the face.

Autonomic Responses Are Elicited by Emotion-Provoking Stimuli

Although the changing expressions of the face are easy to see, the detection of visceral changes requires electronic gadgets. A subject who is connected to devices that measure heart rate, blood pressure, stomach contractions, dilation or constriction of blood vessels, skin resistance, or sweating of the palms or soles exhibits many changes in response to emotional states.

Devices that measure several of these bodily responses are called **polygraphs**, popularly known as "lie detectors." The use of polygraphs to try to detect lying in individuals who are accused of crimes is controversial; most psychophysiologists argue against such use (Cacioppo et al., 1993).

Does the pattern of bodily response indicate the kind of emotion being experienced? This question, arising from the James–Lange theory, continues to intrigue investigators. Experimental studies explore whether people show patterns of reactions that are specific to particular events or stimuli. For example, if we recorded heart activity, stomach contractions, skin temperature, respiration, and blood pressure during states of anger and fear, we would expect to see profiles distinctive for each state. After reviewing a large array of data from studies of the last 30 years, Cacioppo et al. (1993) stated that the evidence on autonomic differentiation of emotions remains inconclusive. Distinct emotional stimuli do not invariably elicit a distinct pattern of autonomic responses. Some autonomic responses, such as changes in heart rate, provide better autonomic differentiation of emotions than others.

However, responses of various bodily systems reveal distinct patterns that are characteristic of the individual. John and Beatrice Lacey (1970) referred to this characteristic as **individual response stereotypy**. Their work involved longitudinal (extending over many years) studies of people, from early childhood to adulthood. The stimuli they used to provoke autonomic responses included stress conditions such as immersion of the hand in ice-cold water, performance of rapidly paced arithmetic calculations, and exposure to intense stimuli on the skin. Across these conditions the investigators observed an individual profile of response that is evident even in newborns. For example, some newborns respond vigorously with heart rate changes, others with gastric contractions, still others with blood pressure responses.

The response patterns are remarkably consistent throughout life. Jerome Kagan and colleagues have classified newborns based on their behavioral responses to cues such as an alcohol-soaked cotton swab. About 20% of the infants are termed "high reactives" because they give especially strong reactions to the stimuli. Later many of these high reactives became extremely shy and, by the time they were old enough for school, about a third of them displayed extreme phobias (compared to fewer than 10% of the other children). Kagan

Jerome Kagan

(1997) suspects that these consistent patterns of reactivity as children grow up reflect inborn differences in temperament that may relate to individual differences in response to stress, which we will discuss at the end of this chapter.

Distinct Brain Circuits Mediate or Control Emotions

Are particular neural circuits for emotions localized in particular regions of the brain? This question has been explored in studies involving either localized brain lesions or electrical stimulation. Neuropharmacological studies have tried to determine the role of specific transmitters in particular emotions. Brain lesion studies, involving clinical observations in humans or experimentally produced lesions in nonhuman animals, have focused on some dramatic syndromes of emotional change, such as the taming of monkeys following lesions of the temporal lobe. Brain stimulation studies have generated brain maps for various emotional responses, especially those involving aggression. In the discussion that follows we will look at both types of studies and their results.

Brain Lesions Affect Emotions

Many studies have explored the brain mechanisms of emotion by investigating how the destruction of brain regions affects behavior. These studies include both clinical investigations of injured humans and surgical experiments with animal subjects.

Decorticate rage. Surgical removal of the neocortex provided the oldest experimental demonstration of brain mechanisms and emotion. Early in the twentieth century, decorticate dogs (dogs from which the cortex has been removed) were shown to respond to routine handling with sudden intense rage—sometimes referred to as "sham rage" because it lacked well-directed attack. Snarling, barking, and growling were provoked by ordinary handling, and this behavior included strong visceral responses. Clearly, emotional behaviors of this type are organized at a subcortical level. These observations suggested that the cerebral cortex helps inhibit emotional responsiveness.

Klüver–Bucy syndrome. Studies of brain mechanisms and emotion were advanced by the work of Klüver and Bucy (1938), who described an unusual syndrome in primates following temporal lobe surgery. During studies on the cortical mechanisms of perception, these investigators removed large portions of the temporal lobe of monkeys. The behavior of these animals changed dramatically after surgery; the highlight was an extraordinary taming effect. Animals that had been wild and fearful of humans prior to surgery became tame and showed neither fear nor aggression. In addition, they showed strong oral tendencies, ingesting a variety of objects, including some

that were inedible. Frequent mounting behavior was observed and was described as hypersexuality.

Because lesions restricted to the cerebral neocortex did not produce these results, deeper regions of the temporal lobe, including sites within the limbic system, were implicated. This syndrome has also been observed in humans following a variety of disorders that damage the temporal lobes, including degenerative hereditary disorders (Lanska and Lanska, 1994), Alzheimer's disease (Forstl et al., 1993), and brain inflammation.

Papez's neural circuit. In 1937, James W. Papez, a neuropathologist, proposed a neural circuit of emotion. Papez (rhymes with "capes") reached his conclusions from brain autopsies of humans with emotional disorders, including psychiatric patients. He also studied the brains of animal subjects, such as rabid dogs. He noted the sites of brain destruction in these cases and concluded that the destruction necessary for impairment of emotional feelings involved a set of interconnected pathways in the limbic system.

According to Papez's circuit model, emotional expressions involve hypothalamic control of visceral organs, and feeling arises from connections to a circuit that includes the hypothalamus, the mammillary bodies, the anterior thalamus, the amygdala, and the cingulate cortex. These and other components of Papez's original circuit are shown in purple in Figure 15.6*a*. As we'll see later, strong evidence suggests that the amygdala is important for both the experience and the recognition of emotions, especially fear, so the modern notion of the limbic system has been expanded to include the amygdala and other regions (Figure 15.6*b*).

Sylvius

The triune brain. A broad, speculative neural model of emotion was presented by Paul MacLean (1970). His model arose from a diverse array of observations, including the study of limbic system seizures in humans, the mapping of behavior elicited by brain stimulation in monkeys, and an interpretation of the research literature on the evolution of the vertebrate brain. According to MacLean, the human brain can be viewed as a three-layered (or triune) system, each layer marking a significant evolutionary development.

The oldest and deepest layer, in the brain stem, represents our reptilian brain heritage. It mediates highly stereotyped acts that are part of a limited repertoire, including acts that all creatures have to perform to survive, such as breathing and eating. Routine maintenance is one way of describing these functions. In time, another layer wrapped around the reptilian core; this two-layered system is seen in some "lower" mammals, such as the platypus. This additional layer, MacLean argues, deals with the preservation of the species and the individual and includes the neural apparatus that mediates emotions, feeding, pain escape and avoidance, fighting, and plea-

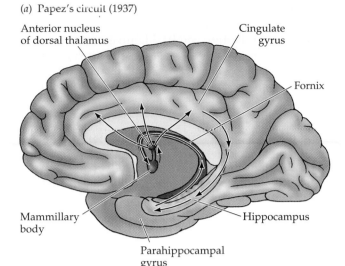

(*a*) Papez's circuit (1937)

Anterior nucleus of dorsal thalamus

Cingulate gyrus

Fornix

Mammillary body

Hippocampus

Parahippocampal gyrus

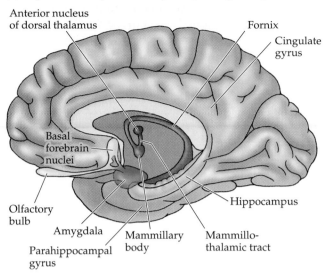

(*b*) Expanded concept of limbic system (1950s–present)

Anterior nucleus of dorsal thalamus

Fornix

Cingulate gyrus

Basal forebrain nuclei

Hippocampus

Olfactory bulb

Amygdala

Mammillary body

Mammillo-thalamic tract

Parahippocampal gyrus

15.6 Papez's Circuit of Emotion

These various components of the limbic system make extensive connections with one another and have been implicated in emotional responses.

sure seeking. The set of relevant structures in this layer is the limbic system, as discussed in the previous section. Further evolution brought a final, third layer, consisting of the dramatic elaboration of the cerebral cortex and providing the substrate for rational thought, according to this speculative model, which has its critics (LeDoux, 1995).

Electrical Stimulation of the Brain Can Produce Emotional Effects

Another productive approach to understanding the neuroanatomy of emotion is electrical stimulation of sites in the brains of awake, freely moving animals and observation of the effects on behavior. Such stimulation may produce either rewarding or aversive effects or may elicit sequences of emotional behavior.

Positive reinforcement. In 1954, psychologists James Olds and Peter Milner reported a remarkable experimental finding: Rats could learn to press a lever when the reward or reinforcement was a brief burst of electrical stimulation of the septal area within the limbic system. Another way to describe this phenomenon is brain "self-stimulation." Heath (1972) reported that patients receiving electrical stimulation in this region feel a sense of pleasure or warmth, and in some instances stimulation in this region provokes sexual excitation.

The report of Olds and Milner (1954) is one of those rare scientific discoveries that starts a new field; many investigators have since employed techniques of brain self-stimulation. Some research has focused on mapping the distribution of

James Olds
(1922–1976)

brain sites that yield self-stimulation responses (Figure 15.7). Other studies have analyzed the similarities and differences between positive responses elicited by brain stimulation and those elicited by other rewarding situations, such as the presentation of food to a hungry animal or water to a thirsty animal (reviewed by N. M. White and Milner, 1992). Perhaps

Peter Milner

electrical stimulation taps into the circuits mediating these more customary rewards.

Research in this area has also moved in a neurochemical direction; many efforts have attempted to identify the relevant transmitters in brain pathways that mediate self-stimulation behavior (P. L. Johnson and Stellar, 1994; Ranaldi and Beninger, 1994; R. A. Wise et al., 1992). Work in this area can be of particular importance in our understanding of the impact of many drugs on the emotional responses of humans.

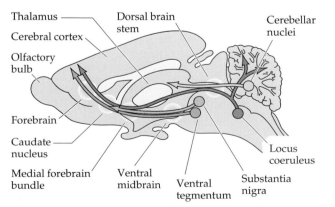

Thalamus

Cerebral cortex

Olfactory bulb

Dorsal brain stem

Cerebellar nuclei

Forebrain

Caudate nucleus

Medial forebrain bundle

Ventral midbrain

Ventral tegmentum

Substantia nigra

Locus coeruleus

15.7 Self-Stimulation Sites in the Rodent Brain

Animals will work very hard pressing a bar in return for a mild electrical stimulation at any of the sites indicated by large, orange circles.

Self-stimulation is observed with electrical stimulation of many different subcortical sites and a few frontal cortical regions (see Figure 15.7). Cerebral cortical stimulation in most regions, however, does not have positive reinforcement properties. Positive brain sites are concentrated in the hypothalamus, although these sites also extend into the brain stem. A large tract that ascends from the midbrain to the hypothalamus—the **medial forebrain bundle**—contains many sites that yield strong self-stimulation behavior. This bundle of axons is characterized by widespread origins and an extensive set of brain regions where terminals of these axons can be found. The anatomical arrangements of self-stimulation sites seem similar in different species, although positive sites are spread more extensively in the rat brain than in the cat brain.

Comparing maps of self-stimulation sites to those of neurotransmitters gave rise to the hypothesis that dopamine is the transmitter for reward circuits (R. A. Wise, 1997). On the other hand, Gallistel et al. (1985) failed to corroborate this conclusion using a metabolic mapping technique with 2-deoxyglucose.

Emotional effects.   Electrical stimulation of the brains of alert cats and monkeys implanted with electrodes has provided maps of the distribution of emotional responses. This work has emphasized limbic system sites and has focused particularly on aggression, which we discuss a little later in the chapter (Kaada, 1967). These maps show that very discrete components of both autonomic and behavioral responses are represented at selected sites in the limbic system and the hypothalamic regions. The types of responses produced by direct electrical stimulation of limbic system sites are described by Panksepp (1982) as "expectancy," "anger," "fear," and "panic."

Observations of the varied behaviors elicited by brain stimulation suggest that the limbic system has three main levels: (1) various zones of the hypothalamus, including critical connecting pathways such as the medial forebrain bundle, which connects to mesencephalic limbic structures; (2) a second level consisting of olfactory zones, septal area, amygdaloid complex, and the hippocampal formation; and (3) the limbic lobe, which consists of the cingulate gyrus and the parahippocampal gyrus. Figure 15.8 shows the effects of electrical stimulation of the limbic system. Stimulation of the cerebral cortex elicits no emotional response.

The Two Cerebral Hemispheres Process Emotion Differently

The fact that the two cerebral hemispheres play different roles in cognitive processes in humans is well established by many experimental and clinical observations (see Chapter 19). Researchers have investigated the possibility that there are hemispheric differences in emotion processing. Differences between the cerebral hemispheres have been explored from several perspectives. One perspective focuses on the special role of the right hemisphere in the perception of emotional states. Another perspective emphasizes the lateralization of emotional expression, especially in facial displays (Fridlund, 1988). Finally, a clinical contribution concerns affective disorders associated with unilateral brain diseases, such as stroke. Contributions from each of these perspectives led to the tentative assertion that emotions involve the hemispheres to different extents.

Emotional syndromes.   A major theme to emerge from studies of patients who have sustained injury or disease confined to one hemisphere is that the hemispheres differ in emotional tone. Patients who have suffered strokes involving the left anterior cerebral hemisphere have the highest frequency of depressive symptoms; the closer the lesion is to the frontal pole, the more intense is the depressive portrait. In these patients, injury-produced language deficits are not correlated with severity of depression (Starkstein and Robinson, 1994). In contrast, patients with right-hemisphere lesions are described as unduly cheerful and apathetic. Table 15.2 lists some of the clinical syndromes that include emotional changes following cerebrovascular disorders.

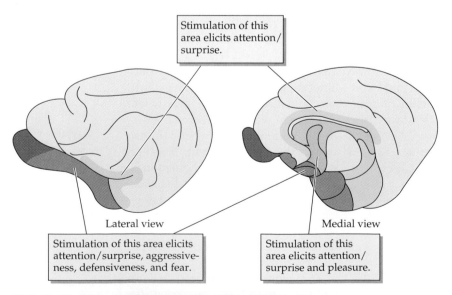

Stimulation of this area elicits attention/surprise.

Stimulation of this area elicits attention/surprise, aggressiveness, defensiveness, and fear.

Stimulation of this area elicits attention/surprise and pleasure.

Lateral view

Medial view

15.8 Brain Sites at Which Electrical Stimulation Can Produce Emotional Responses
Mild electrical stimulation of these various components of the limbic system can elicit specific emotional responses in both cats (shown here) and monkeys.

Results of unilateral injections of sodium amytal into a single carotid artery offer additional data about hemispheric differences in emotion. This procedure, described in Box 19.1, is used to determine the hemisphere that is dominant for language. Generally, injection of sodium amytal into the left hemisphere produces a depressive aftereffect, while an identical injection into the carotid artery on the right side elicits a feeling of euphoria and smiling.

R. J. Davidson (1994) has presented a different view of the role of the cerebral hemispheres in emotion processing. According to this view, anterior regions of the left and right hemispheres are specialized for approach and withdrawal processes, respectively. Thus, damage to the left frontal region results in a deficit in approach, as evident in the loss of interest and pleasure in other people and the difficulty in initiating behavior. The diminished activation of this area is associated with sadness and depression. In contrast, activation of the right anterior region is associated with withdrawal-related emotions, such as fear and disgust.

Deficits in right anterior activation produced by lesions or injury will reduce withdrawal behavior and related negative emotions. Relevant evidence includes the results from an array of electrophysiological experiments with humans. For example, in one study by Richard Davidson and colleagues at the University of Wisconsin (R. J. Davidson et al., 1990), subjects were presented with film clips while their facial expressions and brain electrical activity were recorded. The film excerpts were intended to produce either happiness or disgust. Disgust was associated with greater electrophysiological activation on the right side; the reverse was noted for happiness.

Processing of emotional stimuli. Dichotic listening techniques (see Chapters 9 and 19) have shown that the cerebral hemispheres may function differently in how they recognize emotional stimuli. Ley and Bryden (1982) presented normal subjects with brief sentences spoken in happy, sad, angry, and neutral voices. The sentences were presented through headsets—a different sentence in each ear. Subjects were instructed to attend to one ear and report both the content of the message and its emotional tone.

Subjects showed a distinct left-ear advantage for identifying the emotional tone of the voice and a right-ear advantage for understanding the meaning of the brief message. Since each ear projects more strongly to the opposite hemisphere, these results indicate that the right hemisphere is better than the left in interpreting emotional aspects of vocal messages. Some critics suggest that both hemispheres process emotional stimuli but that stimuli directed to the right hemisphere are more likely to produce emotional reactions (Silberman and Weingartner, 1986).

The presentation of different visual stimuli to each eye has also revealed hemispheric differences in the perception of emotional states or stimuli. The stimuli in these studies usually consist of faces displaying different emotional expressions. In a variety of tasks that emphasize either reaction time or identification, the common finding is that emotional stimuli presented to the left visual field (projecting to the right hemisphere) result in faster reaction times and more accurate identification of emotional states (Bryden, 1982). Likewise, in a split-brain patient, in whom the corpus callosum connecting the two hemispheres had been surgically cut (see Chapter 19), the right cerebral hemisphere was much better than the left at discrim-

TABLE 15.2   *Some Clinical Syndromes Associated with Cerebrovascular Disease*

Syndrome	Clinical symptons	Location of associated lesion
Indifference reaction	Undue cheerfulness or joking, denial of illness, loss of interest, and apathy	Right parietal or temporal lobe
Major depression	Depressed mood, daily mood variation, loss of energy, anxiety, restlessness, worry, weight loss, decreased appetite, early morning awakening, delayed sleep onset, social withdrawal, and irritability	Left frontal lobe; left basal ganglia
Pathological laughing and crying	Frequent, usually brief laughing and/or crying; crying that is not caused by sadness, or that is out of proportion to it; social withdrawal secondary to emotional outbursts	Frequently bilateral hemispheric lesions; can occur with almost any lesion location
Mania	Elevated mood, increased energy, increased appetite, decreased sleep, feeling of well-being, pressured speech, flight of ideas, grandiose thoughts	Right basotemporal or right orbitofrontal region

(a) Left sides

(b) Original

(c) Right sides

15.9 Emotions and Facial Asymmetry
Comparison of the intensity of emotional expression in composite faces. Photographs constructed by using only the left side of the face (a) are judged to be more emotional than either the original face (b) or a composite of the right side of the face (c). (Courtesy of Ruben C. Gur.)

inating emotional facial expressions (V. E. Stone et al., 1996), but the left hemisphere did better when the instructions were changed to emphasize verbal labels for facial expressions.

Asymmetry of facial expressions. By cutting a photograph of the face of a person who is displaying an emotion down the exact middle of the face, we can create two new composite photos, one made by combining two left sides (one of which is printed in mirror image) and the other made by combining two right sides of the face. The results reveal that facial expressions are not symmetric (Figure 15.9). Furthermore, the two photos produced from the same original photo elicit different responses from people looking at them. In several studies subjects judged the left-sides photo as more emotional than the right-sides photo (Sackheim et al., 1978). R. Campbell (1982) showed that composite photos constructed of the left side of the face are judged as happier, and composites of the right side of the face are judged as sadder.

Critics of this type of experiment have noted that such studies fail to distinguish between photographs of posed emotions and those of genuinely emotional expressions (Hager, 1982). The asymmetry of facial expression becomes much less evident when photos of spontaneous, genuine emotions are used as stimuli, although when subjects are asked to relate an emotional experience from their lives, they show more expressive movements on the left side of their face than on the right side (Moscovitch and Olds, 1982). Ekman et al. (1983) emphasize that judgments of facial expression include complex assessments that involve both static features of the face, such as bony landmarks, and dynamic features, such as those produced by facial musculature.

Subjects in some studies have been instructed to produce facial asymmetries by moving parts of one side of their face. Schiff and Lamon (1989) asked subjects to lift one corner of their mouth and describe their emotion when those facial muscles were allowed to relax. Feelings of sadness were associated with left-side facial muscle contraction, and positive feelings were associated with deliberately induced right-side facial muscle contraction.

Fear Is Mediated by Circuitry That Includes the Amygdala

There is nothing subtle about fear. Many animals display similar behavior under conditions that provoke fear, such as danger to one's life posed by either a nonhuman predator or a modern predator that confronts us on a city street. This lack of subtlety and the similarity of fear-related behavior across species may explain why we know much more about the neural circuitry of fear than of any other emotion (LeDoux, 1995). For example, it is very easy to reliably elicit fear using classical conditioning in which the person or animal is presented with a stimulus such as light or sound that is paired with a brief aversive stimulus such as mild electrical shock. After several such pairings, the response to the sound or light is the typical fear portrait, including freezing and autonomic signs such as cardiac and respiratory changes.

Studies of such fear conditioning using an auditory stimulus (Figure 15.10a) have provided a portrait of the neural circuitry that implicates the amygdala as a key structure in the mediation of fear. The amygdala is located at **Neural plasticity** the anterior medial portion of each temporal lobe and is composed of about a dozen distinct nuclei, each with a distinctive set of connections. Some of the connections with the rest of the brain include direct projections from sensory cortex. Lesions of the central nucleus of the *Sylvius* amygdala prevent blood pressure increases and constrain freezing behavior in response to the conditioned fear stimulus. Interconnections within the amygdala form an important part of the story. Information about the conditioned stimulus—the sound—reaches the lateral portion of the amygdala first, is then transmitted to two other small subregions of the amygdala—the basolateral and basomedial portions—and then goes to the cen-

15.10 Conditioning Reveals the Circuitry of Fear
(*a*) In one fear-conditioning procedure, a tone is associated with a mild electrical shock, which causes increased blood pressure and "freezing" (*left* and *middle*); eventually the tone alone will elicit those responses (*right*). (*b*) Proposed circuitry for the mediation of conditioned fear responses. A fear-inducing stimulus reaches the thalamus and is relayed to the cortex and hippocampus. All three regions project to the lateral nucleus of the amygdala. The information reaches the amygdala's central nucleus, which projects to three different brain regions, each of which seems to produce a different component of the fear response. (After LeDoux, 1994.)

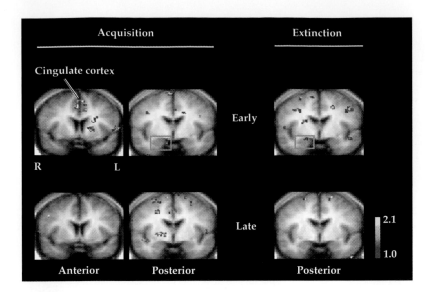

15.11 The Human Amygdala Is Activated by Fear

Subjects given a mild shock when shown a stimulus displayed activation of the anterior cingulate cortex (*top leftmost section*), probably because of the pain. The activation of the right amygdala (*green rectangle on the adjacent row*) may be due to fear. As conditioning acquisition progressed (*lower row*), these regions stopped responding, perhaps due to habituation. After a brief break, the subjects were shown stimuli without shock and, at first (*top rightmost section*), the right amygdala was reactivated when they were shown the stimulus. But as they learned that there were no more shocks, this response faded (*bottom rightmost section*). (From LaBar et al., 1998; courtesy of Kevin LaBar.)

tral nucleus. The central nucleus then transmits information to various brain stem centers to evoke emotional responses (Figure 15.10*b*).

The data from this type of experiment fit well with observations that humans who experience temporal lobe seizures that include the amygdala commonly report intense fear as a prelude or warning about the immediate prospect of a seizure (J. Engel, 1992). Likewise, stimulation of various sites within the temporal lobe of humans—a procedure performed to identify seizure-provoking sites—elicits fear in some patients (Bancaud et al., 1994). Furthermore, when human subjects are shown a visual cue previously associated with shock, blood flow to the amygdala increases (Figure 15.11) (LaBar et al., 1998). Finally, people with bilateral damage to the amygdala rate photos of people showing negative facial expressions to be as trustworthy as photos showing positive emotions (Adolphs et al., 1998), suggesting that the amygdala normally serves to make us wary of people who are in a negative mood.

The role of the amygdala in emotions is more elaborate than mere involvement with fear. Earlier we discussed the Klüver–Bucy syndrome, which is characterized by marked changes in emotional responses. Studies of monkeys show a role for the amygdala in learning the emotional significance of external events, especially social actions (Aggleton, 1993). A case description of a patient without an amygdala illustrates the role of this structure in mediating recognition of emotion in human facial expressions (Adolphs et al., 1994).

This patient suffers from a rare medical condition that results in the bilateral loss of the amygdala without damage to the surrounding hippocampus or overlying neocortex. She was shown photos of facial expressions that represented six basic emotions: happiness, surprise, fear, disgust, sadness, and anger. She showed a marked impairment of the recognition

of fear, although she could select faces of people she knew and learn the identity of new faces. In addition, this patient could not appreciate similarities between emotional expressions; for example, she did not evaluate faces showing surprise and happiness as more alike than faces displaying sadness and happiness. Another patient, with partial bilateral removal of the amygdala, showed similar impairments (A. W. Young et al., 1996). The amygdala thus appears important in mediating features of social cognition in which subtle emotional discriminations are significant.

Neural Circuitry, Hormones, and Synaptic Transmitters Mediate Violence and Aggression

Violence, assaults, and homicide exact a high toll in many human societies; for example, homicide is the most prominent cause of death in young adults in the United States. Many different approaches have investigated the psychological, anthropological, and biological dimensions of aggression. These concerted efforts have clarified many aspects of aggression, including its biological bases in hormonal and neurophysiological mechanisms. In this section we examine the results of these studies.

What Is Aggression?

Surely we all know aggression. Sustained consideration, however, suggests that this all-too-familiar term has many different meanings. In common usage, "aggression" refers to an emotional state that many humans describe as consisting of feelings of hate and a desire to inflict harm. This perspective emphasizes aggression as a powerful inner feeling. However, when we view aggression as an overt response—overt behavior that involves actual or intended destruction of another organism—we see several different forms.

Some investigators view the attack behavior of an animal directed at natural prey as predatory aggression. Glickman (1977), however, has argued that this behavior is more appropriately designated as feeding behavior. Aggression between males of the same species is observed in most vertebrates. The relevance to humans may be the fact that the ratio of males to females arrested on charges of murder in the United States is five to one. Further, aggressive behavior between boys, in contrast to that between girls, is evident early in the form of vigorous and destructive play behavior. Some animals display maternal aggression; an extreme form of this behavior is the cannibalism of young by rodent mothers. Animals that are cornered and unable to escape display fear-induced aggression. Finally, one form of aggression is referred to as irritable aggression; it can emerge from frustration or pain and frequently has the quality described as uncontrollable rage.

Androgens Seem to Increase Aggression

Male sex hormones play a major role in some forms of aggressive behavior, especially in social encounters between males (Nelson, 1995). One set of data relates levels of circulating androgens to different measures of aggressive behavior. At sexual maturity, intermale aggression markedly increases in many species. T. D. McKinney and Desjardins (1973) have shown changes in aggressiveness in mice that start at puberty. Immature mice treated with androgens display increased aggression. Levels of testosterone change seasonally in many species, and seem related to variation in ag-

gression in animals as diverse as birds and primates (Wingfield et al., 1987).

Observations of the behavioral effects of castration give additional evidence for the relation between hormones and aggression. Reductions in the level of circulating androgens produced in this manner are commonly associated with a profound reduction in intermale aggressive behavior. Restoring testosterone by injection in castrated animals increases fighting behavior in mice (Figure 15.12).

The aggressive behavior of female mammals can also depend on reproductive hormones. Although the prevailing view among researchers is that males of most mammalian species are typically the more aggressive sex, in some species such dimorphism is not evident. For example, female hamsters are generally more aggressive than males, but a female becomes transiently less aggressive when in estrus. At present, no clear evidence links hostility changes in women to the menstrual cycle (Brain, 1994).

The idea of a relationship between hormones—especially androgens—and human aggression is very controversial. Arguments summoned in legal briefs frequently cite the literature on nonhuman animals. Some human studies have shown a positive correla-

15.12 Effects of Androgen on Aggressive Behavior of Mice

Counts of the number of biting attacks initiated by males before and after castration (*a*) and by females before and after removal of the ovaries (*b*) reveal significantly higher aggression in males before castration. (*c*) When castrated males are treated with testosterone, aggressive behavior is reinstated. (From G. C. Wagner et al., 1980.)

tion between testosterone levels and the magnitude of hostility, as measured by behavior rating scales. One study of prisoners (Kreuz and Rose, 1972), however, showed no relation between testosterone levels and several measures of aggressiveness; another study (Ehrenkranz et al., 1974) showed positive relations.

Comprehensive studies of military veterans suggest that testosterone is related to antisocial behavior (Dabbs and Morris, 1990). Nonaggressive tendencies in males are associated with satisfaction in family functioning and with low levels of serum testosterone (Julian and McKenry, 1979). Among females, testosterone concentrations are highest in women prisoners convicted of unprovoked violence and lowest among women convicted of defensive violent crimes (Dabbs and Hargrove, 1997; Dabbs et al., 1988).

There are at least two possibly confounding variables in the correlations between testosterone and aggression. First is the observation that experience can affect testosterone levels. In mice and monkeys, the loser in aggressive encounters shows reduced androgen levels (Bernstein and Gordon, 1974; Lloyd, 1971), so low levels of testosterone in nonviolent prisoners may be a result, rather than a cause, of their behavior. In men, testosterone levels rise in the winners and fall in the losers after sporting events or chess matches (Bernhardt, 1997). Even male fans watching a sporting event respond with either an increase or decrease in testosterone levels, depending on whether the team they are rooting for wins or loses, respectively (Bernhardt, 1997).

Neural plasticity

These observations suggest that a second confounding variable between testosterone and aggression is dominance, since chess players could hardly be said to be aggressive. Robert Sapolsky discusses these and other issues concerning the influence of androgen on aggression in his book *The Trouble with Testosterone* (1997).

In spite of the lack of a close relationship between aggression and androgens, people have tried to modify the behavior of male criminals by manipulating sex hormones. Castration studies generally show that violence in sex offenders is reduced by this surgical procedure, especially where "excessive libido" is considered the instigator of sexual assaults (Brain, 1994). The administration of antiandrogen drugs, such as cyproterone acetate, which exerts its impact by competing with testosterone for receptor sites, acts as reversible castration. Several studies on criminals convicted of sexual assault have shown that administration of these substances reduces sexual drive and interest. However, some researchers have suggested that the effects of antiandrogens on aggressive behavior are less predictable than their effects on sexual behavior. Many ethical issues are involved in this approach to the rehabilitation of sex offenders, and the intricacies of such intervention have yet to be worked out.

Serotonin Levels Are Negatively Correlated with Aggression

Aggressive behavior in various animals, including humans, seems especially connected to mechanisms of the synaptic transmitter serotonin. Studies show a negative correlation between brain serotonin activity and aggression. **Animal model** For example, Higley et al. (1992) studied 28 monkeys chosen from more than 4500 monkeys maintained on an island off the coast of South Carolina. These animals roamed freely, and researchers collected observations of aggressive behavior and noted body wounds from fights; animals were ranked from least to most aggressive by researchers who knew nothing of the animals' neurochemical activity. Data from this study show a significant negative correlation between magnitude of aggression and serotonin activity measured in cerebrospinal fluid.

Many other observations support the view that diminished cerebrospinal concentrations of serotonin metabolites such as 5-HIAA (5-*hydroxyindoleacetic acid*) are correlated with human aggression and violence. Diminished serotonin activity (as measured by 5-HIAA concentration in cerebrospinal fluid) is seen in humans who become violent with alcohol use (Virkkunen and Linnoila, 1993), in U.S. Marines expelled for excessive violence (G. L. Brown et al., 1979), in children who torture animals (Kruesi, 1979), and in children whose poor impulse control produces disruptive behavior. Certain types of suicide are also correlated with diminished serotonin activity. Diminished cerebrospinal serotonin metabolite levels are seen in suicides that are violent in character. Similar individuals also show diminished functional serotonergic terminals in the frontal cortex, as revealed by studies of binding by the drug imipramine. Low serotonergic activity also predicted eventual suicide in a group of persons whose initial suicide attempt was unsuccessful.

We must caution that serotonin levels are not inflexible quantities that are indifferent to social stimuli and contexts. Quite the contrary. Examining primate groups, Raleigh et al. (1992) showed that low-ranking male primates have low levels of serotonin but that serotonin levels increase with social ascent. When the dominant male loses his high status, his serotonin levels decline. **Neural plasticity** Further, serotonin is not the "aggression" transmitter. Other substances have been implicated in various forms of aggression in both humans and other animals. The list includes noradrenergic and GABA systems, as well as neuropeptides that might act as modulators of aggression. In addition, a group of knockout mice, in which a gene needed for the production of the neurotransmitter nitric oxide was disabled, are extremely aggressive (Nelson et al., 1995), so this neurotransmitter may normally inhibit or limit aggressive behavior.

The Neurology of Human Violence
Is a Topic of Controversy

Some forms of human violence are characterized by sudden intense physical assaults. In a very controversial book, *Violence and the Brain*, V. H. Mark and Ervin (1970) suggested that some forms of intense human violence are derived from temporal lobe seizure disorders. They offered horrifying examples from newspaper accounts as preliminary evidence. For example, in 1966 Charles Whitman climbed a tower at the University of Texas and murdered by random shooting several passing individuals. Earlier he had killed family members, and letters he left behind revealed a portrait of a bewildered young man possessed by an intense need to commit violence. Postmortem analysis of his brain suggested the presence of a tumor deep in the temporal lobe.

Other, more formal data cited by Mark and Ervin include the common occurrence of aggression in temporal lobe seizure patients and the long-controversial claim that a large percentage of habitually aggressive criminals display abnormal EEGs that indicate likely temporal lobe disease. Mark and Ervin argued that temporal lobe disorders may underlie many forms of human violence and produce a disorder they labeled **dyscontrol syndrome**. They presented several detailed clinical reports of humans with possible temporal lobe seizure disorders. These patients had depth electrodes implanted within the temporal lobe. Electrical stimulation of various sites along the electrode tracks resulted in seizures typical of the patient. Intense assaultive behavior was directly related to elicitation of temporal lobe seizure. In some patients, neurosurgical intervention—the removal of some temporal lobe regions, especially the region of the amygdala—profoundly reduced both seizure activity and reports of assaultive behavior.

Much of the controversy surrounding Mark and Ervin's book has to do with the claim that a large proportion of human violence has this neuropathological origin (Valenstein, 1973). Vigorous controversy is also promoted by the implicit argument that neurosurgery can alleviate forms of violent behavior that many people feel are more readily understood as products of social distress and developmental impairment.

Many other studies have linked violence in humans with some forms of seizure disorders or other clinical neurological pathology (D. O. Lewis, 1990). A high percentage of both juveniles and adults arrested for violent crimes have abnormal EEGs (D. O. Lewis et al., 1979; Williams, 1969). Devinsky and Bear (1984) examined a group of patients with seizures involving emotion-controlling structures of the limbic system. These patients showed aggressive behavior that occurred after the development of an epileptic focus localized within this system. None of these patients had a history that included traditional sociological factors linked to aggression, such as parental abuse, poverty, or use of drugs. In these patients aggression is an event between seizures; directed aggression is seldom seen during an actual seizure involving the limbic system (Delgado-Escueta et al., 1981).

Although the relation of violence and aggression to epilepsy remains controversial, a growing set of clinical observations supports this association in some individuals. Some of these observations are case histories that show an unequivocal link between a seizure and a violent act. For example, studies conducted on a babysitter who had killed the child in her charge in a most violent manner showed that her violent response to the child was elicited during a temporal lobe seizure provoked by the child's laughter—a specific seizure-eliciting stimulus for this person. Many other observations point to complex forms of aggression that might arise as a function of a history of temporal lobe seizures (J. Engel, 1992).

Undoubtedly human violence and aggression stem from many sources. In recent years biological studies of aggression have been vigorously criticized by both politicians and social scientists. These critics argue that emphasizing biological factors such as genetics or brain mechanisms could lead to a failure to focus on the most evident origins of human violence and aggression, as well as to odious forms of biological controls of social dysfunction. However, violence envelops the behavior of relatively few individuals. Furthermore, it is important to understand the possible roles of biological factors, especially since the quality of life of some violent persons might be significantly improved if biological problems such as diminished serotonin activity are addressed. Treatments that enhance serotonin activity in the brain may be an important addition to a social–environmental or psychotherapeutic intervention (Coccaro and Siever, 1995).

Stress Activates Many Bodily Responses

We all experience stress, but what is it? Attempts to define **stress** have always danced around a certain vagueness implicit in this term. Some researchers emphasize that stress is a multidimensional concept that includes the stress stimuli, the processing system including the cognitive assessment of the stimuli, and the stress responses. The early use of the concept "stress" is closely identified with the work of Hans Selye, who popularized the term and defined it in a broad way as "the rate of all the wear and tear caused by life" (Selye, 1956).

Hans Selye
(1907–1982)

In many studies over almost 40 years, Selye described the impact of "stressors" on the responses of different organ systems of the body. He emphasized the connection between stress and disease in his "general adaptation syndrome." According to this scheme, the initial response to stress—called the alarm reaction—is followed by a second stage—the **adaptation stage**—which includes the successful activation of the appropriate response systems and the reestablishment of homeostatic balance. If stress is prolonged or frequently repeated, the exhaustion phase sets in, and it is characterized by increased susceptibility to disease.

In contemporary studies, this concept of stress and disease has been modified; some investigators note that the common ingredient to stressful stimuli is uncertainty or unpredictability about how to gain positive outcomes in response to these stimuli (S. Levine and Ursin, 1980). This model, which considers a broad array of factors relevant to stress and disease, including the roles of coping strategies and learning, emphasizes that stress per se does not inevitably lead to dysfunction or illness, and helps account for the variability in health histories of humans exposed to similar stressful life experiences.

Laboratory studies of human stress have used painful stimuli such as exposure to electrical shock or immersion of the hand in ice-cold water to induce stress. Researchers have frequently criticized the artificiality of such laboratory studies. Placing a hand in a bucket of ice cubes certainly pales in comparison to dangerous situations that threaten life or produce psychological trauma. Some researchers have sought to use real-life situations to explore the biology of stress. Since most human stress situations are not predictable, however, baseline prestress assessments are not available. A few studies avoid this difficulty and offer controlled observations of baseline conditions and prolonged observations during a continuing potentially harmful situation. The most commonly studied real-life stress situation is military training, especially aviator training and parachute training, where stress involves fear of bodily harm and fear of failure.

In what is now considered classic research, Grinker (1963) conducted a comprehensive study of stress in parachute training, involving both tower training and airplane jumps. However, this pioneering study was undertaken long before the development of modern chemical assessments of substances circulating in the body, such as hormones.

Ursin et al. (1978) studied minute changes of hormone levels in blood. A group of young recruits in the Norwegian military were studied by a variety of psychological and physiological measures before and during the early phase of parachute training. In this training period, subjects were propelled down a long sloping wire suspended from a tower 12 m high. Recruits were dressed in a suit equipped with a hook to the guide wire, and they slid along its course. This parachute training evokes an experience somewhat like that of free fall. Initial apprehension is high, and at first the sense of danger is acute, although recruits know that they are not likely to lose their lives in this part of the training.

Physiological measures were obtained during a basal period prior to training and with successive jumps. On each jump day, samples of blood were before and after the jump. Autonomic activation in this situation (Figure 15.13) resembles the pituitary activation of the adrenal cortex during stress that is observed in many animal experiments (see Topic 15.1, Endocrine Changes Accompany Emotions). Initially, cortisol levels were elevated in the blood, but successful jumps during training quickly led to a decrease in the pituitary–adrenal response. **Special topic** On the first jump, testosterone levels in the plasma fell below those of controls, but these levels also returned to normal with subsequent jumps. Other substances that showed marked increases in concentration at the initial jump included urinary epinephrine, norepinephrine, and growth hormone (see Figure 15.13b).

Less dramatic real-life situations also evoke clear endocrine responses, as shown by the research of Frankenhaeuser (1978). For example, riding in a commuter train was found to provoke the release of epinephrine; the longer the ride and the more crowded the train, the greater the hormonal response (Figure 15.14a). Factory work also leads to the release of epinephrine; the shorter the work cycle—that is, the more frequently the person has to repeat the same operations—the higher are the levels of epinephrine. The stress of a Ph.D. oral exam was shown to lead to a dramatic increase in both epinephrine and norepinephrine (Figure 15.14b).

Stress experienced by animals in the wild has become an interesting area of study for investigators who are trying to understand the stress response of humans. Robert Sapolsky (1992) studied baboons living freely in a natural reserve in Kenya. At first appearance, these animals seem to have a good life; food is abundant, predators are rare. The stresses they experience are the impacts they exert on each other. For males, this stress is the vigorous competition that surrounds courtship and the establishment of dominance hierarchies. An animal's place in the dominance hierarchy influences the physiology of the stress response, as seen in the animal's response to anesthesia produced by a dart gun syringe. In general, the testosterone levels of dominant males recover more rapidly after a stressful event than do those of subordinate males. Likewise the subordinates display a more prolonged increase in levels of circulating cortisol.

Robert Sapolsky

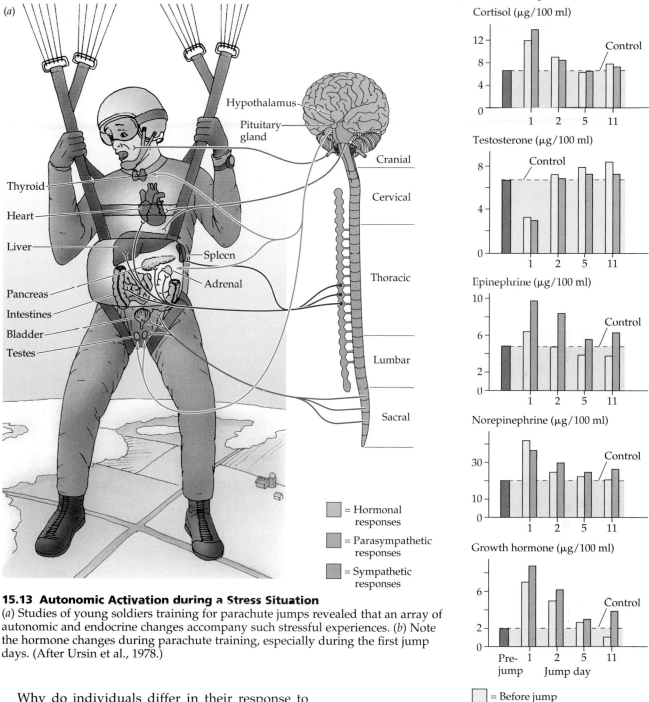

15.13 Autonomic Activation during a Stress Situation
(a) Studies of young soldiers training for parachute jumps revealed that an array of autonomic and endocrine changes accompany such stressful experiences. (b) Note the hormone changes during parachute training, especially during the first jump days. (After Ursin et al., 1978.)

Why do individuals differ in their response to stress? One hypothesis focused on early experience. Rat pups clearly find it stressful to have a human experimenter pick them up and handle them. Yet Seymour Levine et al. (1967) found that rats that had been handled as pups were less susceptible to adult stress than rats that had been left alone as pups. For example, the previously handled rats secreted less corticosteroid in response to a wide variety of adult stressors. This effect was termed **stress immunization**, because a little stress early in life seemed to make the animals more resilient to later stress.

A follow-up study has suggested that there is more to the story. When pups are returned to their mother

after a separation, she spends considerable time licking and grooming them. In fact, she will lick the pups much longer if they were handled by humans during the separation. Michael Meaney and colleagues suggest that this gentle tactile stimulation is crucial for the stress immunization effect. They found that, even among undisturbed litters, the offspring of mother rats that exhibited more licking and grooming behavior were more resilient in their response to adult stress than other rats were (D. Liu et al., 1997).

(a)

(b)

15.14 Hormone Changes in Humans in Response to Social Stresses
(a) Effects of small changes in crowding on a morning commuter train ride. A 10% increase in the number of passengers during a period of gasoline rationing (*right*) resulted in a much higher increase in epinephrine secretion. (b) Levels of epinephrine and norepinephrine in a graduate student during a 2-week period before, during, and after a thesis exam. (After Frankenhaeuser, 1978.)

Stress and Emotions Are Related to Some Human Diseases

During the past 50 years many psychiatrists and psychologists have strongly emphasized the role of psychological factors in disease. This field came to be known as **psychosomatic medicine** after an eminent psychoanalyst, Thomas French, suggested that particular diseases arise from distinctive sets of psychological characteristics or personality conflicts. From this perspective ulcers are related to frustration of "oral" needs and the development of "oral dependency," hypertension is seen as arising from hostile competitive activities, and migraine headaches represent repressed hostile needs or impulses. Each disease

state or illness is thought to be associated with a specific set of psychological characteristics—those that generate some form of unresolved conflict. Although these ideas were prominent in the early development of psychosomatic medicine, current views make fewer claims for highly particular associations. Instead they emphasize that emotional responsiveness is only one factor among many that determine the onset, maintenance, and treatment of bodily disorders.

Emotional stimuli activate a diversity of neural and hormonal changes that influence pathological processes of body organs. Studies in psychosomatic medicine have broadened in scope and now range from evaluating emotions, stress, and sickness on a global scale to unraveling particular relations between emotions and bodily responses or conditions. A field called health psychology (or behavioral medicine) has developed from this interest (Adler and Matthews, 1994; Sapolsky, 1994). Figure 15.15 shows the interaction of the many factors that result in human disease.

One global approach to linking stress and human disease is to study the covariation between precisely defined stressful life events and the incidence of particular diseases over a long period of time. Cancer and heart disease are leading causes of death and misery in human beings. The toll of these diseases in many countries has generated large-scale studies of the health habits, quality of life, and personal adjustment of large samples of people, including whole communities. Most of these studies have been retrospective; that is, participants have been asked to report and rate experiences and emotional responses that occurred prior to the interview. In some instances relatives of deceased subjects provide this information. Behavior scales allow a quantitative assessment of the frequency and number of stressful events that precede an illness.

Although many methodological problems are evident in this approach, some consistent relations between stressful events and illness have been found (N. Adler and Matthews, 1994). For example, men who report frequent and severe stress in a period of 1 to 5 years prior to interviews are more likely to experience heart disease during a 12-year period following the interview than those who report little stress (Rosengren et al., 1991). A study of naval shipboard personnel by Rahe et al. (1972) provides another example. Navy personnel were asked to report major life events associated with stress (such as death of family members or divorce) and a history of illness for a 10-year period. Results showed that subjects who reported few stressful events for a particular period had few episodes of illness in the following year. In contrast, subjects who experienced many stressful events reported a much higher level of illness for the following year. However, some other studies fail to find this association between stressful life events and subse-

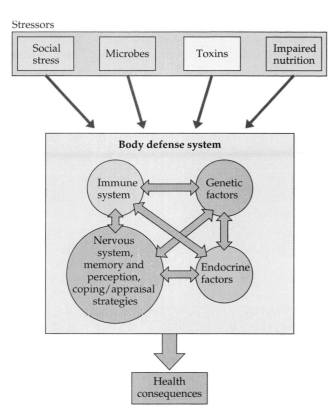

15.15 Factors That Interact during the Development and Progression of Disease

changes in the gastrointestinal system. Secretion of digestive enzymes stops, motility of the gastrointestinal tract is slowed, and blood flow to the stomach is reduced so that more blood is available for skeletal muscular activity. There are many different disorders of the human gastrointestinal system that physicians have long believed to be exacerbated by stress.

During the 1930s psychosomatic medicine focused on a key set of gastrointestinal disorders, especially stomach ulcers, that were believed to be intimately connected to psychological stress. A connection between stress and ulcers was also suggested by observations of a patient known as Tom, by the neurologist Harold Wolff in the 1940s. Tom had swallowed a caustic solution that had seared his esophagus, so he could not eat normally. To enable Tom to take in food, surgeons made a hole through the body wall into his stomach; a tube through this hole provided a route for nutrient fluids. The tube also let Wolff and collaborators directly observe the surface lining of the stomach during the course of interviews that provoked emotional responses. During intensely emotional phases of these interviews, Tom showed marked changes in the gastric mucosa, along with a dramatic buildup of stomach acid.

An ulcer is an erosion in the wall of the stomach itself (gastric ulcer) or in adjacent intestinal areas (peptic ulcer). Ulcers may form because of excessive secretion of acid, which might result from a failure in mechanisms that ordinarily govern the levels of hydrochloric acid secretion in the stomach. Other factors implicated include the dramatic drop in stomach blood flow that accompanies stress that might result in changes in stomach cells. Recently evidence has accumulated that an unusual type of bacterium (*Helicobacter pylori*) is found in the stomachs of people who have ulcers; administering antibiotics to such patients helps heal the ulcers. Stress might change the immune properties of the stomach and allow this bacterium to proliferate (Glavin, 1991).

Emotions and Stress Influence the Immune System

For a long while, researchers viewed the immune system as an automatic mechanism: A pathogen, such as a virus, arrived on the scene, and soon the defense mechanisms of the immune system went to work, usually prevailing with their armory of antibodies and other immunological devices. Few investigators thought of the nervous system as having an important role in this process, although the notion that the mind can influence well-being has been a persistent theme in human history.

In the 1980s a new field, **psychoneuroimmunology** appeared; its existence signals a new awareness that the immune system, with its collection of cells that recognize intruders, interacts with other organs, especially hormonal systems and the nervous system.

Competing hypotheses

quent disease (Hollis et al., 1990). The social network within which stress occurs may be a more important determinant of disease outcome than stress itself is (N. Adler and Matthews, 1994).

Mere frequency of stressful life events may be less related to serious illness than earlier studies emphasized. In a study of stressful events and heart attack, D. G. Byrne and White (1980) compared a group of coronary patients with a "control" group of people who were admitted to emergency rooms with suspected heart difficulties but who were rapidly diagnosed as not being heart attack cases. Questionnaires completed by the patients gave researchers an estimate of the frequency and intensity of stressful life events for the year prior to hospitalization.

Heart attack patients did not have a higher frequency of stressful events during the year prior to illness than did the controls. Nor was the intensity of stress events a factor that distinguished these groups. However, heart attack patients were significantly more distressed by stressful life events and tended to be more anxious. The emotional impact of stress thus appears to have greater significance for future serious illness than does the mere occurrence of stressful events.

Stress Affects the Stomach

Many of us have felt stomach upset during moments of stress and emotion. Stress is accompanied by many

Studies with both human and nonhuman subjects now clearly show psychological and neurological influences on the immune system. These interactions go in both directions: The brain influences responses of the immune system, and immune cells and their products affect brain activities.

The immune system.   To understand this intriguing story we need to note some of the main features of the immune system. There are two basic types of immunological responses, mediated by two different classes of cells called lymphocytes. **B lymphocytes** (or B cells) mediate **humoral immunity**, which occurs when these cells produce proteins called antibodies, or immunoglobulins, that either directly destroy antigens (foreign molecules) such as viruses or bacteria or enhance their destruction by other cells.

A second type of immunological response, **cell-mediated immunity**, is mediated by **T lymphocytes** (T cells). These cells directly attack various antigens. They act as "killer cells," forming a strong part of the body's attack against substances that can cause tumors. T cells are also involved in the rejection of organ transplants. In addition, T cells interact with humoral reactions mediated by B cells. In some of these interactions antibody reactions are enhanced, and this response requires special T lymphocytes called helper T cells. Other T lymphocytes suppress humoral reactions and are referred to as suppressor T cells.

These basic components of the immune system also interact with other body substances and cells in defending the body against disease and harmful substances. The organs of the body where these immune system cells form include the thymus gland, bone marrow, spleen, and lymph nodes. Figure 15.16 illustrates the main components of the immune system and their interactions.

Bidirectional communication.   The potential for interactions between the brain and the immune system is revealed in many anatomical and physiological studies (Ader and Cohen, 1993; Ader et al., 1990; Felten et al., 1993). The nervous system influences the immune system either through the autonomic nervous system or through the hypothalamic–pituitary–neuroendocrine system. Anatomical studies have noted the presence of nerve fibers from the autonomic nervous system in immune organs such as the spleen and thymus gland. Within these organs nerve endings are found among groups of lymphocytes, but the potential impact of their activity is still mysterious. These fibers are usually noradrenergic, sympathetic postganglionic axons.

Other transmitters are also found in immune system tissues, including various neuropeptides. Receptors for neurotransmitters have been found on immune cells such as lymphocytes; these substances probably exert their effects via a second-messenger system. Noradrenergic innervation is claimed to affect antibody production and immune cell proliferation, as well as other aspects of the immune system (Bellinger et al., 1992). The same cells are also affected by the hormones released through the hypothalamic–pituitary–neuroendocrine system. Neural activity in these organs might directly affect the responsiveness of immune system cells either by enhancing or by depressing various immune cell functions (Haas and Schauenstein, 1997).

The bidirectional character of relations between the immune system and the brain is also seen in other studies that show the effects of antibodies on the firing rates of brain neurons, especially in regions within the hypothalamus (Besedovsky and del Rey, 1992; Besedovsky et al., 1985). Other immune system products, such as the hormones interferon and the interleukins, also affect brain activity. Thus the brain seems to be directly informed about the actions of the immune system. In fact, it has been suggested that "the immune system serves as a sensory organ for stimuli not recognized by the classical sensory system" (Blalock, 1984) or as a kind of sensory receptor system (Besedovsky and del Rey, 1992).

Another way to show the role of the brain in immune system responsiveness is to examine the effects of brain lesions on immune responses. Lesions of the hypothalamus in experimental animals can influence immune processes, such as antibody production (M. Stein et al., 1981). Some of these effects are quite specialized, involving responses to some antigens but not others. Furthermore, the specific hypothalamic site of the lesion also determines the character of immune effects. Some ways in which the hypothalamus influences immune system processes involve neuroendocrine mechanisms mediated through the pituitary gland.

Under stressful conditions the hypothalamus produces corticotropin-releasing hormone (CRH), which causes the release of adrenocorticotropic hormone (ACTH) from the pituitary. ACTH causes the release of corticosteroid hormones from the adrenal cortex, and one of the effects of these hormones is to suppress immunological responses by inhibiting the proliferation of some lymphocytes and triggering the death of others.

Psychological stress and immunity.   The anatomical and physiological data described in the previous section suggest some bases for the role of psychological factors in immune system responses. How can we determine whether psychological factors such as emotions and stress affect either susceptibility or responses to infectious diseases? One approach is to examine unusual immunological responses or disease history in emotionally disturbed populations. For example, several lines of evidence suggest that the competence of the immune system is decreased during depression

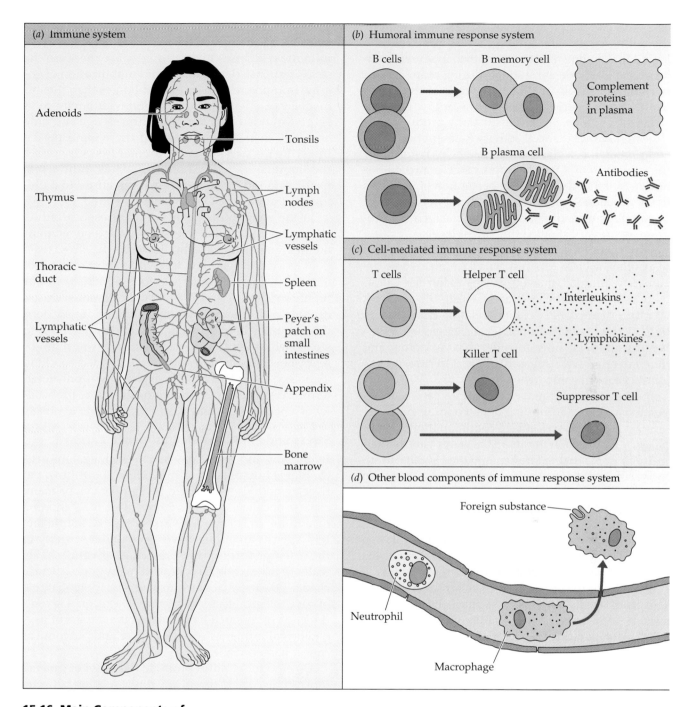

15.16 Main Components of the Human Immune System

The various components of the immune system (*a*) protect us via three classes of cells: B lymphocytes (*b*) produce antibodies to attack invading microbes. T lymphocytes (*c*) release hormones to stimulate B cells to divide. T cells also form killer cells that, together with macrophages (*d*), directly attack foreign tissues or microbes. (Neutrophils are a type of white blood cell.)

(M. Stein et al., 1991). Such a compromise of the immune system would increase susceptibility to infectious diseases, cancer, and autoimmune disorders. Altered immune function is also observed in people who are grieving the death of a relative, especially a spouse (M. Stein and Miller, 1993).

Another way to assess the impact of stress on the immune system is to search for emotional factors in diseases that involve a failure or change in the immune system, especially autoimmune disorders such as arthritis, some types of thyroid disorder, inflammatory bowel disease, and multiple sclerosis, among others. This approach focuses on searching for social and psychological factors that influence the emergence and outcomes of these disorders. For example, psychological factors have been associated with the onset and course of arthritis, which involves a failure of the immune system.

Psychological factors have been related to the susceptibility to and progression of many infectious diseases (Kiecolt-Glaser and Glaser, 1995). For example, the relation between academic stress and immunological functioning has been examined in several studies of medical or dental students during exam periods (which presumably involve high levels of stress) and in subsequent periods of no exams or low levels of stress. Stressful exam periods usually produce a decline in natural killer cell activity (Glaser et al., 1986) and γ-interferon, a glycoprotein that helps regulate the immune system. Of most importance, some studies have noted that the student's perception of the stress of the academic program is a predictor of the level of circulating antibody: Those who perceived the program as stressful showed the lowest levels.

Observations of immune function during marital disruption, such as separation and divorce, show decreases in immune function, as well as increased mortality rates (Kielcolt-Glaser and Glaser, 1995). Indeed, all forms of impaired personal relationships seem to be associated with immunological changes. However, healthy subjects show considerable variability and much overlap with stressed subjects in measures of immunological competence.

Studies of nonhumans allow more precise intervention and yield intriguing data. For example, Ader (1987) was able to condition immunosuppression in rats. This result was demonstrated in studies in which saccharin solution was paired with the administration of a chemical immunosuppressive drug. Continued pairings of this type led to the ability of saccharin alone to reduce the response to pathogens.

Neural plasticity

In similar experiments, Spector (1987) has shown that classical conditioning techniques can enhance the activity of natural killer cells. In his research he exposed mice to the odor of camphor for several hours. This treatment by itself had no impact on the immune system. Some mice were then injected with a chemical that increased the activity of natural killer cells, and this injection was paired with presentation of the camphor odor. After the tenth session of pairings of odor and chemical, mice presented with the odor of camphor alone showed a large increase in natural killer cell activity.

This kind of Pavlovian conditioning of immune system responsiveness might be important as a treatment in some human disorders. It might substitute for injection of drugs that are used to enhance immune system responses and thus enable reduced exposure to toxic treatments. Another connection between the nervous and immune systems was described in Chapter 14, where we learned that sleep deprivation impairs the responsiveness of the immune system.

Immunosuppression as a defense mechanism. In a delightful book entitled *Why Zebras Don't Get Ulcers*, Robert Sapolsky (1994) considers a variety of evolutionary hypotheses about why immunity is suppressed during stress. To the extent that stress might be a sudden emergency, the temporary suppression of immune responses makes some sense, because the stress response demands a rapid mobilization of energy; immune responses extend longer than the immediacy of a demanding situation would require. A zebra wounded by a lion must first escape and hide and only then does infection of the wound pose a threat. So the stress of the encounter first suppresses the immune system, saving resources until a safe haven is found. Then the animal can afford to mobilize the immune system to heal the wound.

In the wild, animals are under stress for only a short while; an animal stressed for a prolonged period dies. So natural selection favored the stress reactions as a drastic effort to deal with a short-term problem. What makes humans unique is that, with our highly social lives and keen analytical minds, we are capable of experiencing stress for prolonged periods—months or even years. The bodily reactions to stress, which evolved to deal with short-term problems, become a handicap when extended too long (Sapolsky, 1994). Perhaps this explains why only long-term stress, lasting over a month, affects the probability of a person's catching a cold (S. Cohen et al., 1998).

Stress and Emotions May Influence Cancer

Every now and then a newspaper or magazine article blares out a warning to readers about links between emotions and cancer. Mystery envelops many aspects of cancer, and its victims often feel "chosen" by evil forces, so it is not surprising that subtle factors, such as emotions, have come under scrutiny in the attempt to discover the cause of cancer. This realm of research is fraught with many contradictory claims. One focus of work concerns the potential role of psychological factors as causes of cancer. A second direction of research has explored the impact of psychological influences on the course and outcome of cancer (Greer, 1983).

Do emotional states promote the onset of cancer? Most studies fail to reveal any direct relation between stressful experiences and the onset of cancer. Some personality studies, however, reveal relations between particular personality attributes and the likelihood of being diagnosed with cancer. One study looked at a large collection of students who entered Johns Hopkins School of Medicine between 1948 and 1964 (Thomas et al., 1979). Psychological tests and yearly questionnaires about health status were given to this population, and the data were related to disorders that appeared many years later. The group of 48 students who ultimately developed cancer were strikingly similar in personality attributes to those who committed suicide. They were described as "low-gear" people with little display of emotion and whose relation to their parents was characterized as cold and remote. In other studies, prior depression and feelings of hopelessness have been associated with cancers even after statistical adjustments for smoking habits. Some researchers have related breast cancer to a life-long suppression of anger (Greer, 1983).

The influence of psychological factors on the course of cancer has been explored in studies of the reactivation of cancer after a long period of dormancy. Some researchers believe that reactivation in these instances can follow a period of severe emotional stress. Debate also surrounds another psychological aspect of outcome that has emerged from studies of survival time following the diagnosis of cancer. Several investigations have shown that long-term survivors had close personal relationships and coped better with illness-related problems; short-term survivors were characterized as responding with passivity, stoic acceptance, and attempts to forget (Weisman and Worden, 1977). The patient's response 3 months after mastectomy for breast cancer is also related to the outcome 5 years after surgery, according to Greer et al. (1979). These investigators believe that survival without recurrence is associated with "fighting spirit or denial." Causal connections are difficult to draw in these efforts to relate psychological factors to the many aspects of cancer. Although methodological problems remain to be tackled, current data clearly point to potentially important psychobiological interactions.

Clues to mechanisms that might account for the links between psychological factors and cancer are found in animal research on stress and the immune system. Research on nonhumans shows that various types of stress produce increased amounts of circulating adrenal cortical hormones, especially corticosterone. Researchers have shown that corticosterone has potent effects on the immune system, including decreased circulating lymphocytes, shrinkage of the thymus gland, and some loss of tissue mass of lymph nodes. Thus, the effectiveness of the immune system in stress states is reduced, and Riley (1981) has suggested that stress enhances vulnerability to cancer-causing agents such as viruses. In one study, this researcher stressed mice into which tumors had been implanted by giving them a brief period of forced body rotation. Following this treatment the tumors grew to four times the size of those in control animals. A similar effect is produced by the direct administration of corticosterone without a stress experience, a finding that lends support to the view that stress-activated release of adrenal cortical hormones can increase susceptibility to cancer or speed its progression.

Emotions and Stress Influence Cardiac Disease

Each day several thousand Americans suffer heart attacks, and many more suffer from other vascular disorders. About one-half of all cardiac-related deaths occur within a few minutes of the onset of symptoms. For many of these individuals, death appears to be caused by the influence of the nervous system on mechanisms that control rhythms of the heart. One part of the story of the origin and progression of heart disease has focused on emotions and psychological stress. Common views of causes of heart attacks emphasize the role of emotions. Many an excited person has heard the admonition, "Calm down before you blow a fuse!"

A major theme instigated by the initial studies of M. Friedman and Rosenman (1974) has focused on differences between two behavior patterns—Type A and Type B—in the development and maintenance of heart disease. Type A behavior is characterized by excessive competitive drive, impatience, hostility, and accelerated speech and movements; in short, life is frantic, hectic, and demanding for such individuals. In contrast, Type B behavior patterns are more relaxed, with little evidence of aggressive drive or an emphasis on getting things done fast. Of course, this is a crude dichotomy; many individuals have some of each pattern in their characteristic style.

For many years research seemed to indicate that Type A individuals show a substantially higher incidence and prevalence of coronary heart disease than do Type B individuals. In the Western Collaborative Group study, which followed subjects for 8.5 years, those who showed Type A behavior at the beginning of the study were twice as likely as Type B subjects to develop heart disease (Rosenman et al., 1975). This difference was evident even after controlling for cigarette smoking, alcohol use, and nutritional differences. However, studies since 1985 have cast doubt on this association, and some researchers have suggested that the Type A concept is too broad (Steptoe, 1993).

A strong association between hostility and heart disease has been noted in these studies (Almada et al., 1991). Excessive expression of hostility may also be related to social isolation, which has been implicated as a risk factor for heart disease in several studies. For example, men who are socially isolated and have experienced significant recent life stress, such as family separation, have a much higher mortality rate than do socially integrated controls (Ruberman et al., 1984). In normal young subjects, the presence of a friend during a demanding task lessens the magnitude of cardiovascular responses to this type of stress.

Laboratory studies in guinea pigs show that stress can markedly reduce the threshold for heart arrhythmias that are elicited by the drug digitalis (Natelson, 1985). (This drug is often used to regulate heart rate, but at toxic levels it can prove fatal.) Abnormal heart rhythms are evident in rats exposed to conflict stress and inescapable shock.

Comparing two different primate species, Hennessy et al. (1995) showed a possible relation between species-characteristic response patterns and disease. They note that squirrel monkeys are excitable, restless, and frequently on the move. In contrast, titi monkeys are more low-key. At rest, the squirrel monkey shows a much higher heart rate and higher levels of the hormone cortisol in blood than does the titi monkey. Long-term studies of these animals reveal that squirrel monkeys are susceptible to heart disease, while titi monkeys, in contrast, are more prone to disorders of the immune system. These and other studies show the role of CNS influences on cardiac arrhythmias. Various hormones and transmitters also influence cardiac rhythms in ways that suggest their role in the emergence of heart disease (Bohus and Koolhaas, 1993).

What Purpose Do Emotions Serve?

Clearly, emotions help us to communicate with one another—to predict, by looking at someone's face, whether he or she is likely to hug us or slug us. But an emotion such as fear can help us even if we are alone, because it reminds us that the world is full of danger and it is our job to stay out of harm's way. One might argue over whether aggression is always an emotional behavior, but it certainly is emotionally driven in many cases and always elicits emotional responses from the victim. And it is easy to see that aggression would be favored by natural selection as males compete for mates and mothers protect their young. The problem, as Konrad Lorenz pointed out, is that today we have the technological capacity to inflict injury on a scale that natural selection could never have anticipated.

The stress response is also adaptive normally, when stressors are either short-lived or fatal, but we must recognize that "civilized" humans are capable of perceiving stress for years and that such a prolonged stress response can be very disadvantageous, even fatal. For these and many other reasons, emotions likely will continue to fascinate researchers and the public alike.

Summary

1. The term "emotion" includes private subjective feelings, as well as expressions or displays of particular somatic and autonomic responses. The three main components of emotions are feeling, physiological arousal, and actions. Psychologists have generated different category systems to account for the varieties of emotions.

2. Whereas the James–Lange theory considered emotions to be the perceptions of stimulus-induced bodily changes, the Cannon–Bard theory emphasized the integration of emotional experiences and responses in the brain. A cognitive theory of emotions argues that activity in a physiological system is not enough to provoke an emotion; rather, the key feature in emotion is the interpretation of visceral activities.

3. Distinct facial expressions represent anger, contempt, happiness, sadness, disgust, fear, surprise, and embarrassment, and these expressions are interpreted similarly across many cultures. Facial expressions are controlled by distinct sets of facial muscles that in turn are controlled by the facial and trigeminal nerves.

4. Studies of brain lesions revealed that particular brain circuits and interconnected regions mediate and control emotions. Relevant regions include limbic system sites described in the Papez circuit and other related regions, including the amygdala.

5. Electrical stimulation of some brain regions is rewarding. Dopamine appears to be an important transmitter at brain sites involved in reward.

6. The left and right cerebral hemispheres process emotions differently. In normal people, the right hemisphere is better at interpreting emotional states or stimuli.

7. Fear is mediated by circuitry that involves the amygdala, which is directly connected to cortical sensory regions.

8. Aggressive behavior is increased by androgens. Brain regions of the limbic system and related sites differ in their relationship to aggressive behavior; stimulation of some regions readily elicits a full, species-typical pattern of aggression. Serotonin levels are negatively correlated with aggression.

9. Assessment of stress in real-life situations shows that stress elevates the levels of several hormones, including cortisol, epinephrine, and norepinephrine, and suppresses other hormones such as testosterone.

10. Stress affects human health and influences the outcome of disease. Incidence of illness tends to be higher in people who sustain prolonged stress, although constitutional factors, as well as strategies for coping with stress, are also important. The nervous system and immune system interact to monitor and maintain health.

Recommended Reading

Ekman, P., and Davidson, R. J. (1994). *The nature of emotion.* New York: Oxford University Press

LeDoux, J. (1995). *The emotional brain.* New York: Simon and Schuster.

Oatley, K., and Jenkins, J. M. (1996). *Understanding emotions.* Oxford, England: Blackwell.

Russell, J. A., and Fernandez-Dols, J. M. (Eds.). (1997). *The psychology of facial expression.* Cambridge, England: Cambridge University Press.

Sapolsky R. (1997). *The trouble with testosterone: And other essays on the biology of the human predicament.* New York: Scribner.

Stanford, S. C., and Gray, J. A. (Eds.) (1993). *Stress—From synapse to syndrome.* San Diego, CA: Academic Press.

Stoff, D. M., and Cairns, R. B. (Eds.). (1996). *Aggression and violence: Genetic, neurobiological, and biosocial perspectives.* Mahwah, NJ: Erlbaum.

16 Psychopathology: Biological Bases of Behavior Disorders

The need to find out more about neurological and psychiatric disorders is urgent because they produce some of the more poignant aspects of human debility. They frequently envelop all aspects of an individual's existence and, in some instances, rob an individual of the precious sense of personal identity. Of most importance, people afflicted with these disorders are not an exotic few. Recent surveys show that at least 50 million to 75 million persons in the United States alone suffer from neurological and psychiatric diseases.

On the optimistic side, in a relatively short time the marriage of neurosciences and psychiatry has yielded new insights into disorders such as schizophrenia, anxiety, epilepsy, and other afflictions that have traveled along with human history. We have had an explosion of information about the "broken brain" (Andreasen, 1984) that gives us the sense that some long-standing mysteries, such as the nature of schizophrenia, are going to be solved and that effective treatments will be based on genuine psychobiological understanding of causes, processes, and mechanisms. Our aim is to focus on some of the advances in this field that promise successful understanding of psychiatric disorders and the ability to treat them. Although no single remedy has been found that cures all who suffer from any of these disorders, recent discoveries have restored millions of people to normal life.

George Tooker, *The Man in the Box*, 1967. Egg tempera on gesso panel

The Toll of Psychiatric Disorders Is Huge

Since the beginning of the twentieth century, the mental health movement has supported large-scale studies that try to determine the number and distribution of psychiatric cases. How many and who among us are or have been psychiatrically ill? All epidemiological studies depend on the clarity of a diagnosis. In psychiatric epidemiology these problems become particularly pressing because there has been much argument about the definition of different psychiatric disorders.

Work by psychiatrists to achieve greater agreement about diagnostic judgments led to a major psychiatric epidemiology study; sponsored by the National Institute of Mental Health, it was titled the "Epidemiologic Catchment Area Study" (Robins and Regier, 1991). The most comprehensive look at the psychiatric health of the United States that had ever been accomplished, this study employed thousands of interviewers, researchers, and respondents. Armed with a carefully developed questionnaire and clearly defined diagnostic categories, interviewers went to five different communities across the country. These communities were selected on the basis of several considerations, including the proximity of a major psychiatric research unit, environmental distinctions including the rural/urban difference, and ethnographic features that enabled attention to mental health issues among minorities.

This extensive survey provides a definitive portrait of the psychiatric problems in the United States. Risk factors such as social class, level of education, race, and sex are exhaustively reported. Prevalence is described for the average 6-month period and lifetime (Table 16.1). About one-third of the U.S. population at some point during a typical lifetime reports symptoms that fulfill the defining features of a major psychiatric disorder. Total rates for mental disorders in men and women are comparable, although the proportions of disorders are slightly different for the two sexes. Depression is far more prevalent among females, and drug dependency and alcoholism are more frequent in males. Certain psychiatric disorders—for example, drug abuse and schizophrenia—tend to appear relatively early in life. The age range 25 to 44 shows peaks for depression and antisocial personality, whereas cognitive impairment occurs especially in people older than 65.

Another national study, of lifetime and 12-month prevalence of psychiatric disorders, offers an even graver portrait of the mental health of the U.S. population (Kessler et al., 1994). According to this study, almost half the population reported at least one lifetime psychiatric disorder; 30% reported at least one disorder in the previous 12-month period.

Clearly, mental disorders exact an enormous toll on our lives. Efforts to understand these disorders depend on research in diverse areas ranging from cell biology to sociology. Some seeds for a biological perspective in psychiatry were sown around the beginning of the twentieth century. At that time, one widely prevalent psychosis accounted for 20 to 25% of the patient population in mental hospitals. Descriptions of these patients emphasized profound delusions, grandiosity and euphoria, poor judgment, impulsive and capricious behavior, and profound changes in thought structure. This disorder was known in all societies of the world and had been noted for centuries. Many people regarded it as a psychosis derived from the stresses and strains of personal and social interactions.

Then, in 1911, the microbiologist Hideyo Noguchi discovered the cause of this profound psychosis. Examining the brains of patients during autopsy, he established that extensive brain changes were wrought by *Treponema pallidum*, a bacterium of the class Spirochaeta. This psychosis was produced by syphilis, a venereal infection that has journeyed through history with humans and has appeared in almost all cultures. The later discovery of drugs that would cure syphilis and prevent this type of psychosis encouraged the development of biological psychiatry and the attempt to find drugs to combat other forms of psychopathology.

Schizophrenia Is the Major Neurobiological Challenge in Psychiatry

Throughout the world, some persons are recognized as unusual because they hear voices, feel intensely frightened, sense persecution from unseen enemies, and act strangely. People with schizophrenia seem to have been a part of all the cultures of the world since the dawn of civilization, although the antiquity of this condition is debated (Bark, 1988; Hare, 1988). For many, this state lasts a lifetime; for others, it appears and disappears unpredictably. Of all the psychiatric disorders, schizophrenia has summoned the most intense public interest because it seems such a cruel exaggeration of the human condition. It is also a "public" disorder, as many schizophrenics become homeless on our streets.

Although most epidemiological surveys of schizophrenia reveal a prevalence of 1 to 2% of the population, this disorder has commanded a huge portion of community health resources because of its chronic and overwhelming character. Its similarity to some disorders that arise from acknowledged brain disease has long contributed to the view that neurobiological research will provide a thorough understanding of schizophrenia.

TABLE 16.1 *Standardized Six-Month and Lifetime Prevalence of DIS/DSM-IV Disorders in Persons 18 Years and Older[a]*

Disorders	Rate (%)	
	Previous 6 months	Lifetime
Any psychiatric disorder covered	19.1	32.2
Substance use disorders	6.0	16.4
Alcohol abuse or dependence	4.7	13.3
Drug abuse or dependence	2.0	5.9
Schizophrenia	0.9	1.5
Affective disorders	5.8	8.3
Manic episode	0.5	0.8
Major depressive episode	3.0	5.8
Minor depression	—	3.3
Anxiety disorders	8.9	14.6
Phobia	7.7	12.5
Panic	0.8	1.6
Obsessive–compulsive	1.5	2.5

[a]The rates are standardized to the age, sex, and race distribution of the 1980 noninstitutionalized population of the United States aged 18 years and older. DIS indicates Diagnostic Interview Schedule.

Schizophrenia Is Characterized by an Unusual Array of Symptoms

The modern story of schizophrenia starts with Emil Kraepelin (1856–1926), a distinguished German psychiatrist whose book *Dementia Praecox and Paraphrenia* (1919) became the cornerstone of this field. Kraepelin searched for coherent patterns in the many symptoms of psychiatric disorders. His description was rich with details, and he argued that the elements of this disorder fit into several distinct clinical forms.

Features common to the varied forms of schizophrenia included bizarre disturbances in thought, paranoid and grandiose delusions, auditory hallucinations, and an odd array of emotional changes. Kraepelin's use of the term "dementia praecox" embodies his view that this disorder begins during adolescence ("praecox" is derived from the Latin for "early") and moves relentlessly to a chronic state of cognitive impairment ("dementia" is derived from the Latin *de*, "away from," and *mens*, "mind"). According to Kraepelin, the cause must be partly genetic, although the relationship to inheritance is not simple.

In the early twentieth century another major work introduced the term **schizophrenia** (from the Greek *schizein*, "to split," and *phren*, "mind"). In 1911, Eugen Bleuler's monograph *Dementia Praecox; or the Group of Schizophrenias* examined more closely the underlying psychological processes of schizophrenia. Although

he agreed with Kraepelin that this disorder was a chronic and persistent condition, he did not consider it a "dementia," and he argued that it did not necessarily arise early in life. And while agreeing with Kraepelin's description of the disease, Bleuler identified the key symptom as **dissociative thinking**, a major impairment in the logical structure of thought. Bleuler also distinguished between primary (fundamental) and secondary (accessory) symptoms. Fundamental symptoms, according to Bleuler, included the four Λ's: loosening of associations, autism (unmindfulness of reality), affective disturbance, and ambivalence. Accessory symptoms included delusions and hallucinations.

The qualitative character of the descriptions offered by Kraepelin and Bleuler left much room for controversy. During the 1980s and 1990s researchers have continued to refine diagnostic and descriptive categories so that both convey a common understanding of the basic features and withstand the rigors of reliability assessments. The need for clearly defined categories is especially keenly felt among researchers such as Irving Gottesman who believe that some of the inconsistency in data is a consequence of diagnostic categories that have ill-defined boundaries (Gottesman, 1995).

Irving Gottesman

Some of the modern reexamination of diagnostic categories is derived from a major shift in diagnostic focus that started with the work of the German psychiatrist Kurt Schneider (1959), whose pragmatic orientation gave primacy to a few major symptoms referred to as "first-rank" symptoms of schizophrenia. These first-rank symptoms included several forms of auditory hallucinations, delusional interpretations that are highly personalized, and changes in affect. This symptom-oriented approach led to efforts to delineate the highly discriminating signs with clear criteria for diagnosis. The *Diagnostic and Statistical Manual IV* (1994) of the American Psychiatric Association incorporates this view.

Some investigators have proposed a major division of schizophrenic symptoms into two separate groups: positive and negative (Andreasen, 1991).

Positive symptoms refer to abnormal states such as hallucinations, delusions, and excited motor behavior. **Negative symptoms** reflect insufficient functioning; some examples are emotional and social withdrawal, blunted affect, slowness, and impoverishment of thought and speech. Although researchers continue to question whether schizophrenia is a single entity or a family of related disorders, biological research is helping to clarify the issue. Defined according to modern criteria, schizophrenia is not distinctive to any particular society; it is a universal disorder found throughout the world (Jablensky et al., 1992; Sartorius et al., 1986).

A Genetic Component Contributes to the Development of Schizophrenia

For many years genetic studies of schizophrenia were controversial, although the notion of inheritance of mental illness is quite old. Data and speculations in this research area sparked vigorous interchanges, some related to the failure of early researchers to appreciate that environments are major modifiers of gene actions. For any genotype there is often a large range of alternative outcomes that are determined by both developmental and environmental factors.

The basic aim of studies in this area is to understand the role of genetic factors in causing and maintaining schizophrenic states. If population studies establish that inheritance plays a significant role, then it becomes important to search for the mechanisms of such effects, including the neurochemical, neurophysiological, and neuroanatomical processes that have gone awry. Genetic studies are also important in the development of preventive programs. For example, if a genetic contribution is established as a significant ingredient in the genesis of schizophrenia, then it will be important to establish programs to aid the population at risk.

Family studies.   If schizophrenia is inherited, then relatives of schizophrenic patients should show a higher incidence of schizophrenia than is found in the general population. In addition, the risk of schizophrenia among relatives should increase with the closeness of the relationship, since close relatives share a greater number of genes. In general, parents and siblings of patients have a higher risk of being or becoming schizophrenic than do individuals in the general population (Figure 16.1). The risk is greater in cases of closer biological relatedness. The conclusion of many family studies is that the mode of inheritance of schizophrenia is not simple; that is, it does not involve a single recessive or dominant gene (Tamminga and Schulz, 1991). Most likely, multiple genes play a role in the emergence of schizophrenia.

It is easy to find fault with family studies. First, they confuse hereditary and experiential factors, since members of a family share both. Second, the data usually depend on the recollections of relatives whose memories are likely to be clouded by zealous efforts to attribute blame for the disorder. "Funny," departed aunts and uncles are easily designated as the agents responsible for the mental disorder. More reliable family studies restrict data to professionally diagnosed cases.

Twin studies.   In twins, nature provides researchers with what seems to be the perfect conditions for a genetic experiment. Human twins can arise either from the same egg (**monozygotic**, or identical, twins) or from two different eggs (**dizygotic**, or fraternal, twins). In addition, many twins have other siblings. Studies of schizophrenia in twins are especially concerned with determining the difference in the rate of occurrence between identical and fraternal twins. When both individuals of a twin pair are schizophrenic, they are described as being **concordant** for this trait. If only one member of the pair is schizophrenic, the pair is described as **discordant**. Whereas about 50% of monozygotic twin pairs are concordant for schizophrenia, the rate of concordance for dizygotic twins is only about 17%. The higher concordance rate among monozygotic twins (who are twice as closely related genetically as dizygotic twins are) is strong evidence of a genetic factor.

Studies of schizophrenia in twins have been criticized on several grounds. For example, some data indicate that twins are unusual from a developmental **Competing hypotheses** perspective in that they usually show lower birth weights and different developmental progress than nontwins. In addition, parental treatment of identical twins differs considerably from their interaction with fraternal twins, thus generating a confounding environmental variable. Despite these weaknesses, studies of twins do indicate the importance of genetic mechanisms in the development of psychotic disorders, particularly schizophrenia. The most striking case of schizophrenia in multiple births may be the Genain quadruplets, who are **Special topic** discussed in Topic 16.1, Four Copies of Schizophrenia: The Genain Quads.

Even with identical twins, however, the concordance for schizophrenia is far less than 100%. Although identical twins have the same genetic constitution, one member of the identical-twin pair may be schizophrenic and the other normal.

Studies of identical twins who are discordant for schizophrenia can provide useful information about the possible factors that lead to schizophrenia and those that protect against its emergence. E. Fuller Torrey notes that the twin that developed schizophrenia tended to be the one who was more abnormal throughout life. The symptomatic twin frequently weighed less at birth and had an early developmental history that included more instances of physiological distress (Torrey et al., 1994; Wahl, 1976). This devel-

General population	1%
Spouses	1%
First cousins (third degree)	2%
Uncles/aunts	2%
Nephews/nieces	4%
Grandchildren	5%
Half siblings	6%
Children	13%
Siblings	9%
Siblings with 1 schizophrenic parent	17%
Dizygotic twins	17%
Parents	6%
Monozygotic twins	48%

No (or distant) relation

Second-degree relatives

First-degree relatives

Lifetime risk of developing schizophrenia (%)

16.1 Schizophrenia Is Heritable
The more closely related a person is to a schizophrenic patient, the greater his or her chances of also developing schizophrenia. (Adapted from Gottesman, 1991.)

opmental history is connected with the parents' view of the symptomatic twin as more vulnerable. During development this twin was more submissive, tearful, and sensitive than the identical sibling. This type of study, still in its infancy, may yet suggest how to prevent schizophrenia. We mention this aspect of genetic studies to show that a genetic tendency does not mean that schizophrenia is inevitable; rather such studies may provide ways of preventing onset of the disorder.

During childhood, the developmental difficulties of twins who would later become schizophrenic are accompanied by behavioral, cognitive, and other neurological signs, such as impairments in motor coordination (Torrey et al., 1994). For example, Elaine Walker showed that observers watching home films of children can pick out the child who became schizophrenic in adulthood with uncanny accuracy (Walker, 1991).

The distinctions between schizophrenics and nonschizophrenics include several neuropsychological characteristics, such as eye tracking. Eye-tracking measurements record eye movements as they follow a

E. Fuller Torrey

Elaine Walker

moving target on a screen. Many studies show abnormal eye tracking in schizophrenic patients (Levy et al., 1993; Stuve et al., 1997). In smooth-pursuit movements, such as those we perform as we follow the slow to-and-fro movements of the pendulum of an old clock, schizophrenic patients are unable to keep up with the moving object and show the intrusion of the rapid, jerky eye movements called saccades (see Chapter 11). Figure 16.2 compares normal and schizophrenic eye tracking.

Important method

Adoption studies. Criticisms of twins studies led to adoption studies, which have produced substantial support for the significance of genetic factors in many psychiatric disorders. Most of the relevant data have come from Denmark, where follow-up studies of adoptees are quite complete. Studies by Kety et al. (1975) identified the biological and adopting parents of all children in Copenhagen, Denmark, who had been given up for adoption early in life during a particular time period, and identified those who were subsequently hospitalized for psychiatric difficulties. Psychiatric disorder was found to a higher degree among the offspring of schizophrenic parents than in a control group of children of nonschizophrenic parents. Further, if we change the point of reference and look at comparisons of the biological and foster parents of schizophrenic adoptees, the evidence is striking. The biological parents of schizophrenic adoptees are far more likely to have been schizophrenic than are the adopting parents (Topic 16.2, Schizophrenic Adoptees).

Special topic

We should emphasize that these patients were reared almost entirely by adopting parents, and therefore social influences from a schizophrenic parent were almost nil. Although parents who give up children for adoption early in life are more likely than the general population to have psychiatric problems, the differences between control and patient groups remain striking. The findings provide conclusive evidence for genetic factors that predispose to schizophrenia (Kety, 1983). Although low socioeconomic status (SES) has been associated with heightened risk of schizophrenia, adoptees who come from biological parents of low SES or are placed in families of low SES are no more likely to develop schizophrenia than are adoptees who are placed in families of higher SES or come from biological parents of higher SES (Kety et al., 1994).

Studies of families, twins, and adoptees provide consistent evidence that genetics contributes to the incidence of schizophrenia. But many questions remain unanswered: (1) How is the disorder transmitted? (2) What is being inherited? (3) What genes are related to this disorder, and what processes do they control? Although the evidence for genetic transmission of a predisposition to schizophrenia is

Genes and behavior

Eye movement recording

Smooth-pursuit response of eyes to pendulum

Schizophrenic tracking

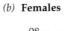

16.2 Eye Tracking in Schizophrenics and Normals
Schizophrenic patients have greater difficulty making smooth-pursuit movements with their eyes. Although watching a clock pendulum works as a test, modern researchers have the subjects view a moving cursor on a computer screen.

clear, alternative genetic models are controversial. Neither single-gene models nor multifactorial models fit all the data (Faraone and Tsuang, 1985), making genetic counseling difficult. A better understanding of the environmental and biological factors that increase the risk of schizophrenia will aid the genetic counseling of individuals who are at risk because of their close relationship to a schizophrenic patient.

The Brains of Some Schizophrenics Show Structural Changes

Since in many patients the symptoms of schizophrenia are so marked and persistent, investigators have wondered whether schizophrenics' brains show a measurable structural change—that is, whether schizophrenia can be localized in the brain (Trimble, 1991). Postmortem investigations of the brains of schizophrenics during the past 100 years occasionally have yielded exciting findings that have been rapidly challenged by better-controlled studies. Studies in this field usually have involved aged patients or those who have been hospitalized for long periods. The advent of CT and MRI scans has enabled the study of brain anatomy in living patients at all stages of their

(a) **Males**

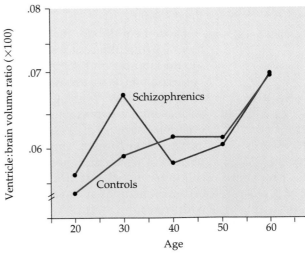

(b) **Females**

16.3 Ventricular Enlargement in Schizophrenia
The volume of the cerebral ventricles, relative to overall brain volume, is greater in schizophrenics than in control subjects. Interestingly, this difference is seen almost exclusively in males.

illness. Within recent years an enormous amount of data from patients at all stages of this disorder have shown that schizophrenic patients do have structural abnormalities of the brain (Hyde and Weinberger, 1990). Furthermore, there is a growing belief that these brain changes are primary to the disease.

Ventricular abnormalities. Studies of schizophrenic patients have consistently revealed an enlargement of cerebral ventricles, especially the lateral ventricles (Figure 16.3) (Hyde and Weinberger, 1990). Ventricular enlargement is not related to length of illness or to duration of hospitalization. D. R. Weinberger et al. (1980) indicated that the degree of ventricular enlargement predicts the patient's response to antipsychotic drugs. Patients with more enlarged ventricles show poorer response to these drugs.

Although many studies have confirmed that schizophrenic patients have enlarged lateral ventricles, the findings must be qualified: Patients with this anatomical characteristic form a distinct subgroup of schizophrenics. Attempts to characterize the patients with enlarged ventricles have revealed other general features, some of them controversial (Gooding and Iacono, 1995). Some researchers have shown that this group is characterized by a high degree of cognitive impairment and social maladjustment (Kemali et al., 1985).

Nancy Andreasen

Neuropsychiatrist Nancy Andreasen has found in MRI studies that enlargement of the ventricles is a static trait in patients, remaining for many years after the initial breakdown (Andreasen, 1994). A study of identical twins discordant for schizophrenia yielded startlingly clear results: The schizophrenic twin had decidedly enlarged lateral ventricles, but the ventricles of the well twin were of normal size (Figure 16.4) (Torrey et al., 1994).

This twin study also revealed that more than 75% of discordant pairs show a marked difference in the size of the hippocampus and the amygdala: These structures are smaller in the schizophrenic twin. This observation suggests that the ventricular enlargement in schizophrenics arises from atrophy or destruction of adjacent neural tissue. When brain cells in the regions adjacent to the cerebral ventricles shrink or die, the ventricles expand to fill those regions. Some of these changes might arise early in development, even in the prenatal period. Another, controversial direction of research suggests a developmental origin for these changes in the schizophrenic brain due to viral exposures during pregnancy (Mednick et al., 1994).

Limbic system abnormalities. Neuropathological studies of the limbic system of schizophrenic patients

(*a*) MRI brain image of twins discordant for schizophrenia

35-year-old female identical twins

Well   Affected

28-year-old male identical twins

Well   Affected

(*b*) Differences in ventricular movements

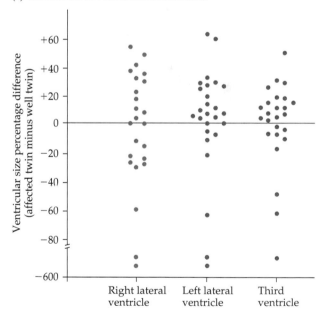

16.4 Identical Genes, Different Fates
(*a*) Although each member of these pairs of monozygotic twins has the same genes, only one of each set of twins (the twin with larger ventricles) developed schizophrenia. (*b*) Measurements of ventricles of many discordant identical twins. (After Torrey et al., 1994; MRIs courtesy of E. Fuller Torrey.)

have revealed differences between patients and controls in several areas, including the hippocampus, amygdala, and parahippocampal regions. Kovelman and Scheibel (1984), comparing the brains of chronic

(f) Normal control

(g) Schizophrenic patient

16.5 Cellular Disarray of the Hippocampus in Chronic Schizophrenia

(a) Horizontally cut cerebral hemispheres, showing the location of the hippocampus. (b) Enlargements of the hippocampus and fornix, showing the location of anterior, middle, and posterior hippocampal segments. (c) Enlargement of a cross section of the hippocampus and the dentate gyrus. (d) Subdivisions of the CA1, CA2, and CA3 regions of the hippocampus. (e) Comparison of pyramidal cell orientation of a normal (upper) and schizophrenic (lower) hippocampal cross section. (f) Histological cross section from a normal control. (g) Histological cross section from a schizophrenic patient. (After Kovelman and Scheibel, 1984; f and g courtesy of Arnold Scheibel.)

schizophrenics with those of medical patients of the same age that did not exhibit brain pathology, noted changes in the hippocampus of chronic schizophrenics.

Figure 16.5 shows an example of cellular differences. The pyramidal cells of chronic schizophrenics were disoriented, in a type of cellular disarray (see Figure 16.5e). Presumably the lack of normal cellular polarity is related to abnormal synaptic linkages, including both inputs and outputs of these cells. The degree of disorientation was positively related to the severity of the disorder. Conrad et al. (1991) extended the earlier work and established that disorientation of hippocampal pyramidal cells is evident in both the right and the left hippocampus. This cellular derangement probably arises during early cell development and might reflect maternal exposure to an influenza infection during the second trimester of pregnancy (Machón et al., 1997). These abnormalities of cellular arrangement in the hippocampus are said to resemble those of mutant mice that show disordered neurogenesis in the hippocampus (Scheibel and Conrad, 1993). Other studies have noted differences between patients and controls in the entorhinal cortex, parahippocampal cortex, and cingulate cortex (R. M. Shapiro, 1993).

Animal model

Some cellular observations have focused on the basal ganglia because schizophrenic patients often show unusual body postures and mannerisms in addition to other abnormal movements. Neurochemical studies of these structures show an increase in dopamine D_2 receptors in the caudate nucleus and putamen of some schizophrenic patients. Unfortunately, traditional antipsychotic drugs drastically modify D_2 receptors; most patients who are not taking antipsychotic drugs do not have elevated levels of D_2 receptors (Hietala et al., 1994). A dramatic sixfold increase in dopamine D_4 receptors in schizophrenic patients has drawn renewed attention to basal ganglia structures, which contain extensive dopaminergic connections (Seeman et al., 1993). A little later in this chapter we will discuss the hypothesis that abnormally high levels of dopamine underlie schizophrenia.

Regional and cellular abnormalities. At one time there were very few reliable findings of brain structural pathology in schizophrenia. Now an overabundance of positive findings overwhelms the effort toward an integrative portrait of the regional and cellular pathology of schizophrenia.

Several studies have noted marked shrinkage of the vermian region of the cerebellum in chronic patients, and have shown that this abnormality is not related to prolonged antipsychotic drug use (Heath et al., 1979; Snider, 1982). Chronic schizophrenics whose disorder started early in life have thicker regions in the corpus callosum, both in anatomical preparations and in some CT scans (Bigelow et al., 1983).

Several hypotheses that link anatomical plasticity of the brain to schizophrenia have a developmental focus (Gooding and Iacono, 1995; D. Weinberger, 1987). One researcher has proposed that a fault in the normal course of synapse elimination (see Chapter 7) during adolescence gives rise to a major rearrangement of brain structures that results in schizophrenia (Feinberg, 1982). Another group, examining postmortem materials, found evidence that neuronal migration during the fetal period had been abnormal in the frontal cortex of schizophrenics (Akbarian et al., 1996).

Deficits shown by schizophrenic patients in tests that are sensitive to frontal cortical lesions have also drawn attention to possible frontal cortical abnormalities. Although some studies show reduced frontal cortical volume in patients, others have failed to show major abnormalities of the frontal cortex (Wible et al., 1995). However, altered gene expression relevant to inhibitory neurons of the frontal cortex has been shown in the prefrontal cortex of schizophrenics without the loss of neurons. These cells show reduced activity for an enzyme involved in GABA synthesis (Akbarian et al., 1995).

Functional Maps Reveal Differences in Schizophrenic Brains

The advent of positron emission tomography (PET), functional magnetic resonance imaging (fMRI), and single-photon emission computerized tomography (SPECT) has provided an abundance of new windows to view the schizophrenic brain. (PET, fMRI, and CT were introduced in Chapter 2; SPECT is much like PET, but can only image a single plane.) The most common measures in these studies have been regional blood flow and cerebral rate of glucose metabolism.

Schizophrenia may involve an alteration in the functional lateralization of the cerebral hemispheres, according to some blood flow imaging studies. The left hemisphere is more active than the right during resting states (Gur et al., 1987), but other data suggest that this effect is restricted to the frontal lobe (K. F. Berman and Weinberger, 1990).

Early observations using PET scan techniques revealed an unusual metabolic feature of schizophrenic brains: Patients show relatively less metabolic activity in frontal lobes as compared with their posterior lobes than do normal subjects (Buchsbaum et al., 1984). This observation, referred to as the **hypofrontality hypothesis**, has generated controversy and has fueled interest in the role of the frontal lobes in schizophrenia (D. R. Weinberger et al., 1994). Some experiments related to this hypothesis show this effect only during difficult cognitive tasks that particularly activate the frontal area (Figure 16.6) and at which frontally damaged patients often fail. Unlike control subjects, schizophrenic patients fail to increase their prefrontal activation above basal levels during the task (D. R. Weinberger et al., 1994).

This deficit is behavior-specific; other tasks do not elicit this phenomenon. This effect does not appear to be the result of drugs used to treat patients and seems especially related to the prominence of negative symptoms (Andreasen et al., 1992). Studies of discordant identical twins show that the frontal blood flow levels are low only in the schizophrenic twin. Changes in frontal lobe structure and function are also found in EEG studies and MRI observations of schizophrenic patients (Andreasen et al., 1986; Morihisa and McAnulty, 1985).

The Brains of Schizophrenics Show Neurochemical Changes

Throughout history, explanations of mental disorder have emphasized biological origins. Bodily factors assumed to be related to schizophrenia have included injury, infection, diet, and brain disease. As knowledge about the neurochemistry of the brain has grown, hypotheses about the bases of schizophrenia have become more precise.

One view holds that schizophrenia arises from faulty metabolic processes in the brain that lead to excesses or insufficiencies of neurochemicals that are nor-

(a) At rest

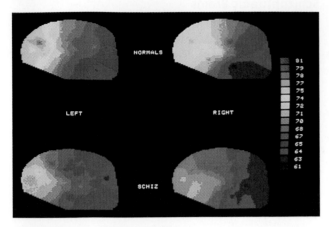

(b) During Card Sort test

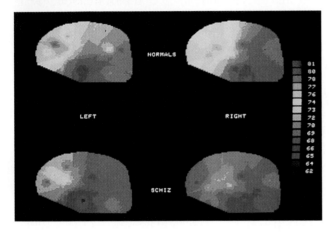

16.6 Hypofrontality in Schizophrenia
The frontal cortex is less activated in schizophrenic patients ("schiz") compared to their non-schizophrenic twins ("normals") either at rest (*top*) or during the Wisconsin Card Sort task (*bottom*). Areas of high activation are shown in red and yellow. (Courtesy of Karen Berman.)

of brain and body. A second major problem in neurochemical research of schizophrenia is the definition of schizophrenia itself. Is it a single disorder, or many disorders with different origins and outcomes?

The dopamine hypothesis. Many clinical and basic experimental findings have suggested that abnormally high levels of dopamine receptor stimulation form the basis of schizophrenia. In Chapter 4 we learned that dopamine is a synaptic transmitter in the brain; in Chapter 15 we discussed its role in brain reward circuits. The first clues suggesting that dopamine plays a role in schizophrenia came from observations of (1) amphetamine psychosis, (2) the effects of antipsychotic drugs, and (3) Parkinson's disease.

Although many drugs, such as LSD and mescaline, produce profound perceptual, cognitive, and emotional changes, some of which resemble aspects of psychoses, several features of the behavioral effects of these drugs are quite dissimilar from symptoms of schizophrenia. Most drug-induced psychoses are characterized by confusion, disorientation, and frank delirium; these are not typical symptoms of schizophrenia. Hallucinations produced by these drugs are usually visual, in contrast to the predominantly auditory hallucinations of schizophrenia. Schizophrenic patients given LSD report that the experience produced by the drug is very different from the experiences of their disorder, and psychiatrists can readily distinguish taped conversations of schizophrenics from those of subjects given hallucinogenic agents. But one drug state—*amphetamine psychosis*—comes close to replicating the schizophrenic state.

Some individuals use amphetamine on an everyday basis as a stimulant. Because tolerance (see Chapter 4) develops, to maintain the same level of euphoria the self-administered dose must be progressively increased and may reach as much as 3000 mg per day. (Contrast this level with the usual 5 mg taken to control appetite or prolong wakefulness.) Many individuals taking these large doses of amphetamine develop symptoms of paranoia, often involving delusions of persecution with auditory hallucinations, and exhibit suspiciousness and bizarre postures.

The similarity of amphetamine psychosis to schizophrenia is also supported by the finding that amphetamine exacerbates symptoms of schizophrenia. Neurochemically, amphetamine promotes the release of catecholamines, particularly dopamine, and prolongs the action of the released transmitter by blocking reuptake. Rapid relief from amphetamine psychosis is

mally found in the brain. In most cases these substances are neurotransmitters or neuromodulators; the most prominent example in current research is dopamine. The functional effect of this type of change would be under- or overactivity of some brain circuits. A second general perspective proposes that schizophrenia develops from faulty metabolic processes in the brain that produce abnormal substances that generate psychotic behavior. Such hypothetical substances, called **psychotogens**, might be similar in some ways to hallucinogenic agents. We will examine each of these two main hypotheses in the sections that follow.

Although exciting ideas and data are apparent in the research, several problems continue to frustrate major progress in our study of schizophrenia. First, it is very hard to separate neurochemical events that are primary causes of psychiatric disorder from those that are secondary effects. Secondary effects arise from the profound impairments of social behavior and may range from dietary limitations to prolonged stress. Treatment variables, especially the long-term use of traditional antipsychotic substances, can mask or distort primary causes, because they frequently produce marked changes in the physiology and biochemistry provided by injection of the dopamine antagonist **chlorpromazine**—a substance that brings us to the second part of the story of the dopamine hypothesis.

Chlorpromazine has had much wider use than merely as an antidote to amphetamine psychosis. In the early 1950s, about half a million people were patients in psychiatric hospitals in the United States. This number has decreased dramatically. Several factors contributed to this reduction, of which the most significant was the introduction of chlorpromazine in the treatment of schizophrenia. In the search for a substance to produce muscle relaxation for surgery, French surgeon Henri Laborit in the 1940s discovered that chlorpromazine not only achieves these effects, but also reduces worry and preoperative tension. An insightful investigator, Laborit collaborated with psychiatrists in trying this substance on psychiatric patients; they found remarkable antipsychotic effects. Chlorpromazine was then introduced on a large scale in psychiatric hospitals around the world, with a profound impact.

By now, a massive number of well-controlled studies point to the fact that chlorpromazine and many other substances related to it (called **phenothiazines**) have a specific antipsychotic effect. These substances act in the brain by blocking postsynaptic receptor sites for dopamine, specifically, the D_2 type. As we noted in Chapter 4, there are several major dopamine-containing pathways. Investigators believe that a major site of action of antipsychotic drugs (also called **neuroleptics** or major tranquilizers) is dopamine terminals in the limbic system. These cells originate in the brain stem, near the substantia nigra (see Figure 4.2). The clinical effectiveness of antipsychotic agents is directly related to the magnitude of postsynaptic receptor blockage of dopamine sites. This result suggests that schizophrenia may be produced either by excessive levels of available dopamine or by excessive postsynaptic sensitivity to dopamine, which might involve a large population of postsynaptic dopamine receptor sites.

Another trail leading to the dopamine hypothesis of schizophrenia is the study of Parkinson's disease (see Chapter 11). Parkinson's disease is caused by the degeneration of nerve cells located in the brain stem (in the substantia nigra). These cells contain dopamine, and administering the substance L-dopa, a precursor for the synthesis of dopamine, increases the amount of released dopamine, which thus provides some relief of parkinsonian symptoms. Two observations of Parkinson's patients connect this disease with schizophrenia and the dopamine hypothesis. First, some patients given L-dopa to relieve parkinsonian symptoms become psychotic. Second, some schizophrenic patients receiving chlorpromazine develop parkinsonian symptoms. In fact, treatment with traditional antipsychotic drugs can result in permanent movement disorders (see Box 16.1). Furthermore, schizophrenic patients with enlarged ventricles show a marked reduction in

levels of dopamine β-hydroxylase, an enzyme that catalyzes the conversion of dopamine into norepinephrine (Sternberg et al., 1982) (see Box 4.1).

The earliest, simplest dopamine model of schizophrenia argued that this disorder arises from the hyperfunctioning of dopamine circuits. This hyperfunctioning could develop from excessive release of dopamine—a presynaptic effect—or an excess of dopamine receptors—a postsynaptic effect. For years, the strongest evidence for this simple hypothesis was the remarkable clinical success of dopamine blockers in treating schizophrenia. Indeed, the clinical effectiveness of the many neuroleptic drugs introduced in the past 40 years has been directly related to their effectiveness in blocking or antagonizing dopamine (Figure 16.7). Drugs that have the opposite effect—increasing dopamine activity—worsen schizophrenic symptoms.

Criticisms of a dopamine model of schizophrenia began to emerge in the 1980s (Alpert and Friedhoff, 1980). Clinical observations revealed that some schizophrenic patients show no changes when treated with drugs that affect dopamine; more recently, some of these patients have been shown to derive benefit from drugs such as **clozapine** that affect serotonin receptors as well as dopamine receptors (see Figure 16.7). Other clinical observations indicate that dopamine antagonists do little to alleviate the negative symptoms of schizophrenia.

More directly related to an assessment of the simple dopamine hypothesis is the fact that studies of dopamine metabolites in blood, cerebrospinal fluid, or urine have provided inconsistent evidence regarding the possible hyperfunctioning of dopamine terminals. For example, many schizophrenic patients have normal levels of dopamine metabolites in their CSF. Some postmortem and PET studies of schizophrenic brains reveal an increase in dopamine receptors, especially the D_2 type (Breier et al., 1997; K. L. Davis et al., 1991). This elevated level of dopamine receptors is evident even in patients who have been off of neuroleptic drugs for some time (Okubo et al., 1997). But PET studies of D_2 receptor density in schizophrenics are inconsistent, as are efforts to relate a D_2 receptor gene to schizophrenia.

One problem may be that the traditional antipsychotics are acting on other, less studied or even undiscovered, dopamine receptors. Another problem with the dopamine hypothesis is the lack of correspondence between the time at which drugs block dopamine (quite rapidly) and the behavior changes that signal the clinical effectiveness of the drug (usually on the order of weeks). Thus, the relation of dopamine to schizophrenia may be more complex than that envisioned in the simple model of hyperactive dopamine synapses. Perhaps dopamine accounts for only some aspects of the schizophrenic syndrome (Carlton and Manowitz, 1984).

BOX 16.1 *Long-Term Effects of Antipsychotic Drugs*

*F*ew people would deny that drugs like chlorpromazine have had a revolutionary impact on the treatment of schizophrenia. With such treatment, many people who might otherwise have been in mental hospitals their whole lives can take care of themselves in nonhospital settings. Drugs of this class can justly be regarded as antipsychotic.

Traditional antipsychotic drugs often have other effects that bring their use into question. Soon after beginning to take these drugs, some users develop maladaptive motor symptoms (**dyskinesia**, which is Greek for "difficulty in moving"). Although many of these symptoms are transient and disappear when the dosage of drug is reduced, some drug-induced motor changes emerge only after prolonged drug treatment—after months, sometimes years. This condition is called **tardive dyskinesia** (the Latin *tardus* means "slow").

The motor effects of tardive dyskinesia include many involuntary movements, especially involving the face, mouth, lips, and tongue. Elaborate uncontrollable movements of the tongue are particularly prominent, including incessant rolling movements and sucking or smacking of the lips.

Some patients show twisting and sudden jerking movements of the arms or legs (D. E. Casey, 1989). Traditional antipsychotic substances affect a large percentage of patients—as much as one-third—in this way. The drugs usually affect females more severely than they do males (J. M. Smith et al., 1979). The relationship between drug parameters and the likelihood of such side effects is complex (Toenniessen et al., 1985). What is alarming is that this motor impairment frequently becomes permanent, even if drug treatment is halted.

The underlying mechanism for tardive dyskinesia continues to be a puzzle. Some researchers claim that it arises from the chronic blocking of dopamine receptors, which results in receptor site supersensitivity. Critics of this view, however, point out that tardive dyskinesia frequently takes a long time to develop and may be irreversible, a time course that is different from dopamine receptor supersensitivity. In addition, there is no difference in D_1 or D_2 receptor binding between patients with tardive dyskinesia and those without these symptoms.

A GABA deficiency hypothesis of tardive dyskinesia was offered by Fibiger and Lloyd (1984). They believed that tardive dyskinesia is the result of drug-induced destruction of GABA neurons in the corpus striatum. Neuroleptic-induced changes in enzymes related to GABA have been observed in experimental animals. A noradrenergic hypothesis of this disorder has also been presented, on the basis of evidence that the concentration of norepinephrine in the cerebrospinal fluid is correlated with tardive dyskinesia (Kaufmann et al., 1986).

Long-term treatment with traditional antipsychotic drugs has another unusual effect: Prolonged blockage of dopamine receptors seems to increase the number of dopamine receptors and lead to **receptor supersensitivity**. In some patients, discontinuation of the drugs or a lowering of dosage results in a sudden, marked increase in positive symptoms of schizophrenia, such as delusions or hallucinations. This "supersensitivity psychosis" can often be reversed by administration of increased dosages of dopamine receptor–blocking agents. A newer generation of antipsychotic drugs has fewer side effects, which may make schizophrenia patients more likely to continue self-medication.

K. L. Davis et al. (1991) speculated that schizophrenia is related to both hypo- and hyperfunctioning of dopamine. They suggested that activity is diminished in the dopamine synapses of the prefrontal cortex, but is excessive in mesolimbic dopamine pathways. Negative symptoms, they suggested, arise from low prefrontal dopamine activity. Still another suggestion is that such changes in dopamine release are a secondary consequence of a loss of glutaminergic stimulation (Carlsson et al., 1997).

The psychotogen hypothesis. The chemical structure of some manufactured hallucinogens resembles that of some endogenous substances of the brain. This finding suggested that the brain accidentally produces a psychotogen—a chemical substance that causes psychotic behavior. Metabolic faults in particular pathways might cause the brain to convert an innocuous molecule into a behaviorally maladaptive substance capable of producing schizophrenic symptoms.

The **transmethylation hypothesis** suggests that the addition of a methyl group (CH_3) to some naturally occurring brain compounds can convert the substances into known hallucinogenic agents. This hypothesis was offered in the 1950s by Humphry Osmond and John R. Smythies who showed hallucinogenic properties for a substance called adrenochrome. This substance was viewed as a possible metabolic product of the neurotransmitter norepinephrine.

One way to test this idea is to administer substances (methyl donors) that provide a good supply of methyl groups. When administered to schizo-

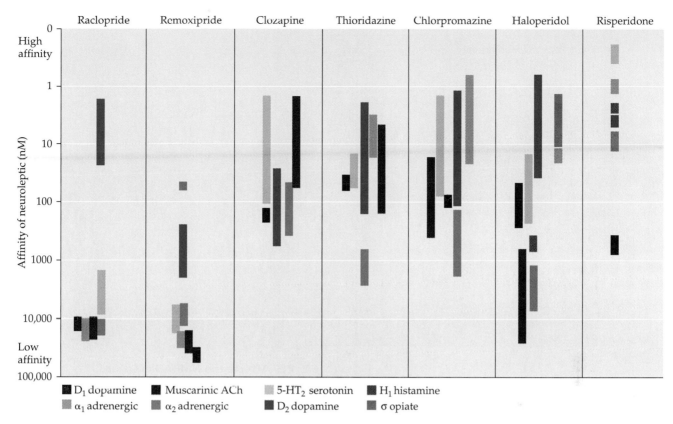

D₁ dopamine   Muscarinic ACh   5-HT₂ serotonin   H₁ histamine
α₁ adrenergic   α₂ adrenergic   D₂ dopamine   σ opiate

16.7 Antipsychotic Drugs That Affect Dopamine Receptors

Drugs vary widely in the affinity with which they bind to various neurotransmitter receptors. Drugs that block dopamine receptors, specifically the D_2 variety, are more effective at combating symptoms of schizophrenia. (After Seeman, 1990.)

phrenic patients, some of these substances exacerbate the symptoms, although the effect is not general to all such substances. This inconsistency, coupled with problems in understanding how the mechanism could account for the effects of antipsychotic drugs, limits the current credibility of the proposal. A modification of the transmethylation hypothesis (Smythies, 1984) suggests that the fault in schizophrenia is an impairment in the transmethylation mechanism itself, rather than the generation of an unusual schizophrenia-producing substance. To support this idea, Smythies presented evidence that the rate of transmethylation in some schizophrenic patients is slower than in normal subjects.

Can the body produce amphetamine-like substances by metabolizing norepinephrine? The amphetamine molecule resembles the molecules of catecholamine transmitters. Since amphetamine psychosis resembles paranoid schizophrenia, an endogenous amphetamine-like substance would be a very interesting discovery. Several investigators have argued that phenylethylamine (PEA)—a substance with amphetamine-like properties—is produced in small quantities by the metabolism of norepinephrine. Current work seeks to assess levels of this metabolite in the bodies of schizophrenics. (Recall that PEA was elevated in the Genain quads; see Topic 16.1, Four Copies of Schizophrenia: The Genain Quads.)

Most drug-induced psychoses do not make good models of schizophrenia, because the psychological

and behavioral changes that they produce do not mimic schizophrenia with great fidelity. One powerful psychotogen, however, comes close to producing a schizophrenia-like state. Initially developed to produce a "dissociative" anesthetic state (one in which an animal is insensitive to pain but shows some types of arousal or responsiveness), this substance, called **phencyclidine** (**PCP**), produces auditory hallucinations, strange depersonalization, disorientation, and intense assaultive behavior. In some cases, prolonged psychotic states can develop from the use of this substance.

Treating monkeys with PCP for 2 weeks produces a schizophrenia-like syndrome, including poor performance on a test that is sensitive to prefrontal damage (Jentsch et al., 1997). This deficit was reversed by treatment with a dopamine-blocking antipsychotic drug, which is further evidence that this drug-induced state is similar to schizophrenia. The mechanism of action of PCP involves the NMDA receptor complex (see Box 4.2), as illustrated in Figure 16.8. Thus PCP can disturb glutamate neurotransmission; a glutamate hypothesis of schizophrenia has been advanced, although research findings about this transmitter in the brains of schizophrenics have been inconsistent.

(a) Effects of PCP on various receptors

Serum PCP concentration (μM)	Mechanisms affected by PCP	Clinical effects
0.01		
	NMDA receptor	Psychosis
0.1		
	NE/DA/5-HT reuptake	Anesthesia
	σ opiate receptor	
1.0		Coma
	K+ channel Na+ channel Nicotinic ACh receptor	
10.0	μ opiate receptor	
	Muscarinic ACh receptor Acetylcholinesterase	
100.0		
	GABA receptors	
1000.0		

(b) A model of PCP action on the NMDA receptor

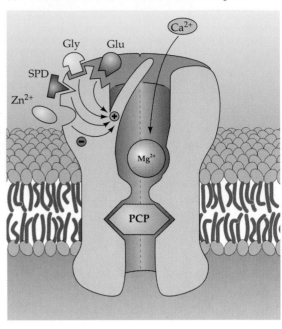

16.8 PCP Affects the NMDA Receptor

(a) The serum concentrations of PCP that elicit clinical effects are the same concentrations that result in PCP binding of the NMDA receptor. (b) A model of PCP action at the NMDA receptor.

An Integrative Psychobiological Model of Schizophrenia Emphasizes the Interaction of Multiple Factors

At times research on schizophrenia seems to have given us many pieces of a large puzzle whose overall appearance is still unknown. Some efforts at integrating the many psychological and biological findings in the field have resulted in important new views about the origins of schizophrenia. One such model, presented by Mirsky and Duncan (1986), views schizophrenia as an outcome of the interaction of genetic, developmental, and stress factors. According to this model, at each life stage specific features contribute to an enhanced vulnerability to schizophrenia.

Genetic influences can be expressed as "brain abnormalities" that provide the basic neurological substrate for schizophrenia. Intrauterine and birth complications—often evident in schizophrenic patients—may also contribute to schizophrenia-generating brain abnormalities. Mirsky and Duncan suggest that through childhood and adolescence, neurological deficits are manifested by behaviors such as impaired cognitive skills, attention deficits, irritability, and delayed gross motor development. Similar neurological deficits are evident in the nonschizophrenic relatives of schizophrenic patients, lending further support to the idea that a genetic factor contributes to schizophrenia (Kinney et al., 1986).

According to the model of Mirsky and Duncan, the emergence of schizophrenia and related disorders depends on the interaction of a compromised biological substrate with environmental stressors (Figure 16.9). The magnitude of brain abnormalities in vulnerable individuals determines how much stress is needed to

produce a schizophrenic disorder. Schizophrenia emerges, according to this model, when the combination of stress and brain abnormalities exceeds a threshold value. People with many schizophrenic brain abnormalities may become symptomatic with relatively minor environmental stresses. Sources of stress may include some types of family interactions, the consequences of impaired attentional or cognitive skills, and the effects of "being different" during development, especially during adolescence.

Models like this one offer the opportunity to appreciate differences among patients. They also suggest the possibility of strategies for decreasing the likelihood of schizophrenia for a child at risk (Hafner, 1998). New biological aids, such as PET scans and genetic tools, might help us identify and understand the at-risk child at a stage early in life, when biological and environmental interventions might reduce the prospects of schizophrenia later in life.

Depression Is a Major Psychiatric Disorder

It seems as though no person now alive nor any of our forebears has been a stranger to depression. Many of us experience periods of unhappiness that we commonly describe as depression. In some people, however, a depressive state is more than a passing malaise

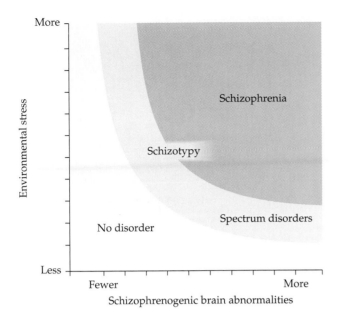

16.9 Model of the Interaction of Stress and Brain Abnormalities in Schizophrenia
Environmental stress and certain brain abnormalities may both contribute to producing a schizophrenic disorder. Disorders ranging from more mild to more severe are called, respectively, spectrum disorders, schizotypy, and schizophrenia. (Adapted from Mirsky and Duncan, 1986.)

and occurs over and over with cyclical regularity. Such people are usually over 40 years old, and women are two to three times more likely than men to suffer from depression.

Depression is characterized by an unhappy mood; loss of interests, energy, and appetite; difficulty in concentration; and restless agitation. Pessimism seems to seep into every act (A. Solomon, 1998). Periods of such unipolar depression (i.e., depression that alternates with normal emotional states) can occur with no readily apparent stress. Without treatment, the depression lasts for several months. Depressive illnesses of this sort afflict 13 to 20% of the population at any one time (Cassens et al., 1990).

Some individuals experience periods of depression alternating with periods of excessively expansive moods that include sustained overactivity, talkativeness, increased energy, and strange grandiosity. This condition is called **bipolar disorder** (also known as manic–depressive psychosis). Men and women are equally affected, and the age of onset is usually much younger than that of unipolar depression. Most people suffering bipolar disorder benefit from treatment with the element **lithium** (Kingsbury and Garver, 1998). No one knows why this metal helps bipolar disorder, and care must be taken to avoid toxic side effects of an overdose. Perhaps the fact that the manic phases blocked by lithium are so exhilarating is the reason that some bipolar clients stop taking the medication. Unfortunately, the depressive episodes return as well.

Inheritance Is an Important Determinant of Depression

Genetic studies of unipolar and bipolar disorders reveal strong hereditary contributions (Moldin et al., 1991). Concordance is much higher for monozygotic (identical) than for dizygotic (fraternal) twins. The concordance rates for monozygotic twins are similar whether the twins are reared apart or together. Adoption studies show high rates of affective illness in the biological parents in comparison to foster parents. Although several early studies implicated specific chromosomes, subsequent linkage studies have failed to identify the locus of any relevant gene.

Genes and behavior

Depression Can Be Lethal

Depression often leads to suicide. Most estimates indicate that about 80% of all suicide victims are profoundly depressed. Unlike the incidence of schizophrenia, suicide rates show great variability across time, age, and places in the world. Although the trend during the twentieth century in the United States and western Europe has shown an overall progressive decline in the incidence of suicide, there is a disturbing trend toward an increase in suicide in younger populations. Several studies have associated the younger age of suicide victims with the frequent use of drugs in this age group (Rich et al., 1986; Sigurdson et al., 1994).

Studies of suicide victims consistently show lower concentrations of serotonin or its metabolites in the brain (Asberg et al., 1986). Low levels of the metabolites of serotonin are also found in the cerebrospinal fluid of people who attempt suicide. Furthermore, suicide attempters who show lower levels of serotonin metabolites are ten times more likely to die of suicide later in their lives than are suicide attempters who show higher levels. Suicide victims also show very high levels of circulating cortisol, which suggests hyperfunction of the hypothalamic–pituitary–adrenal axis (Roy, 1992). (Later in the chapter we will look at the hypothalamic–pituitary–adrenal system in more detail.)

Some Affective Disorders Are Associated with Medical Conditions

In some individuals, depression develops secondarily to other bodily disorders, especially endocrine and brain disorders. For example, **Cushing's syndrome** is characterized by high levels of serum cortisol, which arise from pituitary tumors that produce excessive amounts of ACTH (adrenocorticotropic hormone), from adrenal tumors, or from deliberate therapy involving corticosteroids. In more than 85% of patients with Cushing's syndrome, depression appears quite early in the disorder, even before other signs such as obesity or unusual growth and distribution of body hair (Haskett, 1985; Krystal et al., 1990).

Depression also accompanies brain disorders such as Parkinson's disease (see Chapter 11). Earlier in the chapter we noted that most researchers attribute Parkinson's disease to insufficient production of dopamine. But some investigators argue that Parkinson's patients develop depression in reaction to the motor disabilities of the disorder; others assert that

Competing hypotheses

depression accompanies this disorder because Parkinson's disease affects emotional circuitry and associated transmitters (Sano et al., 1990).

About 50% of Parkinson's patients are in a state of depression that is unrelated to either the duration or the severity of the motor disability. Research suggests that serotonin plays a strong role in their depression. The levels of serotonin metabolites in the cerebrospinal fluid are lower in Parkinson's patients than in controls of the same age (Sano et al., 1990). Administering the precursor for serotonin synthesis alleviates depression in Parkinson's patients. Some of the effects of serotonin in this disorder might arise from a common anatomical lesion in such patients—the loss of large neurons in the dorsal raphe nucleus, which contain large amounts of serotonin.

Functional Maps of the Brain Show Changes with Depression

PET scans of depressed patients show increases in blood flow in the frontal cortex and the amygdala compared with controls (Figure 16.10) (Drevets, 1998). In addition to increasing in the frontal cortex, blood flow decreases in the parietal and posterior temporal cortex—systems that have been implicated in attentional networks and language. The increase in blood flow in the amygdala—a structure involved in mediating fear (see Chapter 15)—persists even after the alleviation of depression over time. Patients treated with antidepressants, however, show normal blood flow in the amygdala.

Several Neurochemical Theories Attempt to Explain Depression

Work on the psychobiology of affective illness has been greatly influenced since the 1960s by a theory offered by Joseph Schildkraut and Seymour Kety (1967)—the monoamine hypothesis of depression. According to this view, depressive illness is associated with a decrease in synaptic activity of connections that employ the monoamine transmitters norepinephrine and serotonin. This decrease is especially characteristic of hypothalamic and associated limbic system circuitry.

Support for this hypothesis comes from the clinical effectiveness of two forms of treatment: antidepressant drugs and electroconvulsive shock therapy. Some antidepressant drugs inhibit **monoamine oxidase**—the enzyme that inactivates norepinephrine, dopamine, and serotonin—thus raising the level of available monoamines. In contrast, the drug **reserpine**, which

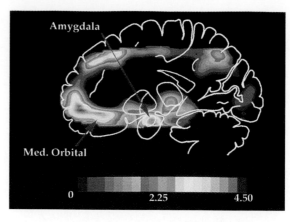

16.10 Brain Activity Patterns in Depression
This PET scan reveals increased activity in the frontal cortex ("Med. orbital") and the amygdala of depressed patients. This image is the result of the subtraction of brain scans of control subjects from those of depressed subjects. Areas of highest activation are shown in red and orange. (Courtesy of Wayne C. Drevets.)

depletes the norepinephrine and serotonin of the brain (by releasing intraneuronal monoamine oxidase, thereby breaking down these transmitters), can result in profound depression. Electroconvulsive shock treatment is effective in many depressed patients, and the seizures produced by this treatment have a strong impact on biogenic amines. The most recent class of antidepressants is the selective serotonin reuptake inhibitors (SSRIs), such as Prozac (Table 16.2).

A very interesting broader view of changes in transmitters like norepinephrine—the dysregulation hypothesis of depression—has been presented by Siever and Davis (1985). These researchers hold that depression is not simply related to depletion of a transmitter, but reflects failure in a regulatory mechanism that governs transmitter operations. This dysregulation results in erratic transmitter activities; they are no longer governed reliably by external stimuli, time of day, or their own actions. Such governance could fail at several different levels in the pathway of noradrenergic system activity. The consequence of impairment of the regulatory devices, according to Siever and Davis, is a transmitter system that is inappropriately responsive to external or internal needs; that is, it becomes maladapted to environmental needs.

Why Do More Females Than Males Suffer from Depression?

Studies all over the world show that more women than men suffer from major depression. The National Institutes of Health (NIH) epidemiological survey mentioned at the start of this chapter documents this sex difference (Robins and Reiger, 1991). All the U.S. sites revealed a twofold difference for major depression. Similar findings have been noted in Sweden. What accounts for these sex differences? The answer

TABLE 16.2 *Drugs Used to Treat Depression*

Drug class	Mechanism of action	Examples[a]
Monoamine oxidase inhibitors (MAOIs)	Inhibit the enzyme monoamine oxidase, which breaks down serotonin, norepinephrine, and dopamine	Marplan, Nardil, Parnate
Tricyclics and heterocyclics	Inhibit the reuptake of norepinephrine, serotonin, and/or dopamine	Elavil, Wellbutrin, Aventyl, Ludiomil, Norpramin
Selective serotonin reuptake inhibitors (SSRIs)	Block the reuptake of serotonin, which is normally removed from the synapse either by degradation by monoamine oxidase or by transport back into presynaptic terminals	Prozac, Paxil, Zoloft

[a]We give here the more commonly used trade names rather than chemical names.

Competing hypotheses

to this question is especially important for achieving an understanding of the causes of depression.

Several hypotheses have been advanced. Some researchers argue that the sex differential arises from differences in how males and females seek help—notably, that women use health facilities more than men do. But even though the NIH survey was a door-to-door survey, not an assessment of appearance at health centers, significant sex differences were apparent. This fact appears to rule out the hypothesis that the sex difference in the incidence of depression is caused by sex differences in help-seeking patterns.

Several psychosocial explanations have been advanced. One view emphasizes that depression in women arises from the social discrimination that prevents them from achieving mastery by self-assertion. According to this view, inequities lead to dependency, low self-esteem, and depression. Another psychosocial focus leans on the learned-helplessness model (which we will discuss shortly). According to this view, stereotypical images of men and women produce in women a cognitive set of classic feminine values, reinforced by societal expectations, of which helplessness is one dimension.

A genetic interpretation of the gender difference in depression is that depression is an inherited disorder linked to the X chromosome. But relatives of male and female depressives show no differences in depression rates (which would be expected with X linking). Thus, although there is a strong genetic determinant for depression in general, there does not seem to be a genetic basis for sex differences in depression.

Some researchers have emphasized gender differences in endocrine physiology. The occurrence of clinical depression often is related to events in the female reproductive cycle—for example, before menstruation, while using contraceptive pills, following child-

birth, and during menopause. Although several hormones have been linked to depression, there is little relation between circulating levels of hormones related to female reproductive physiology and measures of depression.

Epidemiological studies of Amish communities (Egeland and Hostetter, 1983) provide a different slant on the mystery of gender differences in depression. An exhaustive survey of this religious community, which prohibits the use of alcohol and shuns modernity, reveals no sex difference in major depression. This finding suggests that in the general population, heavy use of alcohol masks depression in many males, making it appear as if fewer males than females suffer from depression. Epidemiological data on alcoholism show another major gender difference, which supports this idea: The incidence in males is higher.

The Hypothalamic–Pituitary–Adrenal Axis Is Involved in Depression

For many years researchers have sought easily measurable biochemical, physiological, or anatomical indicators of various mental disorders. These indicators, called **biological markers**, may reflect factors relevant to the causes of a disorder or its current state. The development of such laboratory tests is important especially because some behavioral assessments may not provide clues to genetic mechanisms or differential responses to drugs. Thus, two patients might present a similar portrait of depression but respond differently to antidepressant drugs. An appropriate biological marker could suggest what drug to use for a particular patient.

Of the various mental disorders, research on depression has been especially productive in generating potential biological markers, in particular several that are linked to hormonal responses to stress that involve the hypothalamic–pituitary–adrenal system (Figure

(a)

(b) Normal controls

(c) Depressed patients

(d)

16.11 The Hypothalamic–Pituitary–Adrenal Axis in Depression

(a) The hypothalamic–pituitary–adrenal system. *(b)* The normal circadian rhythm in the secretion of cortisol (day 1) is abolished by treatment with the synthetic glucocorticoid dexamethasone (day 2). *(c)* The same dose of dexamethasone is far less effective in depressed patients. *(d)* Circulating cortisol levels are usually higher in depressed subjects than in psychiatric or normal controls.

16.11*a*). Another reason that investigators studying depression are interested in the hypothalamic–pituitary–adrenal system is that it is activated by stress, which is also believed to activate depression in susceptible individuals (Heit et al., 1997).

Early work in this area focused on the hypothalamic–pituitary–adrenal system because hospitalized depressed patients showed elevated cortisol levels. This finding suggested that ACTH (adrenocorticotropic hormone) is released in excessive amounts by the anterior pituitary. One method for analyzing the pituitary–adrenal function is the **dexamethasone suppression test**. Dexamethasone is a potent synthetic corticoid that ordinarily suppresses the typical early-morning rise in ACTH. Generally given late at night, dexamethasone seems to "fool" the hypothalamus into believing that there is a high level of circulating cortisol (Figure 16.11*b*). In normal individuals, dexamethasone clearly suppresses cortisol levels, but in many depressed individuals it fails to suppress circulating levels of cortisol (Figure 16.11*c*). As depres-

Important method

sion is relieved, dexamethasone again suppresses cortisol normally.

The normalization is claimed to occur no matter what the cause of relief—lapse of time, psychotherapy, pharmacotherapy, or electroconvulsive shock therapy. One possible mediating mechanism is that in depressed people the cells of the hypothalamus are subject to abnormal excitatory drive from limbic system regions, resulting in sustained release of ACTH. Some evidence suggests that depression causes a reduction of cellular corticosteroid receptors, resulting in subnormal negative feedback in this system (Barden et al., 1995).

A provocative proposal is that stress and the attendant release of glucocorticoids reduces brain production of neurotrophic factors, such as brain-derived neurotrophic factor (BDNF; see Chapter 7), leading to neuronal atrophy and therefore depression (Duman et al., 1997). According to this hypothesis, drugs that increase the stimulation of serotonin and/or norepinephrine cause an increase in cyclic AMP in the brain, which causes an increase in the production of CREB (cAMP responsive element–binding) proteins (discussed in Chapter 18) and therefore an increase in BDNF release. The BDNF then maintains other brain neurons to alleviate depression. Favoring this theory is evidence that stress reduces BDNF production in the rat hippocampus and that SSRI drugs block this effect.

Other hormonal systems explored in depression marker research include growth hormone and thyroid hormones. Depressed patients secrete twice as much growth hormone as controls do during a 24-hour period (Kalin et al., 1987). Both hypo- and hyperthyroid conditions have been associated with affective changes. Thyroid hormone supplementation can enhance the responsiveness of patients to antidepressant drugs. However, additional studies are needed to determine whether any components of the hypothalamic–pituitary–thyroid axis are sensitive and reliable markers of depression.

Sleep Characteristics Change in Affective Disorders

The disturbance of sleep that accompanies depression is not news, but the character of the change and the fact that induced changes in sleep might influence depression are new pieces in the puzzle. Difficulty in falling asleep and inability to maintain sleep are common in major depression. In addition, EEG sleep studies of depressed patients show certain abnormalities that go beyond difficulty in falling asleep. The sleep of patients with major depressive disorders is marked by a striking reduction in stages 3 and 4 of slow-wave sleep (SWS) and a corresponding increase in stages 1 and 2 of SWS (Figure 16.12a). Changes in REM sleep include a shortened time from sleep onset to the first REM episode (Figure 16.12b). Furthermore, the temporal distribution of REM sleep is altered; an increased amount of REM sleep occurs during the first half of sleep, as though REM sleep had been displaced toward an earlier period in the night (Wehr et al., 1985). REM sleep in depressives is also more vigorous, marked by very frequent rapid eye movements

Are these sleep abnormalities specific to depression? This question remains steeped in controversy. Some of the abnormalities are seen in other psychiatric states, and most likely some are nonspecific. However, alterations of REM sleep seem to have a special connection to depression; shortened REM sleep latency correlates significantly with the severity of depression. The role of REM sleep in depression is also supported by the clinical effectiveness of various types of sleep therapy. Vogel et al. (1980) focused on the fact that REM sleep seems misplaced and extended in the sleep of depressives; depressives almost seem to start sleep where normals leave off. This analysis inspired studies on the effect of selective REM sleep deprivation on the symptoms of depression.

A marked antidepressant effect of REM sleep deprivation has been noted in several studies of patients suffering from major affective disorders. Patients were awakened as they entered REM sleep, which reduced the overall amounts of REM sleep; the procedure was continued for 2 to 3 weeks. A control group of depressed patients was awakened from non-REM sleep. Depression was evaluated on the basis of a clinical rating scale. At the end of 3 weeks, the REM sleep–deprived group showed a significantly lower depression score than the non-REM sleep–deprived group. Three weeks later the treatments were reversed, and by the end of another 3 weeks, the effect had also switched. Several antidepressant drugs, such as monoamine oxidase inhibitors, suppress REM sleep for extended periods. Vogel asserted that REM sleep deprivation improves severe depression to the extent that it modifies REM sleep abnormalities.

Another sleep therapy approach has emerged from the analysis of circadian rhythms of sleep in depressed patients. Wehr et al. (1983) found that depressed patients show abnormal phase relationships in some body rhythms, in addition to alterations in REM sleep cycles. This analysis generated a type of circadian treatment for depression. Wehr et al. (1982) had patients go to bed 6 hours before their usual time and reported that several patients showed a rapid improvement in their depression. In addition to these links between daily rhythms and depression, seasonal rhythms have been implicated in a particular depressive condition known as seasonal affective disorder (SAD), which is described in Box 16.2.

Seizures Can Relieve Depression in Some Patients

About 50 years ago treatments in psychiatry were few, yet the needs were enormous. The title of a book by

(a) A depressed subject s sleep pattern

(b)

16.12 Sleep and Depression
(a) Depressed subjects spend little or no time in stage 3 or 4 sleep. (Compare with Figure 14.11.) (b) Depressed people also enter their first REM period earlier in the night. Thus REM sleep seems to be distributed differently in depressed people.

Elliot Valenstein (1986)—*Great and Desperate Cures*—captures the general thinking: try anything in the face of an overwhelming absence of knowledge about the brain. During this period several desperate cures were introduced with little rationale. One of them was the induction of seizures to treat schizophrenia.

Initially, convulsions were produced chemically, by use of the convulsant drug Metrazol. Beginning in the late 1930s, convulsions were produced by electricity delivered through two large electrodes placed on the skin over the skull (electroconvulsive shock therapy). Although this treatment had no clinical impact on schizophrenia, frequent use of this technique showed that such induced seizures could rapidly reverse severe depression.

The advent of antidepressant drugs led to the temporary retirement of this clinical tool. However, there proved to be a class of patients for whom antidepressant drugs were relatively ineffective. Furthermore,

patients in imminent danger of committing suicide need a treatment that works faster to relieve depression than do most antidepressant drugs (although new types are constantly being developed and made available for clinical trials). Starting in the 1980s, electroconvulsive shock treatment was resumed to treat suicidal patients who failed to respond to antidepressant drugs. Although somewhat different from its original form, this treatment still elicits a large-scale seizure (R. D. Weiner, 1994). The mechanisms that make electroconvulsive shock therapy an effective treatment of depression remain elusive, although recently developed imaging techniques are being used to gain insight into possible mediating changes in brain function (Nobler et al., 1994).

Animal Models Aid Research on Depression

Because it is difficult to ask a monkey or a cat or a rat if they have delusions of persecution or if they hear voices accusing them of awful crimes, animal models of schizophrenia are limited. But many of the signs of depression are behaviorally overt—such as decreased social contact, problems with eating, and changes in activity. An animal model for the study of depression can provide the ability to evaluate proposed neurobiological mechanisms, a convenient way to screen potential treatments, and the ability to explore possible causes experimentally (Lachman et al., 1993). Table 16.3 lists the characteristics of animal models used in studies of depression.

In one type of stress model—**learned helplessness**—an animal is exposed to a repetitive stressful stimulus, such as an electric shock, that it cannot escape. Like depression, learned helplessness has been linked to a decrease in serotonin function (Petty et al., 1994). Removing the olfactory bulb from rodents creates a model of depression: The animals display irritability, hyperactivity, preferences for alcohol, elevated levels of corticosteroids, and deficiency in passive

BOX 16.2 *The Season to Be Depressed*

Seasonal rhythms characterize the behavior and physiology of many animals, including humans. For some unfortunate people, winter brings a low period, which may become a profound depression. For many such people the winter depression alternates with summer mania (Blehar and Rosenthal, 1989). In wintertime, affected people feel depressed, slow down, generally sleep a lot, and overeat. Come summer they are elated, energetic, active, and become thinner. This syndrome—called **seasonal affective disorder** (**SAD**)—appears predominantly in women and generally starts in early adulthood.

Some studies have reported a positive correlation between latitude and the frequency of SAD, but a recent study in a country at a far northern latitude—Iceland—failed to confirm this relationship (Magnusson and Stefansson, 1993). On the contrary, this study revealed a much lower rate for SAD in Iceland. Perhaps population selection over centuries has tended to diminish the reproductive prominence of individuals susceptible to SAD in Iceland and has led to greater tolerance in this population of prolonged periods of winter darkness. Some support for this idea comes from studies

of SAD in descendants of Icelandic emigrants in Canada. In this population, SAD is lower than in other populations (Magnusson and Axelsson, 1993).

In nonhuman animals, many seasonal rhythms are controlled by the length of the day. For example, migration or hibernation may be triggered by changes in the duration of daylight. Some researchers have suggested that SAD in humans shows a similar dependence. To examine that prospect, researchers have explored whether exposure to light that simulates sunlight can act as an antidepressant. In one investigation (N. E. Rosenthal et al., 1985), a group of patients was secured by a newspaper ad that described the typical features of seasonal affective disorder. The patients selected for the study had at least two winter episodes of depression. Experimental treatment consisted of two 1-week exposures to additional light separated by 1 week of no additional light. During the treatment periods, patients were exposed to bright light twice during the day: from 5:00 A.M. to 8:00 A.M., and from 5:30 P.M. to 8:30 P.M. This distribution extended normal daylight and thus tended to simulate the long daylight period characteristic of summer.

The results indicated that bright lights have a significant antidepressant effect that is reversed upon withdrawal of the lights. No significant effects were noted following exposure to dim lights. The improvement in mood appears after a few days and generally persists through the week of treatment. Removal of light quickly produces relapse (Wehr et al., 1986).

One important biological effect of light is that it suppresses melatonin, a hormone found in the pineal gland that affects gonadotropins and may be of importance in controlling sleep. Whereas exposure to darkness stimulates melatonin synthesis, light suppresses it. People with SAD have been shown to have a high threshold for melatonin suppression. However, oral administration of melatonin did not influence this disorder. Serotonin may be relevant since it has a marked seasonal rhythm in humans, with lower values in winter and spring than in summer or fall (Egrise et al., 1986). Attention to seasonal affective disorder arose primarily because of animal research dealing with photoperiodic behavior and circadian control systems—another example of basic research leading to alleviation of the distresses and diseases of humans.

---

avoidance conditioning—all of which are reversed by many antidepressants. A genetically developed line of rats—the Flinders-sensitive line—has been proposed as a model of depression because these animals show reduced locomotor activity, reduced body weight, increased REM sleep, learning difficulties, and exaggerated immobility in response to chronic stress (Overstreet, 1993). These varied animal models may be useful in finding the essential paths that cause and maintain depression (Lachman et al., 1993).

TABLE 16.3 *Characteristics of Animal Models of Depression*

Model	Activity change	Sensitivity to antidepressants	Decreased social contact
Stress models			
Learned helplessness	+	+	−
Chronic mild stress	−	+	−
Behavorial despair separation models (e.g., primate separations)	+	+	+
Pharmacological models (e.g., reserpine reversal)	+	+	−
Anatomical models (e.g., olfactory bulbectomy)	+	+	−
Genetic models (e.g., Flinders-sensitive line)	+	+	

There Are Several Types of Anxiety Disorders

All of us have at times felt apprehensive and fearful. Some people experience this state with an intensity that is overwhelming and includes irrational fears, a sense of terror, unusual body sensations such as dizziness, difficulty in breathing, trembling, shaking, and a feeling of loss of control. For some, anxiety comes in sudden attacks of panic that are unpredictable and last for minutes or hours. And anxiety can be lethal: A follow-up of patients with panic disorder revealed an increased mortality in men with this disorder resulting from cardiovascular disease and suicide (Coryell et al., 1986)

The American Psychiatric Association distinguishes two major groupings of anxiety disorders: phobic disorders and anxiety states. *Phobic disorders* are intense, irrational fears that become centered on a specific object, activity, or situation that the person feels he or she must avoid. *Anxiety states* include recurrent panic states; generalized, persistent anxiety disorders; and posttraumatic stress disorders.

Panic Can Be Provoked Chemically

Several decades ago psychiatrists observed that some patients experience intense anxiety attacks during or after vigorous physical exercise. This effect was thought to be caused by a buildup of lactate in the blood. This observation inspired Pitts and McClure (1967) to administer sodium lactate to anxiety patients. In some patients the infusions produced immediate panic attacks that resembled the naturally occurring episodes; this chemical treatment did not produce panic attacks in normal people.

Margraf and Roth (1986) contested the study on the grounds that it failed to exclude confounding psychological factors: Patients showed a certain level of panic even when infused with placebo. However, PET scans (which we will discuss in the next section) do support the lactate induction effect. In an attempt to account for chemically induced panic, Liebowitz et al. (1986) suggest that the lactate-induced panic stimulates central noradrenergic mechanisms of the locus coeruleus and its outputs. This suggestion is partially supported by the observation that another locus coeruleus stimulant—inhalation of 5% carbon dioxide—produces panic in clinically vulnerable individuals.

Anxiety and Panic Disorders Are Characterized by Structural and Functional Changes in the Temporal Lobes

Many patients who suffer from recurrent panic attacks have temporal lobe abnormalities, according to MRI studies. Ontiveros et al. (1989) found temporal lobe abnormalities—including small lesions in white matter and dilation of the lateral ventricles—in 40% of patients with panic disorder. The magnitude of neuroanatomical anomalies correlated significantly with the total number of spontaneous attacks and the age of onset of panic (patients whose episodes of panic begin at an earlier age have more anomalies).

Intriguing PET scan observations have provided a portrait of the anatomy of anxiety. Studies by Reiman et al. (1986) revealed abnormalities in the resting, nonpanic state. Reiman et al. compared patients whose panic disorder could be induced by injection of sodium lactate, patients who were not vulnerable to lactate-induced panic, and normal controls. Those who were vulnerable to lactate-induced panic showed a markedly abnormal increase in blood flow in the right parahippocampus. This region contains the major input and output pathways of the hippocampus. Gloor et al. (1982) found that electrical stimulation of this region in awake patients commonly elicits sensations of strong fear and apprehension. In addition to this regional effect, lactate-vulnerable panic patients also had abnormally high oxygen metabolism in the brain.

The work of Reiman and collaborators raises the possibility that a biological indicant—PET scan data—can distinguish two major anxiety groups: those vulnerable to lactate-induced panic and those not vulnerable to this form of induced attack. This distinction might reflect a fundamental difference in underlying biological mechanisms. Although these PET observations were criticized because of the possible confounding factor of temporal muscle activity (Posner and Raichle, 1994), other metabolic studies also point to the role of temporal lobe structures in the elicitation and maintenance of anxiety states (Rauch et al., 1995).

Drug Treatment of Anxiety Provides Clues to Its Mechanisms

Throughout history people have consumed all sorts of substances in the hopes of controlling anxiety. The list includes alcohol, bromides, scopolamine, opiates, and barbiturates. But not until 1960 was a drug introduced that would forever change the treatment of anxiety. Molecular changes in an antibacterial substance produced the drug meprobamate, which, under the trade name Miltown, became famous as a tranquilizing agent. Competition among drug companies led to the development of a class of substances called **benzodiazepines**, which have become the most common drugs used in the treatment of anxiety. One type of benzodiazepine—diazepam (trade name Valium)—is one of the most prescribed drugs in history. These drugs are commonly described as **anxiolytic** ("anxiety relieving"), although at high doses they also have anticonvulsant and sleep-inducing properties.

Early behavioral and electrophysiological data established that the benzodiazepines are associated in some way with the action of GABA synapses (see Chapter 4; recall from Chapter 3 that GABA is the most common inhibitory transmitter in the brain). This interaction with GABA receptors results in enhancement of the action at inhibitory synapses in the brain that use

GABA. Thus GABA-mediated postsynaptic inhibition is facilitated by benzodiazepines. Benzodiazepine receptors are widely distributed throughout the brain and are especially concentrated in the cerebral cortex and some subcortical areas, such as the hippocampus and the amygdala (Figure 16.13).

The ultimate function of the benzodiazepine–GABA receptor complex is to regulate the permeability of neural membranes to chloride ions. When GABA, upon release from a presynaptic terminal, activates its receptor, chloride ions are allowed to move from the outside to the inside of the nerve cell, hyperpolarizing and therefore inhibiting the neuron from firing. Benzodiazepines alone do little to chloride conductance, but in the presence of GABA, they markedly enhance GABA-provoked increases in chloride permeability. Research also suggests that specific anxiety peptides occur naturally in the brain and act in association with the benzodiazepine receptor (J. L. Marx, 1985).

In Posttraumatic Stress Disorder, Horrible Memories Won't Go Away

Some people experience some especially awful moments in their life that seem indelible, resulting in vivid impressions that persist through the remainder of life. Persons exposed to sustained periods of unrelieved horrors, such as the "killing fields" of war, may find it intensely difficult to shut out these events even long after they have passed. The kind of event that seems particularly likely to produce subsequent stress disorders is one that is intense and usually associated with witnessing abusive violence and/or death. Other such events may be the sudden loss of a close friend, torture, kidnapping, and profound social dislocation, such as in forced migration.

Memories of horrible events intrude into consciousness and produce the same intense visceral arousal—the fear and trembling—that the original event caused. These traumatic memories are easily reawakened by stressful circumstances and even by innocuous stimuli. An ever-watchful and fearful stance becomes the portrait of individuals afflicted with what is called **posttraumatic stress disorder** (**PTSD**, once called combat fatigue, war neurosis, or shell shock).

Recent studies on risk factors associated with PTSD in Vietnam War veterans have clarified the interaction of genetic and environmental factors in this disorder. The disorder is particularly prevalent among those who served in the most intense combat areas (True et al., 1993). Familial factors also affect vulnerability, as shown in twins studies of Vietnam era veterans. Researchers compared twins—both monozygotic and dizygotic—who had served in combat zones with other veterans who had not served in Southeast Asia. Monozygotic twins were more similar than dizygotic twins, and the specific contribution of inheritance to PTSD is claimed to account for one-third of the variance.

A comprehensive psychobiological model of the development of PTSD draws connections between the symptoms and the neural mechanisms of fear conditioning, extinction, and behavioral sensitization (Charney et al., 1993). The investigators argue that patients learn to avoid a large range of stimuli associated with the original trauma. A kind of emotional numbing is the consequence of this avoidance, which can also be seen as a type of conditioned emotional response. Work in animals has revealed that this type of memory—fear conditioning—is very persistent and involves the amygdala and some brain stem pathways that are part of a circuit of startle response behavior (see Chapter 15). NMDA receptor–mediated mechanisms in the amygdala are important for the development of fear conditioning.

The persistence of memory and fear in PTSD may also depend on the failure or fragility of extinction mechanisms. In experimental animals, NMDA antagonists delivered to the amygdala prevent the extinction of fear-mediated startle. Sites projecting to the amygdala, such as the hippocampus and prefrontal cortex, may also lose their effectiveness in suppressing learned fear responses.

Animal model

The third element of this model—behavioral sensitization mechanisms—enhances response magnitude after exposure to a stimulus. The neural mechanisms probably involve dopamine, since repeated stressors increase dopamine function in the forebrain. Figure 16.14 presents a large-scale portrait of this in-

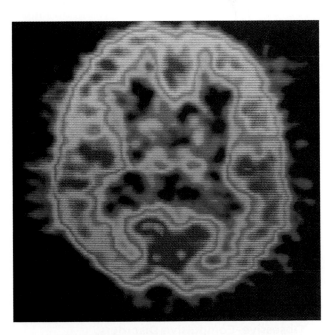

16.13 Distribution of Benzodiazepine Receptors in the Human Brain
PET scan of benzodiazepine receptors, showing their wide distribution in the brain. Highest concentrations are shown in orange and red. (Courtesy of Goran Sedvall.)

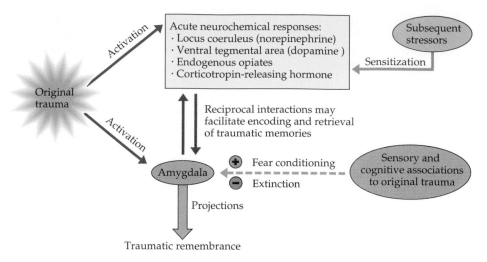

Symptom	Brain region
Flashbacks, intrusive memories	Cortex, hippocampus
Anxiety, fear, hypervigilance	Locus coeruleus, ventral tegmental area
Facial expression of fear	Trigeminal, facial motor nuclei
Anhedonia, depression	Nucleus accumbens
Startle	Reticular formation
Hyperventilation	Medullary respiratory center
Sympathetic activation: rapid heart rate, increased blood pressure	Lateral hypothalamus
Parasympathetic activation: diarrhea, increased urination	Vagal nerve nucleus

16.14 Neural Model of Posttraumatic Stress Disorder

The original trauma activates two systems: one in the brain stem, which sensitizes the subject to related stimuli in the future, and another in the amygdala, which conditions a long-lasting fearful reaction.

triguing neural model. One important implication of this model is that it might direct clinical intervention. For example, it suggests a potentially important use for drugs that block conditioned responses.

Exposure to stress leads to high levels of circulating glucocorticoids, which some researchers have suggested might lead to cell loss in the hippocampus (Sapolsky et al., 1990) or might prevent normal cell gain in the hippocampus (E. Gould et al., 1998). Patients who display combat-related PTSD show (1) memory changes such as amnesia for some war experiences, (2) flashbacks, and (3) deficits in short-term memory (Bremner et al., 1993). Reports of such psychological changes have led to MRI studies of the brains of combat veterans with PTSD. Measurements of the right hippocampus reveal an 8% reduction in the volume of this structure, with no changes in other brain regions (Bremner et al., 1995). Chapter 17 will discuss two research-based methods that have been proposed to prevent or alleviate posttraumatic stress disorder.

In Obsessive–Compulsive Disorders, Thoughts and Acts Keep Repeating

Neatness, orderliness, and similar traits are attributes we tend to admire, especially during those chaotic moments when we realize we have created another tottering pile of papers, bills, or the like. What, then, constitutes what we call **obsessive–compulsive disorder** (**OCD**)? In her book *The Boy Who Couldn't Stop Washing* (1989b), Judith Rapoport, a psychiatrist at the National Institutes of Health with extensive experience in researching and treating people afflicted with OCD, described a remarkable group of people whose lives are riddled with repetitive acts that are carried out without rhyme, reason, or the ability to stop.

Routine acts that we all engage in, such as checking whether the door is locked when we leave our home, are repeated over and over. Recurrent thoughts, such as fears of germs or other potential harms in the world, invade the consciousness. Table 16.4 summarizes the symptoms of OCD. These symptoms progressively isolate a person from ordinary social engagement with the world. For many patients, hours of each day are consumed by compulsive acts such as repetitive hand washing.

Determining the number of persons afflicted with OCD is difficult, especially since many persons with

TABLE 16.4 *Symptoms of Obsessive-Compulsive Disorders*

Symptoms	Percent of patients
Obsessions	
Dirt, germs, or environmental toxins	40
Something terrible happening (fire, death or illness of self or loved one)	24
Symmetry, order, or exactness	17
Religious obsessions	13
Bodily wastes or secretions (urine, stool, saliva)	8
Lucky or unlucky numbers	8
Forbidden, aggressive, or perverse sexual thoughts, images, or impulses	4
Fear of harming others or oneself	4
Household items	3
Intrusive nonsense sounds, words, or music	1
Compulsions	
Excessive or ritualized hand washing, showering, bathing, tooth brushing, or grooming	85
Repeating rituals (going in or out of a door, getting up from or sitting down on a chair)	51
Checking (doors, locks, stove, appliances, emergency brake on car, paper route, homework)	46
Removing contaminants from contacts	23
Touching	20
Preventing harm to self or others	16
Ordering or arranging	17
Counting	18
Hoarding or collecting	11
Cleaning household or inanimate objects	6
Miscellaneous rituals (such as writing, moving, speaking)	26

The basal ganglia, frontal cortex, and OCD. PET scan studies of OCD patients show significantly higher metabolic rates in the left orbital gyrus and bilaterally in the caudate nucleus. The basal ganglia have also been implicated in other disorders related to OCD, such as Tourette's syndrome (see Box 16.3). Studies of regional cerebral blood flow in patients in whom OCD symptoms have been provoked support this finding.

In a recent study, investigators provoked a symptomatic state by using stimuli that patients reported provoked OCD symptoms (Rauch et al., 1994). Brain images obtained in response to an innocuous stimulus were subtracted from those obtained when symptoms were provoked. Statistically significant increases in regional blood flow were seen in the right caudate nucleus, left anterior cingulate cortex, and bilateral orbitofrontal cortex. This pattern of enhanced blood flow supports an anatomical model of obsessive–compulsive disorders proposed by Insel (1992) that emphasizes a circuit involving a loop among frontal, striatal, and thalamic structures.

Serotonin and OCD. The basic observation behind the serotonin hypothesis of obsessive–compulsive disorders is that clomipramine, a tricyclic antidepressant (see Table 16.2), markedly reduces the symptoms of this disorder. Although OCD is classified as an anxiety disorder, some clinicians have long believed that this disorder is related to depression. For example, studies of the incidence of OCD and depression show some overlap between them. OCD patients, like depressed patients, exhibit decreased REM sleep latency.

Comparisons of antidepressants used to treat OCD generally show that clomipramine has greater anti-obsessional effects than most other antidepressants. What sets clomipramine apart? One significant difference between clomipramine and other antidepressants is the potency of its ability to block serotonin uptake. Blocking the reuptake of serotonin has significant anti-obsessional effects.

Neurosurgery Has Been Used to Treat Psychiatric Disorders

Through the ages, the mentally disabled have been treated by methods limited only by the human imagi-

this disorder tend to hide their symptoms. It is estimated that more than 4 million persons are affected by OCD in the United States (Rapoport, 1989a). In many cases, the initial symptoms of this disorder appear in childhood; the peak age group is 25 to 44 years. For a long time, this disorder was thought of as a psychiatric dysfunction associated with psychological conflict. More recently, evidence has accumulated that this disorder is rooted in the neurobiology of the brain. Rapoport (1989a) suggested that the features of this disorder reflect "subroutines" associated with grooming and territoriality that have evolved gradually. Symptoms arise when brain malfunction causes these programs to be executed without the usual provoking stimuli—such as cleaning something that is already clean.

BOX 16.3   *Tics, Twitches, and Snorts: The Unusual Character of Tourette's Syndrome*

Their faces twitch in an insistent way, and every now and then, out of nowhere, they blurt out an odd sound or, quite suddenly, an obscene word. At times they fling their arms, kick their legs, or make violent shoulder movements. Sufferers of Tourette's syndrome also exhibit heightened sensitivity to tactile, auditory, and visual stimuli (A. J. Cohen and Leckman, 1992). Many patients also sense the buildup of an urge to emit verbal or phonic tics; they report that these acts relieve this powerfully felt need. Professionals have long argued about whether this collection of symptoms forms a psychiatric disturbance derived from the stresses of life or emerges from a disturbance in brain structures and/or function.

Tourette's syndrome begins early in life; the mean age of diagnosis is 6 to 7 years (de Groot et al., 1995). Figure A draws a portrait of the chronology of symptoms. Associated behavioral disturbances include attention deficit hyperactivity disorder (ADHD),

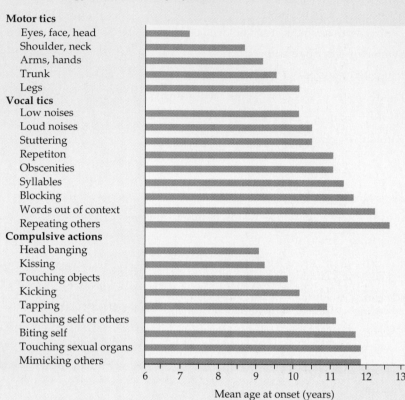

(A) Chronology of Tourette's symptoms

Motor tics
Eyes, face, head
Shoulder, neck
Arms, hands
Trunk
Legs
Vocal tics
Low noises
Loud noises
Stuttering
Repetiton
Obscenities
Syllables
Blocking
Words out of context
Repeating others
Compulsive actions
Head banging
Kissing
Touching objects
Kicking
Tapping
Touching self or others
Biting self
Touching sexual organs
Mimicking others

Mean age at onset (years)

nation. Some methods have been gruesome, inspired by views that people with mental disorders are controlled by demonic forces. Although twentieth-century psychiatry has been purged of such moralistic views, until recently treatment was a trial-and-error affair.

In the 1930s, experiments on frontal lobe lesions in chimpanzees inspired psychiatrist Egas Moniz to attempt similar operations in patients. Moniz was intrigued by the report of a calming influence in nonhuman primates, and at the time he tried frontal surgery little else was available. His observations led to the beginning of **psychosurgery**, defined as the use of surgically produced brain lesions to modify severe psychiatric disorders. Psychosurgery has provoked vigorous debate since the inception of its use, which continues to the present (Valenstein, 1980, 1986).

During the 1940s, **lobotomy** (disconnecting parts of the frontal lobes from the rest of the brain) was forcefully advocated by several neurosurgeons and psychiatrists. A presidential commission on psy-

chosurgery estimated that during this period, 10,000 to 50,000 U.S. patients underwent this surgery (National Commission for the Protection of Human Subjects in Biomedical and Behavioral Research, 1978). During the most intense period of enthusiasm, patients of all diagnostic types were operated on, and different varieties of surgery were employed. Interest in psychosurgery arose from the saddening sight of many people in mental hospitals living empty, disturbed lives without hope of change. Today frontal surgery is rare and generally limited to treatment of intense pain. Its use in psychiatry has practically ended, although the commission on psychosurgery urged further consideration of the role of surgery in psychiatry. (Recall from Chapter 15 that temporal lobe surgery has also been used to treat violent behavior attributed to seizures.)

Assessments of the value of frontal lobe surgery in psychiatric treatment are steeped in controversy. William Sweet (1973) argued that more localized brain lesions might significantly relieve particular problems in school, and obsessive–compulsive disorder (Park et al., 1993).

Genetics appears to play a potent role in this disorder. The most common contemporary view is that Tourette's syndrome is mediated by a single gene inherited in a dominant manner (Eapen et al., 1993). Twins studies of the disorder reveal a monozygotic-twin concordance rate of 53 to 77%, contrasted with a dizygotic-twin concordance rate of 8 to 23% (Hyde et al., 1992; R. A. Price et al., 1985).

An unusual view of genetic factors in Tourette's is provided by a study of a set of triplets who were reared apart after the age of 2 months (Segal et al., 1990). The triplets consisted of a pair of monozygotic female twins and a dizygotic male. They were reunited when they were 47 years old. The male had a history of eye blinking, facial tics, and repetitive arm and finger movements that had begun at age 4. Eye blinking persisted into adulthood. The female twins showed a more severe set of symptoms: frequent motor and phonic tics, head jerks, shoulder jerks, and kicking leg movements.

The symptoms of Tourette's patients resemble some of those seen in patients with basal ganglia disease. MRI studies show subtle changes in basal ganglia structure in Tourette's patients. For example, normal subjects usually show asymmetry in the volumes of left and right basal ganglia structures, but Tourette's patients fail to show this asymmetry, and they show lower overall volumes of basal ganglia such as the caudate nucleus and globus pallidus (B. Peterson et al., 1993).

More persuasive are PET studies of dopamine receptors in monozygotic twins. The twin with more severe symptoms almost always showed significantly higher binding of the D_2 dopamine receptor in the caudate—a correlation of +0.99. In the MRI scan at the bottom of Figure B, the locations of the caudate nuclei are indicated by ovals, which match the areas of highest binding shown in the PET scan above (S. S. Wolf et al., 1996). This finding may explain why drugs that affect dopamine functioning can reduce the frequency of some of the motor features of Tourette's syndrome (A. L. Peterson and Azrin, 1992). Administration of haloperidol, a dopamine

(B) D_2 binding in the brain of a twin with Tourette's syndrome

antagonist, significantly reduces tic frequency and is the primary treatment of this disorder. Unfortunately, side effects limit the duration of this treatment. Behavior modification techniques that aim at reducing the frequency of some symptoms, especially tics, are claimed to help some patients (A. L. Peterson and Azrin, 1992). (Figure B courtesy of Steven Wolf.)

psychiatric disorders. Strong support for this view was offered by Ballantine et al. (1987), who reported on the treatment of depression and anxiety disorders by stereotaxic cingulotomy (lesions that interrupt pathways in the cingulate cortex).

Clinical evaluations reported positive outcomes of this procedure in many chronically depressed patients who were not aided by other treatments. For example, a follow-up study on a group of severely disabled OCD patients (Jenike et al., 1991) indicated that one-third of patients who underwent cingulotomy (Figure 16.15) benefited substantially from this intervention (Martuza et al., 1990). A long-term follow-up study of OCD patients who received ventromedial frontal lesions as a last-resort therapy for OCD indicated significant improvement in obsessive–compulsive symptoms (Irle et al., 1998). This clinical improvement was sustained in some patients for 20 years. However, the use of drugs has overshadowed psychosurgery, especially because neurosurgical interventions are not reversible.

There Are Many Different Hypotheses on the Causes of Mental Disorders

In this chapter we have described several examples of human mental illnesses and some of the biological information that relates to the origins and characteristics of these disorders. Given the vast range of data, it is useful to summarize the different categories of hypotheses, as Table 16.5 does.

The two major categories are anatomical hypotheses and synaptic communication hypotheses. Anatomical hypotheses suggest that mental disorders arise from miswiring of the brain, generally a loss of a particular component. In many cases, such as schizophrenia, the deficiency is suspected to have arisen during early development. Synaptic communication hypotheses suggest that changes in synaptic communication are the basis of mental disorders. These changes include decreased or increased synaptic activity that could arise from the failure of one or more transmitter systems.

(a) Horizontal view

(b) Sagittal view

16.15 Neurosurgery to Treat Obsessive–Compulsive Disorder
Horizontal (a) and sagittal (b) MRIs of a patient who received a cingulotomy, disconnecting cingulate cortex connections (arrows), in an attempt to treat OCD. (From Martuza et al., 1990; courtesy of Robert L. Martuza.)

The two types of hypotheses are not mutually exclusive. Undoubtedly, a full understanding of any mental disorder will reveal both anatomical and neurochemical changes. We can hope that such knowledge will provide a means of relieving or preventing these cruel states.

Summary

1. Biological approaches have enabled better distinctions within large classes of mental disorders, such as schizophrenia and anxiety.

2. There is strong evidence for a genetic factor in the origin of schizophrenia. Consistent evidence comes from studies of the incidence of schizophrenia in families, twins, and adoptees.

3. Structural changes in the brains of schizophrenics may arise from early developmental problems.

4. Biological theories of schizophrenia include two general classes of ideas: (1) the view that schizophrenia comes about because of failure at a particular level in the operation of neurotransmitters at synapses, and

TABLE 16.5 *Some Hypothetical Biological Causes of Mental Disorders*

Hypothesis	Proposed cause(s) of disorders
Anatomical hypotheses	
Destruction/deficiency or loss of neural components	Fault in development produced by genetic mechanisms or exposure to toxins, viruses, or bacteria
	Brain injury
	Vascular interference, such as stroke
	Excessive excitation of nerve cells (excitotoxic effects)
	Deficiency of growth regulators or maintainers
Hyperconnection	Developmental failure of synaptic pruning at any stage
	Failure of cell death in embryonic development
	Perturbed or faulty regenerative events
Cellular disorganization	Developmental errors during early prenatal development
Synaptic communication hypotheses	
Presynaptic interference	Failure to produce or release transmitter
	Excessive release of transmitter
	Failure in feedback regulation
Postsynaptic interference	Failure to terminate action of transmitter
	Reduced or excessive receptors
	Excessive excitation produced by inhibitory failure

(2) the view that schizophrenia develops from a metabolic fault that results in the production of a toxic substance, a psychotogen with properties similar to known hallucinogenic agents.

5. The dopamine hypothesis attributes schizophrenia to excess release of or sensitivity to dopamine. Supporting evidence comes from studies on the effects of antipsychotic drugs, amphetamine psychosis, and Parkinson's disease.

6. According to an integrative psychobiological model, the emergence of schizophrenia depends on the interaction of a vulnerable biological substrate and environmental stressors. The greater the biological vulnerability of an individual, the less stress is needed to precipitate a schizophrenic disorder.

7. Biological studies of affective disorders reveal a strong genetic factor and the importance of levels of various neurotransmitters, including serotonin.

8. People suffering from depression show increased blood flow in the frontal cortex and the amygdala, and decreased blood flow in the parietal and posterior temporal cortex.

9. The hypothalamic–pituitary–adrenal axis is involved in depression. Changes in REM sleep that accompany depression include shortened onset to REM sleep and larger percentages of REM sleep in overall amounts of sleep. Some sleep treatments appear to act as antidepressants.

10. Anxiety states are characterized by functional changes in the temporal lobes that can be revealed by PET scans.

11. Antianxiety drugs affect receptors for the transmitter GABA. These drugs enhance the inhibitory influence of this neurotransmitter.

12. Obsessive–compulsive disorder is characterized by changes in basal ganglia and frontal structures and strongly linked to serotonin activities.

13. Neurosurgery continues to be used as a form of psychiatric treatment in a limited number of instances.

Recommended Reading

Bloom, F. E., and Kupfer, D. J. (Eds.). (1995). *Psychopharmacology: The fourth generation of progress.* New York: Raven.

Fogel, B. S., and Schiffer, R. B. (1996). *Neuropsychiatry: A comprehensive textbook.* New York: Williams and Wilkins.

Gottesman, I. I. (1995). *Schizophrenia genesis: The origins of madness.* New York: Freeman.

Nathan, P. E., and Gorman, J. M. (Eds.). (1998). *A guide to treatments that work.* New York: Oxford University Press.

Torrey, E. F., Bowler, A. E., Taylor, E. H., and Gottesman, I. I. (1994). *Schizophrenia and manic depressive disorder.* New York: Basic Books.

Whybrow, P. C. (1997). *A mood apart.* New York: Basic Books.

Cognitive Neuroscience

*P*lasticity of behavior and the nervous system is the central theme of this book, and Part 6 concentrates on this theme. Learning and memory, language, and cognition are the fascinating focal points of much current research. We start Part 6 with a top-down approach in Chapter 17, describing learning and memory in whole organisms and identifying the associated neural regions and systems. In Chapter 18 we investigate the neuronal and synaptic mechanisms and the neural networks that may underlie learning and memory. Chapter 19 focuses on the most elaborate products of brain function: the biology of language and cognitive states that are so distinctively human.

Striking cases of impaired memory start our discussion. We can discover a great deal about learning and memory by examining how they fail. Clinical cases show that memory can fail in quite different ways, and these observations support the conclusion that there are different kinds of learning and memory. The clinical cases also provide clues about the brain regions that are especially involved in memory. Carefully designed animal research has delved deeper into this question. And now, noninvasive brain imaging is helping investigators acquire new evidence about the brain mechanisms of learning and memory. Together these and other approaches are providing converging evidence to yield a comprehensive picture of the brain mechanisms.

17 Learning and Memory: Biological Perspectives

*I*nvestigating learning and memory and their biological mechanisms is one of the most active and exciting areas of biological psychology. All the distinctively human aspects of our behavior are learned: the languages we speak, how we dress, the foods we eat and how we eat them. Much of our own individuality depends on learning and memory. Research on learning and memory gives us a better understanding of almost all the topics we have taken up so far, because almost every aspect of behavior and cognition requires learning: how we perceive, the skilled acts we perform, our motivations, and the ways we achieve our goals. Conditions that impair memory are particularly frightening; they make it impossible to take part in normal social life and can rob us of our identity.

Valuable research on learning and memory is being done at all the levels of organization of the nervous system, from the intact organism to subcellular mechanisms. A major theme in this chapter is the search for the

Arturo Rodriguez, *Self-Portrait*, 1987

neural regions involved in learning and memory. In this search, investigators use a variety of techniques: studying people with impaired memory; examining the effects of precise, experimental brain lesions in animals on learning and memory; and making noninvasive brain scans of people with normal abilities while they learn or remember tasks that are carefully designed to bring out particular aspects of learning or remembering.

Many Kinds of Brain Damage Can Impair Memory

Many kinds of brain damage, caused by disease or accident, impair learning and memory, and study of such cases is continuing to provide powerful lessons. We'll start by looking at some of these cases before progressing to newer brain imaging techniques that provide novel information about the involvement of brain regions in learning and memory. Study of different types of memory impairment has revealed the existence of different classes of learning and memory, which we will discuss later in the chapter. First, let's look at a few cases of memory impairment that have posed puzzles and have stimulated a great deal of controversy.

For Patient H.M. the Present Vanishes into Oblivion

Henry, known in the literature as *patient H.M.*, had suffered from epileptic seizures since the age of 16. His condition became steadily worse and could not be controlled by medication; he had to stop work at the age of 27. His symptoms indicated that the seizures began in the medial basal regions of both temporal lobes, so in 1953 a neurologist removed this tissue, including much of the amygdala and hippocampus on both sides; this was confirmed in a recent MRI study (Figure 17.1) (Corkin et al., 1997; Hilts, 1995; Scoville and Milner, 1957). (To examine the anatomy of the hippocampus and neighboring structures, see the *Sylvius* brain atlas.) Similar operations had been performed earlier without harmful effects, although in those cases less tissue had been removed. Upon recovery from the operation, Henry's seizures were milder, and they could be controlled by medication. But this relief came at a terrible, unforeseen price: Henry now suffered a peculiar kind of amnesia. **Amnesia** (Greek for "forgetfulness") is a severe impairment of memory; however, most patients with amnesia retain some memories.

Sylvius

Most of Henry's old memories remained intact, but he had difficulty retrieving memories that had formed during the 10 years before the operation. Such memory loss is called **retrograde amnesia** (from the Latin roots *retro-* and *gradi,* "to go backward"). Retrograde amnesia is not rare. What was striking about Henry was an unusual symptom: his apparent inability to retain *new* material for more than a brief period. When he met someone new, almost as soon as that person left the room Henry was unable to recall the person's name or even that he had met someone. The inability to form new memories after the onset of an illness is called **anterograde amnesia** (from the Latin roots *antero-* and *gradi,* "to go forward").

Even now, years after the operation, Henry retains a new fact only briefly; as soon as he is distracted, the newly acquired information vanishes. He doesn't

17.1 Brain Tissue Removed in the Operation on Patient H.M.
(*a*) Approximately corresponding MRI scans of a normal subject (*left*) and patient H.M. (*right*) show that the hippocampus (H) and entorhinal cortex (EC), which are prominent in the normal scan, are absent bilaterally in H.M. (*b*) A more caudal scan (see drawing at top for planes of section) shows some of the hippocampal formation intact (H), but the parahippocampus (PH) is absent, and H.M.'s cerebellum is markedly atrophied. f=fornix, V=lateral ventricle. (From Corkin et al., 1997; courtesy of Suzanne Corkin.)

know his age or the current date, and he doesn't know that his parents (with whom he lived) died years ago. But he converses easily, and his IQ remains a little above average (Corkin et al., 1997).

There are a few indications that Henry has formed some bits of long-term memory in the years since his operation. For example, when asked where he is, he sometimes guesses MIT (the Massachusetts Institute of Technology), the place where he has been interviewed and tested many times in the last 40 years. Henry recognizes that something is wrong with him because he has no memories of the past several years or even of what he did earlier in the same day. His description of this isolation from his past is poignant (B. Milner, 1970, p. 37):

> Every day is alone in itself, whatever enjoyment I've had, and whatever sorrow I've had. . . . Right now,

I'm wondering, have I done or said anything amiss? You see, at this moment everything looks clear to me, but what happened just before? That's what worries me. It's like waking from a dream. I just don't remember.

Henry's short-term memory is normal. For example, if he is given a series of digits and is asked to repeat the list immediately, he, like most people, can usually repeat a list of seven digits without error. But if he is given a list of words to study and is tested on them after other tasks have intervened, he cannot repeat the list; in fact, he does not even remember having studied the list. Thus, Henry's case provides clear evidence that short-term memory (STM) differs from long-term memory (LTM). Psychologists have recognized the distinction between STM and LTM on behavioral and cognitive grounds since the time of William James (1890). Short-term memory is usually considered to last for only about 30 s, or as long as a person rehearses the material; it holds only a limited number of items (J. Brown, 1958; L. R. Peterson and Peterson, 1959). Long-term memory is an enduring form that lasts for hours, days, weeks, or more; it has very large capacity. We will discuss long- and short-term memory in more depth later in this chapter.

After publication of Henry's case, similar cases were reported that resulted not from brain surgery but from disease. On rare occasions, herpes simplex virus destroys tissue in the medial temporal lobe. This destruction can produce a severe failure to form new long-term memories, although acquisition of short-term memories is normal (A. R. Damasio, Eslinger, et al., 1985). Rupture of the anterior cerebral arteries that damages basal forebrain regions, including the hippocampus, can cause amnesia (A. R. Damasio, Graff-Radford, et al., 1985). An episode of reduced blood supply to the brain (ischemia), such as can be produced by a heart attack, can also damage the medial temporal lobe and memory formation. Within this general region of the brain, can we pinpoint a specific site as the cause of these memory problems?

At first, Henry's memory deficit was ascribed to bilateral destruction of much of the hippocampus, because other surgery patients who had received the same type of damage to more anterior structures, including the amygdala, but less damage to the hippocampus, did not exhibit memory impairment. To test this hypothesis, investigators began to remove the hippocampus from experimental animals to reproduce H.M.'s deficit. But after a decade of research, brain scientists had to confess failure: Neither in rats nor in monkeys did widespread failure of memory consolidation follow bilateral destruction of the hippocampus; the effects that were observed could not be distinguished from possible effects of motivational or perceptual factors (Isaacson, 1972).

Different investigators attempted to account for this puzzling discrepancy between human and animal

results in different ways. Some investigated the roles of various structures in the medial temporal lobe and the diencephalon; others looked more carefully into the behavioral tests used to measure memory. This broadened research produced major gains in knowledge—about amnesia in people and ways to test memory, about functions of the hippocampus and neighboring structures, and about brain mechanisms of memory. Later in this chapter we will review research with both human and animal subjects that reveals more precisely the structures in the medial temporal lobe where damage causes symptoms like those of Henry. Before such research could yield useful results, however, it was necessary to define more exactly what was impaired and what was spared in Henry's memory.

An early, incorrect hypothesis to explain why human results differed from those in other animals was that the impairment caused by damage to the medial temporal lobe in humans involves chiefly *verbal* material and that animals, of course, cannot be tested for such deficits. An interesting finding suggested that Henry's memory deficit was restricted mainly to verbal material and might not hold for motor learning. Brenda Milner (1965) presented a mirror-tracing test to Henry (Figure 17.2*a*), and he showed considerable improvement over ten trials. The next day the test was presented again. When asked if he remembered it, he said no, but his performance was better than at the start of the first day (Figure 17.2*b*). Over three successive days, Henry never recognized the problem, but his improved tracings showed memory. If an animal subject with the same type of brain damage showed similar proof of memory, we would have no doubt that the animal had normal memory, because we do not ask animal subjects whether they *recognize* the test.

Brenda Milner

Two other types of findings, however, indicated that the memory problems of Henry and similar patients could not be attributed solely to difficulties with verbal material. First, such patients also have difficulty in reproducing or recognizing pictures and spatial designs that are not recalled in verbal terms. Second, although the patients have difficulty with the specific content of verbal material, they can learn some kinds of information *about* verbal material (N. J. Cohen and Squire, 1980). For example, they can learn to read words printed mirror-reversed. The requirement for this task is not motor skill, but rather the ability to deal with abstract rules or procedures. If some words are used repeatedly, normal subjects come to recognize them and to read them easily. Patients of several kinds—those with temporal lobe amnesia, those who suffer from Korsakoff's syndrome (which we will de-

Competing hypotheses

scribe shortly), and those who have recently received electroconvulsive shock therapy—learn the *skill* of mirror reading well but show impaired learning of the specific words.

Thus, the important distinction is probably not between motor and verbal performances but between two kinds of memory: (1) **Declarative memory** is what we usually think of as memory: facts and information acquired through learning. It is memory we are aware of accessing. (2) **Nondeclarative memory** is shown by performance rather than by conscious recollection. It is sometimes called **procedural memory**. Examples of nondeclarative memory are memory for the mirror-tracing task and for the skill of mirror reading, as we just described. The two kinds of memory can be distinguished as follows: Declarative memory deals with *what*; nondeclarative memory deals with *how*. Thus, an animal's inability to speak is probably not what accounts for its apparent immunity to the effects of medial temporal lesions on memory storage. Rather, the culprit is the difficulty in measuring declarative memory in animals.

Different types of tests measure declarative and nondeclarative memories. *Direct* (or explicit) tests of memory refer to a specific prior episode. Examples of direct tests include requests for information such as

(a) The mirror-tracing task

(b) Performance of H.M. on mirror-tracing task

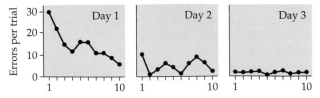

17.2 H.M.'s Performance on a Mirror-Tracing Task
(a) Mirror-tracing task. (b) Performance of H.M. at this task on three successive days shows progressive improvement and thus long-term memory. (After B. Milner, 1965.)

"Repeat the list of words you studied 10 minutes ago" or "What did you eat for dinner yesterday?" They also have been defined as requiring conscious recognition of the material. *Indirect* (or implicit) tests of memory do not refer to a specific prior episode and do not require conscious recognition; the memory is inferred from performance. For example, memory for the recent presentation of certain words may be inferred from ease of recognizing them, versus control words, in blurred or very rapid presentation or from the probability of using them in a word completion test.

Damage to the Medial Diencephalon Can Also Prevent Formation of New Memories

The medial temporal lobe is not the only brain region involved in the formation of declarative memories. For example, the case of *patient N.A.* indicates that damage to the dorsomedial thalamus can impair memory formation (Squire and Moore, 1979; Teuber et al., 1968). N.A. became amnesic as a result of a bizarre accident in which a miniature fencing foil entered his brain through the nostril. N.A. is markedly amnesic, primarily for verbal material, and he can give little information about events since his accident in 1960, but he shows almost normal recall for events of the 1940s and 1950s.

An MRI study of N.A. (Figure 17.3) shows damage to the left dorsal thalamus, bilateral damage to the mammillary nuclei, and probable damage to the mammillothalamic tract (Squire et al., 1989). The devastating effects of this deficit on N.A.'s daily life are described in Topic 17.1, How Do You Live When You Can't Form New Memories? Like H.M., N.A. shows normal short-term memory but impaired long-term memory, and the **Special topic** difficulty in long-term memory is in forming declarative, but not nondeclarative, memories. The similarity in symptoms raises the question of whether the medial temporal region and the midline diencephalic region are parts of a larger system. We will return to this question in Chapter 18.

Patients with Korsakoff's Syndrome Show Damage to Midline Diencephalic Structures and to the Frontal Cortex

In the 1880s a Russian neurologist published a paper about a syndrome in which impaired memory was a major feature. This paper became a classic, and the condition was subsequently named after him: **Korsakoff's syndrome**. Sufferers of Korsakoff's syndrome fail to recall many items or events of the past; if such an item is presented again or if it happens to be recalled, the patient does not feel familiar with it. Korsakoff's patients frequently deny that anything is wrong with them. They often show disorientation as to time and place, and they may **confabulate**—that is, fill a gap in memory with a falsification that they seem to accept as true.

The main cause of Korsakoff's syndrome is lack of the vitamin thiamine. Alcoholics who obtain most of their calories from alcohol and neglect their diet often exhibit this deficiency. Treating such a person with thiamine can prevent further deterioration of memory functions. Animal models of Korsakoff's syndrome are created through either drug-induced thiamine deficiency (Langlais et al., 1992) or surgical lesions.

Mair et al. (1979) examined two Korsakoff's patients for several years, using a battery of behavioral tests; later they examined the brains of these patients in detail. Both brains showed shrunken, diseased mammillary bodies, as well as some damage in the dorsomedial thalamus. Temporal lobe structures, including the hippocampus and the temporal stem, were normal. Thus these cases confirm the less precise, earlier studies. Mair et al. (1979, p. 778) characterize the mammillary bodies as "a narrow funnel through which connections from the midbrain as well as the temporal lobe neocortex and limbic system gain access to the frontal lobes." Damage to the basal frontal lobes, also found in Korsakoff's patients, is probably what differentiates them from other amnesia patients, such as H.M.

Patient K.C. Shows That Damage to the Cerebral Cortex Can Impair Retention or Retrieval of Memories

Damage to the cerebral cortex impairs memory in many cases, perhaps by destroying some memory stores or by preventing access to memories. Sensory maps in the cortex change with experience (see Chapter 8), and some investigators believe that these changes reflect cortical storage of memories. Cortical damage may destroy the ability to recognize certain kinds of stimuli. One example is the loss of ability to recognize faces (prosopagnosia) after damage to the inferotemporal cortex; another is the specific inability to understand words after damage to cortical language areas (see Chapter 19). Each region of the cerebral cortex may store the kinds of information it processes.

A striking case involving cortical damage shows profound effects on memory. It also supports an important distinction between two kinds of declarative

Endel Tulving

memory that cognitive psychologist Endel Tulving (1972) had defined: semantic memory and episodic memory. **Semantic memory** is generalized memory, such as knowing the meaning of a word without knowing where or when you learned that word. **Episodic memory** is autobiographical memory that pertains to a person's particular history; you show episodic memory when you recall a specific episode or relate an event to a particular time and place (such as remembering where and when you last saw a certain friend).

17.3 MRI Images Show Brain Damage in Amnesia Patient N.A.

Successive scans were made through the diencephalic region (*top*); note that right and left are reversed in these scans, as if you were face-to-face with the patient. A prominent lesion on the left side of the brain is indicated by the blue arrows. The floor of the third ventricle also appears to be missing throughout much of the caudal two-thirds of the hypothalamus, as indicated by the red arrows in scans A through C. Where the mammillary nuclei should be present in B and C, there is no indication of intact tissue. (From Squire et al., 1989; MRI scans courtesy of Larry Squire.)

Evidence for the distinction between semantic and episodic memory appeared in studies of a man known as *patient K.C.*, who suffered extensive damage to the left frontal-parietal and the right parietal-occipital cerebral cortex in a traffic accident. He can no longer retrieve any personal memory of his past, although his general knowledge remains good (Tulving, 1989). He converses easily and plays a good game of chess, but he cannot remember where he learned to play chess or from whom. K.C. has difficulty acquiring new semantic knowledge, but he can acquire some, if care is taken to space out the trials to prevent interference among items (Tulving et al., 1991). But even with this method he cannot acquire new episodic knowledge.

Studies of normal human subjects indicate increased blood flow in the anterior regions of the cortex during recall of episodic memories, and increases in posterior regions during recall of semantic materials, so the anterior cortical damage may be what robs K.C. of episodic memory (Tulving, 1989).

There Are Several Kinds of Memory and Learning

By now we have mentioned the distinctions between declarative and nondeclarative memories and between semantic and episodic memories. We will also be discussing some other kinds of memories and seeking to find the brain regions that are especially involved in them, so Figure 17.4 presents a classification of some of the main kinds of long-term memory. In addition, Box 17.1 reviews some basic definitions of learning.

In **skill learning**, subjects perform a challenging task on repeated trials in one or more sessions. The mirror-tracing task performed by H.M. (see Figure 17.2) is an example. Learning to read mirror-reversed text, also mentioned earlier, is a kind of perceptual skill learning.

Priming, or repetition priming, is a change in the processing of a stimulus, usually a word or a picture, as a result of prior exposure to the same stimulus or related stimuli. For example, if a person is shown the word "stamp" in a list and later is asked to complete the word stem STA__, he or she is more likely to reply "stamp" than is a person who was not exposed to that word. Even patients like H.M., who do not recall being shown the list of words, nevertheless show the effect of prior presentation or priming.

Conditioning, shown at lower right in Figure 17.4, is defined in Box 17.1. Different brain areas are re-

sponsible for conditioning depending on the complexity of the conditioning situation.

Even "Simple" Learning May Be Complex

It is important to keep in mind that even relatively simple learning situations may be rather complex. A few examples will illustrate. For a fuller treatment of this topic, see Topic 17.2, Even "Simple" Learning May Be Complex.

⬛ **Special topic**

Conditional Learning Depends on Context

Typical examples of learning have multiple dimensions, as conditional learning reveals. In **conditional learning**, the subject learns that a particular response to a particular stimulus is appropriate in one setting but not in another. More formally, the conditioned stimulus (CS) or unconditioned stimulus (US) becomes associated with the context in which it occurs. A CS evokes a conditioned response (CR) in one context but evokes no response (or not as strong a response) in another. For example, if you are playing a game and a ball flies toward your face, you catch it if you are playing on a basketball court, but you give it a header if you are playing on a soccer field. Conditional learning does not require a big brain, or any brain at all; the relatively simple mollusk *Aplysia* can do it, as described in an experiment in Topic 17.2, Even "Simple" Learning May Be Complex (Colwill et al., 1988).

⬛ **Special topic**

The investigators point out that their "findings highlight the potential complexity of Pavlovian conditioning processes. Moreover, they demonstrate the inadequacy of accounts of associative learning that appeal exclusively to close temporal proximity of the CS and the US for learning to occur" (Colwill et al., 1988, p. 4443). In the next section we will see further evidence that temporal proximity of CS and US is not necessary for conditioning.

Close Temporal Pairing of Stimuli Is Not Necessary for Conditioning

Neuroscientists have often assumed that close temporal proximity of CS and US is required for conditioning, but several experiments during the 1960s demonstrated that such pairing is neither necessary nor sufficient. Although proximity is important in some experiments, such as the eyeblink conditioning of mammals that we will describe shortly, it would be wrong to overgeneralize from these examples. Proximity does not guarantee conditioning, and conditioning does not

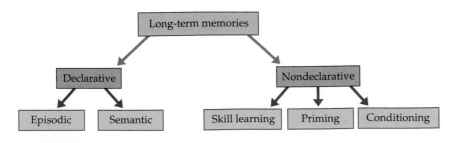

17.4 Kinds of Long-Term Memory

necessarily require proximity, as experiments going back to Pavlov (1927) demonstrate. In order for conditioning to occur, the CS must be a reliable *predictor* of the US—in fact, the most reliable predictor available (Rescorla, 1988).

Several kinds of conditioning have an optimal CS–US interval, but the optimum varies considerably depending on the task. For conditioning the eye-blink reflex in mammals, the interval is about 200 ms; for the siphon- or gill-withdrawal reflex in *Aplysia*, about 0.5 s; for operant-conditioned bar pressing in rats, about 2 s; and for taste aversion in rats (see Chapter 13), an hour or more. This wide variation in optimal CS–US interval raises the question of whether temporal pairing of stimuli is a general requirement for conditioning.

Conditioned Responses Have Many Dimensions

In conditioning, both the response and the stimulus tend to have multiple dimensions. Consider the example of eye-blink conditioning, which is studied in both human and animal subjects. In these experiments a tone or buzzer (the conditioned stimulus) precedes a puff of air to the eye (the unconditioned stimulus) that causes the subject to blink. After a few trials, the subject begins to blink in response to the CS, *before* the puff of air is delivered. Blinking early protects the eye from the mildly unpleasant air puff. But even before subjects develop the specific conditioned response (CR) of blinking to the CS, they show some unspecific CRs that may include increases in heart rate and blood pressure, changes in respiration, and changes in electrical resistance of the skin. These nonspecific autonomic responses develop earlier than the appearance of the specific CR in many situations, especially if the US is aversive; perhaps they help prepare the subject to respond to a novel or threatening situation.

Do Animals Learn Stimulus–Response Chains or Form Cognitive Maps?

Many psychologists in the 1930s and 1940s were searching for the laws that govern all learning. Psychologists such as Clark L. Hull held that animals form stimulus–response associations reinforced by rewards or punishments, and they applied this to behavior such as that of rats in runways or mazes (Hull, 1943). An opposing position was that of Edward C. Tolman (1932/1949b), who held that when rats explore a maze, they are not learning a series of turns, but instead forming a **cognitive map**. For example, after rats had run a maze several times, the experimenters removed a section of wall, thus opening up a shortcut to the goal area. Most rats took the shortcut as soon as it became available, thus showing their knowledge of the overall layout of the maze.

Edward Tolman
(1886–1959)

Tolman and his students also demonstrated that rats' performance may not reveal all they know unless the test situation is appropriate to reveal the knowledge. One kind of evidence for this is the phenomenon called **latent learning**, described in the following experiment (Blodgett, 1929; Tolman and Honzik, 1930). Rats were divided into two groups and were allowed to gain experience in a maze. One group received food when they reached the goal area of the maze; they ran to that area more and more quickly in successive daily trials. Animals of the other group were allowed to explore the maze for a few daily sessions without receiving any reward. Then, in one session, they found food in the goal area. On the next trial, they raced to the goal, reaching it just as rapidly as the rats that had been rewarded on every trial. If the experimenter hadn't offered the reward, he would not have realized that the previously unrewarded group had learned the maze as well as the uniformly rewarded rats; until the reward was introduced, the learning was latent, just as an image on photographic film is latent until the film is developed.

Later, from his surveys of research on learning, Tolman accepted, at least provisionally, the observations of a variety of researchers; he proposed that there are different kinds of learning and that each may have its own laws. He stated these views in an article entitled "There Is More than One Kind of Learning" (Tolman 1949a). A quarter century passed before many workers began to follow the suggestion to look for separate laws for different kinds of learning.

Memory Has Temporal Stages: Short, Intermediate, and Long

The terms "learning" and "memory" are so often paired that it sometimes seems as if one necessarily implies the other. We cannot be sure that learning has occurred unless a memory can be elicited later. (Here we are using "memory" in the common meaning of anything that shows that learning has occurred.) Even demonstrating that *something* has been learned, however, does not guarantee that the memory for the learned material will be retrievable again in the future. A memory may later be absent for a variety of reasons: It may never have formed, it may have decayed with time, it may have been impaired by injury to the brain, or it may be temporarily unretrievable because of the particular state of the subject.

Investigators often contrast short-term and long-term memories, but like many twofold distinctions, this differentiation is probably too simple. The multiple-trace hypothesis of memory classifies different types of memory by duration (Figure 17.5). The briefest memories are called **iconic memories** (from the Greek *eikon*, "image"). An example would be impressions of a scene that is illuminated for only an instant. You may be able to grasp one part of the display,

BOX 17.1 *Learning and Memory: Some Basic Concepts and Definitions*

Since you probably have studied learning and memory in one or more psychology courses, here we only briefly review some of the basic concepts and definitions. Basic experiments on learning and memory, as described for neuroscientists by Rescorla (1988), examine the organism's experience and behavior at two separate times. At the first time (t_1), the organism is exposed to a particular experience—a sensory stimulus or another opportunity to learn. At a later time (t_2), the investigator assesses the organism to determine whether the t_1 experience has modified its behavior. The aim is to determine whether a particular t_1 experience produces an outcome at t_2 that would be absent without the t_1 experience. Therefore, studies of learning usually compare two organisms (or two groups of organisms) at t_2: those that were exposed to the t_1 experience and those that did not have that experience but instead had a "control" experience at t_1. The basic learning paradigms can be organized in terms of the different types of experience provided at t_1 and the different techniques of assessment used at t_2.

There are three main experimental paradigms:

1. A single stimulus (S1), without any other event or constraint, is presented to the organism. The result may be habituation, dishabituation, or sensitization (defined below).
2. One stimulus (S1) is presented in relation with another stimulus (S2). This paradigm (called Pavlovian, or classical, conditioning; see below) allows us to study how the organism learns about the structure of its environment and the relations among stimuli in its world.
3. A single stimulus (S1) is delivered in such a way as to reinforce a certain behavior. Called instrumental, or operant, conditioning (see below), this paradigm allows us to study how an organism learns about the impact of its own actions on the world.

Nonassociative learning involves only a single stimulus at t_1. Three kinds of nonassociative learning are habituation, dishabituation, and sensitization. **Habituation** is a decrease in response to a stimulus as the stimulus is repeated (when the decrement cannot be attributed to sensory adaptation or motor fatigue). When the response to a stimulus has become habituated, a strong stimulus (of the same sort or even in another sensory modality) will often cause the response to the habituated stimulus to increase sharply in amplitude; it may become even larger than the original response. The increase in response amplitude over the baseline level is called **dishabituation** (the habituation has been removed). Even a response that has not been habituated may increase in amplitude after a strong stimulus. This effect is known as **sensitization**: The response is greater than its baseline level because of prior stimulation.

Learning that involves relations between events—for example, between two or more stimuli, between a stimulus and a response, or between a response and its consequence—is called **associative learning**. In one form, **classical conditioning** (also called **Pavlovian conditioning**), an initially neutral stimulus comes to predict an event. At the end of the nineteenth century, Ivan Pavlov (Figure A) found that a dog would salivate when presented with an auditory or visual stimulus if the stimulus came to predict an event that normally caused salivation. Thus, if the experimenter rang a bell just before putting meat powder in the dog's mouth, repeating this sequence a few times would cause the dog to respond to the bell itself by salivating. In this case the sound is called the **conditioned stimulus** (**CS**) and the meat powder in the mouth is the **unconditioned stimulus** (**US**); the meat powder already evokes an **unconditioned response** (**UR**), and the acquired response to the CS (salivation in response to the bell in this example) is called the **conditioned response** (**CR**).

In **instrumental conditioning** (also called **operant conditioning**), an association is formed between the animal's behavior and its consequence(s). The first investigation of instrumental learning was Edward L. Thorndike's report (1898) of cats learning to escape from a puzzle box (Figure B). When placed in a small box with

but the rest vanishes in seconds. (A very brief auditory memory is called echoic, as if you could still hear it ringing in your ears.) These brief memories are thought to reflect the continuation of sensory neural activity, the so-called sensory buffers (see Figure 17.5).

Somewhat longer than iconic memories are **short-term memories** (**STMs**). For example, suppose you want to call a person on the telephone using a number that you have never used before. You look up the number, and if nothing distracts or interrupts you, you call the number successfully, displaying an STM of the telephone number. If the line is busy, however, and you want to call back a minute later, you may have to look the number up again unless you have been repeating it to yourself in the meantime. If you rehearse or use the number, then it can remain in STM until you turn to another activity.

Unfortunately, the label "STM" is not used consistently among investigators from different fields. Cognitive psychologists, who first used the term, found that if subjects are not allowed to rehearse, STM lasts only about 30 s (J. Brown, 1958; L. R. Peterson and Peterson, 1959). Many biologists define STM as memory that is not permanent but that lasts for minutes or

(A) Pavlov and spectators in his laboratory

(B) Thorndike's puzzle box

stimulus (the bell) and the meat powder, but also many other aspects of the situation. They learned the location of the test apparatus and the rewarding features of the test situation, so when the dogs came into the test room they would eagerly leap onto the test stand. They also learned when in the day to expect to be tested. Thorndike's cats learned sensory aspects of the test situation, as well as the correct motor responses.

Different brain regions may process different dimensions or attributes of a learning or memory situation: space, time, sensory dimensions, response, and emotional aspects (Kesner et al., 1993; McDonald and White, 1993). Later in the chapter we will consider some experiments performed to test this so-called **attribute model of memory**.

(C) A "Skinner box"

a latch inside, a cat would initially engage in a variety of behaviors and take quite a bit of time to free itself. But after several trial-and-error sequences, the cat learned to perform skillfully and economically the specific response (the conditioned instrumental response) that permitted escape (the reward). A modern example of an apparatus designed to study instrumental learning is an operant conditioning apparatus, often called a *Skinner box* after its orginator, B. F. Skinner (Figure C). Here the conditioned instrumental response is pressing a bar to gain the reward of a food pellet.

Some investigators emphasize that typical learning events have multiple dimensions or attributes. For example, Pavlov's dogs learned not only the relation between the conditioned auditory

hours, even up to a day. Thus, Kandel et al. (1987) wrote that in the sea slug *Aplysia*, "a single training trial produces short-term sensitization that lasts from minutes to hours" (p. 17), and long-term memory is "memory that lasts more than one day" (p. 35). The lack of agreement on the duration of short-term and long-term memory undermines attempts to find biological mechanisms of the temporal stages of memory.

Some memories last beyond the short term but fall short of long-term memories. For example, suppose you drive to school or work and park your car in a different place each day. If things go well, you remember each afternoon where you parked your car that morning, but you may not recall where you parked your car yesterday or a week ago. You are also likely to recall today's weather forecast, but not that of a few days ago. These are examples of what is sometimes called **intermediate-term memory** (**ITM**)—that is, a memory that outlasts STM but that is far from being permanent (McGaugh, 1966; Rosenzweig et al., 1993).

Beyond ITM are memories that last for weeks, months, and years; these are called **long-term memories** (**LTMs**). Because many memories that last for days or weeks do, however, become weaker and may even fade out completely with time, some investigators use the term **permanent memory** to designate memories that appear to continue without decline for the rest of the life of an organism, or at least as long as the organism remains in good health.

The fact that some memories last only for seconds and others for months is not proof that short-term memories are based on cognitive or biological mechanisms that differ from those of long-term memories. The scientist's task is to find out whether these memories are based on the same or different processes and mechanisms. As we will see, there are good reasons—both clinical and experimental—to conclude that the cognitive processes and biological mechanisms that underlie STM storage are different from those that underlie LTM storage.

Early behavioral evidence for differences between short-term and long-term memory stores came from the performance of subjects who learned lists of words or numbers. If you see or hear a list of ten words presented one at a time, and then 30 s later you try to repeat the list, you will probably remember best the first and the last items of the list. Figure 17.6 shows typical results from such an experiment—a U-shaped serial position curve. The superior performance for the start of the list is called the **primacy effect**. The superior performance for the end of the list, is called the **recency effect**. If subjects try to recall the list a few minutes after having seen or heard the items, there is no recency effect; it is short-lived and thus attributed to STM. The primacy effect, however, lasts longer and is usually attributed to LTM.

Experimental animals also show U-shaped serial position functions. These results provide one type of behavioral evidence to separate STM from a longer-lasting memory store (or stores) in animal subjects, and they offer the possibility of relating behavioral and biological mechanisms of memory stages in the same subjects. Wright et al. (1985) gave similar recog-

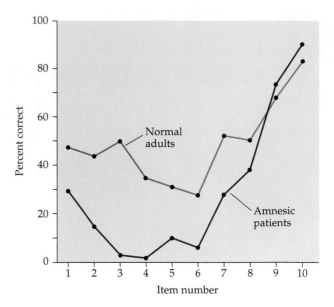

17.6 Serial Position Curves Characterize the Results of Immediate-Recall Experiments
These curves show the percentage of correct responses for immediate recall of a list of ten words. The amnesic patients perform as well on the most recent items (8 through 10) as do the normal adults, but they perform significantly worse on earlier items. (After Baddeley and Warrington, 1970.)

nition memory tests to pigeons, monkeys, and humans. For each test, the material consisted of four sequentially presented color slides. Each slide was presented for 1 s to monkeys and humans and 2 s to pigeons, with a 1 s interval between items for all groups. After a delay, a probe item was presented; on half the trials the probe item matched one of the four test patterns. Subjects demonstrated their memory by making one response if the probe matched a test item and another response if it was new.

All three species showed primacy and recency effects in their serial position curves (Figure 17.7). The human subjects showed both primacy and recency effects when the delay between presentation of the items and the test varied from 10 to 60 s. If the test was administered earlier than 10 s after the items were seen, no primacy effect was found; this result was attributed to retroactive interference from the test items. If the test was administered later than 60 s after the items were seen, then no recency effect was present, but the primacy effect still occurred. Monkeys showed both primacy and recency effects for delays from 1 to 10 s, and pigeons showed both effects at delays of 1 and 2 s, but not at shorter or longer delays. Thus, results for all three species provide evidence of two distinct memory processes: a transient STM that accounts for the short-lived recency effect, and a longer-lasting memory store that accounts for the primacy effect.

Brain lesion studies corroborate the parallel between humans and experimental animals: Rats with

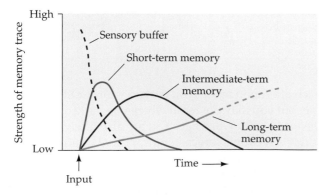

17.5 Multiple-Trace Hypothesis of Memory
According to this hypothesis, an initial brief sensory buffer is followed by a short-term memory trace, which may be followed by an intermediate-term memory trace. If the learning is sufficiently strong, a long-term memory trace may also result. (After McGaugh, 1968.)

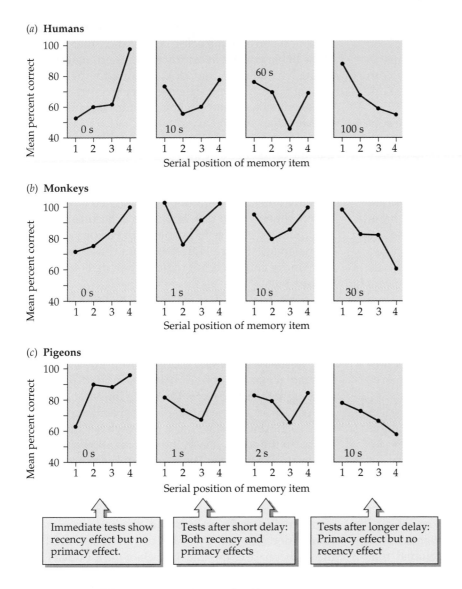

(a) Humans

(b) Monkeys

(c) Pigeons

Immediate tests show recency effect but no primacy effect.

Tests after short delay: Both recency and primacy effects

Tests after longer delay: Primacy effect but no recency effect

17.7 Recognition Memory Curves for Humans, Monkeys, and Pigeons
The curves show the percentage of correct responses to a probe item for four positions in the stimulus series, for humans (a), monkeys (b), and pigeons (c). "Novel" indicates an item that matched none of the four list items. (After Wright et al., 1985.)

of most people hold huge numbers of memories and can acquire enormous amounts more. For example, American college students can recognize, on the average, about 50,000 different words. Many people who master several languages readily acquire even vaster vocabularies. Beyond the words, a person who speaks a language knows its grammar and grammatical forms, its idioms, and its familiar phrases; it is estimated that learning a language means acquiring on the order of 100,000 items of knowledge. Most of us recognize hundreds or thousands of faces and countless visual scenes and objects, hundreds of voices and many other familiar sounds, and hundreds of different odors. Depending on our interests, we may be able to recognize and sing or play many tunes and identify and supply information about a great many athletes, actors, or historical characters.

Such memories can be acquired rapidly and retained well. For example, Canadian psychologist Lionel Standing (1973) presented subjects with color slides for 5 s each in blocks of 20 to 1000 or more slides. A few days later he tested recognition memory by presenting pairs of slides, one previously seen and one new, and requiring sub-

hippocampal lesions exhibit the recency but not the primacy effect, as though, like H.M., they cannot form new LTMs (Figure 17.8) (Kesner and Novak, 1982). Similarly, amnesia patients, particularly those whose amnesia is caused by impairment of the hippocampus, show a reduced primacy effect but retain the recency effect (see Figure 17.6).

The Capacity of Long-Term Memory Is Enormous

A fascinating case study of a man who remembered almost everything he had experienced from childhood on and was burdened by his total recall is presented by Russian psychologist Alexander Luria in *The Mind of a Mnemonist* (1987). Even the fallible memory stores

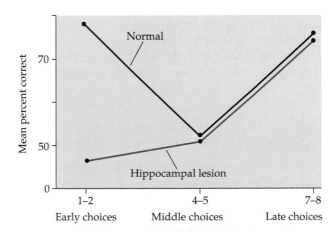

17.8 Hippocampal Lesions in Rats Eliminate the Primacy Effect in the Serial Position Curve
Normal rats and those with hippocampal lesions were tested for memory of early, middle, and late choices in an eight-arm radial maze. (After Kesner and Novak, 1982.)

jects to indicate which of the pair they had seen before. After an early study showed 90% recognition for 2560 items, Standing increased the number of items to 10,000 and found little decrease in scores. He concluded that, for all practical purposes, "there is no upper bound to memory capacity" (Standing, 1973).

Of course, these results do not mean that the subjects learned all the details of the pictures; the two-alternative, forced-choice procedure guarantees only that *something* about the picture makes it more familiar than the paired item. Nevertheless, the amount of information acquired and the rapidity of acquisition are impressive. And it doesn't require a human brain to accomplish such a task; pigeons readily learned 320 slides in a picture recognition test with no indication that this amount approached their capacity, and they retained many of the discriminations for 2 years (Vaughan and Greene, 1984). An example of such memory retention in nature is displayed by Clark's nutcracker, a bird that can locate several thousand cache sites months after hiding food in them (Vander Wall, 1982). What kind of memory mechanisms provide for the enormous capacity of long-term memory?

Can Memories Be Lost or Distorted?

Although the capacity of long-term memory is enormous, we all experience instances of forgetting and inaccurate memory. Early in the twentieth century, investigators supposed that the **memory trace** (the record laid down in memory, and presumably in the central nervous system, by a learning experience) decays or fragments with time. But then other workers studied how memories suffer interference from events before or after their formation, and many concluded that memories do not deteriorate with disuse. Further research showed that each time a memory trace is activated during recall, it is subject to changes and fluctuations, so with successive activations it may deviate more and more from its original form. Furthermore, new information that is provided at the time of recall can add new aspects to the memory trace, so a later evocation of the memory is likely to reactivate the newer traces along with the older, and produce distorted or false memories. (See Estes, 1997, for a review of research on memory loss, recovery, and distortion.)

Different Regions of the Brain Process Different Aspects of Memory

Any particular memory is composed of features or aspects that are specific and unique to that learning experience, as investigators of human memory noted decades ago (Spear, 1976; Underwood, 1969). Some of the main features (or attributes) of memories are *space, time, sensory perception, response,* and *affect* (i.e., emotional tone or content). For example, as you look at this book, you are aware of spatial aspects of your experience—where the book is in relation to you and where

you are; you know the approximate or even the exact time; you perceive the color, shape, and other aspects of the book; you are aware of making certain responses, such as holding the book, turning the page, and writing notes; and you are experiencing a particular affect or emotional state—feeling content, eager, and happy (we hope), not sad.

Biological psychologists have tested the hypothesis that the different attributes of memory are processed by different regions of the brain. For example, Raymond Kesner (1980, 1991, 1998), drawing on the reports of many other investigators, has designed a program of experiments with rats, as well as experimental and observational studies of people with various kinds of brain damage. Figure 17.9 shows some basic attributes of memory and the brain regions that are believed to process them.

Kesner tried to design a series of tasks, each of which would make animals focus especially on a particular attribute of experience. Only working, short-term memory was tested. Thus, for a *spatial recognition task*, Kesner et al. (1993) used the well-known eight-arm radial maze (Figure 17.10*a*). Appropriate pretraining taught the rat to expect to find a bit of food at the end of each arm of the maze. For the spatial recognition task, each trial consisted of a study phase and a test phase. In the study phase, the rat was allowed to run down any arm. When it returned to the central platform, all doors to the arms were closed, confining the rat for a period of 1 to 30 seconds. Next, two doors were opened, allowing the rat a choice between the arm it had recently entered and another arm; the rat found food only if it chose the arm it had entered on the study phase of the trial. In each of the four daily trials, different arms were used. Different groups of ani-

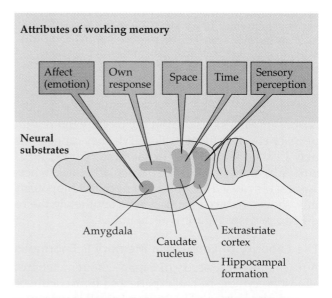

17.9 Basic Attributes of Memory and the Region of the Rat Brain Thought to Process Each (After Kesner, 1980, 1981.)

(a) Spatial location recognition memory

In the study phase of each trial, the rat can choose any of the eight arms. In the test phase, doors block all but two arms: the arm entered on the study phase and one other. The rat obtains food only if it chooses the arm it entered on the study phase.

0 ——— 184 cm

Brain region lesioned

- ● Hippocampus
- ■ Control
- ▲ Caudate nucleus
- ◇ Extrastriate visual cortex

Only rats with hippocampal lesions make significantly more errors than controls.

(b) Response recognition memory

In the first part of each trial, the rat is placed in the middle compartment on one side (2), and it finds food if it enters the compartment either to its right (1) or left (3). In the second part of the trial, it is placed in the middle compartment on the other side (5), and it finds food only if it turns to the same side as it had in the first part.

0 ——— 36 cm

Brain region lesioned

- ● Hippocampus
- ■ Control
- ▲ Caudate nucleus
- ◇ Extrastriate visual cortex

Only rats with caudate nucleus lesions make significantly more errors than controls.

(c) Object recognition memory

In the study phase of each trial, the rat obtains food by displacing a sample object over a small food well (top). In the test phase (bottom), the rat chooses between two objects and obtains food only if it chooses the object that does *not* match the sample.

0 ——— 35.5 cm

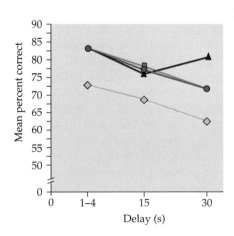

Brain region lesioned

- ● Hippocampus
- ■ Control
- ▲ Caudate nucleus
- ◇ Extrastriate visual cortex

Only rats with lesions of the extrastriate visual cortex make significantly more errors than controls.

17.10 Experiments to Test Specific Attributes of Animals' Memory

The experimental setups (left) and results (right) of different brain lesion experiments. (*a*) Spatial location recognition. (*b*) Response recognition. (*c*) Object recognition. (After Kesner et al., 1993.)

mals were tested after having received a sham lesion or a lesion in the hippocampus, the caudate nucleus, or the extrastriate cortex (visual cortex outside the primary visual area). The results of this experiment showed that only the animals with hippocampal lesions made more mistakes than the controls (the animals with sham lesions) on this predominantly spatial task.

To emphasize memory for the animal's own *response,* the investigators ran trials in a different apparatus (Figure 17.10*b*). On the study phase of a trial, the rat was placed in the middle arm on one side (e.g., 2), where it could make an initial turn to its left (3) or right (1). Then it was placed in a different starting location (5), and was rewarded only if it made a turn to the same side of its body as before, not to the same direction in space. Performance on this task, which depends on memory of the previous response, was impaired by lesions of the caudate nucleus, but not by lesions of the other regions.

A task that emphasizes *sensory perception* is the object recognition (or non-matching-to-sample) test. Using the experimental setup shown in Figure 17.10*c*, the rat was first rewarded each time it pushed aside the sample object over the center depression (top). In the test phase of the experiment (Figure 17.10*c*, bottom), the rat was presented with two objects, one like the sample object that had been presented during the study phase and one novel object; the rat was rewarded only if it chose the object that did *not* match the sample. Only lesions of the extrastriate visual cortex significantly impaired performance on this visual memory task.

Thus, Kesner et al. (1993) found a triple **dissociation** among brain regions and the tests. That is, lesions of each of three brain regions affected memory performance on only one of the three tests, and performance on each test was affected by lesions in only one of the three brain regions. This dissociation is good evidence that these different aspects of working memory are processed separately and, in part at least, by the brain regions indicated. Of course, an even more complete set of brain regions remains to be tested, if only to try to exclude them as important in processing these aspects of memory. Further work by Kesner and Williams (1995) on memory involving *affect* indicated that this attribute of memory is impaired by lesions of the amygdala, but not by lesions in the hippocampal formation or in the cerebral cortex dorsal to the hippocampus.

A similar research project in another laboratory found similar results. McDonald and White (1993) used three different problems, all run in the radial maze. They also found a triple dissociation of three neural memory systems: (1) a neural system that includes the hippocampus, which acquires information about relationships among stimuli and events (declarative memories); (2) a different neural system that includes the dorsal striatum, which mediates the formation of rein-

forced stimulus–response associations (habits, or non-declarative memories); and (3) another system that includes the amygdala, which mediates rapid acquisition of behaviors based on biologically significant events with affective properties.

Place Cells in the Hippocampus Process Spatial Memory

One of the clues that led investigators to test for the processing of spatial memory in the hippocampus was the discovery that some cells in the rat hippocampus seem to encode spatial location (O'Keefe and Dostrovsky, 1971). That is, these neurons produce action potentials preferentially when the rat is in a particular location or is moving toward that location, so they have been called **place cells**. This discovery led to a great deal of research, which continues to the present, to understand the properties of place cells and how they form.

The monkey hippocampus also contains some place cells that respond like those of rats, but in monkeys these cells are relatively less numerous than in rats (Rolls and O'Mara, 1995). More cells in the monkey hippocampus respond to the part of the environment the monkey is looking at, so investigators researching them refer to them as "spatial view cells" and suggest that they reflect the importance of vision for monkeys. Perhaps there are place or spatial cells in the hippocampus of bird species that cache and retrieve food, since they have larger hippocampal formations than species that do not cache, as we reported in Chapter 6.

Memory Processes Extend from Acquisition to Retrieval

Psychologists who study learning and memory suggest that several successive processes are necessary to guarantee recall of a past event: **encoding**, **consolidation**, and **retrieval** (Figure 17.11). The original information must enter sensory channels and then be *encoded* rapidly into a form that passes into short-term memory. Some of this information may then be *consolidated* in long-term storage. The final stage of processing is *retrieval*—that is, the use of information that was stored earlier.

Some cognitive psychologists hold that there is no essential difference between short-term and long-term memory storage; they claim that more deeply processed information is stored longer. Others claim that the neural processes for short-term and long-term memory storage differ; we will see both neurological and neurochemical evidence for this hypothesis. For example, patients with brain damage like H.M. retain new items in short-term storage but show no long-term memory for them. With the three stages outlined here in mind, investigators have tried to determine whether particular examples of "forgetting" in normal

Competing hypotheses

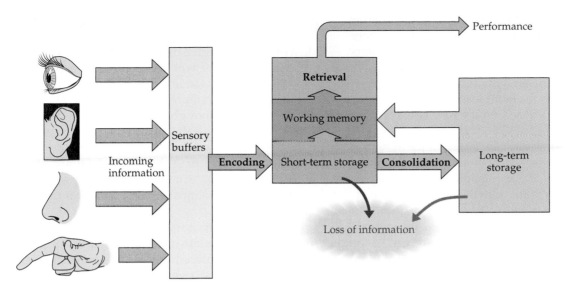

17.11 Hypothesized Memory Processes: Encoding, Consolidation, and Retrieval

subjects involve failure of encoding, of consolidation, or of retrieval, and whether pathological impairments of memory selectively involve one or another of these main processes. Experimental studies show that performance on a memory test can be either enhanced or impaired if the conditions of acquisition, of consolidation, or of retrieval are varied.

Brain regions involved in encoding. Evidence that activation of particular brain regions underlies encoding declarative memories comes from research in which separate activations are recorded for each stimulus in a series. When memory for the stimuli is tested later, the activations can be analyzed separately for stimuli remembered (and thus encoded successfully) and for stimuli fogotten (not encoded). Advances in fMRI now permit the measurement of event-related brain responses to individual brief stimuli, such as a picture or a word presented for as little as 1 second (Bruckner et al., 1996). In one experiment, subjects looked at a series of photographs and classified each scene as indoors or outdoors; they were not told that they would be asked later to remember the pictures (Brewer et al., 1998). Thirty minutes later they were shown these pictures mixed in with novel ones and were asked to identify which they had seen previously and which they had not. In a similar experiment, subjects saw words one at a time and were asked to classify them as abstract or concrete (A. D. Wagner, Schacter, et al., 1998).

When the activations were classified according to later success or failure of recognition, it was found that, although the stimuli activated many brain areas, only a few areas predicted success of recognition. In the case of the pictures, the critical areas were the right prefrontal cortex and the parahippocampal cortex in both hemispheres. In the case of the words, the critical areas were the *left* prefrontal cortex and the *left* parahippocampal cortex. These findings are compatible with results we will discuss in Chapter 19 showing that the left hemisphere is mainly responsible for language, while the right hemisphere is more involved in spatial perception.

Consolidating declarative information. Studies of brain-injured patients suggest that consolidation of declarative long-term memories takes considerable time and involves the hippocampus. To study this problem, four groups of investigators recently and independently designed experiments in which animals learned equivalent material at various times before they sustained lesions of the hippocampal formation. These studies were done with rats (Kim and Fanselow, 1992; Winocur, 1990), mice (Cho et al., 1993), and monkeys (Zola-Morgan and Squire, 1990). Psychologist-neuroscientist Larry Squire has studied this problem and many other aspects of memory with both human and nonhuman subjects.

Larry Squire

In the monkey experiment, animals learned to discriminate between two objects in 20 different pairs at each of five periods (16, 12, 8, 4, and 2 weeks before surgery)—a total of 100 pairs. Eleven of the monkeys were then given bilateral lesions of the hippocampal formation, including the subicular complex and the entorhinal cortex; seven monkeys formed the control group, receiving no lesions. Two weeks after surgery, the investigators showed the animals each of the 100 previously presented pairs in a mixed order. The control monkeys remembered more of what they had learned most recently than of what they had learned earlier (Figure 17.12). The lesioned monkeys, however, performed significantly worse than the controls on the object pairs they had learned 2 and 4 weeks before surgery; they did not differ from the controls for pairs learned earlier. Note also that the lesioned monkeys performed worse on items learned 2 and 4 weeks before surgery than on the items learned earlier. Experiments with rodents yielded similar results, except that the time course is measured in days rather than weeks.

These results show that the hippocampal system is not a repository of long-term memory. In each of the animal experiments, it was possible to identify a time after learning when damage to this system had no effect on memory for the learning. Thus, the information that initially depends on the medial temporal system for processing does not depend on it for long-term (or permanent) storage. Permanent storage is thought to occur in regions of the neocortex where the information is first processed and held in short-term memory; after further processing that involves the medial temporal region (and probably the midline diencephalic region as well), the permanent memory storage becomes independent of the medial temporal–diencephalic region.

The fact that memories require consolidation for long-term storage may help explain the retrograde amnesia that is common with injury to the brain. Memories that have not yet been completely consolidated in the cortex may be seriously impaired by interruption of processing. Conditions that follow learning can also modulate the strength of memory, as we will see in the next section.

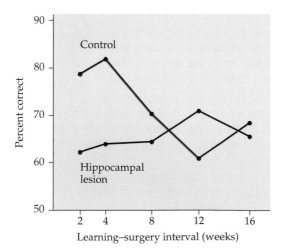

17.12 Retention by Monkeys of Object Discrimination Problems
An equal number of items was learned 2, 4, 8, 12, and 16 weeks before the experimental animals had hippocampal surgery. For the control animals memory was best for the most recently learned items; for the lesioned animals memory was significantly worse for the items learned 2 and 4 weeks prior to surgery. (After Zola-Morgan and Squire, 1990.)

Emotion Can Modulate Memory Formation

Most of us would agree that emotionally arousing experiences tend to be well remembered—sometimes too well. Descartes (1662) wrote, "The usefulness of all the passions [emotions] consists in their strengthening in the soul thoughts which are good for it to conserve. . . . And all the harm they can do consists in their strengthening and prolonging these thoughts more than is necessary." Similarly, William James (1890, p. 670) wrote, "An experience may be so exciting emotionally as almost to leave a scar on the cerebral tissues."

Recently investigators have found evidence that emotions can modulate memory formation in several ways. For example, emotions often enhance memory for aspects of an event or story that are closely tied to the emotional aspects, but they can also weaken memories that are not central to the emotional theme (Reisberg and Heuer, 1995). Animal research starting in the 1960s (e.g., McGaugh, 1992; McGaugh et al., 1993) has attempted to find the neural mechanisms involved in emotional modulation of memory, and recently this research has extended to include human memory (Pitman and Orr, 1995).

An emotionally arousing story is remembered significantly better than a closely matched but more emotionally neutral story; this emotional enhancement of memory may be caused by activation of beta-adrenergic stress hormones (Cahill et al., 1994). In an experiment designed to test the relation between emotion and memory, some subjects were given an emotional version of a story, and some were given a neutral version; both versions were accompanied by the same 12 slides. The first four items of both stories were identical, with four slides showing a mother and son going to visit the father's workplace in a hospital. In the second phase the two narratives differed, but the same five slides were shown: In the neutral version, the boy saw wrecked cars in a junkyard and then witnessed a disaster drill at the hospital; in the emotional version, the boy was badly injured in a traffic accident and was treated in the emergency room and in surgery. In the third phase (three slides), the mother went to pick up her other child at preschool. The subjects heard the narratives and saw the slides while connected to heart rate and blood pressure monitors and were told that the study concerned physiological responses to different types of stimuli. One hour before the story presentation, all subjects received injections; some received a control injection of physiological saline solution, while the others received propranolol, a beta-adrenergic receptor antagonist. (Propranolol and other so-called beta-blockers are used to combat high blood pressure.) A week later, without expecting any further contact with the stories, the subjects were asked to recall as many of the slides as possible and then took an 80-item multiple choice recognition memory test that assessed memory for both visual and narrative story elements.

Subjects who had received the control injection remembered the second, emotionally arousing phase of the story significantly better than the first or third phases. But subjects who had received the propranolol injection did not show better memory for the second, "emotional" phase than for the first and third phases. Control and propranolol-treated subjects scored about the same on the first and third phases of the story. Thus, the drug did not affect memory in general but blocked only the enhancement related to emotional arousal.

Competing hypotheses

Did the propranolol affect memory strength by preventing the subjects from having an emotional reaction to the stories? To test this question, the investigators had each subject rate his or her degree of emotion in response to the story just after it was presented. The "emotional" version was rated significantly more arousing than the neutral version by subjects given the beta-blocker as well as by subjects given the control injection, so it was not the failure of emotional experience that prevented enhancement of memory.

Another hypothesis was that propranolol acted *after* training to block enhancement of the processes of memory formation. This hypothesis is supported by animal research that we will review in Chapter 18. In fact, the human experiment just described was based directly on earlier animal research. In research with humans, it is difficult to separate effects on memory formation from effects on attention at the time of learning, or on rehearsal after the learning session. Research with animal subjects has clarified these effects and the neurochemical systems involved in emotional enhancement of memory formation, as we will see in Chapter 18 (see reviews by McGaugh et al., 1993, 1995).

Can Modulation of Learning Help in Understanding, Alleviating, or Preventing Posttraumatic Stress Disorder?

When some people are exposed to life-threatening events or other catastrophic experiences, they develop a syndrome known as posttraumatic stress disorder (PTSD), as discussed in Chapter 16. One set of symptoms is "reliving experiences such as intrusive thoughts, nightmares, dissociative flashbacks to elements of the original traumatic event, and . . . preoccupation with that event" (Keane, 1998, p. 398).

A hypothesis to help explain this phenomenon is that PTSD patients are caught in a positive feedback loop in which each episode of reexperiencing (intrusive memory, flashback) produces a stress hormone response, especially involving adrenergic hormones. This hormonal response then acts to strengthen the memory that produced it, thereby increasing the likelihood of reexperiencing the memory (Pitman, 1989).

On the basis of this hypothesis, Cahill (1997) has proposed a strategy to prevent PTSD formation by suppressing adrenergic activity with drugs either shortly before a traumatic experience or as quickly as possible after it. Thus, rescue workers could take an appropriate drug on their way to the scene of a disaster, and rape victims could be given an antiadrenergic drug such as propranolol as part of their treatment as soon as possible after the attack. This treatment would not delete memories of the event but would diminish the traumatic aspects. Experiments to test this hypothesis are under way (Cahill, 1997, p. 244).

Already established traumatic memories might also have some of their impact diminished, according to results of a recent animal experiment. As we noted earlier, a variety of treatments are amnestic (memory-impairing) if they are given shortly before or shortly after original learning; such treatments include electroconvulsive shock and drugs, such as inhibitors of protein synthesis or NMDA receptor antagonists. A recent study with rats has shown that when a previously formed memory is reactivated, it can be weakened by administration of propranolol up to 2 hours after reactivation of the memory (P. Roullet, J. Przybyslawski, and S. Sara, personal communication, 1998). Roullet and colleagues suggest that "adrenoreceptor antagonists may be promising pharmacological agents for attenuating debilitating memories"; that is, the drug could be given when the memory is recalled, and it might weaken the strength of the memory.

Brain Imaging Provides New Insights about Regions Involved in Different Kinds of Memories

Studies of brain lesions, both naturally occurring and experimentally induced, yield a great deal of information about the brain regions involved in different kinds of memories, as we have seen. But examination of brain-injured patients and animals with experimental lesions does not reveal what functions are served by the injured or missing tissue. Rather, the behavior shows what the intact brain regions can accomplish after the lesion. Brain-imaging techniques are providing evidence about memory processes in the healthy brain. These techniques include positron emission tomography (PET) and functional magnetic resonance imaging (fMRI), as described in Chapter 2.

Before examining some results of imaging studies, we should note that imaging techniques, as powerful as they are, have their limitations. Gabrieli (1998) points out that a great deal of psychological interpretation is involved in trying to understand what mental process is signified by activation of a brain region. Most reports state the *differences* in the activations caused by two tasks, as we noted in Box 2.3. Such differences are open to a variety of interpretations, and they are often affected by variables such as task difficulty or trial duration. In addition, the tasks must be designed around limitations of the imaging techniques: At present a homogeneous behavioral condition must be maintained for about 2 minutes in PET and for 1 second in fMRI recordings.

The combination of lesion and neuroimaging studies helps overcome the limitations of each of these sources of evidence, and each provides constraints on data from the other source. For example, a memory task may activate several different brain regions, but some of these regions can be injured without affecting performance on that task. So some of the activations may represent correlated memory processes that are not required for the form of memory being measured. The lesion evidence makes it possible to discriminate between activations that are essential or nonessential for a specific form of memory. In the sections that follow, we will take up the kinds of memory included in Figure 17.4.

Imaging Studies of Declarative Memory

Imaging studies confirm and extend the conclusions from lesion studies that implicated the medial temporal and diencephalic systems in the formation of new declarative long-term memories. Imaging studies show activation of these regions during both encoding of new material (e.g., Stern et al., 1996; Tulving et al., 1996) and retrieval (e.g., D. L. Schacter et al., 1996; Squire et al., 1992). A recent survey of 53 PET studies of memory revealed that encoding and retrieval activations are focused in somewhat different medial temporal brain regions (Figure 17.13) (Lepage et al., 1998).

17.13 Encoding and Retrieval Activate Different Medial Temporal Regions of the Brain

(*a*) This reference figure shows the position of a sagittal slice 25 mm from the midline. (*b*) Locations of peak activities in the hippocampal formation in 22 experiments on encoding (red) and 34 experiments on retrieval (blue). (Part *a* after Talairach and Tournoux, 1988; *b* after Lepage et al., 1998.)

Activations in the hippocampal region associated with *encoding* episodic memories are located primarily in the rostral portions of the region. Activations associated with *retrieving* episodic memories are located primarily in the caudal portions. The figure shows only the peak of activity in each study. Both retrieval and encoding activated both regions, but encoding activated the subiculum significantly more than did retrieval, and retrieval activated the parahippocampal cortex significantly more than did encoding. These results were unexpected. Thus, the imaging studies are beginning to provide information about the specific contributions of different components of the medial temporal region to declarative memory.

While the medial temporal region is necessary for *processing* information for long-term storage, the neocortex has been considered to be the site of *storage* of long-term declarative memories. Patients like H.M., who no longer have a hippocampus, nevertheless retain memories that were stored before brain lesion. On the other hand, some patients with lesions of the neocortex can no longer retrieve the names of specific categories of objects—for example, living things such as animals, manufactured things such as tools, or even more specific categories such as flowers or motor vehicles. Neuroimaging studies of normal subjects provide data consistent with specific localizations for such categories. For example, asking subjects to name tools or animals yields cortical activations that overlap in some areas but differ in others (A. Martin et al., 1996). These results with normal subjects indicate that the surprising regional specificity of representations of knowledge in patients reflects the localized cortical geography of the normal brain.

Gabrieli (1998, p. 94) points out two principles that emerge from the neuroimaging studies of cortical locations of declarative memory: "First, knowledge in any domain (e.g., for pictures or words, living or manufactured objects) is distributed over a specific, but extensive, neural network that often extends over several lobes. Injury to any component of that network could affect performance in that domain, with the specific effect reflecting what aspect of that knowledge is represented in that component of the network. Second, some localization appears to be a consequence of how various classes of knowledge interact with different perceptual and motor systems." For example, naming tools causes activation in the left prefrontal regions near motor cortex.

Several imaging studies have shown relatively greater activation in the left hemisphere during encoding of information and in the right hemisphere during retrieval (Nyberg et al., 1996; Tulving, 1998; Tulving and Markowitsch, 1997). Figure 17.14 shows an example of this asymmetry. Note that this is an asymmetry but not an absolute difference; the frontal and temporal regions of both hemispheres are active during both encoding and retrieval. Tulving (1998) sug-

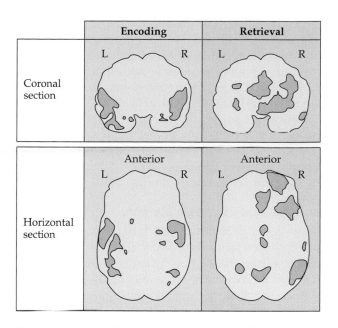

17.14 Hemispheric Asymmetry in Encoding and Retrieval
These representations of the brain, based on data from four different experiments, show that encoding evokes greater activity in the left temporal lobe, whereas retrieval evokes greater activity in the right frontal lobe. (After Tulving and Markowitsch, 1997.)

gests that this effect—known as the **hemispheric encoding retrieval asymmetry (HERA)** effect—can be used to answer the question, Are encoding and retrieval processes basically similar or basically different?

One current point of view is that encoding and retrieval are distinct processes, as indicated in Figure 17.11. On the other hand, many investigators hypothesize that retrieval involves reactivation of the same patterns of mental or neural activity that occurred in the original experience. Tulving (1998) concludes that the HERA effect points to basic differences in the neuroanatomy of the encoding and retrieval systems, thereby confirming that they are distinct processes. Buckner (1996) points out that while a model like HERA attempts to find a unifying principle for activity across multiple areas of the frontal lobes, it is also important to investigate the specific functions of the different cortical regions in learning and memory. Further research (reviewed by D. L. Schacter and Buckner, 1998, and by Tulving, 1998) indicates that activation of the right frontal cortex may reflect primarily the *effort* involved in attempting to recall past events, as opposed to retrieval itself.

The distinction between semantic (general) memory and episodic (autobiographical) memory was supported by the case of patient K.C., discussed earlier; after an accident that caused extensive neocortical damage, K.C. could no longer access any memories about his life, although he retained much general knowledge. But, as in many cases of brain lesions caused by accident or disease, the damage was widespread and did not offer much information about the site(s) of episodic memories. In an attempt to localize episodic memory processes better, experimenters had subjects listen to autobiographical passages and to passages written by others (Fink et al., 1996). The autobiographical passages, relative to the others, caused greater activation of right frontal and temporal lobe regions, as Figure 17.15 shows. So it appears that autobiographical episodic memory is processed in a separate location from semantic memories.

Imaging Studies of Skill Memory

Imaging studies have been made of learning and memory for different kinds of skills: (1) *sensorimotor skills,* such as mirror tracing (see Figure 17.2) and rotary pursuit, in which the subject tries to maintain contact between a handheld stylus and a small target on a rotating disc; (2) *perceptual skills,* such as learning to read mirror-reversed text (mentioned earler); and (3) *cognitive skills,* such as the Tower of Hanoi problem and other tasks that require planning and problem solving. All three kinds of skill learning are impaired in patients with injury to the basal ganglia or with Huntington's disease, which attacks the basal ganglia. Other brain regions, such as the motor cortex and the cerebellum, are involved in some examples of skill learning. Here we discuss briefly only sensorimotor skills, the variety that has been studied the most. For a review of other kinds of skill learning, see Gabrieli, 1998.

Neuroimaging studies support the importance of both the basal ganglia and the cerebellum, as well as of motor neocortex, for sensorimotor skill learning. Rotary pursuit learning activated the primary and secondary motor cortices (Grafton et al., 1992). Learning specific sequences of finger movements activates the primary and secondary motor cortices and the basal ganglia (Doyon et al., 1996; Hazeltine et al., 1997). Some studies also show activation of the cerebellum, which appears to be related to correction of errors in finger movements (Flament et al., 1996). Often the activations shift among brain regions as performance changes during the course of learning, so learning appears to involve a complex set of interacting neural networks.

Imaging Studies of Repetition Priming

Repetition priming (which we will call simply priming, as described earlier) is a change in processing of a stimulus due to prior exposure to the same or a related stimulus. Priming does not require declarative memory of the stimulus—H.M. and other amnesic patients show priming for words they don't remember having seen—so priming does not require the medial temporal or diencephalic regions. In addition, patients who suffer from Huntington's disease show normal priming, so intact basal ganglia are not required.

Priming tasks can be distinguished as perceptual or conceptual. *Perceptual* priming reflects prior processing of the *form* of the stimulus; *conceptual* priming reflects the *meaning* of the stimulus. Perceptual priming, such as priming on word stem completion tasks, is related to *reduced* activity, relative to baseline activity during word stem completion, in bilateral occipitotemporal cortex (D. L. Schacter et al., 1996). Presumably the activity is reduced for the primed words because responding to them requires less effort than responding to nonprimed words does. Conceptual priming is related to reduced activity in left frontal neocortex (Blaxton et al., 1996; Gabrieli et al., 1996; A. D. Wagner, Desmond, et al., 1997).

Imaging Studies of Conditioning

Research on brain circuits involved in classical conditioning will be taken up in Chapter 18. That work

17.15 My Story versus Your Story

Autobiographical passages (*a*) caused greater activation of the right frontal and temporal lobes than nonautobiographical passages (*b*). (After Fink et al., 1996; courtesy of Gereon Fink.)

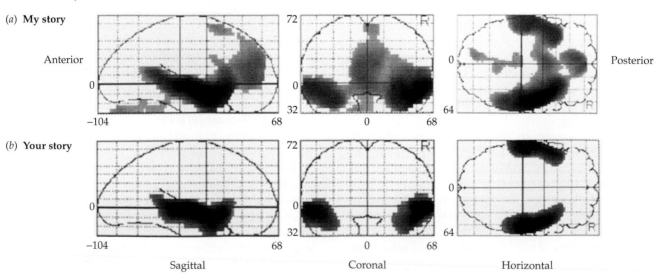

(*a*) **My story**

Anterior · · · · Posterior

Sagittal · · · Coronal · · · Horizontal

(*b*) **Your story**

shows that cerebellar circuits are responsible for simple delay conditioning (where there is no time gap between the conditioned stimulus and the unconditioned stimulus). Delay conditioning occurs normally even if the hippocampus has been lesioned, but for trace conditioning (where the CS ends before the US starts), the hippocampus is required, as it is also for discrimination reversal conditioning (where the stimulus that signals reward [CS+] and the stimulus that does not signal reward [CS–] are reversed).

A PET study of human eye-blink conditioning used both behavioral intervention and the correlational approach (Logan and Grafton, 1995). During the first (control) session of the experiment, PET scans were made while subjects received an unpaired tone and puff of air to the right eye. In the second session, 1 to 6 days later, the stimuli were paired. In the third session, 2 to 7 days after the first, PET scans were made while the subjects received paired stimuli. Comparison of the scans from this third session with the first showed increased activity in several regions of the brain (Figure 17.16*a*). Activity in some of these regions correlated significantly with conditioning behavior (Figure 17.16*b*).

Thus the neural network activated during human eye-blink conditioning includes not only the cerebel-lar and brain stem regions found in animal research, but also the hippocampus, the ventral striatum, and regions of the cerebral cortex. But activity in these other areas may not be *essential* for eye-blink conditioning. For example, patients with hippocampal damage can acquire the conditioned eye-blink response, whereas patients with unilateral cerebellar damage can acquire a conditioned eye-blink response only on the side where the cerebellum is intact (Papka et al., 1994).

The Brain Regions Involved in Different Kinds of Learning and Memory: A Summary

Figure 17.17 summarizes the findings we have reviewed about brain regions involved in different kinds of learning and memory. This is not a complete picture of the subject—there are other kinds of learning and other brain areas involved—but it underscores some major points:

1. Many regions of the brain are involved in learning and memory.
2. The kinds of learning and memory that have been distinguished from each other on cognitive grounds—such as declarative versus nondeclarative, or semantic versus episodic—are mediated by

17.16 A PET Study of Human Eye-Blink Conditioning

(*a*) Areas showing metabolic changes in conditioning versus the control condition; areas of increased activity are shown in yellow. (*b*) Areas where metabolic change during conditioning is significantly correlated with learning performance; positive correlations are shown in yellow. Note the negative correlation (blue) in the left occipitotemporal fissure. (From Logan and Grafton, 1995.)

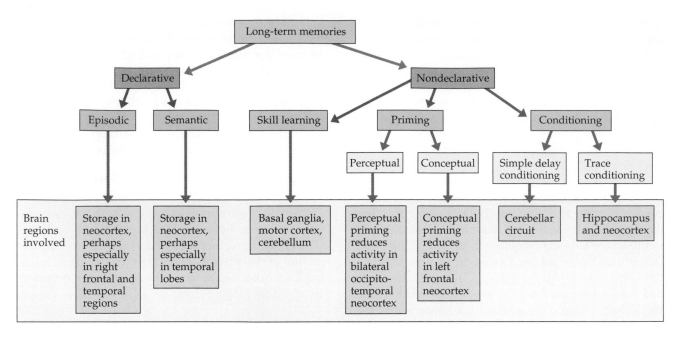

17.17 Brain Regions Involved in Different Kinds of Learning and Memory

different, or at least partially different, brain structures and regions.

3. The same brain structure may be involved in different kinds of learning and memory; for example, the cerebellum is involved in both sensorimotor learning and delay conditioning.

4. A given kind of learning may require activity of a circuit involving several different brain regions.

5. Some kinds of learning that appear rather similar, such as delay and trace conditioning, may nevertheless involve different structures.

Comparative Approaches Yield Insights about the Evolution of Learning and Memory

Animal model

Learning and memory exist throughout the animal kingdom—from short-term learning in single-celled animals through all the variety of learning we have noted in multicellular animals. Although there has been a good deal of speculation about the early evolution of abilities to learn and remember, we cannot research this subject directly, since we cannot measure the behavior of extinct animals. The fact that learning is so widespread throughout the animal kingdom suggests that it was an early evolutionary development, with changes occurring as animals evolved to occupy new niches and meet new challenges. A fruitful approach is to compare the learning and memory of related species in which differences in ecological niche and lifestyle have caused different selection pressures for specific kinds of learning and therefore changes in brain structure.

As we consider attempts at comparing learning ability among existing species, we will see that it is not a simple matter. Just as it is difficult, perhaps impossible, to devise a "culture-free" intelligence test for human beings, so has it been difficult to devise tests for animals that do not favor the sensory and/or motor capacities of some species and work against others. The problem has become even more complicated now that research has shown that relatively simple animals are capable of a greater variety of learning than was suspected only a few years ago (Carew and Sahley, 1986; Krasne and Glanzman, 1995).

In part, these findings have come from attempts to use "simple systems" to investigate the basic neural processes involved in learning and memory formation. Thus, associative learning and conditional learning have been found in the mollusk *Aplysia*, as we noted earlier, and complex conditioning has been found in the garden slug. On the other hand, many kinds of animals show specialized kinds of learning that seem to be restricted to particular events and are not able to encompass other relations. The wide distribution of learning throughout the animal kingdom, as well as restrictions on these abilities, has implications for the evolution of learning.

Learning Abilities Are Widely Distributed throughout the Animal Kingdom

Nonassociative learning appears to be very widespread in the animal kingdom. Simple animals with small nervous systems readily habituate to repeated mild stimuli and become sensitized to strong stimuli. Furthermore, the time courses and other features of habituation and sensitization are similar, whether studied in an earthworm, a mollusk, or a mammal. Some investigators have reported nonassociative learning even in paramecia and bacteria, single-celled animals that do not have a nervous system. Apparently all animals show some kinds of learning and memory.

The fact that learning and memory are so widespread among animal species has led to attempts to study basic mechanisms of learning and memory in animals without nervous systems or with relatively simple nervous systems. It is tempting to suppose that all animals share some basic processes of learning and memory storage, so that relatively simple animals can be taken as models to study processes that all animals use. However, learning may have arisen separately in some of these diverse animal forms; similar learning behaviors may represent convergent evolution in the face of common demands of the environment, but perhaps not all animals use the same mechanisms to accomplish learning and memory storage. We will have to examine critically claims that findings with relatively simple animals can be extrapolated directly to other forms. Neuroscientist Seymour Kety (1976, p. 321) urged the search for varieties of mechanisms in learning and memory:

> So profound and powerful an adaptation as learning and memory is not apt to rest upon a single modality. Rather, I suspect that advantage is taken of every opportunity provided by evolution. There were forms of memory before organisms developed nervous systems, and after that remarkable leap forward it is likely that every new pathway and neural complexity, every new neurotransmitter, hormone, or metabolic process that played upon the nervous system and subserved a learning process was preserved and incorporated.

Until recently associative learning was believed to have a more restricted distribution than nonassociative learning in the animal kingdom. For example, *Aplysia* had been used for many years to investigate the neural mechanisms of habituation, and investigators had sought in vain for evidence of associative learning in *Aplysia* until it was discovered in 1980. Evidence for learning in the fruit fly, *Drosophila*, was long sought in order to try to relate learning to genetic factors, which are very well known in *Drosophila*, but only in 1974 did investigators first announce successful training in these animals. Part of the difficulty in assessing the capacity of a species to learn and remember is that these capacities may be highly specific. Certain species can learn particular associations well even though they are very poor at other tasks that do not seem more difficult to us. Evidence for specificity has accumulated since the 1960s and has led to two successive and quite different concepts.

First came the concept of **genetic constraints on learning**, which became prominent in the 1960s. This formulation held that species-typical genetic factors restrict the kinds of learning that a species can accomplish, or at least accomplish readily. For example, bees readily learn to come to a particular station to feed on a 24-hour schedule, which of course occurs in nature, but they cannot learn to come on an 8- or 12-hour schedule. Birds of some species do not learn the pattern of markings or even the color of their eggs even though they turn the eggs over frequently, yet they learn to recognize their young individually within 3 days after they hatch, just the time when the chicks begin to wander about.

The interpretation of such observations changed in the 1980s. Rather than supposing that the genes of certain species constrain their general ability to learn and thus make them selectively stupid, investigators now believe it more likely that **specific abilities to learn and remember** evolve in response to selective pressures in particular ecological niches (J. L. Gould, 1986; Sherry and Schacter, 1987). Let's consider an example of a specific learning ability.

Selection for Spatial Memory Is Associated with Increased Hippocampal Size in Mammals and Birds

A current research program uses both naturalistic observations and experimental studies with birds and rodents to find out what effects natural or artificial selection for spatial ability may have on brain measures: "If a particular neuroanatomical feature occurs in different species exposed to the same selective pressure, and is better accounted for by this selective pressure than by the phylogenetic relations among the species, then it is reasonable to conclude that the feature is indeed an adaptation—the result of convergent evolution in response to natural selection" (Sherry et al., 1992, p. 298).

We saw one example of this research in Chapter 6: Species of birds that store or cache food for retrieval days or weeks later have hippocampal regions larger than those of related species that do not cache food (see Figure 6.4). The differences in size of hippocampus among these species could not be accounted for by other factors, including migratory behavior, social organization, diet, mode of development, nest dispersion, or habitat (Krebs et al., 1989; Sherry et al., 1989). Furthermore, surgical removal of the hippocampus in a food-storing species disrupts the birds' ability to retrieve cached food and to solve other spatial problems, without obvious effects on other behaviors (Sherry and Vaccarino, 1989). Thus, the larger hippocampus in food-storing species of birds seems to be an adaptive modification that makes it possible for them to retrieve cached food.

Comparison of two related species of kangaroo rats provided an independent test of this hypothesis. Both species are small, nocturnal, seed-eating, desert rodents from the same genus. One species, Merriam's kangaroo rat (*Dipodomys merriami*) hoards food in scattered locations and requires spatial memory to relocate its caches. In contrast, the bannertail kangaroo rat (*Dipodomys spectabilis*) hoards seeds in its burrow and thus needs no specialized spatial memory to retrieve them. As expected on the basis of the results with food-storing versus non-food-storing birds, *D. merriami* has a significantly larger hippocampus than does *D. spectabilis* (L. F. Jacobs and Spencer, 1994).

People have long bred animals selectively to enhance certain traits; such artificial selection can produce results similar to those of natural selection, and more rapidly. For example, pigeons have been bred for their ability to fly rapidly and accurately to their home lofts. Pigeons of these strains have larger hippocampi than breeds of pigeons not selected for homing ability (Rehkamper et al., 1988).

In interweaving information about the hippocampus of birds and mammals, we have to recognize that the hippocampus differs in its location and connections in these two classes of animals. Nevertheless, comparative neuroanatomists consider the hippocampus to be homologous in birds and mammals, and the results of recent behavioral–anatomical research appear to bear this assumption out (Bingman, 1993).

Investigators who test the spatial learning and memory of laboratory rats and mice have often observed that males perform better than females, and human males perform better than human females on many spatial tasks (D. F. Halpern, 1986). Some researchers have suggested that males in general are superior in spatial learning and memory, but others have hypothesized that the behavioral roles of the two sexes determine whether a sex difference in spatial memory exists in a given species, and if it does, which sex is superior in this behavior.

An instructive comparison has been made between two species of North American voles (Figure 17.18). Pine voles (*Microtus pinetorum*) are monogamous, and field observations show that the males and females travel over ranges that are equal in size. In contrast, meadow voles (*Microtus pennsylvanicus*) are highly polygynous (i.e., a male mates with several females), and the ranges of males are several times larger than those of females. In this polygynous mating system, males compete in order to include within their home range as many female ranges as possible. The polygynous male meadow voles, in comparison with females of the same species, have significantly better scores on laboratory tests of spatial learning and memory. The monogamous pine voles show no sex differences on these tests. Furthermore, the polygynous male meadow voles have a significantly larger hippocampus than do the females, whereas among the monogamous pine voles, there is no significant difference in hippocampal size between the sexes (L. F. Jacobs et al., 1990).

(a) **Sizes of home range**

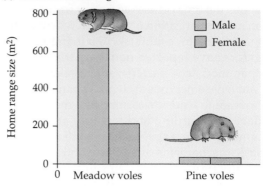

(b) **Ranking in spatial learning**

(c) **Relative hippocampal size**

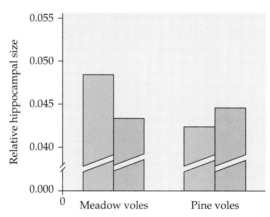

17.18 Sex, Memory, and Hippocampal Size
Comparison of males and females of two species of voles on three variables: (*a*) size of home range; (*b*) score on spatial learning task; (*c*) hippocampal size divided by brain size. (After L. F. Jacobs et al., 1990.)

When the size of the hippocampus differs between the sexes of a species, it is not invariably the male that shows the larger size. For example, the hippocampus of the female brown-headed cowbird (*Molothrus ater*) is significantly larger than that of the male, as investigators predicted on the basis of the breeding behavior of this species (Sherry et al., 1993). The female cowbird is parasitic: She lays her eggs in the nests of other species, who then do the work of hatching and feeding the cowbird chick. In order to do this, the female cowbird has to find and keep track of nests so that she can slip in and lay an egg when the other birds are away. The male cowbird does not participate in this spatial sleuthing and gets along with a smaller hippocampus. No sex difference in hippocampal size was found in two closely related species that are not parasitic.

This example is one of the few indications that spatial ability can influence the size of the hippocampus when other factors—such as sex, breeding system, or foraging behavior—have been ruled out. Other differences in learning and memory among species have contributed to speculation about the evolution of learning and intelligence, as discussed in Topic 17.3, How Learning Ability and Intelligence May Have Evolved.

Special topic

Learning and Memory Change throughout Life

It is easier for us to form some kinds of new memories when we are in the middle of our lives, as young or mature adults, than when we are infants or elderly. Can these changes in ability over the life span be explained in neural terms? Do they provide clues about the neural mechanisms of learning and memory? To answer these and other questions, investigators conduct developmental studies of learning and memory with a variety of species, ranging from humans to mollusks.

Many kinds of animals must be ready to learn as soon as they are born or hatch. For example, newly hatched chicks eagerly sample objects in their environment to find what is edible. Their yolk sacs provide nourishment, so they can sample small bits without having to ingest much. By the time the yolk sac is used up 3 to 4 days after hatching, the chicks need to have learned what is safe and good to eat. Thus, chicks are good subjects for some kinds of learning experiments.

Chicks are precocial—able to locomote and care for themselves from the time they emerge—but even altricial animals (those that are helpless at birth) must learn to adapt to their environment. For example, even though rat pups' eyes and ears are closed for about the first 2 weeks after birth, each pup in a litter learns which of the mother's nipples is "its own." In laboratory experiments, young rat pups learn rapidly which of two artificial nipples provides milk; they can use cues of texture or odor to learn this distinction (Woo and Leon, 1987). Human infants learn quickly to distinguish the faces of their main caregivers from those of others. And human infants can be conditioned to turn their heads to one side or the other at the sound of a tone in order to find the nipple of a nursing bottle (Papousek, 1992). Learning can thus be studied in newly born or newly hatched animals without the complicating effects of prior learning.

Careful recent testing shows that young nervous systems can accomplish some kinds of learning that we used to think only older animals could.

Some kinds of learning are not required until an animal passes the stage of infancy. We mentioned that food-storing species of birds have a larger hippocampus than do related species that do not store food. A recent study measured hippocampal size in nestlings (5 to 25 days after hatching) and adult birds of two species in the crow family (Healy and Krebs, 1993): the food-storing black-billed magpie (*Pica pica*) and the non-food-storing jackdaw (*Corvus monedula*). In the nestlings, the relative volume of the hippocampus did not differ between the two species, but in the adults, the food-storing black-billed magpies had significantly greater hippocampal volume and cell number than the non-food-storing jackdaws. Healy and Krebs (1993) suggested that the differences between adults of the two species are related to the *use* of spatial memory in retrieving stored food. This hypothesis was tested by Clayton and Krebs (1994), who raised crows in the laboratory, giving some birds the opportunity to store and retrieve food while other birds ate from feeders and had no opportunity to store food. The birds who stored and retrieved food developed hippocampal formations that were larger than those of the birds who did not store and retrieve food.

Three different kinds of learning—habituation, dishabituation, and sensitization—emerge successively during the development of the sea slug *Aplysia* (Carew, 1989). Furthermore, electrophysiological correlates of these kinds of learning emerge in parallel with the behavioral states. Details of this story are given in Topic 17.4, Habituation, Dishabituation, and Sensitization Appear Successively during Development in *Aplysia*.

 Special topic

Does Immaturity of Certain Brain Regions Prevent Some Kinds of Learning?

Young animals have difficulty learning certain kinds of problems. Investigators have tried to determine whether these difficulties are related to the immaturity of the specific brain regions. Some hypotheses have been verified, but experiments have forced the abandonment of other hypotheses, as the following examples show.

A classic test of cognitive development devised by Swiss psychologist Jean Piaget now appears to require development of the dorsolateral prefrontal cortex. This "A not B" test requires an infant to uncover a toy that she sees hidden in one of two possible locations (A or B); both locations are used in a series of trials. After the toy is hidden, the infant's visual fixation is broken so that she cannot look at the location during the delay. Human infants will not reliably reach for a hidden object until they are 7 to 8 months old.

Competing hypotheses

Before this age, an infant will reach correctly to either location only if there is no delay (except for breaking visual fixation) between the hiding and the reaching. But with a delay of only 1 to 5 s during which the infant is prevented from reaching, she tends to reach for the object in the last location where she reached successfully, even if that is not the location where she just saw the toy hidden.

These observations might suggest that with a short delay, the *habit* of successful reaching is stronger than the *representational memory* of the hidden object. No long-term memory is required in either case; only short-term working memories are involved. Testing of infants every 2 weeks shows a steady rise in their ability to perform successfully at longer delays. This improvement is due to maturation, not experience, because infants of a given age test equally well whether or not they were given prior tests. By age 12 months, most infants perform successfully with a delay of 10 s

between seeing the object hidden and reaching for it. In the next section we'll see that some adult amnesia patients fail the "A not B" test.

Patricia Goldman-Rakic

A. Diamond and Goldman-Rakic (1989), who confirmed these observations with human infants, also studied monkeys, using a similar test. They used both intact monkeys and monkeys with lesions of either dorsolateral prefrontal cortex or inferior parietal cortex (Figure 17.19). The dorsolateral prefrontal cortex was chosen because other research had shown impairment in performance after a delay with lesions in this area. The inferior parietal cortex was chosen because it has been implicated in spatial processing and because it is large enough that lesions of comparable size could be made in the two regions.

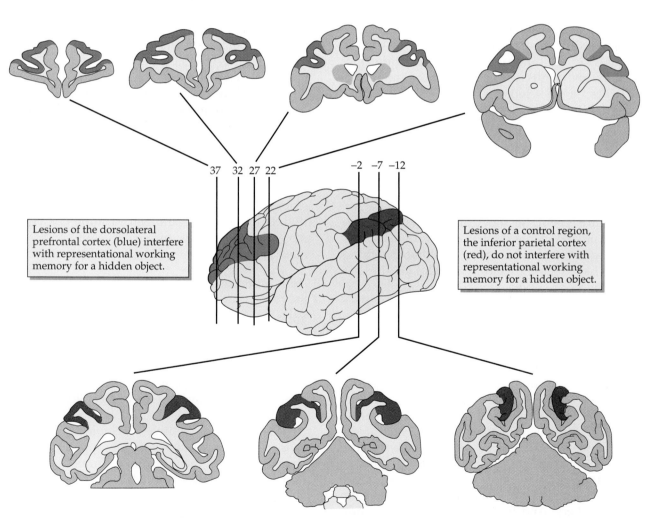

17.19 Cortical Regions Tested for Roles in Representational Memory
Sites of brain lesions in monkeys, in experiments on cortical regions involved in representational memory. (*a*) Dorsolateral prefrontal cortex. (*b*) Inferior parietal cortex. (After A. Diamond and Goldman-Rakic, 1989.)

Normal monkeys performed well on the test at delays of 10 s and more, as did monkeys with lesions of parietal cortex, but monkeys with lesions of prefrontal cortex made errors similar to those of 7- to 8-month-old human infants. Thus, a normal, relatively mature dorsolateral prefrontal cortex appears to be required for representational memory of the hidden object to be retained as long as 10 s. Further research on the roles of prefrontal cortex in memory will be discussed in Chapter 18.

In the 1980s, several investigators proposed that young primates do not have access to declarative memories, because the hippocampus is not yet sufficiently mature. Subsequent research showed that young primates show recognition memory (a form of declarative memory) by selective looking, even at ages when they cannot readily combine the two operations of looking and reaching. We conclude that success on the delayed visual paired-comparison test depends on the hippocampus, because hippocampal lesions seriously impaired performance on this test.

 Special topic For further detail on this story, see Topic 17.5, Does Hippocampal Immaturity Explain Lack of Some Abilities in Primate Infants?

Aging Impairs Some Aspects of Learning and Memory

The capacity of older people to learn and remember has become a topic of heightened interest in recent years. This awareness stems in part from the growing proportion of elderly people in the population of developed countries and the recognition that some reductions in capacity accompany normal aging. It also reflects attention to pathological forms of cognitive impairment that are more likely to affect older people, such as Alzheimer's disease (see Chapter 7).

Most investigators agree that older people in normal health show some decrements in abilities to learn and remember (Craik, 1986), and reviews of both human and animal studies show declines with age in both abilities (Gallagher and Rapp, 1997; Gallagher et al., 1995; Kubanis and Zornetzer, 1981). Accurate comparisons of learning and memory in people of different ages are difficult because of confounding factors. For example, differences in learning ability may be caused not by age alone, but by other factors, such as educational level, how recently the subjects have experienced formal learning, or motivation. After correcting for such factors, differences related to age usually accompany only some tasks, not all.

What kinds of tasks usually show decrements in performance with aging? Normal elderly people tend to show some memory impairment in tasks of conscious recollection that require effort (Hasher and Zacks, 1979) and that rely primarily on internal generation of the memory rather than on external cues (Craik, 1985). Giving elderly subjects easily organized

task structures, or cues, or both can often raise their performance to the level of the young. Thus the type of task helps determine whether impairment is observed. Recent neuroimaging studies show impairment in both the encoding and the retrieval of information in old subjects compared with young. There is greater variability among old subjects than among young, and for many tasks some elderly subjects perform as well or almost as well as the young.

In cases of pathological forms of aging, such as Alzheimer's disease, some memory systems deteriorate, and it has been suggested that what remains are memory processes similar to those of infants. In fact, testing the implications of this idea led Morris Moscovitch (1985) to discover a cognitive disability in amnesia patients similar to the failure on the "A not B" test that Piaget had described for 8-month-old infants. Most amnesia patients, shown a familiar object in a new location, B, continue to search for it at A, even passing by the object in plain sight in order to search for it at A. They appear to remember the search procedure and not the object being sought.

Studies of the effects of aging on memory are difficult with human subjects, partly because of the variability among people resulting from genetic and environmental factors. Therefore, some investigators use animal subjects to obtain an intimate and detailed understanding of how aging affects memory. Here again experiments must be designed in such a way as to overcome the effects of potentially confounding variables, such as differences in strength of motivation with age or differences in sensory acuity (Ingram, 1985). Evidence of slower learning with advanced age has been reported by some of these investigators (e.g., Gallagher et al., 1995). We will see in Chapter 18 that certain neurochemical and neuroanatomical changes correlate closely with the impairments in behavior. Further research may suggest effective therapeutic measures.

Summary

1. The abilities to learn and remember affect all behaviors that are characteristically human. Since every animal species appears capable of some learning and memory, the ability to learn must be required for survival. Whereas evolution by natural selection brings about adaptation over successive generations, learning permits prompt adaptation within the lifetime of the individual.

2. Individuals whose learning or memory capacities are impaired as a result of brain damage may provide valuable information about how different regions of the brain are involved in these processes.

3. Patients with Korsakoff's syndrome show gaps in memory, which they may attempt to fill by confabulation; this syndrome involves severe retrograde as well as anterograde amnesia and impairment in encoding new information. Patients show damage to the mammillary nuclei, midline thalamus, and frontal cortex.

4. Declarative memory tends to be flexible—accessible to many response systems. Nondeclarative memory tends to be inflexible: The information is not readily expressed by response systems that were not involved in the original learning.

5. Learning includes both nonassociative forms, such as habituation, dishabituation, and sensitization, and associative forms, such as classical (Pavlovian) conditioning and instrumental conditioning.

6. Conditioning involves learning relations and predictability among events. Close temporal pairing of stimuli is neither necessary nor sufficient for successful conditioning.

7. Some learning results in the formation of habits (gaining nondeclarative knowledge, or "learning how"); other learning results in the formation of representational memories (gaining declarative knowledge, or "learning what"). Abilities to form habits and memories appear to depend on different brain circuits.

8. Memories are often classified by how long they last. Frequently used classifications include iconic, short-term, intermediate-term, and long-term. Some disorders prevent the formation of long-term declarative memory while not impairing short-term memory.

9. Although the capacity of long-term memory is huge, most of what we experience is not remembered. Attention, reinforcement, and emotional responses help determine what is held in memory beyond the short term.

10. Recall of a past event requires three memory processes: encoding, consolidation, and retrieval.

11. Memory strength can be modulated by emotional state and other conditions in the period following learning.

12. Some patients with damage to the medial temporal lobe or medial diencephalon show particular impairment in consolidation of long-term representational memories. Recent research has focused both on the type of memory test and on the sites of brain damage. Hippocampal lesions in people and animals impair the formation of representational long-term memories but spare the formation of habits (nondeclarative or procedural memories).

13. The hippocampal region is required for processing but not for storage of long-term declarative memory. Long-term (or permanent) memory is stored in the neocortex.

14. Brain imaging is helping to identify brain regions involved in various aspects of learning and remembering. Encoding of information evokes greater activity in the left frontal region; retrieval evokes greater activity in the right frontal region. Sensorimotor skill learning is accompanied by activation in the basal ganglia, the cerebellum, and the motor cortex.

15. The capacities for associative as well as nonassociative learning are very widespread among animal species. The evolution of powerful and flexible brain mechanisms of learning and memory may have resulted from the earlier development of precise and elaborate systems to handle specific sensorimotor adjustments and then from the extension of these systems for more general use.

16. Abilities to learn and remember change throughout life. For some aspects of these changes, biological correlates have been found; other aspects continue to pose questions.

Recommended Reading

Baddeley, A. (1990). *Human memory: Theory and practice.* Needham Heights, MA: Allyn and Bacon.

Baudry, M., and Zola, S. (Eds.). (1998). Brain and Memory: From Genes to Behavior. Proceedings of the Sixth Conference on the Neurobiology of Learning and Memory. *Neurobiology of Learning and Memory, 70,* 1–103.

Cohen, N. J., and Eichenbaum, H. (1993). *Memory, amnesia, and the hippocampal system.* Cambridge, MA: MIT Press.

Gabrieli, J. D. E. (1998). Cognitive neuroscience of human memory. *Annual Review of Psychology, 49,* 87–115.

Luria, A. R. (1987). *The mind of a mnemonist.* Cambridge, MA: Harvard University Press.

Squire, L. R., Knowlton, B., and Musen, G. (1993). The structure and organization of memory. *Annual Review of Psychology, 44,* 453–495.

Zola-Morgan, S., and Squire, L. R. (1993). Neuroanatomy of memory. *Annual Review of Neuroscience, 16,* 547–563.

18 Learning and Memory: Neural Mechanisms

Whereas Chapter 17 stressed behavioral aspects of learning and memory and the general regions of the nervous system where plastic changes that underlie learning and memory occur, this chapter deals mainly with detailed sites and neural mechanisms. We will focus on four main topics:

1. What are the basic biological mechanisms—at the molecular, synaptic, and cellular levels—for long-term storage of information in the nervous system?
2. At the level of neural circuits, how do the formation and modification of circuits function in memory?
3. What is the sequence of neurochemical events that underlies the storage of long-term memory?
4. Are parts of the cascade of neurochemical events correlated with stages in memory formation?

In reviewing the neural mechanisms of learning and memory, we must be careful not to overgeneralize. Some investigators have been so happy to find a specific site or precise mechanism of change for one kind of memory that they have erroneously proposed their finding to account for many or all other kinds of memory too. Careful work is needed to determine which mechanisms may be common among different forms of learning and which mechanisms are specific to particular forms of learning.

Ellen Carey, *Untitled*, 1987

New Experimental Techniques Are Enabling Rapid Progress in Research on Mechanisms of Memory

Only in the twentieth century, and especially in the last few decades, have investigators discovered how to use behavioral intervention, coupled with biological measures, to study the mechanisms of learning and memory—that is, to study changes in the nervous system as a result of training (see Figure 1.3 for definitions of somatic and behavioral intervention). A variety of techniques, with a steady increase in their spatial and temporal resolution, have become available. Now the combined use of somatic and behavioral interventions is yielding rapid progress in our understanding of the neural mechanisms of learning and memory. This approach is revealing how a brief experience can lead to a cascade of neurochemical events that may, in some cases, include protein synthesis and structural changes at synapses. Newer methods are also enabling investigators to determine how neural circuits are established or altered in ways that serve memories.

Changes in Synapses May Be Mechanisms of Memory Storage

Soon after experiments on memory began in the 1880s, and as information accumulated on the physiology and anatomy of the nervous system, investigators began to speculate that changes in neuronal junctions could be a mechanism to store memories. British neurophysiologist Charles S. Sherrington (1897, p. 1117), in the same publication in which he proposed the term "synapse," stated that changes in neural connections were likely to be important for learning:

> Shut off from all opportunity of reproducing itself and adding to its number by mitosis or otherwise, the nerve cell directs its pent-up energy towards amplifying its connections with its fellows, in response to the events which stir it up. Hence, it is capable of an education unknown to other tissues.

The great Spanish neuroanatomist Santiago Ramón y Cajal (1894) also suggested that neurons extend their axons and dendrites to make new connections with other neurons in both development and learning.

Early in the twentieth century, when Ivan Pavlov sought to explain conditioning in neural terms, it was natural to think that neurons in the sensory cortex, representing the conditioned stimulus (CS), developed or strengthened their connections to neurons in the motor cortex, where the unconditioned response (UR) is represented; thus CS–UR linkages would develop. These linkages would form or strengthen neural chains, such as we saw in Figure 3.16. Later, however, it was discovered that cortical lesions that should have interrupted such cross-cortical connections did not abolish conditioned responses or memories for

other kinds of learning. This finding appeared to invalidate the hypothesis that memories depend on direct neural chains, or at least cross-cortical chains. Investigators then began to consider other kinds of neural circuits and even to speculate about other mechanisms, such as the interaction of electrical fields in the brain.

Different Kinds of Neural Circuits May Underlie Memories

It will be helpful for us to organize the varied and active research on neural mechanisms of learning and memory according to the kinds of neural circuits that investigators consider, which range from simple neural chains to parallel distributed circuits (Figure 18.1). We will define each kind of circuit briefly here; these definitions will become more meaningful as we discuss research related to them. Most theorizing about circuits locates the site(s) of memory storage in one or more plastic synapses (shown in Figure 18.1 in orange).

The neural chain (see Figure 18.1a), at its simplest, can be a monosynaptic reflex arc, as in the knee jerk reflex (see Figure 3.15). Some studies indicate that even the simplest variety—a monosynaptic neural circuit—can show some learning, as we will see a little later. In this case, learning is said to cause *intrinsic change* in the circuit.

Many simple neural circuits also receive input from superordinate circuits (see Figure 18.1b), also called modulatory circuits. We saw an example in the case of

(a) Plasticity in a neural chain

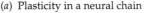

(b) Plasticity in a superordinate circuit

(c) Plasticity in a cell assembly

18.1 Sites of Synaptic Plasticity in Neural Networks (a) A neural chain with a plastic synapse. (b) Plasticity in a higher-order segment of a circuit. (c) A cell assembly with many plastic sites. Changes at such sites may underlie memory storage.

the motor system, where the activity of spinal reflex circuits is modulated by higher-order circuits at the level of the brain stem, basal ganglia, and motor cortex (see Chapter 11). In this chapter we will see an example (eye-blink conditioning) of plasticity in a higher-order modulatory circuit; the basic reflex circuit itself, however, shows no change during training.

Many kinds of learning may require the establishment of relatively complex networks of neurons—cell assemblies, as psychologist Donald O. Hebb called them in his influential book, *The Organization of Behavior* (1949). In Figure 18.1c, several plastic synapses help form a neural network.

Many current hypotheses suggest that the same group or ensemble of neurons can encode many different memories, each neuron participating to a greater or lesser extent in a particular memory, just as a person may belong to several different clubs or groups. In this case, each unit change may be too small to affect behavior significantly by itself, but the aggregate of changes in many neurons can produce large effects. The encoding of memories in an ensemble of neurons also depends on plasticity of the synapses involved.

In addition, new neurons formed in adults may participate in storing memories. Adult mice living in an enriched environment produce additional cells in the hippocampus, compared to mice housed in standard cages (Kempermann et al., 1997). The production of new neurons in the hippocampus declines with age in the mouse, but even in senescent (20-month-old) mice, experience in an enriched environment resulted in a threefold increase in new neurons, as compared with animals in standard housing. A recent paper also reports the formation of new granule cells in the hippocampus of adult monkeys (E. Gould et al., 1998). Perhaps as the hippocampus processes the many incoming memories for storage, it needs new cells to deal with the flood of information.

Before we look at the research on different kinds of neural circuits, we will consider two topics that provide important background: First we will examine the ways in which synapses can change and thereby store information. Then we will discuss technological developments beginning in the 1940s that encouraged research on the neural mechanisms of memory: the ability to measure changes in electrical activity, neurochemistry, and neuroanatomy in response to training. Finding such changes encouraged research on the neural mechanisms of memory.

The Nervous System May Form and Store Memories in Various Ways

As knowledge of synaptic anatomy and chemistry increased, hypotheses about plastic synaptic changes became more numerous and precise. Changes in existing synapses and changes in numbers of synapses

have been proposed as mechanisms of information storage (see Figure 18.2).

Physiological Changes at Synapses May Store Information

Some of the changes that may store information can be measured physiologically. The changes could be presynaptic, postsynaptic, or both. One possibility is that the number of transmitter molecules released per nerve impulse could increase, thus altering the response of the postsynaptic cell (Figure 18.2a). A change in release of transmitter could be caused by chemical changes within the end bouton.

The responsiveness or sensitivity of the postsynaptic endings could also change—for example, by an increase in the number of receptor molecules—so that the same amount of transmitter release would initiate a larger effect (Figure 18.2b). Changes in the rate of inactivation of the transmitter could produce a similar effect.

The amount of neurotransmitter released could also be affected by the influence of terminals from other neurons on the end boutons (Figure 18.2d). That is, impulses from other neurons could alter the polarization of the boutons and thus affect the amount of neurotransmitter released.

Because synapses in the central nervous system are not as reliable as neuromuscular junctions, changes such as those described here could have important influences on the activity of the nervous system.

Structural Changes at Synapses May Provide Long-Term Storage

Many investigators believe that long-term memories require changes in the nervous system so dramatic that they can be seen by microscopic techniques. Structural changes resulting from use are apparent in other parts of the body. For example, exercise changes the mass and/or shape of muscles and bone. In a similar way, the synaptic contact area could increase or decrease as a function of training (Figure 18.2c).

We do not have to limit ourselves to existing synapses. Training could lead to an increase in the number of terminals for the pathway being used (Figure 18.2e), or it could cause a more used pathway to take over endings formerly occupied by a less active competitor (Figure 18.2f).

What Conditions Are Required to Induce Memory-Related Changes at Synapses?

Psychologist Donald O. Hebb suggested conditions that might be required to produce changes at synapses that could account for the development of the nervous system and for learning. Hebb (1949, p. 62) proposed that the functional rela-

Donald O. Hebb
(1904–1985)

Before training

After training

(a)

Axon terminal

Dendritic spine

PSP

More transmitter released

Increased PSP

(b)

More sensitive postsynaptic region

PSP

Increased PSP

(c)

Larger pre- and postsynaptic areas

PSP

Increased PSP

(d)

Interneuron modulation causes increased transmitter release

PSP

Increased PSP

(e)

New synapses formed

(f)

Shift in synaptic input

18.2 Synaptic Changes That May Store Memories

(a) After training, each nerve impulse in the relevant neural circuit causes increased release of transmitter molecules (red dots). The postsynaptic potential (PSP) therefore increases in size (as indicated by the graphs). (b) An increase in size of the postsynaptic receptor membrane causes a larger response to the same amount of transmitter release. (c) The size of the synaptic contact area increases with training. (d) An interneuron modulates the polarization of the axon terminal and causes the release of more transmitter molecules per nerve impulse. (e) A neural circuit that is used more often increases the number of synaptic contacts. (f) A more frequently used neural pathway takes over synaptic sites formerly occupied by a less active competitor.

tionship between a presynaptic neuron (A) and a postsynaptic neuron (B) could change if A frequently took part in exciting B:

> When an axon of cell A is near enough to excite a cell B and repeatedly or persistently takes part in firing it, some growth process or metabolic change takes place in one or both cells such that A's efficacy, as one of the cells firing B, is increased.

Investigators have sought to determine whether Hebb's hypothesis is correct, and positive examples have been found. For example, Kelso and Brown (1986) followed the pattern of differential conditioning in slices of rat hippocampus. They placed three stimulating electrodes in a tract running to the CA1 region. (We will discuss specific regions of the hippocampus later in the chapter.) One electrode was set to deliver a strong, suprathreshold shock, and the other two delivered weak, subthreshold shocks. Stimulation of one weak electrode was paired with the strong electrode, occurring just before stimulation of the strong electrode; the other weak electrode was not paired with the strong stimulus. After a few minutes of such stimulation, the response to the paired weak stimulus was significantly increased in amplitude, whereas the response to the unpaired weak stimulus was unchanged.

Thus, in the absence of a complex circuit, hippocampal synapses show the kinds of conditional changes that could mediate aspects of associative learning. Synapses that show such properties are called **Hebbian synapses**. Hebb later expressed some amusement that his formulation had attracted so much attention, because he thought it was only a formal expression of ideas that many theorists had held for many years and that other aspects of his theory were more original (P. M. Milner, 1993, p. 127).

Hebb (1949, p. 70) also restated what he called the old idea "that any two cells or systems of cells that are repeatedly active at the same time will tend to become 'associated,' so that activity in one facilitates activity in the other." Thus two cells, C and D, that send impulses simultaneously to the same region will tend to make connections to intermediate cells in common, and then no longer act independently of each other. This is an extension of the preceding hypothesis, and it can be used to explain phenomena such as sensori-sensory conditioning and conditional learning (see Chapter 17). Both of these mechanisms can be summed up by the expression: "Neurons that fire together wire together" (Löwell and Singer, 1992, p. 211).

To explain how neural activity could lead to the formation of new synaptic connections as a result of experience, Hebb proposed the dual-trace hypothesis. According to this hypothesis, formation of a memory involves first a relatively brief transient process: Learning experience sets up activity that tends to reverberate through the activated neural cir-

cuits. This activity holds the memory for a short period. If sufficient, the activity helps build up a stable change in the nervous system—a long-lasting memory trace.

Negative Changes May Also Store Information in the Nervous System

We have mentioned only increases in synaptic effects with training, and Hebb wrote only about strengthening synaptic connections, never about weakening them. Changes in the opposite direction, however, could just as well mediate learning and memory, since both making and breaking contacts alter circuits. Later theorists added "weakening connections" to Hebb's formulations, thus greatly increasing their power to account for features of learning and memory. Thus, our list of the ways of increasing synaptic activity or numbers (see Figure 18.2) should be considered shorthand notation for "increasing or decreasing."

Computing What to Remember Requires Circuits of Neurons

For many aspects of learning and memory it may not be possible to find correlates in the responses of individual neurons or synapses; it may be necessary to study the activities of sets or ensembles of neurons. Consider, for example, the cards that a cheering section at a football game holds up: Looking at one or a few cards cannot reveal the pattern made by all the cards. Hebb therefore proposed the concept of cell assemblies—that is, large groups of cells that tend to be active at the same time because they have been activated simultaneously or in close succession in the past. Such groups would include cells that are widely dispersed in the brain and that do not necessarily show any orderly spatial arrangement. Excitation of cells in one part of the assembly would tend to activate other cells in the assembly and so to excite the whole assembly. Such cell assemblies could represent "perceptual elements" that could be grouped into more complex ensembles to give rise to perceptions. Certainly the behavior of neural ensembles depends on unit activity, but it may not be entirely reducible to the activity of units.

In Chapter 17 we found that various kinds of learning require specialized circuits to compute particular features of what is to be remembered. For example, some experiments have demonstrated that different regions of the brain are necessary to process and store different attributes of memory. Each of these brain regions possesses its own particular anatomy of circuits, which differs from that of the other regions, and each region processes an aspect of information that the other regions do not. Several experiments revealed that the temporal pairing of stimuli is neither necessary nor sufficient for conditioning to occur; here, too, complex networks are necessary to process the information, and monosynaptic circuits do not suffice. The distinction between *computation* by neural networks and *storage* of information is stressed by Gallistel (1990), who notes that neuroscientists have been much more concerned with storage than with neural computation.

Cerebral Changes Result from Training

Training and Experience Cause the Brain to Change Chemically and Anatomically

In the early 1960s two experimental programs announced they could show that the brain can be altered by training or differential experience. First was the demonstration by an interdisciplinary team (Figure 18.3) that either formal training or informal experience in varied environments leads to measurable changes in the neurochemistry and neuroanatomy of the rodent brain (E. L. Bennett et al., 1964; Renner and Rosenzweig, 1987; Rosenzweig, 1984; Rosenzweig et al., 1961). Soon thereafter came the announcement by Hubel and Wiesel that depriving one eye of light in a young kitten, starting at the age at which the eyes open, reduces the number of cortical cells responding to that eye (see Chapter 7) (Hubel and Wiesel, 1963, 1965; Wiesel and Hubel, 1965). Although depriving an eye of light is a severe condition, whereas giving animals different degrees of experience without depriving them of any sensory modality is a mild and natural treatment, both approaches lead to measurable changes in the nervous system.

In some experiments, animals have differential opportunities for informal learning. In several experiments, for example, littermates of the same sex were assigned by a random procedure to various laboratory environments. The following three environments were the most common:

1. The **standard condition** (**SC**). Three animals were kept in a standard laboratory cage and provided with food and water (Figure 18.4a). This is the typical environment for laboratory animals.
2. The **impoverished** (or isolated) **condition** (**IC**). A single animal was housed in an SC-sized cage (Figure 18.4b).

3. The **enriched condition** (**EC**). A group of 10 to 12 animals was kept in a large cage containing a variety of stimulus objects, which were changed daily (Figure 18.4c). This environment is considered enriched because it provides greater opportunities for informal learning than does the SC.

In the initial experiments of this series, rats were assigned to the different conditions at weaning (about 25 days after birth), and they were kept in these conditions for 80 days.

At the end of the period of differential experience, each brain was dissected into standard samples for chemical analysis. In the initial experiments, animals in the enriched condition (EC) were found to have developed significantly greater activity of the enzyme acetylcholinesterase (AChE) in the cerebral cortex than their IC littermates had. (Recall that AChE breaks down the synaptic transmitter ACh and clears the synapse for renewed stimulation.) Control experiments showed that this effect could not be attributed to either greater handling of the EC animals or greater locomotor activity in the EC situation (Rosenzweig et al., 1961). Scrutiny of the data then revealed that the experimental groups differed not only in total enzymatic activity but also in weight of the cortical samples: The EC animals developed a significantly heavier cerebral cortex than did their IC littermates (Rosenzweig et al., 1962). This result was a real surprise, because since the beginning of the twentieth century brain weight had been considered a very stable characteristic and not subject to environmental influences. The differences in brain weight were extremely reliable, although small. Moreover, these differences were not distributed uniformly throughout the cerebral cortex. They were largest in the occipital cortex and smallest in the adjacent somesthetic cortex.

Later experiments demonstrated that shorter periods could produce cerebral changes and that brains of adult rats also responded to differential experience.

18.3 Pioneer Investigators of the Effects of Training and Differential Experience on Brain Chemistry and Anatomy
From left to right: Edward L. Bennett, neurochemist; Marian C. Diamond, neuroanatomist; David Krech, biological psychologist; Mark R. Rosenzweig, biological psychologist. (Photograph taken around 1965.)

(a)

(b)

(c)

18.4 Experimental Environments to Test Effects of Enrichment on Learning and Brain Measures
(*a*) Standard condition. (*b*) Impoverished condition. (*c*) Enriched condition. Interaction with an enriched environment has measurable effects on brain measures, on stress reactions, and on learning.

The differences in cortical weights among groups were caused by differences in cortical thickness: Animals exposed to the EC environment developed slightly but significantly thicker cerebral cortices than their SC or IC littermates (M. C. Diamond, 1967; M. C. Diamond et al., 1964). More refined neuroanatomical measurements were then undertaken on pyramidal cells in the occipital cortex, including size of cell bodies, counts of dendritic spines, measurements of dendritic branching, and measurements of the size of synaptic contacts. Each of these measurements showed significant effects of differential experience, as we will see shortly.

Neural plasticity

Experience in the EC environment promotes better learning and problem solving in a variety of tests. It also aids recovery from or compensation for brain damage (Galani et al., 1997; Hamm et al., 1996; Johansson and Ohlsson, 1996; Will et al., 1977). In some cases, a combination of transplanting fetal cells and giving enriched experience is significantly more effective in restoring function than either treatment is alone (Kelche et al., 1995). As we will see later in this chapter, enriched experience also appears to protect against age-related declines in memory, both in laboratory animals and in humans.

Learning Can Produce New Synaptic Connections

The idea that learning and memory can be mediated by the formation of new synaptic contacts has had its ups and downs during the last century. Proposed as early as the 1870s by Alexander Bain, this idea was supported by such eminent neurobiologists as Ramón y Cajal (1894) and Sherrington (1897). Because no concrete evidence was produced to back it up, however, support for the hypothesis waned. Hebb (1949) helped to revive the synaptic hypothesis of learning, but in 1965 John C. Eccles (the neurophysiologist who shared the 1963 Nobel prize in physiology or medicine) remained firm in his belief that learning and memory storage involve "growth just of bigger and better synapses that are already there, not growth of new connections" (Eccles, 1965, p. 97). Not until the 1970s did experiments with laboratory rats assigned to enriched or impoverished environments provide evidence that learning can produce new synaptic connections.

We saw in Chapters 2 and 5 that growth of dendritic spines is a late aspect of the development of neurons and is affected by experience. When dendritic spines were counted in experiments testing EC versus IC, the number of spines per unit of length of dendrite was found to be significantly greater in EC than in IC animals (Globus et al., 1973). This effect was not uniform over the dendritic tree; it was most pronounced for basal dendrites. Different aspects of the dendritic tree receive inputs from different sources, and the basal dendrites of pyramidal cells receive input especially from adjacent neurons in the same region. Thus enriched experience appears to lead to the development of increased numbers of synaptic contacts and richer, more complex intracortical networks.

Psychologist William Greenough also placed laboratory rats in SC, EC, and IC environments, and he quantified dendritic branching by the methods shown in Figure 18.5. EC animals developed dendritic branching significantly greater than that of IC animals (Greenough and Volkmar, 1973; Volkmar and Greenough, 1972). The SC values fell between the IC and EC values and tended to be closer to the IC values. With enriched experience, each cell did not send its dendrites out farther, but instead tended to fill its allotted volume more densely with branches. These results, together with the dendritic spine counts, indicate that the EC animals develop more elaborate information-processing circuits.

More direct measures of numbers of synapses and neurons were then made by more refined techniques (Turner and Greenough, 1985). In layers I to IV of the occipital cortex, the EC rats had about 9400 synapses per neuron versus about 7600 for the IC rats—a difference of more than 20%. The value for SC rats was

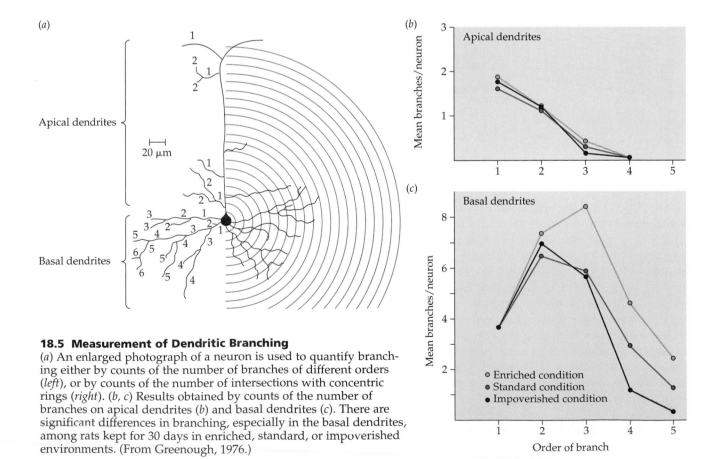

18.5 Measurement of Dendritic Branching
(*a*) An enlarged photograph of a neuron is used to quantify branching either by counts of the number of branches of different orders (*left*), or by counts of the number of intersections with concentric rings (*right*). (*b, c*) Results obtained by counts of the number of branches on apical dendrites (*b*) and basal dendrites (*c*). There are significant differences in branching, especially in the basal dendrites, among rats kept for 30 days in enriched, standard, or impoverished environments. (From Greenough, 1976.)

intermediate, but closer to the IC level. A period of 4 days in EC cages was enough to produce significant increases in dendritic lengths, compared to those of rats kept in individual cages (Wallace et al., 1992).

A study on the effects of formal training used split-brain rats, administering training to only one eye so that it involved only a single cerebral hemisphere (Chang and Greenough, 1982); effects of training on dendritic branching appeared mainly in the trained hemisphere. These results provide strong support for the view that new synaptic contacts form in the cerebral cortex in response to learning and the formation of long-term memory.

The *size* of synaptic contacts also changes as a result of differential experience. The mean length of the postsynaptic thickening in synapses of the occipital cortex is significantly greater in EC rats than in their IC littermates (M. C. Diamond et al., 1975; Greenough and olkmar, 1973). Such increased size and number of synaptic contacts may increase the certainty of synaptic transmission in the circuits where changes occur. The fact that these changes, related to long-term memory, are found in the cerebral cortex is consistent with the hypothesis that much long-term memory is *stored* in the cortex, whereas information is *processed* for memory storage in other brain regions, such as the hippocampus, depending on the attributes of the particular memory (see Chapter 17).

Experiments with several strains of rats showed similar effects of EC and IC environments on both brain values and problem-solving behavior. Similar effects on brain measurements have been found in several species of mammals: mice, gerbils, ground squirrels, cats, and monkeys (Renner and Rosenzweig, 1987, pp. 54–59); effects of training on brain measurements have also been found in birds. Thus, the cerebral effects of experience that were surprising when first found in rats have been generalized to several mammalian and avian species.

The fruit fly *Drosophila* also shows greater branching of neuronal processes when placed in an enriched environment with leafy branches and other *Drosophila*, in comparison with *Drosophila* kept in isolation in small vials (Technau, 1984). Further work confirmed the effects of experience in the *Drosophila* brain, although the roles of different environmental factors have not yet been determined (Heisenberg et al., 1995). Heisenberg et al. (1995, p. 1951) concluded that most regions of the *Drosophila* brain that show extensive neuronal branching "are continuously reorganized throughout life in response to specific living conditions."

The finding that measurable changes could be induced in the brain by experience, even in adult animals, was one of several factors that led increasing numbers of investigators to ask in more detail how the nervous system reacts to training and how new information can be stored by the nervous system.

Invertebrate Nervous Systems Show Plasticity

The relative simplicity of the central nervous systems of some invertebrates led several investigators to try to find in them the neural circuits necessary and sufficient for learning, with the goal of studying plastic synaptic changes in these circuits. Invertebrate preparations, such as the large sea slug *Aplysia* (Figure 18.6), appeared to offer certain advantages for this research, although some of these advantages were overestimated:

1. The number of nerve cells in an *Aplysia* ganglion is relatively small compared with that in a mammalian brain or even brain region, although the number in the invertebrate ganglion is still on the order of 1000.

2. Many individual cells in invertebrate ganglia can be recognized, both because of their shapes and sizes and because the cellular structure of the ganglion is uniform from individual to individual. Thus it is possible to identify certain cells and to trace their sensory and motor connections. The neurotransmitters in some of these large, identifiable cells are also known.

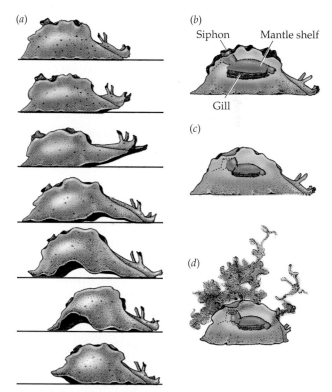

18.6 Characteristic Behaviors of *Aplysia*
(*a*) Locomotion. (*b*) In the usual posture, the siphon is extended and the gill is spread out on the back. Ordinarily only the tip of the siphon would be visible in a lateral view; here the rest of the siphon and the gill are shown as if the animal were transparent. (*c*) The siphon and the gill retract in response to light touch. (*d*) The head retracts and the animal releases ink in response to a strong stimulus. (After Kandel, 1976.)

Eric R. Kandel

A well-known program of research on neural plasticity in invertebrates was initiated by Eric R. Kandel. He investigated sites and mechanisms of plasticity for both nonassociative and associative learning in *Aplysia* (Kandel et al., 1987). Much of Kandel's research indicated that learning takes place within a simple sensorimotor chain that controls the behavior being studied (see Figure 18.1*a*). Many interesting results have been reported from this program, but since the mid-1980s some investigators have voiced reservations about its methods and findings.

Both the number and the size of synaptic junctions have been found to vary with training in *Aplysia* (Bailey and Chen, 1984). This finding is similar to previous findings with mammals (M. C. Diamond et al., 1975; West and Greenough, 1972). It refutes the earlier claim of some investigators that neurochemical events at existing synapses are sufficient to account for learning and long-term memory.

The similarity in results obtained with *Aplysia* and with rats indicates that over a wide range of species, information can be stored in the nervous system by changes in both size and number of synaptic contacts. These findings confirm the hypotheses diagrammed in Figure 18.2*d* and *f*. Thus, even in a relatively simple animal like *Aplysia*, the structural remodeling of the nervous system that we considered early in development (see Chapter 7) probably continues to some extent throughout life and can be driven by experience.

Kandel and his associates have also studied the cascade of neurochemical events that accompany learning in *Aplysia*, as we will note later in this chapter. For a fuller account of the research on *Aplysia*, see Topic 18.1, Plasticity in Invertebrate Nervous Systems.

Special topic

Invertebrate Learning Uses a Variety of Neural Circuits

Reviewing research on learning in invertebrates, Krasne and Glanzman (1995) pointed to evidence for a variety of circuits. Although several studies focus on changes intrinsic to simple circuits, these authors pointed out that the role of higher-level control circuits may be underestimated in these studies because the circuits are likely to be impaired in restrained or partially dissected animals. In both *Aplysia* and crayfish, there is evidence of modulation by higher-level circuitry in freely behaving animals. Furthermore, in both *Aplysia* and crayfish, evidence suggests that learned changes in defensive behavior are due to changes in synaptic efficacy distributed over large numbers of synaptic sites; in other words, there appears to be parallel distributed processing.

Could Long-Term Potentiation Be a Model for Studying Mechanisms of Learning and Memory?

Investigators have long sought a way of isolating a vertebrate brain circuit in which learning occurs so that they could study the mechanisms in detail, much as invertebrate "reduced preparations" are being studied. Some researchers claim that long-term potentiation in the mammalian brain has the advantages necessary for studying mechanisms of synaptic plasticity that may also be important for memory. **Long-term potentiation (LTP)** is a stable and enduring increase in the magnitude of the response of neurons after afferent cells to the region have been stimulated with bursts of electrical stimuli of moderately high frequency (Figure 18.7*a*).

LTP was first discovered in 1973 in the hippocampus of the intact rabbit by British neurophysiologist Timothy Bliss and Norwegian Terje Lømo, then a psychology student. The surprising aspect of their finding was the long-lasting nature of the increase in response magnitude. A shorter-term effect of this sort had long been known under the name of posttetanic potentiation (PTP), which occurs at neuromuscular junctions (see Chapter 11). The 1973 report of Bliss and Lømo has become one of the most frequently cited papers on brain mechanisms of memory. Soon after this report, other investigators demonstrated that LTP could also be studied in slices of rat hippocampus maintained in a tissue chamber (Schwartzkroin and Wester, 1975). LTP can be observed in awake and freely moving animals, in anesthetized animals, or in

Timothy Bliss

Terje Lømo

tissue slices, on which most of the research is now being done. Although most of the work on LTP has been done in the hippocampus of the rat (Figure 18.7*b*), LTP has been observed in many other brain areas in several species of mammals, and even in fishes. LTP can also be studied in sensorimotor synapses of the sea slug *Aplysia* in a cell culture (X. Y. Lin and Glanzman, 1994).

Bliss and Lømo (1973) were cautious as to whether LTP bears any relation to normal behavior. However, LTP does resemble memory in several ways: LTP can be induced within seconds, it may last for days or weeks (Bliss and Gardner-Medwin, 1973), and it shows a labile consolidation period that lasts for several minutes after induction (Barrionueveo et al., 1980). Such properties attracted many investigators to the study of LTP. After reviewing some other findings

(a)

(b)

**18.7 Long-term Potentiation (LTP)
in the Hippocampus**
(a) An example of LTP. After brief tetanic stimulation, the slope of excitatory postsynaptic potential (EPSP) responses increases markedly and remains high throughout the recording period. *(b, top)* Location of the hippocampal formation in whole rat brain and a horizontal section. *(b, bottom)* Diagram of the right hippocampal formation, showing input fibers from the entorhinal cortex via the perforant pathway.

about LTP, we will consider more critically how well LTP may serve as a mechanism of memory. We'll follow our discussion of LTP by looking at an opposite phenomenon, the weakening of synaptic responses, which may also be important as a mechanism of learning.

Different Kinds of LTP Occur at Different Sites in the Hippocampal Formation

Even within the hippocampal formation, there is more than one kind of LTP, although for some time LTP was

assumed to be a unitary phenomenon. The different forms of LTP occur in different sites in the hippocampal formation (see Figure 18.7b). The hippocampal formation consists of two interlocking C-shaped regions, the hippocampus and the **dentate gyrus**, and includes the adjacent **subiculum** (also called the subicular complex or hippocampal gyrus).

The strange shapes of the structures in the hippocampal formation earned them picturesque names: "Hippocampus" itself comes from the Greek *hippokampos,* "seahorse," as we noted in Chapter 2. But other neuroanatomists called it by the Latin name *cornu ammonis* ("Ammon's horn"), referring to the horn of the ram that represented the Egyptian deity Ammon. One region where LTP is investigated is known as CA1 (cornu ammonis 1), another as CA3. The dentate gyrus got its name from its toothlike projections (the Latin *dens* means "tooth"). The Latin *subex* means "underlayer" or "support"; the subiculum can be seen as a support for the rest of the hippocampal formation.

Main inputs to the hippocampal formation come from the nearby entorhinal cortex via the axons of the perforant pathway that push through ("perforate") the subiculum (see Figure 18.7b). The site at which LTP was originally demonstrated consists of synapses from the perforant path to the dentate gyrus. From the dentate gyrus, so-called mossy fibers run to the hippocampus, where they synapse in area CA3. Until recently, LTP was not much studied at these CA3 synapses, possibly because this projection has relatively few synapses, and induction of LTP there requires special conditions, as we will see later. Neurons in CA3 send their axons, called Shaffer collaterals, to area CA1; LTP has been studied intensively at these synapses. The CA1 and CA3 regions also receive inputs from the corresponding regions of the hippocampus in the other hemisphere of the brain via commissural fibers (fibers that cross over through the corpus callosum).

The discovery of selective agonists for different kinds of glutamate receptors in the 1980s allowed investigators to characterize the pharmacology of synaptic transmission in the hippocampus and to study the neurochemistry of hippocampal LTP. LTP in area CA1 was found to require the kind of glutamate receptors that respond to the glutamate agonist *N*-methyl-D-aspartate (the NMDA receptors that we introduced in Box 4.2). Blocking of these receptors by antagonists of NMDA made it impossible to induce LTP in CA1, even though the NMDA antagonists did not affect other glutamate receptors, the AMPA receptors (also introduced in Box 4.2).

Although NMDA antagonists prevent the induction of LTP, they do not affect LTP that has already been established. For a time it appeared that induction of all hippocampal LTP and many kinds of learning

(a) **Normal synaptic transmission**

(b) **Induction of LTP**

18.8 Roles of the AMPA and NMDA Receptors in the Induction of LTP in the CA1 Region

(a) Normally the NMDA channel is blocked by a Mg^{2+} molecule and only the AMPA channel functions in excitation of the neuron. *(b)* With repeated activation of AMPA receptors, depolarization of the neuron drives Mg^{2+} out of the NMDA channel, and Ca^{2+} ions enter. The rapid increase of Ca^{2+} ions triggers processes that lead to LTP. CREB, cAMP response element–binding protein; Glu, glutamate.

might depend on NMDA receptors, but then NMDA antagonists were found not to prevent induction of LTP in some afferents of the dentate gyrus or CA3. Both of these regions obtain their inputs from the lateral perforant path, whereas the NMDA receptor–dependent form of LTP receives its input via the medial perforant path.

NMDA Receptors and AMPA Receptors Play Separate Roles in the Induction of LTP in the CA1 Region

When the neurotransmitter glutamate is released at a synapse that has both AMPA and NMDA receptors, a moderate level of stimulation activates only the AMPA receptors, which handle most of the normal traffic of

messages at these synapses. The NMDA receptors do not respond, because magnesium ions (Mg^{2+}) block the NMDA receptor channel (Figure 18.8*a*) such that few Ca^{2+} ions can enter the neuron. Sufficient activation of AMPA receptors or other excitatory receptors in the same neuron can partially depolarize the membrane to less than –35 millivolts. This partial depolarization removes the Mg^{2+} block (Figure 18.8*b*); the NMDA receptors now respond actively to glutamate and admit large amounts of Ca^{2+} through their channels. Thus, the NMDA receptors are fully active only when they are gated by a combination of voltage and the ligand. The large influx of Ca^{2+} can lead to the next steps in the induction of LTP, as we will see shortly.

Opioid Peptides Modulate the Induction of LTP in the CA3 Region

At the synapses between mossy fibers and CA3 neurons (see Figure 18.7*b*), LTP can be induced even in the presence of an NMDA antagonist, so NMDA receptors are not needed here (E. W. Harris and Cotman, 1986). On the other hand, the induction of LTP in region CA3 can be blocked by the presence of the opioid antagonist naloxone (Derrick and Martinez, 1994). The amount of inhibition depends on the dose: The greater the dose of the opioid receptor antagonist, the greater the blockage of LTP.

In other regions of the hippocampus, opioid receptor–dependent LTP occurs in perforant-pathway fibers arising from the lateral entorhinal cortex and projecting to several regions (see Figure 18.7*b*)—the dentate gyrus, area CA3, and possibly area CA1—via the lateral temperoammonic tract, as well as in the mossy-fiber projection from the dentate region to area CA3. Thus the opioid-dependent form of LTP may be the predominant form of LTP in fibers that convey information from cortex to hippocampus (Derrick, 1993).

LTP in the CA3 region differs markedly from LTP in CA1, both in the rate of induction—that is, the time over which the responses rise in amplitude—and in the duration of the enhancement. LTP rises more slowly but lasts longer in the CA3 region than in CA1. Thus these two forms of LTP differ in their temporal characteristics as well as in their neurochemical mechanisms.

In other parts of the brain too, LTP can be induced without NMDA receptors being activated. For example, in the visual cortex of adult rats, LTP can be induced in the presence of a strong antagonist of NMDA (Aroniadou et al., 1993). But administering blockers of other Ca^{2+} channels prevents the induction of LTP. NMDA activity is known to diminish in the mature neocortex. Aroniadou et al. (1993) concluded that with maturity, the role of the NMDA receptors becomes less important, whereas voltage-gated Ca^{2+} channels assume increasing importance in maintaining synaptic plasticity.

LTP Is Induced via a Cascade of Neurochemical Steps

Several neurochemical steps have been identified in the induction of LTP, and we will see that some of these steps have also been implicated in other kinds of memory formation. In fact, many of these steps are seen whenever a signal leads cells to change the kind of compounds they synthesize or the rate of synthesis.

As Figure 18.9 shows, the entry of Ca^{2+} ions into neurons activates some protein kinases, which are enzymes that catalyze phosphorylation, the addition of phosphate groups (PO_4) to protein molecules. Phosphorylation changes the properties of many protein molecules. Several protein kinases are present in relatively large amounts in neurons, including protein kinase A (PKA), protein kinase C (PKC), calcium–calmodulin kinase (CaM kinase), and tyrosine kinase. Blockage of any of these kinases can prevent the induction of LTP. CaM kinase has the interesting property of remaining activated once it is put into that state by Ca^{2+}, even if the level of Ca^{2+} subsequently falls; only a specific enzyme can cause CaM kinase to revert to its inactive state. Thus CaM kinase could play a role in maintaining LTP.

Research on learning in vertebrates shows that inhibitors of CaM kinase inhibit the formation of intermediate-term memory (ITM), whereas inhibitors of PKC prevent the formation of long-term memory (LTM; Rosenzweig et al., 1992, 1993; Serrano et al., 1994). Recently Huang and Kandel (1994) reported a similar finding concerning LTP in the CA1 region of the hippocampus: One train of 100 Hz stimuli induces a form of LTP that lasts 1 to 3 hours and is blocked by an inhibitor of CaM kinase, but not by an inhibitor of PKA or of protein synthesis; three trains of 100 Hz stimuli induce LTP that lasts 6 to 10 hours and is blocked by inhibitors of PKA or of protein synthesis. Thus, what Huang and Kandel (1994) call two kinds of LTP resemble, respectively, ITM and LTM (see Chapter 17 to review the definitions of the different types of memory).

The activated protein kinases, in turn, not only catalyze the phosphorylation of proteins but also trigger the synthesis of proteins. First they activate cAMP responsive element–binding protein (CREB), a compound we will discuss later in this chapter that occupies a strategic position in the neurochemical cascade underlying memory formation. Mutant mice that lack the main forms of CREB show an intermediate-term potentiation but lack LTP (Bourtchuladze et al., 1994). The activation of CREB recruits transcription factors and leads to increases in immediate early genes (IEGs), a class of genes that are rapidly but transiently expressed in response to extracellular signals such as neurotransmitters and growth factors.

Many IEGs code for transcription factors that govern the growth and differentiation of cell types by regulating the expression of other genes. Only a few studies to date have sought to relate IEGs to the induction of LTP. Some investigators have reported that LTP induction is accompanied by increases in IEGs (W. C. Abraham et al., 1991; Demmer et al., 1993), but others have concluded that activation of IEGs is neither necessary nor sufficient for the induction of LTP (Schreiber et al., 1991). This point remains to be settled.

It is clear that the induction of LTP involves protein synthesis. The earlier stages of LTP, lasting an hour or so, appear not to require protein synthesis, but thereafter inhibition of protein synthesis prevents longer-lasting LTP (Frey et al., 1993; Krug et al., 1984). Three hours after the induction of LTP, certain proteins increase while others decrease, indicating a complex pattern of changes in proteins (Fazeli et al., 1993). Some of these changes may be involved in structural changes in synapses.

In spite of the considerable amount of research devoted to LTP, there are still many disagreements about the processes involved. Some investigators suggest that the main changes occur in the *presynaptic* terminals—increased release of the transmitter glutamate after LTP (Dolphin et al., 1982; Skrede and Malthe-Sorenssen, 1981).

Competing hypotheses

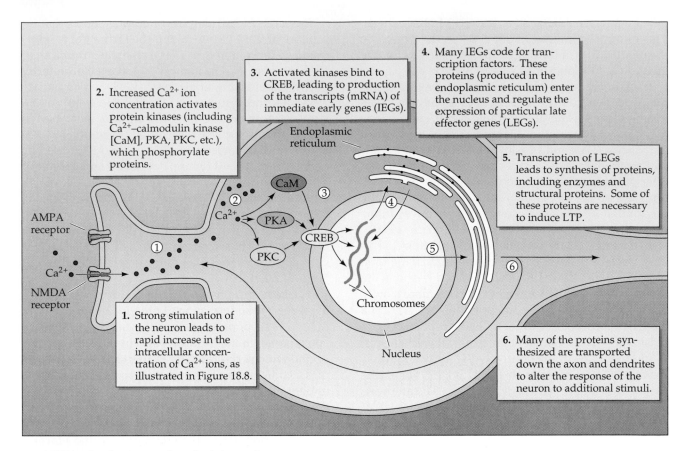

2. Increased Ca^{2+} ion concentration activates protein kinases (including Ca^{2+}–calmodulin kinase [CaM], PKA, PKC, etc.), which phosphorylate proteins.

3. Activated kinases bind to CREB, leading to production of the transcripts (mRNA) of immediate early genes (IEGs).

4. Many IEGs code for transcription factors. These proteins (produced in the endoplasmic reticulum) enter the nucleus and regulate the expression of particular late effector genes (LEGs).

5. Transcription of LEGs leads to synthesis of proteins, including enzymes and structural proteins. Some of these proteins are necessary to induce LTP.

1. Strong stimulation of the neuron leads to rapid increase in the intracellular concentration of Ca^{2+} ions, as illustrated in Figure 18.8.

6. Many of the proteins synthesized are transported down the axon and dendrites to alter the response of the neuron to additional stimuli.

Endoplasmic reticulum

AMPA receptor

Ca^{2+}

NMDA receptor

CaM

PKA

PKC

CREB

Chromosomes

Nucleus

18.9 Steps in the Neurochemical Cascade during the Induction of LTP
This illustration is based on LTP induction in the CA1 region of the hippocampus.

Others hold that the main events are *postsynaptic,* involving increased intracellular levels of Ca^{2+} (Bekkers and Stevens, 1990; Malinow and Tsien, 1990) and exposure of greater numbers of glutamate receptors (G. Lynch and Baudry, 1984). Both presynaptic and postsynaptic processes may participate in LTP, and at present there seems to be no compelling evidence for the exclusive location of changes at either site.

Recently evidence has accumulated that induction of LTP requires a retrograde signal, from the postsynaptic neuron to the presynaptic neuron (see Figure 18.8b). The postsynaptic site is thought to release the signal when conditions of LTP are met, and the presynaptic neuron responds to the signal by increasing transmitter release. Thus, Colley and Routtenberg (1993) speak of the pre- and postsynaptic neurons as being engaged in a "synaptic dialogue" in forming LTP. Both nitric oxide (Schuman and Madison, 1991) and arachidonic acid (M. A. Lynch et al., 1989) are possible retrograde messengers.

Changes in synapse morphology have also been reported when LTP is induced both in intact animals (K. S. Lee et al., 1980) and in slice preparations (Chang and Greenough, 1984; Fifkova et al., 1982). An inhibitor of protein synthesis, anisomycin, was re-

ported not to affect the initiation of LTP in freely moving rats but to prevent LTP from continuing more than a few hours (Krug et al., 1984). This result is consistent with studies suggesting that long-term memory, but not short-term or intermediate-term memory, depends on the synthesis of proteins in the brain, a topic we will consider later in this chapter.

Some of the complexity of and discrepancies in the results of experiments on LTP may come from the fact that several different phenomena seem to be involved. Reviews of the evidence suggest the existence of four or five overlapping but separable effects of prior stimulation on the amplitude of responses of hippocampal cells (W. C. Abraham and Goddard, 1985; Bliss and Collingridge, 1993). Depending on how and when the experimenter measures the responses and on the treatments that are used to affect them, one or another phenomenon may predominate in the results. We have also seen significant differences between LTP induced in region CA1 and LTP in CA3. Further work is needed to sort out these complex phenomena and to decide the extent to which any of them can help us understand the mechanisms of various kinds of learning.

Is LTP a Mechanism of Memory Formation?
Several reviewers support the claim that LTP is a mechanism of memory formation, because of similarities between LTP and examples of learning and memory (G. Lynch et al., 1991; Staubli, 1995; Teyler and

DiScenna, 1986). As we have noted, LTP can be induced within seconds, it may last for days or weeks, and it shows a labile consolidation period that lasts for several minutes after induction. These properties of LTP have suggested to some investigators that LTP is a kind of synaptic plasticity that underlies certain forms of learning and memory. They have therefore sought to test this hypothesis by examining (1) whether other properties of LTP are reflected in properties of learning and memory, and vice versa, and (2) whether various treatments (e.g., drugs) have similar effects on LTP and on learning and memory.

Recent research on this topic has studied both LTP and conditioning in the same neural circuit. One study recorded LTP while an *Aplysia* preparation was being conditioned (G. G. Murphy and Glanzman, 1997). The strength of responses was studied in the abdominal ganglion at a synapse between a sensory neuron from the siphon and a siphon motor neuron. For a cellular analog to sensori-sensory classical conditioning, the conditioned stimulus (CS) was brief intracellular stimulation of the sensory siphon neuron, and the unconditioned stimulus (US) was extracellular stimulation of the nerve from the tail to the abdominal ganglion. Some preparations received a series of paired stimuli: CS followed immediately by US. Then, 60 minutes later, a test shock to the sensory neuron evoked a larger response in the motor neuron than had a test shock before the pairing. The larger response was evidence that LTP had been induced.

In preparations that received a series of unpaired presentations of CS and US, no enhancement occurred. In addition, if the pairing occurred when the NMDA antagonist APV (aminophosphonovalerate) was added to the solution bathing the preparation, no enhancement occurred, although synaptic transmission was not blocked (presumably because AMPA receptors continued to respond to the glutamate). It has not yet been shown whether APV blocks behavioral conditioning in *Aplysia*, and this demonstration will be an obvious next step to test further whether conditioning is mediated, in part at least, by LTP involving activation of NMDA receptors.

In a study involving fear conditioning in rats (Rogan et al., 1997), presentation of a CS (tone) was followed by the US (foot shock), which produced characteristic "freezing" behavior. After a few pairings of CS and US, the tone alone evoked freezing. The amount of freezing during a 20 s period was quantified for a measure of strength of learning. Extracellular potentials were measured in the lateral amygdala, a region where information from the CS and the US converge. As conditioning developed, the responses to the CS in the lateral amygdala increased in amplitude, showing the presence of LTP. In animals that were given the CS and the US unpaired, neither conditioning nor induction of LTP resulted.

Important method

In another study of fear conditioning (McKernan and Shinnick-Gallagher, 1997), rats were trained in much the same way, but with bursts of noise as the CS and a startle response as the CR. Twenty-four hours later, coronal slices through the amygdala were prepared from the brains. Slices were also prepared from animals given unpaired CS and US or given only noise stimuli. LTP was found in the slices from animals that had received paired training but not in slices from rats in the other conditions. Thus, the experimenters were able to study and analyze the synaptic effects of whole-animal fear learning in an in vitro slice, employing the techniques traditionally used in the study of LTP. Potentiation was found only in synapses in the fear-conditioning circuit and not in other nearby synapses, providing additional evidence that LTP serves as a substrate for this kind of learning.

Other evidence for a similarity between LTP and learning comes from experiments in which a particular gene is disrupted to produce so-called knockout mice—mice in which one gene has been made nonfunctional (see Box 7.3). Some laboratories have produced knockout mice lacking one of the enzymes crucial to the LTP cascade, then studied the animals to assess their ability to learn a maze. Kandel's group (Grant et al., 1992) disrupted four different kinases in four different groups of mice. They found that hippocampal LTP was reduced only in the mice missing the kinase gene *fyn*, and that these were the only mice that showed a deficit in maze learning. This result strongly suggests that the fyn protein is important in both LTP and maze learning, and that the electrophysiological phenomenon of LTP is related to learning. Another group of investigators (A. J. Silva et al., 1992) produced knockout mice lacking the CaM kinase II gene; these mice were also slower at learning spatial relations. Interestingly, all of the knockout mice were able to learn the task eventually, indicating that none of these genes is absolutely necessary for learning.

Such findings support the idea that LTP is a kind of synaptic plasticity that underlies or is similar to certain forms of learning and memory and that it can therefore be used to investigate the mechanisms of those forms of learning and memory. The variety of forms of LTP, however, shows that it cannot serve as a general model for learning and memory; rather, certain kinds of LTP may be important for certain kinds of learning and memory, but even this supposition has yet to be proved. Thus some investigators maintain the prudent doubt expressed by Bliss and Lømo in their initial paper that LTP has anything to do with normal behavior.

Joe L. Martinez and Brian Derrick (1996, p. 198) concluded a review about whether LTP is a memory mechanism by conceding that convincing proof that LTP is involved in memory does not exist; nevertheless, they believe that after more than 20 years of research, "LTP remains the best single candidate for the

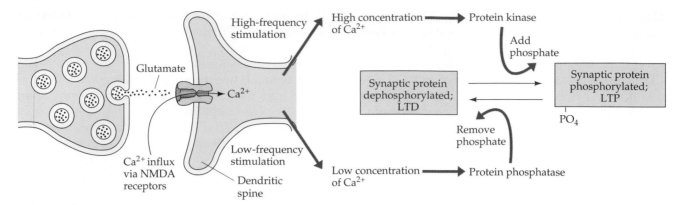

18.10 Model of the Induction of LTP and LTD

High-frequency stimulation causes phosphorylation of a synaptic protein; low-frequency stimulation causes dephosphorylation of the same synaptic protein. The state of phosphorylation of this protein helps control synaptic strength. (After M. F. Bear and Malenka, 1994.)

primary cellular process of synaptic change that underlies learning and memory in the vertebrate brain." On the other hand, A. J. Silva, Giese, et al. (1998) find that while "LTP may be a key contributor to the synaptic changes that encode . . . memories in hippocampal circuits," other cellular mechanisms complement and interact with LTP, and LTP may be necessary but not sufficient for processing and encoding information in the hippocampus.

Long-Term Depression May Be a Reversal of LTP

We noted early in this chapter that negative as well as positive changes can store information in the nervous system. Recently several investigators have shown that **long-term depression** (**LTD**) may play a role in memory (M. F. Bear and Malenka, 1994; Linden, 1994). LTD is the converse of LTP: a lasting *decrease* in the magnitude of responses of neurons after afferent cells have been activated with electrical stimuli of relatively *low* frequency.

In the CA1 region of the hippocampus, induction of LTD appears to require the entry of Ca^{2+} through NMDA receptors, just as the induction of LTP does. How can the entry of Ca^{2+} call for the induction of both LTP and LTD? The critical factor is the amount of change of Ca^{2+}. A large surge of Ca^{2+} in the postsynaptic neuron appears to trigger the induction of LTP by activating Ca^{2+}-dependent protein kinases. In contrast, small increases of postsynaptic Ca^{2+} induce LTD by selectively activating the opposite kind of enzyme—protein phosphatases that catalyze the removal of phosphate groups (Lisman, 1989; Mulkey et al., 1993).

Figure 18.10 diagrams the symmetric nature of this model, in which high-frequency stimulation causes phosphorylation of a synaptic protein and low-frequency stimulation causes dephosphorylation of the same synaptic protein. The state of phosphorylation of this protein helps control synaptic strength.

The Mammalian Cerebellum Houses the Brain Circuit for a Simple Conditioned Reflex

While many investigators studied learning in the apparently simpler nervous systems of invertebrates and others probed the phenomenon of LTP, some tried to define a circuit for learning in intact mammals. Psychologist Richard F. Thompson and his colleagues have been studying the neural circuitry of eye-blink conditioning in the rabbit since the 1970s (Lavond et al., 1993; R. F. Thompson, 1990; R. F. Thompson et al., 1998). Their research has produced a great deal of knowledge about how the eye-blink reflex of the rabbit becomes conditioned, and it has encouraged other neuroscientists to investigate the neural circuits involved in other kinds of learning.

Richard F. Thompson

When a puff of air to the cornea (US) follows an acoustic tone (CS), a stable conditioned response (CR) develops rapidly: The rabbit comes to blink when the tone is sounded. The basic circuit of the eye-blink reflex is simple, involving two cranial nerves and some interneurons that connect their nuclei (shown in black on Figure 18.11). Sensory fibers from the cornea run along cranial nerve V (the trigeminal nerve) to its nucleus in the brain stem. From there some interneurons go to the nucleus of cranial nerve VII (the facial nerve), which is also in the brain stem. Motor fibers in nerves VI and VII activate the muscle fibers that cause the eyelids to close.

Early in their work, Thompson and colleagues found that during conditioning, the hippocampus develops neural responses whose temporal patterns resemble closely those of the eye-blink responses. Although the hippocampal activity closely parallels the course of conditioning, this result does not prove that the hippocampus is required for conditioning. In fact, destruction of the hippocampus has little effect on the acquisition or retention of the conditioned eye-blink response in rabbits (Lockhart and Moore, 1975). Therefore the hippocampus is not *required* for this con-

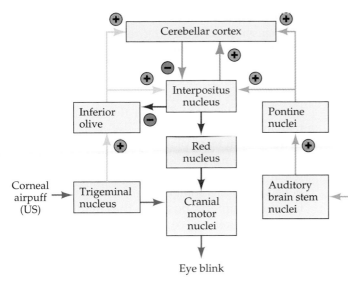

Eye blink

18.11 Sites in the Neural Circuit for Conditioning of the Eye-Blink Reflex

The pathway for the unconditioned eye-blink reflex is at the left in blue. When a tone (CS) regularly precedes a corneal airpuff (US), the inputs from the CS and US converge at the cerebellar cortex and the interpositus nucleus of the cerebellum, where new connections are formed. (After Thompson and Krupa, 1994.)

ditioning. It may, however, participate in the conditioning, as indicated by the finding that abnormal hippocampal activity can disrupt the acquisition of conditioning.

Thompson and his coworkers then searched further, mapping in detail the brain structures where neurons are electrically active during conditioning. They found that learning-related increases in the activity of individual neurons are prominent in the cerebellum, in both its cortex and deep nuclei, and in certain nuclei in the pons (see Figure 18.11).

Deep Cerebellar Nuclei Are Necessary for Eye-Blink Conditioning

In the cerebellum there are only negligible responses to the CS and the US before the stimuli are paired, but a neuronal replica of the learned behavioral response emerges during conditioning. These responses, which precede the behavioral eye-blink responses by 50 ms or more, are found in the deep cerebellar nuclei on the same side as the eye that is trained. The interpositus nucleus appears to be particularly involved. The cerebellar response predicts and corresponds with the form of the CR (McCormick and Thompson, 1984).

Lesion experiments were undertaken to determine whether the cerebellar responses are required for conditioning or whether, like the hippocampal responses, they only correlate with the CR. In an animal that had already been conditioned, destruction of the interpositus nucleus on the side that had been trained abolished the CR. (Whereas the cerebral cortex and the basal ganglia govern activity on the *opposite* side, each hemisphere of the cerebellum governs motor activity on the *same* side of the body.) The CR could not be relearned on the same side, but the opposite eye could be conditioned normally. In a naive animal, prior destruction of the interpositus nucleus on one side prevented conditioning on that side. The effect of the cerebellar lesions could not be attributed to interfer-

ence with sensory or motor tracts, because the animal still showed a normal unconditioned blink when a puff of air was delivered to its eye.

The circuit of the conditioned reflex was mapped in further detail by a combination of methods: electrophysiological recording, localized lesions, localized stimulation of neurons, localized infusion of small amounts of drugs, and tracing of fiber pathways. For example, prior work showed that the inhibitory synaptic transmitter GABA (gamma-aminobutyric acid) is the main transmitter in the deep cerebellar nuclei. Using well-conditioned rabbits, the investigators injected a small amount of a blocking agent for GABA into the deep cerebellar nuclei on the side of the CR. The injection resulted in the disappearance of the behavioral CR and of its electrophysiological neuronal replica. This effect was reversible: As the blocking agent wore off, the CR returned.

On the basis of these and other experiments, Thompson proposed a simplified schematic circuit for the conditioned eye-blink response (see Figure 18.11). This circuit includes the input and output parts of the eye-blink reflex circuit, shown with blue arrows at the lower left of the figure. This pathway ensures the eye-blink reflex, but additional pathways are required to bring together information about the US and the CS.

The pathway that carries information about the corneal stimulation (the US), shown in yellow on Figure 18.11, goes to the inferior olivary nucleus of the brain stem, from where it is carried into the cerebellum by way of axons called climbing fibers, which go to the deep cerebellar nuclei and to cells of the cerebellar cortex, including granule cells and Purkinje cells. The same cerebellar cells also receive information about the auditory CS by a pathway (orange in Figure 18.11) through the auditory nuclei in the brain stem and the pontine nuclei; the latter send axons called mossy fibers into the cerebellum. Efferent information controlling the CR travels along another pathway (purple in Figure 18.11), which runs from the interpositus nucleus of the cerebellum to the red nucleus. From there it goes to the cranial motor nucleus of nerves VI and VII, which control the eye-blink response.

Studies on human subjects are consistent with the animal research on eye-blink conditioning, as we noted in Chapter 17 (see Figure 17.16).

The role of the cerebellum in conditioning is not restricted to eye-blink conditioning. The cerebellum is also needed for the conditioning of leg flexion; in this task, an animal learns to withdraw its leg when a tone sounds in order to avoid a shock to the paw (Donegan et al., 1983; Voneida, 1990). On the other hand, the cerebellum is not required for all forms of conditioning of skeletal muscular responses; cerebellar lesions do not prevent operant conditioning of a treadle-press response in the rabbit (L. Holt, M. D. Mauk, and R. F. Thompson, unpublished, cited in Lavond et al., 1993, p. 328).

The Hippocampus Is Required for Some Kinds of Eye-Blink Conditioning

The hippocampus is not required for animals to acquire a simple form of eye-blink conditioning—specifically, delay conditioning—when little or no time passes between the end of the CS and the US. When the time intervals are longer (in what is called trace conditioning), however, animals from which the hippocampus has been removed are not able to form conditioned eye-blink responses (Moyer et al., 1990). Removal of the hippocampus also prevents the formation of discrimination reversal conditioning—that is, as we stated in Chapter 17, conditioning in which the stimulus that previously served as CS+ is now CS–, and vice versa (Berger and Orr, 1983). The roles of the hippocampus and the cerebellum in this conditioning could be interpreted as follows: The cerebellum represents the direct or obligatory circuitry required for conditioning, and the hippocampus is a modulatory circuit that can facilitate the conditioning. (Later in this chapter we will discuss how learning and memory formation are modulated.)

Features of the Investigation of Brain Substrates of Classical Conditioning

Richard Thompson and colleagues stress three points about investigations of mammalian brain substrates of classical conditioning (Lavond et al., 1993); here we add two others:

Important method

1. The investigation was deliberately restricted to a relatively simple form of conditioning, in the hope that a good understanding of simple conditioning would aid in the study of more complex forms of learning.
2. Learning involves regions of the brain other than just the cerebellum. At the least, the hippocampus and the cerebral cortex are important in more complex learning, and the amygdala appears to be involved in the learning of fear; all three regions probably are involved in aversive classical conditioning.

3. The evidence for localization of plasticity in aversive classical conditioning relies not on a single technique, but on converging results from various techniques.
4. Research using electrophysiological recording demonstrates that brain circuits involved in learning can be located even in the complex mammalian brain.
5. In this case at least, plasticity does not occur in the circuit of the unconditioned reflex; the reflex circuit remains unaffected, but the response can be conditioned through a somewhat complex circuit that is, in a sense, superimposed on the circuit of the unconditioned reflex (see Figure 18.11).

Training Changes Receptive Fields

Training can encode highly specific information in neural circuits. This fact is shown by rapid, precise, and long-lasting changes in the receptive fields of neurons in the auditory centers, either for pure tones or for complex signals such as the vocalization of an individual animal. In research using pure-tone stimuli, receptive fields were determined for cells in the auditory cortex of adult guinea pigs; that is, the response of each cell was measured as the tone was varied in frequency (N. M. Weinberger, 1995, 1998). The blue curve in Figure 18.12 shows the pretraining response of one cell. In this case, the "best frequency" was 0.7 kHz; that is, the largest response occurred for a tone of 0.7 kHz. Then, in the training period, each pulse of a particular tone was followed by a brief foot shock.

The tone used as the CS was chosen to be a few hundred hertz away from the pretraining best frequency of the cell. Within five to ten trials, the animals showed signs of conditioned fear when the tone sounded. When the receptive field of the cell was measured again after conditioning, the receptive field was found to have changed to "favor" processing the CS (as shown by the red curve in Figure 18.12), whereas the response to the previous best frequency was reduced. Moreover, the change in receptive field lasted at least for weeks or months. The changes are associative; they occur only with pairing of CS and US. Thus, the receptive fields in the primary auditory cortex of normal, adult animals are not fixed but can readily be modified by training.

Weinberger and his associates have devised a model of the brain circuit involved in this plasticity and are testing it. Signals from the CS and the US converge at the medial geniculate body (the thalamic auditory center), and training causes transient plasticity of receptive fields in the geniculate, but this change dissipates within an hour. The medial geniculate projects axons not only to the auditory cortex but also to the amygdala; some connections from the amygdala run
Neural plasticity

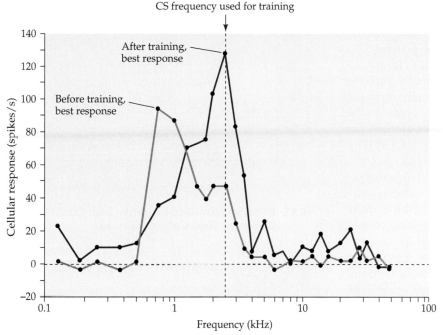

18.12 Long-term Retention of a Trained Shift in Tuning of an Auditory Receptive Field
Before training, the best frequency of this auditory cortex cell of an adult guinea pig was about 0.7 kHz. After training with a 1.1 kHz tone as the CS, the best frequency shifted to 1.1 kHz. Two and 4 weeks after training, the shift remained stable. (From N. M. Weinberger, 1998, Figure 5B.)

to the nucleus basalis. The nucleus basalis sends fibers to the auditory cortex and furnishes cholinergic modulation to the cortex. Recording from each of these areas shows that during conditioning, plastic changes begin in succession in the medial geniculate, amygdala, nucleus basalis, and auditory cortex. Only in the cortex, presumably because of the modulation from the nucleus basalis, are the learned changes preserved in long-term form.

Some auditory neurons in the forebrain of the white-crowned sparrow and the zebra finch respond preferentially to the bird's own song in comparison with the songs of other birds of its species (Margoliash, 1986; Margoliash and Fortune, 1992). The individual bird learns its song from a tutor and could learn a different song, within the range of its species, from a different tutor, so the specificity of tuning of these neurons reveals the accuracy of the learning. Recent work shows that these song-specific neurons respond only when the songs are reproduced within 98% accuracy (Theunissen and Doupe, 1998). We'll consider birdsong and its learning further in Chapter 19.

Memories of Different Durations Form by Different Neurochemical Mechanisms

Memories differ markedly in how long they last, from iconic and short-term memories to long-term and permanent memories, as we saw in Chapter 17. Behavioral evidence suggests that memories of different lengths reflect the operation of different neural processes. For example, individuals like H.M. (see Chapter 17), who have no trouble forming short-term memories, may have an impaired ability to form long-term memories. With habituation and sensitization,

the formation of relatively short-term memories in *Aplysia* involves mainly neurochemical changes at existing synapses, whereas the formation of long-term memories also involves structural changes in existing synapses and changes in the number of synapses.

Since the 1950s, pharmacological agents have been used extensively to study memory formation; this approach has led to many interesting discoveries and to new concepts. Unlike brain lesions or other permanent interventions, many chemical treatments are advantageous for this research because they are reversible. Chemical treatments can produce relatively brief, accurately timed effects, and subjects can be tested in their normal state both before and after treatment. Chemical agents can be given systemically or locally. Systemic administration permits the study of a whole system of widely separated neurons, such as neurons that employ a particular synaptic transmitter. Local injection into a specific brain site can be used to investigate localized processes.

Different agents appear to affect different stages of memory formation. This result has given rise to the concept of sequential neurochemical processes in memory formation. Since about 1960, much research on the formation of long-term memory has centered on the hypothesis that long-term memory cannot form without increased protein synthesis during the minutes (perhaps hours) that follow training (e.g., H. P. Davis and Squire, 1984; Flood et al., 1977; Rosenzweig, 1984). More recently investigators have studied the neurochemical processes involved in earlier stages of memory formation—short-term and intermediate-term memories (M. E. Gibbs and Ng, 1977; Mizumori et al., 1985; Rosenzweig et al., 1992).

Australian psychologists Marie Gibbs and Kim Ng (1977) found evidence that short-term, intermediate-term, and long-term memory in chicks reflect three sequentially linked neurochemical processes. Their experiments studied chicks trained with a single-trial peck avoidance response: The chicks pecked at a small, shiny bead coated with an aversive liquid; after making a single peck, the chicks usually avoided a similar bead whether it was presented minutes, hours, or days later. (Some investigators refer to the aversive bead as "bitter," but bitter taste alone is not enough to cause chicks to form a strong LTM [P. J. Colombo, personal communication].)

The formation of memory for the unpleasant experience could be impaired if an amnestic (amnesia-causing) agent was administered close to the time of training. Gibbs and Ng reported that different families of amnestic agents caused memory to fail at different times after training (Figure 18.13). The agents that caused memory failure by about 5 minutes after training were considered to prevent the formation of STM, those that caused failure about 15 minutes after training were thought to prevent the formation of ITM, and those that caused memory to fail by about 60 minutes after training were thought to be affecting LTM.

Here are some examples of effects caused by different agents: Both the NMDA receptor antagonist APV and lanthanum chloride, which inhibits the influx of Ca^{2+} ions, prevent the formation of STM (and therefore of the succeeding ITM and LTM stages). Ouabain, which inhibits $Na^+–K^+$ ATPase, prevents the formation of ITM (and therefore also of LTM). Protein synthesis inhibitors, such as anisomycin, prevent the formation of only LTM. Some **calcium-dependent enzymes** that have been investigated in regard to memory are **protein kinases**—that is, enzymes that catalyze the addition of a phosphate group to certain proteins.

Protein kinase inhibitors were known to be amnestic, but at first it was not known which stage(s) of memory formation they affected. Peter Serrano found that two classes of protein kinase inhibitors affect two different stages of memory formation (Rosenzweig et al., 1993; Serrano et al., 1994): Those that act on calcium–calmodulin kinase (CaM kinase) but not on protein kinase C (PKC) impair the formation of ITM; those that act on PKC but not on CaM kinase impair the formation of LTM. (As noted earlier, these two kinds of protein kinase inhibitors have a similar differential effect on long-term potentiation in the hippocampus [Huang and Kandel, 1994].)

Not all effects of amnestic agents conform to the three predicted times of the onset of amnesia or to the stage they would be expected to affect (Rosenzweig et al., 1993). For example, the opioid leu-enkephalin causes amnesia beginning more than 4 hours after training, which is later than the LTM stage as defined by other findings. MK801, an inhibitor of NMDA receptors, causes amnesia 3 to 4 hours after training, in contrast to the almost immediate effect of the NMDA receptor antagonist APV. Thus, unsettled issues re-

18.13 Different Amnestic Agents Take Effect at Different Times after Training
Different amnestic agents are thought to impair different stages of memory. They therefore provide a means of observing the duration of each stage. (After M. E. Gibbs and Ng, 1977.)

main, but most of the data confirm at least three stages of memory formation.

The Formation of Long-Term Memory Requires Protein Synthesis

Experiments to test the hypothesis that the formation of long-term memory (LTM) requires protein synthesis have employed both behavioral intervention (in the form of training) and somatic intervention (in the form of agents that inhibit protein synthesis). Training increases the branching of dendrites and the number of synaptic contacts (Black and Greenough, 1998). The enlarged outgrowths of the neurons are made, in part, of proteins. Furthermore, direct measures of protein in the cerebral cortex of rats showed a significant increase with enriched experience (E. L. Bennett et al., 1969). Experiments in the laboratory of neurochemist Steven Rose (Schliebs et al., 1985) have shown that after a chick is trained briefly, parts of its brain can be removed and the training-induced increase in protein synthesis can be followed within a tissue chamber; brain samples from control (untrained) chicks show a significantly lower rate of protein synthesis.

The other side of the story is that inhibiting the synthesis of proteins in the brain at the time of training can prevent the formation of LTM, even though this inhibition does not interfere with acquisition or retrieval during tests of STM or ITM. This field of investigation is a good example of the rigorous testing and elimination of alternatives that characterize an advancing area of research.

Of the many new antibiotic drugs that are created each year, some have been found to inhibit the formation of memory by inhibiting protein synthesis, but many have been abandoned for memory research because of toxic side effects. Furthermore, even strong inhibition of protein synthesis seemed to prevent memory only for rather weak training, so investigators wondered whether there was a real effect of inhibition on memory formation. Use of the protein synthesis inhibitor anisomycin helped overcome previous problems.

Anisomycin was first used in memory experiments when J. H. Schwartz et al. (1971), studying *Aplysia,* showed that inhibiting more than 95% of protein synthesis did not affect neuronal functioning and did not affect *short-term* neural correlates of habituation or sensitization. Then anisomycin was found to prevent LTM storage in mice, although it did not affect STM (E. L. Bennett et al., 1972; Flood et al., 1973). This inhibitor is an effective amnestic agent at low doses; 25 times the effective amnestic dose is nonlethal. Because anisomycin is safe, it can be given in repeated doses; administering it every 2 hours keeps cerebral protein synthesis at about 10% of normal. It may seem strange that the brain can get along with protein synthesis almost completely blocked for hours, but cells contain large supplies of proteins; existing enzymes, for example, can continue directing the cell's metabolism. With repeated administration of anisomycin, Flood et al. (1975, 1977) demonstrated that even relatively strong training could be overcome by inhibition of protein synthesis; the stronger the training, the longer the inhibition had to be maintained to cause amnesia.

Inhibition of protein synthesis prevents the formation of LTM for positive as well as negative reinforcements. When rats ran a radial maze for food rewards, pretrial administration of anisomycin did not prevent the acquisition of STM, but it did prevent the formation of LTM (Mizumori et al., 1985). Similarly, when mice ran a maze for water rewards, inhibition of protein synthesis prevented LTM (Patterson et al., 1987). Thus, inhibition of protein synthesis during the period following learning prevents the formation of LTM for a wide variety of training situations, including learning for both positive and negative reinforcements and situations that involve active and passive avoidance.

Protein synthesis involved in the formation of LTM appears to occur in two successive waves—the first about 1 hour after training, the second about 5 to 8 hours after training (reviewed by Matthies, 1989). Administering inhibitors of protein synthesis so they were effective at either of these periods prevented the formation of LTM. Among the proteins synthesized at these two time periods are synaptic glycoproteins—neural cell adhesion molecules (NCAMs) that are involved in synaptic remodeling. Administration of an antiserum prepared against chick brain glycoprotein prevented LTM formation, not only in chicks but also in rats, and for tasks using either positive or negative reinforcements (Roullet et al., 1997). Thus in general, at least part of the necessity of protein synthesis for establishing LTM seems to involve changes in synaptic membranes.

Additional Evidence Supports the Idea That Memory Forms in Stages

M. E. Gibbs and Ng (1979) reported dips in the strength of memory of untreated chicks at about 15 minutes and 55 minutes after training. They suggested that the dips marked the times of transition between STM and ITM, and between ITM and LTM, respectively. They also found that preventing the formation of one stage of memory inhibited the formation of the following stage(s). These results support the concepts that memory forms in stages and that each stage of memory depends on the preceding one(s).

Further evidence for successive stages of memory formation comes from experiments with relatively weak training. After weak training, achieved by use of a weak solution of the aversive substance, the retention function for control chicks (with no drug treatment) shows four components (Figure 18.14), which may reflect, successively, the sensory buffer (the immediate continuation of sensory input; see Figure 17.5), STM, ITM, and LTM (Rosenzweig et al., 1993).

If these components do represent successive stages, then it should be possible to inhibit each of them with specific agents. The final rise in memory strength, beginning about 60 minutes after training and hypothesized to reflect LTM, was abolished by inhibitors of protein synthesis, in conformity with the hypothesis. Inhibitors of STM abolished all stages after the initial descending limb of the function (the presumptive sensory buffer), thus supporting the hypothesis that the stages are sequentially dependent. So far, it has not been possible with an amnestic agent to inhibit the formation of the presumptive ITM stage after weak training.

In *Drosophila*, Each Stage in Memory Formation Depends on a Different Gene

Because much is known about its genetics, the fruit fly *Drosophila* brings distinct advantages to the study of

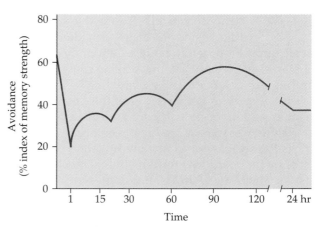

18.14 Four Components of Retention Strength after Weak Training in Chicks
The components of this smoothed curve may reflect, successively, the sensory buffer, STM, ITM, and LTM. (After Rosenzweig et al., 1993.)

mechanisms of learning and memory, even though its central nervous system (which has about 100,000 very small neurons) is more complex than that of the mollusk *Aplysia*. Research with *Drosophila* has corroborated findings obtained with *Aplysia*, as well as adding new information about stages of memory formation and the genetics of these stages.

Research on mechanisms of memory in *Drosophila* began when geneticist William Quinn et al. (1974) developed a method to condition groups of *Drosophila*. They put about 40 flies in a glass tube and let them move upward toward one of two odors that normally are equally attractive. Reaching the upper part of one tube brought an electrical shock; the other odor was not associated with shock. The group could then be tested after various time intervals for approach to each of the odors. As the procedure was refined, about 90% avoided the odor associated with shock (Jellies, 1981). The geneticists then tested mutant strains of *Drosophila*. In 1976 they announced the isolation of the first mutant that failed to learn to discriminate the odors, and they named it *dunce* (Dudai et al., 1976).

Important method

Tests showed that *dunce* had a real problem with learning; its deficiency was not in olfaction, locomotion, or general activity. Three more learning mutants were isolated and named *cabbage, turnip,* and *rutabaga;* another mutant, *amnesiac,* learned normally but forgot more rapidly than normal flies (Quinn et al., 1979). Mutants found in other laboratories were also deficient in learning. Tests with other procedures showed that the failures of these mutants were not restricted to odor–shock training but occurred as well in other tests of associative learning, although the mutants appeared normal in nonlearning behaviors.

The investigators determined which genes were disrupted in each of these mutants (Dudai, 1988; Tully, 1987). Each of the deficiencies can be related to the schema of Eric Kandel, discussed earlier in the chapter. The finding that these genetic defects all fit into the schema of Kandel and associates provides independent support for their hypotheses about mechanisms of plasticity. In evaluating this striking convergence of findings, remember that these mutants were isolated *behaviorally* without knowledge of their genetic deficiencies and independently of Kandel's hypotheses.

Genes and behavior

Further research showed that memory in *Drosophila* has four stages, which the investigators call short-term memory, middle-term memory, anesthesia-resistant memory (ARM), and long-term memory (Dubnau and Tully, 1998). Each stage can be canceled by deficiency in one or more genes specific to that stage. Thus, this genetic research provides independent support for the existence of separate stages of memory. Although ARM has not been reported in other animals, Dubnau and Tully (1998, p. 438) suggest that, given the many similarities between learning in

Drosophila and other animals, "it seems likely that ARM and LTM will be shown to exist as parallel forms of long-lasting memory in vertebrates as well."

The Basic Neurochemical Cascade Extends from Stimulus to LTM

A cascade of neurochemical processes extends all the way from the initial stimulation of a neuron, through conduction of nerve impulses, to short-term changes in responsiveness, and in some cases to intermediate-term changes, or even long-term storage of information. Here we will review some of the processes we have already discussed, adding some further information.

In Chapter 3 we discussed the steps in the activation of membrane ion channels and the flow of ions in conduction of the nerve impulse (see Figure 3.8), as well as the sequence of events in chemical transmission at synapses (see Figure 3.11). More recently we noted the roles of the AMPA and NMDA receptors in the first steps of LTP induction (see Figure 18.8), and then later steps (see Figure 18.9). Figures 18.8 and 18.9 showed that several protein kinases are activated, including PKA, PKC, and calcium–calmodulin kinase (CaM kinase).

Recent research has concentrated on steps that intervene between activation of the protein kinases, in some cases by cyclic AMP (cAMP), and production of the transcripts (mRNA) of immediate early genes (IEGs). A large family of transcription factors bind to cAMP responsive element (CRE) promoter sites (i.e., lengths of DNA adjacent to various genes). When transcription factors bind to such sites, they can increase or decrease the expression of the adjacent genes. One of the best-known factors binding to CRE sites is cAMP responsive element–binding protein (CREB). Several studies have now indicated that CREB is necessary for the formation of long-term memory in both invertebrates and mammals (see the review by A. J. Silva, Kogan, et al., 1998).

In *Drosophila*, genetic studies had implicated the cAMP–PKA pathway, because mutant *Drosophila* strains with disruptions in these compounds showed impaired memory (Tully, 1991). To see whether CREB is required, experimenters inserted a repressor of CREB activity that could be turned on when they wished, by an increase in temperature. Induction of the CREB repressor 3 hours before behavioral training prevented the formation of LTM without affecting the formation of other memory stages (Yin et al., 1994).

In mice, genetic deletion of the main forms of CREB impaired LTM but not STM for training involving both reward (Kogan et al., 1996) and punishment (Bourtchuladze et al., 1994). Thus, mutation of CREB has rather general effects on memory. The possible significance of CREB for human memory is indicated by the fact that a mutation of CREB results in a syndrome characterized by mental retardation (Petrij et al., 1995).

As research continues, we can expect to see the emphasis shift to other steps of the neurochemical cascade. But even though some steps may be easier to investigate or manipulate, it is important to realize that the entire cascade is normally activated to form long-term memory.

Neurochemical Effects of Learning Can Be Used to Trace Changes in Neural Circuits

As well as helping to reveal the processes that lead to the storage of information in the nervous system, neurochemical compounds produced after training trials can serve as tracers for new or altered neural circuits. Here we will briefly mention two examples of such research.

A recent article by Gall et al. (1998) entitled "Mapping brain networks engaged by and changed by learning" reports how changes in expression of the immediate early gene c-*fos* are differentially activated in the amygdala and the hippocampus in successive stages of learning of an odor discrimination task by rats. The balance of activity shifts during the course of learning, both within and between these structures, and the investigators are seeking to relate the shifts to the behavioral output.

Other investigators are studying the regional distribution of a later product of training—neural cell adhesion molecules (NCAMs) (K. J. Murphy and Regan, 1998). NCAMs are produced both during development of the nervous system and beginning about 6 to 8 hours after learning trials in both chicks and rats. NCAM production is associated with the appearance or stabilization of new dendritic spines. The distribution of the NCAMs can be traced within hippocampal–neocortical pathways, suggesting that they play a role in reciprocal connections that underlie the eventual storage of information in the cortex (Figure 18.15).

Neural plasticity

Several Models for the Study of Learning and Memory Show Similar Cascades of Neurochemical and Anatomical Processes

Several other models have been proposed for studying the mechanisms of neural plasticity, including (1) changed responsiveness to drugs, including both tolerance and sensitization (Nestler and Duman, 1995); (2) increased susceptibility to epileptic seizures ("kindling") (Post and Weiss, 1995); and (3) change in the timing of circadian rhythms by exposure to a brief light (Taylor, 1990). Without going into detail about research on these models, we should note here that the resulting findings about cellular mechanisms of plasticity show some of the same neurochemical processes as those obtained from research on conditioning in invertebrate systems, the formation of memory in vertebrates, and long-term potentiation (see Figure 18.9).

Memory Formation Can Be Modulated

Many agents and conditions in addition to those we have already discussed also affect the formation of memory. For example, the general state of arousal of an organism affects its ability to form memories; a moderate state of arousal is optimal (Bloch, 1976). Rapid-eye-movement (REM) sleep in the hours following learning has long been known to improve the formation of LTM in animals (Bloch, 1976), and investigators have recently demonstrated a similar effect in human perceptual learning (Karni et al., 1994). The emotional state immediately following the learning experience also affects the formation of memory for that experience. Specific agents that affect memory formation include stimulants (such as amphetamine and caffeine), depressants (such as phenobarbital and chloral hydrate), neuropeptides, so-called neuromodulators that affect the activity or "gain" of neurons (including agents that elsewhere serve as neurotransmitters, such as acetylcholine and norepinephrine), drugs that affect the cholinergic transmitter system or the catecholamine

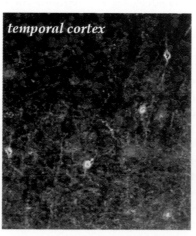

18.15 Neural Cell Adhesion Molecules Are Increased by Training

Ten to 12 hours after rats are trained in either spatial or nonspatial problems, increased expression of neural cell adhesion molecules (NCAMs) is seen transiently in the dentate gyrus of the hippocampus (left) and in the temporal cortex (right). The NCAMs appear, stained green, in the dendrites; the cell nuclei are stained red. (From K. J. Murphy and C. M. Regan, 1998; courtesy of Ciaran Regan.)

transmitters, opioid peptides, and hormones. Experiments with such agents and conditions have suggested that the formation of memory can be modulated—that is, that the strength of memory can be altered.

Many conditions or agents can either enhance or impair memory formation, depending on the time or strength of treatment or other conditions. This variation implies that some biological processes are essential in the formation of memories and that others are modulatory, superimposed on the basic processes. The fact that many treatments that follow training affect memory formation supports other evidence that the cascade of events underlying memory formation takes considerable time.

Emotions Can Affect Memory Storage

Emotion appears to enhance the formation of memory, as we saw in Chapter 17. In research with humans, however, it is difficult to separate effects on memory formation from effects on attention at the time of learning or on rehearsal after the learning session. Research with animal subjects has clarified these effects and has investigated the neurochemical systems and the brain regions involved in the emotional enhancement of memory formation (see reviews by McGaugh et al., 1993, 1995).

Considerable experimental research dating back to the 1960s and 1970s shows that postlearning treatments affect memory storage in rodents. For example, posttraining electrical stimulation of the brain (McGaugh, 1968) and administration of some drugs (McGaugh and Herz, 1972) cause retrograde amnesia. Retention can be enhanced by posttraining electrical stimulation of some brain regions (Bloch, 1970), as well as by some drugs that affect neuromodulatory systems that can be activated by training experiences (Denti et al., 1970). Usually such treatments are effective if administered within minutes after training, but not if given an hour or longer after training. Effects on memory do not require that the treatments act as rewards or punishments. Substances effective in modulating memory storage include neurotransmitters and hormones such as acetylcholine, epinephrine, norepinephrine, vasopressin, the opioids, and GABA, as well as agonists and antagonists of these agents.

James L. McGaugh

Several lines of evidence suggest that epinephrine affects memory formation by influencing the amygdala. Posttraining electrical stimulation of the amygdala can enhance or impair memory formation, depending on the experimental conditions. Lesions of the amygdala induced by the excitotoxin NMDA block the memory-enhancing effects of systemic injections of epinephrine (Cahill and McGaugh, 1991). Injection of epinephrine into the amygdala enhances

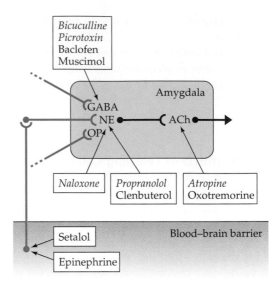

18.16 Model of Neuromodulatory Interactions in the Regulation of Memory Storage
This diagram shows sites of activity of drugs that affect different neuromodulatory and neurotransmitter systems in the amygdala. Antagonists of the transmitters are italicized; agonists are not. ACh, acetylcholine; GABA, gamma-aminobutyric acid; NE, norepinephrine; OP, opioids. (Adapted from McGaugh, 1992.)

memory formation at doses too small to be effective elsewhere in the brain. This treatment appears to cause the release of norepinephrine within the amygdala, as do emotional experiences. Injections of propranolol, a blocker of beta-adrenergic receptors, into the amygdala block the memory-enhancing effects. Opioid peptides also block the release of norepinephrine in the amygdala and elsewhere in the brain.

On the basis of a variety of experimental findings on the effects and interactions of several families of agents—adrenergic, opioid, GABA-ergic, and cholinergic—on memory storage, McGaugh et al. (1993) propose the following model (Figure 18.16): The amygdala influences memory formation in certain brain regions to which it sends axons, including the hippocampus and the caudate nucleus. The amygdala integrates the influences of several neuromodulatory systems that act on it, including adrenergic, opioid, GABA-ergic, and cholinergic. Because several different neurotransmitter systems are involved in this model, multiple agents can affect the influences of emotion on memory formation; some of these agents and their synaptic sites of activity are shown in Figure 18.16. An intact amygdala is not required for either the acquisition or the long-term storage of memory, although it may be a temporary locus of memory storage for a few days after training. Long-term memory may be stored in brain regions influenced by amygdala activity.

The amygdala appears to play more than one role in memory formation. We saw in Chapter 15 evidence that the amygdala is required for fear conditioning. In Chapter 17 we saw that the amygdala appears to play a special role in learning about rewards and punishments. In addition to having these direct roles in some kinds of learning, the amygdala can modulate learning in which other brain regions play more direct roles. Thus, it can enhance declarative learning mediated by the hippocampus, and it can enhance nondeclarative learning mediated by the caudate nucleus.

It is possible that the amygdala can, reciprocally, be modulated in its memory-forming activity by regions such as the hippocampus (Izquierdo and Medina, 1997). Earlier we saw indications that the hippocampus, as well as playing a direct role in the formation of declarative memories, can modulate the activity of the cerebellum in eye-blink conditioning.

Some Brain Measures Correlate with Age-Related Impairments of Memory

In Chapter 17 we saw that some measures of learning and memory decline with aging, even when there is no obvious impairment of the nervous system. Investigators are trying to find changes in the nervous system that may explain such age-related declines in learning and memory. Some of this work is being done with laboratory animals, in which both behavioral measures and brain measures can be obtained from the same individuals (Gallagher and Rapp, 1997). This method is much more powerful than obtaining behavioral and brain measures in separate groups and trying to draw inferences from group means, as earlier studies had done. The animal research on aging also benefits from the shorter life spans of animals, compared to that of humans.

The *ApoE4* Gene Is a Menace to the Mind

A gene that predisposes individuals to Alzheimer's disease also makes people more vulnerable to other conditions that damage the nervous system and impair learning and memory. The *ApoE* (*apolipoprotein E*) gene, which we mentioned in Chapter 7, controls a protein that plays a central role in the homeostasis of lipids in the nervous system and in other organs. The gene exists in three forms: *ApoE2*, *ApoE3*, and *ApoE4*.

The *ApoE2* and *ApoE3* genes have been found to be associated with lower-than-normal risk of developing Alzheimer's and with later age of onset if the disease occurs, but the 15 to 20% of the population that has one copy of *ApoE4* has a greater-than-normal risk of the disease (Strittmatter and Roses, 1996). The 2% of the population who inherit *ApoE4* from both parents are at strong risk of Alzheimer's disease. *ApoE4* is associated with the deposition of β-amyloid protein in the brain, and this protein appears to play a role in Alzheimer's. The exact mechanism by which *ApoE4*,

in conjunction with other factors, causes the neuroanatomical bases of Alzheimer's disease is not yet known, although several research groups are working on this problem and several hypotheses are being tested (Strittmatter and Roses, 1996). The involvement of *ApoE4* in several kinds of brain disorder shows the importance of this research.

Head injury leads to the deposition of β-amyloid in the brain, and this effect is magnified in individuals with the *ApoE4* gene (Nicoll et al., 1996). This deposition is associated with increased mortality following head injury. For persons who survive the head injury, *ApoE4* and the deposition of β-amyloid are associated with increased risk of developing Alzheimer's disease. Nicoll et al. (1996) found that recovery from strokes caused by brain hemorrhages is also influenced by *ApoE4*. They reported that a higher percentage of people who have the *ApoE4* version of the gene died of their strokes, compared to those who lacked that version of the gene (Nicoll et al., 1997).

Head injuries caused by boxing show similar effects. The severity of neurological syndromes in boxers increases in relation to the duration of their careers (see Box 19.4), and recent work suggests that a genetic factor is also important. An exploratory study of 30 boxers found that those who had boxer's dementia or other brain damage tended to be the ones who had the *ApoE4* gene (B. D. Jordan et al., 1992).

A further risk related to *ApoE4* is brain damage following open-heart surgery (Tardiff et al., 1997). Many patients who undergo bypass surgery complain that their minds are not as sharp afterward; some recover from this condition, and some do not. Investigators gave 65 patients memory tests before and after open-heart surgery. Those who had the *ApoE4* gene were more likely to suffer memory impairments.

Even among community-dwelling nondemented elders, free of stroke or other apparent neurological disability, the presence of the *ApoE4* gene is associated with functional limitations. In 158 subjects who did not have the *ApoE4* allele, 50% reported no functional limitations, whereas in the 60 subjects who had the allele, only 28% reported no limitations (Albert et al., 1995). The only known benefit related to the *ApoE4* gene is that it appears to be a protective factor against the development of an age-related visual defect, macular degeneration (Souied et al., 1998).

Beyond identifying people who are genetically susceptible to brain damage, the recent findings about the *ApoE4* gene raise the prospect of being able to prevent such damage. Once the mechanism by which *ApoE4* works to cause or increase brain damage is known, it may be possible to find pharmacological means to prevent or reduce this activity. In the longer run, genetic therapy may make it feasible to introduce healthful genes into the body to replace or counteract genes that cause disorders.

Various Mechanisms Have Been Investigated to Explain the Decline of Learning and Memory with Aging

A variety of possible mechanisms have been examined as potential causes of declines in learning and memory during aging. They include loss of neurons, impairment of the cholinergic system in the basal forebrain, and impaired representation of information by neural circuits. We'll consider each of these possible mechanisms in turn.

Loss of neurons. The brain as a whole shows a gradual loss of weight after the age of 30 (see Figure 7.1), and some parts of the brain may lose a larger proportion of weight or volume than would be expected on the basis of their contribution to the overall brain. We saw in Chapter 7 that shrinkage of the hippocampus in older people correlates significantly with impairment of memory (see Figure 7.22) (Golomb et al., 1994). Alzheimer's patients show significant loss of neurons in the hippocampus compared with age-matched controls.

Although earlier studies suggested loss of neurons in the hippocampus with normal aging, newer, more accurate methods of counting cells show no loss of neurons in the hippocampus during normal aging in humans, monkeys, or rats. The paradox of loss of hippocampal volume without loss of neurons may be explained by several factors—decrease of size of neurons, decrease of neural branching, and/or decrease of glial cells. Any or all of these changes may be related to decreased activity.

Decline in the acetylcholine system. Some studies of age-related changes focus on brain regions that provide inputs to the hippocampal formation. One such region is the **septal complex**, which provides input from subcortical structures to the hippocampus. The neurons of the septal complex are located in the medial septal nucleus and the vertical limb of the diagonal band (Figure 18.17). Many of these neurons use acetylcholine as their transmitter. These regions of the septohippocampal pathway, along with neurons of the nucleus basalis, appear to be involved in the neuropathology of Alzheimer's disease (McGeer et al., 1984; Rossor et al., 1982), and they have also been implicated in declines of memory associated with normal aging (Drachman and Leavitt, 1972).

Experiments by Michela Gallagher and colleagues (1995) compared brain measures in two groups of aged rats: (1) those that perform about as well as young rats on tests of learning and memory, and (2) those that show impairment on these tests. Rats of three age groups—young (4 to 7 months), middle-aged (16 to 18 months), and aged (25 to 29 months)—were trained on a water maze. Special measures of performance taken on every fifth trial showed the number of animals that had reached a designated level of performance (the criterion) by that trial (Figure 18.18). Most young rats reached criterion by the second trial, most middle-aged rats by the third trial, and most aged rats by the fourth trial. No young rat required more than four trials, but some aged rats did not reach criterion even by the sixth trial. However, more than one-fourth of the aged rats reached criterion by the second trial and thus performed as well as the young rats. The aged rats showed much greater variability in their scores than did the young rats, as has been found in many other studies.

Michela Gallagher

Animal model

The investigators then measured the activity of the enzyme choline acetyltransferase (ChAT) in the septal complex; this enzyme catalyzes the synthesis of acetylcholine. Any rats that showed pathology in the gross anatomy of the nervous system were eliminated from the study. ChAT activity in the septal complex was as high in aged rats that performed well as it was in young rats, but the aged rats that performed poorly showed significantly lower ChAT activity than the unimpaired aged rats or the young rats. ChAT activi-

Frontal section through the septal complex

Corpus callosum

Cerebral cortex

Caudate-putamen

Septal complex

Diagonal band

Optic nerve

18.17 The Septal Complex in the Rat
The septal complex is a site at which changes related to defects in memory that occur with aging are studied.

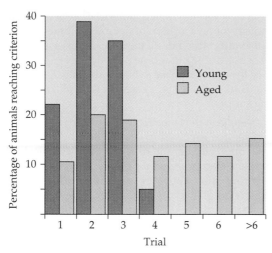

18.18 Performance of Young and Aged Rats in a Water Maze

All young rats reached criterion by the fourth test trial; many aged rats required more trials to reach criterion, but some were as quick to learn as the young rats. (After Gallagher et al., 1995.)

ty decreased not intrinsically with age, but only when aging was associated with impaired performance. This study thus suggests (but does not prove) that the decrease in ChAT *causes* impaired performance with age. Further research may reveal more conclusively the factors that lead to impairment and may suggest interventions that can preserve cognitive functions during aging.

Impaired coding by place cells. Experiments on so-called place cells in the hippocampus (cells that respond when the animal is in a particular location in its environment) show differences in the encoding of information related to aging in rats. In aged rats that showed poorer spatial learning in behavioral tests, the number of hippocampal neurons that responded to spatial cues was not different from that in young rats, but the neurons encoded a smaller amount of spatial information (Tanila, Shapiro, et al., 1997). When the visual cues surrounding a radial maze were changed, the spatial selectivity of place cells decreased considerably in memory-impaired aged rats, compared with that of young rats and that of aged rats with intact memory (Tanila, Sipila, et al., 1997). As noted earlier, the aged rats showed greater interindividual variability than did the younger rats.

Can the Effects of Aging on Memory Be Prevented or Alleviated?

The hippocampus is more susceptible than most brain regions to some kinds of pathology. It can be attacked by certain kinds of encephalitis, and it is easily injured by hypoxia (lack of oxygen), which may occur during major surgery. In Chapter 15 we saw that glucocorti-

coids—adrenal hormones secreted during stress—can damage the hippocampus, which is particularly rich in glucocorticoid receptors. Experiments with rats show that early handling, as opposed to isolation, lowers the concentration of glucocorticoids in adults and retards signs of aging of the hippocampus (Sapolsky, 1993). Rats raised in an enriched condition (EC), as opposed to those in an impoverished (isolated) condition (IC), have lower basal levels of corticosterone and, when challenged by a stressful situation, show a more rapid return of glucocorticoids to low basal levels (Black et al., 1989; Mohammed et al., 1993). Thus, adequate early experience may help protect the hippocampus.

Some research focuses on whether decreased production of nerve growth factor (NGF) causes decline of the hippocampus (Hefti and Mash, 1989). Rats with EC experience show greater expression of NGF in the hippocampus than do IC rats (Mohammed et al., 1993; Ottoson et al., 1995). On the basis of these results, investigators in some clinical studies are infusing NGF into the brains of Alzheimer's patients (Nordberg, 1996; Seiger et al., 1993) in an attempt to prevent or alleviate impairment to the hippocampus and thus preserve memory.

Although it does not pinpoint the hippocampus, longitudinal research on humans indicates that enriched experience throughout life can help reduce the risk of cognitive decline in old age. Schaie (1994), summarizing a 35-year-long study of more than 5000 individuals, listed the following among seven factors that reduce the risk of "normal" cognitive decline:

1. Living in favorable environmental circumstances (e.g., having received above-average education, pursuing occupations that involve high complexity and low routine, earning above-average income, and maintaining intact families).
2. Being involved in activities typical of complex and intellectually stimulating environments (e.g., extensive reading, travel, attendance at cultural events, continuing-education activities, and participation in clubs and professional associations).
3. "Being married to a spouse with high cognitive status" (Schaie, 1994, p. 310).

Enriched experience may also cushion the brain and intellectual function against decline in old age. Masliah et al. (1991) report that loss of synapses correlates strongly with the severity of symptoms in Alzheimer's disease. Enriched experience produces richer neural networks in the brains of all species that have been studied in this regard, as we noted earlier in this chapter. If humans experience similar effects, as seems likely, then enriched experience may set up reserves of connections that protect intellectual function from Alzheimer's.

Summary

1. Memory storage has long been hypothesized to involve changes in neural circuits. Research since the 1960s has demonstrated both functional and structural synaptic changes related to learning.

2. Much current research on neural changes related to learning and memory is based on two hypotheses stated by D. O. Hebb in 1949: (1) The functional relationship between two neurons changes when one frequently takes part in exciting the other. (2) Any two cells or systems of cells that are repeatedly active at the same time tend to become "associated"; that is, activity in one facilitates activity in the other.

3. An early indication that training affects brain measures was the finding that formal training or enriched experience in rats leads to structural changes in the cerebral cortex, including alterations in the number and size of synaptic contacts and in the branching of dendrites.

4. Research on the mollusk *Aplysia* and other invertebrates has demonstrated the existence of plasticity in invertebrate nervous systems.

5. Long-term potentiation (LTP) of neural responses is a lasting increase in amplitude of the response of neurons caused by brief high-frequency stimulation of their afferents. It can be studied in intact animals or in isolated slices of brain tissue. Some of the many different forms of LTP may be components of or models for various kinds of learning. Long-term depression (LTD) may be a reversal of LTP.

6. Conditioning of the eye-blink response in the rabbit is crucially dependent on the cerebellum on the same side of the head; the hippocampus may facilitate acquisition of this response. The cerebellar cells show little initial response to the US or the CS, but during conditioning a neuronal replica of the learned behavioral response emerges along with the CR. Inactivation of the cerebellum on the same side of the head as the stimulus during training prevents conditioning. Eye-blink conditioning in humans involves not only cerebellar and brain stem regions, but also the hippocampus and regions of the cerebral cortex.

7. Neurochemical mechanisms are being investigated for successive stages of memory formation: short-term memory (STM), intermediate-term memory (ITM), and long-term memory (LTM). Each stage appears to be linked to a different part of the cascade of neurochemical events that underlie memory formation. LTM appears to require protein synthesis in the posttraining period: Training induces increased synthesis of protein in certain brain regions, and blocking protein synthesis prevents the formation of LTM, although it does not prevent learning, or the formation of STM or ITM.

8. STM and ITM formation may depend on two different mechanisms of polarization of neurons. Different drugs that affect these mechanisms can cause specific failure at one or the other time period. The stages of memory formation appear to be sequentially linked, because failure of one stage causes failure of the succeeding stage(s).

9. Findings suggest that numerous neural structures and mechanisms are involved in learning and memory. Different brain circuits and different neurochemical mechanisms may be found for different stages of memory formation. Among the species in which neural mechanisms of memory storage have been studied, the mechanisms have been found to be similar, though not identical. This similarity suggests that learning and memory formation use parts of the basic cascade of neurochemical events that extends from initial stimulation of neurons to protein synthesis.

10. Memory formation can be modulated (facilitated or impaired) by neural states and by a variety of agents, including stimulants, depressants, certain neurotransmitters, opioid peptides, hormones, and sensory stimulation.

11. A form of the *ApoE* gene is associated with greater risk of Alzheimer's disease and with greater impairment of brain function caused by strokes, boxing, and open-heart surgery. In elderly people who do not show neurological symptoms, this gene is associated with functional limitations.

12. Some neurochemical and neuroanatomical measures correlate with declines in learning and memory that occur in some, but not all, elderly subjects. The biological changes occur only in subjects who show behavioral decline. The incidence of memory impairments in old age can be reduced by adequate early environment and continuing enriched experience.

Recommended Reading

Baudry, M., and Zola, S. (Eds.). (1998). *Brain and memory: from genes to behavior*. Proceedings of the Sixth Conference on the Neurobiology of Learning and Memory. *Neurobiology of Learning and Memory, 70*, 1–303.

Gallagher, M., and Rapp, P. R. (1997). The use of animal models to study effects of aging on cognition. *Annual Review of Psychology, 48*, 339–370.

Martinez, J. L., and Kesner, R. P. (Eds.). (1998). *Learning and memory: A biological view* (3rd ed.). New York: Academic Press.

McGaugh, J. L., Weinberger, N. M., and Lynch, G. (Eds.). (1995). *Brain and memory: Modulation and mediation of neuroplasticity*. New York: Oxford University Press.

Silva, A. J., Kogan, J. H., Frankland, P. W., and Kida, S. (1998). CREB and memory. *Annual Review of Neuroscience, 21*, 127–148.

19 Language and Cognition

Courtesy of Los Angeles County Museum of Art, Museum Purchase, Art Museum Council Fund

*I*nspection of the week's best-seller list confirms the impression that only humans write books, though chimps may dabble in paint and rats may occasionally eat books. By this and many other measures, human mental life is distinctive in the animal world, and the biological foundations of these abilities, especially language, are beginning to be known. Clues to the relation between the brain and human cognition come from individuals with brain disorders and from hemispheric differences in the brain function of normal people. Specific brain regions are related to particular classes of cognitive disorders, especially language. Imaging techniques such as PET and functional MRI provide confirmation in clinically normal individuals.

In the mid-nineteenth century, the neurologist Paul Broca discovered that lesions in the left hemisphere impair speech and language. More than 100 years later, studies of normal and neurologically impaired humans of all ages continue to inform us about brain organ-

Stuart Davis, *Premiere*, 1957. Oil on canvas

ization and cognition. One of the most fascinating conclusions offered from these studies is that the left and right sides of the brain may perform different but complementary functions. The advent of structural and functional brain imaging has expanded our understanding of brain processes and structures involved in human mental life.

Speech and Language May Have Evolved from Gestures

There are about 10,000 languages in the world and countless local dialects. All these languages have similar basic elements, and each is composed of a set of sounds and symbols that have distinct meanings. These elements are arranged in distinct orders according to rules characteristic of that language. Thus, anyone who knows the sounds (**phonemes**), symbols, and rules (**grammar**) of a particular language can generate sentences that convey information to others who have similar knowledge of the language. The acquisition of language in children is remarkably consistent across all human languages. Indeed, the production of language seems to be inherent in the biological structure of human brains.

Over the centuries, scholars have speculated about the origins of language, but data are scarce. The oldest written records available are clay tablets only about 6000 years old. The absence of older records has promoted a sense of mystery and the creation of elaborate tales about the beginnings of language. For many years, scholars suggested that speech and language originally developed from gestures, especially those involving facial movements. Even today, hand movements often accompany speech. Anthropologist Gordon Hewes (1973) suggested that gestures came under voluntary control early in human history and became an easy mode of communication before the emergence of speech. Other speculations emphasize human imitation of sounds produced by other animals. Many of the ideas about the evolution of the human brain center on the development of language (Corbal-

lis, 1998; Deacon, 1997). Speculation about the evolution of human speech is discussed in Topic 19.1, Some Aspects of Speech Mechanisms Might Form Fossils.

Special topic

Some Nonhumans Engage in Elaborate Vocal Behavior

Chirps, barks, meows, songs, and other sounds are among the many vocalizations produced by nonhuman animals. Many of these sounds, especially calls that distinguish species or signal readiness to mate, accompany reproductive behavior. Other vocalizations alert the group to danger. Could the vocal behavior of nonhuman animals be related to the biological history of human speech and language? Are some attributes of nonhuman vocal behavior akin to human speech? We will explore these questions by focusing on the songs of birds and the sounds of nonhuman primates.

Birdsong. Many birds sing pleasant tunes, and these songs offer some intriguing analogies to human speech. Birdsongs vary in complexity: Some repeat a simple basic unit; others are more elaborate (Figure 19.1). The principal roles of birdsong are territory defense and mate selection (Ball and Hulse, 1998). The intricate patterning of some songs suggests a connection to **Animal model** human speech. Parallels between human speech and birdsong include the importance of early experience and the similarities of neural mechanisms controlling

19.1 Songs of Three Bird Species
For each species, the top trace shows the exact sound pattern detected by a sensitive microphone. The bottom trace shows the same pattern analyzed by a sound spectrograph, which reveals the amount of energy in different sound frequencies at each moment. (After Greenewalt, 1968.)

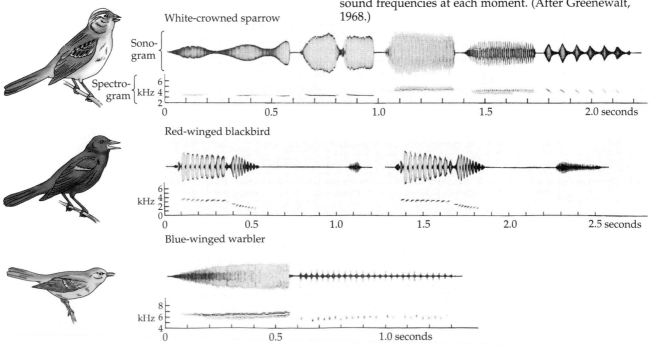

sound production. No investigator believes that bird-song is an evolutionary precursor to human speech. Peter Marler (1970) and other scientists have shown that birdsong can provide an interesting analogy and a useful experimental tool.

Peter Marler

It has long been known that vocal behavior in songbirds can be affected by experience, although some birds have simple vocal behavior that is not affected by early deafening or by rearing in isolation (Baptista, 1996). Song development in canaries, zebra finches, and white-crowned sparrows, as well as many other species, depends on exposure to sounds at particular developmental stages—much as human speech does (DeVoogd, 1994). In contrast, the vocal behavior of ringdoves is unaffected by experience.

Masakazu Konishi

In songbirds, only males of the species sing, and song is acquired in several distinct stages: (1) an initial exposure to the song of a tutor, (2) a period of successive approximation of the produced song to the stored model, and (3) the fixing, or **crystallization**, of the song in a permanent form. Normally, song learning is complete by sexual maturity (90 days). Masakazu Konishi (1985) demonstrated that songbirds show quite abnormal song if they are deafened during the

second stage before they have learned how to produce the final song. Male songbirds raised in acoustic isolation also fail to develop normal song (Figure 19.2). However, if such isolated birds are exposed to tape recordings of species-typical vocalizations during an early **sensitive period**, they acquire normal song; if the birds are exposed to taped songs only later in life, the song acquired is abnormal.

When a bird is exposed to synthetic songs, composed of notes both of the same species and of another, it copies only the song of its own species (Baptista, 1996; Marler, 1991; Marler and Peters, 1982). So the birds show a preference for the species' own song. Interestingly, a bird is more likely to sing the song of another species if its tutor is a live bird rather than a recording. Use of such tutors can also extend the apparent "sensitive period" of otherwise isolated birds (Baptista and Petrinovich, 1986; Morrison and Nottebohm, 1993), suggesting that social stimuli direct the attention of developing birds to an appropriate "mentor," whose song they copy. In isolated zebra finches, the sensitive period can extend well into adulthood, and may be terminated by exposure to a male tutor (Eales, 1985).

The brain birdsong system has been well described as a series of brain nuclei and their connections that control the neural output to the vocal production organ, the **syrinx** (Figure 19.3) (Arnold and Schlinger, 1993; DeVoogd, 1994). A direct pathway, extending from the higher vocal center (HVC) to the nucleus robustus of the archistriatum (RA) to the brain stem twelfth nucleus, seems to control the vocal organ. Le-

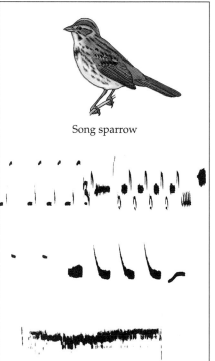

Swamp sparrow · Song sparrow

(*a*) Normal song

(*b*) Reared in isolation, hearing intact

(*c*) Reared in isolation, deafened before singing

19.2 Effects of Isolation on Birdsong
(*a*) Sonograms of the typical adult song patterns of two sparrow species. (*b*) Songs produced by males reared in isolation. (*c*) Songs produced by males deafened in infancy. Either early auditory isolation or deafening results in abnormal song, but the two species still produce different patterns. Deafening has a more profound effect because the animal is prevented from hearing its own song production, as well as that of other males. (After Marler and Sherman, 1983, 1985.)

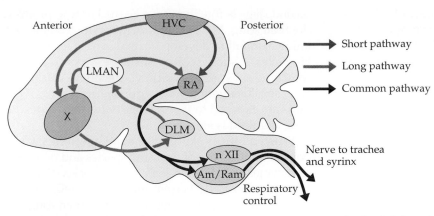

19.3 Vocal Control Centers of the Songbird Brain
Two neural pathways control birdsong. A direct route
from the higher vocal center (HVC) to the nucleus robustus of the archistriatum (RA) to the nucleus of the twelfth
cranial nerve (n XII) is crucial for song; lesions of any of
these areas will disrupt song. The indirect path that
includes the lateral magnocellular nucleus of the anterior
neostriatum (LMAN) may play a role in song learning:
Lesions of the LMAN halt the development of song in
young birds, but lesions of LMAN in adult zebra finches
do not affect singing. X, area X of the locus parolfac-
torium. (From Arnold, 1980.)

This observation indicates left
dominance of vocal control
mechanisms in these birds. Peripheral dominance is matched
by differences in brain hemispheres. Fernando Nottebohm
(1980) has mapped the vocal control centers of the canary brain
(see Figure 19.3), showing that lesions of the direct vocal control
pathway (HVC
to RA to twelfth
nerve nucleus)

in the left hemisphere markedly impair the production of song; singing
becomes unstable and monotonous.
But minimal changes are seen following lesions in right-hemisphere
structures. However, structures of
the brain vocalization system show
no clear anatomical lateralization
(Ball and Hulse, 1998).

Fernando Nottebohm

sions along this direct pathway at any stage of development will disrupt song. A less direct pathway extends from the HVC to the brain stem, and lesions of
one of its components, the lateral magnocellular nucleus of the anterior neostriatum (LMAN), will stop song
development, but similar lesions during adulthood do
not affect song performance (Bottjer et al., 1984).

These results suggest that components of the indirect pathway help sculpt the direct pathway so that it
alone can mediate singing. In Chapter 12 we discussed the role of hormones in the neural development of birdsong circuitry. Song development is par-
alleled by changes in the sizes and organization of
these nuclei. Regions of the brain that control song are
larger in individual canaries that have more elaborate
songs. Furthermore, comparisons of different species
of songbirds reveal that larger song repertoires are related to larger control regions in the brain (Brenowitz
and Arnold, 1986).

Some birds show a striking similarity to humans in
the neurology of vocal control. Changes in membranes of the syrinx are produced by adjacent muscles
innervated by the right and left twelfth nerves—cranial nerves that control the musculature of the neck.
When these nerves are cut, the effects on song differ
markedly depending on whether the right or the left
nerve is cut. Cutting the right twelfth nerve produces
almost no change in song. Cutting the left twelfth
nerve produces an almost entirely silent bird; such
birds "look like actors in silent cinema film" (Nottebohm, 1987). All the correct body movements are
made, but no sound comes out.

Vocalization in nonhuman primates. The calls of
nonhuman primates have been examined intensively
in both field and laboratory studies (Seyfarth and
Cheney, 1997). Many nonhuman primate vocalizations
seem preprogrammed, including infant crying and the
emotional vocalizations of adults, such as shrieking in
pain and moaning. Ploog and his collaborators (Ploog,
1992) studied the vocal behavior of squirrel monkeys,
cataloging the calls they produce and the communication properties of those sounds in a social context. The
monkeys' calls include shrieking, quacking, chirping,
growling, and yapping sounds. Many of these calls can
penetrate a forest for some distance, communicating
alarm, territoriality, and other emotional statements.

Direct electrical stimulation of subcortical regions
can elicit some calls, but stimulation of the cerebral
cortex generally fails to elicit vocal behavior (Figure
19.4). Brain regions that elicit vocalizations also seem
to be involved in defense, attack, feeding, and sex behaviors. These regions include sites in the limbic lobe
and related structures. Changes in electrical potential
are recorded from monkey cortical areas homologous
to human speech areas prior to actual vocalization
(Gemba et al., 1995). However, some investigators
have shown that removing parts of the cerebral cortex
of nonhuman primates has little effect on vocalization,
whereas in humans it can dramatically affect language. Thus we conclude that human speech requires
the cortex, whereas animal cries probably do not.

Nonhuman primate vocalizations differ from human speech in several other ways. In most cases these
vocalizations seem to be elicited by emotional stimuli
and are bound to particular situations. Further, even
in the most talkative nonhuman primate, the number
of distinct sounds is small.

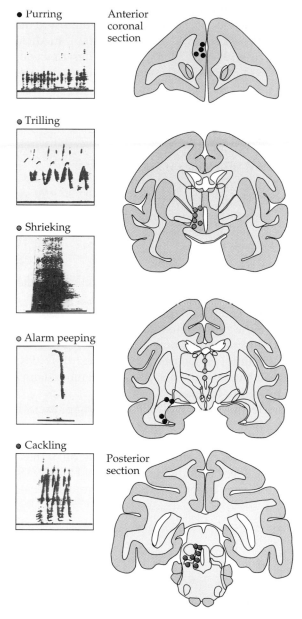

19.4 Electrical Stimulation of the Monkey Brain Elicits Vocalizations

Stimulation at different sites in the monkey brain results in different, species-typical vocalizations. The left column shows spectrograms of different vocalizations, and the coronal sections in the right column show brain sites at which the different vocalizations are elicited. (After Ploog, 1992; spectrograms courtesy of Uwe Jürgens.)

Can Nonhuman Primates Acquire Language with Training?

Throughout history people have tried to teach animals to talk. In most cases, however, any communication between animal and human resulted because the person learned to meow, grunt, or bark rather than because the animal learned to produce human speech. Since both the vocal tracts and the vocal repertoires of nonhuman primates are different from those of humans, scientists have given up attempting to train an-

imals to produce human speech. Can nonhuman primates be taught other forms of communication that have features similar to human language, including the ability to represent objects with symbols and to manipulate these symbols according to rules of order? Can animals other than humans generate a novel string of symbols, such as a new sentence?

R. Allen Gardner and Beatrice Gardner (1969, 1984) trained chimpanzees to learn American Sign Language (ASL)—the sign language used by the deaf in the United States. The chimps mastered many signs and appear to be able to use them spontaneously and to generate new sequences of signs. F. G. Patterson (1978) claims to have taught a gorilla a vocabulary of several hundred ASL words. David Premack (1971) used another approach. He taught chimpanzees a system based on an assortment of colored chips (symbols) that could adhere to a magnetic board. After extensive training, the chimpanzees could manipulate the chips in ways that may reflect an acquired ability to form short sentences and to note various logical classifications.

At the Yerkes Regional Primate Research Center at Emory University, Project Lana has focused on teaching "Yerkish" to chimpanzees (Rumbaugh, 1977). Yerkish is a computer-based language in which different keys on a console represent words. Apes are quite good at acquiring many words in this language, and they appear to string together novel, meaningful chains. Savage-Rumbaugh (1990) claims that pygmy chimpanzees do much better than other chimps in learning the meaning of symbols and in using them to communicate. On the basis of studies such as these, Savage-Rumbaugh et al. (1993) claim that ability to comprehend language preceded the appearance of speech by several million years. Thus, although nonhuman primates (at least those as intelligent as the chimpanzee) do not have a vocal system that permits speech, they appear to have a capacity for learning at least some components of language (Figure 19.5).

Debate about the extent to which chimpanzees learn language has been vigorous, including both methodological and theoretical issues. One of the main critics of the conclusion that chimps can acquire language is Herbert Terrace (1979), who raised a young chimp and taught it many signs. Terrace tested carefully to see whether his chimp or others could construct sentences. According to linguists, grammar is the essence of language, so investigators look for the ability of sign-using chimps to generate meaningful and novel sequences of signs. As we noted, the studies by Gardner and Gardner suggested that sign-using chimps make distinctive series of signs, just as though they were using words in a sentence. Terrace, however, argues that strings of signs have been explicitly presented to the chimps and that the animals merely imitate rather than generate new combinations. He suggests that the imitation is quite subtle

19.5 Chimpanzee Using Symbols
While there is no doubt that chimpanzees can learn to
use arbitrary signs and/or symbols to communicate,
some researchers still question whether this usage is
equivalent to human language. (Courtesy of Sue Savage-
Rumbaugh.)

and may involve cuing practices of which the experimenter is unaware.

Savage-Rumbaugh et al. (1998) have opened a
broader debate emphasizing the nature of language.
True symbolization, they argue, is something more
than the representation of objects or ac-

**Competing
hypotheses**

tion. True symbolization involves an intention to communicate an internal representational process akin to thought.
This process may not be a component of language
learning in chimpanzees, although, of course, questioning the animals about this feature of language use
is difficult. Savage-Rumbaugh (1993) has argued that
apes can comprehend spoken words, produce novel
combinations of words, and respond appropriately to
sentences arranged according to a syntactic rule. She
now believes that the ape's linguistic capacity has
been underestimated. We'll learn later about a brain
asymmetry in humans (the planum temporale) that
has been related to language; a similar asymmetry is
seen in chimpanzee brains (Gannon et al., 1998).

This debate is far from settled, but the accomplishments of the trained chimpanzees have at least forced
investigators to sharpen their criteria of what constitutes language. Pinker (1994) asserts, "Even putting
aside vocabulary, phonology, morphology, and syntax, what impresses one the most about chimpanzee
signing is that fundamentally, deep down, chimps just
don't get it.'"

Language Disorders Result from
Region-Specific Brain Injuries

Much of our early understanding of the relationship
between brain mechanisms and language was derived
from observation of language impairments following

brain injury resulting from accidents, diseases, or
strokes. The history of this topic extends almost to the
earliest written records. Early Egyptian medical
records, written at least 3000 years ago, describe people who became speechless after blows to the temporal bone (Finger, 1994).

The modern era of the study of language impairments following brain injury started in the nineteenth
century. Particularly important was
the observation by the French neurologist Paul Broca of a man who
had lost the ability to speak. Postmortem study of this patient revealed damage to the left inferior
frontal region—a region now known
as *Broca's area* (Figure 19.6). In
approximately 90 to 95% of the cases
of language impairment due to brain
injury—called **aphasia**—the damage
is to the left cerebral hemisphere.
Damage to the right hemisphere is

Paul Broca
(1824–1880)

responsible for the remaining 5 to 10% of the cases of
aphasia. Techniques such as the Wada test (Box 19.1)
also reveal that most of us use our left cerebral hemisphere to control language.

Newer techniques involving brain imaging have
begun to challenge some of the traditional discussion
of language areas of the brain. For example, language-
activated cortical regions are found outside of these
areas noted in lesion studies (e.g., Bavelier et al., 1997).
In addition, some lesion studies (e.g., Dronkers et al.,

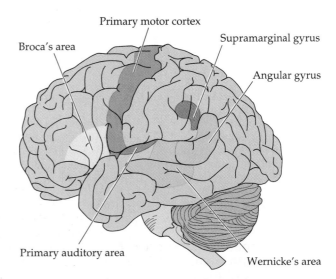

**19.6 Cortical Speech and Language Areas
         in Humans**
Lesions in the anterior frontal region called Broca's area
interfere with speech production; injury to an area of
temporoparietal cortex called Wernicke's area interferes
with language comprehension; injury to the supramarginal gyrus interferes with repetition of heard speech. For
most individuals, these functional regions are found only
in the left hemisphere.

BOX 19.1   *The Wada Test*

Although clinical observations of brain-injured humans indicate that about 95% of us show left-hemisphere specialization for verbal activities, typical psychological tests would have led us to expect a smaller percentage. A technique to produce effects similar to those of brain injury without inflicting permanent damage would be very valuable for neurosurgeons who seek to minimize language impairments from brain operations. Wada and Rasmussen (1960) provided such a tool: injection of a short-acting anesthetic (sodium amytal) into a single carotid artery, first on one side and then, several minutes later, on the other.

Recall from Chapter 2 that the circulation of the anterior two-thirds of the cerebral hemisphere comes from branches of the carotid artery. Most of the anesthetic in the first pass through the vascular system remains on the side of the brain where it was injected. The patient shows arrest of speech for a brief period when injected in the hemisphere specialized for language processing. After a few minutes the effects wear off, so the injection is much like a reversible brain lesion.

The sodium amytal test (sometimes called the **Wada test**, after its discoverer) confirms stroke data indicating that about 95% of humans have a left-hemisphere specialization for language. The Wada test also confirms that while most left-handed people show left dominance for language, the reverse pattern (right-hemisphere dominance for language) is more common in left-handed than in right-handed people.

1995) reveal impacts on language that are not predicted by usual maps of language impairments. With these warnings in mind we present the traditional description, followed by some recent observations from imaging studies.

Several Defining Signs Characterize Aphasia

Distinctive signs of language impairment distinguish several types of aphasia. The most prominent sign of aphasia is the substitution of a word by a sound, an incorrect word, or an unintended word. This characteristic is called **paraphasia**. At times an entirely novel word—called a **neologism**—may be generated by the substitution of a phoneme. Paraphasic speech in aphasic patients is evident both in spontaneous conversation and in attempts to read aloud from a text.

Conversational speech reveals another important aspect of speech: its fluency or ease of production. **Nonfluent speech** is talking with considerable effort, in short sentences, and without the usual melodic character of conversational speech. In some cases of aphasia, fluent speech is *more* abundant than normal. Many patients with aphasic syndromes also show disturbances in the ability to repeat words or sentences.

Almost all aphasic patients show some impairment in writing (**agraphia**) and disturbances in reading (**alexia**). Finally, the brain impairments or disorders that produce aphasia also produce a distinctive motor impairment called *apraxia* (see Chapter 11). Apraxia is characterized by an impairment in the execution of learned movements that is unrelated to paralysis, coordination problems, sensory impairments, or the comprehension of instructions. The patients are unable to imitate some common gestures, such as sticking out the tongue or waving goodbye, although these acts might appear in their spontaneous behavior.

Different Types of Aphasia Result from Injury to Particular Brain Regions

Among the neurologists and researchers who have sought to classify the many different types of aphasia, a prime concern has been the relation between the particular form of language disorder and the region of brain destruction or impairment. Figure 19.6 shows the main brain regions of the left hemisphere that are related to language abilities. Studies of brain-damaged people indicate that language abilities depend on the left hemisphere in almost all right-handed and most left-handed individuals. Damage to the right hemisphere produces major language incapacity in some left-handed individuals. Table 19.1 summarizes the main features of various types of aphasia.

Broca's aphasia.   As we noted earlier, in 1861 Paul Broca submitted postmortem evidence that a large frontal lesion in the left hemisphere produced loss of speech in a patient. This type of aphasia has come to be known as **Broca's aphasia**; it is also described as a nonfluent aphasia. Patients with Broca's aphasia have considerable difficulty with speech, talking only in a labored and hesitant manner. Frequently they have lost the ability of readily naming persons or objects—an impairment referred to as *anomia*. Both reading and writing are also impaired. However, the ability to utter automatic speech is often preserved. Such speech includes greetings ("hello"); short, common expressions ("oh, my God"); and swear words. Although writing is impaired, comprehension remains relatively intact. Most patients with this disorder have apraxic difficulties and right hemiplegia—a partial paralysis involving the right side of the body.

Broca's aphasia is usually associated with lesions of the left frontal lobe, especially the third frontal gyrus and nearby regions of the lower end of the motor cortex. Figure 19.7c shows CT scans of patients

TABLE 19.1 *Language Symptomology in Aphasia*

Type of aphasia	Brain area affected	Spontaneous speech	Comprehension	Paraphasia	Repetition	Naming
Broca s aphasia		Nonfluent	Good	Uncommon	Poor	Poor
Wernicke s aphasia		Fluent	Poor	Common	Poor	Poor
Conduction aphasia		Fluent	Good	Common	Poor	Poor
Global aphasia		Nonfluent	Poor	Variable	Poor	Poor
Subcortical aphasia		Variable	Variable	Common	Good	Variable

with Broca's aphasia. Seven years after a stroke, one Broca's patient (Figure 19.7*b*) still spoke slowly, used mainly nouns and very few verbs or function words, and spoke only with great effort. When asked to repeat the phrase "go ahead and do it if possible," she could say only, "Go to do it," with pauses between each word. Her CT scan revealed a large left frontal lesion and destruction of subcortical areas, including the left caudate nucleus and internal capsule. Broca's patients with brain lesions as extensive as these show little recovery of speech with the passing of time.

Several investigators have argued that lesions restricted solely to the third frontal gyrus on the left side do not produce persistent and severe Broca's aphasia and have suggested that the characteristic aphasic syndrome named after Broca invariably involves a more extended part of the frontal cortex (A. Damasio, 1989; Friedland et al., 1993), such as the frontal operculum and insula (see Figure 19.7*c*). In fact, the initial case presented by Broca in support of his view of localization of function extended well beyond the third frontal gyrus.

Wernicke's aphasia. German neurologist Carl Wernicke (1848–1905) described several syndromes of aphasia following brain lesions. The syndrome now known as **Wernicke's aphasia** includes a complex array of signs. Patients with this syndrome have very fluent verbal output, but what they say contains many paraphasias that often make their speech unintelligible. Sound substitutions (e.g., "girl" becomes "curl") and word substitutions (e.g., "bread" becomes "cake") are common, as are neologisms. Word substitutions and speech errors occur in a context that preserves syntactical structure, although sentences seem empty

of content. The ability to repeat words and sentences is impaired, and patients are unable to understand what they read or hear. In some cases, reading comprehension is more impaired than comprehension of spoken speech; in other cases the reverse is true. Unlike patients with Broca's aphasia, Wernicke's patients usually have no other major neurological disabilities; that is, they do not display partial paralysis.

In Wernicke's aphasia the most prominent brain lesions are in posterior regions of the left superior temporal gyrus and extend partially into adjacent parietal cortex, including the supramarginal and angular gyri (see Figure 19.7*d*) (H. Damasio, 1995). When word deafness (inability to understand spoken words) is more evident than reading impairment, patients show greater involvement of the first temporal gyrus, especially tracts from the auditory cortex. In contrast, when word blindness (inability to understand written words) predominates, greater destruction of the angular gyrus is evident.

Some researchers argue that Wernicke's aphasia may be related to more widespread damage to the temporal lobe than is depicted in usual maps. They note damage in some patients that extends to the deep white matter of the posterior temporal cortex and middle temporal gyrus (Dronkers et al., 1993).

Global aphasia. In some patients brain injury or disease results in total loss of the ability to understand language or to speak, read, or write. This syndrome is called **global aphasia**. Global aphasic patients retain some ability for automatic speech, especially emotional exclamations. They can utter very few words, and no semblance of syntax is evident in their speech. The area of abnormality in the brain is broad, encompass-

19.7 Brain Lesions That Produce Aphasia
(*a*) Levels of the CT scan slices in parts *b–e*. Each level is labeled according to brain language regions shown by that slice: B, Broca's area; SM, supramarginal gyrus; W, Wernicke's area. (*b*) CT scans for a patient with Broca's aphasia, aged 51, 7 years after stroke. (*c–e*) Composite CT scan lesion sites for four cases of Broca's aphasia (*c*), four cases of Wernicke's aphasia (*d*), and five cases of global aphasia (*e*). In *c*, large lesions (blue) were located in Broca's area on slices B and B/W, and the peak amount of tissue damage occurred in the frontoparietal areas on slices SM and SM + 1. In *d*, lesions were located in Wernicke's area on slice W and in the supramarginal gyrus area on slice SM. In *e*, large lesions were present in every language area. (After Naeser and Hayward, 1978; CT scans courtesy of Margaret Naeser.)

ing large realms of frontal, temporal, and parietal cortex, including Broca's area, Wernicke's area, and the supramarginal gyrus (see Figure 19.7*e*). The prognosis for language recovery in these patients is quite poor.

Conduction aphasia. Patients with **conduction aphasia** are characterized by fluent speech and minimal

changes in the comprehension of spoken words, but a major impairment in the repetition of words and sentences. When these patients attempt to repeat words, they offer **phonemic paraphasias**—words with incorrect phonemes substituting for correct sounds. The description of the brain lesion that underlies this form of aphasia is still controversial. Some researchers claim that the key ingredient is destruction of the arcuate fasciculus, a bundle of fibers that connects Wernicke's area to Broca's area. Some cases involve the primary auditory cortex, as well as the insula and supramarginal gyrus.

The Wernicke–Geschwind Model of Aphasia Represents Some Features of Speech and Language Anatomically

Aphasic disturbances span a wide range of language impairments—some quite general in character and others quite specialized—such as the inability to understand spoken language. One traditional approach to understanding aphasic disturbances, begun by Wernicke in the early twentieth century, uses a "connectionist" perspective. According to this view, deficits can be understood as breaks in an interconnected network of components, each of which is involved with a particular feature of language analysis or production. The theory was developed in great detail by Norman Geschwind (1972).

Norman Geschwind
(1926–1984)

Geschwind's view is often referred to as "disconnection theory" to emphasize that symptoms of language impairment following brain injury may result from the loss of connections among brain regions in a network. According to this perspective, when a word or sentence is heard, the results of analysis by the auditory cortex are transmitted to Wernicke's area. In order to say the word, outputs must be transmitted from Wernicke's area to Broca's area, where a speech plan is activated and then transmitted to adjacent motor cortex, which controls the relevant articulatory muscles (Figure 19.8a). The angular gyrus (see Figure 19.8) links the auditory and visual regions. If a spoken word is to be spelled, the auditory pattern is transmitted to the angular gyrus, where the visual pattern is activated.

According to the Wernicke–Geschwind model, saying the name of an observed object involves the transfer of visual information to the angular gyrus, which contains the rules for arousing the auditory pattern in Wernicke's area. From Wernicke's area the auditory form is transmitted via the arcuate fasciculus to Broca's area. In this region the model for the spoken form is activated and transmitted to the face area of the motor cortex, and the word is then spoken (Figure 19.8b). Thus, lesions involving the angular gyrus have the effect of disconnecting the systems involved in auditory and visual language.

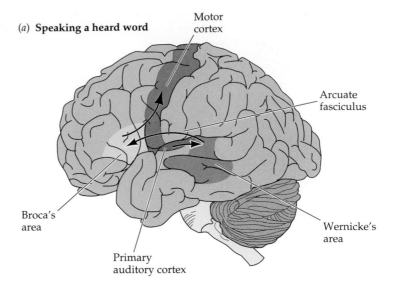

(a) **Speaking a heard word**

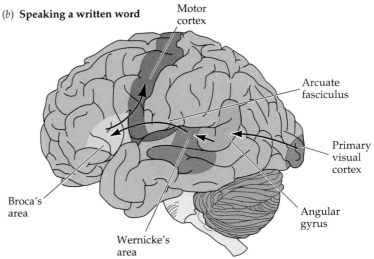

(b) **Speaking a written word**

19.8 The Wernicke–Geschwind Connectionist Model (a) When a word is heard, the sensation from the ears is received by the primary auditory cortex, but the word cannot be understood until the signal has been processed in Wernicke's area nearby. If the word is to be spoken, a representation of it is transmitted from Wernicke's area to Broca's area through a bundle of nerve fibers called the arcuate fasciculus. In Broca's area the word evokes a detailed program for articulation, which is supplied to the face area of the motor cortex. The motor cortex in turn drives the muscles to produce speech. (b) When a written word is read, the sensation is first registered by the primary visual cortex. It is then thought to be relayed to the angular gyrus, which associates the visual form of the word with the corresponding auditory pattern in Wernicke's area. Speaking the word then draws on the same systems of neurons as described in a. (After Geschwind, 1976.)

Patients with lesions in this region would be expected to have difficulty with written language, but they should be able to speak and understand speech. A lesion in Broca's area should disturb speech production but have little impact on comprehension. Many aspects of language disturbances following cor-

Feeling

Be quiet

Secret

19.9 American Sign Language
Aphasia patients who are deaf show deficits in understanding and/or producing sign language that are analogous to language deficits in hearing patients.

tical lesions can be understood from this perspective, which has become the major model for the anatomical analysis of aphasias.

Users of Sign Language Show Aphasia Following Brain Injury

Human hands and arms have remarkable abilities to move in many different and elaborate ways. Some gestures of the hand convey meanings that seem almost universal; some have been used for centuries. Formal hand and arm gestures with specific rules of arrangement form the basis of nonvocal languages of the deaf, such as American Sign Language (ASL). ASL consists of an elaborate code and grammar; Figure 19.9 shows some examples of ASL signs. An exhaustive analysis of ASL by two linguists (Klima and Bellugi, 1979) clearly establishes this gesture-based set of symbols as a language that is as elaborate as its vocal counterparts. In fact, sign languages show features as subtle as dialect. Adding to the complexity of ASL is its heavy reliance on visuospatial differences to convey differences in meaning (Poizner et al., 1990).

Given the unique features of sign language, investigators have been interested in determining whether it is similar to spoken language in its neural organization. Is there hemispheric specialization for a language system based on hand signals, most of which are formed by the right hand, although some involve both hands?

Meckler et al. (1979) described a young man who was raised by deaf-mute parents and who became aphasic after an accident. Previously he had used both spoken and sign language for communication. Afterward, impairments in his spoken language, sign language, and writing were equally severe. He could copy complicated hand and finger movements when he was provided with the model of the experimenter's gestures, but he could not produce gestures in a spontaneous manner.

Chiarello et al. (1982) analyzed sign language deficits in an older deaf-mute. She had well-developed sign language skills until, following a stroke at age 59, she became unable to generate hand signals with either hand. CT scans indicated extensive damage in the left temporal cortex, including Wernicke's area.

Bellugi et al. (1983) described aphasia in three deaf signers who had damage to the left hemisphere. In these patients, differential damage in the left hemisphere impaired different components of sign language. Damage in one region affected grammatical features; damage elsewhere affected word production.

These cases indicate that the neural mechanisms of spoken and sign languages are similar. Cerebral injury in these cases affects a mechanism that controls rules for the ordering of symbolic information, whether conveyed by speech or by hand. Deaf patients with damage to the right hemisphere are like hearing patients with the same type of injury; they show impairments in various visuospatial tasks (described later in the chapter), but their signing is appropriate and includes all linguistic categories of expression. Functional imaging work shows that both hearing and deaf people process their language in the typical areas of the left hemisphere (Neville et al., 1998). However, signers also show extensive activation of homologous areas of the right hemisphere. What contribution the right hemisphere makes to sign language, and why damage there does not obviously impair ASL fluency, are questions that remain unanswered.

Dyslexia Is Characterized by Difficulty with Reading

Some students never seem to learn to read. Their efforts are laden with frustration, and prolonged practice produces only small improvements. The inability to read is called **dyslexia** (from the Greek *dys,* "bad," and *lexis,* "word"). Some dyslexic children have a high

(*a*) Planum temporale, viewed
from above in isolation

L   R

Heschl's gyrus

Area of
micropolygyria

Left   Right

Red dots indicate ectopias and dysplasias

(*b*) Micropolygyria

(*c*) Ectopias

19.10 Neural Disorganization in a Dyslexic's Brain
(*a, left*) Drawings of the left and right planum temporale
(see Figure 19.16) from the brain of a dyslexic show these
regions as nearly symmetrical; in most people the left
planum temporale is considerably larger. The dots and
the shaded area represent regions where microscopic
anomalies called ectopias, dysplasias, and micropolygyr-
ias have been found in the brains of dyslexic individuals.
(*a, right*) Anomalies in dyslexics are much more common
in the left hemisphere, which is primarily responsible for
language function. (*b, c*) Micrographs of (*b*) micropolygyria (literally, "many tiny gyri") and (*c*) ectopias, clusters of neurons in unusual locations, such as this cluster
in cortical layer I (arrow), which is normally devoid of
neuronal cell bodies. (After Galaburda, 1994; micrographs courtesy of Albert Galaburda.)

IQ. The diagnosis of dyslexia includes many different
groups of people who cannot read. It is more common
in boys and left-handed people. Some controversy
surrounds this syndrome, and its characteristics are
probably broader than a reading disorder and encompass other aspects of language dysfunction. Some
people regard dyslexia as a sensory-processing problem; others see it as a memory disorder. Clearly,
dyslexia is a fuzzy clinical category, but it has been
connected to interesting anatomical and physiological
findings (Tallal et al., 1993).

Studies summarized by Galaburda (1994) have
shown various pathological features in the brains of
dyslexic patients. These postmortem observations analyzed four patients who had died from acute disease
or trauma associated with injury that did not involve
the brain. All the brains showed striking anomalies

in the arrangement of cortical cells, especially in areas
of the frontal and temporal cortical regions.

These anomalies consisted of unusual groupings of
cells in outer layers of the cerebral
cortex that distorted the normal layered arrangements and columnar organization (Figure 19.10). Some cells
were disoriented, and excessive cortical folding (micropolygyria) was
observed. Nests of extra cells were
seen. The researchers argue that
these anomalies of cerebral cortical
cell arrangements probably arose
quite early, perhaps during the middle of gestation, a period during

Albert Galaburda

which active cell migration occurs in cerebral cortex.
The result of these deficits might be the production of
unusual patterns of connectivity in language-related
regions of the temporal cortex.

Atypical asymmetries of a specific region near the
Sylvian sulcus within the temporal lobes has been described in boys with impairments of language skills
(Plante et al., 1991). This anatomical finding is also
found in family members of impaired boys, suggesting that it may be a transmissible factor (Plante, 1991).
Although the anatomical asymmetry of brain language areas is clear (as we'll see later in this chapter),
the presence or absence of asymmetry in dyslexic
brains (Rosen et al., 1993) is controversial.

A study by Schultz et al. (1994) cautions that age
and sex have a potent impact on these data. These re-

searchers show that differences found between dyslexics and nondyslexics might be due to small age differences in various studies between control and patient populations. The investigators failed to see anatomical distinctions between dyslexics and controls when differences in overall brain size, age, and sex were controlled. Shaywitz et al. (1998), using functional MRI, found that the pattern of brain activation during a reading task was different between dyslexics and controls. Dyslexic subjects showed relatively little activation of the posterior regions, including Wernicke's area, while showing a relative overactivation of anterior regions. Compared to controls, dyslexics also show less activation of visual cortex in response to written words (Demb et al., 1998).

Sometimes people who have not displayed developmental dyslexia become dyslexic in adulthood as a result of disease or injury, usually to the left hemisphere. This **acquired dyslexia** (or alexia) also tells us about how the brain processes language. One type, known as **deep dyslexia** is characterized by errors in which patients read a word as another word that is related in meaning; for example, the printed word "cow" is read as "horse." These patients are also unable to read aloud words that are abstract as opposed to concrete, and they make frequent errors in which they seem to fail to see small differences in words. It's as though they grasp words whole, without noting the details of the letters, so they have a hard time reading nonsense words.

In another acquired dyslexia, **surface dyslexia**, the patient makes different types of errors when reading. These patients can read nonsense words just fine, indicating that they know the rules of which letters make which sounds. But they find it difficult to recognize words where the letter-to-sound rules are irregular; *The Tough Coughs As He Ploughs the Dough* by Dr. Seuss (1987) would confound them. In contrast to deep dyslexics, surface dyslexics seem restricted to the details and sounds of letters.

These two syndromes suggest that we have two different brain systems for reading—one focused on the sounds of letters, the other on the meanings of whole words (McCarthy and Warrington, 1990).

Many Patients Show Some Recovery from Aphasia

Many people with brain disorders that produce aphasia recover some language abilities. For some people language recovery depends on specific forms of speech therapy. The particular forms of speech therapy are mainly improvisations supported by some degree of clinical success rather than being generated by theories.

The relative extent of recovery from aphasia can be predicted from several factors. For example, recovery is better in survivors of brain damage due to trauma, such as a blow to the head, than in those whose brain damage is caused by stroke. Patients with more severe language loss recover less. Left-handed people show better recovery than those who are right-handed. In fact, right-handed individuals with near relatives who are left-handed recover from aphasia better than right-handed individuals without a family history of left-handedness.

Kertesz (1979) reported that the largest amount of recovery usually occurs during the initial 3 months following brain damage (Figure 19.11). In many instances, little further improvement is noted after 1 year, although this result may reflect impoverished therapeutic tools rather than a property of neural plasticity. In general, Broca's aphasics have the highest rate of recovery. Kertesz suggested that there is a sequence of stages of recovery that are distinguished by linguistic properties and that patients show a transformation of type of aphasia. According to Kertesz, a common end point, no matter what the initial diagnosis, is anomic aphasia, a difficulty in "finding" words, although comprehension and ability to repeat words are normal. Anomic aphasia frequently stands as the residual symptom.

Improvement in language abilities following stroke might involve a shift to right-hemisphere control of language. A case presented by Cummings et al. (1979) lends some support to the hypothesis of a change from left-hemisphere to right-hemisphere control **Neural plasticity**

of language in an adult. CT scans showed total destruction of Wernicke's and Broca's areas in the left hemisphere. Immediately after the stroke, language was limited to small groups of words bereft of meaning. Furthermore, verbal comprehension was severely impaired. Three years later the patient was able to produce comprehensible short phrases and correctly identify objects. Since the left-hemisphere language areas of this patient had been totally destroyed, the investigators concluded that the elements of recovered language were mediated by right-hemisphere mechanisms. Studies on cerebral blood flow following stroke that results in aphasia offer some support for this view. One such study showed that patients with nearly complete recovery of language showed widespread right-hemisphere increases in cerebral blood flow. Those with incomplete recovery showed increases only in the right frontal region.

It is important to note that a concern for remediation following brain injury is relatively recent. For many years researchers regarded the nervous system as a rigidly organized organ without prospects of structural or functional plasticity. We are now in the midst of a major change toward more optimistic views about the prospects of a rational basis for rehabilitation following brain injury. Recovery of language is a top priority of these renewed efforts. One unusual innovation, called melodic intonation therapy, draws attention to the differences between song and speech. Aphasics can frequently sing words and phrases even though they show major handicaps in

(a)

(b)

(c)

19.11 Courses of Recovery of Aphasia Patients
(*a, b*) The course of recovery from Broca's aphasia (*a*), compared with that from Wernicke's aphasia (*b*). These graphs depict the aphasia quotient (AQ), a score derived from a clinical test battery. Higher scores indicate better language performance. (*c*) The course of recovery of auditory comprehension of speech after a stroke in which Wernicke's area was damaged compared with that after a stroke in which Wernicke's area was spared. (Parts *a* and *b* after Kertesz, 1979; *c* after Naeser, 1990.)

the ability to speak words. Melodic intonation therapy attempts to enhance communication by having patients sing sentences they would ordinarily attempt to deliver in conversational form. Therapists have experienced some success in slowly transforming the communication of such subjects from a song mode to a nonmelodic speech pattern. Pharmacotherapy for aphasia also holds some promise for the future (Small, 1994). Drugs that enhance catecholamine functioning have been used to hasten improvement or extend the time for behavioral intervention.

Brain Plasticity Related to Language Development Lasts Several Years

Both external and internal processes direct language acquisition. The internal aspect of language develop-

ment is evidenced by the considerable regularity across all human languages in the timing of its stages. During the first year of life, the babbling of all children sounds similar, regardless of the culture in which they are reared (Stromswold, 1995). The highly specialized attributes of specific languages require learning during early development. Rare cases of children profoundly isolated during early development point to the importance of experience during critical periods early in language development. Restoration of hearing in an adult who had been deaf most of her life supports this critical-period hypothesis for the acquisition of language: She did not learn to speak (Curtiss, 1989).

The notion of the special importance of childhood for language acquisition is also supported by the difficulty postadolescents experience in learning a second language. Imaging studies indicate that people who learn a second language early in life activate the same brain region when using either language. But people learning a second language later than age 11 seem to use different brain regions when using each language (K. H. Kim et al., 1997). This difference in brain organization may be related to the greater fluency of people who learn another language by the age of 6 or 7 (J. S. Johnson and Newport, 1989).

The hemispheric asymmetry of language areas of the brain that is characteristic of adults is also evident in human fetal brains (described later in the chapter). Synaptic development of language areas in the left hemisphere, such as Broca's area, is slower than that of the same region in the right hemisphere (Scheibel, 1982). One research focus is the development of lateralization in children, as seen in structures of the brain and functions such as dichotic listening (which we will describe a little later). Newborn babies turn their heads far more often to the right than to the left (Turkewitz, 1988). Electrophysiological asymmetry of the infant cerebral hemispheres is evident in the response of babies to speech sounds. Thus, from quite early in development, the human brain is structurally and functionally lateralized.

BOX 19.2   *Childhood Loss of One Hemisphere*

During early development the brain is a vulnerable organ—a fact that is especially apparent when we look at the effect of a prolonged, difficult birth involving a period of oxygen loss: Some such children sustain lateralized brain injury involving a single cerebral hemisphere. Early in development such a child may show paralysis on one side of the body and frequent seizures. These seizures can be difficult to control with medication, and they may occur so often that they endanger life.

Surgical removal of the malfunctioning hemisphere reduces seizures. Although at first some severe effects of the surgery are evident, over a long period of time the restoration of behavior is practically complete. This result is strikingly illustrated in a case presented by A. Smith and Sugar (1975). The boy in this study showed paralysis on his right side as an infant, and by 5 years of age he was experiencing 10 to 12 seizures a day. Although the boy's verbal comprehension was normal, his speech was hard to understand. To treat the problem, doctors removed all the cerebral cortex of the left hemisphere. Long-term follow-up studies extended to age 26, when the patient had almost completed college.

Tests revealed an above-normal IQ and superior language abilities; thus the early loss of most of the left hemisphere had not precluded language development. This patient also had remarkable development of nonverbal functions, including visuospatial tasks and manual tasks.

Whereas adult hemispherectomy of the left side usually results in drastic impairment of language, affecting both speech and writing, this case shows that childhood hemispherectomy can be followed by extensive functional recovery. This demonstrates the additional plasticity of the young brain.

Language commonly develops after childhood aphasia resulting from brain injury. In childhood, language recovery is possible even after the removal of a hemisphere (see Box 19.2). These observations suggest that the right hemisphere can take over the language functions of the left hemisphere if impairment occurs early in life. As we grow older, the brain slowly loses the ability to compensate for injury.

Electrical Stimulation of the Brain Provides Information about Brain Organization of Language

Electrical stimulation of the brain is used to explore language functions of the human cerebral cortex. Subjects in these studies are patients undergoing surgery for the relief of seizures. Electrical stimulation helps neurosurgeons locate—and thus avoid damaging—language-related cortical regions. By observing language interference produced by the electrical stimuli, the surgeon can identify these regions. Patients are given only local anesthesia, so that they can continue to communicate verbally.

Pioneering work by Penfield and Roberts (1959) provided a map of language-related zones of the left hemisphere (Figure 19.12a). Pooled data from many patients showed that stimulation anywhere within a

19.12 Electrical Stimulation of Some Brain Sites Can Interfere with Language
(a) Summary of data obtained from many patients, showing the brain sites where stimulation interferes with speech production. (b) Map of stimulation sites that affected the speech of a patient who was bilingual—fluent in Spanish and English. Different regions interfere with either one language or the other, but not both. (Part *a* after Penfield and Roberts, 1959; *b* after Ojemann and Mateer, 1979.)

(*a*) Sites where stimulation interferes with speech in monolingual patients

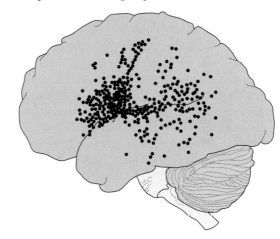

(*b*) Sites where stimulation affects speech in a bilingual patient

○   No naming errors
●   Naming errors in English only
◐   Naming errors in Spanish only
M   Motor response
S   Sensory response

1 cm

large anterior zone arrests speech. Speech simply stopped during the period of applied stimulation. Other forms of language interference, such as misnaming or impaired repetition of words, were evident from stimulation of both this region and more posterior temporoparietal cortex regions. More recent intensive studies of the effects of electrical stimulation of Broca's area add other features to the list of effects (Schaffler et al., 1993). During stimulation, patients in these studies were unable to comprehend auditory or visual semantic material; the impairment included the inability to follow oral commands, point to objects, or understand written questions.

The investigation of language organization during neurosurgical procedures has been a special focus of George Ojemann and collaborators (summarized in Calvin and Ojemann, 1994). These researchers examined the effects of electrical stimulation within a wide extent of cerebral cortex, focusing on the possible compartmentalization of linguistic systems such as naming, reading, speech production, and verbal memory. An interesting example of the effects of cortical stimulation on naming is shown in Figure 19.12*b*, which shows the different loci of naming errors in English and Spanish in a subject who spoke both languages.

Ojemann and Mateer (1979) present more detailed cortical maps, which reveal several different systems. Stimulation of one system arrests speech and impairs all facial movements. This system, located in the inferior premotor frontal cortex, was regarded as the cortical, final motor pathway for speech. Stimulation of a second system alters sequential facial movements and impairs phoneme identification. This system included sites in the inferior frontal, temporal, and parietal cortex. A third system was defined by stimulation-induced memory errors; it surrounds the sites of the systems that impair phoneme identification. Reading errors are elicited by stimulation of yet other cortical positions.

Ojemann also noted that stimulation of the thalamus at the time of verbal input increases the accuracy of subsequent recall (as late as 1 week after stimulation). He suggests that a thalamic mechanism specifically modulates the recall of verbal information. This conclusion fits with the description of patient N.A. in Chapter 17, in whom damage to the thalamus impaired verbal memory.

Functional Neuroimaging Portrays Brain Organization for Speech and Language

The advent of PET and functional-MRI techniques has allowed researchers to obtain portraits of the activity of the brain during periods of activation by various language tasks. A series of studies, summarized by Posner and Raichle (1994), examined PET activation

during different levels of the processing of words. These levels include (1) passive exposure to visually presented words, (2) passive exposure to spoken words, (3) oral repetition of words, and (4) generation of a semantic association to a presented word. The successive levels of these experiments and the accompanying PET scans are presented in Figure 19.13.

◿ **Important method**

Passive viewing of words activates a posterior area within the left hemisphere (Figure 19.13*a*). Passive hearing of words shifts the focus of maximum brain activation to the temporal lobes (Figure 19.13*b*). Repeating the words orally activates the motor cortex of both sides, the supplementary motor cortex, and a portion of the cerebellum and insular cortex (Figure 19.13*c*). During word repetition or reading aloud, activity was relatively absent in Broca's area. But when subjects were required to present a verb that was an appropriate semantic association for a presented noun, language-related regions in the left hemisphere, including Broca's area, were markedly activated (Figure 19.13*d*).

Functional brain imaging also suggests that different parts of the brain are used to store the names of different types of objects. Hanna Damasio et al. (1996), using PET scans in neurologically normal people, found that different regions of the left hemisphere (other than Broca's or Wernicke's areas) were activated differentially depending on whether the subjects were asked to name tools, animals, or unique persons. Close scrutiny of stroke patients confirmed the idea: Damage in one area affected recognition of animals but not tools or people, damage to another area affected recognition of tools but not the other categories, and so on (Tranel et al., 1997). Later studies in neurologically normal people indicated that word retrieval in these three different categories (tools, animals, people) also activates three different regions in the frontal lobes (Grabowski et al., 1998).

Finally, event-related potentials (ERPs; see Chapter 3) also confirm the activation of different brain regions depending on which aspect of language is being performed. Subjects are asked to read a sentence in which they encounter a word that is grammatically correct but, because of its meaning, doesn't fit. "The man started the car engine and stepped on the pancake." About 400 ms after the patient reads the word "pancake," a negative wave is detected on the scalp (Kutas and Hillyard, 1980). Such "N400" responses ("N" denotes "negative," and the number represents the response time in milliseconds) to word meanings seem to be centered over the temporal lobe (Neville et al., 1992) and therefore may originate from Wernicke's area. But *grammatically* inappropriate words elicit a positive potential about 600 ms after encountering the word (a P600 response) (Osterhout et al., 1997), and this potential seems to originate from another part of the brain.

(*a*) Passively viewing words

Level = 40 20 0 −12 −20

(*b*) Listening to words

(*c*) Speaking words

(*d*) Generating a verb associated with each noun shown

19.13 Subtractive PET Scans of Brain Activation in Progressively More Complex Language Tasks
(*Left*) For clarity concerning the tasks, we depict the subjects at a desk, but when the PET scans were made, the subjects reclined with their heads in a PET scanner and viewed a specially mounted display. (*Right*) PET scans corresponding to the tasks at left; see text for details on these results. (After Posner and Raichle, 1994; PET scans courtesy of Marcus Raichle.)

The Left Brain Is Different from the Right Brain

By the early twentieth century, it was firmly established that the cerebral hemispheres are not equivalent in mediating language functions (Finger, 1994, pp. 386–399). The left hemisphere seemed to control this function and was commonly described as the dominant hemisphere. However, the right hemisphere does not just sit within the skull awaiting the call to duty when the left side of the brain is injured. In fact, many researchers have slowly drifted from notions of cerebral dominance to ideas of hemispheric specialization, or **lateralization**. This newer emphasis implies that some functional systems are connected more to one side of the brain than the other—that is, that functions become lateralized—and that each hemisphere is specialized for particular ways of working.

Lateralization of function is not a surprising idea; a broad look at the distribution of body organs shows considerable asymmetry between the right and left sides. For example, the heart is on the left and the liver is on the right. Almost all species, even very simple ones, show such lateral differences (see Topic 19.2, Handedness in Toads). Nevertheless, at the level of brain processing in normal individuals, the interconnections of the hemispheres ordinarily mask evidence of hemisphere specialization. But by studying patients whose interhemispheric pathways have been disconnected—**split-brain individuals**—researchers have been able to see cerebral hemispheric specialization in cognitive, perceptual, emotional, and motor activities.

Special topic

Are There Two Minds in One Head?

The differential properties of the cerebral hemispheres are best illustrated in a series of studies by Roger Sperry and collaborators at the California Institute of Technology, which we mentioned briefly in Chapter 1. In the 1960s, a small group of human patients underwent a surgical procedure designed to provide relief from frequent, disabling epileptic seizures (Bogen et al., 1988). In these patients epileptic activity that was initiated in one hemisphere spread to the other hemisphere via the corpus callosum, the large bundle of fibers that connect the two hemispheres. Surgically cutting the corpus callosum appreciably reduces the frequency and severity of such seizures.

Studies in the 1930s seemed to show that this remedy for seizures caused no apparent changes in brain function, as assessed by general behavioral tests such as IQ tests. But the human corpus callosum is a huge bundle of more than a million axons, and it seemed strange that the principal connection between the cerebral hemispheres could be cut without producing detectable changes in behavior. The eminent physiological psychologist Karl Lashley, with characteristic sardonic humor, suggested that perhaps the only function of the corpus callosum was to keep the two hemispheres from floating apart in the cerebrospinal fluid. Subsequent animal research has shown, however, that careful testing does reveal deficits in behavior as consequences of hemispheric disconnection.

Results of hemispheric disconnection were first studied extensively in animals in the 1950s. For example, in one study on cats, both the corpus callosum and the optic chiasm were sectioned, so that each eye was connected only to the hemisphere on its own side. Such cats learned with their left eye that a particular symbol stood for reward but that the inverted symbol did not, while with the right eye they were able to learn the opposite—that the inverted symbol was rewarded rather than the upright symbol. Thus, each hemisphere was ignorant of what the other had learned (Sperry et al., 1956).

Beginning in the 1960s, split-brain subjects were studied extensively, both pre- and postoperatively, through a series of psychological tests devised by Sperry and coworkers. In research on this group of patients, stimuli can be directed to either hemisphere by being presented to different places on the surface of the body. For example, objects the patient feels with the left hand result in activity in nerve cells of the sensory regions in the right hemisphere. Since the corpus callosum is cut in these patients, most of the information sent to one half of the brain cannot travel to the other half. By controlling stimuli in this fashion, the experimenter can present stimuli selectively to one hemisphere or the other and thus can test the capabilities of each hemisphere.

In some of Sperry's studies, words were projected to either the left or the right hemisphere; that is, visual stimuli were presented in either the right or the left side of the visual field. Split-brain subjects can easily read and verbally communicate words projected to their left hemisphere, but no such linguistic capabilities were evident when the information was directed to the right hemisphere (Figure 19.14). Zaidel (1976) showed that the right hemisphere has a small amount of linguistic ability; for example, it can recognize simple words. In general, however, the vocabulary and grammatical ca-

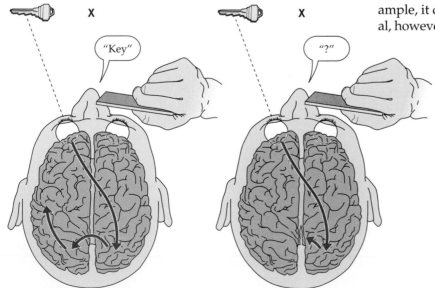

(a) Normal individual   (b) Split-brain individual

19.14 Testing of a Split-Brain Individual
Words or pictures projected to the left visual field activate the right visual cortex. (a) In normals, activation of the right visual cortex excites corpus callosum fibers, which transmit verbal information to the left hemisphere, where the information is analyzed and language is produced. (b) In split-brain patients, the severing of callosal connections prevents language production in response to stimuli in the left visual field.

pabilities of the right hemisphere are far less developed than they are in the left hemisphere.

Sperry's findings not only confirmed the animal research, but they were more dramatic, since they showed that only the processes taking place in the left hemisphere could be described verbally by the patients. Thus, in most people the left hemisphere possesses language and speech mechanisms. For our present concern, the important result is that each hemisphere by itself can process and store information without any participation by the other hemisphere.

The ability of the "mute" right hemisphere was tested by nonverbal means. For example, a picture of a key might be projected to the left visual field and so reach only the right visual cortex. The subject would then be asked to touch a number of objects that she could not see and hold up the correct one. Such a task could be performed correctly by the left hand (controlled by the right hemisphere) but not by the right hand (controlled by the left hemisphere). In such a patient, the left hemisphere literally does not know what the left hand is doing.

Whereas the left hemisphere controls speech, the right hemisphere seems to be somewhat better at processing spatial information, especially if the response is manual rather than simple recognition of a correct visual pattern.

The Two Hemispheres Process Information Differently in Normal Humans

Almost all the research concerning differences between the hemispheres in the processing of information has concentrated on two modalities: hearing and vision. In each modality, psychologists can detect differences in behavioral response to confirm that, in most people, the left cerebral hemisphere processes language.

The right-ear advantage.   Through earphones, we can present different sounds to each ear at the same time; this process is called the **dichotic listening technique**. The subject hears a particular speech sound in one ear and, at the same time, a different vowel, consonant, or word in the other ear. The task for the subject is to identify or recall these sounds.

Although this technique may seem to be a program designed to produce confusion, in general, data from dichotic listening experiments indicate that right-handed persons identify verbal stimuli delivered to the right ear more accurately than stimuli presented simultaneously to the left ear. This result is described as a right-ear "advantage" for verbal information. In contrast, about 50% of left-handed individuals reveal a reverse pattern, showing a left-ear advantage—more accurate performance for verbal stimuli delivered to the left ear.

Doreen Kimura argues that auditory information exerts stronger neural effects on the opposite side than on the same side (Figure 19.15). That is, auditory stimuli presented to the right ear produce stronger effects on the left auditory cortex than on the right auditory cortex, and vice versa. Thus, whereas sounds presented to the right ear exert stronger control over language mechanisms in the left hemisphere, speech sounds presented to the left ear are less potent in activating language-processing regions in the left cerebral hemisphere (D. Kimura, 1973). Several studies have shown that the right-ear advantage for speech sounds in right-handed individuals is restricted to particular kinds of speech sounds (Tallal and Schwartz, 1980). The right-ear advantage is evident with simultaneously presented consonants such as b, d, t, and k, but not with vowel sounds.

Doreen Kimura

Visual perception of linguistic stimuli.   We can study hemispheric specialization in normal humans by briefly exposing visual half-fields to stimuli (see Figures 10.13 and 19.15). If the stimulus exposure lasts less than 100 to 150 ms, input can be restricted to one hemisphere, because this amount of time is not sufficient for the eyes to shift their direction. Of course, in intact humans further processing may involve the transmission of information through the corpus callosum to the other hemisphere.

Most studies show that verbal stimuli (words and letters) presented to the right visual field (going to the left hemisphere) are better recognized than the same input presented to the left visual field (going to the right hemisphere). On the other hand, nonverbal visual stimuli (such as faces) presented to the left visual field are better recognized than the same stimuli presented to the right visual field. Simpler visual processing, such as detection of light, hue, or simple patterns, is equivalent in the two hemispheres. But for more complex materials, in vision as well as audition, most verbal stimuli are processed better in the left hemisphere of most individuals.

Does the Left Hemisphere Hear Words and the Right Hemisphere Hear Music?

The left and right auditory cortical areas appear to play somewhat different roles in human perception of speech and music. An early clue to this difference came from a study of the anatomy of the temporal lobes in adults (Geschwind and Levitsky, 1968); in 65% of the brains examined, the upper surface of the lobe—a region known as the **planum temporale**—was larger in the left hemisphere than in the right (Figure 19.16b). In only 11% of adults was the right side larger. The region examined includes part of the area known as Wernicke's area; damage to this area impairs the perception of speech. Perhaps the difference in size of this region between the two hemispheres reflects the left-hemisphere dominance (as is discussed in further detail in Topic 19.3, Related Asymmetries).

 Special topic

"ma"

Wernicke's area

ma ma

ma

Information to left ear goes to right auditory cortex and then to Wernicke's area in left hemisphere. Subject repeats word.

"pa"

pa

pa

Information to right ear goes to left auditory cortex, then directly to Wernicke's area. Subject repeats word.

"pa"

pa ma ma

ma pa

When conflicting information goes to both ears, that to the right ear reaches Wernicke's area first. Subject repeats only the right ear information.

19.15 Kimura's Model of the Right-Ear Advantage (*a*) A word delivered to the left ear results in stronger stimulation of the right auditory cortex. (*b*) A word delivered to the right ear results in stronger input to the left hemisphere. (*c*) When words are delivered to both ears simultaneously, the one to the right ear is the one usually perceived, because it has more direct connections to the left hemisphere. (After D. Kimura, 1973.)

We saw earlier that left-hemisphere dominance for speech is less common in left-handed people than in right-handed people, and MRI studies show that the asymmetry of the planum temporale is also reduced in left-handed people (Steinmetz et al., 1991), reinforcing the idea that the planum temporale is involved in speech. The difference in size of the planum temporale is even more evident in newborns than in adults; it appeared in 86% of the infant brains examined. The difference in size develops in about the thirtieth week of gestation (Witelson and Pallie, 1973).

This evidence suggests an innate basis for cerebral specialization for language and speech perception, since the asymmetry is established before any experience with speech. The planum temporale of chimpanzees also tends to be larger on the left (Gannon et al., 1998), suggesting that either the asymmetry of this region preceded its involvement in language, or that chimpanzees already possess a precursor to language, as we discussed at the start of this chapter. As Box 19.3 shows, even more dramatic structural asymmetry is evident in other vertebrates.

In the case of music, studies indicate a major role for the auditory areas of the right hemisphere. These studies show that musical perception is impaired particularly by damage to the right hemisphere (Samson and Zatorre, 1994) and that music activates the right hemisphere more than the left (Zatorre et al., 1994). But a recent study indicates that perfect pitch (the ability to identify any musical note without comparing it to a reference note) involves the left rather than the right hemisphere.

Schlaug et al. (1995) made MRI measurements of the planum temporale in three kinds of subjects, all right-handed (because the larger size of the left planum temporale is seen especially in right-handed individuals): (1) musicians with perfect pitch, (2) musicians without perfect pitch, and (3) nonmusicians. The size of the left planum temporale was twice as large in musicians with perfect pitch than in nonmusicians (see Figure 9.16c). The size of the left planum temporale in musicians without perfect pitch was intermediate, but closer to that of nonmusicians. Since perfect pitch requires both verbal ability (to name the pitch) and musical ability, perhaps it is not surprising to find that, like language, it is associated with the left hemisphere.

Despite these data, we cannot assign the perception of speech and pitch entirely to the left hemisphere and the perception of music entirely to the right hemi-

19.16 Structural Asymmetry of the Human Planum Temporale

(*a*) Orientation diagram for the brain section in part *b*. (*b*) The planum temporale (green and blue) on the upper surface of the human temporal lobe. (*c*) MRI images from the brain of a musician with perfect pitch (*top*) and the brain of a nonmusician (*bottom*). In the musician, the left planum temporale is larger. (After Schlaug et al., 1995; *c* courtesy of Gottfried Schlaug.)

sphere. We have seen that the right hemisphere can play a role in speech perception even in people in whom the left hemisphere is speech-dominant. Furthermore, although damage to the right hemisphere can impair the perception of music, it does not abolish it, but damage to both sides of the brain can completely wipe out musical perception (Samson and Zatorre, 1991). Thus, even though each hemisphere plays a greater role than the other in different kinds of auditory perception, the two hemispheres appear to collaborate in these as well as in many other functions.

Are Left-Handed People Different?

Anthropologists speculate that the predominance of right-handedness goes back a long time into prehistory. People portrayed in cave paintings held things in their right hand, and Stone Age tools seem to be shaped for the right hand. Skull fractures of animals preyed on by ancient humans are usually on the animal's left side, so anthropologists conclude that most attackers held an implement in the right hand.

Throughout history many unusual attributes have been ascribed to the left-handed person—from an evil

personality to an "abnormal" cortical organization of language. (Indeed, the term "sinistral," which means "left-handed," comes from the same Latin root as the word "sinister.") Left-handed people make up a small percentage of human populations. A figure of around 10% is commonly reported, although this percentage may be lower in parts of the world where teachers actively discourage left-handedness. For example, there is a higher percentage of left-handed Chinese-Americans in U.S. schools, which are generally more tolerant of left-handedness, than among Chinese in China. Surveys of left-handed writing in American college populations reveal an incidence of 13.8% (Spiegler and Yeni-Komshian, 1983). This percentage is viewed as a dramatic increase over prior generations, perhaps reflecting a continuing decline in the social pressures toward right-handedness and an increase in the acceptability of left-handedness. Interestingly, other primates also show a preference for using the right hand (Westergaard et al., 1998).

Hardyck et al. (1976) examined more than 7000 children in grades 1 through 6 for school achievement, intellectual ability, motivation, socioeconomic level,

BOX 19.3   *Structural Asymmetry in the Vertebrate Nervous System*

*A*quick glance in the mirror and equally fleeting views of other vertebrates suggest that bilateral symmetry of the body is commonplace among animals. But a closer look reveals important exceptions. Among flatfishes—including such well-known edible fish as sole, flounder, and halibut—there are startling examples of body asymmetry that also include the brain (Rao and Finger, 1984).

In adult flatfishes (Figure A), both eyes are on the same side of the head (Picasso wasn't the first to think of this arrangement). This structural oddity emerges during development. When the fish hatches from an egg, it has an ordinary fishlike symmetrical form, but as it develops, one eye migrates across the top of the head (Figure B). Some flatfishes are right-eyed, with both eyes on the right side of the head; others are left-eyed. Most flatfishes spend a large part of their time lying on the bottom of the sea, often cov-

ered with a light layer of sand, with only their eyes and nostrils exposed. When prey come near, the flatfish darts out to capture it. Having both eyes on the same side allows the fish to remain inconspicuous while retaining full vision to look for prey.

All flatfishes belong to the order Pleuronectiformes, and all fish in this order are asymmetrical as adults. Although both eyes are on one side of the head in these animals, the visual regions within the brain are symmetrical. However, the olfactory system in some flatfishes reveals a striking brain anatomical asymmetry (Figure C). The right nostril lies above the left, and the right olfactory receptor and pathways, including the olfactory regions of the brain, are distinctly larger than their counterparts on the left.

We've seen in this chapter that human language is heavily represented in the left hemisphere in most people and that structural asymmetry of the planum tempo-

rale may be related to this asymmetry. Structural asymmetry is evident in the brains of other nonhuman vertebrates, although it is not as pronounced as in flatfishes. The right hippocampas is larger than the left in male rats. Nonhuman primates show anatomical asymmetries in the region of the temporal lobe analogous to those found in humans (Gannon et al., 1998). Functional studies in nonhuman vertebrates reveal many examples of lateralization, including the effects of lesions of the brain. Earlier in this chapter we saw that a surgical cut of the left twelfth cranial nerve in an adult male bird results in the loss of song, whereas damage to the right side has little impact on the bird's vocal behavior (Nottebohm, 1981). These examples support the notion that lateral specialization confers an important advantage, but in most instances the advantages are not as easy to understand as in the flatfish.

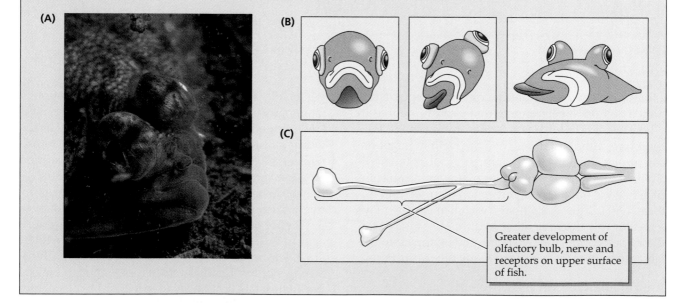

Greater development of olfactory bulb, nerve and receptors on upper surface of fish.

and the like. A detailed analysis of the data showed that left-handed children do not differ from right-handed children on any measure of cognitive performance. However, the idea that left-handed people are "damaged" humans has been common in the past and has even found occasional support in research.

D. A. Silva and Satz (1979) note that several studies show a higher incidence of left-handedness in clinical

populations than in the general population. They examined handedness in more than 1400 patients in a school for the mentally retarded and showed an incidence of 17.8% left-handedness, nearly twice the level in the general population. In this population more left-handers than right-handers had abnormal EEGs. Investigators have suggested that brain injury explains the high rate of left-handedness in this retarded population. Early brain injury, these investigators argue, can cause a shift in handedness. Since most people are right-handed, early one-sided brain injury is more likely to effect a change from right-handedness to left-handedness than the reverse.

Many Theories Attempt to Explain the Evolutionary Origins of Hemispheric Asymmetry and Specialization

Some scientists believe that hemispheric specialization originated in the differential use of the limbs for many routine tasks. Picture early humans hunting. One hand holds the weapon and provides power; the other is used in more delicate guidance or body balance. Archaeological studies of human skulls imply differential use of the limbs in attacking other humans. Proof offered for this idea is the greater frequency of left skull fracture in fossilized specimens of ancient people. In time the evolutionary successes offered by handedness might have been used in the emergence of language and speech.

Some theories about the emergence of speech and language focus on the motor aspects of speech, others on the cognitive properties of language. **Competing hypotheses** The speech motor apparatus involves many delicate muscle systems situated in the midline of the body, such as the tip of the tongue. Sensitivity and precision of stimulus analysis on the body surface are reduced in the exact midline. Perhaps this result reflects the mutual antagonism of right and left axon terminals in the skin. For speech this peculiarity of the midline would be catastrophic for precise control. Asymmetry of motor control of speech production might then offer better unchallenged control of relevant parts of the speech apparatus. Such sidedness in the motor production of sound is seen even in the control of singing in birds, as we discussed earlier.

Arguments that propose a fundamental difference in cognitive style between the hemispheres suggest other connections to language and evolutionary advantages of cerebral specialization. According to this view, the left hemisphere provides processing that is analytical, and the right hemisphere offers a more holistic or general analysis of information (Table 19.2). Some theorists suggest that hemisphere specialization allows for separate cognitive modes that are mutually incompatible. Any linguistic or cognitive response involves different analyses for different kinds of tasks, and hemisphere specialization, it is argued, is a good solution to this need (Ivry and Robertson, 1998). But the notion, now **Special topic** common among the public, that the two hemispheres are so different that they need separate instruction, is not supported by the data, as we discuss in Topic 19.4, There Are Several Models of Cognitive Differences between the Human Cerebral Hemispheres.

TABLE 19.2 *Proposed Cognitive Modes of the Two Cerebral Hemispheres in Humans*

Left hemisphere	Right hemisphere
Phonetic	Nonlinguistic
Sequential	Holistic
Analytical	Synthetic
Propositional	Gestalt
Discrete temporal analysis	Form perception
Language	Spatial

The Frontal Lobes of Humans Are Related to Higher-Order Aspects of Cognitive and Emotional Functions

Because the complexity of human beings far exceeds that of other animals, researchers have sought characteristics of the brain that might account for human preeminence. Among the most striking differences is the comparative size of the human prefrontal cortex. In part because of its size, the frontal region has been regarded as the seat of intelligence and abstract thinking. Adding to the mystery of frontal lobe function is the unusual assortment of behavioral changes that follows surgical or accidental lesions of this region.

The Anatomy of the Frontal Lobe Forms a Basis for Understanding Its Complex Roles

The boundaries of the frontal lobes are not precisely defined, but the human frontal cortex occupies almost one-third of the entire cerebral cortical surface. At the posterior portion the frontal cortex includes motor and premotor regions (see Chapter 11). The anterior part is often referred to as **prefrontal cortex**, which is a critical component of a widespread neuronal network, with extensive linkages throughout the brain (Fuster, 1990; Mega and Cummings, 1994). The prefrontal cortex is further subdivided into a dorsolateral area and an orbitofrontal region (Figure 19.17a). In other animals the frontal cortex, especially prefrontal regions, is a smaller portion of the cerebral cortex (Figure 19.17b).

Frontal Lobe Injury in Humans Leads to Emotional, Motor, and Cognitive Changes

The complexity of change following prefrontal damage is best epitomized by the classic case of Phineas Gage. In 1848, Mr. Gage accidentally exploded gunpowder that sent an iron rod through his skull, producing a massive lesion of the prefrontal cortex. Sober and reliable before his accident, Gage became moody and uninhibited, unconcerned about other people's reactions or the future consequences of his behavior. The last sentence of the physician's report reads, "His

(a) The prefrontal cortex in humans

(b) Relative prefrontal cortex size in several mammals

Squirrel monkey   Cat

Rhesus monkey

Chimpanzee

Human

19.17 The Prefrontal Cortex
(a) The human prefrontal cortex can be subdivided into a dorso-lateral region (blue) and an orbitofrontal region (green). Lesions in these different areas of prefrontal cortex have different effects on behavior. (b) The relative percentage of prefrontal cortex is greatest in humans and decreases successively in other primates, carnivores, and rodents (not shown). The brains here are drawn to different scales. (Photographs courtesy of S. Mark Williams and Dale Purves, Duke University Medical Center.)

mind was radically changed, so decidedly that his friends and acquaintances said that he was 'no longer Gage.'" Attempts to account for Gage's syndrome in neurological terms have undergone successive changes. In the latter part of the nineteenth century, neurologists began to realize that the bases of speech and motor behavior are localized in specific brain regions, but they were still reluctant to believe that moral reasoning and social behavior have localized neural mechanisms. We'll soon see, however, that Gage's symptoms are indeed related to damage to specific brain regions.

Now, a century and a half after Phineas Gage's accident, measurement of his skull and modern imaging techniques indicate that his injury was probably

confined to the orbitofrontal region of both frontal lobes, sparing the dorsolateral region (Figure 19.18). Having made these measurements, Hanna Damasio and Antonio Damasio and colleagues searched their extensive roster of neurological cases and found that Gage's syndrome matches that of several other patients with known brain damage in the region of Gage's probable injury (H. Damasio et al., 1994). Thus, the mysteries of frontal lobe function are gradually being solved.

The clinical portrait of humans with frontal lesions reveals an unusual collection of emotional, motor, and cognitive changes. The emotional reactivity of these patients shows a persistent strange apathy, broken by bouts of euphoria (an exalted sense of well-being).

19.18 Phineas Gage Reconstructed

Computer reconstruction, based on measurements of Phineas Gage's skull, showing from several perspectives the brain areas that are most likely to have been damaged in his famous accident. The red cylinder shows the path of the tamping iron, which entered the skull below the left eye and exited through the top of the head, severely damaging both frontal lobes. (From Damasio et al., 1994; courtesy of Hanna Damasio.)

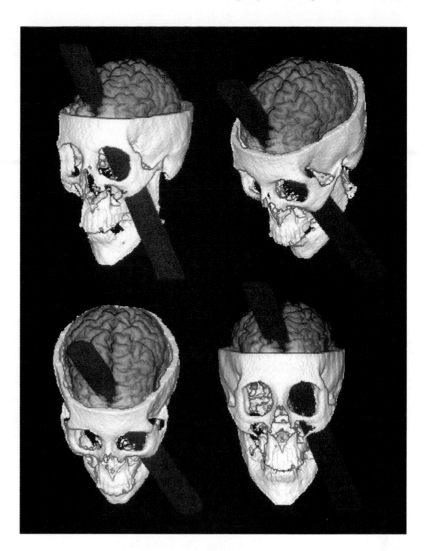

Ordinary social conventions are readily cast aside by impulsive activity. Concern for the past or the future is rarely evident (J. D. Duffy and Campbell, 1994; Petrides and Milner, 1982). Frontal patients show shallow emotions, even including reduced responsiveness to pain. Frequently, though, they exhibit episodes in which this apathy is replaced by boastfulness and silliness and, sometimes, unbridled sexual activity.

Cognitive changes in human frontal patients are very complicated and difficult to pinpoint, although something very different seems to characterize the frontal patient. Standard IQ test performance shows only slight changes after injury or stroke. Forgetfulness is shown in many tasks requiring sustained attention. In fact, some of these patients even forget their own warnings to "remember."

Clinical examination of frontal patients also reveals an array of strange impairments in motor activities, especially in the realm of "plans" for action. The patients seem to perseverate (continue beyond a reasonable degree) in any activity. For example, if the patient is asked to open and then close the fist, once the activity has begun—and it is difficult to initiate such acts in frontal patients—the patient continues a persistent sequence of fist opening and closing. The overall level of motor activity—especially ordinary, spontaneous movements—is quite diminished in frontal patients. For example, facial expression becomes blank, and head and eye movements are markedly reduced. Some reflexes that are evident only very early in life, such as the infantile grasp reflex of the hand, reappear in frontal cases.

Many clinical assessments of these patients have emphasized an impairment in goal-directed behavior, especially an inability to plan acts and use foresight. Daily activities of these patients seem disorganized and without a clear program for successive activities. Table 19.3 lists the main clinical features of patients with lesions of various portions of the frontal lobes.

Formal psychological tests are an important aspect of the assessment of the brain, but sometimes less formal behavioral assessments highlight a feature of brain impairment with striking clarity. This point was underscored by Lhermitte et al. (1986), who described an unusual phenomenon in patients with damaged frontal lobes—a syndrome characterized by spontaneous imitation of the gestures and behavior of the examiner. Lhermitte et al. see this syndrome as related to one they identified as "utilization behavior," defined as an exaggerated dependence on the environment for behavioral cues. The syndrome was observed during clinical exams in which the examiner made body gestures or engaged in writing or handling of objects. All patients with disease involving the frontal lobes spontaneously imitated the gestures of the examiner in detail. Patients were aware of their imitative behavior.

Patient behavior in complex social situations also reflected the extraordinary environmental dependency of the behavior of frontal lobe patients. The social situations included interactions in a home environment and in a doctor's office. In the latter situation, a patient saw a blood pressure gauge and immediately took the physician's blood pressure. After eyeing a tongue depressor, she placed it in front of the doctor's mouth. Upon walking into a bedroom, one patient proceeded

TABLE 19.3 *Core Characteristics of the Regional Prefrontal Syndromes*

Dysexecutive type (dorsolateral)	Disinhibited type (orbitofrontal)	Apathetic type (mediofrontal)
Diminished judgment, planning, insight, and temporal organization	Stimulus-driven behavior	Diminished spontaneity
Cognitive impersistence	Diminished social insight	Diminished verbal output (including mutism)
Motor programming deficits (may include aphasia and apraxia)	Distractibility	Diminished motor behavior (including akinesis)
Diminished self-care	Emotional lability	Urinary incontinence
		Lower-extremity weakness and sensory loss
		Diminished spontaneous prosody
		Increased response latency

to get undressed and go to bed. He hurried out of bed when the examiner picked up a piece of his clothing. In these acts there is a certain mechanical character; Lhermitte describes these patients as powerless in the face of influences from the outside world. The loss of self-criticism is another aspect of the behavior of these patients, as is evident in the act of calmly urinating against a public building in plain view.

Prefrontal Lesions in Nonhumans Produce Distinct Deficits

The study of prefrontal cortical function in animals began with the work of Carlyle Jacobsen in the 1930s. In his experiments with chimpanzees, Jacobsen employed delayed-response learning. The animals were shown where food was hidden, but they had to wait before being allowed to reach for it. This simple test situation revealed a remarkable impairment in chimpanzees with prefrontal lesions. These animals performed this task very poorly, in contrast with animals that sustained lesions in other brain regions. In interpreting this phenomenon, Jacobsen emphasized the memory function of the frontal cortex. Now, however, it seems more likely that the animals were unable to direct their attention properly to solve these tasks.

Deficits in Spatial Perception Follow Some Types of Brain Injury

Injury to the parietal lobe produces impairments such as these: Objects placed in the hand cannot be recognized by touch alone. One side of the body may be completely neglected, even to the point of being rejected as one's own. Faces cannot be recognized from photographs. Spatial orientation can become severely disturbed.

The diversity of behavioral changes following injury to this region is related partly to its large expanse and its critical position adjacent to occipital, temporal, and frontal regions. The anterior end of the parietal region includes the postcentral gyrus, which is the primary cortical receiving area for somatic sensation. Brain injury in this area does not produce numbness; rather, it produces sensory deficits on the opposite side that seem to involve complex sensory processing. For example, objects placed in the hand opposite the injured somatosensory area can be felt but cannot be identified by touch and active manipulation. This deficit is called **astereognosis** (from the Greek *a-*, "not," *stereos*, "solid," and *gnosis*, "knowledge").

In some cases the deficit occurs on the same side as the brain injury (Corkin et al., 1970). More extensive injuries in the parietal cortex, not restricted to the somatosensory cortex, affect interactions between or among sensory modalities, such as visual or tactile matching tasks, which require the subject to identify visually an object that is touched or to reach for an object that is identified visually.

In Prosopagnosia, a Face Is No Longer a Face

Suppose one day you look in the mirror and you see someone who is not familiar to you. As incredible as this scenario might seem, some individuals do suffer this fate after brain damage. This rare syndrome is called **prosopagnosia** (from the Greek *pros-* and *ops*, "face," and *gnosis*, "knowledge"). Such patients fail to recognize not only their own face but also the faces of relatives and friends. No amount of remedial training restores their ability to recognize anyone's face. In contrast, the ability to recognize *objects* is retained, and the patient readily identifies familiar people by the sounds of their voices. Faces simply lack meaning in the patient's life. No cognitive impairments, such as disorientation or confusion, accompany this condition. There is no evidence of diminished intellectual abilities. Visual acuity is maintained, although most patients have a small visual-field defect—that is, an area of the visual field where they are "blind."

The anatomical and neuropsychological features of this syndrome have been elegantly explored by Tranel and Damasio (1985). They noted that although earlier work focused on right-hemisphere lesions as the cause of the deficit, contemporary studies provide a more thorough anatomical picture of this disorder. Both postmortem examination and CT or MRI scans suggest that bilateral lesions, usually at the junction of the parietal, temporal, and occipital lobes, are necessary for the syndrome to appear.

Detailed analysis of these patients provides insights into the underlying mechanisms (Rizzo et al., 1987). The patients retain some complex perceptual abilities, including the ability to draw figures seen in photographs. Furthermore, prosopagnosia often involves other perceptual categories besides faces. Some prosopagnosic patients cannot recognize their own car and do not recognize common makes of cars in general, although they can distinguish between cars and trucks. Some are also unable to recognize types of clothes or distinctive foods. Bird-watchers are no longer able to recognize distinctive birds, and farmers may no longer recognize a particular animal, although they recognize animals as animals. Subfeatures of complex percepts can be pointed out, such as parts of a face. In addition, eye movements of patients recorded during their examination of a picture of a face are like those of controls, indicating that some basic perceptual processes proceed normally.

PET studies indicate that different patterns of brain activation are seen in normal subjects depending on whether they are distinguishing the gender of a face, recognizing a new face, or recognizing a familiar face (Andreasen et al., 1996), which suggests that there are three different systems subserving these different attributes. Topic 19.5, More on Prosopagnosia, discusses further the details of this fascinating syndrome.

Special topic

Neglect of One Side of the Body and Space Can Result from Parietal Lobe Injury

Brain damage involving the right inferior parietal cortex produces an unusual set of behavioral changes (Rafal, 1994). The key feature is neglect of the left side of both the body and space. Patients may fail to dress the left side of their body and may even disclaim "ownership" of their left arm or leg. In some instances familiar people presented on the left side of the patient are completely neglected, although no visual-field defect is apparent. This phenomenon, called **hemispatial neglect**, can also be seen in simple test situations. A common test requires the patient to copy drawings of familiar objects. In a typical result, a patient who is asked to draw the face of a clock, for example, draws numbers only on the right side of the clock face (Figure 19.19) (Schenkerberg et al., 1980).

Associated with this dramatic change is a feature called extinction of simultaneous double stimulation. Most people can readily report the presence of two

19.19 Diagnostic Test for Hemispatial Neglect When asked to duplicate drawings of common, symmetrical objects, patients suffering from hemispatial neglect will ignore the left side of the model they are copying. (From Kolb and Whishaw, 1990.)

stimuli when stimulated simultaneously on both sides of the body. Patients with right inferior parietal lesions, however, are unable to note the double nature of the stimulation and usually report only the stimulus presented to the right side. This syndrome extends to visual imagery as well; when dreaming, for example, these patients scan only one side of dream scenes (Doricchi et al., 1991). Although many patients with injury to this region show recovery from unilateral neglect, the feature of extinction is quite persistent.

Yet another dramatic feature of this syndrome is the frequent denial of illness. Patients may adamantly maintain that they are capable of engaging in their customary activities and do not recognize the impressive signs of unilateral neglect. Remarkably, having these patients wear prisms to shift their visual field 10° to the right for a few minutes eases their symptoms: For a few hours they are less neglectful of the left visual field (Rossetti et al., 1998).

Many hypotheses have been offered to account for these symptoms. Some investigators have regarded the disorder as a consequence of the loss of the ability to analyze spatial patterns; this hypothesis is consistent with the fact that unilateral neglect occurs with lesions of the right hemisphere but not with lesions of the left hemisphere. Others regard the syndrome as an attentional deficit. The neurologist Marek-Marsel Mesulam (1985) noted that recordings of single cells from posterior parietal cortex in monkeys show firing patterns that are sensitive to manipulations of attention. For example, some nerve cells in this area increase their discharge rates when the animal's eyes follow or track a meaningful object—frequently one that has been associated with reward.

Anatomical studies of the sources of inputs to the posterior parietal region show origins in several distinct cortical sectors, including polymodal cortical sensory areas, cingulate cortex, and frontal cortex, especially the frontal eye fields (Rafal, 1994). In turn, outputs from the posterior parietal cortex extend to these regions. Mesulam proposed that each of these regions has a distinctive role in a network that governs attention. The posterior parietal component involves processes that yield an internal sensory map; frontal cortex governs relevant searching movements, and cingulate cortex processing provides motivational values.

Some Functions Show Recovery Following Brain Injury

The course of behavior following brain injury often reveals conspicuous changes. Striking examples of language recovery following stroke have been observed in many adults. Amazing examples of language recovery have been described in children following the removal of a diseased cerebral hemisphere. Many theories are offered to describe the mechanisms mediating the recovery of function after lesions. Current research on the recovery of brain functions provides an exciting array of ideas and data that reveal several forms of brain plasticity. Studies in this area offer striking prospects for rehabilitation. Perhaps many different mechanisms together contribute to the patterns of recovery, so no single explanation can be offered as the sole basis.

In spite of these encouraging developments, prevention is clearly better than the cure. Motor vehicle accidents, horseback riding, diving, and contact sports are major causes of injuries to the brain and spinal cord. Box 19.4, for example, describes the effects of boxing on the brain.

Some Recovery from Brain Injury Follows Relief from Generalized Physiological Abnormalities

Any brain injury destroys particular collections of nerve cells and produces more generalized disturbances that temporarily affect the responsiveness of other nerve cells. For example, in the region of a brain injury, frequently the properties of the blood–brain barrier change. Some researchers have suggested that the time course of functional deficits following structural damage to nerve cells reflects the inhibitory impact of blood-borne substances that ordinarily are prevented from reaching the environment of nerve cells (Seil et al., 1976). In time, the changes in the blood vessels around a site of injury reestablish the blood–brain barrier and increase blood flow to transiently distressed but intact tissue.

Many years ago the anatomist Monakow (1914) coined the term **diaschisis** to describe the distant inhibitory effects of brain lesions that seemed to be reversible. With time, usage of this term has expanded to include a host of potentially reversible, nonspecific effects that make the immediate consequences of a brain lesion more intense than persistent deficits.

The Brain Regrows and Reorganizes Anatomically After Being Injured

Anatomical dogma for many years declared that changes in the adult central nervous system are solely destructive. The intricate structure and connections of nerve cells were considered to be structurally fixed once adulthood was reached. Injury, it was thought, could lead only to the shrinkage or death of nerve cells. Many impressive contemporary demonstrations to the contrary have now led us to emphasize the structural plasticity of nerve cells and their connections.

Regeneration of the axons of the peripheral nervous system has always been accepted, but now comparable structural regrowth has been observed in the brain and spinal cord (Veraa and Grafstein, 1981). For example, injury to catecholamine-containing fibers in the medial forebrain bundle leads to regrowth of axonal portions connected to nerve cells. Dendrites **Neural plasticity** in the brain may also grow back following injury. Figure 19.20 illustrates one form of regrowth after injury: collateral sprouting.

This change has been described in the peripheral nervous system, and the story goes like this: If a peripheral sensory or motor fiber is injured, the terminal portions degenerate and sensory or motor function in the affected region is immediately lost. Nerve fibers adjacent to the injured fibers recognize this injury (perhaps by a chemical signal delivered from the injured site), and they respond by developing sprouts or branches from intact axons. In time, usually weeks, these sprouts connect to denervated skin or muscle and acquire functional control of these regions on the periphery of the body (J. Diamond et al., 1976). This mechanism seems to result in functional compensation for a loss of neuronal connections. Incidentally, the injured nerve fiber (axon) slowly regrows, and as it approaches the skin or muscles to which it had been connected, the sprouts retract. Again, chemical signals from the regrowing original fiber probably produce this change.

R. F. Mark (1980) has suggested that a stage prior to physical withdrawal of the fiber includes the cessation of synaptic effectiveness of the sprout-borne

BOX 19.4   *A Sport That Destroys the Mind*

*B*oxing has a long history, much of it unpleasant. In ancient Greece and Rome, some boxers were admired for their courage and strength, but others, wearing leather wrappings studded with metal nuggets, bludgeoned each other to death for the entertainment of spectators. Although rules developed during the eighteenth century in England, including the use of padded gloves, the goal of prizefighting has always been not to display grace and agility, but to knock the opponent out. A bout usually ends when one fighter has sustained a brief loss of consciousness.

To achieve that goal, boxers aim relentlessly at the head, which sustains blow after blow—a history that comes to exact a price from the contestants. The result of so many blows to the head has been called **dementia pugilistica**, a fancy term used by neurologists to identify a state that is commonly known as punch-drunk. Punch-drunk boxers lead a life with markedly impaired cognitive abilities. Even a boxer as loquacious and talented at dodging blows as Muhammad Ali is today unable to utter more than a word or two at a time.

Deaths in the ring have also drawn attention to the dangers of boxing. Most boxing deaths are due to brain injuries, especially brain hemorrhage. Several professional societies, including the American Psychological Association and various medical and neurological societies, have urged the banning of this sport.

CT scan data have indicated that very few boxers escape unscathed. Casson et al. (1982) studied ten active professional boxers who had been knocked out. These fighters ranged in age from 20 to 31 years, and the number of bouts per boxer ranged from 2 to 52. The group included those of championship caliber, as well as mediocre or poor boxers. None of the knockouts sustained by the fighters involved a loss of consciousness lasting more than 10 s. Yet at least five of the group had definitely abnormal CT scans. The abnormalities included mild generalized cortical atrophy, which in some cases included ventricular dilation. Only one boxer had a clearly normal brain picture. The age of the boxers was not related to the degree of cortical atrophy.

The most successful boxers were the ones with the most profound cortical atrophy. In fact, the total number of professional fights correlated directly with the magnitude of brain changes. During a career of boxing, a fighter accumulates many blows to the head; the most "successful" boxers thus frequently sustain the most punishment (A. H. Roberts, 1969). A Parkinson's-like syndrome of tremors or paralysis may result from boxing. A large-scale CT study of 338 active boxers showed that scans were abnormal in 7% (brain atrophy) and borderline in 12% (B. D. Jordan et al., 1992).

Amateur boxing presents a slightly more optimistic portrait. While some studies report that amateur boxers show neither EEG abnormality nor brain structural changes as measured by MRI or CT (Haglund and Bergstrand, 1990; Haglund and Persson, 1990), others have revealed a high incidence of abnormal EEGs after amateur boxing matches (Busse and Silverman, 1952). It is not surprising that significant neurological impairments are found in amateur boxers as well as in professionals—no small reason that many believe boxing is a sport whose time has passed.

---

connections—a phenomenon he has labeled synaptic repression. This result implies that synapses can be turned off even though the structural connection is still present. This ability of synapses to be switched off is probably a significant feature of neural plasticity.

Demonstrations of collateral sprouting in the brain and spinal cord, once rarely observed, are now reported with regularity. Some investigators suggest that collateral sprouting in the brain offers hope for functional repair following injury (Raisman, 1978). A growing view is that injury of the nervous system might release nerve growth factors. One group of researchers has reported that chemicals in the area of tissue surrounding brain injury contain a growth-promoting substance (Nieto-Sampedro and Cotman, 1985). Grafting specialized glial cells from the olfactory bulb can aid regeneration in the rat spinal cord, a finding discussed in Topic 19.6, A Means for Regeneration?

Special topic

Observations of this sort indicate that brain connections are not as rigid anatomically as was once thought. The response of the brain to injury does include structural modifications. However, are these anatomical changes relevant to the processes of functional repair? Around this question controversy swirls. Although structural repair in the brain in the form of collateral sprouting is now generally accepted, the evidence that links this change with functional recovery following injury to the brain or spinal cord is scarce. In fact, some investigators (e.g., P. D. Wall, 1980) suggest that collateral sprouting might generate behavioral abnormalities, since nerve cells come under the control of unusual inputs. This axonal regeneration in the spinal cord has been linked to spasticity in reflexes elicited below the level of a spinal injury (C. N. Liu and Chambers, 1958). Intensive research currently in progress is aimed at evaluating the functional value of brain regrowth such as collateral sprouting.

Rehabilitation and Retraining Can Help Recovery from Brain and Spinal Cord Injury

Training can restore some functions after brain or spinal cord injury. The range of restorative opportunities following damage to the nervous system broad-

(*a*) Septal nucleus is normally innervated by fimbria and medial forebrain bundle

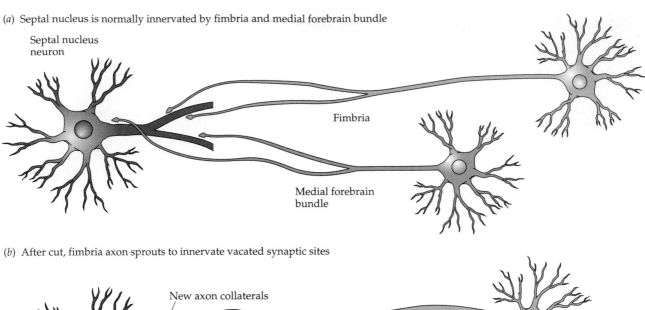

Septal nucleus
neuron

Fimbria

Medial forebrain
bundle

(*b*) After cut, fimbria axon sprouts to innervate vacated synaptic sites

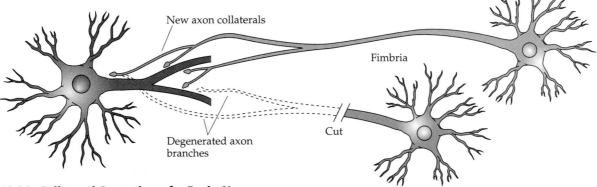

New axon collaterals

Fimbria

Degenerated axon
branches

Cut

19.20 Collateral Sprouting of a Brain Neuron
(*a*) Normal connections of fimbria and medial forebrain
bundle to a septal nucleus cell. (*b*) After severing of the
medial forebrain bundle, a fimbria axon develops sprouts
that occupy synaptic sites formerly occupied by axon terminals from the medial forebrain bundle. (After Raisman,
1978.)

ens with new research reports about neural plasticity that are more encouraging than ever. For example,
although we have long been led to believe that paralysis produced by injury to the spinal cord is untreat-
able, some new reports offer cautious optimism about
the prospects that training can restore some walking
ability in such patients (Wickelgren, 1998). Contemporary work with humans follows in the path of research on animals and shows some restoration of
walking in spinal cord–injured humans following
training (Barbeau et al., 1998).

Cognitive and/or perceptual handicaps that develop from brain impairments can also be modified by
training. It is important at this point to distinguish between the role of experience in compensating for brain
injury and its role in restoring behavior lost after
injury. It is well known that experiences significantly
reduce the impact of brain injury by fostering compensatory behavior. For example, vigorous eye movements can make up for large scotomata (blind spots in
the visual field) that result from injury to the visual

pathways. Behavior strategies can be changed after a
brain injury to enable successful performance on a variety of tests.

The role of experience in the possible reorganization of pathways following a lesion was noted in
Chapter 11, where we described how an individual
whose arm afferents have been cut can recover control
of the limbs. D. Berman et al. (1978) described a striking phenomenon of recovery that involves a change
in feedback signals governing behavior. Several studies performed with brain-lesioned rats have demonstrated that postlesion experience in a complex environment can improve subsequent problem-solving
behavior (Will et al., 1977).

Animals were placed in impoverished or enriched
environments of the same kinds that had been shown
to lead to changes in brain measures (see Chapter 18).
Although the brain-injured animals still made more errors than did intact rats, those in the enriched environments made significantly fewer errors than those in the
impoverished environments. Simply placing a group
of animals together in a large cage had a measurable
beneficial effect; giving the animals access to varied
stimuli was even more helpful (Rosenzweig, 1980).
Thus, even an injured brain can profit from experience.

In the case of human patients, some rehabilitation
experts have questioned the wisdom of placing cer-

tain patients in sensory isolation (coma patients, or patients kept in fixed positions in isolated rooms for intravenous therapy). Such patients, even if they cannot respond, might be aided by visitors, music, and changing visual stimuli. Some current programs of rehabilitation are putting these insights into effect.

Brain Structures That Remain Intact after Injury Can Substitute for Damaged Structures

Recovery following brain injury demonstrates that remaining neural tissue can mediate required behaviors. One perspective suggests that neural systems contain appreciable redundancy and that recovery involves the use of redundant pathways. However, what appears to be redundancy may arise from the complexity of the neural substrates of behavior and the simple ways in which recovery is assessed. Thus if the neural substrate for some behavior is broadly represented in the brain, behavior may be reinstated because of the extensiveness of neural controls rather than because of redundant or repeated systems.

Neural plasticity

One type of unusual substitution has been described by Patrick Wall (1980), who studied the receptive-field properties of dorsal column and thalamic cells following peripheral denervation. Wall noted that sizes of receptive fields of cells in this system change with denervation, tending especially to grow larger. Cells may also become responsive to bilateral inputs. This change is rapid, and Wall suggests that denervation unmasks weakly excitable paths that come to control some neurons. Wall refers to this effect as a "homeostatic adjustment" of nerve cell excitability.

Switching of nerve cell responsiveness in sensory paths is also evident in the vestibular system. Cutting the vestibular nerve or removing the labyrinth on one side results in head tilting or deviation and other signs of postural asymmetry. In time, these effects abate, illustrating a phenomenon known as vestibular compensation. Some of this recovery depends on inputs from the spinal cord (Jensen, 1979). Another independent aspect of recovery is a change in the activity of brain stem vestibular neurons. The dynamic character of cortical sensory systems was shown by J. T. Wall and Kaas (1986): Cutting a peripheral nerve to one digit enlarged the receptive fields of some cortical neurons.

Functional imaging studies of stroke patients provide additional evidence about the role of substituted structures in mediating recovery. PET studies on hemiplegic patients show that whereas movement of the unaffected hand activates motor cortex only on the opposite side of the body, attempted movement of the affected hand activates motor cortex on both sides (Chollet and Weiller, 1994). These results suggest that motor cortex on the same side as the injury mediates recovered movements. Studies of activation in such patients have revealed that the cerebellum also plays a role in recovery.

Slow-Developing and Rapid-Developing Brain Lesions Have Different Effects

The impairment caused by a brain lesion increases with the rate at which the lesion develops. Some investigators refer to this phenomenon as **lesion momentum**, or mass × velocity (Finger, 1978). Investigators experimenting with animals have studied lesion momentum by removing a given amount of tissue all at once or in stages separated by a few weeks. A lesion in the brain stem that incapacitates animals when made all at one time may have only slight effect if done in two successive stages. The partial lesion may stimulate regrowth or relearning or both, so that some compensation has already been achieved by the time the rest of the tissue is removed.

Some experimenters have reported that sensory stimulation or retraining during the interval between successive lesions is necessary for the reduced impairment observed with staged destruction, but not all studies agree. Experimental findings suggest a mechanism for the staged-lesion effect: A lesion that causes loss of synaptic connections may result in the release of chemical signals that facilitate the sprouting of terminals. When a small lesion precedes a larger lesion by 4 days to 2 weeks, the recovery from the second lesion is significantly faster and more extensive than if the earlier lesion had not occurred. Thus the earlier lesion primes the system to respond to the subsequent lesion (Scheff et al., 1978).

Clinical cases also reveal effects of lesion momentum. For example, an adult patient with a brain tumor encroaching on the speech areas of his left hemisphere had several operations, spaced many months apart (Geschwind, 1976). Each time the tumor regrew, it was necessary to remove more of the cortical speech areas, and each time the patient recovered his speech. In the end he was still speaking, even though only a fragment of the speech areas remained. Aging can also be thought of as a slowly developing condition, which probably helps mitigate its effects on the brain.

Summary

1. Humans are distinct in the animal kingdom for their language and associated cognitive abilities. Possible evolutionary origins of human speech may be seen in aspects of gestures.

2. Studies of communication among nonhumans provide analogies to human speech. For example, the control of birdsong is lateralized in the brains of some species of songbirds. Further, in some of these species early experience is essential for proper song development.

3. Limitations of the vocal tract in nonhumans are proposed as one reason that they do not have speech, but nonhuman primates like the chimpanzee can learn to use signs of the American Sign Language. However, controversy surrounds claims that these animals can arrange signs in novel orders to create new sentences.

4. Ninety to 95% of human language impairments involve injuries of the left hemisphere. Left anterior lesions produce an impairment in speech production called Broca's aphasia. More posterior lesions involving the temporoparietal cortex affect speech comprehension, as seen in Wernicke's aphasia.

5. Left-hemisphere lesions in users of sign language produce impairments in the use of sign language that are similar to impairments in spoken language shown by nondeaf aphasics.

6. Split-brain patients show striking examples of hemispheric specialization. Most words projected only to the right hemisphere cannot be read, while the same stimuli directed to the left hemisphere can be read. Verbal abilities of the right hemisphere are also reduced; however, spatial-relation tasks are performed better by the right hemisphere than by the left.

7. Normal humans show many forms of cognitive specialization of the cerebral hemispheres, although these specializations are not as striking as those shown by split-brain patients. For example, most normal humans show a right-ear advantage and greater accuracy for verbal stimuli in the right visual field.

8. Anatomical asymmetry of the hemispheres is seen in some structures in the human brain. Especially striking is the large size difference in the planum temporale (which is larger in the left hemisphere of most right-handed individuals).

9. Broad theoretical statements about different cognitive modes of the two hemispheres exceed confirmations from current experimental and clinical data. In most cases mental activity depends on interactions between the cerebral hemispheres.

10. The frontal lobes of humans are quite large compared with those of other animals. Injury in parts of this region produces an unusual syndrome of profound emotional changes, including reduced responsiveness to many stimuli. Tasks that require sustained attention show drastic impairment after frontal lesions.

11. In most patients, parietal cortex injuries produce many perceptual changes. A dramatic example after bilateral damage is the inability to recognize familiar objects and the faces of familiar people. Some patients with right parietal injury neglect or ignore the left side of both the body and space.

12. Many functional losses following brain injury show at least partial recovery. Most recovery from aphasia occurs in the year following stroke, with fewer changes evident after that. Mechanisms of functional recovery may involve structural regrowth of cell extensions—dendrites and axons—and the formation of new synapses.

13. Retraining is a significant part of functional recovery and may involve both compensation, by establishing new solutions to adaptive demands, and reorganization of surviving networks. Greater recovery is evident in young individuals. Less impairment occurs when lesions are produced over a period of time—that is, when lesion momentum is reduced.

Recommended Reading

Banich, M. T. (1997). *Neuropsychology: The neural bases of mental function.* Boston: Houghton Mifflin.

Bradbury, J. W., and Vehrencamp, S. L. (1998). *Principles of animal communication.* Sunderland, MA: Sinauer.

Deacon, T. (1997). *The symbolic species: The coevolution of language and the brain.* New York: Norton.

Gazzaniga, M. S. (Ed.). (1995). *The cognitive neurosciences.* Cambridge, MA: MIT Press.

Hauser, M. (1996). *The evolution of communication.* Cambridge, MA: MIT Press.

Hellige, J. B. (1993). *Hemispheric asymmetry.* Cambridge, MA: Harvard University Press.

Ivry, R. B., and Robertson, L. C. (1998). *The two sides of perception.* Cambridge, MA: MIT Press.

Kertesz, A. (Ed.). (1994). *Localization and neuroimaging in neuropsychology.* San Diego, CA: Academic Press.

Ogden, J. A. (1996). *Fractured minds.* New York: Oxford University Press.

Pinker, S. (1994). *The language instinct.* New York: Morrow.

Savage-Rumbaugh, S., Shanker, S., and Talbot, T. (1998). *Apes, language and the human mind.* New York: Oxford University Press.

Afterword: The Ever-Changing Brain

*A*s a student, you are of course relieved to reach, at last, the final pages of a textbook. As authors, we too were relieved to arrive here. But we feel moved to have a final word with you to emphasize an overall theme that runs throughout the book and to discuss the importance of that theme explicitly before you go.

Plasticity Is a Defining Feature of the Brain

Sometimes in this book we have likened the brain to a machine, and that analogy is useful up to a point—the brain is a physical object whose parts must obey the laws of a material world. For example, in the early chapters we described how the various parts of the brain communicate using physical media such as neurotransmitters, hormones, and action potentials. However, we have also described a nervous system that is remarkably plastic, and in a constant state of flux. When we described psychological phenomena such as learning, perception, and cognition, it was implicit that these aspects of the mind were a product of the physical machine called the brain. But this machine is unlike any man-made machine because it is continually remodeling itself—rearranging the relationships between its parts—in a manner that (normally) improves its function. As you know from bitter experience, all man-made machines reach their peak performance once they are assembled and simply tumble downhill after that. Computer scientists struggle and yearn to develop systems that can truly learn from experience, something that is accomplished quite easily when an egg and a sperm combine.

The study of behavior is psychologists' special domain, and their research has illuminated how behavior may change. Since the nineteenth century it has been assumed that changes in behavior must be reflections of some physical changes in the brain. (The only alternative would have been a regression to nonphysical explanations—spirits or demons—to explain why people or other animals change their behavior.) But the complexity of the brain is so daunting that, until recently, few researchers even attempted to find out what part of the brain had been altered when some behavior changed. During the past few decades, however, psychologists and other neuroscientists have produced many concrete demonstrations that changes in behavior are due to brain changes. Indeed, it is now clear that constant change is one of the brain's defining features. Just as important, there is now abundant evidence that the relationship between brain changes and changes in behavior is bidirectional: Experience also can alter neural structure. Brain imaging techniques such as PET and fMRI are now enabling us to see changes in the responses of the brain that take place during the course of a single experiment, as examples in the learning research described in Chapters 17 and 18 demonstrate. Here we will briefly recap some of the topics discussed in the book where plasticity plays a particularly dramatic role.

Plasticity and Neural Development

Of course the nervous systems of developing individuals are even more plastic than those of adults—that's why infants learn new languages and recover from brain injuries so much more readily than we adults. In Chapter 7 we reviewed the many processes that occur as the brain puts itself together and showed how cell–cell interactions play a crucial role in all of those processes: The notochord induces cells to become motoneurons; targets secrete neurotrophic factors to attract and maintain neurons; radial glial cells guide migrating cells to their final destination. Based on what their neighboring cells are doing, developing cells take on an assigned role and make the appropriate connections to fulfill that role. Thus the cells of the developing nervous system are in constant communication with one another, and direct and constrain each other's fate. Because some of the neurons communicating these directions are sensory neurons that respond to stimuli in the environment, experience itself shapes the brain. The best-studied example of environmental effects on crucial aspects of development is in the visual system. As you will recall, early experience is crucial for maintaining the connections between the eye and brain that are needed to detect exactly those stimuli that surround us as adults.

Plasticity at the Molecular Level

Even at the molecular level, plasticity and change are the norm. Remember from Chapter 3 that the number of neurotransmitter receptors in the postsynaptic region of a given synapse can increase or decrease depending on the amount of activity at that synapse. Usually this activity serves to regulate the activity of a particular pathway: cells in the basal ganglia that receive too little dopamine stimulation start making more receptors to compensate, until they become supersensitive. Conversely, overstimulation leads to "down-regulation" of the receptors so that the signal is attenuated. Since experience can clearly affect which of our brain cells are firing, it must also indirectly affect the number and distribution of neurotransmitter receptors.

Plasticity in Endocrine Regulation

Chapter 5 presented many examples of the complicated feedback systems in the endocrine system that regulate secretion to maintain relatively steady hormone levels. But experience also modulates patterns of hormone secretion—losing an aggressive encounter can lower testosterone levels, stress can augment ACTH secretion and kill hippocampal cells, and exposure to pheromones can accelerate or delay puberty. While there are no data to indicate that pheromones play a role in human puberty, over the past century the average age at which individuals undergo puberty in our society has declined markedly, which indicates that some environmental factors—perhaps better nutrition or greater exposure to sexual stimuli—have affected our reproductive systems, too.

Sensory Plasticity

As noted above, research on sensory systems has been especially fruitful in demonstrating experiential effects on brain development and structure. In Chapter 8 we learned that changes in tactile stimulation, even in adulthood, can alter the projection patterns of information from the skin to the brain. This was first demonstrated in monkeys, and new, noninvasive techniques are now confirming that these same effects occur in humans.

For example, in a recent study (Yang et al., 1994), people who had lost a hand in accidents were examined. On the side of the brain receiving information from the remaining hand, stimulation of that hand excited a region of the somatosensory cortex sandwiched between brain regions responding to the face and upper arm; as the map of primary somatosenso-

ry cortex in Figure 8.16 shows, this is normal. However, on the side of the brain that was no longer receiving information because of the lost hand, regions sensitive to the face and upper arm were found to be immediately adjacent to each other—connections from the face and upper arm had shifted on that side of the brain to take over the region which had formerly been excited by stimuli from the hand. These data suggest that sensory information is constantly competing not only for our attention, but for space in the brain—space to analyze and process the information that is most relevant to the business of surviving and reproducing. We also saw in Chapter 18 that even in an adult animal the receptive fields of auditory cortical neurons could be changed by conditioning.

Plasticity and Psychopathology

Our bodies and brains constantly make adjustments for the time of day and time of year, as detailed in Chapter 14. In non-human animals, body weight and many other parameters are affected by whether an individual is exposed to summerlike long days or winterlike short days. Similarly, in humans, the short days of winter exacerbate some bouts of depression, so it seems that our nervous systems may also be carefully measuring the seasons. In Chapter 16 we saw that even severe psychopathologies such as schizophrenia are not entirely concordant in identical twins, so something other than genes can influence these disorders, and the best candidate for that "something" is differences in experience. Hopes are blossoming that recovery from brain accidents may be accomplished with grafts of genetically manipulated cells. These procedures clearly work in some cases, and may be feasible one day in others. But to the extent that these transplants work at all, it is because the rest of the brain is capable of changing to integrate these new cells into an existing network, so the underlying plasticity of the brain will prove to be of vital practical importance in this arena.

Plasticity, Learning, and Memory

In Chapters 17 and 18 we dealt with the phenomena that most explicitly depend upon structural alterations in the adult nervous system—learning and memory. If our adult brains could not change, then we could not learn anything, and this college course and all others would be a waste of time. (Please save opinions on this matter for course evaluation forms!) But we can learn, and scientists have made remarkable progress in finding structural changes that may underlie learning and memory.

Again we find that even the number or kind of neurotransmitter receptors can be altered by experience, as one of the foremost models of learning, long-term potentiation (LTP), illustrates. Recall that in a synapse that is activated in a particular way, the NMDA receptor will allow ions to enter the postsynaptic cell; these ions then change the synapse so that it will transmit its signal more forcefully in the future. In other words, "neurons that fire together wire together." LTP is a very active research area, and the details of the process are still being worked out, but based on inferences from behavior and what was known of neuroscience, psychologist Donald Hebb predicted in 1949 that strengthening of synaptic action is the foundation of learning ("the Hebbian synapse").

As work with simple model systems such as *Aplysia* proceeds, we continue to find evidence corroborating Hebb's basic idea that both the strength of existing synapses and the number and pattern of synaptic connections can be altered by the learning experience. This area of work also illuminates the reciprocal relationship between experience and brain structure that we discussed above and described in the first chapter: Experience alters the brain and the brain seeks out particular experiences.

Plasticity over the Life Span

Currently, much attention is being given to changes in the brain during early development and the importance of early experience for children's later development. These aspects of plasticity are certainly important, but we shouldn't forget that learning occurs over the whole life span, which makes the study of adult plasticity an equally valuable endeavor.

In Chapter 18 we saw that two major models of neural plasticity were discovered in the 1960s: (1) The work of Hubel and Wiesel (1963, 1965) showed that preventing a kitten's eye from receiving light during early development reduced the number of cortical cells that respond to that eye later in life. However, if a kitten is a few months old, depriving an eye of light does not affect its adult cortical representation, so the kind of plasticity necessary for "wiring" of the visual cortex occurs only during an early critical period. (2) As discussed in Chapter 17, Rosenzweig and colleagues (1961; Bennett et al., 1964) found that exposing rats to enriched environments alters neurochemical and neuroanatomical aspects of the cortex. In contrast to Hubel and Wiesel's findings, successive extensions of the initial work showed that such effects could be induced not only in young rats but also in juveniles (Zolman and Morimoro, 1962), in young adults (Rosenzweig et al., 1963; Bennett et al., 1964), and in old rats (Riege, 1971), although the size of the effects was greatest in the young animals. Thus, this research demonstrated that some forms of neural plasticity persist throughout the life span.

The Diversity of Temporal Constraints on Plasticity

The many examples of neural plasticity that we have presented and discussed in this book are not limited to these two contrasting possibilities. Several different models are needed to encompass them all. Furthermore, even kinds of learning and/or neural plasticity that seem to be similar may in fact follow different time courses over the life span. For example, LTP can be evoked in the supragranular visual cortex of rats only to day 30, whereas it can be evoked in the infragranular layers into adulthood (Perkins and Teyler, 1988). You will recall from Chapter 17 that a person who can no longer form certain kinds of memories because of brain damage or disease can still form other kinds perfectly well.

Plasticity Can Be Limited to an Early Critical or Sensitive Period

Ocular dominance columns in the visual cortex form early and do not change later in life (Figure 1*a*; Hubel and Wiesel, 1963).

> In cats, plasticity appears to be maximal at about 1 month of age and then declines over the next 3 months, after which time the visual pathways are virtually immutable. During this plastic period, every major response property of cortical cells (ocular dominance, orientation selectivity, direction selectivity, disparity sensitivity) can be modified by manipulation of the visual environment.
>
> G. Mower et al., 1983, p. 178

It is not clear what normally terminates plasticity in these aspects of the visual system. Baer and Singer (1986) suggested one possibility: They reported that they could restore plasticity in the visual cortex of adult cats by perfusing the area with acetylcholine and noradrenaline, so perhaps localized developmental decreases in synthesis of these transmitters is responsible for the decline in plasticity.

Another example of learning that seems to be limited to an early critical period is learning a first language with complete mastery. Investigators are not in complete agreement about the age limits, but such learning appears to be possible up to about 3 years of age, with a gradual falloff thereafter (Morford and Mayberry, in press). Fortunately, very few children with normal hearing are deprived of the possibility of acquiring speech in their first years, so most of the research in this area is based on acquisition of sign language by deaf children.

More than one language can be acquired at the start in infancy. Or, after a first language has been acquired, a second language can be acquired with complete native mastery if the learner starts the age of 6 or 7 years (Johnson and Newport, 1989). As we will discuss below, it has recently been discovered that learning a second language during the teen years leads to development of a second Broca's area in the left hemisphere, adjacent to the original Broca's area (Kim et al., 1997).

In Chapter 7 we saw that early handling by experimenters and early maternal stimulation help to make rat pups more resilient to stress later in life. Similarly,

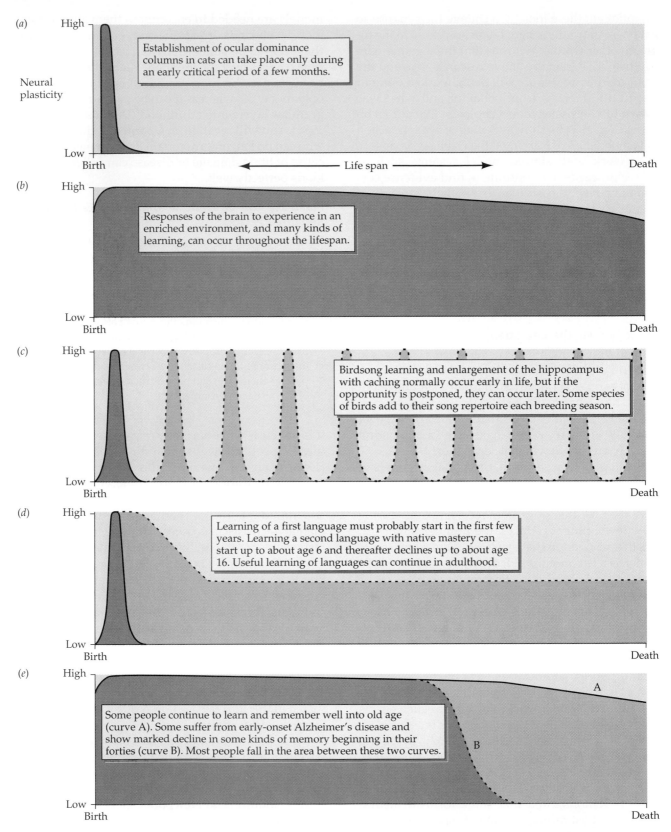

Figure 1 Some Patterns of Neural Plasticity across the Life Span

we saw in Chapter 18 that early handling or experience in a complex environment lowers the concentration of glucocorticoids in the rat brain, and causes more rapid return of glucocorticoids to the basal level, which protects the hippocampus from signs of aging.

Plasticity Can Extend over the Life Span

As we noted in Chapter 18, the research of the Rosenzweig and colleagues at Berkeley extended early findings of post-weaning brain plasticity using enriched environments in juvenile, adult, and aged animals (Figure 1*b*). Related results with aged rats were reported by Cummins et al. (1973), and by Greenough, McDonald, et al. (1986). Life-long plasticity accounts for many of the learning experiences we have in life, such as learning a musical instrument as an adult, learning to use another language, and so forth.

Experimental demonstrations of life-long plasticity include remapping the somesthetic cortex in adults by altering experience (Kaas, 1995), mentioned in Chapter 8, and remapping auditory receptive fields (N. Weinberger, 1998), mentioned in Chapter 18. Sexual behavior can also leave its mark on the nervous system, even in adulthood (Figure 2; Breedlove, 1997). Thus it is possible that structural differences between the sexes (or between people of differing sexual orientation) are the result of behavioral differences rather than the cause of them, as we discussed in Box 12.3.

Figure 2
(From "Science Classics" by Larry Gonick; courtesy of Larry Gonick and *Discover* magazine.)

Plasticity Occurs at the First Opportunity

Some kinds of plasticity occur as soon as the opportunity occurs. The limit is not a matter of age or maturity but of opportunity. For example, despite the comments above, the critical period for plasticity of the visual system can be extended if cats are reared in the dark. Interestingly, however, if dark-reared cats are exposed to light for only 6 hours, the light exposure triggers the developmental process, and once triggered, it runs to completion in the absence of further input (Mower et al., 1983).

Birdsong learning provides another example in which learning occurs at the first opportunity, as mentioned in Chapter 19. Normally a male bird learns its song from its father, but if a bird is prevented from hearing song at the usual age, it can still learn later, provided it is given an accurate model (Eales, 1987). For many years it was believed that it is not possible for a bird to acquire a normal song after a critical period had passed, a conclusion that was based on experiments with a taped song tutor. However, when live tutors or naturalistic taped tutors are used, later acquisition of song can take place. This finding fits in well with the observation that some species of songbirds add to their repertoire during each breeding season, which requires recurring periods of neural plasticity (Figure 1*c*).

In species of birds that cache food, such as nutcrackers, the hippocampus is larger than in related species that do not cache. If one of these birds is denied the opportunity to cache, the hippocampus does not show this size difference. The opportunity to cache can be postponed well beyond the usual age in laboratory-raised birds, but once the birds have the opportunity to cache, they do so promptly, and the hippocampus reflects this experience by enlarging (N. Clayton, 1994), as we mentioned in Chapter 17.

Some Forms of Plasticity are Greatest at an Early Age, but Remain in Later Life in Some Form

Aligning the two eyes to prevent amblyopia (or "lazy eye") is usually thought to be effective only for the first 5 to 6 years of life. But considerable improvement in amblyopia can be shown even by adults, if the condition is not too severe and if they exercise the weak eye sufficiently. As we mentioned in Chapter 10, one study reported considerable recovery from long-standing amblyopia after the normal eye was lost or severely damaged (Romero-Apis et al., 1982).

Chow and Stewart (1972) deprived kittens of pattern vision in one eye for about 20 months after birth. When the kittens were tested for pattern perception with the previously deprived eye, they showed almost no discrimination on formal tests and were not able to guide locomotion with the previously deprived eye, although they performed well with the other eye. As we described in Chapter 10, the investigators then undertook an intensive program of rehabilitation with some of the kittens, and over time, the kittens developed some pattern discrimination in the previously deprived eye, and they could use it to guide their locomotion. Furthermore, the kittens' recovery was accompanied by morphological changes in the lateral geniculate nucleus, and electrophysiological recording showed increased numbers of binocular cells in the visual cortex. Here again, learning to see and plasticity of the visual system occurred after the usual developmental period had ended.

The literature on human recovery from congenital blindness is mixed, but it has been studied in people born with dense cataracts that were removed in adulthood. Gregory (1987) notes that "often the eye takes a long time to settle down after a cataract operation," which may partially explain why many of the historical cases show slow development of vision. A patient studied by Gregory and Wallace (1963) received corneal grafts that provided good retinal images immediately after the operation, and the patient could quickly recognize objects he already knew by touch, but his vision never became fully normal. Learning to see is slow in adults, as it is in infants, but it appears to be possible to learn to see as an adult. The question is complicated by the fact that a person who has not seen until adulthood has learned other ways to adjust to the environment, and it may be difficult to abandon these compensatory behaviors.

In Some Cases, Later Plasticity Depends on Early Training

Eric Knudsen has found that the development of auditory–visual neurons in the optic tectum of the barn owl can be can be finely manipulated in the young bird. In Chapter 9 we saw that a young owl equipped with prismatic lenses that displace the visual image learns to adapt to the lenses and locate objects accurately. If the prisms are fitted to an adult bird, the range of adjustment is normally quite restricted. However, in recent work (Knudsen, 1998) it was shown that if an owl learns an abnormal auditory–visual adjustment as a juvenile and is then returned to the normal condition, it can easily reacquire the abnormal adjustment as an adult. It appears that the early learning leaves a neural trace that, even if not used for an extended period, can be reestablished later, when needed.

The ability to learn a second language with native mastery is possible if the learner starts the second language by the age of 6 or 7, provided the first language was begun during the first year or two (Figure 1*d*). Mastery of the second language shows increasing departures from full native skill as the starting age increases from 7 to 16. Furthermore, people who started their second language in their teens form a second Broca's area adjacent to the Broca's area for their first language (Kim et al., 1997). Nevertheless, even people who start to learn a second (or third, or fourth) language as an adult can gain conversational fluency, provided they work hard enough at it.

The Decline in Plasticity in the Latter Part of the Life Span Takes Many Forms

As we noted in Chapter 18, abilities to learn and remember decline on the average in the latter part of the life span, although some older people and animals perform as well as younger conspecifics (Figure 1*e*, curve A). On the other hand, some individuals suffer from early-onset Alzheimer's disease, and show a marked decline in the formation of declarative memories in their forties (curve B). Most people fall into the area between these two curves as they age. In those older individuals who show declines in ability with age, some studies show changes in neuroanatomy (such as shrinkage of the hippocampus) or in neurochemistry that may explain the decline. The *ApoE4* gene, which intensifies the effects of conditions that impair the brain, also shows its influence mainly in older individuals. Thus, all the observed declines in ability shown in Figure 1*e* may be pathological rather than normal, and it may become possible to counteract or prevent them. It has been proposed that the decline of abilities to learn and remember in the latter part of the life span occurs because there has been no evolutionary pressure to maintain these abilities after the reproductive period (Baltes, 1997), which may indicate why special interventions are required to prevent them. In Chapter 18 we saw that enriched experience early in life and continued throughout the life span helps to reduce the risk of cognitive decline in old age. At an international symposium on cognitive decline in old age, one of us summarized the research in this way (Rosenzweig and Bennett, 1996, p. 63):

> It's a fortunate person whose brain
> Is trained early, again and again,
> And who continues to use it
> To be sure not to lose it,
> So the brain, in old age, may not wane.

Future Directions

To the extent that certain types of neural plasticity are limited to parts of the life span, it will be important to find the mechanisms that enable plasticity and those that inhibit it. One possibility—a decline in neurotransmitter production—was mentioned in regard to plasticity of the visual system (Baer and Singer, 1986), and another is age-related shrinkage of neural structures such as the hippocampus. Other mechanisms remain to be identified, but identifying such mechanisms may allow us to improve our capacity for learning and memory in the future and to extend some kinds of learning further over the life span.

The perspective we hope to have imparted to you concerning the neurosciences is that the brain is indeed dynamic—changing, malleable, and adaptable. Of course this emphasis reflects our biases, since we are both psychologists and neuroscientists. But it also reflects a central problem in understanding the nervous system, and that is the control of behavior. What is most impressive about the behavior of both humans and other animals is its variety: individuals of a given species use many behavioral routes to accomplish the same goals; they display diverse behaviors across the span of their lifetimes; they develop many strategies to solve life's basic problems of survival and reproduction.

We hope that you already had an appreciation for the diversity of behaviors within and across species, but few people on the street understand that this diversity of behaviors requires a plastic brain and that the changes to the brain that underlie this plasticity must be physical—such as changes in receptor or type, neurotransmitter levels, cell numbers, or neuronal connections. The remaining challenge—and it is a formidable one—is to try to understand exactly how experience molds the nervous system and exactly how neural changes alter later behaviors. We and the other 22,000 or so other neuroscientists at work in the United States, as well as our colleagues around the world, hope to tell you more about these issues in the future.

Molecular Biology: Basic Concepts and Important Techniques

Genes Carry Information That Encodes the Synthesis of Proteins

The most important thing about **genes** is that they are *pieces of information,* inherited from parents, that affect the development and function of our cells. The information carried by the genes is a very specific sort: Each gene codes for the construction of a specific string of amino acids to form a **protein** molecule. The various proteins, each encoded by its own gene, make up the physical structure and most of the constituents of cells, including enzymes. **Enzymes** are molecules that allow particular chemical reactions to occur in our cells. For example, only cells that have liver-typical proteins will look like a liver cell and be able to perform liver functions. Neurons are cells that make neuron-typical proteins so that they can look and act like neurons. The genetic information for making these sorts of proteins is crucial for an animal to live and for a nervous system to work properly.

One thing we will hope this book will help you understand is that everyday experience can affect whether and when particular genetic recipes for making various proteins are used. But first let's review how genetic information is stored and how proteins are made. Our discussion will be brief because we assume that you've been exposed to this material before in an introductory biology course.

Genetic Information Is Stored in Molecules of DNA

The information for making all of our proteins could, in theory, be stored in any sort of format—on sheets of paper, magnetic tape, a CD-ROM—but all living creatures on this planet store their genetic information in a chemical called **deoxyribonucleic acid,** or **DNA**. Each molecule of DNA consists of a long strand of chemicals called **nucleotides** strung one after the other. There are only four nucleotides: guanine, cytosine, thymine, and adenine (abbreviated "G," "C," "T," and "A"). The particular sequence of nucleotides (for example, GCTTACC or TGGTCC or TGA) holds the information that will eventually make a protein. Because many millions of these nucleotides can be joined one after the other, a tremendous amount of information can be stored in very little space—on a single molecule of DNA.

A set of nucleotides that has been strung together can snuggle tightly against another string of nucleotides if it has the proper sequence: T nucleotides can fit across from A nucleotides, and Gs can fit across from Cs. Thus, T's are said to be complementary to As, while Cs are complementary to Gs. In fact, most of the time our DNA consists not of a single strand of nucleotides, but of two complementary strands of nucleotides wrapped around one another. The two strands of nucleotides are said to **hybridize** with one another, coiling slightly to form the famous double helix (Figure A.1). The double-stranded DNA twists and coils further, becoming visible in microscopes as **chromosomes,** which resemble twisted lengths of yarn. We and many other organisms are known as **eukaryotes** because we store our chromosomes in a membranous sphere called a **nucleus** inside each cell. You may remember that the ability of DNA to exist as two complementary strands of nucleotides is crucial for the duplication of the chromosomes, but that story will not concern us here. Just remember that, with very few exceptions, every cell in your body has a faithful copy of all the DNA you received from your parents.

DNA Is Transcribed to Produce Messenger RNA

The information from DNA is used to assemble another molecule—**ribonucleic acid,** or **RNA**—that serves as a template or guide for later steps. Like DNA, RNA is made up of a long string of four different nucleotides. For RNA, those nucleotides are G and C (which, you recall, are complementary to each other), and A and U (uracil), which are also complementary to each other. Note that the T nucleotide is found only in DNA and the U nucleotide is found only in RNA. When a particular gene becomes active,

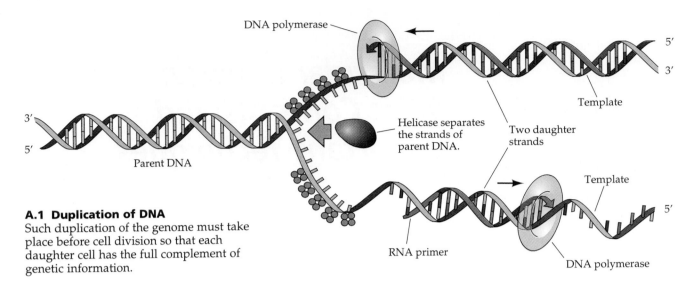

A.1 Duplication of DNA
Such duplication of the genome must take place before cell division so that each daughter cell has the full complement of genetic information.

the double strand of DNA unwinds enough so that one strand becomes free of the other and becomes available to special cellular machinery (including an enzyme called transcriptase) that begins **transcription**—the construction of a specific string of RNA nucleotides that are complementary to the exposed strand of DNA (Figure A.2). This length of RNA, sometimes called the message, or messenger RNA (mRNA), is also sometimes called a **transcript** because it contains a faithful transcript of the information in the DNA. Each DNA nucleotide has encoded for a specific RNA nucleotide (an RNA G for every DNA C, an RNA C for every DNA G, an RNA U for every DNA A, an RNA A for every DNA T). This transcript is made in the nucleus where the DNA resides; then the mRNA molecule moves to the cytoplasm, where protein molecules are assembled.

RNA Molecules Direct the Formation of Protein Molecules

In the cytoplasm are special organelles, called **ribosomes**, that attach themselves to a molecule of RNA, "read" the sequence of RNA nucleotides, and using that information, begin linking together amino acids to form a protein molecule. The structure and function of a protein molecule depend on which particular amino acids are put together and in what order. The decoding of an RNA transcript to manufacture a particular protein is called **translation** (see Figure A.2), as distinct from transcription, the construction of the mRNA molecule. Each trio (or "triplet") of RNA nucleotides encodes for one of about 20 different amino acids. Special molecules associated with the ribosome recognize the trio of RNA nucleotides and bring the appropriate amino acid so that the ribosome can fuse that amino acid to the previous one. If the resulting

string of amino acids is short (say, 50 amino acids or so), it is called a **peptide**; if it is long, it is called a protein. Thus the ribosome assembles a very particular sequence of amino acids at the behest of a very particular sequence of RNA nucleotides, which were themselves encoded for in the DNA inherited from our parents. In short, the secret of life is: DNA makes RNA, and RNA makes protein.

There are fascinating amendments to this short story. Often the information from separate stretches of DNA is spliced together to make a single transcript; so-called "alternate splicing" can create different transcripts from the same gene. Sometimes a transcript is modified extensively before translation begins; special chemical processes can cleave long proteins to create one or several active peptides. But we will not consider those processes in this book. An important point to keep in mind is that each cell has the complete library of genetic information (collectively known as the **genome**), but makes only a fraction of all the proteins encoded for in that DNA. In modern biology we say that each cell **expresses** only some genes; that is, the cell transcribes certain genes and makes the corresponding gene products (protein molecules). Thus, each cell must come to express all the genes needed to perform its function. Modern biologists refer to the expression of a particular subset of the genome as cell differentiation: The process differentiates the appearance and function of different types of cells. During development, individual cells appear to become more and more specialized, expressing progressively fewer genes. Many molecular biologists are striving to understand what cellular and molecular mechanisms "turn on" or "turn off" gene expression in order to understand development and pathologies such as cancer.

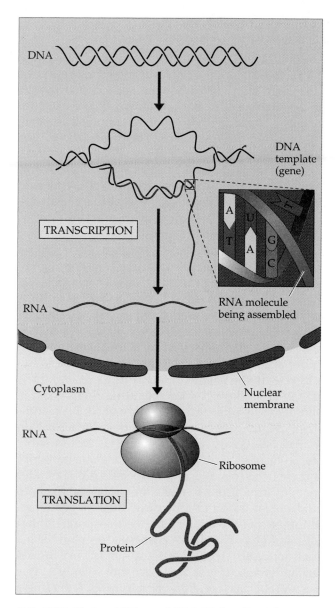

A.2 DNA Makes RNA, and RNA Makes Protein

Molecular Biologists Have Craftily Enslaved Microorganisms and Enzymes

Many basic methods of molecular biology are not explicitly discussed in the text, so we will not describe them in detail here. However, you should understand what some of the terms *mean*, even if you don't know exactly how the methods are performed. Molecular biologists have found ways to incorporate foreign DNA from other species into the DNA of microorganisms such as bacteria and viruses. After incorporating the foreign DNA, the microorganisms are allowed to reproduce rapidly, producing more and more copies of the (foreign) gene of interest. At this point the gene is said to be **cloned**, because the researcher can make as many copies as she likes. To ensure that the right gene

is being cloned, the researcher generally clones many, many different genes, each into different bacteria, and then "screens" the bacteria rapidly to find the rare one that has incorporated the gene of interest.

When enough copies of the DNA have been made, the microorganisms are ground up and the DNA extracted. If sufficient DNA has been generated, chemical steps can then determine the exact sequence of nucleotides found in that stretch of DNA, a process known as **sequencing**. Once the sequence of nucleotides has been determined, the sequence of complementary nucleotides in the messenger RNA for that gene can be inferred. The sequence of mRNA nucleotides tells the investigator the sequence of amino acids that will be made from that transcript, because biologists know which amino acid is encoded for by each triplet of DNA nucleotides. In this manner scientists have discovered the amino acid sequence of neurotransmitter receptors, including the structure of photoreceptors that allows us to see.

In the past few years the business of obtaining many copies of DNA has been boosted by a technique called the **polymerase chain reaction**, or **PCR**. This technique exploits a special type of polymerase enzyme that, like other such enzymes, induces the formation of a DNA molecule that is complementary to an existing single strand of DNA. Because this particular polymerase enzyme evolved in bacteria that inhabit geothermal hot springs, it can function in a broad range of temperatures. By heating double-stranded DNA, we can cause the two strands to separate, making each strand available to polymerase enzymes which, when the temperature is cooled down enough, construct a new "mate" for each strand so that they are double-stranded again. The first PCR yields only double the number of DNA molecules you began with; repeating the process results in four times as many molecules as at first. Repeatedly heating and cooling the DNA of interest in the presence of this heat-resistant polymerase enzyme soon yields millions of copies of the original DNA molecule.

Thus PCR amplifies even tiny amounts of DNA into amounts that are large enough for chemical analysis or other manipulations, such as introducing DNA into cells. For example, you might inject some of the DNA encoding a protein of interest into a fertilized mouse egg (a zygote) and then return the zygote to a pregnant mouse to grow. Occasionally the injected DNA becomes incorporated into the zygote's genome so the **transgenic** mouse that results carries and uses this foreign gene.

Southern Blots Identify Particular Genes

Since all cells contain a complete copy of the genome, if we want to know whether a particular individual or a particular species carries a certain gene, we can gather DNA from just about any cell population (for humans, blood is drawn; for rodents, the tip of the tail may be used). Then we can grind up the cells and use chemical extraction procedures to isolate the DNA (discarding the RNA and protein). Finding a particular gene in that DNA really boils down to finding *a particular sequence of DNA nucleotides*. To do that, we can exploit the tendency of nucleic acids to hybridize with one another. If we were looking for the DNA sequence GCT, for example, we could manufacture the sequence CGA (there are machines to do that readily), which will then stick to (hybridize with) any DNA sequence of GCT. The manufactured sequence CGA is called a **probe** because it is made to include some radioactive molecules so that we can follow the radioactivity to find out where the sequence goes. Of course, such a short length of nucleotides will be found in many genes. In order for a probe to recognize one particular gene, it has to be at least 15 nucleotides long. When we extract DNA from an individual, it's convenient to let enzymes cut up the very long stretches of DNA into more manageable pieces of 1 to 20 thousand nucleotides each. A process called **gel electrophoresis** uses electrical current to separate those millions of pieces more or less by size. Large pieces move slowly through a tube of gelatinlike material, and small pieces move rapidly. The tube of gel is then sliced and placed on top of a sheet of paperlike material called nitrocellulose. When fluid is allowed to flow through the gel and nitrocellulose, DNA molecules are pulled out of the gel and deposited on the waiting nitrocellulose. This process of making a "sandwich" of gel and nitrocellulose and using fluid to move molecules from the former to the latter is called **blotting** (Figure A.3).

If the gene we are looking for is among those millions of DNA fragments sitting on the nitrocellulose, our radiolabeled probe should recognize and hybridize to the sequence. The nitrocellulose sheet is soaked in a solution containing our radiolabeled probe; we wait for the probe to find and hybridize with the gene of interest (if it is present), and rinse the sheet to remove probe molecules that did not find the gene. Then photographic film is placed next to the nitrocellulose. The particles emitted by the radioactive molecule will expose the film just as light does. If the radiolabeled probe found the gene, the film will be dark at one particular place, corresponding to the size of DNA fragment that contained the gene (see Figure A.3). This process of looking for a particular sequence of DNA is called **Southern blotting**, named after the man who developed the technique, Edward Southern, and the final film is often called a Southern blot. Southern blots are useful for determining whether related individuals share a particular gene or for assessing the evolutionary relatedness of different species.

Northern Blots Identify Particular RNA Transcripts

A more relevant method for our discussions is the **Northern blot** (whimsically named as the opposite of a Southern blot). A Northern blot can identify which tissues make use of a particular gene. If liver cells are making a particular protein, for example, then some transcripts for that gene should be present. So we can take the liver, grind it up, and use chemical processes to isolate most of the RNA (throwing the DNA and protein away). Unlike purified DNA, this mixture consists of RNA molecules of many different sizes—long, medium, and short transcripts. Gel electrophoresis will separate the transcripts by size, and we can blot the size-sorted mRNAs onto nitrocellulose sheets. To see whether the particular transcript we are looking for is among the mRNAs, we construct a radiolabeled probe (of either DNA nucleotides or RNA nucleotides) that is complementary to the transcript of interest and long enough that it will hybridize only to that particular transcript. We incubate the nitrocellulose in the probe, allow time for the probe to hybridize with the targeted transcript (if present), rinse off any unused probes, lay the nitrocellulose next to photographic film, and wait a day or so. If the transcript of interest is present, we should see a band on the film (see Figure A.3). Several bands indicates that our probe has hybridized to more than one transcript and we need to make a more specific probe or alter chemical conditions to make the probe less likely to bind similar transcripts. Because different gene transcripts are of different lengths, the transcript of interest should have reached a particular point in the gel electrophoresis; small transcripts should have moved far, large transcripts should have moved only a little. If our probe has found the right transcript, the single band of labeling should be at the point that is appropriate for a transcript of that length.

In Situ Hybridization Identifies Which Cells Possess a Particular Transcript

Northern blots can tell us whether a particular *organ* has transcripts for a particular gene product. For example, Northern blot analyses have indicated that there are thousands of genes that are transcribed only in the brain. Presumably the proteins encoded by these genes are used exclusively in the brain. But such results alone are not very informative because the brain consists of so many different kinds of glial and neuronal cells. We can refine Northern blot analyses somewhat by dissecting out a particular part of the brain, say the hippocampus, to isolate mRNAs. Sometimes, though, it is important to know *exactly which cells* are making the transcript. In that case we use **in situ hybridization**.

With in situ hybridization we use the same sort of labeled probe, constructed of nucleotides that are

Gel electrophoresis

Wells are filled with DNA solutions.

Gel support

Gel

Buffer solution

DNA samples

Later

Still later

Bands of DNA fragments, bearing negative charge, move toward positive electrode.

Smaller fragments movemore rapidly than larger ones.

Movement continues as long as electric field is maintained.

Southern blotting

Weight

Absorbent paper

Wick

Nitrocellulose filter

Buffer solution (to transfer DNA)

Support

Gel (with DNA fragments)

Hybridization

Add labeled probe

Rinse off unattached probe and make chemical marker visible.

Chemical labels

Nitrocellulose filter

A.3 Southern Blotting

complementary to (and will therefore hybridize with) the targeted transcript, as in Northern blots. Instead of using the probe to find and hybridize with the transcript on a sheet of nitrocellulose, however, we use the probe to find the transcripts "in place" (in situ)—that is, on a section of tissue. After rinsing off the probe molecules that didn't find a match, we can look for the probe in the tissue section. Any cells in the section that were transcribing the gene of interest will have transcripts in the cytoplasm and should have some of our labeled probe (Figure A.4). In situ hybridization can tell us exactly which cells are using a particular gene.

Western Blots Identify the Organ or Tissue Region Where a Particular Protein Is Made

Sometimes we may wish to identify a particular protein rather than its transcript. In that case we can use antibodies. **Antibodies** are large, complicated molecules (proteins, in fact) that our immune system makes and releases into the bloodstream to fight invading microbes, thereby arresting and preventing disease (see Figure 15.16). By injecting a rabbit or mouse with the protein of interest, the animal can be induced to create antibodies that recognize and attach to that particular protein. Because there are ways to label such antibodies, they can be used to tell us whether the targeted protein is present. We can grind up an organ, isolate the proteins (throwing the DNA and RNA away), and separate them via gel electrophoresis. Then we can blot these proteins out of the gel and onto nitrocellulose. Next we use the antibodies to tell us whether the targeted protein is among those made by that organ. If our antibodies are identifying only the protein we care about, there should be a single band of labeling (if there are two then the antibodies recognize more than one protein). Because proteins come in different sizes, the single band of label should be at the position corresponding to the size of the protein we are studying. Such blots

Bead of solution covering brain section, contains labeled probe.

Labeled probe hybridyzing to RNA

Rinse off unattached probes and make chemical label visible.

Chemical label identifies hippocampal regions which had been making targeted RNA.

RNA in cytoplasm of cell

A.4 In Situ Hybridization

Rat brain section covered with solution containing antibodies

Labeled antibody attached to targeted protein in brain cell

Rinse off unattached antibodies and make chemical label visible.

Labeled cells in paraventricular nucleus which had produced target protein

A.5 Immunocytochemistry

are called **Western blots**. (To review, Southern blots identify particular DNA pieces [genes], Northern blots identify particular RNA pieces [transcripts], and Western blots identify particular proteins [sometimes called products].)

Antibodies Can Also Tell Us Which Cells Possess a Particular Protein

If we need to know which particular cells within an organ such as the brain are making a particular protein, we can use the same sort of antibodies as we use in Western blots, but in this case directed at that protein in tissue sections. We slice up the brain, expose the sections to the antibodies, allow time for them to find and attach to the protein, rinse off unattached antibodies, and use chemical treatments to visualize the antibodies. Cells that were making the protein will be labeled from the chemical treatments (Figure A.5). Because antibodies from the *immune* system are used to identify *cells* with the aid of *chemical* treatment, this method is called **immunocytochemistry**, or **ICC**. This technique can even tell us where, within the cell, the protein is found. Such information can provide important clues about the function of the protein. For example, if the protein is found in axon terminals, it may be a neurotransmitter.

Glossary

Aδ fiber   A moderately large, myelinated and therefore fast-conducting axon, usually transmitting pain information. See Table 8.2.

absolute refractory phase   See *refractory phase.*

accommodation   The process of focusing by the ciliary muscles and the lens to form a sharp image on the retina.

acetylcholine (ACh)   One of the best known synaptic transmitters. Acetylcholine acts as an excitatory transmitter at synapses between motor nerves and skeletal muscles but as an inhibitory transmitter between the vagus nerve and the heart muscle.

acetylcholinesterase (AChE)   An enzyme that inactivates the transmitter acetylcholine both at synaptic sites and elsewhere in the nervous system.

achromatopsia   Lack of color (but not black-and-white) vision.

acquired immune deficiency syndrome (AIDS)   A disease characterized by the loss of immune function that is spread by the human immunodeficiency virus (HIV).

acquired dyslexia (alexia)   Dyslexia that occurs as result of injury or disease.

act   Complex behavior, as distinct from a simple movement. Also called action pattern.

ACTH   See *adrenocorticotropic hormone.*

actin   A protein that, along with myosin, mediates muscle contraction. See Figure 11.7.

action pattern   See *act.*

action potential   The propagated electrical message of a neuron that travels along the axon to adjacent neurons. Also called the nerve impulse. See Figure 3.5.

activational effect   A temporary change in behavior resulting from the administration of a hormone to an adult animal. Contrast with *organizational effect.*

acupuncture   The insertion of needles at designated points on the skin to alleviate pain.

adaptation   The progressive loss of receptor sensitivity as stimulation is maintained. See Figure 8.7.

adenohypophysis   See *anterior pituitary.*

adequate stimulus   The type of stimulus for which a given sense organ is particularly adapted. Light energy is the adequate stimulus for photoreceptors.

ADH   See *antidiuretic hormone.*

adipose tissue   Tissue made up of fat cells.

adipsia   A condition in which an individual refuses to drink.

adrenal cortex   The outer covering of the adrenal gland. Each of the three cellular layers of the adrenal cortex produces different hormones. See Table 5.2.

adrenal gland   An endocrine gland adjacent to the kidney. See Figure 5.15.

adrenaline   See *epinephrine.*

adrenal medulla   The inner core of the adrenal gland. The adrenal medulla secretes epinephrine and norepinephrine. See Figure 5.15.

adrenocorticoids   A class of steroid hormones that are secreted by the adrenal cortex.

adrenocorticotropic hormone (ACTH)   A tropic hormone secreted by the anterior pituitary gland that controls the production and release of hormones of the adrenal cortex. See Figure 5.16.

adrenosteroids   See *adrenocorticoids.*

afferent fiber   An axon that carries nerve impulses from a sense organ to the central nervous system, or from one region into another region of interest. Contrast with *efferent fiber.*

affinity   Theoretically, the length of time a transmitter or drug molecule binds to a receptor molecule. Practically, the concentration of transmitter or drug molecule that is required to bind half of the receptors at equilibrium.

afterpotential   The positive or negative change in membrane potential that may follow a nerve impulse.

agnosia   The inability to recognize objects, despite being able to describe them in terms of form and color; may occur after localized brain damage.

agonist   A molecule, usually a drug, that binds a receptor and initiates a response like that of another molecule, usually a neurotransmitter. Contrast with *antagonist* (definition 1). Of muscles, a muscle that moves a body part in the same general way as the muscle of interest; a synergistic muscle.

agraphia   The inability to write.

AI   See *androgen insensitivity.*

AIDS   See *acquired immune deficiency syndrome.*

aldosterone   A mineralocorticoid hormone, secreted by the adrenal cortex, that helps maintain homeostasis in the concentrations of ions in blood and extracellular fluid by inducing the kidneys to conserve sodium.

alexia   The inability to read.

alkaloids   A class of chemicals, found in plants, that includes many psychoactive agents, such as curare, the opium alkaloids (morphine and codeine), and lysergic acid (to which LSD is related).

allele A particular version of a gene.

allomone A chemical signal that is released outside the body by one species and affects the behavior of other species. Contrast with *pheromone*. See Figure 5.4.

all-or-none Referring to the fact that the amplitude of the nerve impulse is independent of the magnitude of the stimulus. Stimuli above a certain threshold produce nerve impulses of identical magnitude (although they may vary in frequency); stimuli below this threshold produce no nerve impulses. Contrast with *graded potential*. See Figure 3.7.

alpha motoneuron A motoneuron that controls the main contractile fibers (extrafusal fibers) of a muscle. See Figure 11.8.

alpha rhythm A brain potential that occurs during relaxed wakefulness, especially at the back of the head; its frequency is 8 to 12 Hz. See Figure 14.10.

ALS See *amyotrophic lateral sclerosis*.

altricial Referring to animals that are born in an undeveloped state and depend on maternal care, as human infants do. Contrast with *precocial*.

Alzheimer's disease A type of dementia that occurs in middle age or later.

amacrine cells Cells in the retina that contact both the bipolar cells and the ganglion cells, and are especially significant in inhibitory interactions within the retina. See Figure 10.7.

amblyopia Reduced visual acuity that is not caused by optical or retinal impairments.

amine hormones A class of compounds that are composed of a single amino acid that has been modified into a related molecule, such as melatonin or epinephrine. Also called monoamine hormones.

amnesia Severe impairment of memory.

amnestic An amnesia-causing agent.

AMPA receptor A glutamate receptor that also binds the glutamate agonist AMPA (alpha-amino-3-hydroxy-5-methyl-4-isoxazole-propionic acid). The AMPA receptor is responsible for most of the activity at glutaminergic synapses. See Box 4.2 and Figure 18.8.

amphetamine A molecule that resembles the structure of the catecholamine transmitters and that enhances their activity.

ampulla (pl. ampullae) An enlarged region of each semicircular canal that contains the receptor cells (hair cells) of the vestibular system. See Figure 9.14.

amygdala A group of nuclei in the medial anterior part of the temporal lobe. See Figure 2.15.

β-amyloid A protein that accumulates in senile plaques in Alzheimer's disease.

amyotrophic lateral sclerosis (ALS) A disease in which motoneurons and their target muscles waste away.

analgesic Pain-killing.

analogy A resemblance between two species that is due to convergence rather than to common ancestry.

anandamide An endogenous substance that binds the cannabinoid receptor.

androgen insensitivity (AI) The inability to respond to androgenic hormones; caused by a defect in the gene for the androgen receptor.

androgens A class of hormones that includes testosterone and other male hormones. See Table 5.2.

androstenedione The chief sex hormone secreted by the human adrenal cortex. Responsible for the adult pattern of body hair in men and women.

angiography A noninvasive technique for examining brain structure in humans by taking X-rays after special dyes are injected into cerebral blood vessels. Inferences about adjacent tissue can be made from examining the outline of the principal blood vessels.

angiotensin II A substance that is produced in the blood by the action of renin and that may be involved in control of thirst.

angular gyrus A brain region in which strokes can lead to word blindness.

anion A negatively charged ion, such as a protein or chloride ion. Contrast with *cation*.

anomia The inability to name persons or objects readily.

anomic aphasia Difficulty in recalling words, although comprehension and ability to repeat words are normal.

anorexia The absence of appetite.

anorexia nervosa A syndrome in which individuals severely deprive themselves of food.

anosmia Inability to smell.

antagonist 1. A molecule, usually a drug, that interferes with or prevents the action of a transmitter. Contrast with *agonist*. 2. A muscle which counteracts the effect of another muscle. Contrast with *synergist* or *agonist*.

anterior pituitary The front lobe of the pituitary gland; secretes tropic hormones. Also called adenohypophysis. See Figure 5.13.

anterograde amnesia The inability to form new memories beginning with the onset of the disorder.

anterograde degeneration The loss of the distal portion of an axon resulting from injury to the axon. Also called Wallerian degeneration. See Box 7.1.

anterolateral system (spinothalamic tract) Somatosensory system which carries most of the pain information to the brain. See Figure 8.22.

antidiuretic hormone (ADH) A hormone from the posterior pituitary that controls the removal of water from blood by the kidneys. Also called vasopressin.

antigen A substance that stimulates the production of antibodies.

antipsychotic drug A drug that alleviates schizophrenia.

anxiety states A class of psychological disorders that include recurrent panic states, generalized persistent anxiety disorders, and posttraumatic stress disorders.

anxiolytics A class of substances that are used to combat anxiety; examples include alcohol, opiates, barbiturates, and the benzodiazepines.

aphagia The refusal to eat; often related to damage to the lateral hypothalamus.

aphasia An impairment in language understanding and/or production that is caused by brain injury.

apical dendrite The dendrite that extends from a pyramidal cell to the outermost surface of the cortex. Contrast with *basal dendrite*.

apoptosis See *cell death*.

appetitive behavior The second stage of mating behavior; helps establish or maintain sexual interaction. See Figure 12.2.

apraxia An impairment in the ability to begin and execute skilled voluntary movements, although there is no muscle paralysis.

arachnoid   The thin covering of the brain that lies between the dura mater and pia mater.

archicortex   Evolutionarily old cortex, such as the hippocampus in mammals. Thought to be more ancient than paleocortex.

arcuate fasciculus   A tract connecting Wernicke's speech area to Broca's speech area. See Figure 19.10.

arcuate nucleus   An arc-shaped hypothalamic nucleus.

area postrema   One of the circumventricular nuclei which have weak blood–brain barriers. See Figure 13.17.

arginine vasopressin   See *vasopressin*.

aromatase   An enzyme that converts many androgens into estrogens.

aromatization   The chemical reaction that converts testosterone to estradiol and other androgens to other estrogens.

aromatization hypothesis   The hypothesis that testicular androgens enter the brain and are there converted into estrogens to masculinize the developing nervous system of some rodents.

aspartic acid   Thought by many investigators to be a major excitatory synaptic transmitter in the central nervous system.

associative learning   A type of learning in which an association is formed between two stimuli or between a stimulus and a response; includes both classical and instrumental conditioning. Contrast with *nonassociative learning*.

astereognosis   The inability to recognize objects by touching and feeling them.

astrocyte   A star-shaped glial cell with numerous processes, or extensions, that run in all directions. The extensions of astrocytes provide structural support for the brain and may isolate receptive surfaces. See Figure 2.6.

ataxia   An impairment in the direction, extent, and rate of muscular movement; often caused by cerebellar pathology.

attribute model of memory   Model in which different brain regions process different dimensions or attributes of a learning/memory situation—space, time, sensory dimensions, response, and emotional aspects.

audiologist   Person who measures hearing abilities.

auditory cortex   A region of the temporal lobe that receives input from the medial geniculate nucleus. See Figure 9.7.

auditory evoked potential   A change in EEG potential that follows presentation of an auditory stimulus. See Figure 3.18*c*.

auditory nerve   The VIII cranial nerve; it runs from the cochlea to the brain stem auditory nuclei. See Figure 9.1.

autism   A disorder arising during childhood, characterized by social withdrawal and stereotypy.

autocrine   Referring to a signal that is secreted by a cell into its environment and that feeds back to the same cell. See Figure 5.4.

autonomic ganglia   One of the three main divisions of the peripheral nervous system; includes the two chains of sympathetic ganglia and the more peripheral parasympathetic ganglia.

autonomic nervous system   The part of the peripheral nervous system that supplies neural connections to glands and to smooth muscles of internal organs. Composed of two divisions (sympathetic and parasympathetic) that act in opposite fashion. See Figure 2.11.

autonomic response specificity   Patterns of bodily response governed by the autonomic nervous system that are characteristic of an individual.

autoradiography   A histological technique that shows the distribution of radioactive chemicals in tissues.

autoreceptor   A receptor for a synaptic transmitter that is located in the presynaptic membrane. Autoreceptors tell the axon terminal how much transmitter has been released.

autosome   One of a pair of chromosomes that are identical. All chromosomes except the sex chromosomes are autosomes.

axon   A single extension from the cell that carries nerve impulses from the cell body to other neurons. See Figures 2.3, 2.4, 2.5.

axonal transport   The transportation of materials from the neuron cell body to distant regions in the dendrites and axons, and from the axon terminals back to the cell body.

axon collateral   A branch of an axon from a single neuron.

axon hillock   A cone-shaped area from which the axon originates out of the cell body. Depolarization must reach a critical threshold at the axon hillock for the neuron to transmit a nerve impulse. See Figure 2.4.

axon terminal   The end of an axon or collateral, which forms a synapse upon a neuron or other target.

axoplasmic streaming   The process that transports materials synthesized in the cell body to distant regions in the dendrites and axons.

B cell   A lymphocyte, including those that produce antibodies. See Figure 15.16.

B lymphocyte   An immune-system cell that mediates humoral immunity.

ballism   An uncontrollable violent tossing of the limbs. Lesions in the subthalamic nucleus can produce this syndrome in humans and monkeys.

ballistic movement   A rapid muscular movement that is thought to be organized or programmed by the cerebellum. Contrast with *ramp movement*.

baroreceptor   A pressure receptor in the heart or a major artery that detects a fall in blood pressure and communicates that information to the brain via the autonomic nervous system.

basal dendrite   One of several dendrites on a pyramidal cell that extend horizontally from the cell body. Contrast with *apical dendrite*.

basal forebrain   A ventral region in the forebrain that has been implicated in sleep and Alzheimer's disease. See Figure 4.1.

basal ganglia   A group of forebrain nuclei found deep within the cerebral hemispheres. See Figures 2.14, 2.15, 11.15.

basal metabolism   The rate of metabolism when a body is at rest.

base   A component of a DNA or RNA molecule. DNA contains four bases (adenine, thymine, cytosine, and guanine), a pair of which forms each rung of the molecule. The order of these bases determines the genetic information of a DNA molecule.

basic neuroglial compartment   A level of brain organization that includes a single nerve cell with all its synaptic endings, associated glial cells, surrounding extracellular space, and vascular elements.

basic rest–activity cycle   A cycle of repeating periods of rest and activity that occur both in waking hours and during sleep.

basilar artery   An artery formed by the fusion of the vertebral arteries; its branches supply blood to the brain stem and to posterior portions of the cerebral hemispheres. See Figure 2.20.

basilar membrane   A membrane in the cochlea that contains the principal structures involved in auditory transduction. See Figures 9.2, 9.4.

BDNF   See *brain-derived neurotropic factor.*

behavioral intervention   An approach to finding relations between bodily variables and behavioral variables that involves intervening in the behavior of an organism and looking for resultant changes in bodily structure or function. See Figure 1.3.

behavioral teratology   Study of impairments in behavior that are produced by embryonic or fetal exposure to toxic substances.

behavioral toxicology   Study of effects of toxic substances on behavior and use of behavioral measures to assay toxicity of substances.

benzodiazepines   A class of anti-anxiety drugs that bind with high affinity to receptors in the central nervous system; one example is diazepam (Valium).

bigamy   Having two mates or spouses.

binaural detection   Detection using two ears. See Figure 9.11.

binaural interaction   The interaction of signals from two ears; especially important for localizing auditory stimuli.

binocular deprivation   Depriving both eyes of form vision, as by sealing the eyelids.

binocular disparity   The slight difference between the views from the two eyes; important in depth perception.

biofeedback   A technique in which a bodily variable such as skin temperature or the gross electrical activity of the brain is monitored. The resulting information allows the subject to gain some control over the bodily variable and may be used in the treatment of various disorders.

biological markers   Biological variables that accompany psychological disorders, irrespective of whether they directly cause the disorder.

bipolar cells   Interneurons of the retina that receive information from rods and cones and pass the information to retinal ganglion cells.

bipolar disorder   A psychiatric disorder characterized by depressed periods that alternate with excessive, expansive moods. Also called manic-depressive psychosis. Contrast with *unipolar depression.*

bipolar neuron   A nerve cell that has a single dendrite at one end and a single axon at the other end; found in some vertebrate sensory systems. See Figures 2.3, 10.25.

blastocyst   An early developmental stage in which the organism is a hollow sphere whose wall is one cell thick.

blind spot   The place through which blood vessels enter the retina. Because there are no receptors in this region, light striking it cannot be seen. See Figure 10.1.

blood–brain barrier   The mechanisms that make the movement of substances from capillaries into brain cells more difficult than exchanges in other body organs, thus affording the brain greater protection from exposure to some substances found in the blood.

brain-derived neurotrophic factor (BDNF)   A protein purified from the brain of many animals that can keep some classes of neurons alive. Resembles nerve growth factor.

brain electrical activity mapping (BEAM)   A system of analysis and display of electrical brain signals. See Figure 3.18.

brain explant   A small piece of brain tissue isolated from the body.

brain stem   The region of the brain that consists of the midbrain, the pons, and the medulla.

Brattleboro rat   A rat that has a mutation in the gene for vasopressin that keeps the animal from producing functional hormone. Brattleboro rats show the symptoms of diabetes insipidus.

brightness   One of the basic dimensions of light perception; varies from dark to light. See Figure 10.5.

Broca's aphasia   An impairment in speech production; related to damage in Broca's area.

Broca's area   An area in the frontal region of the left hemisphere of the brain that is involved in the production of speech. See Figure 19.7.

brown fat   Tissue made up of fat cells that is found especially around vital organs in the trunk and around the cervical and thoracic levels of the spinal cord; is capable of intense metabolism and therefore can generate heat. Also called brown adipose tissue.

bulimia   A syndrome in which individuals believe themselves fatter than they are and periodically gorge themselves, usually with "junk food," and then either vomit or take laxatives to avoid weight gain. Also called bulimia nervosa.

C fiber   A small, unmyelinated axon that conducts pain information slowly and adapts slowly. See Table 8.2.

caffeine   A stimulant compound found in coffee, cocoa, and other plants which may have evolved to protect plants against insect predators. Caffeine stimulates and causes uncoordinated behavior in insects and inhibits their growth and reproduction.

calcitonin   A hormone released by the thyroid gland.

calcium-dependent kinase   An enzyme that, in the presence of calcium, adds phosphate groups (PO_4) to protein molecules. Calcium-dependent kinase has been investigated in regard to memory.

calorie   The amount of energy required to raise the temperature of 1 milliliter of water by 1° C.

cAMP   See *cyclic adenosine monophosphate.*

cannabinoids   Substances that bind the same endogenous receptors as are bound by the active ingredient in marijuana, THC.

carotid arteries   The major arteries that ascend the left and right sides of the neck to the brain. The branch that enters the brain is called the internal carotid artery. See Figure 2.20.

castration   Removal of the gonads, usually the testes.

CAT   See *computerized axial tomography.*

cataplexy   The sudden loss of muscle tone, leading to collapse of the body without loss of consciousness.

catecholamine   A class of monoamines that serve as neurotransmitters, including dopamine and nor-epinephrine.

cation   A positively charged ion, such as a potassium or sodium ion. Contrast with *anion*.

caudal   An anatomical term referring to structures toward the tail end of an organism. Contrast with *rostral*.

caudate nucleus   One of the basal ganglia that has a long extension or tail. See Figure 2.15.

cell adhesion molecule (CAM)   A protein found on the surface of a cell that serves to guide cell migration and/or axonal pathfinding.

cell assembly   A large group of cells that tend to be active at the same time because they have been activated simultaneously or in close succession in the past.

cell body   The region of a neuron that is defined by the presence of the nucleus. See Figures 2.2, 2.3.

cell death   The developmental process during which "surplus" nerve cells die. Also called apoptosis.

cell differentiation   The developmental stage in which cells acquire distinctive characteristics, such as those of neurons, as the result of expressing particular genes. See Figure 7.4.

cell-mediated immunity   An immunological response that involves T lymphocytes.

cell migration   The movement of nerve cells from their site of origin to their final location. See Figures 7.4, 7.5.

cell proliferation   The production of cells by mitotic division. See Figure 7.5.

cellular fluid   See *intracellular fluid*.

central deafness   A hearing impairment that is related to lesions in auditory pathways or centers, including sites in the brain stem, thalamus, or cortex.

central nervous system (CNS)   The portion of the nervous system that includes the brain and the spinal cord. See Figure 2.8.

central pattern generator   Neural circuitry that is responsible for generating a rhythmic pattern of behavior, such as walking.

central sulcus   A major groove that divides the frontal lobe from the parietal lobe.

cephalic   See *rostral*.

cerebellar cortex   The outer surface of the cerebellum. See Figure 2.16.

cerebellum   A structure located at the back of the brain, dorsal to the pons, which is involved in the central regulation of movement. See Figure 2.16.

cerebral cortex   The outer covering of the cerebral hemispheres; consists largely of nerve cell bodies and their branches. See Figure 2.17.

cerebral hemispheres   The right and left halves of the forebrain. See Figure 2.12.

cerebral ventricle   A cavity in the brain that contains cerebrospinal fluid. See Figure 2.19.

cerebrospinal fluid (CSF)   The fluid that fills the cerebral ventricles. See Figure 2.19.

cerveau isolé   An animal in which the nervous system has been cut in the upper midbrain, dividing the brain from the brain stem. Contrast with *encéphale isolé*. See Figure 14.19.

cervical   Referring to the neck region.

chemical transmitter   See *synaptic transmitter*.

chemoaffinity hypothesis   Notion that each cell has a chemical identity that directs it to synapse upon the proper target cell during development. See Box 7.2.

chlorpromazine   An antipsychotic drug, one of the class of phenothiazines.

cholecystokinin (CCK)   A hormone that is released from the lining of the duodenum and that may be involved in the satiation of hunger.

cholinergic   Referring to cells that use acetylcholine as their synaptic transmitter.

choreic movement   An uncontrollable, brief, and forceful muscular movement that is related to basal ganglia dysfunction.

choroid plexus   A highly vascular portion of the lining of the ventricles that secretes cerebrospinal fluid.

chromosome   A complex of condensed strands of DNA and associated protein molecules; found in the nucleus of cells.

ciliary muscle   One of the muscles that controls the shape of the lens inside the eye, focusing an image on the retina.

cilium (pl. cilia)   Hair like extensions, such as those in the hair cells of the cochlea. See Figure 9.2*d*.

cingulate cortex   A region of medial cerebral cortex That lies dorsal to the corpus callosum. Also called the cingulum. See Figures 2.15, 16.15.

cingulate gyrus   A cortical portion of the limbic system, found in the frontal and parietal midline. See Figure 2.15*b*.

circadian oscillator   A theoretical circuit with an output that repeats about once per day.

circadian rhythms   A pattern of behavioral, biochemical, and physiological fluctuations that have a 24-hour period.

circannual   Occurring on a roughly annual basis.

circle of Willis   A structure at the base of the brain that is formed by the joining of the carotid and basilar arteries. See Figure 2.20.

circuit   Includes an arrangement of neurons and their interconnections. These assemblages often perform a particular limited function. In a local circuit, all the neurons are contained within a A level of brain organization that particular region. Contrast with *system*.

circumvallate papillae   A type of small structure on the tongue that contains taste receptors. See Figure 9.16.

circumventricular organ   An organ that lies in the wall of a cerebral ventricle. Circumventricular organs contain receptor sites that can be affected by substances in the cerebrospinal fluid. See Figure 13.17.

classical conditioning   A type of associative learning in which an originally neutral stimulus (the conditioned stimulus, or CS)—through pairing with another stimulus that elicits a particular response (the unconditioned stimulus, or US)—acquires the power to elicit that response when presented alone. A response elicited by the US is called an unconditioned response (UR); a response elicited by the CS alone is called a conditioned response (CR). Also called Pavlovian conditioning.

clitoris   A small mound of tissue just anterior to the vaginal opening. Stimulation of the clitoris produces orgasm in most women.

cloaca (pl. cloacae)   The sex organ in many birds, through which sperm are discharged (in the male) and eggs are laid (in the female). This is the same passage through which wastes are eliminated.

clones   Asexually produced organisms that are genetically identical.

closed-loop control mechanism   A control mechanism that provides a flow of information from whatever is being controlled to the device that controls it. Contrast with *open-loop control mechanism*. See Figure 11.3.

clozapine   An antipsychotic.

CNS   See *central nervous system*.

CNV   See *contingent negative variation*.

coactivation   A central nervous system control program that activates or inhibits the skeletal motoneurons at the same time as it alters the sensitivity of the muscle spindles.

cocaine   A drug of abuse, derived from the coca plant, that acts by potentiating catecholamine stimulation.

cochlea   A snail-shaped structure in the inner ear that contains the primary receptors for hearing. See Figure 9.2.

cochlear implant   An electromechanical device that detects sounds and selectively stimulates nerves in different regions of the cochlea via surgically implanted electrodes.

cochlear microphonic potential   An electrical potential, produced by hair cells, that accurately copies the acoustic wave form of the stimulus.

cochlear nuclei   Brain stem nuclei that receive input from auditory hair cells and send output to the superior olivary complex. See Figure 9.7.

coding   The rules by which action potentials in a sensory system reflect a physical stimulus.

codon   A sequence of three bases on a DNA molecule. Each codon specifies a particular amino acid.

cognitive map   A mental representation of a spatial relationship.

coitus   The sexual act, copulation.

colliculus (pl. colliculi)   A small elevation. Two pairs of colliculi are found on the dorsal surface of the midbrain. The rostral pair (the superior colliculi) receive visual information (see Figure 10.13); the caudal pair (the inferior colliculi) receive auditory information (see Figure 9.7).

colloid   A large, gluelike molecule that cannot pass through the cell membrane. When injected into the peritoneum, colloids attract and retain water by osmotic pressure.

command neuron   A higher-level nerve cell that can selectively activate specific behaviors such as walking.

commissural fiber   An axon that crosses the sagittal midline.

complex cortical cell   Neurons in the visual cortex that respond best to a bar of a particular size and orientation anywhere within a particular area of the visual field. See Figure 10.16.

computerized axial tomography (CAT)   A noninvasive technique for examining brain structure in humans through computer analysis of X-ray absorption at several positions around the head; affords a virtual direct view of the brain. The resulting images are referred to as CAT, or CT, scans. See Figure 2.21.

concentration gradient   A region in which the concentration of a substance of interest varies.

concordant   Referring to any trait that is seen in both individuals of identical twins. Contrast with *discordant*.

conditional learning   A type of learning that teaches that a particular response to a particular stimulus is appropriate in one setting but not in another.

conditioned response (CR)   See *classical conditioning*.

conditioned stimulus (CS)   See *classical conditioning*.

conditioned taste aversion   The behavior in which an animal refuses to eat a food if it previously became ill after eating that food.

conditioning   A form of learning in which an organism comes to associate two stimuli or a stimulus and a response. See Box 17.1

condom   A rubber sheath that is fitted over the penis to trap semen during sexual intercourse in order to prevent pregnancy and the transmission of disease.

conduction aphasia   A language disorder in which comprehension remains intact but repetition of spoken language is impaired; related to damage of the pathways connecting Wernicke's area and Broca's area.

conduction deafness   A hearing impairment that is associated with pathology of the external-ear or middle-ear cavities.

cone   One of the receptor cells in the retina that are responsible for color vision. The three types of cones have somewhat different sensitivities to light of different wavelengths. See Figure 10.7.

confabulate   To fill in a gap in memory with a falsification, often seen in Korsakoff's syndrome.

congenital   Present at birth.

congenital adrenal hyperplasia (CAH)   Any of several genetic mutations that can result in exposure of a female fetus to androgen, which results in a clitoris that is larger than normal at birth.

congenital insensitivity to pain   Syndrome of being born without pain perception.

consolidation   A stage of memory formation in which information in short-term or intermediate-term memory is transferred to long-term memory. See Figure 17.11.

consolidation hypothesis   See *perseveration/consolidation hypothesis*.

constraints on learning   Factors that restrict the ease of different kinds of learning in different species.

contingent negative variation (CNV)   A slow, event-related potential that is recorded from the scalp. A CNV arises in the interval between a warning signal and a signal that directs action.

convergence   The phenomenon of neural connections in which many cells send signals to a single cell. Contrast with *divergence*. See Figure 3.15.

convergent evolution   The evolutionary process by which responses to similar ecological features bring about similarities in behavior or structure among animals that are only distantly related (i.e., that differ in genetic heritage).

Coolidge effect   Propensity of an animal that, having appeared sexually satiated with a present partner, resumes sexual activity when provided with a novel partner.

copulatory behavior   Coitus.

copulation   The sexual act, coitus.

copulatory lock   Reproductive behavior in which the male's penis swells after ejaculation so that the male and female are forced to remain joined for five to ten minutes; occurs in dogs and some rodents, but not in humans.

cornea   The transparent outer layer of the eye, whose curvature is fixed, bends light rays, and is primarily responsible for forming the image on the retina.

coronal plane   The plane that divides the body or brain into front and back parts. Also called frontal plane or transverse plane. See Box 2.2.

corpus callosum   The band of axons that connects the two cerebral hemispheres. See Figure 2.18.

correlation   The covariation of two measures.

correlational approach   An approach to finding relations between bodily variables and behavioral variables that involves finding the extent to which a particular bodily measure covaries with a particular behavioral measure. See Figure 1.3.

cortex   Outer layers. 1. The cerebral cortex consists of the outer layers (gray matter) of the cerebral hemispheres. See Figure 2.13. 2. The cerebellar cortex consists of the outer layers of the cerebellum. See Figure 2.16. 3. The adrenal cortex consists of the outer layers of the adrenal gland. See Figure 5.15.

cortical barrel   A barrel-shaped portion of somatosensory cortex. Each barrel receives input from receptors from an individual whisker. See Figure 7.20.

cortical column   One of the vertical columns that constitute the basic organization of the neocortex. See Figure 8.17.

cortical deafness   Deafness caused by a fault or defect in the cortex.

cortical plate   A structure arising from the early proliferation of cells at the rostral end of the neural tube; the beginnings of the cerebral cortex.

corticospinal system   See *pyramidal system.*

corticosteroids   A class of steroid hormones secreted from the adrenal cortex, including glucosteroids and mineralocorticoids.

corticotropin-releasing hormone (CRH)   A releasing hormone, produced by the hypothalamus, that controls the daily rhythm of adrenocorticotropic hormone release.

cortisol   A glucocorticoid hormone of the adrenal cortex.

Courtship   The period during which two potential sexual partners increase their attractiveness toward each other.

CR   See *conditioned response.*

cranial   Referring to the skull (cranium).

cranial nerves   One of the three main subdivisions of the peripheral nervous system, composed of a set of pathways concerned mainly with sensory and motor systems associated with the head. See Figure 2.9.

cretinism   Reduced stature and mental retardation caused by thyroid deficiency.

CRH   See *corticotropin-releasing hormone.*

crib death   See *sudden infant death syndrome.*

critical range   The range within which a particular biological measure must remain to ensure good health.

cross-tolerance   A condition in which the development of tolerance for an administered drug causes the individual to develop tolerance for another drug.

crystallization   The final stage of birdsong formation, in which the fully formed adult song is achieved.

CS   See *conditioned stimulus.*

CSF   See *cerebrospinal fluid.*

CT scan   See *computerized axial tomography.*

cupula (pl. cupulae)   A small gelatinous column that forms part of the lateral-line system of aquatic animals and occurs within the vestibular system of mammals. See Figure 9.14.

Cushing's syndrome   A condition in which levels of adrenal glucocorticoids are high, often arising from pituitary tumors, adrenal tumors, or deliberate therapy involving corticosteroids.

cyclic adenosine monophosphate   A second messenger that is involved in the synaptic activities of dopamine, norepinephrine, and serotonin.

cyclic AMP   See *cyclic adenosine monophosphate.*

cytoarchitectonics   The study of anatomical divisions of the brain based on the kinds and spacing of cells and the distribution of axons.

cytokine   A protein that induces the proliferation of other cells, as in the immune system. Examples include interleukins and interferons.

DA   See *dopamine.*

deafferentation   Removal of sensory (afferent) input.

death gene   A gene that is expressed only when a cell becomes committed to natural cell death (apoptosis).

decibel (dB)   A measure of sound intensity. See Box 9.1.

declarative memory   A memory that can be stated or described. Contrast with *nondeclarative memory.*

decomposition of movement   Difficulty of movement in which gestures are broken up into individual segments instead of being executed smoothly; a symptom of cerebellar lesions.

deep dyslexia   A form of dyslexia in which patients read a word as another word that is semantically related.

degradation   Here, the process by which neurotransmitter molecules are broken down into inactive metabolites.

dehydration   Excessive loss of water.

delta-sleep-inducing peptide (DSIP)   A naturally occurring peptide that is reported to induce slow-wave sleep.

delta wave   The slowest EEG waves, characteristic of stage 3 and 4 SWS. See Figure 14.10.

dementia   Drastic failure of cognitive ability, including memory failure and loss of orientation.

dementia pugilistica   The dementia that develops in boxers, especially prominent in successful boxers because they participate in more bouts.

dendrite   One of the extensions of the cell body that are the receptive surfaces of the neuron. See Figures 2.2, 2.3.

dendritic branching   The pattern and quantity of branching of dendrites. See Figure 18.5.

dendritic knob   A portion of olfactory receptor cells present in the olfactory epithelium. See Figure 9.18.

dendritic spine   An outgrowth along the dendrite of a neuron. See Figures 2.2, 2.4. Also called dendrite thorn.

dendritic tree   The full arrangement of dendrites of a single cell.

denervation supersensitivity Condition in which target cells, upon losing neural input, produce more than the normal number of receptors, resulting in an exaggerated response when synaptic transmitter is applied.

dentate gyrus A strip of grey matter in the hippocampal formation.

2-deoxyglucose (2-DG) A molecule that resembles glucose. When injected into an animal, 2-DG accumulates more readily in active neurons than in inactive neurons, so it can indicate which parts of the brain are active during a given task.

deoxyribonucleic acid (DNA) A nucleic acid that is present in the chromosomes of cells and codes hereditary information.

depolarization A reduction in membrane potential (the inner membrane surface becomes less negative in relation to the outer surface); caused by excitatory neural messages. Contrast with *hyperpolarization.* See Figure 3.3.

depression A psychiatric condition characterized by such symptoms as an unhappy mood; loss of interests, energy, and appetite; and difficulty in concentration. See bipolar depression, unipolar depression.

derepression The mechanism through which regions of the DNA molecule that are repressed from transcription become unblocked. This process allows for the selection of genetic information that will be used by a particular cell.

dermatome A strip of skin innervated by a particular spinal root. See Figure 8.15.

dermis The layer of skin beneath the outermost layer (the epidermis). See Figure 8.3.

dexamethasone suppression test A test of pituitary–adrenal function in which the subject is given dexamethasone, a synthetic glucocorticoid hormone, which should cause a decline in the production of adrenal corticosteroids.

diabetes insipidus Excessive urination, caused by the failure of vasopressin to induce the kidneys to conserve water.

diabetes mellitus Excessive glucose in urine, caused by the failure of insulin to induce glucose absorption by the body.

diaschisis A temporary period of generalized impairment following brain injury.

dichotic listening technique A test in which different sounds are presented to each ear at the same time; used to determine hemispheric differences in processing auditory information. See Figure 19.15.

dichotic stimuli Stimuli that differ at the two ears.

dichromat An organism that has only two classes of wavelength-sensitive light receptor cells.

diencephalon The posterior part of the forebrain, including the thalamus and hypothalamus. See Figure 2.14.

differential classical conditioning Classical conditioning in which two conditioned stimuli are used in the same animal; one (CS+) is *paired* with the unconditioned stimulus, and the other (CS–) is *unpaired* and has no consequence for the animal.

differentiation See *cell differentiation.*

diffuse bipolar cell A type of retinal bipolar neuron that receives input from several receptors. See Figure 10.9.

digestion Process by which food is broken down to provide energy and nutrients.

discordant Referring to any trait that is seen in only one individual of identical twins. Contrast with *concordant.*

dishabituation The restoration of response amplitude following habituation.

dissociation Here, the loss of one function with damage to brain region A but not B, and the loss of a different function with damage to brain region B but not A.

dissociative thinking A condition, seen in schizophrenia, that is characterized by disturbances of thought and difficulty relating events properly.

distal An anatomical term referring to structures toward the periphery or toward the end of a limb. Contrast with *proximal.* See Box 2.2.

diurnal Active during the day.

divergence The phenomenon of neural connections in which one cell sends signals to many other cells. Contrast with *convergence.* See Figure 3.15.

dizygotic Referring to twins derived from separate eggs. Such twins are no more closely related genetically than are other full siblings. Contrast with *monozygotic.*

DNA See *deoxyribonucleic acid.*

dopamine (DA) A synaptic transmitter produced mainly in the basal forebrain and diencephalon that is active in the basal ganglia, the olfactory system, and limited parts of the cerebral cortex. See Figure 4.2.

dopaminergic Referring to cells that use dopamine as their synaptic transmitter.

dorsal An anatomical term referring to structures toward the back of the body or the top of the brain. Contrast with *ventral.* See Box 2.2.

dorsal column system Somatosensory system delivering most touch stimuli via the dorsal columns of spinal white matter to the brain. See Figure 8.14.

dorsal root See *roots.*

double-blind test Test of a drug or treatment in which neither the subjects nor the attending researchers know which subjects are receiving the drug/treatment and which are receiving the placebo/control treatment.

double dissociation The phenomenon in which condition or treatment A causes impairment on behavioral test X but no impairment on test Y, whereas condition B causes impairment on test Y but not on X.

Down syndrome Mental retardation that is associated with an extra copy of chromosome 21.

DSIP See *delta-sleep-inducing peptide.*

dualism The notion, promoted by Descartes, that the mind is subject only to spiritual interactions while the body is subject only to material interactions.

dual trace hypothesis The hypothesis that formation of a memory involves first a relatively brief transient memory storage process followed by a stable change in the nervous system, which is a long-lasting memory trace.

duplex theory A theory of sound localization that combines place theory and volley theory.

dura mater The outermost of the three coverings that embrace the brain and spinal cord.

dynamic phase of weight gain The initial period following destruction of the ventromedial hypothalamus during which the animal's body weight increases rapidly. Contrast with *static phase of obesity*. See Figure 13.25.

dyscontrol syndrome   A condition consisting of temporal lobe disorders that may underlie some forms of human violence.

dyskinesia   See *tardive dyskinesia*.

dyslexia   A reading disorder attributed to brain impairment.

dyspareunia   Discomfort during intromission.

dysregulation hypothesis of depression   The hypothesis that depression reflects a failure in regulation of (dopamine) transmitter operations, resulting in erratic transmitter activities ungoverned by external stimuli.

dystrophin   A gene product that is needed for normal muscle function. Dystrophin is defective in some forms of muscular dystrophy.

eardrum   See *tympanic membrane*.

EC   See *enriched condition*.

ectoderm   The outer cellular layer of the developing fetus. The ectoderm gives rise to the skin and to the nervous system.

ectotherm   An animal whose body temperature is regulated by, and that gets most of its heat from, the environment. Contrast with *endotherm*.

edema   The swelling of tissue, especially in the brain, in response to injury.

EEG   See *electroencephalography*.

effective dose 50 (ED$_{50}$)   The dose of a drug that produces the desired effect in 50% of subjects. Contrast with lethal dose 50.

efferent fiber   An axon that carries information from the nervous system to the periphery. Contrast with *afferent fiber*.

ejaculation   The forceful expulsion of semen from the penis.

electrical force   Here, the tendency of like-charged particles to repel each other while opposite-charged particles are attracted to each other.

electrical synapse   The region between neurons where the presynaptic and postsynaptic membranes are so close that the nerve impulse can jump to the postsynaptic membrane without first being translated into a chemical message. See Box 3.1.

electroencephalography (EEG)   The recording and study of gross electrical activity of the brain recorded from large electrodes placed on the scalp. See Figure 14.10.

electromyography (EMG)   The technique of recording electrical activity of muscles. See Figure 11.22.

electroretinography (ERG)   The electrical recording of responses of the retina to flashes of different stimuli.

embryo   The earliest stage in a developing animal; humans are considered embryos until eight to ten weeks after conception.

EMG   See *electromyography*.

encéphale isolé   An experimental preparation in which an animal's brain stem has been separated from the spinal cord by a cut below the medulla. Contrast with *cerveau isolé*. See Figure 14.19.

encephalization factor   A measure of brain size relative to body size.

encoding   A process of memory formation in which the information entering sensory channels is passed into short-term memory. See Figure 17.11.

endocast   A cast of the cranial cavity of a skull, especially useful for studying fossils of extinct species.

endocrine   Refers to glands that release chemicals to the interior of the body. These glands secrete the principal hormones.

endocrine gland   A gland that secretes products into the bloodstream to act on distant targets. Contrast with *exocrine gland*. See Figure 5.1.

endogenous   Produced inside the body. Contrast with exogenous.

endogenous opioids   A family of peptide transmitters that have been called the body's own narcotics. See Table 4.1, under opioid peptides.

endogenous oscillator   A circuit that generates regularly repeating sequences of neural activity or behavior.

endorphins   One of three kinds of endogenous opioids. See Table 4.1, under opioid peptides.

endotherm   An animal whose body temperature is regulated chiefly by internal metabolic processes. Examples include mammals and birds. Contrast with *ectotherm*.

end-plate potential   The action potential that is induced at the neuromuscular junction when the axon terminal releases its neurotransmitter, which in vertebrates is acetylcholine.

enkephalins   One of the three kinds of endogenous opioids. See Table 4.1, under opioid peptides.

enriched condition (EC)   An experimental condition with a complex environment. See Figure 18.4.

entrainment   The process of synchronizing a biological rhythm to an environmental stimulus. See Figure 14.1.

enzyme   A complicated protein which increases the probability of a specific chemical reaction.

EOAE   See *evoked otoacoustic emission*.

ependymal layer   See *ventricular layer*.

epidermis   The outermost layer of skin, over the dermis. See Figure 8.3.

epididymis   A crescent-shaped structure next to the testis, in which sperm are stored.

epilepsy   A brain disorder marked by major sudden changes in the electrophysiological state of the brain that are referred to as seizures. See Box 3.3.

epinephrine   A compound that acts both as a hormone (secreted by the adrenal medulla) and as a synaptic transmitter. Also called adrenaline.

episodic memory   Memory of a particular incident or a particular time and place.

EPSP   Excitatory postsynaptic potential.

equilibrium potential   The state in which the tendency of ions to flow from regions of high concentration is exactly balanced by the opposing potential difference across the membrane.

erectile dysfunction   Failure to achieve a penile erection.

ERG   See *electroretinography*.

estradiol   The primary type of estrogen that is secreted by the ovary.

estrogens   A class of steroid hormones produced by female gonads. See Figure 5.14, Table 5.2.

estrus   The period during which female animals are sexually receptive.

event-related potential   A large change in electrical potential in the brain that is elicited by a discrete sensory or motor event. Also called evoked potential. See Figure 3.18.

evoked otoacoustic emission (EOAE)   A sound produced by the cochlea in response to acoustic stimulation. Contrast with *spontaneous otoacoustic emission.*

evoked potential   See *event-related potential.*

evolution by natural selection   The Darwinian theory that evolution proceeds by differential success in reproduction.

excitatory postsynaptic potential (EPSP)   A depolarizing potential in the postsynaptic neuron that is caused by excitatory presynaptic impulses. Contrast with *inhibitory postsynaptic potential.*

excitotoxicity   The property of neurons to die when overly stimulated, as with large amounts of glutamate.

excitotoxin   A poison that overexcites neurons so much that it kills them.

exocrine gland   A gland that secretes products through ducts to the site of action. Contrast with *endocrine gland.*

exogenous   Arising from outside the body. Contrast with endogenous.

external capsule   A light-colored band of fibers lateral to the putamen.

external ear   The part of the ear that we readily see (called the pinna) and the canal that leads to the eardrum. See Figure 9.1.

external fertilization   Reproductive fertilization that takes place outside the female's body, as in many fishes and amphibians. Contrast with *internal fertilization.*

extinction   A feature of conditioning in which the learned response wanes when not reinforced.

extracellular fluid   The fluid in the spaces between cells (interstitial fluid) and in the vascular system.

extracellular space   The space between cells.

extrafusal fiber   One of the ordinary muscle fibers that lie *outside* the spindles and provide most of the force for muscle contraction. Contrast with *intrafusal fiber.* See Figure 11.9.

extraocular muscle   One of the muscles attached to the eyeball that control its position and movements.

extrapyramidal system   A motor system that includes the basal ganglia and some closely related brain stem structures.

extrastriate cortex   Visual cortex outside of area 17 (primary visual cortex or striate cortex). See Figure 10.8.

facial nerve   A cranial nerve that innervates facial musculature and some sensory receptors. See Figures 2.9, 15.5.

factor S   Name given to a sleep-inducing substance extracted from the cerebrospinal fluid of sleep-deprived goats.

fallopian tube   The structure between the ovum and the uterus where fertilization takes place in humans. Also called the oviduct. See Figure 12.7.

fast muscle fiber   Class of striated muscle which contracts rapidly but fatigues readily.

fat   A large, complex carbohydrate that provides long-term energy storage. A lipid.

fatal familial insomnia   An inherited disorder in which humans sleep normally at the beginning of their life, but in midlife stop sleeping, and 7 to 24 months later die.

feature detector model   A model of visual pattern analysis in terms of linear and angular components of the stimulus array. Contrast with *spatial frequency filter model.*

feedback circuit   A circuit in which output information is used to modulate the input of that same circuit.

fertilization   The fusion of sperm and egg to produce a zygote.

fetal alcohol syndrome   A disorder, including mental retardation and characteristic facial anomalies, that affects children exposed to alcohol (through maternal ingestion) during fetal development.

α fetoprotein   A protein found in the plasma of fetuses. In rodents (fetoprotein binds estrogens and prevents them from entering the brain.

fetus   A developing individual after the embryo stage. Humans are considered to be fetuses from ten weeks after fertilization until birth.

fictive locomotion   A walking pattern that is elicited by a treadmill from the hind limbs of cats with spinal cord section.

filial imprinting   A type of learning in which precocial animals in their first few days approach and follow the first relatively large moving object they see, usually their mother.

filopodium (pl. filopodia)   A very fine, tubular outgrowth from the growth cone.

final common pathway   The motoneurons, because they direct all the activity of the spinal cord and brain to the muscles.

fission   The process of splitting in two. Some unicellular organisms reproduce by fisson; that is, they simply split into two daughter cells.

fixed action pattern   Complex preprogrammed species-specific behavior that is triggered by particular stimuli and carried out without sensory feedback. See also *modal action pattern.*

flaccid paralysis   A loss of reflexes below the level of transection of the spinal cord.

flexion reflex   The abrupt withdrawal of a limb in response to intense stimulation of the foot.

folia (sing. folium)   The folds or convolutions of the cerebellar cortex.

foliate papillae   A type of small structure on the tongue that contains taste receptors. See Figure 9.16.

follicle-stimulating hormone (FSH)   A tropic hormone, released by the anterior pituitary, that controls the production of estrogen and progesterone. See Figure 5.17.

forebrain   The frontal division of the neural tube that contains the cerebral hemispheres, the thalamus, and the hypothalamus. Also called the prosencephalon.

fornix   A fiber tract that extends from the hippocampus to the mammillary body. See Figure 2.15.

Fourier analysis   The analysis of a complex pattern into the sum of sine waves. See Box 9.1.

fourth ventricle   The passageway within the pons that receives cerebrospinal fluid from the third ventricle and releases it to surround the brain and spinal cord. See Figure 2.19.

fovea   A small depression in the center of the retina that has a dense concentration of cones and maximal visual acuity.

fragile X syndrome   A condition that is a frequent cause of inherited mental retardation; produced by a fragile site on the X chromosome that seems prone to breaking because the DNA there is unstable.

free-running period   The natural period of a behavior that is displayed if external stimuli do not provide entrainment.

frequency   The number of cycles per second in a sound wave; measured in hertz (Hz). See Box 9.1.

frontal lobe   The most anterior portion of the cerebral cortex.

frontal plane   See *coronal plane.*

FSH   See *follicle-stimulating hormone.*

functional MRI (fMRI)   MRI that detects changes in blood flow and therefore regions of the brain which are particularly active during a given task.

fungiform papillae   A type of small structure on the tongue that contains taste receptors. See Figure 9.16.

G protein   A class of proteins which reside next to the intracellular portion of a receptor and which are activated when the receptor binds an appropriate ligand on the extracellular surface.

GABA   See *gamma-aminobutyric acid.*

gamete   A sex cell, sperm or egg, which contains only unpaired chromosomes and therefore has only half the total number of autosomal chromosomes.

gamma-aminobutyric acid (GABA)   Probably the major inhibitory transmitter in the mammalian nervous system; widely distributed in both invertebrate and vertebrate nervous systems.

gamma efferent   A motor neuron that controls muscle spindle sensitivity. See Figure 11.9.

ganglion (pl. ganglia)   A collection of nerve cell bodies outside the central nervous system. See also *nucleus.*

ganglion cells   Cells in the retina whose axons form the optic nerve. See Figure 10.7.

gating current   Tiny electrical current related to opening or closing gates in ion channels. See Figure 3.6.

gender identity   The way that one identifies oneself, and is identified by others, as a male or a female.

generalization   A feature of conditioning in which stimuli similar to the conditioned stimulus can elicit a conditioned response.

generalized seizure   An epileptic seizure that arises from pathology at brain sites and projects to widespread regions of the brain. Generalized seizures include loss of consciousness and symmetrical involvement of body musculature. See Box 3.3.

generator potential   A local change in the resting potential of a receptor cell that mediates between the impact of stimuli and the initiation of nerve impulses. See Figure 10.8.

genetic constraints on learning   A concept, prominent from the 1960s to the early 1980s, that held that species-typical factors restrict the kinds of learning that a species can accomplish readily. Contrast with *specific abilities to learn and remember.*

genetic mosaic   An animal in which the cells of one part of the body have a different chromosomal makeup from the cells in another part. For example, the head of a male fruit fly can be induced to develop on the body of a female fruit fly.

genetics   Study of inheritance, including the genes encoded in DNA.

genome   The sum of all the genetic information an individual has inherited.

genotype   The sum of all the genetic information an individual has inherited.

GH   See *growth hormone.*

giant axon   A large-diameter axon; found in some invertebrates. The size of giant axons facilitates research on the properties of neural membrane structure and function. See Figure 3.7.

glia   See *glial cells.*

glial cells   Nonneural brain cells that provide structural, nutritional, and other supports to the brain. Also called glia or neuroglia. See Figure 2.6.

glioma   A brain tumor resulting from the aberrant production of glial cells.

global aphasia   The total loss of ability to understand language, or to speak, read, or write.

globus pallidus   One of the basal ganglia. See Figure 2.15.

glomerulus (pl. glomeruli)   A complex arbor of dendrites from a group of olfactory cells.

glossopharyngeal nerve   The ninth cranial nerve which serves taste receptors in the tongue. See Figure 2.9.

glucagon   A hormone, released by alpha cells in the islets of Langerhans, that increases blood glucose. See Figure 5.19.

glucocorticoids   A class of hormones, released by the adrenal cortex, that affect carbohydrate metabolism.

glucodetector   A cell that detects and informs the nervous system about levels of circulating glucose. Also called glucostat.

glucose   An important sugar molecule used by the body and brain for energy.

glucose transporter   A molecule that spans the external membrane of a cell and transports glucose molecules from outside the cell to the inside for use.

glucostat   See *glucodetector.*

glutamic acid   Thought by many investigators to be a major excitatory synaptic transmitter in the central nervous system.

glycogen   A complex carbohydrate made by the combining of glucose molecules for a short-term store of energy.

GnRH   See *gonadotropin-releasing hormone.*

goiter   Hypertrophied thyroid gland caused by iodide deficiency.

Golgi stain   A stain which fills a small proportion of neurons with a dark silver-based precipitate. See Box 2.1, Figure A.

Golgi tendon organ   One of the receptors located in tendons that send impulses to the central nervous system when a muscle contracts. See Figure 11.9.

Golgi type I cell   A type of large nerve cell.

gonadotropin-releasing hormone (GnRH)   A hypothalamic hormone that controls the release of luteinizing hormone and follicle-stimulating hormone from the pituitary. Also called luteinizing hormone–releasing hormone. See Figure 5.17.

gonads   The sexual organs (ovaries in females, testes in males), which produce gametes for reproduction.

graded potential   An electrical potential that is initiated at a postsynaptic site and can vary continuously in size. Also called local potential or postsynaptic potential. Contrast with *all-or-none.* See Figure 3.3.

grammar   The rules for usage of a particular language.

grand mal seizure A type of generalized epileptic seizure in which nerve cells fire in high-frequency bursts. Grand mal seizures cause loss of consciousness and sudden muscle contraction. See Box 3.3.

grandmother cell An extrapolation of the feature detector model suggesting that if there were enough levels of analysis, a unit could be constructed that would enable a person to recognize his or her grandmother.

granule cell A type of small nerve cell.

gray matter Areas of the brain that are dominated by cell bodies and are devoid of myelin. Contrast with *white matter*.

growth cone The growing tip of an axon or a dendrite. See Figure 7.12.

growth hormone (GH) A tropic hormone, secreted by the anterior pituitary, that influences the growth of cells and tissues. Also called somatotropic hormone. See Figure 5.14.

guevedoces "Eggs at twelve" A nickname for individuals who are raised as girls but, at puberty change in appearance and begin behaving as boys.

gustatory system The taste system. See Figure 9.17.

gut hormone A hormone that is released by the stomach or intestines, sometimes in response to food.

gyrus (pl. gyri) A ridged or raised portion of a convoluted brain surface. Contrast with *sulcus*. See Figure 2.12.

habit A stimulus–response bond that is acquired automatically, and often gradually, through occurrences of stimulus–response–reinforcement contingencies.

habituation A form of nonassociative learning characterized by a reduction in response strength following repeated presentations of a stimulus. See Box 17.1.

hair cell One of the receptor cells for hearing in the cochlea. Displacement of these cells by sound waves generates nerve impulses that travel to the brain. See Figure 9.2.

hallucinogens A class of drugs that alter sensory perception and produce peculiar experiences.

Hebbian synapse A synapse that is strengthened when it successfully drives the postsynaptic cell.

hemispatial neglect A syndrome in which the patient ignores objects presented to one side and may even deny connection with that side of the body.

hemispheric encoding retrieval asymmetry (HERA) Hypothesis that one hemisphere is especially active during the encoding of a memory while the other hemisphere is especially active during the retrieval of the memory.

hermaphrodite An individual that can reproduce as either a male or a female.

hertz (Hz) Cycles per second, as of an auditory stimulus.

heterogametic Referring to the sex that has two different sex chromosomes. Male mammals and female birds are heterogametic. Contrast with *homogametic*.

hindbrain The rear division of the brain; in the mature vertebrate, the hindbrain contains the cerebellum, pons, and medulla. Also called the rhombencephalon. See Figure 2.14.

hippocampal gyrus See *subiculum*.

hippocampus A portion of the cerebral hemispheres found curled in the basal medial part of the temporal lobe that is thought to be important for learning and memory. See Figures 2.15, 17.1, 18.7.

histology The study of tissue structure.

HIV See *human immunodeiciency virus*.

homeostasis The tendency for the internal environment to remain constant.

homeotherm An animal that maintains a relatively constant body temperature. Examples include birds and mammals. Contrast with *poikilotherm*.

hominid A primate of the family Hominidae, of which humans are the only living species.

homogametic Referring to the sex that has two copies of the same sex chromosome. Female mammals and male birds are homogametic. Contrast with *heterogametic*.

homology A structural or behavioral resemblance between two species that is based on common ancestry.

horizontal cells Specialized retinal cells that contact both the receptor cells and the bipolar cells.

horizontal plane The plane that divides the body or brain into upper and lower parts. See Box 2.2.

hormone A chemical secreted by an endocrine gland that is conveyed by the bloodstream and regulates target organs or tissues. See Table 5.2.

horseradish peroxidase (HRP) An enzyme found in horseradish and other plants that is used to determine the cells of origin of a particular set of axons. See Box 2.1.

5-HT See *serotonin*.

hue One of the basic dimensions of light perception. Hue varies around the color circle through blue, green, yellow, orange, and red. See Figure 10.5.

human immunodeficiency virus (HIV) The virus that can be passed through genital, anal, or oral sex and causes acquired immune deficiency syndrome (AIDS).

humoral immunity The type of immunity in which B lymphocytes produce antibodies that either directly destroy antigens, such as viruses or bacteria, or enhance their destruction by other cells.

hunger The internal state of an animal seeking food. Contrast with *satiety*.

Huntingtin A gene that, when containing too many trinucleotide repeats, will result in Huntington's disease in a carrier.

Huntington's disease A progressive genetic disorder characterized by choreic movements and profound changes in mental functioning. Also called Huntington's chorea.

hypercomplex 1 Cells in the visual cortex that respond best to visual stimulation by bars of a given orientation and of limited length.

hypercomplex 2 Cells in the visual cortex that respond best to visual stimulation by two line segments meeting at a particular angle.

hypercomplex cortical cell Visual cortical cells that respond to an elongated stimulus anywhere within a particular region of the visual field and that have inhibitory areas at both sides.

hyperphagia A condition involving increasing food intake, often related to damage to the ventromedial hypothalamus.

hyperpolarization An increase in membrane potential (the inner surface of the membrane becomes more negative in relation to the outer surface); caused by inhibitory neural messages. Contrast with *depolarization*. See Figure 3.3.

hypertonic   Referring to a solution with a higher concentration of salt than that found in interstitial fluid and blood plasma (more than about 0.9% salt). Contrast with *hypotonic*.

hypnogen   A sleep-producing substance that might accumulate in the brain and/or body.

hypofrontality hypothesis   The hypothesis that schizophrenia may reflect underactivation of the frontal lobes.

hypothalamic–pituitary portal system   System of capillaries that transport releasing hormones from the hypothalamus to the anterior pituitary.

hypothalamus   Part of the diencephalon, lying ventral to the thalamus. See Figures 2.12, 2.14.

hypotonic   A solution with a lower concentration of salt than that found in interstitial fluid and blood plasma (less than about 0.9% salt). Contrast with *hypertonic*.

hypovolemic thirst   The response to a reduced volume of extracellular fluid. Contrast with *osmotic thirst*.

hypoxia   A transient lack of oxygen.

IC   See *impoverished condition*.

iconic memory   A very brief type of memory that stores the sensory impression of a scene.

ideational apraxia   An impairment in the ability to carry out a *sequence* of actions even though each element or step can be done correctly.

identifiable neurons   Neurons that are large and similar from one individual to the next, enabling investigators to recognize and give code names to them.

ideomotor apraxia   The inability to carry out a simple motor activity in response to a verbal command even though this same activity is readily performed spontaneously.

immediate early genes (IEGs)   A class of genes that show rapid but transient increases in response to extracellular signals such as neurotransmitters and growth factors. Examples include *fos* and *jun*.

immunocytochemistry   A method for detecting a particular protein in tissues in which an antibody recognizes and binds to the protein, and chemical methods are then used to leave a visible reaction product around each antibody. See Box 5.1, Figure C.

impermeable   Referring to a barrier that does not allow the substance of interest to pass through.

impoverished condition (IC)   An experimental condition with a drastically simplified environment. See Figure 18.4.

imprinting   A form of learning in which young animals learn to follow the first relatively large moving object they see, usually their mother.

in estrus   Description of a female animal that is receptive to copulation, usually as a result of steroid hormone exposure.

in heat   Sexually receptive; in estrus.

incus   One of three tiny bones in the middle ear, between the malleus (attached to the tympanic membrane) and the stapes (attached to the cochlea).

individual response stereotypy   The tendency of individuals to show the same response pattern to particular situations throughout their lifespan.

indoleamines   Monoamine transmitters or hormones such as serotonin and melatonin.

induction   The process by which one set of cells influences the fate of neighboring cells, usually by secreting a chemical factor that changes gene expression in the target cells.

inferior colliculi   See *colliculus*.

infradian   Referring to biological rhythms that have a frequency of less than once per day.

infundibulum   The stalk of the pituitary gland.

inhibitory postsynaptic potential (IPSP)   A hyperpolarizing potential in the postsynaptic neuron that is caused by inhibitory connections. IPSPs decrease the probability that the postsynaptic neuron will fire a nerve impulse. Contrast with *excitatory postsynaptic potential*. See Figure 3.9.

inner ear   The cochlea and vestibular canals.

inner hair cell   One of the receptor cells for hearing in the cochlea. See Figure 9.2.

innervate   To provide neural input.

innervation   The supply of neural input to an organ or a region of the nervous system.

innervation ratio   The ratio expressing the number of muscle fibers innervated by a single motor axon. The fewer muscle fibers an axon innervates (that is, the lower the ratio), the finer the control of movements.

insomnia   Lack of sleep or of sufficient sleep.

instrumental conditioning   A form of associative learning in which the likelihood that an act (instrumental response) will be performed depends on the consequences (reinforcing stimuli) that follow it. Also called operant conditioning.

instrumental response   See *instrumental conditioning*.

insulin   A hormone, released by beta cells in the islets of Langerhans, that lowers blood glucose. See Figure 5.19.

intention tremor   A tremor that occurs only during voluntary movement, such as reaching out to grasp an object.

intermediate-term memory (ITM)   A form of memory that lasts longer than short-term memory and requires no rehearsal, but does not last as long as long-term memory.

internal capsule   The fiber band that extends between the caudate nucleus on its medial side and the globus pallidus and putamen on its lateral side.

internal carotid artery   See *carotid arteries*.

internal fertilization   The process in which sperm fertilize eggs inside the female's body. All mammals, birds, and reptiles have internal fertilization. Contrast with *external fertilization*.

interneurons   A neuron that is neither a sensory neuron nor a motoneuron.

interstitial cell-stimulating hormone (ICSH)   See *luteinizing hormone*.

interstitial fluid   See *extracellular fluid*.

intracellular fluid   Water within cells. Also called cellular fluid.

intracellular signal   A chemical signal that conveys information within a single cell.

intrafusal fibers   One of the small muscle fibers *within* each muscle spindle. Contrast with *extrafusal fiber*.

intromission   Insertion of the erect penis into the vagina during copulatory behavior.

inverted U-shaped curve   A drug dose–response curve in which increasing doses first elicit increasing responses, but at higher doses, response declines with increasing dose.

in vitro   Literally "in glass," usually a laboratory dish; outside the body.

in vivo Literally "in life"; within a living body.

ion An atom or molecule that has acquired an electrical charge by gaining or losing one or more electrons.

ion channel A pore in the cell membrane that permits the passage of certain ions through the membrane when the channels are open. See Figures 3.4, 3.5.

ionotropic receptor A receptor protein that includes an ion channel that is opened when the receptor is bound by an agonist. See Figure 3.13a.

IPSP See *inhibitory postsynaptic potential.*

iris The circular structure of the eye that provides an opening to form the pupil.

islets of Langerhans Clusters of cells in the pancreas that release two hormones (insulin and glucagon) with opposite effects on glucose utilization. See Figure 5.19.

isotonic Having the same concentration of salt as mammalian fluids have.

ITM See *intermediate-term memory.*

karyotype Complement of chromosomes held by a particular individual.

kinase A class of enzymes that catalyze the addition of a phosphate group to certain proteins.

kindling A method of experimentally inducing an epileptic seizure by repeatedly stimulating a brain region.

knee-jerk reflex A variant of the stretch reflex, in which stretching of the tendon beneath the knee leads to an upward kick of the leg. See Figure 3.14.

knockout organism An individual in which a particular gene has been disabled by an experimenter.

Korsakoff's syndrome A memory disorder, related to a thiamine deficiency, that is generally associated with chronic alcoholism.

Krause's end bulb A skin receptor cell type.

kuru A slow virus of the brain that produces trembling and eventually paralysis of the limbs.

labia (sing. labium) The folds of skin that surround the opening of the human vagina. See Figures 12.7, 12.15.

labile memory An early stage of memory formation during which the formation of a memory can be easily disrupted by conditions that influence brain activity.

laminar organization The horizontal layering of cells found in some brain regions. See Figures 2.17, 8.17.

latency The time delay before a subject displays the behavior of interest.

latent learning Learning which has taken place but has not (yet) been demonstrated by performance.

lateral An anatomical term meaning toward the side. Contrast with *medial.* See Box 2.2.

lateral geniculate nucleus (LGN) The part of the thalamus that receives information from the optic tract and sends it to visual areas in the occipital cortex. See Figure 10.15.

lateral hypothalamus (LH) A hypothalamic region that may be involved in eating. Lesions of the LH result in fasting and weight loss. See Figures 13.24, 13.29.

lateral inhibition The phenomenon in which interconnected neurons inhibit their neighbors, producing contrast at the edges of regions. See Figure 10.6.

lateralization Tendency for the right and left halves of a system to differ from one another.

lateral-line system A sensory system, found in many kinds of fish and some amphibians, that informs the animal of water motion in relation to the body surface.

lateral ventricle A complexly shaped lateral portion of the ventricular system within each hemisphere of the brain. See Figure 2.19.

learned helplessness Learning paradigm in which individuals are subjected to inescapable, unpleasant conditions.

learning set The ability to solve a particular type of problem efficiently after prolonged experience with that type of problem.

lens A structure in the eye that helps form an image on the retina. The shape of the lens is controlled by the ciliary muscles inside the eye. See Figure 10.2.

lentiform nucleus The lens-shaped region in the basal ganglia that encompasses the globus pallidus and the putamen. Also called lenticular nucleus. See Figure 2.15.

leptin A protein manufactured and secreted by fat cells, that may communicate to the brain the amount of body fat stored. Leptin is defective in *obese* mice.

lesion Damage, as to a brain region, caused by disease or experimental design.

lesion momentum The phenomenon in which the brain is impaired more by a lesion that develops quickly than by a lesion that develops slowly.

lethal dose 50 (LD$_{50}$) The dose of a drug that would be lethal for 50% of subjects. Contrast with *effective dose 50.*

LGN See *lateral geniculate nucleus.*

LH See *lateral hypothalamus or luteinizing hormone.*

ligand A substance that binds to receptor molecules, such as those at the surface of the cell.

ligand-gated ion channel An ionotropic neurotransmitter receptor. Contrast with the *voltage-gated channel.*

limbic system A loosely defined, widespread group of brain nuclei that innervate each other to form a network; involved in mechanisms of emotion and learning. See Figure 2.15.

lithium An element which often relieves the symptoms of manic-depression.

lobotomy The detachment of a portion of the frontal lobe from the rest of the brain. Now largely discredited, once a treatment for schizophrenia and many other ailments.

local circuit See *circuit.*

localization of function The concept that specific brain regions are responsible for various types of experience, behavior, and psychological processes.

local potential See *graded potential.*

local potential change A change in potential that is initiated at a postsynaptic site.

local potentiation See *graded potential.*

locus coeruleus A small nucleus in the brain stem whose neurons produce norepinephrine and modulate large areas of the forebrain. See Figure 14.21.

long-term depression (LTD) A lasting *decrease* in the magnitude of responses of neurons after afferent cells have been stimulated with electrical stimuli of relatively *low* frequency. Contrast with *long-term potentiation.*

long-term memory (LTM) An enduring form of memory that lasts for days, weeks, months, or years and has a very large capacity.

long-term potentiation (LTP) A stable and enduring increase in the magnitude of the response of neurons after afferent cells to the region have been stimulated with bursts of electrical stimuli of moderately high frequency. Contrast with *long-term depression*. See Figures 18.7, 18.9.

lordosis A female receptive posture in quadrupeds in which the hindquarters are raised and the tail is turned to one side, facilitating intromission by the male. See Figures 12.3, 12.6.

LSD (lysergic acid diethylamide) A hallucinogenic drug.

lumbar Referring to the lower part of the spinal cord or back.

luteinizing hormone (LH) A tropic hormone, released by the anterior pituitary, that influences the hormonal activities of the gonads.

luteinizing hormone–releasing hormone See *gonadotropin-releasing hormone*.

lymphocytes Immune-system cells. Two different classes of lymphocytes (B and T) mediate two types of immunological responses. See Figure 15.16.

lysergic acid diethylamide See *LSD*.

macrocolumn A column of neurons that is thought to be the functional module of cortical operations. The human cerebral cortex is estimated to contain about a million macrocolumns.

magnetic resonance imaging (MRI) A noninvasive technique that uses magnetic energy to generate images that reveal some of structural details in the living brain. See Figures 1.9, 2.21.

magnocellular layers The two ventral or inner layers of the lateral geniculate nucleus, so called because their cells are large. See Figures 10.15, 10.26.

magnocellular nucleus of the basal forebrain A region of the basal forebrain that modulates the activity of many areas of the neurocortex and is implicated in Alzheimer's disease. Also called Meynert's nucleus, basal nucleus of Meynert, or nucleus basalis of Meynert. See Figure 7.23.

magnocellular system The division of primate visual pathways that appears to be mainly responsible for the perception of depth and movement. See Figures 10.15, 10.26.

malleus A middle-ear bone that is connected to the tympanic membrane; one of the chain of three ossicles that transmits sound across the middle ear. See Figure 9.1.

mammillary body One of a pair of nuclei at the base of the brain that are slightly posterior to the pituitary stalk; a component of the limbic system. See Figure 2.12.

mammillothalamic tract The fiber bundle that connects the mammillary bodies to the thalamus.

manic–depressive psychosis See *bipolar depression*.

MAO Monoamine oxidase. An enzyme that breaks down and thereby inactivates monoamine transmitters.

MAO inhibitor An antidepressant drug that inhibits the enzyme monoamine oxidase, thus prolonging the action of catecholamine transmitters.

marijuana A drug of abuse, usually smoked. The active ingredient is the chemical known as THC.

marsupial An animal that is born at a very early developmental stage and that spends a period of its development in the maternal pouch.

MDMA A drug of abuse, also known as "ecstasy."

medial An anatomical term referring to structures toward the middle of an organ or organism. Contrast with *lateral*. See Box 2.2.

medial forebrain bundle A collection of axonal tracts traveling in the midline region of the forebrain. See Figure 4.2*a*.

medial geniculate nucleus A nucleus in the thalamus that receives input from the inferior colliculus and sends output to the auditory cortex. See Figure 9.7.

medulla The caudal part of the hindbrain. Also called myelencephalon. See Figures 2.12, 2.14.

meiosis The process of forming gametes in which each new cell receives half the chromosomes, therefore not requiring duplication of DNA.

Meissner's corpuscle A skin receptor cell type. See Figures 8.3, 8.13.

melatonin An amine hormone that is released by the pineal gland.

membrane potential A difference in electrical potential across the membrane of a nerve cell during an inactive period. Also called the resting potential. See Figures 3.1, 3.2.

memory A cognitive representation that is often acquired rapidly and that may last a long time.

memory trace A persistent change in the brain that reflects the storage of memory.

meninges The three protective sheets of tissue that surround the brain and spinal cord, called the dura mater, pia mater, and arachnoid.

menstruation A visible flow of cells and blood that exits through the vagina between ovulations in some mammals, including humans and dogs.

Merkel's disc A skin receptor cell type. See Figures 8.3, 8.13.

mesencephalon See *midbrain*.

mesolimbocortical system A set of dopaminergic axons arising in the midbrain and innervating the limbic system and cortex. See Figure 4.2.

mesostriatal system A set of dopaminergic axons arising from the midbrain and innervating the basal ganglia, including those from the substantia nigra to the striatum. See Figure 4.2

messenger RNA (mRNA) A strand of RNA that carries the code of a section of a strand of DNA to the cytoplasm. See the Appendix.

metabolic rate The rate of the use of energy during a given period; measured in terms of kilocalories per day.

metabolism The breakdown of complex molecules into smaller molecules.

metabotropic receptor A type of transmitter receptor that does not contain an ion channel, but may, when activated, use a G-protein system to open a nearby ion channel. See Figure 3.13*b*.

metencephalon A subdivision of the hindbrain that includes the cerebellum and the pons. See Figure 2.14.

Meynert's nucleus The collection of neurons in the basal forebrain which provides cholinergic innervation to much of the cortex. See Figure 7.23.

microelectrode   An especially small electrode, such as the fine, fluid filled glass electrodes used to record the membrane potential of neurons.

microfilament   A very small filament (7 nanometers in diameter) found within all cells. Microfilaments determine cell shape.

microglia   Extremely small glial cells that remove cellular debris from injured or dead cells.

microspectrophotometry   A technique for measuring the light absorption and therefore the chemical content of very small samples, such as the pigment in individual photoreceptors.

microtubule   A small hollow cylindrical structure (20 to 26 nanometers in diameter) in axons that is involved in axoplasmic transport. See Figure 2.5.

midbrain   The middle division of the brain. Also called the mesencephalon. See Figures 2.12, 2.14.

middle canal   The central of the three spiraling canals inside the cochlea.

middle ear   The cavity between the tympanic membrane and the cochlea. See Figure 9.1.

midget bipolar cells   Retinal bipolar cells that connect to just one cone. See Figure 10.9.

milk letdown reflex   The reflexive release of maternal oxytocin in response to suckling, or to stimuli associated with suckling. See Figure 5.12.

mineralocorticoids   A class of steroid hormone, released by the adrenal cortex, that affects ion concentrations in body tissues.

minicolumn   A narrow column of cerebral cortical cells; a subdivision of the macrocolumn.

minimal discriminable frequency difference   The smallest change in frequency that can be detected reliably between two tones.

mitosis   The process of division of somatic cells that involves duplication of DNA.

modal action pattern   A modification of the concept of a fixed action pattern that allows for some variability of the response between different individuals and within the same individual at different times.

modulation of memory formation   Facilitation or inhibition of memory formation by factors other than those directly involved in memory formation.

modulatory role   The role that some hormones play in maintaining the sensitivity of neural circuits and other structures to hormonal influences.

monaural detection   Sound detection using only one ear.

monoamine hormones   See *amine hormones.*

monoamine hypothesis of depression   The theory that depressive illness is associated with a decrease in the synaptic activity of connections that employ monoamine synaptic transmitters.

monoamine oxidase (MAO)   An enzyme that breaks down and thereby inactivates monoamine transmitters.

monoamines   A class of synaptic transmitters that contain a single amine group, NHs. Examples include the catecholamines and indoleamines. See Table 4.1.

monoclonal antibodies   Highly purified and specialized antibodies that enable investigators to identify a particular kind of cell.

monocular deprivation   The deprivation of light to one eye.

monogamy   A mating system in which a female and a male form a breeding pair that may last for one breeding period or for a lifetime. A durable and exclusive relation between a male and a female is called a pair bond.

monopolar neuron   A nerve cell with a single branch that leaves the cell body and then extends in two directions: one end is the receptive pole, the other end the output zone. See Figure 2.3.

monotreme   A mammal belonging to an order that contains only two species, the echidna and the platypus.

monozygotic   Describing twins derived from a single fertilized eggs. Such individuals have the same genotype. Contrast with dizygotic.

mossy fiber   One of the fibers that extend from the dentate gyrus to the hippocampus, where they synapse in area CA3. See Figure 18.7.

motion sickness   The experience of nausea from unnatural passive movement, as in a car or boat.

motivated behavior   Behavior that an organism displays even in the face of barriers or contingencies.

motoneuron   A nerve cell in the spinal cord that transmits motor messages from the spinal cord to muscles. Also called a motor neuron. See Figure 11.8.

motor cortex   A region of cerebral cortex that sends impulses to motoneurons. See Figures 11.12, 11.14.

motor plan   A plan for action in the nervous system.

motor unit   A single motor axon and all the muscle fibers that it innervates.

movement   A brief, unitary activity of a muscle or body part; less complex than an act.

MRH   See *müllerian regression hormone.*

MRI   See *magnetic resonance imaging.*

mRNA   See *messenger RNA.*

müllerian duct   A duct system in the embryo that will develop into female reproductive structures (fallopian tubes, uterus, and upper vagina) if testes are not present in the embryo. Contrast with *wolffian duct.* See Figure 12.15.

müllerian regression hormone (MRH)   The hormone that causes shrinkage of the müllerian ducts during development.

multiple sclerosis   "Many scars," a disorder characterized by the widespread degeneration of white matter.

multipolar neuron   A nerve cell that has many dendrites and a single axon. See Figure 2.3.

muscarinic   Referring to cholinergic receptors that respond to the chemical muscarine as well as to acetylcholine. Muscarinic receptors mediate chiefly the inhibitory activities of acetylcholine. Contrast with *nicotinic.*

muscle fiber   See *extrafusal fiber.* See Figure 11.7.

muscle spindle   A muscle receptor that lies parallel to a muscle and sends impulses to the central nervous system when the muscle is stretched. See Figure 11.9.

muscular dystrophy   A disease that leads to degeneration and functional changes in muscles.

mutation   A change in the nucleotide sequence of a gene as a result of unfaithful replication.

myasthenia gravis   A disorder characterized by a profound weakness of skeletal muscles; caused by a loss of acetylcholine receptors.

myelencephalon   See *medulla.* See Figures 2.12, 2.14.

myelin   The fatty insulation around an axon, formed by accessory cells. This myelin sheath improves the speed of conduction of nerve impulses. See Figures 2.6, 3.8.

myelination The process of formation of myelin. See Figures 2.6, 7.16.

myopia "Near-sightedness," the inability to focus the retinal image of objects that are far away.

myosin A protein which, with actin, mediates the contraction of muscle fibers. See Figure 11.7.

naloxone A potent antagonist of opiates that is often administered to people who have taken drug overdoses. Naloxone binds to receptors for endogenous opioids.

narcolepsy A disorder that involves frequent, intense episodes of sleep, which last from 5 to 30 minutes and can occur anytime during the usual waking hours.

natural selection See *evolution by natural selection*.

NE See *norepinephrine*.

negative feedback system A control system in which some of the output is used to reduce the effect of input signals. See Figure 3.16.

negative symptom In psychiatry, a symptom that reflects insufficient functioning. Examples include emotional and social withdrawal, blunted affect, slowness and impoverishment of thought and speech. Contrast with *positive symptom*.

nematocyst A tiny but effective animal weapon to deliver poison.

neocortex The relatively recently evolved portions of the cerebral cortex. All of the cortex seen at the surface of the human brain is neocortex.

neologism An entirely novel word, sometimes produced by aphasic patients.

neonatal Of or relating to newborns.

neophobia The avoidance of new things.

Nernst equation An equation used to calculate the equilibrium potential at a membrane.

nerve cell See *neuron*.

nerve growth factor (NGF) A substance that markedly affects the growth of neurons in spinal ganglia and in the ganglia of the sympathetic nervous system. See Figure 7.15.

nerve impulse The propagated electrical message of a neuron that travels along the axon to adjacent neurons. Also called the action potential. See Figures 3.5, 3.7.

nerves A collection of axons bundled together outside the central nervous system. Contrast with *tract*. See Figures 2.8, 2.9.

neural chain A simple kind of neural circuit in which neurons are attached linearly, end to end. See Figure 3.15.

neural folds In the developing embryo, ridges of ectoderm that form around the neural groove and come together to form the neural tube in the embryo. These neural folds will give rise to the entire nervous system. See Figure 7.2.

neural groove In the developing embryo, the groove between the neural folds. See Figure 7.2.

neural plasticity The property of the nervous system to change in response to experience or the environment.

neural tube An embryonic structure with subdivisions that correspond to the future forebrain, midbrain, and hindbrain. The cavity of this tube will include the cerebral ventricles and the passages that connect them. See Figure 7.2.

neuroblast An early form of a cell, during the stage of cell migration. See Figure 7.5.

neurocrine Referring to synaptic transmitter function.

neuroendocrine cell A neuron that releases hormones into local or systemic circulation.

neurofibrillary tangle An abnormal whorl of neurofilaments within nerve cells. Neurofibrillary tangles are especially apparent in people suffering from dementia. See Figure 7.23.

neurofilament A small rodlike structure found in axons. Neurofilaments are involved in the transport of materials. See Figure 2.5.

neurogenesis The mitotic division of nonneuronal cells to produce neurons.

neuroglia See *glial cells*.

neurohypophysis See *posterior pituitary*.

neuroleptics Antipsychotic drugs, traditionally dopamine receptor blockers.

neuromodulator A substance that influences the activity of synaptic transmitters.

neuromuscular junction The region where the motoneuron terminal and the adjoining muscle fiber meet; where the nerve transmits its message to the muscle fiber.

neuromuscular synapse elimination In postnatal development, the withdrawal by motoneurons of some of their terminal branches until every muscle fiber is innervated by only a single motoneuron.

neuron The basic unit of the nervous system. Each neuron is composed of a cell body, receptive extension(s) (dendrites), and a transmitting extension (axon). Also called a nerve cell. See Figures 2.1, 2.3.

neuronal cell death The selective death (apoptosis) of many nerve cells.

neuron doctrine The hypothesis that the brain is composed of separate cells that are distinct structurally, metabolically, and functionally.

neuropathy Peripheral nerve destruction.

neuropeptide A peptide that is used by neurons for signaling.

neuropeptide Y A peptide neurotransmitter that may carry some of the signals for feeding.

neuropil The conglomeration of dendrites and the synapses upon them.

neurosecretory cell See *neuroendocrine cell*.

neurospecificity A theory of nervous system development which states that each axon grows to a particular site. See Box 7.2.

neurotoxicology The study of the effects of toxins and poisons on the nervous system.

neurotransmitter See *synaptic transmitter*.

neurotrophic factor A target-derived chemical that acts as if it "feeds" certain neurons to help them survive.

NGF See *nerve growth factor*.

nicotinic Referring to cholinergic receptors that respond to nicotine. Nicotine receptors mediate chiefly the excitatory activities of acetylcholine, including at the neuromuscular junction. Contrast with *muscarinic*.

night terror A sudden arousal from stage 3 or stage 4 slow-wave sleep that is marked by intense fear and autonomic activation.

nightmare A long, frightening dream that awakens the sleeper from REM sleep.

nigrostriatal bundle (NSB)   A dopaminergic tract that extends from the substantia nigra of the midbrain to the lateral hypothalamus, the globus pallidus, and the caudate putamen.

Nissl stain   A histological stain that outlines all cell bodies because the dyes are attracted to RNA, which encircles the nucleus.

NMDA receptor   A glutamate receptor that also binds the glutamate agonist NMDA (*N*-methyl-D-aspartate). The NMDA receptor is both ligand-gated and voltage-sensitive, which enables it to participate in a wide variety of information processing. See Box 4.2 and Figure 18.8.

nociceptor   A receptor that responds to stimuli that produce tissue damage or pose the threat of damage.

nocturnal   Active during the dark periods of the daily cycle.

node of Ranvier   A gap between successive segments of the myelin sheath where the axon membrane is exposed. See Figures 2.6, 3.8.

nonassociative learning   A type of learning in which presentation of a particular stimulus alters the strength or probability of a response according to the strength and temporal spacing of that stimulus; includes habituation and sensitization. Contrast with *associative learning.*

noncompetitive   Describing a drug that affects a transmitter receptor while binding that at a site other than that bound by the endogenous ligand.

nondeclarative memory   A memory that is shown by performance rather than by conscious recollection. Also called procedural memory. Contrast with *declarative memory.*

nonequivalence of associations   A constraint on learning, stating that a given association is learned with differential ease by different species.

nonequivalence of responses   A constraint on learning, stating that the rapidity of learning a given instrumental behavior varies between species.

nonequivalence of stimuli   A constraint on learning, stating that the same stimulus has a differential ability to be learned by different species.

nonfluent speech   Talking with considerable effort, short sentences, and the absence of the usual melodic character of conversational speech.

nonprimary motor cortex   Frontal lobe regions adjacent to primary motor cortex that contribute to motor control and modulate the activity of the primary motor cortex. See Figure 11.14.

noradrenergic   Of or relating to systems using norepinephrine (noradrenaline) as a transmitter.

norepinephrine (NE)   A synaptic transmitter that is produced mainly in brain stem nuclei and in the adrenal medulla. Also called noradrenaline. See Table 4.1.

notochord   A midline structure arising early in the embryonic development of vertebrates. See Figure 7.11.

NSB   See *nigrostriatal bundle.*

nucleotide   A portion of a DNA or RNA molecule that is composed of a single base and the adjoining sugar/phosphate unit of the strand. See Appendix Figure 2.

nucleus (pl. nuclei)   An anatomical collection of neurons within the central nervous system (e.g., the caudate nucleus). See also *ganglion.*

nucleus basalis of Meynert   See *magnocellular nucleus of the basal forebrain.*

nucleus of the solitary tract (NST)   A brainstem nucleus that receives information from the parasympathetic vagus (tenth) cranial nerve. See Figure 13.28.

nucleus ruber   See *red nucleus.*

nutrient   A chemical that is needed for growth, maintenance, and repair of the body, but is not used as a source of energy.

nystagmus   An abnormal to-and-fro movement of the eye during attempts to fixate.

obsessive–compulsive disorder (OCD)   A syndrome in which the affected individual engages in recurring, repetitive acts that are carried out without rhyme, reason, or the ability to stop.

occipital cortex   The cortex of the occipital lobe of the brain. Also called visual cortex. See Figures 2.12, 10.13.

occipital lobe   The posterior lobe of the brain.

ocular dominance column (ODC)   An elongated band of cortical cells that respond preferentially to stimulation of one eye. See Figures 10.21, 10.22.

ocular dominance histogram   A graph that portrays the strength of response of a brain neuron to stimuli presented to either the left eye or the right eye. Used to determine the effects of manipulating visual experience. See Figure 7.19.

odorant   Molecule that elicits a perceived odor.

off-center bipolar cell   Retinal cell that is inhibited by light to the center of its receptive field and excited by light in the surround. See Figure 10.14.

off-center/on-surround   Describing a concentric receptive field in which the center inhibits the cell of interest while the surround excites it. See Figure 10.14.

olfactory bulb   An anterior projection of the brain that terminates in the upper nasal passages and, through small openings in the skull, provides receptors for smell.

olfactory cilium   hair-like structures in arising from the olfactory receptor cells. See Figure 9.18.

olfactory epithelium   A sheet of cells, including olfactory receptors, that lines the dorsal portion of the nasal cavities and adjacent regions, including the septum that separates the left and right nasal cavities.

oligodendrocyte   A type of glial cell that is commonly associated with nerve cell bodies; some oligodendrocytes form myelin sheaths. See Figure 2.6.

on-center bipolar cell   retinal cell that is excited by light to the center of its receptive field and inhibited by light in the surround. See Figure 10.14.

on-center/off-surround   describing a concentric receptive field in which the center excites the cell of interest while the surround inhibits it. See Figure 10.14.

ontogeny   The process in which an individual changes in the course of its lifetime—that is, grows up and grows old.

Onuf's nucleus   human homologue of the spinal nucleus of the bulbocavernosus (SNB) in rats.

open-loop control mechanism   A control mechanism in which feedback from the output of the system is not provided to the input control. Contrast with *closed-loop control mechanism.*

operant conditioning   See *instrumental conditioning.*

opiates   A class of compounds that exert an effect like that of opium, including reduced pain sensitivity. See Table 4.1.

opioids   Peptides produced in various regions of the brain that bind to opiate receptors and act like opiates. See Table 4.1.

opium   A heterogenous extract of the juice of the seed pod of the opium poppy, *Papaver somniferum.*

opponent-process hypothesis   The theory that color vision depends on systems that produce opposite responses to light of different wavelengths. See Figures 10.24, 10.25.

opsin   One of the two components of photopigments in the retina. The other component is RETINAL.

optic chiasm   The point at which the two optic nerves meet. See Figure 10.13.

optic disc   The region of the retina devoid of receptor cells because ganglion cell axons and blood vessels exit the eyeball there. See Figure 10.2.

optic nerve   The collection of ganglion cell axons that extend from the retina to the optic chiasm.

optic radiation   Axons from the lateral geniculate nucleus that terminate in the primary visual areas of the occipital cortex. See Figure 10.13.

optic tectum   The optical center of the midbrain. See Box 7.2.

optic tract   The axons of retinal ganglion cells after they have passed the optic chiasm; most terminate in the lateral geniculate nucleus. See Figure 10.13.

optokinetic system   A closed-loop system that controls eye movement and keeps the gaze on target.

orexin   A group of proteins expressed in the lateral hypothalamus that trigger feeding.

organum vasculosum of the lamina terminalis (OVLT)   One of the circumventricular organs. See Figure 13.17.

organizational effect   The permanent alteration of the nervous system, and thus permanent change in behavior, resulting from the action of a steroid hormone on an animal early in its development. Contrast with *activational effect.*

organizational hypothesis   The hypothesis that early testicular steroids masculinize the developing brain to alter behavior permanently.

organ of Corti   A structure in the inner ear that lies on the basilar membrane of the cochlea. It contains the hair cells and the terminations of the auditory nerve. See Figure 9.2.

orgasm   The climax of sexual experience, marked by extremely pleasurable sensations.

orientation column   A column of visual cortex that responds to rod-shaped stimuli of a particular orientation. See Figure 10.22.

oscillator circuit   A neural circuit that produces a recurring, repeating pattern of output. See Figure 3.17.

osmolality   The number of solute particles per unit volume of solvent.

osmoreceptor   One of the cells in the hypothalamus that are hypothesized to respond to changes in osmotic pressure.

osmosis   The passive movement of molecules from one place to another. The motive force behind osmosis is the constant vibration and movement of molecules.

osmotic pressure   The force produced by osmosis.

osmotic thirst   The response to increased osmotic pressure in brain cells. Contrast with *hypovolemic thirst.*

ossicles   One of three small bones that transmit sound across the middle ear, from the tympanic membrane to the oval window. See Figure 9.1.

otolith   A small bony crystal on the gelatinous membrane in the vestibular system.

otologist   Person who studies the outer, middle and inner ear.

ototoxic   Toxic to the ears, especially the middle or inner ear.

outer hair cell   One of the receptor cells of the cochlea. See Figure 9.2.

oval window   The opening from the middle ear to the inner ear.

ovaries   The female gonads, which produce eggs for reproduction.

overshoot   Here, the portion of the action potential during which the cell is transiently positive with relation to the extracellular medium. See Figure 3.3.

oviparity   Reproduction through egg laying. Contrast with *viviparity.*

ovulation   The production and release of an egg.

ovulatory cycle   The periodic occurrence of ovulation. See Figure 12.5.

ovum (pl. ova)   An egg, the female gamete.

oxytocin   A hormone, released from the posterior pituitary, that triggers milk letdown in the nursing female. See Figures 5.11, 5.12.

Pacinian corpuscle   A skin receptor cell type. See Figures 8.3, 8.4, 8.13.

pair bond   See *monogamy.*

paleocortex   Evolutionarily old cortex, such as the hippocampus. Thought to have evolved more recently than the archicortex.

pancreas   An endocrine gland, located near the posterior wall of the abdominal cavity, that secretes insulin and glucagon. See Figures 5.1, 5.19.

papilla (pl. papillae)   A small bump that projects from the surface of the tongue. Papillae contain most of the taste receptor cells.

parabiotic   Referring to a surgical preparation that joins the peripheral circulation of two animals.

paracrine   Referring to cellular communication in which a chemical signal diffuses to nearby target cells through the intermediate extracellular space. See Figure 5.4.

paradoxical sleep   See *rapid-eye-movement sleep.*

parallel fibers   One of the axons of the granule cells that form the outermost layer of the cerebellar cortex. See Figure 2.16.

parallel processing   The use of several different circuits at the same time to process the same stimuli. A novelty in computers, but an ancient property of nervous systems.

paraphasia   A symptom of aphasia that is distinguished by the substitution of a word by a sound, an incorrect word, an unintended word, or a neologism (a meaningless word).

parasympathetic nervous system   One of the two systems that compose the autonomic nervous system. The parasympathetic division arises from both the cranial nerves and the sacral spinal cord. Contrast with *sympathetic nervous system.* See Figure 2.11 for the different functions of the two systems.

paraventricular nucleus   A nucleus of the hypothalamus. See Figures 5.11, 13.24.

parietal lobe   A major sector of the cerebral hemispheres.

Parkinson's disease   A degenerative neurological disorder that involves dopaminergic neurons of the substantia nigra.

parthenogenesis   "Virgin birth"; the production of offspring without the contribution of a male or sperm.

partial seizure   An epileptic seizure that arises from pathological foci that are not widespread. Partial seizures include focal-repetitive motor spasms and do not involve loss of consciousness.

parvocellular layer   One of the four dorsal or outer layers of the primate lateral geniculate nucleus, so called because their cells are relatively small.

parvocellular system   The division of primate visual pathways that appears to be mainly responsible for analysis of color and form and for recognition of objects. See Figure 10.26.

passive avoidance response   A response that an organism has learned *not* to make, (e.g., learning not to enter a compartment where it has been given a shock).

patch clamp technique   The use of very narrow pipette microelectrodes, clamped by suction onto tiny patches of the neural membrane, to record the electrical activity of a single square micron of membrane, including single ion channels.

Pavlovian conditioning   See *classical conditioning*.

PCP   See *phencyclidine*.

penis   The male genital organ, which enters the female's vagina to deliver semen.

perforant path   The route of axons that "perforate" the subiculum to provide the main inputs to the hippocampal formation.

periaqueductal gray   The neuronal body-rich region of the midbrain surrounding the cerebral aqueduct connecting the third and the fourth ventricles.

period   The interval of time between two similar points of successive cycles, such as sunset to sunset.

peripheral nervous system   The portion of the nervous system that includes all the nerves and neurons outside the brain and spinal cord.

permanent memory   A type of memory that lasts without decline for the life of an organism.

perseveration/consolidation hypothesis   The hypothesis that information passes through two stages in memory formation. During the first stage the memory is held by perseveration (repetition) of neural activity and is easily disrupted. During the second stage the memory becomes fixed, or consolidated, and is no longer easily disrupted.

PET   See *positron emission tomography*.

petit mal seizure   A type of generalized epileptic seizure that is characterized by a spike-and-wave electrical pattern. A person having a petit mal seizure is unaware of the environment and later cannot recall what happened.

PGO wave   An EEG wave of activity from the pons to the lateral geniculate and on to the occipital cortex, usually seen only during REM sleep in cats.

phantom limb   The experience of sensory messages that are attributed to an amputated limb.

phase shift   A shift in the activity of a biological rhythm, typically provided by a synchronizing environmental stimulus.

phasic receptor   A receptor that shows a rapid fall in nerve impulse discharge as stimulation is maintained.

phencyclidine (PCP)   An anesthetic agent that is also a psychedelic drug. Phencyclidine makes many people feel dissociated from themselves and their environment.

phenothiazines   A class of antipsychotic drugs which reduce the positive symptoms of schizophrenia.

phenotype   The sum of an individual's physical characteristics at one particular time.

phenylketonuria (PKU)   An inherited disorder of protein metabolism in which the absence of an enzyme leads to a toxic buildup of certain compounds, causing mental retardation.

pheromone   A chemical signal that is released outside the body of an animal and that affects other members of the same species. Contrast with *allomone*. See Figure 5.4.

phobic disorder   An intense, irrational fear that becomes centered on a specific object, activity, or situation that a person feels he or she must avoid.

phoneme   A sound that is produced for language.

phonemic paraphasias   A symptom of aphasia in which incorrect phonemes are substituted for correct sounds.

phosphene   A perceived flash of light that is provoked by electrical or mechanical stimulation of the eyeball or visual cortex.

phosphorylation   The addition of phosphate groups (PO_4) to proteins.

photon   A quantum of light energy.

photopic system   A system in the retina that operates at high levels of light, shows sensitivity to color, and involves the cones. Contrast with *scotopic system*. See Table 10.1.

phrenology   The belief that bumps on the skull reflect enlargements of brain regions responsible for certain behavioral faculties. See Figure 1.14.

phylogeny   The evolutionary history of a particular group of organisms.

physical dependence   The state of an individual that has frequently taken high doses of a drug and will encounter unpleasant withdrawal symptoms if he or she stops.

physiological nystagmus   Small, rapid movement of the eyes which prevents retinal adaptation and permits sustained viewing of a scene.

physiological saline   A mixture of water and salt in which the concentration of salt is 0.9%, approximately equal in osmolarity to mammalian extracellular fluid.

pia mater   The innermost of the three coverings that embrace the brain and spinal cord.

pineal gland   Secretory gland in the brain midline, source of melatonin release. See Figure 2.12*b*.

pinna (pl. pinnae)   See *external ear*.

pitch   A dimension of auditory experience in which sounds vary from low to high.

pituitary gland   A small, complex endocrine gland located in a socket at the base of the skull. The anterior pituitary and posterior pituitary are separate in function. See Figures 5.11, 5.13.

PKU   See *phenylketonuria*.

place cell   Neuron within the hippocampus which selectively fires when the animal is in a particular location.

placebo   Drug given to a patient which is known to be ineffective or inert, but which sometimes brings relief.

placebo effect   A response to an inert substance (a placebo) that mimics the effects of an actual drug. For example, people suffering pain frequently experience relief from sugar tablets presented as medicine.

placenta   The specialized organ produced by the mammalian embryo that attaches to the walls of the uterus to provide nutrients, energy, and gas exchange to the fetus.

placental mammal   A mammal that produces a highly specialized placenta; includes all mammals except the marsupials and the monotremes.

place theory   A theory of frequency discrimination according to which pitch perception depends on the place of maximal displacement of the basilar membrane produced by a sound. Contrast with *volley theory*.

planum temporale   A region of superior temporal cortex adjacent to the primary auditory area. See Figure 19.16.

plasticity   Malleability. Here, the property by which the nervous system changes in response to environmental conditions and/or experience.

pneumoencephalography   A technique for examining brain structure in humans by taking X rays after a gas is injected into the cerebral ventricles.

poikilotherm   An animal whose body temperature varies with the environment. Examples include reptiles. Contrast with *homeotherms*.

polyandry   A mating system in which one female mates with more than one male. Contrast with *polygyny*.

polygamy   A mating system in which an individual mates with more than one other animal.

polygraph   A device that measures several bodily responses, such as heart rate and blood pressure; popularly known as a "lie detector."

polygyny   A mating system in which one male mates with more than one female. Contrast with *polyandry*.

polymodal   Involving several sensory modalities.

pons   A portion of the metencephalon. See Figures 2.12, 2.14.

positive feedback   The property by which the output of a system feedsback to increase the input. A rarity in biological systems. Contrast with *negative feedback*.

positive reward model   A model of addictive behavior that emphasizes the rewarding attributes of drug ingestion.

positive symptom   In psychiatry, an abnormal state. Examples include hallucinations, delusions, and excited motor behavior. Contrast with *negative symptom*.

positron emission tomography (PET)   A technique for examining brain function in intact humans by combining tomography with injections of radioactive substances used by the brain. Analysis of the metabolism of these substances reflects regional differences in brain activity. See Figure 2.21.

postcentral gyrus   The strip of parietal cortex, just behind the central sulcus, which receives somatosensory information from the entire body.

postcopulatory behavior   The final stage in mating behavior. Species-specific postcopulatory behaviors include rolling (in the cat) and grooming (in the rat).

posterior pituitary   The rear division of the pituitary gland. Also called neurohypophysis. See Figure 5.11.

postganglionic cell   A cell in the autonomic nervous system that resides in the peripheral ganglia and sends its axons to innervate target organs.

postsynaptic   Referring to the region of a synapse that receives and responds to neurotransmitter. Contrast with *presynaptic*.

postsynaptic potential   See *graded potential*.

posttetanic potentiation   A well-known example of neural plasticity in which a rapid series of action potentials (a tetanus) is induced in a nerve, with the result that subsequent single action potentials cause a stronger postsynaptic potential in the target.

posttraumatic stress disorder (PTSD)   Disorder in which memories of an unpleasant episode repeatedly intrude upon the victim.

postural tremor   A tremor that occurs when a person attempts to maintain a posture such as holding an arm or leg extended, often resulting from pathology of the basal ganglia or cerebellum.

potassium equilibrium potential   See *equilibrium potential*.

precentral gyrus   The strip of frontal cortex, just in front of the central sulcus, that is crucial for motor control.

precocial   Referring to animals that are born in a relatively developed state and who are able to survive without maternal care. Contrast with *altricial*.

preferred temperature   The environmental temperature at which an animal chooses to spend most of its time.

prefrontal cortex   The anteriormost region of the frontal lobe.

preganglionic cells   A cell of the autonomic nervous system that resides in the CNS and sends its axons to innervate autonomic ganglia. See Figure 2.11.

premature ejaculation   Ejaculation before the man and/or his partner have achieved the level of excitement desired.

premotor cortex   A region of nonprimary motor cortex, just anterior to the primary motor cortex. See Figure 11.14.

prenatal   Before birth.

preoptic area   A region of the hypothalamus, just anterior to the level of the optic chiasm.

presynaptic   Referring to the region of a synapse that releases neurotransmitter. Contrast with *postsynaptic*.

primacy effect   The superior performance seen in a memory task for items at the start of a list. Contrast with *recency effect*.

primary motor cortex   The apparent executive region for initiation of movement; primarily the precentral gyrus.

primary sensory ending   The axon transmitting information from the central portion of a muscle spindle. See Figure 11.9c.

primary visual cortex   The region of the occipital cortex where most visual information first arrives. Also called striate cortex, area 17, or V1. See Figures 10.12, 10.13, 10.18.

priming   In pheromones, the ability of a pheromone to slowly alter the physiology of a conspecific. In memory, the phenomenon by which exposure to a stimulus facilitates subsequent responses to the same or similar stimulus.

procedural memory   See *nondeclarative memory.*

proceptive behavior   A behavior displayed by an animal that prompts its partner to initiate mating behaviors.

progesterone   The primary type of progestin secreted by the ovary.

progestins   A major class of steroid hormones that are produced by the ovary, including progesterone. See Table 5.2.

projection neuron   A large neuron that transmits messages between widely separated parts of the brain.

prolactin   A protein hormone, produced by the anterior pituitary, that promotes mammary development for lactation in female mammals.

promiscuity   A mating system in which animals mate with several members of the opposite sex and do not establish durable associations with sex partners.

proprioceptive   Referring to information from the periphery about the body's position and movement.

prosencephalon   See *forebrain.*

prosopagnosia   A condition characterized by the inability to recognize faces.

prostate gland   A male secondary sexual gland that contributes fluid to semen.

prosthetic device   An artificial replacement of a body part lost by accident or disease.

protein hormone   A class of hormones that consists of protein molecules.

protein kinase   An enzyme that adds phosphate groups (PO_4) to protein molecules.

proximal   An anatomical term referring to structures near the trunk or center of an organism. Contrast with *distal.* See Box 2.2.

psychedelic   Referring to a mental state with intensified sensory perception and distortions or hallucinations. Psychedelic drugs produce such states.

psychoneuroimmunology   The study of the immune system and its interaction with the nervous system and behavior.

psychopharmacology   The study of the effects of drugs on the nervous system and behavior.

psychosocial dwarfism   Reduced stature caused by stress early in life that inhibits deep sleep. See Box 5.2.

psychosomatic medicine   A field of study that emphasizes the role of psychological factors in disease.

psychosurgery   Surgery in which brain lesions are produced to modify severe psychiatric disorders.

psychotogen   A substance that generates psychotic behavior.

pupil   The aperture, formed by the iris, that allows light to enter the eye.

pure tone   A tone with a single frequency of vibration. See Box 9.1.

Purkinje cell   A type of large nerve cell in the cerebellar cortex.

pursuit movement   A type of eye movement in which your gaze smoothly and continuously follows a moving object.

putamen   One of the basal ganglia. See Figure 2.15.

pyramidal cell   A type of large nerve cell that has a roughly pyramid-shaped cell body; found in the cerebral cortex. See Figure 2.17.

pyramidal system   The motor system that includes neurons within the cerebral cortex and their axons, which form the pyramidal tract. Also called the corticospinal system. See Figure 11.11.

pyramidal tract   The path of axons arising from the motor cortex and terminating in the spinal cord.

pyrogen   A chemical, released by cells of the immune system, that elevates body temperature.

quantum (pl. quanta)   A unit of radiant energy.

radial glial cells   Glial cells that form early in development, spanning the width of the emerging cerebral hemispheres, and guide migrating neurons. See Figure 7.8.

radioimmunoassay (RIA)   A technique that uses antibodies to measure the concentration of a substance, such as a hormone in blood.

ramp movement   A slow, sustained motion that is thought to be generated in the basal ganglia. Also called smooth movement. Contrast with *ballistic.*

range fractionation   A hypothesis of stimulus intensity perception stating that a wide range of intensity values can be encoded by a group of cells, each of which is a specialist for a particular range of stimulus intensities. See Figure 8.5.

raphe nucleus   A group of neurons in the midline of the brain stem that contains serotonin and is involved in sleep mechanisms. See Figure 14.21.

rapid-eye-movement (REM) sleep   A stage of sleep characterized by small-amplitude, fast-EEG waves, no postural tension, and rapid eye movements. Also called paradoxical sleep. Contrast with *slow-wave sleep.* See Figure 14.10.

Raynaud's disease   A circulatory disorder in which blood supply to the fingers may be shut off upon exposure to the cold and sometimes in response to emotional states.

recency effect   The superior performance seen in a memory task for items at the end of a list; attributed to short-term memory. Contrast with *primacy effect.*

receptive field   The stimulus region and features that cause the maximal response of a cell in a sensory system. See Figures 8.10, 10.14, 10.16.

receptivity   The state of readiness in the female to show responses that are necessary for the male to achieve intromission.

receptor   The initial element in a sensory system, responsible for stimulus transduction. Examples include the hair cells in the cochlea or the rods and cones in the retina. See also *receptor molecule.*

receptor cell   A specialized cell that responds to a particular energy or substance in the internal or external environment. The receptor cell converts this energy into a change in the electrical potential across its membrane.

receptor molecule   A protein that captures and reacts to molecules of the transmitter or hormone. Also called a receptor.

receptor site   A region of specialized membrane that contains receptor molecules located on the postsynaptic surface of a synapse. Receptor sites receive and react with chemical transmitters.

red nucleus   A brain stem structure related to the basal ganglia. Also called the nucleus ruber.

reductionism   The scientific strategy of breaking a system down into increasingly smaller parts in order to understand it completely.

reflex   A simple, highly stereotyped, and unlearned response to a particular stimulus (e.g., an eyeblink in response to a puff of air). See Figures 3.14, 11.10.

reflex ovulation   Ovulation that in certain species is induced by copulation, thus not restricting successful mating to a regular ovulatory period of the female's cycle.

refraction   The bending of light rays by a change in the density of a medium, such as the cornea and the lens of our eyes.

refractory phase   1. A period during and after a nerve impulse in which the responsiveness of the axon membrane is reduced. A brief period of complete insensitivity to stimuli (absolute refractory phase) is followed by a longer period of reduced sensitivity (relative refractory phase) during which only strong stimulation produces a nerve impulse. 2. A period following copulation during which an individual cannot recommence copulation. The absolute refractory phase of the male sexual response is illustrated in Figure 12.8.

regulation   An adaptive response to early injury, as when developing individuals compensate for missing or injured cells.

reinforcing stimulus   See *instrumental conditioning.*

relative refractory phase   See *refractory phase.*

releasing hormone   A hormone produced in the hypothalamus, that traverses the hypothalamic–pituitary portal system to control the pituitary's release of tropic hormones.

REM sleep   See *rapid-eye-movement sleep.*

renin   Hormone released by the kidneys when they detect reduced blood flow.

resting potential   A difference in electrical potential across the membrane of a nerve cell during an inactive period. Also called the membrane potential. See Figures 3.1, 3.2.

rete mirabile   A network of fine blood vessels located at the base of the brain in which blood coming from the periphery reduces the temperature of arterial blood before it enters the brain.

reticular formation   An extensive region of the brain stem (extending from the medulla through the thalamus) that is involved in arousal. See Figure 14.20.

reticulospinal tract   A tract of axons arising from the brain stem reticular formation and descending to the spinal cord to modulate movement.

retina   The receptive surface inside the eye that contains the rods and cones. See Figure 10.7.

RETINAL   One of the two components of the photopigment found in the eye. The other component is called opsin.

retrieval   A process in memory during which a stored memory is used by an organism. See Figure 17.11.

retroactive amnesia   A type of memory loss in which events immediately preceding a head injury are not recalled.

retrograde amnesia   Difficulty in retrieving memories formed before the onset of amnesia.

retrograde degeneration   Destruction of the nerve cell body following injury to its axon. See Box 4.1.

retrograde signal   A signal that is thought to be released by the postsynaptic region that instructs the presynaptic neuron to increase subsequent transmitter release.

reuptake   The process by which released synaptic transmitter molecules are taken up and reused by the presynaptic neuron, thus stopping synaptic activity.

rhodopsin   The photopigment in rods that responds to light.

rhombencephalon   See *hindbrain.*

RIA   See *radioimmunoassay.*

ribonucleic acid (RNA)   A nucleic acid that implements information found in DNA. Two forms of RNA are transfer RNA and messenger RNA.

ribosomes   Structures in the cell body where the translation of genetic information (the production of proteins) takes place.

RNA   See *ribonucleic acid.*

rod   One of the light-sensitive receptor cells in the retina that are most active at low levels of light. See Figure 10.7.

roots   The two distinct branches of a spinal nerve, each of which serves a separate function. The dorsal root carries sensory information from the peripheral nervous system to the spinal cord. The ventral root carries motor messages from the spinal cord to the peripheral nervous system. See Figure 2.10.

rostral   An anatomical term referring to structures toward the head end of an organism. Also called cephalic. Contrast with *caudal.* See Box 2.2.

round window   A membrane separating the cochlear duct from the middle-ear cavity.

rubrospinal tract   Axons arising from the red nucleus in the midbrain and innervating neurons of the spinal cord. See Figure 11.15.

Ruffini's ending   A skin receptor cell type. See Figures 8.3, 8.13.

saccade (saccadic movement)   A series of rapid movements of the eyes that occur regularly during normal viewing. Also called a saccadic movement.

saccule   A small, fluid-filled sac under the utricle that responds to static positions of the head. See Figure 9.14.

sacral   Referring to the lower part of the back or spinal cord.

sagittal plane   The plane that bisects the body or brain into right and left portions. See Box 2.2.

saltatory conduction   The form of conduction characteristic of myelinated axons, in which the nerve impulse jumps from one node of Ranvier to the next.

satiety   A feeling of fulfillment or satisfaction. Contrast with *hunger.*

saturation   One of the basic dimensions of light perception. Saturation varies from rich to pale (e.g., from red to pink to gray in the color solid of Figure 10.5).

saxitoxin (STX)   An animal toxin that blocks sodium channels when applied to the outer surface of the cell membrane.

Schaffer collateral   An axon branch from a neuron in area CA3 that projects to area CA1 in the hippocampus.

schema   In terms of actions, a high-level program for movement.

schizophrenia   A severe psychopathology characterized by negative symptoms such as emotional withdrawal and impoverished thought, and by positive symptoms such as hallucinations and delusions.

schizotoxin A hypothesized toxic substance that causes schizophrenia.

Schwann cell The accessory cell that forms myelin in the peripheral nervous system.

SCN See *suprachiasmatic nucleus*.

scotoma A region of blindness caused by injury to the visual pathway or brain.

scotopic system A system in the retina that operates at low levels of light and involves the rods. Contrast with *photopic system*. See Table 10.1.

second messenger A slow-acting substance in the postsynaptic cell that amplifies the effects of nerve impulses and can initiate processes that lead to changes in electrical potential at the membrane.

secondary sensory ending The axon transmitting information from the ends of a muscle spindle.

secretin A hormone that is released from the small intestine during digestion.

seizure An epileptic episode. See Box 3.3.

selective permeability The property of a membrane to allow some substances to pass through, but not others.

selective potentiation The enhancement of the sensitivity or activity of certain neural circuits.

selectivity of reinforcement The idea that across species, different reinforcements are differentially effective in strengthening associations.

semantic memory Generalized memory—for instance, knowing the meaning of a word without knowing where or when you learned that word.

semen A mixture of fluid, including sperm, that is released during ejaculation.

semicircular canal One of the three fluid-filled tubes in the inner ear that are part of the vestibular system. Each of the tubes, which are at right angles to each other, detects angular acceleration. See Figure 9.14.

seminal vesicle A gland that stores fluid to contribute to semen.

semipermeable membrane A membrane that allows some but not all molecules to pass through.

senile dementia (Alzheimer's disease) A neurological disorder of the aged that is characterized by progressive behavioral deterioration, including personality change and profound intellectual decline.

senile plaques A neuroanatomical change that correlates with senile dementia. Senile plaques are small areas of the brain that have abnormal cellular and chemical patterns. See Figure 7.23.

sensitive period The period during development in which an organism can be permanently altered by a particular experience or treatment.

sensitization 1. A form of nonassociative learning in which an organism becomes more responsive to most stimuli after being exposed to unusually strong or painful stimulation. See Box 17.1. 2. A process in which the body shows an enhanced response to a given drug after repeated doses. Contrast with *tolerance*.

sensorineural deafness A hearing impairment that originates from cochlear or auditory nerve lesions.

sensory conflict theory A theory of motion sickness that suggests that discrepancies between vestibular information and visual information may simulate food poisoning and therefore trigger nausea.

sensory neuron A neuron that is directly affected by changes in the environment, such as light, an odor, or a touch.

sensory receptor organ Organ specialized to receive particular stimuli, such as the eye and the ear.

sensory transduction The process in which a receptor cell converts the energy in a stimulus into a change in the electrical potential across its membrane.

septal complex A brain region that provides subcortical input to the hippocampal formation.

serotonergic Referring to neurons that use serotonin as their synaptic transmitter.

serotonin (5-HT) A synaptic transmitter that is produced in the raphe nuclei and is active in structures throughout the cerebral hemispheres. See Figures 4.4, 14.21.

set point The point of reference in a feedback system. An example is the setting of a thermostat.

set zone The range of a variable that a feedback system tries to maintain.

sex chromosome One of a pair of chromosomes that in female mammals are identical (XX) but in males are different (XY). Contrast with *autosomes*.

sex-determining region on the Y (SRY) gene A gene on the Y chromosome that directs the developing gonads to become testes.

sex steroids Steroid hormones secreted by the gonads: androgens, estrogens and progestins.

sexual attraction The first step in the mating behavior of many animals, in which animals emit stimuli that attract members of the opposite sex.

sexual determination The developmentally early event that normally decides whether the individual will become a male or a female.

sexual differentiation The process by which individuals develop either malelike or femalelike bodies and behavior.

sexual dimorphism A structural difference between the sexes.

sexual imprinting A kind of imprinting in which early experience influences the choice of a mate later in life.

sexual receptivity See *receptivity*.

sexual selection Darwin's theoretical mechanism for the evolution of anatomical and behavioral differences between males and females.

sexually dimorphic nucleus of the preoptic area (SDN-POA) A region of the preoptic area which is 5–6 times larger in volume in male rats than in females. See Figure 12.21.

short-term memory (STM) Memory that usually lasts only for seconds or as long as rehearsal continues.

SIDS See *sudden infant death syndrome*.

simple cortical cell A cell in the visual cortex that responds best to an edge or a bar of a particular width and with a particular direction and location in the visual field. See Figure 10.14.

sinistral Left-handed.

skill learning Learning to perform a task that requires motor coordination.

sleep apnea A sleep disorder that involves the slowing or cessation of respiration during sleep, which wakens the patient. Excessive daytime somnolence results from the frequent nocturnal awakening.

sleep cycle   A period of slow-wave sleep followed by a period of REM sleep. In humans, a sleep cycle lasts approximately 90 minutes.

sleep deprivation   The partial or total prevention of sleep.

sleep enuresis   Bed wetting.

sleep epoch   A period of one episode of short-wave sleep followed by an episode of REM sleep.

sleep-maintenance insomnia   Difficulty in staying asleep. Contrast with *sleep-onset insomnia.*

sleep-onset insomnia   Difficulty in getting to sleep. Contrast with *sleep-maintenance insomnia.*

sleep paralysis   A state in which the ability to move or talk is temporarily lost.

sleep recovery   The process of sleeping more than normally after a period of sleep deprivation, as though in compensation.

sleep spindle   A characteristic 14 to 18 Hz wave in the EEG of a person said to be in stage 2 sleep. See Figure 14.10.

slow muscle fiber   A type of striated muscle fiber that contracts slowly but does not fatigue readily.

slow-wave sleep (SWS)   Sleep, divided into stages 1 through 4, that is defined by the presence of slow-wave EEG activity. Contrast with *rapid-eye-movement sleep.* See Figure 14.10.

smooth movement   See *ramp movement.*

smooth muscle   type of muscle fiber, as in the heart, that is controlled by the autonomic nervous system rather than voluntary control. Contrast with *striated muscle.*

SOAE   See *spontaneous otoacoustic emission.*

sodium equilibrium potential   See *equilibrium potential.*

solute   The solid compound that is dissolved in a liquid. Contrast with *solvent.*

solvent   The liquid (often water) in which a compound is dissolved. Contrast with *solute.*

somatic intervention   An approach to finding relations between bodily variables and behavioral variables that involves manipulating bodily structure or function and looking for resultant changes in behavior. See Figure 1.3.

somatomedins   group of proteins, released from the liver in response to growth hormone, that aid body growth and maintenance.

somatosensory   Touch and pain sensation.

somatosensory cortex   The portion of parietal cortex that receives tactile stimuli from the body.

somatotropic hormone   See *growth hormone.*

somnambulism   Sleepwalking.

spatial-frequency filter model   A model of pattern analysis that emphasizes Fourier analysis of visual stimuli. Contrast with *feature detector model.*

spatial summation   The summation at the axon hillock of postsynaptic potentials from across the cell body. If this summation reaches threshold a nerve impulse will be triggered. See Figure 3.10. Contrast with *temporal summation.*

specific abilities to learn and remember   The concept that specific abilities to learn and remember evolve where needed. Contrast with *genetic constraints on learning.*

specific hunger   The temporary, unlearned increase in preference for a particular food; related to a specific need.

specific nerve energies   The doctrine that the receptors and neural channels for the different senses are independent and operate in their own special ways, and can produce only one particular sensation.

spectrally opponent cell   A visual receptor cell that has opposite firing responses to different regions of the spectrum. See Figures 10.24, 10.25.

sperm   The gamete produced by males for fertilization of eggs (ova).

spinal animal   An animal whose spinal cord has been surgically disconnected from the brain to enable the study of behaviors that do not require brain control.

spinal nerve   A nerve that emerges from the spinal cord. There are 31 pairs of spinal nerves. See Figure 2.10.

spinal nucleus of the bulbocavernosus (SNB)   Group of motoneurons in spinal cord that innervated striated muscles controlling the penis. See Figure 12.22.

spinal root   See *roots.*

spinal shock   A period of decreased synaptic excitability in the neurons of the spinal cord after it is isolated surgically from the brain.

spindle cell   A type of small, rod-shaped nerve cell.

spinothalamic system (anterolateral system)   System delivering pain information from the body to the brain. See Figure 8.14.

split-brain individual   Referring to an individual whose corpus callosum has been severed, halting communication between the right and left hemispheres.

spontaneous otoacoustic emission (SOAE)   A sound that is produced by the ears of many normal people. Contrast with *evoked otoacoustic emissions.*

spontaneous recovery   A feature of classical conditioning in which, if there is no testing after extinction, the conditioned stimulus may again elicit a response.

***SRY* gene**   Sex-determining Region of the Y chromosome, the gene responsible for the indifferent gonad developing as a testis.

S-shaped curve   A common dose–response function.

stage 1 sleep   The initial stage of slow-wave sleep, which is characterized by small-amplitude EEG waves of irregular frequency, slow heart rate, and reduced muscle tension. See Figure 14.10.

stage 2 sleep   A stage of slow-wave sleep that is defined by bursts of regular 14 to 18 Hz EEG waves (called sleep spindles) that progressively increase and then decrease in amplitude. See Figure 14.10.

stage 3 sleep   A stage of slow-wave sleep that is defined by the spindles seen in stage 2 sleep mixed with larger-amplitude slow waves. See Figure 14.10.

stage 4 sleep   A stage of slow-wave sleep that is defined by the presence of high-amplitude slow waves of 1 to 4 Hz. See Figure 14.10.

stapedius   A middle-ear muscle that is attached to the stapes.

stapes   A middle-ear bone that is connected to the oval window. One of the three ossicles that conduct sounds across the middle ear.

static phase of obesity   A later period following destruction of the ventromedial hypothalamus during which an animal's weight stabilizes at an obese level and food intake is not much above normal. See Figure 13.25. Contrast with *dynamic phase of weight gain.*

stellate cell   A type of small nerve cell that has many branches.

stereocilium (pl. stereocilia)   A relatively stiff hair that protrudes from a hair cell in the auditory or vestibular system. See Figure 9.2.

stereopsis   The ability to perceive depth, using the slight difference in visual information from the two eyes. See Figure 10.26.

steroid hormones   A class of hormones that are composed of four interconnected rings of carbon atoms.

stimulation-elicited behavior   A motivational behavior, such as eating, drinking, or fearful escape, that is elicited by electrical stimulation of sites in the brain.

STM   See *short-term memory.*

stress   Any circumstance that upsets homeostatic balance. Examples include exposure to extreme cold or heat or an array of threatening psychological states.

stress immunization   The concept that mild stress early in life makes an individual better able to handle stress later in life.

stretch reflex   The contraction of a muscle in response to stretch of that muscle. See Figure 11.10.

striate cortex   See *primary visual cortex.*

striate region   The region of the brain that contains the basal ganglia, called striate because the external capsule and internal capsule appear as light-colored stripes across the gray matter.

striated muscle   Muscle with a striped appearance, generally under voluntary control. Contrast with *smooth muscle.*

striatum   The caudate nucleus and putamen together.

stroke   A disorder of blood vessels—either a block or a rupture of a vessel—that destroys or cripples particular brain regions.

subcutaneous   Beneath the skin.

subfornical organ   One of the circumventricular organs. See Figure 13.17.

subiculum   A region adjacent to the hippocampus that contributes to the hippocampal formation. Also called the hippocampal gyrus.

substantia nigra   A brain stem structure in humans that is related to the basal ganglia and named for its dark pigmentation. Depletion of dopaminergic cells in this region has been implicated in Parkinson's disease.

subventricular zone   A region around the brain ventricle that continues to manufacture the precursors of glial cells after birth.

sudden infant death syndrome (SIDS)   The sudden, unexpected death of an apparently healthy human infant who simply stops breathing, usually during sleep. SIDS is not well understood. Also called crib death.

sulcus (pl. sulci)   A furrow of convoluted brain surface. Contrast with *gyrus.* See Figure 2.12.

superior colliculi   See *colliculus.*

superior olivary nuclei   A brain stem structure that receives input from both right and left cochlear nuclei, and provides the first binaural analysis of auditory information. See Figure 9.7.

superordinate circuit   A neural circuit that is hierarchically superior to other, simple circuits.

supplementary motor cortex   A region of nonprimary motor cortex that receives input from the basal ganglia and modulates the activity of the primary motor cortex.

suprachiasmatic nucleus (SCN)   A small region of the hypothalamus above the optic chiasm that is the location of a circadian oscillator. See Figure 14.4.

supraoptic nucleus   A nucleus of the hypothalamus. See Figure 5.11.

surface dyslexia   A form of acquired dyslexia in which patient seems to attend only to the fine details of reading.

SWS   See *slow-wave sleep.*

Sylvian sulcus   A deep fissure that demarcates the temporal lobe. See Figure 2.12.

sympathetic chain   A chain of ganglia that runs along each side of the spinal column; part of the sympathetic nervous system. See Figure 2.11.

sympathetic nervous system   One of two systems that compose the autonomic nervous system. The sympathetic nervous system arises from the thoracic and lumbar spinal cord. See Figure 2.11 for the different functions of the two systems. Contrast with *parasympathetic nervous system.*

synapse   An area composed of the presynaptic (axonal) terminal, the postsynaptic (usually dendritic) membrane, and the space (or cleft) between them. The synapse is the site at which neural messages travel from one neuron to another. Also called the synaptic region. See Figure 2.4.

synapse rearrangement   The loss of some synapses and development of others; a refinement of synaptic connections that is often seen in development.

synaptic assembly   A level of brain organization that includes the total collection of all synapses on a single cell.

synaptic bouton   The presynaptic swelling of the axon terminal from which neural messages travel across the synaptic cleft to other neurons.

synaptic cleft   The space between the presynaptic and postsynaptic elements. This gap measures about 20 to 40 nanometers. See Figures 2.4, 3.11.

synaptic region   See *synapse.*

synaptic transmitter   The chemical in the presynaptic bouton that serves as the basis of communication between neurons. The transmitter travels across the synaptic cleft and reacts with the postsynaptic membrane when triggered by a nerve impulse. Also called neurotransmitter or chemical transmittter. See Figure 3.11, Table 4.1.

synaptic vesicle   A small, spherical structure that contains molecules of synaptic transmitter. See Figure 2.4.

synaptogenesis   The establishment of synaptic connections as axons and dendrites grow.

synergist   A muscle that acts together with another muscle. Contrast with *antagonist* (definition 2).

synthetic   Here, a chemical that is man-made.

syrinx   The vocal organ in birds.

system   A high level of brain organization that includes specialized circuits (e.g., the visual system). Contrast with *circuit.*

T cell   type of lymphocyte that direct cell-mediate immune responses. See Figure 15.16.

T lymphocyte   An immune-system cell that attacks foreign microbes or tissue; "killer cell."

tardive dyskinesia   A disorder characterized by involuntary movements, especially involving the face, mouth, lips, and tongue. Related to prolonged use of antipsychotic drugs, such as chlorpromazine. See Box 16.1.

tastant   A substance that can be tasted.

taste aversion   See *conditioned taste aversion*.

taste bud   A cluster of 50 to 150 cells that detects tastes. Taste buds are found in papillae on the tongue.

taxonomy   The classification of organisms.

tectorial membrane   A structure in the cochlear duct. See Figure 9.2.

tectum   The dorsal portion of the midbrain, including the inferior and superior colliculi.

telencephalon   The frontal subdivision of the forebrain which includes the cerebral hemispheres when fully developed. See Figure 2.14.

temporal lobe   A major sector of the cerebral hemispheres. See Figure 2.12.

temporal summation   The summation of postsynaptic potentials that reach the axon hillock at different times. The closer together the potentials are, the more complete the summation. Contrast with *spatial summation*.

tendon   Strong tissue that connects muscles to bone.

TENS   See *transcutaneous electrical nerve stimulation*.

tensor tympani   The muscle attached to the malleus and the tympanic membrane that modulates mechanical linkage to protect the delicate receptor cells of the inner ear from damaging sounds.

testes (sing. testis)   The male gonads, which produce sperm and androgenic steroid hormones.

testosterone   A hormone, produced by male gonads, that controls a variety of bodily changes that become visible at puberty. See Figure 5.17, Table 5.2.

tetrodotoxin (TTX)   Toxin from puffer fish ovaries that blocks the voltage-gated sodium channel, preventing action potential conduction.

thalamus   The brain regions that surround the third ventricle. See Figures 2.12, 2.14.

third ventricle   The midline ventricle that conducts cerebrospinal fluid from the lateral ventricles to the fourth ventricle. See Figure 2.19.

thirst   The internal state of an animal seeking water.

thoracic   Referring to the level of the chest, here the vertebrae that have ribs attached and the spinal cord segments originating from those vertebrae.

threshold   The stimulus intensity that is just adequate to trigger a nerve impulse at the axon hillock.

thyroid gland   An endocrine gland located below the vocal apparatus in the throat that regulates metabolic processes, especially carbohydrate use and body growth. See Figure 5.1.

thyroid-stimulating hormone (TSH)   A tropic hormone, released by the anterior pituitary gland, that increases the release of thyroxine and the uptake of iodide by the thyroid gland. See Figure 5.10.

thyrotropin-releasing hormone (TRH)   A hypothalamic hormone that regulates the release of thyroid-stimulating hormone. See Figure 5.10.

thyroxine   A hormone released by the thyroid gland.

tinnitus   A sensation of noises or ringing in the ears.

tip link   A fine, threadlike fiber that runs along and connects the tips of stereocilia. See Figure 9.5.

tolerance   A condition in which, with repeated exposure to a drug, the individual becomes less responsive to a constant dose. Contrast with *sensitization*.

tomography   A technique for revealing the detailed structure of a particular tissue using radiation. Examples include computerized axial tomography (CAT or CT), and positron emission tomography (PET).

tonic receptor   A receptor in which the frequency of nerve impulse discharge declines slowly or not at all as stimulation is maintained.

tonotopic organization   A major organizational feature in auditory systems in which neurons are arranged as an orderly map of stimulus frequency, with cells responsive to high frequencies located at a distance from those responsive to low frequencies.

torpor   The condition in which animals allow body temperature to fall drastically. During torpor, animals are unresponsive to most stimuli.

Tourette's syndrome   A heightened sensitivity to tactile, auditory, and visual stimuli that may be accompanied by the buildup of an urge to emit verbal or phonic tics.

toxin   A poisonous substance, especially one that is produced by living organisms.

tract   A bundle of axons found within the central nervous system. Contrast with *nerves*.

transcription   The process during which mRNA forms bases complementary to a strand of DNA. This message is then used to translate the DNA code into protein molecules.

transcutaneous electrical nerve stimulation (TENS)   The delivery of electrical pulses through electrodes attached to the skin, which excite nerves that supply the region to which pain is referred. TENS can relieve the pain in some instances.

transducer   A device that converts energy from one form to another (e.g., sensory receptor cells).

transduction   The process of converting one form of energy to another.

transfer RNA (tRNA)   A small molecule of RNA that conveys amino acids to ribosomes for translation.

transgenic   Describing animals in which a new or altered gene has been deliberately introduced into the genome.

translation   The process by which amino acids are linked together (directed by an mRNA molecule) to form protein molecules.

transmethylation hypothesis   A hypothesized explanation of schizophrenia suggesting that the addition of a methyl group to some naturally occurring brain compounds can convert them to hallucinogenic agents, or psychotogens.

transmitter   See *synaptic transmitter*.

transporter   Specialized receptors in the presynaptic membrane that recognize transmitter molecules and return them to the presynaptic neuron for reuse.

transverse plane   See *coronal plane*.

tremor   A rhythmic, repetitive movement caused by brain pathology.

tremor-at-rest   A tremor that occurs when the affected region, such as a limb, is fully supported; a symptom of Parkinson's disease.

trichromatic hypothesis   A theory of color perception that there are three different types of cones, each excited by a different region of the spectrum and each having a separate pathway to the brain.

tricyclic antidepressants   A class of compounds whose structure resembles that of chlorpromazine and of related antipsychotic drugs. Tricyclic antidepressants may relieve depression but only after two to three weeks of daily administration.

trigger feature   A particular stimulus characteristic that is most effective in evoking responses from a particular cell.

triiodothyronine (T3)   A thyroid hormone.

trinucleotide repeat   A repetition of the same three nucleotides within a gene, which can lead to dysfunction, as in the case of Huntington's disease and fragile X syndrome.

triplet code   A code for an amino acid specified by three successive bases of a DNA molecule.

tRNA   Transfer RNA.

tropic hormone   An anterior pituitary hormone that affects the secretion of other endocrine glands. See Figure 5.14.

TRH   See *thyrotropin-releasing hormone.*

TSH   See *thyroid-stimulating hormone.*

tuning curve   A graph of the responses of a single auditory nerve fiber or neuron to sounds that vary in frequency and intensity.

turbinates   Complex shapes underlying the olfactory mucosa directing inspired air over receptor cells. See Figure 9.20.

Turner's syndrome   seen in individuals carrying a single X chromosome but no other sex chromosome.

tympanic canal   One of three principal canals running along the length of the cochlea. See Figure 9.2.

tympanic membrane   The partition between the external ear and the middle ear. Also called the eardrum. See Figure 9.1.

ultradian   Referring to a rhythmic biological event whose period is shorter than that of a circadian rhythm, usually from several minutes to several hours.

umyelinated axons   Fine-diameter axons that lack a myelin sheath.

unconditioned response (UR)   See *classical conditioning.*

unconditioned stimulus (US)   See *classical conditioning.*

unipolar depression   Depression that alternates with normal emotional states. Contrast with *bipolar depression.*

urethra   The duct that carries urine from the bladder to outside the body.

uterus   The organ in which the fertilized egg implants and develops in mammals. See Figures 12.7, 12.15.

utricle   A small, fluid-filled sac in the vestibular system that responds to static positions of the head. See Figure 9.14.

vagina   The opening in female genitalia that permits entry of the penis during copulation and later releases the fetus or egg. See Figures 12.7, 12.15.

vagus nerve   The tenth cranial nerve. See Figures 2.9, 13.28.

vas deferens (pl. vasa deferentia)   A duct that connects the epididymis to the seminal vesicles. See Figures 12.7, 12.15.

vasopressin   A peptide hormone that promotes water conservation and increases blood pressure. Also called arginine vasopressin or antidiuretic hormone.

ventral   An anatomical term referring to structures toward the belly or front of the body or the bottom of the brain. Contrast with *dorsal.* See Box 2.2.

ventral root   See *roots.*

ventricles   See *cerebral ventricles.*

ventricular system   A system of fluid-filled cavities inside the brain. See Figure 2.19.

ventricular zone   Region lining the ventricles which displays mitosis, providing neurons early in development and glia throughout life. See Figure 7.5c.

ventromedial hypothalamus (VMH)   A hypothalamic region involved in inhibiting eating, among other functions. See Figures 12.6, 13.24.

vertebral arteries   Arteries that ascend the vertebrae, enter the base of the skull, and join together to form the basilar artery. See Figure 2.20.

vestibular canal   One of three principal canals running along the length of the cochlea. See Figure 9.14.

vestibular nuclei   Brain stem nuclei which receive information from the vestibular organs through the eighth cranial nerve.

vestibular system   A receptor system in the inner ear that responds to mechanical forces, such as gravity and acceleration. See Figure 9.14.

vestibulo-ocular reflex   A rapid response that adjusts the eye to a change in head position.

visual acuity   Sharpness of vision.

visual agnosia   A condition, following stroke, in which the ability to identify familiar objects visually is lost.

visual cortex   See *occipital cortex.*

visual field   The whole area that you can see without moving your head or eyes.

viviparity   Reproduction in which the zygote develops extensively within the female until a well-formed individual emerges; "live birth." Contrast with *oviparity.*

VMH   See *ventromedial hypothalamus.*

VNO   See *vomeronasal organ.*

volley theory   A theory of frequency discrimination that emphasizes the relation between sound frequency and the firing pattern of nerve cells. For example, a 500-Hz tone would produce 500 neural discharges per second by a nerve cell or group of nerve cells. Contrast with *place theory.*

voltage-gated channnel   An ion channel that opens or closes in response to the voltage difference across the membrane, as the voltage-gated Na+ channel that mediates the action potential.

voltametry   A technique in which electrical current is monitored to measure biochemical levels in a brain region.

vomeronasal organ (VNO)   A collection of specialized receptor cells near but separate from the olfactory epithelium. These sensory cells detect pheromones and send electrical signals to the accessory olfactory bulb in the brain.

vomeronasal system   Specialized chemical detection system to detect pheromones and transmit information to the brain.

vulva   The region around the opening of the vagina.

W cells   A retinal ganglion cell that has sluggish and variable responses to visual stimuli.

Wallerian degeneration   See *anterograde degeneration.*

Wada test   Test in which a short-lasting anesthetic is delivered into one carotid artery to determine which cerebral hemisphere mediates language. See Box 19.1.

wavelength   Here, the length between two peaks in a repeated stimulus such as a wave or light or sound. See Box 9.1.

Wernicke's aphasia   A language impairment that is characterized by fluent, meaningless speech and little language comprehension; related to damage to Wernicke's area.

Wernicke's area   A region of the left hemisphere that is involved in language comprehension. See Figures 19.6, 19.8.

whisker barrel   A barrel-shaped column of somatosensory cortex that receives information from a particular whisker. See Figure 7.20.

white matter   A shiny layer underneath the cortex that consists largely of axons with white myelin sheaths. See Figures 2.12, 2.13. Contrast with *gray matter.*

Williams syndrome   A disorder characterized by largely intact, even fluent linguistic function, but clear mental retardation on standard IQ tests. Individuals suffering from this syndrome have great difficulty in copying a pattern of blocks, or assembling a picture from its parts.

withdrawal symptom   An uncomfortable symptom that arises when a person stops taking a drug that he or she has used frequently, especially at high doses.

Wolffian duct   A primitive duct system in the embryo that will develop into male structures (the epididymis, vas deferens, and seminal vesicles) if testes are present in the embryo. Contrast with *müllerian duct.* See Figure 12.15.

word blindness   The inability to recognize written words.

word deafness   Specific inability to hear words although other sounds can be detected.

X cell   A retinal ganglion cell that continues to respond to maintained visual stimuli.

Y cell   Retinal ganglion cell that responds strongly initially, but rapidly decreases its frequency of response as the visual stimulus is maintained.

zeitgeber   Literally "time-giver"; the stimulus that entrains circadian rhythms, usually the light/dark cycle.

Zucker strain   A strain of rats that display obesity.

zygote   The fertilized egg.

References

Aarons, L. (1976). Sleep-assisted instruction. *Psychological Bulletin, 83,* 1–40.

Aaronson, S. T., Rashed, S., Biber, M. P., & Hobson, J. A. (1982). Brain state and body position. A time-lapse video study of sleep. *Archives of General Psychiatry, 39,* 330–335.

Abdullaev, Y. G., & Posner, M. I. (1998). Event-related brain potential imaging of semantic encoding during processing single words. *Neuroimage, 7,* 1–13.

Abel, E. L. (1982). Consumption of alcohol during pregnancy: a review of effects on growth and development of offspring. *Human Biology, 54,* 421–453.

Abel, E. I. (1984). Prenatal effects of alcohol. *Drug and Alcohol Dependence, 14,* 1–10.

Abraham, S. F., Baker, R. M., Blaine, E. H., Denton, D. A., & McKinley, M. J. (1975). Water drinking induced in sheep by angiotensin—a physiological or pharmacological effect? *Journal of Comparative and Physiological Psychology, 88,* 503–518.

Abraham, W. C., Dragunow, M., & Tate, W. P. (1991). The role of immediate early genes in the stabilization of long-term potentiation. *Molecular Neurobiology, 5,* 297–314.

Abraham, W. C., & Goddard, G. V. (1985). Multiple traces of neural activity in the hippocampus. In N. M. Weinberger, J. L. McGaugh, & G. Lynch (eds.), *Memory systems of the brain* (pp. 62–76). New York: Guilford.

Adelson, E. H. (1993). Perceptual organization and the judgment of brightness. *Science, 262,* 2042–2044.

Ader, R. (1985). Conditioned immunopharmacological effects in animals: Implications for a conditioning model of pharmacotherapy. In L. White, B. Tursky, & G. E. Schwartz (eds.), *Placebo* (pp. 306–332). New York: Guilford.

Ader, R., & Cohen, N. (1993). Psychoneuroimmunology: Conditioning and stress. *Annual Review of Psychology, 44,* 53–85.

Ader, R., Felten, D., & Cohen, N. (1990). Interactions between the brain and the immune system. *Annual Review of Pharmacology & Toxicology, 30,* 561–602.

Adler, N., & Matthews, K. (1994). Health psychology: why do some people get sick and some stay well? *Annual Review of Psychology, 45,* 229–259.

Adolphs, R., Tranel, D., & Damasio, A. R. (1998). The human amygdala in social judgment. *Nature, 393,* 470–474.

Adolphs, R., Tranel, D., Damasio, H., & Damasio, A. (1994). Impaired recognition of emotion in facial expressions following bilateral damage to the human amygdala. *Nature, 372,* 669–672.

Aggleton, J. P. (1993). The contribution of the amygdala to normal and abnormal emotional states. *Trends in Neurosciences, 16,* 328–333.

Ahlgren, J. A., Cheng, C. C., Schrag, J. D., & DeVries, A. L. (1988). Freezing avoidance and the distribution of antifreeze glycopeptides in body fluids and tissues of Antarctic fish. *Journal of Experimental Biology, 137,* 549–563.

Akbarian, S., Kim, J. J., Potkin, S. G., Hagman, J. O., Tafazzoli, A., Bunney, W. E. Jr., & Jones, E. G. (1995). Gene expression for glutamic acid decarboxylase is reduced without loss of neurons in prefrontal cortex of schizophrenics. *Archives of General Psychiatry, 52,* 267–278.

Akbarian, S., Kim, J. J., Potkin, S. G., Hetrick, W. P., Bunney, W. E. Jr., & Jones, E. G. (1996). Maldistribution of interstitial neurons in prefrontal white matter of the brains of schizophrenic patients. *Archives of General Psychiatry, 53,* 425–436.

al-Barazanji, K. A., Buckingham, R. E., Arch, J. R., Haynes, A., Mossakowska, D. E., McBay, D. L., Holmes, S. D., McHale, M. T., Wang, X. M., & Gloger, I. S. (1997). Effects of intracerebroventricular infusion of leptin in obese Zucker rats. *Obesity Research, 5,* 387–394.

Albert, S. M., Gurland, B., Maestre, G., Jacobs, D. M., Stern, Y., & Mayeux, R. (1995). APOE genotype influences functional status among elderly without dementia. *American Journal of Medical Genetics, 60,* 583–587.

Alberts, J. R. (1978). Huddling by rat pups: Multisensory control of contact behavior. *Journal of Comparative and Physiological Psychology, 92,* 220–230.

Alberts, J. R., & Brunjes, P. C. (1978). Ontogeny of thermal and olfactory determinants of huddling in the rat. *Journal of Comparative Physiology & Psychology, 92,* 89–906.

Aldrich, M. A. (1993). The neurobiology of narcolepsy-cataplexy. *Progress in Neurobiology, 41,* 533–541.

Alexander, B. K., & Hadaway, P. F. (1982). Opiate addiction: The case for an adaptive orientation. *Psychological Bulletin, 92,* 367–381.

Alho, H., Varga, V., & Krueger, K. E. (1994). Expression of mitochondrial benzodiazepine receptor and its putative endogenous ligand diazepam binding inhibitor in cultured primary astrocytes and C-6 cells: relation to cell growth. *Cell Growth and Differentiation, 5,* 1005–1014.

Almada, S. J., Zonderman, A. B., Shekelle, R. B., Dyer, A. R., Daviglus, M. L., Costa, P. T. Jr., & Stamler, J. (1991). Neuroticism and cynicism and risk of death in middle-aged men: The Western Electric Study. *Psychosomatic Medicine, 53,* 165–175.

Alpert, M., & Friedhoff, A. J. (1980). An un-dopamine hypothesis of schizophrenia. *Schizophrenia Bulletin, 6,* 387–390.

American Academy of Ophthalmology. (1994). Amblyopia: etiology, diagnosis, and treatment. *Journal of Ophthalmic Nursing and Technology, 13,* 273–275.

American Psychiatric Association. (1994). *Diagnostic and statistical manual of mental disorders: DSM-IV. 4th Ed.* Washington, D.C.: American Psychiatric Association.

Amos, L. A., & Cross, R. A. (1997). Structure and dynamics of molecular motors. *Current Opinion in Structural Biology, 7,* 239–246.

Anand, B. K., & Brobeck, J. R. (1951). Localization of a "feeding center" in the hypothalamus of the rat. *Proceedings of the Society for Experimental Biology and Medicine, 77,* 323–324.

Andersen, P. M., Nilsson, P., Ala-Hurula, V., Keranen, M. L., Tarvainen, I., Haltia, T., Nilsson, L., Binzer, M., Forsgren, L., & Marklund, S. L. (1995). Amyotrophic lateral sclerosis associated with homozygosity for an Asp90Ala mutation in CuZn-superoxide dismutase. *Nature Genetics, 10,* 61–66.

Andreasen, N. C. (1991). Assessment issues and the cost of schizophrenia. *Schizophrenia Bulletin, 17,* 475–481.

Andreasen, N. C. (1984). *The broken brain: the biological revolution in psychiatry*. New York: Harper & Row.

Andreasen, N. C. (1994). Changing concepts of schizophrenia and the ahistorical fallacy. *American Journal of Psychiatry, 151*, 1405–1407.

Andreasen, N. C. (1989). Neural mechanisms of negative symptoms. *British Journal of Psychiatry (Supplement), Nov(7)*, 93–99.

Andreasen, N. C., Flaum, M., Swayze 2d, V. O. D. S., Alliger, R., Cohen, G., Ehrhardt, J., & Yuh, W. T. (1993). Intelligence and brain structure in normal individuals. *American Journal of Psychiatry, 150*, 130–134.

Andreasen, N. C., O'Leary, D. S., Arndt, S., Cizadlo, T., Hurtig, R., Rezai, K., Watkins, G. L., Ponto, L. B., & Hichwa, R. D. (1996). Neural substrates of facial recognition. *Journal of Neuropsychiatry and Clinical Neurosciences, 8*, 139–146.

Andreasen, N. C., Rezai, K., Alliger, R., Swayze, V. W.2d, Flaum, M., Kirchner, P., Cohen, G., & O'Leary, D. S. (1992). Hypofrontality in neuroleptic-naive patients and in patients with chronic schizophrenia. Assessment with xenon 133 single-photon emission computed tomography and the Tower of London. *Archives of General Psychiatry, 49*, 943–958.

Andreasen, N., Nassrallah, H. A., Dunn, V., Olson, S. C., Grove, W. M., Ehrhardt, J. C., Coffman, J. A., & Crossett, J. H. W. (1986). Structural abnormalities in the frontal system in schizophrenia. *Archives of General Psychiatry, 43*, 136–144.

Angier, N. (1992). A potent peptide prompts an urge to cuddle. *The New York Times*.

Anholt, R. R. (1993). Molecular neurobiology of olfaction. *Critical Reviews in Neurobiology, 7*, 1–22.

Arbas, E. A., Meinertzhagen, I. A., & Shaw, S. R. (1991). Evolution in nervous systems. *Annual Review of Neuroscience, 14*, 9–38.

Arendt, J., Skene, D. J., Middleton, B., Lockley, S. W., & Deacon, S. (1997). Efficacy of melatonin treatment in jet lag, shift work, and blindness. *Journal of Biological Rhythms, 12*, 604–617.

Arnold, A. P. (1980). Sexual differences in the brain. *American Scientist, 68*, 165–173.

Arnold, A. P., & Schlinger, B. A. (1993). Sexual differentiation of brain and behavior: The zebra finch is not just a flying rat. *Brain, Behavior, and Evolution, 42*, 231–241.

Aroniadou, V. A., Maillis, A., & Stefanis, C. C. (1993). Dihydropyridine-sensitive calcium channels are involved in the induction of N-methyl-D-aspartate receptor-independent long-term potentiation in visual cortex of adult rats. *Neuroscience Letters, 151*, 77–80.

Asberg, M., Nordstrom, P., & Traskman-Bendz, L. (1986). Cerebrospinal fluid studies in suicide. An overview. *Annals of the New York Academy of Sciences, 487*, 243–255.

Aserinsky, E., & Kleitman, N. (1953). Regularly occurring periods of eye motility, and concomitant phenomena, during sleep. *Science, 118*, 273–274.

Ashmore, J. F. (1994). The cellular machinery of the cochlea. *Experimental Physiology, 79*, 113–134.

Atkinson, M. A., Bowman, M. A., Campbell, L., Darrow, B. L., Kaufman, D. L., & Maclaren, N. K. (1994). Cellular immunity to a determinant common to glutamate decarboxylase and coxsackie virus in insulin-dependent diabetes. *Journal of Clinical Investigation, 94*, 2125–2129.

Atkinson, M. A., & Maclaren N. K. (1994). The pathogenesis of insulin-dependent diabetes mellitus. *New England Journal of Medicine, 331*, 1428–1436.

Avan, P., Loth, D., Menguy, C., & Teyssou, M. (1992). Hypothetical roles of middle ear muscles in the guinea-pig. *Hearing Research, 59*, 59–69.

Azar, B. (1995). NIAAA: 25 years of alcohol research. *American Psychological Association Monitor, 26*, 5, 23.

Azar, B. (1998). Why can't this man feel whether or not he's standing up? *American Psychological Association Monitor*, 18–20.

Bach-y-Rita, P. (1992). Recovery from brain damage. *Journal of Neurologic Rehabilitation, 6*, 191–199.

Baddeley, A. D., & Warrington, E. K. (1970). Amnesia and the distinction between long- and short-term memory. *Journal of Verbal Learning & Verbal Behavior, 9*, 176–189.

Bailey, J. M., & Bell, A. P. (1993). Familiality of female and male homosexuality. *Behavior Genetics, 23*, 313–322.

Ball, G. F., & Hulse, S. H. (1998). Birdsong. *American Psychologist, 53*, 37–58.

Ballantine, H. T., Bouckoms, A. J., Thomas, E. K., & Giriunas, I. E. (1987). Treatment of psychiatric illness by stereotactic cingulotomy. *Biological Psychiatry, 22*, 807–820.

Baltes, P. B. (1997). On the incomplete architecture of human ontogeny: selection, optimization, and compensation as foundation of developmental theory. *American Psychologist, 52*(4), 366–380.

Bancaud, J., Brunet-Bourgin, F., Chauvel, P., & Halgren, E. (1994). Anatomical origin of deja vu and vivid 'memories' in human temporal lobe. *Brain, 117*, 71–90.

Bannon, A. W., Decker, M. W., Holladay, M. W., Curzon, P., Donnelly-Roberts, D., Puttfarcken, P. S., Bitner, R. S., Diaz, A., Dickenson, A. H., Porsolt, R. D., Williams, M., & Arneric, S. P. (1998). Broad-spectrum, non-opioid analgesic activity by selective modulation of neuronal nicotinic acetylcholine receptors. *Science, 279*, 77–81.

Baptista, L. F. (1996). Nature and its nurturing in avian vocal development. In D. E. Kroodsma & E. H. Miller (eds.), *Ecology and evolution of acoustic communication in birds*. (pp. 39–60). Cornell University Press, Ithaca, NY.

Baptista, L., & Petrinovich, L. (1986). Song development in the white-crowned sparrow: social factors and sex differences. *Animal Behaviour, 34*(5), 1359–1371.

Barbour, H. G. (1912). Die Wirkung unmittelbarer Erwärmung und Abkühlung der Warmenzentren auf die Korpertemperatur. *Archiv Fur Experimentalle Pathologie Und Pharmakologie, 70*, 1–26.

Barden, N., Reul, J. M., & Holsboer, F. (1995). Do antidepressants stabilize mood through actions on the hypothalamic-pituitary-adrenocortical system? *Trends in Neurosciences, 18*, 6–11.

Bark, N. M. (1988). On the history of schizophrenia. Evidence of its existence before 1800. *New York State Journal of Medicine, 88*, 374–383.

Barkow, J. H., Cosmides, L., & Tooby, J. (1992). *The adapted mind: Evolutionary psychology and the generation of culture*. New York: Oxford University Press.

Barlow, H. B. (1953). Summation and inhibition in the frog's retina. *Journal of Physiology (London), 119*, 69–88.

Barnes, B. M. (1989). Freeze avoidance in a mammal: body temperatures below 0°C in an Arctic hibernator. *Science, 244*, 1593–1595.

Barnett, S. A. (1975). *The rat: A study in behavior*. Chicago: University of Chicago Press.

Barr, E., & Leiden, J. M. (1991). Systemic delivery of recombinant proteins by genetically modified myoblasts. *Science, 254*, 1507–1509.

Barrionuevo, G., Schottler, F., & Lynch, G. (1980). The effects of repetitive low frequency stimulation on control and "potentiated" synaptic responses in the hippocampus. *Life Sciences, 27*, 2385–2391.

Bartoshuk, L. M. (1993). Genetic and pathological taste variation: what can we learn from animal models and human disease? In D. Chadwick, J. Marsh, & J. Goode (eds.), *The molecular basis of smell and taste transduction* (pp. 251–267). New York: John Wiley & Sons.

Bartoshuk, L. M., & Beauchamp, G. K. (1994). Chemical senses. *Annual Review of Psychology, 45*, 419–449.

Bartoshuk, L. M., Fast, K., Karrer, T. A., Marino, S., Price, R. A., & Reed, D. A. (1992). PROP supertasters and the perception of sweetness and bitterness. *Chem.Senses, 17*, 594.

Basbaum, A., & Fields, H. L. (1978). Endogenous pain control mechanisms: Review and hypothesis. *Annals of Neurology, 4*, 451–462.

Basbaum, A., & Fields, H. L. (1984). Endogenous pain control systems: Brainstem spinal pathways and endorphin circuitry. *Annual Review of Neuroscience, 7*, 309–339.

Basil, J. A., Kamil, A. C., Balda, R. P., & Fite, K. V. (1996). Differences in hippocampal volume among food storing corvids. *Brain, Behavior, and Evolution, 47*, 156–164.

Baskerville, K. A., Schweitzer, J. B., & Herron, P. (1997). Effects of cholinergic depletion on experience-dependent plasticity in the cortex of the rat. *Neuroscience, 80*(4), 1159–1169.

Baumgardner, T. L., Green, K. E., & Reiss, A. L. (1994). A behavioral neurogenetics approach to developmental disabilities: gene-brain-behavior associations. *Current Opinion in Neurology, 7*, 172–178.

Bavelier, D., Corina, D., Jezzard, P., Padmanabhan, S., Clark, V. P., Karni, A., Prinster, A., Braun, A., Lalwani, A., Rauschecker, J. P., Turner, R., & Neville, H. (1997). Sentence reading: A functional MRI study at 4 tesla. *Journal of Cognitive Neuroscience, 9*, 664–686.

Beach, F. A. (1971). Hormonal factors controlling the differentiation, development, and display of copulatory behavior in the ramstergig and related species. In E. Tobach, L. R. Aronson, & E. Shaw (eds.), *The Biopsychology of Development* (pp. 249–296). New York: Academic Press.

Beach, F. A. (1977). *Human sexuality in four perspectives.* Baltimore: Johns Hopkins University Press.

Beach, F. A., & Holz, A. M. (1946). Mating behavior in male rats castrated at various ages and injected with androgen. *Journal of Experimental Zoology, 101*, 91–142.

Bear, M. F., & Malenka, R. C. (1994). Synaptic plasticity. *Current Opinion in Neurobiology, 4*, 389–399.

Beauchamp, G. K., Cowart, B. J., Mennella, J. A., & Marsh, R. R. (1994). Infant salt taste: developmental, methodological, and contextual factors. *Developmental Psychobiology, 27*, 353–365.

Beggs, W. D., & Foreman, D. L. (1980). Sound localization and early binaural experience in the deaf. *British Journal of Audiology, 14*, 41–48.

Bekkers, J. M., & Stevens, C. F. (1990). Presynaptic mechanism for long-term potentiation in the hippocampus. *Nature, 346*, 724–729.

Bellinger, D. C., Stiles, K. M., & Needleman, H. L. (1992). Low-level lead exposure, intelligence and academic achievement: a long-term follow-up study. *Pediatrics, 90*, 855–861.

Bellinger, D. L., Ackerman, K. D., Felten, S. Y., & Felten, D. L. (1992). A longitudinal study of age-related loss of noradrenergic nerves and lymphoid cells in the rat spleen. *Experimental Neurology, 116* , 295–311.

Bellugi, U., Poizner, H., & Klima, E. S. (1983). Brain organization for language: clues from sign aphasia. *Human Neurobiology, 2*, 155–171.

Belluscio, L., Gold, G. H., Nemes, A., & Axel, R. (1998). Mice deficient in G(olf) are anosmic. *Neuron, 20*, 69–81.

Bennett, A. F., & Ruben, J. A. (1979). Endothermy and activity in vertebrates. *Science, 206*, 649–654.

Bennett, E. L., Diamond, M. L., Krech, D., & Rosenzweig, M. R. (1964). Chemical and anatomical plasticity of brain. *Science, 146*, 610–619.

Bennett, E. L., Orme, A. E., & Hebert, M. (1972). Cerebral protein synthesis inhibition and amnesia produced by scopolamine, cycloheximide, streptovitacin A, anisomycin, and emetine in rat. *Federation Proceedings, 31*, 838.

Bennett, E. L., Rosenzweig, M. R., & Diamond, M. C. (1969). Rat brain: effects of environmental enrichment on wet and dry weights. *Science, 163*, 825–826.

Bennett, W. (1983). The nicotine fix. *Rhode Island Medical Journal, 66*, 455–458.

Berger, T. W., & Orr, W. B. (1983). Hippocampectomy selectively disrupts discrimination reversal conditioning of the rabbit nictitating membrane response. *Behavioural Brain Research, 8*, 49–68.

Berman, D., Derasmo, M. J., Marti, A., & Berman, A. J. (1978). Unilateral forelimb deafferentiation in the monkey: purposive movement. *Journal of Medical Primatology, 7*, 106–113.

Berman, K. F., & Weinberger, D. R. (1990). The prefrontal cortex in schizophrenia and other neuropsychiatric diseases: *in vivo* physiological correlates of cognitive deficits. *Progress in Brain Research, 85*, 521–536.

Bernhardt, P. C. (1997). Influences of serotonin and testosterone in aggression and dominance: Convergence with social psychology. *Current Directions in Psychological Science, 2*, 44–48.

Bernstein-Goral, H., & Bregman, B. S. (1993). Spinal cord transplants support the regeneration of axotomized neurons after spinal cord lesions at birth: a quantitative double-labeling study. *Experimental Neurology, 123*, 118–132.

Bernstein, I. S., & Gordon, T. P. (1974). The function of aggression in primate societies. *American Scientist, 62*, 304–311.

Besedovsky, H. O., & del Rey, A. (1992). Immune-neuroendocrine circuits: integrative role of cytokines. *Frontiers of Neuroendocrinology, 13*, 61–94.

Besedovsky, H. O., del Rey, A. E., & Sorkin, E. (1985). Immune-neuroendocrine interactions. *Journal of Immunology, 135*, 750s–754s.

Bigelow, L., Nasrallah, H. A., & and Rauscher, F. P. (1983). Corpus callosum thickness in chronic schizophrenia. *British Journal of Psychiatry, 142*, 284–287.

Binder, J. R., Rao, S. M., Hammeke, T. A., Yetkin, F. Z., Jesmanowicz, A., Bandettini, P. A., Wong, E. C., Estkowski, L. D., Goldstein, M. D., Haughton, V. M. et al. (1994). Functional magnetic resonance imaging of human auditory cortex. *Annals of Neurology, 35*, 662–672.

Bingman, V. P. (1993). Vision, cognition, and the avian hippocampus. In H. P. Zeigler, & J.-J. Bischof (eds.), *Vision, brain, and behavior in birds* (pp. 391–408). Cambridge, MA: MIT Press.

Birnbaumer, L., Abramowitz, J., & Brown, A. M. (1990). Receptor–effector coupling by G proteins. *Biochimica Et Biophysica Acta, 1031*, 163–224.

Bjorklund, A., Hokfelt, T., & Kuhar, M. J. (1992). *Neuropeptide receptors in the CNS.* Amsterdam, New York: Elsevier.

Black, J. E., & Greenough, W. T. (1986). Developmental approaches to the memory process. In J. L. Martinez, & R. P. Kesner (eds.), *Learning and memory: A biological view.* New York: Academic Press.

Blakemore, C. (1976). The conditions required for the maintenance of binocularity in the kitten's visual cortex. *Journal of Physiology (London), 261*, 423–444.

Blakemore, C., & Campbell, F. W. (1969). On the existence of neurones in the human visual system selectively sensitive to the orientation and size of retinal images. *Journal of Physiology (London), 203*, 237–260.

Blalock, J. E. (1984). The immune system as a sensory organ. *Journal of Immunology, 132*, 1067–1070.

Blaxton, T. A., Bookheimer, S. Y., Zeffiro, T. A., Figlozzi, C. M., Gaillard, W. D., & Theodore, W. H. (1996). Functional mapping of human memory using PET: Comparisons of conceptual perceptual tasks. *Canadian Journal of Experimental Psychology, 50*, 42–56.

Blaxton, T. A., Bookheimer, S. Y., Zeffiro, T. A., Figlozzi, C. M., William, D. D., & Theodore, W. H. (1996). Functional mapping of human memory using PET: Comparisons of conceptual and perceptual tasks. *Canadian Journal of Experimental Psychology, 50*, 42–56.

Blehar, M. C., & Rosenthal, N. E. (1989). Seasonal affective disorders and phototherapy Report of a National Institute of Mental Health-sponsored workshop. *Archives of General Psychiatry, 46*, 469–474.

Bleuler, E. (1952). *Dementia praecox; or, The group of schizophrenias.* New York: International Universities Press.

Bliss, T. V. P., & Collingridge, G. L. (1993). A synaptic model of memory: long-term potentiation in the hippocampus. *Nature, 361*, 31–39.

Bliss, T. V. P., & Gardner-Medwin, A. R. (1973). Long-lasting potentiation of synaptic transmission in the dentate area of the unanaesthetized rabbit following stimulation of the perforant path. *Journal of Physiology, 232*, 357–374.

Bliss, T. V. P., & Lømo, T. (1973). Long-lasting potentiation of synaptic transmission in the dentate area of the anaesthetized rabbit following stimulation of the perforant path. *Journal of Physiology (London), 232*, 331–356.

Bliwise, D. L. (1989). Neuropsychological function and sleep. *Clinics in Geriatric Medicine, 5*, 381–394.

Bloch, V. (1976). Brain activation and memory consolidation. In M. R. Rosenzweig, & E. L. Bennett (eds.), *Neural mechanisms of learning and memory.* Cambridge: MIT Press.

Bloch, V. (1970). Facts and hypotheses concerning memory consolidation processes. *Brain Research, 24*, 561–575.

Blodgett, H. C. (1929). The effect of the introduction of reward upon the maze performance of rats. *University of California Publications in Psychology, 4*, 113–134.

Blue, M. E., & Parnavelas, J. G. (1983). The formation and maturation of synapses in the visual cortex of the rat. II. Quantitative analysis. *Journal of Neurocytology, 12,* 697–712.

Blumberg, M. S., Sokoloff, G., & Kirby, R. F. (1997). Brown fat thermogenesis and cardiac rate regulation during cold challenge in infant rats. *American Journal of Physiology, 272,* R1308–R1313.

Bodnar, R. J., Kelly, D. D., Brutus, M., & Glusman, M. (1980). Stress-induced analgesia: Neural and hormonal determinants. *Neuroscience and Biobehavioral Reviews, 4,* 87–100.

Bogen, J. E., Schultz, D. H., & Vogel, P. J. (1988). Completeness of callostomy shown by magnetic resonance imaging in the long term. *Archives of Neurology, 45,* 1203–1205.

Bohus, B., & Koolhaas, J. M. (1993). Stress and the cardiovascular system: Central and peripheral physiological mechanisms. In S. C. Stanford, & P. Salmon (eds.), *Stress: From synapse to syndrome* (pp. 75–117). London: Academic Press.

Bonese, K. F., Wainer, B. H., Fitch, F. W., Rothberg, R. M., & Schuster, C. R. (1974). Changes in heroin self-administration by a rhesus monkey after morphine immunisation. *Nature, 252,* 708–710.

Bonhoeffer, F., & Huf, J. (1985). Position-dependent properties of retinal axons and their growth cones. *Nature, 315,* 409–410.

Bonhoeffer, T., & Grinvald, A. (1991). Iso-orientation domains in cat visual cortex are arranged in pinwheel-like patterns. *Nature, 353,* 429–431.

Boolell, M., Allen, M. J., Ballard, S. A., Gepi-Attee, S., Muirhead, G. J., Naylor, A. M., Osterloh, I. H., & Gingell, C. (1996). Sildenafil: An orally active type 5 cyclic GMP-specific phosphodiesterase inhibitor for the treatment of penile erectile dysfunction. *International Journal of Impotence Research, 8,* 47–52.

Bothwell, M. (1995). Functional interactions of neurotrophins and neurotrophin receptors. *Annual Review of Neuroscience, 18,* 223–253.

Bottjer, S. W., Miesner, E. A., & Arnold, A. P. (1984). Forebrain lesions disrupt development but not maintenance of song in passerine birds. *Science, 224,* 901–903.

Bourtchuladze, R., Frenguelli, B., Blendy, J., Cioffi, D., Schutz, G., & Silva, A. J. (1994). Deficient long-term memory in mice with a targeted mutation of the cAMP-responsive element-binding protein. *Cell, 79,* 59–68.

Bowmaker, J. K. (1984). Microspectrophotometry of vertebrate photoreceptors. A brief review. *Vision Research, 24,* 1641–1650.

Brain, P. F. (1994). Hormonal aspects of aggression and violence. In A. J. Reiss Jr., K. A. Miczek, & J. A. Roth (eds.), *Understanding and preventing violence, Vol. 2: Biobehavioral influences* (pp. 173–244). Washington, D. C.: National Academy Press.

Brasel, J. A., & Blizzard, R. M. (1974). The influence of the endocrine glands upon growth and development. In R. H. Williams (ed.), *Textbook of endocrinology.* Philadelphia: Saunders.

Bray, G. A. (1969). Effect of caloric restriction on energy expenditure in obese patients. *Lancet, 2,* 397–398.

Breier, A., Su, T. P., Saunders, R., Carson, R. E., Kolachana, B. S., De Bartolomeis, A., Weinberger, D. R., Weisenfeld, N., Malhotra, A. K., Eckelman, W. C., & Pickar, D. (1997). Schizophrenia is associated with elevated amphetamine-induced synaptic dopamine concentrations: Evidence from a novel positron emission method. *Proceedings of the National Academy of Sciences U.S.A., 94,* 2569–2574.

Bremner, J. D., Randall, P., Scott, T. M., Bronen, R. A., Seibyl, J. P., Southwick, S. M., Delaney, R. C., McCarthy, G., Charney, D. S., & Innis, R. B. (1995). MRI-based measurement of hippocampal volume in patients with combat-related posttraumatic stress disorder. *American Journal of Psychiatry, 152,* 973–981.

Bremner, J. D., Scott, T. M., Delaney, R. C., Southwick, S. M., Mason, J. W., Johnson, D. R., Innis, R. B., McCarthy, G., & Charney, D. S. (1993). Deficits in short-term memory in posttraumatic stress disorder. *American Journal of Psychiatry, 150,* 1015–1019.

Brennan, P., Kaba, H., & Keverne, E. B. (1990). Olfactory recognition: a simple memory system. *Science, 250,* 1223–1226.

Brenowitz, E. A. (1991). Altered perception of species-specific song by female birds after lesions of a forebrain nucleus. *Science, 251,* 303–305.

Brenowitz, E. A. (1991). Evolution of the vocal control system in the avian brain. *Seminars in the Neurosciences, 3,* 399–407.

Brenowitz, E. A., & Arnold, A. (1986). Interspecific comparisons of the size of neural song control regions and song complexity in dueting birds: Evolutionary implications. *Journal of Neuroscience, 6,* 2875–2879.

Brewer, J. B., Zhao, Z., Desmond, J. E., Glover, G. H., & Gabrieli, J. D. E. (1998). Making memories: Brain activity that predicts how well visual experience will be remembered. *Science, 281,* 1185–1187.

Brien, J. A. (1993). Ototoxicity associated with salicylates. A brief review. *Drug Safety, 9,* 143–148.

Broberg, D. J., & Bernstein, I. L. (1989). Cephalic insulin release in anorexic women. *Physiology and Behavior, 45,* 871–874.

Brodmann, K. (1909). *Vergleichende Lokisationslehre der Grosshirnrinde in ihren Prinzipien dargestellt auf Grund des Zellenbaues.* Leipzig: Barth.

Brook, J. S., Cohen, P., Whiteman, M., & Gordon, A. S. (1992). Psychosocial risk factors in the transition from moderate to heavy use or abuse of drugs. In M. D. Glantz, & R. W. Pickens (eds.), *Vulnerability to drug use* (pp. 359–388). Washington, D.C.: American Psychological Association.

Brooks, V. B. (1984). Cerebellar function in motor control. *Human Neurobiology, 2,* 251–260.

Broughton, R. (1985). Slow-wave sleep awakenings in normal and in pathology: A brief review. In W. P. Koella, E. Ruther, & H. Schulz (eds.), *Sleep '84* (pp. 164–167). Stuttgart: Gustav Fischer Verlag.

Brown, G. L., Goodwin, F. K., Ballenger, J. C., Goyer, P. F., & Major, L. F. (1979). Aggression in humans correlates with cerebrospinal fluid amine metabolites. *Psychiatry Research, 1,* 131–139.

Brown, J. (1958). Some tests of the decay theory of immediate memory. *Quarterly Journal of Experimental Psychology, 10,* 12–21.

Brown, T. H., Zador, A. M., Mainen, Z. F., & Claiborne, B. J. (1992). Hebbian computations in hippocampal dendrites and spines. In T. M. McKenna, J. Davis, & S. F. Zornetzer (eds.), *Single neuron computation. Neural nets: Foundations to applications* (pp. 81–116). Boston: Academic Press.

Brown, W. L. (1968). An hypothesis concerning the function of the metapleural gland in ants. *American Naturalist, 102,* 188–191.

Brownell, W. E., Bader, C. R., Bertrand, D., & de Ribaupierre, Y. (1985). Evoked mechanical responses of isolated cochlear outer hair cells. *Science, 227,* 194–196.

Brownlee, S., & Schrof, J. M. (1997). The quality of mercy. Effective pain treatments already exist. Why aren't doctors using them? *U.S. News and World Report, 122,* 54–67.

Brunet, L. J., Gold, G. H., & Ngai, J. (1996). General anosmia caused by a targeted disruption of the mouse olfactory cyclic nucleotide-gated cation channel. *Neuron, 17,* 681–93.

Bryden, M. P. (1982). *Laterality: Functional asymmetry in the intact brain.* New York: Academic.

Buchsbaum, M., Mirsky, A., DeLisi, L. E., Morihisa, J., Karson, C., Mendelson, W., Johnson, J., King, A., & Kessler, R. (1984). The Genain quadruplets: Electrophysiological, positron emission and X-ray tomographic studies. *Psychiatry Research, 13,* 95–108.

Buck, L. B. (1996). Information coding in the mammalian olfactory system. *Cold Spring Harbor Symposia on Quantitative Biology, 61,* 147–155.

Buck, L., & Axel, R. (1991). A novel multigene family may encode odorant receptors: a molecular basis for odor recognition. *Cell, 65,* 175–187.

Buckner, R. L., Bandettini, P. A., O'Craven, K. M., Savoy, R. L., Petersen, S. E., Raichle, M. E., & Rosen, B. R. (1996). Detection of cortical activation during averaged single trials of a cognitive task using functional magnetic resonance imaging. *Proceedings of the National Academy of Sciences U.S.A., 93,* 14878–14883.

Buckner, R. L. (1996). Beyond HERA: Contributions of specific prefrontal brain areas to long-term memory retrieval. *Psychonomic Bulletin & Review, 3,* 149–158.

Buhrich, N., Bailey, J. M., & Martin, N. G. (1991). Sexual orientation, sexual identity, and sex-dimorphic behaviors in male twins. *Behavior Genetics, 21*, 75–96.

Bullock, T. H. (1984). Comparative neuroscience holds promise for quiet revolutions. *Science, 225*, 473–478.

Buss, D. M., & Malamuth, N. M. (1996). *Sex, power, conflict: Evolutionary and feminist perspectives.* New York: Oxford University Press.

Busse, E. W., & Silverman, A. J. (1952). Electroencephalographic changes in professional boxers. *Journal of the American Medical Association, 149*, 1522–1525.

Butcher, L. L. & Woolf, N. J. (1986). Central cholinergic systems: Synopsis of anatomy and overview of physiology and pathology. In A. B. Scheibel, A. F. Weschler, & M. A. B. Brazier (eds.), *The biological substrate of Alzheimer's disease* (pp. 73–86). Orlando: Academic Press.

Butler, R. A., Diamond, I. T., & Neff, W. D. (1957). Role of auditory cortex in discrimination of changes in frequency. *Journal of Neurophysiology, 20*, 108–120.

Byrne, D. G., & Whyte, H. M. (1980). Life events and myocardial infarction revisited. *Psychosomatic Medicine, 42*, 1–10.

Cabelli, R. J., Hohn, A., & Shatz, C. J. (1995). Inhibition of ocular dominance column formation by infusion of NT-4/5 or BDNF. *Science, 267*, 1662–1666.

Cacioppo, J. T., Klein, D. J., Berntson, G. G., & Hatfield, E. (1993). The psychophysiology of emotion. In M. Lewis, & J. M. Haviland (eds.), *Handbook of emotions* (pp. pps. 119–142). New York: Guilford Press.

Cadoret, R. J., O'Gorman, T., Troughton, E., & Heywood, E. (1986). An adoption study of genetic and environmental factors in drug abuse. *Arch. Gen. Psychiatry, 43*, 1131–1136.

Cahill, L. (1997). Influenced memory: Implications for understanding traumatic memory. In R. Yehuda, & A. C. McFarlane (eds.), *Psychobiology of traumatic stress disorder, Annals of the New York Academy of Sciences* Vol. 41 (pp. 238–246). New York: New York Academy of Sciences.

Cahill, L. (1997). The neurobiology of emotionally influenced memory. Implications for understanding traumatic memory. *Annals of the New York Academy of Sciences, 821*, 238–246.

Cahill, L., Prins, B., Weber, M., & McGaugh, J. L. (1994). Beta-adrenergic activation and memory for emotional events. *Nature, 371*, 702–704.

Cahill, L., & McGaugh, J. L. (1991). NMDA-induced lesions of the amygdaloid complex block the retention-enhancing effect of posttraining epinephrine. *Psychobiology, 19*, 206–210.

Calvert, G. A., Bullmore, E. T., Brammer, M. J., Campbell, R., Williams, S. C., McGuire, P. K., Woodruff, P. W., Iversen, S. D., & David, A. S. (1997). Activation of auditory cortex during silent lipreading. *Science, 276*, 593–596.

Calvin, W. H., & Ojemann, G. A. (1994). *Conversations with Neil's brain: the neural nature of thought and language.* Reading, MA: Addison-Wesley.

Campbell, F. W., & Robson, J. G. (1968). Application of Fourier analysis to the visibility of gratings. *Journal of Physiology London), 197*, 551–566.

Campbell, R. (1982). The lateralisation of emotion: A critical review. *International Journal of Psychology, 17*, 211–219.

Campbell, S. S., & Murphy, P. J. (1998). Extraocular circadian phototransduction in humans. *Science, 279*, 396–399.

Campbell, S. S., & Tobler, I. (1984). Animal sleep: A review of sleep duration across phylogeny. *Neuroscience and Biobehavioral Reviews, 8*, 269–301.

Campfield, L. A., Smith, F. J., Guisez, Y., Devos, R., & Burn, P. (1995). Recombinant mouse OB protein: evidence for a peripheral signal linking adiposity and central neural networks. *Science, 269*, 546–549.

Cannistra, L. B., Davis, S. M., & Bauman, A. G. (1997). Valvular heart disease associated with dexfenfluramine. *New England Journal of Medicine, 337*, 636.

Cannon, S. C. (1996). Ion-channel defects and aberrant excitability in myotonia and periodic paralysis. *Trends In Neurosciences, 19*(1), 3–10.

Cannon, W. B. (1929). *Bodily changes in pain, hunger, fear and rage.* New York: Appleton.

Cao, Y. Q., Mantyh, P. W., Carlson, E. J., Gillespie, A. M., Epstein, C. J., & Basbaum, A. I. (1998). Primary afferent tachykinins

are required to experience moderate to intense pain. *Nature, 392*, 390–394.

Capretta, P. J., Petersik, J. T., & Stewart, D. J. (1975). Acceptance of novel flavours is increased after early experience of diverse tastes. *Nature, 254*, 689–691.

Carew, T. J. (1989). Development assembly of learning in *Aplysia. Trends in Neurosciences,* (12), 389–394.

Carew, T. J., & Sahley, C. L. (1986). Invertebrate learning and memory: From behavior to molecule. *Annual Review of Neuroscience, 9*, 435 487.

Carlsson, A., Hansson, L. O., Waters, N., & Carlsson, M. L. (1997). Neurotransmitter aberrations in schizophrenia: New perspectives and therapeutic implications. *Life Sciences, 61*, 75–94.

Carlton, P. L., & Manowitz, P. (1984). Dopamine and schizophrenia: An analysis of the theory. *Neuroscience and Biobehavioral Reviews, 8*, 137–153.

Carter, C. S. (1992). Oxytocin and sexual behavior. *Neuroscience and Biobehavioral Reviews, 16*, 131–44.

Cartwright, R. D. (1979). The nature and function of repetitive dreams: a survey and speculation. *Psychiatry, 42*, 131–137.

Casey, D. E. (1989). Clozapine: neuroleptic-induced EPS and tardive dyskinesia. *Psychopharmacology, 99*, S47-S53.

Cassens, G., Wolfe, L., & Zola, M. (1990). The neuropsychology of depressions. *Journal of Neuropsychiatry and Clinical Neurosciences, 2*, 202–213.

Casson, I. R., Sham, R., Campbell, E. A., Tarlau, M., & Didomenico, A. (1982). Neurological and CT evaluation of knocked-out boxers. *Journal of Neurology, Neurosurgery, and Psychiatry, 45*, 170–174.

Caterina, M. J., Schumacher, M. A., Tominaga, M., Rosen, T. A., Levine, J. D., & Julius, D. (1997). The capsaicin receptor: A heat-activated ion channel in the pain pathway. *Nature, 389*, 816–24.

Caviness, V. S. (1980). The developmental consequences of abnormal cell position in the reeler mouse. *Trends in Neuroscience, 3*, 31–33.

Caza, P. A., & Spear, N. E. (1984). Short-term exposure to an odor increases its subsequent preference in preweanling rats: a descriptive profile of the phenomenon. *Developmental Psychobiology, 17*, 407–422.

Challamel, M. J., Lahlou, S., & Jouvet, M. (1985). Sleep and smiling in neonate: A new approach. In W. P. Koella, E. Ruther, & H. Schulz (eds.), *Sleep '84.* Stuttgart: Gustav Fischer Verlag.

Chang, F.-L., & Greenough, W. T. (1982). Lateralized effects of monocular training on dendritic branching in adult split-brain rats. *Brain Research, 232*, 283–292.

Chang, F. L., & Greenough, W. T. (1984). Transient and enduring morphological correlates of synaptic activity and efficacy change in the rat hippocampal slice. *Brain Research, 309*, 35–46.

Chapman, C. R., Casey, K. L., Dubner, R., Foley, K. M., Gracely, R. H., & Reading, A. E. (1985). Pain measurement: an overview. *Pain, 22*, 1–31.

Charney, D. S., Deutch, A. Y., Krystal, J. H., Southwick, S. M., & Davis, M. (1993). Psychobiologic mechanisms of posttraumatic stress disorder. *Archives of General Psychiatry, 50*, 295–305.

Chase, J. E., & Gidal, B. E. (1997). Melatonin: Therapeutic use in sleep disorders. *Annals of Pharmacotherapy, 31*, 1218–1226.

Chen, D. Y., Deutsch, J. A., Gonzalez, M. F., & Gu, Y. (1993). The induction and suppression of c-fos expression in the rat brain by cholecystokinin and its antagonist L364,718. *Neuroscience Letters, 149*, 91–94.

Cheng, H., Cao, Y., & Olson, L. (1996). Spinal cord repair in adult paraplegic rats: Partial restoration of hind limb function. *Science, 273*, 510–513.

Chiarello, C., Knight, R., & Mundel, M. (1982). Aphasia in a prelingually deaf woman. *Brain, 105*, 29–52.

Cho, Y. H., Berachochea, D., & Jaffard, R. (1993). Extended temporal gradient for the retrograde and anterograde amnesia produced by ibotenate entorhinal cortex lesions in mice. *Journal of Neuroscience, 13*, 1759–1766.

Chollet, F., & Weiller, C. (1994). Imaging recovery of function following brain injury. *Current Opinion in Neurobiology, 4*, 226–230.

Chow, K. L., & Stewart, D. L. (1972). Reversal of structural and functional effects of long-term visual deprivation in cats. *Experimental Neurology, 34,* 409–433.

Clark, W. W. (1991). Noise exposure from leisure activities: a review. *Journal of the Acoustical Society of America, 90,* 175–181.

Clayton, N. S. (1995). The neuroethological development of food-storing memory: a case of use it, or lose it. *Behavioural Brain Research, 70*(1), 95–102.

Clayton, N. S., & Krebs, J. R. (1994). Hippocampal growth and attrition in birds affected by experience. *Proceedings of the National Academy of Sciences, U.S.A., 91,* 7410–7414.

Clemens, L. G., Gladue, B. A., & Coniglio, L. P. (1978). Prenatal endogenous androgenic influences on masculine sexual behavior and genital morphology in male and female rats. *Hormones and Behavior, 10,* 40–53.

Cloninger, C. (1987). Neurogenetic adaptive mechanisms in alcoholism. *Science, 236*(4800), 410–416.

Clutton-Brock, T. H., & Harvey, P. H. (1980). Primates, brains and ecology. *Journal of Zoology, 190,* 309–323.

Coccaro, E. F., & Siever, L. J. (1995). Personality disorders. In F. E. Bloom, D. J. Kupfer, B. S. Bunney, R. D. Ciaranello, K. L. Davis, G. F. Koob, H. Y. Meltzer, C. R. Schuster, R. I. Shater et al. (eds.), *Psychopharmacology: The fourth generation of progress: An official publication of the American College of Neuropsychopharmacology* (pp. 1567–1679). New York: Raven Press.

Cohen, D. B. (1979). *Sleep and dreaming: Origin, nature and functions.* Oxford: Pergamon.

Cohen, N. J., & Squire, L. R. (1980). Preserved learning and retention of pattern-analyzing skill in amnesia: Dissociation of knowing how and knowing what. *Science, 210,* 207–210.

Cohen, S., Frank, E., Doyle, W. J., Skoner, D. P., Rabin, B. S., & Gwaltney, J. M. Jr. (1998). Types of stressors that increase susceptibility to the common cold in healthy adults. *Health Psychology, 17,* 214–223.

Cohen, S., Lichtenstein, E., Prochaska, J. O., Rossi, J. S., Gritz, E. R., Carr, C. R., Orleans, C. T., Schoenbach, V. J., Bierner, L., Abrams, D., DiClemente, C., Curry, S., Marlatt, G. A., Cummings, K. M., Emant, S. L., Giovino, G., & Ossip-Klein, D. (1989). Debunking myths about quitting: Evidence from 10 perspective studies of persons who attempt to quit smoking by themselves. *American Psychologist, 44,* 1355–1365.

Colangelo, W., & Jones, D. G. (1982). The fetal alcohol syndrome: A review and assessment of the syndrome and its neurological sequelae. *Progress in Neurobiology, 19,* 271–314.

Colley, P. A., & Routtenberg, A. (1993). Long-term potentiation as synaptic dialogue. *Brain Research Review, 18,* 115–122.

Collingridge, G. L., & Watkins, J. C. (1994). *The NMDA receptor.* New York: Oxford University Press.

Collings, V. B. (1974). Human taste response as a function of locus of stimulation on the tongue and soft palate. *Perception and Psychophysics, 16,* 169–174.

Colwill, R. M., Absher, R. A., & Roberts, M. L. (1988). Conditional discrimination learning in *Aplysia californica. Journal of Neuroscience, 8,* 4440–4444.

Conel, J. L. (1939). *The postnatal development of the human cerebral cortex. Volume 1. The cortex of the newborn.* Cambridge: Harvard.

Conel, J. L. (1947). *The postnatal development of the human cerebral cortex. Volume 3. The cortex of the three-month infant.* Cambridge, MA: Harvard University Press.

Conel, J. L. (1959). *The postnatal development of the human cerebral cortex. Volume 6. The cortex of the twenty-four-month infant.* Cambridge, MA: Harvard University Press.

Conrad, A. J., Abebe, T., Austin, R., Forsythe, S., & Scheibel, A. B. (1991). Hippocampal pyramidal cell disarray in schizophrenia as a bilateral phenomenon. *Archives of General Psychiatry, 48,* 413–417.

Constantine-Paton, M., Cline, H. T., & Debski, E. (1990). Patterned activity, synaptic convergence, and the NMDA receptor in developing visual pathways. *Annual Review of Neuroscience, 13,* 129–154.

Convit, A., de Leon, M. J., Golomb, J., George, A. E., Tarshish, C. Y., Bobinski, M., Tsui, W., De Santi, S., Wegiel, J., & Wisniewski, H. (1993). Hippocampal atrophy in early Alzheimer's disease: anatomic specificity and validation. *Psychiatric Quarterly, 64,* 371–387.

Corbett, S. W., & Keesey, R. E. (1982). Energy balance of rats with lateral hypothalamic lesions. *American Journal of Physiology, 242,* E273-E279.

Corkin, S., Amaral, D. G., Gonzalez, R. G., Johnson, K. A., & Hyman, B. T. (1997). H. M.'s medial temporal lobe lesion: Findings from magnetic resonance imaging. *Journal of Neuroscience, 17,* 3964–3979.

Corkin, S., Milner, B., & Rasmussen, T. (1970). Somatosensory thresholds: Contrasting effects of postcentral-gyrus and posterior parietal-lobe excisions. *Archives of Neurology, 23,* 41–58.

Corwin, J. T., & Oberholtzer, J. C. (1997). Fish n'chicks: Model recipes for hair-cell regeneration? *Neuron, 19,* 951–954.

Coryell, W., Noyes, R. Jr., & House, J. D. (1986). Mortality among outpatients with anxiety disorders. *American Journal of Psychiatry, 143,* 508–510.

Costanzo, R. M. (1991). Regeneration of olfactory receptor cells. *Ciba Foundation Symposium, 160,* 233–242.

Cotanche, D. A. (1987). Regeneration of hair cell stereociliary bundles in the chick cochlea following severe acoustic trauma. *Hearing Research, 30,* 181–195.

Courtney, S., Ungerleider, L., Keil, K., & Haxby, J. (1996). Object and spatial visual working memory activate separate neural systems in human cortex. *Cerebral Cortex, 6*(1), 39–49.

Cowan, W. M. (1979). The development of the brain. *Scientific American, 241*(3), 112–133.

Cragg, B. G. (1975). The development of synapses in the visual system of the cat. *Journal of Comparative Neurology, 160,* 147–166.

Craig, A. D., Reiman, E. M., Evans, A., & Bushnell, M. C. (1996). Functional imaging of an illusion of pain. *Nature, 384,* 258–260.

Craik, F. I. M. (1986). A functional account of age differences in memory. In F. Klix, & H. Hogendorf (eds.), *Human memory and cognitive capabilities. Vol. A* (pp. 409–422). Amsterdam: North-Holland.

Craik, F. I. M. (1985). Paradigms in human memory research. In L.-G. Nilsson, & T. Archer (eds.), *Perspectives on learning and memory* (pp. 197–221). Hillsdale, NJ: Lawrence Erlbaum Associates.

Crews, D. (1994). Temperature, steroids and sex determination. *Journal of Endocrinology, 142,* 1–8.

Crick, F., & Mitchison, G. (1983). The function of dream sleep. *Nature, 304,* 111–114.

Crouch, R. (1997). Letting the deaf be deaf. Reconsidering the use of cochlear implants in prelingually deaf children. *Hastings Center Report, 27*(4), 14–21.

Cruce, J. A. F., Greenwood, M. R. C., Johnson, P. R., & Quartermain, D. (1974). Genetic versus hypothalamic obesity: Studies of intake and dietary manipulation in rats. *Journal of Comparative and Physiological Psychology, 87,* 295–301.

Cummings, J. L. (1995). Dementia: the failing brain. *Lancet, 345,* 1481–1484.

Cummings, J. L., Benson, D. F., Walsh, M. J., & Levine, H. L. (1979). Left-to-right transfer of language dominance: A case study. *Neurology, 29,* 1547–1550.

Curcio, C. A., Sloan, K. R., Packer, O., Hendrickson, A. E., & Kalina, R. E. (1987). Distribution of cones in human and monkey retina: individual variability and radial asymmetry. *Science, 236,* 579–582.

Curtiss, S. (1989). The independence and task-specificity of language. In M. H. Bornstein, & J. S. Bruner (eds.), *Interaction in human development* (pp. 105–137). Hillsdale, NJ: Lawrence Erlbaum Associates.

Czeisler, C. A., Zimmerman, J. C., Ronda, J. M., Moore-Ede, M. C., & Weitzman, E. D. (1980). Timing of REM sleep is coupled to the circadian rhythm of body temperature in man. *Sleep, 2,* 329–346.

D'Amato, R. J., Alexander, G. M., Schwartzman, R. J., Kitt, C. A., Price, D. L., & Snyder, S. H. (1987). Evidence for neuromelanin involvement in MPTP-induced neurotoxicity. *Nature, 327,* 324–326.

Dabbs, J. M. Jr., & Hargrove, M. F. (1997). Age, testosterone, and behavior among female prison inmates. *Psychosomatic Medicine, 59,* 477–480.

Dabbs, J. M., & Morris, R. (1990). Testosterone, social class, and antisocial behavior in a sample of 4,462 men. *Psychological Science, 1,* 209–211.

Dabbs, J. M., Ruback, R. B., Frady, R. L., Hopper, C. H. et al. (1988). Saliva testosterone and criminal violence among women. *Personality & Individual Differences, 9,* 269–275.

Daly, M., & Wilson, M. (1978). *Sex, evolution and behavior.* North Scituate, MA: Duxbury Press.

Damasio, A. R., Chui, H. C., Corbett, J., & Kassell, N. (1980). Posterior callosal section in a non-epileptic patient. *Journal of Neurology, Neurosurgery, and Psychiatry, 43,* 351–356.

Damasio, A. R., Eslinger, P. J., Damasio, H., Van Hoesen, G. W., & Cornell, S. (1985). Multimodal amnesic syndrome following bilateral temporal and basal forebrain damage. *Archives of Neurology, 42,* 252–259.

Damasio, A. R., Graff-Radford, N. R., Eslinger, P. J., Damasio, H., & Kassell, N. (1985). Amnesia following basal forebrain lesions. *Archives of Neurology,* (42), 263–271.

Damasio, H. (1995). *Human brain anatomy in computerized images.* New York: Oxford University Press.

Damasio, H., Grabowski, T. J., Tranel, D., Hichwa, R. D., & Damasio, A. R. (1996). A neural basis for lexical retrieval [published erratum appears in *Nature* 1996 *381:*810]. *Nature, 380,* 499–505.

Damasio, H., Grabowski, T., Frank, R., Galaburda, A. M., & Damasio, A. R. (1994). The return of Phineas Gage: clues about the brain from the skull of a famous patient. *Science, 264,* 1102–1105.

Damasio, H., Tranel, D., Spradling, J., & Alliger, R. (1989). In A. M. Galaburda (ed.), *From Reading To Neurons; Conference, Florence, Italy, June 8–12.* (pp. 307–330). Cambridge, MA: MIT Press.

Dantz, B., Edgar, D. M., & Dement, W. C. (1994). Circadian rhythms in narcolepsy: studies on a 90 minute day. *Electroencephalography and Clinical Neurophysiology, 90,* 24–35.

Darian-Smith, I., Davidson, I., & Johnson, K. O. (1980). Peripheral neural representations of the two spatial dimensions of a textured surface moving over the monkey's finger pad. *Journal of Physiology, 309,* 135–146.

Dark, J., Miller, D. R., & Zucker, I. (1994). Reduced glucose availability induced torpor in Siberian hamsters. *American Journal of Physiology, 267,* R496-R501.

Darwin, C. (1872). *The expression of the emotions in man and animals.* London: J. Murray.

Darwin, C. (1859). *On the origin of species by means of natural selection, or, The preservation of favoured races in the struggle for life.* (pp. ix, 502 p., [1] folded leaf of plates). London: J. Murray.

Darwin, F. (1888). *Life and letters of Charles Darwin. Vol 3.* London: John Murray.

Davenport, J. W. (1976). Environmental therapy in hypothyroid and other disadvantaged animal populations. In R. N. Walsh, & W. T. Greenough (eds.), *Environments as therapy for brain dysfunction.* New York: Plenum.

Davey Smith, G., Frankel, S., & Yarnell, J. (1997). Sex and death: are they related? Findings from the Caerphilly Cohort Study. *British Medical Journal. Clinical Research Edition, 315,* 1641–1644.

Davidson, J. M., Camargo, C. A., & Smith, E. R. (1979). Effects of androgen on sexual behavior in hypogonadal men. *Journal of Clinical Endocrinology and Metabolism, 48,* 955–958.

Davidson, R. J. (1994). Asymmetric brain function, affective style, and psychopathology: The role of early experience and plasticity. *Development & Psychopathology, 6,* 741–758.

Davidson, R. J., Ekman, P., Saron, C. D., Senulis, J. A. et al. (1990). Approach-withdrawal and cerebral asymmetry: Emotional expression and brain physiology: I. *Journal of Personality & Social Psychology, 58,* 330–341.

Davis, H. P., & Squire, L. R. (1984). Protein synthesis and memory: A review. *Psychological Bulletin, 96,* 518–559.

Davis, K. L., Kahn, R. S., Ko, G., & Davidson, M. (1991). Dopamine in schizophrenia: a review and reconceptualization. *American Journal of Psychiatry, 148,* 1474–1486.

Daw, N. W., Brunken, W. J., & Parkinson, D. (1989). The function of synaptic transmitters in the retina. *Annual Review of Neuroscience, 12,* 205–225.

Daw, N. W., Stein, P. S., & Fox, K. (1993). The role of NMDA receptors in information processing. *Annual Review of Neuroscience, 16,* 207–22.

Dawson, D., & Encel, N. (1993). Melatonin and sleep in humans. *Journal of Pineal Research, 15,* 1–12.

de Groot, C. M., Janus, M. D., & Bornstein, R. A. (1995). Clinical predictors of psychopathology in children and adolescents with Tourette Syndrome. *Journal of Psychiatric Research, 29,* 59–70.

de Leon, M. J., Golomb, J., George, A. E., Convit, A., Tarshish, C. Y., McRae, T., De Santi, S., Smith, G., Ferris, S. H., Noz, M. et al. (1993). The radiologic prediction of Alzheimer disease: the atrophic hippocampal formation. *American Journal of Neuroradiology, 14,* 897–906.

de Paiva, A., Poulain, B., Lawrence, G. W., Shone, C. C., Tauc, L., & Dolly, J. O. (1993). A role for the interchain disulfide or its participating thiols in the internalization of botulinum neurotoxin A revealed by a toxin derivative that binds to ectoacceptors and inhibits transmitter release intracellularly. *Journal of Biological Chemistry, 268,* 20838–20844.

De Valois, K. K., De Valois, R. L., & Yund, E. W. (1979). Responses of striate cortex cells to grating and checkerboard patterns. *Journal of Physiology, 291,* 483–505.

De Valois, R. L., Albrecht, D. G., & Thorell, L. G. (1977). Spatial tuning of LGN and cortical cells in the monkey visual system. In H. Spekreijse, & H. van der Tweel (eds.), *Spatial contrast* (pp. 60–63). Amsterdam: Elsevier.

De Valois, R. L., & De Valois, K. K. (1993). A multi-stage color model. *Vision Research, 33,* 1053–1065.

De Valois, R. L., & De Valois, K. K. (1980). Spatial vision. *Annual Review of Psychology, 31,* 309–341.

De Valois, R. L., & De Valois, K. K. (1988). *Spatial vision.* New York: Oxford University Press.

Deacon, T. W. (1997). What makes the human brain different? In W. H. Durham (ed.), *Annual Review of Anthropology, Vol. 26.* (pp. 337–357). Palo Alto, CA: Annual Reviews, Inc.

Dearborn, G. V. N. (1932). A case of congenital general pure analgesia. *Journal of Nervous & Mental Disease, 75,* 612–615.

DeArmond, S., Fusco, M., & Dewey, M. (1989). Structure of the human brain: a photographic atlas. (p. 202 p.) New York: Oxford University Press.

Dekaban, A. S., & Sadowsky, D. (1978). Changes in brain weights during the span of human life: Relation of brain weights to body heights and body weights. *Annals of Neurology, 4,* 345–356.

Delgado-Escueta, A. V., Mattson, R. H., King, L., Goldensohn, E. S., Spiegel, H., Madsen, J., Crandall, P., Dreifuss, F., & Porter, R. J. (1981). The nature of aggression during epileptic seizures. *New England Journal of Medicine, 305,* 711–716.

DeLong, M. R., Georgopoulos, A. P., Crutcher, M. D., Mitchell, S. J., Richardson, R. T., & Alexander, G. E. (1984). Functional organization of the basal ganglia: Contributions of single-cell recording studies. *Ciba Foundation Symposium, 107,* 64–82.

Demb, J. B., Boynton, G. M., & Heeger, D. J. (1998). Functional magnetic resonance imaging of early visual pathways in dyslexia. *Journal of Neuroscience, 18,* 6939–6951.

Demb, J., Boynton, G., & Heeger, D. (1998). Functional magnetic resonance imaging of early visual pathways in dyslexia. *Journal of Neuroscience, 18*(17), 6939–6951.

Dement, W. C. (1974). *Some must watch while some must sleep.* San Francisco: W. H. Freeman.

Demmer, J., Dragunow, M., Lawlor, P. A., Mason, S. E., Leah, J. D., Abraham, W. C., & Tate, W. P. (1993). Differential expression of immediate early genes after hippocampal long-term potentiation in awake rats. *Brain Research, 17,* 279–286.

Dennis, S. G., & Melzack, R. (1983). Perspectives on phylogenetic evolution of pain expression. In R. L. Kitchell, H. H. Erickson, E. Carstens, & L. E. Davis (eds.), *Animal pain* (pp. 151–161). Bethesda: American Physiological Society.

Denti, A., McGaugh, J. L., Landfield, P. W., & Shinkman, P. (1970). Effects of posttrial electrical stimulation of the mesencephalic reticular formation on avoidance learning in rats. *Physiology and Behavior, 5,* 659–662.

Denton, D. A. (1982). The hunger for salt: an anthropological, physiological, and medical analysis. (pp. xix, 650 p). Berlin. New York: Springer-Verlag.

Deol, M. S., & Glueckschn-Waelsch, S. (1979). The role of inner hair cells in hearing. *Nature, 278,* 250–252.

Derrick, B. (1993). *Opioid receptor-dependent long-term potentiation.* Unpublished doctoral dissertation, University of California, Berkeley, CA.

Derrick, B. E., & Martinez, J. L. (1994). Frequency-dependent associative long-term potentiation at the hippocampal mossy fiber-CA3 synapse. *Proceedings of the National Academy of Sciences, U.S.A., 91,* 10290–10294.

Descartes, R. (1662). *De homine.* Paris: Petrvm Leffen & Franciscvm Moyardvm.

Desimone, R., Albright, T. D., Gross, C. G., & Bruce, C. (1984). Stimulus-selective properties of inferior temporal neurons in the macaque. *Journal of Neuroscience, 4,* 2051–2062.

Devane, W. A., Dysarz, F. A., Johnson, M. R., Melvin, L. S., & Howlett, A. C. (1988). Determination and characterization of a cannabinoid receptor in rat brain. *Molecular Pharmacology, 34,* 605–613.

Devane, W. A., Hanus, L., Breuer, A., Pertwee, R. G., Stevenson, L. A., Griffin, G., Gibsdon, D., Mandelbaum, A., Etinger, A., & Mechoulam, R. (1992). Isolation and structure of a brain constituent that binds the cannabinoid receptor. *Science, 258,* 1946–1949.

Devinsky, O., & Bear, D. (1984). Varieties of aggressive behavior in temporal lobe epilepsy. *American Journal of Psychiatry, 141,* 651–656.

DeVoogd, T. J. (1994). Interactions between endocrinology and learning in the avian song system. *Annals of the New York Academy of Sciences, 743,* 19–41.

Dewsbury, D. A. (1972). Patterns of copulatory behavior in male mammals. *Quarterly Review of Biology, 47,* 1–33.

Diamond, A., & Goldman-Rakic, P. S. (1989). Comparison of human infants and rhesus monkeys on Piaget's AB task: evidence for dependence on dorsolateral prefrontal cortex. *Experimental Brain Research, 74,* 24–40.

Diamond, J., Cooper, E., Turner, C., & Macintyre, L. (1976). Trophic regulation of nerve sprouting. *Science, 193,* 371–377.

Diamond, M. C. (1967). Extensive cortical depth measurements and neuron size increases in the cortex of environmentally enriched rats. *Journal of Comparative Neurology, 131,* 357–364.

Diamond, M. C., Krech, D., & Rosenzweig, M. R. (1964). The effects of an enriched environment on the histology of the rat cerebral cortex. *Journal of Comparative Neurology, 123,* 111–119.

Diamond, M. C., Lindner, B., Johnson, R., Bennett, E. L., & Rosenzweig, M. R. (1975). Differences in occipital cortical synapses from environmentally enriched, impoverished, and standard colony rats. *Journal of Neuroscience Research, 1,* 109–119.

Dichgans, J. (1984). Clinical symptoms of cerebellar dysfunction and their topodiagnostical significance. *Human Neurobiology, 2,* 269–279.

Dlugos, C., & Pentney, R. (1997). Morphometric evidence that the total number of synapses on purkinje neurons of old f344 rats is reduced after long-term ethanol treatment and restored to control levels after recovery. *Alcohol and Alcoholism, 32*(2), 161–72.

Dolphin, A. C., Errington, M. L., & Bliss, T. V. P. (1982). Long-term potentiation of the perforant path in vivo is associated with increased glutamate release. *Nature, 297,* 496–498.

Domjan, M., & Purdy, J. E. (1995). Animal research in psychology: More than meets the eye of the general psychology student. *American Psychologist, 50,* 496–503.

Domjan, M., & Purdy, J. (1995). Animal research in psychology: more than meets the eye of the general psychology student. *American Psychologist, 50*(7), 496–503.

Donegan, N. H., Lowery, R. W., & Thompson, R. F. (1983). Effects of lesioning cerebellar nuclei on conditioned leg-flexion responses. *Society for Neuroscience Abstracts, 9,* 331.

Doricchi, F., & Guariglia, C. P. S. P. L. (1991). Disappearance of leftward rapid eye movements during sleep in left visual hemi-inattention. *Neuroreport, 2,* 285–288.

Doyle, K., Burggraaff, B., Fujikawa, S., Kim, J., & Macarthur, C. (1997). Neonatal hearing screening with otoscopy, auditory brain stem response, and otoacoustic emissions. *Otolaryngology and Head and Neck Surgery, 116*(6 Pt 1), 597–603.

Drachman, D. A., & Leavitt, J. (1972). Memory impairment in the aged: Storage versus retrieval deficit. *Journal of Experimental Psychology, 93,* 302–308.

Drevets, W. C. (1998). Functional neuroimaging studies of depression: The anatomy of melancholia. *Annual Review of Medicine, 49,* 341–361.

Drickamer, L. C. (1992). Behavioral selection of odor cues by young female mice affects age of puberty. *Developmental Psychobiology, 25,* 461–470.

Dronkers, N. F., Redfern, B., & Shapiro, J. K. (1993). Neuroanatomic correlates of production deficits in severe broca's aphasia. *Journal of Clinical and Experimental Neuropsychology, 15*(1), 59–60.

Druckman, D., & Bjork, R. A. (1994). *Learning, remembering, believing: enhancing human performance.* Washington, D. C.: National Academy Press.

Dubnau, J., & Tully, T. (1998). Gene discovery in *Drosophila*: New insights for learning and memory. *Annual Review of Neuroscience, 21,* 407–444.

Dudai, Y. (1988). Neurogenic dissection of learning and short term memory in *Drosophila*. *Annual Review of Neuroscience, 11,* 537–563.

Dudai, Y., Jan, Y.-N., Byers, D., Quinn, W. G., & Benzer, S. (1976). Dunce, a mutant of *Drosophila* deficient in learning. *Proceedings of the National Academy of Sciences, U.S.A., 73,* 1684–1688.

Duffy, F. H., Burchfiel, J. L., & Lombroso, C. T. (1979). Brain electrical activity mapping (BEAM): A method for extending the clinical utility of EEG and evoked potential data. *Annals of Neurology, 5,* 309–321.

Duffy, F. H., Jones, K., Bartels, P., McAnulty, G., & Albert, M. (1992). Unrestricted principal components analysis of brain electrical activity: Issues of data dimensionality, artifact, and utility. *Brain Tomography, 4,* 291–307.

Duffy, J. D., & Campbell, J. J. 3rd. (1994). The regional prefrontal syndromes: a theoretical and clinical overview. *Journal of Neuropsychiatry and Clinical Neurosciences, 6,* 379–387.

Duman, R. S., Heninger, G. R., & Nestler, E. J. (1997). A molecular and cellular theory of depression. *Archives of General Psychiatry, 54,* 597–606.

Eales, L. A. (1985). Song learning in zebra finches (*Taeniopygia gyttata*): Some effects of song model availability on what is learnt and when. *Animal Behaviour, 33,* 1293–1300.

Eapen, V., Pauls, D. L., & Robertson, M. M. (1993). Evidence for autosomal dominant transmission in Tourette's syndrome. United Kingdom cohort study. *British Journal of Psychiatry, 162,* 593–596.

Eccles, J. C. (1965). Possible ways in which synaptic mechanisms participate in learning, remembering and forgetting. In D. P. Kimble (ed.), *The anatomy of memory* (pp. 12–87). Palo Alto: Science and Behavior Books, Inc.

Egaas, B., Courchesne, E., & Saitoh, O. (1995). Reduced size of corpus callosum in autism. *Archives of Neurology, 52,* 794–801.

Egaas, B., Courchesne, E., & Saitoh, O. (1995). Reduced size of corpus callosum in autism. *Archives of Neurology, 52*(8), 794–801.

Egeland, J. A., & Hostetter, A. M. (1983). Amish study, 1: Affective disorders among the Amish, 1976–1980. *American Journal of Psychiatry, 140,* 56–71.

Ehrenkranz, J., Bliss, E., & Sheard, M. H. (1974). Plasma testosterone: correlation with aggressive behavior and social dominance in man. *Psychosomatic Medicine, 36,* 469–475.

Ekman, P. (1973). *Darwin and facial expression; a century of research in review.* New York: Academic Press.

Ekman, P. (1981). Methods for measuring facial action. In K. Scherer, & P. Ekman (eds.), *Handbook on methods of nonverbal communications research.* New York: Cambridge University Press.

Ekman, P., Levenson, R. W., & Friesen, W. V. (1983). Autonomic nervous system activity distinguishes among emotions. *Science, 221*, 1208–1210.

Ekstrand, B. R., Barrett, T. R., West, J. M., & Maier, W. G. (1977). The effect on human long-term memory. In R. Drucker-Colin, & J. L. McGaugh (eds.), *Neurobiology of sleep and memory*. New York: Academic.

Elliott, T., Howarth, C. I., & Shadbolt, N. R. (1996). Axonal processes and neural plasticity. Ii: adult somatosensory maps. *Cerebral Cortex, 6*(6), 789–793.

Engel, A. G. (1984). Myasthenia gravis and myasthenic syndromes. *Annals of Neurology, 16*, 519–535.

Engel, J. Jr. (1992). Recent advances in surgical treatment of temporal lobe epilepsy. *Acta Neurologica Scandinavica (Supplementum), 140*, 71–80.

Epelbaum, M., Milleret, C., Buisseret, P., & Dufier, J. L. (1993). The sensitive period for strabismic amblyopia in humans. *Ophthalmology, 100*, 323–327.

Epstein, A. N., Fitzsimons, J. T., & Rolls, B. J. (1970). Drinking induced by injection of angiotensin into the brain of the rat. *Journal of Physiology (London), 210*, 457–474.

Epstein, C. J. (1986). Developmental genetics. *Experientia, 42*, 1117–1128.

Erhardt, V. R., & Goldman, M. B. (1992). Adverse endocrine effects. In M. S. Keshavan, & J. S. Kennedy (eds.), *Drug-induced dysfunction in psychiatry*. New York: Hemisphere.

Erickson, J. T., Conover, J. C., Borday, V., Champagnat, J., Barbacid, M., Yancopoulos, G., & Katz, D. M. (1996). Mice lacking brain-derived neurotrophic factor exhibit visceral sensory neuron losses distinct from mice lacking NT4 and display a severe developmental deficit in control of breathing. *Journal of Neuroscience, 16*, 5361–5371.

Estes, W. K. (1997). Processes of memory loss, recovery, and distortion. *Psychological Review, 104*, 148–169.

Evans, C. J., Keith, D. E., Morrison, H., Magendzo, K., & Edwards, R. H. (1992). Cloning of a delta opioid receptor by functional expression. *Science, 258*, 1952–1955.

Evarts, E. V., Shinoda, Y., & Wise, S. P. (1984). *Neurophysiological approaches to higher brain functions*. New York: Wiley.

Eybalin, M. (1993). Neurotransmitters and neuromodulators of the mammalian cochlea. *Physiological Reviews, 73*, 309–373.

Falk, D. (1993). Sex differences in visuospatial skills: Implications for hominid evolution. In K. R. Gibson, & T. Ingold (eds.), *Tools, language and cognition in human evolution* (pp. 216–229). Cambridge, England: Cambridge University Press.

Faraone, S. V., & Tsuang, M. T. (1985). Quantitative models of the genetic transmission of schizophrenia. *Psychological Bulletin, 98*, 41–66.

Farbman, A. I. (1994). The cellular basis of olfaction. *Endeavour, 18*, 2–8.

Fazeli, M. S., Corbet, J., Dunn, M. J., Dolphin, A. C., & Bliss, T. V. (1993). Changes in protein synthesis accompanying long-term potentiation in the dentate gyrus *in vivo*. *Journal of Neuroscience, 13*, 1346–1353.

Feder, H. H., & Whalen, R. E. (1965). Feminine behavior in neonatally castrated and estrogen-treated male rats. *Science, 147*, 306–307.

Feinberg, I. (1982). Schizophrenia: Caused by a fault in programmed synaptic elimination during adolescence. *Journal of Psychiatry Research, 17*, 319–334.

Feldman, R. S., Meyer, J. S., & Quenzer, L. F. (1997). *Principles of neuropsychopharmacology, 2nd ed.* Sunderland, MA: Sinauer Associates.

Felten, D. L., Felten, S. Y., Bellinger, D. L., & Madden, K. S. (1993). Fundamental aspects of neural-immune signaling. *Psychotherapy and Psychosomatics, 60*, 46–56.

Fernald, R. D. (1995). Social control of cell size: Males and females are different. *Progress in Brain Research, 105*, 171–177.

Ferster, D., Chung, S., & Wheat, H. (1996). Orientation selectivity of thalamic input to simple cells of cat visual cortex [see Comments]. *Nature, 380*(6571), 249–252.

Fibiger, H. C., & Lloyd, K. G. (1984). The neurobiological substrates of tardive dyskinesia: the GABA hypothesis. *Trends in Neurosciences, 8*, 462.

Fields, S. (1990). Pheromone response in yeast. *Trands in Biochemical Sciences, 15*, 270–273.

Fifkova, E., Anderson, C. L., Young, S. J., & Van Harreveld, A. (1982). Effect of anisomycin on stimulation-induced changes in dendritic spines of the dentate granule cells. *Journal of Neurocytology, 11*, 183–210.

Finger, S. (1994). *Origins of neuroscience: a history of explorations into brain function*. New York: Oxford University Press.

Finger, S. Ed. (1978). *Recovery from brain damage: Research and theory*. New York: Plenum.

Fink, G. R., Markowitsch, H. J., Reinkemeier, M., Bruckbauer, T., Kessler, J., & Heiss, W. D. (1996). Cerebral representation of one's own past: Neural networks involved in autobiographical memory. *Journal of Neuroscience, 16*, 4275–4282.

Finlay, B. L., & Darlington, R. B. (1995). Linked regularities in the development and evolution of mammalian brains. *Science, 268*, 1578–1584.

Fischer, M., Kaech, S., Knutti, D., & Matus, A. (1998). Rapid actin-based plasticity in dendritic spines. *Neuron, 20*, 847–854.

Fishman, R. B., Chism, L., Firestone, G. L., & Breedlove, S. M. (1990). Evidence for androgen receptors in sexually dimorphic perineal muscles of neonatal male rats. Absence of androgen accumulation by the perineal motoneurons. *Journal of Neurobiology, 21*, 694–704.

Fitts, P. M., & Posner, M. I. (1967). *Human performance*. Belmont, CA: Brooks/Cole.

Flament, D., Ellermann, J. M., Kim, S. G., Ugurbil, K., & Ebner, T. J. (1996). Functional magnetic resonance imaging of cerebellar activation during the learning of a visuomotor dissociation task. *Human Brain Map, 4*, 210–226.

Flood, J. F., Bennett, E. L., Orme, A. E., & Rosenzweig, M. R. (1975). Relation of memory formation to controlled amounts of brain protein synthesis. *Physiology and Behavior, 15*, 97–102.

Flood, J. F., Bennett, E. L., Rosenzweig, M. R., & Orme, A. E. (1973). The influence of duration of protein synthesis inhibition on memory. *Physiology and Behavior, 10*, 555–562.

Flood, J. F., Jarvik, M. E., Bennett, E. L., Orme, A. E., & Rosenzweig, M. R. (1977). The effect of stimulants, depressants and protein synthesis inhibition on retention. *Behavioral Biology, 20*, 168–183.

Forger, N. G., & Breedlove, S. M. (1987). Seasonal variation in mammalian striated muscle mass and motoneuron morphology. *Journal of Neurobiology, 18*, 155–165.

Forger, N. G., & Breedlove, S. M. (1986). Sexual dimorphism in human and canine spinal cord: role of early androgen. *Proceedings of the National Academy of Sciences, U.S.A., 83*, 7527–7531.

Forger, N. G., Roberts, S. L., Wong, V., & Breedlove, S. M. (1993). Ciliary neurotrophic factor maintains motoneurons and their target muscles in developing rats. *Journal of Neuroscience, 13*, 4720–4726.

Forger, N., Howell, M., Bengston, L., Mackenzie, L., Dechiara, T., & Yancopoulos, G. (1997). Sexual dimorphism in the spinal cord is absent in mice lacking the ciliary neurotrophic factor receptor. *Journal of Neuroscience, 17*(24), 9605–9612.

Forstl, H., Burns, A., Levy, R., Cairns, N., Luthert, P., & Lantos, P. (1993). Neuropathological correlates of behavioural disturbance in confirmed Alzheimer's disease. *British Journal of Psychiatry, 163*, 364–368.

Foster, N. L., Cahse, T. N., Mansi, L., Brooks, R., Fedio, P., Patronas, H. J., & Di Chiro, G. (1984). Cortical abnormalities in Alzheimer's disease. *Annals of Neurology, 16*, 649–654.

Fox, H. E., White, S. A., Kao, M. H., & Fernald, R. D. (1997). Stress and dominance in a social fish. *Journal of Neuroscience, 17*, 6463–6469.

Francis, R. C. (1992). Sexual lability in teleosts developmental factors. *Quarterly Review of Biology, 67*, 1–18.

Frank, L. G., Glickman, S. E., & Licht, P. (1991). Fatal sibling aggression, precocial development, and androgens in neonatal spotted hyenas. *Science, 252*, 702–704.

Frankenhaeuser, M. (1978). Psychoneuroendocrine approaches to the study of emotion as related to stress and coping. *Nebraska Symposium on Motivation, 26*, 123–162.

Franz, S. I. (1902). On the functions of the cerebrum: I. The frontal lobes in relation to the production and retention of simple sensory-motor habits. *American Journal of Physiology, 8,* 1–22.

Frazier, W. T., Kandel, E. R., Kupfermann, l., Waziri, R., & Coggeshall, R. E. (1967). Morphological and functional properties of identified neurons in the abdominal ganglion of *Aplysia californica. Journal of Neurophysiology, 30,* 1288–1351.

Freund, H.-J. (1984). Premotor areas in man. *Trends in Neuroscience, 7,* 481–483.

Frey, U., Huang, Y.-Y., & Kandel, E. R. (1993). Effects of cAMP simulate a late stage of LTP in hippocampal CA1 neurons. *Science, 260,* 1661–1664.

Fridlund, A. (1988). What can asymmetry and laterality in EMG tell us about the face and brain? *International Journal of Neuroscience, 39,* 53–69.

Fridlund, A. J. (1994). *Human facial expression: an evolutionary view.* San Diego: Academic Press.

Fried, I., Wilson, C. L., MacDonald, K. A., & Behnke, E. J. (1998). Electric current stimulates laughter. *Nature, 391,* 650.

Friedland, R. P., Koss, E., Lerner, A., Hedera, P., Ellis, W., Dronkers, N., Ober, B. A., & Jagust, W. J. (1993). Functional imaging, the frontal lobes, and dementia. *Dementia, 4,* 192–203.

Friedman, L., & Jones, B. E. (1984). Study of sleep-wakefulness states by computer graphics and cluster analysis before and after lesions of the pontine tegmentum in the cat. *Electroencephalography and Clinical Neurophysiology, 57,* 43–56.

Friedman, M. B. (1977). lnteractions between visual and vocal courtship stimuli in the neuroendocrine response of female doves. *Journal of Comparative and Physiological Psychology, 91,* 1408–1416.

Friedman, M. I. (1978). Hyperphagia in rats with experimental diabetes mellitus: a response to a decreased supply of utilizable fuels. *Journal of Cmparative and Physiological Psychology, 92,* 109–117.

Friedman, M., & Rosenman, R. H. (1974). *Type A behavior and your heart.* New York: Knopf.

Froehlich, J., Harts, J., Lumeng, L., & Li, T. (1990). Naloxone attenuates voluntary ethanol intake in rats selectively bred for high ethanol preference. *Pharmacology, Biochemistry and Behavior, 35*(2), 385–390.

Fuster, J. M. (1990). Prefrontal cortex and the bridging of temporal gaps in the perception-action cycle. *Annals of the New York Academy of Sciences, 608,* 318–336.

Gabrieli, J. D. E. (1998). Cognitive neuroscience of human memory. *Annual Review of Psychology, 49,* 87–115.

Gabrieli, J. D. E., Sullivan, E. V., Desmond, J. E., Stebbins, G. T., Vaidya, C. J. et al. (1996). Behavioral and functional neuroimaging evidence for preserved conceptual implicit memory in global amnesia. *Society for Neuroscience, 22,* 1449.

Galaburda, A. M. (1994). Developmental dyslexia and animal studies: at the interface between cognition and neurology. *Cognition, 56,* 833–839.

Galaburda, A. M., Wang, P. P., Bellugi, U., & Rossen, M. (1994). Cytoarchitectonic anomalies in a genetically based disorder: Williams syndrome. *Neuroreport, 5,* 753–757.

Galani, R., Jarrard, L. E., Will, B. E., & Kelche, C. (1997). Effects of postoperative housing conditions on functional recovery in rats with lesions of the hippocampus, subiculum, or entorhinal cortex. *Neurobiology of Learning and Memory, 67,* 43–56.

Gall, C. M., Hess, U. S., & Lynch, G. (1998). Mapping brain networks engaged by—and changed by—learning. *Neurobiology of Learning and Memory, 70,* 1–2, 14–32.

Gallagher, M., Nagahara, A. H., & Burwell, R. D. (1995). Cognition and hippocampal systems in aging: Animal models. In J. L. McGaugh, N. M. Weinberger, & G. Lynch (eds.), *Brain and memory: Modulation and mediation of neuroplasticity* (pp. 103–126). New York: Oxford University Press.

Gallagher, M., & Rapp, P. R. (1997). The use of animal models to study the effects of aging on cognition. *Annual Review of Psychology, 48,* 339–370.

Gallant, J. L., Braun, J., & Van Essen, D. C. (1993). Selectivity for polar, hyperbolic, and Cartesian gratings in macaque visual cortex. *Science, 259,* 100–103.

Gallistel, C. R. (1990). *The organization of learning.* Cambridge, MA: MIT Press.

Gallistel, C. R., Gomita, Y., Yadin, E., & Campbell, K. A. (1985). Forebrain origins and terminations of the medial forebrain bundle metabolically activated by rewarding stimulation or by reward-blocking doses of pimozide. *Journal of Neuroscience, 5,* 1246–1261.

Gannon, P. J., Holloway, R. L., Broadfield, D. C., & Braun, A. R. (1998). Asymmetry of chimpanzee planum temporale: Humanlike pattern of brain language area homolog. *Science, 279,* 220–222.

Gaoni, Y., & Mechoulam, R. (1964). *Journal of the American Chemical Society, 86,* 1646.

Garcia, J., Kimmeldorf, D. J., & Koelling, R. A. (1955). Conditioned aversion to saccharin resulting from exposure to gamma radiation. *Science, 122,* 157–158.

Gardner, L. l. (1972). Deprivation dwarfism. *Scientific American, 227*(1), 76–82.

Gardner, R. A., & Gardner, B. T. (1969). Teaching sign language to a chimpanzee. *Science, 165,* 664–672.

Gardner, R. A., & Gardner, B. T. (1984). A vocabulary test for chimpanzees (*Pan troglodytes*). *Journal of Comparative Psychology, 98,* 381–404.

Gazzaniga, M. S. (1992). *Nature's mind: the biological roots of thinking, emotions, sexuality, language, and intelligence.* New York: Basic Books.

Gemba, H., Miki, N., & Sasaki, K. (1995). Cortical field potentials preceding vocalization and influences of cerebellar hemispherectomy upon them in monkeys. *Brain Research, 697*(1–2), 143–151.

Georgopoulos, A. P., Kalaska, J. F., Caminiti, R., & Massey, J. T. (1982). On the relations between the direction of twodimensional arm movements and cell discharge in primate motor cortex. *Journal of Neuroscience, 2,* 1527–1537.

Georgopoulos, A. P., Taira, M., & Lukashin, A. (1993). Cognitive neurophysiology of the motor cortex. *Science, 260,* 47–52.

Gerard, C. M., Mollereau, C., Vassart, G., & Parmentier, M. (1991). Molecular cloning of a human cannabinoid receptor which is also expressed in testis. *Biochemical Journal, 279,* 129–134.

Gerkema, M. P., & Daan, S. (1985). Ultradian rhythms in behavior: The case of the common vole (*Microtus arvalis*). In H. Schulz, & P. Lavie (eds.), *Ultradian rhythms in physiology and behavior* (pp. 11–32). Berlin: Springer-Verlag.

Geschwind, N. (1976). Language and cerebral dominance. In T. N. Chase (ed.), *Nervous system. Vol.2. The clinical neurosciences* (pp. 433–439). New York: Raven.

Geschwind, N. (1972). Language and the brain. *Scientific American, 226*(4), 76–83.

Geschwind, N., & Levitsky, W. (1968). Human brain: left-right asymmetries in temporal speech region. *Science, 161,* 186–187.

Geyer, M. A., & Markou, A. (1995). Animal models of psychiatric disorders. In F. E. Bloom, & D. J. Kupfer (eds.), *Psychopharmacology: the fourth generation of progress* (pp. 787–798). New York: Raven Press.

Ghez, C., Hening, W., & Gordon, J. (1991). Organization of voluntary movement. *Current Opinion in Neurobiology, 1,* 664–671.

Gibbs, J., & Smith, G. P. (1986). Satiety: the roles of peptides from the stomach and the intestine. *Federation Proceedings, 45,* 1391–1395.

Gibbs, M. E., & Ng, K. T. (1979). Neuronal depolarization and the inhibition of short-term memory formation. *Physiology & Behavior, 23,* 369–375.

Gibbs, M. E., & Ng, K. T. (1977). Psychobiology of memory: Towards a model of memory formation. *Biobehavioral Reviews, I,* 113–136.

Gilbert, A. N., & Wysocki, C. J. (1987). The smell survey results. *National Geographic, 172,* 514–525.

Gilbert, A. N., Yamazaki, K., Beauchamp, G. K., & Thomas, L. (1986). Olfactory discrimination of mouse strains (*Mus musculus*) and major histocompatibility types by humans (*Homo sapiens*). *Journal of Comparative Psychology, 100,* 262–265.

Gilchrist, I. D., Brown, V., & Findlay, J. M. (1997). Saccades without eye movements. *Nature, 390,* 130–131.

Gillingham, J. C., & Clark, D. L. (1981). An analysis of prey-searching behavior in the western diamondback rattlesnake *Crotalus atrox. Behavioral & Neural Biology, 32,* 235–240.

Gitelman, D. R., Nobre, A. C., Meyer, J. R., Parrish, T.B., Callahan, C, Russell, E. J., & Mesulam, M. M. (1996). Functional magnetic resonance imaging of covert spatial attention. *Neuroimage, 3,* S180.

Glantz, M. D. (1992). A developmental psychopathology model of drug abuse vulnerability. In M. D. Glantz, & R. W. Pickens (eds.), *Vulnerability to drug abuse* (pp. 389–418). Washington, D.C.: American Psychological Association.

Glantz, M., & Pickens, R. (1992). *Vulnerability to drug abuse.* Washington, D.C.: American Psychological Association.

Glaser, R., Rice, J., Speicher, C. E., Stout, J. C., & Kiecolt-Glaser, J. K. (1986). Stress depresses interferon production by leukocytes concomitant with a decrease in natural killer cell activity. *Behavioral Neuroscience, 100,* 675–678.

Glavin, G. B. (1991). Dopamine and gastroprotection. The brain-gut axis. *Digestive Diseases and Sciences, 36,* 1670–1672.

Glickman, S. E. (1977). Comparative psychology. In P. Mussen, & M. R. Rosenzweig (eds.), *Psychology: An introduction, second edition.* Lexington, MA: D. C. Heath.

Glickman, S. E., Frank, L. G., Davidson, J. M., Smith, E. R., & Siiteri, P. K. (1987). Androstenedione may organize or activate sex-reversed traits in female spotted hyenas. *Proceedings of the National Academy of Sciences, U.S.A., 84,* 344–347.

Globus, A., Rosenzweig, M. R., Bennett, E. L., & Diamond, M. C. (1973). Effects of differential experience on dendritic spine counts in rat cerebral cortex. *Journal of Comparative and Physiological Psychology, 82,* 175–181.

Gloor, P., Olivier, A., Quesney, L. F., Andermann, F., & Horowitz, S. (1982). The role of the limbic system in experiential phenomena of temporal lobe epilepsy. *Annals of Neurology, 12,* 129–144.

Goldsmith, T. H. (1986). Interpreting trans-retinal recordings of spectral sensitivity. *Journal of Comparative Physiology. a. Sensory, Neural, and Behavioral Physiology, 159,* 481–487.

Golomb, J., de Leon, M. J., George, A. E., Kluger, A., Convit, A., Rusinek, H., de Santi, S., Litt, A., Foo, S. H., & Ferris, S. H. (1994). Hippocampal atrophy correlates with severe cognitive impairment in elderly patients with suspected normal pressure hydrocephalus. *Journal of Neurology, Neurosurgery and Psychiatry, 57,* 590–593.

Goodale, M. A., & Haffenden, A. (1998). Frames of reference for perception and action in the human visual system. *Neuroscience and Biobehavioral Reviews, 22,* 161–72.

Gooding, D., & Iacono, W. (1995). Schizophrenia through the lens of a developmental psychopathology perspective. In *Developmental Psychopathology, Vol. 2: Risk, Disorder, and Adaptation. Wiley Series on Personality Processes* (pp. 535–580). New York: Wiley.

Goodman, C. (1979). Isogenic grasshoppers: Genetic variability and development of identified neurons. In X. O. Breakefeld (ed.), *Neurogenetics.* New York: Elsevier.

Goodman, C. S. (1996). Mechanisms and molecules that control growth cone guidance. *Annual Review of Neuroscience, 19,* 341–377.

Goodman, M., Tagle, D. A., Fitch, D. H., Bailey, W., Czelusniak, J., Koop, B. F., Benson, P., & Slightom, J. L. (1990). Primate evolution at the DNA level and a classification of hominoids. *Journal of Molecular Evolution, 30,* 260–266.

Gorelick, D. A., & Balster, R. L. (1995). Phencyclidine. In F. E. Bloom, & D. J. Kupfer (eds.), *Psychopharmacology, the fourth generation of progress* (pp. 1767–1776). New York: Raven Press.

Gorman, M. R. (1994). Male homosexual desire: neurological investigations and scientific bias. *Perspectives in Biology and Medicine, 38,* 61–81.

Gorski, R. A., Gordon, J. H., Shryne, J. E., & Southam, A. M. (1978). Evidence for a morphological sex difference within the medial preoptic area of the rat brain. *Brain Research, 148,* 333–346.

Gottesman, I. I. (1991). *Schizophrenia genesis.* New York: Freeman.

Gottesman, I. L. (1995). *Schizophrenia genesis: The origins of madness.* New York: W.H. Freeman.

Gottlieb, G. (1976). The roles of experience in the development of behavior and the nervous system. In G. Gottlieb (ed.), *Studies on the development of behavior and the nervous system (Volume3) Neural and behavioral specificity.* New York: Academic.

Gould, E., Tanapat, P., McEwen, B. S., Flugge, G., & Fuchs, E. (1998). Proliferation of granule cell precursors in the dentate gyrus of adult monkeys is diminished by stress. *Proceedings of the National Academy of Sciences U.S.A., 95,* 3168–3171.

Gould, J. L. (1986). The biology of learning. *Annual Review of Psychology, 37,* 163–192.

Gould, S. J. (1981). *The mismeasure of man.* New York: Norton.

Grabowski, T. J., Damasio, H., & Damasio, A. R. (1998). Premotor and prefrontal correlates of category-related lexical retrieval. *Neuroimage, 7,* 232–243.

Grafton, S. T., Mazziotta, J. C., Presty, S., Friston, K. J., Frackowiak, R. S., & Phelps, M. E. (1992). Functional anatomy of human procedural learning determined with regional cerebral blood flow and pet. *Journal of Neuroscience, 12,* 2542–2548.

Grant, S. G., O'Dell, T. J., Karl, K. A., Stein, P. L., Soriano, P., & Kandel, E. R. (1992). Impaired long-term potentiation, spatial learning, and hippocampal development in fyn mutant mice. *Science, 256 ,* 1903–1910.

Graybiel, A. M. (1995). The basal ganglia. *Trends in Neurosciences, 18,* 60–62.

Graybiel, A. M., Aosaki, T., Flaherty, A. W., & Kimura, M. (1994). The basal ganglia and adaptive motor control. *Science, 265,* 1826–1831.

Graziano, M. S., Hu, X. T., & Gross, C. G. (1997). Coding the locations of objects in the dark. *Science, 277,* 239–241.

Green, W. H., Campbell, M., & David, R. (1984). Psychosocial dwarfism: A critical review of the evidence. *Journal of the American Academy of Child Psychiatry, 23,* 39–48.

Greenewalt, CH. (1968). Bird song: acoustics and physiology. (p. 194 p). Washington: Smithsonian Institution Press.

Greenough, W. T. (1976). Enduring brain effects of differential experience and training. In M. R. Rosenzweig, & E. L. Bennett (eds.), *Neural mechanisms of learning and memory* (pp. 255–278). Cambridge: MIT Press.

Greenough, W. T., & Volkmar, F. R. (1973). Pattern of dendritic branching in occipital cortex of rats reared in complex environments. *Experimental Neurology, 40,* 491–504.

Greer, S. (1983). Cancer and the mind. *British Journal of Psychiatry, 143,* 535–543.

Greer, S., Morris, T., & Pettingale, K. W. (1979). Psychological response to breast cancer: effect on outcome. *Lancet, 2,* 785–787.

Gregory, R. L. (1987). Blindness, recovery from. In R. L. Gregory (Ed.), *The Oxford companion to the mind* (pp. 94–96). Oxford, U.K.: Oxford.

Gregory, R. L., & Wallace, J. G. (1963). *Recovery from early blindness: a case study.* Cambridge, U.K.: Cambridge.

Grevert, P., Albert, L. H., & Goldstein, A. (1983). Partial antagonism of placebo analgesia by naloxone. *Pain, 16,* 129–143.

Grevert, P., & Goldstein, A. (1985). Placebo analgesia, naloxone, and the role of endogenous opioids. In L. White, B. Tursky, & G. E. Schwartz (eds.), *Placebo* (pp. 332–351). New York: Guilford.

Grill, R., Murai, K., Blesch, A., Gage, F. H., & Tuszynski, M. H. (1997). Cellular delivery of neurotrophin-3 promotes corticospinal axonal growth and partial functional recovery after spinal cord injury. *Journal of Neuroscience, 17,* 5560–5572.

Grillner, P., Hill, R., & Grillner, S. (1991). 7-Chlorokynurenic acid blocks NMDA receptor-induced fictive locomotion in lamprey —evidence for a physiological role of the glycine site. *Acta Physiologica Scandinavica, 141,* 131–132.

Grillner, S. (1985). Neurobiological bases of rhythmic motor acts in vertebrates. *Science, 228,* 143–149.

Grosof, D. H., Shapley, R. M., & Hawken, M. J. (1993). Macaque V1 neurons can signal "illusory" contours. *Nature, 365,* 550–552.

Grunt, J. A., & Young, W. C. (1953). Consistency of sexual behavior patterns in individual male guinea pigs following castration and androgen therapy. *Journal of Comparative and Physiological Psychology, 46,* 138–144.

Gudermann, T., Schoneberg, T., & Schultz, G. (1997). Functional and structural complexity of signal transduction via G-protein-coupled receptors. *Annual Review of Neuroscience, 20,* 399–427.

Gulevich, G., Dement, W., & Johnson, L. (1966). Psychiatric and EEG observations on a case of prolonged (264 hours) wakefulness. *Archives of General Psychiatry, 15,* 29–35.

Gur, R. E., Resnick, S. M., Alavi, A., Gur, R. C., Caroff, S., Dann, R., Silver, F. L., Saykin, A. J., Chawluk, J. B., Kushner, M. et al. (1987). Regional brain function in schizophrenia. I. A positron emission tomography study. *Archives of General Psychiatry, 44,* 119–125.

Gurney, M. E., & Konishi, M. (1979). Hormone induced sexual differentiation of brain and behavior in zebra finches. *Science, 208,* 1380–1382.

Gurney, M. E., Pu, H., Chiu, A. Y., Dal Canto, M. C., Polchow, C. Y., Alexander, D. D., Caliendo, J., Hentati, A., Kwon, Y. W., Deng, H. X. et al. (1994). Motor neuron degeneration in mice that express a human Cu,Zn superoxide dismutase mutation. *Science, 264,* 1772–1775.

Gusella, J. F., & MacDonald, M. E. (1993). Hunting for Huntington's disease. *Molecular Genetic Medicine, 3,* 139–158.

Häfner, H. (1998). Neurodevelopmental disorder and psychosis: One disease or major risk factor? *Current Opinion in Psychiatry, 11,* 17–18.

Haas, H. S., & Schauenstein, K. (1997). Neuroimmunomodulation via limbic structures —the neuroanatomy of psychoimmunology. *Progress in Neurobiology, 51,* 195–222.

Hadley, M. E. (1992). *Endocrinology, 3rd edition.* Englewood Cliffs, NJ: Prentice-Hall.

Hadley, M. E. (1996). Endocrinology. (pp. xxi, 518 p) Englewood Cliffs, NJ: Prentice Hall.

Hager, J. (1982). Asymmetries in facial expression. In P. Ekman (ed.), *Emotion in the human face* (pp. 318–352). New York: Cambridge University Press.

Haglund, Y., & Bergstrand, G. (1990). Does Swedish amateur boxing lead to chronic brain damage? 2. A retrospective study with CT and MRI. *Acta Neurologica Scandinavica, 82,* 297–302.

Haglund, Y., & Persson, H. E. (1990). Does Swedish amateur boxing lead to chronic brain damage? 3. A retrospective clinical neurophysiological study. *Acta Neurologica Scandinavica, 82,* 353–360.

Hakansson, M. L., Brown, H., Ghilardi, N., Skoda, R. C., & Meister, B. (1998). Leptin receptor immunoreactivity in chemically defined target neurons of the hypothalamus. *Journal of Neuroscience, 18,* 559–72.

Halaas, J. L., Gajiwala, K. S., Maffei, M., Cohen, S. L., Chait, B. T., Rabinowitz, D., Lallone, R. L., Burley, S. K., & Friedman, J. M. (1995). Weight-reducing effects of the plasma protein encoded by the obese gene. *Science, 269,* 543–546.

Hall, J. C., & Greenspan, R. J. (1979). Genetic analysis of *Drosophila* neurobiology. *Annual Review of Genetics, 13,* 127–195.

Hall, W. G., & Oppenheim, R. W. (1987). Developmental psychobiology: Prenatal, perinatal, and early postnatal aspects of behavioral development. *Annual Review of Psychology, 38,* 91–128.

Halpern, D. F. (1986). A different answer to the question, "Do sex-related differences in spatial abilities exist?" *American Psychologist, 41,* 1014–1015.

Halpern, M. (1987). The organization and function of the vomeronasal system. *Annual Review of Neuroscience, 10,* 325–62.

Halpern, M., Halpern, J., Erichsen, E., & Borghjid, S. (1997). The role of nasal chemical senses in garter snake response to airborne odor cues from prey. *Journal of Comparative Psychology, 111,* 251–60.

Halsband, U., Matsuzaka, Y., & Tanji, J. (1994). Neuronal activity in the primate supplementary, pre-supplementary and pre-motor cortex during externally and internally instructed sequential movements. *Neuroscience Research, 20,* 149–55.

Hamburger, V. (1975). Cell death in the development of the lateral motor column of the chick embryo. *Journal of Comparative Neurology, 160,* 535–546.

Hamburger, V. (1958). Regression versus peripheral control of differentiation in motor hypoplasia. *American Journal of Anatomy, 102,* 365–410.

Hamer, D. H., Hu, S., Magnuson, V. L., Hu, N., & Pattatucci, A. M. (1993). A linkage between DNA markers on the X chromosome and male sexual orientation. *Science, 261,* 321–327.

Hamm, R. J., Temple, M. D., O'Dell, D. M., Pike, B. R., & Lyeth, B. G. (1996). Exposure to environmental complexity promotes recovery of cognitive function after traumatic brain injury. *Journal of Neurotrauma, 13,* 41–7.

Hammond, P. (1974). Cat retinal ganglion cells: size and shape of receptive field centres. *Journal of Physiology, 242,* 99–118.

Hampton, R. R., Sherry, D. F., Shettleworth, S. J., Khurgel, M., & Ivy, G. (1995). Hippocampal volume and food-storing behavior are related in parids. *Brain, Behavior and Evolution, 45,* 54–61.

Hardyck C., Petrinovich, L., & Goldman R. (1976). Left-handedness and cognitive deficit. *Cortex, 12,* 226–279.

Hare, E. (1988). Schizophrenia as a recent disease. *British Journal of Psychiatry, 153,* 521–531.

Harris, E. W., & Cotman, C. W. (1986). Long-term potentiation of guinea pig mossy fiber responses is not blocked by N-methyl D-aspartate antagonists. *Neuroscience Letters, 70,* 132–137.

Harris, R. M., & Woolsey, T. A. (1983). Computer-assisted analyses of barrel neuron axons and their putative synaptic contacts. *Journal of Comparative Neurology, (220),* 63–79.

Hartmann, E. (1984). *The nightmare: The psychology and biology of terrifying dreams.* New York: Basic Books.

Hartmann, E. (1973). Sleep requirement: long sleepers, short sleepers, variable sleepers, and insomniacs. *Psychosomatics, 14,* 95–103.

Hartmann, E. (1978). *The sleeping pill.* New Haven: Yale.

Hartse, K., Zorick, F., Sicklesteel, J., & Roth, T. (1988). Isolated cataplexy: a familial study. *Henry Ford Hospital Medical Journal, 36(1),* 24–7.

Harvey, P. H., & Krebs, J. R. (1990). Comparing brains. *Science, 249,* 140–146.

Hasher, L., & Zacks, R. T. (1979). Automatic and effortful processes in memory. *Journal of Experimental Psychology: General, 108,* 346–288.

Haskett, R. F. (1985). Diagnostic categorization of psychiatric disturbance in Cushing's syndrome. *American Journal of Psychiatry, 142,* 911–916.

Hatten, M. E. (1990). Riding the glial monorail: a common mechanism for glial-guided neuronal migration in different regions of the developing mammalian brain. *Trends in Neuroscience, 13,* 179–184.

Hauser, P., Zametkin, A. J., Martinez, P., Vitiello, B., Matochik, J. A., Mixson, A. J., & Weintraub, B. D. (1993). Attention deficit-hyperactivity disorder in people with generalized resistance to thyroid hormone. *New England Journal of Medicine, 328,* 997–1001.

Hazeltine, E., Grafton, S. T., & Ivry, R. (1997). Attention and stimulus characteristics determine the locus of motor-sequence encoding. A PET study. *Brain, 123–40.*

Healy, S. D., & Krebs, J. R. (1993). Development of hippocampal specialisation in a food-storing bird. *Behavioural Brain Research, 53,* 127–130.

Heath, R. G. (1972). Pleasure and brain activity in man. *Journal of Nervous and Mental Diseases, 154,* 3–18.

Heath, R. G., Franklin, D. E., & Shraberg, D. (1979). Gross pathology of the cerebellum in patients diagnosed and treated as functional psychiatric disorders. *Journal of Nervous and Mental Disorders, 167,* 585–592.

Hebb, D. O. (1949). *The organization of behavior.* New York: Wiley.

Heffner, H. E., & Heffner, R. S. (1989). Unilateral auditory cortex ablation in macaques results in a contralateral hearing loss. *Journal of Neurophysiology, 62,* 789–801.

Hefti, F., & Mash, D. C. (1989). Localization of nerve growth factor receptors in the normal human brain and in Alzheimer's disease. *Neurobiology of Aging, 10,* 75–87.

Heisenberg, M., Heusipp, M., & Wanke, C. (1995). Structural plasticity in the *Drosophila* brain. *Journal of Neuroscience, 15,* 1951–1960.

Heit, S., Owens, M. J., Plotsky, P., & Nemeroff, C. B. (1997). Corticotropin-releasing factor, stress, and depression. *Neuroscientist, 3,* 186–94.

Held, R. (1993). Binocular vision —behavioral and neuronal development. *Brain Development and Cognition: A Reader* (pp. 152–166. xi, 734).

Heldmaier, G., & Ruf, T. (1992). Body temperature and metabolic rate during natural hypothermia in endotherms. *Journal of Comparative Physiology. B, Biochemical, Systemic and Environmental Physiology, 162 ,* 696–706.

Helzer, J. E. (1987). Epidemiology of alcoholism. *Journal of Consulting and Clinical Psychology, 55,* 284–292.

Hemmingsen, A. M. (1960). Energy metabolism as related to body size and respiratory surfaces, and its evolution. *Reports of Steno Memorial Hospital, Copenhagen, 9,* 1–110.

Hendrickson, A. (1985). Dots, stripes and columns in monkey visual cortex. *Trends in NeuroSciences, 8,* 406–410.

Hennessy, M. B., Mendoza, S. P., Mason, W. A., Moberg, G. P. et al. (1995). Endocrine sensitivity to novelty in squirrel monkeys and titi monkeys: Species differences in characteristic modes of responding to the environment. *Physiology & Behavior, 57,* 331–338.

Hetherington, A. W., & Ranson, S. W. (1940). Hypothalamic lesions and adiposity in the rat. *Anatomical Record, 78,* 149–172.

Hewes, G. (1973). Primate communication and the gestural origin of language. *Current Anthropology, 14,* 5–24.

Hietala, J., Syvalahti, E., Vuorio, K., Nagren, K., Lehikoinen, P., Ruotsalainen, U., Rakkolainen, V., Lehtinen, V., & Wegelius, U. (1994). Striatal D2 dopamine receptor characteristics in neuroleptic-naive schizophrenic patients studied with positron emission tomography. *Archives of General Psychiatry, 51,* 116–123.

Higley, J. D., Mehlman, P. T., Taub, D. M., Higley, S. B., Suomi, S. J., Vickers, J. H., & Linnoila, M. (1992). Cerebrospinal fluid monoamine and adrenal correlates of aggression in free-ranging rhesus monkeys. *Archives of General Psychiatry, 49,* 436–441.

Hille, B. (1992). *Ionic channels of excitable membranes, 2nd ed.* Sunderland, MA: Sinauer.

Hilts, P. J. (1995). *Memory's ghost: The strange tale of Mr. M. and the nature of memory.* New York: Simon & Schuster.

Hindler, C. G. (1989). Epilepsy and violence. *British Journal of Psychiatry, 155,* 246–9.

Hingson, R., Alpert, J., Day, N., Dooling, E., Kayne, H., Morelock, S., Oppenheimer, E., & Zuckerman, B. (1982). Effects of maternal drinking and marijuana use on fetal growth and development. *Pediatrics, 70,* 539–546.

Hirsch, E., Moye, D., & Dimon, J. H. 3rd. (1995). Congenital indifference to pain: Long-term follow-up of two cases. *Southern Medical Journal, 88,* 851–7.

Hirsch, H. V. B., & Spinelli, D. N. (1971). Modification of the distribution of receptive field orientation in cats by selective visual exposure during development. *Experimental Brain Research, 12,* 509–527.

Hobson, J. A., & McCarley, R. W. (1977). The brain as a dream state generator: an activation-synthesis hypothesis of the dream process. *American Journal of Psychiatry, 134,* 1335–1348.

Hochstein, S., & Shapley, R. M. (1976). Quantitative analysis of retinal ganglion cell classifications. *Journal of Physiology, 252,* 237–264.

Hodgkin, A. L., & Huxley, A. F. (1952). A quantitative description of membrane current and its application to conduction and excitation in nerve. *Journal of Physiology (London) , 117,* 500–544.

Hodgkin, A. L., & Katz, B. (1949). The effect of sodium ions on the electrical activity of the giant axon of the squid. *Journal of Physiology (London), 108,* 37–77.

Hoffman, K.-P., & Stone, J. (1971). Conduction velocity of afferents to cat visual cortex: A correlation with cortical receptive field properties. *Brain Research , 32,* 460–466.

Holcomb, H. H., Links, J., Smith, C., & Wong, D. (1989). Positron emission tomography: Measuring the metabolic and neuro-chemical characteristics of the living human nervous system. In N. C. Andreasen (ed.), *Brain imaging: Applications in psychiatry* (pp. 235–370). Washington, D. C.: American Psychiatric Press.

Hollis, J. R., Connett, J. E., Stevens, V. J., & Greenlick, M. R. (1990). Stressful life events, Type A behavior, and the prediction of cardiovascular and total mortality over six years. MRFIT Group. *Journal of Behavioral Medicine, 13,* 263–280.

Horai, S., Hayasaka, K., Kondo, R., Tsugane, K., & Takahata, N. (1995). Recent African origin of modern humans revealed by complete sequences of hominoid mitochondrial DNAs. *Proceedings of the National Academy of Sciences, U.S.A., 92,* 532–536.

Huang, Y. Y., & Kandel, E. R. (1994). Recruitment of long-lasting and protein kinase A-dependent long-term potentiations in the CA1 region of the hippocampus requires repeated tetanization. *Learning and Memory,* (1), 74–82.

Hubbard, A. (1993). A traveling-wave amplifier model of the cochlea. *Science, 259,* 68–71.

Hubel, D. H., & Wiesel, T. N. (1965). Binocular interaction in striate cortex kittens reared with artificial squint. *Journal of Neurophysiology, 28,* 1041–1059.

Hubel, D. H., & Wiesel, T. N. (1959). Receptive fields of single neurones in the cat's striate cortex. *Journal of Physiology (London), 148,* 573–591.

Hubel, D. H., Wiesel, T. N., & LeVay, S. (1977). Plasticity of ocular dominance in monkey striate cortex. *Phil. Trans. Roy. Soc. (London) Ser. B, 278,* 377–409.

Hudspeth, A. J. (1992). Hair-bundle mechanics and a model for mechanoelectrical transduction by hair cells. *Society of General Physiologists Series, 47,* 357–370.

Hudspeth, A. J. (1989). How the ear's works work. *Nature, 341,* 397–404.

Hull, C. L. (1943). *Principles of behavior.* New York: D. Appleton-Century.

Huntington, G. (1872). On chorea. *Medical and Surgical Reporter, 26,* 317–321.

Huttenlocher, P. R., deCourten, C., Garey, L. J., & Van der Loos, H. (1982). Synaptogenesis in the human visual cortex-evidence for synapse elimination during normal development. *Neuroscience Letters, 33,* 247–252.

Hyde, T. M., Aaronson, B. A., Randolph, C., Rickler, K. C., & Weinberger, D. R. (1992). Relationship of birth weight to the phenotypic expression of Gilles de la Tourette's syndrome in monozygotic twins. *Neurology, 42,* 652–658.

Hyde, T. M., & Weinberger, D. R. (1990). The brain in schizophrenia. *Seminars in Neurology, 10,* 276–286.

Idzikowski, C. (1984). Sleep and memory. *British Journal of Psychology, 75,* 439–449.

Ignarro, L. J. (1991). Signal transduction mechanisms involving nitric oxide. *Biochemical Pharmacology, 41,* 485–90.

Imperato-McGinley, J., Guerrero, L., Gautier, T., & Peterson, R. E. (1974). Steroid 5 a-reductase deficiency in man: an inherited form of male pseudohermaphroditism. *Science, 86,* 1213–1215.

Indo, Y., Tsuruta, M., Hayashida, Y., Karim Ma, Ohta, K., Kawano, T., Mitsubuchi, H., Tonoki, H., Awaya, Y., & Matsuda, I. (1996). Mutations in the trka/ngf receptor gene in patients with congenital insensitivity to pain with anhidrosis [see comments]. *Nature Genetics, 13*(4), 485–8.

Ingram, D. K. (1985). Analysis of age-related impairments in learning and memory in rodent models. *Annals of the New York Academy of Sciences, 444,* 312–331.

Insel, T. R. (1992). Toward a neuroanatomy of obsessive-compulsive disorder. *Archives of General Psychiatry, 49,* 739–744.

Institute for Health Policy, B. U. (1993). *Substance abuse: The nation's number one health problem.* Princeton, NJ: Robert Wood Johnson Foundation.

Institute of Medicine. (1990). *Broadening the base of treatment for alcohol problems.* Washington, D.C.: National Academy Press.

Irle, E., Exner, C., Thielen, K., Weniger, G., & Ruther, E. (1998). Obsessive-compulsive disorder and ventromedial frontal lesions: Clinical and neuropsychological findings. *American Journal of Psychiatry, 155,* 255–63.

Isaacson, R. L. (1972). Hippocampal destruction in man and other animals. *Neuropsychologia, 10,* 47–64.

Ito, J., Sakakibara, J., Iwasaki, Y., & Yonekura, Y. (1993). Positron emission tomography of auditory sensation in deaf patients and patients with cochlear implants. *Annals of Otology,Rhinology and Laryngology, 102,* 797–801.

Ito, M. (1987). Cerebellar adaptive function in altered vestibular and visual environments. *Physiologist, 30,* S81.

Ivry, R. (1993). Cerebellar involvement in the explicit representation of temporal information. *Annals of the New York Academy of Sciences, 682,* 214–230.

Ivry, R. B., & Robertson, L. C. (1998). The two sides of perception. (p. 315 p). Cambridge, Mass: MIT Press.

Iwamura, Y., & Tanaka, M. (1978). Postcentral neurons in hand region of area 2: Their possible role in the form discrimination of tactile objects. *Brain Research, 150,* 662–666.

Izquierdo, I., & Medina, J. H. (1997). Memory formation: The sequence of biochemical events in the hippocampus and its connection to activity in other brain structures. *Neurobiology of Learning and Memory, 68,* 285–316.

Jablensky, A., Sartorius, N., Ernberg, G., Anker, M., Korten, A., Cooper, J. E., Day, R., & Bertelsen, A. (1992). Schizophrenia: manifestations, incidence and course in different cultures. *Psychological Medicine, Monograph Supplement, 20.*

Jackson, H., & Parks, T. N. (1982). Functional synapse elimination in the developing avian cochlear nucleus with simultaneous reduction in cochlear nerve axon branching. *Journal of Neuroscience, 2,* 1736–1743.

Jacobs, G. H. (1993). The distribution and nature of colour vision among the mammals. *Biological Reviews of the Cambridge Philosophical Society, 68,* 413–471.

Jacobs, G. H. (1984). Within-species variations in visual capacity among squirrel monkeys (*Saimiri sciureus*): color vision. *Vision Research, 24,* 1267–1277.

Jacobs, G. H., Neitz, J., & Neitz, M. (1993). Genetic basis of polymorphism in the color vision of platyrrhine monkeys. *Vision Research, 33,* 269–274.

Jacobs, L. F., Gaulin, S. J., Sherry, D. F., & Hoffman, G. E. (1990). Evolution of spatial cognition: sex-specific patterns of spatial behavior predict hippocampal size. *Proceedings of the National Academy of Sciences, U.S.A., 87,* 6349–6352.

Jacobs, L. F., & Spencer, W. D. (1994). Natural space-use patterns and hippocampal size in kangaroo rats. *Brain, Behavior & Evolution, 44,* 125–132.

Jacobson, M. (1991). *Developmental neurobiology.* New York: Plenum Press.

James, W. (1890). *Principles of psychology.* New York: Holt.

Jellies, J. A. (1981). Associative olfactory conditioning in *Drosophila melanogaster* and memory retention through metamorphosis. Unpublished doctoral dissertation, Master's thesis, Illinois State University, Normal, IL.

Jenike, M. A., Baer, L., Ballantine, T., Martuza, R. L., Tynes, S., Giriunas, I., Buttolph, M. L., & Cassem, N. H. (1991). Cingulotomy for refractory obsessive-compulsive disorder. A long-term follow-up of 33 patients. *Archives of General Psychiatry, 48,* 548–555.

Jenkins, J., & Dallenbach, K. (1924). Oblivescence during sleep and waking. *American Journal of Psychology, 35,* 605–612.

Jensen, C. (1979). Learning performance in mice genetically selected for brain weight: Problems of generality. In M. E. Hahn, C. Jensen, & B. C. Dudek (eds.), *Development and evolution of brainsize.* New York: Academic.

Jentsch, J. D., Redmond, D. E. Jr., Elsworth, J. D., Taylor, J. R., Youngren, K. D., & Roth, R. H. (1997). Enduring cognitive deficits and cortical dopamine dysfunction in monkeys after long-term administration of phencyclidine. *Science, 277,* 953–5.

Jerison, H. J. (1991). *Brain size and the evolution of mind.* New York: American Museum of Natural History.

Jernigan, T. L., Bellugi, U., Sowell, E., Doherty, S., & Hesselink, J. R. (1993). Cerebral morphologic distinctions between Williams and Down syndromes. *Archives of Neurology, 50,* 186–191.

Johansson, B. B., & Ohlsson, A. L. (1996). Environment, social interaction, and physical activity as determinants of functional outcome after cerebral infarction in the rat. *Experimental Neurology, 139,* 322–7.

Johnson, E. M. Jr., & Deckwerth, T. L. (1993). Molecular mechanisms of developmental neuronal death. *Annual Review of Neuroscience, 16,* 31–46.

Johnson-Greene, D., Adams, K., Gilman, S., Koeppe, R., Junck, L., Kluin, K., Martorello, S., & Heumann, M. (1997). Effects of abstinence and relapse upon neuropsychological function and cerebral glucose metabolism in severe chronic alcoholism. *Journal of Clinical and Experimental Neuropsychology, 19(3),* 378–385.

Johnson, J. S., & Newport, E. L. (1989). Critical period effects in second language learning: The influence of maturational state on the acquisition of English as a second language. *Cognitive Psychology, 21,* 60–99.

Johnson, L. C. (1969). Psychological and physiological changes following total sleep deprivation. In A. Kales (ed.), *Sleep: Physiology and pathology.* Philadelphia: Lippincott.

Johnson, P. L., & Stellar, J. R. (1994). Effects of accumbens DALA microinjections on brain stimulation reward and behavioral activation in intact and 6-OHDA treated rats. *Psychopharmacology, 114,* 665–671.

Jones, K. E., Lyons, M., Bawa, P., & Lemon, R. N. (1994). Recruitment order of motoneurons during functional tasks. *Experimental Brain Research, 100,* 503–508.

Jordan, B. D., Jahre, C., Hauser, W. A., Zimmerman, R. D., Zarrelli, M., Lipsitz, E. C., Johnson, V., Warren, R. F., Tsairis, P., & Folk, F. S. (1992). CT of 338 active professional boxers. *Radiology, 185 ,* 509–512.

Jordan, B., Relkin, N., Ravdin, L., Jacobs, A., Bennett, A., & Gandy, S. (1997). Apolipoprotein e epsilon4 associated with chronic traumatic brain injury in boxing. *Jama, 278(2),* 136–40.

Jordan, C. L., Breedlove, S. M., & Arnold, A. P. (1991). Ontogeny of steroid accumulation in spinal lumbar motoneurons of the rat: implications for androgen's site of action during synapse elmination. *Journal of Comparative Neurology, 313,* 441–448.

Jordan, C. L., Letinsky, M. S., & Arnold, A. P. (1988). Synapse elimination occurs late in the hormone-sensitive levator ani muscle of the rat. *Journal of Neurobiology, 19,* 335–356.

Jouvet, M. (1967). Neurophysiology of the states of sleep. In G. C. Quarton, T. Melnechuk, & F. O. Schmitt (eds.), *The Neurosciences* (pp. 529–544). New York: Rockefeller University.

Julian, T., & McKenry, P. C. (1979). Relationship of testosterone to men's family functioning at mid-life: A research note. *Aggressive Behavior, 15,* 281–289.

Julien, R. J. (1992). *A primer of drug action, 6th ed.* New York: Freeman.

Kölmel, H. W. (1988). Pure homonymous hemiachromatopsia. Findings with neuro-ophthalmologic examination and imaging procedures. *European Archives of Psychiatry and Neurological Sciences, 237,* 237–243.

Kaada, B. (1967). Brain mechanisms related to aggressive behavior. In C. D. Clemente, & D. B. Lindsley (eds.), *Aggression and defense.* Berkeley: University of California.

Kaas, J. H. (1991). Plasticity of sensory and motor maps in adult mammals. *Annual Review of Neuroscience, 14,* 137–167.

Kaas, J. H., Nelson, R. J., Sur, M., Lin, C. S., & Merzenich, M. M. (1979). Multiple representations of the body within the primary somatosensory cortex of primates. *Science, 204,* 521–523.

Kadekaro, M., Cohen, S., Terrell, M. L., Lekan, H., Gary, H. Jr., & Eisenberg, H. M. (1989). Independent activation of subfornical organ and hypothalamo-neurohypophysial system during administration of angiotensin II. *Peptides, 10,* 423–429.

Kagan, J. (1997). Temperament and the reactions to unfamiliarity. *Child Development, 68,* 139–43.

Kales, A. (1973). Treating sleep disorders. *American Family Physician, 8,* 158–168.

Kales, A., & Kales, J. (1970). Evaluation, diagnosis and treatment of clinical conditions related to sleep. *Journal of the American Medical Association, 213,* 2229–2235.

Kales, A., & Kales, J. D. (1974). Sleep disorders. Recent findings in the diagnosis and treatment of disturbed sleep. *New England Journal of Medicine, 290,* 487–499.

Kalin, N. H., Dawson, G., Tariot, P., Shelton, S., Barksdale, C., Weiler, S., & Thienemann, M. (1987). Function of the adrenal cortex in patients with major depression. *Psychiatry Research, 22,* 117–125.

Kamil, A. C. (1994). A synthetic approach to the study of animal intelligence. In L. A. Real (ed.), *Behavioral mechanisms in evolutionary ecology* (pp. 11–45). Chicago: University of Chicago Press.

Kandel, E. R. (1976). *Cellular basis of behavior.* San Francisco: Freeman.

Kandel, E. R., Castellucci, V. F., Goelet, P., & Schacher, S. (1987). 1987 cell-biological interrelationships between short-term and long-term memory. *Research Publications, Association for Research in Nervous and Mental Disease, 65,* 111–132.

Kandel, E. R., Schacher, S., Castellucci, V. F., & Goelet, P. (1986). The long and short of memory in *Aplysia*: a molecular perspective. *Fidia Research Foundation Neuroscience Award Lectures* (pp. 7–47). Padova: Liviana Press.

Kandel, E. R., Schwartz, J. H., & Jessell, T. M. (1991). *Principles of neural science, 3rd edition.* New York: Elsevier.

Karni, A., Tanne, D., Rubenstein, B. S., Askenasy, J. J., & Sagi, D. (1994). Dependence on REM sleep of overnight improvement of a perceptual skill. *Science, 265,* 679–682.

Karp, L. E. (1976). Genetic engineering, threat or promise? (pp. xvii, 235 p). Chicago: Nelson-Hall.

Katz, L. C., & Shatz, C. J. (1996). Synaptic activity and the construction of cortical circuits. *Science, 274,* 1133–8.

Kaufmann, C. A., Jeste, D. V., Shelton, R. C., Linnoila, M., Kafka, M. S., & Wyatt, R. J. (1986). Noradrenergic and neuroradiological abnormalities in tardive dyskinesia. *Biological Psychiatry, 21,* 799–812.

Kavanau, J. L. (1997). Memory, sleep and the evolution of mechanisms of synaptic efficacy maintenance. *Neuroscience, 79,* 7–44.

Keane, T. M. (1998). Psychological and behavioral treatments of post-traumatic stress disorder. In P. E. Nathan, J. M. Gorman et al. (eds.), *A guide to treatments that work* (pp. 398–407). New York: Oxford University Press.

Keele, S. W., & Summers, J. J. (1976). The structure of motor programs. In G. E. Stelmach (ed.), *Motor control: Issues and trends.* New York: Academic.

Keesey, R. E. (1980). A set-point analysis of the regulation of body weight. In A. J. Stunkard (ed.), *Obesity.* Philadelphia: Saunders.

Keesey, R. E., & Boyle, P. C. (1973). Effects of quinine adulteration upon body weight of LH-lesioned and intact male rats. *Journal of Comparative and Physiological Psychology, 84,* 38–46.

Keesey, R. E., & Corbett, S. W. (1984). Metabolic defense of the body weight set-point. *Research Publications - Association for Research in Nervous and Mental Disease, 62,* 87–96.

Keesey, R. E., & Powley, T. L. (1986). The regulation of body weight. *Annual Review of Psychology, 37,* 109–133.

Kelso, S. R., & Brown, T. H. (1986). Differential conditioning of associative synaptic enhancement in hippocampal brain slices. *Science, 232,* 85–7.

Keltner, D., & Buswell, B. N. (1996). Evidence for the distinctness of embarrassment, shame, and guilt: A study of recalled antecedents and facial expressions of emotion. *Cognition & Emotion, 10,* 155–171.

Kemali, D., Galderisi, M. S., Ariano, M. G., Cesarelli, M., Milici, N., Salvati, A., Valente, A., & Volpe, M. (1985). Clinical and neuropsychological correlates of cerebral ventricular enlargement in schizophrenia. *Journal of Psychiatric Research, 19,* 587–596.

Kemp, D. T. (1979). The evoked cochlear mechanical responses and the auditory microstructure: Evidence for a new element in cochlear mechanics. *Scand. Audiol. Suppl., 9,* 35–47.

Kempermann, G., Kuhn, H. G., & Gage, F. H. (1997). More hippocampal neurons in adult mice living in an enriched environment. *Nature, 386,* 493–495.

Kertesz, A. (1979). Recovery and treatment. In K. M. Heilman, & E. Valenstein (eds.), *Clinical neuropsychology.* New York: Oxford.

Kesner, R. P. (1980). An attribute analysis of memory: The role of the hippocampus. *Physiological Psychology, 8,* 189–197.

Kesner, R. P. (1996). An exploration of the neural bases of memory representations of reward and context. In K. H. Probram, & J. King (eds.), *The amygdala: Neurobiological aspects of emotion, memory, and mental dysfunction.* New York: Wiley-Liss.

Kesner, R. P. (1991). Neurobiological views of memory. In J. L. Martinez, & R. P. Kesner (eds.), *Learning and memory: A biological view* 2nd ed., (pp. 499–547). New York: Academic Press.

Kesner, R. P. (1998). Neurobiological views of memory. In J. L. Martinez Jr., & R. P. Kesner (eds.), *Neurobiology of learning and memory* (3rd ed., pp. 361–416). San Diego, CA: Harcourt Brace.

Kesner, R. P., Bolland, B. L., & Dakis, M. (1993). Memory for spatial locations, motor responses, and objects: triple dissociation among the hippocampus, caudate nucleus, and extrastriate visual cortex. *Experimental Brain Research, 93,* 462–470.

Kesner, R. P., & Novak, J. M. (1982). Serial position curve in rats: Role of the dorsal hippocampus. *Science, 218,* 173–175.

Kesner, R. P., & Williams, J. M. (Manuscript). Memory for magnitude of reinforcement: Dissociation between the amygdala and hippocampus.

Kessler, R. C., McGonagle, K. A., Zhao, S., Nelson, C. B., Hughes, M., Eshleman, S., Wittchen, H. U., & Kendler, K. S. (1994). Lifetime and 12-month prevalence of DSM-III-R psychiatric disorders in the United States. Results from the National Comorbidity Survey. *Archives of General Psychiatry, 51,* 8–19.

Kety, S. (1976). Biological concomitants of affective states and their possible role in memory processes. In M. R. Rosenzweig, & E. L. Bennett (eds.), *Neural mechanisms of learning and memory.* Cambridge: MIT Press.

Kety, S. (1983). Mental illness in the biological and adoptive families of schizophrenic adoptees: Findings relevant to genetic and environmental factors in etiology. *American Journal of Psychiatry, 140,* 720–727.

Kety, S. S., Wender, P. H., Jacobsen, B., Ingraham, L. J., Jansson, L., Faber, B., & Kinney, D. K. (1994). Mental illness in the biological and adoptive relatives of schizophrenic adoptees. Replication of the Copenhagen Study in the rest of Denmark. *Archives of General Psychiatry, 51,* 442–455.

Kety, S., Rosenthal, D., Wender, P. H., Schulsinger, F., & Jacobsen, B. (1975). Mental illness in the biological and adoptive families of adopted individuals who have become schizophrenic. A preliminary report based on psychiatric interviews. In R. R. Fieve, D. Rosenthal, & H. Brill (eds.), *Genetic research in psychiatry.* Baltimore: Johns Hopkins University.

Keynes, R. J., & Cook, G. M. (1992). Repellent cues in axon guidance. *Current Opinion in Neurobiology, 2,* 55–59.

Kiang, N. Y. S. (1965). *Discharge patterns of single fibers in the cat's auditory nerve.* Cambridge, MA: MIT Press.

Kiecolt-Glaser, J. K., & Glaser, R. (1995). Psychoneuroimmunology and health consequences: data and shared mechanisms. *Psychosomatic Medicine, 57,* 269–274.

Killiany, R. J., Moss, M. B., Albert, M. S., Sandor, T., Tieman, J., & Jolesz, F. (1993). Temporal lobe regions on magnetic resonance imaging identify patients with early Alzheimer's disease. *Archives of Neurology, 50,* 949–954.

Kim, J. J., & Fanselow, M. S. (1992). Modality-specific retrograde amnesia of fear. *Science, 256,* 675–677.

Kim, K. H., Relkin, N. R., Lee, K. M., & Hirsch, J. (1997). Distinct cortical areas associated with native and second languages. *Nature, 388,* 171–174.

Kimura, D. (1973). The asymmetry of the human brain. *Scientific American, 360,* 368.

Kingsbury, S. J., & Garver, D. L. (1998). Lithium and psychosis revisited. *Progress in Neuro-Psychopharmacology and Biological Psychiatry, 22,* 249–63.

Kinney, D. K., Woods, B. T., & Yurgelun-Todd, D. (1986). Neurologic abnormalities in schizophrenic patients and their families. II. Neurologic and psychiatric findings in relatives. *Archives of General Psychiatry, 43,* 665–668.

Kinsey, A. C., Pomeroy, W. B., & Martin, C. E. (1948). *Sexual behavior in the human male.* Philadelphia: Saunders.

Kinsey, A. C., Pomeroy, W. B., Martin, C. E., & Gebhard, P. H. (1953). *Sexual behavior in the human female*. Philadelphia: Saunders.

Klüver, H., & Bucy, P. C. (1938). An analysis of certain effects of bilateral temporal lobectomy in the rhesus monkey, with special reference to "psychic blindness". *Journal of Psychology, 5*(33–54).

Kleiber, M. (1947). Body size and metabolic rate. *Physiological Reviews, 15*, 511–541.

Kleitman, N. (1969). Basic rest-activity cycle in relation to sleep and wakefulness. In A. Kales (ed.), *Sleep: Physiology and pathology*. Philadelphia: Lippincott.

Kleitman, N., & Engelmann, T. (1953). Sleep characteristics of infants. *Journal of Applied Physiology, 6*, 269–282.

Klima, E. S., & Bellugi, U. (1979). *The signs of language*. Cambridge: Harvard.

Kluckhohn, C. (1949). *Mirror for man*. New York: Whittlesey House.

Knibestol, M., & Valbo, A. B. (1970). Single unit analysis of mechanoreceptor activity from the human glabrous skin. *Acta Physiologica Scandinavica, 80*, 178–195.

Knudsen, E. I. (1982). Auditory and visual maps of space in the optic tectum of the owl. *Journal of Neuroscience, 2*, 1177–1194.

Knudsen, E. I. (1998). Capacity for plasticity in the adult owl auditory system expanded by juvenile experience. *Science, 279*, 1531–1533.

Knudsen, E. I. (1985). Experience alters the spatial tuning of auditory units in the optic tectum during a sensitive period in the barn owl. *Journal of Neuroscience, 5*, 3094–3109.

Knudsen, E. I. (1984). The role of auditory experience in the development and maintenance of sound localization. *Trends in NeuroScience, 7*, 326–330.

Knudsen, E. I., Knudsen, P. F., & Esterly, S. D. (1984). A critical period for the recovery of sound localization accuracy following monaural occlusion in the barn owl. *Journal of Neuroscience, 4*, 1012–1020.

Knudsen, E. I., & Konishi, M. (1978). A neural map of auditory space in the owl. *Science, 200*, 795–797.

Knudsen, E., & Knudsen, P. (1985). Vision guides adjustment of auditory localization in young barn owls. *Science, 230*, 545–548.

Knudsen, E. (1998). Capacity for plasticity in the adult owl auditory system expanded by juvenile experience. *Science, 279*(5356), 1531–1533.

Kobatake, E., & Tanaka, K. (1994). Neuronal selectivities to complex object features in the ventral visual pathway of the macaque cerebral cortex. *Journal of Neurophysiology, 71*, 856–867.

Kobilka, B. (1992). Adrenergic receptors as models for G protein-coupled receptors. *Annual Review of Neuroscience, 15*, 87–114.

Kogan, J. H., Frankland, P. W., Blendy, J. A., Coblentz, J., Marowitz, Z., Schutz, G., & Silva, A. J. (1997). Spaced training induces normal long-term memory in CREB mutant mice. *Current Biology, 7*, 1–11.

Kolb, B., & Whishaw, I. Q. (1990). *Fundamentals of human neuropsychology*. San Francisco: Freeman.

Kolodny, E. H., & Cable, W. J. L. (1982). Inborn errors of metabolism. *Annals of Neurology, 11*, 221–232.

Kondo, Y., Sachs, B. D., & Sakuma, Y. (1997). Importance of the medial amygdala in rat penile erection evoked by remote stimuli from estrous females. *Behavioural Brain Research, 88*(2), 153–160.

Koob, G. F. (1995). Animal models of drug addiction. In F. E. Bloom, & D. J. Kupfer (eds.), *Psychopharmacology, the fourth generation of progress* (pp. 759–772). New York: Raven Press.

Koob, G. F., Sandman, C. A., & Strand, F. L. (1990). *A decade of neuropeptides: past, present, and future*. New York: New York Academy of Sciences.

Kopin, I. J., & Markey, S. P. (1988). MPTP toxicity: Implications for research in Parkinson's disease. *Annual Review of Neuroscience, 11*, 81–96.

Korenman, S. G., & Barchas, J. D. (1993). *Biological basis of substance abuse*. New York: Oxford University Press.

Kosslyn, S. M., Chabris, C. F., Marsolek, C. J., & Koenig, O. (1992). Categorical versus coordinate spatial relations: computational analyses and computer simulations. *Journal of Experimental Psychology: Human Perception and Performance, 18*, 562–577.

Kovelman, J. A., & Scheibel, A. B. (1984). A neurohistological correlate of schizophrenia. *Biological Psychiatry, 19*, 1601.

Kraepelin, E. (1919). *Dementia praecox and paraphrenia*. Edinburgh: Livingstone.

Kramer, M. S., Cutler, N., Feighner, J., Shrivastava, R. et al. (1998). Distinct mechanism for antidepressant activity by blockade of central substance P receptors. *Science, 281*, 1640–1645.

Krasne, F. B., & Glanzman, D. L. (1995). What we can learn from invertebrate learning. *Annual Review of Psychology, 45*, 585–624.

Kraut, R. E., & Johnston, R. E. (1979). Social and emotional messages of smiling: An ethological approach. *Journal of Personality & Social Psychology, 37*, 1539–1553.

Krebs, J. R., Sherry, D. F., Healy, S. D., Perry, V. H., & Vaccarino, A. L. (1989). Hippocampal specialisation of food-storing birds. *Proceedings of the National Academy of Sciences, U.S.A, 86*, 1388–1392.

Kreuz, L. E., & Rose, R. M. (1972). Assessment of aggressive behavior and plasma testosterone in a young criminal population. *Psychosomatic Medicine, 34*, 321–332.

Kril, J., Halliday, G., Svoboda, M., & Cartwright, H. (1997). The cerebral cortex is damaged in chronic alcoholics. *Neuroscience, 79*(4), 983–998.

Kruesi, M. J. (1979). Cruelty to animals and CSF 5HIAA. *Psychiatry Research, 28*, 115–116.

Krug, M., Lössner, B., & Ott, T. (1984). Anisomycin blocks the late phase of long-term potentiation in the dentate gyrus of freely moving rat. *Brain Research Bulletin, 13*, 39–42.

Krystal, A., Krishnan, K. R., Raitiere, M., Poland, R., Ritchie, J. C., Dunnick, N. R., Hanada, K., & Nemeroff, C. B. (1990). Differential diagnosis and pathophysiology of Cushing's syndrome and primary affective disorder. *Journal of Neuropsychiatry and Clinical Neurosciences, 2*, 34–43.

Kubanis, P., & Zornetzer, S. F. (1981). Age-related behavioral and neurobiological changes: a review with emphasis of memory. *Behavioral and Neural Biology, 31*, 115–172.

Kuffler, S. W. (1953). Discharge patterns and functional organization of mammalian retina. *Journal of Neurophysiology, 16*, 37–68.

Kuljis, R. O., & Rakic, P. (1990). Hypercolumns in primate visual cortex can develop in the absence of cues from photoreceptors. *Proceedings of the National Academy of Sciences, U.S.A., 87*, 5303–5306.

Kutas, M., & Hillyard, S. A. (1980). Reading senseless sentences: Brain potentials reflect semantic incongruity. *Science, 207*, 203–5.

Löwel, S., & Singer, W. (1992). Selection of intrinsic horizontal connections in the visual cortex by correlated neuronal activity. *Science, 255*, 209–212.

LaBar, K. S., Gatenby, J. C., Gore, J. C., Ledoux, J. E., & Phelps, E. A. (1998). Human amygdala activation during conditioned fear acquisition and extinction: A mixed-trial fMRI study. *Neuron, 20*, 937–945.

Lacey, J. I., & Lacey, B. C. (1970). Some autonomic-central nervous system interrelationships. In P. Black (ed.), *Physiological correlates of emotion*. New York: Academic.

Lachman, H. M., Papolos, D. F., Boyle, A., Sheftel G., Juthani, M., Edwards, E., & Henn, F. A. (1993). Alterations in glucorticoid inducible RNAs in the limbic system of learned helpless rats. *Brain Research, 609*, 110–116.

Lack, D. (1968). *Ecological adaptations for breeding in birds*. London: Methuen.

Lajoie, Y., Teasdale, N., Cole, J. D., Burnett, M., Bard, C., Fleury, M., Forget, R., Paillard, J., & Lamarre, Y. (1996). Gait of a deafferented subject without large myelinated sensory fibers below the neck. *Neurology, 47*, 109–115.

Land, M. F., & Fernald, R. D. (1992). The evolution of eyes. *Annual Review of Neuroscience, 15*, 1–29.

Landau, B., & Levy, R. M. (1993). Neuromodulation techniques for medically refractory chronic pain. *Annual Review of Medicine, 44*, 279–287.

Lange, C. S. (1887). Ueber Gemuthsbewegungen. In W. James, & C. G. Lange (eds.), *The emotions* (pp. 33–90). Baltimore: Williams & Wilkins.

Langlais, P. J., Mandel, R. J., & Mair, R. G. (1992). Diencephalic lesions, learning impairments, and intact retrograde memory following acute thiamine deficiency in the rat. *Behavioural Brain Research, 48,* 177–185.

Langston, J. W. (1985). MPTP and Parkinson's disease. *Trends in Neurosciences, 8,* 79–83.

Lanska, D. J., & Lanska, M. J. (1994). Kluver-Bucy syndrome in juvenile neuronal ceroid lipofuscinosis. *Journal of Child Neurology, 9,* 67–69.

Larroche, J. (1977). *Developmental pathology of the neonate.* Excerpta Medica. New York: Elsevier.

Larsson, J., Gulyas, B., & Roland, P. E. (1996). Cortical representation of self-paced finger movement. *Neuroreport, 7,* 463–468.

Laufer, R., & Changeux, J. P. (1989). Activity-dependent regulation of gene expression in muscle and neuronal cells. *Molecular Neurobiology, 3,* 1–53.

Lavie, P. (1996). *The enchanted world of sleep.* New Haven, CT: Yale University Press.

Lavie, P., & Kripke, D. F. (1981). Ultradian circa 1.5-hour rhythms: A multioscillatory system. *Life Sciences, 29,* 2445–2450.

Lavond, D. G., Kim, J. J., & Thompson, R. F. (1993). Mammalian brain substrates of aversive classical conditioning. *Annual Review of Psychology, 44,* 317–342.

Laxova, R. (1994). Fragile X syndrome. *Advances in Pediatrics, 41,* 305–342.

Leber, S. M., Breedlove, S. M., & Sanes, J. R. (1990). Lineage, arrangement, and death of clonally related motoneurons in chick spinal cord. *Journal of Neuroscience, 10,* 2451–2462.

Lebrun, C. J., Blume, A., Herdegen, T., Seifert, K., Bravo, R., & Unger, T. (1995). Angiotensin II induces a complex activation of transcription factors in the rat brain: expression of Fos, Jun and Krox proteins. *Neuroscience, 65,* 93–99.

LeDoux, E. (1995). Emotion: Clues form the brain. *Annual Review of Psychology, 46,* 209–235.

Lee, K. S., Schottler, F., Oliver, M., & Lynch, G. (1980). Brief bursts of high-frequency stimulation produce two types of structural change in rat hippocampus. *Journal of Neurophysiology, 44,* 247–258.

Lefebvre, L., Whittle, P., Lascaris, E., & Finkelstein, A. (1997). Feeding innovations and forebrain size in birds. *Animal Behavior, 53,* 549–560.

Lefebvre, P. P., Malgrange, B., Staecker, H., Moonen, G., & Van de Water, T. R. (1993). Retinoic acid stimulates regeneration of mammalian auditory hair cells. *Science, 260,* 692–695.

Leibowitz, S. F. (1991). Brain neuropeptide Y: an integrator of endocrine, metabolic and behavioral processes. *Brain Research Bulletin, 27,* 333–337.

LeMay, M. (1977). Asymmetries of the skull and handedness. *Journal of the Neurological Sciences, 32,* 243–253.

Lenhoff, H. M., Wang, P. P., Greenberg, F., & Bellugi, U. (1997). Williams syndrome and the brain. *Scientific American, 277,* 68–73.

Lennie, P., Krauskopf, J., & Sclar, G. (1990). Chromatic mechanisms in striate cortex of macaque. *Journal of Neuroscience, 10,* 649–669.

Leon, M., Croskerry, P. G., & Smith, G. K. (1978). Thermal control of mother-young contact in rats. *Physiology and Behavior, 21,* 790–811.

Leonard, B. E. (1992). *Fundamentals of psychopharmacology.* New York: Wiley.

Lepage, M., Habib, R., & Tulving, E. (1998). Hippocampal PET activations of memory encoding and retrieval: The HIPER model. *Hippocampus, 8,* 313–322.

LeRoith, D., Shemer, J., & Roberts, C. T. Jr. (1992). Evolutionary origins of intercellular communication systems: Implications for mammalian biology. *Hormone Research, 38,* 1–6.

LeVay, S. (1991). A difference in hypothalamic structure between heterosexual and homosexual men. *Science, 253,* 1034–1037.

LeVay, S. (1996). Queer science: the use and abuse of research into homosexuality. (pp. x, 364 p). Cambridge, Mass: MIT Press.

Levenson, R. W., Ekman, P., & Friesen, W. V. (1990). Voluntary facial action generates emotion-specific autonomic nervous system activity. *Psychophysiology, 27,* 363–384.

Leventhal, A. G. (1979). Evidence that the different classes of relay cells of the cat's lateral geniculate nucleus terminate in different layers of the striate cortex. *Experimental Brain Research, 37,* 349–72.

Leventhal, A. G., Thompson, K. G., Liu, D., Zhou, Y., & Ault, S. J. (1995). Concomitant sensitivity to orientation, direction, and color of cells in layers 2, 3, and 4 of monkey striate cortex. *Journal of Neuroscience, 15,* 1808–1818.

Levi-Montalcini, R. (1982). Developmental neurobiology and the natural history of nerve growth factor. *Annual Review of Neuroscience, 5,* 341–362.

Levi-Montalcini, R. (1963). In J. Allen (ed.), *The nature of biological diversity.* New York: McGraw-Hill.

Levine, J. D., Gordon, N. C., & Fields, H. L. (1978). The mechanism of placebo analgesia. *Lancet, 2,* 654–657.

Levine, J. S., & MacNichol, E. F. (1982). Color vision in fishes. *Scientific American, 246,* 140–149.

Levine, S., Haltmeyer, G. C., & Karas, G. G. (1967). Physiological and behavioral effects of infantile stimulation. *Physiology & Behavior, 2,* 55–59.

Levine, S., & Ursin, H. (1980). *Coping and health.* New York: Plenum Press.

Levinthal, F., Macagno, E., & Levinthal, C. (1976). Anatomy and development of identified cells in isogenic organisms. *Cold Spring Harbor Symposium on Quantitative Biology, 40,* 321–331.

Levitt, P., Harvey, J., Friedman, E., Simansky, K., & Murphy, E. (1997). New evidence for neurotransmitter influences on brain development. *Trends In Neurosciences, 20*(6), 269–274.

Levy, D. L., Holzman, P. S., Matthysse, S., & Mendell, N. R. (1993). Eye tracking dysfunction and schizophrenia: a critical perspective. *Schizophrenia Bulletin, 19,* 461–536.

Lewin, G. R., & Barde, Y. A. (1996). Physiology of the neurotrophins. *Annual Review of Neuroscience, 19,* 289–317.

Lewis, D. O. (1990). Neuropsychiatric and experiential correlates of violent juvenile delinquency. *Neuropsychology Review, 1,* 125–136.

Lewis, D. O., Shankok, S. S., & Pincus, J. (1979). Juvenile male sexual assaulters. *American Journal of Psychiatry, 136,* 1194–1195.

Lewis, R. (1998). Flies invade human genetics. *The Scientist, 12,* 1, 4–5.

Lewy, A. J., Ahmed, S., Jackson, J. M., & Sack, R. L. (1992). Melatonin shifts human circadian rhythms according to a phase-response curve. *Chronobiology International, 9,* 380–392.

Ley, R. G., & Bryden, M. P. (1982). A dissociation of right and left hemispheric effects for recognizing emotional tone and verbal content. *Brain & Cognition, 1,* 3–9.

Lhermitte, F., Pillon, B., & Serdaru, M. (1986). Human autonomy and the frontal lobes. Part 1. Imitation and utilization behavior: A neuropsychological study of 75 patients. *Annals of Neurology, 19,* 326–335.

Li, X. J., Li, S. H., Sharp, A. H., Nucifora, F. C. Jr., Schilling, G., Lanahan, A., Worley, P., Snyder, S. H., & Ross, C. A. (1995). A Huntingtin-associated protein enriched in brain with implications for pathology. *Nature, 378,* 398–402.

Li, X. J., Sharp, A. H., Li, S. H., Dawson, T. M., Snyder, S. H., & Ross, C. A. (1996). Huntingtin-associated protein (HAP1): Discrete neuronal localizations in the brain resemble those of neuronal nitric oxide synthase. *Proceedings of the National Academy of Sciences U.S.A., 93,* 4839–4844.

Li, Y., Field, P. M., & Raisman, G. (1997). Repair of adult rat corticospinal tract by transplants of olfactory ensheathing cells. *Science, 277,* 2000–2002.

Licht, P., Frank, L. G., Pavgi, S., Yalcinkaya, T. M., Siiteri, P. K., & Glickman, S. E. (1992). Hormonal correlates of 'masculinization' in female spotted hyenas (*Crocuta crocuta*). 2. Maternal and fetal steroids. *Journal of Reproduction and Fertility, 95,* 463–474.

Lichtman, J. W., & Purves, D. (1980). The elimination of redundant preganglionic innervation to hamster sympathetic ganglion cells in early post-natal life. *Journal of Physiology, 301,* 213–228.

Liebowitz, M. R., Gorman, J. M., Fryer, A., Dillon, D., Levitt, M., & Klein, D. F. (1986). Possible mechanisms for lactate's induction of panic. *American Journal of Psychiatry, 143,* 495–502.

Lin, X. Y., & Glanzman, D. L. (1994). Long-term potentiation of *Aplysia* sensorimotor synapses in cell culture: regulation by postsynaptic voltage. *Proceedings of the Royal Society of London, Series B, 255,* 113–118.

Lindemann, B. (1995). Sweet and salty: Transduction in taste. *News in Physiological Sciences, 10,* 166–170.

Linden, D. J. (1994). Long-term synaptic depression in the mammalian brain. *Neuron, 12,* 457–472.

Lindvall, O., Sawle, G., Widner, H., Rothwell, J. C., Bjorklund, A., Brooks, D., Brundin, P., Frackowiak, R., Marsden, C. D., Odin, P. et al. (1994). Evidence for long-term survival and function of dopaminergic grafts in progressive Parkinson's disease. *Annals of Neurology, 35,* 172–180.

Lisk, R. D. (1962). Diencephalic placement of estradiol and sexual receptivity in the female rat. *American Journal of Physiology, 203*(3), 493–496.

Lisman, J. (1989). A mechanism for the Hebb and the anti-Hebb processes underlying learning and memory. *Proc. Natl. Acad. Sci. USA, 86,* 9574–9578.

Liu, C. N., & Chambers, W. W. (1958). Intraspinal sprouting of dorsal root axons. *Archives of Neurology and Psychiatry, 79,* 46–61.

Liu, D., Diorio, J., Tannenbaum, B., Caldji, C., Francis, D., Freedman, A., Sharma, S., Pearson, D., Plotsky, P. M., & Meaney, M. J. (1997). Maternal care, hippocampal glucocorticoid receptors, and hypothalamic-pituitary-adrenal responses to stress. *Science, 277,* 1659–1662.

Livingstone, M. S., & Hubel, D. (1984). Anatomy and physiology of a color system in the primate visual cortex. *Journal of Neuroscience, 4,* 309–356.

Livingstone, M. S., & Hubel, D. (1988). Segregation of form, color, movement, and depth: Anatomy, physiology, and perception. *Science, 240,* 740–749.

Lloyd, J. A. (1971). Weights of testes, thymi, and accessory reproductive glands in relation to rank in paired and grouped house mice (*Mus musculus*). *Proceedings of the Society for Experimental Biology and Medicine, 137,* 19–22.

Lockhart, M., & Moore, J. W. (1975). Classical differential and operant conditioning in rabbits (*Orycytolagus cuniculus*) with septal lesions. *Journal of Comparative and Physiological Psychology, 88,* 147–154.

Loeb, G. E. (1990). Cochlear prosthetics. *Annual Review of Neuroscience, 13,* 357–371.

Loewenstein, W. R. (1971). Mechano-electric transduction in the Pacinian corpuscle. Initiation of sensory impulses in mechanoreception. In *Handbook of sensory physiology: Vol.1. Principles of receptor physiology* (pp. 269–290). Berlin: Springer-Verlag.

Logan, C. G., & Grafton, S. T. (1995). Functional anatomy of human eyeblink conditioning determined with regional cerebral glucose metabolism and positron emission tomography. *Proceedings of the National Academy of Sciences, U.S.A., 92,* 7500–7504.

Luria, A. R. (1987). *The mind of a mnemonist.* Cambridge, MA: Harvard University Press.

Lush, I. E. (1989). The genetics of tasting in mice. VI. Saccharin, acesulfame, dulcin and sucrose. *Genetical Research, 53,* 95–99.

Lynch, E. D., Lee, M. K., Morrow, J. E., Welcsh, P. L., Leon, P. E., & King, M. C. (1997). Nonsyndromic deafness DFNA1 associated with mutation of a human homolog of the *Drosophila* gene *diaphanous. Science, 278,* 1315–1318.

Lynch, G., & Baudry, M. (1984). The biochemistry of memory: A new and specific hypothesis. *Science, 224,* 1057–1063.

Lynch, G., Larson, J., Staubli, U., & Granger, R. (1991). Variants of synaptic potentiation and different types of memory operations in hippocampus and related structures. In L. R. Squire, N. M. Weinberger, G. Lynch, & J. L. McGaugh (eds.), *Memory: Organization and locus of change* (pp. 330–363). New York: Oxford University Press.

Lynch, M. A., Errington, M. L., & Bliss, T. V. (1989). Nordihydroguaiaretic acid blocks the synaptic component of long-term potentiation and the associated increases in release of gluta-mate and arachidonate: an in vivo study in the dentate gyrus of the rat. *Neuroscience, 30,* 693–701.

Macagno, E., Lopresti, U., & Levinthal, C. (1973). Structural development of neuronal connections in isogenic organisms: Variations and similarities in the optic system of *Daphnia magna. Proceedings of the National Academy of Sciences (USA), 70,* 57–61.

Mace, G. M., Harvey, P. H., & Clutton-Brock, T. H. (1981). Brain size and ecology in small mammals. *Journal of Zoology, 193,* 333–354.

Machón, R. A., Mednick, S. A., & Huttunen, M. O. (1997). Adult major affective disorder after prenatal exposure to an influenza epidemic. *Archives of General Psychiatry, 54,* 322–328.

MacLean, P. D. (1970). The triune brain, emotion, and scientific bias. In F. O. Schmitt (ed.), *The neurosciences* (pp. 336–348). New York: Rockefeller University.

Madrazo, I., Franco-Bourland, R., Ostrosky-Solis, F., Aguilera, M., Cuevas, C., Zamorano, C., Morelos, A., Magallon, E., & Guizar-Sahagun, G. (1990). Fetal homotransplants (ventral mesencephalon and adrenal tissue) to the striatum of parkinsonian subjects. *Archives of Neurology, 47,* 1281–1285.

Maffei, L., & Fiorentini, A. (1973). The visual cortex as a spatial frequency analyser. *Vision Research, 13,* 1255–1267.

Magnusson, A., & Axelsson, J. (1993). The prevalence of seasonal affective disorder is low among descendants of Icelandic emigrants in Canada. *Archives of General Psychiatry, 50,* 947–951.

Magnusson, A., & Stefansson, J. G. (1993). Prevalence of seasonal affective disorder in Iceland. *Archives of General Psychiatry, 50,* 941–946.

Mair, W. G. P., Warrington, E. K., & Wieskrantz, L. (1979). Memory disorder in Korsakoff's psychosis. *Brain, 102,* 749–783.

Malinow, R., & Tsien, R. W. (1990). Presynaptic enhancement shown by whole-cell recordings of long-term potentiation in hippocampal slices. *Nature, 346,* 177–180.

Manfredi, M., Bini, G., Cruccu, G., Accornero, N., Berardelli, A., & Medolago, L. (1981). Congenital absence of pain. *Archives of Neurology, 38,* 507–511.

Mantyh, P. W., Demaster, E., Malhotra, A., Ghilardi, J. R., Rogers, S. D., Mantyh, C. R., Liu, H., Basbaum, A. I., Vigna, S. R., Maggio, J. E., & Simone, D. A. (1995). Receptor endocytosis and dendrite reshaping in spinal neurons after somatosensory stimulation. *Science, 268,* 1629–1632.

Mantyh, P. W., Rogers, S. D., Honore, P., Allen, B. J., Ghilardi, J. R., Li, J., Daughters, R. S., Lappi, D. A., Wiley, R. G., & Simone, D. A. (1997). Inhibition of hyperalgesia by ablation of lamina I spinal neurons expressing the substance P receptor. *Science, 278,* 275–279.

Margoliash, D. (1986). Preference for autogenous song by auditory neurons in a song system of the white-crowned sparrow. *Journal of Neuroscience, 6,* 1643–1661.

Margoliash, D., & Fortune, E. S. (1992). Temporal and harmonic combination-sensitive neurons in the zebra finch's HVc. *Journal of Neuroscience, 12,* 4309–4326.

Margraf, J., & Roth, W. T. (1986). Sodium lactate infusions and panic attacks: A review and critique. *Psychosomatic Medicine, 48,* 23–50.

Mariani, J., & Changeaux, J.-P. (1981). Ontogenesis of olivocerebellar relationships. I. Studies by intracellular recordings of the multiple innervation of Purkinje cells by climbing fibers in the developing rat cerebellum. *Journal of Neuroscience, 1,* 696–702.

Mark, R. F. (1980). Synaptic repression at neuromuscular junctions. *Physiological Reviews, 60,* 355–395.

Mark, V. H., & Ervin, F. R. (1970). *Violence and the brain.* New York: Harper & Row.

Marlatt, G. A. (1992). Substance abuse: Implications of a biopsychological model for prevention, treatment, and relapse prevention. In J. Grabowski, & G. R. VandenBos (eds.), *Psychopharmacology: Basic mechanisms and applied interventions* (pp. 131–162). Washington, D.C.: American Psychological Association.

Marler, P. (1991). Song-learning behavior: the interface with neuroethology. *Trends in Neurosciences, 14,* 199–206.

Marler, P., & Peters, S. (1982). Developmental overproduction and selective attrition: new processes in the epigenesis of birdsong. *Developmental Psychobiology, 15*, 369–378.

Marler, P., & Sherman, V. (1985). Innate differences in singing behaviour of sparrows reared in isolation from adult conspecific song. *Animal Behavior, 33*, 57–71.

Marler, P., & Sherman, V. (1983). Song structure without auditory feedback: Emendations of the auditory template hypothesis. *Journal of Neuroscience, 3*, 517–531.

Marsden, C. D., Rothwell, J. C., & Day, B. L. (1984). The use of peripheral feedback in the control of movement. *Trends in Neuroscience, 7*, 253–257.

Marshall, J. F., Richardson, J. S., & Teitelbaum, P. (1974). Nigrostriatal bundle damage and the lateral hypothalamic syndrome. *Journal of Comparative and Physiological Psychology, 87*, 800–830.

Martin, A., Wiggs, C. L., Ungerleider, L. G., & Haxby, J. V. (1996). Neural correlates of category-specific knowledge. *Nature, 379*, 649–652.

Martin, J. V., Wyatt, R. J., & Mendelson, W. B. (1985). Growth hormone secretion in sleep and waking. In W. P. Koella, E. Ruther, & H. Schulz (eds.), *Sleep '84* (pp. 185–188). Stuttgart: Gustav Fischer Verlag.

Martin, W. R., & Hayden, M. R. (1987). Cerebral glucose and dopa metabolism in movement disorders. *Canadian Journal of Neurological Sciences, 14*, 448–451.

Martinez, J. L., & Derrick, B. E. (1996). Long-term potentiation and learning. *Annual Review of Psychology, 47*, 33.

Martuza, R. L., Chiocca, E. A., Jenike, M. A., Giriunas, I. E., & Ballantine, H. T. (1990). Stereotactic radiofrequency thermal cingulotomy for obsessive compulsive disorder. *Journal of Neuropsychiatry and Clinical Neurosciences, 2*, 331–336.

Marx, J. L. (1985). "Anxiety peptide" found in brain. *Science, 227*, 934.

Marzani, D., & Wallman, J. (1997). Growth of the two layers of the chick sclera is modulated reciprocally by visual conditions. *Investigative Ophthalmology and Visual Science, 38*, 1726–1739.

Masliah, E., Salmon, D. P., Butters, N., DeTeresa, R., Hill, R., Hansen, L. A., & Katzman, R. (1991). Physical basis of cognitive alterations in Alzheimer's disease: synapse loss is the major correlate of cognitive impairment. *Annals of Neurology, 30*, 572–580.

Masters, W. H., & Johnson, V. E. (1970). *Human sexual inadequacy*. Boston: Little, Brown.

Masters, W. H., & Johnson, V. E. (1966). *Human sexual response*. Boston: Little, Brown.

Masters, W. H., Johnson, V. E., & Kolodny, R. C. (1994). *Heterosexuality*. New York: HarperCollins.

Masterton, R. B. (1993). Central auditory system. *Journal of Oto-Rhino-Laryngology and Its Related Specialties, 55*, 159–163.

Masterton, R. B., & Imig, T. J. (1984). Neural mechanisms for sound localization. *Annual Review of Physiology, 46*, 275–287.

Mathias, R. (1994). NIDA, the FDA, and nicotine regulation. *NIDA Notes, 9*, 5,7.

Matsuda, L. A., Lolait, S. J., Brownstein, M. J., Young, A. C., & Bonner, T. I. (1990). Structure of a cannabinoid receptor and functional expression of the cloned cDNA. *Nature, 346*, 561.

Matthies, H. (1989). Neurobiological aspects of learning and memory. *Annual Review of Psychology, 40*, 381–404.

McAllister, A. K., Katz, L. C., & Lo, D. C. (1997). Opposing roles for endogenous BDNF and NT-3 in regulating cortical dendritic growth. *Neuron, 18*, 767–778.

McBurney, D. H., Smith, D. V., & Shick, T. R. (1972). Gustatory cross adaptation: Sourness and bitterness. *Perception & Psychophysics, 11*, 2228–2232.

McCall, W. V., & Edinger, J. D. (1992). Subjective total insomnia: an example of sleep state misperception. *Sleep, 15*, 71–73.

McCann, U. D., Seiden, L. S., Rubin, L. J., & Ricaurte, G. A. (1997). Brain serotonin neurotoxicity and primary pulmonary hypertension from fenfluramine and dexfenfluramine. A systematic review of the evidence. *Journal of the American Medical Association, 278*, 666–672.

McCarthy, R. A., & Warrington, E. K. (1990). Cognitive neuropsychology: A clinical introduction. (pp. x, 428 p). San Diego: Academic Press.

McClintock, M. K. (1971). Menstrual synchrony and suppression. *Nature, 229*, 244–245.

McCormick, D. A., & Thompson, R. F. (1984). Cerebellum: Essential involvement in the classically conditioned eyelid response. *Science, 223*, 296–299.

McDonald, R. J., & White, N. M. (1993). A triple dissociation of memory systems: Hippocampus, amygdala and dorsal striatum. *Behavioral Neuroscience, 107*, 3–22.

McFadden, D. (1993). A masculinizing effect on the auditory systems of human females having male co-twins. *Proceedings of the National Academy of Sciences, U.S.A., 90*, 11900–11904.

McFadden, D. (1993). A speculation about the parallel ear asymmetries and sex differences in hearing sensitivity and otoacoustic emissions. *Hearing Research, 68*, 143–151.

McFadden, D., & Champlin, C. A. (1990). Reductions in overshoot during aspirin use. *Journal of the Acoustical Society of America, 87*, 2634–2642.

McFadden, D., & Pasanen, E. G. (1994). Otoacoustic emissions and quinine sulfate. *Journal of the Acoustical Society of America, 96*, 3460–3474.

Mcfadden, D., & Pasanen, E. (1998). Comparison of the auditory systems of heterosexuals and homosexuals: click-evoked otoacoustic emissions. *Proceedings of The National Academy of Sciences of The United States of America, 95*(5), 2709–2713.

McGaugh, J. L. (1995). Emotional activation, neuromodulatory systems, and memory. In D. L. Schacter (ed.), *Memory distortions: How minds, brains, and societies reconstruct the past* (pp. 255–273). Cambridge, MA: Harvard University Press.

McGaugh, J. L. (1968). A multi-trace view of memory storage processes. In D. Bovet (ed.), *Attuali orientamenti della ricerca sull' apprendimento e la memoria*. Rome: Academia Nazionale dei Lincei, Quaderno N. 109.

McGaugh, J. L. (1992). Neuromodulatory systems and the regulation of memory storage. In L. R. Squire, & N. Butters (eds.), *Neuropsychology of memory, 2nd edition* (pp. 386–401). New York: Guilford Press.

McGaugh, J. L. (1966). Time-dependent processes in memory storage. *Science, 153*, 1351–1358.

McGaugh, J. L., & Herz, M. J. (1972). *Memory consolidation*. San Francisco: Albion.

McGaugh, J. L., Introini-Collison, I. B., Cahill, L. F., Castellano, C., Dalmaz, C., Parent, M. B., & Williams, C. L. (1993). Neuromodulatory systems and memory storage: role of the amygdala. *Behavioural Brain Research, 58*, 81–90.

Mcgeer, P., Mcgeer, E., Suzuki, J., Dolman, C., & Nagai, T. (1984). Aging, Alzheimer's disease, and the cholinergic system of the basal forebrain. *Neurology, 34*(6), 741–745.

McKernan, M. G., & Shinnick-Gallagher, P. (1997). Fear conditioning induces a lasting potentiation of synaptic currents in vitro. *Nature, 390*, 607–611.

McKim, W. A. (1991). *Drugs and behavior: An introduction to behavioral pharmacology (2nd ed.)*. Englewood Cliffs, NJ: Prentice Hall.

McKinney, T. D., & Desjardins, C. (1973). Postnatal development of the testis, fighting behavior, and fertility in house mice. *Biology of Reproduction, 9*, 279–294.

McKinney, W. T. (1988). *Models of mental disorders: A new comparative psychiatry*. New York: Plenum Press.

McLaughlin, S. K., McKinnon, P. J., Spickofsky, N., Danho, W., & Margolskee, R. F. (1994). Molecular cloning of G proteins and phosphodiesterases from rat taste cells. *Physiology and Behavior, 56*, 1157–1164.

McMahon, H. T., Foran, P., Dolly, J. O., Verhage, M., Wiegant, V. M., & Nicholls, D. G. (1992). Tetanus toxin and botulinum toxins type A and B inhibit glutamate, gamma-aminobutyric acid, aspartate, and met-enkephalin release from synaptosomes. Clues to the locus of action. *Journal of Biological Chemistry, 267*, 21338–21343.

McNamara, J. O. (1984). Role of neurotransmitters in seizure mechanisms in the kindling model of epilepsy. *Federation Proceedings, 43*, 2516–2520.

Meckler, R. J., Mack, J. L., & Bennett, R. (1979). Sign language aphasia in a non-deaf mute. *Neurology, 29*, 1037–1040.

Meddis, R. (1979). The evolution and function of sleep. In D. A. Oakley, & H. C. Plotkin (eds.), *Brain, behavior and evolution*. London: Methuen.

Meddis, R. (1975). On the function of sleep. *Animal Behavior, 23,* 676–691.

Meddis, R. (1977). *The sleep instinct.* London: Routledge & Kegan Paul.

Mednick, S. A., Huttunen, M. O., & Machon, R. A. (1994). Prenatal influenza infections and adult schizophrenia. *Schizophrenia Bulletin, 20,* 263–267.

Mega, M. S., & Cummings, J. L. (1994). Frontal-subcortical circuits and neuropsychiatric disorders. *Journal of Neuropsychiatry and Clinical Neurosciences, 6,* 358–370.

Meisel, R. L., & Luttrell, V. R. (1990). Estradiol increases the dendritic length of ventromedial hypothalamic neurons in female Syrian hamsters. *Brain Research Bulletin, 25,* 165–168.

Meisel, R. L., & Sachs, B. D. (1994). The physiology of male sexual behavior. In E. Knobil & J. D. Neill (eds.). *The physiology of reproduction, 2nd edition, Vol. 1,* (pp 3–105). Raven: New York.

Melzack, R. (1984). Neuropsychological basis of pain measurement. *Advances in Pain Research,* 323–341.

Melzack, R. (1990). The tragedy of needless pain. *Scientific American, 262*(2), 27–33.

Melzack, R., & Wall, P. D. (1965). Pain mechanisms: a new history. *Science, 150,* 971–979.

Mendelson, W. B. (1997). Efficacy of melatonin as a hypnotic agent. *Journal of Biological Rhythms, 12,* 651–656.

Meredith, M. A., & Stein, B. E. (1983). Interactions among converging sensory inputs in the superior colliculus. *Science, 221,* 389–391.

Merigan, W. H., & Maunsell, J. H. (1993). How parallel are the primate visual pathways? *Annual Review of Neuroscience, 16,* 369–402.

Merzenich, M. M., & Jenkins, W. M. (1993). Reorganization of cortical representations of the hand following alterations of skin inputs induced by nerve injury, skin island transfers, and experience. *Journal of Hand Therapy, 6,* 89–104.

Merzenich, M. M., & Kaas, J. H. (1980). Principles of organization of sensory-perceptual systems in mammals. *Progress in Psychobiology and Physiological Psychology (Vol. 9), 9.*

Merzenich, M. M., Schreiner, C., Jenkins, W., & Wang, X. (1993). Neural mechanisms underlying temporal integration, segmentation, and input sequence representation: some implications for the origin of learning disabilities. *Annals of the New York Academy of Sciences, 682,* 1–22.

Mesulam, M.-M. (1985). Attention, confusional states and neglect. In M.-M. Mesulam (ed.), *Principles of behavioral neurology.* Philadelphia: F. A. Davis.

Mesulam, M. M. (1989). Behavioral neuroanatomy of cholinergic innervation in the primate cerebral cortex. *EXS, 57,* 1–11.

Miaskiewicz, S. L., Stricker, E. M., & Verbalis, J. G. (1989). Neurohypophyseal secretion in response to cholecystokinin but not meal-induced gastric distention in humans. *Journal of Clinical Endocrinology and Metabolism, 68,* 837–843.

Micheva, K., & Beaulieu, C. (1996). Quantitative aspects of synaptogenesis in the rat barrel field cortex with special reference to gaba circuitry. *Journal of Comparative Neurology, 373*(3), 340–354.

Middlebrooks, J. C., & Pettigrew, J. D. (1981). Functional classes of neurons in primary auditory cortex of the cat distinguished by sensitivity to sound location. *Journal of Neuroscience, 1,* 107–120.

Mignot, E., Nishino, S., Sharp, L. H., Arrigoni, J., Siegel, J. M., Reid, M. S., Edgar, D. M., Ciaranello, R. D., & Dement, W. C. (1993). Heterozygosity at the canarc-1 locus can confer susceptibility for narcolepsy: induction of cataplexy in heterozygous asymptomatic dogs after administration of a combination of drugs acting on monoaminergic and cholinergic systems. *Journal of Neuroscience, 13,* 1057–1064.

Mignot, E., Wang, C., Rattazzi, C., Gaiser, C., Lovett, M., Guilleminault, C., Dement, W. C., & Grumet, F. C. (1991). Genetic linkage of autosomal recessive canine narcolepsy with a mu immunoglobulin heavy-chain switch-like segment. *Proceedings of the National Academy of Sciences, U.S.A., 88,* 3475–3478.

Miles, L. E., & Dement, W. C. (1980). Sleep and aging. *Sleep, 3,* 1–220.

Miller, J. M., & Spelman, F. A. (1990). *Cochlear implants: models of the electrically stimulated ear.* New York: Springer-Verlag.

Milner, B. (1970). Memory and the medial temporal regions of the brain. In D. H. Pribram & D. E. Broadbent (eds.), *Biology of Memory.* New York: Academic.

Milner, B. (1965). Memory disturbance after bilateral hippocampal lesions. In P. M. Milner, & S. E. Glickman (eds.), *Cognitive processes and the brain.* Princeton: Van Nostrand.

Milner, P. M. (1992). The functional nature of neuronal oscillations. *Trends in Neurosciences, 15,* 387–388.

Milner, P. M. (1993). The mind and Donald O. Hebb. *Scientific American, 268*(1), 124–129.

Mirsky, A. F., & Duncan, C. C. (1986). Etiology and expression of schizophrenia: Neurobiological and psychosocial factors. *Annual Review of Psychology, 37,* 291–321.

Mishina, M., Kurosaki, T., Tobimatsu, T., Morimoto, Y., Noda, M., Yamamoto, T., Terao, M., Lindstrom, J., Takahashi, T., Kuno, M. et al. (1984). Expression of functional acetylcholine receptor from cloned cDNAs. *Nature, 307,* 604–608.

Mishkin, M., & Ungerleider, L. (1982). Contribution of striate inputs to the visuospatial functions of parieto-preoccipital cortex in monkeys. *Behavioural Brain Research, 6*(1), 57–77.

Miyashita, Y. (1993). Inferior temporal cortex: where visual perception meets memory. *Annual Review of Neuroscience, 16,* 245–263.

Mizumori, S. J. Y., Rosenzweig, M. R., & Bennett, E. L. (1985). Long-term working memory in the rat: Effects of hippocampally applied anisomycin. *Behavioral Neuroscience, 99,* 220–232.

Mohammed, A., Henriksson, B. G., Soderstrom, S., Ebendal, T., Olsson, T., & Sekl, J. R. (1993). Environmental influences on the central nervous system and their implications for the aging rat. *Behavioural Brain Research, 23,* 182–191.

Moldin, S. O., Reich, T., & Rice, J. P. (1991). Current perspectives on the genetics of unipolar depression. *Behavior Genetics, 21,* 211–242.

Monakow, C. von. (1914). *Die lokalisation im grosshirn und der abbau der funktion durch kortikale herde, von dr. med. C. v. Monakow. Mit 268 abbildungen im text und 2 tafeln.* Wiesbaden: J. F. Bergmann.

Moncada, S., Palmer, R. M., & Higgs, E. A. (1991). Nitric oxide: Physiology, pathophysiology, and pharmacology. *Pharmacological Reviews, 43,* 109–142.

Money, J., & Ehrhardt, A. A. (1972). *Man and woman, boy and girl.* Baltimore: Johns Hopkins University.

Montague, C. T., Farooqi, I. S., Whitehead, J. P., Soos, M. A., Rau, H., Wareham, N. J., Sewter, C. P., Digby, J. E., Mohammed, S. N., Hurst, J. A., Cheetham, C. H., Earley, A. R., Barnett, A. H., Prins, J. B., & O'Rahilly, S. (1997). Congenital leptin deficiency is associated with severe early-onset obesity in humans. *Nature, 387,* 903–908.

Monti-Bloch, L., Jennings-White, C., Dolberg, D. S., & Berliner, D. L. (1994). The human vomeronasal system. *Psychoneuroendocrinology, 19,* 673–686.

Moore, C. L., Dou, H., & Juraska, J. M. (1992). Maternal stimulation affects the number of motor neurons in a sexually dimorphic nucleus of the lumbar spinal cord. *Brain Research, 572,* 52–56.

Moore-Ede, M. C. (1982). *The clocks that time us: physiology of the circadian timing system.* Cambridge, MA: Harvard University Press.

Moore, R. Y. (1983). Organization and function of a central nervous system circadian oscillator: The suprachiasmatic nucleus. *Federation Proceedings, 42,* 2783–2789.

Moore, R. Y., & Eichler, V. B. (1972). Loss of circadian adrenal corticosterone rhythm following suprachiasmatic lesions in the rat. *Brain Research, 42,* 201–206.

Moran, D. T., Jafek, B. W., & Rowley 3rd, J. C. (1991). The vomeronasal (Jacobson's) organ in man: ultrastructure and frequency of occurrence. *Journal of Steroid Biochemistry and Molecular Biology, 39,* 545–552.

Moran, E. F. (1981). Human adaptation to arctic zones. *Annual Review of Anthropology, 10,* 1–25.

Morford, J. P., & Mayberry, R. I. (1999). A reexamination of "early exposure" and its implications for language acquisition by eye. In C. Chamberlain, J. P. Morford, & R. I. Mayberry (Eds), *Language acquisition by eye.* Mahwah, NJ: Lawrence Erlbaum.

Mori, E., Hirono, N., Yamashita, H., Imamura, T., Ikejiri, Y., Ikeda, M., Kitagaki, H., Shimomura, T., & Yoneda, Y. (1997). Premorbid brain size as a determinant of reserve capacity against intellectual decline in Alzheimer's disease. *American Journal of Psychiatry, 154,* 18–24.

Morihisa, J., & McAnulty, G. B. (1985). Structure and function: Brain electrical activity mapping and computed tomography in schizophrenia. *Biological Psychiatry, 20,* 3–19.

Morrell, F. (1991). The role of secondary epileptogenesis in human epilepsy (editorial). *Archives of Neurology, 48,* 1221–1224.

Morrison, A. R. (1983). A window on the sleeping brain. *Scientific American, 248*(4), 94–102.

Morrison, R. G., & Nottebohm, F. (1993). Role of a telencephalic nucleus in the delayed song learning of socially isolated zebra finches. *Journal of Neurobiology, 24,* 1045–1064.

Moruzzi, G. (1972). The sleep-waking cycle. *Ergebnisse Der Physiologie, Biologischen Chemie Und Experimentellen Pharmakologie, 64,* 1–165.

Moscovitch, M. (1985). Memory from infancy to old age: Implications for theories of normal and pathological memory. *Annals of the New York Academy of Sciences, 444,* 78–96.

Moscovitch, M., & Olds, J. (1982). Asymmetries in spontaneous facial expressions and their possible relation to hemispheric specialization. *Neuropsychologia, 20,* 71–81.

Mott, F. W. (1895). Experimental inquiry upon the afferent tracts of the central nervous system of the monkey. *Brain, 18,* 1–20.

Mountcastle, V. B. (1984). Central nervous mechanisms in mechanoreceptive sensibility. In I. Darian-Smith (ed.), *Handbook of physiology, Section 1, Volume 3, Sensory Processes* (pp. 789–878). Bethesda: American Physiological Society.

Mountcastle, V. B. (1979). An organizing principle for cerebral function: the unit module and the distributed system. In F. O. Schmitt, & F. G. Worden (eds.), *The neurosciences: fourth study program.* Cambridge: MIT Press.

Mountcastle, V. B., Andersen, R. A., & Motter, B. C. (1981). The influence of attentive fixation upon the excitability of the light-sensitive neurons of the posterior parietal cortex. *Journal of Neuroscience, 1,* 1218–1235.

Movshon, J. A., & van Sluyters, R. C. (1981). Visual neural development. *Annual Review of Psychology, 32,* 477–522.

Moyer, J. R. Jr., Deyo, R. A., & Disterhoft, J. F. (1990). Hippocampectomy disrupts trace eye-blink conditioning in rabbits. *Behavioral Neuroscience, 104,* 243–252.

Mukhametov, L. M. (1984). Sleep in marine mammals. In A. Borbely, & J. L. Valatx (eds.), *Sleep mechanisms (Experimental Brain Research Supplement 8).* Berlin: Springer-Verlag.

Mulkey, R. M., Herron, C. E., & Malenka, R. C. (1993). An essential role for protein phosphatases in hippocampal long-term depression. *Science, 261,* 1051–1055.

Murasugi, C. M., Salzman, C. D., & Newsome, W. T. (1993). Microstimulation in visual area MT: effects of varying pulse amplitude and frequency. *Journal of Neuroscience, 13,* 1719–1729.

Murphy, G. G., & Glanzman, D. L. (1997). Mediation of classical conditioning in *Aplysia californica* by long-term potentiation of sensorimotor synapses. *Science, 278,* 467–71.

Murphy, K. J., & Regan, C. M. (1998). Contributions of cell adhesion molecules to altered synaptic weightings during memory consolidation. *Neurobiology of Learning and Memory, 70,* 1–2, 73–81.

Nader, K., Bechara, A., & Van Der Kooy, D. (1997). Neurobiological constraints on behavioral models of motivation. *Annual Review of Psychology, 48,* 85–114.

Naeser, M., Gaddie, A., Palumbo, C., & Stiassny-Eder, D. (1990). Late recovery of auditory comprehension in global aphasia. Improved recovery observed with subcortical temporal isthmus lesion vs wernicke's cortical area lesion. *Archives of Neurology, 47*(4), 425–32.

Naeser, M., & Hayward, R. (1978). Lesion localization in aphasia with cranial computed tomography and the boston diagnostic aphasia exam. *Neurology, 28*(6), 545–51.

Natelson, B. H. (1985). Neurocardiology: An interdisciplinary area for the 80s. *Archives of Neurology, 42,* 178–184.

Nathan, P. E., & Gorman, J. M. (1998). *A guide to treatments that work.* New York: Oxford University Press.

Nathans, J. (1987). Molecular biology of visual pigments. *Annual Review of Neuroscience, 10,* 163–194.

Nathanson, J. A. (1984). Caffeine and related methylxanthines: Possible naturally occurring pesticides. *Science, 226,* 184–187.

National Research Council. Commission on Life Science. (1988). *Use of laboratory animals in biomedical and behavioral research.* Washington, D. C.: National Academy Press.

National Research CouncilCommittee on Animals as Monitors of Environmental Hazards. (1991). *Animals as sentinels of environmental health hazards.* Washington, D. C.: National Academy Press.

Neitz, J., Geist, T., & Jacobs, G. H. (1989). Color vision in the dog. *Visual Neuroscience, 3,* 119–125.

Neitz, J., & Jacobs, G. H. (1984). Electroretinogram measurements of cone spectral sensitivity in dichromatic monkeys. *Optics and Image Science, 1,* 1175–1180.

Nelson, R. J. (1995). *Introduction to behavioral endocrinology.* Sunderland, MA: Sinauer.

Nelson, R. J., Demas, G. E., Huang, P. L., Fishman, M. C., Dawson, V. L., Dawson, T. M., & Snyder, S. H. (1995). Behavioural abnormalities in male mice lacking neuronal nitric oxide synthase. *Nature, 378,* 383–386.

Nestler, E. J., & Duman, R. S. (1995). Intracellular messenger pathways as mediators of neural plasticity. In F. E. Bloom, & D. J. Kupfer (eds.), *Psychopharmacology: the fourth generation of progress* (pp. 695–704). New York: Raven Press.

Neville, H. J., Bavelier, D., Corina, D., Rauschecker, J., Karni, A., Lalwani, A., Braun, A., Clark, V., Jezzard, P., & Turner, R. (1998). Cerebral organization for language in deaf and hearing subjects: Biological constraints and effects of experience. *Proceedings of the National Academy of Sciences U.S.A., 95,* 922–929.

Neville, H. J., Mills, D. L., & Lawson, D. S. (1992). Fractionating language: Different neural subsystems with different sensitive periods. *Cerebral Cortex, 2,* 244–258.

Newsome, W. T., Wurtz, R. H., Dursteler, M. R., & Mikami, A. (1985). Deficits in visual motion processing following ibotenic acid lesions of the middle temporal visual area of the macaque monkey. *Journal of Neuroscience, 5,* 825–840.

Nicoll, J. A., Burnett, C., Love, S., Graham, D. I., Dewar, D., Ironside, J. W., Stewart, J., & Vinters, H. V. (1997). High frequency of apolipoprotein E epsilon 2 allele in hemorrhage due to cerebral amyloid angiopathy. *Annals of Neurology, 41,* 716–721.

Nicoll, J. A., Roberts, G. W., & Graham, D. I. (1996). Amyloid beta-protein, APOE genotype and head injury. *Annals of the New York Academy of Sciences, 777,* 271–275.

Nieto-Sampedro, M., & Cotman, C. W. (1985). Growth factor induction and temporal order in central nervous system repair. In C. W. Cotman (ed.), *Synaptic plasticity* (pp. 407–457). New York: Guilford.

Nobler, M. S., Sackeim, H. A., Prohovnik, I., Moeller, J. R., Mukherjee, S., Schnur, D. B., Prudic, J., & Devanand, D. P. (1994). Regional cerebral blood flow in mood disorders. III. Treatment and clinical response. *Archives of General Psychiatry, 51,* 884–897.

Nobre, A. C., Sebestyen, G. N., Gitelman, D. R., Mesulam, M. M., Frackowiak, R. S., & Frith, C. D. (1997). Functional localization of the system for visuospatial attention using positron emission tomography. *Brain, 120,* 515–533.

Noguchi, H. (1911). Serum diagnosis of syphilis and the butyric acid test for syphilis. (pp. ix, 238 p). Philadelphia & London: J. B. Lippincott company.

Nordberg, A. (1996). Functional studies of new drugs for the treatment of Alzheimer's disease. *Acta Neurologica Scandinavica. Supplementum, 165,* 137–44.

Nordeen, E. J., Nordeen, K. W., Sengelaub, D. R., & Arnold, A. P. (1985). Androgens prevent normally occurring cell death in a sexually dimorphic spinal nucleus. *Science, 229,* 671–673.

Norman, A. W., & Litwack, G. (1987). *Hormones.* Orlando: Academic Press.

Norsell, U. (1980). Behavioral studies of the somatosensory system. *Physiological Reviews, 60,* 327–354.

Nottebohm, F. (1981). A brain for all seasons: Cyclical anatomical changes in song control nuclei of the canary brain. *Science, 214,* 1368–1370.

Nottebohm, F. (1980). Brain pathways for vocal learning in birds: A review of the first 10 years. *Progress in Psychobiology and Physiological Psychology, 9.*

Nottebohm, F. (1987). Plasticity in adult avian central nervous system: possible relations between hormones, learning, and brain repair. In F. Plum (ed.), *Higher functions of the nervous system, Section 1, Vol 5 Handbook of physiology.* Washington D.C.: American Physiological Society.

Nottebohm, F. (1991). Reassessing the mechanisms and origins of vocal learning in birds. *Trends in Neurosciences, 14,* 297–304.

Nottebohm, F., & Arnold, A. P. (1976). Sexual dimorphism in vocal control areas of the songbird brain. *Science, 194,* 211–213.

Nottebohm, F., Stokes, T. M., & Leonard, C. M. (1976). Central control of song in the canary, *Serinus canarius. Journal of Comparative Neurology, 165,* 457–486.

Nougier, V., Bard, C., Fleury, M., Teasdale, N., Cole, J., Forget, R., Paillard, J., & Lamarre, Y. (1996). Control of single-joint movements in deafferented patients: Evidence for amplitude coding rather than position control. *Experimental Brain Research, 109,* 473–82.

Novikov, S. N. (1993). The genetics of pheromonally mediated intermale aggression in mice: current status and prospects of the model. *Behavior Genetics, 23,* 505–508.

Nozza, R., Sabo, D., & Mandel, E. (1997). A role for otoacoustic emissions in screening for hearing impairment and middle ear disorders in school-age children. *Ear and Hearing, 18*(3), 227–39.

Nyberg, L., Cabeza, R., & Tulving, E. (1996). PET studies of encoding and retrieval: The HERA model. *Psychonomic Bulletin & Review, 3,* 135–148.

O'Keefe, J., & Dostrovsky, J. (1971). The hippocampus as a spatial map. Preliminary evidence from unit activity in the freely-moving rat. *Brain Research, 34,* 171–5.

Oatley, K., & Jenkins, J. M. (1996). Understanding emotions. (pp. xxvi, 448 p). Cambridge, Mass: Blackwell Publishers.

Ojemann, G., & Mateer, C. (1979). Human language cortex: Localization of memory, syntax, and sequential motor-phoneme identification systems. *Science, 205,* 1401–1403.

Okubo, Y., Suhara, T., Suzuki, K., Kobayashi, K., Inoue, O., Terasaki, O., Someya, Y., Sassa, T., Sudo, Y., Matsushima, E., Iyo, M., Tateno, Y., & Toru, M. (1997). Decreased prefrontal dopamine D1 receptors in schizophrenia revealed by PET. *Nature, 385,* 634–6.

Olds, J., & Milner, P. (1954). Positive reinforcement produced by electrical stimulation of septal area and other regions of the rat brain. *Journal of Comparative and Physiological Psychology, 47,* 419–427.

Ontiveros, A., Fontaine, R., Breton, G., Elie, R., Fontaine, S., & Dery, R. (1989). Correlation of severity of panic disorder and neuroanatomical changes on magnetic resonance imaging. *Journal of Neuropsychiatry and Clinical Neurosciences, 1,* 404–408.

Oppenheim, R. W. (1991). Cell death during development of the nervous system. *Annual Review of Neuroscience, 14,* 453–501.

Orban, G., Dupont, P., Vogels, R., De, B. B., Bormans, G., & Mortelmans, L. (1996). Task dependency of visual processing in the human visual system. *Behavioural Brain Research, 76*(1–2), 215–23.

Osterberg, G. (1935). Topography of the rods and cones in the human retina. *Acta Ophthalmologica (Supplement 6).*

Osterhout, L. (1997). On the brain response to syntactic anomalies: manipulations of word position and word class reveal individual differences. *Brain & Language, 59*(3), 494–522.

Ott, A., Slooter, A. J., Hofman, A., Van Harskamp, F., Witteman, J. C., Van Broeckhoven, C., Van Duijn, C. M., & Breteler, M. M. (1998). Smoking and risk of dementia and Alzheimer's disease in a population-based cohort study: the Rotterdam Study. *Lancet, 351,* 1840–3.

Ottoson, D. (1995). Wenner-Gren International Series, Vol. 66. Challenges and perspectives in neuroscience. D. Ottoson et al. (eds.). *Challenges and perspectives in neuroscience. Wenner-Gren International Series, Vol. 66.* Amsterdam: Elsevier.

Overstreet, D. H. (1993). The Flinders sensitive line rats: a genetic animal model of depression. *Neuroscience and Biobehavioral Reviews, 17,* 51–68.

Panksepp, J. (1982). Toward a general psychobiological theory of emotions. *Behavioral & Brain Sciences, 5,* 407–467.

Pantev, C., Oostenveld, R., Engelien, A., Ross, B., Roberts, L. E., & Hoke, M. (1998). Increased auditory cortical representation in musicians. *Nature, 392,* 811–14.

Pantle, A., & Sekuler, R. (1968). Size detecting mechanisms in human vision. *Science, 162,* 1146–1148.

Papez, J. W. (1937). A proposed mechanism of emotion. *Archives of Neurology and Psychiatry, 38,* 725–745.

Papka, M., Ivry, R., & Woodruff-Pak, D. S. (1994). Eyeblink classical conditioning and time production in patients with cerebellar damage. *Society of Neuroscience Abstracts, 20,* 360.

Papousek, H. (1992). Experimental studies of appetitional behavior in human newborns and infants. *Advances in Infancy Studies, 7,* xix–liii.

Paradiso, S., Andreasen, N. C., O'Leary, D. S., Arndt, S., & Robinson, R. G. (1997). Cerebellar size and cognition: Correlations with IQ, verbal memory and motor dexterity. *Neuropsychiatry, Neuropsychology, and Behavioral Neurology, 10,* 1–8.

Park, S., Como, P. G., Cui, L., & Kurlan, R. (1993). The early course of the Tourette's syndrome clinical spectrum. *Neurology, 43,* 1712–1715.

Parkes, J. D. (1985). *Sleep and its disorders.* Philadelphia: Saunders.

Patterson, F. G. (1978). The gestures of a gorilla: language acquisition in another pongid. *Brain and Language, 5,* 72–97.

Patterson, T. A., Rosenzweig, M. R., & Bennett, E. L. (1987). Amnesia produced by anisomycin in an appetitive task is not due to conditioned aversion. *Behavioral and Neural Biology, 47,* 17–26.

Paulson, H. L., & Fischbeck, K. H. (1996). Trinucleotide repeats in neurogenetic disorders. *Annual Review of Neuroscience, 19,* 79–107.

Pavlov, I. P. (1927). *Conditioned reflexes.* Oxford: Oxford University Press.

Pearson, K. G. (1993). Common principles of motor control in vertebrates and invertebrates. *Annual Review of Neuroscience, 16,* 265–297.

Pechura, C. M., & Martin, J. B. (1991). Mapping the brain and its functions: integrating enabling technologies into neuroscience research. In C. M Pechura & J. B. Martin (eds.). *Mapping the brain and its functions: Integrating enabling technologies into neuroscience research.* National Academy Press: Washington, D.C.

Peele, S., & Brodsky, A. (1991). *The truth about addiction and recovery.* New York: Simon & Schuster.

Penfield, W., & Roberts, L. (1959). *Speech and brain-mechanisms.* Princeton, NJ: Princeton University Press.

Pennisi, E. (1997). The architecture of hearing [news; comment]. *Science, 278*(5341), 1223–4.

Peris, J., Boyson, S. J., Cass, W. A., Curella, P., Dwoskin, L. P., Larson, G., Lin, L. H., Yasuda, R. P., & Zahniser, N. R. (1990). Persistence of neurochemical changes in dopamine systems after repeated cocaine administration. *Journal of Pharmacology and Experimental Therapeutics, 253,* 38–44.

Perkins, A. T., & Teyler, T. J. (1988). A critical period for long-term potentiation in the developing rat visual cortex. *Brain Research, 439*(1–2), 222–229.

Perl, E. R. (1980). Afferent basis of nociception and pain: evidence from the characteristics of sensory receptors and their projections to the spinal dorsal horn. *Research Publications - Association for Research in Nervous and Mental Disease, 58,* 19–45.

Perry, V. H. O. R., & Cowey, A. (1984). Retinal ganglion cells that project to the dorsal lateral geniculate nucleus in the macaque monkey. *Neuroscience, 12,* 1101–1123.

Pert, C. B., & Snyder, S. H. (1993). Properties of opiate-receptor binding in rat brain. *Proceedings of the National Academy of Sciences, U.S.A., 70,* 2243–2247.

Peschanski, M., Defer, G., N'Guyen, J. P., Ricolfi, F., Monfort, J. C., Remy, P., Geny, C., Samson, Y., Hantraye, P., Jeny, R. et al. (1994). Bilateral motor improvement and alteration of L-dopa effect in two patients with Parkinson's disease following intrastriatal transplantation of foetal ventral mesencephalon. *Brain, 117*, 487–499.

Peter, M. E., Medema, J. P., & Krammer, P. H. (1997). Does the *Caenorhabditis elegans* protein CED-4 contain a region of homology to the mammalian death effector domain? *Cell Death and Differentiation, 4*, 51–134.

Peterhans, E., & von der Heydt, R. (1989). Mechanisms of contour perception in monkey visual cortex. II. Contours bridging gaps. *Journal of Neuroscience, 9*, 1749–1763.

Peters, A., Palay, S. L., & Webster, H. de F. (1991). *The fine structure of the nervous system: neurons and their supporting cells.* New York: Oxford University Press.

Peterson, A. L., & Azrin, N. H. (1992). An evaluation of behavioral treatments for Tourette syndrome. *Behaviour Research and Therapy, 30*, 167–174.

Peterson, B., Riddle, M. A., Cohen, D. J., Katz, L. D., Smith, J. C., Hardin, M. T., & Leckman, J. F. (1993). Reduced basal ganglia volumes in Tourette's syndrome using three-dimensional reconstruction techniques from magnetic resonance images. *Neurology, 43*, 941–949.

Peterson, L. R., & Peterson, M. J. (1959). Short-term retention of individual verbal items. *J. Exp. Psychol., 58*, 193–198.

Petre-Quadens, O. (1972). Sleep in mental retardation. In C. D. Clemente, D. R. Purpura, & F. E. Mayer (eds.), *Sleep and the maturing nervous system* (pp. 1–2). New York: Academic.

Petrides, M., & Milner, B. (1982). Deficits on subject-ordered tasks after frontal- and temporal-lobe lesions in man. *Neuropsychologia, 20*, 249–262.

Petrij, F., Giles, R., Dauwerse, H., Saris, J., Hennekam, R., Masuno, M., Tommerup, N., Van, O. G., Goodman, R., Peters, D., & Et, A. (1995). Rubinstein-taybi syndrome caused by mutations in the transcriptional co-activator cbp [see comments]. *Nature, 376*(6538), 348–51.

Pettigrew, J. D., & Freeman, R. D. (1973). Visual experience without lines: Effect on developing cortical neurons. *Science, 182*, 599–601.

Petty, F., Kramer, G., Wilson, L., & Jordan, S. (1994). In vivo serotonin release and learned helplessness. *Psychiatry Research, 52*, 285–293.

Pfaff, D. W. (1997). Hormones, genes, and behavior. *Proceedings of the National Academy of Sciences U.S.A., 94*, 14213–6.

Pfaff, D. W. (1980). Estrogens and brain function: neural analysis of a hormone-controlled mammalian reproductive behavior. (pp. x, 281 p). New York: Springer-Verlag.

Pfaffmann, C., Frank, M., & Norgren, R. (1979). Neural mechanisms and behavioral aspects of taste. *Annual Review of Psychology, 30*, 283–325.

Pfefferbaum, A., Sullivan, E. V., Mathalon, D. H., Shear, P. K., & and Others. (1995). Longitudinal changes in magnetic resonance imaging brain volumes in abstinent and relapsed alcoholics. *Alcoholism: Clinical & Experimental Research, 19*(5), 1177–1191.

Phoenix, C. H., Goy, R. W., Gerall, A. A., & Young, W. C. (1959). Organizing action of prenatally administered testosterone propionate on the tissues mediating mating behavior in the female guinea pig. *Endocrinology, 65*, 369–382.

Pickens, R., & Thompson, T. (1968). Drug use by U.S. Army enlisted men in Vietnam: A followup on their return home. *Journal of Pharmacology and Experimental Therapeutics, 161*, 122–129.

Pines, J. (1992). Cell proliferation and control. *Current Opinion In Cell Biology, 4*(2), 144–8.

Pinker, S. (1994). *The language instinct.* New York: W. Morrow and Co.

Pitman, R. K. (1989). Post-traumatic stress disorder, hormones, and memory. *Biological Psychiatry, 26*, 221–223.

Pitman, R. K., & Orr, S. P. (1995). Psychophysiology of emotional memory networks in posttraumatic stress disorder. In J. L. McGaugh, N. M. Weinberger, & G. Lynch (eds.), *Brain and memory: modulation and mediation of neuroplasticity* (pp. 75–83). New York: Oxford University Press.

Pitts, J. W., & McClure, J. N. (1967). Lactate metabolism in anxiety neurosis. *New England Journal of Medicine, 277*, 1329–1336.

Plante, E. (1991). Mri findings in the parents and siblings of specifically language-impaired boys. *Brain and Language, 41*(1), 67–80.

Plante, E., Swisher, L., Vance, R., & Rapcsak, S. (1991). Mri findings in boys with specific language impairment. *Brain and Language, 41*(1), 52–66.

Plante, E. (1991). Mri findings in the parents and siblings of specifically language-impaired boys. *Brain & Language, 41*(1), 67–80.

Plautz, J. D., Kaneko, M., Hall, J. C., & Kay, S. A. (1997). Independent photoreceptive circadian clocks throughout *Drosophila. Science, 278*, 1632–1635.

Ploog, D. W. (1992). Neuroethological perspectives on the human brain: From the expression of emotions to intentional signing and speech. In A. Harrington (ed.), *So human a brain: Knowledge and values in the neurosciences* (pp. 3–13). Boston: Birkhauser.

Plutchik, R. (1994). *The psychology and biology of emotion.* New York: HarperCollins College Publishers.

Poinar, G. O. Jr. (1994). The range of life in amber: significance and implications in DNA studies. *Experientia, 50*, 536–542.

Poizner, H., Bellugi, U., & Klima, e. S. (1990). Biological foundations of language: clues from sign language. *Annual Review of Neuroscience, 13*, 283–307.

Polymeropoulos, M. H., Lavedan, C., Leroy, E., Ide, S. E., Dehejia, A., Dutra, A., Pike, B., Root, H., Rubenstein, J., Boyer, R., Stenroos, E. S., Chandrasekharappa, S., Athanassiadou, A., Papapetropoulos, T., Johnson, W. G., Lazzarini, A. M., Duvoisin, R. C., Di Iorio, G., Golbe, L. I., & Nussbaum, R. L. (1997). Mutation in the alpha-synuclein gene identified in families with Parkinson's disease. *Science, 276*, 2045–2047.

Poritsky, R. (1969). Two and three dimensional ultrastructure of boutons and glial cells on the motoneuronal surface in the cat spinal cord. *Journal of Comparative Neurology, 135*(4), 423–452.

Posner, M. I., & Raichle, M. E. (1994). *Images of mind.* New York: Scientific American Library.

Post, R., Weiss, S., Smith, M., Rosen, J., & Frye, M. (1995). Stress, conditioning, and the temporal aspects of affective disorders. *Annals of The New York Academy of Sciences, 771*, 677–696.

Premack, D. (1971). Language in a chimpanzee? *Science, 172*, 808–822.

Preti, G., Cutler, W. B., Garcia, C. R., Huggins, G. R., & Lawley, H. J. (1986). Human axillary secretions influence women's menstrual cycles: the role of donor extract of females. *Hormones and Behavior, 20*, 474–482.

Price, J. L., Carmichael, S. T., & Drevets, W. C. (1996). Networks related to the orbital and medial prefrontal cortex; a substrate for emotional behavior? *Progress in Brain Research, 107*, 523–536.

Price, M. A., & Vandenbergh, J. G. (1992). Analysis of puberty-accelerating pheromones. *Journal of Experimental Zoology, 264*, 42–45.

Price, R. A., & Gottesman, I. I. (1991). Body fat in identical twins reared apart: roles for genes and environment. *Behavior Genetics, 21*, 1–7.

Price, R. A., Kidd, K. K., Cohen, D. J., Pauls, D. L., & Leckman, J. F. (1985). A twin study of Tourette syndrome. *Archives of General Psychiatry, 42*, 815–820.

Pugh, E. N. Jr., & Lamb, T. D. (1993). Amplification and kinetics of the activation steps in phototransduction. *Biochimica Et Biophysica Acta, 1141*, 111–149.

Pugh, E. N. Jr., & Lamb, T. D. (1990). Cyclic GMP and calcium: the internal messengers of excitation and adaptation in vertebrate photoreceptors. *Vision Research, 30*, 1923–1948.

Purdy, R. H., Moore, P. H. Jr., Morrow, A. L., & Paul, S. M. (1992). Neurosteroids and GABAA receptor function. *Advances in Biochemical Psychopharmacology, 47*, 87–92.

Purves, D. (1988). *Body and brain: a trophic theory of neural connections.* Cambridge, MA: Harvard University Press.

Purves, W. K., Orians, G. H., & Heller, H. C. (1995). *Life: The science of biology* (5th ed.). Sunderland, MA: Sinauer.

Quinn, W. G., Harris, W. A., & Benzer, S. (1974). Conditioned behavior in *Drosophila melanogaster*. *Proceedings of the National Academy of Sciences, U.S.A., 71*, 708–712.

Quinn, W. G., Sziber, P. P., & Booker, R. (1979). The *Drosophila* memory mutant amnesiac. *Nature, 277*, 212–214.

Raab, D. H., & Ades, H. W. (1946). Cortical and midbrain mediation of a conditioned discrimination of acoustic intensities. *American Journal of Psychology, 59*, 59–83.

Rafal, R. D. (1994). Neglect. *Current Opinion in Neurobiology, 4*, 231–236.

Rahe, R. H., Biersner, R. J., Ryman, D. H., & Arthur, R. J. (1972). Psychosocial predictors of illness behavior and failure in stressful training. *Journal of Health and Social Behavior, 13*, 393–397.

Rainville, P., Duncan, G. H., Price, D. D., Carrier, B., & Bushnell, M. C. (1997). Pain affect encoded in human anterior cingulate but not somatosensory cortex. *Science, 277*, 968–971.

Raisman, G. (1978). What hope for repair of the brain? *Annals of Neurology, 3*, 101–106.

Raisman, G., & Field, P. M. (1971). Sexual dimorphism in the preoptic area of the rat. *Science, 173*, 731–733.

Rajendra, S., Lynch, J. W., Pierce, K. D., French, C. R., Barry, P. H., & Schofield, P. R. (1994). Startle disease mutations reduce the agonist sensitivity of the human inhibitory glycine receptor. *Journal of Biological Chemistry, 269*, 18739–18742.

Rakic, P. (1971). Guidance of neurons migrating to the fetal monkey neocortex. *Brain Research, 33*, 471–476.

Rakic, P. (1985). Mechanisms of neuronal migration in developing cerebellar cortex. In G. M. Edelman, W. M. Cowan, & E. Gull (eds.), *Molecular basis of neural development*. New York: Wiley.

Rakic, P., Bourgeois, J.-P., Eckenhoff, M. F., Zecevic, N., & Goldman-Rakic, P. S. (1986). Concurrent overproduction of synapses in diverse regions of the primate cerebral cortex. *Science, 232*, 232–235.

Raleigh, M. J., Brammer, G. L., McGuire, M. T., Pollack, D. B., & Yuwiler, A. (1992). Individual differences in basal cisternal cerebrospinal fluid 5-HIAA and HVA in monkeys. The effects of gender, age, physical characteristics, and matrilineal influences. *Neuropsychopharmacology, 7*, 295–304.

Ralph, M. R., Foster, R. G., Davis, F. C., & Menaker, M. (1990). Transplanted suprachiasmatic nucleus determines circadian period. *Science, 247*, 975–978.

Ralph, M. R., & Lehman, M. N. (1991). Transplantation: a new tool in the analysis of the mammalian hypothalamic circadian pacemaker. *Trends in Neurosciences, 14*, 362–366.

Ralph, M. R., & Menaker, M. (1988). A mutation of the circadian system in golden hamsters. *Science, 241*, 1225–1227.

Ramon y Cajal, S. (1894). La fine structure des centres nerveus. *Proceedings of the Royal Society of London, 55*, 444–468.

Ramsay, D. J., & Booth, D. A. (1991). *Thirst: Physiological and psychological aspects*. New York: Springer-Verlag.

Ranaldi, R., & Beninger, R. J. (1994). The effects of systemic and intracerebral injections of D1 and D2 agonists on brain stimulation reward. *Brain Research, 651*, 283–292.

Rand, M. N., & Breedlove, S. M. (1987). Ontogeny of functional innervation of bulbocavernosus muscles in male and female rats. *Brain Research, 430*, 150–152.

Randolph, M., & Semmes, J. (1974). Behavioral consequences of selective subtotal ablations in the postcentral gyrus of *Macaca mulatta*. *Brain Research, 70*, 55–70.

Rao, P. D. P., & Finger, T. E. (1984). Asymmetry of the olfactory system in the brain of the winter flounder *Pseudo-pleuronectes americanus*. *Journal of Comparative Neurology, 225*, 492–510.

Rapoport, J. L. (1989). The biology of obsessions and compulsions. *Scientific American, 260*, 82–89.

Rasmussen, P. (1996). The congenital insensitivity-to-pain syndrome (analgesia congenita): Report of a case. *International Journal of Paediatric Dentistry, 6*, 117–122.

Rauch, S. L., Jenike, M. A., Alpert, N. M., Baer, L., Breiter, H. C., Savage, C. R., & Fischman, A. J. (1994). Regional cerebral blood flow measured during symptom provocation in obsessive-compulsive disorder using oxygen 15-labeled carbon dioxide and positron emission tomography. *Archives of General Psychiatry, 51*, 62–70.

Rauch, S. L., Savage, C. R., Alpert, N. M., Miguel, E. C., Baer, L., Breiter, H. C., Fischman, A. J., Manzo, P. A., Moretti, C., & Jenike, M. A. (1995). A positron emission tomographic study of simple phobic symptom provocation. *Archives of General Psychiatry, 52*, 20–28.

Recanzone, G. H., Schreiner, D. E., & Merzenich, M. M. (1993). Plasticity in the frequency representation of primary auditory cortex following discrimination training in adult owl monkeys. *Journal of Neuroscience, 13*, 87–103.

Rechtschaffen, A., & Kales, A. (1968). *A manual of standardized terminology, techniques and scoring system for sleep stages of human subjects*. Bethesda, MD: U.S. National Institute of Neurological Diseases and Blindness, Neurological Information Network.

Redfern, P. A. (1970). Neuromuscular transmission in newborn rats. *Journal of Physiology, 109*, 701–709.

Redican, W. K. (1982). An evolutionary perspective on human facial displays. In P. Ekman (ed.), *Emotion in the human face, 2nd edition* (pp. 212–280). Elmsford, NY: Pergamon.

Reedy, F. E. J., Bartoshuk, L. M., Miller, I. J. J., Duffy, V. B., Lucchina, L., & Yanagisawa, K. (1993). Relationships among papillae, taste pores, and 6-n-propylthiouracil (prop) suprathreshold taste sensitivity. *Chemical Senses, 18*(5), 618–619.

Rehkamper, G., Haase, E., & Frahm, H. D. (1988). Allometric comparison of brain weight and brain structure volumes in different breeds of the domestic pigeon, *Columba livia* f. d. (fantails, homing pigeons, strassers). *Brain, Behavior & Evolution, 31*, 141–149.

Reichardt, L. F., & Tomaselli, K. J. (1991). Extracellular matrix molecules and their receptors: functions in neural development. *Annual Review of Neuroscience, 14*, 531–570.

Reid, M. S., Tafti, M., Nishino, S., Siegel, J. M., Dement, W. C., & Mignot, E. (1994). Cholinergic regulation of cataplexy in canine narcolepsy in the pontine reticular formation is mediated by M2 muscarinic receptors. *Sleep, 17*, 424–435.

Reiman, E. M., Raichle, M., Robins, E., Butler, F. K., Herscovitch, P., Fox, P., & Perlmutter, J. (1986). The application of positron emission tomography to the study of panic disorder. *American Journal of Psychiatry, 143*, 469–477.

Reisberg, D., & Heuer, F. (1995). Emotion's multiple effects on memory. In J. L. McGaugh, N. M. Weinberger, & G. Lynch (eds.), *Brain and memory: modulation and mediation of neuroplasticity* (pp. 84–92). New York: Oxford University Press.

Reisenzein, R. (1983). The Schacter theory of emotion: two decades later. *Psychological Bulletin, 94*, 239–264.

Rende, R., & Plomin, R. (1995). Nature, nurture, and the development of psychopathology. In D. Ciccheti, & D. J. Cohen (eds.), *Developmental psychopathology, Vol. 1: Theory and methods* (pp. 291–314). New York: John Wiley & Sons.

Renner, M. J., & Rosenzweig, M. R. (1987). *Enriched and impoverished environments: effects on brain andb ehavior*. New York: Springer-Verlag.

Reppert, S. M. (1985). Maternal entrainment of the developing circadian system. *Annals of the New York Academy of Science, 453*, 162–169.

Reppert, S. M., Perlow, M. J., Tamarkin, L., & Klein, D. C. (1979). A diurnal melatonin rhythm in primate cerebrospinal fluid. *Endocrinology, 104*, 295–301.

Rescorla, R. A. (1988). Behavioral studies of Pavlovian conditioning. *Annual Review of Neuroscience, 11*, 329–352.

Ressler, K. J., Sullivan, S. L., & Buck, L. B. (1994). A molecular dissection of spatial patterning in the olfactory system. *Current Opinion in Neurobiology, 4*, 588–596.

Reynolds, C. F., Kupfer, D. J., Taska, L. S., Hoch, C. H., & Sewitch, D. E. (1985). Sleep of healthy seniors: A revisit. *Sleep, 8*, 20–29.

Rhode, W. S. (1984). Cochlear mechanics. *Annual Review of Physiology, 46*, 231–246.

Ribeiro, R. C., Kushner, P. J., & Baxter, J. D. (1995). The nuclear hormone receptor gene superfamily. *Annual Review of Medicine, 46*, 443–453.

Rich, C. L., Young, D., & Fowler, R. C. (1986). San Diego suicide study. I. Young vs. old subjects. *Archives of General Psychiatry, 43*, 577–582.

Richard, F., & Dutrillaux, B. (1998). Origin of human chromosome 21 and its consequences: a 50-million-year-old story. *Chromosome Research, 6*(4), 263–268.

Richter, C. (1967). Sleep and activity: their relation to the 24-hour clock. *Proceedings of the Association for Research in Nervous and Mental Diseases, 45,* 8–27.

Ridley, R. M., & Baker, H. F. (1991). Can fetal neural transplants restore function in monkeys with lesion-induced behavioural deficits? *Trends in Neurosciences, 14,* 366–370.

Riley, V. (1981). Psychoneuroendocrine influences on immunocompetence and neoplasia. *Science, 212,* 1100–1110.

Rinn, W. E. (1984). The neuropsychology of facial expression: A review of the neurological and psychological mechanisms for producing facial expressions. *Psychological Bulletin, 95,* 52–77.

Roberts, A. H. (1969). *Brain damage in boxers.* London: Pitman.

Roberts, W. W., & Mooney, R. D. (1974). Brain areas controlling thermoregulatory grooming, prone extension, locomotion, and tail vasodilation in rats. *Journal of Comparative and Physiological Psychology, 86,* 470–480.

Robertson, D., & Irvine, D. R. (1989). Plasticity of frequency organization in auditory cortex of guinea pigs with partial unilateral deafness. *Journal of Comparative Neurology, 282,* 456–471.

Robins, L. N., & Regier, D. A. (1991). *Psychiatric disorders in America: the epidemiologic catchment area study.* New York: Free Press.

Rocca, W. A., Hofman, A., Brayne, C., Breteler, M. M., Clarke, M., Copeland, J. R., Dartigues, J. F., Engedal, K., Hagnell, O. H. T. J. et al. (1991). The prevalence of vascular dementia in Europe: facts and fragments from 1980–1990 studies. *Annals of Neurology, 30,* 817–824.

Rochlin, M. W., Wickline, K. M., & Bridgman, P. C. (1996). Microtubule stability decreases axon elongation but not axoplasm production. *Journal of Neuroscience, 16,* 3236–3246.

Roelink, H., Augsburger, A., Heemskerk, J., Korzh, V., Norlin, S., Ruiz i Altaba, A., Tanabe, Y., Placzek, M., Edlund, T., Jessell, T. M. et al. (1994). Floor plate and motor neuron induction by vhh-1, a vertebrate homolog of hedgehog expressed by the notochord. *Cell, 76,* 761–775.

Roffwarg, H. P., Muzio, J. N., & Dement, W. C. (1966). Ontogenetic development of the human sleep-dream cycle. *Science, 152*(3722), 604–619.

Rogan, M. T., Staubli, U. V., & Ledoux, J. E. (1997). Fear conditioning induces associative long-term potentiation in the amygdala. *Nature, 390,* 604–607.

Roland, E., & Larson, B. (1976). Focal increase of cerebral blood flow during stereognostic testing in man. *Archives of Neurology, 33,* 551–558.

Roland, P. E. (1984). Metabolic measurements of the working frontal cortex in man. *Trends in Neuroscience, 7,* 430–436.

Roland, P. E. (1980). Quantitative assessment of cortical motor dysfunction by measurement of the regional cerebral blood flow. *Scandinavian Journal of Rehabilitation Medicine, 7,* 27–41.

Rolls, E. T., & O'Mara, S. M. (1995). View-responsive neurons in the primate hippocampal complex. *Hippocampus, 5,* 409–424.

Romero-Apis, D., Babayan-Mena, J. I., Fonte-Vazquez, A., Gutierrez-Perez, D., Martinez-Oropeza, S., & Murillo-Murillo, L. (1982). Perdida del ojo fijador en adulto con ambliopia estrabica. *Anales Sociedad Mexicana De Oftalmologia, 56,* 445–452.

Rorabaugh, W. J. (1976). Estimated U. S. alcoholic beverage consumption, 1790–1860. *Journal of Studies on Alcohol, 37,* 357–364.

Rosen, G. D., Sherman, G. F., & Galaburda, A. M. (1993). Neuronal subtypes and anatomic asymmetry: changes in neuronal number and cell-packing density. *Neuroscience, 56,* 833–839.

Rosenbaum, D. A. (1991). *Human motor control.* San Diego: Academic Press.

Rosengren, A., Tibblin, G., & Wilhelmsen, L. (1991). Self-perceived psychological stress and incidence of coronary artery disease in middle-aged men. *American Journal of Cardiology, 68,* 1171–1175.

Rosenman, R. H., Brand, R. J., Jenkins, C. D., Friedman, M., Straus, R., & Wurm, M. (1975). Coronary heart disease in the Western Collaborative Group Study: final follow-up experience of 8 1/2 years. *Journal of the American Medical Association, 233,* 872–877.

Rosenthal, N. E., Sack, D. A., Carpenter, C. J., Parry, B. L., Mendelson, W. B., & Wehr, T. A. (1985). Antidepressant effects of light in seasonal affective disorder. *American Journal of Psychiatry, 142,* 606–608.

Rosenzweig, M. R. (1980). Animal models for effects of brain lesions and for rehabilitation. In P. Bach-y-Rita (ed.), *Recovery of function: Theoretical considerations for brain injury rehabilitation.* Bern: Hans Huber.

Rosenzweig, M. R. (1946). Discrimination of auditory intensities in the cat. *American Journal of Psychology, 59,* 127–136.

Rosenzweig, M. R. (1984). Experience, memory, and the brain. *American Psychologist, 39,* 365–376.

Rosenzweig, M. R., & Bennett, E. L. (1977). Effects of environmental enrichment or impoverishment on learning and on brain values in rodents. In A. Oliveno (ed.), *Genetics, environment, and intelligence* (pp. 1–2). Amsterdam: Elsevier/North-Holland.

Rosenzweig, M. R., & Bennett, E. L. (1978). Experimental influences on brain anatomy and brain chemistry in rodents. In G. Gottlieb (ed.), *Studies on the development of behavior and the nervous system. Vol. 4. Early influences* (pp. 289–327). New York: Academic.

Rosenzweig, M. R., Bennett, E. L., Colombo, P. J., Lee, D. W., & Serrano, P. A. (1993). Short-term, intermediate-term, and long-term memory. *Behavioural Brain Research, 57,* 193–198.

Rosenzweig, M. R., Bennett, E. L., Martinez, J. L., Colombo, P. J., Lee, D. W., & Serrano, P. A. (1992). Studying stages of memory formation with chicks. In L. R. Squire, & N. Butters (eds.), *Neuropsychology of memory (2nd edition)* (pp. 533–546). New York: Guilford.

Rosenzweig, M. R., Krech, D., & Bennett, E. L. (1961). Heredity, environment, brain biochemistry, and learning. In *Current trends in psychological theory* (pp. 87–110). Pittsburgh: University of Pittsburgh Press.

Rosenzweig, M., Krech, D., Bennett, E. L., & Diamond, M. (1962). Effects of environmental complexity and training on brain chemistry and anatomy: A replication and extension. *Journal of Comparative and Physiological Psychology, 55,* 429–437.

Rosenzweig, M. R., & Bennett, E. L. (1996). Psychobiology of plasticity: effects of training and experience on brain and behavior. *Behavioural Brain Research, 78*(1), 57–65.

Rossetti, Y., Rode, G., Pisella, L., Farné, A., Li, L., Boisson, D., & Perenin, M.-T. (1998). Prism adaptation to a rightward optical deviation rehabilitates left hemispatial neglect. *Nature, 395,* 166–169.

Rossor, M., Garrett, N., Johnson, A., Mountjoy, C., Roth, M., & Iversen, L. (1982). A post-mortem study of the cholinergic and gaba systems in senile dementia. *Brain, 105*(Pt 2), 313–330.

Rothschild, A. J. (1992). Disinhibition, amnestic reactions, and other adverse reactions secondary to triazolam: a review of the literature. *Journal of Clinical Psychiatry, 53,* 69–79.

Rothwell, J. (1994). *Control of human voluntary movement (2nd ed.).* London: Chapman and Hall.

Roullet, P., Mileusnic, R., Rose, S. P. R., & Sara, S. J. (1997). Neural cell adhesion molecules play a role in rat memory formation in appetitive as well as aversive tasks. *NeuroReport, 8,* 1907–1911.

Roullet, P., Mileusnic, R., Rose, S. P. R., & Sara, S. J. (1997). Neural cell adhesion molecules play a role in rat memory formation in appetitve as well as aversive tasks. *Neuroreport: An International Journal for the Rapid Communication of Research in Neuroscience, 8,* 1907–1911.

Roy, A. (1992). Hypothalamic-pituitary-adrenal axis function and suicidal behavior in depression. *Biological Psychiatry, 32,* 812–816.

Rozin, P. (1976b). The psychobiological approach to human memory. In M. R. Rosenzweig, & E. L. Bennett (eds.), *Neural mechanisms of learning and memory.* Cambridge: MIT Press.

Ruberman, W., Weinblatt, E., Goldberg, J. D., & Chaudhary, B. S. (1984). Psychosocial influences on mortality after myocardial infarction. *New England Journal of Medicine, 311,* 552–559.

Rumbaugh, D. M. (1977). *Language learning by a chimpanzee: The LANA project.* New York: Academic.

Rusak, B., & Boulos, Z. (1981). Pathways for photic entrainment of mammalian circadian rhythms. *Photochemistry and Photobiology, 34,* 267–273.

Rusak, B., & Zucker, I. (1979). Neural regulation of circadian rhythms. *Physiological Reviews, 59,* 449–526.

Russell, J. A. (1994). Is there universal recognition of emotion from facial expressions? A review of the cross-cultural studies. *Psychological Bulletin, 115*(1), 102–141.

Rymer, R. (1993). *Genie: An abused child's flight from silence.* New York: HarperCollins.

Sack, R. L., Blood, M. L., & Lewy, A. J. (1992). Melatonin rhythms in night shift workers. *Sleep, 15,* 434–441.

Sackheim, H., Gur, R. C., & Saucy, M. C. (1978). Emotions are expressed more intensely on the left side of the face. *Science, 202,* 434–436.

Sacks, O., & Wasserman, R. (1987). The case of the colorblind painter. *New York Review of Books, November 19,* 25–34.

Sahu, A. (1998). Evidence suggesting that galanin (GAL), melanin-concentrating hormone (MCH), neurotensin (NT), proopiomelanocortin (POMC) and neuropeptide Y (NPY) are targets of leptin signaling in the hypothalamus. *Endocrinology, 139,* 795–798.

Sahu, A., Kalra, P. S., & Kalra, S. P. (1988). Food deprivation and ingestion induce reciprocal changes in neuropeptide Y concentration in the paraventricular nucleus. *Peptides, 9,* 83–86.

Salzman, C. D., Murasugi, C. M., Britten, K. H., & Newsome, W. T. (1992). Microstimulation in visual area MT: effects on direction discrimination performance. *Journal of Neuroscience, 12,* 2331–2355.

Samson, S., & Zatorre, R. J. (1994). Contribution of the right temporal lobe to musical timbre discrimination. *Neuropsychologia, 32,* 231–240.

Samson, S., & Zatorre, R. J. (1991). Recognition memory for text and melody of songs after unilateral temporal lobe lesion: evidence for dual encoding. *Journal of Experimental Psychology; Learning, Memory, and Cognition, 17,* 793–804.

Sanacora, G., Kershaw, M., Finkelstein, J. A., & White, J. D. (1990). Increased hypothalamic content of preproneuropeptide Y messenger ribonucleic acid in genetically obese Zucker rats and its regulation by food deprivation. *Endocrinology, 127,* 730–737.

Sano, M., Stanley, M., Lawton, A., Cote, L., Williams, J., Stern, Y., Marder, K., & Mayeux, R. (1991). Tritiated imipramine binding. A peripheral marker for serotonin in Parkinson's disease. *Archives of Neurology, 48,* 1052–1054.

Sano, M., Stern, Y., Cote, L., Williams, J. B., & Mayeux, R. (1990). Depression in Parkinson's disease: a biochemical model. *Journal of Neuropsychiatry and Clinical Neurosciences, 2,* 88–92.

Sapolsky, R. M. (1993). Potential behavioral modification of glucocorticoid damage to the hippocampus. Special Issue: Alzheimer's disease: Animal models and clinical perspectives. *Behavioural Brain Research, 57,* 175–182.

Sapolsky, R. M. (1992). *Stress, the aging brain, and the mechanisms of neuron death.* Cambridge, MA: MIT Press.

Sapolsky, R. M. (1997). *The trouble with testosterone: and other essays on the biology of the human predicament.* New York: Scribner.

Sapolsky, R. M. (1994). *Why zebras don't get ulcers.* New York: W. H. Freeman.

Sapolsky, R. M., Uno, H., Rebert, C. S., & Finch, C. E. (1990). Hippocampal damage associated with prolonged glucocorticoid exposure in primates. *Journal of Neuroscience , 10,* 2897–2902.

Sartorius, N., Jablensky, A., Korten, A., Ernberg, G., Anker, M., Cooper, J. E., & Day, R. (1986). Early manifestations and first-contact incidence of schizophrenia in different cultures. A preliminary report on the initial evaluation phase of the WHO Collaborative Study on determinants of outcome of severe mental disorders. *Psychological Medicine, 16,* 909–928.

Sartucci, F., Bonfiglio, L., Del Seppia, C., Luschi, P., Ghione, S., Murri, L., & Papi, F. (1997). Changes in pain perception and pain-related somatosensory evoked potentials in humans produced by exposure to oscillating magnetic fields. *Brain Research, 769*(2), 362–366.

Satinoff, E. (1978). Neural organization and evolution of thermal regulation in mammals. *Science, 201,* 16–22.

Satinoff, E., & Rutstein, J. (1970). Behavioral thermoregulation in rats with anterior hypothalamic lesions. *Journal of Comparative and Physiological Psychology, 71,* 77–82.

Satinoff, E., & Shan, S. Y. (1971). Loss of behavioral thermoregulation after lateral hypothalamic lesions in rats. *Journal of Comparative and Physiological Psychology, 77,* 302–312.

Savage-Rumbaugh, E. S. (1990). Language acquisition in a non-human species: implications for the innateness debate. *Developmental Psychobiology, 23,* 599–620.

Savage-Rumbaugh, E. S., Murphy, J., Sevcik, R. A., Brakke, K. E., Williams, S. L., & Rumbaugh, D. M. (1993). Language comprehension in ape and child. *Monographs of the Society for Research in Child Development, 58,* 1–222.

Savage-Rumbaugh, E. S., Rumbaugh, D. M., & Boysen, S. (1980). Do apes use language? *American Scientist, 68,* 49–61.

Scalaidhe, S. P. O., Wilson, F. A. W., & Goldman-Rakic, P. S. (1997). Areal segregation of face-processing neurons in prefrontal cortex. *Science, 278*(5340), 1135–1138.

Schachter, S., & Singer, J. (1962). Cognitive, social, and physiological determinants of emotional state. *Psychological Review, 69*(5), 379–399.

Schacter, D. L., Alpert, N. M., Savage, C. R., Rauch, S. L., & Albert, M. S. (1996). Conscious recollection and the human hippocampal formation: Evidence from positron emission tomography. *Proceedings of the National Academy of Sciences U.S.A., 93,* 321–325.

Schacter, D., & Buckner, R. (1998). Priming and the brain. *Neuron, 20*(2), 185–195.

Schacter, S. (1975). Cognition and peripheralist-centralist controversies in motivation and emotion. In M. S. Gazzaniga, & C. Blakemore (eds.), *Handbook of psychobiology.* New York: Academic.

Schaffler, L., Luders, H. O., Dinner, D. S., Lesser, R. P., & Chelune, G. J. (1993). Comprehension deficits elicited by electrical stimulation of Broca's area. *Brain, 116,* 695–715.

Schaie, K. W. (1994). The course of adult intellectual development. *American Psychologist, 49,* 304–313.

Scheff, S. W., Bernardo, L. S., & Cotman, C. W. (1978). Decrease in adrenergic axon sprouting in the senescent rat. *Science, 202,* 775–778.

Scheibel, A. B. (1982). Age-related changes in the human forebrain. *Neurosciences Research Program Bulletin, 20,* 577–583.

Scheibel, A. B., & Conrad, A. S. (1993). Hippocampal dysgenesis in mutant mouse and schizophrenic man: is there a relationship? *Schizophrenia Bulletin, 19,* 21–33.

Scheibel, M. E., Tomiyasu, U., & Scheibel, A. B. (1977). The aging human Betz cells. *Experimental Neurology, 56,* 598–609.

Schenkerberg, T., Bradford, D. C., & Ajax, E. T. (1980). Line bisection and unilateral visual neglect in patients with neurologic impairment. *Neurology, 30,* 509–518.

Schiff, B. B., & Lamon, M. (1989). Inducing emotion by unilateral contraction of facial muscles: a new look at hemispheric specialization and the experience of emotion. *Neuropsychologia, 27,* 923–935.

Schiffman, S. S., Simon, S. A., Gill, J. M., & Beeker, T. G. (1986). Bretylium tosylate enhances salt taste. *Physiology and Behavior, 36,* 1129–1137.

Schildkraut, J. J., & Kety, S. S. (1967). Biogenic amines and emotion. *Science, 156,* 21–30.

Schiller, P. H. (1996). On the specificity of neurons and visual areas. *Behavioural Brain Research, 76*(1–2), 21–35.

Schlaug, G., Jancke, L., Huang, Y., & Steinmetz, H. (1995). In vivo evidence of structural brain asymmetry in musicians. *Science, 267,* 699–701.

Schliebs, R., Rose, S. P. R., & Stewart, M. G. (1985). Effect of passive-avoidance training on in vitro protein synthesis in forebrain slices of day-old chicks. *Journal of Neurochemistry, 44,* 1014–1028.

Schlupp, I., Marler, C., & Ryan, M. J. (1994). Benefit to male sailfin mollies of mating with heterospecific females. *Science, 263,* 373–374.

Schmidt-Nelson, K. (1960). *Animal physiology*. Englewood Cliffs, NJ: Prentice-Hall.

Schnapf, J. L., & Baylor, D. A. (1987). How photoreceptor cells respond to light. *Scientific American, 256*(4), 40–47.

Schnapp, B. J. (1997). Retroactive motors. *Neuron, 18*, 523–526.

Schneider, G. E. (1969). Two visual systems. *Science, 163*(3870), 895–902.

Schneider, K. (1959). *Clinical psychopathology*. New York: Grune & Stratton.

Schreiber, S. S., Maren, S., Tocco, G., Shors, T. J., & Thompson, R. F. (1991). A negative correlation between the induction of long-term potentiation and activation of immediate early genes. *Brain Research, 11*, 89–91.

Schuckit, M. A., & Smith, T. L. (1997). Assessing the risk for alcoholism among sons of alcoholics. *Journal of Studies On Alcohol, 58*(2), 141–145.

Schulteis, G., & Martinez, J. L. Jr. (1992). Peripheral modulation of learning and memory: enkephalins as a model system. *Psychopharmacology, 109*, 347–364.

Schultz, R. T., Cho, N. K., Staib, L. H., Kier, L. E., Fletcher, J. M., Shaywitz, S. E., Shankweiler, D. P., Katz, L., Gore, J. C., Duncan, J. S. et al. (1994). Brain morphology in normal and dyslexic children: the influence of sex and age. *Annals of Neurology, 35*, 732–742.

Schuman, E. M., & Madison, D. V. (1991). A requirement for the intercellular messenger nitric oxide in long-term potentiation. *Science, 265*, 1503–1506.

Schuster, C. R. (1970). Psychological approaches to opiate dependence and self-administration by laboratory animals. *Federation Proceedings, 29*, 1–5.

Schutz, F. (1965). Sexuelle pragung bei anatiden. *Zeitschrift fur Tierpsychologie, 22*, 50–103.

Schwartz, J. H., Castellucci, V. F., & Kandel, E. R. (1971). Functioning of identified neurons and synapses in abdominal ganglion of *Aplysia* in absence of protein synthesis. *J. Neurophysiology, 34*, 939–963.

Schwartz, L. M. (1992). Insect muscle as a model for programmed cell death. *Journal of Neurobiology, 23*, 1312–1326.

Schwartz, W. J., Smith, C. B., Davidsen, L., Savaki, H., Sokoloff, L., Mata, M., Fink, D. J., & Gainer, H. (1979). Metabolic mapping of functional activity in the hypothalamo-neuro-hypophysial system of the rat. *Science, 205*, 723–725.

Schwartzkroin, P. A., & Wester, K. (1975). Long-lasting facilitation of a synaptic potential following tetanization in the in vitro hippocampal slice. *Brain Research, 89*, 107–119.

Schwenk, K. (1994). Why snakes have forked tongues. *Science, 263*, 1573–1577.

Sclafani, A., Springer, D., & Kluge, L. (1976). Effects of quinine adulteration on the food intake and body weight of obese and nonobese hypothalamic hyperphagic rats. *Physiology and Behavior, 16*, 631–640.

Scoville, W. B., & Milner, B. (1957). Loss of recent memory after bilateral hippocampal lesions. *Journal of Neurology, Neurosurgery and Psychiatry, 20*, 11–21.

Seeley, R. J., & Schwartz, M. W. (1997). The regulation of energy balance: Peripheral hormonal signals and hypothalamic neuropeptides. *Current Directions in Psychological Science, 6*, 39–44.

Seeman, P., Guan, H. C., & Van Tol, H. H. (1993). Dopamine D4 receptors elevated in schizophrenia. *Nature, 365*, 441–445.

Segal, N. L., Dysken, M. W., Bouchard, T. J. Jr., Pedersen, N. L., Eckert, E. D., & Heston, L. L. (1990). Tourette's disorder in a set of reared-apart triplets: genetic and environmental influences. *American Journal of Psychiatry, 147*, 196–199.

Seiger, A., Nordberg, A., von Holst, H., Backman, L., Ebendal, T., Alafuzoff, I. et al. (1993). Intracranial infusion of purified nerve growth factor to an Alzheimer patient: the first attempt of a possible future treatment strategy. *Behavioural Brain Research, 57*, 255–261.

Seil, F. J., Kelly 3rd, J. M., & Leiman, A. L. (1974). Anatomical organization of cerebral neocortex in tissue culture. *Experimental Neurology, 45*, 435–450.

Seil, F. J., Leiman, A. L., Herman, M. M., & Fisk, R. A. (1977). Direct effects of ethanol on central nervous system cultures: An electrophysiological and morphological study. *Experimental Neurology, 55*, 390–404.

Seil, F. J., Leiman, A. L., & Kelly, J. (1976). Neuroelectric blocking factors in multiple sclerosis and normal human sera. *Archives of Neurology, 33*, 418–422.

Selkoe, D. J. (1991). Amyloid protein and Alzheimer's disease. *Scientific American, 265*(5), 68–71.

Selye, H. (1956). *The stress of life*. New York: McGraw-Hill.

Sendtner, M., Holtmann, B., & Hughes, R. A. (1996). The response of motoneurons to neurotrophins. *Neurochemical Research, 21*, 831–841.

Serrano, P. A., Beniston, D. S., Oxonian, M. G., Rodriguez, W. A., Rosenzweig, M. R., & Bennett, E. L. (1994). Differential effects of protein kinase inhibitors and activators on memory formation in the 2-day-old chick. *Behav. Neural. Biol., 61*, 60–72.

Serviere, J., Webster, W. R., & Calford, M. B. (1984). Isofrequency labelling revealed by a combined [14C]-2-deoxyglucose, electrophysiological, and horseradish peroxidase study of the inferior colliculus of the cat. *Journal of Comparative Neurology, 228*, 463–477.

Seuss Dr. (1987). *The tough coughs as he ploughs the dough: Early writings and cartoons by Dr. Seuss*. New York: W. Morrow.

Seyfarth, R. M., & Cheney, D. L. (1997). Behavioral mechanisms underlying vocal communication in nonhuman primates. *Animal Learning & Behavior, 25*, 249–267.

Shapiro, R. M. (1993). Regional neuropathology in schizophrenia: Where are we? Where are we going? *Schizophrenia Research, 10*, 187–239.

Shaywitz, S. E., Shaywitz, B. A., Pugh, K. R., Fulbright, R. K., Constable, R. T., Mencl, W. E., Shankweiler, D. P., Liberman, A. M., Skudlarski, P., Fletcher, J. M., Katz, L., Marchione, K. E., Lacadie, C., Gatenby, C., & Gore, J. C. (1998). Functional disruption in the organization of the brain for reading in dyslexia. *Proceedings of the National Academy of Sciences U.S.A., 95*, 2636–2641.

Sherrington, C. S. (1898). Experiments in examination of the peripheral distribution of the fibres of the posterior roots of some spinal nerves. *Philosophical Transactions, 190*, 45–186.

Sherrington, C. S. (1897). Part III. The central nervous system. In M. Foster (ed.), *A text-book of physiology*. London: Macmillan.

Sherry, D. F. (1992). Memory, the hippocampus, and natural selection: Studies of food-storing birds. In L. R. Squire, & N. Butters (eds.), *Neuropsychology of memory* 2nd ed., (pp. 521–532). New York: Guilford Press.

Sherry, D. F., Jacobs, L. F., & Gaulin, S. J. (1993). "The hippocampus and spatial memory": Reply. *Trends in Neurosciences, 16*, 57.

Sherry, D. F., Jacobs, L. F., & Gaulin, S. J. (1992). Spatial memory and adaptive specialization of the hippocampus. *Trends in Neurosciences, 15*, 298–303.

Sherry, D. F., & Schacter, D. L. (1987). The evolution of multiple memory systems. *Psychological Review, 94*, 439–454.

Sherry, D. F., & Vaccarino, A. L. (1989). Hippocampus and memory for food caches in black-capped chickadees. *Behavioral Neuroscience, 103*, 308–318.

Sherry, D. F., Vaccarino, A. L., Buckenham, K., & Herz, R. S. (1989). The hippocampal complex of food-storing birds. *Brain Behav. Evol., 34*, 308–317.

Shiang, R., Ryan, S. G., Zhu, Y. Z., Hahn, A. F., O'Connell, P., & Wasmuth, J. J. (1993). Mutations in the alpha 1 subunit of the inhibitory glycine receptor cause the dominant neurologic disorder, hyperekplexia. *Nature Genetics, 5*, 351–358.

Shoulson, I. (1992). Neuroprotective clinical strategies for Parkinson's disease. *Annals of Neurology, 32*, S143-S145.

Siarey, R. J., Coan, E. J., Rapoport, S. I., & Galdzicki, Z. (1997). Responses to NMDA in cultured hippocampal neurons from trisomy 16 mice. *Neuroscience Letters, 232*, 131–134.

Sibley, C. G., & Ahlquist, J. E. (1987). DNA hybridization evidence of hominoid phylogeny: results from an expanded data set. *Journal of Molecular Evolution, 26*, 99–121.

Sibley, C. G., & Ahlquist, J. E. (1990). *Phylogeny and classification of birds: a study in molecular evolution*. New Haven: Yale University Press.

Sibley, C. G., Comstock, J. A., & Ahlquist, J. E. (1990). DNA hybridization evidence of hominoid phylogeny: a reanalysis of the data. *Journal of Molecular Evolution, 30*, 202–236.

Siegel, J. M. (1994). Brainstem mechanisms generating REM sleep. In M. H. Kryger, T. Roth, & W. C. Dement (eds.), *Principles and practice of sleep medicine, 2nd ed.*(pp. 125–144). Philadelphia: Saunders.

Siegel, R. K. (1989). *Intoxication: Life in pursuit of artificial paradise.* New York: E. P. Dutton.

Sierra-Honigmann, M. R., Nath, A. K., Murakami, C., García-Cardeña, G., Papapetropoulos, A., Sessa, W. C., Madge, L. A., Schechner, J. S., Schwabb, M. B., Polverini, P. J., & Flores-Riveros, J. R. (1998). Biological action of leptin as an angiogenic factor. *Science, 281,* 1683–1686.

Siever, L. J., & Davis, K. L. (1985). Overview: Toward a dysregulation hypothesis of depression. *American Journal of Psychiatry, 142,* 1017–1031.

Sigurdson, E., Staley, D., Matas, M., Hildahl, K., & Squair, K. (1994). A five year review of youth suicide in Manitoba. *Canadian Journal of Psychiatry, 39,* 397–403.

Silberman, E. K., & Weingartner, H. (1986). Hemispheric lateralization of function related to emotion. *Brain and Cognition, 5,* 322–353.

Silva, A. J., Giese, K. P., Fedorov, N. B., Frankland, P. W., & Kogan, J. H. (1998). Molecular, cellular and neuroanatomical substrates of place learning. *Neurobiology of Learning and Memory, 70,* 1–2, 44–61.

Silva, A. J., Kogan, J. H., Frankland, P. W., & Kida, S. (1998). CREB and memory. *Annual Review of Neuroscience, 21,* 127–148.

Silva, A. J., Paylor, R., Wehner, J. M., & Tonegawa, S. (1992). Impaired spatial learning in alpha-calcium-calmodulin kinase II mutant mice. *Science, 257,* 206–211.

Silva, D. A., & Satz, P. (1979). Pathological left-handedness. Evaluation of a model. *Brain and Language, 7,* 8–16.

Silver, R., Lesauter, J., Tresco, P., & Lehman, M. (1996). A diffusible coupling signal from the transplanted suprachiasmatic nucleus controlling circadian locomotor rhythms. *Nature, 382*(6594), 810–813.

Skinner, M., Holden, L., & Holden, T. (1997). Parameter selection to optimize speech recognition with the nucleus implant. *Otolaryngology and Head and Neck Surgery, 117*(3 Pt 1), 188–195.

Skrede, K. K., & Malthe-Sorenssen, E. (1981). Increased resting and evoked release of transmitter following repetitive electrical tetanization in hippocampus: A biochemical correlate to long-lasting synaptic potentiation. *Brain Research, 208,* 436–441.

Smale, L., Lee, T. M., Nelson, R. J., & Zucker, I. (1990). Prolactin counteracts effects of short day lengths on pelage growth in the meadow vole, *Microtus pennsylvanicus. Journal of Experimental Zoology, 253,* 186–188.

Small, S. L. (1994). Pharmacotherapy of aphasia. A critical review. *Stroke, 25,* 1282–1289.

Smith, A., & Sugar, O. (1975). Development of above normal language and intelligence 21 years after hemispherectomy. *Neurology, 25,* 813–818.

Smith, C. (1985). Sleep states and learning. A review of the animal literature. *Neuroscience and Biobehavioral Reviews, 9,* 157–169.

Smith, J. M., Kucharski, L., Oswald, W. T., & Waterman, L. J. (1979). A systematic investigation of tardive dyskinesia in inpatients. *American Journal of Psychiatry, 136,* 918–922.

Smith, P. B., Compton, D. R., Welch, S. P., Razdan, R. K., Mechoulam, R., & Martin, B. R. (1994). The pharmacological activity of anandamide, a putative endogenous cannabinoid, in mice. *Journal of Pharmacology and Experimental Therapeutics, 270,* 219–227.

Smythies, J. (1984). The transmethylation hypotheses of schizophrenia re-evaluated. *Trends in Neuroscience, 7,* 48–53.

Snider, S. R. (1982). Cerebellar pathology in schizophrenia-Cause or consequence? *Neuroscience and Biobehavioral Reviews, 6,* 47–53.

Snyder, A. Z., Abdullaev, Y. G., Posner, M. I., & Raichle, M. E. (1995). Scalp electrical potentials reflect regional cerebral blood flow responses during processing of written words. *Proceedings of the National Academy of Sciences U.S.A., 92,* 1689–1693.

Snyder, F. (1969). Sleep and REM as biological enigmas. In A. Kales (ed.), *Sleep: Physiology and pathology* (pp. 266–280). Philadelphia: Lippincott.

Snyder, S. H., & D'Amato, R. J. (1986). MPTP: a neurotoxin relevant to the pathophysiology of Parkinson's disease. *Neurology, 36,* 250–258.

Snyder, S. H., & D'Amato, R. J. (1985). Predicting Parkinson's disease. *Nature, 317,* 198–199.

Sobel, N., Prabhakaran, V., Desmond, J. E., Glover, G. H., Goode, R. L., Sullivan, E. V., & Gabrieli, J. D. E. (1998). Sniffing and smelling: Separate subsystems in the human olfactory cortex. *Nature, 392* , 282–286.

Solomon, A. (1998). Personal history: Anatomy of melancholy. *New Yorker, 73,* 46–61.

Song, H.-J., Ming, G.-L., He, Z., Lehmann, M., McKerracher, L., Tessier-Lavigne, M., & Poo, M.-M. (1998). Conversion of neuronal growth cone responses from repulsion to attraction by cyclic nucleotides. *Science, 281,* 1515–1518.

Sorensen, P. W., & Goetz, F. W. (1993). Pheromonal and reproductive function of F prostaglandins and their metabolites in teleost fish. *Journal of Lipid Mediators, 6,* 385–393.

Souied, E. H., Benlian, P., Amouyel, P., Feingold, J., Lagarde, J. P., Munnich, A., Kaplan, J., Coscas, G., & Soubrane, G. (1998). The epsilon4 allele of the apolipoprotein E gene as a potential protective factor for exudative age-related macular degeneration. *American Journal of Ophthalmology, 125,* 353–359.

Spear, N. F. (1976). Retrieval of memories: A psychobiological approach. In W. K. Estes (ed.), *Handbook of learning and cognitive processes.Volume 4. Attention and memory.* Hillsdale, NJ: Lawrence Erlbaum.

Spector, N. H. (1987). Old and new strategies in the conditioning of immune responses. *Annals of the New York Academy of Sciences, 496,* 522–531.

Sperry, R. W. (1974). Lateral specialization in the surgically separated hemispheres. In F. O. Schmitt, & F. G. Worden (eds.), *Neuroscience 3rd study program.* Cambridge: MIT Press.

Sperry, R. W., Stamm, J., & Miner, N. (1956). Relearning tests for interocular transfer following division of optic chiasma and corpus callosum in cats. *Journal of Comparative and Physiological Psychology, 49,* 529–533.

Spiegler, B. J., & Yeni-Komshian, G. H. (1983). Incidence of left-handed writing in a college population with reference to family patterns of hand preference. *Neuropsychologia, 21,* 651–659.

Squire, L. R., Amaral, D. G., Zola-Morgan, S., & Kritchevsky, M. P. G. (1989). Description of brain injury in the amnesic patient N. A. based on magnetic resonance imaging. *Experimental Neurology, 105,* 23–35.

Squire, L. R., Knowlton, B., & Musen, G. (1993). The structure and organization of memory. *Annual Review of Psychology, 44,* 453–495.

Squire, L. R., & McKee, R. (1992). Influence of prior events on cognitive judgments in amnesia. *Journal of Experimental Psychology. Learning, Memory, and Cognition, 18,* 106–115.

Squire, L. R., & Moore, R. Y. (1979). Dorsal thalamic lesion in a noted case of chronic memory dysfunction. *Annals of Neurology, 6,* 503–506.

Squire, L. R., & Slater, P. C. (1975). Forgetting in very long-term memory as assessed by an improved questionnaire technique. *Journal of Experimental Psychology: Human Learning in Memory, 104,* 50–54.

Standing, L. G. (1973). Learning 10,000 pictures. *Quarterly Journal of Experimental Psychology, 25,* 207–222.

Stanley, B. G., Anderson, K. C., Grayson, M. H., & Leibowitz, S. F. (1989). Repeated hypothalamic stimulation with neuropeptide Y increases daily carbohydrate and fat intake and body weight gain in female rats. *Physiology and Behavior, 46,* 173–177.

Starkstein, S. E., & Robinson, R. G. (1994). Neuropsychiatric aspects of stroke. In C. E. Coffey, J. L. Cummings, M. R. Lovell, & G. D. Pearlson (eds.), *The American Psychiatric Press textbook of geriatric neuropsychiatry* (pp. 457–477). Washington, D. C.: American Psychiatric Press.

Starmer, G. A. (1994). *Drugs and traffic safety.* Canberra: Federal Office of Road Safety.

Staubli, U. V. (1995). Parallel properties of long-term potentiation and memory. In J. L. McGaugh, N. M. Weinberger, & G. Lynch (eds.), *Brain and memory: modulation and mediation of neuroplasticity* (pp. 303–318). New York: Oxford University Press.

Staubli, U., Le, T. T., & Lynch, G. (1995). Variants of olfactory memory and their dependencies on the hippocampal formation. *Journal of Neuroscience, 15,* 1162–1171.

Stein, B., & Meredith, M. A. (1993). *The merging of the senses.* Cambridge, MA: The MIT Press.

Stein, M., Keller, S., & Schleifer, S. (1981). The hypothalamus and the immune response. In H. Weiner, A. Hofer, & A. J. Stunkard (eds.), *Brain behavior and bodily disease* (pp. 45–63). New York: Raven.

Stein, M., & Miller, A. H. (1993). Stress, the hypothalamic-pituitary-adrenal axis, and immune function. *Advances in Experimental Medicine and Biology, 335,* 1–5.

Stein, M., Miller, A. H., & Trestman, R. L. (1991). Depression, the immune system, and health and illness. Findings in search of meaning. *Archives of General Psychiatry, 48,* 171–177.

Steinmetz, H., Volkmann, J., Jancke, L., & Freund, H. J. (1991). Anatomical left-right asymmetry of language-related temporal cortex is different in left- and right-handers. *Annals of Neurology, 29,* 315–319.

Stella, N., Schweitzer, P., & Piomelli, D. (1997). A second endogenous cannabinoid that modulates long-term potentiation. *Nature, 388*(6644), 773–778.

Stephan, F. K., & Zucker, I. (1972). Circadian rhythms in drinking behavior and locomotor activity of rats are eliminated by hypothalamic lesions. *Proceedings of the National Academy of Sciences, USA, 69,* 1583–1586.

Stephan, H., Frahm, H., & Baron, G. (1981). New and revised data on volumes of brain structures in insectivores and primates. *Folia Primatologica, 35,* 1–29.

Steptoe, A. (1993). Stress and the cardiovascular system: A psychosocial perspective. In S. C. Stanford, & P. Salmon (eds.), *Stress: From synapse to syndrome* (pp. 119–141). London: Academic Press.

Stern, C. E., Corkin, S., Gonzalez, R. G., Guimaraes, A. R., Baker, J. R., Jennings, P. J., Carr, C. A., Sugiura, R. M., Vedantham, V., & Rosen, B. R. (1996). The hippocampal formation participates in novel picture encoding: Evidence from functional magnetic resonance imaging. *Proceedings of the National Academy of Sciences U.S.A., 93,* 8660–8665.

Stern, K., & Mcclintock, M. (1998). Regulation of ovulation by human pheromones [see Comments]. *Nature, 392*(6672), 177–179.

Sternberg, D. E., VanKammen, D. P., Lerner, P., & Bunney, W. E. (1982). Schizophrenia: dopamine beta-hydroxylase activity and treatment response. *Science, 216,* 1423–1425.

Stoerig, P., & Cowey, A. (1997). Blindsight in man and monkey. *Brain, 120,* 535–559.

Stone, J., Dreher, G., & Leventhal, A. (1979). Hierarchical and parallel mechanisms in the organization of visual cortex. *Brain Research, 180,* 345–394.

Stone, V. E., Nisenson, L., Eliassen, J. C., & Gazzaniga, M. S. (1996). Left hemisphere representations of emotional facial expressions. *Neuropsychologia, 34,* 23–9.

Stricker, E. M. (1977). The renin-angiotensin system and thirst: a reevaluation. II. Drinking elicited in rats by caval ligation or isoproterenol. *Journal of Comparative and Physiological Psychology, 91,* 1220–1231.

Strittmatter, W. J., & Roses, A. D. (1996). Apolipoprotein E and Alzheimer's disease. *Annual Review of Neuroscience, 19,* 53–77.

Stromswold, K. (1995). The cognitive and neural bases of language acquisition. In M. S. Gazzaniga (ed.), *The cognitive neurosciences* (pp. 855–870). Cambridge, MA: MIT Press.

Stroud, R. M., & Finer-Moore, J. (1985). Acetylcholine receptor structure, function, and evolution. *Annual Review of Cell Biology, 1,* 317–351.

Stuve, T. A., Friedman, L., Jesberger, J. A., Gilmore, G. C., Strauss, M. E., & Meltzer, H. Y. (1997). The relationship between smooth pursuit performance, motion perception and sustained visual attention in patients with schizophrenia and normal controls. *Psychological Medicine, 27,* 143–152.

Sullivan, R. M., & Leon, M. (1986). Early olfactory learning induces and enhanced olfactory bulb response in young rats. *Brain Research, 392,* 278–282.

Sweet, W. H. (1973). Treatment of medically intractable mental disease by limited frontal leucotomy-Justifiable? *New England Journal of Medicine, 289,* 1117–1125.

Takagi, S. F. (1989). Standardized olfactometries in Japan—a review over ten years. *Chemical Senses, 14,* 25–46.

Takahashi, J. S. (1995). Molecular neurobiology and genetics of circadian rhythms in mammals. *Annual Review of Neuroscience, 18,* 531–554.

Takahashi, Y. (1979). Growth hormone secretion related to the sleep and waking rhythm. In R. Drucker-Colin, M. Shkurovich, & M. B. Sterman (eds.), *The functions of sleep.* New York: Academic.

Tallal, P., Galaburda, A. M., Llinas, R. R., & von Euler, C. (1993). *Temporal information processing in the nervous system: special reference to dyslexia and dysphasia.* New York: New York Academy of Sciences.

Tallal, P., & Schwartz, J. (1980). Temporal processing, speech perception and hemispheric asymmetry. *Trends in Neuroscience, 3,* 309–311.

Tamminga, C. A., & Schulz, S. C. (1991). *Schizophrenia research.* New York: Raven Press.

Tanaka, K. (1993). Neuronal mechanisms of object recognition. *Science, 262,* 685–688.

Tanaka, Y., Kamo, T., Yoshida, M., & Yamadori, A. (1991). 'So-called' cortical deafness. Clinical, neurophysiological and radiological observations. *Brain, 114,* 2385–2401.

Tandan, R., & Bradley, W. G. (1985). Amyotrophic lateral sclerosis: Part I. Clinical features, pathology, and ethical issues in management. *Annals of Neurology, 18,* 271–281.

Tang, N. M., Dong, H. W., Wang, X. M., Tsui, Z. C., & Han, J. S. (1997). Cholecystokinin antisense RNA increases the analgesic effect induced by electroacupuncture or low dose morphine: Conversion of low responder rats into high responders. *Pain, 71,* 71–80.

Tanila, H., Shapiro, M., Gallagher, M., & Eichenbaum, H. (1997). Brain aging: Changes in the nature of information coding by the hippocampus. *Journal of Neuroscience, 17,* 5155–5166.

Tanila, H., Sipila, P., Shapiro, M., & Eichenbaum, H. (1997). Brain aging: Impaired coding of novel environmental cues. *Journal of Neuroscience, 17,* 5167–5174.

Tardiff, B. E., Newman, M. F., Saunders, A. M., Strittmatter, W. J., Blumenthal, J. A., White, W. D., Croughwell, N. D., Davis, R. D. Jr., Roses, A. D., & Reves, J. G. (1997). Preliminary report of a genetic basis for cognitive decline after cardiac operations. The neurologic outcome research group of the Duke Heart Center. *Annals of Thoracic Surgery, 64,* 715–720.

Taub, E. (1976). Movement in nonhuman primates deprived of somatosensory feedback. *Exercise and Sport Sciences Reviews, 4,* 335–374.

Taylor, R. (1990). Immediate-early genes may offer a new key to the circadian clock. *Journal of NIH Research, 2,* 49–53.

Technau, G. M. (1984). Fiber number in the mushroom bodies of adult *Drosophila melanogaster* depends on age, sex and experience. *Journal of Neurogenetics, 1,* 113–126.

Teitelbaum, P., & Stellar, E. (1954). Recovery from failure to eat produced by hypothalamic lesions. *Science, 120,* 894–895.

Tenn, W. (1968). *The seven sexes.* New York: Ballantine Books.

Terman, G. W., Shavit, Y., Lewis, J. W., Cannon, J. T., & Liebeskind, J. C. (1984). Intrinsic mechanisms of pain inhibition: Activation by stress. *Science, 226,* 1270–1277.

Terrace, H. S. (1979). *Nim.* New York: Knopf.

Tessier-Lavigne, M., & Placzek, M. (1991). Target attraction: are developing axons guided by chemotropism? *Trends in Neurosciences, 14,* 303–310.

Tessier-Lavigne, M., Placzek, M., Lumsden, A. G., Dodd, J., & Jessell, T. M. (1988). Chemotropic guidance of developing axons in the mammalian central nervous system. *Nature, 336,* 775–778.

Tetrud, J. W., Langston, J. W., Irwin, I., & Snow, B. (1994). Parkinsonism caused by petroleum waste ingestion. *Neurology, 44,* 1051–1054.

Teuber, H.-L., Milner, B., & Vaughan, H. G. (1968). Persistent anterograde amnesia after stab wound of the basal brain. *Neuropsychologia, 6,* 267–282.

Teyler, T. J., & DiScenna, P. (1986). Long-term potentiation. *Annual Review of Neuroscience, 10,* 131–161.

Theunissen, F. E., & Doupe, A. J. (1998). Temporal and spectral sensitivity of complex auditory neurons in the nucleus HVc of male zebra finches. *Journal of Neuroscience, 18,* 3786–3802.

Thibos, L. N. L. W. R. (1985). Orientation bias of brisk-transient y-cells of the cat retina for drifting and alternating gratings. *Experimental Brain Research, 58,* 1–10.

Thomas, C. B., Duszynski, K. R., & Shaffer, J. W. (1979). Family attitudes reported in youth as potential predictors of cancer. *Psychosomatic Medicine, 41,* 287–302.

Thompson, G. N., & Halliday, D. (1990). Significant phenylalanine hydroxylation in vivo in patients with classical phenylketonuria. *Journal of Clinical Investigation, 86,* 317–322.

Thompson, R. F. (1992). Memory. *Current Opinion in Neurobiology, 2,* 203–208.

Thompson, R. F. (1990). Neural mechanisms of classical conditioning in mammals. *Philosophical Transactions of the Royal Society of London, Series B, 329,* 161–170.

Thompson, R. F., & Krupa, D. J. (1994). Organization of memory traces in the mammalian brain. *Annual Review of Neuroscience, 17,* 519–549.

Thompson, R. F., Thompson, J. K., Kim, J. J., Krupa, D. J., & Shinkman, P. G. (1998). The nature of reinforcement in cerebellar learning. *Neurobiology of Learning and Memory.*

Thompson, T., & Schuster, C. R. (1964). Morphine self-administration, food reinforced and avoidance behaviour in rhesus monkeys. *Psychopharmacologia, 5,* 87–94.

Thurber, J., & White, E. B. (1929). *Is sex necessary? or, Why you feel the way you do.* New York: Harper.

Timberlake, W. (1993). Animal behavior: A continuing synthesis. *Annual Review of Psychology, 44,* 675–708.

Tobias, P. V. (1980). L'evolution du cerveau humain. *La Recherche, 11,* 282–292.

Toenniessen, L. M., Casey, D. E., & McFarland, B. H. (1985). Tardive dyskinesia in the aged. Duration of treatment relationships. *Archives of General Psychiatry, 42,* 278–284.

Tolman, E. C. (1949). *Purposive behavior in animals and men.* Berkeley: University of California Press.

Tolman, E. C., & Honzik, C. H. (1930). Introduction and removal of reward, and maze performance in rats. *University of California Publications in Psychology, 4,* 257–275.

Tolman, E. C. (1949). There is more than one kind of learning. *Psychological Review, 56,* 144–155.

Tootell, R. B. H., Hadjikhani, N. K., Vanduffel, W., Liu, A. K., Mendola, J. D., Sereno, M. I., & Dale, A. M. (1998). Functional analysis of primary visual cortex (V1) in humans. *Proceedings of the National Academy of Sciences, USA, 95,* 811–817.

Tootell, R. B., Silverman, M. S., Hamilton, S. L., De Valois, R. L., & Switkes, E. (1988). Functional anatomy of macaque striate cortex. III. Color. *Journal of Neuroscience, 8,* 1569–1593.

Tootell, R. B., Silverman, M. S., Switkes, E., & De Valois, R. L. (1982). Deoxyglucose analysis of retinotopic organization in primate striate cortex. *Science, 218,* 902–904.

Tordoff, M., Rawson, N., & Friedman, M. (1991). 2,5-anhydro-d-mannitol acts in liver to initiate feeding. *Am J Physiol, 261*(2 Pt 2), R283–R288.

Torrey, E. F., Bowler, A. E., Taylor, E. H., & Gottesman, I. I. (1994). *Schizophrenia and manic depressive disorder.* New York: Basic Books.

Tranel, D., & Damasio, A. R. (1985). Knowledge without awareness: An autonomic index of facial recognition by prosopagnosics. *Science, 228,* 1453–1454.

Tranel, D., Damasio, H., & Damasio, A. R. (1997). A neural basis for the retrieval of conceptual knowledge. *Neuropsychologia, 35,* 1319–1327.

Travis, J. (1992). Can 'hair cells' unlock deafness? *Science, 257,* 1344–1345.

Treisman, M. (1977). Motion sickness-Evolutionary hypotheses. *Science, 197,* 493–495.

Trimble, M. R. (1991). Interictal psychoses of epilepsy. *Advances in Neurology, 55,* 143–152.

Trivers, R. (1985). Social evolution. (pp. xvii, 462 p). Menlo Park, Calif: Benjamin/Cummings Pub. Co.

True, W. R., Rice, J., Eisen, S. A., Heath, A. C., Goldberg, J., Lyons, M. J., & Nowak, J. (1993). A twin study of genetic and environmental contributions to liability for posttraumatic stress symptoms. *Archives of General Psychiatry, 50,* 257–264.

Truman, J. W. (1983). Programmed cell death in the nervous system of an adult insect. *Journal of Comparative Neurology, 216,* 445–452.

Ts'o, D. Y., Frostig, R. D., Lieke, E. E., & Grinvald, A. (1990). Functional organization of primate visual cortex revealed by high resolution optical imaging. *Science, 249,* 417–420.

Tully, T. (1987). *Drosophila* learning and memory revisited. *Trends in Neuroscience, 10,* 330–335.

Tully, T. (1991). Physiology of mutations affecting learning and memory in *Drosophila* —the missing link between gene product and behavior. *Trends in Neurosciences, 14,* 163–164.

Tulving, E. (1998). Brain/mind correlates of human memory. In M. Sabourin, F. Criak, & M. Robert (eds.), *Advances in psychological science, Vol. 2:Biological and cognitive aspects* (pp. 441–460). Hove, East Sussex, U.K.: Psychology Press.

Tulving, E. (1972). Episodic and semantic memory. In E. Tulving, & W. Donaldson (eds.), *Organization of memory* (pp. 381–403). New York: Academic Press.

Tulving, E. (1989). Memory: Performance, knowledge, and experience. *European Journal of Cognitive Psychology, 1,* 3–26.

Tulving, E., Hayman, C. A., & Macdonald, C. A. (1991). Long-lasting perceptual priming and semantic learning in amnesia: a case experiment. *Journal of Experimental Psychology: Learning, Memory, and Cognition, 17,* 595–617.

Tulving, E., & Markowitsch, H. J. (1997). Memory beyond the hippocampus. *Current Opinion in Neurobiology, 7,* 209–216.

Tulving, E., Markowitsch, H. J., Craik, F. E., Habib, R., & Houle, S. (1996). Novelty and familiarity activations in PET studies of memory encoding and retrieval. *Cerebral Cortex, 6,* 71–79.

Turek, F. (1985). Circadian neural rhythms in mammals. *Annual Review of Physiology, 47,* 49–64.

Turkewitz, G. (1988). A prenatal source for the development of hemispheric specialization. In D. L. Molfese, & S. J. Segalowitz (eds.), *Brain lateralization in children: Developmental implications* (pp. 73–81). New York: Guilford Press.

Turner, A. M., & Greenough, W. T. (1985). Differential rearing effects on rat visual cortex synapses. I. Synaptic and neuronal density and synapses per neuron. *Brain Research, 329,* 195–203.

U.S. Department of Health and Human Services. (1991). *Drug abuse and drug abuse research: the third triennial report to Congress.* Rockville, MD: National Institute on Drug Abuse.

Underwood, B. J. (1969). Attributes of memory. *Psychology Review, 76,* 559–573.

Ungerleider, L. G., Courtney, S. M., & Haxby, J. V. (1998). A neural system for human visual working memory. *Proceedings of the National Academy of Sciences, USA, 95,* 883–890.

United States CongressJoint Economic Committee. (1988). *The 1987 economic report of the president: hearings before the Joint Economic Committee, Congress of the United States, 1987.* Washington, D.C.: G.P.O.

Ursin, H., Baade, E., & Levine, S. (1978). *Psychobiology of stress: A study of coping men.* New York: Academic.

Valbo, A. B., & Johansson, R. S. (1984). Properties of cutaneous mechanoreceptors in the human hand related to touch sensation. *Human Neurobiology, 3,* 3–15.

Valenstein, E. S. (1973). *Brain control.* New York: Wiley-Interscience.

Valenstein, E. S. (1986). *Great and desperate cures: the rise and decline of psychosurgery and other radical treatments for mental illness.* New York: Basic Books.

Valenstein, E. S. (1980). *The psychosurgery debate: Scientific, legal, and ethical perspectives.* San Francisco: Freeman.

Vallbona, C., Hazlewood, C., & Jurida, G. (1997). Response of pain to static magnetic fields in postpolio patients: a double-blind pilot study. *Archives of Physical Medicine and Rehabilitation, 78*(11), 1200–1203.

van Bergeijk, W. A. (1967). The evolution of vertebrate hearing. In W. D. Neff (ed.), *Contributions to sensory physiology, Vol. 3.* New York: Academic.

Van Essen, D. C., Anderson, C. H., & Felleman, D. J. (1992). Information processing in the primate visual system: An integrated systems perspective. *Science, 255,* 419–423.

Van Essen, D. C., & Drury, H. A. (1997). Structural and functional analyses of human cerebral cortex using a surface-based atlas. *Journal of Neuroscience, 17,* 7079–7102.

van Valen, L. (1974). Brain size and intelligence in man. *American Journal of Physical Anthropology, 40,* 417–424.

Van Valen, L. (1974). Brain size and intelligence in man. *American Journal of Physical Anthropology, 40*(3), 417–423.

van Zoeren, J. G., & Stricker, E. M. (1977). Effects of preoptic, lateral hypothalamic, or dopamine-depleting lesions on behavioral thermoregulation in rats exposed to the cold. *Journal of Comparative and Physiological Psychology, 91,* 989–999.

Vander Wall, S. B. (1982). An experimental analysis of cache recovery in Clark's nutcracker. *Animal Behaviour, 30,* 84–94.

Vassar, R., Ngai, J., & Axel, R. (1993). Spatial segregation of odorant receptor expression in the mammalian olfactory epithelium. *Cell, 74,* 309–318.

Vaughan, W., & Greene, S. L. (1984). Pigeon visual memory capacity. *Journal of Experimental Psychology: Animal Behavior Processes, 10,* 256–271.

Veraa, R. P., & Grafstein, B. (1981). Cellular mechanisms for recovery from nervous system injury: A conference report. *Experimental Neurology, 71,* 6–75.

Villringer, A., & Chance, B. (1997). Non-invasive optical spectroscopy and imaging of human brain function. *Trends In Neurosciences, 20*(10), 435–442.

Virkkunen, M., & Linnoila, M. (1993). Brain serotonin, type II alcoholism and impulsive violence. *Journal of Studies on Alcohol (Supplement), 11,* 163–169.

Vitaterna, M. H., King, D. P., Chang, A. M., Kornhauser, J. M., Lowrey, P. L., McDonald, J. D., Dove, W. F., Pinto, L. H., Turek, F. W., & Takahashi, J. S. (1994). Mutagenesis and mapping of a mouse gene, Clock, essential for circadian behavior. *Science, 264,* 719–725.

Vogel, G. (1997). Cocaine wreaks subtle damage on developing brains [news]. *Science, 278*(5335), 38–39.

Vogel, G. W., Vogel, F., McAbee, R. S., & Thurmond, A. J. (1980). Improvement of depression by REM sleep deprivation: New findings and a theory. *Archives of General Psychiatry, 37,* 247–253.

Volkmar, F. R., & Greenough, W. T. (1972). Rearing complexity affects branching of dendrites in the visual cortex of the rat. *Science, 176,* 1445–1447.

Voneida, T. J. (1990). The effect of rubrospinal tractotomy on a conditioned limb response in the cat. *Society for Neuroscience Abstracts, 16,* 279.

Vries, H. d. (1901). Die Mutationen und die Mutationsperioden bei der Entstehung der Arten: Vortrag, gehalten in der allgemeinen Sitzung der Naturwissenschaftlichen Hauptgruppe der Versammlung Deutscher Naturforscher und Aerzte in Hamburg am 26. September 1901. (p. 63 p). Leipzig: Veit.

Wada, J. A., & Rasmussen, T. (1960). Intracarotid injection of sodium amytal for the lateralization of cerebral speech dominance: Experimental and clinical observations. *Journal of Neurosurgery, 17,* 266–282.

Wagner, A. D., Desmond, J. E., Demb, J. B., Glover, G. H., & Gabrieli, J. D. E. (1997). Semantic repetition priming from verbal and pictorial knowledge: A functional MRI study of left inferior prefrontal cortex. *Journal of Cognitive Neuroscience, 9,* 714–726.

Wagner, A. D., Gabrieli, J. D. E., & Verfaellie, M. (1997). Dissociations between familiarity processes in explicit recognition and implicit perceptual memory. *Journal of Experimental Psychology. Learning, Memory, and Cognition, 23,* 305–323.

Wagner, A. D., Schacter, D. L., Rotte, M., Koutstaal, W., Maril, A., Dale, A. M., Rosen, B. R., & Buckner, R. L. (1998). Building memories: Remembering and forgetting of verbal experiences as predicted by brain activity. *Science, 281,* 1188–1191.

Wagner, A. D., Desmond, J. E., Demb, J. B., Glover, G. H., & Gabrieli, J. D. E. (1997). Semantic repetition priming for verbal and pictorial knowledge: A functional MRI study of left inferior prefrontal cortex. *Journal of Cognitive Neuroscience, 9,* 714–726.

Wagner, G. C., Beuving, L. J., & Hutchinson, R. R. (1980). The effects of gonadal hormone manipulations on aggressive target-biting in mice. *Aggressive Behavior, 6,* 1–7.

Wahl, O. F. (1976). Monozygotic twins discordant for schizophrenia: A review. *Psychological Bulletin, 83,* 91–106.

Wald, G. (1964). The receptors of human color vision. *Science, 145,* 1007–1016.

Walker, E. F. (1991). *Schizophrenia: a life-course developmental perspective.* San Diego: Academic Press.

Wall, J. T., & Kaas, J. H. (1986). Long-term cortical consequences of reinnervation errors after nerve regeneration in monkeys. *Brain Research, 372,* 400–404.

Wall, P. D. (1991). *Defeating pain: The war against a silent epidemic.* New York: Plenum Press.

Wall, P. D. (1980). Mechanisms of plasticity of connection following damage of adult mammalian nervous systems. In P. Bach-y-Rita (ed.), *Recovery of function: Theoretical considerations for brain injury rehabilitation* (pp. pp.1–2). Bern: Hans Huber.

Walls, G. L. (1942). *The vertebrate eye, Vol. 1.* Bloomfield Hills, MI: Crankbrook Institute of Science.

Walsh, R. N., Cummins, R. A., & Budtz-Olsen, O. E. (1973). Environmentally induced changes in the dimensions of the rat cerebrum: a replication and extension. *Developmental Psychobiology, 6*(1), 3–7.

Wang, F., Nemes, A., Mendelsohn, M., & Axel, R. (1998). Odorant receptors govern the formation of a precise topographic map. *Cell, 93,* 47–60.

Wang, J. B., Imai, Y., Eppler, C. M., Gregor, P., Spivak, C. E., & Uhl, G. R. (1993). μ opiate receptor: cDNA cloning and expression. *Proceedings of the National Academy of Sciences, U.S.A., 90,* 10230–10234.

Ward, I. L. (1969). Differential effect of pre- and postnatal androgen on the sexual behavior of intact and spayed female rats. *Hormones and Behavior, 1,* 25–36.

Warrington, E. K., & Silberstein, M. (1970). A questionnaire technique for investigating very long term memory. *Quarterly Journal of Experimental Psychology, 22,* 508–512.

Watkins, J. C., & Collingridge, G. L. (1989). *The NMDA receptor.* Oxford and New York: IRL Press at Oxford University Press.

Waxman, S. G., & Kocsis, J. D. (1997). Spinal cord repair: Progress towards a daunting goal. *Neuroscientist, 3,* 263–269.

Webb, W. B. (1992). *Sleep, the gentle tyrant.* Bolton, MA: Anker Publishing.

Weeks, J. C., & Levine, R. B. (1990). Postembryonic neuronal plasticity and its hormonal control during insect metamorphosis. *Annual Review of Neuroscience, 13,* 183–194.

Wehling, M. (1997). Specific, nongenomic actions of steroid hormones. *Annual Review of Physiology, 59,* 365–393.

Wehr, T. A., Goodwin, F. K., Wirz-Justice, A., Breitmaier, J., & Craig, C. (1982). 48-hour sleep-wake cycles in manic-depressive illness: naturalistic observations and sleep deprivation experiments. *Archives of General Psychiatry, 39,* 559–565.

Wehr, T. A., Jacobsen, F. M., Sack, D. A., Arendt, J., Tamarkin, L., & Rosenthal, N. E. (1986). Phototherapy of seasonal affective disorder. *Archives of General Psychiatry, 43,* 870–875.

Wehr, T. A., Sack, D. A., Duncan, W. C., Mendelson, W. B., Rosenthal, N. E., Gillina, J. C., & Goodwin, F. K. (1985). Sleep and circadian rhythms in affective patients isolated from external time cues. *Psychiatry Research, 15,* 327–339.

Wehr, T., Sack, D., Rosenthal, N., Duncan, W., & Gillin, J. C. (1983). Circadian rhythm disturbances in manic-depressive illness. *Federation Proceedings, 42,* 2809–2814.

Weil, A., & Rosen, W. (1993). *From chocolate to morphine: everything you need to know about mind-altering drugs.* Boston: Houghton Mifflin.

Weinberger, D. R., Aloia, M. S., Goldberg, T. E., & Berman, K. F. (1994). The frontal lobes and schizophrenia. *Journal of Neuropsychiatry and Clinical Neurosciences, 6,* 419–427.

Weinberger, D. R., Bigelow, L. B., Kleinman, J. E., Klein, S. T., Rosenblatt, J. E., & Wyatt, R. J. (1980). Cerebral ventricular enlargement in chronic schizophrenia. An association with poor response to treatment. *Archives of General Psychiatry, 37*, 11–13.

Weinberger, D. R., Zigun, J. R., Bartley, A. J., Jones, D. W., & Torrey, E. F. (1992). Anatomical abnormalities in the brains of monozygotic twins discordant and concordant for schizophrenia. *Clinical Neuropharmacology, 15*, 122A-123A.

Weinberger, D. R. (1985). Clinical-neuropathological correlations in schizophrenia: theoretical implications. *Controversies In Schizophrenia: Changes and Constancies: Proceedings of The 74th Annual Meeting of The American Psychopathological Association, New York City, March 1–3, 1984* (pp. 92–106. ix, 432).

Weinberger, D. (1987). Implications of normal brain development for the pathogenesis of schizophrenia. *Archives of General Psychiatry, 44*(7), 660–669.

Weinberger, N. M. (1995). Dynamic regulation of receptive fields and maps in the adult sensory cortex. *Annual Review of Neuroscience, 18*, 129–159.

Weinberger, N. M. (1998). Physiological memory in primary auditory cortex: Characteristics and mechanisms. *Neurobiology of Learning and Memory, 70*, 1–2, 226–251.

Weiner, H. (1992). *Perturbing the organism: The biology of stressful experience.* Chicago: University of Chicago Press.

Weiner, R. D. (1994). Treatment optimization with ECT. *Psychopharmacology Bulletin, 30*, 313–320.

Weingarten, H., Chang, P., & Mcdonald, T. (1985). Comparison of the metabolic and behavioral disturbances following paraventricular- and ventromedial-hypothalamic lesions. *Brain Research Bulletin, 14*(6), 551–559.

Weiskrantz, L. (1986). *Blindsight: A case study and implications.* New York: Oxford University Press.

Weisman, A. D., & Worden, J. W. (1976–1977). The existential plight in cancer: Significance of the first 100 days. *International Journal of Psychiatry in Medicine, 7*, 1–15.

Weitzman, E. D. (1981). Sleep and its disorders. *Annual Review of Neurosciences, 4*, 381–417.

Weitzman, E. D., Czeisler, C. A., Zimmerman, J. C., & Moore-Ede, M. C. (1981). Biological rhythms in man: Relationship of sleep-wake, cortisol, growth hormone, and temperature during temporal isolation. In J. B. Martin, S. Reichlin, & K. L. Bick (eds.), *Neurosecretion and brain peptides.* New York: Raven.

Welker, W. (1976). Mapping the brain. Historical trends in functional localization. *Brain, Behavior and Evolution, 13*(4), 327–343.

Weller, L., & Weller, A. (1993). Human menstrual synchrony: a critical assessment. *Neuroscience and Biobehavioral Reviews, 17*, 427–439.

West, R. W., & Greenough, W. T. (1972). Effect of environmental complexity on cortical synapses of rats: Preliminary results. *Behavioral Biology, 7*, 279–284.

Westergaard, G. C., Kuhn, H. E., & Suomi, S. J. (1998). Bipedal posture and hand preference in humans and other primates. *Journal of Comparative Psychology, 112*, 55–64.

Westheimer, G. (1984). Spatial vision. *Annual Review of Psychology, 35*, 201–226.

Wever, E. G. (1974). The evolution of vertebrate hearing. In *Handbook of sensory physiology Vol. 1. Audition.* New York: Springer-Verlag.

Wever, R. A. (1979). Influence of physical workload on freerunning circadian rhythms of man. *Pflugers Archiv. European Journal of Physiology, 381*, 119–126.

Wexler, B. E., & Heninger, G. R. (1979). Alterations in cerebral laterality during acute psychotic illness. *Archives of General Psychiatry, 36*, 278–284.

Wexler, N. S., Rose, E. A., & Housman, D. E. (1991). Molecular approaches to hereditary diseases of the nervous system: Huntington's disease as a paradigm. *Annual Review of Neuroscience, 14*, 503–529.

White, L. E., & Hain, R. F. (1959). Anorexia in association with a destructive lesion of the hypothalamus. *Archives of Pathology, 68*, 275–281.

White, N. M., & Milner, P. M. (1992). The psychobiology of reinforcers. *Annual Review of Psychology, 43*, 443–471.

Wible, C. G., Shenton, M. E., Hokama, H., Kikinis, R., Jolesz, F. A., Metcalf, D., & McCarley, R. W. (1995). Prefrontal cortex and schizophrenia. A quantitative magnetic resonance imaging study. *Archives of General Psychiatry, 52*, 279–288.

Wiesel, T. N., & Hubel, D. H. (1965). Extent of recovery from the effects of visual deprivation in kittens. *Journal of Neurophysiology, 28*, 1060–1072.

Wikler, K. C., & Rakic, P. (1990). Distribution of photoreceptor subtypes in the retina of diurnal and nocturnal primates. *Journal of Neuroscience, 10*, 3390–3401.

Wiklund, C., & Sillén-Tullberg, B. (1985). Why distasteful butterflies have aposematic larvae and adults, but cryptic pupae: evidence from predation experiments on the monarch and the European swallowtail. *Evolution, 39*, 1155–1158.

Will, B. E., Rosenzweig, M. R., Bennett, E. L., Hebert, M., & Morimoto, H. (1977). Relatively brief environmental enrichment aids recovery of learning capacity and alters brain measures after postweaning brain lesions in rats. *Journal of Comparative and Physiological Psychology, 91*, 33–50.

Willerman, L., Schultz, R., Rutledge, J. N., & Bigler, E. D. (1991). In vivo brain size and intelligence. *Intelligence, 15*(2), 223–228.

Williams, D. (1969). Neural factors related to habitual aggression. *Brain, 92*, 503–520.

Willner, P. (1991). *Behavioural models in psychopharmacology.* New York: Cambridge University Press.

Wilson, M. A., & McNaughton, B. L. (1994). Reactivation of hippocampal ensemble memories during sleep. *Science, 165*, 676–679.

Winberg, S., Winberg, Y., & Fernald, R. D. (1997). Effect of social rank on brain monoaminergic activity in a cichlid fish. *Brain, Behavior and Evolution, 49*, 230–236.

Wingard, D. L., & Berkman, L. F. (1983). Mortality risk associated with sleeping patterns among adults. *Sleep, 6*, 102–107.

Wingfield, J. C., Ball, G. F., Dufty, A. M., Hegner, R. E., & Ramenofsky, M. (1987). Testosterone and aggression in birds. *American Scientist, 75*, 602–608.

Winocur, G. (1990). Anterograde and retrograde amnesia in rats with dorsal hippocampal or dorsomedial thalamic lesions. *Behavioural Brain Research, 38*, 145–154.

Wise, R. A. (1997). Drug self-administration viewed as ingestive behaviour. *Appetite, 28*, 1–5.

Wise, R. A. (1984). Neural mechanisms of the reinforcing action of cocaine. In J. Grabowski (ed.), *Cocaine: Pharmacology, effects and treatment of abuse, NIDA Research Monograph 50* (pp. 15–33). National Institute on Drug Abuse.

Wise, R. A., Bauco, P., Carlezon, W. A. Jr., & Trojniar, W. (1992). Self-stimulation and drug reward mechanisms. *Annals of the New York Academy of Sciences, 654*, 192–198.

Wise, S. P., & Strick, P. L. (1984). Anatomical and physiological organization of the non-primary motor cortex. *Trends in Neuroscience, 7*, 442–447.

Witelson, S. F., & Pallie, W. (1973). Left hemisphere specialization for language in the newborn. Neuroanatomical evidence of asymmetry. *Brain, 96*, 641–646.

Wolf, S. S., Jones, D. W., Knable, M. B., Gorey, J. G., Lee, K. S., Hyde, T. M., Coppola, R., & Weinberger, D. R. (1996). Tourette syndrome: Prediction of phenotypic variation in monozygotic twins by caudate nucleus D2 receptor binding. *Science, 273*, 1225–1227.

Wolinsky, E., & Way, J. (1990). The behavioral genetics of *Caenorhabditis elegans. Behavior Genetics, 20*, 169–189.

Woo, C. C., & Leon, M. (1987). Sensitive period for neural and behavioral response development to learned odors. *Developmental Brain Research, 36*, 309–313.

Wood, J. M., Bootzin, R. R., Kihlstrom, J. F., & Schacter, D. L. (1992). Implicit and explicit memory for verbal information presented during sleep. *Psychological Science, 3*, 236–239.

Woolsey, C. N. (1981). *Cortical sensory organization: Multiple auditory areas.* Crescent Manor, NJ: Humana.

Woolsey, T. A., Durham, D., Harris, R. M., Simous, D. T., & Valentino, K. (1981). Somatosensory development. In R. S. Aslin, J. R. Alberts, & M. R. Peterson (eds.), *Sensory and perceptual development: Influence of genetic and experiential factors.* New York: Academic.

Woolsey, T. A., & Wann, J. R. (1976). Areal changes in mouse cortical barrels following vibrissal damage at different postnatal ages. *Journal of Comparative Neurology, 170,* 53–66.

Wright, A. A. et al. (1985). Memory processing of serial lists by pigeons, monkeys, and people. *Science, 229,* 287–289.

Xerri, C., Coq, J., Merzenich, M., & Jenkins, W. (1996). Experience-induced plasticity of cutaneous maps in the primary somatosensory cortex of adult monkeys and rats. *Journal de Physiologie, 90*(3–4), 277–287.

Yahr, P., & Gregory, J. E. (1993). The medial and lateral cell groups of the sexually dimorphic area of the gerbil hypothalamus are essential for male sex behavior and act via separate pathways. *Brain Research, 631,* 287–296.

Yanagisawa, K., Bartoshuk, L. M., Karrer, T. A. et al. (1992). Anesthesia of the chorda tympani nerve: insights into a source of dysgeusia. *Chemical Senses, 17,* 724.

Yasuda, K., Raynor, K., Kong, H., Breder, C., Takeda, J., Reisine, T., & Bell, G. I. (1993). Cloning and functional comparison of kappa and delta opioid receptors from mouse brain. *Proceedings of the National Academy of Sciences, U.S.A., 90,* 6736–6740.

Yin, J. C., Wallach, J. S., Del Vecchio, M., Wilder, E. L., Zhou, H., Quinn, W. G., & Tully, T. (1994). Induction of a dominant negative CREB transgene specifically blocks long-term memory in *Drosophila. Cell, 79,* 49–58.

Young, A. B. (1993). Role of excitotoxins in heredito-degenerative neurologic diseases. *Research Publications - Association for Research in Nervous and Mental Disease, 71,* 175–189.

Young, A. W., Hellawell, D. J., Van De Wal, C., & Johnson, M. (1996). Facial expression processing after amygdalotomy. *Neuropsychologia, 34,* 31–39.

Yu, S., Pritchard, M., Kremer, E., Lynch, M., Nancarrow, J., Baker, E., Holman, K., Mulley, J. C., Warren, S. T., Schlessinger, D. et al. (1991). Fragile X genotype characterized by an unstable region of DNA. *Science, 252,* 1179–1181.

Zaidel, E. (1976). Auditory vocabulary of the right hemisphere following brain bisection or hemidecortication. *Cortex, 12,* 191–211.

Zantua, J. B., Wasserstrom, S. P., Arends, J. J., Jacquin, M. F., & Woolsey, T. A. (1996). Postnatal development of mouse "whisker" thalamus: Ventroposterior medial nucleus (VPM), barreloids, and their thalamocortical relay neurons. *Somatosensory and Motor Research, 13,* 307–322.

Zatorre, R. J., Evans, A. C., & Meyer, E. (1994). Neural mechanisms underlying melodic perception and memory for pitch. *Journal of Neuroscience, 14,* 1908–1919.

Zecevic, N., & Rakic, P. (1976). Differentiation of Purkinje cells and their relationship to other components of developing cerebellar cortex in man. *Journal of Comparative Neurology, 167,* 27–48.

Zeki, S. (1993). *A vision of the brain.* London: Blackwell.

Zeki, S., Watson, J. D., Lueck, C. J., Friston, K. J., Kennard, C., & Frackowiak, R. S. (1991). A direct demonstration of functional specialization in human visual cortex. *Journal of Neuroscience, 11,* 641–649.

Zhang, L. I., Tao, H. W., Holt, C. E., Harris, W. A., & Poo, M.-M. (1998). A critical window for cooperataion and competition among developing retinotectal synapses. *Nature, 395,* 37–44.

Zhang, Y., Proenca, R., Maffei, M., Barone, M., Leopold, L., & Friedman, J. M. (1994). Positional cloning of the mouse obese gene and its human homologue. *Nature, 372,* 425–432.

Zhao, H., Ivic, L., Otaki, J. M., Hashimoto, M., Mikoshiba, K., & Firestein, S. (1998). Functional expression of a mammalian odorant receptor. *Science, 279,* 237–242.

Zihl, J., von Cramon, D., & Mai, N. (1983). Selective disturbance of movement vision after bilateral brain damage. *Brain, 106,* 313–340.

Zola-Morgan, S. M., & Squire, L. R. (1990). The primate hippocampal formation: Evidence for a time-limited role in memory storage. *Science, 250,* 288–290.

Zola-Morgan, S., & Squire, L. R. (1993). Neuroanatomy of memory. *Annual Review of Neuroscience, 16,* 547–563.

Zucker, I. (1976). Light, behavior, and biologic rhythms. *Hospital Practice, 11,* 83–91.

Zucker, I., Boshes, M., & Dark, J. (1983). Suprachiasmatic nuclei influence circannual and circadian rhythms of ground squirrels. *American Journal of Physiology, 244,* R472-R480.

Zucker, L. M., & Zucker, T. F. (1961). "Fatty," a mutation in the rat. *Journal of Heredity, 52,* 275–278.

Zuker, C. S. (1994). On the evolution of eyes: would you like it simple or compound? *Science, 265,* 742–731.

Zurek, P. M. (1981). Spontaneous narrowband acoustic signals emitted by human ears. *Journal of the Acoustical Society of America, 69,* 514–523.

Author Index

A

Aarons, L., 400
Aaronson, S. T., 388
Abdullaev, Y. G., 78
Abel, E. L., 181–182
Abraham, S. F., 364
Abraham, W. C., 507, 508
Adelson, E. H., 253
Ader, R., 430, 432
Ades, H. W., 232
Adler, N., 428, 429
Adolphs, R., 422
Aggleton, J. P., 422
Ahlquist, J. E., 136, 140, 142
Akbarian, S., 443
al-Barazanji, K. A., 376
Albert, S. M., 519
Alberts, J. R., 358
Aldrich, M. A., 405
Alexander, B. K., 100
Alho, H., 95
Almada, S. J., 433
Alpert, M., 445
Amos, L. A., 33
Anand, B. K., 373
Andersen, P. M., 307
Andreasen, N. C., 21, 43, 51, 435, 437, 441, 443, 549
Angier, N., 120
Anholt, R. R., 242
Arbas, E. A., 73
Arendt, J., 404
Aristotle, 17, 107, 181–182
Arnold, A., 526
Arnold, A. P., 342, 344, 525, 526
Aroniadou, V. A., 507
Asberg, M., 449
Aserinsky, E., 386
Ashmore, J. F., 224, 225, 226
Atkinson, M. A., 369, 370
Avan, P., 223
Axel, R., 242
Axelsson, J., 455
Azar, B., 101
Azrin, N. H., 461

B

Bach-y-Rita, P., 282
Baddeley, A. D., 476
Bailey, C. H., 504
Bailey, J. M., 345

Bain, A., 502
Baker, H. F., 10
Ball, G. F., 524, 526
Ballentine, H. T., 460
Balster, R. L., 97
Banchaud, J., 422
Bannon, A. W., 213
Baptista, L. F., 525
Barasa, A., 148
Barbour, H. G., 359
Barchas, J. D., 101
Bard, P., 411, 412
Barde, Y. A., 170
Barden, N., 453
Bark, N. M., 436
Barkow, J. H., 333
Barlow, H. B., 265, 279
Barnes, B. M., 351
Barnett, S. A., 320
Barr, E., 306
Barrionuevo, G., 504
Bartoshuk, L. M, 239, 240
Basbaum, A., 213, 214
Basil, J. A., 141
Baskerville, K. A., 207
Bateson, W, 139
Baudry, M., 508
Baumgardner, T. L., 181
Bavelier, D., 528
Baylor, D., 257
Beach, F. A., 319, 339
Bear, D., 425
Bear, M. F., 510
Beauchamp, G. K., 238, 240
Beaulieu, C., 207
Beggs, W. D., 233
Bekkers, J. M., 508
Bell, A. P., 345
Bellinger, D., 430
Bellugi, U., 533
Beluscio, L., 242
Beninger, R. J., 417
Bennett, A. F., 352
Bennett, E. L., 176, 500, 514, 515
Bennett, W., 96, 104
Berger, T. W., 512
Bergstrand, G., 551
Berkman, L. F., 403
Berman, D, 552
Berman, K. F., 443, 444
Bernard, C., 107
Bernhardt, P. C., 424

Bernstein-Goral, H., 307
Bernstein, I. L., 377
Bernstein, I. S., 424
Berthold, A. A., 107, 108, 115
Besedovsky, H. O., 430
Bigelow, L., 443
Binder, J. R., 230
Bingman, V. P., 490
Birnbaumer, L., 72
Bjork, R. A., 400
Björklund, A., 111
Black, J. E., 514, 521
Blakemore, C., 178, 269
Blaxton, T. A., 486
Blehar, M. C., 455
Bleuler, E., 437
Bliss, T. V. P., 504, 508
Blizzard, R. M., 123
Bloch, V., 402, 517, 518
Blodgett, H. C., 473
Blue, M. E., 169
Blumberg, M. S., 357, 358
Bodnar, R. J., 215
Bogen, J. E., 540
Bohus, B., 434
Bonese, K. F., 104
Bonhoeffer, F., 173, 275
Bonhoeffer, T., 273
Bonilla, E., 312
Boolell, M., 326
Bothwell, M., 170
Bottjer, S. W., 526
Bourtchuladze, R., 516
Bowmaker, J. K., 279
Boyle, P. C., 373
Bradley, W. G., 307
Brain, P. F., 423, 424
Brasel, J. A., 123
Bray, G. A., 368
Breedlove, S. M., 169, 343, 344
Bregman, B. S., 307
Breier, A., 97, 445
Bremer, F., 395
Bremner, J. D., 458
Brennan, P., 326
Brenowitz, E. A., 142, 526
Brewer, J. B., 481
Bridgman, P., 168
Brien, J. A., 235
Brobeck, J. R., 373
Broberg, D. J., 377
Broca, P., 528, 529, 530

Brodmann, K., 48
Brodsky, A., 103
Brook, J. S., 102, 103
Brooks, V. B., 313
Broughton, R., 385
Brower, L., 371
Browman, L. G., 245
Brown, G. L., 424
Brown, J., 469, 474
Brown, T. H., 167, 499
Brown, W. L., 109
Brownell, W. E., 226
Brownlee, S., 213
Brunet, L. J., 242
Brunjes, P. C., 358
Bryden, M. P., 419
Buchsbaum, M., 443
Buck, L., 242
Buckner, R. L., 485
Bucy, P. C., 416
Buhrich, N., 345
Bullock, T. H., 143, 144
Buss, D. M., 333
Busse, E. W., 551
Buswell, B. N., 413
Butler, R. A., 232
Byrne, D. G., 429

C

Cable, W. J. L., 181
Cacioppo, J. T., 411, 415
Cadoret, R. J., 102
Cahill, L., 482, 483, 518
Calvert, G. A., 232
Calvin, W. H., 538
Campbell, F. W., 269
Campbell, J. J., III, 546
Campbell, R., 420
Campbell, S. S., 383, 390
Campfield, L. A., 374
Cannistra, L. B., 376
Cannon, S. C., 61
Cannon, W. B., 107, 411, 412
Cao, Y. Q., 211
Capretta, P. J., 371
Carew, T. J., 488, 491
Carlsson, A., 446
Carlton, P. L., 445
Carter, C. S., 120
Cartwright, R. D., 389
Casey, D. E., 446
Cassens, G., 449

Index

Illustration Credits

Chapter 1
1.1 "How Biology Affects Behavior and Vice Versa," "In Hope of Averting Learning Problems, an Early Test for Infant Ears," "Hormone Is Clue to Control of Weight," "Severe Trauma May Damage the Brain as Well as the Psyche," all ©1995 by The New York Times Company. "Studies Find Brain Grows New Cells" ©1997 by The New York Times Company. "Don't Worry. A Brain Still Can't Be Cloned," ©1998 by The New York Times Company. Reprinted with permission. *National Geographic* cover courtesy of Joseph McNally/NGS Image Sales. "The Battle Over Marijuana" ©1997, Newsweek, Inc. All rights reserved. Reprinted with permission. "How a Child's Brain Develops," ©1997 Time Inc. Reprinted by permission.
1.12 Reproduced with gracious permission of Her Majesty Queen Elizabeth II, copyright reserved.
1.13 The Bettmann Archive.
1.14 The Bettmann Archive.

Chapter 2
2.8 From *Gray's Anatomy*, 35th ed, Figure 2.9, page 807. Reprinted with permission of the publisher Churchill Livingstone. (Dissection by M. C. E. Hutchinson, photograph by Kevin Fitzpatrick, Guy's Hospital Medical School, London.)
2.21 *Top*: CT scans © Dan McCoy/Rainbow. *Middle*: MRIs © Hank Morgan, Science Source/Photo Researchers, Inc. *Bottom*: Courtesy of Jamie Eberling.

Chapter 4
4.6 Biological Photo Service.
4.9 © Ken M. Highfill/National Audubon Society Collection, Photo Researchers, Inc.

Chapter 6
Box 6.1 Photographs © Art Wolfe.

Chapter 8
8.1 (*a*) ©1986 Scott Camazine/Photo Researchers Inc.; (*b*) © Art Wolfe; (*c*) © Tom McHugh/Photo Reserachers, Inc.; (*d*) © Art Wolfe.
8.18 Culver Pictures, Inc.

Chapter 11
11.1 Courtesy of Peak Performance Technology.

Chapter 12
12.1 Courtesy of James Thurber Literary Properties.
12.11 Yorgos Nikas/Tony Stone Images.
12.14 Doug Wechsler/VIREO.
Box 12.2 Stephen Glickman; © Lawrence Frank.

Chapter 13
13.2 (*a*) Steinhart Aquarium, ©Tom McHugh/Photo Researchers, Inc.; (*b*) © Tim Davis/Photo Researchers, Inc.
13.5 (*a*) © Wm. Bacon III/Photo Researchers, Inc.; (*b*) © 1989 G. J. James/Biological Photo Service.
13.6 © Art Wolfe.
13.19 Photograph by Mr. E. Slater, CSIRO Wildlife Division, Canberra.
13.27 Photograph by John Sholtis, The Rockefeller University.
13.30 (*a*) AP/Wide World Photos. Photographed by Monika Graff. (*b*) Kunsthistorisches Museum, Vienna.

Chapter 17
Box 17.1 (A) The Bettmann Archive; (C) © Richard Wood/The Picture Cube.

Chapter 19
Box 19.3 (A) H. W. Pratt/Biological Photo Service.

Scientist photographs
Chapter 6: Charles Darwin, Alfred Russel Wallace, Karl Lashley: The Bettman Archive; Theodore Bullock: Neuroscience History Archives, Brain Research Institute, University of California, Los Angeles.

Chapter 9: Georg von Békésy: courtesy of Harvard University Press.

Chapter 10: Torsten Wiesel: Robert Reichert.

Chapter 11: Sir Charles Sherrington: Neuroscience History Archives, Brain Research Institute, University of California, Los Angeles.

Chapter 13: John Garcia: Neuroscience History Archives, Brain Research Institute, University of California, Los Angeles.

Chapter 15: Paul Ekman: © John McDermott; James Olds and Hans Selye: Neuroscience History Archives, Brain Resarch Institute, Unversity of California, Los Angeles.

Chapter 16: Elaine Walker: Annemarie Poyo, © Emory University Photography.

Chapter 17: Edward Tolman: Department of Pyschology, Unversity of California, Berkeley.

Chapter 18: Eric Kandel: Rene Perez.

Chapter 19: Fernando Nottebohm: Robert Reichert; Paul Broca: The Bettmann Archive/Corbis; Norman Geschwind: Neuroscience History Archives, Brain Research Institute, University of California, Los Angeles.